Cyclopedia
of
Literary Characters II

Serp-Z

CYCLOPEDIA
of
LITERARY
CHARACTERS II

VOLUME FOUR—SERP-Z

Edited by
FRANK N. MAGILL

Salem Press
Pasadena, California   Englewood Cliffs, New Jersey

Library of Congress Cataloging-in-Publication Data

Magill, Frank Northen, 1907-
    Cyclopedia of literary characters II / edited by
Frank N. Magill.
    p.   cm.
    Includes index.
    1. Literature—Stories, plots, etc. 2. Literature—Dic-
tionaries. 3. Characters and their characteristics in literature. I. Title. II. Title: Cyclopedia of literary characters two. III. Title: Cyclopedia of literary characters 2.
  PN44.M28   1990
  809 ' .927 ' 03—dc20   90-8550
                                        CIP

  ISBN 0-89356-517-2 (set)
  ISBN 0-89356-521-0 (volume 4)

LIST OF TITLES IN VOLUME 4

	page
Key to Pronunciation	lxxvii
Serpent and the Rope, The—*Raja Rao*	1377
Setting Free the Bears—*John Irving*	1378
Setting Sun, The—*Osamu Dazai*	1379
Settlers of the Marsh—*Frederick Philip Grove*	1380
Seven Ages, The—*Eva Figes*	1381
Seven Days of Creation, The—*Vladimir Maximov*	1383
Seven Madmen, The—*Roberto Arlt*	1384
Severed Head, A—*Iris Murdoch*	1385
Sexual Perversity in Chicago—*David Mamet*	1386
Shadow of a Gunman, The—*Sean O'Casey*	1387
Shakespeare's Dog—*Leon Rooke*	1388
Shame—*Salman Rushdie*	1389
Sheltering Sky, The—*Paul Bowles*	1390
Shikasta—*Doris Lessing*	1391
Shining, The—*Stephen King*	1393
Shipyard, The—*Juan Carlos Onetti*	1394
Short Letter, Long Farewell—*Peter Handke*	1395
Shosha—*Isaac Bashevis Singer*	1396
Shrouded Woman, The—*María Luisa Bombal*	1397
Shuttlecock—*Graham Swift*	1398
Sibyl, The—*Pär Lagerkvist*	1399
Siddhartha—*Hermann Hesse*	1400
Siege of Krishnapur, The—*J. G. Farrell*	1401
Sigismund—*Lars Gustafsson*	1403
Sign in Sidney Brustein's Window, The—*Lorraine Hansberry*	1404
Silence—*Shusaku Endō*	1405
Silent Cry, The—*Kenzaburō Ōe*	1407
Silesian Tetralogy, The—*Horst Bienek*	1408
Silmarillion, The—*J. R. R. Tolkien*	1410
Silver Dove, The—*Andrey Bely*	1413
Silver Tassie, The—*Sean O'Casey*	1413
Simple Story, A—*Shmuel Yosef Agnon*	1415
Singapore Grip, The—*J. G. Farrell*	1416
Sirens of Titan, The—*Kurt Vonnegut, Jr.*	1418
Sister Mary Ignatius Explains It All for You—*Christopher Durang*	1419
62: A Model Kit—*Julio Cortázar*	1420
Slaughterhouse-Five—*Kurt Vonnegut, Jr.*	1421

page

Slave, The—*Isaac Bashevis Singer* 1422
Sleepless Days—*Jurek Becker* 1423
Sleuth—*Anthony Shaffer* 1424
Slow Homecoming—*Peter Handke* 1425
Small Changes—*Marge Piercy* 1426
Small Room, The—*May Sarton* 1427
Small World—*David Lodge* 1429
Snail on the Slope, The—*Arkady Strugatsky* and *Boris Strugatsky* 1430
Snooty Baronet—*Wyndham Lewis* 1432
Snow Country—*Yasunari Kawabata* 1433
Snow Was Black, The—*Georges Simenon* 1434
Solaris—*Stanisław Lem* 1435
Soldiers' Pay—*William Faulkner* 1437
Solid Mandala, The—*Patrick White* 1438
Some Prefer Nettles—*Jun'ichirō Tanizaki* 1439
Something Happened—*Joseph Heller* 1440
Something Wicked This Way Comes—*Ray Bradbury* 1441
Sometimes a Great Notion—*Ken Kesey* 1442
Son of Man—*Augusto Roa Bastos* 1444
Song of a Goat—*John Pepper Clark* 1444
Song of Solomon—*Toni Morrison* 1445
Sophie's Choice—*William Styron* 1446
Sorrow Beyond Dreams, A—*Peter Handke* 1448
Souls and Bodies—*David Lodge* 1448
Sound of the Mountain, The—*Yasunari Kawabata* 1450
Sour Sweet—*Timothy Mo* 1451
Source, The—*James A. Michener* 1452
Southpaw, The—*Mark Harris* 1455
Space Trilogy, The—*C. S. Lewis* 1456
Speed-the-Plow—*David Mamet* 1458
Speedboat—*Renata Adler* 1459
Spell, The—*Hermann Broch* 1460
Speranza—*Sven Delblanc* 1461
Spire, The—*William Golding* 1462
Splendors and Miseries of Courtesans, The—*Honoré de Balzac* 1463
Sport of the Gods, The—*Paul Laurence Dunbar* 1465
Sporting Club, The—*Thomas McGuane* 1466
Spy in the House of Love, A—*Anaïs Nin* 1468
Spy Who Came in from the Cold, The—*John le Carré* 1469
Stand, The—*Stephen King* 1470
Stanley and the Women—*Kingsley Amis* 1472
Staring at the Sun—*Julian Barnes* 1472

page

Tent of Miracles—*Jorge Amado* 1526

Tents of Wickedness, The—*Peter De Vries* 1528

Terms of Endearment—*Larry McMurtry* 1529

Terra Nostra—*Carlos Fuentes* 1530

That Awful Mess on Via Merulana—*Carlo Emilio Gadda* 1532

That Voice—*Robert Pinget* 1532

Thaw, The—*Ilya Ehrenburg* 1533

Their Eyes Were Watching God—*Zora Neale Hurston* 1534

them—*Joyce Carol Oates* 1535

Theophilus North—*Thornton Wilder* 1536

There Is a Tree More Ancient Than Eden—*Leon Forrest* 1538

Thérèse Raquin—*Émile Zola* 1539

These Thousand Hills—*A. B. Guthrie, Jr.* 1541

Thin Red Line, The—*James Jones* 1542

Things Fall Apart—*Chinua Achebe* 1544

Third and Oak: The Laundromat—*Marsha Norman* 1546

Third Factory—*Viktor Shklovsky* 1546

Third Life of Grange Copeland, The—*Alice Walker* 1547

Third Policeman, The—*Flann O'Brien* 1548

This Side of Paradise—*F. Scott Fitzgerald* 1550

This Sporting Life—*David Storey* 1551

This Sunday—*José Donoso* 1552

Thousand Cranes—*Yasunari Kawabata* 1554

Three-Cornered World, The—*Sōseki Natsume* 1555

Three Lives—*Gertrude Stein* 1555

Three Marias, The—*Rachel de Queiroz* 1557

Three Sisters, The—*May Sinclair* 1558

Three Trapped Tigers—*Guillermo Cabrera Infante* 1559

Threepenny Opera, The—*Bertolt Brecht* 1560

Ticket to the Stars, A—*Vassily Aksyonov* 1561

Tidings Brought to Mary, The—*Paul Claudel* 1563

Tieta, the Goat Girl—*Jorge Amado* 1564

Till We Have Faces—*C. S. Lewis* 1565

Tilted Cross, The—*Hal Porter* 1566

Time and the Conways—*J. B. Priestley* 1567

Time of Indifference, The—*Alberto Moravia* 1568

Time of the Hero, The—*Mario Vargas Llosa* 1569

Time of Your Life, The—*William Saroyan* 1571

Tiny Alice—*Edward Albee* 1572

Tirra Lirra by the River—*Jessica Anderson* 1573

Titan—*Jean Paul* 1574

To Have and Have Not—*Ernest Hemingway* 1577

page

Steppe, The—*Anton Chekhov* 1474
Stone Angel, The—*Margaret Laurence* 1475
Stormy Weather—*August Strindberg* 1476
Strait Is the Gate—*André Gide* 1477
Stranger in a Strange Land—*Robert A. Heinlein* 1478
Strangers and Brothers—*C. P. Snow* 1480
Streamers—*David Rabe* 1483
Strike the Father Dead—*John Wain* 1484
Strong Wind—*Miguel Ángel Asturias* 1485
Subject Was Roses, The—*Frank D. Gilroy* 1486
Such Is My Beloved—*Morley Callaghan* 1487
Suddenly Last Summer—*Tennessee Williams* 1488
Suicide's Wife, The—*David Madden* 1489
Sula—*Toni Morrison* 1490
Summer and Smoke—*Tennessee Williams* 1492
Summer of the Seventeenth Doll—*Ray Lawler* 1493
Sunday of Life, The—*Raymond Queneau* 1494
Sunlight Dialogues, The—*John Gardner* 1495
Surfacing—*Margaret Atwood* 1498
Survivor, The—*Thomas Keneally* 1499
Sutter's Gold—*Blaise Cendrars* 1500
Suttree—*Cormac McCarthy* 1501
Swamp Angel—*Ethel Wilson* 1503
Swan Villa, The—*Martin Walser* 1504
Sweet Bird of Youth—*Tennessee Williams* 1505
Sweet Dove Died, The—*Barbara Pym* 1507
Sword of Honour—*Evelyn Waugh* 1508
System of Dante's Hell, The—*Amiri Baraka* 1510

Take a Girl Like You—*Kingsley Amis* 1511
Takeover, The—*Muriel Spark* 1513
Talley's Folly—*Lanford Wilson* 1514
Tango—*Sławomir Mrożek* 1515
Tartar Steppe, The—*Dino Buzzati* 1516
Taste of Honey, A—*Shelagh Delaney* 1517
Tea and Sympathy—*Robert Anderson* 1518
Teahouse of the August Moon, The—*John Patrick* 1519
Tell Me That You Love Me, Junie Moon—*Marjorie Kellogg* 1520
Temple of the Golden Pavilion, The—*Yukio Mishima* 1522
Temptation—*Václav Havel* 1523
Ten North Frederick—*John O'Hara* 1524
Tennis Players, The—*Lars Gustafsson* 1525

page

To Have and to Hold—*Mary Johnston*. 1578
To Kill a Mockingbird—*Harper Lee* 1580
To the Land of the Cattails—*Aharon Appelfeld* 1581
Tobacco Road—*Jack Kirkland* 1582
Tobias Trilogy, The—*Pär Lagerkvist* 1583
Told by an Idiot—*Rose Macaulay* 1585
Tomb for Boris Davidovich, A—*Danilo Kiš* 1586
Tonight We Improvise—*Luigi Pirandello* 1588
Tooth of Crime, The—*Sam Shepard* 1589
Top Girls—*Caryl Churchill*. 1591
Torch Song Trilogy—*Harvey Fierstein* 1592
Torrents of Spring, The—*Ernest Hemingway* 1593
Torrents of Spring, The—*Ivan Turgenev* 1594
Tortilla Flat—*John Steinbeck*. 1595
Towers of Trebizond, The—*Rose Macaulay*. 1596
Tragedy of King Christophe, The—*Aimé Césaire* 1598
Transfiguration of Benno Blimpie, The—*Albert Innaurato* 1599
Translations—*Brian Friel* 1600
Transposed Heads, The—*Thomas Mann*. 1602
Travelling North—*David Williamson* 1603
Travels of Lao Ts'an, The—*Liu E*. 1604
Travesties—*Tom Stoppard*. 1606
Tree Climber, The—*Tawfiq al-Hakim* 1607
Tree of Knowledge, The—*Pío Baroja* 1608
Tremor of Intent—*Anthony Burgess* 1609
Trial Begins, The—*Abram Tertz* 1610
Trick of the Ga Bolga, The—*Patrick McGinley* 1612
Triptych—*Claude Simon*. 1613
Triton—*Samuel R. Delany*. 1614
Tropic of Cancer—*Henry Miller* 1615
Trouble in Mind—*Alice Childress* 1616
Troubles—*J. G. Farrell* 1617
Trout Fishing in America—*Richard Brautigan* 1619
True Story of Ah Q, The—*Lu Hsün* 1620
True West—*Sam Shepard* 1621
Tubby Schaumann—*Wilhelm Raabe* 1622
Turvey—*Earle Birney*. 1623
Twenty-seven Wagons Full of Cotton—*Tennessee Williams* 1624
Two for the Seesaw—*William Gibson* 1625
Two Solitudes—*Hugh MacLennan* 1625
2001: A Space Odyssey—*Arthur C. Clarke*. 1627
Two Thousand Seasons—*Ayi Kwei Armah* 1628

CYCLOPEDIA OF LITERARY CHARACTERS II

        page

Typhoon—*Joseph Conrad* 1629
Tzili—*Aharon Appelfeld* 1630

Ubu Roi—*Alfred Jarry* 1631
Ultramarine—*Malcolm Lowry* 1632
Unbearable Lightness of Being, The—*Milan Kundera* 1633
Under the Sun of Satan—*Georges Bernanos* 1634
Underground Man, The—*Ross Macdonald* 1636
Unholy Loves—*Joyce Carol Oates* 1637
Unicorn, The—*Iris Murdoch* 1639
Union Street—*Pat Barker* 1640
Universal Baseball Association, Inc., J. Henry Waugh, Prop., The—
    Robert Coover 1642
Unnamable, The—*Samuel Beckett* 1643
Untergeher, Der—*Thomas Bernhard* 1644

V.—*Thomas Pynchon* 1646
Vagabond, The—*Colette* 1649
Valley of Decision, The—*Edith Wharton* 1650
Vein of Iron—*Ellen Glasgow* 1651
Vendor of Sweets, The—*R. K. Narayan* 1653
Venusberg—*Anthony Powell* 1654
Victoria—*Knut Hamsun* 1655
Vienna: Lusthaus—*Martha Clarke* 1655
Violins of Saint-Jacques, The—*Patrick Leigh Fermor* 1656
Vipers' Tangle—*François Mauriac* 1657
Virgin and the Gipsy, The—*D. H. Lawrence* 1658
Visit, The—*Friedrich Dürrenmatt* 1659
Visitants—*Randolph Stow* 1661
Vivisector, The—*Patrick White* 1662
Voices in Time—*Hugh MacLennan* 1663
Volunteers—*Brian Friel* 1665
Voss—*Patrick White* 1666
Voyage Out, The—*Virginia Woolf* 1667
Voyage Round My Father, A—*John Mortimer* 1668
Voyage to Tomorrow—*Tawfiq al-Hakim* 1669

Waiting for the Barbarians—*J. M. Coetzee* 1671
Walk in the Night, A—*Alex La Guma* 1672
Walk on the Wild Side, A—*Nelson Algren* 1673
Wall, The—*John Hersey* 1674
Wall Jumper, The—*Peter Schneider* 1676

page

Woman of the Pharisees, A—*François Mauriac* 1730
Woman on the Edge of Time—*Marge Piercy* 1732
Women at the Pump, The—*Knut Hamsun*............................... 1733
Women of Brewster Place, The—*Gloria Naylor* 1734
Women of Messina—*Elio Vittorini* 1736
Women of Trachis—*Sophocles*, translated by *Ezra Pound* 1736
Women's Room, The—*Marilyn French*................................ 1737
Wonder-Worker, The—*Dan Jacobson* 1738
Wonderful Fool—*Shusaku Endō*..................................... 1740
Wonderland—*Joyce Carol Oates*...................................... 1741
Woodcutters—*Thomas Bernhard* 1742
Woods, The—*David Mamet* 1743
Word Child, A—*Iris Murdoch* 1744
Words and Music—*Samuel Beckett*................................... 1745
Words upon the Window-Pane, The—*William Butler Yeats*................. 1746
Workhouse Ward, The—*Lady Augusta Gregory* 1748
Works of Love, The—*Wright Morris*.................................. 1749
World According to Garp, The—*John Irving*............................ 1749
World My Wilderness, The—*Rose Macaulay* 1752
World of Love, A—*Elizabeth Bowen*.................................. 1753
World of Strangers, A—*Nadine Gordimer* 1754
Wreath for Udomo, A—*Peter Abrahams*............................... 1755
Wreath of Roses, A—*Elizabeth Taylor* 1756
Wreckage of Agathon, The—*John Gardner* 1758

Xala—*Ousmane Sembène*.. 1759

Year of Living Dangerously, The—*C. J. Koch* 1760
Year of the Dragon, The—*Frank Chin* 1761
Yellow Back Radio Broke-Down—*Ishmael Reed*........................ 1762
Yonnondio—*Tillie Olsen*.. 1763
You Can't Take It with You—*George S. Kaufman* and *Moss Hart* 1764
Young Lions, The—*Irwin Shaw* 1765
Young Törless—*Robert Musil* 1766

Zazie in the Metro—*Raymond Queneau*................................ 1767
Zero—*Ignácio de Loyola Brandão* 1769
Zone, The—*Sergei Dovlatov*... 1770
Zoo—*Viktor Shklovsky*... 1771
Zoo Story, The—*Edward Albee* 1772
Zoot Suit—*Luis Miguel Valdez* 1773
Zuckerman Unbound—*Philip Roth*.................................... 1774

page

Wanderers, The—*Ezekiel Mphahlele*............................... 1677

War and Remembrance—*Herman Wouk*............................. 1678

War Between the Tates, The—*Alison Lurie*........................ 1681

War of the End of the World, The—*Mario Vargas Llosa*................. 1682

Wars, The—*Timothy Findley* 1683

Watch on the Rhine—*Lillian Hellman*............................ 1684

Watch That Ends the Night, The—*Hugh MacLennan* 1685

Watchmaker of Everton, The—*Georges Simenon* 1686

Water Hen, The—*Stanisław Ignacy Witkiewicz*...................... 1687

Waterfall, The—*Margaret Drabble*.............................. 1688

Waterfalls of Slunj, The—*Heimito von Doderer* 1689

Waterland—*Graham Swift* 1691

Watership Down—*Richard Adams* 1692

Watt—*Samuel Beckett*....................................... 1694

Wave, The—*Evelyn Scott* 1695

Way West, The—*A. B. Guthrie, Jr.* 1698

We—*Yevgeny Zamyatin* 1700

Weather in the Streets, The—*Rosamond Lehmann* 1701

Weeds—*Edith Summers Kelley*................................. 1702

Well, The—*Elizabeth Jolley* 1703

What a Beautiful Sunday!—*Jorge Semprun* 1704

What I'm Going to Do, I Think—*Larry Woiwode*..................... 1705

What Price Glory?—*Maxwell Anderson* and *Laurence Stallings* 1706

What the Butler Saw—*Joe Orton* 1707

What's Bred in the Bone—*Robertson Davies* 1708

When I Whistle—*Shusaku Endō*................................ 1709

When You Comin' Back, Red Ryder?—*Mark Medoff* 1710

Where Has Tommy Flowers Gone?—*Terrence McNally* 1711

Who Has Seen the Wind—*W. O. Mitchell*......................... 1712

Wide Sargasso Sea—*Jean Rhys* 1714

Widower's Son, The—*Alan Sillitoe*.............................. 1715

Wielopole/Wielopole—*Tadeusz Kantor*........................... 1717

Wind, The—*Claude Simon*.................................... 1717

Wind from the Plain, The; Iron Earth, Copper Sky; *and* The Undying Grass—
    Yashar Kemal... 1718

Winds of War, The—*Herman Wouk* 1720

Wine of Astonishment, The—*Earl Lovelace*........................ 1723

Wings—*Arthur Kopit* 1725

Winners, The—*Julio Cortázar* 1726

Wise Virgin—*A. N. Wilson* 1727

Woman from Sarajevo, The—*Ivo Andrić*.......................... 1728

Woman in the Dunes, The—*Kōbō Abe* 1729

KEY TO PRONUNCIATION

â	pare, stair	o͝o	book, push
ă	man, rang	o͞o	moor, move
ā	ale, fate	ou	loud, round
ä	calm, father	p	put, stop
b	bed, rub	r	red, try
ch	chin, reach	s	see, pass
d	day, bad	sh	she, push
ĕ	ten, ebb	t	to, bit
ē	equal, meat	th	thin, path
ė	fern, bird	th̸	then, mother
f	fill, off	ŭ	up, dove
g	go, rug	ū	use, cube
h	hot, hear	û	surge, burn
ĭ	if, hit	v	vast, above
ī	ice, right	w	will, away
j	joy, hedge	y	yet, yam
k	keep, take	z	zest, amaze
l	let, ball	zh	azure, seizure
m	man, him	ə	is a vowel occurring in an unaccented
n	now, ton		syllable, as
ng	ring, English		a *in* above
ŏ	lot, box		e *in* chapel
ō	old, over		i *in* veracity
ô	order, shorn		o *in* connect
oi	boy, oil		u *in* crocus

FOREIGN SOUNDS

à	pronounced as in the French *ami*
k̲	pronounced as in the German *ich*
ll	usually pronounced like *y* in *yes* in Latin America; in Spain like the *ll* in *million*
ṅ	a nasal *n* pronounced as in the French *bon*
ñ	pronounced like the *ny* in *canyon*
œ	pronounced as in the French *feu* or the German *böse*
r̅r̅	pronounced as in the Spanish *barranco*
ü	pronounced as in the French *du* or the German *grün*
x	pronounced as in the German *nacht*

Cyclopedia
of
Literary Characters II

Serp-Z

THE SERPENT AND THE ROPE

Author: Raja Rao (1908-   )
Type of work: Novel
Time of action: The late 1940's and the early 1950's
First published: 1960

K. R. Ramaswamy, or **Rama,** the narrator and protagonist. He is a South Indian Brahmin, a research scholar and historian who is living in France while writing his doctoral dissertation on the Albigensian heresy. Twenty-six years old, this handsome, consumptive, gentle, sensitive, and self-conscious intellectual leisurely recounts the story of his family background, his stay in Europe from 1946 to 1954, his marriage with a Frenchwoman at the age of twenty-one, his two trips to India, his discovery of a soul mate in a young Hindu woman studying at Cambridge, his subsequent estrangement from his French wife resulting in divorce, and his determination to go back to India to seek "Truth" under the spiritual guidance of his guru. Deeply rooted in Indian culture and tradition and equally conversant with the philosophies of the West, Rama has chosen the abstract dialectical path in his quest for Truth. He revels in abstruse thinking, metaphysical analysis, aphoristic sayings, and mythological ramblings. His two trips to India have reinforced his spiritual heritage and, at the end of the novel, having finished his thesis, he is ready to embark for India to fulfill his spiritual destiny.

Madeleine (Mado) Roussellin (rōō•sə•làn′), Rama's French wife, a teacher of history. Five years older than Rama, this shy, beautiful, golden-haired intellectual woman is attracted to his spiritual heritage and falls in love with him. After marriage, she tries to be a devoted wife and learns to venerate everything that is sacred to him. Though a self-avowed atheist, she turns to Buddhism to understand India and her Brahmin husband. After the death of her two infant children, however, she becomes cold, withdrawn, and aloof, becoming more and more absorbed in meditation and other Buddhist rituals. Unaware of Rama's emotional involvement with Savithri and his brief sexual encounter with

Lakshmi, she initiates divorce proceedings through her cousin Catherine in order to release him from the bondage of marriage.

Savithri Rathor (sä•vĭt′rē), a young modern Hindu girl, daughter of a ruling prince, studying at Cambridge. Endowed with natural grace and intelligence, this idealistic, restless, and unconventional nineteen-year-old princess is a heavy smoker and attracted to communism. Having an aversion to British rule in India, she defies her betrothal to Pratap, because as a civil servant he had served the British government faithfully. She betrays her fiancé by becoming interested in a young Muslim in London. When she meets Rama, she is dazzled by his intellectual brilliance and metaphysical knowledge. She falls in love with him, solemnizes a ritualistic and symbolic marriage, and becomes his true spiritual bride. Eventually, at Rama's persuasion, she marries Pratap and promises to be a good wife to him.

Vishalakshi, or **Little Mother,** Rama's stepmother widowed at the age of twenty-six. A simple loving woman of meager education, she spends her time in religious ceremonies and in taking care of the large household. She provides Rama with an opportunity to accompany her to Benares and other holy places to perform his father's last rites and thus to rediscover his ancient cultural heritage.

Oncle Charles, Madeleine's uncle, a notary public. Fifty-seven years old and always dressed meticulously, he exudes vitality and looks much younger than his age. A paternal figure, he pays annual visits to Rama and Madeleine and looks after Madeleine in Rama's absence.

Georges Khuschbertieff (khōōsh•byĕr′tĭ•yəf), a brilliant and pious Russian refugee teaching Latin at the College de Garcons. Thirty-two years old, with his grave face, deep voice, twisting arm, and gray-blue flashing eyes, Georges looks like an inspired prophet. A devout Catholic, he manifests deep interest in India in his frequent discussions on Christianity and Vedanta philosophy with Rama. Once fascinated by Madeleine, he finally discovers his marital bliss with her cousin Catherine.

Lakshmi (lŭk'shmē), a married Indian woman with whom Rama has a brief adulterous relationship during his two-week stay in Bombay. Neglected by her husband, this sad, unfulfilled, round, and fine-looking woman hungers for male attention and spends several nights of amorous enjoyment in bed with Rama with the connivance of her husband and children.

Pratap Singh, an Indian civil servant be-

trothed to Savithri. When he learns of Savithri's interest in a young Muslim in London, he solicits Rama's help to persuade her to keep her marital commitment to him.

Catherine (Cathy) Roussellin, Madeleine's cousin, daughter of Oncle Charles. Shy, jovial, maternal, and five years younger than Madeleine, she marries Georges. Rama adopts her as his sister, and she helps him obtain the divorce from Madeleine.

Lezo, a young Basque refugee doing linguistics at Aix University. Deeply interested in Buddhism, he initiates Madeleine into Buddhist studies and teaches her Pali, Chinese, and Tibetan to understand the various forms of Buddhism. A close friend of Georges, he also flirts with Catherine before her marriage.

Chaman L. Sahni

SETTING FREE THE BEARS

Author: John Irving (1942-   )
Type of work: Novel
Time of action: Spring and summer of 1967, with flashbacks to the years 1938-1955
First published: 1968

Hannes Graff (gräf), a failed university student who narrates the first ("Siggy") and third ("Setting Them Free") sections of the novel. A naïve, easygoing young man, Hannes first encounters Siggy Javotnik eating salted radishes on a bench in Rathaus Park and later in Herr Faber's motorcycle shop. Hannes is initially a follower, a student in search of order; his experience with Siggy forces him to act according to his own conscience, though his actions cause harm, suffering, and loss.

Siegfried (Siggy) Javotnik (yă·vŏt'nĭk), a university dropout and motorcycle salesman named for his father Vratno's alias, Siegfried Schmidt, under which Vratno successfully eluded Yugoslav partisans and German soldiers to return to free Vienna in the last days of the Third Reich. Siggy always wears a corduroy duck hunter's jacket and affects a

pipe. A carefree and footloose adventurer who entices Hannes on a cross-country tour of Austria on a 700 cc Royal Enfield motorcycle, Siggy narrates the second section, "The Notebook," divided between his "Pre-History" and twenty-two "Zoo Watches." The "Pre-History" chronicles his mother's family's flight from Vienna ahead of the Nazis and their subsequent misfortunes and his father Vratno's adventures hiding out from the war in Yugoslavia; the "Zoo Watches," logged during a night of clandestine after-hours reconnoitering, form the core of a plan to liberate all the animals from the Heitzinger Zoo. On his way back to rejoin Hannes, Siggy crashes his motorcycle into a trailer of beehives and is stung to death on the road.

Gallen von St. Leonhard, a pretty country girl whom Hannes and Siggy meet on the road. After Siggy's death, she and Hannes become lovers, and she assists him in setting free the zoo animals, with calamitous results. Guilty and upset, she leaves Hannes and returns to Vienna alone.

Vratno Javotnik, Siggy's father, an apolitical linguist who runs afoul of the terrorist Slivnika family during the war and heads into the mountains on a motorcycle, accompanied by Gottlub Wut, a German soldier. Vratno is later killed by Todor Slivnika in Vienna.

Hilke Marter, Siggy's mother, who abandons him in Kaprun when he is ten years old.

Gottlub Wut (gŏt′ləb vōōt), leader of Motorcycle Unit Balkan 4 during the German occupation of Yugoslavia. A scarred and practical former champion racing mechanic, he teaches Vratno how to ride his 1939 Grand Prix racer, and the two hide out together in the mountains of Yugoslavia until Gottlub is killed by his old Balkan 4 comrades, stuffed headfirst down the toilet in a men's room in Maribor.

Ernst Watzek-Trummer (vä′chĕk trōōm′ ər), a chicken farmer who, as a patriotic gesture, goes to Vienna on the eve of the Nazi invasion wearing an eagle suit fashioned from chicken feathers, lard, and pieplates. After Hilke's abandonment and Grandfather Marter's death, he becomes guardian to the young Siggy. An autodidact, he records everything, becoming a kind of self-appointed family historian.

Grandfather Marter, Hilke's proper father, who organizes the family's flight from Vienna to Kaprun to escape the Nazis in Zahn Glanz's stolen taxi. In 1956, after Hilke disappears in search of long-lost Zahn Glanz, he dies suicidally, sledding down the Catapult trail wearing the shopworn and heavily symbolic eagle suit.

Grandmother Marter, Hilke's mother. She is machine-gunned to death standing in the kitchen window of her Vienna home while boldly announcing to the neighborhood the birth of her grandson, Siggy.

Zahn Glanz (tsän glänts), a spirited student of politics and journalism and Hilke's boyfriend before the war. On the day of the Austrian plebiscite against German annexation, he wears Watzek-Trummer's eagle suit and in a series of reckless mishaps becomes a fugitive from the police. When Hilke's family flees Vienna, he stays behind to arrange for bank drafts to be sent to Kaprun, then disappears.

Keff, the driver of the tractor and trailer loaded with beehives with which Siggy fatally collides. Though once in love with Gallen, he now engineers her escape with Hannes.

O. Schrutt (shrōōt), the second watchman at the Heitzinger Zoo. He wears jackboots and carries a truncheon and is routinely torturing the small mammals at night. Apparently a former concentration camp guard, he is left trussed up in a cage when Hannes and Gallen free the animals.

Philip Gerard

THE SETTING SUN

Author: Osamu Dazai (Tsushima Shūji', 1909-1948)
Type of work: Novel
Time of action: Shortly after World War II
First published: Shayō, 1947 (English translation, 1956)

Kazuko, the narrator, a twenty-nine-year-old woman living with her mother. From an aristocratic family whose fortunes are dwindling and well-educated in Western culture, she sees herself as a victim. After her marriage ended in divorce, she returned home to live with her mother. She idolizes her mother's elegant manners but, like her mother, is helpless in handling finances. After leaving their Tokyo estate and servants for a humbler life in the country, they await the return of Naoji, her brother. Kazuko becomes hysterical over her mother's waning health and favoritism of Naoji. She sends frantic love letters to a dissolute writer, Uehara, and eventually pursues him in Tokyo to achieve her purpose of becoming pregnant.

Naoji, her brother, a frustrated writer. He is fearful of everyone. As a student, his aristocratic background was a burden. Then, as a soldier in a losing war, his despair led him to opium. He rationalized that under the effects of drugs he could become friendly and brutal like the common people. Nevertheless, the pose of being coarse never won people's approval and never quelled his innate sensibilities. He ruthlessly impoverishes his mother and sister to pretend to start a publishing business. He even fails at declaring his love for a married woman. His mother's death overwhelms him with guilt. In the end, he commits suicide.

The mother of Kazuko and Naoji, an aris-tocratic lady. A creature from an obsolescent society, she only knows how to comport herself. She understands nothing of finances or survival in the postwar world. She is dependent on her brother, Wada, for important decisions about how and where she will live. She never questions the actions of her brother or her son, Naoji, whom she favors over Kazuko. When she falls ill, she abandons the fight to keep on living and dies docilely and quickly.

Uehara, a debauched novelist who becomes Kazuko's lover. He is a friend of Naoji and transmits money from Kazuko to her brother. Uehara leads a dissolute life but criticizes Naoji for not substituting alcohol for drugs, as he himself has done. He is a farmer's son who became educated but is cynical about life. Though he does not reply to Kazuko's love letters, he cannot resist her when she seeks him out in Tokyo.

Uncle Wada, the mother's younger brother who manages the family finances. A miser, he shows little sympathy for his dying sister or her children. He will not even observe his sister's death with the traditional mourning ceremony. Yet he feels righteous in his stern lecture to Kazuko on how she should live.

Lila Chalpin

SETTLERS OF THE MARSH

Author: Frederick Philip Grove (Felix Paul Greve, 1879-1948)
Type of work: Novel
Time of action: The turn of the twentieth century
First published: 1925

Niels Lindstedt, a pioneer farmer from Sweden. Niels likes to conceive a plan and then carry it out. Remembering his mother's poverty, he makes his dreams come true by clearing a homestead near Minor and Balfour, in the marsh area of Manitoba. His first sight of Amundsen's daughter inspires his visions of a wife and children in a comfortable home. He makes a plan to be ready to have Ellen accept his proposal of marriage. This vision motivates Niels, who is ever ready to help neighbors, a steady worker even in winter, and a fair employer who pays his help well. When Ellen makes it clear that she does not want to be married, however, he leaves and works even harder, though despondent. His lapse with Mrs. Vogel causes him, for the rest of his life, to be plagued by a strong sense of sin because he gave way to his passion. Once out of prison, he goes to Ellen to

say he would accept being a brother to her but is quietly overjoyed with her outpouring that she would attempt to be a wife. Both are very happy, for now they share the same vision.

Ellen Amundsen, the daughter of a neighboring pioneer farmer. Ellen actively works like a man for her father but observed her mother lift and work too hard, which brought on many miscarriages. Others see Ellen as unusual, for after her father's death she continues to farm. She even issues neighbors permits to take off hay and, alongside men, plows a fire break. Though always correct and conservative in her behavior, Ellen loves Niels. She expresses a freer spirit in a pastoral romantic scene: They go through the woods and fields to share a vista from the top of a haystack, and then they huddle together in a hollowed-out niche during a downpour. She refuses Niels's offer of marriage, however, unable to overcome her memories of her mother's grief at having to leave two children in Sweden to be reared by grandparents, of her mother's hard life with her father, and her own promise to her mother never to marry. That she loves Niels is very evident, for she wants him to continue to be her one and only friend. Years later, she still loves him, and she attends to his house until he returns from prison. When he calls, she finally tells him that she has been wrong: She will try marriage and wants his children.

Clara Vogel, a widow who later marries Niels. Clara had inherited a farm near his homestead. Portrayed as a well-dressed woman whose eyes look for men and whose voice is ready with repartee, Clara first meets Niels at the Lunds' Sunday gatherings. She chances upon Niels and intercepts him in the hall of the hotel. Just refused by Ellen, he succumbs to Clara's advances. The next morning, he proposes, and Clara, with only a slight hesitation, accepts. In the farmhouse, she gets meals for several months but eventually keeps to her room, which is furnished with her boudoir frills. Her laziness and primping are tolerated by Niels, and, whereas Clara might have responded to being ordered about by Niels, he treats her too well. When she ignores his best friend Nelson and his family during their visit at Christmas, she no longer restrains her disinterest and isolation. Later, she lets herself be found in compromising situations with men, until Niels finally shoots her.

Bobby, Niels's faithful employee and friend. At first, Bobby worked for his foster father, Mr. Lund. Then his brother-in-law Nelson, married to his sister Olga, paid Bobby to work for him, until Niels offers full regular pay. A man yet in his teens, Bobby is happy when his steady work with Niels earns for him wage increases as time and circumstances warrant. On Sundays, he goes visiting, especially after Niels marries Clara, whose presence makes Bobby blush. Young, hardworking, and faithful, Bobby eventually not only takes care of Niels but also establishes his own farm. He marries a capable wife, and they have five children. Though poor, Bobby looks after Niels's farm during the six and a half years Niels is in prison and banks its profits. His honesty and reliability are rewarded by the fair Niels, and Bobby is given comfortable affluence.

Greta McCormick Coger

THE SEVEN AGES

Author: Eva Figes (1932-   )
Type of work: Novel
Time of action: The 1980's, with flashbacks to earlier periods
First published: 1986

The Narrator, a midwife retired after a thirty-five-year practice, the mother of Kate and Sally, the grandmother of Emily and Adam. After years spent dedicated to women in her

work as midwife and in her role as a single mother, the narrator feels newly aware of her solitude. In the quiet darkness of the country she is visited by memories, by women's voices, and by tales from far history.

Granny Martin, a pioneer in family planning, grandmother of the narrator. In Granny Martin the narrator finds precious knowledge, a clever mind, and the example of a woman who has "done things" with her talents. Before the Great War, the young Granny Martin works in a family planning clinic begun by Dora, granddaughter of The Matriarch. Although the clinic is scorned and attacked by men, it is a valuable resource for women dying piecemeal from too much childbirth.

Sophie, The Matriarch, mistress of the manor house and astute manager of family businesses. As Sophie, she is a lonely, timid, and delicate heiress who is restrained by her various guardians. As the black-robed Matriarch, she is respected and feared by her household. When Sophie meets a man who laughs at her strict and dour housekeeper, she marries him. Life with the "Master" ruins her health; in the first seven years of marriage she bears seven children. It is also ruinous to her manor, for the Master sells her meadows and home farm without her knowledge. The semi-invalid Sophie suffers from the local doctor's ignorance, enduring his leeches and bleedings, his Victorian outrage, and his mistaken ideas about the female reproductive system. Freedom and The Matriarch are born together when the doctor and the Master die in a train and carriage collision.

Lady Lucy, a notable descendant of Lady Aethelfrida and mistress of the manor. A capable and resilient woman, Lady Lucy has abilities and family loyalties that prove to be great. During the seventeeth century, Lady Lucy and her sister, Lady Sarah, are caught on opposite sides during the Civil War. Colonel Francis is busy levying troops for Parliament, so Lady Lucy must manage the manor, collect rents, send provisions to her husband, and maintain a constant prepara-

tion for siege. Seven months pregnant, she worries about the three younger children trapped with her in the manor house. She loses her unborn baby when she learns that her eldest son, Edward, has left the University of Oxford to become a captain of horse. Colonel Francis is purged from the House and imprisoned, later returning to the manor as a ghostly figure.

Lady Sarah, sister to Lady Lucy. Pregnant and penniless, Lady Sarah realizes the folly of a civil war and is shaken by constant, hysterical laughter. Lady Sarah's husband supports the royal cause and flees to France. Her home burned, Lady Sarah takes refuge with her sister.

Alice, nun and later mother, great-great-granddaughter of Judith, and inheritor of the family's skill in healing. The simple, hard-working, unlettered Alice labors for the nuns. After the dissolution of nunneries and monasteries under Henry VIII, she is sent home. She marries a priest and bears six children; after the death of Edward and the coming to power of his sister Mary, Alice's husband is deprived of his benefice for falsely marrying a nun. Under Elizabeth her husband returns to her, confused and old.

Judith, a midwife and healer in feudal Britain, granddaughter of Emma-of-the-caul (who was granddaughter in turn of Moriuw). Black-haired and blue-eyed, Judith is as beautiful as Bedda, her wild mother who was drowned for witchcraft. She is successor in herbal medicine to her grandmother Emma. Fearless of danger, she attempts to defend herself from a series of rapes but in turn gives birth to six children, all of whom die during a pestilence. Half-crazed by grief, she succumbs willingly to the advances of a friar and conceives again.

Moriuw (môr′o͞o), midwife and healer in pre-Christian Britain. Regarded by many as a witch because of her herbal skill, Moriuw is under the protection of the Lord Edwin and the Lady Aethelfrida because she oversees the birth of their first living child. Her

female descendants learn Moriuw's skills and, like her, show signs of magical abilities: visionary dreams, cauled birth, and healing powers.

Marlene Youmans

THE SEVEN DAYS OF CREATION

Author: Vladimir Maximov (Lev Samsonov, 1930-   )
Type of work: Novel
Time of action: The Russian Revolution through the 1960's
First published: Sem dnei tvoreniia, 1971 (English translation, 1974)

Pyotr Vasilievich Lashkov, an elderly Communist Party functionary who becomes a Christian. In the winter of his life, Pyotr, a self-righteous autocrat and a faithful Communist, realizes that he is isolated from his relatives and from other people, without any meaningful relationship, and facing bleak emptiness. Deciding to renew his neglected family ties, after all of his six children have abandoned him, he visits one close relative after another, only to discover that most of them have not fared much better. His daughter Antonina fills the void in Pyotr's later life with her religious zeal and with the renewed faith in the future, symbolized by her newborn son. Pyotr belatedly realizes that being an honest but stern Communist, without a genuine rapport with fellow human beings, leads to alienaton and general resentment by others. With the help of several people (Antonina, Gupak, the two grandsons), his empty existence is enriched through love and caring for other people. He is finally able to reconcile his Communist beliefs with an active loving religion. The final words of the novel ("He went, and he knew. He knew, and he believed.") symbolize his spiritual rebirth.

Andrei Lashkov, his brother, a warden in the Kurakin forest. Though driven by the same urge as all the Lashkovs (to bring honor and justice into life and to do what is best for everybody), Andrei chooses a different path. Instead of wielding a political power, he opts for a forest service, for only in closeness with nature and in communion with the forest does he feel at peace. He thus escapes the silent agony his older brother goes through.

Vasilii Lashkov (vä•sĭ′lĭy), another brother, a janitor in Moscow. Vasilii escapes the tutelage and domination of Pyotr by moving to Moscow, but at a price of a drab, joyless life and of his being alienated from everyone and everything. Even though he is his own man, he is so embittered that even a belated visit by Pyotr fails to restore a good relationship that may have brought happiness.

Antonina Lashkov, Pyotr's daughter, whose return home with an infant son reinforces Pyotr's belief in religion. A middle-aged woman who has become an alcoholic, she finds happiness and peace late in life, not so much through actual happenings as through a religious awakening. She is able to convey that message to her influential but frustrated father. Together, they find a new meaning in life through love and genuine concern for each other and for fellow human beings, finally realizing that they are not alone in this world but a part of the unity of all things.

Vadim Lashkov, Pyotr's grandson, a debauched variety artist. At times, Vadim reflects the author's own experiences as a young man. Finding himself in the spiritual and moral desert of Soviet society, Vadim gropes in the dark for a long time, until he, too, finds peace with himself and fulfillment through his art, though not before he suffers through a painful period of heartache, misunderstanding, and alienation. Always surrounded by strangers and always doing the wrong things, constantly on the move and never having time to get attached to things, Vadim finally becomes reconciled with his grandfather (who needs him more than Vadim needs him, as the only male offspring of the family). More important, he, like Antonina and Pyotr, is helped by the religious soul-healer Gupak. Even though the results are not visible yet, Vadim is on his way to total recovery.

Gupak, an elderly friend of the Lashkovs. A

religious fanatic, in a positive sense, Gupak is able to spread his beneficial influence and help several people searching for salvation. His belief in traditional Christian values parallels those of the author himself, which, in turn, indicates the resurgence of a religious life among the Soviet populace thirsty for spiritual rebirth. His stoic acceptance of his impending death from cancer underlines the strength of his faith, which he is able to convey to others as well.

Vasa D. Mihailovich

THE SEVEN MADMEN

Author: Roberto Arlt (1900-1942)
Type of work: Novel
Time of action: The 1920's
First published: Los siete locos, 1929 (English translation, 1984)

Augusto Remo Erdosain (ou•gōōs′tō r̄r̄ĕ′ mō ĕr•dō•sä•ēn′), the protagonist, a hapless dreamer who, at the beginning of the novel, loses both his wife (to a virile military captain) and his low-paying job as a bill collector for a sugar company in Buenos Aires (because he has embezzled funds). Frustrated, humiliated, and emotionally overwrought, Remo surrenders himself to fantasies of amorous and financial success, and to the crackpot schemes of a subversive group that he joins. He fancies himself an inventor, and his desire to fortify his precarious existence is reflected in his project of coating roses with copper to preserve them. Out of resentment, he plans to kill his wife's obnoxious cousin, Barsut, who has turned him in for embezzlement.

The Astrologer, a charismatic charlatan who leads a pseudorevolutionary cell of down-and-outers and plans to take over Argentina in a *coup d'état*. With his rhombus-shaped face and broken nose, his hulking frame, and his kinky, tangled hair, the Astrologer's looks are as bizarre as his ideas. His plan for revolution is elitist in intention: The happy few will benefit from the labor of

the masses, who will be regimented for maximum productivity. The Astrologer's subversive society meets at his house in a wooded suburb of Buenos Aires.

Arturo Haffner, called the **Melancholy Ruffian,** a pimp and member of the Astrologer's activist cell. Haffner despises women, seeing only potential earnings in them. He befriends Erdosain at the Astrologer's house and gives him the money he needs to pay back the funds he has embezzled.

Elsa, Erdosain's wife, a woman brought up in some luxury who has sacrificed herself to live with him but reaches the end of her patience with the poverty and hopelessness of his life. She goes off with Captain Belaúnde after a tense scene with Erdosain at his apartment. Elsa still loves Erdosain and promises to return to him. She leaves the Captain almost immediately, after he makes an offensive pass at her, and ends up in a nervous crisis at a hospital, unbeknown to Erdosain.

Eduardo Ergueta (ĕr•gĕ′tä), a corpulent pharmacist who is a compulsive gambler, religious fanatic, and member of the Astrologer's group. A deluded small-time prophet, Ergueta has married a prostitute, Hipólita, in order to save her. He refuses, however, to save Erdosain from his predicament by lending him money to pay back the sugar company. Ergueta's ravings eventually land him in a mental hospital.

Hipólita (ē·pō′lē·tä), a redheaded prostitute married to Ergueta and befriended by Erdosain. Hipólita is not physically impaired, but she is called the Lame Woman or Lame Whore by Ergueta because she has, as he says, gone astray. This sobriquet sticks to her. Formerly a domestic servant, Hipólita made a calculated decision to become a prostitute and thereby take greater control of her life. She has a prostitute's cynical view of men but seems to adopt an almost motherly attitude toward Erdosain. She plans, however, to betray his confidence—Erdosain has told her about the proposed murder of Barsut—by blackmailing his accomplice, the Astrologer.

Gregorio Barsut, Elsa's cousin, who is locked into an ongoing contest of wills with Erdosain. Barsut's rapacious personality is mirrored in his shaven head, his bony nose like the beak of a bird of prey, and his pointed wolf's ears. He punches Erdosain upon learning of Elsa's departure and then confesses that it was he who denounced Erdosain to the sugar company. Then and there Erdosain resolves to have Barsut killed, and, in fact, the revolutionaries kidnap Barsut on Erdosain's suggestion. Barsut is saved from death by the Astrologer, who arranges with him to simulate the execution in front of Erdosain.

The Gold Seeker, a young member of the activist group whose incongruous physical makeup combines aspects of a cardsharp, a boxer, and a jockey. He mesmerizes the group with (mainly fictional) tales of his expeditions in southern Argentina, and he suggests a southern region for the subversives' training camp. The Seeker makes friends with Erdosain, whom he impresses with his cult of violence and adventure.

The Major, an army officer affiliated with the Astrologer's group who plans to use the revolutionary movement as a provocation for a military coup.

John Deredita

A SEVERED HEAD

Author: Iris Murdoch (1919-   )
Type of work: Novel
Time of action: The early 1960's
First published: 1961

Martin Lynch-Gibbon, the forty-one-year-old, oversensitive, intellectual narrator, a wine tradesman by vocation. Neurotic, misguided, and generally naïve, Martin tells his story of love, romance, lust, incest, and adultery in an aura of 1960's liberalism toward these matters. At the beginning he is happy and in love with both his wife, Antonia, and his mistress, Georgie Hands. This stability ends when Antonia reveals her affair with and coming marriage to Palmer Anderson, Martin's best friend. Martin tries to convince himself that he loves and must have both women, and he pursues this end by complacently and placidly accepting the situation. Meanwhile, Honor Klein, Palmer's half-sister, appears on the scene; consequently, Martin falls in love with her to lose his infatuation for wife and mistress. Thwarted by Klein, he attacks her physically though not sexually, only shortly thereafter to realize that he has homosexual inclinations for Palmer. After Antonia and Palmer decide not to marry, she returns home for a short-lived period of peace and reconciliation, until she announces that she will marry Alexander, Martin's brother and her lover of many years. At the end, Martin is left alone, but with some great though ambiguous hope for capturing Honor Klein.

Antonia, Martin's forty-six-year-old wife. Her most overriding characteristic is her beauty. Graceful, accomplished, and sophisticated, her emotions rule her conduct to blunt her efforts to know and to keep stability and happiness. Antonia, intense and passionate, always professes love for her husband, particularly so on the two occasions when she informs him of her lovers, Palmer and Alexander. After her relationship with Palmer disintegrates, her reunion with Martin is short-lived; at the end she is to marry Martin's brother, Alexander.

Georgie Hands, Martin's twenty-six-year-old lover and an instructor at the London School of Economics. Martin loves her for her nature, which is antithetical to Antonia's in many ways: She is tough, independent, and witty, and possesses a dryness and lack of intensity. During the novel, she becomes lover first to Palmer, then to Alexander. She is insecure because she had aborted Martin's child, a factor that partially contributes to her attempted suicide midway through the novel. She is last seen at the London airport, headed to America with Palmer.

Alexander, Martin's older brother, lover to Antonia and to Georgie, sculptor. Artistic, flamboyant, cunning, and manipulative, Alexander has a history of seducing Martin's lovers, taking them away from his brother. Al-

exander is sculpting a head that has "imagination" rather than an actual head as its model. At the end of the work, Alexander is paired with Antonia.

Palmer Anderson, a psychoanalyst to Antonia, best friend to Martin, and lover to Antonia, Georgie, and Honor Klein, his half sister. Professionally astute and jargonistic, he assumes superiority over all other characters except Honor. He copes with reality by changing it, and, like the other characters, cannot succeed either as a lover or husband or person. The most constant thing in his life seems to be his affair with Antonia.

Honor Klein, an anthropologist who spends about half of her time in Germany, a half sister and lover to Palmer, and the final object of Martin's desire. Martin first describes her as a "middle-aged Germanic spinster," and he is repelled by her until he realizes that he loves her rather than Antonia or Georgie. Shrewd, perceptive, and effectual, Honor repeatedly functions so as to prove disconcerting to other characters, particularly to Martin. She is a woman of intellect and accomplishment, a character never wrong, yet never the better for her astuteness about the motivations of others.

Rosemary, Martin's sister and an emotional eunuch. Rosemary, always stable yet alienated from the other characters, stands in contrast to those who would perpetually love and lose. She is divorced, at once blissfully and bitterly so.

Carl Singleton

SEXUAL PERVERSITY IN CHICAGO

Author: David Mamet (1947-   )
Type of work: Play
Time of action: The 1970's
First produced: 1974

Danny Shapiro, an insecure twenty-year-old assistant office manager who seeks the acceptance of others. He simply wants to be-

long. Therefore, Danny listens with awe to Bernie's tales of sexual prowess and asks questions that feed Bernie's ego. To please

Bernie, his replies are generally nondirective reflections of Bernie's statements. Danny is a loyal friend to both Bernie and Deb. He defends Bernie against their coworkers' verbal assaults, and he refuses to discuss the details of his relationship with Deborah. Danny is unable to open himself to others, however, and retreats from his own emotions into the safety of patterned communication. Consequently, he rejects Deb when she wants to know more about his inner being, and he returns to Bernie. Danny is sensitive enough to recognize the one point at which Bernie appears to have lost himself as well as to accept Bernie's hurried masking of that one vulnerable moment.

Bernard Litko (Bernie), Danny's friend and coworker, a 1970's heterosexual American male stereotype locked into exaggerating his sexual prowess to validate his masculine identity and desirability. He is homophobic. Bernie showers his speech with obscenities to prove his superiority and believes that females should be subordinated and mistreated. He, too, is insecure. Bernie lies about his occupation in order to attract women, deals ineffectively with a confrontive female, and is jealous of Danny and Deb's relationship. He has centered his life on genitalia, female seductiveness and willingness as well as male size and endurance. Bernie focuses totally on appearance and blames women both for his sexual arousal and for his sexual rejections.

Although he once questions the meaning of his words, Bernie immediately reverts to the security of his ritualistic behaviors.

Deborah Soloman (Deb), an attractive, twenty-three-year-old professional illustrator who wants to be loved but habitually feels misunderstood. She enters into a sexual (then cohabitative) relationship with Danny in an effort to establish emotional security but alternates a desire for closeness with alienating behaviors to protect herself. Deb blames herself for their eventual dissolution and uses her friend Joan as her primary psychological support. Deborah is a dependent person in conflict between what she believes that she wants and what she is willing to risk.

Joan Webber, a kindergarten teacher who lives with Deb, a bitter woman who views sexual intercourse as mutually destructive behavior and from which she has withdrawn. She is predominantly hostile toward men (for example, she sees premature ejaculation as a consequence of the male's desire to punish her). As a dramatic foil for Bernie, Joan could be described as a 1970's American castrating female stereotype. Intelligent and witty, Joan uses negative philosophical patter (that she herself interrupts for practical considerations) to fuel her own sense of depression, alienation, and helplessness.

Kathleen Mills

THE SHADOW OF A GUNMAN

Author: Sean O'Casey (John Casey, 1880-1964)
Type of work: Play
Time of action: May, 1920
First produced: 1923

Donal Davoren, an aspiring poet who shares a tenement room with Mr. Shields. A man of about thirty, with a strong romantic streak, Davoren evinces a mixture of weakness and strength. When a rumor begins that he is a "gunman" on the Republican side of the civil war, Davoren proves susceptible to the admiration and flattery that his new reputation brings him. This seemingly innocent deception is the foundation of his romance with Minnie Powell, but when it threatens to bear serious consequences, and the British authorities appear, Davoren weakens and proves unable to face danger.

Seumas Shields, a peddler of shoddy goods, a lazy and superstitious man who loudly voices both nationalist sentiments and condemnation of the Republican gunmen. Shields has pretensions to literary and political ideals, but his ideals are merely catchphrases inserted into his conversation. His chief enemy, in reality, is his landlord, who demands payment of rent past due. Like Davoren, he proves cowardly in the face of British military authority.

Tommy Owens, a resident of the tenement, a small, unexceptional man of roughly age twenty-five. He is a "hero-worshiper," who breaks into patriotic song at any opportunity and who vows that he would die for Ireland. Owens is primarily responsible for creating the false public image of Davoren as a gunman.

Minnie Powell, a working woman who resides in the tenement. She is self-assured, good-looking, and carefully dressed. She is twenty-three years old. Despite her lack of education, she is intelligent and poised: Davoren is attracted as much by these qualities in her as he is flattered by her admiration for the "gunman." She is flirtatious, even frivolous, with Davoren, but ultimately she is the only one who acts bravely and idealistically in the final crisis of the play.

Adolphus Grigson, a resident of the tenement, a well-fed clerk of about forty-five, with a tendency to drink. A domestic tyrant who bullies his wife. Grigson is avowedly anti-Republican. He is, nevertheless, ruthlessly terrorized and humiliated by the British auxiliaries who raid the building, but he denies this fact, claiming to have faced them bravely.

Mrs. Grigson, a worn-out woman looking much older than her forty years, who is in a constant state of worry or panic. It is she who brings the news of Minnie's arrest and death.

Mr. Malone, a business associate of Shields and a genuine Republican gunman who appears only briefly in the play. He leaves in the room of Shields and Davoren a bag that proves to contain bombs, and which Minnie attempts to hide—an action leading to her arrest and death.

Mrs. Henderson, a neighbor and local authority on any topic of conversation. A large, good-natured woman, she helps to spread the rumor of Davoren's political activities.

Mr. Gallogher, a neighbor and friend of Mrs. Henderson. He is a small, nervous man. He is harassed by disorderly neighbors, and, at Mrs. Henderson's request, he writes a letter to the Irish Republican Army asking for assistance, which he gives to Davoren. The possession of this letter becomes a danger during the raid.

Heidi J. Holder

SHAKESPEARE'S DOG

Author: Leon Rooke (1936-   )
Type of work: Novel
Time of action: 1585
First published: 1983

Hooker, a mongrel. He has a long nose, a whitish smear behind the ears, lean haunches, and a sturdy tail. Inquisitive, aggressive, and lecherous, he gets aroused by any bitch, including his twin sister Terry, and even by Anne Hathaway. Adopted by William Shakespeare, Hooker saves him from drowning in the Avon River and provides him with phrases that will become famous in his plays. Considering dogs to be as intelligent and important as humans, Hooker despises Shakespeare's accepting conservative beliefs, such as the chain of being, his lack of compassion, and his exaltation of body over soul. Having killed a deer in Sir Thomas Lucy's park at Charlecote, and therefore being in danger of severe punishment, Hooker is overjoyed when his master decides to leave Stratford for London.

William Shakespeare, an aspiring writer. Highbrowed and balding at age twenty-one, he has been married for three years to Anne Hathaway, whom he impregnated. Now he attempts to write in an upstairs room, but domestic affairs continually interrupt him, and he frequently comes to blows or bed with his wife. He chafes at small-town life but aspires to buy New Place if he can escape to make his fame and fortune in London, seat of the Queen, about which he fantasizes.

Anne Shakespeare, née **Hathaway,** eight years older than her husband, a stocky, lusty, and earthy woman oppressed by the chores of motherhood and unalterably suspicious of and opposed to her husband's plans to leave her in Stratford while he goes to London.

John Shakespeare, William's father. Now white-haried and bloated with dropsy, he used to be a citizen of importance in Stratford, but quarrels and debts have driven him into staying at home. There he drinks Warwickshire brown ale, deplores contemporary trends such as the spread of enclosures and the increase in Hathaways under his roof, and reminisces about his wooing Mary Arden thirty years ago.

Wolfsleach, a dog. He lusts after Marr, Hooker's steady bitch, and is defeated by him in a fight. Apparently dead, he eventually recovers and runs off with Terry, Hooker's twin sister.

Christopher M. Armitage

SHAME

Author: Salman Rushdie (1947-   )
Type of work: Novel
Time of action: c. 1920 through the early 1980's
First published: 1983

Omar Khayyam Shakil, a physician friend of Iskander Harappa and son-in-law of General Raza Hyder. Omar is an antihero, who describes himself as peripheral to his own life. He grows up in a secluded, crumbling palace on what seems to him like the edge of the world, in an unnamed country that has all the attributes of Pakistan. His mother is one of three sisters who reveal to no one, including Omar, which of the three gave birth to him or who his father is. At age twelve, he leaves home for school, becomes a physician, and engages in a life of debauchery with Iskander Harappa. He becomes obsessed with and marries Sufiya Zinobia Hyder, the retarded daughter of General Hyder. His life is always shaped by other actors, by his three mothers and by Iskander, Raza, and Sufiya. He is finally executed at about age sixty-five, accused, wrongly, of having killed General Hyder.

Chhunni (chū′nē),
Munnee, and
Bunny Shakil, Omar's three mothers. They live walled off from the world, receiving supplies into their mansion through a dumbwaiter. After Omar leaves, they have another son, Babar. Babar is killed by General Raza Hyder. Years later, the three women execute General Hyder, which results in Omar's death.

Iskander Harappa, prime minister, a character based on Pakistani Prime Minister Zulfikar Ali Bhutto. Iskander is a rich playboy until his friends and relatives begin to gain high positions in society. Out of competitive sense, not social concern, he becomes serious, giving up his playboy life. He uses his charm and a radical program of "Islamic socialism" to gain power, based on mass support. Cynical and ruthless, he becomes prime minister and places his friend and competitor, General Raza Hyder, in command of the army. Iskander rules for four years, is jailed for two, and is then executed after Raza takes over. He returns as a ghostly adviser to General Hyder, reading to him from Niccolò Machiavelli's works.

Raza Hyder, general and president. Raza, based on Pakistani president Zia-ul-Haq, is a short, mustachioed, proud man, with impeccable manners and a deceiving air of humility. His forehead is marked by the *gatta*, a permanent bruise stemming from fervent praying with his forehead on the floor. After he overthrows Iskander, he rejects the prime minister's social program and creates an Islamic theocratic state. When he loses power, he flees, dressed as a woman, with Omar. Omar's mothers kill him.

Sufiya Zinobia Hyder, daughter of General Raza Hyder and wife of Omar Shakil. Sufiya, called Shame by her mother, is retarded, symbolizing purity and innocence. She is a saintly figure who absorbs the shame of those around her who commit brutal acts. Shame, internalized, emerges as rage and violence, in nations or individuals. At age twelve, the shy, quiet girl kills 218 turkeys, pulling their heads off and their entrails out. After Omar marries her, she erupts in violence again, killing several men, pulling their heads off after having sex with them.

Omar keeps her sedated and chained for months, before she breaks free and turns into a legendary white panther, killing people all over Pakistan, creating part of the uproar that leads to the overthrow of her father, and, indirectly, leading to his and Omar's deaths. The white panther then disappeared, never to be heard from again, and was perhaps, the narrator says, a collective fantasy of an oppressed people.

Maulana Dawood (mä·län′ä), an Islamic divine, a beardy serpent, the narrator says, who becomes a spiritual adviser to General Hyder. When Dawood dies, he joins Iskander as a ghostly presence sitting on General Hyder's shoulders. He pours Islamic fundamentalism into the general's right ear, while Iskander reads Machiavelli into his left.

Bilquìs Hyder and
Rani Harappa, the wives of Raza and Iskander. Both are publicly honored but privately ignored as their husbands begin their rise to power. Both accept their subordination quietly. Bilquìs sinks into eccentricity and madness. Rani knits shawls, recording the memory of her husband, who achieves quasi-sainthood after his death. Her shawl shows him as he really was: a philandering, authoritarian, ruthless man, determined to obliterate his opponents rather than merely defeat them. The wives symbolize their husbands' failures as statesmen. Men cannot create democratic societies, as Iskander wanted, or moral theocracies, as Raza wanted, if they cannot tolerate freedom and justice in their personal lives.

William E. Pemberton

THE SHELTERING SKY

Author: Paul Bowles (1910-   )
Type of work: Novel
Time of action: After World War II
First published: 1949

Port Moresby, an independently wealthy American. Fascinated by maps, he defines himself as a traveler rather than a tourist, feeling that he has no permanent home but instead journeying continuously from one place to another. Married to Kit Moresby for twelve years, he realizes that they are experiencing difficulties and arranges an excursion to Africa with the hope of sorting through their problems. At the last instant, he panics about the trip and invites Tunner, one of his close friends, to join them. Both husband and wife wish Tunner would leave them alone, Port because he longs for intimacy with Kit and she because Tunner continually makes advances toward her, but, because of the lack of communication, neither expresses that desire clearly to the other. Instead, Port turns to prostitutes out of frustration, and Kit is eventually seduced by Tunner. Ironically, Port contracts typhoid and dies, alone, while Kit has a rendezvous with Tunner.

Kit Moresby, Port's wife. An attractive, small blonde with an intense gaze, her white skin draws attention from African men and jealousy from African women. Quite superstitious, she is excellent at interpreting everyday occurrences as good or bad omens. Tunner's presence during the trip bothers her, but she tolerates him because of his friendship with Port. After she is seduced by the young man, the remorse she experiences causes her to refrain from voicing her disgust with the various traumatic circumstances the threesome undergo. After Port's death, she appears to reject Western civilization and hides out in the desert.

Tunner, Port's friend and Kit's paramour. Handsome, sturdy, and young, he is a proud and persistent individual who refuses to acknowledge the hints dropped by both Port and Kit that his companionship is no longer desired. When he and Kit are separated from Port, he offers her several glasses of champagne and then sleeps with her. Kit is overcome by guilt, but Tunner sees the encounter simply as another conquest. After Port's death, however, Tunner becomes greatly distressed by Kit's disappearance.

Mrs. Lyle, a photographer and writer from Australia. Belligerent and boisterous, she is large and sallow-skinned, with expressionless black eyes. Described by Port as the loneliest woman he has ever met, she seems to be motivated primarily by fear of relationships. Even with her son, Eric, she communicates mainly by shrieking at him. Her favorite conversation topics include the stupidity of the French, the laziness of the Arabs, and her own ill health.

Eric Lyle, Mrs. Lyle's spoiled and greedy son. Allusions are made to his probable homosexual tendencies, but one witness claims he has seen mother and son together in bed. Always running low on financial resources, Eric tries to befriend the Moresbys by offering to drive them to their next destination so they will not have to travel by train. In the process, he manages to borrow three hundred francs and to steal Port's and Tunner's passports.

Belqassim (bĕl·kä·sēm′), Kit's second husband. Finding Kit alone in the desert, he rapes her, kidnaps her, then marries her, much to the dismay of his three other wives.

Coleen Maddy

SHIKASTA

Author: Doris Lessing (1919-   )
Type of work: Novel
Time of action: c. 35,000 B.C. to c. A.D. 2000, but mainly the twentieth century
First published: 1979

Johor, incarnated as **George Sherban,** a representative of the galactic empire Canopus to the planet Earth, named Shikasta in the novel. Shikasta is Johor's worst assignment, for he must watch its decline from the golden age when it was named Rohanda to its low point in the twentieth century. Rohanda/ Shikasta/Earth once had two races: the Giants, who live twelve to fifteen thousand years and are sixteen to eighteen feet tall, and the Natives, who live five hundred years and are half the height of the Giants, with the former acting as benevolent guides and teachers to the latter. Johor witnesses and reports on the degeneration of both races as a mystical flow of goodwill called "the Lock" between Canopus and Shikasta breaks down and chaos replaces an idyllic pastoral life. He travels about in various incarnations, including that of a "shaggy" Native, attempting to salvage what he can and opposing the influence of Shammat, a criminal planet allied with the evil empire Puttioria. Johor ultimately resurfaces as George Sherban, a young man tutored by a remarkable series of Canopean influences as he lives with his family in Nigeria, Kenya, Morocco, and Tunisia. George, though basically Scotch-Irish, has an Indian grandfather; he is tall, with ivory skin, black hair, and black eyes, easily passing for an Indian or an Arab. He becomes an international youth leader, helping to organize Children's Camps for refugees and orphans and Youth Armies, which attempt to maintain civilization under the Chinese socialist overlordship now controlling Europe. George's greatest achievement is in his role as prosecutor at the Mock Trial of the white race sponsored by the Combined Youth Armies of the World. George's artful defusing of the hostility against the whites by admitting their culpability for colonial and other misdeeds circumvents a planned genocide of all remaining Europeans by the newly resurgent black, brown, and "golden" races. After the trial, George continues his work for human betterment, developing geometrically organized cities in the Andes in South America and siring his family. When his work is finished, he dies.

Benjamin Sherban, George's fraternal twin, who is always contrasted to George. Benjamin is heavy, tending toward fat, with curly brown hair, blue-gray eyes, and a reddish-brown skin, the result of perpetual sunburn in the North African climate. As an adolescent, he is cynical, sarcastic, surly, and in constant conflict with his sister Rachel. Benjamin the boy is clearly made to feel inferior by the near-perfection of Johor/George; as he grows up, he comes to accept his second-class status, takes on the supervision of the Children's Camps, and makes his peace with George and Rachel. He acts as an assistant to defense counsel Taufiq/John Brent-Oxford in the Mock Trial of the white race. He ends up on a remote Pacific island in a settlement committed to starting over life.

Rachel Sherban, George and Benjamin's younger sister. Her journal, which comprises a substantial part of the middle of the book, gives a quirky, rather earthy point of view of George and Benjamin through the eyes of a somewhat spoiled and petulant teenage sister. Like Benjamin, Rachel is intimidated by George's casual success in all of his many endeavors and by his enormous influence on all around him. Rachel's jealousy is complicated by her schoolgirl crush on George, but she learns tolerance and responsibility, finally sacrificing herself for her brother. Rachel's rich description of life in a tenement in Morocco is a high point in the novel.

Taufiq, like Johor a secret agent of Canopus, born on Earth as **John Brent-Oxford.** He attains success as a lawyer and politician but is corrupted by the malign influences of Earth/Shikasta and begins to live only for his own pleasure, in complete contradiction to the Canopean ideal of service. His neglect of his duties leads to failure and disaster for a number of people, whose unhappy stories are listed by Johor. Taufiq/John Brent-Oxford, at the end a frail, white-haired old man, redeems himself at the Mock Trial by acting as defense counsel for the white race and behaving with wisdom and decency. He is killed by a falling rock when an unidentified airplane bombs the Greek amphitheater where the trial is held.

Andrew Macdonald

THE SHINING

Author: Stephen King (1947-   )
Type of work: Novel
Time of action: The 1970's
First published: 1977

Jack Torrance, a former preparatory school teacher in his early thirties, who has taken the job of winter caretaker for the isolated Overlook Hotel, high in the Colorado Rockies. He hopes to use this time to restore intimacy to his relationships with his wife, Wendy, and his young son, Danny, and also to renew his earlier successes as a writer. These intentions are complicated and threatened by the darker elements in Jack's character: a history of alcoholism, a background of child abuse (learned from his father and already manifested in one episode against Danny), an uncontrolled temper, and self-destructive thoughts and tendencies which, in the past, have led to a serious contemplation of suicide. These flaws make Jack especially vulnerable to the malevolent powers of the Overlook, and he is led eventually to betray loyalties to wife and son. Yet, in the final moment of his life, the strength of his love for Danny overpowers even the evil persona with which the hotel has endowed him, as a final glimpse at Jack's almost lost humanity materializes and then is destroyed in a climactic explosion and conflagration.

Wendy Torrance, Jack's pretty wife, also in her early thirties. Despite past problems, she is committed to her husband, but only when this commitment does not conflict with her loyalty to her young son. She joins Jack at the Overlook with the highest hopes, but when the vicious ghosts of the hotel begin to absorb Jack's personality, she finds unforeseen strength to protect Danny and to survive their encounter with the Overlook.

Danny "Doc" Torrance, Jack and Wendy's five-year-old son gifted with "the shining," a telepathic ability to read the thoughts of other people and to visualize future events. It is Danny's presence and his special abilities that seem to activate the stored-up evils of the Overlook. Danny inspires great love in his father, a love that is Jack's strongest claim to respectability and, ultimately, to his own humanity.

Dick Hallorann, a single black man in his sixties, the summer-season cook at the Overlook Hotel. When he meets the Torrances in the autumn, on closing day, he feels an instant affinity with Danny, because Hallorann, too, has a touch of "the shining." An urgent telepathic message from Danny eventually summons the kindly Hallorann to return from Florida to the Overlook in the depth of winter to rescue Wendy and Danny.

Albert Shockley, a shadowy character, a single man of independent, and perhaps illegally obtained, wealth. During Jack's days at Stovington Prep, Shockley, a board member, was Jack's drinking buddy and fellow alcoholic. More recently, as a part-owner of the Overlook, he is the man responsible for Jack gaining employment as caretaker. By telephone he later discourages Jack's interest in researching and writing the history of the Overlook and its unsavory background.

Stuart Ullman, the short, plump, officious manager of the Overlook. He gives Jack Torrance the caretaker's job, against his better judgment, because of Shockley's influence.

Delbert Grady, the ghost of an earlier Overlook caretaker who murdered his wife and two young daughters many winters before, apparently in a fit of cabin fever. He is one of Jack's hallucinations during the period when the hotel seduces and overpowers Jack's personality.

Laura Stone Barnard

THE SHIPYARD

Author: Juan Carlos Onetti (1909-   )
Type of work: Novel
Time of action: The late 1950's
First published: El astillero, 1961 (English translation, 1968)

E. Larsen, the antihero, a stout, balding, late-middle-aged former pimp with a swagger to match his former trade. He wishes to reintegrate himself legitimately into the area of Santa Maria, the Argentine or Uruguayan river city from which he was exiled five years before for establishing a brothel there. Larsen is named general manager of a bankrupt shipyard nearby at Puerto Astillero and, feeding self-delusion to justify his vitiated existence, tries to make something out of its rusting plant, which has not received an order or paid its managers in years. He even courts the boss's mentally defective daughter in hopes of possessing the seignorial house where she and her father live. Larsen's end comes when he realizes fully, at long last, that his quest for upward mobility has been a farce. Apparently dying, he rides upriver on a ferryboat.

Jeremías Petrus (hĕ•rĕ•mē′äs), the elderly owner of the defunct shipyard. Petrus, too, is self-deluded. He keeps up the role of willful pioneer of industry with his bustling gait, heavy eyebrows, and sideburns. When he is jailed for forgery, Petrus ages further overnight, calls the cell his office, and continues to make empty plans for the business with his visitor, Larsen.

Angélica Inés Petrus, the idiot daughter of the shipyard owner. Tall, blonde, and childlike, she emits involuntary bursts of laughter from her perpetually open mouth and is generally incapable of making coherent conversation. Larsen courts her with comic formality at their proper meetings in the summerhouse of the Petrus estate, but Angélica Inés barely comprehends what is happening.

A. Gálvez, the bald young administrative manager of the shipyard. Receiving no salary in his purely nominal job, with nothing to do but occasionally sell off spare parts from the plant, he lives in poverty with a wife and dogs in a shack on the shipyard grounds. When Larsen first meets him, Gálvez acts the role of the perfect cynic, mimicking Petrus' pomposity and the irony of the nonexistent activities and salaries of the shipyard. He then becomes increasingly humorless, denounces Petrus to the police for forgery, and then commits sucide, as if he were no longer able to live the lie of the shipyard.

Gálvez's wife, a tall, pretty, but unkempt woman who wears a man's overcoat and shoes. At the time of the action, she is pregnant. Larsen is attracted to her, considering her a real woman, perhaps by comparison with the childish Angélica Inés. She is kind and patient, but Larsen realizes that she is spent by her wretched existence. Their relationship is not intimate, although Larsen spends many evening hours alone with her at the shack. He leaves Puerto Astillero after looking through the window of the shack and seeing the woman alone, struggling in labor.

Kunz, the older, corpulent, hairy technical manager of the shipyard, a German immigrant. Like Gálvez, Kunz is cynical and sarcastic about the phantom enterprise and spends his supposed work time looking over his stamp album. He simply yawns and professes ignorance when Larsen asks him about past operations. Kunz is the source of a story about a visit Larsen receives at the shipyard from Angélica Inés, who presumably accuses her aging beau of infidelity with Gálvez's wife.

Dr. Díaz Grey, a middle-aged bachelor physician from Santa Maria, formerly acquainted with Larsen. Díaz Grey lives a life of dull routine: evenings of solitaire, an unvarying program of recorded sacred music, and drugs to put him to sleep. He is happy to break the monotony when Larsen visits him one evening, and Díaz Grey's impressions of Larsen and recollections of the string of predecessors Larsen has had at Petrus Limited provide another perspective on things. Informed of Larsen's absurd engagement to Angélica Inés Petrus, Díaz Grey soberly recommends that they avoid having children.

Josefina (hō•sĕ•fē′nä), Angélica Inés' servant, a short, dark, sturdy country girl whom Larsen bribes and romances in order to get access to Petrus' daughter. He spends his last night in Puerto Astillero with Josefina in a kind of sentimental replay of his past, which, nevertheless, is faceless: Anyone could have had the experience.

John Deredita

SHORT LETTER, LONG FAREWELL

Author: Peter Handke (1942-   )
Type of work: Novel
Time of action: The late 1960's
First published: Der kurze Brief zum langen Abschied, 1972 (English translation, 1974)

The narrator, an Austrian writer. A young man, almost thirty years old, he has just arrived in the United States (in New England). His journey across America makes up the external plot of the novel. The narrator is a strange and introspective figure, often overcome by mood swings that range from pure horror to almost euphoria. He believes that he has a very exaggerated sense of time. He is not very tolerant of other people and does not like to look at them up close. When people tell the narrator stories, the narrator is annoyed because he thinks that "one look at me must have told them I wouldn't like it." Yet, he also thinks that people can see at a glance that he is the kind of person who will put up with anything. Throughout the novel, the narrator reads works of American and German literature and reflects upon his past and his anxieties about death.

Judith, the narrator's estranged wife. Although little is said of her, she seems obsessed with taking revenge on her former husband.

Claire Madison, an American instructor of German and friend of the narrator, with whom she has had an affair on one of his previous trips to the United States. She is a single parent and travels with the narrator to St. Louis. Claire is genuinely concerned about the narrator and, in the course of various conversations, helps him to clarify his feelings.

Delta Benedictine, the two-year-old daughter of the narrator's friend Claire. She is obsessed with having things in order and becomes extremely upset when objects are misplaced. The child seems out of touch with nature and the environment and is only interested in the artificial products and imitations that make up much of modern American life.

John Ford, a seventy-six-year-old American film director. He lives in his Bel Air estate and is visited by the narrator and his wife at the end of the novel. The romantic and optimistic images of nature and America found in the director's films (such as *Young Mr. Lincoln)* have been highly significant for the narrator, in coming to terms both with modern America and with his own life.

Thomas F. Barry

SHOSHA

Author: Isaac Bashevis Singer (1904-   )
Type of work: Novel
Time of action: 1914-1952
First published: Neshome Ekspeditsyes, 1974 (English translation, 1978)

Aaron Greidinger, nicknamed **Tsutsik,** a vegetarian writer who narrates the events of the novel from his humble beginnings as a rabbi's son on Krochmalna Street in Warsaw to post-World War II New York. Young and idealistic despite his poverty and the growing menace of Nazism in Poland, Aaron must grapple with recurring bouts of despair that naturally result when he, his friends, and his country cannot live up to his high illusions. Nevertheless, he maintains his belief in a Supreme Power. Red-haired yet balding, sexually attractive to women of all classes, he engages in a series of brief affairs, finally marrying his childhood sweetheart even though he risks his career and very life to do so. After a temporary stint as an aspiring playwright supported by a wealthy patron, he makes a meager living writing articles and serialized biographies for a Yiddish newspaper, thereby gaining a measure of fame. He escapes from Poland before the Holocaust and relates at the end of the novel the fate of the other characters.

Shosha Schuldiener, Aaron's childhood sweetheart, who becomes his wife. A blonde, blue-eyed beauty, she is nevertheless physically and mentally stunted. An academic failure, she still manages to attract the intellectual boy Aaron with her total acceptance of and devotion to him, and he has never forgotten her, despite their early separation. When they meet as adults, he reaffirms his love for her, and they marry in the face of others' incredulity at this seeming mismatch. She actually matures in the marriage, displaying unusual insight in her philosophical discussions with Aaron and eventually disarming and winning over his friends with her simple charm. She remains compulsively dependent on Aaron, continually voicing fears of separation from him and her family. She

dies while fleeing Poland, having lost her will to live at this violent upheaval.

Morris Feitelzohn, a writer and philosopher who takes an interest in Aaron and whom Aaron greatly admires. Stocky and square-faced with bushy eyebrows and thick lips, he is witty, debonair, and chronically unemployed, constantly borrowing money from his friends. At the Writers' Club and various other meeting places, he engages Aaron in lengthy conversations that explore almost every known philosophy, though to none of which he subscribes. He introduces Aaron to several of the novel's major characters and, thus, initiates much of the plot. He dies in Warsaw in 1941.

Betty Slonim, an American actress in her early thirties. She is in Poland with her wealthy lover to find a play for the Yiddish stage in which she can star. Red-haired and extremely attractive, she is immediately drawn to Aaron, with whom she shares the story of her Russian Jewish background and generally hard life. Aaron is hired to write a play for her, but she sabotages his work by demanding that he spend his time accompanying her around Warsaw; they soon become lovers. Her constant suggestions and revisions concerning the play render it a disaster before it can even open; however, far from abandoning Aaron, she wishes to marry him and thus ensure his safety in America. He rejects her, though, for Shosha. Brittle, cocky, with little self-esteem, she ends up married to an American officer who is instrumental in smuggling Aaron out of Poland. She eventually commits suicide, which she has threatened throughout the story.

Sam Dreiman, an American millionaire who is Betty's lover. A vigorous old man with a shock of white hair and a broad face and body, he is essentially a father figure to Betty. He is alienated from his wife and children, who have disappointed him, and the fortune he has made in construction is now devoted to Betty's happiness. He finances the writing of Aaron's play, and, when it dissolves into chaos, he is incensed at Aaron for Betty's sake. When he falls gravely ill in Warsaw, it is he who proposes that Betty marry Aaron and that they become joint heirs in Sam's will.

Celia Chentshiner, a wealthy, sophisticated intellectual who is an avowed atheist and with whom Aaron has a brief affair. She is severely proper in her appearance but warmly gracious as a hostess.

Haiml Chentshiner, Celia's childlike and independently wealthy husband, who survives the war and remarries several years after his wife's death. Aaron meets up with him in Israel at the story's end, and Haiml delivers the poignant and philosophical last words of the novel.

Dora Stolnitz, Aaron's first mistress. A fanatic Communist, she persists in her ideology even when presented with evidence of its treachery.

Tekla, Aaron's buxom housemaid and mistress, a peasant girl who serves him devotedly and for whom he finds a job at the Chentshiners'.

Caren S. Silvester

THE SHROUDED WOMAN

Author: María Luisa Bombal (1910-1980)
Type of work: Novel
Time of action: The first half of the twentieth century
First published: La amortajada, 1938 (English translation, 1948)

Ana María, a dead woman who alternately views her mourners, the memories they arouse, and the dramatic landscape of death. A passionate woman and mother of three children, Ana María finds that in death her perceptions are amplified; her emotions are fully realized. Her early beauty returns, and she sees herself as pale, slender, and unwrinkled by time. In life she was imaginative, sensitive, intense, and playful. She journeys through the past and relives her adolescent love for Ricardo, his betrayal, and her subsequent herbally induced abortion; her marriage to Antonio, his love for her and the loss of that love, and her passion for him; the adoration of the luckless Fernando in her later years; and the unhappy loves of her three children. Following heart attacks and a stroke, Ana María dies and witnesses her wake, a journey to the family vault, and her fall to surreal subterranean landscapes. Flowing back to the surface, she roots herself to the world and longs for immersion in death.

Ricardo, Ana María's adolescent lover and neighbor. As a young man Ricardo is clear-eyed, tanned, and wiry. A trickster tyrant, he teases Ana María. He is willful, rebellious, and impetuous. Ana María is a childish lover; she does not share his passion but desires his strong arms and the "wild flower" of his kisses. Ricardo deserts Ana María when he goes to study agricultural farming in Europe. On his return he fails to approach her, then says that he is not to blame for her pregnancy. From this time on each avoids the other; when he enters her room of death, Ana María understands that her love for him was a hidden core, that his love for her is the same.

Antonio, Ana María's rich, handsome, and charming husband. For a year Antonio spies on Ana María from the wild black forest adjoining her father's hacienda. After marriage, his young bride feels lost in his sumptuous, labyrinthine house; she resists both his home and the pleasure that Antonio arouses in her. Antonio allows her to visit her father's home, but when she returns, he is indifferent to her presence. Fated now to love a man who seems only to tolerate her, Ana María suffers from Antonio's constant pursuit of other women, just as he suffers from her long, vicarious bond to Ricardo. Antonio weeps for the dead Ana María, who discovers that she neither loves nor hates him.

Fernando, an older man who woos Ana María and becomes her confidant in her later years. Fernando—ill, luckless, unhappy, swarthy, and lean—repulses Ana María, although she needs to confide in him. His dispassionate attitude toward his wife's suicide disturbs Ana María; requited love, he says, eludes him. Fernando, tormented by his love, finds that he can admire, understand, and forgive Ana María after her death. The death releases him to return to his interests in politics, farming, and study.

Alberto, the son of Ana María and Antonio. Handsome and taciturn, he loves only life on his southern hacienda until he meets María Griselda. Her overwhelming beauty and appearance of self-containment drive him to agony and drink. Jealous, he walls her up in the family hacienda, deep in the dark forest.

María Griselda, wife of Alberto. The swanlike María Griselda is lovely, and her beauty causes her to suffer from early childhood. Green eyes, pale skin, black hair, and harmonious gestures draw the adoration of men and women, children, and nature. Left lonely by her husband's searching love, she remains solitary. Only Ana María can forgive her great beauty.

Fred, the son of Ana María and Antonio. Ana María dearly loves this child, who fears mirrors and talks an unknown language in dreams. As a robust young man he falls in love with blonde Silvia, but it is dark María Griselda who awakens his poet's soul.

Silvia, Fred's wife. Tiny, graceful, and golden, Silvia makes the tragic decision to spend her honeymoon at the forest hacienda. The new bride shoots herself in the temple when Fred confesses that he has been transformed by the presence of María Griselda.

Anita, daughter of Ana María and Antonio. Anita is arrogant, private, haughty, and brilliant. When her good-natured sweetheart, don Rodolfo, falls under the spell of María Griselda, Anita seduces him and becomes pregnant.

Sofía, the estranged wife of Ricardo. Lively Sofía envies Ana María's intensity; the two are bound by friendship until Ana María comes to think that Sofía has betrayed her.

Alicia, Ana María's sister. Sad, pale, and religious, Alicia has suffered her husband's brutality and the death of her son.

Luis, Ana María's brother. Commonplace values separate Luis from Ana María, especially after he rejects the vivacious Elena for a conventional woman.

Marlene Youmans

SHUTTLECOCK

Author: Graham Swift (1949-   )
Type of work: Novel
Time of action: c. 1980
First published: 1981

Prentis, the narrator, a senior clerk in a London police bureau that handles information on closed and unsolved cases. In his early thirties, secretive, and self-consciously prickly—almost paranoid—with a tyrannical and sadistic streak, he also has a capacity

1398

and craving for affection that leaves him hurt by his sons' lack of interest and respect and his wife's quiet withdrawal. Unable to live up to his own father's heroic image after reading his wartime memoirs at age eleven, Prentis' confused adult relationship to "Dad," whom he visits religiously every Wednesday and Sunday at a mental home (visits that his family resents), talking to him even though he cannot talk back, is one reason for his own familial failures. His obsession with the past and his father's role in it, especially his father's daring escape from the Gestapo, ultimately dovetails with his professional suspicions about the C-9 case, missing files, and his boss, Quinn. At the opening of the novel, he is surprised to hear that he is to get Quinn's job; at the close, his promotion and his decision quietly to suppress police information that may hurt the innocent allows his rehabilitation as husband and father.

Quinn, the bureau chief. Another problematic father figure with a suspect military background, unsmiling and curt, Quinn is plump and bespectacled, with none of the physical attributes of power, but his position (literally) elevates him above his clerks at work in their semi-basement, on whom an internal window allows him to spy unseen. His silent removal of files, assignment of projects that cannot be completed, and sudden takeovers of cases, generate an aura of mystery and turn his subordinates' jobs into a guessing game. His revelation that "Dad" cracked in the hands of the Gestapo, and stooped not only to betrayals but to perpetuating his impostures in print, releases Prentis from his obsessions—the files are "lost" and the past rewritten, while his retirement and naming of Prentis as his successor ensure Prentis a large chair in a large office, like his father's—the status he needs.

Prentis, Sr. (Dad), codenamed **Shuttlecock,** a World War II espionage agent. He is a retired partner in a successful firm of consultant engineers, and now resident in an institution. A silent and seemingly noble figure, Dad's apparent mental breakdown a few years ago has left him unable or unwilling to talk to his son, in whom he lost interest when, as a boy of eleven, Prentis withdrew from him. His terse, brisk memoirs of daring wartime operations in France made him something of a public figure in the late 1950's. Pages of them fill Prentis' narrative.

Marian, Prentis' wife. Slightly dull, but still sexually attractive, pliant of limb and compliant by disposition, Marian withdraws from domestic battles into caring for her plants; she seems set to transfer her affection from husband to sons.

Martin, Prentis' ten-year-old son. On the verge of growing up, with a rebellious streak and considerable courage, Martin has taken to spying on Prentis from a distance, as he goes to and from work. When his father gets rid of the television set, resentful of both sons' addiction to "heroes" like the Bionic Man, Martin provokes a confrontation and a beating by removing Grandpa's book from the shelves.

Peter, Martin's younger brother. An instinctive conformist with a tendency to snivel, Peter submits to his father's whims and temper.

Joss Lutz Marsh

THE SIBYL

Author: Pär Lagerkvist (1891-1974)
Type of work: Novel
Time of action: The second century A.D. (well after Christ's crucifixion and before the decline of the Delphic oracle in the late third century)
First published: *Sibyllan,* 1956 (English translation, 1958)

The Sibyl, an old woman who occupied the position of pythia, or oracle, at Delphi. She was given by her parents into the service of the Delphic god of prophecy, who, in this story, is a combination of Apollo (represented by serpents) and Dionysus (represented by goats). Having spent her adolescence and much of her young womanhood as the bride of the god, she violates her office by having sexual union with a man whom she loves. The man very shortly meets his death, and the Sibyl gives birth, not to his son, as she had expected, but to the son of the Delphic god. She listens to the story of a male visitor to her mountain hut and then relates her own story, while her son, now an aging idiot, sits silent and perpetually smiling in her presence.

The Sibyl's visitor, a man with the features of early middle age who is recognizable in the story of himself that he relates to the Sibyl as **Ahasuerus** (ä·hä·sōō·ā'rəs), **The Wandering Jew.** He had had a wife and son in the city of his birth. One day he refused to let a man, who was carrying a cross, rest against his house. The man, whom people later identified as God's son, laid upon Ahasuerus the curse of eternal life without rest. Ahasuerus seeks from the Sibyl advice and an answer to the mystery of life and the inscrutability of the deity. Her story impresses him but does not lessen his perplexity, and he departs from her to continue his endless wandering.

The Sibyl's son, who is also to be understood as a son of God. He was conceived by the Sibyl during one of her prophetic trances, when she was invaded by the temple god in the form of a goat. The Sibyl, expelled from the temple for her infidelity to the god, later gives birth to her son in a mountain cave. She is attended by protective goats, who lick clean the newborn boy and his mother. While his mother tells the visitor her story, he (the son) disappears. The Sibyl and her visitor track him by his footprints in the snow. The footprints come to a stop in an open space, and the conclusion is that this son of God has ascended to his Father.

The Sibyl's lover, a man of twenty-five or thirty who has lost one arm as a soldier and has returned to do his family farming. His inability to complete an embrace and his shock at the Sibyl's excessive sensuality combine to indicate the Sibyl's destiny never to live with a human mate. After he and the Sibyl have entered upon their affair, he is found dead in the rapids of a river; he is drained of blood but without visible wounds, and he is clutching a twig of the tree sacred to the Delphic god, the laurel.

The Sibyl's parents, simple farming people. Both die—first the mother, then the father—while the Sibyl serves as the pythia.

The little servant of the oracle, custodian of the temple and its precinct and the Sibyl's only true friend.

The priest of the temple, an unpleasant man. He is often impatient with the Sibyl in her duties as the pythia.

Roy Arthur Swanson

SIDDHARTHA

Author: Hermann Hesse (1877-1962)
Type of work: Novel
Time of action: The sixth century B.C., at the time of the Buddha
First published: 1922 (English translation, 1951)

Siddhartha, a Brahman's son. Tall and handsome, he decides in his youth to seek enlightenment. As a result of this quest, he and his friend Govinda leave their comfortable homes and join a group of wandering ascetics, the Samanas. Later, they go to hear the

Buddha. While Siddhartha admires the man, he feels that the life of this monk is not what he is seeking and he leaves. In his wanderings, he sees a beautiful courtesan and decides that he must know her. She sends him to a merchant to learn the trade, and, while she teaches him about love, the merchant teaches him about business. By the time he reaches age forty, he realizes that he has not found enlightenment. He wanders into the forest, where he meets a ferryman. He stays with him and finally achieves enlightenment by listening to the songs of the river.

Govinda, a monk. A childhood friend of Siddhartha, he insists on accompanying him and joining a group of wandering ascetics. When he hears the Buddha speak, however, he decides that he must remain with this man, and the friends part. Much later, he encounters a wealthy man sleeping in the woods and stands guard over him until he awakes. It is only then that he finds it is his old friend Siddhartha. He is very surprised at the changes he finds but makes no judgments. In old age, after the death of the Buddha, he hears of a ferryman who is considered a sage and a holy man and he goes to see him. Again he finds it is his old friend, who has since found enlightenment, but he does not understand the words Siddhartha uses to try to explain what has happened to him. It is only when Govinda kisses his forehead that he sees that Siddhartha sees and partly understands.

Kamala, a courtesan. An extraordinarily beautiful woman, she is wealthy and experienced. She teaches Siddhartha the ways of love, but she realizes that neither of them is capable of love as they are. After Siddhartha leaves, she finds that she is pregnant, and she closes her house and no longer receives visitors. Eventually, she turns her house over to the followers of the Buddha, and when she hears that he is dying, she takes her son and sets out to see him. On the journey, she is bitten by a snake while near the river, and Siddhartha and his friend find her. She dies in Siddhartha's arms.

Vasudeva, a ferryman. A poor old man, he has found enlightenment listening to the river. He takes Siddhartha in after he leaves his wealth and becomes his friend and adviser. Already an old man, during Siddhartha's stay he begins to lose his strength and can no longer operate the ferry. After Kamala's death, he counsels Siddhartha to allow his son to leave and live his own life, and it is only after Siddhartha finally takes his advice that he reveals all the river's message to his friend. After he is sure that Siddhartha understands, he walks off into the woods to die.

Gotama, the Buddha. He is a wise man living an ascetic life whose words and manner of living have a profound effect on those around him. From all over India, people flock to hear him and many remain as his followers. Siddhartha goes to hear him speak in the hope that he will find enlightenment, but, while he recognizes the Buddha as a very holy man, he does not find the path he seeks.

C. D. Akerley

THE SIEGE OF KRISHNAPUR

Author: J. G. Farrell (1935-1979)
Type of work: Novel
Time of action: 1857
First published: 1973

Mr. Hopkins, "the Collector," chief administrator of the East India Company in the Krishnapur district of the Bengal Presidency in northeastern India. A large, handsome, brown-haired man, with carefully trimmed, low sideburns, he is a fastidious dresser, complete with high collars. Possessed of a public sense of dignity and duty, Hopkins is privately moody and often overbearing toward his family. His wife leaves for England, ostensibly after the death of a child, but it seems the marital relationship was less than happy, for "the Collector" has an eye for the ladies, including a fondness for Miriam Lang. Through Hopkins' roving eye and commentary, the life and position of women in mid-nineteenth century India is illuminated. Hopkins is a well-rounded character capable not only of the highest duty and courage but also of showing grief and fear. Early in the novel, he demonstrates foresight by preparing for the revolt that he believes is coming and fortitude by continuing his actions amid scoffs and general disdain. Hopkins is in command of the defensive operations at Krishnapur once the sepoy revolt. As the British ominously retreat to their second line of defenses, Hopkins symbolically falls ill with cholera but later returns to lead the final retreat and the last stand. Hopkins' character strikes a balance between the "emotionalism and human spirit versus materialism and scientific progress" theme that runs through the novel. By the end of the book, however, Hopkins' faith in either portion of the theme seems shattered.

George Fleury, son of Sir Herbert, who is a director of the East Indian Company. He has only recently come to India. George is fashionably dressed, but his personality is serious, even somber and, as such, represents a contrast to Louise's other, more carefree suitors. A musician, a purported writer, and a poet in the Romantic vein, Fleury originally adopts a strident antimaterialistic tone but, by the end of the novel, acquires an almost unqualified appreciation of modernist ideas and gadgetry. Described as slightly fat and perpetually perspiring, Fleury presents a vulnerable and sometimes humorous character. Fleury is capable of cowardice yet capable of heroism, too. Fleury is a secondary protagonist, for when the mainstream of the novel diverts from Hopkins it is primarily carried along by Fleury. In the end, he marries Louise.

Tom Willoughby, "the Magistrate," the chief judicial officer for the Krishnapur district. Somewhat younger than Hopkins, he sports red hair, with ginger-colored whiskers. Cold, rational, cynical, and pessimistic concerning human nature, Willoughby has no discernible human attachments. Addicted to the science of phrenology (which asserts that the shape of a person's skull reveals his personality), Willoughby makes himself generally detested or, at best, tolerated. Hopkins' decisions are frequently at odds with what Willoughby recommends; the men are antagonists, each being content not to be the other man.

Louise Dunstaple, blonde, fair, pale, remote, the local beauty and a target for aspiring suitors. She is the daughter of Dr. Dunstaple and the sister of Harry. Originally insipid and self-occupied, she learns willpower and how to help others, even the unfortunate Lucy, during the siege.

Dr. Dunstaple, a fat, energetic man, with a rosy complexion and a good-humored face, the civilian surgeon. He is also stubborn, for his hatred for Dr. McNab becomes so pathological that he drinks cholera-infested water to prove a medical point and, subsequently, dies.

Reverend M. Hampton, "the Padre," a lightly built, unassuming man with a healthy manner (a former rower at Oxford) who becomes sickly with cholera during the defense and has his faith tested during the trials. At times, he appears half crazy in a humorous way that contrasts with the grim surroundings.

Dr. McNab, the Scottish military surgeon at odds with Dr. Dunstaple over methods of medical treatment. McNab's practices, though unorthodox for his time, are in fact more correct. He is a young widower with a middle-aged air and is also described as gloomy, formal, and reticent. He eventually marries Miriam Lang.

Harry Dunstaple, brother of Louise, son of

Dr. Dunstaple. He is a young lieutenant of a sepoy infantry regiment who is a "manly" opposite of Fleury, at least originally, but both become friends during ensuing adventures and behave with equal gallantry. Harry falls for Lucy, and, despite gossip that her reputation will damage his future, several years after the siege he makes the rank of general.

Miriam Lang, the widowed elder sister of George Fleury, who often embarrasses her brother in front of Louise and others by referring to him by the childhood nickname of "Dobbin." She represents the more sensible and sure side of feminine nature when compared with the relatively more naïve Louise, who respects her.

Lucy Hughes, a lovely woman "fallen" because of a sexual indiscretion and broken engagement. After comtemplating suicide while drunken, Lucy gradually makes herself acceptable to some polite company, including Hopkins, Louise, Miriam, and Harry, although she never wins respectability with the majority of ladies at Krishnapur.

Hari, the son of the local maharaja. The fat-cheeked, black-eyed, and pale-faced Hari, having been educated by English tutors, is the bridge between native Indian and English colonial society. Hari and Fleury are ironical opposites, Hari embracing all the materialism and scientific advances of the West that Fleury views as irrelevant to human progress; each fails to understand the other.

General Jackson, commanding officer of the garrison at Captainganj, a small, fat, and very forgetful man. At well over seventy years old, Jackson was appointed by circumstance of seniority rather than by virtue of competence. Because of his behavior, confidence in the ability of the military to handle the uprising is diminished. He represents an obstacle for Hopkins to circumnavigate, for Hopkins intends to take precautions, while Jackson supports the alternative opinion that precautions will merely incite the Indians to rebel.

David L. Bullock

SIGISMUND
From the Memories of a Baroque Polish Prince

Author: Lars Gustafsson (1936-   )
Type of work: Novel
Time of action: 1973
First published: Sigismund: Ur en polsk barockfurstes minnen, 1976 (English translation, 1985)

Lars, the narrator, a Swedish writer. He has a wife and children, as well as an alter ego named Sigismund III, King of Poland. Lars apparently writes the novel, entitled *Sigismund*, under direction from the Polish king. In fact, the entire book is made up of the narrator's attempt to describe his writing process and the rationale for the text he produces. The novel encompasses various styles and genres, including science fiction, fantasy, pornography, and realism.

Sigismund III, King of Poland from 1587 to 1632, the narrator's alter ego, who calls Lars his "stand-in." The narrator supposedly writes for this king, who, at the end of the novel, shows up at the narrator's door complaining about the book's composition.

Laura G., friend of the narrator and of his wife. This artist becomes the subject of some of Lars's fanciful writing. Drawing his inspiration from her comment that she would sell her soul to the devil for perfection in her paintings and wealth, Lars creates a narrative in which Laura descends into hell to determine whether she would care to spend eternity there. In Lars's fiction, she requests of hell the opportunity to become another person for one day. The boundary between fantasy and reality breaks down when Lars sees Laura as a young man on a street in Berlin. Apparently, she has signed a contract with the devil.

Uncle Stig, a Marxist, a member of the Sophia Bicycle Club, the narrator's uncle. He is an inventor, and one of his inventions is a bicycle that can go as fast as sixty miles an hour and possibly faster. He believes that he is always "swindled out of" the patents on these inventions. After an accident on his newly crafted bicycle, he gives up inventing altogether.

Aunt Clara, the narrator's mother's sister. She is beautiful and charming; her voice is particularly melodic. As a telephone operator for a government office, she falls in love with a government official. When jilted by him, she is momentarily crushed but then falls madly in love with the neighborhood's blind beggar. The two of them wander off together and become a romantic legend in the area. Aunt Clara dies of lung disease shortly thereafter.

Gottwold, a blind beggar who makes small cloth dolls to sell. Children either love him or hate him. Aunt Clara falls in love with him and the two of them run off together. He has also written two novels, which he has wrapped in waterproof cloth and carries in a wagon filled with various pieces of junk. One of these novels imitates Homer's *Iliad*; the other mirrors the *Odyssey* and is an expression of Gottwold's love for Clara.

Baal B. Zvuvium, one of the emissaries from hell who seek to convince Laura G. to sell her soul to the devil. He is charming and handsome, but Laura realizes that while he is very skilled in rhetoric, he is not truly interested in her well-being. Originally bemused by the painter's request to become another person for one day, he later comes to understand her reasoning. Consequently, these two individuals develop a mutual empathy.

Sally Bartlett

THE SIGN IN SIDNEY BRUSTEIN'S WINDOW

Author: Lorraine Hansberry (1930-1965)
Type of work: Play
Time of action: The early 1960's
First produced: 1964

Sidney Brustein, a cynical, disillusioned intellectual living in a Greenwich Village apartment with his wife, Iris. An idealist in his youth, Sidney had been involved with all manner of causes and active on various committees advocating social change. Now in his early thirties, he epitomizes the alienated white intellectual searching for meaning in his life. As the disappointed disinterested dreamer, Sidney has withdrawn from social and political action to run a failed coffee house and, subsequently, to attempt a community newspaper. Both ventures reflect his efforts to escape to an ideal world. Circumstances force Sidney to realize that his mask of cynical detachment prevents him from seeing life realistically and allows others to manipulate his political naïveté. He learns, as well, that without committed involvement by responsible individuals, chaos, disintegration, and failure may well result.

Iris Parodus Brustein, Sidney's wife, an aspiring but unsuccessful actress. She is a young and pretty woman, with long flowing hair that Sidney is always letting down. Iris is several years younger than Sidney and the realist of the two. She, however, feels stifled in their marriage. The pressure of trying both to conform to and yet escape from Sidney's image of her as a rustic, naïve, unsophisticated woman-child whom he has educated has worn on her nerves. Her own inability to overcome her fear of auditions has also taken its toll. Yet, Iris is capable of rebellion, of making changes, of taking control of her life back into her own hands.

Mavis Parodus Bryson, Iris' traditional, matronly, older sister and the family conservative. Though almost a stereotype of the staid, meddling, racist, and parochial elder sister who cannot understand the life-style of her younger sister or her Jewish husband and their bohemian friends, Mavis manages to escape her limitations by raising challenging questions. She is also a more honest person, a more caring person, and a far stronger person than either her sister or her brother-in-law realizes.

Gloria Parodus, the youngest of the three Parodus sisters, who, collectively, function something like a chorus annotating the play's action. Although Gloria is not introduced until the third act, her presence colors the attitudes and actions of several characters. A beautiful, wholesome-looking young woman, Gloria makes her living by prostitution. Because of her line of work, she has been physically abused by clients and is involved in substance abuse, taking a variety of pills and drinking far too much to enable her to face her life. Gloria resolves to leave prostitution and marry, attempting to escape from a brutal life to an idealized one.

Alton Scales, a black American intellectual, part of Sidney's bohemian circle, and the man Gloria plans to marry. Alton is the lone African American character in the play. He is a fair- or light-skinned Negro whose color permits a discussion of interracial relationships and racism. Serving initially as a goad forcing Sidney to reorganize his obligation to become involved in the political affairs of the community, Alton accuses Sidney of "ostrich-ism" and intimates that hiding his head will not make the problems of the world disappear. Later, however, Alton bungles his own moral problem of individual responsibility and integrity. He had been quite willing to love and cherish Gloria, despite a rebuff by Mavis, until he discovered that she was not a fashion model as he had believed but a prostitute. Unable to accept her as a "commodity," he rejects her without ever speaking to her and vanishes.

David Ragin, a young, struggling but successful, homosexual playwright living upstairs from the Brusteins. As an artist and intellectual, David serves as a catalyst for many of the issues in the play. He provides shock value for Marvis, who does not realize that "gay" implies homosexuality; he helps debate the function of art, the role of the artist, and the integrity of the artist; his life-style illustrates yet another dimension of societal prejudice; and he proves without question that being an artist or intellectual does not necessarily mean that the individual possesses sensitivity.

Wally O'Hara, the corrupt local politician who uses Sidney's idealism to his own advantage. Wally convinces Sidney to get involved and to raise his voice, via editorials in his newspaper, against machine politics. Yet, Wally, it seems, is owned by the political machine he attacks.

Max, a middled-aged, gravel-voiced, scruffy, egotistical, comic type. Max, an artist who may be played by a black or white actor, believes the sole responsibility of the artist is to reflect himself. He designs an obscure masthead for Sidney's newspaper.

Sandra Y. Govan

SILENCE

Author: Shusaku Endō (1923-   )
Type of work: Novel

Time of action: The seventeenth century
First published: Chimmoku, 1966 (English translation, 1969)

Sebastian Rodrigues, a young Portuguese seminarian. Rodrigues, with two other priests, gains permission to journey to Japan to track down his former mentor in order to learn why he has renounced his faith. Because *Silence* is essentially the spiritual odyssey of Rodrigues told through his correspondence, his character is discerned through his sensitive and candid portrayal of the events around him, which are filtered through the eyes of one seeking to understand and exonerate his beloved teacher from his ostensible apostasy. Rodrigues begins as a naïve young priest with textbook theories about crosscultural evangelism with his own vague aspirations toward martyrdom neatly submerged in his self-conscious. As he matures in his understanding of the complexities of the Japanese setting, he confronts Ferreira in his supposed sin and, eventually, undergoes his own apostasy by trampling the *fumie*, or image of Christ. In this act, he comes to reinterpret his actions and those of his fellow apostates as renunciations of only an institutionalized form of Christianity that had no roots in Japan or the original gospel and deserves no allegiance. In his apostasy, Rodrigues has learned to love the unlovely, to forgive and embrace his fallen mentor and the formerly outcast Kichijiro, whom he once rejected as a betrayer.

Christovao Ferreira, a Jesuit missionary priest to Japan. Ferreira, held in the highest respect by his peers, is an intellectual and theologian who attains the high position of provincial. Having spent thirty years building the church in Japan, Ferreira has written glowingly back to his Portuguese colleagues from Japan of the indomitable courage of his converts and the steadfastness of his fellow priests undergoing intense persecution. Inexplicably, a report comes back that he has apostatized, sending his colleagues into a quandary. Ferreira remains a shadowy, noncompelling figure in the story known only through his reputation and the rumors about him until his confrontation with Rodrigues.

Here, he emerges as a pragmatist who has renounced his faith not so much to save the Japanese from martyrdom as to salve his own theological conscience for bringing a faith unsuitable to the Japanese psyche. Ultimately, Ferreira is more anthropologist than missionary, ironically sharing this rather momentous conclusion with the one man presumably most at odds with his vision of Christian faith and love: Inoue, the chief persecutor of Japanese converts.

Kichijiro, Rodrigues' Japanese guide during his search for Ferreira. Kichijiro is a lapsed Christian convert whose drunkenness and shifty, mercenary spirit mark him initially as the "chief of sinners" in Rodrigues' eyes. Despite his slovenly character and apparently loose moral standards, Kichijiro emerges as a maternal, forgiving creature, moved in compassion for the suffering of his fellow Japanese converts to betray the foreign priests who have come to his native shores. At the novel's end, Kichijiro has returned to gain absolution at the hands of Rodrigues, reembracing the faith he had intermittently denounced previously.

Yuki, a Christian convert in Japan. Yuki demonstrates her courage and bravery by willingly interposing herself between her non-Christian lover and his captors when they demand that he step on the *fumie* to demonstrate his contempt for the faith of Christianity. In his rufusal to step on her or the fumie, both are condemned and executed.

Inoue, the fierce Japanese magistrate who pursues and compels the Japanese Christians under torture to apostatize. Cool, calm, and relentlessly detached from the human suffering about him, Inoue unwittingly raises the key issues of the confrontation between East and West in this piercing intellectualized questions about the appropriateness of Christianity for the Orient.

Francisco Garpe, Rodrigues' fellow seminarian and traveling companion to Japan. Garpe drowns while swimming after a boat from which bound Christians will be cast into the sea to their deaths.

Bruce L. Edwards

THE SILENT CRY

Author: Kenzaburō Ōe (1935-   )
Type of work: Novel
Time of action: The early 1960's
First published: Man' en san' nen no futtoboru, 1967 (English translation, 1974)

Mitsusaburo (Mitsu) Nedokoro, a young academic aristocrat. A stoical man, he is depressed by two events: the suicide of a friend and the birth of his first child, who is mentally retarded. He notes the details of his wife's depression and her alcoholic consumption, but he feels powerless to change their situation. Upon the return to Japan of Taka, his younger brother, he consents to a return to their native village to begin life anew. There they are both swept up by a peasant revolt in 1860 led by an ancestor. They are also overwhelmed by an awareness of their two dead siblings, S., an older brother, and a young retarded sister. Mitsu tries to balance Taka's romantic versions of their family's deaths by logic and cynicism.

Takashi (Taka) Nedokoro, a reformed student-activist. A charismatic young man in his twenties, Taka returns from the United States determined to seek his roots in his native village. With a small band of followers and his brother and sister-in-law, they complete the arduous journey. Once there, Taka sells the homestead and unilaterally decides to invest the money in a football team. Prone to violence and distortion of events, past and present, he seduces Natsumi without remorse, murders a young woman senselessly, and finally confesses to his brother his incestuous relationship with their sister. He feels responsible for her death and commits suicide.

Natsumi Nedokoro, Mitsu's wife, who has become an alcoholic since the birth of her retarded son. Natsumi is an intelligent, sensitive young woman who is suffering from her thwarted motherhood and collapsing marriage. She becomes an ardent follower of Taka and eventually becomes pregnant with his child.

Paek Sun-gi (The Emperor), a Korean former laborer and now owner of a supermarket chain. He buys the Nedokoro homestead and outbuildings. Though Taka paints him as a villain, he appears to be civilized.

Great-Grandfather's younger brother, leader of a peasant revolt in 1860. Thought to have been a deserter and to have brought shame on the clan, he is finally exonerated through Mitsu's research.

Momoko, a young woman who becomes a follower of Taka. At first, she is an enthusiastic follower, but, when Taka organizes the riot at the supermarket, she becomes disenchanted.

Hoshio, a young boy who becomes a bodyguard of Taka. In the course of Taka's treachery and violence, Hoshio tells Mitsu that Taka has seduced Natsumi. He, too, is disenchanted and wants only to leave the village and return to normal life.

Jin, a grossly overweight family retainer. Because of her uncontrollable appetite, her husband and children are undernourished. Both Mitsu and Taka respect her and make a provision for her shelter even though they sell the homestead. After the riot, Jin's appetite decreases markedly.

Lila Chalpin

THE SILESIAN TETRALOGY

Author: Horst Bienek (1930-   )
Type of work: Novels
Time of action: 1939-1945
First published: 1975-1982: *Die erste Polka*, 1975 (*The First Polka*, 1978); *Septemberlicht*, 1977 (*September Light*, 1987); *Zeit ohne Glocken*, 1979 (*Time Without Bells*, 1988); *Erde und Feuer*, 1982

Valeska Piontek (pē·ŏn′tĕk), a piano teacher, wife of Leo Maria Piontek, and mother of Irma and Josel. She is a strong, domineering mother figure, an overbearing and thus oppressive wife who suffocates her family with her love. As a shrewd businesswoman she provides for her family by speculating in real estate. During the trying days of the war and the subsequent chaos of the flight from the approaching Russians, her most important goal is to keep her family together. She is able to fuse her own brand of Catholicism with opportunism without being bothered by the inherent contradiction. Unaware of the burden her restrictive love places on her family, she is often bewildered by their actions. Rigidly set in her ways, she does not react well to change and social upheaval.

Leo Maria Piontek, the ailing husband of Valeska, a former photographer. He came from a family where the women (mother and five older sisters) decided what was to be done. Leo Maria's father had saved his hard-earned money to leave this henhouse and take his son away with him, but then his wife died and he had to spend the money on the funeral. Just as the father was unsuccessful at becoming independent from the women in his life, Leo Maria, the youngest child, dominated by his mother and older sisters, never becomes a free person. Leo Maria, who always wanted to become a photographer, became an apprentice in a laboratory against his will. When he married Valeska, she allowed him to open a photography studio despite the fact that it is not commercially successful. After his wife meddles in his studio, he becomes an invalid, takes to his bed, and dies a few years later. His true identity, his feelings, and his political convictions re-mained hidden from his wife behind his silence. Only a few objects betray his identity after his death.

Josel Piontek, the son of Valeska and Leo Maria. He is fifteen years old in the first novel and later becomes a soldier. As an adolescent he displays curiosity in sexual matters and at the same time combines it with some of his mother's entrepreneurial skills when he rents a dilapidated shed by the river to soldiers and their girls for thirty minutes each. Through a hole in the wall he observes the couples making love. With the profits of this "business," he hopes to take his sweetheart Ulla, who aspires to be a great pianist, to Warsaw to the Church of the Holy Cross where Frédéric François Chopin's heart is buried. He is relieved to leave his overbearing mother when he is called up to be a soldier. In the last book he lies wounded in a hospital in Dresden with Ulla by his side.

Irma Piontek, the daughter of Valeska and Leo Maria. She marries a German soldier, becomes widowed soon after the wedding, and is remarried to a cabdriver. Irma rebels in silence; she withdraws emotionally from her mother who—among other things—had secretly interfered with her relationship to a man whom Irma had known since childhood and with whom she was going for drives in the country. While her mother had high hopes for Irma to marry up socially, she, in turn, tries to escape the suffocating love of her mother by first sleeping with a cretin and then marrying a German soldier in a civil ceremony against the will of her pious mother. Her husband dies shortly after the wedding. Even after she remarries, however, she and her two daughters remain with Valeska, and they flee to Dresden together. She is unable to liberate herself from her mother's influence and become a free and independent person.

Ulla Ossadnik (ŏs•säd′nĭk), Valeska's most promising piano student, childhood sweetheart of Josel. She later becomes a famous pianist. Along with Andreas, Josel's cousin, she becomes a witness to the feigned attack on the transmitter Gleiwitz (Gliwice), which was used by the Germans to claim provocation by Polish guerrillas. Despite the fact that her parents are from the working class and can barely afford the tuition, she is sent to piano lessons and excels as a brilliant student. She loves the music of the romantics, especially Chopin. Her dedication to her art remains strong even though she has to perform the duties of a nurse as the war nears its end.

Franz Ossadnik, the father of Ulla and her four brothers, a railroad engineer for the German Railway. While he is essentially content with his lot in life, his wife, who is socially ambitious and who points out that the family could stand a higher income, pushes him to join the Nazi Party in order to gain the benefits associated with it, such as a promotion. He agrees because it means that he can support the musical talent of his daughter better and can send her away for more advanced training. As he realizes that he is transporting Jews to the concentration camps, he suddenly understands how much of his soul he had to sell for the advancement.

Anna Ossadnik, wife of Franz and mother of Ulla, Paulek, Tonik, Kotik, and Andreas (Squintok). Although she married beneath her own social position, she is socially ambitious and prods her husband to act less like a common laborer and more like a person of the middle class. Despite having five chil-

dren, she always takes time to read tomes of trashy novels. She acts on the principle that the children should rear one another. All the sons have to help run her five-room household; only Ulla, her father's favorite, is exempt from these household duties, so that she can pursue her interests in music.

Willi Wondrak, Valeska's brother, a lawyer and her closest business associate. As a closet homosexual, he is bound to Valeska not only by brotherly love but also because she is aware of his secret. Without ever mentioning the subject of his homosexuality, she is able to influence him through some internalized value system that she adheres to and he intuitively comprehends. He even lets his sister pressure him into marrying a woman he obviously does not love. Despite his social position, he is unable to escape her well-intended but stifling love.

Georg Montag, a magistrate with Jewish ancestry who lives in Valeska's garden shed. He is working on a biography of the Polish politician Wojciech Korfanty. He became interested in Korfanty after reading vicious attacks on him in Polish newspapers. After his politically motivated early retirement, Montag intellectually and spiritually returns more and more to his Jewish roots, which he had buried deeply during his life. After seeing troops and equipment being transported away, he decides not to leave his home anymore and commits suicide when he hears German soldiers in the yard.

Arthur Silbergleit (zīl′bĕr•glīt), a Jewish poet, friend of Georg Montag. Although he is married to an Aryan woman, Ilse, he is trying to leave Germany after the events of "Kristallnacht," when Jewish synagogues and stores were destroyed. After unsuccessfully seeking asylum abroad, Silbegleit is transported to a concentration camp and gassed.

Karin A. Wurst

THE SILMARILLION

Author: J. R. R. Tolkien (1892-1973)
Type of work: Novel
Time of action: A mythical past
First published: 1977

Ilúvatar, also known as **Eru** (the one), his name meaning "father of all." He is the creator of Ea (the universe) and of Arda (the earth). He first sang into being the Ainur, a race of angelic beings who then helped him to sing into existence the universe and finally the earth. Although all the Ainur (except Melkor the rebel) know part of his thoughts, no single Ainu knows them all; their amazement at his creativity and compassion never ceases, and they love best his newest creation, the Children of Ilúvatar: humanity. All things involving Arda are woven into the ultimate design of Ilúvatar; nothing, not even Melkor's rebellion, happens without his foreknowledge or permission.

Manwë, chief of the Valar (those Ainur who came to dwell on earth either permanently or temporarily) and ruler of Arda. His special delight is winds, clouds, and the regions of the air. He takes to himself no kingly power in the sense of forcing men or Elves (created before man on earth and therefore called the Firstborn) to serve him, but he is wisest of the Valar, so they seek his counsel, and he submits always to the will of Ilúvatar. He and his spouse dwell in Valimar, the home of the Valar on Arda, upon Mt. Oiolosse (Mount Everwhite), the tallest mountain on earth, from which they can behold almost everything that occurs in Arda.

Varda, also called **Elbereth** (lady of the stars), one of the Valar. Spouse of Manwë, she dwells with him in the halls of Taniquetil on Mt. Oiolosse and bends her thoughts always upon both Elves and men. She knows all regions of Ea and loves light above all creations of Ilúvatar. With his blessing, she creates the stars and is often invoked by both Elves and men, who revere her above all other Valar, as "star-kindler." She also creates the mighty lamps that first light Middle Earth (where men and Elves dwell) and places several especially bright constellations in the sky when those lamps are thrown down by Melkor. He fears her power above that of her peers because his strength lies in darkness.

Melkor (he who arises in might), originally the mightiest and most favored of the Ainur, renamed **Morgoth** (dark enemy) after his theft of the Silmarils. Lucifer-like, he turns his power to selfish ends and eventually loses his surpassing beauty, rebelling against Ilúvatar and seeking to destroy the Music. After eons of undermining and perverting the works of the Valar, he is taken captive and imprisoned for centuries in the halls of Mandos, the realm of Namo, keeper of the houses of the dead. When he eventually "repents," he is paroled by Manwë, who is incapable of understanding evil; eventually he escapes, enlists the aid of the ferocious spider-creature Ungoliant, and destroys the Two Trees that light the Blessed Lands of Valimar. After he steals the Silmarils, jewels of incredible beauty in which the light of the Trees is preserved, the Valar join forces with Elves and men to overthrow his kingdom at tremendous cost: Ainur, Maiar, Elves, and men die; the earth itself is rent and twisted by the tremendous forces unleashed in the battle. Like Lucifer, however, Melkor has corrupted others of the Ainur and multitudes of the Maiar, a lesser order of angelic beings, in addition to seducing many men, so his evil cannot be fully eradicated from Arda. Able only to pollute or imitate, he perverts captured Elves into Orcs, which become some of Sauron's most terrible servants. His most terrible "creations" are the ferocious demons called Balrogs, which may be twisted Maiar. His most powerful and deadly convert is Sauron.

Sauron, one of the Maiar perverted by Melkor, once as beautiful as Melkor. Originally the lieutenant of Morgoth (the Valar refuse to call Melkor by any other name), he becomes a Dark Lord himself after the downfall of Melkor, taking the Black Land of Mordor for his own and building the mighty Barad-dur (Dark Tower) as his chief fortress. Desiring to rule all Middle Earth, he seduces many men and a few Maiar, as well as drawing to himself sundry dark creatures devised by Melkor in imitation of Iluvatar's true powers. Sauron's deadliest weapon is the One Ring, which he forges in the fires of Orodruin (Mount Doom), pouring into the ring much of his own power. It controls the nine rings, which he gives to mortal men to enslave them, and exerts some power even over the seven rings of the Dwarves and the three rings of the Elves. Cut from his hand by Isildur during the Last Alliance of Elves and Men, it is lost for an age in the river Anduin, found first by Gollum and then by Bilbo Baggins, and is finally destroyed by Frodo, Bilbo's heir, thus casting down Sauron and bringing the Third Age to an end.

Ulmo, one of the Valar, lord of waters. Close to Manwë in might, he comes seldom to the councils of the Valar, preferring to roam the seas, streams, lakes, fountains, and rivers of Arda. Because water is ubiquitous, all the news, needs, and griefs of earth come to Ulmo, who conveys what might be otherwise hidden to Manwë. Earth dwellers say that the sound of his great horns, the Ulumuri, can be heard during storms and high tides; once heard, it implants the sea-longing forever in the heart of the hearer.

Aule, one of the Valar, lord of all substances of which earth is made. He is a smith and master of all crafts; jealous of his skill, Melkor takes special delight in marring his works. Weary of battling Melkor and desiring to make something marvelous, Aule creates the hardy race of Dwarves, unwittingly usurping the prerogative of Ilúvatar. When he humbly submits his creation to Ilúvatar and repents of his audacity, offering to destroy his creations, Ilúvatar forgives him and casts the Dwarves into a deep sleep until

their proper time to join the other races on earth.

Yavanna, also called **Kementari** (queen of the earth), spouse of Aule. She loves all growing things, both animals and plants, especially trees. She sings into being the Two Trees that light Valinor until Melkor destroys them. At her request, Ilúvatar creates the Ents, giant shepherds of trees, to protect the forests.

Fëanor (spirit of fire), son of the Elven king Finwë and Miriel, who fades into death soon after his birth. He is greatest among the race of Elves called Noldor, skillful craftsmen whom he later leads into rebellion. Marvelously gifted but prone to jealousy, he creates the Silmarils, the three most beautiful jewels in the universe, and the Palantiri, the "seeing stones" of Numenor. Corrupted by Melkor, he is used to destroy the bliss of the Elves who have migrated from Middle Earth to Valinor.

Thingol (grey-cloak), also called **Elwë,** an Elven lord who marries the Maia Melian, the father of Luthien. His Hidden Kingdom of Doriath is one of the few refuges for Elves in Middle Earth during the depredations of Melkor.

Luthien Tinuviel (nightingale), daughter of Thingol, the most beautiful of Elvenkind. Relinquishing immortality for love of Beren, a human, she chooses mortality in order to join him in the afterlife. They help to overthrow Melkor and rescue one Silmaril from his iron crown.

Beren One-hand, a mortal, husband of Luthien Tinuviel. After helping to overthrow Melkor, he loses a hand to Carcharoth, a demon-wolf from Angband, who bites it off to devour the Silmaril, which Beren holds. Eventually slain by the same wolf, which has been driven mad by the power of the Silmaril (and from whose body the Silmaril is recovered), he alone of mortal men is allowed to return from the dead to help in later battles. He and Luthien are the ancestors of Elrond, Elros, and the Kings of Numenor.

Eärendil (lover of the sea) **the Mariner,** a half-elven who weds Elwing, the granddaughter of Beren and Luthien. His doom is to sail the heavens forever with the one remaining Silmaril on his brow, as a light and a hope for earth dwellers.

Ar-Pharazôn (the golden), last king of Numenor, a great island within sight of Valinor prepared by the Valar to be the dwelling of the Edain (men of the west) as a reward for their struggles against Sauron. Captor of Sauron, by whom he is seduced, he leads a great fleet in rebellion against the Valar, seeking eternal life. At the moment when his fleet touches the Blessed Lands, they are removed forever from the confines of earth; the fleet is swallowed by a huge abyss. Numenor is destroyed by a gigantic tidal wave from which only nine ships of loyal Numenoreans, led by Isildur, escape.

Elrond Half-elven, a descendant of Beren and Luthien who chooses to belong to the Elven kindred. Wise and revered, he rules Imladris (Rivendell), in which the heirs of Isildur dwell until the time for the final battle with Sauron. He is the keeper of Vilya, the Ring of Air, bequeathed to him by Gil-galad the Elven king, and is the father of Arwen Undomiel, the "Evenstar" of her people, in whom the likeness of her great-grandmother, Luthien, has come again to Middle Earth. To Elrond's grief, she also chooses mortality in order to marry Aragorn, heir of Isildur.

Gandalf, also called **Mithrandir** (the grey pilgrim), a Maia, one of the Istari (wizards) sent by the Valar to battle Sauron. Ancient, wise, and fearless, he is the keeper of the Elven ring Narya, the Ring of Fire, which he wields in his long struggle against Sauron. Long aware that the One Ring resides in the Shire with Bilbo Baggins, he is instrumental in preserving it until Frodo can undertake the quest to destroy it.

Círdan, the Lord of the Havens, from which homesick Elves may depart Middle Earth for Valinor. A shipwright, he was keeper of the Elven ring Narya, which he surrenders to Gandalf for use in the war against Sauron.

Elendil (star lover), called the tall, descended from Earendil and Elwing but not of the direct line of the Kings of Numenor. He leads the fleet of the faithful who escape the downfall of Numenor and founds the realms of the Numenoreans in Middle Earth. Although he is slain in the overthrow of Sauron at the end of the Second Age, the shards of his sword, Narsil, which broke beneath him when he fell, are preserved by his heirs throughout the Third Age until the time for their reforging for the final battle against Sauron.

Isildur, son of Elendil. He cuts the One Ring from Sauron's hand at the end of the Second Age and keeps it as weregild for his father and brother instead of throwing it into the fires of Orodruin to destroy it. The ring later betrays him to his death in the River Anduin, where it remains hidden for most of the Third Age.

Aragorn, called **Elfstone** and **Estel** (hope) by the Elves, son of Arathorn. Disguised as a Ranger of the North, he has been reared in Rivendell, where he falls in love with the Elven maiden Arwen Evenstar. Isildur's heir through generations unbroken, he inherits the shards of Narsil and bears the sword reforged into the final battle against Sauron in order to inherit his kingship and earn his right to wed Arwen. He becomes the first king of the Fourth Age, the age of men.

Frodo Baggins, a Hobbit, who inherits the One Ring from Bilbo. He and his servant Samwise help to bring about the final downfall of Sauron as well as the fading of the three Elven rings. As a reward for valor, he is allowed to join the last Elves who sail from the Havens.

Sonya H. Cashdan

THE SILVER DOVE

Author: Andrey Bely (Boris Nikolayevich Bugaev, 1880-1934)
Type of work: Novel
Time of action: c. 1900
First published: Serebryanny golub, 1909-1910 (English translation, 1974)

Pyotr Daryalsky, a poet who makes a summer visit to the small Russian village of Tselebeyevo. The handsome young Daryalsky, who has no obvious intellectual gifts or notable background, soon falls in love with Katya Gugolevo, who lives nearby with her grandmother, the Baroness Todrabe-Graaben. The dreamily impractical Daryalsky is an innocent romantic weakling, who is soon identified by the revolutionary leader Kudeyarov as an appropriate potential father of the messiah who will lead thehoped-for overthrow of the government. Thus, Daryalsky is paired off by Kudeyarov with Matryona, a peasant woman whose earthiness contrasts with the vaguely spiritual beauty of Katya Gugolevo. His plight—torn between the two women— represents allegorically the plight of Russia at the turn of the century: looking West to European culture while looking East at its Asian heritage.

Katya Gugolevo, a lovely young aristocrat who lives with her grandmother and falls in love with Daryalsky. Katya has no special qualities; she is an allegorical embodiment of what many Russian intellectuals at the time saw as a waning European civilization. She contrasts physically and spiritually with Matryona.

Matryona, the peasant woman chosen to be the mother of the messiah of the revolution. The earthy Matryona is Mother Russia, a clichéd incarnation of the vitality of Russia's Tolstoyan peasantry. She is cloaked in a mystique that is aptly symbolized by the hypnotic appeal she exerts on Daryalsky—the same kind of mythic force that the peasantry represented for European Romantic intellectuals throughout the nineteenth century. She is also apparently Kudeyarov's common-law wife.

Kudeyarov, a carpenter who lives with Matryona and leads the group of political revolutionaries known as the "Doves." Kudeyarov is the most interesting of the four characters who carry the story. His face is described as split into opposed halves, a peculiarity that suggests the ambivalence of his personality. He is eager to pander for Daryalsky in inciting an affair with Matryona, but he is at the same time distressed by jealousy. The response is understandable enough on the simplest level, but his jealousy perhaps also betrays his envy of the role he sees Daryalsky playing in the revolution. His heavy allegorical burden is further weighted by the New Testament allusions that enrich his role: his carpenter's occupation, his anticipation of a messiah, and the ritual sharing of bread and wine that introduces the meetings of the Doves. Matryona and Daryalsky produce no child, and the disappointed Kudeyarov has Daryalsky murdered by the Doves when the poet realizes how he is being used. Kudeyarov is a provocative harbinger of much that was to follow in Russia.

Frank Day

THE SILVER TASSIE

Author: Sean O'Casey (John Casey, 1880-1964)
Type of work: Play
Time of action: During and after World War I
First published: 1928

Harry Heegan, a boisterous and athletic young man. He is established as a local hero early in the play, winning the cup, the "silver tassie," for his football club while he is on leave from the army. In love with Jessie, Harry is a rather unthinking man, devoted to the senses. He takes for granted his own strength and health and the adoration of others. When he is wounded in battle and his legs are paralyzed, he loses his standing at home as well as Jessie's love, and he becomes a bitter outcast, haunting his former friends and ultimately renouncing them.

Teddy Foran, a neighbor and comrade of Harry who is married to a woman who prefers to have him away at war. He is large and powerful and is first seen chasing his battered wife into the Heegan's home. Physical dominance over others is his most notable trait: He breaks all the crockery in his home before his leave is ended. He is rendered powerless, and dependent on his wife, when he is blinded in battle.

Barney Bagnal, a friend and comrade of Harry, a pleasant, unexceptional young man. He is clearly in Harry's shadow when they are home on leave, and he is tied to a gunwheel throughout the entire second act as punishment for stealing a chicken. Despite his unheroic character in much of the play, it is Barney who is the hero at home after the war. He has come home unscathed, and decorated; he is the latest hero of the football club and Jessie's new lover. He comes to represent all that Harry has lost and finally rejects.

Jessie Taite, a spirited, young local woman who is in love with Harry. When he is injured, she refuses even to visit him in the hospital. Her attachments are based on physical attraction and public esteem, and she easily transfers her love to Barney after the war. While at first she is disapproved of by other characters, she comes to represent the prevailing ethos—selfish and utilitarian—of the whole community.

Sylvester Heegan, Harry's father, a retired dockworker who spends his free time drinking and bragging about his son's exploits. He is a strong, stocky man of a humorous and argumentative temper. Ultimately he cares little for his son, and his comic exploits with his friend Simon Norton begin to appear grotesque when they are removed from their earlier, jovial context.

Mrs. Heegan, Harry's mother, a nervous, worn-out woman. Her conversation tends to revolve around money. Her worries that Harry might miss his boat after his leave-time is ended mask a concern that the family might then lose money from the government. She is oblivious to Harry's pain after he is crippled, and reproaches Jessie not with her betrayal of Harry, but with the money that he had spent on her when courting.

Simon Norton, a friend and former colleague of Sylvester Heegan. He is a slightly less robust and loud man than Sylvester. A caricature of a petty, self-centered man, Simon maintains a running debate with his friend, intent on preserving an air of authority. Their trivial wrangling endures throughout the play, in increasing contrast to the situation around them.

Susie Monican, an attractive young woman who is in love with Harry and extremely jealous of Jessie. She hides her infatuation behind a rigid sense of propriety and loud religious fervor. A stint as a wartime nurse ironically liberates her, and she enters a romance with Harry's doctor while treating Harry with impersonal pity.

Mrs. Foran, Teddy's wife. She is indifferent to her husband, who beats her when she appears to be too happy to see him return to war. She is heartbroken over Teddy's destruction of her household goods but less concerned over his blindness.

Heidi J. Holder

A SIMPLE STORY

Author: Shmuel Yosef Agnon (Shmuel Yosef Czaczkes, 1888-1970)
Type of work: Novella
Time of action: The late nineteenth and early twentieth centuries
First published: Sipur pashut, 1935 (English translation, 1985)

Hirshl Hurvitz (hûr'shəl), the weak-willed son of a wealthy shopkeeper. He falls madly in love with the family servant, Blume, who is also his cousin. His domineering mother manipulates him into a more suitable marriage, which he spinelessly accepts, although his feelings for his wife range from detached tolerance to hatred. In the first year of his marriage, he falls into a deep depression that culminates in insanity. With the help of Dr. Langsam, he slowly returns to health and is able to find a measure of happiness within the conventions of family life and the traditions of the Jewish community.

Blume Nacht (blōō'·mĕ näk̲t), Hirshl's very beautiful, penniless cousin, who becomes a servant in his household after the death of her parents. She is a paragon housekeeper and cook, yet quiet and retiring and as mysterious as her name, "Night Flower," suggests. She secretly returns Hirshl's love, but when she learns of his betrothal, she leaves her employment with the Hurvitzes. Deeply hurt, idealistic, and proud, she remains loyal to her secret love although two other men want her. By the novel's end, she has faded from sight.

Mina Ziemlich (zēm'lĭk̲), the daughter of a wealthy tavern keeper of a nearby town. She has been educated in a city boarding school and is considered cultured and fashionable. Although her betrothal to Hirshl is a product of matchmaking and misunderstanding, she admires her groom and is attracted to him. She knows in her heart that her husband does not love her, however, and though she tries to make the best of their joyless and incommunicative marriage, her pregnancy debilitates her and she gives birth to a sickly child. Her second child, conceived after Hirshl's return to mental health, is a healthy product of her newly happy marriage.

Tsirl Hurvitz (tsėr'əl), Hirshl's mother, clever, determined, forceful, and a consummate diplomat. She is able to implement her will in her business dealings, her social relationships, and her family. She steers Hirshl in the direction she wants in everything—his diet, his occupation, even his exercise habits—and she chooses Mina to be his wife.

Baruch Meir Hurvitz (bä·rōōk' mä·yĕr'), Hirshl's father, a completely conventional man who wants nothing more from life than that it run smoothly. He performs his duties, and somewhat more than his duties, to his family, his community, and his business; quarrels with no one; and, though he is always ready to help his son in any way he can, finds his son's unhappiness and depression to be beyond his understanding.

Gedalia Ziemlich, Mina's father, a wealthy innkeeper and manager of the count's estate. He worries continuously that his good fortune will be reversed, plunging him back into his former destitution. His daughter's marriage to a Hurvitz seems another undeserved stroke of good luck, while his son-in-law's insanity seems one piece of expected catastrophe.

Bertha Ziemlich, Mina's mother, an industrious woman who continues to work hard and prides herself on putting on no airs, although her husband has attained a high place in their town. She and Hirshl's mother form a bulwark of tradition for the young couple, and, at the end of the novel, she nurses her sickly infant grandson back to health while her daughter and Hirshl begin to be happy.

Yona Toyber, the matchmaker who arranges the marriage of Hirshl and Mina. For himself, long after the death of his first wife, he chooses a no-longer-young, shrewish hunchback who, after their marriage, becomes a good-natured angel of domesticity.

Getzel Stein, a clerk in the Hurvitz store, political activist, idealist, and ambitious founder of the local chapter of Workers of Zion. He is in love with Blume.

Dr. Langsam, a neurologist who uses no drugs and administers no psychological tests. He nurses Hirshl back to health with gentle conversations and a peaceful environment.

Lolette Kuby

THE SINGAPORE GRIP

Author: J. G. Farrell (1935-1979)
Type of work: Novel
Time of action: 1938-1942, 1976
First published: 1978

Walter Blackett, the protagonist, the ambitious co-owner and acting director of the Singapore firm of Blackett and Webb. Walter is a commanding figure, with pale blue eyes and white hair and mustache; his large head looms over a compact body and short legs. An entrepreneur convinced of his own worth, for years Walter has greedily exploited the native economy to advance company interests and has used the law and corrupt officials to undermine local competition. As the Japanese invade and Singapore falls, he remains contemptuous of Orientals in general and is more concerned with his company's simple-minded allegorical Jubilee pageant and with his rivals, the Langfields, than with historical inevitability. A prototype of the uprooted British imperialist, he is held tightly by the "Singapore grip," the dream of greater and greater financial coups, and is farcically blind to the realities of his and the British position in Malaya. He considers collaborating with the Japanese more acceptable than forgoing his long-held tyrannical power.

Monty Blackett, Walter's spoiled and insensitive thirty-year-old son and heir apparent. With blue, bulging eyes and poor judgment, he is clearly his father's son. Totally amoral and mindlessly exuberant, Monty thinks of the natives only in terms of sexual encounters and amusement potential. As a second-generation colonial convinced of British superiority and native inferiority, he implements his father's plans for exploitation with

self-assured aplomb, no matter how injurious to the locals.

Joan Blackett, Walter's bumptious, headstrong, and coldly calculating daughter, a femme fatale who toys with the sensitive Ehrendorf and who then tries to capture Matthew and his half of the business. A product of a Swiss finishing school, healthy and solidly built in the English manner, Joan is contemptuous of provincial Singapore and her youthful, rebellious affairs are a trial to her parents, though her pursuit of Matthew wins their blessing. Having forced him, while weak from fever, to consent to her marriage proposal, she is affronted by his later forceful rejection of the engagement. She and her brother share an unquestioning belief in their own superiority and in their right to manipulate and exploit those around them. They are both overwhelmingly materialistic; matters of the soul and conscience are unknown to them. Joan relies on sexual allure to tightly grip the men under her spell; she is self-serving, predatory, grasping, and ruthless, as her attempts to escape from Singapore with her unexpectedly acquired husband (Nigel Langfield) confirm.

Matthew Webb, the conscience-ridden son and heir of Walter Blackett's deceased partner, whom Joan and Walter pursue as a marital alliance. He is stooped and shortsighted, with rounded shoulders and an unhealthy complexion. At age thirty-three an otherworldly

Oxford innocent who believed in and worked for the League of Nations and who arrives in Singapore anxious to apply socialistic solutions easily and painlessly, Matthew is deeply bothered by racial abuse and by his own ineffectuality; stricken with a tropical disease that he imagines is the "Singapore Grippe," he finds Singapore a surreal nightmare and, throughout half the book, sees and hears life swirl around him through the veil of high fever and possible hallucination. Through Vera Chiang he sees a Malay that many foreigners do not, and his incredulous and then horrified reaction to traditional colonial attitudes and behavior provides the moral cornerstone of the book. He is an idealist amid opportunists, a slightly comic, muddled figure, made sympathetic by good intentions. Refusing to believe that the "Singapore Grip" is the sexual technique certain Singapore prostitutes use to improve trade, he asserts that it is the European stranglehold on the Orient.

Vera Chiang, Matthew's mistress and his father's protégée, an exotic Eurasian (the reputed daughter of a Russian princess and a Cantonese tea-merchant), a social activist who fled Shanghai police oppression, a survivor. Initially befriended by a thrill-seeking Joan, she becomes Joan's rival for Matthew, with her stunning Oriental beauty and sexuality proving the more intoxicating. Following the elder Webb's program of strenuous acrobatic nude exercise, she lives in the Webb home and nurses Matthew until forcibly removed. She is enigmatic but human, visiting and sympathizing with the aged and dying, giving English lessons, nursing those injured by the Japanese invasion, an Oriental earth mother offering understanding, calm, practical assistance, and hope.

Major Brendan Archer, a well-meaning and kindly retired British officer, an ineffectual liberal, sympathetic to the natives and appalled at their racist exploitation. Major Archer is always in the background, listening to Blackett's theories and plans, helping with civil service war preparation, sympathizing with refugees (in pidgin), caring for the cast-off people and animals of his associates, and indignantly protesting tragedy, disgrace, and injustice. A cynic and an optimist, the Major, like Matthew, provides an outsider's critical commentary on Singapore insiders. "What fools those men are!" he exclaims at one point, and then adds humbly, "Of course, they may know things that we don't."

François Dupigny, an old friend of Major Archer from World War I days, a cynical French rationalist who is continually appalled at the inanities and rudeness of the local British and who has watched his friend become more and more private and eccentric in his habits. "Stranded in an alien culture, surrounded by British dog-lovers," he longs for prewar days in Hanoi or Saigon, but instead finds himself fleeing Japanese bombers. Dupigny debates Major Archer on the nature of man, and concludes that self-interest negates any possibility of brotherhood and a community of races.

Captain Jim Ehrendorf, an American officer from Kansas City, longtime school chum of Matthew, and rejected suitor of Joan. Ehrendorf contradicts all the British stereotypes of Americans; He is a Rhodes scholar, soft-spoken, cultured, well-educated, well-mannered, tactful, polished, and well-informed: in sum a complete gentleman, pale and handsome with an attractive smile. He is hopeless in love and suffers Joan's torments without complaint: throwing himself (fully clothed) into a pool or thrusting his hand into an open fire at her whim. He becomes introspective and quiet, and finally yields the field to his friend, Matthew. As the Japanese advance, he provides an American perspective on British defense and is practical and commonsensical about war in a way the British are not. He observes the confirmation of Ehrendorf's Second Law: "In human affairs things tend inevitably to go wrong. Things are slightly worse at any given moment than at any preceding moment."

Cheong, an embittered Blackett family servant whose father and uncles had been shipped to Singapore as indentured coolies under appalling conditions and who incarnates their anger and sense of outrage. He finds the strange mixture of exploitation, general cruelty, and personal kindness of whites inscrutable. Summing up the native perspective, he muses, "How strange these people are!" At-

tuned to the Chinese grapevine, he always has the news before his masters and fears the worst.

Gina Macdonald

THE SIRENS OF TITAN

Author: Kurt Vonnegut, Jr. (1922-   )
Type of work: Novel
Time of action: The near future
First published: 1959

Malachi Constant (Unk), the world's richest and luckiest playboy, whose name means "faithful messenger." Having inherited from his father, Noel, a previously infallible system for stock investment, Malachi is told by Winston Niles Rumfoord that he will lose his money, marry Rumfoord's wife (Beatrice), have a child, and move to Saturn's largest moon. Despite all of his efforts to the contrary, these events occur. Lawsuits deplete his capital; he is impressed into the army of Mars and fitted with a radio control; he rapes Mrs. Rumfoord while drunk; he engenders a son, Chrono; he is lost on Mercury; he returns to Earth, where he is vilified by Rumfoord's new Church of God, the Utterly Indifferent; and he is forced to retreat with his wife and son to Titan.

Winston Niles Rumfoord, former millionaire, member of the social elite, and explorer. He is now, with his dog Kazak, a collection of particles that materialize at regular intervals. Stylish, elderly, and possessing a winning smile, Rumfoord has had the power to foresee the future ever since he drove his spaceship into a time tunnel, or "chronosynclastic infundibulum." In an attempt to manipulate Earth's history, he creates a suicidal army on Mars, whose destruction engenders global remorse and the formation of a new religion. All of this is done in order to force his wife and Malachi to marry and create a son whose good-luck piece must be transported to Titan, where it is needed by a visiting alien.

Beatrice Rumfoord (Bee), the reserved,

privileged, and too-proper virgin wife of Winston. A tall and beautiful woman in her late thirties at the story's start, her central desire is to remain chaste and so frustrate her husband's predictions. Her rape by Malachi defeats both wishes and makes her the mother of Chrono. During the story's forty years, she loses her affectation as well as teeth and one eye. In the end, she loves both Malachi and her son.

Chrono, son of Malachi and Beatrice. This juvenile delinquent unknowingly carries the secret of earth's history. Born on Mars after his mother's rape, Chrono, a dark and sociopathic player of German bat ball, picks up a piece of scrap metal in a flamethrower factory. This good-luck charm is the key to the story. As the reader discovers in the end, all the plot's involutions only serve to take Chronos' talisman to Titan, where it is needed as a replacement part for an alien spaceship.

Salo, an interstellar robot from the small Magellanic Cloud. A sentient and ultimately caring machine, the orange Salo has a head on gimbals, three inflatable feet, no arms, and three eyes. Carrying the single word "Greetings" across the galaxy, his spaceship's breakdown has forced the members of his home planet, Tralfamadore, to use their "Universal Will to Become" to influence Earth's history such that it would produce, in the form of Chronos' good-luck charm, the piece needed for his saucer's repair. In the end, Salo learns to love Rumfoord more than his robot mission, and it is this emotion more than the absurd machinations of planetary fate that becomes his triumph.

Stony Stevenson, Malachi's best and only friend and one of the commanders of the army of Mars. Stony is an admirer of Unk because Unk resists the brainwashing to which he is repeatedly subjected. Ironically, Unk (or Malachi) strangles Stony to death after a final and effective mind cleansing. This execution takes place under radio control and in complete ignorance. It demonstrates yet again how little human wishes have to do with personal or collective fate.

Daniel D. Fineman

SISTER MARY IGNATIUS EXPLAINS IT ALL FOR YOU

Author: Christopher Durang (1949-   )
Type of work: Play
Time of action: The late 1970's
First produced: 1979

Sister Mary Ignatius, a nun and fifth-grade teacher at what she calls Our Lady of Perpetual Sorrow School. Sister Mary appears in an old-fashioned nun's habit; her age is uncertain, but she might be anywhere from forty to sixty. While she displays many quite human characteristics, Sister Mary is a caricature of an earnest but oppressive parochial school teacher, more concerned with doctrine than truth. One of her chief assertions is that God answers all prayers, but that sometimes the answer is no. She lectures directly to the audience, occasionally answering questions that she has on file cards, but the information she presents is often confused. When questioned, Thomas, her assistant, gets the commandments wrong, but Sister nevertheless approves his answers and rewards him with cookies. She claims to come from a large family, some twenty-six children, of whom five became priests, seven nuns, three brothers. The others, as well as her mother, she says, were placed in institutions. When four students from her 1959 fifth-grade class arrive and perform a Christmas pageant, she becomes even more confused. The pageant, presumably written by Mary Jean Mahoney, a fifth-grade student from 1948, clearly reflects Sister Mary's teachings and marks the turning point of the play. After the performance, Sister Mary questions her former students and discovers that they have all abandoned her teaching and that each has sinned in some way. Sister Mary immediately dislikes Diane, who has had two abortions. When Diane accuses Sister Mary of being insane and threatens her with a gun, Sister tricks her, and, drawing her own gun from beneath her habit, kills her. After learning that Gary, a homosexual, has been to confession just that morning, Sister kills him, too, so that he may go directly to Heaven. She allows Philomena to leave quietly but finally takes Thomas on her lap and directs him to keep the gun aimed at Aloysius while she naps.

Thomas, a seven-year-old boy, in the second grade at Our Lady of Perpetual Sorrow School, serves as Sister's assistant and is an example of her latest victim. He wears a tie and a school blazer. When he first enters, Sister explains that, having achieved the age of seven, he is capable of choosing to sin or not to sin. In reciting his lessons, and his catechism, Thomas illustrates Sister Mary's warped teaching. He remains loyal to her when she is attacked by her former pupils and in the end happily recites his catechism.

Diane Symonds, a student in Sister Mary Ignatius' 1959 fifth-grade class who plays the Blessed Mother in the pageant. At the age of eighteen, on the same day that her mother died of cancer, Diane was raped by a maniac who broke into her house, and she subsequently had an abortion. Depressed for many years afterward, she had a second abortion after she was raped by her psychiatrist. She organizes her classmates to present the Christmas pageant as a means of getting even with Sister Mary Ignatius for having instilled in her a false view of the world. Her death at the hands of Sister Mary illustrates Sister's continuing strength and Diane's own ineptitude.

Gary Sullavan, another member of Sister Mary's 1959 fifth-grade class, a homosexual, who joins with Diane to embarrass their former teacher. Seduced when he was in the seminary, Gary afterward went to New York, where he reports having slept with five hundred different people. Gary, who portrays St. Joseph in the pageant, lives with Jeff Hannigan, another of Sister Mary's former fifth-grade students.

Philomena Rostovitch and
Aloysius Busiccio, who together perform the role of the camel, Misty, in the pageant. Philomena is an unwed mother with a daughter age three. She was beaten by Sister Mary for being stupid. Aloysius is married and has two children but recently has become an alcoholic and has taken to beating his wife. He attributes his bladder problems to Sister Mary never having allowed him to go to the bathroom.

Robert M. Bender

62: A MODEL KIT

Author: Julio Cortázar (1914-1984)
Type of work: Novel
Time of action: The 1950's or the 1960's
First published: 62: Modelo para armar, 1968 (English translation, 1972)

Juan, an Argentine interpreter who works for an international agency. He has a humorous and unprejudiced character and an almost surrealist vision of the world, which he shares with most of the characters, all of whom are among a group of friends that meet habitually in the café Cluny. Juan is interested in metaphysical matters, especially in the ways in which reality is perceived. He has much imagination and looks for secret keys or symbols to understand the universe or what happens to him. He shares the keys, the dreams, and the imaginary realms ("the city," "the zone") with his friends. He usually travels with his partner, Tell, but he is desperately in love with Hélène. During his stay in Vienna, as he works at an international conference and shares his life with Tell, he is obsessed with the story of a bloody countess, the Basilisk House, and an old and disgusting woman, Frau Marta, who vampirizes an English girl who is touring Vienna. Always mixing fantasies with real life, he tries to save the English girl from an imaginary danger, and everything becomes a metaphor of his relationship with Hélène. Back in Paris, he has an intense encounter with Hélène but is unable to keep her after she tells her story of a dead patient who resembled Juan and her affair with Celia. He desperately intends to reach her and to follow her but he loses her in a scenery where dreams and symbols are mixed and become real.

Hélène, a young French anesthetist, aloof and distant but a sensible and tender person. Unlike Juan, she is unable to share everything with her friends in the Cluny. She is really touched when a young man, almost a boy, with a close resemblance to Juan, dies without awakening from anesthesia. She leaves the hospital very disturbed, goes to the Cluny, and meets Celia, who has just run away from her parents' home. She invites Celia to her small apartment and, that night, having no control of her feelings and senses, forces Celia to make love with her. After this disturbing experience, she has a sexual encounter with Juan, but she cannot forgive herself for the disgraceful incident of the night spent with Celia.

Marrast, a French sculptor with an extraordinary sense of humor who travels to London to get a stone to carve a statue of Vercingetorix, commissioned by the mayor of Arcueil. In order to forget that his lover, Nicole, has revealed to him her love for Juan, he invents absurd situations in a museum, situations in which almost all the members of the group, now in London, are engaged. He teaches French to Austin but then, when Nicole betrays him with Austin, comes back to Paris and works on the sculpture. All the members of the group are together in the inauguration of the Vercingetorix statue, and Nicole, too, is there. He continues loving Nicole and tries to get her back.

Nicole, a French illustrator of children's books. She has a good relationship with Marrast, but their happiness is destroyed when she confesses that she is in love with Juan. They live together for a while, but she decides to go to bed with Austin in order to destroy Marrast's love. She is not able to gain another's love nor to forget Marrast or destroy his affection for her.

Tell, Juan's lover. She is a young, beautiful, and independent Danish woman. She shares Juan's friends and travels with him, trying to enjoy their relationship even when she knows that Juan is in love with Hélène. She participates joyfully in the surrealistic games in which Juan is engaged, such as following Frau Marta and the English girl in their wanderings across Vienna and trying to protect the girl from impending danger.

Calac and
Polanco, two Argentines, the first a writer and critic, the second a worker in unusual jobs. Both have a ludicrous sense of life and are always engaged in absurd dialogues, in which they have nothing to say. Sometimes, they use a language of their own, which irritates conformist people. They are, in some respects, as Juan is in others, the alter ego of the author.

Celia, the youngest member of the group. She is rich and spoiled and decides to leave her parents' home. She runs into Hélène in the Cluny. They are alone because Juan and Tell are in Vienna and the others are in London. She has no place to spend the night and accepts Hélène's invitation to her place with curiosity, because Hélène is a mystery to most members of the group. She suffers a tremendous shock when she accepts Hélène's sexual assault, and she decides to go to London to join the others. She meets Austin and falls in love with him.

Austin, a young English lute player who receives French lessons from Marrast and joins the group. He is handsome and self-confident, having a casual affair with Nicole and initiating Celia into the delights of heterosexual love. He meets the group in London and travels to Paris, attending with them the inauguration of Marrast's statue in Arcueil.

The paredros, abstract entities that sometimes function as an alter ego of the main characters.

Feuille Morte (fœy mōrt), an indefinite entity, a feminine voice that only says "bisbis bisbis."

Leda Schiavo

SLAUGHTERHOUSE-FIVE
Or, The Children's Crusade

Author: Kurt Vonnegut, Jr. (1922-   )
Type of work: Novel
Time of action: 1922-1976
First published: 1969

Billy Pilgrim, a conservative, middle-aged optometrist living in upstate Ilium, New York. Born in 1922, Billy leads a very bland life—except for the fact that at the end of World War II he came "unstuck in time" and began to jump back and forth among past, present, and future, and, in 1967, was captured by a flying saucer from the planet Tralfamadore. (The novel's jerky structure mirrors his interplanetary and time travel.) Billy is thus a schizophrenic character: An apathetic, almost autistic widower in the present, he is also a crackpot visionary who claims to have visited another planet and to speak as a prophet. The cause of Billy's schizoid behavior, as Vonnegut makes clear, is the horror he has witnessed in Dresden as a prisoner of war (along with Vonnegut) when this beautiful old German city was systematically incinerated by American bombers.

Kurt Vonnegut, Jr., the author of the novel, living on Cape Cod, Massachusetts, but also a character in it. The first and last chapters of the novel form a frame around the narrative proper, and, in them, Vonnegut describes his trip with his wartime buddy, Bernard V. O'Hare, back to Dresden, Germany, where they were imprisoned during World War II, as well as current events (for example, the assassinations of Martin Luther King, Jr., and Robert Kennedy). The persona of this narrator is naïve, idealistic, and fixated on World War II, especially on the fire-bombing of Dresden, a city of no apparent military significance. As he tells us, Vonnegut himself was one of the few survivors of the destruction of Dresden, when he and other prisoners of war—including Billy Pilgrim in the novel itself—were entombed in a slaughterhouse below the city and thus survived the holocaust above. Vonnegut surfaces several other times in the narrative he is telling of Billy Pilgrim, so history and fiction, author and fictional characters intermingle freely in Vonnegut's pages, as past and present and future similarly do.

Montana Wildhack, a voluptuous movie star who is captured and put in a zoo on Tralfamadore along with Billy Pilgrim, and who becomes his lover and bears his child while they are living in captivity there.

Valencia Merble Pilgrim, Billy's wife, a rich, overweight woman who is later killed rushing to Billy's aid after a plane crash in which Billy is the only survivor.

Howard W. Campbell, Jr., an American collaborator working for the Nazis who tries to convince Billy and his fellow prisoners to defect to the German side.

Edgar Derby, an older, idealistic American soldier and former high-school teacher who stands up to Howard Campbell but then is executed at the end of the war for the trivial act of stealing a teapot.

Roland Weary, a pathetic and tiresome comrade of Billy Pilgrim who dies in the boxcar taking the prisoners to Dresden.

Paul Lazzaro, a mean and ugly member of the band of prisoners being shipped to Dresden who vows to kill Billy after the war in revenge for the death of Roland Weary, and eventually does, in 1976.

Kilgore Trout, a science-fiction writer living in Ilium (and a character who figures in other Vonnegut novels as well).

David Peck

THE SLAVE

Author: Isaac Bashevis Singer (1904-   )
Type of work: Novel
Time of action: The mid- and late seventeenth century
First published: Der Knekht, 1961 (English translation, 1962)

Jacob, a devout, scholarly Jew, aged twenty-nine. A survivor of a massacre, he is sold as a slave to Polish peasant Jan Bzik, who uses him as a cowherd. He is tall, with brown hair and blue eyes, and he is descended from rabbis. He resists the temptation to commit adultery with Wanda, Jan's daughter, in a mountain village in which diseased sexuality is rampant, but finally succumbs and is tormented by shame and desire. After five years, Jacob is ransomed by fellow Jews, and their account of Cossack atrocities in his village and of the death of his wife and children increases his guilt. Yet, he returns to Wanda after seeing her in a dream. It is Jacob's faithful nature that makes him return to Pilitz twenty years after her death, and there he dies, faithful to the last.

Wanda Bzik, widowed daughter of Jan. She is almost pagan but comparatively civilized, a fair-haired, good-looking, capable, and healthy woman. Managing her father's household, she falls in love with Jacob and helps him by bringing him food and treating a snakebite. She pursues him passionately and is anxious to learn his doctrine. When he is ransomed, she falls sick and is in this condition when he rescues her. She accompanies him to Pilitz, pretending to be a deaf-mute, Dumb Sarah, and trying to behave as a Jewish married woman should. She dies giving birth to a son, revealing, in her agony, the truth about her origins. She appears to Jacob in dreams for the rest of his life.

Adam Pilitzky, the fifty-four-year-old overlord of the village of Pilitz, whose youth was spent in the West. He is ruthless with his peasantry but is a poor manager, with corrupt bailiffs. Against his declared intent, a Jewish community forms in Pilitz. He hangs himself when Pilitz passes to a creditor.

Theresa Pilitzky, Adam's wife. She is small, plump, sprightly, and as loose-living as her husband. For her own amusement, she tries to tempt Jacob. She dies alone after giving her remaining wealth to an impoverished nobleman, her last lover.

Jan Bzik, Wanda's father and Jacob's master. He has a certain innate intelligence that prevents him from ridiculing Jacob. Once a man of importance in the village, he is now old, sick, and morose, so that his wife wishes him dead. He dies, leaving Wanda, his favorite daughter, unprotected.

Gershon, a powerful man in Pilitz who has leased the manorial fields. A cunning dealer and a leader of the Jewish community who collects (and embezzles) their taxes, he dresses like a rabbi, looks like a butcher, and dislikes Jacob and all scholars. He is a stickler for the forms of religion and is loud in condemning Jacob when the truth emerges.

Dziobak, a Catholic priest in the mountain village, where pagan superstitions prevail. He is short, broad, clumsily built, lame, dirty, and drunk, and the father of many children.

Miriam, Jacob's sister who survived the massacre. Formerly handsome and well to do, she is now toothless and ragged and shrilly enumerates the atrocities.

Tirza Temma, a Jewish woman forced into marriage with a Cossack. Hearing that her first husband will be allowed to divorce her, she berates the community in Cossack, having forgotten her Yiddish.

W. Gordon Cunliffe

SLEEPLESS DAYS

Author: Jurek Becker (1937-   )
Type of work: Novel
Time of action: The 1970's
First published: Schlaflose Tage, 1978 (English translation, 1979)

Karl Simrock, an East Berlin high-school teacher. Soon after his thirty-sixth birthday, he examines his past life and finds it wanting. His marriage is empty, and his work as a teacher is governed by authoritarian regimentation. He leaves his wife, Ruth (root), and daughter, Leonie (lā·ō′nē·ä), and enters into a relationship with Antonia Kramm. At work he starts to measure the difference between East German ideology and reality. He tries to teach his students to question and doubt, not merely to accept. This emphasis causes him to lose his position, however, and he takes work as a bakery truck driver with Boris (bô′rĭs).

Ruth Simrock, a part-time insurance agent and Karl's wife. Karl complains that she will not accept certain matters as "women's business." Very controlled, she never cries, even when her husband suddenly leaves her. She admits that marriage to him has been "hellish." She accuses him of leaving her because school authorities "broke his back."

Kabitzke (kä·bĭts′kə), the vice-principal at Simrock's school. A timid sycophant, he cannot understand Karl's rebelliousness and warns him that it is self-destructive. He refuses to support Karl publicly.

Antonia Kramm, age twenty-eight, a former physics student, now a free-lance typist. When younger, she was a textbook socialist until she became embittered by the hypocrisy of her society. Accepted at a university, she studies physics to avoid politics, but after three semesters she is nevertheless exmatriculated for political reasons. She attempts to create the greatest possible independence for herself, dreaming of "islands of solitude" in a society of enforced community. On vacation in Hungary with Simrock, she attempts, without first informing him, to escape to Austria, but she is caught and imprisoned for at least nineteen months.

Boris, age twenty-two, physically strong, a bakery truck driver with "charming long hair"; his dream is to see Liverpool. No heroic worker, he believes that anyone who claims to derive satisfaction from delivering bread is a liar or a fool. He goes through the motions of political commitment, not out of conviction, but in order to be left in peace; thus he destroys Karl Simrock's remaining illusions about his society.

Thomas C. Fox

SLEUTH

Author: Anthony Shaffer (1926-   )
Type of work: Play
Time of action: The 1970's
First published: 1970

Andrew Wyke, a writer of detective stories. A tall, well-built man of fifty-seven, he has written many old-fashioned mystery novels featuring the fictional detective Inspector Merridrew. Disdaining the modern detective shows one sees on television, he favors the golden age of mystery fiction, the 1930's, with stories featuring complex plots and elaborate puzzles. In the first act, Andrew amicably invites Milo Tindall over to his home to discuss Milo's plan to marry his wife, Marguerite. Yet, Andrew's real intention in inviting Milo over is to teach him a lesson in humility. He persuades Milo to participate in a game to steal Marguerite's jewels from a safe in the house; Milo can fence the jewels and keep the money to support Marguerite. The game turns nasty, however, when Andrew pulls a gun and threatens to shoot Milo. He explains that he will tell the police that he heard a burglar in the house and shot and killed the man. Andrew has no intention of letting Milo marry Marguerite. When he points the gun at Milo's head and shoots, the bullet is a blank. When Milo faints at the shot, Andrew wins the game; he has humiliated Milo.

Milo Tindall, Marguerite Wyke's lover. A slim, handsome man of thirty-five, of medium height, with a Mediterranean complexion inherited from his half-Italian, half-Jewish father, Milo is in the travel business at Dulwich. Humiliated by Andrew's game, Milo seeks revenge by disguising himself and reappearing at Andrew's house as Inspector Doppler, pretending to investigate the possible murder of Milo Tindall. Much to Andrew's surprise, Milo, as Inspector Doppler, discovers certain clues that incriminate Andrew in the so-called murder. Milo wins his game as he tells the horrified Andrew that the most time he will serve is seven years for manslaughter. When Milo

finally unmasks himself, Andrew knows he has found a worthy opponent. Yet, Milo has not yet completed his revenge.

Milo tells Andrew that he gained access to the house with the help of Andrew's lover, whom, Milo says, he raped and strangled and then buried in the yard. Furthermore, Milo planted evidence in the house that will incriminate Andrew in the murder. Through a series of riddles, Andrew finds the evidence before the police come to arrest him. In fact, the police do not arrive, because there has been no murder: Milo has humiliated Andrew a second time. When Milo tells Andrew that he plans to take Marguerite away and marry her, Andrew is desperate. Believing that he can make the burglar plan work in reality, and not simply as a hoax, he shoots Milo. As Milo dies, however, he has achieved his ultimate revenge on Andrew, for, as the play closes, the police do arrive.

Dale Davis

SLOW HOMECOMING

Author: Peter Handke (1942-   )
Type of work: Novel
Time of action: The mid-1970's
First published: Langsame Heimkehr, 1979 (*The Long Way Around*, 1985); *Die Lehre der Sainte-Victoire*, 1980 (*The Lesson of Mont-Sainte-Victoire*, 1985); *Kindergeschichte*, 1981 (*Child Story*, 1985)

The Long Way Around

Valentin Sorger, an Austrian geologist working in Alaska, above the Arctic Circle. He is in early middle age. His work consists of making geological sketches of the Alaskan terrain. Sorger begins to feel estranged from existence and decides to return to Austria. He flies to San Francisco and spends time with a married couple he knows. The colors and forms of nature become the object of his meditations, and he longs to find some kind of spiritual law, an experience of salvation, that will redefine his existence. He then flies to Denver and, finally, to New York, where he engages in a long and intense conversation with a stranger. Ultimately, he takes a plane for Europe.

The Lesson of Mont-Sainte-Victoire

The narrator, a writer who wanders in the South of France in order to see the various scenes that had been painted by the artist Paul Cézanne, especially the Mont-Sainte-Victoire. The narrator reflects upon the shapes of nature and the artist's task of transforming these landscapes into the transcendent forms of art. After a bizarre encounter with a half-crazed guard dog in a Foreign Legion camp, he realizes the extent of the hate and violence that permeates the world, and he longs even more for the existential salvation of art.

Child Story

The adult, an Austrian man, a simple parent living in Paris with his young daughter. He is in his late thirties. After the birth of his child, the parents' marriage breaks up, and the man and his daughter move to Paris. The adult constantly reflects upon his relationship to his child and often tends to view her as a kind of symbol of the innocence and spontaneity that he has lost in his own life.

One night, he loses his temper and strikes the child. He feels great guilt over his act.

The child, a girl around six years old. She is an average child and must deal with the consequences of her father's move to Paris. She attends a special school and must learn to make new friends.

Thomas F. Barry

SMALL CHANGES

Author: Marge Piercy (1936-   )
Type of work: Novel
Time of action: The late 1960's through the early 1970's
First published: 1973

Beth Phail Walker, a high school graduate who works as a secretary in Boston. Slight, quiet, and introverted, she is an omnivorous reader and a perceptive observer of her surroundings. Made to feel inferior by the traditional expectations of her family and husband and trapped in an early marriage with no possibility of attending college, she runs away, finds a job and room of her own, and audits classes at the Massachusetts Institute of Technology. Encounters with Miriam Berg and communal life lead to a series of "small changes." She becomes a vegetarian, forms a women's commune, divorces, and works intensely in women's theater. In her liaison with its leader, Wanda Rosario, she gains political awareness, speaks out, and discovers her sexuality and the joys of physical labor. Forming a lesbian family with Wanda brings her fulfillment.

Miriam Berg, a graduate student and researcher in computer science. She is an intelligent young Jewish woman with glossy black hair, full-bodied, vivacious, and outgoing. She pours her considerable energies equally into her academic studies and her stormy love relationship with Phil. Her search is for the love and support missing during her Flatbush years as a fat teenager with braces and thick glasses. The experiences of college in Wisconsin, the ordeal of her moth-

er's slow death, and her sexual awakening with Phil and Jackson give her self-confidence and new goals. Frustrated, however, by the transitory nature of communal life and the sexism that impedes her academic life and professional work at Logical Systems Development, she finds temporary security in marriage to Neil Stone and motherhood. That role fails to satisfy her energy. Her desire to reenter the job market and maintain her ties with Phil, Beth, and friends in local communes creates tension and misunderstanding with her husband.

Phil, a Vietnam veteran, woman chaser, and would-be poet. He is extremely handsome, with blue-green eyes and an ingratiating manner especially attractive to women. He works at a series of menial jobs to support his constant use of drugs. Rejecting the alcoholic father and battered mother who scarred his Boston childhood, he finds primary support in the strong friendship forged with Jackson during their war service. He is Miriam's first lover and constant friend. Only after a jail term does he find a vocation as a carpenter and a partner, Dorine.

Jackson, an older, long-haired fringe academic, Phil's roommate and mentor. A lined, sad face characterizes the complex, sardonic loner who never mentions his cultured background and later misfortunes. Shielding himself with constant banter, he manipulates human beings as if they were pawns in his favorite game, chess. Only Miriam and Beth penetrate his reserve briefly. He is finally graduated and teaches political science at the University of Massachusetts.

Neil Stone, a director of Logical Systems Development, a small research corporation in Cambridge. He is a precise, methodical, attractive man with traditional family values. As Miriam's husband, he encourages her role of model homemaker and pressures her to have children, but he resents her attempts at financial and social independence. At the novel's end, he is seeking companionship with a lonely female colleague and considering divorce.

Wanda Rosario, a chunky, gray-haired Italian-Polish woman in her late thirties who is married to Joe, a radical political organizer who deserts her and their two young sons. She is a hardworking, wise, earthy woman who finds

a new vocation as director of a traveling women's theater troupe and is joined by Beth, who becomes her lover. A political activist before her marriage, she is jailed for refusing to testify against former comrades. After her release, she steals her children from custody and begins a new life, disguised and fugitive, with Beth in Ohio.

Dorine, a frizzy-haired, timid girl who performs the role of maid, doormat, and bedmate for Phil and Jackson's circle of friends. Finally tiring of their ridicule and insensitivity, she moves to a women's commune. Through the support and love of her friends, she gains respect for herself, attends graduate school, becomes a strong leader in the women's movement, and works out an equal relationship with Phil.

Jim Walker, Beth's hard-drinking and sports-loving young husband, who expects his wife to cater to his demands and uses physical force to keep her in line.

Jo C. Searles

THE SMALL ROOM

Author: May Sarton (1912-   )
Type of work: Novel
Time of action: The 1950's
First published: 1961

Lucy Winter, a twenty-seven-year-old Harvard graduate who has recently experienced the collapse of her engagement and is beginning her first year of teaching American literature at Appleton, a small New England college for women. She is abruptly initiated into the twisting relationships of academe when she accidentally discovers indisputable plagiarism in the paper of an outstanding student who is the protégée of one of the most powerful and respected professors on campus. Confronted with issues of honesty, loyalty, pride, confusion, and commitment, Lucy maintains her integrity during the ensuing arguments about the situation and grows steadily in respect from and for her

colleagues and students. Simultaneously, she sharpens her awareness of teaching as a challenging profession and a demanding art.

Carryl Cope, a brilliant, indomitable scholar and professor of medieval history. Totally devoted to her profession and the college, she cares little for appearances and is passionately committed to academic excellence. Upon discovering the dishonesty of a student in whom she has invested countless hours and enormous energy, Professor Cope at first hopes to cover up the incident. When it becomes clear that exposure is inevitable, she maintains her self-respect and that of others by admitting her mistakes in pressuring the student and concentrating too exclusively on cultivating the mind. In the painful resolution, Carryl not only faces her own pride directly, but also risks the dissolution of her intimate twenty-year friendship with Olive Hunt.

Harriet (Hallie) Summerson, a secure, honest, well-liked woman and a superb teacher of British literature. A generation older than Lucy and unfailingly generous, Hallie welcomes her into the college community and consistently offers her valuable advice and support. In her characteristically unself-conscious way, Hallie also models for Lucy, a teacher accomplished in her art.

Olive Hunt, a wealthy, influential, generous trustee of Appleton College. Once elegant but now somewhat faded with age, she is proudly rigid in her ideas and beliefs. Convinced that people are responsible for managing their own lives independently, she violently opposes the college's hiring a resident psychiatrist and vows to withdraw her financial support if her views are dismissed. An irreparable consequence of her adamant resolve is alienation from Carryl Cope, whom she has loved for years.

Jennifer Finch, an apparently unassuming but wise professor, who inserts a quiet objectivity and compassion into frequently heated discussions of campus affairs. Bound tightly to an extraordinarily dominating mother, she still maintains an inner freedom that gives her unique influence among her peers and students.

Jane Seaman, a brilliant student whose plagiarized essay on Homer's *The Iliad* is published in the college magazine. When Lucy Winter confronts her, Jane admits that the pressures to excel academically and to fulfill the demanding expectations of Professor Cope have driven her to dishonest scholarship. Softened by Lucy's genuine, loving concern, Jane eventually agrees to see a psychiatrist for assistance in dealing with her problems.

Blake Tillotson, president of Appleton College. He maintains an honest, intelligent, and compassionate attitude throughout debate over the plagiarism incident, despite conflicting demands: from Carryl Cope and Olive Hunt, whose financial support depends upon his decisions; from students who are angered that their governing councils were ignored in handling a student's dishonesty; and from faculty members who express opposing views on both the Seaman case and the proposed mental health committee.

Jack Beveridge, an intense and seasoned professor of Romance languages, whose ironic, cynical attitude masks a deep kindness and compassion. His defense of Carryl Cope and Olive Hunt leads him to unaccustomed anger and alienates him from his wife.

Maria Beveridge, an ample, commanding, straightforward woman, wife of Jack and mother of three young boys. Disagreements with several of her husband's views, and particularly her jealousy of Carryl Cope and Olive Hunt, move the couple close to divorce.

Henry Atwood, a young assistant professor, completing his dissertation on Henry Fielding. Initially naïve about the complexities of the college scene, he grows into a new sense of himself and his profession during his first semester at Appleton.

Deborah Atwood, a somewhat immature young woman, wife of Henry, who also develops as she finds her way into a new academic environment.

Pippa Brentwood, a student who especially needs encouragement and affirmation following the death of her father. She questions Lucy about the plagiarism issue and tests the young teacher's developing, ambivalent convictions about the nature of teacher-student relationships.

Sara McAlpin

SMALL WORLD

Author: David Lodge (1935-   )
Type of work: Novel
Time of action: 1979
First published: 1984

Persse McGarrigle, a poet and lecturer in English literature at Limerick University, Ireland. A "conference virgin," he is as ignorant of the structuralist and poststructuralist theories, which have come to dominate literary criticism in the twentieth century, as he is of sex. At his first conference, this "hopeless romantic" falls in love with the elusive Angelica Pabst. He uses the poetry prize he wins to finance his international, conference-to-conference quest for her hand in marriage. He finally catches up with her at a mammoth meeting of the Modern Language Association in New York, where Persse, playing the part of grail knight, asks the question that frees the small world of academic critics from their sexual and intellectual impotence. He saves them but loses Angelica; ever hopeful, he is last seen about to set off in pursuit of yet another grail/girl, Cheryl Summerbee.

Angelica Pabst, age twenty-seven, the brilliant and beautiful graduate student who is the object of Persse's chaste desire. Adept in the field of contemporary literary theory, she is writing a dissertation on romance from Heliodorus to Barbara Cartland. A foundling, she has been reared by a KLM executive who has bestowed on her the gift of unlimited air travel.

Lily Papps, Angelica's twin sister. Their only distinguishing feature is the birthmark high upon one thigh, which, when they stand together in their bikinis, makes them look as if they are inside quotation marks. Not knowing that Angelica has a twin sister, least of all one who works as a stripper and porn star, Persse mistakenly believes that the face he sees outside Soho clubs, in porn theaters, and in Amsterdam's red-light district is Angelica's. Only after he has made love to Lily (believing that she is Angelica) does Persse learn that Angelica has not only a twin but a fiancé, named Peter McGarrigle.

Philip Swallow, head of the English department at Rummidge University and author of *Hazlitt and the Amateur Reader.* Since his initial appearance in Lodge's 1975 novel, *Changing Places,* Swallow has become professionally and sexually more assertive. During one of his lecture trips he resumes his affair with Joy Simpson, whom he believed dead. He loses her later as a result of his very British preoccupation with appearances. At the MLA session devoted to literary theory, Swallow is asked at the last minute to stand in for Rudyard Parkinson and represent the naïvely conventional approach.

Morris Zapp, professor of English at Euphoric State in California. He exemplifies the new international scholar, jetting from conference to conference. His latest book is appropriately entitled *Beyond Criticism.* Kidnapped by an Italian terrorist group, which mistakenly believes that his former wife will pay the ransom, he decides to give up Deconstruction (and his "Textuality as Striptease" lecture) in order to pursue the more domestic pleasures of life with Thelma Ringbaum, soon to be ex-wife of a former colleague.

Fulvia Morgana, professor of cultural studies at the University of Padua and, with her husband, well-to-do supporter of Marxist radicals, including the ones who kidnap Zapp. She seduces Zapp, mistakenly confusing him with the sexual animal that his ex-wife, Desiree Byrd, villifies in her best-selling book about their marriage.

Siegfried von Turpitz, an ex-Panzer commander and currently a German scholar specializing in reception theory. He is caught plagiarizing Persse's unpublished dissertation and mystifying one of his perfectly normal hands by concealing it inside an enigmatic black glove.

Michel Tardieu, a homosexual professor of narratology at the Sorbonne.

Rudyard Parkinson, a South African who has turned himself into the quintessential English academic, the Oxford don, stuffy, conventional, celibate, snide, and malicious. He damns Zapp's book and praises Swallow's in a *Times Literary Supplement* review solely to promote his own name and position among the possible candidates for the newly created UNESCO chair of literary studies.

Rodney Wainwright, an instructor at the University of North Queensland whose efforts to get beyond the opening of his paper for Zapp's Future of Criticism conference in Jerusalem repeatedly fail. At the moment of truth, he is saved by an outbreak of Legionnaire's disease.

Arthur Kingfisher, the major literary theorist of his time. He has had no new ideas and no new erections in years. At novel's end, this fisher king (Klingelfischer) is freed from his sterility by Persse, confers the coveted UNESCO chair of literary studies upon himself, and announces his intention to marry his Korean assistant, Ji-Moon Lee. Kingfisher is also exposed as the natural father of Angelica and Lily.

Ronald Frobisher, the British novelist who has been blocked ever since, six years earlier, Robin Dempsey showed him a computer analysis of his style. He has a brief affair with Desiree Byrd.

Desiree Byrd, Zapp's ex-wife and author of *Difficult Days*, about her marriage. Currently blocked in the writing of *Men*, she has an affair with Ronald Frobisher at the Reception Theory conference in Heidelberg.

Miss Sibyl Maiden, a retired professor and former pupil of Jessie Weston (author of *From Ritual to Romance*). Twenty-seven years before, when she was forty-six, she bore Arthur Kingfisher's twin daughters, Angelica and Lily, abandoning them in the restroom aboard a KLM airliner.

Robin Dempsey, demoralized professionally and sexually, he carries on a lengthy, obsessive conversation with Eliza, a computer program modeled on the psychiatric interview, never realizing that a colleague is manipulating Eliza's responses.

Cheryl Summerbee, the blonde and cheerful checker for British Air at Heathrow who livens up her job by making seat selections according to her perception of passengers' characters. She is responsible for Zapp meeting Fulvia Morgana and for Frobisher missing the MLA meeting. She loses her job but unknowingly gains Persse's love.

Peter McGarrigle, the McGarrigle with whom Angelica is in love and to whom the University of Limerick thought it was offering the job that mistakenly went to Persse.

Robert A. Morace

THE SNAIL ON THE SLOPE

Authors: Arkady Strugatsky (1925-   ) and Boris Strugatsky (1933-   )
Type of work: Novel
Time of action: The near future
First published: Ulitka na sklone, 1966-1968 (English translation, 1980)

Pepper, the central figure, a linguist, who tries to escape the Kafkaesque bureaucracy of the Directorate and seek illumination from a distant contemplation of the primal forest that the Directorate strives to contain and destroy. Intellectually superior, he is nevertheless treated with condescending tolerance as a bumbling, naïve incompetent. He flees one nightmarish situation after another: wrestling with the illogic of a Forest Study Group bent on eradication and with the jargonate nonsense of Directorate communications, encountering blindfolded men seeking a lost classified machine whose sight is forbidden, being caught up in meaningless bureaucratic processes (such as room repairs scheduled at midnight), overhearing machines debating when to demonstrate their dominance over man, and finally finding himself inexplicably supplanting the old Director. Faced with the mechanistic, he feels compelled to exercise reason and to seek explanations. For him hope lies in the human decency of "considerate" and "hospitable" people, but his peregrinations never reveal any. After a lifetime of senseless activities performed at the bequest of nonsensical directives, Pepper so accommodates himself to the system that, when he can bring change, he is trapped by a historical accumulation of absurdities that determine the course of his own directives, ones as cruel, chaotic, and meaningless as those of his much deplored predecessors. Pepper is the prototype of the intellectual who theorizes about life (the Forest) from a distance, is repulsed by closer contact with it, and is, in the end, content to be seduced by power. His "yearning for understanding" (what he calls "his sickness") is cured at the cost of his humanity.

Kandid, Pepper's counterpart, a scientist who, after ejecting from his crashing helicopter, finds himself trapped in the alien and ever-changing forest among primitive villagers. Assumed dead by his colleagues, Kandid spends his time seeking a way back to "civilization." Kandid, like Voltaire's Candide, travels amid alien peoples and, while seeking vainly to comprehend the incomprehensible, furthers his creators' satiric purpose. Unlike Pepper, Kandid is immersed in the Forest and lives amid the chaos and disorder of nature, facing bandits and organic anomalies (faceless men, disappearing villages, mer-maids and Amazonian Maidens, "Swampings," "Harrowings," and "deadlings"). Nicknamed "Dummy" by the narrowminded villagers, who find him eccentric and slightly mad, he is later feared for his power to wield a scalpel to destroy "deadlings," odd forest creatures whose touch burns. Kandid is metaphorically too close to the trees to see the forest (the other extreme from Pepper) and, consequently, suffers from a strange inability to retain ideas or to find meaningful patterns or relationships. With heart and head in conflict, Kandid refuses to succumb to his situation. His conclusion that annihilating populations for the sake of some nebulous theory about progress is wrong, that nature may be outside of concepts of good and bad but that man is not, and that one must look at the Authority and the Forest both "from the side" seems to voice the Strugatskys' views.

Nava, Kandid's chattering, clinging child-wife, who pressures him to accept the monotonous "vegetable way of life" of her village and who complains of the dangers inherent in escape. Her mother, kidnapped by "deadlings," has become one of the matriarchal Maidens, whose generative power is responsible for the peculiarities of the Forest. Though she saves Kandid's life, clearly Nava will join the Maidens as a parthenogenetic power, a regenerative and reproductive force methodically directing the burgeoning growth and change of the Forest in its progress toward a future clear to the Maidens but not to others.

Claudius-Octavian Hausbotcher, the quintessential bureaucrat, ignorant and narrowminded. With dark, piercing eyes and a long, stony face, Hausbotcher records deviant statements and actions and is obsessed with paperwork, permits, and regulations. He meets chaos with regimen, dismisses the unfamiliar as mysticism, and supports the party line as inviolate. He intimidates subordinates and toadies up to superiors.

Acey, a sexually obsessed Directorate driver convicted of passport violations and theft, a neanderthal who guzzles yogurt and speculates on the peculiar characteristics of the

Forest. He has a darkly handsome, Italianate face, with bushy eyebrows, lively eyes, and flashing teeth. His feet smell, and his narrations focus on sexual exploits. His hairy arms are tattooed with the phrases "What destroys us" and "Ever onward," cryptic comments on Directorate goals. As Pepper's driver, Acey provides a sense of how much Pepper has capitulated to power when Pepper regrets not being able to castrate him for his own good.

Alevtina, a photo lab worker determined to become Pepper's mistress, despite his aversion to sex. She helps Pepper take over as Director, and becomes the guiding power behind the scenes, suggesting the direction his orders should take, theorizing about the historical continuity of bureaucratic power and praising his new measures (orders to the Eradication Group to self-eradicate).

Gina Macdonald

SNOOTY BARONET

Author: Wyndham Lewis (1882-1957)
Type of work: Novel
Time of action: c. 1930
First published: 1932

Sir Michael Kell-Imrie (Snooty, Snoots), the author-narrator, almost age forty. Though poor, he is the seventeenth baronet of his Scottish family. He was wounded five times during World War I. His artificial leg is removed by his mistress before sex; afterward he suffers illness from head wounds. A writer of scientific books about behaviorism, he is celebrated most for his fictional skills. He got his interest in animals after catching a huge fish and reading *Moby Dick*. Persuaded to pretend to be captured by a Persian bandit while researching Mithra religious cults, he reads D. H. Lawrence on animal worship. Though he despises Persia, he cooperates with Humph, allowing Val to pay his passage and accompany him; finally he shoots Humph to death for pleasure, abandons Val to smallpox, and finds solace in the arms of a Persian harem girl on the Bosphorus.

Captain Humphrey (Humph) Cooper Carter, Snooty's literary agent in London. He has a big head, large chin, and short legs. He met Snooty in the Scots Guards during World War I. He held down a desk job for most of the war, while Snooty was in the trenches and wounded many times. He concocts the scheme for Snooty to be kidnapped by a Persian bandit in order to extract ransom money and publicity. He is shot and

killed by Snooty during the rendezvous with Mirza Aga's bandits.

Mrs. Valerie (Val) Ritter, Snooty's first girlfriend, whom he visits in Chelsea as soon as he returns to London from America. With a double-chin, thinning hair, and pocked skin, she is somewhere between thirty and forty years old. She has the annoying habit of giggling constantly, but she knows how to please Snooty in bed. She writes pornographic novels, which are never published, and she pays for Snooty's passage to Persia to accompany him and Humph. Though she dislikes Humph, she is appalled when she sees Snooty shoot him, and she tries unsuccessfully to blackmail Snooty into marrying her. When she contracts smallpox while a guest of Mirza Aga, she is abandoned by Snooty. She recovers and sends him a telegram of indignation.

Lily Tayle, Snooty's second girlfriend. She works at a tobacco kiosk at Victoria Station, London. She is two months past twenty-four. She does not know that he is a baronet until she reads it in the gossip columns of newspapers while he is in America. She writes him letters while he is in Persia.

Rob McPhail, a poet and a close friend of

Snooty. He has lived for four years with his wife and children on the French coast near Marseilles, at Faujas de Saint Riom, where he fishes and sometimes fights bulls. He was born in China, where his father was employed by the Chinese government. A tall man dressed in white, he drinks heavily. After he tells Snooty that he will go to Persia with him, Rob is killed by a bull during the prefighting sticking ceremony.

Pat Bostock, a source of information about Persia. He causes Humph to think of the kidnapping caper.

Mirza Aga, the Persian bandit contracted to kidnap Snooty for ransom. He speaks perfect English with a Chicago accent. When he discovers that Snooty shot Humph, he thinks it was done so that Snooty would not have to share the ransom. He orders his men to kill all the muleteers and guides who accompanied Snooty, Humph, and Val. Acting as host to Snooty and Val, he waits in vain for the ransom but escorts Snooty back to civilization, while Val lingers with smallpox.

Ali Akbar, the leader of the Persian muleteers who carry Snooty, Humph, and Val to the point of the kidnapping. He is impressed with Snooty's skill with a rifle and he is indignant when he sees Snooty shoot Humph.

He and his men are slaughtered by Mirza Aga's bandits.

Mortimer, who pays rent for Val's Chelsea rooms.

Mr. Willis, a forty-one-year-old tobacconist whom Lily introduces to Snooty as her "Uncle."

Vieuxchange (vyū·chänzh'), Rob McPhail's brother-in-law and fishing partner. He is a big, leonine, ex-marine who leaps with Rob into the bull-fighting arena to stick the bulls.

Mrs. Laura McPhail, Rob's wife. She has black-violet eyes and talks to Snooty of her Communist brother in Leningrad.

Juanito, the Spanish manager/owner of the bull-fight at Faujas de Saint Riom; he dresses as Charlie Chaplin for pre-fight entertainment.

Shushani (shū·shä'nē), Snooty's Persian harem girl, who helps him hide from Humph and stays with him at the Bosphorus.

Kafi, a Persian harem girl. Her name means "enough."

Hasan, a Persian muleteer who sneezes at Humph to frighten him.

Richard D. McGhee

SNOW COUNTRY

Author: Yasunari Kawabata (1899-1972)
Type of work: Novel
Time of action: The mid-1930's
First published: Yukiguni, 1935-1937, serial; 1947, book (English translation, 1956)

Shimamura, an idle man from Tokyo, perhaps in early middle age, who makes a series of visits to a village in Japan's "snow country." There, he takes advantage of the hot springs and breathtaking scenery. He also strikes up an ambiguously spiritual and sensual relationship with Komako, a very young apprentice geisha. Married with children,

Shimamura is unable to make a lifetime commitment to Komako. More to the point, he is unable to invest himself emotionally in their affair such as it is, or, it seems, in any aspect of his life. An amateur writer on classical Western dance, which he experiences only through books, Shimamura notes the "wasted effort" of Komako's life but seems unaware of his own emptiness until the novel's final scene.

Komako, a young geisha with whom Shimamura has a relationship stretching over several years. Komako begins the novel as something less than a full geisha, though in ways she seems older than her years. By the novel's end, the example of another geisha has been used to suggest that Komako will age quickly in her role as a professional entertainer of men. In addition, Komako's personality is undergoing change. She is becoming cynical and acutely sensitive, as when Shimamura says she is a "good woman." Komako's life has, indeed, been sad. She is forced by financial necessity to give up her interest in dance and work as a geisha. Aside from Shimamura, she has no lover for whom she feels deeply. In addition, a man to whom she may have been engaged becomes ill and dies young. These difficulties never kill Komako's spirit. She faithfully keeps her diary and hones her musical skills. Yet, she also has a tendency to drink too much sake and is often confused in her feelings, particularly regarding Shimamura.

Yukio, the son of Komako's music teacher.

Rumored to have been Komako's fiancé (which she vehemently denies), Yukio returns to the village to die. As he is about to expire, he calls for Komako to be at his side. Komako is seeing Shimamura off at the train station and refuses to return when Yukio's request is brought to her, even though Shimamura urges her to be at the dying man's side. Yukio dies before Komako's return.

Yoko, Yukio's nurse and Komako's friend. Yoko is much younger and more innocent than Komako. She remains devoted to Yukio until his death and, afterward, spends considerable time mourning at his grave side. Shimamura is captivated by Yoko's voice and her apparent purity. Yet, Yoko, too, is considering a trip to Tokyo so that she might be trained as a geisha. Komako refuses to answer Shimamura's questions about Yoko, and relations between the two women become strained after Yukio's death. In the final scene, Yoko dies in a fire. Komako rushes forward to carry her lifeless body from the ruins. This display of naked passion finally brings Shimamura face to face with his own emptiness.

Ira Smolensky

THE SNOW WAS BLACK

Author: Georges Simenon (1903-1989)
Type of work: Novel
Time of action: 1940-1945
First published: La Neige était sale, 1948 (English translation, 1950)

Frank Friedmaier, an idler, robber, and killer. Son of a former prostitute, now a madam, and of an unknown father, Frank is short and boyish (he is nineteen years old when the story begins); his outward lack of emotion, disconcerting to others and terrifying to his mother, conceals an intense desire to find a stable place in the chaos of Nazi-occupied Europe. Craving attention, he nevertheless despises those who demonstrate affection for him. He bullies his mother, who fears him, even while he lives off of her earnings; he is contemptuous of the source

of his money, of his mother's pliable morality, and of himself for taking advantage of both. He kills a woman who had befriended him in his childhood; he assaults Sissy Holst, who adores him; he loathes the prostitutes who satisfy his physical needs. Imitating his wealthy and obviously criminal friend, Fred Kromer, Frank determines on murder as a way of self-assertion, but, even as he kills, he realizes that what he is really trying to do is to attract the attention of his respectable neighbor, Gerhardt Holst, who is, for Frank, a father figure. In prison Frank finally finds the structured life he craves. When Holst and Sissy visit him, the former treats him with paternal affection despite his abuse of Sissy, and Sissy, despite his cruel tests of her, asserts her lasting love. Now fulfilled, Frank is ready to die; he confesses his two murders and is shot.

Lotte Friedmaier, former prostitute, madam, and the mother of Frank. A blowsy, reddish-blonde, overweight woman with a youthful face, Lotte runs a manicure parlor on the third floor of a boardinghouse; it actually is a brothel. She hires very young girls, trains them to wait on her, and fires them rapidly to provide new excitements for jaded appetites. Her job provides the luxuries that others lack during the German occupation. Well fed, warm, and amply clothed, Lotte and Frank are hated by most of their neighbors except for the Holsts.

Gerhardt Holst, a former art critic forced under the occupation to be a streetcar conductor. Despite his quiet, colorless appearance, Holst possesses unmistakable integrity. Although he is thin, weak, and prematurely aged from hunger and cold, he neither hates Lotte and Frank nor envies them their comforts, although he lives across the hall from them and can smell them cooking food. After Frank and Kromer assault his daughter, Sissy, Holst gives up his job to do bookkeeping at home and to nurse his daughter. Aware of Sissy's love for Frank, he takes the girl to visit Frank in prison, where Holst admits that Frank reminds him of his own lost son, first a thief and later a suicide.

Sissy Holst, the sixteen-year-old daughter of Gerhardt. She adores Frank despite his clear contempt for her efforts to attract him. She senses, or Frank fears she does, the unhappiness he is unwilling to admit to anyone. As a result of her childish flirtatiousness, she is sexually assaulted by Kromer with Frank's help. After this attack, she falls seriously ill but does not renounce her love for Frank, and, visiting him in prison, voices this love with her father's consent.

Annie Loeb, an elegant prostitute. As lazy and insolent as Frank himself is, Annie attracts him by the way she refuses to do Lotte's housework. She demands service and reads and smokes her days away. Unknown to Frank, she is waiting for death; the daughter of a captured Resistance worker, she herself is serving as a prostitute in order to spy on German officers.

Fred Kromer, age twenty-two, bull-like and shiny in his corrupt sensuality. Boasting a fur-lined coat and expensive cigars as a result of his drug dealing, Kromer is Frank's pipeline to occupation forces. Kromer enjoys pursuing the young, hungry, miserable girls made vulnerable by the occupation and thus is attracted by Sissy and cooperates in Frank's desire to contaminate her innocence.

The "Old Gentleman," a professorial man in glasses who smokes constantly, carefully rolling his own cigarettes. Another father figure to Frank, although he represents the occupying forces, he questions Frank repeatedly in prison, moving him toward the confession and death that are precipitated by Holst and Sissy's visit.

Betty Richardson

SOLARIS

Author: Stanisław Lem (1921-   )
Type of work: Novel
Time of action: The distant future
First published: 1961 (English translation, 1970)

Kris Kelvin, a scientist who has just arrived at the Solaris station. In his early thirties, Kelvin descends from space to find that the experimental work station he has reached is in chaos. He feels fearful and disoriented when he discovers that his previous teacher, Gibarian, has just committed suicide and that the station's two other scientists appear to be insane: Snow and Sartorius often hide in their rooms and speak in a cryptic and paranoid fashion. Upon waking from a much-needed sleep, Kelvin finds himself confronted with the reincarnation of his girlfriend, Rheya, who committed suicide ten years earlier after he had left her. While he is repulsed by this replica of a past love, he also appreciates the opportunity to expiate his guilt over her death and continue, if only in a sham, the experience of their relationship. As he talks to the other scientists, reads the station's library, and performs experiments, he gradually understands that she is a projection of his own memories created by the planetary entity he has come to study. When she dissolves at the novel's end, he is left with the desire to get her back again but little hope that this event will occur.

Solaris, the protoplasmic creature that covers the planet of the same name. For more than a hundred years, Earth missions have attempted to understand this as yet inscrutable multibillion-ton gelatinous oceanic entity. While the myriad shapes that form on this global creature suggest sentience, no previous attempts at contact and communication have been successful. Hundreds of theories are alluded to that have attempted to account for this blob, but all are flawed. At the time of the story, however, an illegal dose of X rays has caused the mass to express itself in a new way. Reaching into the minds of the station's occupants, it has created, out of neutrinos, perfect replicas of remembered or imagined people. While these models, phi-creatures, are palpable, they are no more intelligible to the crew than any other phenomenon. While Solaris' human simulacra are destroyed at the story's end, neither they nor the planet itself is understood.

Rheya, the most important of the human incarnations created by the planetary entity called Solaris. Rheya is an almost perfect duplicate of Kris's girlfriend, who was nineteen years old when she committed suicide ten years before. She has no self-consciousness of her own artificiality and differs from the original woman mentally only in her knowledge of some facts she should not know and in an undeniable compulsion to stay in Kris's proximity. Physically, she is exactly the same except at the subatomic level: Because she is composed of neutrinos, she heals rapidly. As she gradually understands that she is not who she thinks she is, she, like the original, attempts suicide. This effort fails, but by gaining the help of two other scientists, she is able to dissolve herself and leave a suicide note that unintentionally parodies that of the original ten years before.

Snow (Ratface), a cybernetics expert and Gibarian's deputy. Drunk and half mad from his recent experiences on Solaris, Snow tries to help Kelvin understand the situation without appearing to be crazy. His mental struggles have left him haggard, gray, and sunken. He is reticent and only semifunctional. Nevertheless, he understands the situation to some degree and aids Kelvin.

Sartorius, the most reclusive and yet insistently professional scientist at the station. Tall, thin, and distracted, Sartorius attempts, despite his own phi-creature, to maintain the scientific method. It is largely through his efforts that the scientists attempt direct communication with Solaris, and it is he who develops the antineutrino device that dissolves the replicas, including Rheya.

Gibarian, a dead scientist scholar and Kelvin's teacher. At the story's start, Gibarian has just committed suicide because of his inability to deal with the Solaris projections. He is still active in the narrative, however, through Kelvin's memories, his publications, and, finally, in an embodiment that may have been a dream or another phi-creature.

Daniel D. Fineman

SOLDIERS' PAY

Author: William Faulkner (1897-1962)
Type of work: Novel
Time of action: April and May, 1919
First published: 1926

Donald Mahon, a flyer dying of wounds suffered in World War I. Wild like a faun in his youth, he was shot down and now is going blind, has lost most of his memory, is not fully conscious, and says little. His face is so dreadfully scarred that it shocks people, revealing their natures. He brings out the best and the worst in others. As the novel begins, he is coming back from the war by train to his home in a small town in Georgia, where he is engaged to a prominent Southern belle. At the end, his death, like the war, significantly changes the lives of some characters while not affecting others at all.

Margaret Powers, a young war widow on the train who nurses and, shortly before his death, marries Mahon. Tall, slim, dark, and pallid, with a mouth like a red scar, she is an independent woman of twenty-four, self-contained, unconventional, and the most intelligent, perceptive character in the novel. Some intend to insult her by calling her a black woman. Her compassion for Mahon is motivated to some extent by guilt about the way she broke off with her first husband, also a young officer, shortly before he was killed at the front by one of his own men. At the end, she declines a marriage proposal from Joe Gilligan and sets out on her own.

Joe Gilligan, a discharged American soldier who serves as Donald Mahon's guardian throughout the novel, regarding him as the kind of son he would have liked to have. An easygoing, talkative man of thirty-two, with a sense of humor and a capacity for self-sacrifice, he is almost the only person to whom Mahon speaks. He is a strong, mature man, and when Margaret Powers declines his proposal he is not wounded for long.

Julian Lowe, an air cadet whose anticipation of glory as a flyer is disappointed by the armistice. An inexperienced boy on the train with Mahon and Gilligan, traveling back to his home in San Francisco, he naïvely envies Mahon. He is infatuated with Margaret Powers, whose feeling toward him is maternal, and throughout the rest of the novel he writes her ungrammatical love letters. His expectation of marrying her is frustrated like his equally absurd dream of becoming a hero in the war.

Joseph Mahon, the rector, an Episcopalian priest who is Donald's father. A hopeful clergyman inclined to illusion, he sustains a faith that his son will recover and rise again. He grows increasingly realistic as Donald's condition worsens, but he transcends disappointment. In the end, after the death of Donald and the departure of Margaret, he consoles Joe Gilligan and leads him to some inspiration from black culture.

Cecily Saunders, the local belle engaged to Donald. A shallow flirt with reddish dark hair and green-blue eyes, she has a conventional perfection but is spoiled and petulant. She is jealous of Margaret (she calls her a black woman) and forces herself to kiss Donald on the side of his face that is not scarred, but she cannot go through with a marriage. She consorts with other men and, finally, elopes with George Farr.

George Farr, an ordinary, gullible young man in love with Cecily Saunders. Duped by the superficial, he suffers with jealousy and at last succeeds in eloping with Cecily, who continues to make him miserable.

Emmy, the housekeeper at the rectory in love with Donald. A poor, loyal, and passionate young woman with a wild face and dark eyes, she gave her virginity to Donald before he became engaged to Cecily and went to war. She is distraught that, as a result of his wounds, he has forgotten her. In wounded pride, she declines the opportunity to marry him offered her by Margaret after Cecily runs away.

Januarius Jones, a fat, coldhearted Latin teacher who pursues women like a satyr. Baggy in gray tweeds, the antithesis of Donald, he has eyes the color of urine and the morals of a goat. Margaret rejects him, while Cecily, to some extent his moral counterpart, teases him, and Emmy, as an escape from grief, submits to him.

Michael Hollister

THE SOLID MANDALA

Author: Patrick White (1912-   )
Type of work: Novel
Time of action: c. 1900-1960
First published: 1966

Arthur Brown, the fraternal twin brother of Waldo Brown. Arthur is a huge, simple-minded, kindly man who is entirely devoted to his brother Waldo. In fact, he considers himself Waldo's protector, although Waldo is always trying to dissociate himself from his dull-witted brother. Arthur lives by intuition and instinct; he is a noble primitive who sees into the essence of people and things. He is also capable of building meaningful, platonic relationships with women such as Mrs. Poulter and Dulcie Feinstein, both of whom value his innate wisdom. Despite his apparent handicap, Arthur proves himself capable of reading classics such as Fyodor Dostoevski's *The Brothers Karamazov* and of writing symbolic poetry. Although he loves dogs and simple things like tables and chairs, Arthur prizes his collection of glass marbles most of all. In particular, he considers four to be his solid mandalas, or symbols of totality and wholeness. Arthur keeps these with him always, until he decides to give them away to the people who mean the most to him: Waldo, Dulcie, and Mrs. Poulter. Waldo refuses his mandala, a rejection that makes Arthur ineffably sad. In the end, though, it is Arthur who endures.

Waldo Brown, the fraternal twin brother of Arthur. Waldo is Arthur's opposite in every way; thin, moody, and self-centered, Waldo is capable of great anger and cruelty toward his well-meaning sibling. Arthur is a big em-barrassment to Waldo, and he is burdened with him throughout their lives. Waldo considers himself an intellectual: He has some schooling and works for years in the local library. He also has literary ambitions and actually starts work on a novel. Yet Waldo's writing is uninspired because his mind is so disconnected from his emotions. He remains half a man, and that is why Arthur's unwitting successes so infuriate him. Waldo, like Arthur, pursues both Dulcie and Mrs. Poulter, not because he loves them, but because he believes that they should love him. Waldo never succeeds in getting close to another human being; he cannot even enjoy the dogs that he and his brother adopt. Waldo's resentment of his twin increases as the two of them grow up and grow old together in their parents' house. He is particularly incensed because Arthur always seems to know so much about him: Waldo despairs that he can never have secrets from his blundering, perceptive brother. Finally, Waldo's murderous resentment builds to the point where it explodes.

Mrs. Poulter, the Browns' neighbor from across the street. Mrs. Poulter and her husband move into the suburb of Sarsaparilla shortly after the Browns become residents. An uneducated, nosey sort, she is also well-meaning enough to take an interest in Waldo and Arthur after their parents die. Having lost a baby at one time herself, she bonds with Arthur in a maternal way. He spends a good amount of time with her, until her husband objects, after which Arthur and Mrs. Poulter see each other only infrequently. In the end, it is Mrs. Poulter who takes Arthur in; because of his simplicity, goodness, and innocence, he comes to seem a kind of savior to her, and she comforts him in his misery. She also remains keeper of one of his solid mandalas.

Dulcie Feinstein, a Jewish girl, friend to both Arthur and Waldo. Despite Arthur's eccentricities, the Feinsteins invite him into their home and enjoy his surprising insights. Waldo meets Dulcie by chance at a party and is most annoyed to find his brother already ensconced in her home the first time he goes to call on her there. The Feinsteins are a cultured family, but somewhat adrift emotionally because Dulcie's father rejects Judaism. Eventually, the horrible fact of World War II has a profound effect on the Feinsteins. Dulcie ends up marrying a Jewish carpet merchant named Leonard Saporta

and having two children, one of whom she names after Arthur. Dulcie is also keeper of one of Arthur's solid mandalas.

George Brown and
Anne Brown, father and mother to Waldo and Arthur. Anne marries below herself when she chooses George. They set out from England for Australia with their two boys and end up in an ugly house in a drab suburb named Sarsaparilla. Yet, they are still possessed of ideas of grandeur: George has a classical pediment built onto the front of the house. The incongruous addition makes the domicile something of a curiosity down Terminus Road and keeps others at a distance from the Brown family. George works in a bank; it is said that he is sadly disappointed in Arthur, the son for whom he had high hopes. Anne stays on in the house following her husband's death, frequently indulging in flights into the past and declining into an alcoholic end.

Susan Whaley

SOME PREFER NETTLES

Author: Jun'ichirō Tanizaki (1886-1965)
Type of work: Novel
Time of action: March through June, 1929
First published: Tade kuu mushi, 1928-1929, serial; 1936, book (English translation, 1955)

Kaname, a sinecurist in his father's company. A quiet, unassuming man in his mid-forties, he and his wife, Misako, agree that their marriage has ended in all but name (they still live together), but neither has the necessary decisiveness to obtain a divorce. Although the basic reason for the marriage's failure is Kaname's lack of sexual interest in his wife, he is equally put off by her modern ways and extreme interest in the latest fads of Western culture. Kaname, though somewhat Westernized himself, becomes increasingly interested in traditional Japanese culture, as evidenced by his growing enthusiasm for the Osaka puppet theater and in the model provided for him by the apparently satisfying relationship his father-in-law has

with a young, very old-fashioned mistress. The concluding implication is that he will turn away from his wife and become more interested in "doll-like" women, but it is uncertain if he can overcome his indecisiveness.

Misako, Kaname's wife. Estranged from her husband but still living with him, Misako is a woman who has turned her back on traditional culture and ideals and tries to make herself a modern, Westernized woman. She shares her husband's indecisiveness completely, partly for the sake of their ten-year-old son, and for solace has been having an affair for the past two years. It is her interest in shallow and insubstantial Western objects and fads, as much as her sexual unattractiveness, which propels Kaname toward his increasing interest in traditional Japanese culture and women. Kaname becomes aware that Misako's lover is not permanently committed to her, which increases his anxiety about divorcing her and setting her adrift.

Hiroshi, the ten-year-old son of Kaname and Misako. Hiroshi is a sensitive boy who has been living in a constant state of anxiety because his parents have concealed their marital problems from him, forcing him to guess what their intentions might be. He thinks, for example, that his parents may be intending to abandon him and lives in a constant state of torment until he is finally informed by a relative that his parents are getting a divorce (supposedly) and he will not be abandoned by them. This news apparently serves to calm his fears.

Misako's father, a man in his early sixties. He is a conservative, old-fashioned man who is very interested in all aspects of traditional Japanese culture, especially the Osaka puppet theater. He has a mistress in her mid-twenties, a traditional-looking and -acting woman who resembles one of the theater puppets herself. Kaname grows to admire the older man and his style of living, especially his interest in traditional Japanese arts and his successful relationship with his doll-like mistress.

O-hisa, mistress of Misako's father, a woman in her mid-twenties. She is the exact opposite of Misako, the modern woman. O-hisa is not only young and pretty, she is also old-fashioned and docile, quite content to wait hand and foot on Misako's father. She serves as the model for the type of woman to whom Kaname may be beginning to turn, and, in fact, she serves as a living counterpart to the Osaka puppets to which Kaname is also increasingly finding himself attracted.

Hideo Takanatsu, a businessman who is a cousin of Kaname. Divorced himself, while on a visit to Kaname and his wife he tries to talk them into going ahead with the divorce and is astonished to discover that they have procrastinated and never gotten around to saying anything to their son. He takes it upon himself to inform their son, who is actually relieved at getting some hard facts.

Louise, a Eurasian prostitute who is Kaname's sometime lover. She is a sex object for Kaname and also satisfies his woman-worshiping tendencies and flirtation with Western erotica. He loses interest in her as he becomes more interested in Japanese culture.

James V. Muhleman

SOMETHING HAPPENED

Author: Joseph Heller (1923-   )
Type of work: Novel
Time of action: The late 1960's or early 1970's
First published: 1974

Robert (Bob) Slocum, a middle-level corporate executive. In his early forties, he works in New York City and lives with his wife and three children in Connecticut. At his office, Slocum is fearful and cynically prudent in dealing with his superiors. At home, he is often competitive and abrasive with his two older children, or he retreats from them to the isolation of his study. He recalls with enthusiasm his earlier, insatiable lust for his wife, but he feels threatened by her increasing sexual assertiveness, and he scrutinizes her carefully for signs of alcoholism and marital infidelity. Slocum himself is a philanderer who is joyless and emotionally numb with prostitutes and his girlfriends. He is preoccupied with death, disintegration, and fear of the unknown, and he ruminates obsessively upon unresolved emotional experiences, such as his adolescent flirtation with a girl who later committed suicide and his neglect of his mother before her death in a nursing home. At the end of the novel, following the death of his nine-year-old son, Slocum is promoted to the head of the Sales Department of the company.

His wife, unnamed, four years younger than Slocum, a tall, slender, well-dressed woman. She is bored and unhappy, and she has recently become a secretive drinker. In the years since marrying Slocum, she has lost self-confidence. She feels unloved by Slocum and their children, and she is beginning, awkwardly, to use obscenities and to flirt with other men at parties.

His daughter, unnamed, an unhappy, fifteen-year-old high school student. Overweight and anxious about her appearance, she both fears and provokes arguments between her parents. Rebellious in her use of obscenity and her insistence upon smoking cigarettes, she expresses fear of her parents' dying or divorcing with abrasive assertions of indifference. Her eagerness for a car and her delight in the prestige of a new house express her pleased participation in the economic upward mobility of the family.

His older son, unnamed, a bright and agreeable nine-year-old. As a young child, he had exasperated and delighted his parents by giving money to other children and by his lack of competitiveness. This family peacemaker has numerous irrational fears, however, and he is physically delicate. Slocum loves and identifies with this boy but inadvertently suffocates him after he is injured in a minor, freak auto accident.

Derek, Slocum's brain-damaged younger son. This child is a focus of concern and conflict between the characters. A major issue is deciding whether to keep Derek at home or send him to an institution.

Andrew (Andy) Kagle, head of the Sales Department in the unnamed company for which Slocum works. A middle-aged man with a limp, Kagle wears the wrong clothes for his executive position, and he is not comfortable in dealing with his superiors or the salesmen who work under him. He trusts Slocum and has been good to him; at the end of the novel, Slocum is promoted to Sales Manager, and Kagle is shunted into Special Projects.

Donald Vanouse

SOMETHING WICKED THIS WAY COMES

Author: Ray Bradbury (1920-   )
Type of work: Novel
Time of action: A week before one Halloween in the early 1930's
First published: 1962

Will Halloway, a boy of almost fourteen, the best friend of Jim Nightshade, born one minute before midnight on October 30. The less adventuresome of the two, he is frightened by the hypnotically attractive carnival that appears in Green Town, Illinois, just before Halloween. He is still very much a young boy, in contrast to Jim. His experience with the evil Cooger and Dark's Pandemonium Shadow Show helps to teach him about the value of friendship, the importance of his father, and the nature of evil. He brings down the wrath of Cooger and Dark by jamming the carousel's controls in the forward position while Cooger is riding the machine, thus turning the man into an ancient, dying being.

Will eventually gains the courage necessary to fight off the sideshow freaks and help his father save Jim Nightshade.

Jim Nightshade, Will Halloway's best friend, born one minute after midnight on October 31. His father has died. In contrast to Will, Jim is the dark side of youth and is very much attracted to the carnival and its mysterious and threatening sideshow and rides. Jim is eager to grow up and falls under the spell of the promise of adulthood held out to him by the carousel, which ages a person a year for every one of its forward revolutions. By the novel's conclusion, he has learned that growing up takes time and is content to let time run its course naturally.

Charles Halloway, Will's father. He married late in life and considers himself an unworthy man. He works as a janitor in the Green Town library and is a man of tremendous intellectual curiosity and learning. Despite his negative self-image, he loves his family and wants to protect his son from the dangers he perceives in Cooger and Dark's carnival. Halloway discovers that the carnival is as old as time, that it has kept itself alive by feeding on others' dissatisfactions, hopes, and foolish wishes. It is Halloway who discovers how to defeat the dark forces of the carnival: by means of laughter and love.

G. M. Dark, a man covered in sinister tattoos and one of the owners of Cooger and Dark's Pandemonium Shadow Show. Dark is intent on capturing as many gullible persons as he can because the people of the carnival feed on human suffering. Dark and Cooger depend on people's fear of death and suffer-

ing to bring them willing victims. He, like his followers, fears death and, thus, exists in a perpetual limbo between living and dying. He manages to entice Miss Foley into meeting her end on the carousel and nearly captures Jim.

J. C. Cooger, the other carnival proprietor. He first rides the carousel in reverse to become Robert, the phoney nephew of Miss Foley. Eventually he rides the machine forward and is trapped in the body of a dying old man because Will prevents him from getting off the machine. He becomes a grisly parody of old age, kept alive by G. M. Dark's black electric chair. He serves as the horrible example of what results from falling prey to the carnival's dark promise of eternal life.

Tom Fury, the enigmatic lightning rod salesman. He sells Jim a lightning rod just before the carnival appears in town.

Miss Foley, an unhappy Green Town spinster in her fifties, Will and Jim's seventh-grade teacher. She is a well-intentioned woman who is kind to the local children. Because she has no family, she is empty and dissatisfied with her life. Cooger and Dark's carnival holds out to her the promise of recapturing her lost youth, and another chance to lead a fulfilled life. Because she is so intent on attaining her goal, she betrays Jim and Will to the carnival owners and to the police. She becomes lost in the carnival's mirror maze and is trapped as a member of the carnival, an adult woman in the body of a young child.

Melissa E. Barth

SOMETIMES A GREAT NOTION

Author: Ken Kesey (1935-)
Type of work: Novel
Time of action: 1961
First published: 1964

Hank Stamper, the head of a small family logging operation in Oregon. He has all the virtues of the traditional hero: self-reliance,

physical strength, endurance, courage, determination, and the ability to do the job. His strength of character, in particular his emphasis on independence, creates conflicts not only with the local community but also within the family itself, especially with his wife and younger half brother. He lives by the motto his father nailed over his bed: Never Give an Inch. His independence has been fostered by his lifelong struggle with nature, which he sees as his principal opponent. An element of rivalry is present in all of his relations with people as well. Hank's determination to fulfill the contract to deliver logs to the mill in spite of a strike by local loggers puts him at odds with the town. Time is running out; the river is rising. Not enough men are available to cut the trees, and the machinery is breaking down as usual. Moreover, dissension from a variety of sources breaks out within the family. Hank perseveres.

Leland (Lee) Stamper, a graduate student at Yale who returns to help the family fulfill the logging contract. Lee is Hank's younger half brother, the son of Hank's father's second wife, who took Lee to the East after an affair with Hank. Moody, apprehensive, self-destructive, self-conscious, and willing to play upon his own weakness, Lee returns to Oregon with hopes of getting revenge on Hank, on whom he blames his sense of alienation. Lee seduces Hank's wife. In the meantime, he is initiated into the logging business. He has to prove himself as a logger. The rivalry with Hank is conducted in the woods and in the house.

Henry Stamper, the patriarch of the Stamper family. An independent, stubborn old man, he is the living link with the pioneer spirit of the Stamper past. When Henry's father Jonas gave up the battle with nature in Oregon and abandoned the family, Henry dug in his heels and made the family business a success. His toughness is his heritage to Hank; however, his intolerance of the weakness of others contributes to Lee's alienation. Only age defeats Henry Stamper. He loses his arm in the desperate attempt to deliver the logs and dies in the hospital, a major source of suffering for Hank and thereby a contributing factor to Hank's development of tolerance.

Vivian (Viv) Stamper, the attractive, spirited wife of Hank, a woman with a will of her own, with a great capacity for love, with dreams of her own self-realization, and with the ability to manage the houseful of cantankerous males. Viv's vulnerability to Lee derives from their mutual sense of alienation. Hank brought her to Oregon from Colorado, and she has never felt at home. Their inability to have children contributes to her lack of fulfillment. She believes that Lee needs her more than Hank does, because Hank is unable to express his needs and unable to see that she has needs of her own. After the two men fight over her, she leaves them both, in spite of her love for them, to seek an identity of her own.

Joe Ben Stamper, Hank's cousin and fellow logger. Joe Ben's spirit is one of the positive aspects of the family struggles. He is cocky, optimistic, full of humor and fun. Married, with two young children, Hank's friend since childhood, Joe Ben remains Hank's principal ally amid all the controversies and problems in the woods. His accidental death by drowning during the fight to fill the contract is another strong blow to Hank's spirit.

Jonathon Draeger, the union president, sent in to direct the local strike, another outsider. Draeger believes in communal action and values. He thinks that any man will give up his principles to protect someone he loves. He cannot understand the independent values of Hank but eventually comes to appreciate him. Draeger is in conflict with Hank because if Hank delivers the logs the strike will be jeopardized.

Floyd Evenwrite, the local union representative. Floyd fancies himself a rival of Hank and resents the presence of Jonathon Draeger. Unlike the rationalist Draeger, Floyd operates by his emotions. He is ambivalent about Hank's success because that means Draeger's failure. In the face of Hank's determined independence, Floyd, and with him the strikers, is finally reduced to passivity.

William J. McDonald

SON OF MAN

Author: Augusto Roa Bastos (1917-   )
Type of work: Novel
Time of action: 1910-1935
First published: Hijo de hombre, 1960 (English translation, 1965)

Miguel Vera, narrator of the odd-numbered chapters, a member of the educated upper middle class in Paraguay. Characterized by his utter lack of direction in life, he can never seem to make a commitment to any cause. He joins the military at an early age and becomes an official but later sneaks away to help a group of rebel peons whom he subsequently betrays. Later, when fighting in the Chaco war, he and his men become stranded and are dying of thirst. When, after a treacherous journey, Cristóbal Jara arrives with a water truck, Vera, delirious with thirst, shoots him down. In the end, Vera is killed by a bullet from his own gun in an apparent suicide.

Cristóbal Jara (hä'rä), a rebel leader of the Paraguayan campesinos. A brave, silent young man, he works selflessly to better the lives of the peons, of which he is one. He organizes a peon rebellion to fight for their rights in the Chaco war. After Vera's betrayal, he ingeniously escapes the persecution of the military. He later embarks on a final selfless mission of carrying water across the enemy lines to a group of isolated soldiers, one of whom is Vera, who shoots at the water truck, killing Jara.

Casiano Jara, an indentured worker in the yerba mate plantations. Weakened from abuse, he and his wife Nati escape with their infant son, Cristóbal, from the forced labor they were subjected to on the plantation. They flee to their hometown of Sapukai, where they make their home in an old train car.

Demented by their harrowing experiences, they continue their flight by pushing the car up and down old and forgotten rails.

Gaspar Mora, a leper who has isolated himself in the woods, away from the townspeople so as not to contaminate them with his disease. To assuage his loneliness, he busies himself by carving a life-size wooden image of himself. After his death, this statue is cherished by the townspeople as a Christlike symbol of Mora's sacrifice for his fellowmen.

Alexis Dubrovsky, an exiled Russian doctor. He comes to live in the town of Sapukai and establishes a ranch for the lepers of the town. He begins caring for the sick, from whom he rarely accepts payment until one day, when he discovers a coin in the neck of an ancient image he receives from a patient. He begins demanding these images from his patients and ultimately breaks them all open, goes on a drinking spree financed with the coins from within the images, and disappears from the village, never to be seen again.

Crisanto Villalba (vē'yäl•bä), a soldier who fought in the Chaco war. After the war, he returns to his hometown of Itapé a broken man. Although he is reunited with his son and is now able to return to his ranch, he is depressed and dejected. He no longer wants to be a farmer. He had found his identity and his purpose in life as a soldier. He returns to his ranch with his son and blows it up with hand grenades.

Gaston F. Fernandez

SONG OF A GOAT

Author: John Pepper Clark (1935-   )
Type of work: Play

Time of action: 1960
First published: 1961

Zifa, the protagonist of the play, a fisherman and ship pilot who is a proud man unable to accept his impotence. He blames his inability to father a child on his wife, Ebiere, and on everyone else. He consults the experts but to no avail. When his younger brother, Tonyá, replaces him as surrogate father, Zifa, in a rage, ritually slaughters a goat, which foreshadows Tonyá's suicide and Zifa's act of atonement—his own suicide.

Tonyá, Zifa's younger brother. He attempts to take Zifa's place in fathering a child, a tradition accepted by Nigerian people, but finds that he cannot live with what he has done in good faith and commits suicide. Tonyá is, therefore, a victim of tragic circumstances.

Ebiere, Zifa's wife. She is told by the Masseur that she should have a child by Tonyá, Zifa's younger brother, because Zifa is impotent. Ebiere follows this advice, thinking that Zifa would believe the child to be his. After Zifa's violent reaction to the act, Ebiere loses her child in a miscarriage, but she accepts the child's death as punishment for her sin. This incident takes place in a sequel to *Song of a Goat,* entitled *Masquerade.*

The Masseur, the most important person in the community. The Masseur is the symbol of strength and stability to the people of the village. He serves as the family doctor, the confessor, and the oracle. The Masseur acts as the sage. He attempts to convince Zifa that infertility will bring ruin to a family and that Zifa must accept Tonyá as a surrogate father. Zifa, in his pride, refuses to follow the Masseur's advice.

Orukorere (ō′r̄ōō•kô•r̄ĕ′r̄ĕ), Zifa's half-possessed aunt. When she hears of Ebiere and Tonyá's plan to conceive a child without Zifa's knowledge, she makes a prophecy of tragic consequences. Her warning, however, is disregarded by all; Orukorere, because of her half-crazed personality, is not taken seriously by the members of her family. Actually, her warnings of disaster, which become a reality, echo the myths and superstitions that have been a large part of the people's consciousness. Throughout the drama, she acts as chorus and conscience.

Dode, Zifa's young son. He appears briefly in the Second Movement as an innocent child who questions his mother, Ebiere, about the differences in animals' sizes.

Three neighbors, who act as chorus. They warn the members of Zifa's family of the tragic consequences that will take place if Tonyá and Ebiere conceive Zifa's child.

Robert J. Willis

SONG OF SOLOMON

Author: Toni Morrison (1931–   )
Type of work: Novel
Time of action: The first half of the twentieth century, the days immediately after the Civil War, and particularly the late 1950's and early 1960's
First published: 1977

Macon Dead III, known also as **Milkman,** the protagonist, a young black male in his twenties who grows up when he discovers his connection with his ancestors, especially the founder of his family, his great-grandfather, Solomon. At first, Milkman is a spoiled, self-centered, confused, and immature boy affected greatly by the tense atmosphere of his unhappy home and family. Milkman's family is ruled by his domineering and unsympathetic father, who has no interest in his past and his family heritage; Milkman, however, with the help of his aunt, Pilate, and his friend, Guitar, manages to complete his journey of cultural, historical, and personal discovery with satisfaction even though it puts his life in jeopardy at the conclusion of the novel.

Macon Dead II, Milkman's materialistic and unsympathetic father. He is the richest black man in town and cares nothing for people in general, including his wife, daughters, and sister. He rules his household autocratically, his primary interest is in obtaining money and land, and he admonishes Milkman to make this his primary goal also.

Ruth Dead, Milkman's mother. She is dominated first by her father and then by her husband, Macon Dead, who rejects her and physically and mentally abuses her. She is a spiritually frail and weak personality, and her primary focus in life centers on a water mark on her dining room table and clandestine visits to her father's grave. She is the reason that her son acquires the name Milkman—from her extended nursing of him in an attempt to hold on to her son in some way.

Pilate, the sister of Macon Dead and the Aunt of Milkman. Her outstanding physical feature is the absence of a navel, supposedly because her mother died before Pilate was born. She lives with her daughter and grandmother in complete absence of all the material things that her brother finds so necessary. Her value system is in complete opposition to all that her brother and her nephew, at first, find important. She represents family and folk values and aids Milkman in his quest for identity. She also symbolizes humanistic values in that she aids Ruth before the birth of Milkman, enabling her through folk charms to achieve a third pregnancy in spite of the past rejection of her husband, and aids Ruth in bringing about Milkman's safe birth.

Reba, Pilate's daughter, a lesser version of her mother. Unlike her mother, Reba has little strength of character and no folk wisdom. Like her mother, she has little regard for the materialistic and is unselfish and giving. In the household of Pilate, Reba, and Hagar, Milkman finds warmth, love, and a safe harbor until he can begin his quest.

Hagar, Pilate's granddaughter, who becomes Milkman's lover. Like her mother and grandmother, she is totally unmaterialistic and gives Milkman her complete love and devotion. She is finally spurned by Milkman and attempts to kill him, but she can never carry out her murderous intentions. Finally, she becomes mad and dies of unrequited love.

Guitar Baines, a young black man who is a bit older than Milkman and befriends Milkman as a young boy. Guitar and Milkman become best friends, and their friendship grows throughout their youth and young adulthood. Guitar becomes a member of the Seven Days, a racial consciousness group that takes revenge for the unjust murder of blacks by killing white people. He and Milkman become enemies during their search for gold that they believe was hidden by Milkman's ancestor. At the conclusion of the novel, Guitar is trying to murder Milkman.

**Magdelena (Lena) and
First Corinthians,** Milkman's boring and dominated sisters. Lena eventually rebels and leaves her parents' household.

Betty Taylor Thompson

SOPHIE'S CHOICE

Author: William Styron (1925-   )
Type of work: Novel

Time of action: 1947 and World War II
First published: 1979

Stingo, a twenty-two-year-old transplanted Southerner and would-be novelist living in New York City, where he struggles to find himself and write. He is oversensitive, intellectual, and astute. The novel is a record of Stingo's pursuits in the big city, which primarily include his employment at McGraw-Hill, his attempts to write, and his relationship with Sophie Zawistowska and Nathan Landau. Stingo—a moderately disguised Styron—becomes more and more involved with these two characters to the extent that he becomes the third point of a love triangle. As the plot unfolds, the reader learns of Sophie's history, and concurrently, Stingo falls helplessly in love with her. After Nathan goes violently crazy, Stingo takes Sophie to the South, to his home region, for one night of passionate lovemaking. Subsequently, Sophie and Nathan commit suicide, leaving Stingo unable to comprehend evil in human nature, primarily embodied in Auschwitz but more immediately in these two deaths.

Sophie Zawistowska, née **Biegańska,** a stunningly beautiful Polish survivor of Auschwitz, lover to Nathan Landau and later to Stingo. The essential aspect of her character is that, though a survivor of the worst atrocities of World War II, she remains a victim of it. In terms of the immediate plot, Sophie is the object of Stingo's infatuation turning to love, a fact that presents problems to all because of her long-standing affair with Nathan Landau. More important, though, Sophie is the focus of the novel in that the gradual revelation of her history is the main thrust of the work. She feels guilty for having survived Auschwitz, a point with which the demented Nathan repeatedly taunts her. In fact, Sophie had been complicit in the terrors of Auschwitz because her father and husband had favored the Nazi cause. Sophie had been arrested in Poland and sent to the prison camp because, out of depression, she smuggled meat and was caught. Also, in the prison camp she survives as private secretary to the camp director. Sophie, upon her arrival at Ausch-

witz, had been given a choice: One of her two children would live; the other would die. She saves her son, who later disappears. Finally, Sophie chooses death over life when she kills herself.

Nathan Landau, Sophie's Jewish lover and Stingo's New York friend. Extremely manipulative and cruel, vainly intellectual and accomplished, perceptive and articulate, Nathan's two main characteristics are his Jewishness and his dementia. Seemingly, he can exist only in love-hate relationships: He persecutes Sophie for being a Gentile and a survivor of Auschwitz; at the same time he persecutes Stingo, making him feel guilty for Southern slavery in the past and racism in the present. Nathan is vain, moody, and violent. Through indulgence in his insanity, Nathan entices Sophie into the suicide pact that ends the novel.

Zbigniew Biegański (zbĭg′nyĕv), Sophie's father and a law professor. Dictatorial and authoritative, Sophie's father had abetted the Nazis by writing a political tract arguing for the extermination of the Jews; hence, Sophie feels guilt for what happens even though the Nazis later arrested and imprisoned her father in a concentration camp, where he eventually died.

Rudolph Franz Höss, Sophie's employer, director of the prison camp/extermination center at Auschwitz. An actual historical figure, Höss had tried to maintain his humanity (particularly his family relations) even while supervising the atrocities at Auschwitz. As camp commandant, he is the object of Sophie's sexual advances while she is working as his secretary and translator (she would sell herself for survival); the advances fail and Höss returns Sophie to work camp.

Fritz Jemand von Niemand, an SS officer at Auschwitz. Totally devoid of any compassion or morality, Niemand determines which new arrivals at Auschwitz will survive temporarily as workers and which will proceed to immediate death. As Sophie confronts him, she professes herself a Roman Catholic and not a Jew. Niemand is then the agent of evil who afflicts her with the heinous crime of choosing which of her children will live, the other die. (*Jemand von Niemand* is German for "somebody from nobody," a phrase that has several applications in this situation.)

Carl Singleton

A SORROW BEYOND DREAMS

Author: Peter Handke (1942-   )
Type of work: Novel
Time of action: The early 1920's to the early 1970's
First published: Wunschloses Unglück, 1972 (English translation, 1974)

The Narrator, a young Austrian writer whose mother has recently committed suicide. He is in his early thirties. His mother's death comes as a shock, and he deals with his grief by attempting to write a memoir, a chronicle of her life. He struggles with the problems of writing this difficult book, that is, with both his own painful feelings and the inherent tendency of all language to fictionalize—and therefore distort—its subject. He is committed to trying to write the most honest, authentic account of her life and death that he can. He reflects upon the various strategies that he might pursue in composing this work; finally, he decides to look at the kind of language used to describe a woman's life—a typical woman's biography—and to see where his mother's life is both similar to and different from that of the prototypical woman. He composes a sensitive and touching portrait of his mother but is unable, in the end, to overcome the horror of her death. He is left with his guilt and anxiety.

His mother, an Austrian woman born in the early 1920's. She is an intelligent and good-looking woman with a winning smile. Her existence is, in certain crucial ways, dictated by the traditional expectations and limitations imposed upon a female's life by the rural and conservative society into which she is born. Although she does well in school, she is not supposed to continue her education because a woman's "place" is to get married and have children. Her grandfather finally allows her to study cooking since this is useful for a "girl." When the Nazis annex Austria in 1938, she, like many others, embraces the festive spirit engendered by the propaganda machine of the Germans. She falls in love with a married German soldier and gives birth to an illegitimate child: the narrator. In order to fulfill her duty as a "mother," she marries another German, who does not really love her. He eventually becomes an abusive alcoholic and repeatedly beats her. Their marriage becomes a prolonged war of silence, and the mother's friendly smile is slowly—and literally—beaten out of her. Her life becomes more solitary and desperate and she becomes chronically depressed. Despite the narrator's efforts to renew her interest in life through literature, she grows worse, and one night, she takes an overdose of sleeping pills.

Thomas F. Barry

SOULS AND BODIES

Author: David Lodge (1935-   )
Type of work: Novel

Time of action: 1952-1978
First published: 1980, in Great Britain as *How Far Can You Go?* (U.S. edition, 1982)

Adrian, one of nine characters whose fortunes and growth from late adolescence to early middle age the novel traces. They are representative not of English youth in general but of young Anglo-Catholics. Collectively, they are sexually ignorant and quite accepting of Church doctrine. Their development is profoundly influenced by the changes then sweeping through Western society and more specifically through the Catholic church as a result of Vatican II. Adrian is a particularly repressed, unquestioning young man. During his military service, this dogmatist of the political and religious right becomes disillusioned with British foreign policy (the Suez crisis). He marries Dorothy ("of course" a virgin) and later continues to move leftward, eventually becoming chairman of Catholics for an Open Church.

Angela, a shopkeeper's daughter and devout Catholic who has been "conditioned" to do all the right things. She and Dennis are the last of their college set to marry and the first to experience tragedy (one daughter is afflicted with Down's syndrome, another is struck and killed by a van); as a result, their marriage begins to dissolve.

Dennis, not a devout Catholic; he is, however, devoted to Angela. After a long, ardent, but entirely chaste courtship, they marry and, as dutiful Catholics, multiply. Domestic tragedies lead Dennis to break first with the Church and then with his wife. After a brief affair with his secretary, Lynn, Dennis returns to Angela.

Edward, a medical student with large ears and a funny face. He marries Tessa, an Anglican willing to convert to Catholicism in order to have a Catholic nuptial mass. Ignorance and inexperience rather than promiscuous intention account for her being pregnant with their first child at the time of the wedding. As a Midlands general practitioner, Edward counsels his patients to use the Church-approved rhythm method until he comes to

realize its negative consequences. Shunned by his Catholic colleagues and in need of some support, the conservative Edward finds himself joining Catholics for an Open Church in spite of its liberal ideas.

Michael, obsessed by sex, eventually in love with Miriam, a Protestant, who, despite her doubts concerning certain Catholic doctrines, becomes a convert. He becomes a lecturer in English literature at a Catholic college, finds himself shocked yet fascinated by the new sexual openness, participates in the 1960's counterculture, moves on to a more liberal Catholic college, and publishes a book entitled *Moving the Times: Religion and Culture in the Global Village.* He worries that he may have cancer, and when he learns that he does not, he almost has a heart attack as he tries too hard to participate in Polly and her husband, Jeremy Elton's, liberated "lifestyle."

Miles, tall and thin, effeminate in appearance and homosexual in orientation. A graduate of an English public school, he knows considerably more about sex than any of the others. A recent convert to Catholicism when the novel begins, this religious conservative (and later Cambridge don) rejects the liberalizing of the Catholic church and eventually returns to the Church of England.

Polly, cheerful, sexy, and considerably less chaste than the others. After numerous affairs she marries a philandering television producer, Jeremy Elton, in a civil ceremony. She later writes an advice column for a women's magazine (at first as "Ann Field"). Sexually liberated and financially well off, she nevertheless remains at least superstitiously Catholic, baptizing her children when one of them becomes seriously ill. She divorces Elton when she discovers his infidelities.

Ruth, plain looking. She becomes a nun, later questions her calling as well as the

Church's authority, goes to the United States as part of her research on changes in the convents, and in the middle of a spiritual crisis recovers her faith at a meeting of charismatics in California.

Violet, small, dark-haired, and neurotic. Easy prey for several men who take advantage of her sexually and emotionally, she suffers several nervous breakdowns. Desperately, she turns from Catholicism to psychoanalysis, which she in turn gives up to become first a Jehovah's Witness and later still a Sufist.

Austin Brierley, young curate and unofficial chaplain of the University of London Catholic study group to which all the above characters belong and on whom he depends for human contact. Theologically naïve, he gradually realizes and attempts to overcome

his ignorance. He is suspended for questioning the wisdom and validity of the papal encyclical on birth control, *Humanae Vitae*; while on leave he studies sociology and psychology, and, after saving Dennis and Angela's marriage, he leaves the priesthood and marries Lynn, Dennis' former lover.

Narrator, an anonymous professor of English at a redbrick university who writes novels in his spare time. He interrupts the story to comment on it, to acknowledge its fictiveness, to provide background information, to refer to relevant literary theories (especially those of Gerard Genette), and to point to his own limited omniscience—indeed to his own inability to keep pace with a reality that changes so swiftly.

Robert A. Morace

THE SOUND OF THE MOUNTAIN

Author: Yasunari Kawabata (1899-1972)
Type of work: Novel
Time of action: The early 1950's
First published: Yama no oto, 1949-1954, serial; 1954, book (English translation, 1970)

Shingo, an elderly businessman. At roughly sixty-three years old, a year younger than his wife, he is preoccupied with some of the principal concerns of aging. His unreliable memory at one point makes him forget momentarily how to knot his tie, while his longing for his beautiful, long-dead sister-in-law is disturbingly fresh. It is right before her death that he first hears the sound of the mountain. Concerned that the problems of his son and daughter point to his failure as a father, he feels equally inept trying to straighten out their lives as adults. Unable to sleep soundly, he dreams frequently and is forced to remember his old friends as they pass away. A man sensitive to the beauty of nature, especially of flowers, he takes refuge in a subtly erotic but platonic friendship with his daughter-in-law, who seems to care more about him than his own children do.

Yasuko, Shingo's wife of some forty years.

She is a plain woman who grew up in the shadow of her beautiful sister. When her sister died, Yasuko, in love with both her sister and her brother-in-law, went to live in her sister's home, willingly becoming a handy maid. Rescued from this domestic slavery by her marriage to Shingo, Yasuko has settled into a comfortable matronly role. She annoys her husband with her snoring and her habit of collecting newspapers for several days before reading them, sometimes aloud, to her family. Her relationship with her daughter is strong, while her long marriage has made her indifferent to her husband.

Shuichi, Shingo's son and a coworker in the same office. He appears to be suffering from his traumas as a soldier during the war, and perhaps it is for this reason that, though married to the beautiful and loving Kikuko, he finds a mistress soon after the wedding. With his mistress, he drinks excessively and becomes violent, but with his wife he seems to show his softer, hurting side. He and his wife share a love of French songs.

Fusako, Shingo's daughter and the mother of two children. Only thirty years old, she has left her husband and come to live with her parents but appears to be in touch with her abusive failure of a husband until he commits suicide with another woman. Somewhat defensive about her plain looks, she perceives her father's attraction to her sister-in-law and is jealous.

Kikuko, Shuichi's wife. The youngest of eight children, she retains a delicate, fragile, child-like quality about her, a quality that her father-in-law describes as "clean." She is the only beautiful woman in Shingo's household but is childless. Though an ideal daughter-in-law and a loving and forgiving wife, she quietly rebels against her husband's philandering by aborting her long-awaited pregnancy.

Tanizaki Eiko, a secretary in Shingo's office for three years. A slight, petite woman recommended to Shingo by an acquaintance, Eiko has a passing fling with Shuichi and has to leave her job. She visits Shingo briefly but regularly and is the chief go-between who brings the father and the son's mistress together to negotiate a breakup.

Kinuko, also called **Kinu,** Shuichi's mistress. A large woman with a round and cheerful face, she is a war widow resentful of women whom she perceives to be pampered wives, those who still have their husbands. She is determined to have a child, even illegitimately. Though Shuichi beats her up trying to get her to have an abortion, she breaks up with him and is determined to carry her pregnancy through. She soothes everyone's conscience by avowing that the baby is not Shuichi's.

Shakuntala Jayaswal

SOUR SWEET

Author: Timothy Mo (1950-   )
Type of work: Novel
Time of action: The 1960's
First published: 1982

Chen, a Chinese émigré to England, a stocky, pale, unprepossessing man with a round, bun-like face and a chubby torso atop short legs. He is only modestly ambitious and works his way up from menial jobs to the ownership of a tiny restaurant in a rundown suburb, where he settles down to create the perfect vegetable garden and to hide from a Triad family. Earlier, Chen had turned to the Triad society of the Chinese underworld for help in paying off his father's debts; in return, he has "helped" the society as a drug runner. His wife's stubbornness reveals his whereabouts to the society, and Chen is murdered.

Lily, Chen's strong-willed and ambitious wife. Taller than the average Chinese woman (and possessed of large hands and feet), Lily was trained by her father as a temple boxer and a traditional herbalist. Very much a tra-

ditionalist, she clings to her Chinese ways, arrogantly assuming that anything unfamiliar to her is inferior. She insulates herself from English culture with both ridiculous and disastrous results. When her son obeys her instructions to kick and bite the bullies at school, he is reprimanded for fighting dirty; worse, her refusal to learn about English law gets her into trouble with the district tax office. Her arrogance is Chen's death sentence: Refusing to obey his request that she omit their address on her monthly check to his father, she inadvertently informs the Triad society of Chen's location. Unfortunately, she never finds out what has happened to Chen; she never discovers that she has sent her husband to his death.

Mui, Lily's older sister, and initially very much the dutiful, submissive, compliant traditional Chinese woman. Paralyzed by culture shock when she is brought to England to help Lily and Chen, Mui learns English quickly and adjusts rapidly to English ways. Eventually Mui bears a daughter out of wedlock (she refuses to identify the father), and later she marries Lo, a friend of the family.

Man Kee, the young son of Chen and Lily, educated in both English and Chinese schools. His ambition to be a gardener when he grows up infuriates Lily, who dreams of more impressive careers for her son.

Mrs. Law, a rich widow who takes an interest in Lily and Mui, whom she entertains frequently at lavish teas and dinners in restaurants. An old-fashioned Chinese, she views home hospitality as inferior to restaurant meals.

Lo, a barbecue chef who is Chen's only friend. The quiet and withdrawn Lo (whose wife ran off with another man) becomes a regular guest at the Chen home; eventually he marries Mui.

Red Cudgel, the leader of a Triad gang that

functions in London. A short, ugly, harsh-voiced man—his face is pockmarked, his knuckles are calloused, and he is missing some fingers—he prefers expensive clothes and a chauffeured car. He believes in Chinese tradition (he insists on eating peasant food) and in the use of force.

White Paper Fan, Red Cudgel's deputy leader. A mild, scholarly man, White Paper Fan speaks French, English, and four Chinese dialects—all of which he learned in his travels around the world.

Grass Sandal, a former jet-setting model, now a Triad officer. Born to wealthy parents as Miranda Lai, she speaks a heavily accented English learned in convent and finishing schools. She is highly ambitious and single-minded; her only real interests are money, power, and sex.

Night Brother, once a foundling and street urchin, now the Triad officer in charge of public relations. He is amiable and cheerful, and possessed of abundant self-confidence.

E. D. Huntley

THE SOURCE

Author: James A. Michener (1907-   )
Type of work: Novel
Time of action: 1964, with flashbacks covering approximately twelve thousand years of Israel's history, beginning c. 9831 B.C.E. (before common era)
First published: 1965

Dr. John Cullinane, a forty-year-old Irish American archaeologist from a museum in Chicago, the leader of an expedition to excavate one of the mounds in Galilee known as Tell Makor. He is exceptionally well educated for the job, having learned to read Aramaic, Arabic, and ancient Hebrew script, as well as Mesopotamian cuneiform and Egyptian hieroglyphs. He is also trained in ceramics, metallurgy, ancient coins, and problems of biblical research. Although he is Catholic, his religiousness is not so much a matter of ardent participation as another intellectual

interest. Nevertheless, he is moved by some of the Jewish religious ceremonies he observes in Israel. Cullinane's easy religious tolerance and ecumenical spirit contrast with the religious passions that emerge in the history of this area, particularly the fanatical devotion to Jewish law that survived multiple disasters.

Jemail Tabari, an Arab trained at Oxford, a first-rate scientific archaeologist. When the Jews threatened to capture Palestine from the Arabs, young Jemail, then twenty-two, fought the Jews vigorously. After his army was crushed, however, he chose to stay in Israel and work with the Jews to rebuild the war-torn area. He is actually the last of an unbroken line of the ancient family of Ur, which originally occupied Makor. He and his Jewish friend Eliav are the ones who make the final breakthrough to the ancient, long-buried well that was the source of water for Makor, a Hebrew word meaning "source."

Dr. Ilan Eliav, Jewish statesman and archaeologist, official watchdog of the dig, whose job is to see that the valuable tell is not mutilated. Cullinane finds out early that Eliav is Vered's fiancé, but this fact does not prevent the rivals from enjoying mutual respect. The former history of Eliav is not revealed to either Cullinane or the reader until the last flashback dated 1948, when the Jews drove the Arabs from the area, then called Safad. Eliav had been a German Jewish immigrant named Isidore Gottesmann. His father had shipped him to Amsterdam during the rise of the Nazis, where he became part of the Jewish underground operating along the German border. English agents spotted his abilities and turned him into an excellent soldier. They then sent him to Syria with a secret unit to keep Damascus out of German hands. There, he met members of the Jewish Brigade from Palestine and acquired their vision of a free Israel. When the British left the Galilee, virtually handing over power to the Arab majority, Gottesmann and a small band of Jews rose up and took over the town, fighting against great odds. Gottesmann's seventeen-year-old wife died in this action. The bitter Gottesmann, worn down by many years of warfare, changed his name to the Hebrew Ilan Eliav and vowed to devote his life to the new Israel.

Dr. Vered Bar-El, a Jewish archaeologist and Israel's top expert in dating pottery. She is an extremely attractive, thirty-three-year-old widow, about whom the reader knows little of a personal nature. She was a young girl in those fateful days when Jewish men, women, and even children launched their desperate assault against the Arabs. Later in that war, she, with gun blazing, rescued Eliav when he was captured. Few details emerge, however, about her attachment to Eliav. When legal complications in traditional Jewish marriage law concerning widows threaten to endanger Eliav's political career, Vered surprises everyone by marrying the rich American Jew Paul Zodman, who financed the dig.

Paul J. Zodman, a Chicago businessman and a thoroughly Americanized Jew who has little patience for the old rigid religious laws of Orthodox Judaism. He still considers the State of Israel as the source and preserver of Jewish heritage, however, and willingly pours money into projects that confirm the Jewish homeland.

Ur, a caveman and hunter of the prehistoric period that first saw some attempts to domesticate plants and animals. Ur himself would never have deviated from the familiar hunting pattern of his ancestors had it not been for his wife, who was responsible for gathering wild plants. She conceived their idea of planting seed near the cave and, later, tricked Ur into neglecting the hunt in order to protect their wheat fields. She is also credited with the beginnings of religion, and her daughter first domesticated a wild dog.

Urbaal, Ur's descendant, a farmer who, in 2202 B.C.E., prayed to a father-god El, as well as Baal-of-the-Storm, Baal-of-the-Waters, Baal-of-the-Sun, and the love goddess Astarte. In spite of the vehement objections of his second wife, Timna, he dutifully allowed her firstborn son to be sacrificed to Melak, god of death and war. Ultimately, however, unruly passions overcame the law-abiding farmer. He fell in love with a priestess of Astarte and killed a herdsman who was a rival for the privilege of lying with her in the temple for seven days and nights—part of an institutionalized fertility ritual. He fled from the city and took refuge at the altar of an approaching desert nomad.

Joktan, that desert nomad, who was thought to be the forerunner of the Hebrews and was the first Habiru to see Makor. He worshiped only the one god, El. After the death of Ur-baal, Joktan married his widow, Timna. Ur-baal, Joktan, and Timna became parts of later religious myth. Joktan was a heavenly stranger, who arrived from the east. Urbaal became the god Ur-baal, the principal god of Makor, and Timna became an aspect of Astarte. Amalek, the herdsman Urbaal killed, was transformed into Melak, god of war. Timna/Astarte rescued Baal from the realm of darkness by killing Melak and scattering his fragmented body over the fields. This ritual brings the wheat to germination and the olive trees to blossom. In later times, Ur-Baal became simply Baal, the dying and resurrected earth god of the Canaanites.

Uriel, the astute Canaanite governor of Makor in 1419 B.C.E., also a descendant of Ur. He allows a large group of Hebrews led by an old man, Zadok, to settle outside the town.

Zadok, a man who calls himself "the right arm of El-Shaddai," the god of "the mountain that no man ever sees." Though both Zadok and Uriel were men of integrity and generally tolerant of each other's religion, Zadok was shocked by the temple prostitution involved in the worship of Astarte. When Zadok's daughter married Uriel's son and began to worship the fertility goddess, Zadok declared the town an abomination. El-Shaddai spoke to Zadok and ordered him to kill every man of the town, take the children as his own, and distribute the women among his men. Zadok objected to this cruel assignment, but his hot-blooded sons slaughtered the Canaanites, as well as their sister, and burned Makor.

Jabaal, called the **Hoopoe,** a man who, in 963 B.C.E., accepts Yahweh as the great diety of the outer heavens while continuing to worship the earth god Baal as the local deity. Hoopoe is a descendant of Governor Uriel but a rather ridiculous figure—a short, stocky man with an oversized bottom that wiggles as he walks and a large, bald head covered with freckles. Children and most other people call him Hoopoe, the name of a common bird that seldom flies but runs from place to place poking into holes for insects. Actually, the man is an excellent architect, who rebuilds the walls of Makor and creates a remarkable tunnel to the well, which is vulnerable to attackers because it is outside the city walls. He then buried the well in an underground chamber so that no one could see where their source of water was. This chamber is the hidden well found by Tabari and Eliav so many years later.

Jehubabel, a pudgy, middle-aged wise man living in 171 B.C.E. Mediocre in talent, Jehubabel is a master of commonplace knowledge. He is tediously prone to quoting old Jewish proverbs but is neither forceful nor particularly religious. He does, however, confront the Canaanite Governor Tarphon, though Tarphon is not very impressed by Jehubabel's objections to the ban against circumcision. Yet, driven by forces that he does not understand, Jehubabel risks his life to perform the circumcision ritual in secret. His greatest trial, however, is when his son Benjamin has his foreskin reconstructed so that he can participate in the Greek games. Appalled at his son's betrayal and heresy, Jehubabel crushes his son's skull with the knotted walking stick of a nearby cripple.

Abd Umer, a man born a slave but now a servant of Muhammad in 635 C.E. He achieves an almost bloodless conquest of Makor. Neither Jews, Christians, nor pagans offer any resistance.

Rabbi Laki, the shoemaker, the most beloved of three rabbis who come to Safed in 1559 C.E. A short, grossly fat, neither brave nor learned man, but full of goodwill, he is a buffoon of the spirit. His people had fled the Inquisition from Spain to Portugal, then from Lisbon to Italy. Rabbi Laki senses the hatred of the Christians there as well and foresees a Jew-burning in a vision. Years later, after he had become a beloved leader in Safed, his vision came to pass, and he returned to the congregation he had abandoned. He was honored thereafter as a martyr.

Rabbi Eliezer bar Zadok, the leader of the

Jewish community of Gretz, Germany, where his ancestors had come from Babylonia a thousand years before. When both Catholics and Protestants were castigating Jews as well-poisoners, ritual murderers, practitioners of black magic, Rabbi Eliezer started on the long and dangerous journey to Turkey. In Safed, he became famous for codifying Jewish law.

Dr. Abulafia, a distinguished medical man in Avaso, Spain, whose Jewish ancestors had become Christian in 1391. The Avaro Inquisition had begun ferreting out thousands of persons of Jewish background who had accepted baptism, claiming they were secret Jews. They tortured and burned some six thousand on flimsy evidence. After watching a personal friend die in the fire, the sickened Abulafia circumcised himself with a pair of scissors, cried "I am a Jew," and fled Spain. He became a noted Kabbalist scholar in Safed.

Katherine Snipes

THE SOUTHPAW

Author: Mark Harris (1922-   )
Type of work: Novel
Time of action: 1952
First published: 1953

Henry Whittier Wiggen, left-handed pitcher for the New York Mammoths. The twenty-one-year-old rookie is an innocent reluctant to be corrupted by a cynical world, cocky about his pitching prowess, and unashamedly cowardly when confronted by violence. Henry grows up in Perkinsville, New York, believing he will be the greatest pitcher of all time, wins twenty-six games in his first season, is named the league's most valuable player, and leads his team to the world championship. His controversial year includes taunts for having a black roommate, back pain caused by the tension of the pennant race, refusal to take a postseason tour to Korea because of his opposition to the war, and an obscene gesture at hecklers during the World Series.

Holly Webster Wiggen, Henry's wife. A rebel, unable to live with her parents in Baltimore, she lives with her uncle next door to Henry, seduces him, and reads him poetry. Her husband's moral conscience, Holly finally accepts his fourth proposal once he has proven he is an individual.

Pop Wiggen, Henry's father. Despite great promise, he quits professional baseball after two years in the minor leagues, never explaining why. He drives a school bus, is caretaker at Aaron Webster's observatory, pitches semi-professional baseball, and rears his son alone after his wife dies when the boy is two.

Aaron Webster, Holly's uncle. An eighty-year-old intellectual, he runs an observatory he refuses to allow the government to use during World War II, also declining to pay taxes that promote war. Aaron convinces Pop, his best friend, not to force the young Henry to become a right-hander.

Mike Mulrooney, Henry's minor league manager. He wins Henry's admiration by treating all his players as human beings and teaches the youngster more about baseball than even Pop has.

Herman H. Schnell (Dutch), the Mammoth manager. Alternately a stern disciplinarian and a kindly grandfather, Dutch will do anything to motivate his players, though he resents that they have different personalities.

Samuel Delbert Yale (Sad Sam), the Mammoths' longtime star pitcher. Soured on life, Sam does not enjoy baseball, money, or sex. As a boy, Henry worships Sam, talking to his photograph and rereading his autobiography, only to discover years later that his idol is a phony.

Berwyn Phillips Traphagen (Red), the Mammoth catcher. The smartest player in baseball, Red is a Harvard graduate, an atheist, and a pacifist. He helps guide Henry's development as a pitcher, worrying that the youngster will hurt his arm by throwing the screwball.

Robert Stanley Jones (Ugly), the Mammoth shortstop. Unattractive because of a misaligned jaw, Ugly is nevertheless a ladies' man, married to a film actress. He ends his salary holdout only when Patricia Moors goes to bed with him. His jaw is fixed after it is broken in a fistfight.

Perry Garvey Simpson, a rookie second baseman. The only black on the team for most of the season, he is not allowed in hotels and restaurants during spring training in Florida. A hustler and student of the game, he is Henry's roommate until a second black player joins the Mammoths.

Bruce William Pearson, Jr., the third-string catcher and Henry's second roommate. Unsophisticated and slow-witted, he is the butt of his teammates' jokes. He gets drunk once a year en route to spring training because he knows he will play less than he desires.

Patricia Moors, vice president of the team owned by her father. Beautiful, bored, and alcoholic at thirty, she will do anything for the good of the Mammoths, including sleeping with the players, but she resists Henry's schoolboy advances.

Krazy Kress, a sports columnist. Grossly overweight, self-serving, and opportunistic, he attacks Henry as an ungrateful, unpatriotic, obnoxious whiner, giving the young pitcher the impetus to write an honest book about baseball.

John Llewellyn Roguski (Coker) and **Earle Banning Smith (Canada),** other Mammoth rookies. With Henry and Perry, they form a locker room quartet invited to sing on television.

Lester T. Moors, Jr., an automobile manufacturer who owns the Mammoths.

Michael Adams

THE SPACE TRILOGY

Author: C. S. Lewis (1898-1963)
Type of work: Novel
Time of action: The late 1930's and the 1940's
First published: 1975: *Out of the Silent Planet,* 1938; *Perelandra,* 1943; *That Hideous Strength,* 1945

Ransom, a philologist and reluctant hero, the protagonist of the three novels that form the trilogy. Kidnapped to Mars in the opening novel, Ransom is forced to draw upon all of his wit and cunning as an intellectual Englishman to defeat the evil Dr. Weston and his accomplice, Dick Devine. Thus drawn into interplanetary intrigue and rescue, Ransom redeems his heretofore less-than-adventurous life. Consisting chiefly of long walking tours and classroom lectures on obscure languages, Ransom's sedentary existence is transformed into continual confrontation with the supernatural and with fearful alien life-forms. By nature somewhat of a loner and terrified of strange and foreign settings, he is the least likely victor over diabolical forces. As a deeply moral man, Ransom is ashamed of his own planet's rebellion against God and becomes passionate in his determination to keep free other planets from the rebellion of Earth, lest it spread. His single most distinguishing trait is his unabashed Christian faith, a faith that sustains him in thwarting interplanetary villains and plots against Martians, Venutians, and, in the final novel of the trilogy, the humanity of Earth. Ransom's name links him symbolically with the messianic, rescuer mission of the historical Jesus, while his exploits with Merlin in the last of the three novels align him with the Arthurian tradition. On Perelandra, or Venus, his wounded heel—retained in his battle with the un-man—recalls both Achilles and Christ; there, he learns that intellectual prowess alone cannot secure a cause but rather that physical strength must sometimes be employed to make a crafty man more resourceful. Back on Earth in *That Hideous Strength*, the now-wizened Ransom moves to the background as an adviser and referee for the final victory against the supernatural evil represented in the National Institute of Coordinated Experiments (N.I.C.E.).

Dick Devine, later, **Lord Feverstone,** a wealthy eccentric and former schoolmate of Ransom. Devine is the accomplice of the evil Dr. Weston in *Out of the Silent Planet*, who drugs Ransom so that he can be hijacked to Mars. In the last novel of the trilogy, Devine also reemerges as the calculating Lord Feverstone, a fellow of Bracton, the nefarious college that houses N.I.C.E. There, he recruits the impressionable Mark Studdock for the diabolical organization. By the novel's climax he is killed by a timely earthquake, a just end for a reprehensible and antihuman figure.

Dr. Weston, a wicked physicist who serves as a dual adversary in two of Ransom's adventures, in both *Out of the Silent Planet* and *Perelandra*. In the first book of the trilogy, Weston emerges as an unscrupulous, avaricious scientist willing to kidnap Ransom and offer him as a human sacrifice in exchange for riches on Malacandra, or Mars. When he is defeated along with his accomplice, Devine, he is banished from the planet by its angelic overlord, the Oyarsa. Weston returns in the second novel of the trilogy as the "unman," a no-longer-human, satanic figure bent

on seducing the unfallen Eve of Perelandra to sin against God. Here, Ransom kills him, sparing the planet from Earth's fate.

Mark Studdock, a young sociologist in *That Hideous Strength*. Studdock, filled with a naïve enthusiasm for the ability of science to improve nature and the human race, unwittingly makes common cause with the Nazi-like N.I.C.E. Eventually, he is persuaded that N.I.C.E. is science gone mad and is captured and sentenced to death by N.I.C.E. lest he desecrate a crucifix. Studdock is finally delivered from his illusions about the organization and saved from death only by the faithfulness and heroic intervention of his wife, Jane.

Jane Studdock, the graduate-student-turned-housewife of Mark, and a determined foe of N.I.C.E. in *That Hideous Strength*. Jane is a spiritually sensitive young woman whose dreams lead her to recognize the evil of N.I.C.E. Her marriage with Mark is dry and empty; she loves him but cannot be the support and helpmate of one so arrogant and blinded by ambition. As she seeks the meaning of her dreams and counsel for her disintegrating marriage, she discovers the underground group seeking to undermine the villainy of N.I.C.E. She becomes, allied with Ransom, a key operative in defeating Feverstone and his conspirators. Her native skepticism of value-free scientific inquiry and her dutiful care for Mark's destiny serve to unravel the sinister plot of her husband's captors.

The Green Lady, the unfallen Eve of Perelandra. Like the biblical Eve, the Green Lady is callow, innocent, and blithely ignorant of the danger posed by the serpentine Weston, who has come specifically to cause the Fall of her world just as Earth had been condemned. She is beautiful and buoyantly alive, but her trusting nature makes her susceptible to cunning and guile. In the absence of her husband, the King, the Green Lady ultimately turns to Ransom as her teacher and protector to learn how to resist the subtle temptations of the un-man that would turn Eden into Hell.

Maleldil the Younger, the deity/ruler of the universe and head of the eldila, or angelic beings, who govern both Malacandra and Perelandra in the first two books of the trilogy. It is he, as a Christ figure, who ultimately has called Ransom into these interplanetary battles and who serves as the moral center of its universe.

The King, husband of the Green Lady, and rightful ruler of Perelandra, who returns to welcome his triumphant Queen at the end of the novel.

Merlin, the sorcerer of Arthurian legend. The cynical, curmudgeonly Merlin appears at the appropriate moment in Belbury, the setting of *That Hideous Strength*, to assist Ransom in bringing N.I.C.E. to its proper end and setting things aright spiritually.

Lewis, friend of Ransom and the narrator of *Out of the Silent Planet* and *Perelandra*. This fictional "Lewis" reveals to the reader the frame and setting of Ransom's first two adventures.

Hyoi, a friendly hross, hrossa being the tall, furry creatures who populate Malacandra. Hyoi befriends the lost and fearful Ransom upon his escape from the treachery of Devine and Weston in *Out of the Silent Planet*. He and other hrossa teach Ransom their language and generally prepare him with their historical and geographical instruction for his mission on the planet.

Oyarsa, the angelic planetary ruler of Malacandra. The Oyarsas are angelic beings made of light who serve Maleldil the Younger. In exposing Devine and Weston for who they are, the Malacandra Oyarsa explains to Ransom the history of Earth's fall, "the silent planet," whose bent Oyarsa (Satan) had broken communication with other unfallen, intelligent beings throughout the universe. The Oyarsas of the other planets close to Earth descend upon Earth at the end of *That Hideous Strength* to assure the victory of the righteous resistance.

Cecil Dimble, Jane Studdock's tutor in *That Hideous Strength*. Mr. Dimble serves, along with his wife, as an important confidant and a source of spiritual strength in Jane's rocky marriage with Mark and her role as a combatant against N.I.C.E.

Mrs. Dimble, Cecil Dimble's wife. Mrs. Dimble routes Jane Studdock to the people in the Bracton College underground who can help her interpret her dreams and point her to Ransom.

Fairy Hardcastle, the brutal security force director of N.I.C.E. A sadist and probable lesbian, Fairy Hardcastle tortures Jane to uncover what she might know about the plots against N.I.C.E. She meets her end with other N.I.C.E. officials when Merlin and Ransom bring the judgment of God upon the dastardly clan of conspirators.

Bruce L. Edwards

SPEED-THE-PLOW

Author: David Mamet (1947-   )
Type of work: Play
Time of action: The 1980's
First produced: 1988

Bobby Gould, the number-two man in a Hollywood production office, who at almost forty years of age is still immature, guided by the "street smarts" learned in his youth. Bobby has earned his position by honoring the principle that a film is good only if it makes money. By following this standard, he has been rewarded with an office redolent of success. Gould is primarily concerned with his own self-image, with his maleness, and with the appearance of success. He dresses expensively, probably drives a flashy car off-stage, and utilizes special, irreverent, and vulgar insiders' language with ease and fluidity. For a brief period, because he is starving for love and affection, he tries to impress a good-looking girl, his temporary secretary Karen. He allows himself to pretend that scruples were always important to him. He almost produces an "art for art's sake" film, seemingly abandoning Hollywood's "money rules" credo. His lack of faith in his ability to sustain a caring relationship proves justified when the good-looking secretary is found to have been interested in him only for what he could do for her career. A misogynist from the start, Bobby has no qualms or thoughts about what happens to her when he dumps her.

Charlie Fox, of a similar age to Bobby Gould and an old pal of his as well, a hanger-on in the film industry, continually flattering all those in a position to help him, while waiting for his big break to come along, which occurs when a hot property (film star or director) agrees to sign on his team, thereby making him a producer. Using friendship as motivation, he presents his new deal to his old buddy, knowing that his friend will remain faithful to him. Charlie uses language riddled with clichés. He has no pretensions—

neither intelligence, charm, nor wit—and he seems proud of his coarseness. He will stop at nothing, let nothing get in the way of his success, which is defined by Hollywood's rules. He will even use the street behavior learned as a kid, physically bullying to get his way. Charlie probably lacks a family, as indicated by his own sense of mistrust, impotence, and misogyny. Suspecting that everyone is, like himself, motivated by self-interest, Charlie will use and abuse, all the time pretending long-term affection and trust for those who have been more monetarily successful than he.

Karen, a good-looking, seemingly sweet, temporary secretary in her twenties who has the makings of an opportunist. While working for Bobby Gould, Karen sees a chance to make a difference in the type of film produced while furthering her career. Using earnestness as a cover-up, she is unfortunately honest enough to admit that she used sex with her boss only to get ahead; she did not care for him as a person. While pretending a certain amount of naïveté, she nevertheless relies on the stereotype that the man will take care of her, ironically proving herself to be actually naïve as well as stupid, manipulative, plotting, power-hungry, and whorish.

Marjorie J. Oberlander

SPEEDBOAT

Author: Renata Adler (1938-   )
Type of work: Novel
Time of action: Chiefly the 1970's
First published: 1976

Jen Fain, the thirty-five-year-old narrator and protagonist of a novel that is, like her life, at once highly discontinuous and yet all of a piece. Currently living in New York and working as a reporter on a tabloid, the *Standard Evening Sun*, she has held a variety of jobs—speech writer, grants rewriter, investigative reporter, gossip columnist, member of a congressional select committee, teacher, librarian, and worker at a university infirmary.

She has also traveled extensively and in fact describes her life as a series of idle periods interspersed with travel. She grew up in the country in, or near, a New England mill town (her account is not entirely consistent) and has been educated in progressive schools as well as American, English, and French universities. Neither her education nor her psychoanalysis, however, has prepared her either to order her life or to overcome her fears. She has, she says, led several lives, successively, of course, but also to a degree concurrently. She is attracted to situations that involve risk and have a "moral edge." This is true of her writing and, more especially, her relationships with the men with whom she intermittently lives. At the end of the novel Jen, uncertain whether to tell her lover that she is pregnant, looks for reassurance, including whatever reassurance illusions and clichés can provide. She is, however, too self-conscious not to realize how false such a position would be.

Aldo, a "gentle, orderly, soft-spoken" writer from St. Louis who lives with Jen when he is not living alone. They attended graduate school together in England and have visited Venice and a Caribbean island together. He is currently back in New York "doing a political essay."

Jim, a lawyer from Atlanta who used to work for the Office of Strategic Services (OSS) but who now runs a political campaign for a man whom Jen has never liked and who dies near the end of the narrative. Jim has known Jen for a long time and lives with her occasionally, always careful that any calls he makes from her apartment are made collect. He does not know what Jen knows: that he has begun to talk like a politician and that he is the father of the child she is carrying.

Will, a lawyer at the foundation where Jen once worked rewriting grants applications. Although they have slept together on occasion, he is presently "gone."

Stewart, a thirty-two-year-old tennis instructor from whom Jen takes lessons on her weekends in the country. "A good, confused," quiet man, he considers himself both a humanitarian and a bohemian.

Jen's group, the people who, like Jen, wanted to live safely and successfully but who now find themselves quietly and desperately "fighting for their lives." Collectively they are urban, ambitious, financially well-off, international, well-meaning (or at least meaning no harm), and capable of issuing "a qualified no." They have had their share of breakdowns, divorces, abortions, homosexuality, and long, sad affairs. Although they exercise and do yoga, they are, Jen says, "really a group of invalids, hypochondriacs, and misfits."

Ned, a representative member of Jen's group. He is a young uptown doctor who, until the change in the abortion law, made an extra two thousand dollars per week, tax-free, performing illegal operations in his office. He now finds himself in a financial bind. His wife is in analysis, his daughters in therapy; he prefers not to talk about his son.

Robert A. Morace

THE SPELL

Author: Hermann Broch (1886-1951)
Type of work: Novel
Time of action: The twentieth century
First published: Die Verzauberung, 1976 (English translation, 1987)

The Narrator, a country doctor, formerly an obstetrician and deputy director on the staff of a large urban hospital. This aging physician has settled in Kuppron, a remote Alpine village, to get over a failed love affair with a fellow doctor named Barbara (whom he reminisces about at length) and in search of a purer life-style. He is fascinated by the archaic mountain madness that he witnesses and by the atavistic surfacing of primal drives and delusions among the inhabitants. In various ways the doctor attempts to atone for a certain guilt incurred by allowing himself to get caught up in the mass hysteria.

Marius Ratti, a mysterious stranger in his

thirties whose appearance one spring marks the beginning of something sinister, barbaric, and demonic in the isolated mountain community. The embodiment of a malevolent mysticism, this Pied Piper with Italianate curly hair and mustache is a curiously charismatic catalyst as he inveighs against the corrupt capitalistic cities and preaches a primordial purity, chastity, misogyny, metaphysical machismo, and regressive social structure based on hate-filled power. Ratti urges the abandonment of such devilish devices as radios and assures the impoverished villagers that gold may once again be mined from the mountain. After civilization reasserts itself, Ratti extends his triumph by becoming a member of the municipal council.

Wetchy, a weak and ineffectual insurance agent and salesman of agricultural machinery and other merchandise, including radios. Though not a Jew, he is the quintessential outsider and a scapegoat for the villagers' frustrations and problems. "Wireless Wretchy" becomes the chief target of Ratti's hatred, and he, his wife, and their two children are attacked in their home and hounded out of the village. In a final encounter with his persecutor, Wetchy temporarily abandons his downtrodden and obsequious stance.

Irmgard Miland, the Mountain Bride, who believes that she is in love with Ratti, yet has premonitions of her doom. During the bacchanalian revelry of the mountain kermis, the murder of this young girl marks the climax (or nadir) of the rustic frenzy. This expiatory ritual sacrifice is intended to appease the earth and provide the villagers with strength-giving knowledge of death. Irmgard's killer, the innkeeper Theodor Sabest, perishes among the rocks.

Mother Grisson, Irmgard's grandmother and the guardian of the earth spirit. Her name is an anagram of *gnosis* (a Greek word meaning knowledge). This matriarch of the community is securely rooted in her thisworldly faith and provides a counterpoise of sanity. Her warnings having gone unheeded, Ratti's triumph leads to her mystically experienced death, but first she imparts her "knowledge of the heart" to Agatha, a young woman expecting a child.

Wenzel, a clownish dwarf, a "wenching runt," and Ratti's henchman. This Joseph Goebbels (Nazi propagandist) figure compensates for his small size by affecting an aggressive virility. Concentrating on the harassment of Wetchy, he becomes the leader of a band of young lads. Wenzel almost loses his life in a mining mishap.

Harry Zohn

SPERANZA

Author: Sven Delblanc (1931–   )
Type of work: Novel
Time of action: 1794
First published: 1980 (English translation, 1983)

Count Malte Moritz von Putbus (mäl'tə mō'rīts fŏn püt'bŭs), known as **Mignon** (mē•nyōn'), a callow Swedish aristocrat who both relates the story and serves as its protagonist. A self-professed idealist and political visionary, this naïf has embraced the liberal creed of the Enlightenment and dedicated himself to extending the effects of the French Revolution. The novel consists entirely of his diary, which, after summarizing the inept radical activism and erotic misadventure that have led his parents to exile the young man to the New World, reflects upon events during his journey aboard the *Speranza*, a slaver vessel. In effect, Mignon's mind, not the ship itself, is the story's stage, and the drama is defined through his transition from the presumption of his own goodness and a delusive faith in mankind to the realization that human corruption is complete and unredeemable.

Roustam (rōō·stäm′), the Count's black valet. Dressed in European finery and displaying European manners, he is regarded as only an entertaining clown by the court at Putbus, but on the *Speranza* he quickly tests his master's egalitarian posture and eventually emerges as the leader of the slaves during their insurrection. The diary's last entries, in relating Roustam's execution, indicate the terrible secret that impels Mignon to wish him dead: a homosexual liaison which occurred the night the former valet called upon the aristocrat to side with the slaves once they rebelled.

Hoffmann, Mignon's tutor, who has reveled in Putbus' pleasures of the flesh while pretending to covet the superior rewards of the liberated intellect. After boarding the slave ship, however, he drops his philosopher's pose and shamelessly tries to satisfy his base appetites. To the extent that *Speranza* alludes to *Candide*, Hoffmann is a grim elaboration of Pangloss.

Doctor Rouet (rü·ā′), an embittered humanist who pitches his charity and solidarity with the oppressed in futile defiance of civilization's rampant depravity. The ship's physician assumes the role of tutor to Mignon that Hoffmann has abandoned; instead of the philosopher's hypocrisy, however, the severe truths of reality issue from Rouet's instruc-

tion. If he represents the best qualities that Europe has developed since the Renaissance, his retreat into cynicism bespeaks the failure of society to act according to the very virtues it has exalted.

Abbe Marcello (mär·chĕl′lō), appointed by the Jesuits to oversee their financial investment in the human cargo of the *Speranza*, the opposite of Dr. Rouet. A man wholly without emotion, he perverts reason in order to justify any cruelty or any injustice as an instrument of the soul's salvation.

The Black Aphrodite, later called **Eve,** the surpassingly beautiful slave whose erotic appeal shatters Mignon's illusions about himself as an apostle of the Age of Reason. Once he sees her in her naked voluptuousness, he will resort to any means to ravish her. The Aphrodite's blackness is not only a mark of her race but also, and more profoundly, a manifestation of the dark powers that mock the faculties emphasized by the Enlightenment.

Grethel, the parish clerk's daughter, whom Mignon seduced, reminiscent of Johann Wolfgang von Goethe's simple, betrayed innocent in *Faust I*. Her lover promises liberation from outmoded strictures, but it is the gratification of an adolescent's itch that motivates his arguments, not the logic of political freedom.

Frank Gado

THE SPIRE

Author: William Golding (1911-   )
Type of work: Novel
Time of action: The fourteenth century
First published: 1964

Jocelin, the Dean of the Cathedral Church of Our Lady, somewhere in England. He obtained the position through the influence of his aunt, mistress to a previous king. Despite this connection, Jocelin appears a spiritual man, full of visionary faith, feeling called by

God to construct a tower and spire for the cathedral. At first, the vision is seen by Jocelin as an act of faith over material impossibilities, such as inadequate foundations. He feels tremendous joy and love as this act of faith begins to take shape and sees his vision as providing the willpower to motivate those who doubt the feasibility of the project. As opposition and difficulties mount, however, he finds that his will becomes more naked. He realizes that self-sacrifice may not be cost enough; he starts to "sacrifice" those around him, for example, making no move to protect Goody or her husband. Eventually both die. He learns, too, to shut difficult people and situations out of his consciousness, to become indifferent to them. This enables him to remain totally uncompromising, whatever the consequences. His will becomes all-consuming and obsessive, and he neglects all of his other duties as he drives the workmen on.

Roger Mason, the master builder, the only person, as far as Jocelin is concerned, who has the skill and the workers to build so ambitiously. Roger cannot respond to Jocelin's faith and, when he discovers how insufficient the foundations are, tries to compromise with merely a tower. In this battle of wills, Roger loses, undermined by his own infatuation with Goody. He fears heights, too, and in the end is broken by the tensions, becomes alcoholic, walks off the job, and ultimately attempts an unsuccessful suicide.

Rachel, Roger's wife and one of the four "pillars," people around him whom Jocelin views as equivalent to the four pillars supporting the new building. Her unconsummated marriage to Roger is a complex affair, full of power struggles yet held together by a brother-and-sister compatibility. Under the growing tensions, she talks incessantly and hysterically, and is left at the end to look after an imbecile husband.

Pangall, another of Jocelin's "pillars," being the church caretaker and odd-job man, a position held by his family since the first building of the cathedral. He has a limp and is impotent. He is made the scapegoat to ward off bad luck by the workmen, is persecuted, and is finally ritually murdered, his pleas to Jocelin for protection having remained unanswered.

Goody Pangall, the last of Jocelin's "pillars." She was married off to Pangall by Jocelin previously, to keep her nearby. Her youthful innocence and dutifulness are finally destroyed by Roger Mason's lust for her. She may or may not know the manner of her husband's death. She dies in a sordid childbirth, just as Jocelin is bringing her money to go to a convent to have Roger's child. Jocelin has allowed the affair to go on to keep Roger working on his project, and she dies feeling both accused and betrayed by the church.

Father Anselm, the Lord Sacristan of the cathedral and one of its "Principal Persons." Previously he was master of novices, one of whom was Jocelin. Among other things, he is embittered by Jocelin's rise to power and the masterful way in which Jocelin squashed his opposition to the spire. He ceases to be either Jocelin's friend or his confessor, which relationships, he claims, he never wanted in the first place.

Father Adam, or **Father Anonymous,** as Jocelin calls him, a cathedral chaplain. He neither supports nor opposes Jocelin, but as Jocelin lies dying, he tries in his patient, orthodox way to minister to him, without ever understanding the complexities of Jocelin's mind or motivation.

David Barratt

THE SPLENDORS AND MISERIES OF COURTESANS

Author: Honoré de Balzac (1799-1850)
Type of work: Novel
Time of action: 1824-1830

First published: Splendeurs et misères des courtesanes, 1838-1847 (English translation, 1895):
Comment aiment les filles, 1838, 1844 (*The Way That Girls Love*, 1895); *À combien
l'amour revient aux vieillards*, 1844 (*How Much Love Costs Old Men*, 1895); *Où mènent
les mauvais chemins*, 1846 (*The End of Bad Roads*, 1895); *La Dernière Incarnation de
Vautrin*, 1847 (*The Last Incarnation of Vautrin*, 1895)

Jacques Collin, alias **Vautrin** (vō•trăń'), a brilliant professional criminal posing as a Spanish priest, the **Abbé Carlos Herrera.** Collin appears an impressive man, short but broad and powerful. He is one of Balzac's most memorable creations, a figure of menace who figures prominently in two previous novels: *Le Père Goriot* (1835; *Daddy Goriot*, 1860; better known as *Père Goriot*) and *Illusions perdues* (1837-1843; *Lost Illusions*, 1913). In *Père Goriot* (set in 1819-1820), he appears as Vautrin, is about forty years old, and lives on money provided by his criminal followers. He is a cynical rogue and an aggressive homosexual whose only human sympathies are devoted to the two young men whom he loves, Théodore Calvi and Lucien de Rubempré. He meets Calvi in *Père Goriot* when they are chainmates in prison but, when they escape and become separated, Vautrin, or Collin, shifts his affections to the feckless Lucien de Rubempré. In Lucien he sees, in Balzac's words, "a Jacques Collin, handsome, youthful, ennobled, in the position of an ambassador." It is in *Lost Illusions* that Collin murders the Abbé Carlos Herrera, assumes his identity, and scars his face with vitriol to disguise himself. Collin's satanic manipulativeness shows up well in *The Splendors and Miseries of Courtesans* in his schemes to bilk Baron Nucingen and shape the lives of Lucien and Esther Gobseck. He is a man of great intelligence, who devotes his powers to subverting the lives of others. His motives perhaps are rooted in the deep alienation that he feels at being a homosexual and in his resentment at not having been born to a station in life commensurate with his talents.

Lucien de Rubempré (rü•bĕm•prā'), a charming but weak young man whom Collin loves and schemes to place in a high social position. Born Lucien Chardon, Lucien takes his mother's maiden name, de Rubempré, when he undertakes Collin's scheme for his grand career. When he first appears in *Lost Illusions,* Lucien is roughly twenty years old, handsome, and given to scribbling verse. With these slight recommendations, Lucien attracts a host of society women of literary pretensions, and he flees from Angoulême to Paris with Mme de Bargeton, about twice his age. At the end of this affair, Lucien becomes the kept lover of an actress named Coralie. After Coralie dies and Lucien becomes depressed at forging some letters of credit that ruin his brother-in-law, he decides to commit suicide but is saved by the false Abbé, who is seeking his beloved chainmate, Théodore Calvin. These events precede Lucien's appearance in *The Splendors and Miseries of Courtesans.* The plasticity of Lucien's characters makes him a perfect pawn for Collin to deploy in his venal intrigues.

Esther Gobseck, also known as **La Torpille** (tôr•pē'), a prostitute whom Collin uses for devious purposes of his own. A beautiful young woman known spitefully as La Torpille (the torpedo), Esther is victimized by her hapless love for the shallow Lucien. When Collin realizes her obsession with Lucien, he sets Esther up in an apartment where Lucien may visit her and thereby keeps Lucien in his power. Esther later becomes the bait in Collin's scheme to bilk the rich but foolish Baron Nucingen, who suffers an unappeasable passion for Esther. She is a silly, trivial person, used by everyone.

Baron Frédéric de Nucingen (nü•săn•jĕń'), a wealthy banker. A ruthless, aging financier who speaks in a ridiculous accent, the Baron is a wonderful comic figure, a figure of worldly power and substance who is reduced to a buffoon by his desire for a common prostitute. The Baron, in the helplessness of his besotted lust, is a perfect target for the unscrupulous Collin.

Jacqueline Collin, Jacques Collin's aunt. Known as **Asia** in recognition of her birth in Java, she is Collin's most trusted accomplice. The sinister and malicious Asia does much of Collin's dirty work, such as blackmailing the vapid ladies of society, Mme de Maufrigneuse and Mme de Sérisy, by means of their romantic letters to Lucien. She appears in other novels.

Corentin (kō·rĕn·tăn´), a corrupt policeman. Actually no more than a spy, or a stool pigeon, Corentin has a mercenary temperament that recognizes no loyalties. He is vicious and contemptible, on the side of justice only by virtue of greed and calculation.

Peyrade (pā·răd´), a good-natured sensual-ist in the pay of Corentin. Although Peyrade is without morals, he sincerely loves his daughter, and it is this one redeeming feature of his character that ultimately leads to his death at the hands of Collin.

Contenson (kŏn·tĕn·sŏn´), or **Bernard-Polydor Bryond, Baron des Tours-Minières,** despite the pretentious name and lineage, contemptible and corrupt. He is anybody's man for a few francs, ready to do anybody's dirty work. With Corentin and Peyrade, Contenson completes a trio of despicable instruments of the law, useful tools but no more admirable than the felons and scoundrels whom they pursue.

Frank Day

THE SPORT OF THE GODS

Author: Paul Laurence Dunbar (1872-1906)
Type of work: Novel
Time of action: The late Reconstruction period, c. 1900
First published: 1901, serial; 1902, book

Maurice Oakley, a wealthy Southern businessman. Kind and generous, especially to his younger half-brother, Francis, Maurice becomes a hardened man after making an example of Berry Hamilton, his black butler and trusted servant, who has been accused of stealing a sizable sum of money from Francis. Largely through Oakley's efforts, Berry is sentenced to a long prison term, and his family is evicted from the Oakley estate. Years later, after Francis admits Berry's innocence and his own duplicity, Maurice Oakley becomes reclusive and obsessed with hiding this secret. When the truth is exposed by a Northern newspaper, Maurice goes completely insane.

Berry Hamilton, the trusted butler to Maurice Oakley. Through thrift and industry, Berry has gained a high standing in the community, but his fortune changes drastically and immediately when he is convicted—falsely—of having stolen more than eight hundred dollars from Maurice Oakley's half-brother, Francis. After spending almost ten years at hard labor, Berry is pardoned after a New York newspaper exposes the truth. He goes to New York to find his family in shambles and his wife remarried. After reclaiming his wife, Berry and Fannie Hamilton return to the South to their old cottage on the Oakley estate, where they live out the rest of their days.

Fannie Hamilton, Berry's proud and illiterate, but thrifty and industrious wife, who has served as the Oakleys' housekeeper. After Berry's false conviction, she and her children are evicted from the Oakley estate and make their way to New York. Here Fannie helplessly witnesses her family's disintegration. In order to survive, she marries Tom Gibson, a gambler. When Tom is killed in a fight, Fannie reunites with Berry and they move back South.

Leslie Oakley, Maurice Oakley's wife. Kindhearted and long-suffering, she nurses her husband in his insanity and makes amends to the Hamiltons by refurnishing their former cottage and inviting them to return to the Oakley estate following Berry's pardon.

Francis (Frank) Oakley, an artist. As the younger half-brother of Maurice Oakley, he is pampered and spoiled. He gambles away a large sum of money that his brother has provided for him to go to Paris, and his fabrication to cover this loss precipitates the charge against Berry Hamilton and his ultimate imprisonment. Years later, when Francis learns of Berry's fate, he confesses his duplicity to his brother, which in turn leads to Maurice's madness.

Joe Hamilton, a barber, Berry and Fannie's son. After Berry is convicted, he loses his job and is unable to find work. When his family is evicted from the Oakley estate, Joe takes his mother and sister to New York. In the city, Joe is defeated by life in the fast lane. He begins drinking heavily and becomes estranged from his mother and sister. Finally, in a drunken stupor, he strangles his lover to death and is sent to prison.

Kit Hamilton, a dancer, Berry and Fannie's daughter. She is beautiful, charming, and condescending. Upon arriving in New York, she begins going out with William Thomas, a married man, though this fact is unbeknown to her. Afterward, she becomes a showgirl in "Martin's Blackbirds."

Hattie Sterling, a dancer. As one of "Martin's Blackbirds," she becomes Joe Hamilton's lover and is instrumental in helping Kit obtain a job in the troupe. Finally tiring of Joe's constant drunkenness, she puts him out. Later that night, he kills her in an act of retaliation.

Skaggs, a newspaper reporter. As a frequent visitor to Harlem, Skaggs is acquainted with Joe Hamilton. Upon hearing Joe's account of his father's innocence, Skaggs goes South to the Hamilton's hometown. Here he forcibly obtains Maurice Oakley's secret about the missing money and his subsequent exposé in the New York *Universe* leads to Berry's pardon and Maurice's insanity.

Minty Brown, a visitor to New York. Originally from the Hamiltons' hometown, Minty calls on the Hamiltons upon her arrival. Having shunned Minty at home, Fannie and Kit Hamilton condescendingly refuse to accept her visit. In retaliation, Minty exposes the Hamiltons' predicament, which results in their eviction from their apartment and being dismissed from their jobs.

Tom Gibson, a racehorse gambler. As a boarder in Fannie Hamilton's flat, he convinces her that Berry's conviction and imprisonment nullified their marriage and convinces her to marry him. After their marriage, Tom frequently beats Fannie. Finally, he is killed in a fight at the racetrack.

Warren J. Carson

THE SPORTING CLUB

Author: Thomas McGuane (1939-   )
Type of work: Novel
Time of action: The 1960's
First published: 1969

James Quinn, a young Michigan businessman who has recently assumed control of his father's tool and die business. Quinn has retreated to the Centennial Club in the Michigan woods for rest and relaxation. To his dismay, he learns that his old friend and rival, Vernor Stanton, has also arrived. Reluctantly at first, but then with some of his old enthusiasm, Quinn joins Stanton in duels and in his attempts to bring chaos to the

Club and its members, eventually participating in the Club's abrupt demise. Throughout the novel he is in a quandary between fighting Stanton's influence or playing along wholeheartedly and between being the responsible businessman or a fomenter of discord.

Vernor Stanton, a mad, extremely wealthy, and bored man who finds pleasure in disrupting his environment with practical jokes and outright cruelty. Using the Centennial Club as his stage, Stanton enlists the help of Quinn to disrupt and destroy the Club in less than a month. His "jokes" include such acts as dueling with antique pistols loaded with wax bullets in his cellar (a relatively harmless but very painful experience for Quinn), stealing a dignitaries' bus from a bridge dedication ceremony, fomenting the move to fire the Club's manager, and constantly irritating and antagonizing fellow Club members. He eventually goes officially mad, threatening and controlling the assembled Club members with a tripod-mounted machine gun. Some months later, he apparently partially recovers, buys the Club property, returns, and is watched over by Janey and "attendants" who carefully control his activities.

Janey, Stanton's girlfriend, who sticks by him in spite of his cruelty and madness. A physically attractive, concerned, and mild-mannered woman, Janey unintentionally attracts Quinn, who wants to rescue her from Stanton. She is completely loyal to Stanton, however, dismayed by many of his antics but at the same time fascinated by the charm and strength of the man. Her presence forces Quinn to see a side of Stanton that he would rather ignore, and this knowledge forces him to remain concerned and interested in what Stanton does.

Jack Olson, the Club's manager and an accomplished outdoorsman. He is a member of one of the families dispossessed when the Club acquired its extensive acreage, and he has spent a lifetime poaching on and managing Club property. So adept at hunting and fishing that he embarrasses the wealthy Club members who associate hunting and fishing with masculinity, he becomes a target for their ire as they plot with Stanton to get rid of him, even though they know that he is irreplaceable as a manager. When he realizes what their plans are, he hires Earl Olive as his replacement and disappears.

Earl Olive, an uneducated crook and purveyor of live bait. He is hired by Olson as the Club's manager, a move designed by Olson to avenge himself for the treatment he has received. Olive, who has no respect for the Club's "reputation," brings in his crowd of rowdy friends, who party and fornicate openly. Painfully beaten and embarrassed by Stanton in a duel, he dynamites the dam, which drains the lake, and in the resulting chaos he dynamites the main lodge, the lifeguard's platform, and the flagpole. Finally captured by angry Club members, he is freed by Stanton, wielding a machine gun.

Fortescue, an old-time Club member and collector of military miniatures. When the Club is "at war" with Earl Olive and his crowd, Fortescue assumes command as they attempt to handle Olive without the intervention of the law. He becomes a little despot as he attempts to live out his military fantasies, even to the point of outfitting his "army" at his own expense. As inept as he is enthusiastic, he is ultimately caught and tarred and feathered by Earl Olive and his gang.

Spengler, the Club chronicler. As a means of celebrating the first hundred years of the Club's existence, he has written a history of the Club and the surrounding area, focusing on the illustrious founding fathers and claiming to base all of this on what he calls "solid research." Eventually disillusioned by the antics of the present members, he burns his chronicle before the centennial celebration, which includes the unearthing of the capsule buried by the Club's founders. This capsule contains information that destroys any notion that the founders were illustrious.

Scott, an old-time Club member and obsequious professor. He is basically a non-person, often present and speaking but always ignored.

Charles Murray, an old-time Club member. He is a homosexual, alternately chasing the heavy-set daughter of Fortescue, Quinn, and others. He is also basically ignored by the other members, except when they are escaping his advances.

David E. Huntley

A SPY IN THE HOUSE OF LOVE

Author: Anaïs Nin (1903-1977)
Type of work: Novel
Time of action: The late 1940's and early 1950's
First published: 1954

Sabina, a thirty-year-old woman who is looking for the ultimate bliss of true love. Extremely attractive, highly sexual, but continuously thwarted by guilt, she wastes her energy desperately looking for a satisfying psychosexual relationship. She assumes a variety of fictive roles, ranging from the prostitute to the spiritual mother, but finds all of them frustrating. She consistently finds herself an onlooker rather than a participant in life and uses her sexual addiction as a means to avoid accepting her inner purity and goodness. She defines herself, then, as a spy in the house of love and, therefore, incapable of sharing in its joys.

The "Lie Detector," a mysterious stranger whom Sabina randomly calls on the telephone at the beginning of the novel. They meet from time to time throughout the narrative as he becomes Sabina's confessor and absolver. He delineates for her the variety and levels of guilt and atonement and tells her that they are stratagems by which she avoids uncovering her true nature. Sabina eventually discovers that he is a creation of her own imagination.

Alan, Sabina's thirty-five-year-old amiable husband. Tall, extremely handsome with graying sideburns, he protects her from the realities of life. Completely devoted to her, he is the only fixed point in her life and gives her fatherly solicitude. Although sexually desirable, he is passive and does not possess the kind of passionate desire that Sabina finds in other men; he is her guardian angel from whom she wishes absolution because she has been unfaithful to him so often.

Philip, a Wagnerian tenor and sometime lover of Sabina. He is a large, powerfully built, broad-shouldered, handsome man in his thirties. Although he is relentlessly pursued by many women, he finds Sabina an exceptional lover, although his athletic lovemaking fails initially to bring her to climax. After successive tries, he finally breaks through her frigidity and names her "Dona Juana"; that is, he makes her the feminine counterpart of his own role as an infamous Don Juan.

Donald, a slender, beautiful, and delicate young homosexual who loves Sabina in a passionate but platonic fashion. His seductive voice and passive indolence, combined with his penchant for satirizing everything and everybody, entertain Sabina enormously and relieve her temporarily from her chronic boredom. Sabina becomes for Donald a loving maternal figure and consoles him for the indifferent and shallow mother who never gave him love. He names her "The Firebird" and makes her feel innocent.

John, a young man in his twenties who has been grounded as a rear gunner from the British Air Corps. Sabina meets him on Long Island and they are immediately drawn to each other because of their shared incipient madness. He has experienced the hell of war and cannot blot it out. He is an elusive and gentle lover but manages to melt her frigidity. He, too, suffers from sexual guilt, which Sabina wants to help him overcome.

Mambo, a black jazz musician from the Caribbean in his twenties. He and Sabina become lovers for a while, although he distrusts all white women because he has been their sexual toy for years. He claims that they only want to experience the darkly romantic energy of the tropics but want nothing to do with bearing him black children and living as natives do.

Jay, a painter and former lover of Sabina. They met earlier, in the Montparnasse sec-

tion of Paris, and experienced an open, sexual relationship. The war forced him back to the United States, however, where he does not seem to be able to produce anything but fragmentary, satiric paintings. He is half bald, has narrow eyes, and resembles Lao Tze.

Djuna, a beautiful, exotic, and highly accomplished dancer in her thirties. Her dancing enables her to distinguish illusion from reality, and she tries to convince Sabina that she is innocent and that it is Sabina's inability to love herself that drives her to fabricate the Lie Detector who, in turn, exacerbates her guilt.

Patrick Meanor

THE SPY WHO CAME IN FROM THE COLD

Author: John le Carré (David John Moore Cornwell, 1931-   )
Type of work: Novel
Time of action: The early 1960's
First published: 1963

Alec Leamas, a British spy, about fifty, a loner. The former head of a network of undercover agents operating out of Berlin, Leamas is directed by British Intelligence to stage a fake defection and bring about the downfall of Hans-Dieter Mundt, a top East German agent. Tough-minded and cynical, Leamas has long avoided the moral and ethical questions raised by his work, adopting the unspoken philosophy of his profession that any action is justified if it achieves the desired results. Divorced and the father of children he rarely sees, Leamas is a case-hardened and emotionally isolated man until he begins a relationship with Liz Gold.

Liz Gold, a young woman in her early twenties, naïve, idealistic, a member of the Communist Party. Liz is working in a London library when she meets Leamas and becomes his lover. Tall, awkward, intelligent, and serious, Liz believes passionately in the future of world communism. She is warm and loving toward Leamas, and remains ignorant of the true nature of his work until she be-

comes an unwitting participant in the espionage plot. Her journey to East Germany forces her to confront the realities of life in a communist state and ends with her death at the Berlin Wall.

Control, the head of British Intelligence. Known only by his code name, Control is a mixture of old school manners and ruthless tactics. Detached and enigmatic, he is the master manipulator who pulls the strings that hold the complex espionage operation together, often risking the lives of his agents to achieve the results he wants.

Hans-Dieter Mundt, the Deputy Director of Operations for the East German intelligence community. A onetime Nazi, Mundt is a cruel, ruthless man who has brought about the death of several agents and is disliked and feared even by his own people. He is also, as Leamas at last learns, a highly placed double agent working for the British.

Fiedler, Mundt's second-in-command and a

committed Communist. Fiedler, too, is mistrusted by his own people and is infamous among British agents for his savage interrogation techniques. A Jew, Fiedler has long hated the anti-Semitic Mundt and sees Leamas as the key to his superior's downfall.

Miss Crail, the head librarian at the Bayswater Library for Psychic Research. Spinsterish, sour-tempered, and a stickler for details, Miss Crail takes an immediate dislike to Leamas, who spends a brief period working in the library.

William Ashe, a low-level Eastern bloc agent operating in England. Effete and homosexual, it is Ashe who first makes contact with Leamas regarding a possible defection.

Peters, Ashe's superior. Peters is assigned to handle Leamas' defection and to bring him to East Berlin.

Karl Riemeck, an East German official who has been acting as a British double agent. Riemeck is the last surviving member of Leamas' Berlin network of spies. He is killed in the book's opening pages as he attempts to cross over to the Western side.

Janet Lorenz

THE STAND

Author: Stephen King (1947-   )
Type of work: Novel
Time of action: June 16, 1985, to summer, 1986
First published: 1978

Stuart Redman, a widowed factory worker. Big and strong, Stu is quiet and competent. As a survivor of the superflu, he serves as a lab rat until his captors, government employees, die. He escapes, joins with others, and leads them to Mother Abigail's and on to Colorado, where he becomes a leader, eventually taking a group to the West to take on Flagg. Injured and left on the way, he is the only survivor of the expedition to Las Vegas.

Frannie Goldsmith, a pregnant, unmarried college student. Tall and leggy with long chestnut hair, Frannie is "prime stuff." The object of Stu Redman's affection as well as Harold Lauder's, she is gentle and understanding, a helpmate and colleague to Stu. Frannie's son is the first child born who contracts and survives the superflu.

Harold Emery Lauder, later called **Hawk,** an exceptionally bright, socially inept teenager. The unwashed, overweight, and unpleasant spoiled child gives way to a hard, determined young man who winds up with the unlikely sobriquet "Hawk." His intelligence guides him and those who follow safely to Mother Abigail's and Colorado, but he becomes twisted because he wants Frannie, who loves Stu. He teams with Nadine Cross to destroy the town leaders. After their escape from Boulder, he is injured and abandoned by Nadine Cross. Realizing that he has been and done wrong, he writes an apology (later found by the Las Vegas expedition) and commits suicide.

Larry Underwood, a rock-and-roll singer. Larry is not a nice guy until he confronts himself after his companion's accidental death. After an infatuation with Nadine Cross, he grows to love Lucy Swann, who supports him. First as group leader then as community leader, he finds the strength to do the right thing in refusing Nadine and later finds the strength again in Las Vegas to not give in to fear or to Randall Flagg, even in the face of death.

Nick Andros, a deaf and mute wanderer. Small, dark, thin, and younger looking than his twenty-two years, Nick is bright, responsible, honest, generous, and compassionate. He looks after victims of the superflu and after Tom Cullen and is an organizer as well as a leader because of his native intelligence. His death at the hands of Harold Lauder and Nadine Cross demoralizes the people of the Free Zone.

Tom Cullen, a mentally deficient man. Near forty but with the mind of a child, Tom is youthful and Nordic looking. Under hypnosis he becomes God's Tom, cognizant and righteous, and he is sent to spy on Flagg and the evil in Las Vegas. He is the only man of the Free Zone to enter Las Vegas and survive, finding Stu and helping him on his way back to Colorado.

Glendon Pequod Bateman, an aging sociology professor. Gray-haired and sixtyish, Glen is a scholar and adviser. He helps to organize the people of Boulder into a community; he goes to Las Vegas to confront and confound Flagg.

Kojak, a friendly Irish setter. Kojak is Stu Redman's guardian after his injury. He keeps Stu alive until Tom Cullen comes along to help him return to Boulder. The only dog found alive after the superflu, Kojak is a reminder of destruction until a bitch is found, and then they become the hope of a species.

Nadine Cross, a virgin schoolteacher. Pretty, with dark hair turning prematurely white, Nadine is enigmatic. She is destined to bear Flagg's child, dreaming of him and keeping herself for him. A desperate, rebuffed, last-minute bid for Larry convinces her that she is not wanted. She turns wholly to the evil of Flagg, planning the demise of Boulder's leaders, only to discover her grave mistake when she meets Flagg. Her death at his hands is a turning point for evil.

Leo Rockaway (Joe), a disturbed boy. First appearing as the feral "Joe" in the care of Nadine Cross, Leo begins to blossom, first

as a musical prodigy, then as a clairvoyant. He senses evil about Harold Lauder and refuses to go near him; he knows what is happening elsewhere. Nadine Cross's defection sets him back, and he turns to Larry Underwood for care.

Mother Abigail Freemantle Trotts, an old, religious black woman. Mother Abigail, at age 108, is thin with thinning white hair. She is the spiritual leader of the group in Colorado. Survivors have dreamed of her and sought her out. She is the voice of God and the voice of reason, setting people on the paths chosen for them. She dies after a sojourn in the wilderness.

Randall Flagg, a wicked creature. He is dark, not identifiable as black or white; people dream of Flagg and see no face, only burning red eyes. Flagg is evil. He draws his followers, keeping them with fear, punishing dissidents with crucifixion. The evil he unleashes goes beyond his control, undermining his power.

Lloyd Henreid, a thief, murderer, and Flagg's right-hand man. Flagg saves Lloyd from having to resort to cannibalism in his jail cell, and Lloyd becomes his first "convert." Never very bright but easily persuaded, Lloyd is swept along with Flagg until he realizes that he has become smarter. This knowledge comes at about the same time that he notices that things are going wrong.

Donald Merwin "Trashcan Man" Elbert, an imbalanced arsonist. With strange, muddy eyes and one arm a mass of burn scars, Trash is Randall Flagg's secret weapon. He is drawn to instruments of destruction, finally finding the ultimate hardware: a nuclear warhead. He brings it to Flagg in atonement for blowing up his air force. The resultant explosion destroys Las Vegas, Flagg's followers, and some of the surviving members of the expedition from the Free Zone.

Terry Hays Jackson

STANLEY AND THE WOMEN

Author: Kingsley Amis (1922-   )
Type of work: Novel
Time of action: The mid-1980's
First published: 1984

Stanley Duke, the narrator, the advertising manager of a London newspaper. He is a balding, middle-aged man now in his second marriage. He is intelligent and perceptive; still, he has little understanding of women, at least of the women in his own life. When his son falls ill, he is beleaguered by three women—his former wife, his current wife, and the doctor treating his son—all of whom, he believes, are behaving toward him in a hostile and irrational manner.

Steve Duke, Stanley's nineteen-year-old son by his first marriage. He is believed to be traveling in Spain with his girlfriend, but he turns up suddenly at Stanley's door. He is talking and behaving in a bizarre fashion and is eventually diagnosed as schizophrenic and committed to a hospital for treatment. He is released into his father's care for a time but is recommitted after his stepmother alleges that he attacked and slightly wounded her with a knife.

Nowell Hutchinson, Stanley's first wife, to whom he was married for thirteen years. She is a fading television actress now married to a television producer. She is a selfish woman, who has the facility for creating an alternate reality, which always suits her own interests. She attempts to take care of Steve for a day or so but quickly concludes that his illness is his father's fault and that she bears no responsibility.

Susan Duke, Stanley's second wife. She is an assistant literary editor for a London newspaper. A tall brunette, thirty-eight years of age, she is on the surface a perfect wife. She subtly attempts to force Stanley to choose between his son and her. Finally, she charges that Steve attacked her, but her wound may well have been self-inflicted.

Trish Collings, the psychiatrist in charge of Steve's case. She is a nervous, restless young woman who takes an instant dislike to Stanley. She seems less interested in curing Steve than in proving that Stanley is vaguely responsible for his son's condition.

Bert Hutchinson, Nowell's second husband, the man for whom she left Stanley. He is a television producer. In one scene, he and Stanley get drunk together. They come to share an unspoken camaraderie, based upon their common experience of being married to an exceedingly difficult woman.

Lindsey Lucas, a women's page columnist for a London daily. She is a fair, attractive woman with a Northern Ireland accent. She is an exact contemporary of Susan, and Stanley had an affair with her between his marriages. He gets on with her well, probably because he is not married to her.

Lady Daly, Stanley's mother-in-law, the widow of a Conservative Member of Parliament. In her middle or late sixties, she is yet another woman with whom Stanley has a tenuous relationship. She is not very bright and is totally lacking in humor. The distant quality of their relationship is characterized by his term of address for her, "lady."

Patrick Adcock

STARING AT THE SUN

Author: Julian Barnes (1946-   )
Type of work: Novel

1472

Time of action: c. 1930-2020
First published: 1986

Jean Serjeant, wife of Michael Curtis and mother of Gregory. Jean lives to be ninety-nine, and her preoccupation with the wonders of the world and life's disappointments make her a major voice in the discussion of the significance of human existence in this novel. She is reared as the daughter of a grocer in Bryden and comes to maturity during World War II. As a young woman, Jean is much impressed by the speculations on death, fear, and heroism uttered by the Royal Air Force (RAF) officer who is billeted with her family, but she settles for a marriage to Michael, a police constable. Her life sours as Michael's traditional notions of domestic life and sexuality become increasingly onerous, and, after almost two decades of married life, Jean leaves her husband when she is thirty-nine years old and seven months pregnant with her first child. She subsequently takes on a number of temporary jobs in pubs and cheap restaurants in an effort to support herself and her son, Gregory. In late middle age, Jean experiences a brief lesbian relationship with Rachel, one of her son's girlfriends, and she becomes much preoccupied with foreign travel, particularly with her own list of the seven wonders of the world. In her old age, she turns her attention to the wonders of her life and to the pattern presented by her experiences. At the end of the novel, she joins Gregory in a final airplane ride, which allows them both to confront the brilliant image of the sun.

Sergeant-Pilot Thomas Prosser, a short, slim man with brilliantined black hair and a small mustache. Originally from somewhere near Blackburn in Lancashire, Prosser is a Hurricane IIB fighter pilot in the RAF during World War II, but he is temporarily grounded when he is billeted with the Serjeants. Nicknamed "Sun-UP" by his fellow fliers, Prosser is something of a battle ace who has increasingly lost his nerve. In his conversations with Jean, Prosser describes watching the sun rise twice in an early morning flight over the English Channel and the

possibility of committing suicide by flying straight into the sun. Prosser later dies by committing suicide in this fashion during a combat mission.

Uncle Leslie, the eccentric brother of Jean's mother. With his well-styled hair and his dark blazer with its regimental badge, Uncle Leslie affects a faded gentility, but he supports himself by gambling, sponging, and various undisclosed employments. Leslie is very fond of Jean, and his sleight-of-hand tricks and ironic gifts introduce her to life's illusions and its disappointments. Before World War II breaks out, he flees to America, but when he returns after the cessation of hostilities, Leslie provides the same introduction to life's absurdities for his nephew Gregory. Leslie dies an old man, and, though he alternately rages and trembles at his own mortality, his sense of the absurdity and irony of human existence is well appreciated by Gregory and Jean.

Michael Curtis, a tall man with a fleshy head and a schoolboy's neck. Michael is a police constable and Jean's husband. He first appears to be a charming and unusual figure, much like Uncle Leslie, but he proves to be a stolid and unexceptional husband. He becomes increasingly frustrated with what he describes as his wife's stupidity, and eventually he even strikes her; he is unwilling ever to consider the prospect of his own shortcomings. Curiously, he leaves his house and all of his money to his estranged wife at his death.

Gregory Curtis, the son of Jean and Michael. Gregory begins life as a quiet, passive boy who grows into a studious, melancholy, and methodical adult. He builds numerous model airplanes when a boy, but his ambition is limited; he never marries; he becomes the unremarkable employee of a life insurance company who lives in the same house as his mother. Like his mother, however, Gregory is much concerned with death and the existence of God; he becomes a fervent interrogator of the state computer information system, and his persistent questions lead him to seek the absolute truth through this system, though without much success.

Rachel, a sometime girlfriend of Gregory and briefly Jean's lesbian lover. After leaving home at age sixteen and drifting through several large cities, Rachel has become a militant feminist who works in a neighborhood law center. She is ideologically committed, and her forceful insights are appreciated by Jean, though they often seem discomforting and somewhat distasteful to the older woman.

Thomas Carmichael

THE STEPPE
The Story of a Journey

Author: Anton Chekhov (1860-1904)
Type of work: Novella
Time of action: The 1870's
First published: "Step: Istoriya odnoi poezdki," 1888 (English translation, 1915)

Yegorushka Knyazev (knyà′zəf), called **Georgie,** a boy on the way to his first boarding school. Georgie has been reared by his widowed mother and has thus been, to a degree, sheltered from the world. His unworldliness has been further nurtured by the provincial town in which he has grown up. His journey across the seemingly endless Russian steppe, then, greatly expands his knowledge of both the world and human nature, although he is often frightened or repulsed by his experiences. The boy has a good heart though; he sympathizes with the carters, whose difficult lives cause him vicarious pain. On the whole, however, Yegorushka is understandably bored by the lengthy trip and made lonely by the separation from his mother.

Ivan Kuzmichov, a provincial merchant and Yegorushka's uncle. Continually preoccupied with business, reserved, with the air of a civil servant, Kuzmichov is ambivalent about his nephew. Although he clearly has affection for the boy, the practical businessman has little time for Yegorushka's sensitivity. His chief concern is to settle on a good price for his wool, and his secondary errand, escorting the boy to school, is bothersome to him. He grudgingly admits, however, that the boy's education will reflect well on his family.

Father Christopher Siriysky, a Russian Orthodox priest. Father Christopher, a kindly, gentle man, is Yegorushka's parish priest. His benign, optimistic worldview contrasts favorably with Kuzmichov's hard practicality. Himself the father of a family, Father Christopher understands Yegorushka's homesickness and does his best to lighten the boy's journey. A sincere Christian, he finds authentic delight in the sights of the steppe, making him the only character to do so. His one vanity is his learning, which, with age, he has largely forgotten.

Panteley, an old carter. His age and his air of wisdom make him the unofficial leader of the wagon train to which Yegorushka becomes attached when his uncle is pressed to hurry on. He befriends the boy, taking Yegorushka into his confidence, explaining the histories of the other carters, and pointing out the wonders of the steppe. Panteley is in some ways a mirror image of Father Christopher and acts as his surrogate with Yegorushka: Both men are saintly, calm, and wise in the ways of the world. Short, gaunt men, they even look much alike.

Yemelyan, a carter, formerly a singer. Having lost his once-beautiful voice as the result, he claims, of bathing in a cold river,

Yemelyan is a melancholy figure. Despite his almost constant *sotto voce* singing, his voice does not improve. As a former professional chorister, however, he still retains his religious devotion.

Dymov, a young carter. Dymov is rough, gregarious, handsome, a natural leader—he is also something of a troublemaker. His very real ennui prompts him to torment Yemelyan and to taunt the other carters. His "rude" behavior, in turn, sparks a confrontation with Yegorushka.

Moses, a peasant innkeeper. Motivated by equal parts of greed and authentic hospitality, Moses alternates between giddiness over the arrival of his guests (Yegorushka, his uncle, and Father Christopher) and despair over the behavior of his brother, Solomon. To an extent, Chekhov's portrait is drawn from nineteenth century stereotypes of Jewish merchants; Moses' dialect, his sycophancy, and, of course, his thrift are all caricatured.

Solomon, Moses' brother. Sardonic and embittered, Solomon is considered mad by the other characters. He neither respects his social superiors nor demonstrates affection toward his brother. His role in the story is enigmatic: His half-insane behavior is perhaps a reaction to the rampant anti-Semitism of the period.

Varlamov, a rich peasant. Varlamov is the stereotype of the self-made man. During his brief and almost mythic appearance in the story, the responses of the other characters to him make it abundantly clear that he is a man whom others naturally respect, and possibly fear. Short, powerfully built, mature, he awes the carters.

Deniska, Kuzmichov's coachman. A simple, good-humored peasant, Deniska shares Yegorushka's boyishness.

Constantine, a newly married man. Constantine appears briefly at the carter's campfire; he has been on a hunting expedition, although his entire attention is centered on his happiness.

John Steven Childs

THE STONE ANGEL

Author: Margaret Laurence (1926-1987)
Type of work: Novel
Time of action: The mid-1870's to the early 1960's
First published: 1964

Hagar Shipley, née **Currie,** the protagonist, a ninety-year-old woman. She has become too much of a burden to her son and his wife and even a hazard, for, bored at eighty, she took up smoking. Daily matters make her aware of her aging body, but her mind is prompted by objects or sounds, such as in her room or at the doctor's, to recall episodes of her life filled with her enormous pride and inwardness. More clever than Matt and Dan at school, her father drills her about her Scottish heritage and sends her to an Ontario girls' finishing school. Then she works in her father's Manawaka store until she disdains his plan to have her marry well. At age twenty-four, she arranges her own wedding without his consent, for she responds to Bram Shipley's dancing and is attracted to his passion. Only once does she nearly express her deep feelings to Bram, whose speech and manners embarrass her. When she can no longer rear her two sons with dignity, she saves money from selling eggs in town and takes the boys to Vancouver. There she keeps house for retired Mr. Oakley, only returning when Bram is dying. Another year she visits John in Manawaka until his accident. With Mr. Oakley's bequest, she buys a house in Vancouver, which she later signs over when Marvin and his wife care for her. Rather than be put in Silverthreads nursing home, she runs away, but becomes disoriented after alighting from the bus at Shadow Point. As she rests in the abandoned cannery near the beach, she drinks wine with vagrant Murray Lees, after whose story she shares her similar loss of a son. Her collapse comes the next morning. Dying in the hospital, she emerges somewhat from her lifelong inwardness enough to help the girl in the next bed; later she can even lie to Marvin that he has always been her favorite. Aware that her pride has interfered with her doing more than two independent acts in her life, she expires.

Marvin Shipley, Hagar's eldest son who, in consideration of his wife's health, drives Hagar out to Silverthreads to get her accustomed to the place. Her flashbacks reveal that he knew his parents always liked his younger brother more. Yet he dutifully did farm chores for his father, enlisted in the war, returned to succeed as a salesman, and reliably cared for Hagar, not merely because she had signed over her house and property. Just after Hagar says that he was "a better son than John," realist Marvin tells the nurse, "She's a holy terror."

Doris Shipley, Marvin's wife who, in her seventies, has difficulty caring for Hagar. She talks to her, keeps her favorite things near her, takes her to the doctor, and has the minister come. She is pleased when Hagar, in the hospital, gives her sapphire ring to Tina.

Bram Shipley, a tall, big, handsome widower with a black beard, Hagar's husband. He deteriorated from a sensuous dancer in courtship to alcoholism. Though he gives her a crystal and silver decanter as a wedding gift, he provides few amenities on the farm. Though coarse, he continues to evoke a primal response from Hagar, but he embarrasses her by driving down the main street to the hospital for Marvin's birth and in the general store. Increasingly repulsive, he drinks heavily with the town halfbreed and with his son John, until his liver gives out.

John Shipley, Hagar's younger and favorite son, who learned to lie about Vancouver school friends' social status to please her. He returns to Manawaka to his father. Upset by his death, John continues his heavy drinking and wildness. Then he brings Arlene Telford home often and drinks less until enraged that Hagar and Lottie plot to send Arlene to Ontario. John and Arlene die in a dare: He drives his car across the trestle but a special train comes.

Murray Ferney Lees, the stranger whom Hagar meets in the abandoned cannery, who willingly shares his bottle of wine and life story. He had loved the Advocate tabernacle of his grandfather who was ignored by his mother and father, of the United Church and owners of a shoe store in Blackfly. Marrying Lou from Bible camp, he continued to sell insurance but misplaced his faith though he prayed with her. He blames his drinking and smoking in the basement for their house fire, where son Donnie died. This prompts Hagar, previously unable, to express her own loss of a son, John. After a drafty night and Hagar's collapse, Murray calls Marvin, whose number was in her purse.

Greta McCormick Coger

STORMY WEATHER

Author: August Strindberg (1849-1912)
Type of work: Play
Time of action: The early 1900's
First produced: Oväder, 1907 (English translation, 1913)

The Gentleman, an aging civil servant living on a pension. Having lost his wife and daughter, he seeks only peace and order in his old age and resists intrusions in his life. He is so inflexible and set in his ways that his desire for peace can be taken as a rationalization based more on a fear of change than on principle. When his young wife and daughter reappear, he remains aloof, even to the point of assuming no responsibility for his child, whom he claims to love. He stresses that he himself urged his wife to leave him; although the matter remains unclear. He is cynical, somewhat misanthropic, and intolerant.

Karl Fredrik, the Gentleman's brother, a lawyer. He criticizes his brother's isolation and helps Gerda, his brother's former wife, in her flight from her new husband, Fischer. He also defended Gerda during her divorce from the Gentleman, which remains a sore spot in the brothers' relationship. He is a more reasonable and less soured man than his brother.

Gerda, the Gentleman's former wife, his junior by many years. She is rather emotionally unstable and suffers from her inability to judge men. She marries the sinister Fischer a few years after divorcing the Gentleman, but finally leaves him as well because of his lowly life-style.

Louise, the Gentleman's young domestic. Her relationship with the Gentleman verges on romance, although it is carefully controlled by the latter to preclude that possibility. She is loyal and devoted to the Gentleman; she spends much of her time playing chess with him.

Fischer, a sinister character, Gerda's new husband. He runs a shady gambling joint in the apartment building where he, Gerda, and the Gentleman live. When Gerda decides to leave him, he abducts her child, Anne-Charlotte, and runs off with a young girl, Agnes, the confectioner's daughter.

Agnes Starck, the confectioner's daughter, an innocent young woman yearning for romance who runs off with Fischer, although she soon returns home.

Starck, a confectioner who lives next door to the Gentleman. He is resigned to his life and content in his resignation. He lives for simple pleasures and has few grand illusions.

Louis Gallo

STRAIT IS THE GATE

Author: André Gide (1869-1951)
Type of work: Novel
Time of action: The late nineteenth century
First published: La Porte étroite, 1909 (English translation, 1924)

Jérôme Palissier (pä·lē·syā´), the narrator and a scholar. A sensitive, romantic, but passive child (and then young man), he is obsessed with his love for his first cousin Alissa. This love issues from a fascination with virtue and self-abnegation, and a desire to protect Alissa from life. He is, however, continually frustrated by Alissa's delaying tactics and refusals and by his own inability to overcome his passivity and act. Like Alissa, he fears the physical side of love. After Alissa's death, he remains faithful to her memory.

Alissa Bucolin (bü·kō·lăn´), Jérôme's first cousin, a serious, gentle, artistic young girl who, repulsed by her mother's sexuality and infidelity, seeks to repress her own love for Jérôme by insisting on the necessity of pure spiritual love and self-sacrifice. Her goal becomes nothing less than sainthood, an unmediated relationship with God. To that end, she abandons all nonspiritual concerns (music and literature), devotes herself to an ascetic existence (simple food and dress), and refuses to accept Jérôme's timid advances. After her death, her diary reveals the despair that came from her inability to transcend her earthly love for Jérôme.

Juliette Bucolin, Alissa's younger sister, an attractive and vivacious girl. Although less religiously oriented than Alissa, she shows an equally strong capacity for self-sacrifice, when, despite her love for Jérôme, she agrees to marry Édouard Teissières. She does, however, succeed in finding a form of happiness in motherhood and domesticity.

Lucile Bucolin, the adopted daughter of Pastor Vautier, Alissa's mother. She is a strikingly beautiful woman of Créole origin, whose languid, sensual nature makes her feel stifled by the strict Protestant society in which she lives. Toward the start of the novel, she runs off with a lover. Her blatant infidelity to her husband shocks Alissa and Jérôme and reinforces their fear of sexuality.

Abel Vautier (vō•tē•yā′), son of the Pastor Vautier and friend of Jérôme, who falls in love with Juliette. He later writes a novel that Alissa finds shocking.

Félicie Plantier (plän•tyā′), the cousins' aunt, a good-hearted, but slightly scatterbrained,

woman who tries, with disastrous results, to bring Alissa and Jérôme together.

Monsieur Bucolin, Alissa's father and Jérôme's maternal uncle. A passive and gentle man, he is crushed by his wife's departure and seeks support and consolation from Alissa, who lives with him until his death.

Madame Palissier, Jérôme's mother. A widow who wears only black, she is a strong-willed and conservative woman who regards Lucile Bucolin's nontraditional behavior as both shocking and immoral. She dies while Jérôme is still a student.

Robert Bucolin, the younger brother of Alissa and Juliette, a relatively uninteresting boy whom Jérôme temporarily takes under his wing in Paris out of a sense of duty.

Pastor Vautier, the father of Abel Vautier and (through adoption) of Lucile Bucolin. The sermon he pronounces after Lucile's desertion of her family contains the biblical verse (Luke 13:24, "Strait is the gate and narrow is the way . . .") from which the novel's title is taken and which so strongly influences Alissa and Jérôme's conduct.

Miss Flora Ashburton, Jérôme's mother's former tutor and now her companion.

Édouard Teissières (tĕ•syĕr′), a winegrower from Nîmes who marries Juliette.

Raymond Bach

STRANGER IN A STRANGE LAND

Author: Robert A. Heinlein (1907-1988)
Type of work: Novel
Time of action: After World War III, in the near future
First published: 1961

Valentine Michael Smith (Mike), the protagonist, who was born on Mars of two human scientists but was reared by Martians. "Rescued" and taken to earth in his mid-

twenties, he appears weak and underdeveloped, but his grave eyes reveal his intense curiosity and desire to behave "rightly." Trained by the Martian "Old Ones," he is, at least mentally, more Martian than human and has totally alien concepts of social and moral relationships. Because water is so scarce on Mars, for example, to share it with another creates an unbreakable bond of trust and mutual responsibility with one's "water brothers." Death, sex, property, lying, guilt, jealousy, and money are all unknown to Martians, whose sole purpose appears to be to "grok" (Martian for "to totally comprehend") everything in the universe. Mike's Martian heritage thus makes him appear extremely innocent to other humans, but, in fact, he has many superhuman powers. These allow him to manipulate, or even separate himself from, his body, to levitate or destroy objects simply with the power of his mind, and to retain and digest immense amounts of information. As the sole survivor of the first, ill-fated expedition to Mars, Mike is both heir to fabulous wealth and the legal "owner" of the entire planet Mars. This makes him a political hot potato for the world government of the Federation, which attempts to keep him incommunicado at the Bethesda hospital complex near Washington, D.C. With the help of newfound human friends, however, he escapes from the clutches of the Federation and begins an odyssey of self-discovery and self-education in the nature of the human condition. He eventually uses his new awareness and Martian powers to develop and propagate a religious philosophy that combines Martian wisdom with sexual ecstasy and openness, as well as a revelation of the universal "Godhood" and individual responsibility of all creatures who "grok" the cosmos.

Ben Caxton, a well-known free-lance investigative reporter. Caxton is streetwise, cynical, persistent, and ruggedly handsome. Extremely hostile to the current political leadership, he attempts to gain Mike's release from Bethesda but is foiled, drugged, and held captive by the evil police forces of the Federation. Later released, he becomes one of Mike's "waterbrothers" and champions but remains skeptical about Smith's new faith. In the end, however, he, like others who become close to Mike, accepts Mike's vision and becomes an important supporter of it.

Gillian (Jill) Boardman, an extremely attractive registered nurse at Bethesda, dedicated both to her profession and to Ben Caxton. Asked by Caxton to spy on Smith, she discovers that the minions of the Federation plan to eliminate him. She dresses Mike up as a nurse and escapes with him to the estate of Jubal Harshaw. As Mike's first "waterbrother," as well as his nurse and teacher in the customs of earth folk, Jill accompanies the "Man from Mars" on his voyage of self-discovery and ultimately becomes a high priestess in his universal religion.

Jubal E. Harshaw, a rich and eccentric recluse. Though a paunchy, curmudgeonly septuagenarian, Harshaw effortlessly churns out an unending series of popular literary works under a variety of pseudonyms. He is also both a brilliant doctor and an incisive lawyer but has refused to involve himself in the affairs of the outside world until Jill and Mike arrive at his compound as refugees. Intensely interested in Mike's Martian mentality, especially after he learns of the latter's superhuman powers, Harshaw slyly defeats the government's attempts to recapture Smith. He becomes yet another "water-brother," as well as Mike's spiritual father, and guides the young man's education, expressing a philosophy of skeptical agnosticism and rugged individualism. He then sends Mike and Jill out into the world to experience it at first hand. Though initially distressed by reports that Mike has started a new church, Harshaw ultimately realizes that he himself inspired it and becomes its leader after Mike's sacrificial death.

The Honorable Joseph Edgerton Douglas, the Secretary General of the Federation. A middle-aged but handsome politician dominated by his ambitious wife, Douglas stakes his political future on controlling Mike, yet does not approve of the violent and underhanded methods used by his subordinates. He is relieved of the need to resolve this conflict by Harshaw, who negotiates to gain Mike's freedom by giving Douglas general control over both Mike's wealth and future relations with Martians.

The Reverend Doctor Daniel Digby, Supreme Bishop of the Fosterite Church of the New Revelation. The leader of a politically powerful religion, Digby is both cynical con man and sincere proselyte. The Fosterites combine high-technology showmanship, hard-sell commercialism, and a revivalist theology to convert the masses and dominate politics.

Digby attempts to win the "Man from Mars" to the faithful, but Mike senses a great "wrongness" in the Supreme Bishop and sends him directly to the Fosterite heaven. The Fosterites later declare an unsuccessful holy war against Mike and his followers.

Thomas C. Schunk

STRANGERS AND BROTHERS

Author: C. P. Snow (1905-1980)
Type of work: Novel
Time of action: 1914-1968
First published: 1972: *George Passant* (originally *Strangers and Brothers*), 1940; *The Light and the Dark*, 1947; *Time of Hope*, 1949; *The Masters*, 1951; *The New Men*, 1954; *Homecomings*, 1956 (U.S. edition, *Homecoming*, 1956); *The Conscience of the Rich*, 1958; *The Affair*, 1960; *Corridors of Power*, 1964; *The Sleep of Reason*, 1968; *Last Things*, 1970

Lewis Eliot, later **Sir Lewis,** the narrator of the novel sequence, whose life is traced from youth to old age. His character and experiences partially reflect those of the author. He is the elder son of Bertie and Lena Eliot and brother of Martin. Eliot rises from humble origins in a small provincial town to be a clerk in a local government office, a barrister, and a Cambridge fellow. He later becomes a consultant to industry and a civil servant in the government. His government service includes involvement with England's wartime development of atomic weapons. Eliot is an ambitious man who prides himself on his judgment and who is perceived by his friends as a man with great sympathy for others. He is emotional but is highly regarded by some for his ability to control his emotions, a talent that leads others to view him as cold and manipulative. His first marriage, to Sheila Knight, proves disastrous, as he is forced to see the mental deterioration of someone he once loved deeply. His second marriage, to Margaret Davidson, is a far more mutually supportive relationship and one in which Lewis learns to accept that he cannot control the lives of those whom he loves. In the course of the sequence, Eliot comes to better terms with himself and his ambitions, forced to do so by events (including near death while undergoing an eye operation) and by the support of those around him.

Martin Eliot, Lewis' younger brother. There is strong affection between the two but also conflict, since for a long time Lewis has greater hopes and ambition for Martin than Martin himself has. Martin is a physicist and a fellow of the same Cambridge college with which Lewis is affiliated. He is the principal character in *The New Men*, in which he becomes involved in the nation's nuclear weapons research. Lewis believes that his brother is unscrupulous in climbing over friends during an investigation to root out a subversive scientist, but, when Martin is offered the post of administrator of the nuclear establishment at Barford, he turns it down and returns to academic life, eventually becoming senior tutor at the Cambridge college. He works closely with Lewis in seeking a reversal of the judgment against Donald Howard in *The Affair*.

Sheila Knight, the daughter of the Reverend Lawrence and Mrs. Knight, who becomes Lewis Eliot's first wife. She is described as very handsome rather than pretty, with magnificent eyes and a dramatic presence. The young Lewis loves her deeply and persuades her to marry him, though she is reluctant because she realizes a personal flaw that makes her incapable of reciprocating that love. She becomes increasingly neurotic, and Lewis must curtail his ambitions so as to pursue a life-style that allows him to devote considerable energy to caring for her. The marriage becomes an imprisonment, which ends when Sheila dies of an overdose of drugs.

Margaret Davidson, the younger daughter of art critic Austin Davidson. She becomes Lewis Eliot's second wife. Lewis meets her at a London clinic during the war and romances her, though she is still married to Geoffrey Hollis. After her divorce, she marries Eliot. She is the mother of Maurice Hollis and Charles Eliot.

Bertie Eliot, the father of Lewis and Martin. A mild, self-centered man, he has no great ambitions. He cares more for his position as organist for a church choir than he does for his family and never appreciates the success of his sons.

Lena Eliot, the wife of Bertie and the mother of Lewis and Martin. She is the dominant figure in the Eliot household and invests young Lewis with much of her ambition and drive for betterment.

George Passant, a solicitor's managing clerk in the town of Lewis Eliot's birth and a part-time lecturer in the local technical college. Passant, who is brilliant and unconventional, attracts and inspires a coterie of free-thinking young men and women who are anxious to extend themselves and challenge the order of the day. Lewis gives Passant much credit for shaping his early career. Passant's influence on others is less beneficial; he is implicated in a fraud with two members of the group, Jack Cotery and Olive Calvert, and the sexual license that he encourages provides a backdrop for the crimes (including murder) committed by Cora Ross and Kitty Patemen, who were associated with the group after Eliot left town. Lacking discipline and sub-

ject to paranoia, Passant fails to achieve the greatness of which Eliot thought him capable.

Roy Calvert, the central figure in *The Light and the Dark*. A brilliant oriental scholar, he is a fellow at the brothers' Cambridge college and Lewis' closest friend there. Calvert is a romantic who wants to believe in God but cannot, and who is also subject to manic-depression. He can be very caring about others but is reluctant to commit himself in love until he marries Rosalind Wykes. He enlists and serves in bombers during World War II, deliberately choosing that most dangerous job. He is killed on a mission over Germany.

Francis Getliffe, later **Sir Francis** and then **Lord Getliffe,** one of Lewis Eliot's oldest friends and a close confidant throughout his career. Getliffe is a brilliant physicist and fellow of the Cambridge college. He is noted for his strong moralism and total personal integrity. He is left-wing in his politics. During the war he is a key figure in England's application of scientific knowledge to develop new weapons and plays a key role in the development of radar. In devoting his energies to the nation, he sacrifices his chance at great scientific discoveries. In the postwar decades, he emerges as a voice against Great Britain's nuclear armament. He is married to Katherine March.

Herbert Getliffe, the half brother of Francis Getliffe. He is a barrister whose chambers Lewis Eliot entered as a young man. Getliffe gives the appearance of being befuddled but is a shrewd, capable man. He is leading counsel for the defense in the trial for fraud of George Passant, Jack Cotery, and Olive Calvert.

Charles March, the son of Leonard March, who is the patriarch of a wealthy Anglo-Jewish family which befriends Lewis Eliot. *The Conscience of the Rich* is the story of Charles March's gradual repudiation of his background as he gives up the law to become a medical general practitioner and then marries outside the Jewish faith. His actions cause his father to disinherit him at great personal cost to both.

Leonard March, the father of Charles March. He is a wealthy Anglo-Jewish banker who has great ambitions for his son and heir, Charles. He is unbending in his opposition to Charles's efforts to carve out his own life, and the clash between them leads to a permanent estrangement.

Ann Simon, an avowed Communist with whom Charles March falls in love and marries. She is a friend of Lewis Eliot, though critical of him for not being as advanced as she would like on various political positions. She is a contributor to the *Note*, a political newsletter.

Donald Howard, the central figure in *The Affair*. He is a fellow of the Cambridge college and is unpopular with many of his colleagues because of his strong communist views. He is dismissed when it is discovered that he incorporated fraudulent data in the scientific publication that earned for him his fellowship. His wife, Laura, forces a reconsideration of the dismissal. Lewis and Martin Eliot, Francis Getliffe, and others defend Howard, whom they dislike, because they believe that an injustice has been done. Lewis is able to persuade the Court of Seniors of the college that Howard's mistake was not fraud but uncritically accepting falsified data offered to him by the aged professor under whom he had been working.

Walter Luke, later **Sir Walter** and then **Lord Luke of Salcombe,** a brilliant physicist and fellow of the Cambridge college. He spearheads the drive for nuclear weapons during the war and becomes chief superintendent of the Atomic Energy Establishment and later chief scientist in the Ministry for Defense. Intensely patriotic, he is also brash and impulsive and not well adapted to the compromises of political life.

Roger Quaife, a Conservative Member of Parliament who becomes parliamentary secretary in the Ministry for Defense and then

is elevated to the post of minister. He is the central figure in *Corridors of Power*. With the support of Lewis Elliot and Francis Getliffe, he tries to turn England away from a policy of nuclear armament, but his career is brought to an end by an extramarital affair with Ellen Smith, the wife of a fellow Member of Parliament, whom Quaife eventually marries.

Paul Jago, the senior tutor of the Cambridge college in the years before World War II. He is Lewis Eliot's candidate for master when Vernon Royce dies. His wife, Alice, is socially inept and a political liability. His devotion to her contributes to his defeat in the election and to his eventual withdrawal from college affairs.

Arthur Brown, junior tutor at the time of the mastership election. He considers Lewis a protégé and has much affection for the younger man. He is an extremely shrewd political tactician whom Lewis respects. He becomes senior tutor after Jago leaves the position. Lewis believes that his role in the Howard affair (supporting the original dismissal) was one of his few political misjudgments.

R. T. A. Crawford, a distinguished scientist who is elected master in preference to Paul Jago. Lewis later acknowledges that Crawford was a good choice because his international scientific reputation contributed to the college's visibility and stature.

Godfrey Winslow, another fellow of the college, served as Bursar. He is a man embittered by personal tragedies and a difficult person with whom to get along.

R. E. A. Nightingale, a priggish and contentious fellow to whom Eliot is invariably opposed when he appears in *The Masters*. He succeeds Winslow as Bursar after Crawford becomes master and seems to be revitalized, doing much good for the college. At the conclusion of *The Affair*, however, he is found to have destroyed evidence that would have helped Howard, acting to preserve the reputation of the college.

Kitty Pateman and
Cora Ross, residents of the provincial town of Lewis Eliot's youth. They were once affiliated with George Passant's group. They are lesbian lovers who abduct, torture, and kill a young boy in *The Sleep of Reason.*

Francis J. Bremer

STREAMERS

Author: David Rabe (1940-   )
Type of work: Play
Time of action: The 1960's
First produced: 1976

Richie Douglas, an enlisted man who shares army quarters with Roger Moore, Billy Wilson, and Martin. Richie is effeminate and open about his homosexuality and his attraction to Billy, though the other men refuse to take him seriously. Deserted by his father at the age of six, Richie is almost paternally protective of the troubled Martin, trying to cover up the suicide attempt and to deal with the problem himself. Richie is immediately suspicious of Carlyle and warns the others that he is dangerous.

Carlyle, a newcomer just out of basic training. An angry black man from the streets, Carlyle is dressed in filthy fatigues and is nervous, fidgety, and suspicious. Drunken and reckless, he takes Roger Moore and Billy to a brothel, then later makes sexual overtures to Richie, who is strangely uncomfortable with these advances. Carlyle starts a fight with Billy, cutting him on the hand and then fatally stabbing him in the stomach. When he is discovered by Sergeant Rooney, Carlyle murders Rooney as well.

Billy Wilson, an enlisted man. White, trim, blond, in his mid-twenties, Billy is the only one greatly bothered by Richie's jokes about homosexuality. He is also very serious about the army and the war, though he has a morbid fear of the snakes in Vietnam. A complex, sensitive thinker, Billy has always felt out of place, especially while growing up in Wisconsin, where at the age of sixteen, he wanted to be a priest in order to help others.

Because Billy refuses to leave Richie and Carlyle alone, Carlyle attacks Billy and kills him.

Roger Moore, an enlisted man and the moral leader of the group. A tall, well-built black man, Roger displays much loyalty to the group and to the army. Confessing that he cries upon hearing the national anthem, Roger is, nevertheless, acutely aware of the oppression of blacks by his country. He is also unsure about the justification of the army's presence in Vietnam. Having been treated for headaches in the past by a psychiatrist, Roger is consciously trying to be more open and communicative with others. He is close friends with Billy.

Cokes, a sergeant and old army buddy of Sergeant Rooney. Cokes is in his fifties, overweight, with short, whitish hair. A bit neater than Rooney, his jacket is tucked in, even when he is drunk. He wears canvas jungle boots, as he has just returned from Vietnam. He wants to return there, but the army has denied his request since he has been diagnosed with leukemia, an illness that Cokes denies. After the murders of Billy and Rooney, however, Cokes explains to Richie that the fatal disease has made him more tolerant, and he is surprisingly sensitive when he learns of Richie's homosexuality. With Rooney, Cokes teaches the young men the parody of the song "Beautiful Dreamer," called "Beautiful Streamers," legendarily sung by a soldier whose parachute would not open. Cokes sings another version in a mock Korean as the play closes. One minute Cokes is drunk and boisterous, bragging about wartime exploits in Korea; the next minute he is sad and haunted by the memory of a Korean he killed, an incident that he compares to a Charlie Chaplin film.

Rooney, a sergeant in his fifties, with short, whitish hair and a big belly. Rooney, usually drunk and disheveled, is fond of reliving memories of his airborne missions with Cokes in the Korean War. Rooney discovers Billy's body and is then murdered by Carlyle.

Martin, an enlisted man. Thin, dark, and young, Martin is more openly disturbed than the others by the army and the prospect of going to Vietnam. Attempting suicide by cutting his wrists, Martin is shipped home.

Lou Thompson

STRIKE THE FATHER DEAD

Author: John Wain (1925-   )
Type of work: Novel
Time of action: The 1940's and 1950's
First published: 1962

Alfred Coleman, a middle-aged professor of the classics. The son of a minister, Alfred has inherited his father's sense of duty, if not his faith. Except for his wife, Mary, who died after ten years of marriage, Alfred has never permitted himself to become close to anyone. Although he is secretly troubled by the memory of his own wartime weakness, he projects an image of certainty, insisting that everyone accept his values, which are chiefly the suppression of emotion and dedication to learning, particularly to the classics. It is his inflexibility that drives his son, Jeremy Coleman, from home and causes a seventeen-year break in their relationship. Finally, while visiting his son in a hospital, Alfred admits his own vulnerability, enabling father and son to be reconciled.

Jeremy Coleman, the only son of Alfred Coleman and his dead wife. Of average stature, Jeremy is healthy but not athletic. He is bright but not scholarly, tending to drift into daydreams or toward the piano, his chief source of pleasure. Jeremy has always tried to please his father, but at age seventeen he realizes that he can find no happiness in Greek books, only in jazz. Running away from school, he eventually becomes a jazz pianist, first in London, then in Paris. After a ten-year period of stagnation, Jeremy once again meets his friend Percy Brett and is inspired to return to his music. Defending Percy in a fight against racist thugs, Jeremy is injured and taken to a hospital. There he and his father are reconciled. At the end of the novel, even though the new popularity of rock and roll means that Jeremy may no longer be able to make a living from jazz, he realizes that even if there is no audience to hear and applaud him, his music makes his life meaningful.

Eleanor Coleman, the sister of Alfred Coleman, his housekeeper. A tender-hearted, gentle, motherly person, Eleanor loves Jeremy as if he were her own child. Because she is in awe of her older brother Alfred, she rarely disagrees with him, but whenever Jeremy is threatened, she will fight like a tigress. It is at her insistence that Alfred goes to visit Jeremy in the hospital.

Percy Brett, a black musician. Of medium height but massive in stature, he has large, expressive eyes and a melodious voice. When Jeremy meets him in London, he is in the U.S. Air Force, but after World War II, Percy has no desire to return to his native Maryland or to anywhere else in the United States, where he would face racial discrimination. Percy, a brilliant trombonist, introduces Jeremy to real jazz. After Jeremy has been sidetracked by Diana, Percy persuades him to return to his music.

Tim, a friend of Jeremy, an inveterate womanizer, sponger, and scoundrel. Although he is roughly twenty-five when he first meets Jeremy, Tim successfully evades wartime service by his facility at lying and scheming and by his total lack of shame. Eventually he sets himself up as Jeremy's public relations man. When Jeremy meets the pathetic wife and young children whom Tim has deserted and who have followed him to Paris, however,

Jeremy loses all respect for Tim and breaks off their friendship.

Diana, an English girl. Pretty but discontented, she has a grudge against men because her parents spent all of their money educating her brother so that he could move upward in society. After she has become Jeremy's mistress in Paris, she goes to London, where for eight years she uses him to relieve her sexual frustrations while she seeks a husband. Jeremy blames her physical demands and her psychological attacks for the loss of his musical powers. After she finds her husband and discards Jeremy, he is able to return to his piano.

Rosemary M. Canfield Reisman

STRONG WIND

Author: Miguel Ángel Asturias (1899-1974)
Type of work: Novel
Time of action: The early twentieth century
First published: Viento fuerte, 1950 (*The Cyclone*, 1967; better known as *Strong Wind*)

Lester Mead (Cosi, Lester Stoner), the green-eyed millionaire organizer of a banana growers' cooperative in an unnamed Latin American country. He left his life as a millionaire for adventure in the tropics. Under the name of Cosi, he is an itinerant salesman of sewing supplies. After his marriage to Leland Foster, he is known as Lester Mead. He buys land and becomes an independent banana grower. When the Tropical Banana Company refuses to buy the independent growers' bananas, he organizes them into a cooperative to sell their crop elsewhere. He goes to Tropbanana headquarters to try to convince company executives to stop exploiting the banana growers. When members of his cooperative are jailed for heading an uprising against Tropbanana, he bribes an official to release them. Under his true identity as Lester Stoner, millionaire and major stockholder in Tropbanana, he travels to New York to urge other stockholders to pressure the company to treat the growers justly and

honestly and thereby ensure for themselves a profitable and stable investment. While in New York, he prepares his will, in which he names his wife as beneficiary and the cooperative as the second beneficiary in the event of her decease. When he returns to his banana farm, he is killed by the strong wind conjured up to destroy Tropbanana.

Adelaido Lucero, overseer on a banana plantation. He saves his money to buy land for his sons. They become Mead's partners in the independent banana growers' cooperative. His son Juan is imprisoned for leading an uprising against Tropbanana. He does not agree with Mead's calls to the cooperative's members to live frugally and save their money in order to win their struggle for just treatment from Tropbanana.

Leland Foster, the greenish-golden-haired wife of Lester Mead. She divorced John Pyle to marry Foster and dies with him in the strong wind. She does not realize that her husband is a millionaire until their trip to New York.

Sarajobalda (sä·rä·hō·bäl′dä), an old witch, godmother of Lino Lucero. Her beating and rape at the hands of representatives of Tropbanana trigger the uprising led by Juan Lucero and Bastiancito Cojubul.

Rito Perraj (pĕ·r̄äh′), the shaman who conjures up the strong wind to satisfy Hermenegilo Puac's desire for vengeance on Tropbanana for refusing to buy his crop.

Bastiancito Cojubul (bäs·tyän·sē′tō kō·hō̄·

bōōl′), a highlander who migrated with his wife to the coast to become a banana grower. He is arrested with Juan Lucero for rebellion against Tropbanana.

The Green Pope, president of Tropical Banana Company, visited by Lester Mead in Chicago. He ordered the company's representatives to stop buying bananas from the growers. He maintains that the stockholders are only interested in dividends and would not be upset if they knew that the company profits came from the merciless, inhuman exploitation of the growers.

Evelyn Toft

THE SUBJECT WAS ROSES

Author: Frank D. Gilroy (1925-   )
Type of work: Play
Time of action: May, 1946
First produced: 1964

John Cleary, a fifty-year-old coffee merchant. John is deeply disappointed with the course his life has taken. He had the opportunity, years ago, to relocate in Brazil, but his wife, Nettie, did not want to make the move. Instead they settled in the Bronx, near Nettie's mother, while the man who took the position in Brazil became rich. Having failed to achieve the American dream, John now turns his frustration toward others, particularly Nettie and Timmy, his son. John's unhappiness also reveals itself in his rigidity (particularly about morality and religion) and reticence. He is unable to speak about those things that are deeply meaningful to him. He drinks to excess, though he does not approve of his son's drunkenness. John's long-standing estrangement from his wife has intensified during Timmy's absence from home. Now, with Timmy's return, he finds himself both jealous of and frustrated by his son. Though he reaches tentative agreement with his son at the end of the play, his deeper problems are unresolved.

Nettie Cleary, John's wife, a bitter, estranged

woman. At forty-five, she contrasts her present life with a happier past. She recalls (or imagines) her childhood at home, a world of gentility, culture, and love. Though she had several suitors, she chose John as the most energetic and ambitious of them. He alone would be able to give her the life she sought. His failure to do so disappointed her, and her love diminished. To replace her expectations, she has created a life of service to her husband, her mother, her son, and her retarded cousin, but it is a life that has left her unfulfilled. The day that she walks out of the house and spends hours wandering around the city is, she says, "the only real freedom I've ever known." Like her husband, Nettie is caught in a self-created worldview, unable to appreciate the different reality of others and unable to communicate with those others. Timmy's return home is yet another failure of reality to meet her expectations.

Timmy Cleary, their son, who left home at eighteen to fight in World War II. Now twenty-one, he returns to his parents' house an adult, precipitating the family crisis for all three characters. Timmy is now better able to perceive his parents' relationship with each other, as well as his relationship with each, though his insight is colored by his own quest for independence. While he attempts to meet each parent's separate expectations of him, he cannot alter the person he has become. When he tries to reconcile John and Nettie, for instance by buying her roses, he fails. Like his father, Timmy drinks excessively, providing a convenient escape from the shattered home he is trying to reenter. His behavior, though, merely makes the situation worse, and while he almost manages some moments of communication, first with Nettie and then with John, his decision to leave home at the end is the only resolution for the family conflict.

Bruce H. Leland

SUCH IS MY BELOVED

Author: Morley Callaghan (1903-   )
Type of work: Novel
Time of action: The 1930's
First published: 1934

Father Stephen Dowling, a large, handsome young priest, dark-haired and fresh faced, one year out of the Seminary. He serves the Roman Catholic cathedral under the pastor, Father Anglin. Father Dowling is interested in social causes, and his fervent sermons frequently disturb the wealthier parishioners. Returning from a deathbed, Father Dowling is accosted by two young prostitutes who do not see the clerical collar under his coat. Initially ignoring them in anger and confusion, he decides to return and speak to them, ashamed of his lack of pity for their wretchedness. Motivated at first by a sense of duty to his parishioners, Father Dowling decides to help the two girls, visiting them repeatedly and giving them whatever money he can spare or borrow, even the money he sends to help support his mother and brother. Although at rare moments he is tempted physically, his feelings for the girls are dominated by a Christian love for the weak and unfortunate. Realizing that one of the girls is sick, and that in spite of all that he can give them they continue to work as prostitutes, Father Dowling impulsively appeals to the richest and most powerful of his parishioners, James Robison, to find the girls honest work. The meeting with Mr. Robison is a failure as the girls insult him and his wife, and he feels compelled to report Father Dowling's involvement with the girls to the Bishop. Father Dowling continues to visit the girls at the hotel where they live and work until, shortly after the meeting with Mr. Robison, the girls are arrested and ordered to leave town. Father Dowling is called to see the Bishop and told that he has behaved wrongly. He refuses to agree with the Bishop that his love for the girls is inappropriate, and while he awaits the Bishop's discipline, he becomes increasingly withdrawn and depressed. He is unable to reconcile his strong love for the girls and his belief that it is his duty to save them with the Bishop's contention that he loved the girls for themselves rather than for the sin from which he might save them. Confined to a sanatarium at the end of the novel, he prays that God will accept his illness as a sacrifice to save the souls of the two girls.

Veronica Olsen (Ronnie), a tall, fair girl, who has become a prostitute after losing her job in a shop. She is stubborn and determined not to let life defeat her, eager to travel, and defiant when she feels attacked, as she does by Mrs. Robison. Ronnie cares for Midge, her partner, and especially for Lou, her pimp and occasional lover.

Catherine Bourassa (Midge), smaller than Ronnie and more fragile both physically and emotionally. She is a dark-haired French Canadian from a typical large Montreal family.

She had left home with a man who promised to marry her and has passed from man to man since. Her illness intensifies Father Dowling's desire to help the girls by any means possible.

James Robison, the wealthiest and most influential parishioner to remain at the Cathedral while other important families have moved to the suburbs. He is sympathetic to Father Dowling in spite of the priest's sermons attacking the bourgeois world for its lack of Christian values. Mr. Robison is generous in charitable giving but demands recognition for his gifts. After Father Dowling brings the prostitutes to his house, however, he feels threatened and, at the urging of his wife, complains to the Bishop about Father Dowling, precipitating the arrest of the two girls and Father Dowling's breakdown.

Charlie Stewart, a young medical student, Father Dowling's closest friend, the only person with whom Father Dowling feels completely relaxed. He is concerned with social justice and believes in reform through secular means. He and his fiancée, however, ask Father Dowling to marry them in the church. Father Dowling feels uneasy about lying to Charlie and his fiancée about the two girls he has befriended when he asks for their help. Charlie notices and is frightened by the change in Father Dowling after the girls are forced to leave town.

Lou Wilenski, Ronnie's lover. He procures men for her and takes part of her earnings. Lou is a small man who looks and acts tough. He is jealous and suspicious of the girls' involvement with the priest and makes fun of him in his absence, but he is unable to prevent the girls from seeing Father Dowling.

Father Jolly, another young priest at the Cathedral. He has a room with bookshelves that Father Dowling had wanted. When Father Jolly leaves, he offers Father Dowling the room, but Father Dowling is too depressed by his failure with the girls to care.

Bishop Foley, a shrewd politician who is more concerned with protecting the church against scandal than with the soul of a young priest or those of two prostitutes. He is presented as a good administrator but not a deeply religious person.

Katherine Keller

SUDDENLY LAST SUMMER

Author: Tennessee Williams (Thomas Lanier Williams, 1911-1983)
Type of work: Play
Time of action: The mid-twentieth century
First produced: 1958

Violet Venable, a wealthy Southern matron of the New Orleans Garden District, mother of the late Sebastian Venable, an aging woman of fading beauty. She has light orange or pink hair, wears a lavender lace dress, and has a starfish of diamonds pinned over her "withered bosom." She has devoted her life to her late son, even refusing to return to her critically ill husband in order to stay with her son and keep him from becoming a Buddhist monk. She and her son traveled every summer, and with her encouragement he wrote one poem each summer. Having suffered a stroke that slightly paralyzed one side of her face, she was rejected as a traveling companion on her son's last and fatal summer voyage and replaced by her husband's niece, Catharine Holly. Violet is devastated by Sebastian's rejection and death and most of all by Catharine's story of what happened that last summer, a story that is destroying the legend of everything for which Violet has lived. She has proposed to fund young Doctor Cukrowicz's experimental work in exchange for his performing a lobotomy on Catharine to silence her horrible stories. Violet has been accustomed to getting her own way and will use any means at her disposal to get it.

Catharine Holly, the young and beautiful cousin of Sebastian Venable. She wears a suit that was bought for her by her cousin Sebastian, and her hair has been done in a beauty parlor. She is quite nervous, moving about with quick, dancelike movements, attempting to smoke cigarettes, which her nun attendant does not allow but the doctor permits. She is the niece of Mrs. Venable's husband and is strongly disliked by Mrs. Venable. She and her mother and brother are dependent upon Mrs. Venable for financial support. Ignored by a weak, indulgent mother and egotistical, self-indulgent brother, Catharine is starved for attention and affection. She is outgoing, aggressive, and unconventional. When her cousin Sebastian shows an interest in her, she accepts his invitation to travel with him. When Sebastian is killed while on their excursion, Catharine tells a story of horror to authorities and is flown home by Mrs. Venable and committed to a mental hospital. When Catharine continues to repeat her story, despite shock therapy, injections, and other treatments to cure insanity, she is brought to her aunt's home with the intention of having her committed to another sanatorium to have a new experimental treatment, a lobotomy, which Doctor Cukrowicz would perform. In Sebastian's jungle garden, she tells her story of moral degradation and cannibalism to the doctor and her family, including Violet.

Doctor Cukrowicz (kōō·krō′vĭts, meaning "sugar" in Polish), a young, blond physician, dressed in white, "glacially brilliant," extremely handsome with icy charm. He tells Mrs. Venable that she can call him "Doctor Sugar." He is engaged in experimental brain surgery on mental patients but has a very small budget. He needs money for a separate ward for his patients, for trained assistants, and for a large enough salary to support a wife. He also wants patients in addition to the criminal psychopaths that the state sends to him. He attempts to be fair; he is kind and listens to all sides with an open mind. Mrs. Venable offers him a subsidy from the Sebastian Venable Memorial Foundation to perform the lobotomy on Catharine Holly, plainly stating: no operation, no subsidy.

George Holly, Catharine's brother. A typically handsome man, he has the best looks in the family, tall with an elegant figure. He is ambitious, petulantly spoiled, and concerned about what people will think when they learn that his sister is in a mental hospital. He is also very much afraid that he will not get his share of Sebastian's money.

Mrs. Holly, the mother of Catharine and George and sister-in-law of Violet Venable. Mrs. Holly is a "fatuous Southern lady who requires no other description." She is upset with her daughter's behavior because she is afraid that Mrs. Venable will break Sebastian's will, which left money to them. She asks Catharine not to "invent" terrible stories about what happened to Sebastian.

Miss Foxhill, a private nurse for Mrs. Venable. She moves about nervously in rubber-soled white oxfords and fears displeasing her employer.

Sister Felicity, an attendant nun for Catharine from the mental hospital. She is dressed in a starched white habit and has difficulty keeping Catharine under her control.

Bettye Choate Kash

THE SUICIDE'S WIFE

Author: David Madden (1933-   )
Type of work: Novel

Time of action: 1968, from the time of Martin Luther King, Jr.'s, assassination to Robert Kennedy's assassination
First published: 1978

Ann Harrington, the protagonist, a housewife and mother of three small children. Having grown up in a Polish ghetto in Pittsburgh, Ann attended college only after being urged repeatedly by her high school home economics teacher. At the University of Pittsburgh, she met and later married Wayne Harrington, her English professor. After Wayne commits suicide during a visit to his vacant family home in upstate New York, Ann returns to San Francisco, West Virginia, fearing that Wayne has abandoned her. When the news of his death reaches Ann, she finds herself unable to cope with her new status: the suicide's wife. As she tries to make sense of her life without Wayne, Ann realizes that she was completely dependent on him to fix everything around the house or to make sure that the bills were paid; she cannot even drive Wayne's dilapidated car. Ann starts to grow into an independent woman as she learns to make repairs around the house and as she begins to teach herself how to drive. She soon realizes, though, that she knows very little about Wayne's life. Turning to Max Crane, she learns that Wayne was not admired by his students or his colleagues at the university. In fact, he was regarded as a boring teacher. Ann comes to understand that if Wayne had not committed suicide, she would have continued to live her life in his shadow.

Max Crane, a poet and former colleague of Wayne Harrington. Witty and egotistical, successful as a poet, Max is popular with his students and faculty coworkers. After Max meets Ann, he tells her much that she never knew about Wayne: that his students found him boring and that the other professors at the university found his work mediocre. While Max relates this information, he also proposes the idea that Wayne may have been killed by Anson Kellor, a radical student who criticized both Wayne and Max. Max wonders if Kellor, a homosexual, may have been attracted to Wayne and may have followed him to New York, killing him because Wayne rejected Kellor's advances. Max even tells Ann that he found himself attracted to Wayne because Wayne's body image contrasted to Max's image of his own body and how others perceived him. Eventually, Max invites Ann to a faculty party, but they wind up at his apartment when Ann cannot face meeting the people who knew her husband. The two go to bed, but Ann cannot make love to Max. While lying together, Ann demonstrates how Wayne made her feel sexually violated before he left her to commit suicide. The next day, Max writes a poem entitled "The Suicide's Wife," which tries to capture Ann's feelings about her ordeal. The poem, however, leaves Ann angry and confused about her own feelings.

Mark Harrington, Ann's eleven-year-old son. A sensitive boy, Mark writes an imaginative biography about his father. Because Ann cannot answer Mark's questions about Wayne's life, the boy makes up most of the details. When Ann later finds the biography, she reads it and discovers that Mark has written nothing about her. Mark becomes openly hostile toward Ann, refusing to complete his chores around the house or to baby-sit his younger brother and sister, Wayne and Annie. Mark eventually fails the sixth grade, which makes Ann realize that while she has worked so hard to make sure everything in her house runs smoothly, she has neglected her children's emotions.

Dale Davis

SULA

Author: Toni Morrison (1931-   )
Type of work: Novel

Time of action: 1919-1965
First published: 1973

Sula Peace, the protagonist. Sula is different from the other women of the town of Medallion, as willing to feel pain and pleasure as she is to give them. Having lost her best friend, Nel, she looks in vain for friendship in men. After leaving Medallion to go to college and to travel, she returns as a pariah and is blamed for all the town's misfortunes. Contrary to the beliefs of the townspeople, who believe that a brighter day will dawn after she dies, her death is followed by a severe ice storm and the catastrophic cave-in of the tunnel.

Nel Wright, Sula's best friend. Reared in an oppressive household, she decides to be her own person, not her mother's daughter. Nel marries Jude because she wants to be needed; she blames Sula when he leaves her. Unlike Sula, she fears change so much that she refuses to buy a car. Long after her marriage breaks up, Nel realizes that she has been mourning for Sula all of her life, not for Jude.

Eva Peace, the crippled matriarch of the Peace family, Sula's grandmother. She is so preoccupied with her hatred of her womanizing husband and with keeping herself and her family alive that she is unable to show much love to her children. When her husband leaves her, she leaves her children with a neighbor, returns eighteen months later with one leg, and builds a new home. Her arrogance is apparent in the fancy shoe she wears on her one foot. Strangely, she murders her own son and almost bleeds to death trying to save her daughter.

Shadrack, a shell-shocked veteran of World War I. When he returns to Medallion after the war, he earns the reputation of town character, spending most of his time catching fish to sell, cussing people out, acting obscene, and getting drunk. In 1920, he proclaims January 3 as National Suicide Day, and he commemorates the event every year thereafter by carrying around a hangman's

noose and ringing a cowbell. On January 3, 1941, he leads a parade of townspeople to the tunnel, where many of them die in a cave-in.

The Deweys, Eva's three adopted sons. Surly and unpredictable, they resist all attempts to distinguish between them. They speak with one voice and think with one mind. After Eva is sent to a nursing home, they live wherever they want. Their bodies are never found after the tunnel collapses.

Hannah Peace, Sula's beautiful and self-indulgent mother. After the death of her husband, Rekus, she takes a series of lovers because of her need to be touched every day. As a result, she is despised by all the women in town. She teaches Sula that sex is pleasurable but otherwise unremarkable. Hannah burns to death while trying to light the yard fire.

Tar Baby, an alcoholic half-white who rents a room from Eva. He is arrested for causing a wreck involving the mayor's niece. Tar Baby dies in the cave-in.

Jude, Nel's handsome husband and Sula's lover. Frustrated in his attempt to find work building the New River Road, he marries Nel in his determination to take on a man's role. Even after ten years of marriage, he still feels belittled by white society. Jude leaves Nel shortly after she catches him making love to Sula.

Ajax (Albert Jacks), the one true love in Sula's life. Son of a conjure woman, Ajax loves women, airplanes, and hot baths. He is the only one of Sula's lovers who actually talks to and listens to her. After he is arraigned for arguing with the police, he goes to an air show in Dayton, Ohio, and walks out of Sula's life forever.

Helene Wright, the domineering mother of Nel. She moves to Medallion to get as far away from the brothel where she was born as possible. In the absence of a Catholic church, she joins the most conservative black church in town and spends her time forcing her daughter to be obedient and polite. Helene saves her own life by refusing to march in the parade to the tunnel.

Plum, Eva's shiftless, spoiled son, to whom she had planned to bequeath everything. He almost dies as a baby because he shoves pebbles up his anus. When he returns to Medallion after serving in World War I, he steals, takes trips to Cincinnati, and sleeps for days in his room with the record player going. Believing that Plum is trying to return to the womb, Eva sets him afire while he is asleep.

Alan Brown

SUMMER AND SMOKE

Author: Tennessee Williams (Thomas Lanier Williams, 1911-1983)
Type of work: Play
Time of action: c. the early 1900's and 1916
First produced: 1947

Alma Winemiller, daughter of a minister in Glorious Hill, a small town in Mississippi. In the Prologue, she and John Buchanan are shown as children at a fountain of Eternity in the town in the early years of the century. The scene shows their pattern as children to foreshadow their pattern as adults: attracted to each other but unable to achieve true communication because she is sensitive and primarily spiritual (as she says, Alma means soul) and he, while capable of a degree of sensitivity, is primarily physical, and hence is representative, in a sense, of the anatomy chart that he shows Alma near the end of the play. As an adult, Alma is given to panic attacks and frequently goes to John's father for help, even in the middle of the night.

John Buchanan, son of a physician, frequently at odds with his father and, as an adult and physician, uncertain that he wants to join his father's practice. The Buchanans and Winemillers are next-door neighbors. In the end, however, John achieves an understanding of "soul" and will be a successful and empathic physician and husband.

Reverend Winemiller, Alma's father. Incapable of empathy and lacking genuine faith, he is successful as neither minister nor father nor husband.

Mrs. Winemiller, Alma's mother, who is, as Williams says, in a permanent psychological state of "perverse childishness." She is primarily interested in eating ice cream.

Dr. Buchanan, John's father. Early in the play he correctly calls his son a drunkard and a lecher, though it becomes clear that they do feel an affection for each other. He treats Alma with great sympathy and does not object to her middle-of-the-night visits.

Rosa Gonzalez, a young Mexican woman whose father owns the gambling casino on Moon Lake and who has a relationship with John.

Nellie Ewell, a younger woman and vocal student of Alma. Her mother goes to trains to attract traveling salesman, and therefore, as the daughter of a loose woman, Nellie is unaccepted in the community.

Mrs. Bassett, a member of a not-very-successful book club, which has an abortive meeting at Alma's house.

Mr. Gonzalez, Rosa's father. He enters the Buchanan house, seeking Rosa. Dr. Buchanan enters, is insulted at seeing the Gonzalezes in his house, orders them out, and attacks Gonzalez with a cane. Gonzalez shoots and kills him.

Jacob H. Adler

SUMMER OF THE SEVENTEENTH DOLL

Author: Ray Lawler (1921-   )
Type of work: Play
Time of action: December, 1952, to January, 1953, during the five-month layoff season for sugarcane workers
First produced: 1955

Olive Leech, thirty-seven years old, cynical, a barmaid at the same hotel as Pearl. She has an "eagerness that properly belongs to extreme youth." She appears to have no frustrations about her dull job and seems to take life as it comes. Yet in adjusting to the unconventional relationship she has with a man who only comes to town for five months out of every year, she has blocked off the other seven months of the year, becoming, as she realizes, "blind to what I want to be." A chance to change the situation with a more conventional arrangement leaves her with a sense of loss and betrayal that borders on the psychotic.

Roo Webber, a sugarcane worker, tall, thirty-seven years old, with light hair starting to gray. "He is a man's man with a streak of gentleness, a mixture that invites confidence." He has had a bad working season, however, because of a pretended back injury which he uses as an explanation of his failure to maintain his position as a champion ganger. In his frustration, he fights with his major competitor, Johnny Dowd. He then quits work before the end of the term and returns to the city, eventually getting a job as a painter in a factory, an employment he considers degrading. During his annual layoff, he always returns from the fields to live with Olive, to whom he brings, as symbol of affection, a kewpie doll. This is the seventeenth year for such a present. For him the relationship with Olive is only a vacation from his real career in the cane fields, where he enjoys a strong sense of community with his fellow workers. He fears making any commitments that will end such bonding but now comes to realize that those days are over. He decides to stay in the city and marry Olive, falsely hoping that such stability will redeem his life.

Barney Ibbot, also a canecutter, Roo's best friend. He is about medium height and of solid build with the beginning of a pot belly, "his manner is assertive, confident, and impudently bright, perhaps a little overdone as defiance to his forty years." He is a heavy drinker. He has had numerous affairs with women and has fathered three children out of wedlock. As he is getting older, his conquests are more in the telling than in the observance. He cannot admit that the fun is over, however, and lies as a cover-up. His attempt to re-create the past ends in failure.

Pearl Cunningham, "a biggish woman, well corseted, with dyed red hair," a widow and mother who earns her living as a barmaid. She feels demeaned by her job and would like to get something more classy. Her friend Olive wants to fix her up with Barney Ibbot, but she is hesitant, blaming it on her responsibility in bringing up a teenage daughter. Her suspicious, tentative nature changes to possessiveness when she becomes his lover. Yet Barney does not conform to her idea of respectability. She breaks off the relationship, believing that life should be lived without daydreams.

Emma Leech, the seventy-year-old mother of Olive. She owns the house where they live, and Olive pays the bills. Emma is "a wizened, life-battered wisp of a woman . . . with no illusions about humanity, expecting the worse from it, and generally crowing with cynical delight when her expectations are fulfilled." She is fond of her daughter's friend Roo and offers to lend him money; yet, wiser than her daughter, she knows the falsity and fragility of a relationship maintained only during a five-month layoff season.

Bubba Ryan, "a dark, shy-looking girl of

twenty-two." A next-door neighbor of Olive. She drops in from time to time to help for plot exposition, but she also becomes involved with a young canecutter, Johnny Dowd. Life with him, she is convinced, will turn out differently from that lived by Olive and Roo. "Some way I can have it safe and know that it's going to last," she says self-assuringly.

Johnny Dowd, another canecutter, "a big, boyish, friendly-looking fellow of twenty-five." In asking Bubba to go with him to the races, he provides evidence that seasonal relationships will survive into a new generation.

Wm. Laird Kleine-Ahlbrandt

THE SUNDAY OF LIFE

Author: Raymond Queneau (1903-1976)
Type of work: Novel
Time of action: The late 1930's and the 1940's
First published: Le Dimanche de la vie, 1951 (English translation, 1976)

Valentin Brû, an army private. Valentin is a very average young man whose real desire in life is to be a street sweeper. He allows himself to be courted by the middle-aged Julia and goes into shopkeeping when he marries her. They move to Paris, where Valentin runs a picture frame shop and then knows much success when, disguised as a woman, he becomes a fortune-teller. He is drafted again as World War II approaches, and the novel's last image presents him at a train station helping young girls into the crowded train and fondling them as he does so. Valentin would like to be a saint, but he is quintessentially a petit bourgeois character who is quite satisfied with the little pleasures of life.

Julia Julie Antoinette Segovie, a middle-aged provincial haberdasher. The novel begins with her deciding to marry Valentin, a young soldier whom she has merely seen passing on the street. She succeeds in arranging this marriage, though she cannot take time away from business, so she sends Valentin on a honeymoon trip alone. She inherits a business in Paris from her mother but prefers to become a medium and allows Valentin to run the shop. She becomes ill and allows Valentin to replace her as "Madame Sophie." Julia is a petit bourgeois character incarnating all the comic vices of her class: brashness, vulgarity, avarice, and scheming.

Chantal, Julia's sister. She helps her sister

in her marriage schemes, even going so far, apparently, as to sleep with Valentin's commanding officer in order to get Valentin's name. She is an attractive woman, loyal to her family, and her main desire is to see her daughter get her share of the inheritance that Nanette, her mother, leaves to Julia and Valentin.

Paul Bolucra, also **Botucat, Brodago,** and **Batraga,** Chantal's husband. Queneau systematically changes the spelling of this functionary's last name, an inspector of weights and measures, whose main concerns are whether he is a cuckold, the future of his daughter, and his promotions. He is promoted and is sent from Bordeaux to Paris, where he can consort with Valentin and worry if his wife is doing the same.

Marinette, the daughter of Chantal and Paul.

Nanette, Julia and Chantal's mother. She is a lively old woman, which Valentin learns when he meets her, accidentally, on the return trip from Bruges, in Paris, where she is attending her lover's funeral. She leaves her Parisian shop to Valentin and Julia.

Captain Bordeille (bôr-dā'), Valentin's commanding officer. He is a representative of the gallant French soldier and seduces Chantal.

Sergeant Bourrelier (boo-rĕl-yā'), another

1494

soldier. This friend of Valentin shares frequent drinks with him and comes to visit him in Paris.

Didine, a waitress. She gives Valentin advice about marriage and later wants to come to Paris.

Jean-sans-tete, or **Jack-Lackwit** in translation, an idiot. This mindless inhabitant of the eleventh arrondissement in Paris carries a broom and is a double for Valentin in his attempt to meditate on nothingness.

Allen Thiher

THE SUNLIGHT DIALOGUES

Author: John Gardner (1933-1982)
Type of work: Novel
Time of action: August, 1966
First published: 1972

Taggert Faeley Hodge, a gifted man of forty years, plagued by bad luck, which transforms a gentle idealist into the cynical, fire-scarred **Sunlight Man.** Having failed in all of his efforts to save his wife from insanity and his children from death, he returns to his native Batavia, New York; is arrested for painting the word "love" on a city street; and begins using magic tricks to undermine man's faith in law and order and in love. His four "dialogues" with Police Chief Fred Clumly, following the Sunlight Man's escape, are at once seriously learned and blackly humorous, intelligent and insane. Set apart from the rest of mankind as much by his despair and nihilism as by his stench and blasted appearance, he chooses in the end to give himself up, only to be shot dead by a nervous police officer.

Fred Clumly, Batavia's sixty-four-year-old police chief. His beady eyes, large nose, and white, completely hairless body make him a particularly conspicuous figure, especially at the funerals he likes to attend. One year short of retirement, he has become increasingly critical of the modern age. As the crime rate soars, his frustrations, weariness, and paranoia grow, fueled by his noble but decidedly old-fashioned belief in personal responsibility. In a highly irregular maneuver, he agrees to meet secretly with the Sunlight Man following the latter's escape. As a result, he loses his job but gains a deeper understanding of who and what the Sunlight

Man is. This understanding culminates in the speech Clumly delivers at the end of the novel, which enables him to rise above the merely personal and to affirm those "connections" that bind self to community and the individual to the ideal.

Arthur Hodge, Sr., a congressman and patriarch, builder of Stony Hill, the now-ruined family estate. He was a man of superior mind and virtue blessed by good fortune. His absolutism, perfection, and idealism come to tyrannize his survivors as they try to live in a less pastoral, more ambiguous age, which the congressman himself foresaw. His wholeness of being and vision lives on in fragmented form, in the specializations of each of his children.

Will Hodge, Sr., oldest of the congressman's five children. A country lawyer and inveterate toggler committed to shoring up the fragments against last year's ruins, he is a dependable, rueful man, "comfortable in the cage of his limitations" but burdened by guilt and the responsibility he feels for his former wife, his two sons, and his brother Tag, indeed for all mankind.

Millie Jewel Hodge, Will's former wife. Born poor, she tries to win the love of Ben Hodge, drawn by his strength and freedom. Rejected, she takes her revenge by marrying Will (whom she does come to love briefly) and destroying Stony Hill and the Hodges with it. Imprisoned by the Sunlight Man, she struggles to maintain her existential autonomy—"I exist, no one else"—but fails. Seeing Tag and hearing the news of her son Luke's death restores this Circe to the world of forgiveness and love.

Luke Hodge, Millie and Will's twenty-two-year-old son. He has an enormous tolerance for the pain caused by his own histamine headaches and his having witnessed his parents' endless bickering. His elephantine ears undermine his romantic tragic-hero pose, just as his will to believe undermines his hard-earned yet nevertheless not-entirely-convincing cynicism. Kept a prisoner in his own house by the Sunlight Man (his uncle), Luke undergoes a significant change. He transforms his adolescent rage into a selfless but suicidal act that will put a stop to the Sunlight Man's madness and Nick Slater's murders. Although Luke dies alone (Tag and Nick having jumped from the truck sometime before Luke drove it off the bridge), it is Luke's death that prompts Tag to give himself up.

Ben Hodge, age fifty, a large but gentle dairy farmer and lay preacher. Married to Vanessa, a cartoonishly fat but very friendly schoolteacher, he finds his freedom in his visionary sermons and in riding his motorcycle. In his youth he betrayed Millie Jewel's love but as an adult has been both faithful and generous toward others.

Will Hodge, Jr., Luke's older brother, a Buffalo lawyer specializing in legal collection. His earlier idealism—largely destroyed by what he learned when he ran his father's unsuccessful political campaign and by his discovery that the legal system deals with technicalities rather than truth—survives in attenuated form in his commitment to his work and to the Civil Rights movement. He spends much of his time futilely and obsessively tracking down the enigmatic (and, Will believes, dangerous) R. V. Kleppmann.

Esther Clumly, the police chief's blind wife. She met Fred while he was on leave from the Navy and she a student at the Batavia Blind School and before the onset of the disease that has made him "grublike" and before the failure of the operation she underwent to restore her sight. Aging, childless, and emotionally estranged from her husband, she takes refuge in religion, tippling, and self-pity. Her attempt to protect Fred from an imagined conspiracy backfires and contributes to his losing his job. When officials come to the house to collect the tape recordings he has made of the Sunlight Man's dialogues (evidence that will incriminate Fred), Esther comically yet nobly tries to hold them off.

Dominic Sangirgonio, "Miller," a police captain whom Clumly thinks of both as a son and as a rival. An ex-Marine, he tries as best he can to help Clumly, only to be rebuffed. Eventually (or so the mayor claims) he believes that he can no longer trust the chief.

Stan Kozlowski, who has joined the police force in order to escape his father's farm. Although he may at times be working outside the law (in protecting a prostitute and in accepting free meals), Clumly is nevertheless drawn to Kozlowski, whose ambiguous silence and apparent imperturbability, Clumly says, makes a man think. As the story progresses, he becomes more and more Clumly's sole companion and confidant.

John Figlow, Clumly's desk sargeant, who dreams of escaping his unhappy marriage. When the Sunlight Man returns to surrender, it is Figlow who shoots and kills him, understanding only as he fires that the Sunlight Man is not dangerous this time, only once again clowning.

Mickey Salvador, the young, overly trusting police officer who is shot and killed by Nick Slater during the jail break.

Walter Benson, a short, fat, slightly hunchbacked man who his enormously fat wife, Marguerite, believes is a traveling salesman but who in fact has for the past twenty-two years been the small-time professional thief Walter Boyle. Witness to all that is said and done during his pretrial term in the Batavia jail, he chooses not to become involved, despite the price others must pay for his passivity. He and the Sunlight Man know each other's actual identities (Tag once defended Boyle). Miller, too, discovers Boyle's real identity, but Clumly refuses to use Miller's evidence in court. Returning to Buffalo, Boyle, now Benson, learns that his wife is having an affair with their boarder, whom Benson, taking heart from the kitsch poetry he loves to read, decides not to kill.

Ollie Nuper, Benson's boarder, a man with a silly face, a passion for radical causes, and a distaste for the hypocrisy of others but a self-pitying tolerance for his own. His civil rights activities bring him into contact with Will Hodge, Jr. He is murdered by local neo-Nazis and secretly buried by Benson, who once again chooses not to become involved.

Nick Slater, an eighteen-year-old Indian who first comes under Luke Hodge's guardianship and then under Ben's. He and his oafish younger brother, Verne, are in jail for their part in a fatal traffic accident. When the Sunlight Man returns to free the prisoners, Nick alone chooses to go, giving up his cell only to become the Sunlight Man's prisoner and slave. He kills a guard during the break and later, more deliberately, murders Will Sr.'s landlady, Mrs. Palazzo, and Luke's friendly neighbor, Mr. Hardesty.

Kathleen Paxton, the beautiful only daughter of Clive Paxton, whose overprotection made her both gentle and ill-tempered. She became a teacher, married Taggert Hodge against her father's wishes, and gradually lost her mind, coming to prefer the voices she imagined from the past to the harsh reality of her present. Tag and her brothers have spirited her from sanatorium to sanatorium in order to keep her from again coming under the tyrannical influence of the father who refuses to admit his responsibility for her illness. It was apparently Kathleen who set the

fire in which Taggert was badly burned while trying to rescue their two sons.

Clive Paxton, a merciless, self-made businessman and domestic tyrant, feared and hated by most, including his wife, their sons, and the Hodges. He dies at age seventy-six on the night before the arrest of the Sunlight Man, who may be implicated in the death.

Elizabeth Paxton, the invalid wife of Clive Paxton, from whose tyranny she took refuge in the love of Professor Combs.

Walt Mullen, Batavia's mayor, an advocate of the time-cost factor in all government affairs, including policework. He is a small man who speaks in clichés and likes to tell off-color jokes. He turns an informal investigation into the formal hearing that ends with Clumly's ouster. He and Phil Uphill (city fire chief and another of Clumly's critics), however, are the first to congratulate the ex-police chief for his powerful end-of-the-novel speech.

Sam White, "the oldest judge in the world." He gives Clumly two of Taggert Hodge's essays to read, one on "Policework and Alienation," the other on Harry Houdini, without, however, divulging that Taggert is the Sunlight Man. Asked by Uphill to help depose Clumly, the judge retreats into silence, acting neither for nor against him.

R. V. Kleppmann, the tall, well-mannered son of Polish Jews whom Will Hodge, Jr., obsessively tries to make live up to his financial responsibilities. His cultivated appearance masks his strong dislike of people, whom he tolerates only insofar as he can use them.

Freeman, a young drifter who appears briefly in Batavia wearing a black coat and an Amish hat, accompanying Will Hodge, Sr., as he trails Clumly. He is "the encourager," but he is also (as Will Sr. realizes) the one without responsibilities and commitments, who can just pack and leave.

Robert A. Morace

SURFACING

Author: Margaret Atwood (1939-   )
Type of work: Novel
Time of action: The late 1960's
First published: 1972

The narrator, the main protagonist, an un-named commercial artist and illustrator. At the beginning of the novel, the narrator is returning to the island on the U.S.-Canadian border, where she will look for her father, a "voluntary recluse," who has disappeared. David and Anna are doing the narrator a favor by driving her and her boyfriend, Joe, to the remote island, inaccessible by boat or trains. The narrator is disoriented, intro-verted, and fearful, trying to recover from the shock of an abortion and a broken love affair with a married man. After the four have stayed on the island a week, the narra-tor hides from the group and remains on the island when the others leave. There she en-gages in a ritual of grieving for her parents and of shedding off the garments and other vestiges of civilization.

Joe, her boyfriend, an avant-garde potter who teaches night school. Joe and David are doing a makeshift film, including Anna and the narrator in much of the footage. They plan to put the miscellaneous clips together and call it "Random Samples." After Joe asks the narrator to marry him and she re-fuses, a series of conflicts unfolds. In the final scene of the novel, Joe has returned to the island with Paul to look for her. He calls to her and waits for her response. The novel ends with the narrator on the brink of mak-ing this decision.

Anna, her so-called best friend, though the narrator has known her for only two months. She is somewhat older than the narrator. In-secure in her marriage of nine years to David, Anna dyes her hair, hides behind a coat of makeup, and worries about getting fat and losing David. To make her week on the island away from the city and civilization tolerable, she reads many detective novels and rations her cigarettes. Though Anna

laughs about David's film behind his back and calls it "Random Pimples," she tells on the narrator to David and Joe for throwing their film and camera into the lake at the end of their weeklong stay on the island.

David, Anna's husband, a former radio an-nouncer and Bible salesman, now a teacher of communications at the same night school at which Joe works. He was studying for the ministry when he met Anna. The oldest member of the group, David fears aging, worries about becoming unattractive, and ar-ranges his hair to conceal his balding. He is the first to suggest that the group stay a full week rather than just the two days that they originally planned. He is angry and dis-traught when he learns that the narrator has dropped his camera and the film for "Ran-dom Samples" into the lake.

Paul, a neighbor of the narrator's father, a truck farmer. Paul writes to the narrator when her father disappears. Though Paul speaks only broken English and the narrator speaks only academic French, they commu-nicate through the ritual of exchanging vege-tables. Early in the week, Paul brings Bill Malmstrom to the island and delivers "a huge wad of vegetables from his garden." Later he comes to the island with Claude to bring word that the narrator's father had been found drowned. Finally, it is Paul who brings Joe to the island in a last search for the narrator.

Madame, Paul's wife, a sturdy woman who has never learned English. She remains nameless and in the background.

Bullhead Evans, "a bulky laconic Ameri-can" who runs the Blue Moon Cabins. He delivers the group to the island and picks up Joe, Anna, and David a week later.

Bill Malmstrom, a graying executive for "Teenie Town: Togs for Toddlers 'n Tots" in Detroit, Michigan. He identifies himself to the narrator as a "member of the Detroit branch of the Wildlife Protection Association of America." He is looking for a place where the members can meditate, observe, hunt, and fish because the place on Lake Erie is "giving out."

The narrator's former lover, a teacher of lettering, he appears only in the narrator's memories. Married, with children, he insists that the narrator have an abortion when she

becomes pregnant. The narrator ultimately says of him that he was "only a normal man, middle-aged, second-rate, selfish and kind in the average proportions. . . . "

The narrator's brother, who explores mineral rights in Australia. The narrator has sent him a letter but believes that he has not yet received it.

Madame, an old woman who formerly ran the local store. The narrator observes that "none of the women had names then."

Carol Franks

THE SURVIVOR

Author: Thomas Keneally (1935-   )
Type of work: Novel
Time of action: The mid-1960's
First published: 1969

Alexander Ramsey, the director of Extension studies at a provincial Australian university and a former Antarctic explorer. A large, homely man of sixty-two, Ramsey is debilitated with guilt at having survived Stephen Leeming, leader of his Antarctic expedition, and having slept with Leeming's wife before the journey. Oversensitive to references to Leeming, Ramsey begins the novel by walking out of a Rotary Club meeting because of a casual inquiry. Preoccupied and neglectful of his university work, Ramsey thinks that he is approaching madness when informed that Leeming's body has been found and is to be excavated. He flies to the Antarctic to watch the dig, and, once it is completed, he achieves a new sense of mental well-being.

Ella Ramsey, Ramsey's wife and a part-time lecturer in the department of history at his university. She is forty-five and has an attractive Mediterranean appearance. Her life is dominated by the knowledge of her own infertility; her one pregnancy ended in a stillbirth. From that time she abandoned her doctoral thesis and has redirected her ener-

gies into pottery and sparring with her husband. She has little patience for Ramsey's fixation on Leeming, though she grudgingly supports him otherwise.

The poet, an Australian man of letters. Small and intense, the poet is writing an extended poem about the Leeming expedition. The poet delivers the information of the discovery of Leeming's body to Ramsey, thereby precipitating Ramsey's crisis. Despite some initial distrust, he and Ramsey become friends.

Belle Leeming, the widow of Stephen Leeming. An elderly but still attractive and quick-witted woman, Belle led an unconventional earlier life that included affairs with many men. Her memory of Leeming is practical where Ramsey's is mystical. She goes to the Antarctic to watch the excavation.

Denis Leeming, a doctoral student and the nephew of Belle. In his early thirties, Denis has an impressive academic background, but his thesis cannot be approved. An eccentric, dilettantish man, Denis is excited by the idea of the recovery and reburial of Leeming's body. This plan brings him into conflict with Ramsey. Eventually Leeming's thesis is accepted for publication as a book.

Stephen Leeming, the leader of the Antarctic expedition. A thin, slight man from a rich family, Leeming was a self-confessed fanatic for polar exploration. Intelligent though atavistic, he led a largely successful exploration but was eventually crippled by a stroke while crossing a glacier.

Morris Pelham, the senior lecturer under Ramsey. A Yorkshire man with a Cambridge education, Pelham is Ramsey's chosen successor to the directorship. Pelham covers up for much of Ramsey's administrative neglect.

Eric Kable, the assistant director of Extension. An ambitious, unscrupulous man who wants the directorship, Kable plays departmental politics in an attempt to tarnish Ramsey. He supports Denis Leeming.

Valerie Kable, Kable's wife. An attractive woman and amateur actress, she is best known in the university for her promiscuity, which sometimes serves to advance her husband's career.

Arthur Lloyd, a doctor and former Antarctic explorer. Now a dying man, Lloyd accompanied Leeming and Ramsey on the fatal leg of their Antarctic journey. Two weeks before his death, Lloyd tells Ramsey that when they left Leeming, he was not quite dead.

Sir Byron Mews, the vice-chancellor of the university, a phlegmatic and political man widely, if secretly, known by his old rugby name, **"Chimpy."** Lord Byron controls the university machinations behind Ramsey, especially with regard to Denis Leeming.

Lady Sadie Mews, Lord Byron's wife, an attractive, girlish, older woman who confides in Ramsey her distrust of her husband.

Brian Sanders, a professor of physics. A handsome age fifty, Sanders is a pleasant and honest man but given to sexual adventuring. As Denis Leeming's supervisor, he tries to prevent him from going to the Antarctic. He almost succeeds in seducing Ella Ramsey, and he makes a student, Sally Bourke, pregnant.

David Hammond, a journalist. A thin, tanned thirty-five, Hammond is the Australian journalist assigned to cover the excavation of Leeming. He meets Ramsey in New Zealand on the way to the pole and becomes his confessor, if not friend.

Barbara, Ramsey's secretary. An overweight, pretentious, but loyal woman, she runs Ramsey's office for him with motherly efficiency.

Paul Budra

SUTTER'S GOLD

Author: Blaise Cendrars (Frédéric Louis Sauser, 1887-1961)
Type of work: Novel
Time of action: 1834-1880
First published: L'Or: La Merveilleuse Histoire du général Johann August Suter, 1925
   (English translation, 1926)

John Augustus Sutter, a Swiss emigrant to America, a magnificent dreamer and methodical man of action who builds and loses an empire in California. In 1834 a penniless Swiss fugitive, vagabond, and swindler named Johann August Suter, he deserts his wife and four children and sails for America. His family has no news of him until he becomes famous as General John Augustus Sutter, one of the richest men in the world, lord of a vast domain in California. Shrewd in maneuvers and a skillful diplomat, he steers a careful course and maintains good relations both with the Mexican authorities who rule California when he arrives and with the forces of American expansion, which will soon claim California as a new state. By the time of statehood, Sutter owns the largest domain in the United States. His vision realized, his vast farms flourishing with cotton, rice, indigo, livestock, orchards, and vineyards, Sutter longs to settle back into calm and peaceful cultivation of his choice European vinestocks. At last, he is ready to send for his wife and children, to live out the fulfillment of his grand agrarian dream of New Helvetia in the garden of America. Then gold is discovered on his land; the ensuing chaos, the inundation of his lands by gold-mad prospectors, settlers, and squatters, shatters his dream, destroys his farms, forts, estates, and villages, decimates his family, and leaves him a ruined, broken man. Aside from the character traits that mark Sutter with a genius for colonization, he possesses a "profound knowledge of the human heart" and a certain "moral ascendancy." When his estates are overrun and the filth of gold hunger seems to have polluted all California, Sutter wonders whether he is guilty of setting it all in motion, whether it is not somehow his fatal flaw, his overweening ambition, that has caused everything. In this phase of his life, Sutter takes on a certain tragic grandeur. He lives out his final years in Washington, D.C., where he is viewed as something of a joke, as the eccentric old madman seeking an impossible justice. In Cendrars' version, even General Sutter's death is monumental and symbolic: He dies on the steps of the Capitol and its "gigantic shadow" falls over his corpse. Sutter is one of the most compelling exemplars of the glory and the tragedy of the American Dream. His presence in this novel is so all-engulfing that he is not merely the only principal character but also, strictly speaking, the only character developed at all.

Anna Sutter, Sutter's wife, abandoned by him, left without word from him for fourteen years. She makes the long difficult journey to join him, with their children, only to find her husband a ruined man. She dies shortly after her arrival in California.

Judge Thompson, a California magistrate who pronounces Sutter's claims valid. One of the few just and civilized men in the raw territory, Thompson befriends the ruined Sutter, understands and feels compassion for the general's plight.

Jean Marchais, Sutter's loyal blacksmith. One of the very few employees of the general who remains faithful through everything, the Frenchman is finally hanged by the gold-seeking rabble.

Father Gabriel, a missionary and protector of the Indians. Eloquent, just, and firm, he is a friend to Sutter and possesses an intelligent and compassionate understanding of the historical anguish of California and Sutter's role in these events.

Johannes Christitsch, leader of the Herrenhütter of Lititz, Pennsylvania. A relentless intriguer and self-appointed manager of Sutter's affairs in his last years, he schemes to take advantage of the old general.

H. R. Stoneback

SUTTREE

Author: Cormac McCarthy (1933-)
Type of work: Novel
Time of action: 1951-1955
First published: 1978

Cornelius Suttree, also called **Buddy** by his family, **Sut** by his friends, and **Young-** blood by Abednego Jones, an intelligent and well-educated man of approximately thirty who, for reasons never explicitly divulged, has left his wife and child and gone to live in a houseboat moored to the banks of the Tennessee River. Born with a dead identical twin, Suttree suffers from a sort of double vision: He lives half in this world and half in the next, and he views each from the perspective of the other. He makes a meager living by fishing and spends the rest of his time either taking care of or getting drunk with an assortment of mostly homeless and alcoholic outcasts who are his friends. In the course of his disjointed but thematically coherent adventures, Suttree undergoes a series of encounters with the dead and with death, from the floating corpse that opens the novel to the corpse in his bed that closes it. Not only do many of Suttree's friends die (through violence, neglect, or disaster), but Suttree is himself hospitalized three times in the novel, twice as a result of barroom brawls and once for an advanced and untreated case of tuberculosis. Suttree makes three excursions from Knoxville: The first is to attend the funeral of his son; the second is into the Smoky Mountains, where he wanders without food or shelter for more than a month in an effort to lay his demons to rest; the third is to the French Broads of the Tennessee River, with Reese, in an ill-fated attempt to make money by gathering mussel shells and freshwater pearls. At the end of the novel, Suttree (most of his friends dead or gone and his already tenuous ties to the material world loosened still further by his lengthy and near-fatal illness) leaves McAnally Flats one step ahead of the death that hounds him.

Gene Harrogate, also called the **City Mouse,** who meets Suttree in the workhouse, to which he has been sent for the unusual crime of melon-mounting. Harrogate is a misfit even among misfits and serves as Suttree's comic twin; his harebrained get-rich-quick schemes provide some of the novel's lighter moments.

Abednego (Ab) Jones, a huge black man, one of Suttree's closest friends. With his wife Doll, Ab runs an unlicensed tavern in his houseboat. Ab tells Suttree that the police "don't like no nigger walkin' around like a man," and, as Ab refuses to be intimidated, he is frequently and violently incarcerated. Suttree is involved in Ab's two unsuccessful attempts to get Mother She to destroy his enemies for him and is present during Ab's last epic battle with the police. Ab is finally beaten to death in jail.

Reese, a raft-dwelling ne'er-do-well. He persuades Suttree to undertake his only experiment with earning a living through hard work; the experiment is a miserable failure, and the expedition culminates in death and destruction.

Wanda, Reese's daughter and one of Suttree's lovers. She is killed in a rockfall at the French Broads camp.

Joyce, Suttree's lover after Wanda. Joyce is a prostitute from Chicago who supports Suttree in lavish style until his dependency embitters him, and his bitterness drives her temporarily mad.

Mother She (Miss Mother), an ancient black witch who takes a particular interest in Suttree and, in a hallucinatory episode toward the end of the novel, gives him "the second sight."

Billy Ray "Red" Callahan, a bully and a petty thief who rescues Harrogate from an assailant in the workhouse, generally wreaks havoc, and is finally shot in the head by a bartender, after which he lingers on in a vegetable state until a hospital orderly pours rubbing alcohol into his wound.

The ragpicker, also called **the ragman,** Suttree's most philosophical friend. Asked whether he believes in God, the ragman replies, "I got no reason to think he believes in me."

Michael, an Indian fisherman. He and Suttree become friends when Suttree defends him from a racist attack. He returns to seek help from Suttree during the latter's brief period of prosperity with Joyce, but Suttree ignores his knock.

Daddy Watson, a retired and senile railroad engineer. Until he is committed to an asylum, Daddy lives in an abandoned railroad car near Suttree's houseboat.

Leonard, a male prostitute. Suttree is recruited by Leonard to assist in disposing of the corpse of Leonard's father, which the family has been hiding for months in order to continue collecting his Social Security payments.

Grace Suttree, Suttree's mother. Grace appears only once in the novel, when she visits Suttree in the workhouse, but she is one of several characters, such as Suttree's dead twin, who are more important than they are visible.

John Merritt Unsworth

SWAMP ANGEL

Author: Ethel Wilson (1888-1980)
Type of work: Novel
Time of action: The early 1950's
First published: 1954

Maggie Vardoe, also known as **Maggie Lloyd,** a young widow, married for the second time, to a man whom she detests. Her beauty is not immediately apparent and she makes no effort to look beautiful, but her eyes are large, gray, and "tranquil," and her body is characterized by "large easy curves." Maggie is self-sufficient, even secretive, and confides very little about her present unhappiness or the pain of losing her first husband and her daughter, even to her closest friends Hilda and Nell Severance. Having decided to leave her second husband, Eddie Vardoe, she ties fishing flies in secret for more than a year in order to earn money and slips away one night after dinner so unobtrusively that it takes several hours for her husband to notice her absence. Maggie seeks escape and peace away from the city of Vancouver in the mountains of British Columbia, where she tries to re-create the happy setting of her childhood and first marriage at an East Coast fishing lodge. A naturally nurturing and competent woman, Maggie becomes cook and eventually manager of a fishing lodge owned by Haldar and Vera Gunnarsen at Three Loon Lake. Maggie, who had hoped to escape not only her husband but also all emotional involvement with people, finds that she is faced with several crises caused by Vera's jealousy of Maggie's competence and increasing influence with Haldar and their son, Alan.

Nell Severance, now in her seventies and with her movement limited by obesity, had been a beautiful circus performer who married into an aristocratic but eccentric English family. Nell has kept the Swamp Angel, a revolver that she used in her juggling act, as a reminder of her lost power. She sends the revolver to Maggie when she realizes that she is no longer independent physically and fears that she is close to death. Nell's powerful personality enables her to control Eddie Vardoe after Maggie's disappearance. Nell's unconventional life and her love of drama contrast with both her daughter's conventionality and with Maggie's search for tranquillity and disengagement. Despite her nonconformity, Nell provides wisdom and stability to Maggie.

Hilda Severance, later **Hilda Cousins,** an attractive young working woman, daughter of Nell and Maggie's only friend of her own age. She accepts and respects Maggie's reticence. She cares for her mother, whom she both loves and resents for the irregularity of her childhood, but she is drawn away from her and from Maggie by her marriage to Albert Cousins and the birth of her child.

Edward Vardoe (Eddie, E. Thompson Vardoe), a crude, boorish man with "spaniel eyes," a real estate agent with aspirations

1503

to own his own business. Eddie's uncouth behavior and his petty tyrannizing about money and the running of the household humiliate Maggie and cause her to leave him as quietly as possible, so as not to be subjected to one of his scenes. Having taken Nell's advice to forget Maggie and find someone else, Eddie becomes involved with "a blonde" who manipulates and humiliates him.

Haldar Gunnarsen, the owner of the Lodge at Three Loon Lake. He is passionately attached to the land and determined to keep his lodge in spite of a crippling accident that breaks his hip. Haldar is insensitive to his wife's jealousy of the land and her fear of the future, and, as he depends more and more on Maggie in the running of the Lodge, he also fails to understand Vera's jealousy of her. His anger at Vera for precipitating Maggie's departure leads to Vera's suicide attempt and the final reconciliation between the Gunnarsens and Maggie.

Vera Gunnarsen, Haldar's wife, a woman reared in the city and unable to understand the reality of running a lodge. She has grandiose dreams of immediate success and wealth. Vera appears to prefer unhappiness to happiness, and focuses the blame for all of her misery on Maggie. Maggie's patience with her only increases her sense of resentment and jealousy, and finally she forces a confrontation that causes Maggie to leave the lodge temporarily.

Katherine Keller

THE SWAN VILLA

Author: Martin Walser (1927-   )
Type of work: Novel
Time of action: A summer in the 1970's
First published: Das Schwanenhaus, 1980 (English translation, 1982)

Gottlieb Zürn (tsürn), a real estate broker living in the Lake Constance area of Southern Germany. He is almost fifty years old and is haunted by a sense of failure and inadequacy in business and family life. He feels harassed by the details of everyday living (such as car insurance) and troubled by inopportune lust: Is his real age fourteen? He likes to speculate about the real ages of his acquaintances. People and events in the novel are seen through his eyes, although this is a third-person narrative. His rival realtors seem far wealthier, more stylish, enterprising, and successful than he is and likely to obtain the coveted sole agency to sell a magnificent art-nouveau villa on the Lake where Gottlieb, who writes poetry, likes to linger in useless melancholy. At parties he is likely to lose his head in efforts to entertain the company, so that his indiscretions haunt him afterward. On one occasion he makes extravagant purchases while failing to call on a client through loss of nerve. In family affairs he believes that he is an inadequate father to his four daughters. He is hot-tempered and impatient in his dealings with them and fails to provide support in their times of need (for example, pregnancy or a wish to "drop out"). He observes that his wife, who bears the brunt of family difficulties, is also more effective than he is at selling real estate. The final discovery that the villa is being demolished at the hands of a rival agent leaves him battered and resigned.

Anna Zürn, wife to Gottlieb, burdened with family cares, which include tending a daughter (one of four) inexplicably ill. She has a tenacious memory for detail and is perhaps a better agent than her husband. She fends off Gottlieb's amorous advances, often using sobering information for this purpose.

Regina, their daughter, mysteriously ill, often in the hospital, a constant worry to her parents.

Rosa, another daughter. At a university as a student of law, she returns home pregnant by Max, a married man, and decides against an abortion.

Magdalena, or **Magda,** another daughter. Approaching her final examinations at school, she is conscientious but not at the top of the class. A vegetarian and a violin-player, often listless, she plans, for a time, to drop her studies.

Julia, another daughter. She plays the piano when her sister plays the violin. She takes the family dog to training classes without success and often seems irritated by her family.

Hortense Leistle, the wife of a wealthy manufacturer, responsible for the sale of Swan Villa now that her sister has been declared legally incompetent. Gottlieb is eager to get the sole listing, but she refuses to commit herself and ends by allowing the old house to be demolished.

Lissi Reinhold, the wife of a prosperous businessman and a prospective client to Gottlieb, a former tennis partner. She appears everywhere without her husband, accompanied by a bearded young sociologist. A formidable woman with a powerful voice, in her presence Gottlieb is likely to behave foolishly.

Jarl F. Kaltammer, a rival real estate agent. A former student activist with aristocratic pretensions, he finds the local dialect "vulgar." A constructor of shoddy buildings, he prides himself on dealing only in Burgundian chateaus. It is he who outwits all the other agents by arranging for the demolition of Swan Villa.

Paul Schatz, Gottlieb's principal rival in the real estate business. An autodidact of Hungarian origins, his life, to the envious Gottlieb, seems carefree, and his advertising, flamboyant. He is prominent in environmental causes and is a painter whose work Mrs. Reinhold admires.

Rudi W. Eitel, another rival to Gottlieb. Rarely in Germany, he cultivates a surrealist appearance and imitates Southern California business methods.

Helmut Maier, nicknamed **Claims-Maier,** a real estate claims consultant and Gottlieb's drinking companion. He proves to be a competent bidder at the final auction and is good at repartee but is of little assistance to Gottlieb.

Baptist Rauh (rou), a composer from the Lake Constance region and a prospective purchaser easily moved to enthusiasm, although his wife prefers Hamburg.

Max Stöckl (shtœk'l), a cameraman with ambitions to be a director, Rosa's married boyfriend by whom she is pregnant. He talks incessantly in a Bavarian accent, trying to organize Rosa's life (she should drop law studies, he thinks) and preaching a doctrine of self-assertion. Rosa sends him away.

Eberhard Banzin, son of the original owner of Swan Villa, Gottlieb's former schoolmate. Once a brilliant mathematician, he relapsed into eccentricity and was declared legally incompetent.

W. Gordon Cunliffe

SWEET BIRD OF YOUTH

Author: Tennessee Williams (Thomas Lanier Williams, 1911-1983)
Type of work: Play
Time of action: 1959
First produced: 1956

Chance Wayne, a handsome would-be actor who did not "make it" in Hollywood and is now a gigolo. He has maneuvered his traveling companion, Princess Kosmonopolis, to visit his birthplace, a small town on the Gulf of Mexico. His plan is to get the Princess, who is really a faded film star, Alexandra Del Lago, to help him and Heavenly Finley, the youthful sweetheart he had deserted, begin careers in the motion picture industry. During their short stay, however, he learns that Heavenly has had a hysterectomy, because of his having given her a venereal disease, and that her father, Boss Finley, and her brother, Tom Junior, are waiting to castrate Chance if he ever shows his face in St. Cloud again. As the play ends, Chance has recognized that his youth has passed, that his dreams of stardom and Heavenly will never materialize, and that he must wait for the inevitable with what the playwright calls "deathbed dignity."

Princess Kosmonopolis, also known as **Alexandra Del Lago,** a film star traveling incognito after fleeing from a preview showing of her "comeback" film. She uses every service Chance offers, from oxygen, pills, liquor, and hashish to sex. She cannot forget, however, what she believes to be her failed attempt to return to pictures as a middle-aged woman. Toward the end of the play, she learns that her film is a success, and she offers to take Chance with her on the return trip to Hollywood, but he declines. She, too, has lost the "sweet bird of youth," but time has allowed her a slight reprieve.

Boss Finley, the father of Heavenly and Tom Junior, a caricature of a "redneck" pre-civil rights politician. His concern for his daughter stems from his fear of what gossip about her will do to his election campaign; he has bullied his son into complete compliance; even his mistress, Miss Lucy, has neither respect nor love for him. As Heavenly reminds him, it was he who drove the young, clean Chance away years ago because he wanted his daughter to marry an older man from whom he hoped to profit. His character becomes clear when he tells his daughter how he had bought her mother a diamond clip as she lay dying—to prove to her that she was going to recover—and then had gotten a refund before the funeral.

Miss Lucy, Boss Finley's mistress for years. She is disloyal to him, secretly encouraging the Heckler, who has interrupted Finley's Youth rallies before, by asking questions about Heavenly's operation, and who has now appeared at the television rally to be broadcast from St. Cloud on Easter Sunday. She also tries unsuccessfully to urge Chance to escape his fated castration by leaving with the Princess while he has the opportunity.

Aunt Nonnie, the sister of Heavenly's dead mother, dependent on Boss, who had a part in the original love affair between the teenagers. Now she reminds Chance that time has passed for Heavenly, too, and that nothing can come of his "plans" for them to win a Youth Search in Hollywood. She warns him to leave St. Cloud while he can.

Heavenly Finley, Chance's sweetheart, who blames her father for much of what has happened to her. She does, however, appear at his side in "virginal white" at his television rally and has agreed to marry Dr. George Scudder, although she threatens going into a convent. She is a very weak person whose only chance for happiness ended when she was not allowed to marry her young lover.

Tom Finley, Jr., Heavenly's brother, a wild young man whose indiscretions have been paid for by his father.

Dr. George Scudder, the chief surgeon at St. Cloud Hospital, put up by Boss Finley, who operated on Heavenly. He will marry her, but he wants nothing to do with plans for the castration, even though he agrees in principle that it is deserved.

Hatcher, the assistant manager of the Royal Palms Hotel, who tries without success to get the Princess to leave St. Cloud.

The Heckler, who has taken a number of beatings but continues to appear whenever Boss Finley holds a rally.

Scotty and
Bud, ex-friends of Chance Wayne. They will

participate with Tom Junior in the final *coup de grâce* at the end of the play.

Stuff, a bartender in the hotel who remembers Chance from the old days and hates him.

Edythe M. McGovern

THE SWEET DOVE DIED

Author: Barbara Pym (Mary Crampton, 1913-1980)
Type of work: Novel
Time of action: The 1960's
First published: 1978

Leonora Eyre, an aristocratic spinster who lives in London, does not work, and is nearing the age of fifty. She is an attractive brunette, especially in the right kinds of light, dresses well, and entertains herself by buying Victorian *objets d'art et de vertu* and by reading. She rather complacently thinks of her life as passion spent and emotion recollected in tranquillity, although she cannot remember just where and when she spent the passion. On a number of occasions, she is faced with the fact that some of her friends think her cold and formidable. She does not accept this judgment, preferring to think her responses to life properly measured and rigorously tasteful.

Humphrey Boyce, the owner of an antique shop in London. Nearing sixty and a widower of many years, Humphrey is tall, slender, and, he thinks, bald in the most distinguished kind of way. He is rather fussy in the shop with Miss Caton, his typist, and with his nephew and employee James Boyce. Having met Leonora in the book's first chapter at an auction in Bond Street, he finds himself in a contest for her affections with his nephew.

James Boyce, a twenty-four-year-old graduate of the University of Oxford. Recently orphaned by the death of his mother, he has gone to work for his uncle. He is attractive, well-mannered, and rather passive, falling, as he does, into and out of relationships in a casual and mildly guilt-ridden fashion. Installed by Leonora in a flat above hers, James engages first in a somewhat colorless

affair with Phoebe Sharp and, later, in a more spirited liaison with Ned, an American whom he meets in a Spanish post office. Leonora does what she can to end these affairs but is successful only with respect to the former.

Phoebe Sharp, a recent graduate of an undesignated English university. She is brown-eyed, tall, shy, and not overly attractive. Her casual manner of dress is made to look slovenly when she comes up against the immaculate Leonora. She likes James more than he does her but does not have the necessary resources to fight Leonora for his attentions.

Ned, a twenty-nine-year-old, small, neat, fair-haired, blue-eyed American college English professor. Ned becomes James's lover in Spain and returns to England with him. He is described as having a thin, gnatlike voice, and, indeed, he becomes gnatlike in the extreme in his struggle with Leonora. He breaks off the affair with James and prepares to return to his mother in Cambridge, Massachusetts, but not before going to Leonora and announcing his bequeathing of James back to her in a meretricious, cruel, and finally, unrewarded play for a show of emotion and of gratitude.

Miss Foxe, a kindly, fragile, white-haired woman of seventy who plays what Leonora considers to be distasteful programs on her radio and whose flat Leonora commandeers to rent to James.

Liz, a neighbor of Leonora whose love of

cats has been occasioned by a ruinous marriage.

Meg, a friend of Leonora who is also nearing fifty. She has a homosexual friend named Colin, who occasionally leaves her for lovers. She commiserates with Leonora when Ned enters James's life.

Miss Caton, a typist in the employ of Humphrey Boyce. She is admirable, prim, and middle-aged. She takes her tea from a "monstrosity" of a cup and is reproved by Humphrey for so doing.

Johnny Wink

SWORD OF HONOUR

Author: Evelyn Waugh (1903-1966)
Type of work: Novel
Time of action: 1931-1951
First published: 1965: *Men at Arms*, 1952; *Officers and Gentlemen*, 1955; *Unconditional Surrender*, 1961 (*The End of the Battle*, 1962)

Guy Crouchback, an emotionally maimed expatriate Englishman who has lived in Italy for the eight years since his divorce. As a Roman Catholic, he cannot marry again, nor has he recovered from his wife's desertion of him for another man. He welcomes the coming of war in 1939, for he sees it as an opportunity to do battle with the evils of the modern age, represented by the hateful combination of Nazism and Communism. He returns to England and, despite his advanced age of thirty-six, secures a commission in the Royal Corps of Halberdiers. He loves army life from the very start, but the trilogy chronicles his disillusionment with the war. First, the Russian-German alliance falls apart, and Britain immediately embraces the Soviets as allies. Next, he is a part of the humiliating British rout on Crete. Finally, he observes the Allies' coldblooded betrayal of Royalist officers in Yugoslavia. He concludes that the two sides are morally indistinguishable, that his country has won the war at the cost of its honor.

Virginia Troy, Guy's former wife. She is an amoral, not evil, woman whose only two real interests are pleasing men and pleasing herself. She left Guy for Tommy Blackhouse and still later was married to Hector Troy, an American. She goes from one affair to another until she is eventually impregnated by one of the most loathsome characters in the

trilogy. Guy remarries her so that her unborn child will have a lawful father.

Gervase Crouchback, Guy's saintly father. He represents what is best in the old Catholic families of England. As others are being either corrupted or disillusioned by the war, his life is the ideal of Christian and civilized behavior in times of trial. He thus serves as the moral center of the novel.

Apthorpe, like Guy, an aging subaltern in the Halberdiers. Also like Guy, who once farmed in Kenya, he has an African background, although a murkily imprecise one. He is Guy's alter ego—at one point, both men suffer knee injuries and go hobbling about with sticks, like absurd mirror images of each other. He is ardently and ludicrously attached to his thunderbox, a personal chemical toilet, which is in turn fiercely coveted by the eccentric brigade commander.

Frank de Souza, a Halberdier officer. He is one of the Communists with whom the British military mission to Yugoslavia is loaded. He joyously participates in Britain's betrayal of her former allies. British intelligence, which sees right-wing conspiracies everywhere, views him as quite sound politically.

Trimmer, also known as **Gustave** and **Alistair McTavish,** a lazy, incompetent, fraudulent probationary officer in Guy's group. When he was a hairdresser on ocean liners, he used the name Gustave. During his military service, he has assumed the persona of Captain, sometimes Major, Alistair McTavish. He is the manufactured hero of *Operation Popgun*, the bogus invasion of a deserted Channel island. He is also Virginia's lover and the father of the child whom Guy will rear as his own.

Ludovic, a corporal-major in Guy's Commando unit. He is an effete but tough man with disconcerting pink eyes and no documented past. He was once a valet. He murders Brigade Major "Fido" Hound when the latter cracks during combat on Crete, and during the retreat he murders a sapper captain on the getaway boat. After the war, he writes a best-selling novel entitled *The Death Wish*.

Ivor Claire, an aristocratic young Commando officer. In his first appearance, he is seen wiping the face of his beloved Pekingese with a silk handkerchief. This dandy possesses all the traditional virtues of upper-class English society, those virtues that Guy believes are at battle against the Modern Age. In the hour of crisis on Crete, however, he abandons his men to captivity and flees the island. His upper-class friends cover up his act of treachery, thus emphasizing the utter failure of noblesse oblige during Britain's mortal struggle.

Tommy Blackhouse, Virginia Troy's second husband, the man who took her away from Guy. He turns up as Guy's commanding officer when the latter disgraces himself with the Halberdiers and is transferred to X Commando. The two men become good friends again.

Ben Ritchie-Hook, the brigadier-general whose command includes both the Halberdiers and the Commandos. This war lover has lost one eye and most of his right hand during a lifetime spent in "biffing" whatever enemies he could find. His arrival predictably presages Trimmer's departure from the Halberdiers. He engages in a series of wild skirmishes with Apthorpe, his aim being to gain that officer's thunderbox for himself. In the amphibious *Operation Skylark*, he joins his men as they slip onto the coast of Africa. He decapitates a sentry, has the head pickled, and keeps this lugubrious souvenir constantly by his bed.

Ian Kilbannock, an Air Force publicity officer who in peacetime wrote a racing column. He wishes to do well out of the war and believes that the propagandists will be the real profiteers of World War II. He goes along on *Operation Popgun*, the purely-for-publicity invasion of an insignificant Channel island, to chronicle the brave deeds of Trimmer and his sappers. The ten-man invasion force mistakenly lands on the coast of France, from which they make a "heroic" escape after a French housewife fires a shotgun at them.

Grace-Groundling-Marchpole, an army colonel and head of counterintelligence. He believes in a Plan, a great net of conspiracy of which virtually everyone is a part. He accumulates information tirelessly, toward the end of proving this thesis. He is suspicious of Guy, on whom he maintains a thick dossier.

Julia Stitch, the wife of the politician Algernon Stitch. She has accompanied her husband to Egypt, and Guy meets her in Alexandria. She is the darling of the diplomatic and military elite. She enjoys wielding her influence on General Headquarters Middle East, and she is the devoted friend of Ivor Claire. She appeared earlier, as a much more farcical character, in the comic novel *Scoop*.

James Pendennis "Chatty" Corner, an apelike former denizen of the African bush. This man of the tropics has been sent to X Commando to teach the men how to climb the icebound slopes of Scotland. He finally reveals the closely guarded secret of Apthorpe's African past.

General Miltiades, an old Greek who is

attempting to escape from Crete. Unlike the rabble around him, however, he is courageous, uncomplaining, and unfailingly courteous. Captain Crouchback perceives him as the ideal of the gentleman warrior, but the General moves Ludovic to observe in his journal that all gentlemen are now very old.

Peregrine Crouchback, Guy's eccentric, asexual uncle. Virginia is sharing his London flat during Guy's posting to Yugoslavia. He and Virginia are killed by a "doodle" bomb which falls there.

General Whale, the fatuous commander of H.O.O.HQ. He is plagued by the problem of what to do with the repulsive Trimmer and the unmanageable Ritchie-Hook, until the former jumps ship in South Africa, disappearing utterly, and the latter throws his life away in a spurious partisan attack in Yugoslavia.

General Spitz, the American observer whose favor the partisans are currying. This vain and stupid man goes about accompanied by his personal photographer. Ritchie-Hook's senseless death somehow legitimizes the fiasco in his mind, and he recommends an increase in supplies for the gallant partisan forces.

Eloise Plessington, a Catholic friend of the Crouchback family. She takes little Gervase, Virginia's baby, to the country and so saves his life.

Domenica, Eloise Plessington's tomboy daughter. After the war, she becomes Guy's second wife (or technically his third, since he married Virginia twice) and the mother of his two younger sons.

Sir Ralph Brompton, Ludovic's former master and homosexual lover. He is a Communist and Soviet agent who is busily stocking the government with his protégés.

Patrick Adcock

THE SYSTEM OF DANTE'S HELL

Author: Amiri Baraka (Everett LeRoi Jones, 1934-   )
Type of work: Novel
Time of action: Time periods of the author's life: his youth, his adolescence, his 1965 self
First published: 1965

The Narrator, the author's persona, **"Leroi,"** a black intellectual from lower-middle-class origins, attracted to white culture and Western civilization but guilt-ridden and confused by the resultant denial of his black heritage. Jones describes himself as in continual flux—"I don't recognize myself 10 seconds later. Who writes this will never read it"— and empty at "the core." He feels trapped in a Dantesque and nightmarish hell, torn between his black identity, which is violent and promiscuous, and his intellectual quest to rise above it. The entrance to his vision of hell, therefore, is inscribed with "You love these demons and will not abandon them." In a disjointed, stream-of-consciousness-like flow of memories, punctuated by black English slang and expletives, he recalls in long and cryptic catalogs the inhabitants of his childhood streets and the ugliness and squalor of their lives; he relives the bewildering seductions of adolescence and the chain of lovers, male and female, who become momentarily tangled in his posing and his longing. People from his past loom up in memory, people doomed to the various circles of hell, and then fade away ("Powell . . . a lawyer," "Pinckney . . . a teacher," "Dolores Morgan, who had an illegitimate child," "Orlando Davis . . . caught stealing on his scooter," "Michael Scott, made blind by God," and so forth). Jones depicts his youth as a time of excess born of the blues, a time of "violence against others, against one's self, against God, Nature, and Art," a time of hunting and conquest and golden boys, of bisexual use and abuse. He lists the literary greats whose words have lured him toward their value systems (Dylan Thomas, James Joyce, T. S. Eliot, Ezra Pound, and Dante, among others), indicts them as seducers, and cries out in self-disgust: "I am left only with my small words . . . against the day. Against you. Against. My self." Yet he expects even those "small words" to be misinterpreted as he quotes "The Brantley Brothers": "You know we don't understand what you mean by all this!" The Narrator seeks to find some sense in the seemingly meaningless confrontations of his youth: a fight at a party, a homosexual encounter, a rape of an old woman with venereal disease, a "ball" at "The Bottom; where the colored lived," abuse by whites who define him as a "slick city nigger." In the final circle of hell he calls himself "an imitation white boy" and "the young wild virgin of the universe" with an Odysseus or a Vergil-like shade pointing the way toward a wilderness "For Madmen Only," a place where he is enslaved by a white prostitute and prostitutes himself for her approval and where he understands himself a "nobody." Ultimately he claims to have a clearer vision of the "inferno" of his frustation and to have found peace in returning to his black self.

46, a nameless representative of "brittle youth" and "dead America," rootless and disillusioned, ignorant and weak, and easily taken.

He is a middle-class black with delusions of hope, "a smooth faced" black youth who is sexually seduced by 64.

64, or **Herman Saunders,** a tempting exploiter from Morton Street, an underprivileged black youth who sings the blues. The Narrator calls him "a maelstrom of definitions," and places him in the circle of "Drama" and "False Counsellors." He is both a homosexual seducer and a representative of street knowledge.

Peaches, a fat, white, seventeen-year-old prostitute, who tries to rape and then control the Narrator. She has short "baked hair" split at the ends, fat tiny hands full of rings, perspiring flesh, and a purple dress with wrinkles across the stomach. She laughs at the Narrator and his friend in their military uniforms, and when they try to leave after a few dances, she grabs the Narrator's hat so that he will be technically out of uniform if he tries to return to base. She then forces the Narrator to spend the evening drinking with her and to come home with her, only to beat on him and accuse him of being a homosexual when he cannot perform in bed. Later, when they become lovers, she initially makes him feel as though his past was "all fraud and sickness." Being "Peaches' man," however, eventually helps him to understand how he has prostituted himself to white values and leads him to return to his own people, hellish though their lives may be.

Gina Macdonald

TAKE A GIRL LIKE YOU

Author: Kingsley Amis (1922-   )
Type of work: Novel
Time of action: The late 1950's
First published: 1960

Jenny Bunn, a twenty-one-year-old schoolteacher. She is, in most things, an ordinary young woman, pleasant, with average tastes and wants, better than average in the domestic virtues, disciplined and orderly in her habits, and accommodating of others. Yet, she has a resolute moral compass, and here her problem begins. She is strikingly beautiful, but, with the guidance of her dour, pedestrian, north-of-England morality, she has resolved to remain a virgin until she marries. Being sensible, she has learned to deal with the barrage of sexual attention that comes from almost every quarter, from even the most respectable or homely of men and, occasionally, from women. She has more difficulty with her own divided nature, however, which does and does not want to remain firm. This difficulty she surmounts also. She does want to be married, and here she falters. The men whom she finds who will naturally respect her morality do not interest her. They are the pathetic, homely, and absurd men of the town. The men who do interest her are impatient with her reserve. After Jenny has lived for a time in the company of women for whom virginity is no longer even a wistful memory, and had difficulties with almost every character in the novel (those who have no direct designs on her are offended when Jenny attracts people close to them), she falls prey to the less-than-honorable actions of Patrick Standish, with whom she is in love, and whom she had hoped to marry, and becomes his mistress.

Patrick Standish, a master at a local boys' school. Handsome, intelligent, and cosmopolitan, he is a self-styled rake and playboy and devotes much of his energy to womanizing. He also is a conscientious and concerned teacher, in spite of himself, and he has another nature, less avaricious and more self-content. This other nature, hidden behind the playboy at adolescence, has been seen rarely since. In his adult persona he has grasped what he thinks he ought to want, at the expense of what he does want. One look at Jenny is enough to bring out the wolf in him, and their first date establishes the pattern that continues through the novel. Patrick behaves badly and then tries to argue her out of her principles. Later, he regrets his boorishness, tries to make amends, and Jenny, seeing no ready alternatives, forgives him. Their romance goes thus, up and down through the novel, the down moments being many, and the up parts including a long idyll when it looks as though they will marry, during which Patrick begins to feel something like his preadolescent content. Finally

Patrick gives in to his lesser self and, in actions that, if not quite amounting to rape, are certainly more than seduction, makes Jenny his mistress.

Graham McClintoch, a young chemistry instructor and Patrick's roommate. A would-be Patrick Standish, Graham is the prototype for the homely and pathetic men who would respect Jenny's morality but are quite unfit to be her husband. Although he devotes as much energy as Patrick to sexual misadventures, and dotes on Patrick's advice, he has no success. His one date with Jenny falters when he becomes more interested in his own self-pitying fantasies than he is in Jenny. There are good sides to him, and he is not meant to be farcical, except perhaps as a romantic figure. During the crisis at the end of the novel, his natural chivalry proves insufficient to save Jenny from Patrick.

Anna le Page, a French girl who lives in Jenny's boardinghouse. She is a posturing and cosmopolitan woman, the most extreme of the many who appear in the novel. When Jenny makes a sincere try at friendship, she gives back only a large dose of polemics, on the theme of free love and self-expression, and makes a pass at her. By the end of the novel, she has revealed to Jenny that her public persona, by which she was, in her own eyes, a rebel and an outcast, is simple fabrication. Jenny thinks only that in revealing her true self she seems all the more false.

Julian Ormerod, an upper-class friend of the men. He is the master of ceremonies for most of the book's fun and mayhem. He has built up a real charm out of a supercilious manner. He has his own moral compass, and although his north is nowhere near Jenny's, these two are in a way meant for each other. He knows enough not to make an unwelcome proposition, and he knows not to let his desire for a woman run away with his better judgment. He is the prototype of the man who might respect women's virtue, at least in the woman he meant to marry, without being pathetic. As such, he is something of a missing link for the novel, considered a dying breed. At the time of the novel, he is simply not disposed to be married and he and Jenny quickly establish a solid understanding. He and Jenny may be friends, and she gets some of the benefit of his natural chivalry, but their relations end there.

Fritz Monsma

THE TAKEOVER

Author: Muriel Spark (1918-   )
Type of work: Novel
Time of action: 1973-1976
First published: 1976

Maggie Radcliffe, the Marchesa Tullio-Friole (tōō′lē·ō frē·ō′lā), a wealthy American. Charming and egocentric, in her forties, Maggie draws to her a dissolute circle who find her great wealth and her prodigality equally attractive. Exhibiting a frivolous, fickle, and careless temperament, she seems to those around her an easy prey to various criminal schemes. She is, however, relentless in pursuit of those who attempt to bilk her of her fortune and ruthless in meting out her sense of justice against them. Having been deceived into believing that she is the owner of the sacred wood and sanctuary of Diana of Nemi (Nā′mē), she subsequently finds herself dispossessed by a former companion who, having been lent the use of the house, now lays claim to it as a gift. The expulsion of her unwelcome tenant and the pursuit of her unscrupulous business manager, Coco de Renault, who has absconded with her fortune, send her into protracted litigation, and through the financial centers of Europe hunting the elusive confidence man. She plans and has executed a wild kidnapping and ransom scheme to restore all of her money and her rights. Like her ancient predecessor, the goddess of fertility and the hunt, Maggie shows both aspects of Diana in modern society as she seeks to claim what is hers.

Berto, Maggie's devoted and elderly husband. As a descendant of an ancient Italian family, his own vast wealth encourages a predisposition to security. He, consequently, spends much of his time installing electronic alarms, hiring and maintaining guards, and providing impregnable defenses to his various properties. Although somewhat dismayed by his wife's unpredictability, he nevertheless indulges and supports her unflinchingly.

Hubert Mallindaine, an Englishman and a former companion of Maggie, a tenant of one of her houses. A handsome man of forty-five, his charisma and personal appearance draw both men and women to him. He is a charlatan and a thief. An eccentric, he has half-convinced himself, on spurious evidence, that he is the descendant of the goddess Diana and the Roman emperor Caligula, whose ritual marriage took place, according to legend, at Nemi. His imposture as King-of-the-Wood in a quasi-religious cult would deny Maggie, his benefactress, her ownership of the site and make his ownership a claim by divine right. He has also been systematically looting her house by replacing her antique furniture and furnishings with fakes.

Pauline Thin, secretary to Hubert Mallindaine. She is attracted to her employer but is brought to a realization that his sexual preference will not admit a more intimate relationship. She assumes a self-appointed prominence in the pagan cult that Hubert has founded. Despite her name, she is plump, with a flair for the dramatic in dress that ill suits her figure and face. She sees herself as chic and fashionable.

Lauro Moretti, a houseboy, first to Hubert Mallindaine and then to Maggie. He later, through polite blackmail, achieves the status of secretary to her. A handsome, graceful opportunist, he deserts a pregnant servant girl, Agata, to marry a middle-class salesgirl in a Roman boutique. Betty, his wife, provides him, also, with a claim to the properties of Nemi and the distinction to which he aspires.

Michael Radcliffe, Maggie's son. Although recently married, he spends much of his time in Rome with a mistress, leaving his wife to her own devices and pleasures.

Mary Radcliffe, Michael's wife. California-born, she is striking, with long blonde hair. A certain puritanical sense of orderliness and propriety is evident in her continual keeping of lists. At the top of her list is her duty to succeed in marriage, as did her sister. After a sexual encounter with Lauro, this goal becomes somewhat obscured in her mind.

Dr. Emilio Bernadini, a business lawyer and a tenant of Maggie who introduces her to Coco de Renault. He is sophisticated, fashionably slim, and graceful. His glasses lend a scholarly distinction and seriousness to his pale face.

Letizia Bernadini, the eighteen-year-old daughter of Emilio Bernadini. She is full of teenage idealism and good works. She is also a nationalist and a collector of supposed injustices. She enjoys rehabilitating drug addicts and proclaiming Italy for the Italians. Athletic and large of frame, she is also overpowering in her opinions.

Pietro Bernadini, the twenty-year-old son of Emilio Bernadini. He is dark-eyed, with delicate, aristocratic features. His great goal is to become a film star, and he travels with the film set whenever he can.

Maureen W. Mills

TALLEY'S FOLLY

Author: Lanford Wilson (1937-   )
Type of work: Play
Time of action: July 4, 1944
First produced: 1979

Matt Friedman, a forty-two-year-old Jewish accountant from St. Louis. A tall, commanding figure with great warmth and honesty, Matt fell in love with Sally the year before, when he met her during a vacation in her small hometown of Lebanon, Missouri. After having written to her daily for a year and receiving no response, he has returned to her home to face her and ask her to marry him. Matt is not, by his own admission, the romantic type; he is a loner, a European immigrant whose loss of his family in prewar Europe has left him isolated and rootless. He has a strong propensity for mimicry and wit, and he uses these often as a defense mechanism to ward off pain, a talent he adopted in having to assuage the painful memories of his childhood. Undaunted by Sally's rejection and demands that he return home, Matt knows that Sally cares for him and refuses to leave until he can reveal a secret about himself that will affect her marriage decision. With great difficulty, he recounts his life, in the guise of a hypothetical story, detailing the murder of his parents and sister in Europe and his arrival in America. He concludes with revealing the effect that his losses have made on his life: his secret "resolve . . . never to be responsible for bringing into such a world another living soul." He believes that no woman would want a husband who refused to father children, but when Sally finally admits the secret to her life, the secret behind her loneliness and pain, these two displaced and isolated people finally make contact and find love and acceptance.

Sally Talley, a thirty-one-year-old nurse. Born to a wealthy capitalist family, Sally is the outcast, rejected not only because of her socialist beliefs but also because her infertility, brought on by an illness a decade ago, prevented her marriage into another wealthy Lebanon family, a marriage that would have increased her family's fortune during the lean years of the Depression. Sally hates her home life and is eager to move, but, because she believes that her only worth as a woman is her ability to procreate, she has decided never to marry and is content to live her life as a spinster. For this reason, coupled with her low self-esteem, which has been nurtured by her family's ostracism of her, she has sentenced herself to loneliness and, despite her attraction to Matt, discourages his romantic pursuit of her. Acutely sensitive to her infertility, which she deems synonymous with womanhood, Sally flies into a rage when Matt admits his unwillingness to father children, believing his confession to be a mere fabrication in order to manipulate her into marrying him. Outraged at his seemingly patronizing gesture, she rejects him outright and forcefully for the first time. As Matt pursues the reason for her irrational anger, insisting that his secret resolution is true, Sally eventually believes him and finally, in a most stirring and pathetic moment, lets down her guard and admits her secret: her infertility and the isolation and loneliness it has brought her.

B. A. Kachur

TANGO

Author: Sławomir Mrożek (1930-   )
Type of work: Play
Time of action: The mid-twentieth century
First produced: 1965 (English translation, 1968)

Arthur, age twenty-five, neat, handsome, dressed until the last act in a freshly pressed suit, white shirt, and tie, a counterrevolutionary idealist. He rebels against what he considers his family's (and society's) liberalism, ethical relativism, slack permissiveness, disorder, and all-around anarchic individualism. Disgusted by what he regards as their immoral refusal to follow firm rules of conduct, he seeks to map out an orderly and respectable way of life, regulated by old-fashioned ceremonies and submission to absolute principles. He persuades his cousin Ala to marry him rather than simply sleep with him and forces his family, by the beginning of act 3, into ill-fitting, outdated, moth-eaten formal clothes for the wedding. Yet he comes to realize that the old order cannot be reestablished at the point of his pistol. When Ala nonchalantly informs him that she had sex with the servant, Eddie, the morning before the marriage vows are to be exchanged, he breaks down into tears and becomes easy prey for Eddie, who kills him.

Eddie, the family's muscular, sensual, anti-intellectual servant. He is crude, unshaven, slovenly, and sports a small, square mustache. His card playing with Eugene and Eugenia annoys Arthur, but it is his affair with Eleanor that deeply outrages Arthur, who urgently attempts to have his father shoot his mother's lover. When a disillusioned, drunken Arthur raves about the glory of omnipotent power in the final act, Eddie takes him at his word and tries to murder Arthur's uncle Eugene. Ala's declaration of her infidelity causes Arthur to seek Eddie's death. It is the latter, however, who is armed and uses his revolver to stun Arthur, before murdering him with a savage hand blow. Eddie then assumes despotic dominion over the family. The play ends with Eddie dancing all the steps of the tango, "La Cumparsita," with old Eugene.

Stomil, Arthur's father, described as "a large, corpulent man with gray hair like a lion's mane." He prefers to wear pajamas that are unbuttoned, thereby angering his son. Stomil is an aesthetic nonconformist who devotes himself to impractical, avant-garde artistic experiments. When Arthur adjures his father to murder Eddie for having made him a cuckold, Stomil repeatedly refuses to make a tragedy out of what he regards as a farce and ends up playing cards with Eddie instead. In act 3, the disillusioned son begs Stomil's forgiveness: "[T]here's no turning back to the old forms. They can't create a reality for us. I was wrong." After Arthur's death, Stomil does forgive him in a generous eulogy.

Eleanor, the middle-aged mother of Arthur and wife of Stomil. She retains a good figure and is casually open about her affair with Eddie. He delights her by lacking complexes, scruples, or any other sort of sophistication, by what she considers his naturalness and authenticity.

Ala, Arthur's eighteen-year-old cousin. She is pretty, long-haired, flirtatious, and bored by Arthur's long-winded speeches about convention and formal principles. When the dying Arthur tells her that he loved her, she asks him why he had not revealed his heart to her earlier, instead of using her as an audience for his pronouncements.

Eugene, a polite, old ex-officer, Arthur's greatuncle, who is opportunistic enough to accommodate himself to whatever order, or disorder, governs the family. He is impressed by Arthur's purposefulness and becomes his willing lieutenant when Arthur attempts his return to nineteenth century formalism. When Eddie takes power in the play's final minutes, he orders Eugene to take off his, Eddie's, shoes. Eugene obeys this new regime slavishly.

Eugenia, Arthur's grandmother, lively, irreverent, playful, and indifferent to the philosophic debates that volley in the family. In the opening scene, Arthur insists that she lie on her late husband's catafalque. In the last act, she willingly climbs up on it and dies, thereby upsetting no one but Stomil.

Gerhard Brand

THE TARTAR STEPPE

Author: Dino Buzzati (Dino Buzzati Traverso, 1906-1972)
Type of work: Novel
Time of action: The late nineteenth or early twentieth century
First published: Il deserto dei Tartari, 1940 (English translation, 1952)

Giovanni Drogo, a newly commissioned officer posted to Fort Bastiani. Very young when he is first sent to Fort Bastiani, Drogo is sad at leaving the exciting life of the town for the isolated and gloomy fort. Perhaps because of his melancholy and introspective nature, Drogo is self-conscious about every gesture that he makes. As his time at the fort stretches on and on, Drogo loses all contact with the world outside the fort. Like Captain Ortiz, Drogo allows his life to be spent in hope, waiting in vain for the glorious war that seems never to arrive. When it finally does, Drogo is sent away from the fort before the action starts because he is ill. Even though Drogo (now a major) is second in command, he is powerless to prevent his commanding officer, Simeoni, from ignoring his pleas.

Francesco Vescovi, a childhood friend of Drogo. Vescovi has chosen the opposite path to Drogo. Drogo has become an officer; Vescovi has stayed in the "easy elegant life" in town, getting fatter as the years go by, in marked contrast to Drogo's bony frame by the end of the novel. It is Francesco's sister Maria to whom Drogo is unofficially engaged. As the years pass, Drogo drifts apart from both Francesco and Maria.

Captain Ortiz, a soldier (later a lieutenant colonel) whom Drogo meets on his first trip to the fort. A man of about forty when he first appears in the novel, Ortiz has a "thin, aristocratic face." He stays at Fort Bastiani his entire career, waiting for war and only leaving when he is forced to retire because of his age.

Angustina, a lieutenant who is Drogo's friend. Angustina is a pale, sickly man whose pride and arrogance are seen as positive reflections of his strength of character. Though he is described by Buzzati as having a "usual expression of detachment and boredom," Angustina differs from Drogo in that he stays at Fort Bastiani out of pride, rather than be-cause staying is a habit that has become impossible to break. Angustina dies a heroic death, which inspires Drogo when it is his turn to die.

Simeoni, another lieutenant at Fort Bastiani. It is Simeoni who first spots the approaching invaders building their road. He relinquishes his telescope and theories easily, however, when they threaten his career. Though he professes to be Drogo's friend, Simeoni sends Drogo away just when it looks as if the long-awaited war will become a reality and justify Drogo's thirty-year wait.

T. M. Lipman

A TASTE OF HONEY

Author: Shelagh Delaney (1939-   )
Type of work: Play
Time of action: The late 1950's
First produced: 1958

Josephine (Jo), about sixteen, in high school but preparing to drop out, attractive but without the instinctive sexuality of her mother, with whom she lives in squalor in the tenement slums of Manchester, England. The illegitimate daughter of (according to her mother) a retarded man, Jo is self-contained, more mature than her years, with an acerbic wit that more than matches her mother's hardness, and with some signs of artistic talent. Unable to concentrate on her possibilities because of the transient nature of her upbringing, she tries to avoid succumbing to her mother's life-style. She seeks affection in a brief affair with a black sailor, who leaves her pregnant. Fearing that her own father's idiocy will be passed on to the child, she lives through her pregnancy dreading motherhood, cared for only by a homosexual friend.

Helen, Josephine's mother, a "semi-whore" in her mid- to late thirties but looking younger. Harsh, independent, bruised by life's experiences but capable of sustaining herself, a constant and serious drinker, she lives off a series of male friends, moving from place to place to flee more complex relationships, dragging Jo with her from slum to slum. Her motherly instincts are confined to unemotional retreats from real contact, coupled with loud, sarcastic, scourging reprimands laced with indifference and self-indulgence, only occasionally alleviated by real but inarticulate concern. In her mind there are no moral reservations about her way of life; it is a matter of survival. At her first opportunity she marries a fairly affluent car salesman, leaving her daughter behind to fend for herself, as she has had to do. Only after he throws her out does she return to help her daughter give birth.

Peter Smith, a successful car salesman, a heavy drinker who is younger than Helen, his lover. When he makes his offer of marriage to her, it is with the understanding that she will desert her daughter, a source of shame to him. Flippant and disdainful when drunk, wearing a patch over one eye, he becomes vicious and dangerous when approaching sobriety (a state that he never reaches).

In his hatred for Jo, which stems partly from repressed sexual attraction to her and partly from jealousy of the mother-daughter bond, he twice forces Helen to choose him over her daughter.

The Boy, "a colored naval rating," Jo's boyfriend, who calls himself "the lascivious Moor," young and handsome, romantic, caring. He has a poetic nature and an unrealistic impression of their chances. On leave at Christmas, he courts Jo by carrying her books from school, offering her a Woolworth engagement ring, kissing her hand, quoting Shakespeare and reciting nursery rhymes: giving her the attention her mother never did.

He dances with her, sings to her, and leaves her pregnant after the Christmas fair.

Geoffrey Ingram, a young, effeminate boy whom Jo, several months pregnant, has picked up and brought home, calling him "a big sister." Sensitive and loving without making any sexual demands, organized, a calming influence on Jo, he moves in and stays with her for the final months of her pregnancy, cooking, cleaning, and preparing to assist in the delivery itself. He leaves reluctantly when Helen returns for the actual birth, not because he is offended by her insults, but because Jo, repeating the patterns of her mother, insulates herself against all men and lets him go.

Thomas J. Taylor

TEA AND SYMPATHY

Author: Robert Anderson (1917-   )
Type of work: Play
Time of action: A few days in early June in the 1950's
First produced: 1953

Laura Reynolds, a young woman in her mid-to late twenties. She has been married for less than a year to Bill Reynolds. Sensitive and compassionate, she is trying to adjust to life at the boys' school where her husband teaches, but she is not one for vigorous outdoor activity or small-minded gossip, both of which seem to be prerequisites for acceptance there. She is also worried by what she perceives as Bill's growing distance from her— physical as well as emotional distance. She is generally cheerful, however, and carries an air of maturity and wisdom about her. When she takes steps to protest an injustice done to Tom Lee, one of the students, she does so thoughtfully and decisively, without histrionics.

Tom Lee, one of the boys living in the house of which Bill Reynolds is housemaster. Almost eighteen years old, midway between boy and man, he is in love with Laura without fully realizing it. Laura, in turn, is touched by Tom's intensity, especially because he reminds her of her first husband, now deceased. The son of divorced parents, reared by a father who does not understand him and scorned by classmates who do not respect him, Tom is very lonely and very sensitive. He spends afternoons listening to his phonograph and playing the guitar. He plans on becoming a folk singer. Although he is the school's tennis champion, that show of athletic prowess fails to help him fit in: He is criticized for winning on technique and control rather than power and strength. Naïve and innocent, Tom has trouble at first understanding why a scandal has erupted over the afternoon he spent sunbathing nude with one of his favorite teachers.

Bill Reynolds, Laura's husband and a teacher at the school. He is large and strong, about forty years old. He has a tendency to be gruff. It is difficult for him to admit any weaknesses of character, although it was his honesty during an unguarded moment that attracted Laura to him originally. He claims that he was like Tom as a boy, seeking solace for his loneliness in music, but was able to pull himself together to become the outdoorsy man he is today. When Tom is swept up in scandal, Bill worries not about Tom but about how it will reflect upon his friendship with Tom's father and his chances of becoming headmaster one day.

Herbert (Herb) Lee, Tom's divorced father and a Boston businessman. He took custody of Tom to ensure that Tom grew up to become a "regular guy." Extroverted and deeply concerned over appearances, he has no rapport with Tom and is extremely critical of him. Herb confides his concerns to Bill Reynolds, who is an old friend.

Al Thompson, Tom's roommate and captain-elect of the baseball team. A big, brawny athlete and one of the popular guys on campus, Al is everything that Bill and Herb would like Tom to be. Al is also kind and caring, and Tom considers him his closest friend. Al is able to stand up to his peers when they urge him not to room with Tom the next year, but when his father calls with the same advice, Al feels compelled to switch houses.

David Harris, a good-looking young teacher who is kind to Tom. The dean suspects him of homosexual tendencies and informs him that he will not be reappointed for the next year because he was seen sunbathing nude with Tom.

Lilly Sears, a faculty wife in her late thirties. Flashy, almost gaudy, she is entertained by the crushes she engenders among the boys. She takes Laura as her confidante.

Liz Marshall

THE TEAHOUSE OF THE AUGUST MOON

Author: John Patrick (John Patrick Goggan, 1905-   )
Type of work: Play
Time of action: The late 1940's
First produced: 1953

Sakini, a middle-aged Okinawan interpreter for U.S. occupation forces following World War II. His skillful use of native Okinawan customs, oriental folk wisdom, parody of Western ways, naïveté, and the like reveal his perceptions of the American. Sakini effectively bridges cross-cultural barriers.

Colonel Purdy, a stout U.S. Army officer assigned to democratize Okinawa following World War II. He is a single-minded individual who follows orders without question. He has rules and signs for the most trivial of situations; when alone, however, Purdy reads *Adventure Magazine* on work time. Outwardly he guards his reputation, especially because of what his wife might say, but he is not above reversing orders to suit the whims of his superiors.

Captain Fisby, a U.S. Army officer in his late twenties, assigned as aide to Colonel Purdy. Although he had been an associate professor of humanities, he is regarded as a misfit in military matters. Sakini constantly manipulates him into making all sorts of compromises and changes. Gradually, Fisby becomes so acculturated that he disobeys virtually every order that he is given, but in so doing he succeeds in making Tobiki a model village. His role demonstrates that a system is only a framework within which ideal and reality may differ.

Lotus Blossom, a beautiful, petite Okinawan geisha girl. She has difficulty performing her duties as a geisha since Captain Fisby, to whom she has been given, is ignorant of the true role of the well-trained geisha and assumes her to be a prostitute.

Captain McLean, a psychiatrist in the U.S.

1519

Army. He is short and rather fat. His assignment is to make a psychological report on Captain Fisby, whose assimilation of the native ways is interpreted as a sign of mental imbalance. While he is working with Fisby, he is won over by Fisby and his cultural insights.

Sergeant Gregovich, a U.S. Army enlisted man, aide to Colonel Purdy. He goes through the motions of appearing to be efficient.

Old Woman, an Okinawan villager and grandmother of Tobiki's mayor, who rides, over protest, atop a loaded wagon that conveys Captain Fisby to his Tobiki assignment. Not to allow her to ride would make the mayor lose face; thus, she outmaneuvers those in command.

Old Woman's daughter, an Okinawan villager who, along with her three children, rides on the wagon to Tobiki.

Mr. Hokaida, a villager of Tobiki. A stout man in tattered peasant clothes, he presents Captain Fisby with a cricket cage when he arrives in Tobiki.

Mr. Omura, a villager of Tobiki. He welcomes Captain Fisby to Tobiki with chopsticks. He wears a white coat to distinguish himself from the rest of the villagers.

Mr. Sumata, a skilled carpenter in Tobiki. He brings Captain Fisby a geisha girl as a gift, providing a chance to see how cross-cultural misunderstanding can strain relationships.

Mr. Sumata's father, a skilled Tobikian carpenter. He helps to build the five-sided school/teahouse, highlighting the oriental custom of passing on skills from one generation to the next.

Mr. Seiko, a Tobiki villager. He gives Captain Fisby geta, a kind of wooden sandals, when the officer arrives in Tobiki.

Miss Higa Jiga, an Okinawan villager chosen to be the president of a Ladies' League for Democratic Action. A chunky, flat-faced young woman, unmarried, who wears heavy glasses, she makes amusing demands of Fisby in the name of democracy. Thus the Americans see how democracy is perceived by foreigners unaccustomed to the system.

Mr. Keora, an Okinawan villager. He is one of several who are dejected when they cannot sell Okinawan crafts to the U.S. Army personnel because they regard the handcrafted items as inferior to what American technology could produce at lower cost and of lower quality.

Mr. Oshira, an Okinawan villager. A skilled artisan, he cannot sell his lacquer wear cups to soldiers who do not appreciate the time and skill that have gone into making them. He feels that the August moon at the end of summer, the peak between spring, the growing season, and fall, when nature sheds its foliage, symbolizes the maturity and wisdom that the two cultures have attained.

Major McEvoy, a U.S. Army officer. He is to be Captain Fisby's replacement.

Lady Astor, Miss Higa Jiga's goat. If the goat can drink homemade sweet potato brandy without harm, the men will drink it.

Victoria Price

TELL ME THAT YOU LOVE ME, JUNIE MOON

Author: Marjorie Kellogg (1922-   )
Type of work: Novel
Time of action: The 1960's
First published: 1968

Junie Moon, a young woman with her face and hands severely disfigured from having acid poured on her by a sexually disturbed assailant. Although her maimed face masks her emotions and her occasional biting words hide her sensitivity, she is the emotional center for the three disabled friends who leave the hospital to set up housekeeping in a run-down shack. Repulsed by the sight of her own face, she nevertheless is sexually attractive to Arthur, with whom she falls in love and has a brief affair before his death, and Mario, with whom she and Warren live after Arthur's death.

Arthur, a young man with an undiagnosed, progressive neurological disease. Walking with a lurching gait and waving his hands wildly around his face, he disguises his feelings by his nervous tics, yet his expressive eyes reveal his deep sensitivity. Deserted by his parents at a state school for the feebleminded, he runs away after being humiliated by Ramona, a cook he loves. He works for a time as a Western Union messenger and later is the only one of the three friends to look for a job. Rejected by the fishmonger Mario as a sexual pervert, he disappears to the woods before returning to his friends in a weakened state with a pet dog. On a vacation to the beach, he confesses his love for Junie Moon, has a brief affair with her, then dies in her arms when they return home.

Warren, the paraplegic who has the idea and makes the arrangements for the three friends to live together. Abandoned by his mother at birth, he lived with Guiles, a young man who was hit by a delivery truck and killed when Warren is seven years old. For the rest of his life he searches for a man who will love and care for him, thus assuming the role of Guiles. He became a paraplegic at age seventeen, when he was shot in the back by Melvin Coffee in a hunting "accident" after confessing his love for his friend.

Mario, the owner of a fish store who befriends Junie Moon, then the two men. Not repulsed by disfigurement because his grandmother had been seriously burned by hot soup, he helps Junie Moon search for the missing Arthur after making the mistake of not hiring him because of the malicious gossip of a neighbor. He provides a truck and money for the three friends to go on vacation when he realizes that Arthur will soon die, and he later shares his home with Warren, Junie Moon, and Arthur's dog.

Minnie, a fifty-two-year-old roommate of Junie Moon whose greatest desire, to be taken from the hospital to live with the three friends, is fulfilled when a sympathetic resident arranges for an ambulance to take her to their home, then picks her up himself later in the afternoon.

Sidney Wyner, a nosy neighbor who spies on the three friends and calls Mario to tell him that Arthur is a sodomist.

Gregory, a wealthy, voyeuristic woman who takes the three friends to her home and tries to convince Warren that he can walk.

Beach Boy, an employee of the resort hotel Patty's Hideaway, who pampers rich people and temporarily takes the place of Guiles in Warren's mind.

Binnie Farber, a sympathetic social worker who helps the three friends obtain welfare money to enable them to live in their own home.

Miss Oxford, a straight-laced head nurse who jealously believes that sex is at the heart of the friends' plan to live together.

Donna Maples

THE TEMPLE OF THE GOLDEN PAVILION

Author: Yukio Mishima (Kimitake Hiraoka, 1925-1970)
Type of work: Novel
Time of action: The early 1940's through July 2, 1950
First published: Kinkakuji, 1956 (English translation, 1959)

Mizoguchi, a young Zen acolyte at the Temple of the Golden Pavilion and student at Otani University. From a poverty-stricken background, he is a physically frail only child, and he recognizes early that he is ugly and that his speech impediment (a stutter) locks him away from easy communication with the rest of the world. Alienated and isolated, he lives virtually in an inner world, stubbornly proud that no one understands him. From his youth, he is obsessed with the beauty of the Golden Temple. At age twenty-one, in order to become free of that obsession, he sets fire to the beautiful Zen temple, a revered architectural wonder more than five hundred years old.

Kashiwagi, a clubfooted student at Otani University. Misanthropic and selfish, he uses his disability to take advantage of other people's feelings and to promote his own selfish desires. A negative influence, Kashiwagi counsels Mizoguchi to be more active in life, but in a selfish, nihilistic manner. By reporting to Father Dosen that Mizoguchi failed to repay a personal loan, Kashiwagi nearly gets Mizoguchi expelled from the temple.

Tsurukawa, a Zen acolyte at the Golden Temple and student at Otani University. Seemingly cheerful and gentle, he comes from the suburbs of Tokyo, the son of affluent parents. He befriends Mizoguchi, urging him to break out of his quiet isolation. When the two acolytes begin to matriculate at Otani University, their relationship falters. Tsurukawa's death, at first reported as an accident, later is revealed as a probable suicide caused by an unhappy love affair. Letters written by Tsurukawa shortly before his death also call into question his previous seemingly cheerful disposition.

Father Tayama Dosen, a friend of Mizoguchi's father in their seminary days and currently Superior of the Temple of the Golden Pavilion. A plump man, he devotes his free time to various satisfactions of the flesh. Although on the surface a fair and impartial Superior, Father Dosen shows no feelings for Mizoguchi all the time he acts as his mentor. He provides the tuition that allows Mizoguchi to attend Otani University, but after Mizoguchi falters in his studies and increasingly becomes more undisciplined at the temple, Father Dosen tells Mizoguchi that he has lost his opportunity to become the Superior's successor at the temple.

Uiko, a volunteer nurse at a Naval Hospital. This proud young woman from a wealthy family attracts the young Mizoguchi. After she tells her parents of Mizoguchi's watching for her as she bicycles to work at dawn, Mizoguchi wishes for her death, thinking that would end his embarrassment. A few months later Uiko dies when a Navy deserter, whom she had been secretly aiding, shoots her when she leads the military police to his hiding place. After her death, Mizoguchi continues to be preoccupied with her memory, and he often thinks of her when he comes into contact with other women.

Mizoguchi's father, an impoverished country priest. Knowing that he will soon die from tuberculosis, he takes his adolescent son to see the Temple of the Golden Pavilion, to the father a structure of limitless beauty, and to place him under the protection of Father Tayama Dosen.

Mizoguchi's mother, a shabby, impoverished wife, then widow. Her ambition is to see her son as the Superior of the Golden Temple; she berates Mizoguchi for being undutiful while an acolyte at the temple.

Father Kuwai Zenkai, a Zen priest, the head of Ryoko Temple. Strong and healthy in appearance and character, he serves as a contrast to his two friends from seminary days—Mizoguchi's father and Father Dosen. Father Zenkai is candid when he talks to Mizoguchi a few hours before the temple burns, and Mizoguchi yearns for this priest to understand him.

Mariko, a prostitute. A few years older than Mizoguchi, she warns him that he should not frequent the brothel too often.

Marion Boyle

TEMPTATION

Author: Václav Havel (1936-   )
Type of work: Play
Time of action: The 1980's
First produced: 1986

Dr. Henry Foustka, a scientist employed by the scientific research facility called the Institute but who is secretly exploring the occult, burning candles and reciting incantations alone in his study. A Faust figure exploring the possibility that science itself is the worship of the devil, Foustka reluctantly employs the services of Fistula, which are essentially the arguments by which Foustka realizes his own beliefs. He is damned by Fistula's accusations and disappears in clouds of smoke.

Fistula, an invalid in retirement, sinister and philosophical, who is prone to visiting Foustka unannounced. The Mephistopheles character, he second-guesses Foustka, causing him to make admissions that he does not actually believe, then betrays him to the Director, for whom he has been acting as agent provocateur.

The Director, head of the Institute, in constant need of support staff and yes-men, strangely attracted to Foustka until his offer of intimate friendship is rebuffed. Both in his position as the head of the Institute and in his duplicity toward Foustka, he is the embodiment of evil, despite his superficial concern for others and his quiet, self-deprecating attitude.

Vilma, a scientist, Foustka's lover, addicted to elaborately staged role-playing scenarios in her love life and accused by Foustka of being responsible for his exposure to the Director. She loses her respect for Foustka when he lies his way out of trouble. Eventually she acts out what Foustka has always believed to be one her fantasies, taking up with a dancer who brings her violets every night.

The Deputy Director, oily and hypocritical. On the surface the spokesman for the Director, who actually despises him, the Deputy Director acts as facilitator for the Institute. He is always seen with a silent girl, Petruska, who holds his hand at all times, except when she sneaks off to be unfaithful to him with other scientists.

Maggie, a secretary, young and attractive, completely taken in by Foustka's rhetoric. She falls in love with him, believing him to be a clearheaded defender of the world against the devil, and willingly sacrifices herself in his defense when he is condemned by the Director. She goes mad when the Director takes away her job for supporting Foustka.

Lorencova,
Kotrly, and
Neuwirth, scientists, the staff for the Institute's work, and romantically involved in various combinations. They act as the jury during Foustka's "trial" and attend two parties hosted by the Institute.

Mrs. Houbova, Foustka's elderly landlady. Representing the naïve but unpretentious real world, she is sane and protective of Foustka, with natural instincts of repulsion toward Fistula.

Thomas J. Taylor

TEN NORTH FREDERICK

Author: John O'Hara (1905-1970)
Type of work: Novel
Time of action: 1945, with flashbacks to the late nineteenth through mid-twentieth centuries
First published: 1955

Joseph Benjamin (Joe) Chapin, a right-minded snob, born into one of the wealthiest and most socially prominent families of Gibbsville, Pennsylvania. An only child dominated by his mother, Charlotte, who has become cold to his father after two miscarriages, Joe has a strong sense of his place in Gibbsville and returns there after attending Yale. With his closest friend, Arthur McHenry, he builds a law practice and establishes a reputation for propriety and discretion. Haunted by the death of Marie Harrison, with whom he had a brief affair while in college and who later died in the abortion of another man's child, he carries on an emotionally intense but sexually restrained courtship of Edith Stokes, whose family has an equal prominence in Gibbsville. Following his marriage to Edith, Joe is particularly fond of their daughter, Ann. He feels diminished, however, when he misses the experience of serving with the military in World War I. He eventually decides to pursue a career in politics, but he is devastated when he learns that he will not get, and never had a real chance at getting, the nomination for lieutenant governor. This revelation, combined with his increasing sense of his wife's selfishness and of their failures with their children, leads him to become an alcoholic, and he eventually dies of cirrhosis.

Edith Stokes Chapin, the wife of Joe Chapin. Her reserved personality has caused her to be an enigma to almost everyone in Gibbsville. She is actually a very cold person who makes it her purpose in life to "own" her husband emotionally. Jealous of her husband's affection for their daughter and essentially disinterested in their son, she becomes increasingly embittered by the realization that aspects of her husband's life are beyond her control. Physically a very plain woman, she has a very Machiavellian attitude toward sex that is apparent in her lesbian affair with Barbara Dantworth, a schoolmate in board-ing school, and in her adulterous affair with Lloyd Williams, a brash lawyer who eventually becomes District Attorney of Lantenengo County.

Ann Chapin, the beautiful and precocious daughter of Joe and Edith Chapin. She elopes with Charley Bongiorno, a jazz musician, and is permanently scarred when her parents force her to accept an annulment and an abortion. She moves to New York City, works in various offices, and has casual affairs with a number of men until she becomes frightened by her promiscuity. At the time of her father's death, she is living at home, having obtained a separation from her second husband, who is referred to only as Mr. Musgrove.

Joseph (Joby) Chapin, Jr., Edith and Joe's son, a cynic on the verge of becoming an alcoholic. He works with the office of Strategic Services in Arlington, Virginia. In his adolescence, he compensated for his lack of purpose by playing piano with jazz bands. His knowledge of his mother's affair with Lloyd Williams, of the abortion forced on his sister, and of his mother's willingness to let his father die of alcoholism has permanently disillusioned him.

Mike Slattery, a shrewd politician who has extended his influence far beyond his base as a state senator. Proud of his family and of his Irish ancestry, he views Joe Chapin as a political amateur. Unlike Joe, he is happily married and confides in his wife, trusting her instincts on political matters. He initially encourages Joe's political ambitions, but he is too much the pragmatist to compromise his own influence for the sake of those ambitions.

Arthur McHenry, a man influenced on all sides to be the closest friend and law partner of Joe Chapin. He is level-headed and unassuming, a loyal confidant. He probably understands Joe better than anyone. His first wife dies of cancer, but, with Joe's insistent encouragement, he rediscovers contentment married to her sister.

Martin Kich

THE TENNIS PLAYERS

Author: Lars Gustafsson (1936-   )
Type of work: Novel
Time of action: 1974
First published: Tennisspelarna, 1977 (English translation, 1983)

Lars Gustafsson (lärz gŭs•täf′shŭn), a visiting professor of Scandinavian literature at the University of Texas. Sharing, not coincidentally, both the author's name and profession, the professor reveals that he is glad to have escaped his native Sweden in order to divide his time between playing tennis in the hot Texas sun and delivering popular lectures at the University in Austin. Unfortunately, Gustafsson's indolent existence is threatened by the problems presented by two graduate students.

Doobie Smith, the professor's favorite student, an expert on nineteenth century European philosophers. Blonde, blue-eyed, and sensuously plump, Doobie reminds the professor of Friedrich Nietzsche's beloved Lou Salomé. Theoretically a committed Nietzschean, Doobie reverts to her fundamentalist Baptist roots when she discovers that her role as one of the Rhine Maidens in the student production of Richard Wagner's *Das Rheingold* is jeopardized by her refusal to sleep with the conductor. Outraged, Doobie enlists Professor Gustafsson's help in defending her honor.

Bill, a graduate student who has unearthed from the university library a book by Zygmunt I. Pietziewzskoczsky, an obscure Polish writer whose book, *Mémoires d'un chimiste*, if authenticated, will force a reevaluation of August Strindberg's *Inferno*. Tall, black, and intense, Bill disrupts the professor's graduate seminar when he theorizes that Strindberg's

so-called Inferno Crisis is not a product of the author's mad delusions, as Strindberg experts maintain, but stems from a real conspiracy of Polish exiles who were trying to find out the results of Strindberg's chemical experiments.

Chris, a nearsighted computer genius who works part time at the Strategic Air Command near Fort Worth. Having met Gustafsson on the tennis court, Chris invites the professor to his lodgings to drink beer and to meet the psychiatrist under whose care he has been since his nervous breakdown two years before. When Chris learns of Professor Gustafsson's Strindberg problem, he offers to employ the Strategic Air Command's unused memory to collate *Inferno* and *Mémoires d'un chimiste* in order to test whether there is in fact sufficient correlation between the two books to justify an overhaul of Strindberg criticism. Before Chris can complete his task and remove the books from the computer, however, he is arrested during a campus demonstration and fired from his post. As a result, the *Inferno* and the one known copy of *Mémoires d'un chimiste* are frozen in the Early Warning System's memory. At least the professor and other Strindberg authorities are saved from having to go to the trouble of reexamining accepted theories.

Abel, a superb tennis player who has won the Australian open once and reached the finals at Wimbledon twice but who prefers to play pick-up matches on public tennis courts.

From Abel, the professor learns to improve his serve and to refuse to allow the past to taint the present.

Mr. Hugh Frisco, chairman of the Board of Trustees for the University of Texas. Rich and accustomed to getting his own way, Senator Frisco convenes the board in order to fire the university's president for defying Frisco's order to replace Wagner's *Das Rheingold* with Giuseppe Verdi's *Aïda* as the spring concert.

Geoffrey Gore, an oil magnate and vice chairman of the Board of Trustees who sides with Frisco in wanting to fire the president.

Professor John R. Perturber, Jr., a former professor of forestry and the current president of the university. The last four university presidents having lasted less than one year apiece, the timid Perturber appears to be on his way out when he refuses to give in to the Board of Trustees on the matter of the Spring Concert.

Gordon Hugh Smith, a Travis County assistant sheriff who discovers Gore's black Cadillac parked in the middle of the university's baseball field. Smith, sad-faced and rather nondescript, achieves notoriety when he arrests Gore for drunken driving and Frisco for having sex with a waitress, the real scandal being that Frisco chooses for his liaison the batter's box, a spot traditionally reserved for the school's best batter to meet his girlfriend on the night before a big game. As a result of Smith's discovery, Gore and Frisco are fired from the board, President Perturber keeps his job, the Spring Opera goes on as planned, and Sheriff Smith becomes a local hero.

Sandra Hanby Harris

TENT OF MIRACLES

Author: Jorge Amado (1912-　　)
Type of work: Novel
Time of action: 1968-1969 and 1868-1943
First published: Tenda dos milagres, 1969 (English translation, 1971)

Pedro Archanjo (är•shän′zhō), a writer and self-taught anthropologist. A brilliant, light-brown, husky mulatto who loves good conversation, riotous celebration, women, and social justice, he earns his living as a runner at Bahia School of Medicine yet writes four insightful anthropological works about the beloved mulatto culture of his native Bahia. One highly controversial work traces the impurities in the aristocratic bloodlines, which infuriates the white supremacists. He is a font of virtue and humanity to the good, a thorn to the proud and hateful. His tremendous powers of observation and language earn for him the folk titles **Ojuobá** (ō•zhū•bä′) and **Eyes of Xangô** (shäng′ô), titles that imply the supernatural and magical. The 1868-1943 frame of the novel follows his fight against white supremacy, especially the promotion of miscegenation. The 1968-1969 frame relates the perverse whitewashing of his image when it becomes profitable to make the neglected writer a national hero.

Fausta Pena, a poet. The first-person narrator of the 1968-1969 frame, Fausta, with his beard, long hair, and blue jeans, prides himself on the nickname given him by the lady poets—**Wicked Cobra.** When Ana Mercedes betrays him, he experiences severe doubts about his masculinity, literary significance, and political integrity. Fausta accepts a commission from Levenson to research Archanjo's life, which forms the basis for the 1868-1943 frame, but he later realizes that the commission was merely a ruse to clear Levenson's access to Ana Mercedes.

Nilo d'Ávila Argolo de Araújo (ä•rou′zhō), professor of forensic medicine at the Bahia

School of Medicine. Tall, erect, with a spare, dry, black-clad frame and a forbidding voice and bearing, Argolo uses his considerable force of character to advance racial hatred. He persecutes Archanjo, inciting Archanjo's arrest and the destruction of the Tent of Miracles. His arrogant world falls to pieces when Archanjo's research reveals that Argolo is related to Archanjo.

Lídio Corró, miracle painter and printer. Fortyish, short and stocky, a shrewd keen-witted mulatto, Lídio is Archanjo's best friend and owner of the art and print shop called the Tent of Miracles, where Archanjo and his circle gather to celebrate and converse.

Ana Mercedes, a poetess, reporter, Pena's girlfriend. Golden and slender with slightly fleshy lips, greedy white teeth, and loose black hair, the mulatta Mercedes exudes sexiness and voluptuous insouciance. Mercedes seduces Pena into writing poems over her name, then betrays him for a prestigious affair with Levenson.

James D. Levenson, a scholar. Forty-five, more than six feet tall, with blond hair, sky-blue eyes, and a pipe, the famous North American Nobel Prize winner disrupts Bahia in 1968 by declaring that he has arrived to study the neglected writer Archanjo. Everyone suddenly clamors to become Archanjo's champion.

Rosa de Oxalá (ō·shä·lä′), Corró's mistress. With languid Yoruba eyes, blue-black skin that exudes a scent of the night, and her body shining with supple power, she laughs lustily while performing the most seductive dances of the celebrations. Archanjo will not consummate their passionate mutual love because of his loyalty to Corró.

Major Damião de Souza (dä·myouń′), a self-taught lawyer, Archanjo's friend. Always dressed in white, he keeps himself straight and slim as a ramrod with rum and sex. Smoking a cheap cigar, his mouth full of bad teeth, and waving his big knotty mulatto hands, his rough voice rolls out the most exquisite and winning rhetoric in the courtroom, but only in defense of the poor.

Tadeu Canhoto, a professional engineer, one of Archanjo's illegitimate sons. With a fine-featured, frank copper face, gleaming black hair, and dancing yet bashful eyes, he works brilliantly and diligently to succeed and thus gain the acceptance of the rich white family whose daughter he loves. His marriage to the daughter helps incite a six-year campaign of arrest and destruction by the secret police.

Pedrito Gordo, the chief of the secret police. Stoutish, middle-aged, and looking like a dandy, the cane-wielding bully wages brutal war against the mulatto element of Bahia.

Dr. Zèzinho Pinto (zä·zē′nyō), a newspaper publisher. A stolid, wordly man who thinks of nothing but selling newspapers, he spearheads and profits from the new acclamation of Archanjo, and instigates the white-washing of Archanjo's image.

Kirsi the Swede, one of Archanjo's mistresses. Actually a Finn, very blonde, white, and lovely, she happily returns to Finland to bear Archanjo a son.

Dr. Silva Virajá (vē·rä·zhä′), a professor. Good natured and honest, he is Archanjo's friend and mentor within the Bahia School of Medicine.

Professor Azevedo,
Professor Calazans, and
Professor Ramos, scholars. Truly interested in science, these scholars resist Pinto's misrepresentation of Archanjo's person and message.

Timothy C. Davis

THE TENTS OF WICKEDNESS

Author: Peter De Vries (1910-   )
Type of work: Novel
Time of action: The late 1950's
First published: 1959

Charles (Chick) Swallow, a fortyish columnist for the Decency, Connecticut, *Picayune Blade*, whose sympathic pen and ear win him more friends than he wants. His reinvolvement with a girlfriend from adolescence, Sweetie Appleyard, prompts him to apologize for his excessive conventionality, as opposed to her strained and theatrical feeling that she is special and needs special allowances made for her. He is just silly enough and she just barely reasonable enough that there is some plausibility to each case.

Crystal Swallow, Chick's wife and the mother of his three children. Crystal has a sense that she is trapped in a "chintz prison." She is a pre-Women's Liberation example of an educated woman who believes that her abilities are not being well used in her role as wife and mother, however urbane the setting.

Elizabeth (Sweetie) Appleyard, a childhood sweetheart of Chick described by her father as an Emily Dickinson without talent. Hers is a case of arrested development—sexually and otherwise—caused, her father thinks, because Chick's early attempted seduction of her was traumatically interrupted. After she has reentered Chick's life as a baby-sitter, her father asks Chick to complete the seduction mission. Chick fails, and she goes off to the Village to try to live like, if not be, a poet. Damning the bourgeois life, she asks Chick to father a child for her to rear, and temporarily fools him into thinking her pregnancy was caused by him. After being found out, she heads for the West Coast, marries a divorced man with two children, and moves to a Los Angeles suburb.

Charles Appleyard, Sweetie's father, a widower who marries in the course of the novel. A failure at almost everything he has attempted, he nevertheless had the good sense to inherit and invest money through his French connection—his wife's relatives—and thus is able to present himself as a sort of effete Adlai Stevenson. Probably he is the cause of his daughter's holier-than-thou attitude, and he certainly is the cause of her enrichment, since he dies a moment or so before Sweetie's grandmother (both in the same plane crash), thus enabling the fortune to proceed directly to his daughter and not to his newly acquired wife.

Nickie Sherman, Chick's boyhood friend and brother-in-law. Like Chick, Nickie is a failed boulevardier; unlike Chick, however, he has not gone on to find any meaningful work. He cannot come to terms with the ordinariness of life, and his marriage, partly as a result of this failure, is breaking up. After a schizophrenic episode triggered by Chick's well-meaning but ill-conceived intervention, Nickie is shocked back to normality and into responsibility.

Lila Sherman, Chick's intelligent, down-to-earth sister, Nickie's wife. As the mother of two children, she has lost patience with her husband's intellectual philandering, his unwillingness to let his life be "disrupted by routine." When he finally becomes reconciled to reality, however, she accepts him; their lives are normalized, and their marriage saved.

James H. Bowden

TERMS OF ENDEARMENT

Author: Larry McMurtry (1936-   )
Type of work: Novel
Time of action: The 1960's and 1970's
First published: 1975

Aurora Greenway, a middle-aged, fairly prosperous widow in Houston, Texas. Aurora is incurably selfish but charming and spends her time encouraging and then terrifying a host of middle-aged beaus. Her principal vanities are her lovely head of auburn hair, her vocabulary, and her authentic Renoir. Her principal disappointment—in addition to the suitors, who always fall short of her expectations—is her daughter, Emma, who is as ordinary as Aurora is eccentric. She bullies Emma and her suitors to make the most of themselves, to be more alive, to seize the moment; often, though, her encouragements only paralyze them with terror.

Emma Horton, Aurora's only child, who lives in the shadow of her mother. Emma is bright, articulate, and capable of deep emotions, but she is mousy-haired, a little dumpy, and saddled with a bad marriage to a lethargic young English professor, Flap. Emma does not lack a spirit of adventure and has two romantic affairs, but they are without the flair and exuberance of her mother. Her strengths are principally as a mother and surface when she is dying of cancer and must plan for her children's future in the midst of a disintegrating marriage. While Aurora makes trivia into high drama, Emma effaces the great tragedy of her short life into daily domestic detail.

Rosie Dunlop, Aurora's maid, tiny and outspoken, tremendously attached to Emma, and usually at odds with Aurora. Rosie is a counterpoint to the romantic lives of Aurora and Emma. Her perpetual crises with her philandering husband, Royce, are essentially comic because they are forever resolvable. Rosie provides pithy and accurate commentary on the affectations and selfishness of Aurora; like all the others, however, she is under Aurora's spell.

Vernon Dalhart, a Texas oilman, one of Aurora's suitors. Short and unimposing, Vernon's most memorable feature is that he lives in his Lincoln in a parking garage that he owns in downtown Houston. He never quite succeeds in winning Aurora but is perenially there to solve her problems, help her dependents, and provide absolute adoration.

Hector Scott, a retired general who is Aurora's neighbor and her principal suitor. Hector is tall, gray in both hair and dress, and as rigid and conservative as a proper general should be. Hector is alternately floored and infuriated by Aurora's assumption of command of everyone, including him. His persistence, however, pays off; he is the only beau whom Aurora takes to bed.

Thomas "Flap" Horton, Emma's husband. Flap enters the story as a graduate student, later an English professor at small, unremarkable Midwestern universities. His only energy is sexual; academically and emotionally, Flap is a wimp. His philandering breaks apart his family before Emma's cancer does. Yet Flap's lethargy pressures Emma as much as her mother's exuberance does; Flap is an intriguing negative balance to Aurora in this novel, and neither values Emma appropriately.

Evelyn Romig

TERRA NOSTRA

Author: Carlos Fuentes (1928-   )
Type of work: Novel
Time of action: The first century before Christ to 1999
First published: 1975 (English translation, 1976)

Pollo Phoibee (pō′lō foi′bē), in Spanish **Polo Febo** (pō′lō fē′bō), a young man in Paris in 1999 who works as a sidewalk hawker carrying a sandwich board, inquisitive, adventurous, and handsome, with shoulder-length blond hair and only one hand. He is proclaimed in the novel as the seeker of ultimate truth and is perhaps the possessor of some mysterious knowledge. He is transformed into one of the three bastard sons of Felipe the Fair and becomes the lover of Joanna Regina, the widow of Felipe. At times, he seems to be one of the narrators of the novel. At the end of the novel, he performs an ecstatic act of love with Celestina, through which the two become one hermaphroditic being who gives birth to the new creature, the New World of the twenty-first century.

Celestina, a female pimp, a twentieth century transformation of the female procuress of the same name from the Spanish Renaissance play *Comedia de Calisto y Melibea* (1949; the play of Calisto and Melibea), by Fernando de Rojas. Young and beautiful, with firm skin like a china teacup, lips tattooed with violet, yellow, and green snakes, and dressed as a male page, she accompanies Pollo Phoibee on his search through history for eternal truth. At times she seems to be a narrator of the novel as she tells her story, which forms a large part of the narrative. She is also transformed into a bride, raped by Felipe the Fair on her wedding night, who gives birth to one of his three bastard sons, the Pilgrim. She and Pollo Phoibee, in an act of sexual union on the last night of 1999, become transformed into a hermaphroditic creature who produces the new creature, the New World of the twenty-first century.

Felipe, also called **El Señor,** Philip II (1527-1598), King of Spain from 1556 to 1598, portrayed in the novel as the son of Felipe the Fair and the Mad Lady Joanna Regina (though historically their grandson and the son of Charles I, King of Spain from 1516 to 1559 and, as Charles V, Emperor of the Holy Roman Empire from 1519 to 1559). Educated from birth to be a strong monarch, Felipe is a tyrant intent on creating a perfect building, the royal palace and monastery, the Escorial, with the desire to contain in one place all time and space and to preserve an ascetic way of life, shutting out all lasciviousness and evil. He marries Elizabeth I of England (though historically Philip II pursued Elizabeth unsuccessfully after the death of his wife, Elizabeth's sister Mary Tudor). When one of the bastard sons of Felipe the Fair returns from an encounter with the Aztecs in the New World, Felipe refuses to admit the possibility of an unknown world beyond the oceans. Felipe orders his scribe, Guzmán, to transcribe his words exactly to create a definitive text of all experience, a document that will encompass all truth and grant Felipe ultimate power over the world.

Isabel (ē·sä·běl′), also called **La Señora,** Elizabeth I (1533-1603) Queen of England (1558-1603), married to Felipe II (although, historically, she refused his offer of marriage after the death of her sister, Mary Tudor, Queen of England from 1553 to 1558, who was in fact married to Felipe). Frustrated and confused by her husband's attempt to preserve an ascetic way of life within the walls of the royal palace, the Escorial, Isabel remains closeted away in a hidden room of the palace, in which she has created a Moorish pleasure salon furnished with white sand, blue water, and a bed of total sexual abandon. As she cultivates her hedonism, seeking in vain to ward off the devastating effects of the passage of time, she is haunted by a recurring nightmare of a mouse that "knows the truth" and gnaws incessantly at her genitals.

Felipe the Fair, the Archduke Philip of Austria (1478-1506), King Philip I of Spain for several months before his death in 1506, son of the Emperor Maximilian (1459-1519), married to Joanna Regina. He is the father of three bastard sons and of Felipe II (although historically he was the father of Charles V, Emperor of the Holy Roman Empire and, as Charles I, King of Spain, who was in turn the father of Felipe II). In the novel, after his death, his embalmed body, preserved against the ravages of time, is transported throughout Spain in a caravan led by his wife, the Mad Lady.

Joanna Regina (jō·än′ä rä·jīn′ạ), in Spanish **Juana la Loca,** the Mad Lady (1479-1555), daughter of the Catholic monarchs Fernando of Aragón (reigned 1474-1516) and Isabel of Castilla (reigned 1474-1504), a widow of Felipe the Fair. Always dressed in mourning, heavily veiled, she travels in a caravan across Spain bearing the embalmed body of her dead husband and finally takes as her lover one of his bastard sons.

Guzmán (gōōth·män′), the secretary of Felipe (El Señor). He is the principal aide to the king, bureaucratic and opportunistic. He is responsible for recording all the king's words to create a compendium of all knowledge so that the king may gain ultimate power over the world.

Fray Julián (hōō·lyän′), a court artist commissioned to paint royal portraits. He is also a court confessor and knows the secrets of the palace. He travels to the New World and narrates part of the novel.

Don Juan, a handsome and sensuous young man, with a birthmark on his back in the shape of a cross, one of the three bastard sons of Felipe the Fair, born of Isabel, La Señora. He becomes the lover of first the Mad Lady and then of Isabel, who imprisons him in her bedchamber.

The Pilgrim, a handsome young man with a birthmark on his back in the shape of a cross and with six toes on each foot, one of the three bastard sons of Felipe the Fair, born of Celestina. He narrates the second part of the novel as the story of his journey to the New World and his encounter with the Aztecs.

The Idiot Prince, a young man with a birthmark on his back in the shape of a cross and with six toes on each foot, one of the three bastard sons of Felipe the Fair, born of a she-wolf. He is forced by Joanna Regina to be a court jester.

Miguel de Cervantes, the fictionalized representation of the historical author of *Don Quixote de la Mancha* (1605, 1615). He appears as the chronicler in the novel, who narrates a part of the story and transforms it into the story of the knight and his squire, Don Quixote and Sancho Panza.

Ludovico, a flagellant in the Parisian parade. He also appears as a student of theology and finally as the man who plays the role of father of the three mysterious bastard sons of Felipe the Fair.

Tiberius Caesar (42 B.C.-A.D. 37), Emperor of Rome from A.D. 14 to 37, assassinated by the reincarnated Agrippa Postumus, the heir to the throne designated by his father-in-law, the Emperor Augustus. Because Tiberius had himself assassinated Agrippa, Tiberius' death is accompanied by a curse, which dictates that Agrippa would be revived in the form of three Caesars, born from the bellies of she-wolves, represented in the novel as the three young men, each with a red birthmark in the shape of a cross on his back and six toes on each foot.

Gilbert Smith

THAT AWFUL MESS ON VIA MERULANA

Author: Carlo Emilio Gadda (1893-1973)
Type of work: Novel
Time of action: February and March, 1927
First published: Quer pasticciaccio brutto de via Merulana, 1957 (English translation, 1965)

Francesco Ingravallo, Don Ciccio (chē' chyō), a Roman police inspector in charge of a robbery and homicide investigation. Don Ciccio is a bachelor but is perhaps a little in love with his good friend, Liliana Balducci, who is murdered. Don Ciccio is a complex figure; his patience, determination, hidden feelings, and skepticism are only revealed through his struggles to find Liliana's murderer. Despite his cynicism, Don Ciccio does not think like most people at his level in society. He always tries to give the poor a chance to defend themselves, rather than assume that they are automatically guilty because of their class.

Liliana Balducci (bäl·dōō'chē), an emotionally and physically barren middle-aged woman. She is found in her apartment with her throat cut and her jewels stolen. For Don Ciccio, Liliana symbolized perfect femininity. During the murder investigation, however, a surprising side of Liliana is revealed. Unable to have children, Liliana had poured her affection on some young orphan girls, whom she had employed as housemaids and then helped

to make good marriages. Though cheated and disappointed every time by those reprobate young women, Liliana always found the strength to continue in her faith in them, helped by the tacit support of her husband, Remo. It seems probable that Liliana was murdered by one of her former protégées.

Corporal Pestalozzi (pĕs·tä·lō'tsē), a carabiniere, or member of the national police. A coarse and spiteful man, Corporal Pestalozzi mainly succeeds through use of brute force. It is he (and his men) who brings the case to a head when he locates the jewelry stolen from the apartment building on Via Merulana.

Zamira Pàcori (pä'kôr·ē), a laundress. A former prostitute, Zamira is a grotesque old woman whose current occupation is a cover for her activities as a bawd, a sorceress, and a faith healer. She surrounds herself with poor, unfortunate young women just as Liliana did, though for more sinister reasons.

Rosaria Pipia

THAT VOICE

Author: Robert Pinget (1919-   )
Type of work: Novel
Time of action: Unspecified
First published: Cette Voix, 1975 (English translation, 1982)

Alexandre Mortin (môr·tăn'), a failed author and would-be historian. At age twenty he published some poems in the *Fantoniard*, the local newspaper, and then earned a scant living as a hack writer. With his small mustache; old, greasy hat; and pince-nez glasses, he was a common sight in the village of Fantoine as he went about collecting all forms of printed matter—newspapers, advertisements,

catalogs—and gossip in an effort to chronicle the history of his family and region. Given to drink and perhaps senile in his later years, he never organizes all the papers he accumulates. His death is mysterious; various accounts claim that he died of a heart attack, committed suicide, was strangled or poisoned, or was stabbed by his maid, her nephew, or by his own nephew and heir. Alexandre's failure to make sense of the information he has gathered, like the multiple accounts of his death, reveals the impossibility of knowing, the uncertainty of what passes for truth.

Théodore, Alexandre Mortin's godson and nephew, or great-great nephew, and heir. As a child he may have lived with Alexandre, whom he affectionately called Dieudonné or Dodo, because his own mother was too poor to support him or because Alexandre bribed her and kept the boy as his homosexual lover. After Alexandre's death, Théodore attempts to catalog his uncle's papers but fares no better than Mortin. Even wearing his uncle's pince-nez does not help him make sense of the material. His identity fuses with that of his uncle, suggesting again the difficulty of distinguishing fact from fancy, of knowing even oneself.

Alfred Mortin, Alexandre's older brother, the first historian of the family. His wife ran away with a Spanish juggler. Alfred leaves his house, fortune, and papers to his younger brother, whom he had been supporting. The cause of Alfred's death, like that of his brother (with whom he is sometimes confused), is questionable: He may have died of a heart attack or a stab wound.

Léo, Alfred's favorite nephew. Léo goes to America, where he presumably dies, since no one hears from him.

Mademoiselle Moine (mwăṅ), president of the Dieudonné Foundations. After Théodore's death, she oversees the successful cataloging of Mortin's papers. Since Alexandre's will prohibits the removal of his papers from his house, Théodore bequeathed the building to the town for its library. Mademoiselle Moine serves as the local librarian and hence as guardian of the material the Mortins accumulated.

Mademoiselle Francine de Bonne-Mésure (bŏṅ mă·zür'), a bookbinder and supposedly rich. She donates her labor and material to bind the catalog that the Dieudonné Foundation has prepared.

Marie, housekeeper for Alfred and Alexandre Mortin. She may be given to drink and senility like her master, or she may be a teetotaler who tries to help Théodore organize Alexandre's papers.

Louis, Marie's nephew or lover. Perhaps a waiter, he is poor and relies on Marie for money.

Joseph Rosenblum

THE THAW

Author: Ilya Ehrenburg (1891-1967)
Type of work: Novel
Time of action: The early 1950's
First published: Ottepel, 1954 (English translation, 1955)

Elena (Lena) Borissovna Zhuravliov, a Soviet schoolteacher. Attractive, intelligent, and cultured, she is a thirty-year-old wife and mother grown dissatisfied with her life. She finds purpose in her career as a teacher but no emotional satisfaction in her relationship with her husband. She unwittingly falls in love with her husband's coworker, Dmitri Koroteyev, who is also cultured and sensitive. When she realizes the seriousness of her affec-tion, she leaves her husband. Mistakenly believing that her love is unrequited, she lives solitarily until a chance encounter brings her and Dmitri together.

Ivan Zhuravliov, a factory manager. Several years older than Lena, he has grown stout and sedate with marriage. Committed to production growth, he puts machines ahead of workers and his job before his family. Soon after Lena leaves him, a storm destroys shoddily built housing that he constructed for employees. Well-meaning but bewildered by private as well as public humiliation, he loses both family and career.

Dmitri Koroteyev, an engineer in Zhuravliov's factory. Thirty-five years old and regarded as a model worker, he is quiet and somewhat reclusive. His wife was killed in the Great Patriotic War against the Nazis, and he has since resisted any emotional involvement. His friendship with Lena grows from their mutual love of books and ideas. Unaware of the depth of his passion for her or of her passion for him, he hesitates to act after she leaves Ivan. At the end of a long, bitter winter, he can no longer stifle his need for affection and approaches Lena.

Andrey Pukhov, an old schoolmaster. Age sixty-four, he has acted as Lena's mentor, inspiring her with ideals about learning and living. He supports her separation from Ivan.

Vladimir (Volyoda) Andreyevich Pukhov, Andrey's son, an artist. He has grown cynical by painting industrial scenes that sell well to bureaucrats but do not reflect his own aesthetic aspirations. Like Ivan, he has lost the ability to love by concentrating upon his social advancement. Though constantly attracting women, he is unable to find love.

Saburaov, an artist and friend of Volyoda. He and his wife Glasha live miserably on her bookkeeper's salary, but they live contentedly, with passion compensating for poverty.

Sonya, Andrey's daughter, who is studying to be an engineer. Though she loves literature, she is determined to pursue a practical career. At age twenty-five, she has just finished school and taken her first job, though it means breaking off a romance with Savchenko, Dmitri's coworker.

Vera Scherer, a physician at the factory. Like Dmitri, she is a veteran of the war whose lover was killed in the fighting. She dedicates herself to work to stifle her own emotions. Thirteen years older than Lena, she serves as Lena's confidante and supporter.

Robert M. Otten

THEIR EYES WERE WATCHING GOD

Author: Zora Neale Hurston (1891-1960)
Type of work: Novel
Time of action: c. 1897-1921
First published: 1937

Janie Crawford Killicks Starks Woods, the novel's central character, a beautiful, romantic, and hopeful young black girl who, over thirty years and three marriages, grows into an attractive, life-affirming, and independent woman. As an adolescent, Janie imagines life and especially marriage as a blossoming pear tree kissed by singing bees. Her first two marriages end in disappointment, but Tea Cake, her third husband, reminds her of a pear tree blossom in spring. Even after Janie kills Tea Cake in self-defense, he is alive in her memory, associated with sunshine and life's plenty.

Nanny Crawford, Janie's grandma, who rears Janie while keeping house for the white Washburn family. Born into slavery, Nanny flees a Georgia plantation when its white mistress, rightly suspecting Nanny to be her husband's lover, threatens to kill her and sell her daughter Leafy (later Janie's mother). Because experience has taught Nanny that "de nigger woman is de mule uh de world," she forces Janie to marry for protection rather than love. Nanny dies a month after the wedding, unforgiven by Janie.

Logan Killicks, Janie's first husband, an older,

responsible, and well-to-do farmer and land-owner. Janie, at age sixteen, thinks that he looks like "some ole skullhead in de grave yard" and marries him only because Nanny insists. When Logan decides to buy a second mule so that Janie can work in the fields, she runs off with Jody Starks and never sees Logan again.

Joe (Jody) Starks, Janie's ambitious second husband, whose goal is to become rich and powerful. Janie runs off with him because he promises her comfort and position and because he reminds her of rich white people. In the black town of Eatonville, Florida, Joe opens a store and gets himself elected mayor. As he gains power, however, he becomes less loving and less loved: He resents Janie's desire for independence, as well as her youthful beauty, and he is resented by the townspeople because he demands their obedience. Mistakenly persuaded that Janie is poisoning him, he dies a frightened, solitary, and pathetic man.

Vergible "Tea Cake" Woods, Janie's adored third husband, playful, charming, and vital. Although Janie suspects that the much younger Tea Cake might be after her money, she takes a risk, marries him, and never regrets it. Tea Cake not only loves Janie but also, unlike Jody, encourages her growth toward independence by teaching her skills and praising her talents. During a hurricane, Tea Cake is bitten by a rabid dog while protecting Janie, and, when he turns mad himself, Janie must shoot him to save her own life.

Phoeby Watson, Janie's closest friend, a loyal, intelligent, and affectionate woman. Janie tells the story of her life to Phoeby, with the understanding that Phoeby will share it with others. When Janie finishes, Phoeby says, "Ah done growed ten feet higher from jus' listenin' tuh you."

Mrs. Turner, a prideful, thin-lipped, light-skinned black woman who worships Caucasian traits and cannot stand dark-skinned blacks. She tries, but fails, to have her no-account brother win Janie away from Tea Cake.

Donald A. Daiker

THEM

Author: Joyce Carol Oates (1938-   )
Type of work: Novel
Time of action: 1937-1967
First published: 1969

Loretta Wendall, née **Botsford,** the mother of Jules and Maureen. A generally passive and not particularly intelligent woman, she nevertheless has an extravagantly romantic nature that is never satisfied. Her one truly independent gesture, an escape to Detroit from the stifling home of her in-laws, ends in humiliation but does achieve her goal of leaving the country for the city. As she grows older, she becomes more limited in her aspirations and more shrewish in her complaints. She is crudely racist and moralistic but is also a survivor in a brutal and violent environment. She drinks to avoid facing the blankness of much of her life and generally neglects her family, changing character, dreams, lifestyle, and men, depending on her situation. Her children are baffled and frustrated by her inconsistencies in behavior and in her often irrational and unpredictable actions toward them. The Detroit riots, which destroy her home, rather then discouraging or defeating her, actually rekindle some of her old desire for adventure and excitement.

Howard Wendall, Loretta's husband and father of Jules and Maureen. Stolid and unintelligent, Howard is dominated by his mother. A policeman at the start of the book, he is later forced to work at jobs that he hates.

Unable to meet the emotional needs of his wife or of his children, he has become a mere shell by the time of his death.

Jules Wendall, son of Loretta and Howard. He continues the romantic tendencies of his mother, often to his own destruction. Searching for wealth and adventure, he roams Detroit's streets, stealing and living independently even as a child. When older, he runs off with an unstable rich girl, who first abandons and later shoots him. He also becomes involved with a wealthy, bombastic, but ineffectual criminal, who is murdered. A survivor, through each disaster Jules continues a deep love for his family, none of whom, however, can meet his needs. After a period of severe depression, during which he exists as a pimp, the violence of the Detroit riots

serves as a catalyst and reawakens his romantic need for adventure and self-importance.

Maureen Wendall, the daughter of Loretta and Howard. She shares her mother and her brother's romantic nature, but eventually responds to the brutality of the life around her by abandoning her dreams of being a teacher, repudiating her family, and deliberately entrapping and marrying one of her college professors. She then settles into the highly respectable middle-class life of which her mother had dreamed but never achieved, setting up a barrier between herself and her past. This past includes a brutal and almost fatal beating by one of her mother's husbands, who discovered that she had been prostituting herself to earn money to escape her life at home.

Eleanor H. Green

THEOPHILUS NORTH

Author: Thornton Wilder (1897-1975)
Type of work: Novel
Time of action: Summer, 1926
First published: 1973

Theophilus (Teddy) North, the stiff and stuffy narrator. Teddy has recently quit his teaching job at a prestigious boys' preparatory school in Raritan, New Jersey, and has come back to Newport, Rhode Island. Stationed there during World War I (1919-1920), he returns older and wiser, having finished college and lived in Europe for a year, to work for the summer as tennis coach, companion, and tutor to the wealthy residents of Newport. Very conscious of his own middle-class background, Teddy draws clear lines between himself and his employers (refusing, for example, to be entertained in their homes), but his regular interactions with these rich residents of the seaside resort allow him glimpses into their lives of privilege and leisure. Priggish and pedantic, a real "planner," as one character calls him, Teddy is constantly lecturing his employers about what

they should do to change and then setting up elaborate schemes (often involving the wildest stories or lies) in order to bring about the necessary transformations. He is both a savior figure and a cupid, either helping people to transform their lives or matching people who should be together. His means and methods are highly manipulative and usually involve some type of deceit. Teddy North is, at least in background, a thinly disguised portrait of the younger Thornton Wilder, but his formal manners and didactic relations with others seem closer to the seventy-five-year-old author than to his thirty-year-old character. Still, in contrast to some of the cardboard characters in the various stories, Teddy North has a certain three-dimensional, if punctilious, reality.

Diana Bell, the spoiled and headstrong daughter of one of the oldest families of Newport. Teddy is hired by her father to head off her elopement, and he does it in such a way that no one is hurt; other influential people hear of his exploits.

Miss Norine Wyckoff, the last of a line of Newport aristocrats. Her house is supposedly haunted, but Teddy helps her to dispel that rumor so that servants will again stay there at night and she can also. This story demonstrates more about how Teddy the narrator/manipulator operates: He digs into the past, finds out much about the residents and their history (here, about how the story of the haunted house got started), sets up an elaborate scheme (as usual involving, often unknowingly, several other characters), and carries it to its successful conclusion.

Flora Deland, a gossip columnist, originally a part of the Newport colony but now an outsider, digging around trying to uncover juicy items for her national gossip columns. She is not a bad person, but her parties are wild "flapper" affairs at which much liquor and indiscretion may flow. She is the object of gossip herself, but Teddy helps her, as he helps so many others, to gain a better reputation.

Dr. James McHenry Bosworth, a seventy-four-year-old widower who is trapped in his own mansion, Nine Gables, by his family and servants. A former diplomat, Dr. Bosworth is interested in philosophy, which he and Teddy read together. As usual, this job soon turns into more, and Teddy helps to free this bright and vibrant man from the prison of his own estate.

Persis Tennyson, Dr. Bosworth's granddaughter, who lives on his estate with her son in a small cottage. Teddy North is half in love with Persis himself but works instead to fix her up with Bodo Stams. First he must clear her name; a widow, she lost her husband when he shot himself, not out of despondency, but rather, as Teddy proves, because of his own reckless way of living. Persis really loved her husband but was living hidden

under the shadow cast by his tragic death until Teddy proves that it was an accident and not suicide.

Baron Bodo von Stams, an Austrian diplomat who summers with friends in Newport. Convivial and loyal, cultured and intelligent, Bodo gets as close to Teddy as anyone in Newport does, and he helps him in several of his adventures. In return, Teddy helps Bodo to win Persis, with whom he is in love, and the novel closes on the expectation that the two will marry.

Henry Simmons, a British manservant, who first befriends Teddy North in a pool hall and then introduces him to other people in Newport who become his friends and confidants.

Amelia Cranston, the owner of a servants' boardinghouse, the woman who knows more about what is going on in Newport, and about what has gone on in the past, than perhaps anyone else. Her relations with the chief of police and other officials in the town allow her access to information and assistance when she needs either. She helps Teddy in several of his adventures, and the parlor of her boardinghouse acts as the hub of the wheel for Teddy during this summer.

Edweena Wills, Henry Simmons' fiancée, a woman with whom Teddy spent one night at the end of World War I. Neither of them allows Henry to learn of this liaison, and the three remain friends. Edweena is a ladies' maid who has risen to be respected as the epitome of her profession and now also owns several dress shops and has gained financial independence.

Colonel Nicholas Vanwinkle, a World War I flying ace and a classmate of Teddy North at Yale. "Rip" hires Teddy to help him with his German, for his remaining life's desire is to return to Berlin for a reunion of the flyers on both sides in the air wars of World War I. "Rip" Vanwinkle is a prime example of what wealth does to a man, in this case, his wife's. A true war hero, he is trapped by his wife's wealth, but Teddy helps him to begin to free himself.

Charles Fenwick, a shy and precocious teenager whom Teddy frees from his adolescent hangups about sex. Thanks to Teddy's help, Charles is permanently changed and ends his chapter speaking French easily with his tutor and holding sophisticated conversations with his parents.

Myra Granberry, a young woman to whom Teddy reads the classics and slowly gets to read and enjoy them on her own. What Teddy really does in the Granberry household is another one of his miraculous metamorphoses: He gets George Granberry to give up his mistress and recommit himself to his pregnant and insecure wife.

Benjamino (Mino) Matera, a brilliant young man who has lost both feet in a childhood accident and is pretty much confined to the store/house of his Italian family, where he devises clever puzzles for newspapers for

money. Teddy gets Mino to overcome his self-consciousness about his handicap, and, by the end of his chapter, he is relating to others much more easily, particularly to women.

Alice, the unhappy wife of a sailor. Teddy meets her in a restaurant one night; Alice is convinced that her problems will be solved if she has a baby; Teddy tries to oblige her.

Miss Elspeth Skeel, a young girl and heir of The Deer Park, an extensive estate containing myriad examples of animal life, who suffers from terrible migraine headaches. Teddy shows that her attacks are the result, not of medical problems, but rather of the hermetic conditions in which she is kept by her strict Danish father. Teddy "lays hands" on Elspeth and cures her, but his success owes less to any shamanistic abilities than to the honest way in which he treats her and the hope that he gives her for her future.

David Peck

THERE IS A TREE MORE ANCIENT THAN EDEN

Author: Leon Forrest (1937-   )
Type of work: Novel
Time of action: Primarily the 1920's through the 1960's
First published: 1973

Nathaniel (Turner) Witherspoon, the boy who recalls most of the events in the book. He is intelligent and has a vivid imagination. His complexion is lighter than those of some of his black friends because his great grandfather, on his father's side, was a white slaveowner. His father tried to instill in him the cultural myths of both black and white American society; consequently, Nathaniel is torn between both worlds. He painfully tries to reconstruct his own identity as well as understand his role in a world beset by racial strife. Nathaniel's attempts to resolve his internal conflicts form the basis in the book for questions concerned with wider social issues.

Aunt Hattie Breedlove Wordlaw, Nathaniel's aunt, who, aside from his father, is the

greatest influence in Nathaniel's life. She is wise and shrewd and tries to counteract the attempts by Nathaniel's father to make his son into a great, heroic "man." She is gentle with Nathaniel but can be tough when necessary. A devout Christian, she believes that only love and self-sacrifice can better the world. Breedy tries to teach Nathaniel love, dignity, pride, and inner strength.

Jamestown Fishbond, an artist, criminal, and Nathaniel's boyhood friend. He is an Afro-Indian and is described as ebony-black in complexion, and six feet, one inch tall. Extremely intelligent, he is a prodigious reader, a very good painter, and a speaker of several languages. He is also a superior chess player and has published articles dealing with jazz.

As gifted as Fishbond is, he has also been diagnosed as a manic-depressive and paranoic with a personality dislocation crisis. Eventually, he becomes involved with the violence in Mozambique and is killed. His obvious talents make him the perfect idol for the young Nathaniel. Yet, his hatred of the whites and his poor method of dealing with his own identity crisis show Nathaniel how not to be.

Madge Ann Fishbond, Jamestown's older sister. She becomes streetwise at a very young age, as she has to survive the terrible poverty that breaks up her family and kills her mother prematurely. Despite the harshness of her surroundings while growing up, she does not become embittered, as Jamestown does. It is through her that the reader learns more about Jamestown and the Fishbond family.

Hilda Mae Fishbond, Jamestown's mother. She manages to rear her eight children alone after her husband abandons them. Yet, the strain becomes too much, and one night she attempts to burn down the tenement where they live. Luckily, everyone escapes. After that, she continues to support her family by working as a cleaning lady for rich, white families; she dies of a heart attack while at her job.

Jericho Witherspoon, Nathaniel's grandfather, a slave and son of a white slave-owner.

He was intelligent and deft with his hands. Described as six feet, five inches tall, large, with reddish, curly hair and reddish brown in complexion, he was taught to read and write by his father. Jericho ran away from his father in 1850 and was considered dangerous. Although he thought of himself as white, he was also said to have hated white society.

Taylor "Warm-Gravy" James, a pianist. He writes scores for musicals and folk operas, and eventually becomes quite well known for his work as well as for his political views. He joins the Islamic religion, changing his name to Ebn-Allah, Al-Fatir. He is also a health food addict and does not smoke, use alcohol, or take drugs.

Maxwell "Black-Ball" Saltport, Nathaniel's friend. He has minor scrapes with the law, but then seems to become responsible abruptly, eventually becoming a member of the California State Council on prison reforms. He also wins a Medal of Freedom for his drug rehabilitation efforts. Under the influence of his uncle, Grandberry Persons Saltport, he converts to the Nation, receiving his X in spring, 1956.

Goodwin "Stale-Bread" Winters, Nathaniel's friend. He is his high school class valedictorian in 1958. Four years later, Stale-Bread dies of a heroin overdose.

Ruth Hsu

THÉRÈSE RAQUIN

Author: Émile Zola (1840-1902)
Type of work: Novel
Time of action: The Second Empire (1852-1870)
First published: Un Mariage d'amour, 1867, serial; *Thérèse Raquin,* 1867, book (English translation, 1881)

Madame Raquin (rä·kăṅ'), a plump, sixty-year-old, doting mother, who centers her life on her son, Camille, and gratifies his every whim. When he decides to go to Paris to look for a new position, she leaves her comfortable country retirement at Vernon and uses a portion of her savings to rent a miser-

able little haberdashery on a wretched Left Bank alley. Camille, wife Thérèse, and his mother live a life of unbroken plainness and regularity, until enlivened by Camille's vivacious coworker and friend, Laurent. After the seemingly accidental death of Camille, Madame Raquin's sorrow is eventually tempered by her apparently devoted daughter-in-law, Thérèse, and the thoughtful Laurent. She is maneuvered into suggesting their marriage. At first, they guard the secret of their culpability for Camille's death and hide their psychological torment from her. After Madame Raquin suffers a progressively debilitating paralysis, which leaves her unable to move or speak, Laurent, in one of his regular anguished and angry bouts with Thérèse, lets the truth slip out in front of the invalid. Unable to communicate the awful truth to the members of the Thursday night gatherings, Madame Raquin festers in her hatred, relishing the destructive behavior of Thérèse and Laurent, until she has the ultimate satisfaction of witnessing their double suicide.

Thérèse Raquin (tā·rĕz'), the twenty-eight-year-old daughter of Madame Raquin's brother, Captain Degans, whom he left to her aunt's care after the death of the toddler's Algerian mother. Thérèse, a strong and lissome person, has fine features with dark hair and eyes. Madame Raquin decides that her niece and ward should marry her son, Camille, and, though she was deeply repelled by his sickly smell and touch, the passive Thérèse acquiesced. She, too, without protest, gives up the life in the country, which she loved, for the dismal shop and apartment in Paris. She moulders away until her passionate nature is brought to life and unleashed by the advances of Laurent. When their secret but tempestuous affair is threatened by lack of opportunity, it is she who suggests the murder of her husband. After Camille's death their ardor cools, and in its place grows guilt. They hope that their marriage will bring peace; instead, it brings greater guilt and psychological anguish. They cannot stand to touch each other, and the two engage in protracted bouts of hateful recrimination. Unable to find peace in dissipation, Thérèse, in despair, decides to escape Laurent and her own demons by killing him. Laurent, overwrought by guilt and haunted by the specter of Camille, has decided to poison her at precisely the same time. When they discover their mutual intent, they embrace. Thérèse takes the glass of poisoned water, drinks

half, and hands it to Laurent, who consumes the remainder.

Camille Raquin, a thirty-year-old clerk. Camille, Madame Raquin's only son, whom she has overprotected because of his frail health, is a slight, pale, listless creature with colorless hair and an almost beardless but blotchy face. A mentally dull person, devoid of imagination and passion, his only ambition is fulfilled when he obtains a clerical post with the Orleans Railway. He admires the elemental and vivacious Laurent. He introduces him to his wife and mother. Completely unaware that Laurent has seduced Thérèse, Camille continues to bring him into his household. He does not suspect the fate that is in store for him when he suggests a walk in the country. He allows himself, despite his terror of water, to be shamed into a skiff on the Seine. As Laurent wrestles him out of the boat, Camille takes a deep bite out of his attacker's neck, thus leaving a lasting reminder of the deed.

Laurent (lä·rän'), the tall and square-shouldered, earthy son of a peasant, who attended school at Vernon with Camille and Thérèse. He went to Paris to study law, but concentrated rather on his own ease and enjoyment until his father cut off his subsidies. Attracted by the Bohemian life-style, he tried his hand at art. His lack of talent forces him to take a job at the office of the Orleans Railway. When he meets Thérèse, he regards her as an easy and insignificant conquest. Her unleashed animality, however, captivates him and awakens in him a latent sensitivity. After drowning Camille, Laurent goes daily to the morgue to look for his body. When it is finally discovered and displayed, the bloated, decomposing horror of the corpse is deeply etched upon Laurent's mind, and the recurring memory consumes him with guilt.

Michaud (mē·shō'), a retired police superintendent, an old friend of Madame Raquin. He had retired to Paris after having been stationed in Vernon. After a chance meeting with Madame Raquin, the pasty and blotched-faced Michaud becomes a regular guest at her apartment on Thursday evenings, when the Raquins and their guests shared tea, conversation, and dominoes. After the murder of Camille, Laurent goes immediately to Michaud, ostensibly for assistance in breaking the news to Madame Raquin. Michaud, whose primary concern is to continue his comfortable Thursday evenings, suspects nothing and gives his support to Laurent's version of the tragedy. He is manipulated into suggesting to Madame Raquin that the apparently pining Thérèse should marry and that the obvious choice is Laurent.

Grivet (grē·vā'), an old employee of the Orleans Railway, Camille's supervisor, and a regular at the Thursday night gatherings. Grivet has narrow features and thin lips but round eyes. The inner turmoil and growing loathing of Thérèse and Laurent for each other remains hidden from him and from the others.

His lack of perception and self-centeredness are especially evident when he presumes, always erroneously, to be able to understand the unspoken wishes of Madame Raquin after her paralysis.

Olivier, Michaud's son, another habitual participant at the Thursday night gatherings. A thirty-year-old, tall, lean, angular, arrogant, and egotistical chief clerk in the prefecture of police's Department of Public Order and Safety, Olivier unwittingly helps to deflect any possible suspicion from the murderers.

Suzanne, Olivier's small and flabby-faced wife, also a Thursday night regular. An intellectually dull and physically frail person of unattractive appearance, she idolizes Thérèse's vivacity.

Bernard A. Cook

THESE THOUSAND HILLS

Author: A. B. Guthrie, Jr. (1901-   )
Type of work: Novel
Time of action: The 1880's
First published: 1956

Albert Gallatin (Lat) Evans, a ranch hand and later a rancher. Twenty years old as the story begins, he is an only child, strongly influenced by his strict, upright father and by his good, gentle mother but is determined to see life and to make his own way. He is daring, intelligent, and courageous. Although later he passionately desires to be a respectable community leader, he will risk his reputation and even his marriage to save old friends who once helped him.

Tom Ping, Lat's companion. In his late twenties when the novel begins, Tom has dark skin and hair with a forelock that hangs over his forehead, a strong mouth, and even teeth. Having run away from his Texas home when he was ten, Tom is more defiant of society and more experienced in life than Lat. Their friendship deepens on the trail and in Indian captivity, but it breaks when Lat disapproves of Tom's marriage to a prostitute. Resentful

of Lat's prosperity, Tom insults him in bars, even after Lat has saved him from being caught rustling, but he finally acknowledges publicly how much he admires Lat.

Callie Kash, a young prostitute. Sweet-faced and considerate, slim and pretty, with yellow hair and blue eyes, she comes to her aunt's brothel in Montana after having been seduced by her West Virginia lover. Deeply in love with Lat, she becomes his mistress. It is Callie who loans him her life savings so that he can bet on a horse race and make his fortune. Shielding the black servant who had defended her, Callie is herself accused of murder. Although Lat decides to risk everything in order to testify for her, Callie and the servant flee and thus protect him.

Joyce Sheridan, Lat's wife. Her coloring is striking: She has very pale skin, black hair, and black eyes. When Lat meets her, she is nineteen or twenty and has just finished her schooling. The niece of the storekeeper, she has come west from Indiana to be a school-teacher. From the first, Joyce admits that she is frightened by the vastness of the new country. Although she admires and loves Lat, Joyce is unable to tolerate the uncouthness and immorality of his friends or to see the nobility often present beneath the rough surface. The revelation of Lat's former relationship with Callie almost destroys her feelings for her husband; Joyce proves to have depths of love which she had not previously sounded, however, and at the end of the novel welcomes him back to her arms.

Mike Carmichael, a trail rider. Short and wiry, he is already middle-aged when young Lat joins the cattle drive. Later, after Mike has been injured and disabled, Lat gives him a job on the ranch. Although Mike understands Tom Ping's continuing rebellion against a new, tamer society, he is willing to settle down with the country. On the hunt for rus-tlers, Mike keeps quiet about Ping's escape; he points out to Lat that his debt has thus been paid.

Jehu, a wealthy horse-fancier. Tall and immaculately dressed, with a gray hat, a pearl-handled revolver, and spotless boots, he wagers that Lat cannot break his horse, Sugar. Lat wins the bet and begins to work for Jehu. Later, when Jehu cheats him out of his pay, Lat outsmarts him. When Sugar later wins a race against an Indian horse, Lat collects enough money to buy his ranch and begin his upward climb.

Brownie Evans (Pa), Lat's father, a poor Oregon rancher. A straight-laced, respected man, he has always been moody, sometimes frighteningly temperamental. Even though the successful Lat avoids visiting his parents, he is strongly influenced by them. His upbringing will not let him marry Callie; instead, he must seek a respectable girl such as Joyce.

Rosemary M. Canfield Reisman

THE THIN RED LINE

Author: James Jones (1921-1977)
Type of work: Novel
Time of action: 1942-1943
First published: 1962

Edward Welsh, the first sergeant in Charlie Company. He enlisted in the army at the beginning of the Great Depression, believing that he had shrewdly escaped the general economic calamity, but convinced that, as a career soldier, he would not escape the next war because of the pattern of America's becoming involved in wars at roughly twenty-year intervals. His personality is full of paradoxes. Even though he cynically dismisses all ideals as empty and believes that all wars are struggles over property rights, he himself is completely disinterested in acquiring property and respects only the most fatalistic acceptance of the insignificance of the individual. Even though he has no combat experience before the Guadalcanal campaign, he instinctively understands and accepts the demands of battle and the likelihood of death. Even though he takes every opportunity to exhibit his contempt for his subordinates and his superiors alike, he has an underlying pity for their limitations and a desire to compensate for them. He lives up to his nickname of "Mad Welsh," but at bottom it is a posture behind which he can conceal a reflexive compassion to which he will not admit, not even to himself. In particular, he singles out Corporal Fife for verbal abuse, recognizing that Fife is too self-reflective and has too strong a sense of self-preservation to be suited to combat. In the end, when Fife is finally injured seriously enough to be offered evacuation, it is Welsh's further derision that, ironically, makes him decide to accept the offer. In effect, Welsh has saved Fife by allowing

Fife to think that he is spiting him. In another instance, a soldier named Tella is gut-shot and left lying in screaming agony on the open ground cleared by enemy machine-gun fire. When a medic is cut down trying to administer morphine to Tella, Welsh insanely runs across the open ground to the wounded man. Though he cannot rescue Tella, he is able to administer the morphine to relieve his suffering and to quiet the screaming that is unnerving everyone. Afterward, he is so embarrassed at having revealed how much he cares for the men in his company, that he loudly threatens Captain Stein for wanting to recommend him for the Silver Star. When the Guadalcanal campaign is almost over, Welsh contracts malaria but refuses to accept evacuation because it will mean being permanently separated from the company.

Storm, the mess sergeant in Charlie Company. In many ways, he is Welsh's opposite. Whereas Welsh is explosively abusive of his men, Storm tries to be consistently self-controlled and reassuring. Whereas Welsh finds his emotional equilibrium in combat, Storm is appalled by the little combat he sees, in particular, by his participation in the abuse of some Japanese prisoners after an especially fierce hand-to-hand engagement. When he is wounded, he gladly accepts evacuation, wanting only to prepare one last meal for the company before departing. At bottom he believes that the levelheaded performance of his duties is all that he owes the men of Charlie Company.

John Bell, a private, later a sergeant, and finally a lieutenant in Charlie Company. A commissioned officer in the regular army in the years before the war, he resigned his commission when given an assignment that would require a prolonged separation from his wife, Marty. When he is drafted as a private into Charlie Company, the other soldiers regard him as something of an enigma because he exhibits no bitterness or presumptuousness about his having been an officer. Initially, Bell goes into combat with an intense underlying fear that he will be killed in battle and that his death will be as

essentially meaningless as any other small statistic of battle. He suppresses this fear only by recalling vividly erotic moments with his wife. He begins to volunteer for especially dangerous missions and gradually admits to himself that his wife's vibrant sexuality makes it extremely improbable that she will remain faithful to him. He is, then, not entirely surprised when he receives a Dear John letter from his wife, ironically at about the same time that he receives notification of his reinstatement as an officer. Of all the soldiers in Charlie Company, Bell is the most farsightedly thoughtful in his repeated recognition that giving oneself up to the brutality of combat will leave permanent emotional scars.

Geoffrey Fife, a corporal in Charlie Company. Because his very idealistic notions about the nature and purpose of war are essential to his sanity, he is repelled by the continual evidence of the mindless and soulless machinery of war. He cannot accept the notion that his death in battle may be pointless, and he repeatedly confesses his cowardice in the face of such a death, believing that the other men of the company lack the idealism to fear death as he does. In his exaggerated sense of his singular weakness, he begins a homosexual relationship with Private Bead, whom he abuses as a gesture of his self-disgust. When Bead is mortally wounded, he asks Fife to hold his hand, and Fife is very reluctant, afraid that he will confirm any suspicions about their relationship. When Fife himself receives a minor wound, he is appalled that the wound, which to him seems pointed evidence that he has done his part in the battle, does not make him eligible for evacuation. He transfers out of Charlie Company when Welsh, while he is hospitalized for the minor wound, gives his job as company clerk to another soldier. With his new company, Fife participates in the attack on Boola Boola, the last, weakly defended, Japanese stronghold, and all of his desperation releases itself in his wild slaughtering of every Japanese soldier he sees. Still, once the insane exhilaration of the battle has worn off, Fife is haunted by the same anxieties that he has felt since the opening of the campaign.

Don Doll, a private in Charlie Company. In many ways, he is the opposite of Fife. Although he is very afraid of dying pointlessly in combat, he recognizes, as Fife does not, that all the soldiers in the company have assumed postures of one sort or another to hide this same fear. Consequently, he assumes a posture of recklessness that the others ironically come to accept as genuine bravery. Aboard the troopship as the landings are under way, he steals a pistol that he hopes will serve as a sort of talisman for his survival, though he knows that it will not be an especially useful weapon in combat. Later, during a night bombardment, he stands in his foxhole, insanely testing his fate with an outward manner of nonchalance. After his first killing of a Japanese soldier, he feels a genuine guilt, but also the strange elation of knowing that his guilt will not result in any corresponding punishment. He begins a strange competition with another private, Charlie Dale, for the most dangerous assignments. While Dale is looking to move up through the ranks as quickly as possible, Doll is motivated more simply by the need to keep up his adrenaline to avoid reflection. Near the end of the campaign, he is suddenly attracted to the feminine build of Private Abre and assumes that Abre will submit to being buggered. He finds it very disquieting, then, when Abre misinterprets his advances and assumes that Doll himself is more pointedly homosexual and is willing to take on the more degrading sexual role.

Witt, a private in Charlie Company who transfers to another company because he hates Welsh. A free spirit with inexplicable politics, he deserts his new company to rejoin Charlie Company whenever the fighting becomes especially heavy. The men in Charlie Company are reassured by his presence at critical moments, but they cannot understand the loyalty to them that compels him to endanger himself by rejoining them. Witt himself is unable to articulate the code that drives him.

James Stein (Bugger), the captain of Charlie Company in the early stages of the Guadalcanal campaign. Nicknamed Bugger by the men in the company, he is a well-meaning but ineffective leader in combat. His training in the Reserve Officers' Training Corps and his six months in the Army Reserve have not given him an understanding of what his men expect from him. He ends up relying on soldierly clichés that, in themselves, cause his men to lose faith in him. He is replaced as the captain of Charlie Company after an especially disastrous battle. Ironically, he has allowed his superior, Lieutenant Colonel Gordon Tall, to overrule a more effective battle plan that he has devised, and then Tall has him transferred.

George Band (Brass Band), Captain Stein's replacement in Charlie Company. Nicknamed Brass Band by the men of the company, he devises battle plans without any regard for the casualties that will entail. He is eventually replaced when his tactics prove not only costly but also unsuccessful.

Gordon Tall, the battalion commander, a lieutenant colonel. A very Machiavellian personality, he views the Guadalcanal campaign as a career opportunity and has very little empathy for the circumstances of the ordinary soldiers.

Martin Kich

THINGS FALL APART

Author: Chinua Achebe (1930-   )
Type of work: Novel
Time of action: The late nineteenth century
First published: 1958

Okonkwo, the protagonist, one of the leaders of the Ibo community of Umuofia. He struggles from humble beginnings to achieve high status yet is still haunted by feelings of insecurity associated with his former lack of status. He is now a great warrior and wealthy farmer, with two barns full of yams, three wives, and two titles; he is also a lord in the clan. This string of successes is interrupted when he accidentally kills a man and is forced into exile for seven years. His plans for advancement are of necessity put on hold, and he chafes under this banishment. While he is gone, European missionaries establish themselves in the midst of Umuofia, make converts, and subtly undermine the old order. Under the impact of Westernization and modernization, things begin to fall apart. When Okonkwo returns, he finds Umuofia much changed and its former independence and integrity dangerously threatened by the new ways. He tries to rally his people and save his community. He is the most authentic representative and protector of traditional society. He rejects the new values that are subverting the old order and crosses the point of no return by killing a messenger of the Europeans to force his clansmen to make a choice. When they let the other messengers escape, he realizes that his community will not go to war against the Europeans. He commits suicide, which is a great evil and prevents him from being buried among his people. His tragic end underscores that there can be no compromise or halfway house between traditional and modern society. Things must of necessity fall apart.

Unoka, Okonkwo's father. Lazy and shiftless, always in debt, he is a man without title and unable to provide for his family. He is a good storyteller and a fine musician, the life of any party.

Nwoye (n•wŏ′yĕ), Okonkwo's eldest son. Sensitive and deeply troubled by certain Umuofian practices, such as the exposure of twins in the Evil Forest and the sacrifice of his beloved companion, Ikemefuna, he was attracted to the music, hope, and poetry of Christianity, and he converted. His actions remind Okonkwo of the failures of his father and raise the specter that he too might have these flaws.

Chielo, the priestess of Agbala, the Oracle of the Hills and the Caves. Her approval is needed for major decisions, such as going to war. In everyday life, she is an ordinary woman, but as priestess few dare to ignore her divinations.

Ekwefi, Okonkwo's second wife. The village beauty, she was captivated by Okonkwo's victory over the Cat in the greatest wrestling match within living memory. She ran away from her huband to live with Okonkwo. She bears ten childen but loses nine in infancy. A daughter, Ezinma, survives, however, and Ekwefi lavishes special care and affection on her.

Ezinma (ĕ•zĭn′mä), Okonkwo and Ekwefi's daughter. Intelligent and beautiful, she best understands the complex moods of her father and best interprets the appropriate course of action. Okonkwo wishes she were a male. She is his favorite child, and he plans her marriage as a logical part of his rise to power. Chielo calls her "daughter" and is probably training her to be the new priestess.

Ikemefuna (ĭ•kĕ•mĕ•fōō′nä), a fifteen-year-old boy from a neighboring village. Okonkwo treats him like a son, and Nwoye learns under his tutelage and regards him as the older brother he never had. Given to Umuofia in atonement for the murder of a clansman's wife, he is placed under the guardianship of Okonkwo. After about three years the Oracle of the Hills and the Caves orders his sacrifice. Wishing to show his strength and his loyalty to village traditions, Okonkwo strikes the fatal blow.

Obierika (ō•bē•ĕ′rē•kä), a friend of Okonkwo. He manages Okonkwo's affairs while he is in exile, warns him that the law does not require him to participate in Ikemefuna's sacrifice, and has him buried by outsiders when he commits suicide.

Mr. Brown, the first European missionary

in Umuofia. Respectful of Umuofia's traditions, he wisely guides the affairs of the early Christian church, and its membership and power grows.

The Reverend James Smith, a narrow-minded missionary who succeeds Mr. Brown.

He brooks no compromises with native traditions and insists on the rights and privileges of the Christian community over those of Umuofia. His fanaticism and nonbending stance set the stage for the imposition of European rule of government and law.

Maurice P. Brungardt

THIRD AND OAK
The Laundromat

Author: Marsha Norman (1947-   )
Type of work: Play
Time of action: The late twentieth century
First produced: 1978

Alberta Johnson (Bertie), a retired teacher and Herb's recent widow, a white, middle-aged perfectionist who initially keeps her husband's death secret because she cannot yet deal with letting go of Herb. An isolationist, Alberta is lonely and talks to herself for company. Precise and proper, she is at first taken aback by Deedee's spontaneity and is reluctant to accept help from or be close to Deedee. Yet Bertie is a caring person and extends herself to help Deedee with issues ranging from change for the machines to her unfaithful husband. Her approach to her world is predominantly logical.

Deedee Johnson, Joe's lonely wife, who ad-

dresses envelopes for a secret income and wants to be liked but sees herself as essentially inadequate. In fact, Deedee sabotages her own competence by her impulsive behaviors; therefore, she is frequently unprepared for her own actions or for others' reactions to her. Deedee believes that she lacks intelligence. A chocolate lover who belittles herself for responding to her world emotionally, Deedee has tolerated a violent, racist, unfaithful husband because she needs to be with someone and he has been there. Nevertheless, Deedee displays both independent thought and independent action in her final exchanges with Alberta in the laundry.

Kathleen Mills

THIRD FACTORY

Author: Viktor Shklovsky (1893-1984)
Type of work: Novel
Time of action: c. 1900-1926
First published: Tretya fabrika, 1926 (English translation, 1977)

Viktor Borisovich Shklovsky, the author, narrator, and subject of this work. Shklovsky sets forth memories and ideas in an autobiographical sketch that was meant also to present his conception of prose fiction and his assessment of other writers who were prominent during that period. Instead of a conventional self-portrait, Shklovsky pro-

vides a series of anecdotes that illustrate the development of his own views and feelings, which in their turn are arranged according to his own notions of the Formalist novel. The author's conception of himself is refracted by the technical devices he has chosen to employ, and underlying creative concerns may be found alongside some outwardly offhand notes and observations. According to the author, his existence has been lived in a succession of factories: The first was his home and school; the second was Opoyaz, a literary society of innovative predilections; his employment in the Soviet film industry—the "third factory"—provides a backdrop for his reflections and reminiscences. During those passages dealing with the author's early manhood, names and images of writers and theorists flash by along with some blunt and unvarnished recollections of war and revolution. Among many noted figures, Jan Baudouin de Courtenay, a professor of philology and one of Shklovsky's mentors, is mentioned with some respect, while elsewhere important theorists of the author's own generation, including Roman Osipovich Jakobson, Yury Nikolayevich Tynyanov, and Boris Mikhailovich Eikhenbaum, are the recipients of some reflections on life and language in the guise of open letters. His writing features Tatars and sailors, as well as travel notes and hints of homebound affection for the author's native land. Odd, abrupt changes of subject and wildly humorous interjections occur amid musings upon the possibilities and shortcomings of modern literary figures. Through it all, it can hardly be said that the author is prone to take himself too seriously: He calls attention to his prominent bald shining head, and, at times, he recoils from a surfeit of his own wit.

J. R. Broadus

THE THIRD LIFE OF GRANGE COPELAND

Author: Alice Walker (1944-   )
Type of work: Novel
Time of action: 1920 to the early 1960's
First published: 1970

Grange Copeland, the protagonist, a black sharecropper in Georgia. A tall, gaunt man who has worked hard all of his life, Grange is poor, ignorant, and in debt to the white plantation owner. He abuses his wife and son out of his own powerlessness and eventually abandons them to try his luck in the North. On his return, he marries his longtime lover, Josie, but treats her badly and tries in vain to keep his son from making the mistakes that he himself has made. Only his granddaughter, Ruth, receives his love, as he tries to make up for past sins. Grange never loses his hatred of white people, but he comes to realize how his hatred has made him weak. He tries to make a life for himself and for Ruth that will enable them to stay free by never depending on whites for anything.

Margaret Copeland, Grange's first wife and the mother of Brownfield and a bastard son. In the early years of her marriage, Margaret is soft and has sweet breath, and she is as submissive to her husband as a dog. After years of abuse, she becomes hardened and turns to drinking and promiscuity. It is her sexual relationship with the white plantation owner, resulting in the birth of a child, that finally drives Grange away for good. Yet Margaret has never stopped loving Grange, and when he leaves she kills herself and the baby, leaving fifteen-year-old Brownfield to fend for himself.

Brownfield Copeland, the neglected son of Grange and Margaret. As a baby he is unattended, unfed, and unchanged all day because both parents work in the fields. He never attends school and envies his cousins up North. Abandoned by both parents at the age of fifteen, he sets out to find the North but only gets as far as Josie's Dew Drop Inn. After several years of sharing the home and beds of Josie and her daughter, Brownfield falls in love with the beautiful and educated Mem, whom he marries. He comes to resent her accomplishments, however, and to despise her. He begins to repeat his father's life, working long hours as a sharecropper for little reward, beating his wife and children, drinking away his earnings, and spending his nights with Josie. His once-handsome body becomes worn down from hard work and disease. Unlike his father, Brownfield never learns to accept any responsibility for his own failings. He believes that the white man has kept him from being a man, and that the only way to assert his manliness is to abuse his family.

Mem Copeland, Brownfield's wife. Cherry brown, plump, quiet, and demure, Mem has been educated in Atlanta and speaks a dialect that at first sounds wonderful to Brownfield. She is a schoolteacher for several years and teaches Brownfield to read and write. In the early years of her marriage, she is a happy and devoted wife. Brownfield then begins to beat her, makes her give up teaching to become a domestic, makes her speak the way he speaks, and moves her from one ramshackle cabin to another. Mem is resigned to her own fate, but fights back at Brownfield when the children's future is at stake. For a few years, Mem rises to power in the family and there is a surface of domestic harmony, but Brownfield eventually supplants her and chaos and violence are restored.

Ruth Copeland, the youngest daughter of Brownfield and Mem. Born in a frozen cabin while her drunken father sleeps, Ruth receives her first beating from her father at the age of four, and watches him kill her mother at eight. She moves in with Grange and Josie and becomes the center of Grange's life, squeezing out even Josie. She is spoiled and sassy, and her only friend is Grange. At sixteen, she loves to read and wonders about life outside the farm that Grange has established to protect them from white society. Unlike Grange, she believes that white people could change and that hating them for their ancestors' sins against her ancestors is wrong.

Josie Copeland, a prostitute, Grange's second wife and Brownfield's first lover. She is cantaloupe-colored, fat, and a voracious lover. She and Grange have had a relationship since before his first marriage, and it is to her that he returns after ten years in the North. Josie has spent those years as Brownfield's mistress, and she returns to Brownfield after Ruth steals Grange's heart. In fact, both men abuse her, and she is a lonely old woman who realizes that she has never been loved.

Cynthia A. Bily

THE THIRD POLICEMAN

Author: Flann O'Brien (Brian O'Nolan, 1911-1966)
Type of work: Novel
Time of action: The late 1930's
First published: 1967

The Narrator, unnamed, who as a child was sent to a fine boarding school when both of his parents died. At sixteen, he becomes obsessed with the thought of a fictional charlatan, de Selby, who believes that most human experiences are illusory. After the Narrator leaves school, he loses his left leg in an accident and returns home interested only in continuing his study of de Selby. He joins his dishonest caretaker, John Divney, in a crime to finance the publication of his definitive collation of all the interpretations of

de Selby's thought. After Divney murders him, the Narrator, not realizing that he is dead, goes to a strange police barracks in search of the lockbox that contains their loot. Amid strange dialogues and disorienting experiences, he is accused by Sergeant Pluck of murder. He narrowly avoids hanging, and escapes on Pluck's animate and gynecomorphic bicycle, toward which he develops amorous feelings. When he reaches his house, the Narrator finds Divney and discovers that not three days but sixteen years have passed since he began his search for the box.

John Divney, the man hired to take care of the Narrator's farm and tavern while he is at boarding school. Divney is short but well-built, with broad shoulders and thick arms. He is brown haired and roughly handsome with a reassuring face and brooding, brown, and patient eyes. After the Narrator returns home, he does not dismiss the lazy and unprincipled Divney, even after he realizes that Divney was stealing from him. Divney convinces the Narrator to join him in a plot to rob and murder Mathers, who carries his cash box with him when he walks to the village. After the murder, Divney hides the box and will not tell the Narrator where it is. After the Narrator had shadowed him for several years, even to the point of sleeping in the same bed with him, Divney relents. He tells the Narrator that he has hidden the strong box under the floor in Mathers' house, but he had actually planted a bomb there. When the Narrator, who has been killed by the bomb, comes back to his house, Divney, who alone can see him, is frightened to death. The two, unaware that they are dead, then prepare to repeat the forgotten trials of the Narrator.

Phillip Mathers, a wealthy, elderly, retired man who lives alone in a big house three miles from the Narrator's house. On a rainy night, the Narrator and Divney attack him. After Divney strikes him with a bicycle pump and the Narrator finishes him off with a spade, they bury his body in a ditch. He appears to the Narrator after the Narrator's death. Not aware of his own death, the Narrator enters into a conversation with the ghastly and spectral, but apparently alive, Mathers. Mathers directs the Narrator to the weird policemen, whom he sought out in hope that they could help him locate the missing strong box.

Joe, the Narrator's soul, whom the Narrator becomes aware of after his death. Joe is the Narrator's companion and adviser and carries on dialogues with him. He is a voice of common sense in the midst of the Narrator's disorienting experiences and fantastic theories on the nature of all sorts of things expressed by the policemen.

Martin Finnucane, a robber and murderer whom the Narrator encounters on his way to the police barracks. Finnucane also has a wooden left leg and is the leader of a band of one-legged men.

Sergeant Pluck, head of the constabulary at the strange police station. Pluck is a giant of a man, with a bulging neck and an enormous, fat red face sporting a violent red mustache and topped with abundant and unruly straw-colored hair. Believing that people and bicycles are exchanging identities through too much contact, he continually steals and hides bicycles. In order to solve a second murder of the dead Mathers, he blames the—this time—innocent Narrator. After subjecting the Narrator to prolonged interrogations and an escorted tour of an eternity machine, Pluck prepares to hang him but is distracted by the Finnucane gang.

Policeman MacCruiskeen, an inventive policeman who crafts a marvellous but incredible series of Chinese boxes and honed spearpoints, so fine that they are invisible. Dark complexioned with a hook nose, dark whiskers, and a mass of curly black hair, he is as big and fat as Pluck but has a lean and intelligent face with penetrating eyes. He supervises and adjusts the gauges that control their strange world.

Policeman Fox, the third policeman, a mysterious character whom no one ever sees. The Narrator, on his way back home, encounters Fox in his own private station in the walls of Mathers' house. Corpulent and with the face and voice of Mathers, he informs the Narrator that the sought-after box contained 4 ounces of omnium, the essence of everything, which could satisfy his every desire.

Bernard A. Cook

THIS SIDE OF PARADISE

Author: F. Scott Fitzgerald (1896-1940)
Type of work: Novel
Time of action: 1896-1919
First published: 1920

Amory Blaine, a boy born in the Midwest at the beginning of the twentieth century to a prominent family in the process of losing their fortune. He is a pampered, privileged young boy who embarks on a quest for self-discovery that covers his years at preparatory school, Princeton University, the army, and the beginning of a life as an adult as he pursues a career in New York. He arrives in the East full of a kind of idealistic innocence, with untested assumptions about courage, honor, duty, and a man's place in the world, but his natural charm, earnestness, amiability, and obvious intelligence enable him to progress toward a firmer understanding of his essential nature. He is almost six feet tall as he enters Princeton, with light hair and penetrating green eyes, strikingly but not conventionally handsome, with a kind of slender athleticism to his carriage. Often intoxicated with the splendor of his youth and intensely conscious of his reactions to everything, he is fond of outrageous gestures and desperately concerned about his appearance and status in the eyes of those whom he admires and hopes to equal or emulate. He correctly sees himself as a "romantic egotist," and his attitude toward the world—and particularly toward women—has been shaped heavily by his reading, which has tended toward nineteenth century writers with rebellious and ultra-romantic philosophies. His inclinations toward social equality and his sensitivity toward the people whom he likes rescue him from his tendencies to be a prototypical snob with a vastly inflated estimate of his own self-worth.

Beatrice O'Hara Blaine, Amory's mother, an extremely theatrical, self-dramatizing woman of exceptional beauty, almost constantly affected in manner, with no sense of monetary value and no real fundamental understand-

ing of life. She lives as she wishes, with few responsibilities and a casually distant relationship with her husband. She is primarily responsible for rearing Amory through his childhood and for almost sealing him in the mold of a precious young prig fascinated with his own glory. She and Amory come to understand each other very well, but he is hardly affected by the news of her death during World War I.

Thayer Darcy, a Catholic monsignor, forty-four years old when Amory meets him, robust, and somewhat stout. He creates an impressive figure in his religious regalia, much more striking in terms of his warmth, wisdom, and abiding religious faith, which he has won through a test of conscience and experience. He is almost perfect as the surrogate father whom Amory needs: appreciative of Amory's wit, guiding him toward sound moral and aesthetic precepts, showing him gradually the range and depth of life that Amory has not seen yet. He is encouraging, patient, nonjudgmental, incisive, and philosophic—a constant pleasure to know. He gives Amory a sense of his Irish/Celtic heritage, supports his quest, and accepts his egotism. He is a model for Amory to pattern himself after, and his death at the book's end marks the true beginning of Amory's adulthood.

Thomas Parke D'Invilliers, one of Amory's classmates at Princeton, who seems to be eccentrically out of touch with important social customs. He is stoop shouldered, with pale blue eyes. Amory eventually discovers that Thomas is genuinely literary and fundamentally traditional in outlook. He remains one of Amory's best friends and is able to discuss literature with passion and without affectation. He is drawn from the poet John Peale Bishop.

Kerry Holiday and
Burne Holiday, brothers at Princeton, housemates of Amory his freshman year. Kerry, good-natured, easygoing, and completely natural, volunteers for and dies in World War I. Burne seems to emerge during his junior year, when he reaches a position of socialism and pacificism and argues his reformist politics with passion, conviction, and an impressive, lucid logic.

Alec Connage, another of Amory's friends at Princeton, basically decent but essentially nondescript. He lacks the special essence of Amory's closest friends.

Rosalind Connage, Alec's sister, the great love of Amory's life, with "glorious yellow hair," an "eternal kissable mouth, small, slightly sensual," and "an unimpeachable skin with two spots of vanishing color." She is physically stunning and mentally overwhelming. Self-confident and self-possessed, her offhand, casually witty personality tends to distract people from her perceptive view of the world. She has a gift for romantic banter (possibly based on Zelda Sayre), and she and

Amory spend five weeks in an all-consuming relationship. Then, ruled by social expectations, she breaks off the affair and marries for money, comfort, and what she refers to as "background." In spite of her appeal, she exhibits tendencies to be vain, lazy, and self-ish—something that Amory is not aware of, caught up as he is in blind ardor.

Isabelle Borgé, Amory's first love, a girl from his hometown.

Clara Page, Amory's distant cousin, with whom he falls in love briefly. A beautiful, self-composed, mature woman, she is both regal in demeanor and democratic in attitude—too advanced for Amory.

Eleanor Savage, an impetuous eighteen-year-old with whom Amory has a brief summer romance shortly after his break with Rosalind. She is a reckless romantic, with a "gorgeous clarity of mind" and a self-destructive streak that recalls some of Edgar Allan Poe's more exotic heroines. Her incipient madness and her atheism attract and frighten Amory.

Leon Lewis

THIS SPORTING LIFE

Author: David Storey (1933-   )
Type of work: Novel
Time of action: The late 1950's
First published: 1960 (U.S. edition, 1961)

Arthur Machin, a professional rugby league football player for the Primstone Team in Northern England. Muscular, taciturn, self-reliant, in his early twenties, Arthur is grimly determined to succeed. Born in the working class, he seeks social respectability through athletic success. Rugby brings him money (and, thus, a car, a television, even women) that his full-time job as a machinist could never earn. Money and fame also give him a sense of power over others. In confident moments, he treats friends, parents, even his lover, as opposing players who must be knocked

down. On rare occasions, he is a gentle, generous giant.

Valerie Hammond, a widow with two small children, Arthur's landlady. Desperately poor and still grieving for her dead husband, she keeps emotionally and socially distant from Arthur despite his efforts to befriend her. She becomes his mistress when success allows him to treat her and the children to middle-class comforts. She resists Arthur's clumsy efforts at emotional commitment. She breaks off their relationship because of intense neighborhood gossip. Months later, when she suffers an eventually fatal stroke, Arthur is the only visitor.

Johnson, previously committee man for the team and now an aging hanger-on. He gets Arthur a tryout with a team. Though he protests that he wants no reward, he finds that Arthur now treats him contemptibly. As a sop, he is hired as a gardener by one of the team's owners.

Charles Weaver, an industrialist who owns the factory where Arthur works and co-owns the team for which Arthur plays. Annoyed by Arthur's egotism, he constantly votes to dismiss Arthur from the team. Toward the end of the novel, he temporarily succeeds.

Diane Weaver, the wife of Charles. Ostensibly dedicated to charitable works, she pursues handsome, young football players. She propositions Arthur, but he resists; later, she spurns his attempt to start a liaison.

Mr. Slomer, a co-owner of the team. An eccentric, reclusive semi-invalid, he is a mysterious figure to the players. He and Charles Weaver battle to control the team by supporting and promoting different players. His death at the end of the novel is regarded by all the characters as a turning point with unpredictable consequences in their lives and in the history of the team.

Frank, a rugby team captain. Like Arthur, he is a taciturn bull of a man. Unlike Arthur, he is content with working in the mines and with a normal domestic life. He also differs in that he puts no emphasis on the pleasures or powers which fame and money buy.

Maurice Braithwaite, Arthur's teammate and an employee at Weaver's factory. He is a thoughtless pleasure seeker and exhibitionist. Reluctantly he marries Judith, a secretary, when she becomes pregnant by him. Gradually, married life calms his restless instincts.

Robert M. Otten

THIS SUNDAY

Author: José Donoso (1924-   )
Type of work: Novel
Time of action: The late 1950's
First published: Este domingo, 1965 (English translation, 1967)

Josefina Rosas de Vives (hō•sĕ•fē′nä rō′säs dĕ vē′vĕs), called **Chepa,** the well-to-do daughter of Alejandro Rosas and the wife of the lawyer Alvaro, who likens her to a bitch constantly nursing a vast litter. In her preoccupation with giving aid and sustenance to slum dwellers, she assumes the character of an Artemis of Ephesus and even envisions herself as a many-breasted nurturer who, in giving suck to a multitude, is bitten and consumed. Her ostensible charity is actually an obsession with making others completely dependent upon her. In her passion to control others, she develops a strange attachment to a convicted murderer, Maya, whose release from prison she secures and whom she sets up in a leather business. Seeking him in the slums after his desertion of her, she is manhandled by the slum dwellers and loses consciousness. Broken by the experience and by her loss of Maya, she spends the last ten years of her life in silence and sadness and dies at the age of sixty-five.

Alvaro Vives, a fifty-five-year-old lawyer and husband of Chepa, who is the same age. His cancer, evidenced by an enlarging mole above his left nipple, will take his life within five months. His youthful sexual affair with Violeta had been followed by dates with many girls, eight of whom are named in the story, and by his marriage to Chepa when both are age twenty-two. Although he and Chepa have two daughters, his extramarital affairs with Matilde Greene (who later commits suicide), Carmen Méndez, and Picha attest his loveless marriage. Both he and Chepa, each irrefragably self-centered, are incapable of love. They remain married but stop sleeping together after the exposure of Alvaro's affair with Matilde Greene. His grandchildren call the terminally ill Alvaro *la Muñeca* (the Doll) because of his porcelain-like whiteness.

Maya, a convicted murderer. He is tall and ungainly. Like Alvaro, he has a mole, but it is on his upper lip and is not symptomatic of cancer; like Alvaro, again, he is compared to a doll, but, where Alvaro is in metaphor a *muñeca* (female doll), Maya is a *muñeco* (male doll). Maya exploits Chepa's fascination with him by prevailing upon her to secure his release from prison. Once released and set up in a leather business, which Chepa provides for him, he resents his subjection to her: She has arranged lodging for him at Violeta's house and keeps close tabs on him until he breaks with her and leaves Violeta's house. He loses all of his money and subsistence by betting on racehorses. His loss of independence frustrates his desire to be his own person. Ultimately, he can assert his individualism only by committing another murder as a means of being returned to prison.

Violeta, a maid in the household of Don Alvaro and his wife Elena, the parents of Alvaro. She had continued to serve without monetary compensation after a household staff retrenchment and was rewarded upon Elena's death with the legacy of a house. She is four years older than Alvaro (the son), although, on the Sunday that she initiates him in sexual union, she is said to be twenty-two (instead of twenty) to his sixteen. She remains the young Alvaro's sexual partner for six years, until he marries Chepa. She is abandoned by her lover, Marín, whose child she bears out of wedlock. Each Sunday she prepares a batch of *empanadas* (meat pastries) for Alvaro, Chepa, and their grandchil-

dren. Eventually she confesses to Chepa her sexual affair with Alvaro. She is murdered by Maya in his determination to be returned to prison.

Mirella (mē•rĕ′yä), the illegitimate daughter of Violeta and Marín. She marries an automobile mechanic named Fausto, and they have a daughter named Maruxa Jacqueline.

Meche, daughter of Alvaro and Chepa. She and her husband Lucho are the parents of Magdalena, Marta, Luis, and Alberto.

Pina, daughter of Alvaro and Chepa. She is married to a doctor.

The grandson of Alvaro and Chepa. The son of Pina and her husband, he narrates the three shorter sections of the novel (the two major parts are in third-person narrative). He is one year younger than Luis and the coeval of Alberto. He is in his mid-fifties as he gives his account of "this Sunday" at the home of his grandparents when they were in their mid-fifties: He and his four cousins played for the last time, on this particular Sunday, their game of Ueks (good people) and Cuecos (villains); the "funeral" of "Mariola Roncafort," the consummate Uek, was played as prelude to her "resurrection"; but there was to be no "resurrection." The games ended on this Sunday, during which Alvaro learned from his son-in-law, the doctor, about his terminal cancer; Violeta was murdered by Maya; and Chepa, seeking out Maya, was traumatically abused by her slum constituents.

Marujita Bueras (mä•rōō•hē′tä bōō•ĕ′räs), a peddler of shirts, who is married and who both visits Maya in prison and corresponds with him by mail. She proves to be a rival to Chepa for Maya's attentions.

Fanny Rodríguez, companion of Chepa on her visits to the penitentiary. She suggests that Chepa is in love with Maya and provides Chepa with information on how to use influence to gain Maya's release.

Bartolomé Páez, the warden of the penitentiary. He had been a clerk when Chepa's father was president of the supreme court.

Don Pedro Benítez, an official whose aid Chepa solicits in working out the release of Maya.

Gabriel, manager of the Caja de Crédito Industrial (Industrial Credit Bank), who approves Chepa's request to lend Maya the money for an expensive sewing machine. He is a man who has risen from the same poverty that Maya knew. In his success and affluence, he is disappointed that his wife and sister-in-law have gone into a candy-store business without needing to.

Antonia, the maid at the household of Alvaro and Chepa.

Roy Arthur Swanson

THOUSAND CRANES

Author: Yasunari Kawabata (1899-1972)
Type of work: Novel
Time of action: The late 1940's
First published: Sembazuru, 1949-1951, serial; 1952, book (English translation, 1958)

Kikuji Mitani, an orphan and a bachelor in his late twenties. A singularly passive man, he finds himself embroiled in the subtle machinations of his dead father's mistresses without having any clear sense of what he wants. He is given to much reflection about his father's love life and meditations on the utensils of the tea ceremony connected with Mrs. Ota, but he falls into her arms and later into the arms of her daughter without equal thought. He is attracted to the girl proposed as a bride for him, Yukiko Inamura, but seems unable to wring himself away from the women who were involved with his father.

Chikako Kurimoto, a teacher of the tea ceremony. After a few years as the mistress of Mitani's father, she seems to become sexless and appears to be fated to a lonely life because of a repulsively large black birthmark on her breasts. Unable to let go of the Mitani family after the affair, she becomes a family confidante, spewing her jealous resentment of the last mistress. She insists on being the go-between for Mitani and a young woman student of hers and, finding Mitani hesitating between two young women, tries to punish him by reporting that they are both married.

Yukiko Inamura, Chikako's student and a prospective bride for Mitani. Elegant, pleasing, she carries a pink scarf with a pattern of a thousand cranes, an omen that seems very promising for Mitani's future happiness.

Mrs. Ota, the widow of a fellow tea enthusiast of the elder Mitani. She was his mistress in the last years of his life. In her midforties, with a long white neck, small mouth and nose, full shoulders, and a warm, pliant manner, she seems to be attracted to Kikuji as a way of remembering his father. Clinging and affectionate, she is, however, consumed with guilt and commits suicide.

Fumiko Ota, daughter of Mrs. Ota. She inherits her mother's long neck but has a fuller mouth and very sad eyes. Ashamed of her mother's behavior, she nevertheless is also attracted to Mitani. She disappears mysteriously at the end, and there is a hint that she, too, may have committed suicide.

Shakuntala Jayaswal

THE THREE-CORNERED WORLD

Author: Sōseki Natsume (Kinnosuke Natsume, 1867-1916)
Type of work: Novel
Time of action: 1905
First published: Kusamakura, 1906 (*Unhuman Tour,* 1927; better known as *The Three-Cornered World*)

The narrator, a well-educated connoisseur of both Oriental and Western arts, literature, and philosophy. The narrator has fled the capital with its mundane distractions and involvements for a hiking trip to put himself in touch with nature and regain his artistic perspective. As he says, "an artist is a person who lives in the triangle which remains after the angle which we may call common sense has been removed from this four-cornered world." Because the artist lacks common sense, he can approach areas from which the average person shrinks in both the worlds of nature and humanity and find beauty. The narrator spends his time sketching, writing poems, philosophizing about art and life, and soaking up the atmosphere in the Shioda family inn at a small mountain hot spring.

O-Nami Shioda, the beautiful daughter of a wealthy innkeeper. O-Nami was forced to marry the son of a rich man of the local castle town rather than the boy she preferred. When the couple's money evaporated in a business turndown, O-Nami divorced her husband, returned to her father's home, and engaged in increasingly strange behavior. O-Nami entrances the narrator with her bizarre behavior and frank speech. He is awakened by her singing as she strolls through the garden; later, she enters his room while he sleeps and leaves reminders of her presence. She walks the veranda of the inn in her bridal gown and once enters the bathroom naked while the narrator is having a bath, only to run away laughing. O-Nami takes long walks in the mountains alone, writes poems that respond to the narrator's verses, and verbally spars with him as he tries to find out more about her.

The village barber, a rough-speaking village gossip. He provides the village perspective on O-Nami while he gives the narrator a painful shave and shampoo. He relates that a local monk, Taian, fell in love with O-Nami and expressed his affection in a letter. O-Nami responded by disrupting a prayer service and demanding that the monk publicly make love to her in front of the Buddha. He sees her as crazy and warns the narrator against her.

Kyuichi Shioda, a callow young cousin of O-Nami who does amateur paintings in the Western style. Kyuichi is drafted to serve in the army fighting Russians in Manchuria. He is encouraged to die a hero's death on the battlefield by O-Nami, and he has the mark of death already on his countenance as he says good-bye to the Shiodas and the narrator as they see him leave on the same train that takes O-Nami's husband off to Manchuria to begin a new life.

O-Nami's former husband, once a wealthy young man, now a wandering, beaten tramp who meets her in the mountains to beg money to go to Manchuria. The narrator, who secretly observes them from afar, fears that O-Nami seeks to kill him with the dagger she carries, a present from her father to Kyuichi.

Joseph Laker

THREE LIVES

Author: Gertrude Stein (1874-1946)
Type of work: Novel

Time of action: The early twentieth century
First published: 1909

Anna Federner, a middle-aged domestic servant, "the good Anna" who provides the title for the first of the three stories in the book. She is a hardworking, clean, immigrant German woman who fills her life with service to others. Through caring she exercises a measure of control over her employers, her dogs, and the young girls who are her assistants in the domestic sphere. Anna is not sophisticated or educated and is used by others because of her desire to be needed. She literally works herself to death being good to others.

Miss Mary Wadsmith, Anna's initial employer in Bridgeport. She is a large, fair, helpless woman, trying to rear her brother's orphaned children. She lets Anna make all the decisions that pertain to the family. She cannot control her niece, who, as she matures, challenges Anna's control and drives her away.

Miss Mathilda, Anna's second employer. She is a large, careless woman who needs Anna because Anna's willingness to take over the entire domestic sphere frees her to pursue other interests. She listens to Anna's problems and offers the kind of sympathetic understanding proper to a relationship based on class difference. Her interests finally take her to Europe (as Gertrude Stein's did), and Anna is left behind, totally bereaved.

Mrs. Lehntman, Anna's friend and the only love of her life besides her dogs. She is Anna's opposite in her easygoing approach to life and her failure to care about strict codes of behavior. She is a widow who acquires an extra child without thinking about financial responsibilities. She borrows money from Anna and others that she cannot repay and appears to be involved in illegal activities with a local doctor. Although she always lands on her feet, she finally alienates Anna.

Melanctha Herbert, eighteen years old at the beginning of the novella that takes her name in this second story, but somewhat older by the end of her adventures, when she dies, as do all the major women characters of these stories. Melanctha is a mulatto, whose mixed race reflects her difficulty in understanding where she belongs. Melanctha is intelligent, adventuresome, desirous of learning what life means. She lives always in the present in her fearless, apparently undirected way. She naturally accepts the life of feeling and learning as opposed to the life of fixed rules and appearances. As a result, she enters into a number of fluid relationships that bring her disillusionment and disappointment and lead to her death by tuberculosis.

Dr. Jeff Campbell, a hardworking, serious black physician who opposes the fluidity of Melanctha's life and wants to create a life of traditional values for his people. His love affair with Melanctha ends when the conflicts that the two of them represent overwhelm him.

Jane Harden, a hard-drinking, independent, educated mulatto who teaches Melanctha much of what she learns about life. Jane's rebellious understanding takes Melanctha only so far, however, and her influence lessens when Melanctha meets Jeff.

Rose Johnson, a careless, negligent, sullen, childlike, selfish black woman who allows her child to die because of indifference. She is a friend of Melanctha and the opposite of Jane Harden. Rose does not question or seek to learn but accepts things as they are and has her place in the social fabric of the black community. She uses Melanctha until she becomes jealous of Melanctha's friendship with her husband.

Jem Richards, Melanctha's last lover and a gambler, dashing and powerful, honest, and fast in his life. The power attracts Melanctha, but his desire for freedom is greater than hers, and he abandons her.

Lena Mainz, the title character of "The Gentle Lena." She is brought to Bridgeport from Germany by her cousin, who is unable to understand that Lena's gentleness is a result of her passivity. So simple is Lena that she seems to have no desires in this world or concern about autonomy of any kind. Manipulated into an unhappy marriage, she bears three children, who bring her no joy. Lena becomes increasingly lifeless in her marriage until she bears a fourth baby, a stillborn child, and, the birth taking what life she has, she dies.

Herman Kreder, Lena's husband, a German American tailor who works for his father. He is an unimaginative, spoiled mother's boy, who has no will to protect his wife from his mother's interference until he realizes that he will be a father. As Lena becomes more lifeless with each child, Herman becomes more involved in the lives of his childen, loving and caring for them because they are his. After Lena's death, he is very content not to have a woman always around, for he has his three children.

Mrs. Haydon, Lena's cousin, a hard, ambitious, well-meaning German American woman married to a well-to-do-grocer. She exercises power by arranging other people's lives for their own good, and Lena is a victim of her "goodness."

Donna Gerstenberger

THE THREE MARIAS

Author: Rachel de Queiroz (1910-   )
Type of work: Novel
Time of action: The 1930's
First published: As três Marias, 1939 (English translation, 1963)

Maria Augusta (Guta), the narrator, a student in a girls' boarding school and later a typist in the city of Fortaleza, Brazil. Awkward and fearful, she is relieved to find friends during her first days at the nuns' school; she, Maria José, and Glória share one another's hopes, enthusiasms, fantasies, and discouragements. After graduation, Guta tires of the monotony of home life, gets a job in Fortaleza, and soon moves in with Maria José. Guta is intrigued by a middle-aged Bohemian painter, Raul; he paints her portrait and almost seduces her. Guta's father sends her money for a trip to Rio because she is depressed after a friend, Aluísio, commits suicide, and in Rio she meets a young Romanian doctor, Isaac, falls in love, and returns to Fortaleza pregnant. After a miscarriage and illness, she returns home to Crato, in the Cariri region, where her father, her dull and virtuous stepmother, and her younger half brothers and half sisters live.

Maria José, Guta's closest friend and the first girl to befriend her at the nuns' school. After they have left school and are working, Maria José, who teaches school and is devoutly religious, shares her room in her mother's house with Guta.

Maria da Gloria (Glória), Guta's other close friend at the convent school and afterward. An orphan at age twelve, Glória venerated the memory of the poet-father who reared her, and her friends admire her passionate mourning and her talent as a violinist. Soon after they are graduated, she becomes engaged to Afonso, a young college graduate, and she centers her emotional energy upon him. Guta and Maria José attend her wedding. The birth of Glória's son is also an important event for her two friends.

Jandira (zhăṅ·dē·rə'), a friend of the three Marias at the school. The illegitimate daughter of a married man and a prostitute, she has been cared for and sent to school by her father's sisters. She marries a seaman during their last year at school, but the marriage is an unhappy one. Their child is almost blind, and Jandira toils as a seamstress to support him. She is left a house and money by her aunt, takes a lover, and is much happier.

Raul, a middle-aged married painter who fascinates Guta and with whom she imagines herself in love for a while. He seems romantic and mysterious to her, and she goes with Maria José and Aluísio to his studio and agrees to model for a portrait. Alternately repelled and attracted, Guta is almost seduced by him but realizes just in time that she does not want to be sexually involved with Raul. Guta is very disillusioned when she sees him as he really is.

Aluísio, an emotional young student, a friend of Guta and Maria José, who commits suicide and leaves a letter in which he alludes to an unhappy love affair. Everyone assumes that his passion was for Guta. She visits him before he dies and is much distressed, although she knows that his death is not really her fault.

Isaac, a young Romanian Jewish immigrant whom Guta meets at the boardinghouse where she stays when she visits Rio. He is studying to validate his medical diploma and risks being deported if he fails the examination. He talks to Guta about Romania, plays records for her, and encourages her to tell him about her home and memories. She falls in love with him, and they become lovers just before Guta must return to her job in Fortaleza. She never tells him that she is pregnant with his child, and he does not speak to her of plans for a future together, although he writes letters to her.

Mary G. Berg

THE THREE SISTERS

Author: May Sinclair (1863-1946)
Type of work: Novel
Time of action: The early 1900's
First published: 1914

Gwendolyn Cartaret, the defiant and perceptive second daughter of James Cartaret, twenty-five years old when the novel opens. Keenly sensitive to nature, she assumes responsibility for visiting outlying parishioners in the lonely Yorkshire moors and thrives on strenuous hikes in the evenings as well. Slender, with translucent skin and expressive hands, she is a nervous beauty whose inner strength impresses other characters forcibly. She sees through her father's hypocrisy and maintains an intellectual's reverence for truth yet is susceptible to pointless self-sacrifice. She leaves Steven Rowcliffe, who loves her, in hopes that he will marry Alice. Later, she is forced to endure his mistaken choice of Mary, when she returns to Garth to nurse her father after his stroke.

James Cartaret, the Vicar of Garth. His egotism and sensuality oppress his daughters; his fear of public opinion has led him to move to the isolated community of Garth when the novel begins. He is cold, domineering, unsuited for both his profession and the celibate life that he is forced by his wife's desertion to lead. He bullies his daughters endlessly, afraid only of Gwendolyn who opposes him. His control of his daughters' lives relaxes after a stroke, which renders him a gentle, pathetic old man relying on Gwendolyn for daily care.

Mary Cartaret, twenty-seven years old, the oldest daughter of the vicar, responsible for teaching Sunday School. Proud of her own goodness, Mary is a placid, deceptive beauty, who encourages Gwendolyn to leave Garth only to woo Steven Rowcliffe herself. After her marriage, her self-deception turns to hypocrisy, as she increasingly cultivates acquaintance with "good" society. She becomes a neglectful mother of three children and torments Gwendolyn with evidence of her satisfying marriage to Steven.

Alice Cartaret, the youngest daughter of the vicar, responsible for directing the church choir and playing the organ for church service. At twenty-three, with little outlet for her passionate nature, she is subject to hysteria and responds to her father's bullying by starving herself into serious anemia. Believing that she is in love with the doctor, she blossoms into youthful beauty; her graceful manner and golden hair and skin attract Jim Greatorex. She forgets the doctor in her quest to reform Jim and matures during the course of their love affair. Her pregnancy by and subsequent marriage to this farmer from a significantly lower social class precipitate the vicar's stroke. Motherhood turns her into a plump, cheerful matron, completely absorbed in her children.

Steven Rowcliffe, the village doctor, who has left a successful practice in Leeds to minister to the needs of country patients. At thirty, he is stimulated by the rough people and countryside and finds that the outdoor demands of his job appeal to his romantic nature. Handsome, somewhat vain, embracing strenuous activity, he is drawn to Gwendolyn, although he is jealous of her capacity to lose herself in the natural beauty of the moors. His egotism is appeased by Mary's attention after Gwendolyn rejects his proposal of marriage and goes to London. Only after Gwendolyn's return does he realize that Mary bores him and has captured him by appealing to his latent laziness. Sensual and passionate, he urges Gwendolyn to have an affair with him; when she refuses, his love for her gradually wanes over the years.

Jim Greatorex, a young farmer who marries Alice after she is pregnant with his child. He begins the novel dominated by his physical needs, but his drunkenness and his affairs with village serving girls cease when he falls in love with Alice. Despite his brutishness, he is capable of great gentleness and inarticulate appreciation of natural beauty, traits demonstrated by his emotive, powerful baritone voice. Frustrated by a lack of faith, he finds purpose in protecting Alice, and his sensitivity appeals to Gwendolyn, who discovers that he shares her passion for nature.

Essy Gale, a young servant at the vicarage. She is forced to leave her position when the vicar discovers that she is pregnant with Jim Greatorex's child. Despite social ostracism, Essy maintains her dignity by refusing to marry Jim because she knows that he does not love her. She finds solace in the fact that Gwendolyn is genuinely kind to her and later returns to work for the vicar after his stroke has erased the memory of her past mistakes.

Gweneth A. Dunleavy

THREE TRAPPED TIGERS

Author: Guillermo Cabrera Infante (1929-   )
Type of work: Novel
Time of action: Summer, 1958
First published: Tres tristes tigres, 1967 (English translation, 1971)

Bustrófedon (bōōs·tr̄rō′fĕ·dōn), a character who embodies language and its creative potential. His name, of Greek origin, means "to write alternately from right to left and left to right." During his lifetime, he has been fascinated with anything that was reversible, words, numbers, or concepts. He represents an appreciation of the potentiality of language and of the sheer joy of spontaneous and uninhibited creation. He is a character in the process of discovering and creating himself through language. Although he dies, he lives in the minds of many of the novel's characters.

Silvestre, a would-be writer. Estranged from the present, he is obsessed with the past, preferring his memories over experiencing life. He is particularly concerned with ordering the chaos of existence by means of the written word. He is linked to one of the novel's major themes: man's attempt to comprehend the implications of formlessness.

Arsenio Cué, a professional actor, television star, and Silvestre's closest friend. His personal and professional lives merge to such an extent that they seem one and the same. He is so often playing a role that it is difficult to know who he is. His humor, his continual role-playing, and his dark sunglasses protect him from the outside world. His playful excursions into the world of fantasy have a serious purpose; he lives in a society that is wasting its energies in useless dissipation, yet he attempts to channel his activities into creative forces. His view is that the universe is dominated by chance rather than by order.

Códac, a photojournalist. He is first a superficial recorder of the social scene, then later becomes involved in the more realistic and distasteful journalistic duties of photographing political reality during the last months of the dictatorship of Fulgencio Batista. Although sensitive to visual reality, he is also able to appreciate the beauty beneath the superficial appearances, underscoring one of the novel's major themes: the importance of re-creation instead of duplication, creation rather than sterility, change rather than permanence.

Eribó, a lonely mulatto bongo drum player and would-be social climber. He becomes emotionally involved with Vivian Smith Corona, a spoiled and immature member of the upper class, but the relationship leads nowhere. Eribó recognizes the pathos of the situation and views it in ironic terms. His association with Vivian is typical of most of the relationships that exist between men and women in the novel. These relationships, essentially sterile and self-defeating, are also symptomatic of this society.

La Estrella (lä ĕs•tr̄rĕ′yä), a huge mulatta singer of boleros. Although she is obese and generally unattractive, she is an outstanding singer, capable of creating a purity of sound that moves everyone who hears her. La Estrella is a combination of the ugly and the beautiful, a symbol of life itself. She and Bustrófedon's unique use of language and sound represent an attempt to return to origins in order to capture the freshness of a new beginning. They are, however, an anomaly in a society that is committed to artificiality and illusion.

Genevieve Slomski

THE THREEPENNY OPERA

Author: Bertolt Brecht (1898-1956)
Type of work: Play
Time of action: 1837, immediately before and during the coronation ceremonies for Queen Victoria
First produced: Die Dreigroschenoper, 1928 (English translation, 1949)

Macheath, or **Mac the Knife,** head of a gang of London petty criminals. He manages his crooked affairs through "understandings" with Sheriff Brown. An incorrigible philanderer, he is involved with Brown's daughter, Lucy, but also entices Polly, daughter of "Beggar Boss" Peachum, into matrimony. This act outrages Peachum, who vows to undo Macheath by working a deal with Sheriff Brown. Mac's enemies are convinced that, even when warned that a plot has been hatched against him, he will not flee far; soon he is caught while making his habitual turn among the harlots of Turnbridge. Because Mac is an inveterate wheeler and dealer, however, he is able to bribe his way out of the charges and even to obtain recognition for service to the crown, something that becomes very attractive to the Peachums.

Jonathan Jeremiah "Beggar Boss" Peachum, the proprietor of Beggar's Friend, Ltd. He organizes London's beggars quarter by quarter, giving them territories and pitiful roles to play. Although Peachum himself is an obvious opportunist, the destitute figures under him provide a channel to convey the social revolutionary theme of the play. Peachum is distracted from organizing an unprecedented parade of beggars at Queen Victoria's coronation by the troublesome scandal of his daughter's marriage to Mac. A mixture of opportunism and pomposity is revealed in Peachum, whose concern over the poor focuses mainly on how to use them to his benefit.

Polly Peachum, the daughter of Jonathan Peachum. Polly marries Macheath in a ceremony that reflects the milieu to which her father, in obvious hypocrisy, objects: The marriage takes place in a "borrowed" stable; all accessories, including furniture, are stolen. Polly is not timid about her association with Mac's gang, prompting her mother's recollection that "even as a child she had a swelled head like the Queen of England." When Mac is pursued by the law, Polly is asked by Mac to "manage" the gang's affairs. In her dealings with her parents, as well as in her verbal confrontations with Sheriff Brown's daughter Lucy, who also claims Mac's amorous loyalties, Polly demonstrates an uncanny ability to turn vulnerability into moral superiority.

Jack Brown, or **Tiger Brown,** High Sheriff of London, Mac's friend since childhood days and a former fellow soldier with him in the colonial army in India. Brown receives a cut from all profits of Mac's gang. He suffers pangs of conscience over his friend's arrest and is only partially embarrassed when Mac escapes. He is soon caught in a quandary, however, when Peachum threatens to compromise the high sheriff by amassing hundreds of beggars at the queen's coronation. Brown learns that, unless Mac hangs, he will have to undergo the unpleasantness of removing the destitute from the shadow of regal splendor by brute force. On the other hand, the sheriff is worried that, if a public execution is carried out, the crowds that would have cheered the queen will throng to the side of the gallows. Brown outdoes himself arranging a deal, gaining not only a reprieve but also the queen's award of an honorary peerage, a pension, and a castle to Mac the Knife. This device satisfies the Peachums.

Lucy Brown, daughter of High Sheriff Brown. She has been involved amorously with Mac; upon her discovery of Mac's marriage and her first confrontation with Polly, her role is that of a frenetic woman propelled by jealousy. As the plot advances, however, and Mac must flee both women to avoid arrest, Lucy's weaknesses show through. Not only does Mac succeed in making her believe that he loves only her but also (perhaps because she is so gullible as to believe Mac) she comes to commiserate with her rival Polly, whom she now calls "Mrs. Macheath." Both women come to the conclusion that men are not worth the frustration that they cause.

Byron D. Cannon

A TICKET TO THE STARS

Author: Vassily Aksyonov (1932-   )
Type of work: Novel
Time of action: Summer, 1960
First published: Zvyozdnyi bilet, 1961 (*A Starry Ticket*, 1962; better known as *A Ticket to the Stars*)

Dimka, a seventeen-year-old who has recently been graduated from high school. He represents the generation of Russian youth born during World War II, who have little knowledge at first hand of the hardships that their parents experienced. Having completed his secondary education, he is faced with the decision of whether to continue his education or to seek a job. Even though he loves his parents and admires his older brother, Victor, a space scientist, Dimka leaves home and Moscow, mainly because he wants to make his own decisions for the first time in his life. This rebelliousness stems from the fact that young people in the Soviet Union are constantly told what to do instead of being allowed to make their own decisions. Even Dimka's successful brother cannot escape the criticism of being too pliant in acquiescing to the system. That Dimka is not rebellious only for the sake of asserting his independence, justified though it may be, is shown at the end of the novel, when he returns home upon hearing about his brother's fatal accident. Through this act he confirms his integrity and innate sense of responsibility. This attitude bodes well for the young Soviet generation, showing that its individuals can think and act for themselves after decades of submissiveness.

Yurka, Dimka's classmate, who joins him on the postgraduation journey and becomes a "kilometer eater" instead of meekly accepting the will of his elders. With his feet placed firmly on the ground, Yurka shows promise in the sports field and hopes to become a basketball star. Yet he is willing to forgo the best chance of achieving that goal, which would mean that he would have to stay at home. Like Dimka and others, Yurka is a young man whose behavior is typical for his age, as seen in his desire to have fun and in his falling in love with Galya. At the same time, he, too, demonstrates a readiness to make his own decisions and to sacrifice the benefits of going along with the system.

Alik, Dimka's and Yurka's classmate and trip companion. More withdrawn and art-oriented, Alik has writing ambitions, hoping to make writing his career. By asserting his independence and by wasting time in aimless wandering, he risks losing the best chance of learning the writing skills, a continuing education. Yet he is willing to take that risk, knowing intuitively that the best way to become a good writer is to get to know the world outside the benevolent but stifling protection of his parents. Like his friends, Alik shows a remarkable maturity for his age and a fiercely independent spirit.

Galya, Dimka's girlfriend and classmate. Galya asserts her will by leaving on the trip with three classmates, against her parents' wishes. She behaves normally for her age when she flirts with Yurka, even though she is Dimka's girlfriend, and when she falls for the tall tales of a middle-aged actor, a chance acquaintance, who promises to help her in her acting career. She is a perfect companion for the three boys in showing the same desire for independence. She also demonstrates that this desire is genuine and widespread among the Russian youth.

Victor, Dimka's older brother, a space scientist. A member of a prewar generation, Victor displays a more obedient mentality and a willingness to serve the system. Yet he, too, shows signs of independence when, after discovering new material, he refuses to complete his dissertation only for the sake of getting a degree. He is also more understanding of the young people, as he refuses to interfere with Dimka's decision to leave home, even though he disagrees with it. Victor's lasting legacy is "a ticket to the stars" for the younger generations, which prompts Dimka to abandon his quest for a new life of adventure and uncertainty and to follow in his brother's footsteps. Victor can thus be seen as a middleman between the old and the new generations and a guidepost toward a better future.

Vasa D. Mihailovich

THE TIDINGS BROUGHT TO MARY

Author: Paul Claudel (1868-1955)
Type of work: Play
Time of action: The early years of the fifteenth century
First produced: L'Annonce faite à Marie, 1912 (English translation, 1916)

Violaine Vercors (vĕr•côr'), the eighteen-year-old daughter of Anne and Elisabeth, Mara's elder sister. She is engaged to marry Jacques Hury, a farmer. In the prologue, she forgives Pierre de Craon, a mason, who had attempted to rape her. He now suffers from leprosy. As he is about to leave their village for Rheims in order to build a church appropriately named Holy Justice, Violaine gives him her engagement ring as a contribution to the construction costs. She then kisses Pierre as a sign of her forgiveness. She thus becomes infected with leprosy, from which she will die. Although she loves Jacques, her fiancé, she tells him that they can never marry each other. After she leaves their village of Combernon, he marries her younger sister, Mara. When their baby Aubaine dies, Mara implores Violaine to pray to God so that Aubaine may live. Aubaine is miraculously restored to life. As this play ends, Violaine encourages her father, her sister, and her brother-in-law to appreciate God's intense love for humanity.

Pierre de Craon (crä•ōṅ'), a mason who appears only in the prologue to this play. He bitterly regrets his attempted rape of Violaine. He tells her that his leprosy is a divine punishment for his crime. She believes that his repentance is sincere. He is miraculously cured of his leprosy. While in Jerusalem, he meets Violaine's father and gives him her engagement ring.

Anne Vercors, husband to Elisabeth and father of two grown daughters, Violaine and Mara, a farmer. After having arranged Violaine's forthcoming marriage to Jacques Hury, he informs his wife and daughters that God needs him to make a pilgrimage to the Holy Land. Anne believes that he must sacrifice his comfortable life in France in order to serve God. When he returns to his village, he finds Violaine unconscious in the sand. He brings her home and explains to Jacques

and Mara that Violaine freely contracted leprosy in order to serve God through suffering and prayer.

Jacques Hury (hü•rē'), a young and sensible farmer engaged to marry Violaine. When he learns from her that she suffers from leprosy, he agrees with her that they should never marry. He arranges for her to leave Combernon for Chevoche, where she will be cared for. Although he does marry Mara, he never stops loving Violaine. As Violaine is dying, Anne tells Jacques that she was inspired by God to sacrifice happiness so that she could dedicate her life to prayer.

Mara Vercors, Violaine's younger sister, first portrayed as self-centered and manipulative. Mara wanted to marry Jacques; she tells her mother that she will commit suicide if her mother does not prevent Violaine's wedding to Jacques. After Violaine becomes a leper, Mara does marry Jacques. When their baby daughter, Aubaine, dies, Mara implores her sister to intervene with God. While Violaine prays, Mara recites readings from the masses for Christmas Day. Their prayers are answered with Aubaine's miraculous restoration to life. After his return from the Holy Land, Anne helps Mara to understand that altruism can overcome selfishness. Thanks to Anne and Violaine, Mara grows both spiritually and emotionally.

Elisabeth Vercors, wife of Anne and mother of Violaine and Mara, hurt by her husband's sudden decision to leave for the Holy Land and by Mara's threat to commit suicide. She feels abandoned by her husband and she cannot understand Mara's extreme selfishness. Elisabeth dies sometime between the wedding of Jacques and Mara and the birth of her granddaughter, Aubaine.

Edmund J. Campion

TIETA, THE GOAT GIRL
Or, The Return of the Prodigal Daughter

Author: Jorge Amado (1912-   )
Type of work: Novel
Time of action: The mid-1960's
First published: Tiêta do Agreste, 1977 (English translation, 1979)

Antonieta Esteves Cantarelli, also called **Tieta,** the wealthy owner of the Lord's Retreat, a sophisticated bordello in São Paulo. A middle-aged, curly haired brunette who dresses her tall, voluptuous, dark-skinned body in red turbans, blonde wigs, and skin-tight jeans, the sexy Tieta unashamedly lusts for good men, fine food, and unbridled laughter. Her goatlike stubbornness, pragmatism, and flinty hardness sometimes conflict with her genuine loving-kindness but just as often translate her generosity into action. Tieta's arrival in backward Sant'Ana do Agreste to visit her impoverished relatives and birthplace catalyzes changes in the town and crises in many characters. She uses her bordello-related influence to obtain electricity for the town, which attracts the interest of the deadly titanium dioxide industry. Her many acts of goodness earn for her the title of saint, until the town discovers her true profession and her seduction of her nephew.

Ascânio Trindade (əz·kân′yō), Agreste's county clerk. A good-looking, serious-faced official of twenty-eight, Ascânio is frank, friendly, honest, kind, and sometimes excitable in his dreams about a possible bright future for Agreste. He suffers a cruel betrayal by his betrothed, from which he does not recover until he falls in love with Leonora. In his sincere dreams for progress, the innocent Ascânio becomes the pawn of the titanium dioxide industry as the industry's candidate for mayor. This influence gradually corrupts him. His last vestiges of goodness are shattered when he discovers that Leonora is a prostitute.

Ricardo Batista, a seminarian and Perpétua's older son. A tall, dark, muscular, good-looking, husky, and somewhat gangling youth of seventeen with the hint of a mustache, Ricardo exudes innocence and good health

in his black cassock. He is tortured by his lust for Tieta, which finally triumphs over his devotion to God. Through a talk with a wise old holy man, however, he finally realizes that he can be both priest and lover. He consequently pursues both paths with such dedication that Tieta throws him naked into the street when she learns of his other lovers. Ricardo also matures into a radical champion against the titanium dioxide industry.

Perpétua Esteves Batista, Tieta's widowed older sister. A stern-faced, bony-chested, domineering sourpuss with a perpetually constipated face, Perpétua masks her greed and meanness in exaggerated piety. Her covetous wish to have Ricardo become Tieta's heir provides Tieta the chance to seduce him, but Perpétua's wrath abates when Tieta compensates her in cash for the seminarian's lost virginity.

Elisa Esteves Simas, Tieta's younger half sister. A slender, graceful, sensitive brunette whose luxurious hair frames a pretty pale face with full lips, and melancholy eyes, Elisa lives in constant sexual frustration, since her husband insists on treating her high-haunched, firm-breasted body with delicate respect. Elisa longs to move to exciting São Paulo, even if she must become a prostitute, until Tieta persuades Asterio to make love to Elisa with more force and abandon.

Leonora Cantarelli, a prostitute at the Lord's Retreat. A slim, blonde, youthful sylph, charming and sweet with a crystalline laugh, Leonora masquerades as Tieta's stepdaughter. Her impoverished and brutal past has not destroyed a core of innocence and a longing for true love, which she thinks that she has found with Ascânio. When she tearfully confesses her true identity, Ascânio rejects her, and she tries to commit suicide.

Donna Carmosina Sluizer da Consolação (lōō·zĭr′də kŏn·sōō·lə·souṅ′), Agreste's postmistress. Light-skinned, with a freckled, broad face, keen eyes, and a keener wit, Carmosina loves life and laughter but grieves that she is still a virgin at age fifty. She freely reads everyone's mail and controls local gossip, but she does so with benevolent intentions.

Skipper Dário Queluz (kä·lōōsh′), a retired seaman. Athletic but philosophic, Skipper Dário commands love and respect with his integrity and kindly smile. His love for the natural beauty of Agreste makes him sacrifice his reclusive life-style to become an antipollution candidate for mayor.

Doctor Mirko Stefano, a São Paulo industrialist. With his matinee-idol looks, avant-garde clothes, and prissy, affected voice, the unscrupulous Mirko contrives to establish a deadly titanium dioxide factory in Agreste.

Peto Batista, Perpétua's youngest son. A lewd, precocious thirteen-year-old, Peto cannot understand Ricardo's resistance to Tieta's attractions.

Asterio Simas, Elisa's husband. Weak-willed and unambitious since giving up the unorthodox sexual practices of his bachelorhood, Asterio finally heeds Tieta's advice to express his deepest desires with his wife.

Timothy C. Davis

TILL WE HAVE FACES
A Myth Retold

Author: C. S. Lewis (1898-1963)
Type of work: Novel
Time of action: Sometime after the death of Socrates (399 B.C.) and before the birth of Christ
First published: 1956

Orual, or **Maia,** the eldest princess of Glome and finally its queen. The narrator of the story, she is caught between her love of learning as presented in the ideals of Greek philosophy and poetry and her earthy, passionate nature. So ugly as to have no hope of romantic love, Orual attaches herself fiercely to her Greek tutor and her divinely beautiful half sister, Istra/Psyche, while secretly cherishing a love for the soldier who teaches her swordsmanship. Each love is marred by her inability to release its object, a fault most evident with Istra, who is doomed to exile through Orual's possessive jealousy. Orual rules Glome well; she is brave in battle and wise in council. The story is told in her old age, as an accusation against gods and their inscrutable cruelty, and covers Orual's life from childhood. Visions and dreams cause the book to end in understanding and acceptance of the paradox of divinity as Orual dies.

Istra, or **Psyche,** the youngest princess of Glome, the lovely child of the king's second wife. She fills Orual's hungry heart but is too beautiful for a mortal; she is sacrificed to the "Shadow Beast," a manifestation of the son of Glome's patron goddess, Ungit. As Ungit is understood as a cultural alternate form of Aphrodite (Venus), her son is the Glome Eros (Cupid). Thus Istra/Psyche and Ungit's son tie Lewis' tale with the Cupid-Psyche myth of antiquity. The princess' sacrifice is also a wedding, and Psyche lives in an invisible palace with a divine husband whom she must never see. When Orual forces a betrayal of the god-bridegroom, Psyche is doomed to lose her love and home and wander weeping through the world. Before her own death, Orual encounters a shrine where Istra/Psyche is worshiped as a goddess of spring and renewal.

Lysias, the **"Fox,"** a Greek slave bought as a status symbol to teach the children of the king. He stands as an affectionate father to Orual and Istra, teaching them the intellectual ideals of Greek philosophy, yet he is unable to fathom the nature of divinity manifested in Ungit. He renounces his hope of a return to Greece in order to stay with Orual as a councillor when she frees him.

Trom, the brutal, selfish king of Glome, who rejects his daughters in the hope of having a son, railing against the gods and fate in his misfortunes of war, famine, and disease. He uses Orual's intellectual gifts but dies in terror of her, realizing in his last illness the growth of her power in his own decline.

Bardia, captain of the king's guards and councillor to Orual. He teaches her military arts and accompanies her on her first search for the body of the sacrificed Istra. Devoted to martial virtues and common sense, Bardia never sees Orual as a woman or realizes that she loves him. His widow accuses Orual of working her devoted servant to death.

Redival, the middle princess, beautiful in mortal terms, also hungry for love and jealous of

Orual's tie with Istra. She is a flirt and a gossip, whose indiscretions help lead to Istra's sacrifice. Orual marries her to a neighboring king and adopts her second son as heir to the throne of Glome.

Priest of Ungit, the immensely old and inscrutable representative of the abuses and mystery surrounding the worship of the goddess Ungit. It is he who demands the sacrifice of Princess Istra. He dies of a long illness at the same time as does Trom.

Arnom, the successor to the old priest of Ungit. He understands his goddess as a Hellenized and abstract deity, an Aphrodite represented by a Greek statue that displaces Ungit's shapeless, faceless stone. Arnom is a skilled politician, alert to the interests of the temple. His establishment as chief priest is contemporary with Orual's accession to the throne, and they work as allies. He ends the novel with praise of the dead queen.

Anne W. Sienkewicz

THE TILTED CROSS

Author: Hal Porter (1911-1984)
Type of work: Novel
Time of action: The 1840's
First published: 1961; revised, 1971

Judas Griffin Vaneleigh, an artist and former convict. Once a handsome, dashing figure of consequence in London artistic circles, Vaneleigh has lost his aristocratic air and has turned into a broken man, both in appearance and in spirit, even though he is only in his early forties. Vaneleigh's character draws from a historical figure, Thomas Griffiths Wainewright, who, like his fictional counterpart, was convicted of forgery in England and transported to the Australian penal colony, Van Dieman's Land (present-day Tasmania). There Vaneleigh eventually gains release from prison and becomes a "ticket-of-leave man" (parolee), who survives by painting portraits of local socialites. Once Vaneleigh's assignment at Cindermead, the Knight

estate, sets the action in motion, he remains in the background until his death.

Queely Sheill, Vaneleigh's unpaid attendant. In his early twenties, he is strikingly handsome, almost an Adonis-like figure. Although a sex object to women and men of all ages, as well as a guardian angel to the downtrodden, Queely appears somewhat stupid and naïve. The son of an itinerant actor, Queely offers his services to Vaneleigh, partly out of pity, partly out of admiration for this rare "gentleman" in a town of convicts, their keepers, ersatz aristocrats, and wretched hangers-on. He accompanies Vaneleigh to Cindermead and there enters into a sexual liaison with a houseguest, the consequences of which determine what little plot the novel possesses. Falsely accused of theft, Queely goes to prison, where he dies, transformed at that point into a Christ figure.

Sir Sydney Knight, master of Cindermead and a government official. Sir Sydney, approaching middle age, is virile in appearance but in truth is impotent. A caricature of the nineteenth century British colonial civil servant, Sir Sydney is blustering, pompous, petty, ruthless, ambitious, and self-important.

Lady Rose Knight, Sir Sydney's wife. Frustrated by her husband's impotence, Lady Rose takes a series of lovers. In her forties (perhaps fifties), vicious and stupid, overdressed and overwrought, she plays the grand lady of Cindermead to the hilt. Her jealousy of Asnetha Sleep's conquest of the handsome Queely leads her to the action that destroys the young man.

Asnetha Sleep, a wealthy English cousin of Sir Sydney and a houseguest at Cindermead. Roughly thirty years old, she is crippled, wears outlandish clothes and jewelry, drinks too much, and behaves in a bizarre way. Without harm to her reputation, she manages to extricate herself from the affair with Queely and marries a local fortune hunter.

Orfée Maka (Teapot), a West Indian servant to Asnetha Sleep. In his mid-teens, he is inordinately fond of his mistress, who both mistreats him and dotes on him. The exotic, simpleminded Teapot inadvertently becomes involved in Lady Rose's revenge on Asnetha and Queely.

John Death Sheill, father of Queely and an itinerant actor. Monstrously fat, drunken, womanizing, the elder Sheill serves as the antithesis to his son. Otherwise, his main function is to provide a kind of comic relief, though black in nature, and to heighten the decadence that pervades the novel.

Polidorio Smith, also called **"the duchess,"** another actor and housemate of the Sheills. He is of indeterminate age, skinny and angular, drunken, and excessively talkative. A homosexual, he is also known as "the duchess" and has long been in love with Queely. Like his fellow actor, he serves primarily as a background figure to create a milieu of wretchedness and moral depravity.

Robert L. Ross

TIME AND THE CONWAYS

Author: J. B. Priestley (1894-1984)
Type of work: Play
Time of action: 1919 and 1938
First produced: 1937

Mrs. Conway, a widow in a provincial town. She is in her mid-forties at the start of the play, and is well dressed, talkative, and very conscious of her status in local society. She is at her best at parties and other social gatherings; she has little practical knowledge or talent. Her behavior as a mother is a central concern in the play, as the promising lives of her children are shown to be wasted, and she herself faces financial ruin at the end of the play.

Alan Conway, the eldest son and a clerk. Rather shy and silent, he is in his early twenties as the play begins. He stammers and dresses shabbily. Initially, he seems a failure in contrast to the other characters; yet, his sense of futility finally extends to the rest of the family. He is truly good-natured and is the person closest to Kay. It is Alan who elaborates for Kay the theory of time at the heart of the play.

Madge Conway, the eldest sister. She is a well-educated and efficient woman, busy with plans for social and political reform.

She is the least attractive of the sisters but has a romantic interest in Gerald Thornton early in the play, an interest that might be returned. A possible union with Thornton is thwarted by her mother, who treats her ideas with scorn, and Madge ultimately becomes the hostile, defensive headmistress of a girl's school.

Robin Conway, the younger son. His mother's favorite and a loafer with no apparent talent, Robin is returning from World War I as the play begins. He is charming and good-looking and spends much of his time pursuing Joan Helford, to whom he is married and whom he subsequently abandons. He manipulates his mother, who gives him money, but he proves unable to help her when she faces financial difficulties.

Hazel Conway, the most beautiful and popular of the Conway sisters. Fair-haired and elegant, seemingly self-confident, she is at her best at parties and games. She is pursued by and finally married to Ernest Beevers, a social-climbing young man who represents everything that the Conways scorn. She becomes a weak and terrorized wife.

Kay Conway, an aspiring writer. The play begins at her twenty-first birthday party. Not as pretty as Hazel or as serious as Madge, she is sensitive and doubtful of her own talent. Kay's perceptions control the structure of the play; the middle act is her vision of the family's future. Like the other Conways, she fails at what she tries to do: She gives up writing novels for a career as a popular journalist and becomes the mistress of a married man.

Carol Conway, the youngest child. Sixteen as the play begins, she is energetic and charming, without the social affectations seen in most of the family. She is also very morbid and is obsessed with thoughts of death, particularly with memories of her father's drowning. She is the only member of the family who welcomes Ernest Beevers into their social circle. Carol dies young, and her death symbolizes the loss of vitality and goodness in the Conways.

Joan Helford, a local girl. Pretty but unexceptional, Joan is a friend of the Conway family. She is in love with Robin, whom she idolizes. This attachment puts her in conflict with Mrs. Conway, who is jealous of Robin's interest in her. Her difficult marriage only promotes her worst qualities, and she becomes a slovenly and irritable middle-aged woman.

Ernest Beevers, a local businessman. He is approximately thirty as the play begins. Of a somewhat lower social class than the Conways, he is small and shy but with a growing sense of his own authority. Fascinated by the Conways and in love with Hazel, Beevers is at first awkward and out of place in the Conway home. Yet he comes to dominate Hazel and to sneer at the rest of the family. Ultimately, he will deny them the money needed to make Mrs. Conway financially secure.

Gerald Thornton, the family solicitor. A promising young man of roughly thirty years as the play begins, he is good-looking and well-groomed. He carefully maintains an air of gentility and professionalism. Embarrassed by Mrs. Conway's ridicule of Madge, he proves too weak to pursue his interest in her or in her political ideas, and he lapses into a petty provincial by the end of the play, presiding over the inevitable dismantling of the Conway home.

Heidi J. Holder

THE TIME OF INDIFFERENCE

Author: Alberto Moravia (1907-   )
Type of work: Novel
Time of action: 1929
First published: Gli indifferenti, 1929 (English translation, 1953)

Mariagrazia Ardengo (är·dän′yō), a silly, neurotic middle-aged widow. Mariagrazia's main motivation is to keep her love affair with Leo from expiring. Her jealous scenes, however, drive Leo away, and he begins to focus his interest on Mariagrazia's daughter, Carla. Ultimately, Mariagrazia is willing to share Leo with Carla as long as he does not abandon her altogether.

Leo Merumeci (mĕr·ōō·mä′chē), Mariagrazia's forty-two-year-old lover. Leo is a rough and unscrupulous businessman who is trying to appropriate Mariagrazia's money. His interest in having Carla even if it means he has to marry her does not preclude his keeping Mariagrazia as a lover.

Carla Ardengo, Mariagrazia's twenty-four-year-old daughter. Passive and indifferent, Carla is a true victim of the situation who, at times, longs to escape her dreary existence. She witnesses without any sign of rebellion the various events that are used to manipulate her. Carla marries Leo not out of love but out of a desire for change in her life.

Michele Ardengo, Mariagrazia's son, a first-year law student. He has visions of liberation from his indifferent existence, but they are doomed by that very indifference. When Michele realizes that Leo has seduced Carla, Michele believes that he must do something but cannot find any real emotion for the task. As a result, Michele decides to shoot Leo, but his attempt fails miserably as he forgets to load the gun. From the failure of his action, however, Michele gains an understanding of the value of love and honesty and the importance of family and society. Yet this new awareness does not help him break out of his passive life. He agrees to see Lisa and start an affair with her, but he does so with no real enthusiasm.

Lisa, Leo's lover before he met Mariagrazia. After losing Leo first to Mariagrazia and then to Carla, Lisa switches her attentions to Michele, whom she seeks to seduce. Lisa also wants change (as Carla does) and passion (as Michele does) in her life, though Michele's lack of spontaneous emotion will probably not provide either.

Rosaria Pipia

THE TIME OF THE HERO

Author: Mario Vargas Llosa (1936-   )
Type of work: Novel
Time of action: The 1950's
First published: La ciudad y los perros, 1963 (English translation, 1966)

Porfirio Cava, a cadet at the Leoncio Prado Military Academy in Lima, Peru. A highlander with a peasant background, he has chosen to attend the academy because he plans a career in the military. He is one of four members of "the Circle" (also including Jaguar, Boa, and Curly), which is formed for mutual protection and support. After a losing roll of the dice, he is obligated to steal a chemistry examination for the Circle. In a late-night theft of the examination, he accidentally breaks a window. This evidence, coupled with information supplied by the infor-mant Arana, leads to his court-martial and expulsion. It also closes off any chance he had for a career in the military, and for the resulting economic and social mobility.

Ricardo Arana (the Slave), a timid and shy cadet who is ostracized and picked on by the other cadets. He is reared by his mother and his aunt Adelina in the regional town of Chiclayo; his father is absent from his early upbringing. Suddenly he is uprooted from this environment and brought to Lima, where his mother begins to live with his father again.

Terrified at this change, he avoids his father and most social interaction. His father concludes that he is a mama's boy, effeminate and ill-adapted to face the world. He sees the military academy as a remedy for these shortcomings. Ricardo willingly agrees to enroll, but he is not accepted by the other cadets. They make fun of him, abuse him, and exploit his unwillingness to fight back. He does find some solace in his friendship with Alberto and is infatuated with Teresa. Having been confined to the academy, he becomes so desperate for a pass so that he can see her that he informs the authorities that Cava stole the examination. In revenge, he is murdered in a field exercise. The authorities cover up the incident and blame the death on the cadet himself.

Alberto Fernández Temple (the Poet), a cadet whose wit and skill at writing love letters and pornographic stories are admired by the other cadets. His father is a womanizer, and his mother, a complainer. Alberto also is preoccupied with women. First he is infatuated with Helena. When she breaks off their relationship, his grades suffer. His father decides to send him to the academy to teach him discipline. Alberto has his first sexual experience with Golden Toes, the prostitute who has serviced half of his class. At the request of Ricardo, who cannot get a pass, he agrees to meet with Teresa. He takes her to see films, is smitten, and continues to date Teresa. Sustaining a friendship with Ricardo and a relationship with Teresa produces a troubled conscience. When Ricardo is murdered, Alberto is so overwhelmed with guilt that he denounces the murderer before Lieutenant Gamboa. Academy officials ignore the facts, and nothing is done. As the novel ends, he has finished the academy with high marks, has received a gift from his father as a reward, and will probably go to the United States to study engineering. Influenced by his circle of bourgeois friends outside the academy, he drops Teresa and begins dating Marcela. He will probably repeat his father's philandering ways.

Jaguar (hä·gwär'), a violent, fearless cadet who shows his class how to stand up and beat the system. Before entering the academy, he falls in love with Teresa, but after an argument, they go their separate ways. Poor, his father dead, and his mother old, Jaguar lives with the criminal Skinny Higueras and follows a life of crime, until a robbery goes wrong and most of his cohorts are caught. After going without food and sleeping in the open, he finally turns to his godfather, who puts him to work in his store in exchange for room and board. He tries to rise above his situation, and, with the help of his godfather's wife, whom he has to satisfy sexually, he is able to enter the academy. There he is a natural leader and fighter. He organizes the class and his followers to resist the upperclassmen. He teaches them that there are no moral limits to protecting the group; when Cava is betrayed, Jaguar murders the betrayer, Arana. Jaguar's own ostracism from the group, however, makes him aware of how lonely Arana must have been. Remorseful, Jaguar confesses his crime, but the academy is not interested. In the end he marries Teresa.

Boa, a cadet who sexually molests chickens and his dog Skimpy. He is a member of the Circle and a loyal follower of its leader, Jaguar.

Lieutenant Gamboa, a tough, no-nonsense model officer, who believes in a fair and consistent application of the rules and discipline. He reports the murder but finds his career threatened by superiors, who cover up the scandal.

Teresa, a young woman whose interest in Ricardo and Alberto probably results from their higher economic and social background. She marries Jaguar.

Maurice P. Brungardt

THE TIME OF YOUR LIFE

Author: William Saroyan (1908-1981)
Type of work: Play
Time of action: An afternoon and evening in October, 1939
First published: 1939

Joe, a young man with money, the initiator of most of the action of the play. He sits at a table in Nick's bar, near the waterfront in San Francisco, observing and commenting on the activities in the bar and trying to help some of the patrons, particularly Kitty Duval and Mary L. He directs his young flunkey, Tom, to run errands for him, and, when he sees that Tom is falling in love with Kitty, he does everything he can to promote the love affair, including renting a car and making a romantic drive with the two lovers down the Pacific coast and then installing Kitty in a room at a fancy hotel. Joe gets Tom a job driving a truck and at the end of the play sends the two lovers away to get married. Joe also helps to defend Kitty when Blick, the vice cop, tries to arrest her. Joe states the philosophy that gives the play its title, his belief that one should live so that the time of one's life is not wasted in game-playing, frantic pursuit of money and prestige, or regrets.

Tom, Joe's younger friend, who idolizes Joe and does everything that Joe asks him to do. Yet, he is sometimes mystified by his tasks, such as bringing Joe on one occasion a collection of toys and on another a gun. He falls in love with Kitty, and their blossoming romance is the main plot device of the play.

Kitty Duval, a prostitute who wanders into the bar, angry at herself and the world because of her circumstances and occupation. She is revived by Joe, who reminds her that she once had dreams and is still capable of hope.

Nick, the owner of the bar in which most of the action takes place. He is bemused by the actions of most of his patrons but accepts their antics with good nature, although he halfheartedly complains from time to time

that he does not understand what is occurring.

Mary L., a woman who comes into the bar and with whom Joe strikes up a slightly drunken conversation when he notices the initials "M. L." on her bag. They realize that they may have fallen in love with each other, but Mary walks out of the bar and does not return.

Harry, a young song and dance man, who tries (in vain) to entertain the customers with his comedic monologues.

Wesley, a young black man, who plays the piano as entertainment for Nick's customers.

Blick, a vice cop in his middle forties. He harasses the patrons and provides the conflict in the play when he tries to make Kitty perform the burlesque routine that she did before she drifted into prostitution. Nick throws Blick out of the bar, and he is killed in the street.

McCarthy, a good-natured longshoreman who is on the side of ordinary people in spite of the mess made of the world. He tries to convince Krupp that he is in the wrong line of work.

Krupp, his friend, a slightly dim-witted cop in his late thirties who is growing tired of his job and is unable to understand why people keep making what is basically a pleasant world worse.

Dudley R. Bostwick, a young man who continually uses the telephone in the bar to contact a girl; any girl will do, but the one with whom he is in love would be best.

Willie, a young man who plays the pinball

machine in the bar, sometimes with spectacular results, as the machine lights up, displays an American flag, and plays music when he scores a win.

Kit Carson, an old-time cowboy who tells tall tales of his wild adventures fighting Indians; these tales seem to be lies, until he

shoots and kills Blick offstage near the end of the play.

The Arab, who sits at the bar and mutters the recurring line, "No foundation. All the way down the line."

James Baird

TINY ALICE

Author: Edward Albee (1928-   )
Type of work: Play
Time of action: The 1960's
First produced: 1964

Julian, a modest, shy, and benevolent Roman Catholic lay brother and personal secretary to the Cardinal. In his benevolence and his desire to serve, he represents the victim of the Roman Catholic church's avarice. After having become disillusioned with other people's images and uses of God, he loses his faith and therefore commits himself to a mental institution for six years. By the beginning of the play, Julian is Brother Julian, the first lay secretary to a cardinal in Church history. He is sent by the Cardinal to Miss Alice to work out the details of the $20 billion grant that the Church is to receive from Miss Alice. After frequent meetings with Miss Alice, Julian consents to becoming married to her and, after the wedding, is left alone by all other characters, including his wife. He discovers that he did not really marry Miss Alice but rather Tiny Alice, the occupant of a miniature replica of the castle in which most of the play's action takes place. Julian has to learn that Miss Alice is only the physical representation of Tiny Alice. When he refuses to remain in the castle all alone as the trophy that Tiny Alice demanded for her large grant and wants to return to a mental institution, Lawyer shoots him. Now Julian, bleeding to death beside the castle replica, becomes a Christlike figure in a crucifixion pose, thinking initially that he has been forsaken by God but then accepting the sacrifice asked of him and addressing Tiny Alice as God.

Miss Alice, a mysterious young woman apparently hired as a representative by Tiny Alice, the occupant of the miniature of Miss Alice's castle. Although at the beginning of the play Miss Alice seems to be the one giving the grant, and although she likes to order others around, her subordinate role becomes increasingly clear: Like the Lawyer and the Butler, she, too, works for Tiny Alice. She may have had love affairs with the Butler and the Lawyer, whom she seems to be giving up for Julian. Miss Alice likes to joke with Julian and does not want to harm him, but she willingly lures him into marriage in order to make him a sacrifice for Tiny Alice. While she seems to care for Julian, she does not try to prevent his death but follows the orders of the Lawyer, which are implicitly Tiny Alice's orders.

The Lawyer, an aggressive and intimidating man seemingly employed by Miss Alice but ultimately in the service of Tiny Alice. He represents the intelligent and unfeeling leader. He enjoys teasing his former schoolmate, the Cardinal, with whom he starts numerous arguments and whose problematic past he likes to discuss. He plays with the Cardinal's wish to get the $20 billion grant and delights in catching the Cardinal at failing to use the majestic plural. The Butler is another victim of his witty condescension. The Lawyer seems interested in Miss Alice but ultimately does all that he can to serve Tiny Alice, the occupant of the miniature castle. To provide a sacrifice for her, he shoots Julian and refuses to call a doctor for him.

The Butler, a friendly but puzzling servant seemingly working for Miss Alice but ultimately employed by Tiny Alice. He is benevolent and helpful toward Julian and tries to assist him against the Lawyer's intimidations. Although he presents himself as Julian's friend, he refuses to take orders from Julian after the wedding and joins all other characters in avoiding Julian. He also does not try to prevent Julian's murder, reasoning that, since Julian had been chosen as the sacrifice, he might be better off dead than alive.

The Cardinal, the representative of the Roman Catholic church, who is to receive the grant money from Tiny Alice. The Cardinal is used as an illustration of human conduct: The expectation of the grant makes him forget his principles (the use of the majestic plural) and prevents hesitations about sacrificing his secretary Julian. With the Lawyer, the Cardinal shows his command of the art of argument and insult. He justifies sacrificing Julian by noting the good that this sacrifice would bring to the Roman Catholic church, but he does not dare to tell Julian what is awaiting him. When Julian has been shot, the Cardinal does not attempt to rescue him but asks him to die as a martyr.

Josef Raab

TIRRA LIRRA BY THE RIVER

Author: Jessica Anderson (c. 1935-   )
Type of work: Novel
Time of action: The early 1900's to 1970
First published: 1978

Nora Roche Porteous, a retired dressmaker. In her seventies, she returns to her family home in Brisbane, where she recalls her past while recovering from pneumonia. Having lost her father at age six, she grew up yearning for escape from the household of her mother and older sister. Marriage to Colin Porteous took her to the comparatively glamorous world of Sydney, but her husband proved unfeeling and ungenerous, installing her in his mother's house and deriding her few contacts with creative friends. Nora turns an early skill at needlework into a profession; her divorce settlement carries her to London, where she practices her craft for the next thirty-five years. A horrifying illegal abortion and, later, a ruinous face-lift cause greater withdrawal and shyness in a personality always prone to expect loss and disappointment. She concludes, however, that her search for autonomy and self-ratification has been proper and successful.

Grace Roche Chiddy, Nora's older sister.

She remained in Brisbane, hoping that submissiveness and moralizing would bolster her faith; in the end, "she had only opinions." Nora's early resentment of Grace is tempered in the narrative present by admiration for her late sister's improvements in the decorating and landscaping of the house.

Olive Partridge, a childhood friend of Nora. She becomes a successful and worldly novelist. She helps Nora to obtain her abortion in London; Nora criticizes Olive's writing for depicting glamorous affairs without advocating sexual responsibility.

Dorothy Irey Rainbow, Nora's childhood model of grace and charm. Marrying at a young age and giving up elegant dreams to remain in Brisbane, she later attacks her husband and children with an ax. The sole survivor, Dr. Gordon Rainbow, becomes Nora's physician upon her return to Australia.

Colin Porteous, a lawyer. Nora marries him

more to get away than for his particular qualities: He is egotistical and heavy-handed, demanding that Nora think for herself and then deriding her decisions. Ultimately, he deserts Nora for a more submissive, ornamental partner.

Una Porteous, Colin's mother, the archetypal evil mother-in-law. When Nora and Colin move into her house during the Depression, Una attempts a systematic reduction of Nora's self-confidence. Long after the marriage ends, her name is Nora's catchphrase for hypocrisy and manipulation.

Lewie Johns, an artist in Sydney. Nora builds confidence through her friendship with him; she finds discontent at home, too, because her husband does not take her search for identity as seriously as Johns does. The narrowness of the role that Colin has assigned to Nora is strongly revealed in his homophobic reaction to her friend. Nora takes comfort in finding "a lesser Lewie" at almost all phases of her later career.

Ida Mayo, a dressmaker in Sydney who first encourages Nora to turn her skill at needlework into a career. Her professionalism, like Lewie's friendship, helps Nora to find the confidence to seek personal autonomy.

Liza,
Hilda, and
Fred, Nora's fellow tenants at "number six," a house that they rent together in London. Many of Nora's reminiscences follow recalled patterns of discussion among these friends, so that she can almost hear the questions that they might ask her. The collapse of this supportive household and surrogate family precipitates the aging Nora's lonely return to Australia.

John Scheckter

TITAN
A Romance

Author: Jean Paul (Johann Paul Friedrich Richter, 1763-1825)
Type of work: Novel
Time of action: The late eighteenth century
First published: Titan, 1800-1803, 4 volumes (English translation, 1862)

Albano, the Prince of Hohenfliess (hō′ĕn•flēs). Albano is a young, fiery, and handsome aristocrat, prince of the mythical German principality of Hohenfliess. As the novel begins, he is about to meet his assumed father, Gaspar de Cesara, with whom he spent the first three years of his life on the island of Isola Bella. Albano's complicated history is revealed to him in a letter from his mother, the Princess Eleonore, toward the end of the novel: Because his real parents, the rulers of Hohenfliess, feared an attempt on his life by their cunning relatives, the rulers of the neighboring principality of Haarhaar (hàr′hàr), they arranged that their son be reared by the trustworthy burgher Wehrfritz under the supervision of Cesara. Consequently, Albano is educated in the quiet countryside with the help of several tutors and emerges as a noble and serious young man who does not yet know the world. He admires, respects, and loves unusual and great individuals: His assumed father, a knight of the Golden Fleece, has attained superhuman status for him, primarily by his absence and invisibility. Albano is the central character of this novel, on whom all events and occurrences focus. The purpose of his entry into society, beginning with the return to the island where he spent his infancy, is the formation of Albano as a worthy successor to the throne of Hohenfliess. Eventually Albano learns who his true parents and siblings are and becomes acquainted with Roquairol von Froulay, son of the prime minister of Hohenfliess, who had been held up as a model by his teachers. Roquairol proves to be immoral and deceitful, and after the friendship that Albano had sought with him dissolves, Count Cesara sends him on a trip to Rome so that he can learn to appreciate art. Albano, who still does not know that he is next in line to the throne of Hohenfliess, which in the meantime has been claimed by his older and unknown brother Luigi, expresses his republican inclination in his desire to travel to France in order to assist the revolutionaries. In the course of the novel, Albano succeeds in emancipating himself from his complex family background and from the passivity of the young, disinterested aristocrat. When Luigi dies and Albano is told of his true birth, he gives up the planned trip to France and, along with his bride, Idoine, becomes the enlightened ruler of Hohenfliess.

Julienne, Albano's twin sister, of whose existence he does not know until he is an adult. Along with their older brother Luigi, Julienne was reared at the court of Hohenfliess. The young princess, whose best friend is Liane von Froulay, shares the sentimentality and tendency to ecstatic imaginings of her friend. Julienne, who is also Linda's friend, reveals herself to Albano as his sister during his stay in Italy, where she has been visiting with Linda.

Luigi, Albano's older brother. Luigi, heir to the throne of Hohenfliess, is a degenerate who wastes his life and suffers from boredom. His face carries an expression of permanent discontent; his body is bloated from his incontinent eating and drinking habits. When the old prince dies, Luigi, who has married the oldest daughter of the Prince of Haarhaar, becomes ruler of Hohenfliess. He soon dies. Luigi represents the decadent aristocrat who is doomed from birth. Hope lies with Albano, who is not reared at the court and therefore becomes regenerated.

Liane von Froulay (fôn frōō′lä), the daughter of the prime minister of Hohenfliess. Liane is fifteen years old when she first meets Albano, a year and one-half her senior, in the princely gardens of Lilar, where she and her brother are spending some time. Excep-

tionally beautiful, Liane is also an eager student who excels in music and drawing. Liane and Albano fall in love, but Liane renounces her claim on Albano when she is told his true identity. The young woman, sickly and sentimental, soon becomes fatally ill. On her deathbed, she requests one last visit from Albano. After her death, Albano becomes very ill and recovers only with the appearance of Idoine, his later bride, who resembles Liane.

Roquairol von Froulay (rŏ·kī′rŏl), son of the prime minister of Hohenfliess. Roquairol is at first Albano's friend but later becomes his enemy. He has a stormy and uneven personality and a temperament given to excess and enthusiasms. In a letter to Albano, he reveals that he has seduced Rabette, believing that Albano will understand his claim that passion has its own rights. Albano's love for his friend turns to hatred after this incident. In the meantime, Roquairol has fallen in love with Linda, who does not return his feelings. He grows to hate Albano and decides to injure his erstwhile friend by deceiving Linda, which he does by imitating Albano's handwriting in a note inviting Linda to a rendezvous. Linda mistakes Roquairol for Albano (she is unable to see well at night) and allows the seduction to take place. Roquairol, who has written a drama entitled *Der Trauerspieler* (*The Tragedian*), invites everyone to attend its premiere. The script consists of events that have actually occurred in Roquairol's life, with the seduction of Linda as the last scene. As end and part of the play, Roquairol fatally shoots himself.

Falterle (fält′ər·lĕ), Albano's fencing teacher. A Viennese, he praises Roquairol and his sister Liane and awakens in Albano the desire to meet them. Basically insecure, he hides behind fancy dress and polite manners. He survives life in the country by escaping to the city, Pestitz (pĕ′stēts), three times a week.

Wehmeier (vā′mī·ər), Albano's tutor. He is approximately fifty years old and is the father of eight children. His knowledge of science and philosophy is limited, but he knows history well.

Dian (dē·än′), an architect and later tutor of Albano. Dian is a Greek who was educated in Greece and Rome. He introduces Albano to the works of Homer and Sophocles. Dian's methods of education consist of giving Albano a reading list in which no specific order prevails.

Schoppe (shŏ′pĕ), an honorary librarian and also a later tutor of Albano. Albano regards Schoppe, who is outspoken and not easily intimidated, to be his special friend. Schoppe is said to have a southern temperament, which is in conflict with northern culture. Schoppe tries to uncover the secret of Albano's origin and, as the result of his activities, is confined to an insane asylum. There he becomes mentally ill and dies when he sees his friend and double "Siebenkäs."

Augusti, a lecturer employed by the prince. Augusti, who is thirty-seven but appears to be ten years older because of his experience and mode of dress, becomes Albano's chief tutor. His first meeting with Albano occurs on the island of Isola Bella. Together with Schoppe and Dian, who accompanied Albano to the island, he spends several days with him there. Augusti is a member of the court circle and is therefore important for Albano's later education.

Gaspard de Cesara (gàs′pär dā tsä·zär′ə), a knight of the Golden Fleece and Albano's assumed father. The narrator indicates that he himself is not certain whether Gaspard is a Spanish or an Austrian knight of the Golden Fleece. Of advanced age, Gaspard is still extremely vital and active. Gaspard spent his early years traveling from court to court, since one place could not contain his restless energy. As the result of his travels, he became acquainted with important and unimportant individuals and with great and insignificant courts. His attitude toward others is evenhanded and unsentimental; his temperament is composed. When the Prince and Princess of Hohenfliess searched for a safe haven for Albano, he agreed to become his foster father, provided that Albano would eventually marry his daughter Linda. Gaspard spent only the first three years of Albano's life with him, but summons him to return briefly to the island where he spent his infancy when Albano is a young man and ready to enter the world. Gaspard is also responsible for the trip Albano makes to Rome, which is a traditional German motif in the aesthetic education of an artist or nobleman. Only after Albano has seen his assumed father is he allowed to visit Pestitz, the major city in Hohenfliess.

Linda (de Romeiro), Gaspard's daughter. Albano meets Linda in Italy but does not know that she is his assumed sister since they were reared separately. Linda has the tall and aristocratic bearing of a Spanish noblewoman. Dressed in red silk, she covers her face with a white veil, through which Albano can detect black, serious eyes, and a proud, straight nose and forehead. Linda and Albano fall in love. In a letter to Albano, Linda describes her travels, which have taken her, like her father, from country to country and court to court. She becomes tired of this mode of life but suffers from the inactivity society forces upon women. Linda, who fears marriage, which she considers to be the end of a woman's freedom and the death of love, refuses Albano's marriage proposal. When Linda fears that Albano may fall in love with Idoine, who resembles Liane, she decides to marry him after all. When Albano refuses Linda's plea to promise that he never participate in a war, however, Linda leaves. Roquairol, who is also in love with Linda, deceives and seduces her. After Linda, who is now pregnant, discovers her mistake, she leaves, vowing that she hates all men.

Wehrfritz (vär′frīts), a landscape architect. Wehrfritz is a good and honest burgher in whose home in Blumenbühl (blū′mən·byl) Albano is being reared.

Albine, Wehrfritz's wife. She is gentle and concerned about Albano's welfare and loves him like a son.

Rabette, Wehrfritz's daughter. Rabette is a healthy and blooming country girl who loves

Albano like a brother. She is seduced by Roquairol and spends the rest of her life in mourning and unhappiness.

Idoine, the Princess of Haarhaar, a neighboring principality with which Hohenfliess has long been in conflict. Idoine is tall and of noble and majestic appearance. She resembles Liane but has learned self-control and has a well-balanced personality. A friend of Linda and of Julienne, she spent time living in Switzerland, where she improves the economy and life of a village; ultimately, she marries Albano.

Helga Stipa Madland

TO HAVE AND HAVE NOT

Author: Ernest Hemingway (1899-1961)
Type of work: Novel
Time of action: The mid-1930's, during the Great Depression
First published: 1937

Harry Morgan, the owner of a charter fishing boat based in Key West, Florida. He is a big, powerfully built, athletic man in his early forties, ruggedly handsome and scarred by a life of adventure, which has made him even more attractive to women, an attraction enhanced by his indifference to its effect. He knows and loves the sea but has been forced to work as a guide for rich and ignorant tourists, and, when times are hard, he runs liquor on the Caribbean. Although he is scrupulously honest in his dealings with people, he is worried about his responsibilities to his wife and children and, under the pressures of corrupt and immoral local officials, moves beyond the law into a series of dangerous and illegal voyages, which eventually lead to his death. He tries to be decent and honorable according to his own set of principles, but he is overmatched by evil men and an inclination toward violence that finally goes beyond his control. Even during those scenes in the novel in which he is not actively present, his daunting individuality hovers around the other characters as a measure of their courage, wit, and fundamental decency.

Marie Morgan, Harry's wife and the mother of his three daughters, formerly a call girl. She is in her mid-forties, a big and handsome woman, with bleached blonde hair, still attractive in a Rubenesque fashion but on the verge of losing her edge and sliding toward excess. She is very deeply in love with her husband, strongly attracted to him physically and very dependent on him. Although she has the strength to survive on her own, she has committed her life completely to him and, to a lesser extent, to their children.

Albert Tracy, Morgan's right-hand man and first mate. Tracy is roughly middle-aged, nondescript in appearance, not particularly intelligent, not especially strong, and not at all imaginative. He lives on welfare much of the time and tries to keep his complaining wife moderately satisfied. Morgan likes and trusts him because he is reliable, faithful, loyal, and competent at his job: "dumb but straight and a good man in a boat," Morgan says. He tends to be cautious and has no real driving force in his life, but he shows the kind of courage Morgan values and dies absurdly, sticking close to Morgan on his last ride.

Eddy, a "rummy" who sometimes works for Morgan, a man who has lost the courage to act decisively except when fortified by alcohol. Morgan understands him and sympathizes to an extent with his fears, but Morgan is ultimately disgusted with him and regards him as a failure who does not have the character to face death and danger with some degree of grace. His walk, which is described as "sloppy" with "his joints all slung wrong," typifies his lack of control and his absence of style.

Richard Gordon, a successful novelist, still youthful in the manner of a man who can afford the best clothing and care and the privileged existence of a celebrity. He is not a bad writer, but he has sacrificed a part of his soul to maintain his carefree pattern of living. He and his wife have no children, no permanent residence, and many affairs. Whereas Morgan knows who he is and what he must do to protect his honor, Gordon has no clear conception of himself and is disturbed by his uncertainty about how to act in a crisis. His writing is slick but superficial, contrived to exploit commercial opportunities, and he is no real judge of character, a crucial prerequisite for a real artist. When his wife leaves him for a less flashy but more substantial man, he is thrown into a kind of chaos he cannot resolve.

Helen Gordon, his wife, an extremely attractive woman in her early thirties, with dark hair, clear skin, and a need for something beyond the frivolous existence that they have been leading. She is instinctively aware of some deeper aspects of her character that have been suppressed and is willing to give up the brittle pleasures they share to find something of more enduring value. She and her husband form a kind of parallel to the Morgans, a pair of "haves" in contrast to the Morgans, who are "have nots" in the economic sense. The separation may drive both Helen and her husband into closer contact with the exigencies of life that have shaped Morgan and his wife.

Freddy, a saloon keeper, a friend of Morgan, who appreciates his special character and tries to treat everyone with a degree of honesty and respect, one among several minor characters who appear on the streets, wharves, and bars of Key West who are not motivated by selfishness or the pleasures of power and control. He speaks Spanish and English, is worldly and experienced, is basically nonjudgmental, and appears likable in an ordinary way. He is another of the "have nots" who actually has a genuine sense of value and worth.

Wallace Johnston, the owner of a yacht, with a master's degree from Harvard and money from silk mills; at age thirty-eight, he is the epitome of the kind of "have" who is essentially harmless but who lacks any kind of insight, knows nothing of life beyond the club, and in his idle ignorance contributes to the economic conditions of the Depression, which have forced men such as Morgan over the line.

Leon Lewis

TO HAVE AND TO HOLD

Author: Mary Johnston (1870-1936)
Type of work: Novel
Time of action: 1621-1622
First published: 1900

Captain Ralph Percy, a Virginia planter and veteran of the Dutch war for independence. He was among the first settlers at Jamestown. Against his better judgment, he takes the advice of his good friend, John Rolfe, and seeks a wife among the women who arrive in the colony early in 1621. Rescuing her from the rude attentions of some of his fellow colonists, Percy chooses on impulse the haughty but beautiful Jocelyn Leigh. By his marriage, he incurs the wrath of Lord Carnal and risks imprisonment and death to win the respect and eventually the love of his wife. At the end of this quest, Percy saves Jamestown by warning his fellow settlers of the projected slaughter of all the colonists by the united Indian tribes of eastern Virginia.

Jocelyn Leigh, a ward of the English king, James I, who flees to Virginia under an assumed name to escape being forced into an unwanted marriage with Lord Carnal, a man whom she hates. In desperation she weds Captain Ralph Percy to gain his protection. Although she confesses her deception to her husband, her pride will not permit her to love the man whose name and devotion she has accepted. When Carnal pursues her to Virginia, Mistress Percy realizes that her flight may cost Ralph his life. Slowly she falls in love with the man whose loyalty never falters despite arrest, torture, and almost certain death. Surviving the attack on Jamestown, Jocelyn is reunited with the husband whom she now loves as well as respects.

Lord Carnal, one of the favorites of James I. His personality combines all the loathsome qualities associated with those handsome young men who preyed on the English king's weaknesses. There are no redeeming aspects to Carnal: He follows Jocelyn Leigh to Virginia to force her into an unwanted marriage simply to see her suffer, and he marks Captain Percy for death because he thwarts his plan. When an accident robs Carnal of his physical beauty, he escapes from his failure to retain the king's favor and win Jocelyn Leigh by taking poison.

Jeremy Sparrow, a former actor turned minister. He is a close friend of Captain Ralph Percy and is the clergyman who marries him to Jocelyn Leigh. A giant of a man who possesses both great strength and courage, Sparrow saves Ralph and Jocelyn from certain death and effects their eventual reunion. A ventriloquist, he uses his talent both to amuse and to serve his friends when they are in danger.

Diccon, like Percy, a veteran of the Dutch wars. Because of minor criminal offenses, however, he is indentured to his former commander. Unlike the majority of men and women, both real and fictional, who people *To Have and to Hold*, Diccon possesses a personality that has real depth. He is both saint and sinner, a surly, brawling man who attempts at one point to murder Ralph Percy, only to sacrifice himself for that same master whom he loves and hates. A man of the lowest social class, he is nevertheless a very complex individual, a bundle of contradictions.

John Rolfe, the husband of Pocahontas, the close friend of Captain Ralph Percy and his defender from the attacks of Lord Carnal and the authorities of the Virginia Company. A well-known historical personality, Rolfe was one of the early leaders of England's first successful colony in North America. The tragic early death of his wife left him a widower at the time of the attempted slaughter of the English in Virginia, and he moves through the novel, a sad but ever-noble figure. Endowed with all the virtues associated with persons of gentle birth, he is the obvious opposite of Lord Carnal.

Nicolo, Lord Carnal's physician, the personification of evil. His death by self-administered poison is regretted by no one, including his master. A combination of all the bad qualities attributed by seventeenth century Englishmen to all foreigners, and especially to Italians, Nicolo is woven into the fabric of the story like a dark thread twisted into one of the tapestries favored by the early Virginians.

Nantauquas, the son of Powhatan and the brother-in-law of John Rolfe, the noble savage brought to life. A friend of the English settlers and especially of Captain Ralph Percy, he is haunted by the fear of what may happen to his people and their way of life if the number of colonists increases. Although he reluctantly participates in the massive attack by the Indians on the Virginia colony, he spares the lives of Ralph Percy, Jocelyn Leigh, and Jeremy Sparrow. Sorrow and a certain fatalism cling to Nantauquas like the fur mantle he wears.

Clifton W. Potter, Jr.

TO KILL A MOCKINGBIRD

Author: Harper Lee (1926-   )
Type of work: Novel
Time of action: 1932-1935
First published: 1960

Jean Louise "Scout" Finch, a five-year-old girl when the story begins, eight years old when it ends. She is smart and precocious, having learned to read at an early age by studying her father's law books. A hothead, more willing to fight than to think, she is often in trouble. She serves as a willing accomplice to her older brother's escapades. It is in her clear, honest voice that the story is told.

Jeremy "Jem" Atticus Finch, Scout's brother, nine years old when the novel begins. He is thoughtful, with a slower fuse than Scout, and often acts as interpreter to his sister of the world's confusing contradictions and vagaries. He intends to be a lawyer like his father when he grows up.

Atticus Finch, Scout and Jem's father, a lawyer in Maycomb, Alabama. A widower, almost fifty years old, Atticus responds to the challenge of rearing two small children by treating them as equals, with dignity and honesty. Atticus is a rare man, not only because he is a keen judge of human nature but because he is able to forgive his fellow citizens their faults. When he defends a black man charged with raping a white woman, he does so knowing full well what wrath he will draw from the community. Standing up to the town's anger and ridicule requires both physical and moral courage, and Atticus shows that he has both.

Calpurnia, the Finch's cook and housekeeper, a black woman in her fifties. Self-educated, Calpurnia acts as Scout and Jem's substitute mother. It is through Calpurnia that the Finches learn how the black community is responding to the rape charge against Tom Robinson.

Charles "Dill" Baker Harris, a fatherless boy one year older than Scout. Shunted from home to home, Dill comes to Maycomb in the summers to stay with his aunt. A grand storyteller and an inspired actor, he is Scout and Jem's favorite playmate. (Dill is based upon Truman Capote, Harper Lee's lifelong friend from her hometown of Monroeville, Alabama.)

Arthur "Boo" Radley, a recluse in his forties who lives with his brother, next door to the Finches. Boo was put under the equivalent of house arrest by his father years ago as punishment for a teenage prank. Few have seen him since, and many of the children's games revolve around making Boo come out.

Tom Robinson, a twenty-five-year-old black laborer. Married, the father of three, Tom is an honest, well-respected man. Although possessed of a crippled left arm, he is a strong and steady worker. Tom ignores the social dictums that forbid a black man from associating with a white woman, and, out of pity, helps overworked Mayella Ewell with some of her heavier chores. He is killed trying to escape from prison before Atticus can appeal his conviction for rape.

Helen Robinson, Tom's wife.

Robert (Bob) E. Lee Ewell, a cocky, uneducated widower who spends his relief checks on green whiskey and lets his oldest daughter, Mayella, worry about how to feed herself and the other seven children from what she can forage from the town dump. After Atticus implies in court that Bob, not Tom, beat Mayella, Bob vows revenge. He is found dead with a knife in his ribs after Scout and Jem are attacked.

Mayella Violet Ewell, Bob Ewell's nineteen-year-old daughter. She is a stocky, friendless girl more or less resigned to a difficult life.

When her attempt to kiss Tom is discovered, she quickly joins her father in accusing the black man of rape.

Alexandra Finch Hancock, Atticus' married sister. She strongly disapproves of how Atticus is rearing his children, especially Scout. During the trial, she comes to stay with the Finches.

John (Jack) Hale Finch, Atticus' younger brother by ten years, a physician.

Miss Maudie Atkinson, an independent-minded widow who lives near the Finches. Like Atticus, she treats Scout and Jem with respect, and they enjoy her company.

Mrs. Henry Lafayette Dubose, a very old invalid who breaks her addiction to morphine, the painkiller prescribed to her, before she dies.

Miss Stephanie Crawford, the neighborhood busybody.

Liz Marshall

TO THE LAND OF THE CATTAILS

Author: Aharon Appelfeld (1932-   )
Type of work: Novel
Time of action: 1938-1940
First published: 1986

Toni Strauss, née **Rosenfeld,** a Jewish woman who was divorced by her gentile husband when she was only twenty years old; they had been married three years old. A dark, beautiful woman, she has had many lovers. A year after an elderly lover dies and leaves her a legacy, Toni decides that she and her son must return to her birthplace. She is short on education and academic knowledge, which leads her son to think that she is a stupid woman; yet people fall in love with her wherever she goes. An ephemeral woman, Toni almost dies of typhus when they are in Buszwyn. Throughout the book, Toni experiences an ever-growing fear. It is an oppression that grows greater as she and Rudi near her parents' village, just as her craving for coffee also increases. In the end, she is taken by the Nazis, along with her parents, to the concentration camps.

Rudi Strauss, Toni's son by her gentile husband, August Strauss. Rudi loves his mother but cannot stand the way that her mind seems to be a jumble of thoughts clouded with fear. His connection with animals emphasizes the difference between his mother's

hypersensitivity and his insensitivity. After a drunken binge, he recovers to find that his mother has gone to see her parents without him. He follows, but a day behind, to the railway station. Along the way, he meets Arna and takes her with him.

Rosemarie, the dead owner of a tavern. Murdered because she was a Jew, Rosemarie's death is the first real sign of the impending doom that will first engulf Toni and then Rudi.

Tina, a woman at Rosemarie's tavern. At first, Tina is insane with the events that are befalling the Jews for no apparent reason. By the end of Toni and Rudi's stay, she seems to have accepted the fate that is approaching them.

Arna, a young Jewish girl. Arna, while at the railroad station with the other Jews awaiting deportation, was sent by her mother to fetch water. When Arna returned, all the people were gone. Arna takes care of Rudi when he falls ill while they are looking for their mothers. Though she is still very young, Arna is very wise and helps Rudi to accept himself as a Jew. Arna reassures Rudi that "soon we'll find them all" when he despairs of finding his mother, though finding them all will probably be in death.

T. M. Lipman

TOBACCO ROAD

Author: Jack Kirkland (1901-1969)
Type of work: Play
Time of action: The early 1930's
First produced: 1933

Jeeter Lester, a shiftless, starving tobacco farmer living in rural Georgia. He resides in a ramshackle cabin that was once part of a prosperous homestead. The land has since been depleted by generations of tobacco plantings followed by cotton crops. Jeeter has an obsession with the soil, and every spring he promises to plant a cotton crop but somehow never gets around to it. The economic effects of the Depression in the South are too great for him to overcome. He refuses to leave his beloved land to work elsewhere. He says of his plight, "City ways ain't God-given. It wasn't intended for a man with the smell of the land in him to live in a mill in Augusta." Jeeter is a tragic figure who cannot control his own destiny. In the course of the play, Jeeter dramatically demonstrates that he is lazy, selfish, lecherous, and brutally degenerate. Racked by poverty and starvation, lost in reveries over a spring planting that will never come to pass, Jeeter fights desperately to keep his beloved land, and it is that losing struggle that proves to be his one saving grace.

Ada Lester, Jeeter's haggard, pellagra-ridden, and long-suffering wife. Ada, in her mid-fifties, has been married to Jeeter for forty years; she habitually chews on a snuff stick to ease the pangs of hunger. She has given birth to seventeen children, of whom her favorite is the youngest, Pearl, whose real father was not Jeeter. Throughout the play, Ada expresses one modest wish: that she be buried with a stylish dress. Her selfless love for Pearl leads to the daughter's long-desired freedom, her own accidental death by the new automobile, and Jeeter's loss of the land at the end of the play.

Dude Lester, Jeeter's sixteen-year-old son. Dude, as lazy as his father, has no ambition in life except to sit around the yard. Openly contemptuous of his parents and Ellie May, his sister, he is moved only by the prospect of driving a new car. He accepts Sister Bessie Rice's marriage proposal, despite the fact that she is more than twenty years older than he, when she offers him a new Ford automobile as a wedding present. The ignorant Dude proceeds to destroy the car piece by piece and kills two people with it; one of the victims is Ada, his mother.

Ellie May Lester, Jeeter's silent eighteen-year-old daughter, disfigured by a harelip. Ellie May, who is quite self-conscious about her deformity, is secretly in love with her brother-in-law, Lov Bensey, who is married to her much younger and prettier sister, Pearl. She openly flirts with, and attempts to seduce, the love-starved Bensey. Her dearest wish comes true at the tragic conclusion when Jeeter sends her off to live with Lov following Pearl's escape and Ada's death.

Pearl Bensey, Ada's pubescent daughter, the youngest of her children. Her mother's favorite, Pearl was fathered by a passing stranger. Sold in marriage by Jeeter to Lov Bensey for seven dollars, Pearl has refused to accept Lov as a husband; ultimately, she escapes from him and her family. Although offstage for most of the play, she is a pivotal figure in the action.

Lov Bensey, Jeeter's disgruntled son-in-law, Pearl's husband. Lov is the only one of the major characters to hold a job and earn a steady income. He is very unhappy with his child-wife because Pearl absolutely refuses to talk to him or share his bed; he tries to bribe, threaten, and beat her into submission, but to no avail. Lov has always been sexually attracted to the older and more voluptuous Ellie May but has been put off by her facial deformity.

Sister Bessie Rice, an itinerant, self-ordained evangelist. Almost forty years old and widowed, Bessie preaches her own version of the gospel without benefit of a church and will do so whenever the spirit moves her. She prays out loud, carrying on a dialogue with God, and He always agrees with her passionate petitions. When, for example, Sister Bessie lusts after the young Dude, she prays for guidance; according to her account, God replies that "Dude Lester is the man I want you to wed." She persuades the reluctant Dude to wed with the bribe of a new car for his very own. Her primary interest is to turn the aimless Dude into a country preacher like herself, with both of them traveling by car and spreading the gospel.

Terry Theodore

THE TOBIAS TRILOGY

Author: Pär Lagerkvist (1891-1974)
Type of work: Novel
Time of action: The Middle Ages
First published: Pilgrimen, 1966: *Ahasverus död,* 1960 (*The Death of Ahasuerus,* 1962);
   Pilgrim på havet, 1962 (*Pilgrim at Sea,* 1964); *Det heliga landet,* 1964 (*The Holy Land,* 1966)

Tobias, a wanderer who becomes a pilgrim to the Holy Land. He has a Nordic appearance, being fair-complexioned and light-haired. His hands are hairy. He abandons his wealthy parents early in life, after they had arranged an abortion for a girl he had impregnated. He takes up various means of livelihood—scholar, bandit, soldier of fortune, pirate, dweller in a ruined temple—until his pilgrimage brings him to an allegorical holy land, which is Love and Death. At the beginning of the trilogy, he is coarse and brutal, and his childhood is long past. The persons he meets and those with whom he lives in the course of his pilgrimage have successively mysterious and richly moving effects upon him, such that when he dies, his spiritual demeanor is marked by an infinite and radiant tenderness.

Ahasuerus (ä·hä·sōō·ā′rŭs), **The Wandering Jew.** He meets Tobias at an inn for pilgrims to the Holy Land and hears Tobias' accounts of his association with Diana and of his being moved to complete the pilgrimage of a dead woman who bore the stigmata of Christ. He later accompanies Tobias and Diana, witnesses Diana give her life to save Tobias', and sees Tobias off on his sea voyage to the Holy Land. Ahasuerus has been cursed by Jesus to live and wander forever without rest because he had refused to let Jesus, on the way to crucifixion, rest against his house. Persecuted by God, he is a reversal of the figure of Paul, who persecuted Christ; Paul was vanquished by Christ in a blinding light, but Ahasuerus vanquishes God in a blinding light by recognizing that God is what separates humans from the divinity within themselves and beyond all accessibility. With this knowledge, he dies in peace. Tobias proves to be the heir not to the dead woman's pilgrimage but to the wandering of Ahasuerus.

Diana, a woman who hunts in the wilds with bow and arrows. Tobias rapes her and gives her the name "Diana" because of her evocation of the mythic goddess. She remains with Tobias as his consort and, despite his cruelty to her, loves him, even after he has caused her to become a camp follower and prostitute. When an arrow, shot from the hills by unseen hands, speeds toward Tobias, she steps in front of him and dies in his stead. Ahasuerus concludes that the arrow was actually meant for her in that it provided her with a happy death.

Giovanni (jǐ·ō·vän′nē), a defrocked priest turned pirate and would-be atheist. His mother had promised him to the priesthood before he had had any opportunity to grow into his own identity. He falls in love with a married woman, who tells him in the confessional that she has an extramarital lover. She keeps her lover's picture in a locket. Giovanni manages to become her lover. When their affair is exposed, he is unfrocked but has stolen her locket, which proves to be empty and which he wears for the rest of his life. He meets Tobias on the pirate ship, and the two become inseparable. Tobias remains with him when, blind and old, he is marooned by the pirate crew. Giovanni's bitterness toward God, in whom he cannot disbelieve, is resolved in death; Tobias, the heir of Ahasuerus' empty wandering, inherits the empty locket as well.

Elizabeth, an old, lame woman and the manager and housekeeper of the inn for pilgrims. Diana admires her as a person who is truly herself.

The Little Lay-Brother, an old monastic servant who attends the dying Ahasuerus. He is friendly, always smiling, and constantly selfless in his care for others. Ahasuerus looks upon him as an inherently good person.

Ferrante (fâr·än′tā), a pirate. Like Tobias, he has hairy hands, but he is dark-skinned. His viciousness and cruelty win the respect of the pirate captain. His attempt to kill Tobias is thwarted by Giovanni.

The Giant, a pirate. He is a huge and fearfully strong man, voracious in appetite. His vast consumption of liquor never inebriates him. He is exceptionally good-natured and has to be specially goaded into the hostility necessary to pirates. Ferrante controls him in somewhat the same way that John Steinbeck's George controls Lennie (in *Of Mice and Men*).

The Pirate Captain, a cruel and capable leader of brigands and cutthroats. He coolly supervises the robbery and killing of the captain and passengers of a wrecked merchant ship.

The Captain of the Merchant Ship, a proud and dignified ship's master who is subjected to a gruesome execution ordered by the pirate captain.

Giusto (jǐ·ūs′tō), a pirate. He is a small, rat-faced coward who avoids the fight with the merchantmen. He is ordered by the pirate captain to stab to death the captain of the wrecked merchant ship. This order he carries out very clumsily, ineptly, and at consequent great length, causing his victim the agony of a slow death from multiple wounds.

Herdsmen, indeterminately old men who tend sheep and goats on the coastland where Giovanni and Tobias are marooned. They are gentle and kind. Their blissful reception of a baby boy, brought down from the hills by his father after the mother's death, turns to angry distress when the infant dies. Their gentleness changes to incipient cruelty as they witness the rites of augury and animal sacrifice during a plague.

Bald Man, a bird-faced inhabitant of the coastland who is quite unlike the herdsmen. During the plague, in which numerous sheep and goats die and are consumed by equally numerous vultures, he assumes among the herdsmen the function of priest and seer. He vivisects a young vulture in fruitless augury and vainly sacrifices a living lamb.

Father of the Baby, a man much younger than the herdsmen: He is not past middle age. He tells the herdsmen how the baby's mother died after asking that her baby be placed upon her breast in order to learn of death from his own mother. When the baby boy himself is found dead, the father disappears back into the hills.

Woman with a Basket, an allegorical figure of Death. She comes down from the hills, carrying a poisonous snake in a basket, to call on Tobias and Giovanni. The gravely ill Giovanni dies in peace after she removes the locket from his neck. She then places the locket about the neck of Tobias. Tobias learns that, after she had asked him about the baby boy, the infant had died of a snakebite.

The Blue Lady, an allegorical figure of Love. She is a composite of Tobias' young sweetheart and the Virgin Mary. As the young girl, she had made a blue dress, which she wore for Tobias, out of flax that she herself had grown; after the abortion is forced upon her, she drowns herself in this dress. When Tobias ascends the hills from which the father of the baby and the woman with the basket had come, he finds himself in Eveningland. Here, he rests beside a wooden statuette of the Virgin Mary. The blue-painted figure addresses him and reminds him of the love that he had repressed but that had remained in his heart after the death of his childhood sweetheart. The Virgin Mary then becomes this very childhood sweetheart in womanly maturity. She expresses her undying love for Tobias, removes the locket from his neck, places it upon her own, and tells him to sleep as he dies in great peace.

Roy Arthur Swanson

TOLD BY AN IDIOT

Author: Rose Macaulay (1881-1958)
Type of work: Novel
Time of action: 1879 to the early 1920's
First published: 1923

Aubrey Garden, a liberal clergyman. When the story begins, he is fifty, distinguished-looking and melancholy, with bright blue eyes. Earnest and intellectual, he is a spiritual Don Quixote, forever questing after "the truth." His wife and children react with varying degrees of loyalty, sympathy, and ironic tolerance to each spiritual crisis; his switching of faiths usually causes switching of jobs and living situations. In his intense devotion to various religions, he names his children for their symbols. When he dies in 1914, he has realized that for him, only a combination of all religions equals truth.

Mrs. Garden, his loyal, patient wife. In her mid-forties, she is devoted to her family, adapting serenely to Aubrey's perpetual quest for truth until she finally gets her fill of switching and announces her intention of staying at home while he worships. She secretly grieves over Maurice's unhappy marriage and his perpetual war with society but remains remarkably tolerant of her children's quirks. Even at her death from cancer in 1903, she refuses to burden her children with guilt by bequeathing the care of their bereaved father to them.

Victoria Garden, the eldest daughter, named for her father's temporary victory over unbelief. At twenty-three, she is slim and graceful, with thick chestnut hair and gray eyes. Lively and affectionate, she adores parties, dresses, music, beaux, and aesthetics. She marries Charles Carrington, bears five children, and runs with energy and vivacity a warm if not intellectually stimulating household.

Rome Garden, the second daughter, named (ironically, as she vacillates between agnosticism and atheism) for the Catholic church. At twenty, she is pale and slender with fair hair and intense blue-green eyes. Although she never marries, she falls in love with a married man, Francis Jayne. Contemplating adultery from a "civilized" rather than a moral perspective, she witnesses his murder and never loves again. Even when facing death at sixty-four from cancer (she has told none of her family and is planning suicide to forestall the pain and "uncivilized" messiness), she maintains a detached and ironic view of life, bordering on nihilism—it is from her outlook that the novel takes its title.

Stanley Garden, the third daughter, named for a dean whom her father had admired. Vigorous, stocky, athletic, and independent, she is in her teens when the story begins. An avid reader and worker for social causes, she eventually marries Denman Croft, bears two children (neither of whom shares her political interests), and divorces him for infidelity. She embraces social causes with her father's fervor and fluctuation. As the story ends, she is heading eagerly for Geneva to work for the new League of Nations, optimistic that it can save the world from further war.

Una Garden, the youngest daughter, named for the One Person in whom her father had once believed. Fifteen at the outset, she is plump, physically vigorous, cheerful, and attractive, with brown hair and blue eyes. The "least clever and the best balanced of the Gardens," she marries a farmer, settles in the country, bears several healthy children, and remains "attuned to the soil," her contentment a powerful foil for Rome's ironic detachment.

Maurice Garden, the older son, named for a prominent theologian. In his early twen-

ties, Maurice has light, straight hair, a long chin, and thin lips; his glasses make him look scholarly and serious. A rationalist who respects some religions but has no faith, he becomes a radical journalist. He marries the catty Amy Wilbur, fathers two disappointingly shallow children (his son becomes a second-rate novelist whose writing is more esteemed than his intellectual father's erudite prose), and divorces her once they are grown. In late middle age he finally achieves a truce with life.

Irving Garden, the younger son, named "Irving" because Aubrey had been an Irvingite, or member of the Catholic Apostolic Church. Handsome, dark, and urbane, Irving is in his middle teens. With his flair for business, he becomes the only financially successful Garden, sharing wealth and opportunities with his siblings. He marries Lady Marjorie Banister and settles down to rear a family, enjoy life, and make more money. Although he views war and politics only as they affect his finances, he remains genial and affectionate.

Imogen Carrington, Victoria's youngest daughter, one of the "new" generation. Tomboyish and imaginative, she becomes a poet and novelist, never exactly sure what the "proper role" for women should be, and she usually imagines herself as a boy. Like her Aunt Stanley, she is in love with life; like her Aunt Rome, she falls in love with a married man. At the end of the story, she departs with her lover (half in grief, half in joy) to live out her dreams for a year in the South Pacific.

Sonya H. Cashdan

A TOMB FOR BORIS DAVIDOVICH

Author: Danilo Kiš (1935-1989)
Type of work: Novel
Time of action: The 1920's to the 1970's
First published: Grobnica za Borisa Davidoviča, 1976 (English translation, 1978)

Boris Davidovich, a Jew and a Russian revolutionary. Boris has been imbued with a revolutionary zeal from his early youth, fighting against the czarist regime and for the Bolsheviks. As a result, a portrait of a classical revolutionary emerges: brave, resolute, bold, cool, resourceful, loyal to the cause, and blind to questioning of his ideology. Although it is not quite clear whether he joins the revolution out of a sense of justice or in quest of action or adventure, he participates in it without any reservations, which leads to a firmness of character that remains throughout his life. When he falls out of grace and is tortured and threatened with death, he refuses to sign a confession that would implicate others; instead, he prefers to be shot as a traitor rather than to be hanged as a common thief. Through his death in a labor camp during an escape attempt, he epitomizes a revolutionary who dies unjustly at the hands of his comrades. He also resembles the numerous revolutionaries throughout the world who, convinced of the rightness of their cause, are nevertheless stymied in their idealistic expectations and sacrificed to the exigencies of the revolution.

A. L. Chelyustnikov, a Russian revolutionary—another example of a loyal servant of the revolution, yet for entirely different reasons. A boaster and a womanizer, expert at playing cards, he seems to have become a revolutionary out of opportunism or inertia. He is a typical organization man, even to the point of agreeing to be a fall guy in order to serve the cause. It is not surprising that he survives the ups and downs of the revolutionary struggle, even though he is not without scars or close calls.

Fedukin, a secret police investigator. A revolutionary of yet another sort, Fedukin serves the revolution and the state out of a need to do evil and hurt people in order to satisfy his sadistic impulses. A tall, pock-marked, and unbending interrogator, of modest education but of some literary talent, he derives the greatest pleasure when he investigates and tortures his former comrades, guilty or innocent. His motto is, "Even a stone would talk if you broke its teeth," referring to those victims who have passed through his hands. He believes that it is better to destroy one person's truth than to jeopardize "higher" interests and principles and that to sign a confession for the sake of duty is logical and moral and, therefore, deserving of respect. He simply cannot understand the "sentimental egocentricity of the accused, their pathological need to prove their own innocence, their own little truths." Fedukin thus becomes villainy incarnate, without any alleviating circumstances or rational explanations.

Karl Taube, a Hungarian revolutionary. Representative of a well-meaning European intellectual who joins the revolution as a firm believer in just and idealistic goals, Taube eventually dies during the intraparty intrigues in the Soviet Union. He pays the ultimate price, however, in a bizarre way—he is murdered by common criminals in the prison. He thus becomes a victim of blind fate because, had the leadership not imprisoned him for a flimsy reason, he would not have been killed. Refusing to recognize harsh realities and clinging to his dream of a better life, he perishes for trying to solve problems through reason under circumstances that are governed by passion and blind hatred.

Gould Vershoyle, an Irish revolutionary. His disenchanted search for a better place to live takes him to Spain, where he fights for the Republicans in the civil war, and to Moscow, where he is brought because of his suspicions about the Soviet role in the war. His death in a labor camp in 1945 is another example of a juggernaut crushing everything in its way toward a revolutionary goal.

Miksha, a handyman from Bukovina, working for a Jewish shopkeeper, and a member of the underground. Introduced to the underground by another revolutionary, Aimicke, Miksha sets out to find a traitor in their midst. He suspects a certain girl and kills her, but it was Aimicke who was informing the police. After fleeing to the Soviet Union, Miksha is arrested and forced to confess that he was a Gestapo agent, implicating twelve Russian officials as well; they all get twenty years of hard labor. Miksha thus becomes another example of the revolution devouring its own children.

Eduard Herriot, the leader of the French Radical Socialists. Herriot represents the West European politicians who were unclear about the true nature of the Soviet system. Predictably, he visits the Soviet Union to see whether religion is suppressed there, and he returns convinced that it is not. That is all the more surprising since Herriot is a cautious and sensitive person. Chelyustnikov, who masterminds the official cover-up of the truth during Herriot's visit, signs a guest book in Lyons years later as if thanking Herriot for being so gullible.

Baruch David Neumann, a refugee from Germany and a former Jew. Neumann, who lived in fourteenth century France during the pogroms, suffers the same indignities as those suffered in the twentieth century and, eventually, death for a related reason—human intolerance of different creeds and beliefs. Even though he was converted to Christianity in order to save his life, he later recants, finding it impossible to renounce Judaism. Like Fedukin, Neumann's detractors believe that it is better "to slaughter one mangy sheep than to allow the whole flock to become tainted." This aspect relates Neumann's case to other stories in the novel, proving that intolerance and inhumanity are as old as humankind.

A. A. Darmolatov, a Soviet writer. Even though Darmolatov, a minor Soviet poet, is acquainted with Davidovich, a more significant connection is somewhat obscure. It is not quite clear whether his story is included because of his acquaintanceship with Davidovich, or because he develops mental problems trying to be a successful writer under oppressive conditions, or because he becomes a medical phenomenon by developing elephantiasis. His is the only story without victims, Jewish or otherwise, and without enforced confessions.

Vasa D. Mihailovich

TONIGHT WE IMPROVISE

Author: Luigi Pirandello (1867-1936)
Type of work: Play
Time of action: The 1920's
First produced: Questa sera si recita a soggetto, 1930 (English translation, 1932)

Doctor Hinkfuss, stage manager (director) of an improvised dramatic presentation. Dwarfish in size yet gigantic in his assumed authority, Hinkfuss comes on stage to address the audience at the opening of the play, declaring himself, rather than the unidentified author of the play, fully responsible for the evening's performance. Instead of presenting the usual fixed, unmoving drama, he will present a living, changing theater as vital and unpredictable as life itself. Throughout the production, he interrupts scenes with comments of approval or disgust; he maneuvers light and set pieces to create the ambiance he desires with no regard for the actors' needs or responses. At every opportunity, he heedlessly prattles on with his philosophy of the aesthetics of the theater, asserting the superiority of improvisation and spontaneity over fixed dialogue for the creation of the essential fluidity and passion of life on the stage. He asserts that, like life, improvisational theater allows for the unforeseen circumstances that may thwart the best-planned organization of events. Hinkfuss presents to the minds of the audience the Pirandellian conundrum: whether it is life that shapes and defines theater or theater that gives the shape of truth to life.

Leading Man, who plays the part of **Rico Verri,** a young Sicilian aviation officer, and speaks also as himself, **Mr. . . . ,** the leading male performer of the troupe. He testily refuses to be introduced to the audience before the performance of the play-within-the-play, protesting that he must be nonexistent for the audience as anyone but his character part; he must live only as the character Verri for the time he is on stage. He is a temperamental and angry young man, both in himself and as the character he plays, frequently stepping out of his part to berate the stage manager or other actors in the same manner that his character scolds and belittles other characters in the play. The Leading Man is dissatisfied with improvisation, believing that there must be written parts or the actors will begin to speak out of real passions and life will take over where the stage should prevail. He criticizes Hinkfuss, demanding in the third act that he leave the stage entirely and allow the actors to continue without his manipulations and bring meaning solely through their own interactions.

Leading Lady, who plays the part of **Mommina,** oldest daughter of the Le Croce family, and speaks also as herself, **Mrs. . . . ,** the leading female performer. She too resists improvisation, claiming that she requires specific lines and actions to be certain of the quality of her performance. Throughout the first two acts, she manipulates other cast members into following her view of the scenes. In the final act, however, after the stage manager has been forced to leave, she gives herself entirely to identification with her character, Mommina, who has married Rico Verri in order to prove that her family is worthy of a place in acceptable society.

Old Character Man, who plays the part of **Signor Palmiro Le Croce,** nicknamed **Penny Whistle,** and speaks also as himself to Hinkfuss and the other actors. Signor Palmiro is an ineffectual old man, harassed by his society-minded wife and made to appear foolish by the younger men of the village because he is fond of a young singer from the local tavern. In the course of the improvisational script, the character Palmiro is killed while protecting the young singer from an angry suitor.

Character Woman, who plays the part of **Signora Ignatia Le Croce** and speaks also as herself to Hinkfuss and the other actors. The Signora is intent on living an urban style of life in her small country village. Because of this determination, she brings disgrace on her family by allowing her four daughters to entertain young men openly in their home, an action looked on as scandalously brazen by the gossipy villagers.

The Four Le Croce Daughters, Mommina, Totina, Dorina, and **Nenè,** four charming and high-spirited girls who flirt with young aviation officers assigned them as their escorts by their mother. Their actions scandalize Rico Verri, and he marries Mommina to take her away from such circumstances. He then imprisons her in his home, however, to make certain she does not bring scandal on himself.

Five Young Aviation Officers, Mangini, Nardi, Pomarici, Pometti, and **Sarella,** five gentlemen who are guests at parties in the Le Croce home. They escort the Le Croce daughters and their mother to social affairs.

Members of the Audience, various men and women seated among the actual audience. Their purpose is to respond to and occasionally to heckle Dr. Hinkfuss in his lengthy explanations and philosophizing about the aesthetics of the theater.

Gabrielle Rowe

THE TOOTH OF CRIME

Author: Sam Shepard (Samuel Shepard Rogers, 1943-   )
Type of work: Play
Time of action: The future
First produced: 1972

Hoss, a killer, intent on improving his position on the charts, aiming for a gold record. He is indisputably one of the best solo acts in the game and is well aware of the pressure that fame puts on him to continue to play that game in order to become number one. Hoss's problem is that he senses the futility of continuing to perform according to other people's rules instead of to his own instincts. The isolation into which his managers have pushed him is destroying Hoss's confidence and his awareness of what is going on at the fringes of the game. He knows that the real threats to any star come not from the other acts playing within the game but from the Gypsy Markers acting outside the game who use and break the rules to fit their own purposes. This threat is realized in Crow, who is able to defeat Hoss in a shoot-out and to claim all Hoss's territory and entourage.

Becky Lou, Hoss's manager and girlfriend, a woman capable of shaping a renegade killer into a chart-topping solo marker, as she has done with Hoss. Becky, however, is also capable of destroying her creations, because she defines success as playing by the rules of the game. She is an opportunist who apparently joined up with Hoss when he was starting to make a name for himself on the circuit and who knows how to manipulate him to act against the instincts that served him well early in his career. After the fight, she leaves with Crow.

Star-Man, an astrologer, part of Hoss's management team, who, in advising Hoss when to kill and not to kill according to the stars, takes away the unpredictable edge that made Hoss a successful solo marker. By advising Hoss against moving when he is ready, Star-Man helps to leave Hoss in the vulnerable, disheartened, and stagnant state that Crow finds him at the time of the fight.

Galactic Jack, a disc jockey, in the style of Wolfman Jack, who keeps the charts on the game. He informs Hoss of his position on the charts and of movements being made by other participants in the game. Like the other people surrounding Hoss, Galactic Jack believes in the power of the game and the forces that administer the rules. He does not believe in the possibility of a serious threat coming from outside the game, that is, from the Gypsy Markers.

Cheyenne, driver of Hoss's Maserati and long-time companion and friend to Hoss. Because of their years as a team, Cheyenne senses the wavering of Hoss's confidence. Unlike Hoss, however, Cheyenne believes in the game because of the rewards it promises: the gold record and the stability the game has maintained. Following the fight between Hoss and Crow, Cheyenne is the only member of Hoss's management team who does not leave with Crow.

Doc, Hoss's trainer, whose main activities are preparing and dispensing drugs to Hoss and giving him advice about how to prepare for the big fight.

Crow, an arrogant, finely tuned, efficient young killer who comes from the outside to challenge Hoss to a shoot-out. He is a real threat to Hoss's position on the charts as well as to his pride. Crow is a Gypsy Marker and, unlike Hoss, is not restricted in how he plays the game. This freedom is one thing that Hoss has lost, and Crow capitalizes on Hoss's desire once again to be free to act as he wishes. Following Hoss's suicide at the end of their fight, Crow surrounds himself with all Hoss's possessions and entourage and prepares to move on his next target.

Referee, the official who scores the duel between Hoss and Crow.

Eric H. Hobson

TOP GIRLS

Author: Caryl Churchill (1938-   )
Type of work: Play
Time of action: The 1980's
First produced: 1982

Marlene, the thirty-three-year-old recently promoted managing director of the Top Girls Employment Agency. A working-class woman who left behind her illegitimate daughter, she has achieved success in the business world by being as tough, ruthless, and aggressive as any man. Politically conservative and emotionally cold, she represents those women who have made it by incorporating patriarchal standards of success and who are contemptuous of those who have selected more traditional paths.

Joyce, Marlene's older sister and acting mother to Angie. A cleaning woman, she has stayed home to care for her parents and her husband, as well as Angie, after Marlene leaves the country for London. Politically liberal with a hatred for the wealthy who employ her, she rejects Marlene's money, pity, and contempt and accepts without regret the choices she has made.

Angie, Marlene's slow-witted seventeen-year-old daughter. Driven by a murderous hatred of Joyce, she suspects that Marlene is her real mother and runs away to London to join her. She is one of those girls who will not, as Marlene says, "make it."

Pope Joan, disguised as a man, reigned between 854 and 856. Driven by a thirst for knowledge in philosophy, religion, and metaphysics, she had to assume the male role to achieve her goals. At Marlene's imagined promotion celebration, she is one of five historical and mythical dinner guests, all of whom are linked to present-day characters by the dramatic device of having an actress play more than one role. Louise is her contemporary physical analogue, and Marlene, her emotional one.

Dull Gret, the subject of the Pieter Brueghel painting in which she is dressed in armor and an apron, leading a crowd of women through hell to fight the devils. The only lower-class woman at the dinner who accepts her status, she has reared ten children, whom she is willing to go to any lengths to save. She is linked with Angie physically and with Joyce temperamentally.

Lady Nijo, born in 1258, a Japanese emperor's courtesan and later a Buddhist nun, who traveled through Japan on foot. Totally dominated by the patriarchy, she has suffered through the murder of her children because they were not boys and the economic consequences of being out of favor with the court. Win is her counterpart.

Isabella Bird, a Scottish world traveler who lived from 1831 to 1904. She idolizes her sister and her late husband, admitting to having experienced great loneliness. The actress who plays her also plays Louise.

Patient Griselda, the obedient wife of "The Clerk's Tale" in Chaucer's *The Canterbury Tales.* Constantly tested by her husband, she always responds with acceptance. The same actress who plays her also plays Nell and Jeanine.

Jeanine, a client, looking for a job so that she can get married.

Louise, a client, who has devoted her life to her company, only to see men promoted over her.

Win and
Nell, two of Marlene's interviewers.

Lori Hall Burghardt

TORCH SONG TRILOGY

Author: Harvey Fierstein (1954-   )
Type of work: Play
Time of action: The 1970's
First produced: 1981

Arnold Beckoff, a female impersonator. Twenty-five years old, Jewish, and gay, Arnold plays Virginia Hamn, a singer of torch songs. He is proud of his sexuality, and his life revolves around the gay culture. Arnold meets Ed, a bisexual schoolteacher, at a bar called the International Stud. He is devastated when jilted by Ed for a woman. Arnold later meets a young hustler, Alan, and they become lovers. Still in love with Ed and not over his hurt, he is unfaithful to Alan, making routine trips to the back room of the International Stud for indiscriminate sex. When Arnold finally meets the woman in Ed's life (Laurel) at Ed's country home, he tells her that Ed is using her to prove his own normalcy. Arnold and Alan plan to adopt a child, but Alan is killed by a group of homophobic punks before the adoption goes through. Arnold assumes the responsibility alone, caring for a fifteen-year-old juvenile delinquent. Ed finally leaves Laurel and moves onto Arnold's couch until he can find another place to live. Arnold indicates to Ed that there is a good chance that they can renew their relationship.

Ed Reiss, a Brooklyn schoolteacher. He is thirty-five years old, handsome, charming, and, at times, insensitive. Ed claims that he is bisexual; Arnold labels him a closet case. Ed approaches Arnold at a gay bar and, for two weeks, sees him consistently. Confused over his sexuality, he is unable to make a commitment to Arnold or to the homosexual life-style. He becomes involved with a woman named Laurel and, after participating in group therapy, decides to marry her. When Arnold and his new lover, Alan, visit Ed and his wife at their farmhouse near Montreal, Ed experiences pangs of jealousy and seduces Alan. Ed eventually realizes that his relationship with Laurel is not a panacea and decides to leave her. Turning to his only gay friend, Arnold, he moves in and becomes a surrogate father to David. He wants to renew his relationship with Arnold, but Arnold will only accept him if he is willing to confront his sexuality. Ed assures Arnold that he is at least willing to try.

Alan, a former hustler turned model. He is eighteen years old and extremely good looking. When he was fourteen, he arrived in New York with dreams of opening a disco. He quickly learned that the only reason men would give him money was in exchange for sex. These sexual encounters provided connections that led to his career as a model. One evening in a nightclub Alan gets drunk, becomes involved in a fight, and is almost knifed; he is saved by Arnold in full Virginia Hamn attire. As a result, he falls deeply in love with Arnold, even tolerating his infidelity. Alan remains faithful until his trip to the Reiss farm, where he is seduced by Ed. After deciding to adopt a child with Arnold, he is killed by a street gang.

Laurel, Ed's average-looking, liberal-minded wife. She has a history of falling in love with gay men and has numerous gay friends. She attends group therapy and has involved Ed in these meetings. Despite knowing that Arnold is Ed's former lover, she invites him and his new lover up to the Reiss farmhouse. When she learns that Ed has seduced Alan, she leaves him. She returns to him, however, and when Ed finally decides to withdraw from the relationship, Laurel has difficulty letting go.

David, Arnold's adopted son. He is fifteen years old, bright, handsome, and gay. Mistreated in foster homes, he lives on the streets for three years. Although skeptical and streetwise, he has been transformed in his six months with Arnold into a fun-loving prankster, comfortable with both home and school.

At times he is a typical teenager, but he displays an uncanny wisdom. Not wanting Arnold to devote his whole life to him, David would like to see Arnold and Ed back together again.

Mrs. Beckoff, Arnold's mother. She is a widow in her sixties who has retired to Florida. Presented as a stereotypical Jewish mother, she loves to meddle and kvetch, or complain. She rambles constantly, saying very little. She cannot accept Arnold's homosexuality and prefers to deny it. When she meets David, she takes a liking to him but is completely opposed to Arnold's plans of adop-

tion. She is insensitive to her son's feelings about the death of Alan (although the cause of death has been concealed from her) and is incensed that he would dare to compare their affair with her many years of marriage. They quarrel, and Arnold asks her to leave. Before she departs, though, there is a reconciliation, and she tries to comfort Arnold about Alan's death.

Lady Blues, a blues singer employed between scenes. She sings 1920's and 1930's torch songs in the tradition of Helen Morgan or Ruth Etting.

Steven C. Kowall

THE TORRENTS OF SPRING

Author: Ernest Hemingway (1899-1961)
Type of work: Novella
Time of action: The early 1920's
First published: 1926

Scripps O'Neil, who claims to have published two stories in *The Dial* and one in *The Saturday Evening Post*. O'Neil is tall, lean, and claims to be a Harvard man. Deserted by his wife and daughter Lucy in Mancelona, Michigan, O'Neil wanders down the railroad tracks to Petoskey and goes to work in the "pump factory" as a "piston-collarer." It is mentioned that his father was a great composer, that his mother is from Florence, Italy, and that he and his mother had to beg from door to door in Chicago when Scripps was a boy, but much of what is said about Scripps in this satirical work is contradictory. He also claims that his father was a general in the Confederate Army and that his mother, with Scripps clinging to her dress, berated General Sherman as the Yankees burned the O'Neil plantation. O'Neil, who is "literary" and romantically fickle, takes many of his meals in Brown's Beanery, where he falls in love with and marries Diana, an elderly waitress, whom he rejects soon for Mandy, a younger waitress. Scripps inexplicably carries a bird inside his shirt through much of the story. He finally gives the bird to Diana.

Scripps is with Mandy at the story's end, but his mind is wandering.

Yogi Johnson, a World War I veteran. Johnson is of Scandinavian descent and works in a Petoskey, Michigan, "pump factory." He is a chunky, well-built fellow, of the sort one might see anywhere. He claims to have been the first World War I volunteer from Cadillac, Michigan. Yogi is worried because he does not want a woman; he fears that something is wrong. A philosopher, he often remarks on the decay of morality in his time. He meets two Indians and tells them of his experiences, playing center in football and at the front, where he killed five men. Yogi speaks of the stages a soldier goes through as he becomes hard-boiled. The Indians take Yogi to an all-Indian private club, which he is forced to leave hurriedly when it is noticed that Yogi is not an Indian. He takes the Indians to Brown's Beanery, a local restaurant, where he relates his most humiliating experience: In Paris, Yogi had unknowingly participated in a live sex exhibition. Having told his tale, he strides away into the night. Yogi is last seen walking down the railroad tracks with an Indian squaw, at night, stripping off and throwing away all of his clothes.

Diana, an elderly waitress in Brown's Beanery in Petoskey. She wears steel-rimmed glasses and her face is lined and gray. She claims to be from the English Lake Country and she claims furthermore that, as a *jeune fille* on a visit to Paris with her mother, her mother disappeared. The police were unable to find Diana's mother, and it is not until the "Author's Final Note to the Reader" that it is revealed that she died of bubonic plague and that the French authorities concealed the matter in order not to destroy the financial success of the Paris Exposition. After her mother's death, Diana was forced, she explains, to come to America, and she became a waitress. Diana is a constant reader of *The Manchester Guardian.* She and Scripps "fall in love" and are married, but half an hour later she notices that Scripps is eyeing the relief waitress. She worries whether she can hold Scripps. She tries to hold him by reading and relating stories from most of the literary journals of the time: *Scribner's, The Century, The Bookman.* She does lose Scripps, but she asks for and receives the bird. She goes out into the night.

Mandy, a waitress at Brown's Beanery. She is a buxom, jolly-looking girl. Scripps thinks that she is robust and vigorously lovely, with healthy, calm, capable hands. He is "stirred"

by her only thirty minutes after his marriage to Diana. Mandy likes to tell improbable literary anecdotes, the first one being about the death of Henry James, others concerning Edmund Gosse, and more. She wins Scripps, but for how long is questionable. His interest is already wandering to the Indian squaw.

Two Indians, a little one and a big one, who had studied at the Carlisle Indian School. They are on their way, they say, to Petoskey, to join the Salvation Army. They both claim to be veterans, much decorated. One, the little Indian, won the Victoria Cross. He has artificial arms and legs but still shoots excellent pool and can climb ladders. The big Indian was a major and won the Distinguished Service Order. The Indians take Yogi to an all-Indian club; when they are thrown out, the little one loses one of his artificial arms. They are last seen picking up Yogi's discarded clothes to sell.

The squaw, carrying a papoose. She enters the beanery wearing only moccasins. She is joined by Yogi, and they walk out together.

The author, clearly Hemingway, a character. He speaks to the reader from time to time, discussing his progress on the book and what he has had for lunch and with whom.

A drummer, a steady customer at Brown's Beanery.

Donald R. Noble

THE TORRENTS OF SPRING

Author: Ivan Turgenev (1818-1883)
Type of work: Novel
Time of action: 1840
First published: Veshniye vody, 1872 (*Spring Floods,* 1874; better known as *The Torrents of Spring*)

Dimitry Pavlovich Sanin, a young Russian nobleman and the novel's aging narrator. Presented as a reminiscence, *The Torrents of Spring* gives two distinct visions of Sanin: the weak-willed, twenty-one-year-old idealist and the soul-sickened, fifty-two-year-old

narrator. The youthful Sanin is a careless nobleman who is accosted by Gemma Rosselli while walking down a street in Frankfurt. She believes that her brother Emilio has stopped breathing, and when Sanin restores the young man, she and her family consider him their savior. Sanin stays on in Frankfurt and discovers that he is infatuated with Gemma. After winning her affection by fighting a duel in her honor, he meets the predatory Maria Nikolayevna and falls under her sexual spell. Sanin's betrayal of Gemma is worsened by his inability to confess his perfidy to her. After a time in Maria Nikolayevna's retinue, Sanin is cast aside. It is only as a life-sickened, aging man of the world that Sanin seeks out Gemma and is relieved of his guilt when he hears of her happy married state in the United States. The news fills him with a new sense of life, and he begins to make plans to immigrate.

Gemma Rosselli, a beautiful Italian girl living in Frankfurt. Dutiful and innocent, Gemma is willing to sacrifice herself to Klüber's loveless proposal for the financial stability of her family, but Sanin's romantic defense of her honor gives her the courage to break off her engagement to Klüber and openly express her love for Sanin. Her forgiving response to the aging Sanin's letter demonstrates her generosity and virtue.

Karl Klüber, a German businessman, Gemma's fiancé. Reflecting Turgenev's growing disenchantment with Germany, Klüber is a complete materialist, devoid of character or sensitivity. He callously treats love as a business arrangement. When Gemma is insulted by von Dönhof, Klüber tries to ignore the incident.

Maria Nikolayevna Polozov, a wealthy half-Gypsy who seduces Sanin. Predatory and evil, Maria uses sex as a weapon, relishing her sexual victory over Sanin. Her greatest pleasure comes from despoiling the honorable love that was shared by Gemma and Sanin. In the context of nineteenth century Russian culture, Maria's sexual adventuring can be viewed as a sort of apolitical nihilism.

Ippolit Sidorych Polozov, Maria Nikolayevna's phlegmatic husband. Morally impoverished, physically grotesque, and psychologically dominated, Polozov accepts his wife's sexual adventuring as the price he must pay to pursue in peace his own self-centered existence.

Von Dönhof, the German officer with whom Sanin fights a duel for Gemma's honor. A boasting drunkard, von Dönhof insults Gemma, who is defended by Sanin. He later shows little enthusiasm for the duel with Sanin.

Panteleone, an aged, retired opera singer who lives with the Rossellis. At first, Panteleone's pathetic reminiscences of past operatic triumphs playing heroic roles make him a comic figure, but he is the character who effectively confronts Sanin with his unfaithfulness after he has betrayed Gemma.

Emilio Rosselli, Gemma's idealistic younger brother. Impressed by the heroism that he believes Sanin displays, he is encouraged to enlist in the idealistic fight for independence under Giuseppe Garibaldi. He is killed, and his growth from an uncertain boy into a martyr in the cause of national unification contrasts markedly with Sanin's sorry decline into corruption.

Carl Brucker

TORTILLA FLAT

Author: John Steinbeck (1902-1968)
Type of work: Novel
Time of action: The early 1920's
First published: 1935

Danny, a *paisano* in his early thirties. His heritage is a mixture of Spanish, Indian, Mexican, and Caucasian blood, but, like all *paisanos,* he claims to be purely Spanish. He is small, dark, compact in build. Danny is without conventional ambition but is intelligent and capable. He broke mules for the army in Texas all during World War I. Upon his return, Danny inherits two wooden houses from his grandfather, but property brings responsibility and worry, and security brings boredom, brooding, and restlessness: Danny likes women and fighting. He is the King Arthur of this round table of *paisanos* of Monterey.

Pilon (pē·lōn'), one of the *paisanos* who is a tenant in Danny's house. Smarter than most of the others, Pilon is a sentimentalist, though utterly without ambition. He is a cunning thief and rationalizer. Pilon also served in World War I.

Big Joe Portagee, another *paisano* tenant in Danny's house. He had joined the infantry in World War I but spent eighteen of twenty-nine months in jail. He loves women, drinking, and brawling, and is less intelligent than his friends. He has trouble concentrating and often falls asleep at inopportune times. He is nearly without morality because he has trouble remembering right from wrong.

Jesus Maria Corcoran (hā·sōōs'), a *paisano*. Jesus is great-hearted and always tries to relieve suffering whenever he hears of it. He lives in Danny's house and brings home the needy strays he finds.

The Pirate, a huge, broad, slow-witted man with five dogs who cuts twenty-five cents worth of kindling each day and saves the quarters to buy a silver candlestick for Saint Francis. He lives in an abandoned chicken house until taken in by the *paisanos*.

Delores Engracia "Sweets" Ramirez, a *paisana* who belongs to the Native Daughters of the Golden West. "Sweets" is given to fits of lust once or twice a week. Then, her figure has voluptuousness of movement, and her voice has a certain throatiness, though she is lean-faced, lumpy, and not considered pretty most of the time. Sweets desires Danny and is catapulted to the top of the social heap when Danny, a property owner, gives her a vacuum cleaner, though she has no electricity in her house.

Torelli the wine-seller, a man much put upon by the *paisanos*, who try to cheat him as he seeks to take advantage of them. He can be miserly and foul-tempered.

Mrs. Torelli, his wife. A woman with a gentle nature, susceptible to flattery, she is occasionally seduced by one of the *paisanos*.

Señora Teresina Cortez, nearing thirty, the mother of at least nine children, although her own mother is only in her late forties. The Cortez children live exclusively on tortillas and beans, a diet on which, to the astonishment of all, they thrive. The *paisanos* generously provide this family with a year's supply of beans, then Señora Cortez becomes pregnant once again and wonders which of them is responsible.

Cornelia Ruiz, a woman famous for her love of men and fighting. She is a favorite of the *paisanos*, although she is known to take money from men's pockets while they sleep.

The corporal from Torreón, Mexico, a man whose wife had left him for a captain. He hopes his infant son will rise to be a general so that his son can steal some enlisted man's attractive young wife.

Donald R. Noble

THE TOWERS OF TREBIZOND

Author: Rose Macaulay (1881-1958)
Type of work: Novel
Time of action: The mid-1950's
First published: 1956

Laurie, the protagonist, the niece of Dorothea ffoulkes-Corbett. Both her name and her outlook (independent and tomboyish, with a zest for adventure and a love of solitude) keep her androgynous; no details of age or appearance are revealed as she narrates the adventures of the traveling party: Aunt Dot, Father Hugh Chantry-Pigg, herself, and, later, Dr. Halide Tanpinar and Xenophon. Enlisted by Aunt Dot as a sort of companion-cum-secretary on a trip to the Middle East, Laurie agrees to illustrate and contribute to the book about Turkey that her aunt plans to write, in addition to helping with the daily affairs of lodging, luggage, camping, transportation, dining, and caring for the camel. Like her aunt, she loves travel perhaps more than any other occupation, not only because she relishes new sights and experiences but also because she often thus encounters her mother (who had left Laurie's clergyman father when Laurie was young) and her mother's "protector," both of whom are cheerful, lively, generous, and easygoing. Engaged in an affair of ten years' duration with her married cousin Vere, Laurie yearns for the consolations of the Anglican Church (she comments that it is in her family's blood) but cannot relinquish the love that it condemns. Trebizond, with its rich and ancient history encompassing so many religions and cultures, becomes for her a symbol of the mystery at the center of life, and after Vere's death she feels forever alienated both from its mystery and from the comfort of the Church. Laurie's character is partially drawn from Macaulay's own life: fascination with travel, enjoyment of writing and adventure, devotion to/alienation from the Anglican church, and a lengthy affair with a married man, although in Macaulay's case the affair endured for more than twenty years and ended with her lover's death by cancer.

Dorothea ffoulkes-Corbett (Aunt Dot), an eccentric feminist, adventurer, and missionary of sorts, very much her own person. She had become a widow when her missionary husband had tried to shoot her and himself to save them from cannibals; when he missed her, she feigned death to avoid his next shot, saw him kill himself, and then talked her way out of the stewpot by convincing the savages that she was a goddess. She spearheads the trip (taking the camel to make a good impression), greatly concerned about the plight of Middle Eastern women, whose religious beliefs contribute to their oppression. Convinced that only conversion to Christianity (specifically High Church Anglicanism) will liberate them, she takes along Father Chantry-Pigg to legitimize her travels, allowing her to be partially funded as a missionary. Traveling so near to "the curtain" between Turkey and Russia, which she has yearned for many years to visit and into which travel is forbidden because of the Cold War, she yields to temptation: She talks Father Chantry-Pigg into sneaking across the border with her for several months, thus leaving Laurie and the rest of the party to fend for themselves. She returns unscathed, ebullient, and even more notorious than before, accused by both the Russians and the British of spying. As the story closes, she is determined to publish her book and make the world aware of the sufferings of Middle Eastern women.

Father Hugh Chantry-Pigg, a zealous and narrow-minded Anglican clergyman. Now retired, he eagerly accepts Aunt Dot's invitation to accompany her abroad, desiring to enlighten the heathen, visit holy places, and test the miraculous powers of the relics he collects. His pomposity and self-righteousness alienate Laurie, the Moslems, and most of the various government officials with whom the party must deal; he fails to make a single convert and in fact probably sets back the missionary work of the Anglican Church by several years. A willing conspirator in Aunt Dot's clandestine trip across the Russian border, he cares not at all about the plight of women but desires rather to visit shrines and collect or display relics. Like Aunt Dot, he returns notorious and accused of spying, still self-satisfied and inflexible.

Dr. Halide Tanpinar, a female doctor from Istanbul, attractive and strong-minded. While taking medical training in London, she had converted to Anglicanism, primarily to protest the Moslem treatment of women, but

Father Chantry-Pigg pressures her and doubts her motives. Persuaded by Aunt Dot to join their party as translator and part-time missionary, she reveals that she loves a Moslem but will not marry him because of the Moslem oppression of women. Eventually, she comes to realize that change for the better must come from within the country and its people, and that Anglicanism is too alien to be accepted at that time. She reconverts to Islam, marries her beloved, and determines to work for the bettering of the situation of women as a Moslem herself.

Vere, Laurie's cousin and adulterous lover of ten years. He is evidently wealthy enough to travel frequently; Laurie is in love with his wit, intellect, and understanding. He never expresses any regret for betraying his wife or any interest in Anglicanism, a topic vitally important to Laurie. He dies suddenly in an auto accident when Laurie, enraged at a bus driver who is running a red light, attempts to beat the bus across the intersection.

Xenophon Paraclydes, a young Greek student. He joins Aunt Dot's caravan as jeep driver (he "borrows" the jeep from a family member) and as general assistant. After Aunt Dot sneaks into Russia, he regretfully heads back home, losing his zest for travel in the ensuing legal fray.

Charles Dagenham, a writer of travel books. Probably homosexual, he is an acquaintance of Laurie, whom she encounters in Turkey; he has recently had a falling-out with his companion and fellow writer, David Langley. A few days after he insists upon telling Laurie "the real story"—lest she should hear an alternate version from David—he is killed by a shark while swimming in dangerous waters. Laurie, spending the night in a hotel room where he had stayed earlier, finds his manuscript and keeps it to return to his family after his death.

David Langley, Charles's collaborator and (probably) lover. After Charles's death and Aunt Dot's disappearance, Laurie reads a London paper and realizes that David is plagiarizing from a copy of Charles's manuscript, unaware that she possesses the original, and taking full credit for the work. Short of funds and desperate to reach Alexandretta, where Vere awaits, she makes David aware of the original manuscript, thus gently blackmailing him into providing food and transportation. She eventually returns the manuscript, but even back in England he continues to be obliging lest she should reveal what she knows. Although she maintains silence, his plagiarism is eventually discovered.

A camel, called merely **"the camel,"** a gift from a rich Arab to Aunt Dot on one of her earlier adventures. It is a beast of pedigree, a white Arabian Dhalur, and the means of Aunt Dot's escape into Russia. When Laurie is left almost penniless, it provides her transportation to Alexandretta, and it provides comic relief throughout the story.

Sonya H. Cashdan

THE TRAGEDY OF KING CHRISTOPHE

Author: Aimé Césaire (1913-   )
Type of work: Play
Time of action: 1806-1820
First published: La Tragédie du Roi Christophe, 1963 (English translation, 1964)

Henri Christophe, king of the new nation of Haiti, a former slave, cook, and revolutionary soldier with the great liberator, Toussaint-Louverture. He is named a general and commander of the northern province and then offered the presidency of the new republic. He refuses, preferring to have himself crowned king of the northern province, and he sets up a court in imitation of Haiti's former masters, the French. His throne has a gold sun emblazoned on the back to resemble that of Louis XIV, and he puts the crown on his own head at the coronation, as did Napoleon. After fourteen years of trying to make a world power of Haiti, however, he admits defeat and commits suicide.

Pétion, a mulatto who accepts the presidency after Christophe refuses. He rules the other half of Haiti as a republic. He urges the senate to refuse Christophe's offer of unification and later sends the army to destroy his rival.

Hugonin, Christophe's agent and "court jester," who insists that the nobility created by Christophe is a fine way to bestow favors and to secure the king's authority. A buffoon and scoundrel, he is nevertheless appointed as Minister of Public Morality; in this role he is commanded to force marriage upon the promiscuous natives and to reinstate respect for the family. When Christophe at last commits suicide, Hugonin declares himself ready to join the return to former ways and announces the end of the king's dream of a Europe-like kingdom.

Master of Ceremonies, a protocol expert sent by the European nations to set up a court in response to Christophe's request for technical aid. He oversees dress, dancing, and general etiquette at the court.

Corneille Brelle, archbishop of the realm, who crowns Christophe as king, "first crowned monarch of the New World." He later displeases the king, who orders him walled up in the archbishop's palace and left to die.

Metellus, a conspirator who hopes to overthrow both Christophe and Pétion because they have betrayed the revolution and divided the country.

Madame Christophe, a former servant, now the queen. She warns her husband that he is pushing his people too hard in his drive to make Haiti a world power.

Martial Besse, a young European engineer who will oversee the building of Christophe's great stone citadel, a monument to glorify the new Haiti and to inspire its citizens to greater accomplishments.

Richard, Count of the Northern Marches, banished to distant Thomasico after dancing the Bamboola at a court ball.

Franco de Medina, a French diplomat who comes to Christophe's court with a proposal from the French king and is promptly put to death by Christophe.

Juan de Dios, the archbishop replacing the murdered Corneille Brelle. He is forced to accommodate the king and celebrate the Feast of the Assumption at a church near Christophe's palace instead of at the cathedral in the capital city. His intoning of the Mass puts Christophe in a trance that causes him to see the ghost of Corneille Brelle and to collapse.

Lucy Golsan

THE TRANSFIGURATION OF BENNO BLIMPIE

Author: Albert Innaurato (1948-   )
Type of work: Play
Time of action: The 1970's
First produced: 1974

Benno Blimpie, an enormously obese, physically repulsive man of twenty-five. Although relatively short, he weighs more than five hundred pounds and has a splotchy, sickly complexion and greasy, unkempt hair. His shapeless clothes, too large even for him, are wet with his sweat and filthy from his slovenly habits. Although Benno undergoes no physical transformation, he is depicted at the various stages of his unhappy life in a series of scenes in which his age is indicated by gestures and changes in his voice. He otherwise remains inactive, like a large, inert blob. These scenes, like flashbacks in fiction, lead to Benno's transfiguration, or his decision to eat himself to death. Once that decision is made, Benno refers to his previous self in the third person. This former Benno, further revealed through recollections and dreams, is full of longing and desperate for love, but he inspires none, not even in his own family. He is always both frustrated and brutalized by experience. In one episode, he is nearly beaten to death after being sexually abused by three teenage bullies. In another, as a prelude to biting himself on the arm, he imagines himself being cooked in an oven like a fat, pus-basted roast. Although for a time he is able to find solace in art of the Italian masters and his own drawings, and, presumably, some emotional satisfaction in his perpetual eating, he finally resigns himself to his fate. The transfigured Benno will feed upon himself and, nearing death, eat large quantities of poison so that the rats feeding on his body will die and he, in death, will have achieved some purpose.

Girl, a streetwise tease of twelve or thirteen. Her notable characteristic, suggesting her sensuality, is her red hair. She is full of erotic fantasies and uses her sexual attraction to torment Benno's grandfather, who pursues her shamelessly. Although finding him offensive, she is willing to let him fondle her as long as he gives her his social security checks. She eventually tires of the lurid games with the old man and stabs him to death with a broken bottle when he tries to overpower her.

Woman (Mary), the haggard, middle-aged mother of Benno. She is a very coarse, shrewish woman who deeply resents her loss of her youth and good looks. Much of her resentment is taken out on her husband and Benno, both of whom she grows to despise. Loveless and cruel, her frequent tirades include extremely bitter and vicious remarks that help crush Benno's spirit.

Man (Dominick), the middle-aged father of Benno. Like his wife, he is coarse, vulgar, and able to hold his own in the furious family rows. He is a compulsive gambler who is accused by his wife of being a dismal failure both as husband and as father. Although greatly disappointed in Benno, he does not revile him as Benno's mother does and is more patient with him. Yet, he believes his son is a "pansy" who can never measure up to his conception of what it means to be a real man, and, though less vituperative, he wounds Benno just as much as the mother does.

Old Man, Benno's elderly grandfather, called **Pop-Pop** by Benno. He is an old lecher with pedophilic preferences. Over seventy, he ardently pursues the girl, who encourages him, even though she finds him physically disgusting. He often has Benno in his care and seems to be Benno's best hope for familial affection. He, at least, is not cruel to Benno and has some protective concern for his welfare. In one of Benno's fantasies, the old man is transformed into an angelic-appearing butcher who covers Benno with a sheet and marks it like a chart used to designate cuts of meat. The old man's murder is profoundly disturbing for Benno and contributes to his alienation and withdrawal.

John W. Fiero

TRANSLATIONS

Author: Brian Friel (1929-   )
Type of work: Play
Time of action: 1833
First produced: 1980

Hugh Mor O'Donnell, in his early sixties, the master of an Irish hedge school, who persists in educating his charges (most of whom are adults) in the classical languages, despite his growing recognition that English is the language of the future. Fond of his pint, he has usually taken a drop too much, but he is never really drunk. Irascible and arrogant, he, more than anyone else in the play, understands that the translation of Irish place-names into English involves a transition from one world to another. Further, despite his personal regret at the cultural violence done by such translation, he recognizes the inevitability of the transition if Ireland is to avoid being "imprisoned in a linguistic contour which no longer matches the landscape of . . . fact." A poet writing in a language few can read, he understands the extent to which language shapes humankind's understanding of the world and sees clearly the forces sweeping his country from "spiritual" Irish to "commercial" English.

Manus, in his late twenties or early thirties, Hugh's eldest son. He assists Hugh in the hedge school, makes his dinner, and sees him safely through the hours of drink. For all of this, his father pays him no salary and treats him like a footman. Manus loves Maire and would like to marry her, but he has no way to support her and will not go against his father for the job at the new national school the British are building. Lamed when his father, drunk, fell on him while he was a baby, Manus somehow turns the incident into a reason for being responsible for his father. He is a gentle, caring man, hurt by what is happening to Ireland and hurt by Maire's defection but without the capacity to resist either effectively.

Owen, in his later twenties, Hugh's youngest son, who had "escaped" to England and returns now in service to the British, who need him to help remap Ireland because they do not speak Irish but who never get his name right and call him Roland. Initially pleased to have avoided his brother's fate and to be earning a good salary, he is finally appalled by the consequences of the process of which he has been a part.

Lieutenant George Yolland, in his twenties, the officer in charge of translating Irish place-names into English. He speaks only English and relies heavily on Owen. In love with Ireland and with Maire, he longs to learn the language that will open communication with both. His courtship of Maire takes place across the language barrier and illustrates the power of love and nonverbal communication.

Maire, in her twenties, a lively, strong young woman with little sympathy for Manus' reluctance to take steps to escape the dual traps of exploitation by his father and a failing Irish economy. She wants to learn English, a practical language that she knows will serve her well when she emigrates to America. When she falls in love with Yolland, she discovers that feelings are not hindered by language barriers.

Jimmy Jack, the "Infant Prodigy," in his sixties, a dirty, poor student in Hugh's school who does not always distinguish clearly between the mythology he studies in Greek and the "real" world around him. He is at times faintly ridiculous, but his fluency in Greek and Latin indirectly comments on the superiority assumed by the British, who speak only English.

Sarah, in her twenties, a student in Hugh's class whose speech defect is so severe she has always been assumed to be mute. Manus, whom she loves, is teaching her to speak.

Captain Lancey, Lieutenant Yolland's superior officer. He is a stereotypical representation of rigid, self-righteous British imperialism, convinced of his own superiority, with no sympathy or understanding of the country or the people whose land he is dominating and changing.

Helen Lojek

THE TRANSPOSED HEADS
A Legend of India

Author: Thomas Mann (1875-1955)
Type of work: Novella
Time of action: The eleventh century
First published: Die vertauschten Köpfe: Eine indische Legende, 1940 (English translation, 1941)

Shridaman, a merchant well-versed in classical learning, twenty-one years old and of delicate build. His father, also a merchant in the village of Welfare of Cows in the land of Kosala, was of Brahman stock and very familiar with Vedic texts. Shridaman has all the attributes of a man of the mind. It is for this reason that he is attracted to his mental and physical opposite, Nanda. They are friends and inseparable. It is through Nanda that Shridaman is introduced to the pleasures of the flesh and the senses. It is also through him that he comes to know the identity of his future wife. By accident, he and Nanda witness Sita's ritual ablutions near the temple of Kali and Shridaman falls in love with her. Because Nanda and Sita had known each other as children, Nanda is able to bring Sita and his friend together. It is Shridaman's admiration for his friend's physical strength and uncomplicated mind and piety as well as his love for Sita that finally leads him to acknowledge Sita's longing for Nanda by sacrificing himself in the temple of Kali, "the great mother." With the same loyalty and devotion, he accepts his new existence as an amalgam of his former self and that of his friend. His honesty, fair-mindedness, and love for Sita ultimately lead him to agree to a murder-suicide pact that results in a triple funeral pyre in order that the conflict between the friend and the couple may be resolved and to assure their child's future happiness.

Nanda, a shepherd and blacksmith who is eighteen years old. He is dark-skinned, with a big, flat nose and a strong, muscular body. His father is also a smith. Nanda has a "lucky calf lock" on his chest. Nanda is devoted to his friend Shridaman, whom he admires for his learning and slender, "elegant" physique.

Nanda, although loyal to Shridaman and intent on avoiding any hint of an interest in Sita, Shridaman's wife, is nevertheless secretly desirous of her, just as Sita is of him. After his unquestioning immolation before the corpse of his friend in Kali's temple and his cheerful acceptance of a new physical identity, he also accepts willingly the hermit's verdict as to whether he has a right to Sita's affections. Because the judgment goes against him, he decides to live in self-imposed exile and seclusion. He accepts willingly Shridaman's decision that each end the life of the other by mortally wounding his heart, and he agrees to Sita's decision to die on the funeral pyre so that their unhappy union may have a happy resolution and Samadhi a happy future.

Sita, a young maiden who becomes Shridaman's wife. Her appelation is "Sita of the beautiful hips." Her innocence, piety, and devotion to her parents is also the reason for her unquestioning obedience when her parents and Shridaman's agree that she should marry Shridaman. It is her husband who introduces her to the pleasures of the senses although, over time, it is clear to her that he is more of a man of the mind than of the flesh. She, therefore, develops a secret longing for Nanda's arms and body, which seem perfect to her, and she wishes for a combination of her husband's mind and his friend's body. She inadvertently reveals to Shridaman this secret longing. It is her sense of guilt that leads her to implore Kali, the goddess, to restore the friends to their former life, and it is her secret desire for a perfect husband that leads her to transpose their heads. She enjoys a night with Nanda's 'husband-body' during Shridaman's absence, but, in the end, she decides to join in the friends' suicide pact by her self-immolation on a funeral pyre at the feast of burning. She does so because she rejects polyandry and out of concern for the future of her child, whom she wants to grow up not as the child of an abandoned mother but as an orphan and the son of a legendary mother, whose self-sacrifice assures her legend and commemoration through a monument.

Kali (Durga, Devi), Hindu goddess of motherhood, destruction, sacrifice, and bloodshed. These contradictory attributes match those of her victims and followers, Shridaman, Nanda, and Sita. As a disembodied voice, she enters into a dialogue with Sita. In forceful terms, she expresses her displeasure with the disingenuous sacrifices of Nanda and Shridaman and, therefore, is willing to accede to Sita's fervent desire to see the two restored to their former existence with Sita's help.

Kamananda, a pious hermit. He agrees to settle the dispute between Shridaman, Nanda, and Sita. He has no difficulty in deciding that it is the head that is the decisive criterion in determining whether Shridaman with Nanda's body or Nanda with Shridaman's body is now the husband of Sita.

Samadhi (Andhaka, the blind one), the light-skinned and near-sighted son of Shridaman and Sita. As the child of a famous mother, he is reared by "a wise and learned Brahman." His progress is reported at the ages of four, seven, twelve, and twenty. At age twenty, he has become reader to the King of Benares.

Arthur Tilo Alt

TRAVELLING NORTH

Author: David Williamson (1942-   )
Type of work: Play
Time of action: 1969-1972
First produced: 1979

Frank, a retired construction engineer and widower over seventy, from Melbourne, Australia. He has taken his lover Frances north to live in a small cottage in a remote tropical area in Queensland, where he intends to escape people and examine the meaning of his life. A disenchanted former Communist and an atheist, he is an assertively self-assured man governed by his own rationality who sees the world in terms of measurable quantities capable of explanation or analysis. Direct and opinionated, he does not relate to people easily. Estranged from his artist son, Frank still remains on good terms with his daughter Joan. Untroubled by guilt, he dismisses the guilt held by Frances regarding her disapproving daughters, whom he sees as exploitative children. His tall and athletic physique exudes an energetic vitality, which increasingly diminishes as the infirmity of a discovered heart ailment strikes. His illness causes a progressive withdrawal into himself that makes him difficult to live with, but eventually his condition makes him realize his dependence on other human beings. Frank is the initial motivator of the action as the coldly rational and dominant half of a complex love affair with a loving woman whose qualities and temperament contrast sharply with his own. When Frances leaves him temporarily, he arrives at the self-discovery that while he has "always loved mankind in general," he has been ungenerous to some of those he has been "involved with in particular." Effecting a reconciliation with Frances, who has now become the controller of the action, Frank puts aside his anticonventional prejudices for marriage. The play's central figure, Frank before his death has learned from his life with Frances a monumental revelation about himself.

Frances, a slim and attractive woman of about fifty-five whose home has been in Melbourne. She is the divorced mother of two married daughters. With her lover Frank, she has traveled north to distant Queensland. That her daughters, Sophie and Helen, question her relationship with an older man who is taking her to northern isolation distresses her, and, recalling her disinterested mothering of them as children, she feels guilty about their apparent domestic unhappiness. Her loyalty to Frank is in part an effort to compensate for her past irresponsibility. Gentle and reticent as well as restless by nature, Frances is a sensitive, emotional person who holds an undefined openness to life and people. For her, questions exist to be answered. Her temperament complements and contrasts with that of Frank, for she represents the warm and initially passive half of a complicated relationship whose difficult odyssey forces her to become a more complete woman. Restless in the north and dismayed by Frank's irascible self-absorption, exacerbated by his discovered infirmity, Frances returns south to her daughters only to realize that they, and all people, are responsible for their own lives. She reunites with Frank, who also has reached important self-realizations and pleases her by his decision to marry her. Reaching a final fulfillment with Frank shortly before his death, Frances gains a more defined and guilt-free concept of herself.

Helen, Frances' youngest daughter, an attractive housewife in her late twenties with children and a deserting husband. Direct and somewhat neurotic, she has not forgiven her mother for placing her with a relative when a child and considers Frances' departure for Melbourne yet another betrayal. Helen strongly disapproves of her mother's affair with Frank and warns her of becoming an older man's nursemaid. Stimulating Frances' guilt feelings, she functions with her sister as a secondary antagonist to the two major characters.

Sophie, Frances' thirty-year-old daughter, who is a pretty suburban wife with impractical and self-absorbing career expectations that create domestic unhappiness. Gentler and better adjusted than Helen, she is more sympathetic toward her mother's relationship with Frank.

Saul Morgenstein, a disenchanted but wry Queensland physician who correctly diagnoses Frank's illness. His medical advice is vindicated after Frank's stubborn insistence on treating himself runs its course. Affectionate toward Frances and tolerant of Frank, Saul becomes a close family friend.

Freddy Wicks, a jovial widower and neighbor to Frank and Frances in the north. A World War II veteran and a nationalist who supports Australian participation in Vietnam, he proves to be a good neighbor despite Frank's trenchant opposition to his views. His acceptance by Frank, with that of Saul, indicates the latter's realization of his dependent need for other people.

Joan, Frank's daughter. She is an intelligent woman in her early thirties whose liberal ideas support those of her father. She openly accepts Frank's liaison with Frances.

Christian H. Moe

THE TRAVELS OF LAO TS'AN

Author: Liu E (Liu T'ieh-yun, 1857-1909)
Type of work: Novel
Time of action: The 1880's and 1890's
First published: Lao Ts'an youji, 1904-1907 (English translation, 1952)

T'ieh Pu-ts'an, known as **Lao Ts'an** (lou sān), a man who wanders through the North China province of Shantung as an itinerant physician. The nickname "Lao Ts'an" means "Old Vagabond" and fits his unconventional style of life. In his travels, he savors the special character of each place while encountering old friends and making new ones. He is regularly drawn into some human problem and finds wise, just solutions. Lao Ts'an, a vigorous, healthy man of about fifty, has no home but resides in plain inns; in truth, he is a person of modest means but disdains money. He has few possessions beyond simple cotton clothes, a few books, his medicine chest, and a string of bells used by Chinese itinerant healers to attract patients. Lao Ts'an's humble existence hides administrative insight, considerable learning, a cultivated aesthetic sense, and a noble character. In addition to curing his patients, he helps control Yellow River flooding, exposes a ruthless official, shows a new magistrate how to suppress banditry, and prevents a miscarriage of justice. His sagacity leads others to treat him with the highest respect. Once his solutions are set in motion, Lao Ts'an leaves before he is fully thanked to continue his wandering care for humanity.

Kao Shao-yen, secretary to the Governor of Shantung, who seeks Lao Ts'an's treatment for his sick concubine. Through him, Lao Ts'an is brought to the attention of the governor.

Governor Chuang, the highest official in Shantung, who shows great favor to the apparently common medical practitioner Lao Ts'an by seeking advice and accepting his recommendations. This character is modeled on Chang Yao, a governor of Shantung in the 1880's and a mentor to the author.

Yü Tso-ch'en, also known as **Yü Hsien** (ū syěn), a notorious Manchu official who appears under his own name. In the novel, Yü Hsien is pilloried for the harsh justice he meted out as a prefect in Shantung. On his own initiative, Lao Ts'an travels to Yü Hsien's prefecture, where he confirms the reports of Yü Hsien's cruelty and enlightens the governor about Yü Hsien's deficiencies. In real life, Yü Hsien (who died in 1901) was executed for promoting antiforeign attacks during the Boxer uprising of 1900. Also, in reality Liu E and Yü Hsien were enemies.

Shen Tung-tsao, a cautious newly appointed magistrate whom Lao Ts'an encounters. Lao Ts'an advises him on how to suppress banditry without resorting to the cruel and unwise policies of Yü Hsien.

Shen Tzu-p'ing, a nephew of Magistrate Shen Tung-tsao who is sent into the mountains to locate a man whom Lao Ts'an has recommended to his uncle. During this search, the young man encounters a beautiful maiden and a middle-aged recluse who calls himself "Yellow Dragon." In a long fantasy sequence, these two figures introduce the philosophical ideas of the T'ai-chou school, a nineteenth century Chinese syncretic philosophy (combining Buddhism, Taoism, and Confucianism) favored by the author.

Huang Ying-t'u, also called **Huang Jen-jui,** an educated man from a family of high officials who had come to Shantung to offer advice on river control. Huang Jen-jui is about thirty, pleasant but dissolute. Lao Ts'an encounters Huang Jen-jui while traveling and, through him, meets the courtesan Ts'ui-huan, and learns of a tangled and unsolved multiple murder case.

Ts'ui-huan, a young courtesan whose name means "Green Bracelet." With a companion, she is invited to entertain Huang Jen-jui and Lao Ts'an. Ts'ui-huan relates how she fell into prostitution; then, moved by her story, Lao Ts'an devises a means to free her from bondage. She later becomes his concubine. In a continuation of this novel (translated by Lin Yu-tang as *Widow, Nun and Courtesan*), Ts'ui-huan accompanies Lao Ts'an on a pilgrimage to Mountain T'ai, where they befriend a Buddhist nun and Ts'ui-huan decides to enter the nunnery herself.

Kang Pi, a narrow, arrogant judicial official, brought into a multiple murder case. His inhuman use of torture produces a miscarriage of justice. Lao Ts'an, however, intervenes and saves the wrongly convicted widow and exposes the real murderer, a callow nephew. Kang Pi represents another Manchu official, Kang I, who, like Yü Hsien, was a real enemy of Liu E.

David D. Buck

TRAVESTIES

Author: Tom Stoppard (Tomas Straussler, 1937-   )
Type of work: Play
Time of action: 1917-1918 and the 1970's
First produced: 1974

Henry Carr, an elegantly attired character who appears both as a very old man and as his youthful self. The character is modeled on a minor official by the same name who was in the English consulate in Switzerland during the turbulent years of World War I. The events of the play mirror history: As young Carr, he is involved in a quarrel with James Joyce over money for clothes in a production of Oscar Wilde's *The Importance of Being Earnest*, in which Joyce is closely involved. As an old man, Carr narrates the events of the time, and it is his erratic recall of events through which Stoppard filters the events of the play, including a fictional meeting in the Zurich library among Tristan Tzara, James Joyce, and Vladimir Ilich Lenin: Revolutionaries in art, literature, and politics, respectively, who actually lived in Zurich at that time.

James Joyce, aged thirty-six, an inelegant dresser who mixes jackets and trousers from two different suits. At work in the Zurich library on his famous novel *Ulysses*, he conflicts with Tzara and Lenin on the nature of art. As Stoppard's *raisonneur*, he argues that art is its own excuse for being and that whatever meaning is to be found in history is what art makes of it. He uses Homer's poems about the Trojan War to illustrate his theory that art re-creates the shards of history into a "corpse that will dance for some time yet and leave the world precisely as it finds it."

Tristan Tzara, a Romanian Dadaist artist. He is short, dark-haired, charming, and boyish, and wears a monocle. He argues his theories of history and art as pure chance. In demonstration, he tears up a sonnet of Shakespeare, letting the words fall where they will,

in the process arranging themselves into a new poem. Tzara is in love with Gwendolen, and, despite a mix-up of names and identities that parallels the plot of *The Importance of Being Earnest*, he does end up with her. His role unites the two major plot components: Stoppard's debates on art and the romantic intrigues.

Lenin, a forty-seven-year-old revolutionary. Writing in the Zurich library, he sees art as a means to change the world for the good of the masses. In contrast with the brilliantly parodic language of Tzara and Joyce, that of Lenin is pedestrian and pedantic.

Gwendolen, the attractive younger sister of Carr. She is secretary to Joyce but in love with Tzara. With Cecily, she forms the double romantic interest in the plot. Their mix-up of briefcases causes Joyce's latest chapter of *Ulysses* to fall into the hands of Tzara and Lenin's political treatise to come into Joyce's possession, thus creating occasions for romantic complications, as well as for Tzara to criticize Joyce and for Carr to impress Cecily with his pretended admiration of Lenin's views.

Cecily, a young, attractive librarian who appears also as her eighty-year-old self. She is deeply devoted to Lenin's philosophy and is in love with Carr. With Gwendolen, she falls farcically into and out of the mistaken-identity confusion, eventually ending up with her Algernon, Henry Carr.

Nadya (Nadezhda) Krupskaya, the forty-eight-year-old wife of Lenin, a minor character in the play who converses with Lenin about their impending journey to Russia.

Susan Rusinko

THE TREE CLIMBER

Author: Tawfiq al-Hakim (1898-1987)
Type of work: Play
Time of action: The 1960's
First published: Ya tali' al-shajarah, 1962 (English translation, 1966)

The husband, Bahadir Effendi, a retired train conductor ("ticket inspector") sixty-five years of age who has been married for nine years to Madame Behana. During that time and especially since his retirement on a modest pension five years ago, he has devoted exclusive attention to an orange tree in the garden of their home. Underneath his precious orange tree resides a lizard called Lady Green, whom only he can see and for whom he professes love. Bahadir and his wife appear to have no relatives or social acquaintances. He seems content to care for his tree, never disagrees with his wife, and says he has lost the habit of being worried and perturbed. His philosophizing, hypothesizing, and inattention to his wife (he admits to the detective that he has thought about killing her) lead to his arrest at the end of act 1 for the murder of his wife, who has disappeared. In fact, after Behana returns home, a philosophical motive leads him at the end of act 2 to kill her for real. He feels no guilt thereafter and decides to risk ultimate arrest and possible execution for the sake of his tree, which can be much nourished by burying her corpse under it.

The wife, Madame Behana, or **Bihana,** Bahadir Effendi's wife, a woman sixty years of age with white hair who always wears a green dress. Bahadir is her second husband. Behana thinks and talks constantly of Bahiyya, the daughter she can never have. As a young woman of nineteen, she acceded to her first husband's request that she have an abortion. She had named the anticipated girl "Bahiyya" early in that pregnancy. Later, when their circumstances improved and they wanted children, Behana discovered that she could not get pregnant again. At the death of her first husband, who was a real estate broker, she inherited the house in the Zeitoun suburb of Cairo, where she and Bahadir live.

When talking with Bahadir, she speaks only of Bahiyya, and he only of his orange tree. Behana has disappeared for three days when the play begins and returns shortly after the beginning of act 2. As oblivious to Bahadir's needs and character as he is to hers, she refuses to respond to his insistent queries about where she was during her absence from home. Bahadir grabs her by the throat to force words out of her, and she dies. Before Bahadir can bury her under his orange tree, however, her corpse disappears.

The maid, a day servant for nine years to Madame Behana and Bahadir Effendi who returns to her own home each evening to care for her old and blind husband. The play opens with her conversation with the detective, who is investigating Madame Behana's disappearance. The maid recalls for the detective a conversation between Bahadir and Behana, which, when acted out for the detective, gives a sense of the curious relationship of mutual inattention and self-centered misunderstanding between the married couple. In act 2, the maid answers the knock on the door and is startled to see her mistress, Madame Behana, back home after everyone, including the maid, had assumed Bahadir had killed her.

The detective, a plodding police investigator who reaches conclusions on the basis of suspicions and circumstantial evidence. After conversations with the maid and with Bahadir Effendi early in act 1, he concludes that Bahadir must have found his missing wife unbearable and, consequently, killed her. Led further by Bahadir's hypothesizing, a mode of thinking with which he cannot deal, he assumes that Bahadir has buried his wife's corpse beneath the orange tree in their garden. When Bahadir subsequently does kill his wife and calls the detective to inform him of the crime, the latter again misconstrues the ambiguous statements he hears and advises Bahadir to continue with his gardening and to expect his wife to return sooner or later.

The conductor's assistant, a lazy young man from Bahadir's past who used to sleep on the job at every opportunity. He appears in a scene recalled by Bahadir when describing his railway conductor's career for the detective. The assistant tells Bahadir of the latter's own sleeping or fixed gazing on the job. Bahadir used to stare out of the train window and count the trees rushing past, saying that he wanted this tree and that.

Children's Voices, a hundred schoolchildren on the train described by Bahadir for the detective. They sing: "Oh tree climber, bring me a cow with you./ Milk it and feed me with a silver spoon." Bahadir sings also, but changes the second line to "Bring me a tree with you."

The dervish, a wise and prescient man on the train whom the conductor's assistant reports to Bahadir as not having a ticket. When Bahadir accosts him, he presents his birth certificate as his "ticket for the journey." When threatened with arrest, he produces ten valid tickets out of the air. Then, when Bahadir conjures him up in the present while talking with the detective, the dervish states that Behana's fate is to suffer death one day at the hands of her husband for a philosophical reason. The dervish later appears just as Bahadir is about to bury his wife's body beneath the orange tree. He will not turn in Bahadir, however, because he can act, he says, only when Bahadir wants him to.

Lady Green, a beautiful green lizard (unseen by the audience) that Bahadir says he has known for nine years, ever since he set foot into his wife's house and garden. According to Bahadir, she disappeared when his wife did and reappears when his wife does. After killing his wife, Bahadir discovers Lady Green dead also, in a hole under the orange tree.

Michael Craig Hillmann

THE TREE OF KNOWLEDGE

Author: Pío Baroja (1872-1956)
Type of work: Novel
Time of action: The final decades of the nineteenth century
First published: El árbol de la ciencia, 1911 (English translation, 1928)

Andrés Hurtado (o͞ortä′dō), a medical doctor. A permanent feeling of loneliness that became more acute after his mother's death has made Hurtado withdrawn, melancholy, and sad in appearance. He defines himself as a partisan of the Republican Party and as an upholder of the cause of the poor, but his true commitment is to literature and things intellectual. His main concern is to find a rational explanation for the formation of the world and, at the same time, for life and mankind. At the beginning of the novel, Andrés is attending his first medical classes at the Institute of San Isidro in Madrid. In spite of the fact that Hurtado does not show a profound calling for medicine, he continues his studies, completing his internship in the hospitals of Madrid, where he witnesses all forms of abuse and misery, and, finally, he is graduated. After two disappointing and weakening experiences, one as a rural doctor and the other in a Public Hospital in Madrid, he weds an old friend, Lulú, and begins a new job as translator of technical papers for a journal. Later, other personal experiences lead him to the extreme decision to commit suicide.

Lulú, Andrés Hurtado's wife. Lulú is unattractive and has a caustic disposition. Nevertheless, she is intelligent, noble, and progressive in her thinking. Julio Aracil, Hurtado's friend, introduces him to Lulú. From the very first moment, she falls in love with Andrés, but they do not talk about marriage until several years have passed. They are finally married and, after a period of peace and contentment, she becomes pregnant, changing both her mood and the family stability. Her child is stillborn, and, three days later, she dies of internal injuries.

Dr. Iturrioz (ē·tōō·r̄ryōs'), Andrés Hurtado's uncle and mentor. Iturrioz is a medical doctor with a pragmatic attitude toward life. Several times, Iturrioz helps Andrés to succeed, approving his exams and obtaining professional positions. For Andrés, he is one of the few people to whom he can talk about far-reaching topics, in particular, his personal observations on people and everyday life. They usually meet at his home, where they have the opportunity to discuss not only the mean-

ing of life, but also Andrés' personal preoccupations concerning his future.

Montaner (mōn·tä·nĕr'), one of Andrés' classmates. Montaner is lazy and quiet. He belongs to the monarchist party, and he supports the aristocratic and wealthy classes. At the beginning he is always out of step with Andrés, but, after concluding their first courses together, they become friends.

Julio Aracil (hōō'lyō ä·rä'sēl), one of Andrés' old friends and now his classmate at the university. Aracil is opinionated, selfish, and incapable of doing anything for others. Since his family has no means to support him, he has to support himself by gambling. His interest in pleasure and luxury, even false and cheap ones, is the reason he always needs money. Aracil seems finally to succeed in life because he is able to do whatever is necessary to obtain what he wants.

Daniel Altamiranda

TREMOR OF INTENT

Author: Anthony Burgess (John Anthony Burgess Wilson, 1917-   )
Type of work: Novel
Time of action: The mid-1960's, with flashbacks to the 1930's and 1940's
First published: 1966

Denis Hillier, a British secret agent in his mid-forties. His final assignment before retirement is to travel to Yarylyuk, in the Crimea, where he is to persuade or compel the defector Edwin Roper to redefect. Coincidentally—or perhaps not—Hillier and Roper were schoolmates at a Roman Catholic public school, continued to correspond during World War II, and remained friends afterward. As a secret agent, Hillier is sophisticated, capable, and skeptical; he is also overtly sexual and combative. Unlike most spy heroes, however, he keeps discovering his limitations. Traveling aboard a Black Sea cruise ship, for example, his cover is penetrated by a thirteen-year-old whiz kid, he is seduced and drugged by a Eurindian sexual prodigy, he loses a stupid eating contest, and

he discloses major secrets to a double agent. Further, in his attempts to regain the initiative and realize his objective, he keeps learning that things are not as they seem, that dividing the world into "us and them" is a reductive absurdity. By the end of the novel, having "disappeared" himself, he has become a priest.

Edwin Roper, Hillier's former friend, a rocket-fuels scientist who has defected to the Soviets. From the beginning of their friendship, Roper is a doubter of conventional explanations. He begins by rejecting the orthodox Catholic doctrine of his public school chaplain, progresses to questioning the innocence of German culture in the atrocities of World War II, and ends in finding the Cold War a convenient political contrivance for both sides. Although assertive in intellectual confrontations, Roper is hopeless socially. In Germany, after the war, he falls in love with Brigitte, a prostitute by nature. Led apparently by his hormones, he pliantly accepts her excuses for German complicity and marries her, only to find her continuing her trade. When Hillier succeeds in separating them, Roper temporarily adopts the platform of the Labour Party; however, he defects to the Soviet Union in the hope of being reunited with Brigitte. When finally liberated by Hillier, he demonstrates that repatriation would have absolutely no effect on anything but the reputations of certain intelligence operatives and administrators. He remains in Russia.

Theodorescu, a double agent and intelligence broker. A man who makes a positive virtue out of obesity and consumption, he seems simply a gourmand and polysophisticate on first acquaintance; however, he proves to be the most sinister of sensualists, deviants, and amoralists, disclosed first in his conscienceless seduction of the thirteen-year-old Alan. He defeats Hillier in a bet on gluttony, then uses Hillier's own sexual appetites to gain control of and neutralize him. He thus becomes the truly evil element in the political world of the Cold War: one who catalyzes existing tensions solely in order to profit from them, one who believes only in himself and his own gratification.

Richard (Rick or **Ricky) Wriste,** a steward aboard the cruise ship *Polyolbion*. He is apparently quite willing to provide any additional service for the appropriate gratuity. In this respect, he inhabits a moral universe parallel to Theodorescu's: Anything can be bought or sold, regardless of right or wrong. It still comes as a shock, however, to discover that he is a hired assassin, a hit man for a neutral agency, assigned to kill both Hillier

and Roper, and hired by Hillier's own superiors, who feel that he has learned too many Allied secrets during his career. Still, whether as obsequious Cockney waiter or as Harrovian contract murderer, Wriste, like Theodorescu, is one of the soulless neutrals, indifferent to good or evil.

Miss Devi, the seductive and inscrutable companion-assistant of Theodorescu. A stunning, dark, exotic beauty with an encyclopedic repertory of sexual techniques, she confronts Hillier directly, almost impersonally, before he has time to determine his own sexual objectives. She practices sex expertly but indifferently, as a means of gaining control of men. When Hillier later expresses a preference for sex as a simple exchange of intimacy, she immediately disengages.

Alan Walters, a precocious thirteen-year-old game show expert. He is aboard ship with his sister, his self-indulgent father, who suffers a fatal stroke on the voyage, and his indifferent, gold-digging stepmother. Left essentially to rear himself, Alan embarrasses Hillier by breaking his cover, then lets himself be seduced by Theodorescu so that he can get a gun. Ultimately, however, he proves indispensable in saving Hillier. In return, Hillier gives him the direction his father failed to provide.

Clara Walters, Alan's eighteen-year-old sister, an amazingly beautiful blonde, abandoned like her brother to her own devices. At the beginning of the novel, though still a virgin, she spends most of her time studying sex manuals. After their father's death, Hillier takes on the necessity of comforting the survivors; in Clara's case, it leads at first to sexual initiation but finally to a kind of spiritual fatherhood.

James L. Livingston

THE TRIAL BEGINS

Author: Abram Tertz (Andrei D. Sinyavsky, 1925-   )
Type of work: Novella

The Trial Begins

Time of action: Late 1952 until the death of Joseph Stalin in March, 1953; epilogue in 1956
First published: Sad idzie, 1959 (English translation, 1960)

Vladimir Petrovich Globov, a public prosecutor during Soviet tyrant Joseph Stalin's last round of purges. These purges were aimed at Jewish citizens, who were referred to as "rootless cosmopolitans" and "enemies of the people." A man with a "large spreading trunk" and "hands as heavy as oars," Globov is an unquestioning follower of the Master's (Stalin's) will. He discovers that Dr. S. Y. Rabinovich, a Jewish physician he has prosecuted for alleged activities against the Soviet state, had performed an abortion for Marina, Globov's wife, who is having an affair with Yury Karlinsky, a public defense attorney. Globov is severely bothered by this deprivation of his embryonic "daughter," yet he does not protest when his adolescent son, Seryozha, is arrested and sentenced to Siberia for an innocent involvement in political idealism.

Marina, second wife of Prosecutor Globov. She is an "ideally constructed" woman who spends much of her time trying various cosmetics to stop time's inexorable erosion of her beauty. She seeks the attention of her husband's colleagues in order to assure herself of her powers of attraction. In a moment of spite, she announces to him that she has had an abortion. Without any real passion, she submits to Karlinsky's seduction. The arrest of her stepson, Seryozha, does not concern her, although she does later send a box of candy to him in Siberia.

Yury Karlinsky, a public defense attorney whose brilliance is frustrated by the Soviet state's prosecutorial bias. He rationalizes his continual failure by philosophizing that "one man's justice is another man's injustice." To show himself that his words can have an appreciable impact, he sets about to seduce Marina, the prosecutor's wife. At the moment of his success, he is unable to perform. It is Karlinsky who interprets Seryozha's immature notes about a communist utopia to be antistate "Trotskyism" and denounces the youth to the authorities.

Seryozha, the teenage son of Prosecutor Globov. In his classes, he questions whether "the end justifies the means" and disquiets his father with discussions of "just and unjust wars." He confides his doubts about the wisdom of the prevailing political system to his grandmother, Ekaterina Petrovna, and to his admiring schoolmate, Katya, who shows his notes outlining "a new world, communist and radiant," to Karlinsky. To his father's embarrassment, he is arrested and sentenced to prison in Siberia.

Dr. S. Y. Rabinovich, a Soviet gynecologist of Jewish extraction who is sentenced to Siberia for being a "rootless cosmopolitan." The fact that he had performed an abortion on his prosecutor's wife is probably the reason for his continued confinement in Siberia after the "rehabilitation" of others in his plight. In the epilogue, his mind deteriorates, and he rambles on about "God, history, and ends and means."

Ekaterina Petrovna, the mother of Prosecutor Globov's first wife and the grandmother of Seryozha. She is a Communist of the old school who is proud of her revolutionary activity. Globov indulges her daily visits to his office and calls her "mother," but he is frightened by her insistence that he intervene in Seryozha's unjustified arrest and he tells her not to visit him again.

Katya, a young girl and a schoolmate of Seryozha. She shares Seryozha's dream of a new and just communist society, naïvely reporting the matter to Karlinsky. After Seryozha's arrest, she writes a note to Karlinsky protesting his denunciation of Seryozha. She is trampled to death by the crowd surging to view the body of the Master, lying in state after his death.

The Narrator, a Soviet writer whose room is searched by two police agents, who subsequently discover torn-up drafts of this novel in his sewage. He was instructed to write the text that eventually incriminates him by a supernatural vision of Stalin, who requires him to "celebrate" the Master's "beloved and faithful servant," Prosecutor Globov. He is arrested for failing to depict Globov and the others "in the fullness of their many-sided working lives" and sentenced to Siberia, where, as he relates in the epilogue, he encounters Seryozha and Dr. Rabinovich.

Lee B. Croft

THE TRICK OF THE GA BOLGA

Author: Patrick McGinley (1937–   )
Type of work: Novel
Time of action: 1942-1943
First published: 1985

Rufus George Coote, an English expatriate and engineer. A thirty-year-old man with prematurely gray hair and a black beard, he has purchased a farm in the remote village of Garaross in County Donegal, Ireland, to wait out World War II. Ironically, he bears the name of one of Oliver Cromwell's generals and believes that he is living a double existence without control of his destiny. After several sexual affairs and minor social triumphs, he believes that he has become an integral part of the village life. In death, however, he learns that he has always been an outsider, both to himself and others.

Hugh "The Proker" Donnelly, a farmer and one of Coote's neighbors. Tall and thin with an odd, permanently closed eye, he constantly feuds with Salmo and vows revenge for the death of his dog. The original source of his quarrel with Salmo dates to their teens when they both desired and lost the affections of a village girl. When he believes that Coote is trying to take advantage of him, he provokes a fight and is inadvertently killed. Coote arranges his corpse to appear like the remains of some strange mystery.

Manus "Salmo" Byrne, another bachelor neighbor, with a bald, egg-shaped head fringed by fair, curly hair. Large and imposing, he is actually a gentle soul who enjoys lying in a field simply observing nature. Arrested and jailed for Proker's murder, he is innocent but feels oddly responsible for having wished the man dead. Once in jail, he deteriorates markedly, putting up no defense and wishing for his death. He has prescient powers and even predicts the nature of Coote's eventual demise.

Imelda McMackin, another neighbor. She is large, buxom, and sensual and seduces Coote, who is overwhelmed by her sexuality. Although he is warned to avoid her, Coote succumbs to her schemes. She operates as a quietly malevolent force in the village world.

Denis McMackin, a soldier in Africa who suffers from nervous exhaustion and is sent home. He is tall and heavy, with a pallid, triangular face topped with thick, curly hair. He takes an instant dislike to Coote and repeatedly attempts to provoke him. At the novel's close, he kills Coote for kissing his daughter.

Helen McMackin, a bony child with red hair, wide eyes, and taut, pale skin; her appearance is often referred to as otherwordly. Coote saves her from drowning, and the solitary child visits his farm to sweep his floor and listen to stories. When he affectionately kisses her, however, she is horrified, runs out of the house, and is drowned in bog water. Coote soon learns from her father that her parents have never kissed her.

Consolata O'Gara, another neighbor who takes an interest in Coote. Twenty-six years old, pleasant looking, and commonsensical, she becomes Coote's lover and boon companion. One night, she inadvertently finds him with Imelda and then hangs herself without explanation. She warns Coote against involvement with the McMackins.

Master "Timideen" O'Gara, a retired schoolmaster. He is a short, thin man, with a flat head, intent on marrying his daughter to a man of substance. Garrulous and agreeable, he befriends Coote and seriously misleads him with a spurious account of the trick of the Ga Bolga, a tale with origins in Irish mythology.

Father McNullis, the village priest. Short, jowly, roundheaded, and gray-haired, he has a narrow body and self-confident manner. With the three hundred pounds that he finds

on a corpse, he finances the building of a bridge, which he persuades Coote to engineer. As their unlikely friendship grows, Coote confesses to killing Donnelly, though Father McNullis refuses to believe him. Although initially he appears to be an unscrupulous schemer, the priest is actually wise and understanding of human fallibility.

Sergeant Blowick, the village policeman. He is a tall, thin man obsessed with the disappearance of his official caps. When he finds one on the Proker's corpse, he is convinced that it is incriminating evidence of Salmo's guilt, despite Coote's confession. Although well-intentioned, he is largely ineffectual and comical.

David W. Madden

TRIPTYCH

Author: Claude Simon (1913-   )
Type of work: Novel
Time of action: The 1970's
First published: Triptyque, 1973 (English translation, 1976)

Corinne, a middle-aged actress. She spends her time in bed reading about a young man and woman who have recently been married. She is worried about her son, who has problems with drugs and who is under investigation by the police. She asks her friends Brown and Lambert to secure the release of her son.

Lambert, an Englishman who has made love to Corinne with the apparent understanding that he will intervene with the police authorities to assure her son's release from jail.

Brown, an overweight, middle-aged friend of Corinne. He has a conversation with a man in a bar, where he exchanges money for little packages of powder. He later assures Corinne that her son will be freed. He also completes a jigsaw puzzle that represents the boys in the fishing scene and then scatters it.

A clown, who is pictured on a circus adver-

tisement hanging on a barn. He participates in a dumb show with a monkey and another man who torments him. His performance is staged against a background of music that is frequently interrupted by the lion tamer's animals.

Two young boys, who are fishing and take time to examine some film strips that they try to arrange in the proper sequence. Some of their film relates the story of Corinne at the beach. They notice a young mother leave her child to meet her lover in a barn. They then head toward the barn to spy on the love-making.

Young men, part of a boisterous wedding celebration, who accompany the groom into a bar.

Man in a bar who wears a leather jacket and a cap and has a swarthy complexion. After talking with one of the women, he leaves and finds Lily with the young husband on the street. He continues his ride into the country, where, meeting the young married woman in the barn, he repeatedly makes love to her.

Lily, a barmaid. She has a conversation with a young groom on his wedding day in the bar. She apparently has known him for some time. While his friends noisily celebrate the marriage with much drinking and loud music, she leaves the bar to rejoin him in an alley, where the two make love. He has vomited and she tries to clean him up with her rolled-up underwear, and she unsuccessfully tries to keep him from leaving her.

The groom, who abandons his wife to return to a bar at whose entrance he had earlier seen Lily and another woman standing. Once he has become inebriated and has made love to Lily, he returns to his hotel room in clothes now soiled with vomit and dirt. He goes to bed without undressing and falls into a deep sleep.

The young bride, still in her wedding clothes, who has been crying because she has been left alone. When her inebriated husband returns and she finds him asleep in bed, she undresses him and then herself.

An adolescent, who is studying geometry and drawing triangular figures, interested in a photograph of a naked woman that he intermittently takes out from his desk drawer.

A young boy with tow-colored hair, who herds cows in a pasture where, nearby, two other young boys are fishing.

An elderly woman, who crosses the field with a rabbit in hand and walks past the barn where the couple is making love. She had been feeding several rabbits and has just chosen the one that she eventually kills and skins. She belongs to the household of the young woman whose child is missing.

A young married woman, who goes on a walk with her little girl and leaves her with the boys who are fishing when she sees a motorcyclist drive by. She crosses the field to join him in a barn, where they make love. She later discovers that her little girl is missing.

Two young girls, who take a walk in the countryside. They take care of the little girl, who has been turned over to them by the boys who were fishing. They, in turn, abandon her, and she drowns in the river.

Young boys, who try to slip into a barn where a motion picture is being shown. The film features the story of Corinne.

Peter S. Rogers

TRITON

Author: Samuel R. Delany (1942-   )
Type of work: Novel
Time of action: A.D. 2112, after humankind has colonized Mars and several moons of planets in the solar system
First published: 1976

Bron Helstrom, a metalogician from Mars. Bron is an attractive, tall, blond, curly-haired man, with one gold-inlaid eyebrow; the other eyebrow is the normal hairy type, though it grows so constantly that it has to be trimmed regularly, giving it a rough, rumpled look. As a youth, Bron was a male prostitute on Mars, and he has always been highly sexed. Yet, Bron is an indifferent socializer, "emotionally lazy"; people become his friends almost by default, with Bron not really playing an active role in developing the relationships. When he meets The Spike, however, he meets his match; her rejection of him completely undermines his emotional world. His life changes radically as he undergoes a sex change and becomes a woman and as he develops the capacity to care about other people's feelings.

Gene Trimbell, also called **The Spike,** a director and producer of and actress in "microtheater for unique audiences." The Spike is a big-boned, thirty-four-year-old woman with whom Bron falls in love after seeing one of her shows. It is her bluntness in a letter to Bron that motivates him to change his life, though he at first denies the validity of her criticisms of him.

Lawrence, one of Bron's only real friends. Lawrence is a seventy-four-year-old homosexual originally from South Africa, which he left because of the repression of human rights there. Lawrence helps Bron after he becomes a woman, finding for Bron a place to stay and new clothes. Ultimately, Lawrence joins a musical commune and becomes a singer.

Sam, a big black man who has also had a sex change, having formerly been a blonde, sallow waitress. At first, Bron claims to dislike Sam, perhaps out of jealousy, and though Bron originally dismisses Sam as an average, handsome, friendly man, after a while he realizes that "under that joviality there was a rather amazing mind." After Bron has his sex changed, "she" runs into Sam in a bar and propositions him, but Sam refuses, perhaps realizing Bron's unstable emotional state.

Audri, one of Bron's bosses at work. Audri is a lesbian mother with three children and, therefore, though she likes Bron, she is never sexually interested in him. After Bron becomes a woman, however, Audri falls in love with Bron and asks her to move in with her and her family. It is at this point that, for the first time in his/her life, Bron tries to spare someone's feelings. Not wanting to hurt Audri, Bron makes up a story about already being involved with another woman.

T. M. Lipman

TROPIC OF CANCER

Author: Henry Miller (1891-1980)
Type of work: Novel
Time of action: 1930-1931
First published: 1934

"Henry Miller," the narrative consciousness of the novel, a somewhat transformed, semiautobiographical elaboration of the author. He is a man of indeterminate middle age, an indigent, aspiring writer who is visiting Europe to escape from the conditions of life in the United States, which he believes are responsible for his artistic and economic failures. After trying to conform to the conventional rules and requirements of middleclass society in America, he is struggling to survive as a kind of underground man in the bohemian realms of Paris. Convinced that his true nature has been suppressed by his failed attempts at various mundane jobs and two marriages, he has recast himself as an artist/hero, a rebel, and a kind of gangster of erotic aggression. He is mostly sex and stomach, but, although it is not as immediately apparent, he is also a man of feeling and sensitivity. He is essentially an observer; he demonstrates his kinship with the historical tradition of great art in Paris through his extremely inventive use of language; verbal styles of expression charged with the energy of the anger and joy with which he confronts everything. His spirit remains strong in the midst of conditions which crush nearly everyone else with whom he associates, and his heartfelt tributes to the subtle beauties of the city, its architecture, rivers and streets, register his deeper, more humane and more gentle side. As he progresses, crab-like, through the eighteen months or so that the novel covers, the manner in which he skips from one incident, episode and location to another suggests entries in a journal, a record of the final phases of his development as the artist who will write the book.

Van Norden, a newspaperman of sorts, also American, who represents the worst aspects of the society from which Miller is trying to escape and who also exhibits the author's worst traits carried to excess and with no redeeming qualities. He is vain, stupid, consumed by self-pity, and completely oblivious to the extraordinary features of the city in which he feels trapped. His only interest seems to be the seduction of women, whom he regards as little more than versions of sexual mechanisms and to whose human qualities he is completely blind. He "wakes up cursing" and tries to obliterate his psychic numbness with the gratification of sensory demands. Ultimately, he is a homicidal monster, though not in the conventional sense. He is a killer of the soul, and his murderous tendencies destroy every life he touches, including his own. Miller uses him as a powerful contrast to the life to which he aspires, a life that is animated by the "spark of passion" Van Norden lacks. Other characters called Carl, Boris, and Moldorf are variations of Van Norden.

Fillmore, a relatively young American trying to live in the style of the carefree bohemians of legendary Parisian society. Like Van Norden and Carl, he is a case of arrested development, an adolescent who has no real sense of himself, and, like Carl, he is forced into the pitiable retreat from life. At the conclusion of the novel, Miller helps Fillmore onto a boat headed back to England and then to America. Fillmore is a beaten man whose defeat is presented as a contrast with Miller's survival.

Germaine, a prostitute, who is praised by Miller for her lack of pretense and admired for exhibiting some of the same characteristics that the narrator relishes in himself: guts, fire, stamina, courage, and cunning. Although she is primarily presented as another version of the members of an essentially nondistinct conglomerate of women called Tania, Llona, and Irene, some aspects of personality and singularity emerge, suggesting an individual more than a sexual device.

Mona, a beautiful, dark young woman who has been involved with the narrator prior to his arrival in Paris and who has spent some time with him in Paris during his first days there. She is a characterization of Miller's second wife, Jane Smith, and represents a mysterious and valued woman who is still a factor in the narrator's existence.

Leon Lewis

TROUBLE IN MIND

Author: Alice Childress (1920-   )
Type of work: Play
Time of action: The 1950's
First produced: 1955

Wiletta Mayer, a veteran actor beginning rehearsals of a play. She is an attractive middle-aged black woman, with an outgoing personality. She had made a career out of playing stereotypical black roles but aspires to be cast in parts more deserving of her rich talents. Initially, she readily gives advice to a novice actor on how to ingratiate oneself, to stay on good terms with the management no matter how loathsome the production may be. When rehearsals begin, however, she cannot adhere to such a strategy when her white director uses tactics that humiliate her and the script calls for the black characters to make statements and perform actions that offend her racial pride. Consequently, Wiletta becomes an outspoken critic of the production.

Al Manners, a theatrical director working on his first Broadway show. In his early forties, he is an energetic, confident man, with a patronizing manner. He unknowingly triggers Wiletta's critical evaluation of the production by demanding that she find a sense of integrity about her work. Though he considers himself to be a liberal, he treats black and white cast members differently and is insensitive to the objections the blacks have concerning the script. As the racial strife becomes more intense, he exposes his own deep-rooted racial biases.

John Nevins, a novice actor. He is a black college graduate aspiring to rise to the top of his profession. Though he believes his formal training and performances in Off-Broadway plays to be superior to Wiletta's experience, he condescendingly listens to her advice out of deference to her age and her acquaintance with his mother. As the conflict between Wiletta and the director heightens, he becomes embarrassed by what he thinks is a woman too racially sensitive and ignorant of contemporary acting methods. Aligning himself with the director and white cast members, he attempts to appease Wiletta without fully considering the validity of her complaints.

Millie Davis, a veteran actor. She is a well-dressed thirty-five-year-old black woman. Like Wiletta, she has spent her career performing black stock characters, and she readily voices her dissatisfaction concerning dialogue and actions that demean blacks. Unlike Wiletta, she stops short of pursuing her objections with the director even when he chooses to ignore her opinions or provides a patronizing response.

Sheldon Forrester, a veteran actor. An elderly, poorly educated black man, he embodies the Uncle Tom stereotype regardless of whether he is performing. He fawns on the director and criticizes Wiletta for disrupting rehearsals with her racial complaints. He has held such an obsequious posture for so long, Sheldon is numb to the indignities he and other blacks suffer in the profession.

Judith Sears (Judy), a novice actor. She is a young energetic white woman of a privileged background. Thrilled to be in her first professional production since her training at Yale, she is eager to please the director. A liberal, she becomes uncomfortable with some of her dialogue using offensive terms in reference to blacks. She befriends John to the dismay of the director and several black cast members.

Addell Austin

TROUBLES

Author: J. G. Farrell (1935-1979)
Type of work: Novel
Time of action: 1919-1921
First published: 1970

Major Brendan Archer, the protagonist, a shy, well-bred British major who witnesses the fall of the British Empire in Ireland at first hand. Tired, disoriented, and shell-shocked, Archer first comes to Kilnalough to investigate his uncertain engagement to Angela. As he patiently awaits some personal response from her, he becomes fascinated by the uncertainty, decay, and general Irishness of her surroundings, and experiences the frustrations and lunacies of Anglo-Irish life and troubles that provide the satiric edge of the book. Valuing propriety, reason, and detachment, he is amazed at the eccentricity and the vulgar excesses of the Anglo-Irish and, as he seeks to bring order to the chaos about him, gradually takes on hotel responsibilities. He provides a liberal outsider's view on the viciousness of reprisals and a pro-Irish perspective in debates with his host. Except for occasional rather vague sexual fantasies, he is brusque, judicious, responsible: a peacemaker. For his trouble, the Sinn Féin bury him neck-high in sand to let him drown with the tide, and only rescue by the small elderly ladies of the Majestic Hotel allows him to flee Ireland with his life and with the only reward for his effort: the hotel's much-abused statue of Venus.

Angela Spencer, Archer's Anglo-Irish fiancée. A straightforward mine of trivial gossip in letters, Angela is a remote, untouchable model of decorum in person. She finessed a slight acquaintance with Major Archer into an engagement, and her detailed letters provide a graspable reality at odds with the confusion left by the war. She soon disappears into her room, however, only to exit in a coffin, having slowly succumbed to leukemia. Her deathbed letter is as long-winded and embarrassing as her personal presence. It is her tenuous relationship with Archer that motivates his observations on the Anglo-Irish troubles.

Edward Spencer, Angela's eccentric and volatile father, the owner of the Majestic Hotel. "A fierce man in flannels" with a stiff, craggy face, rugged brow, clipped mustache, broken boxing nose, and flattened ears, the stony set to his jaw suggests his hot temper as he fights, with impatience, irascibility, and resignation, a losing battle against decay. A sportsman and dog lover, at times he is overbearing, opinionated, and tyrannical, at times weak and sentimental. He provides an Anglo-Irish view of the reprisals, of mixed marriages (religion and race), and of the Irish (a subhuman and superstitious rabble composed of criminals and fanatics). His hate-filled desire to revenge the English loss of Ireland leads him purposely to shoot a Sinn Féiner for tampering with his provocatively displayed statue of Queen Victoria. He is Archer's opposite, his rival for Sarah, and his burden.

Ripon Spencer, Angela's roguish black sheep brother. Compelled by his glands rather than his mind, Ripon is a lazy, ill-mannered bumpkin who spends his days tossing jackknives and romancing village girls. He finally elopes with the chubby but winsome Maire, the Roman Catholic daughter of the wealthiest man in Kilnalough, to the consternation of both families.

Sarah Devlin, a temperamental Roman Catholic flirt. Charming and cruel, she becomes the second unattainable object of Archer's affection, not only because of her youth, her gray eyes, and her attractive sunburn but also because of her sharp-tongued, aggressively Irish wiles. She is catty and rude, self-pitying and self-deprecating, yet men continue to pay her court, even before she jettisons her wheelchair. Her biting letters of local life and her London visit lure Archer back to Ireland, while the smitten Edward Spencer pays her medical bills. Yet, she spurns them all for a brutish British soldier who scorns her race and beats her regularly. Her scandalous behavior and shocking comments suggest the irrationality of the love/hate relationship between the British and the Irish.

Evans, a prototype of Irish rage, the venomous tutor to Spencer's two frolicsome and mischievous daughters, Faith and Charity. Evans nurses his explosive sense of outrage and injustice. Belligerent and aggressive, he deals the grandmother's attacking cat a crippling blow and then, in an ecstasy of violence and with a "savage rictus in his white pocked face," hurls it against the wall. Later, at the Majestic's final ball he displays open antipathy for guests and hosts alike.

Murphy, a prototype of Irish deceit, the sullen, two-faced hotel butler. Aged and truculent, his face is wrinkled and wizened, with his few teeth discolored. Murphy hides his mad hatred of anything English and his malevolent joy at their suffering behind a façade of loyal subservience. Despite his long years of service, he abuses the defenseless and chuckles at their discomfort and, ultimately, ignites the hotel, its multitude of cats, and himself in an orgy of hate.

Gina Macdonald

TROUT FISHING IN AMERICA

Author: Richard Brautigan (1935-1984)
Type of work: Novel
Time of action: Fall, 1960, through fall, 1961, with flashbacks to the 1940's
First published: 1967

The narrator, unnamed but who may be identified with the author, as he is a writer and has had similar life experiences. That is, he had a fatherless, rather lonely childhood, living in poverty with his mother first in Great Falls, Montana, then later in Portland, Oregon, and Tacoma, Washington. Around age nineteen, he moves to San Francisco, which becomes the center of his life as a writer. A more spiritual element is provided by certain trout streams in the mountains to the north and east, such as Grider Creek, Graveyard Creek, Paradise Creek, Lake Josephus, and Hell-Diver Lake. The narrator tends to describe the people and settings in his brief collection of sketches with an inventive, sometimes even magical poetic surrealism. For example, there is a distant, beautiful waterfall that the narrator recalls having seen as a child. As he draws closer to it, however, he sees that his vision was only a flight of white wooden stairs leading up into some trees. Such disillusionment is an important element in the narrator's worldview. He continually seeks escape from reality yet retains the integrity to be able to admit to doing so.

The narrator's wife, unnamed but usually referred to as "my woman" or "the woman I live with." She corresponds to the author's wife of this period (that is, his first wife), Virginia "Ginny" Adler. Little of the woman's personality is revealed. Her role is simply to cook, have sexual intercourse, conceive and bear a child, and tend it as it grows. Once the narrator and his wife have sexual intercourse in the warm water of Worsewick Hot Springs in the middle of green slime and dead fish: a more or less typical juxtaposition by the narrator of the beautiful and the profane (or of life and death).

The narrator's daughter, an unnamed child. Called only "the baby," she corresponds to the author's daughter, Ianthe, born in 1960. The child, as she grows older, affords a perception of the passage of time. She comes interestingly alive once in Washington Park when a Catholic church is described as towering up behind her red dress.

Trout Fishing in America, a personification that talks and writes but has no corporeal existence. The figure sometimes evokes the distant past, such as the time of the American Revolution, or the day that Meriwether Lewis discovered Great Falls. It acts on the whole as a positive or even romantic vision of America.

Trout Fishing in America Shorty, a legless wino in San Francisco who demands even of strangers that they push him everywhere in his wheelchair. Once, he falls face first, drunk, right out of his chair. The narrator and his acquaintances decide to mail him to Nelson Algren, in honor of the latter's character "Railroad Shorty." He disappears, however, before they can get around to doing it.

Statue of Benjamin Franklin, a statue in Washington Square, San Francisco. This statue is mentioned frequently throughout the book, beginning with the first chapter, in which it is the central figure. In addition, it is an important feature of the cover photograph. It is presented as a symbol of welcome. It is a good place for beatniks and hippies to sit before and drink port wine.

Donald M. Fiene

THE TRUE STORY OF AH Q

Author: Lu Hsün (Chou Shu-Jên, 1881-1936)
Type of work: Novel
Time of action: The early 1900's
First published: Ah Q cheng-chuan, 1921, serial; 1923, book (English translation, 1927)

Ah Q, an impoverished, homeless man in his late twenties who loafs around the village where he lives and earns his living by working at various odd jobs. Lean and weak, he has a bald spot on his head, a physical blemish caused by scabies that often makes him the butt of jokes among the people of the village of Wei. Whenever he suffers humiliation, however, he is always able to find solace and even triumph through his imagination. He leads a relatively quiet, though obscure and insignificant, life in the countryside until one day when the entire village rejects him as a result of his proposition to a maidservant, Wu Ma. Because of this incident, people avoid him and refuse to give him any work. In order to continue his livelihood, he leaves for the city, and, after returning to the village, he is later falsely accused of robbery and is eventually executed.

Chao T'ai-yeh, an influential country squire. Somewhat educated and in middle age, he is greedy and unkind, especially in his treatment of Ah Q, whom he sometimes employs for odd jobs. When the revolution of 1911 breaks out, he safeguards the money of Pai Chü-jen, a gentleman from the city. In the end, some people break into Chao's house and steal Pai's money. Chao has to pay a small fortune to the local official to clear his name so as to avoid being accused by Pai of swindling his money.

Pai Chü-jen, a well-educated man of the gentry class living in the city. After leaving the village of Wei, Ah Q serves in his house for a short period of time. Because of his uncertainty about the revoluton, Pai sends some of his property to the Chao family for safekeeping when the revolutionaries enter the city. He becomes, however, a high official in the city shortly after the revolution.

To his chagrin, his property safeguarded by the Chao family is never retrieved.

Ch'ien Shao-yeh, also known as the **Imitation Foreign Devil,** a son of a gentry family in the village of Wei. Because of the loss of his queue while pursuing his studies away from home, he wears a false queue after his return to the village. Different from the other villagers, he studies in Western schools, first in a neighboring city, later in Japan. His Western education causes him to support the revolution, in the name of which he, along with Chao T'ai-yeh's son, steals an antique incense burner from a Buddhist temple. When Ah Q expresses his interest in becoming a revolutionary, Ch'ien rudely rejects him.

Chao Mao-ts'ai, the son of the country squire, Chao T'ai-yeh. He beats Ah Q and chases him away after Ah Q proposes to sleep with Wu Ma. Later in the story, he becomes a revolutionary and, along with Ch'ien Shao-yeh, steals an antique incense-burner from a local Buddhist temple in the name of the revolution.

Wu Ma, also called **Amah Wu** in some translations, the maidservant for the Chao family. She reacts violently to Ah Q's proposition and tries to hang herself in order to prove her chastity as a widow. On the day of Ah Q's execution, she appears in the watching crowd.

Ti Pao, the local policeman, who takes advantage of Ah Q's misfortunes by extorting money from him.

Hsiao Niku, a nun in the local Buddhist temple. Young and docile, she is the only one whom Ah Q can insult without fear of retaliation. Ironically, after maliciously pinch-

1620

ing her face in public, Ah Q becomes conscious of his sexual desires, which lead to his proposition to Wu Ma.

Wang Lai-hu, another impoverished, homeless man of Ah Q's class. Characterized by a full beard and scabs also caused by scabies, he insults Ah Q at the beginning of the story. After Ah Q returns from the city to the vil-

lage of Wei, Wang regards him with awe because of his experience of living in the city.

Pa Tsong, the commander of the local troops, who has Ah Q arrested and eventually executed as a scapegoat for the robbery of Pai's property.

Vincent Yang

TRUE WEST

Author: Sam Shepard (Samuel Shepard Rogers, 1943-   )
Type of work: Play
Time of action: The 1980's
First produced: 1980

Austin, a self-deprecating but aspiring screenwriter in his early thirties. Somewhat romantic, he works by candlelight in his vacationing mother's house, creating a "simple love story" to complete a film deal with producer Saul Kimmer, toward whom he is respectful and sycophantic. Conventionally educated at an Ivy League college, Austin inhabits a neat world constructed of middle-class values of rationality, self-discipline, and hard work, which is threatened by the arrival of brother Lee, the object of Austin's sibling envy and repressed hostility. As Lee insinuates himself into his territory, Austin becomes increasingly insecure, and, adopting Lee's behavior, speech, and profession in a complete character transformation, he abandons his film project and becomes roaring drunk, thereby unleashing an inventiveness previously stifled by his intellectuality. With a burst of bravado, he steals every toaster in the neighborhood in an attempt to outperform Lee's nefarious activities. Now uncertain of his identity and believing himself unable to exist in modern society, he bargains to return to the desert with Lee. When Lee reneges on the promise, Austin's civilized veneer shatters, exposing a murderous violence beneath.

Lee, Austin's menacing older brother. He is in his forties, scruffily dressed, just returned from several months of nomadic existence in the desert with only a pit bull dog for com-

pany. Austin's opposite, a natural man, lacking education and goals, Lee is without visible morality or scruples (except in the matter of their absent father), but his behavior reveals a jealousy of his brother's life-style; he systematically usurps Austin's time, space, and identity. He is not without insight, and he possesses an imagination unfettered by education, but he lacks discipline and cannot tolerate frustration. What he wants he takes, whether it be a neighbor's television set, Austin's car, or, ultimately, Austin's work, as he gambles with Saul Kimmer for the acceptance of his scenario in preference to his brother's. When he discovers that he lacks the skills necessary to transform his imaginative ideas into art, or his life-style into one of legitimacy, he becomes destructive.

Saul Kimmer, a Hollywood producer in his late forties. Shallow and superficial, dressed in loud flowered shirts and polyester pants, he is a caricature of the Hollywood parasite who, lacking talent himself, survives by marketing the talents of others. His amorality matches Lee's; he is seduced by Lee's manipulations, and rejects Austin's script without a qualm. Lee's insistence upon calling him "Mr. Kipper" labels him accurately as a cold fish.

Mom, a woman in her sixties, the mother of the two brothers. Mom is characterized by

Lee as not liking "even a single tea leaf in her sink," but she is strangely indifferent to the destruction of her home and plants when she returns suddenly in the last scene from her vacation in Alaska. More concerned about what she has interpreted as a visit of Picasso to the local museum than about the primal contest occurring before her eyes, she seems unable to grasp the fact that Picasso is dead, and she is blind to her sons' hatred, thus displaying an inability to distinguish life from art.

Joyce E. Henry

TUBBY SCHAUMANN
A Tale of Murder and the High Seas

Author: Wilhelm Raabe (1831-1910)
Type of work: Novel
Time of action: Probably the 1880's
First published: Stopfkuchen: Eine See- und Mordgeschichte, 1891 (English translation, 1983)

Heinrich "Tubby" Schaumann (shou'män), owner of Red Bank Farm after his father-in-law's death, as a boy very overweight and a slow student. Subject to ridicule because he was such a poor student and so overweight, Heinrich Schaumann comes to be called Tubby by the local townspeople. His dream is to live at Red Bank Farm, which he views as a kind of refuge from the cruelty of the world outside. Because he understands the feelings of an outcast, he is able to befriend young, lonely Valentina and her bitter father. Although he tries to please his parents by going away to school, Schaumann is not suited for that venture. Instead, he finds his true place and a philosophy of peaceful acceptance of his life by marrying Valentina and taking over Red Bank Farm. From this safe haven, he wants to take in the whole of human experience: His fossil hunting represents his look at history in all its depth, and his outsider position gives him a wider perspective on the community. At the end of the story, his capacity for forgiveness and humane understanding allows him to wait until after Störzer's death to reveal that man's identity as the true murderer of Kienbaum.

Edward, boyhood friend of Schaumann and narrator of the story. Although he was Schaumann's closest friend at school, he, too, was often involved in the cruel taunting that the boys aimed at Schaumann. A man who desired travel and adventure, Edward has made his fortune and settled in South Africa. Returning to his boyhood town, he visits his old friend Tubby and comes to admire and appreciate him.

Andreas Quakatz (kvä'käts), owner of Red Bank Farm and falsely blamed for the murder of Kienbaum. At first a bitter old man, he is helped by Schaumann to become somewhat reconciled to the unfair situation that made him an outcast. He dies without seeing his name cleared.

Valentina, daughter of Andreas Quakatz and later Heinrich Schaumann's wife. As a child, she often bears the brunt of her father's bitter anger against the community. Finding love and compassion in Schaumann, she blossoms into a loving, compassionate woman herself, in spite of her difficult childhood. Her care and devotion to Schaumann make Red Bank Farm a true refuge for them both.

Friedrich (Fritz) Störzer (shtœr'tsər), a country postman who often told young Edward stories about exotic places. A mild-mannered worker who never missed a day's work during thirty-one years of service, he is tormented by Kienbaum, until one day he accidentally kills him. Afraid to confess even when Quakatz is unjustly accused, he carries a burden of guilt with him until his death.

Kienbaum (kēn'boum), a prosperous livestock dealer and bully, who constantly mocked and tormented Störzer on his mail route. His death brings the community to label Quakatz a murderer.

Meta, the barmaid who listens to Schaumann's story about how Störzer happened to kill Kienbaum and then spreads the information to the community, as Schaumann had intended.

Schoolmaster Blechhammer, together with the members of the community, a cruel, judgmental force that mocks Schaumann for personal characteristics outside the societal norm and that judges Quakatz guilty without sufficient evidence, using rumor to make him an outcast.

Susan L. Piepke

TURVEY
A Military Picaresque

Author: Earle Birney (1904-   )
Type of work: Novel
Time of action: World War II, 1942-1945
First published: 1949; revised, 1976

Thomas Leadbeater "Tops" Turvey, the somewhat befuddled, persistently cheerful hero of this satire of Canadian military life, backward and painfully lacking in sophistication. He was born in Shookum Falls, British Columbia, on May 13, 1922, went to school only through the ninth grade, and has an employment record that leads nowhere (cucumber pickler, worker in a hat factory, popsicle coater, assistant flavor manager in a candy factory, oiler in a mosquito-control gang). Lured by a spirit of adventure, he desires to become a soldier. His first attempt to enlist in the army, and in the air force, is unsuccessful. When the national need for manpower increases with the outbreak of war, he is finally inducted. The character of this army seems clear: If it can take Turvey, it will take anyone. Turvey hopes to fight in a good regiment, specifically the Kootenay Highlanders, in which his best friend, Gillis MacGillicuddy, serves. This determination propels him through a series of situations in which his incompetence and bumbling depict the military and its leaders in an increasingly nonsensical light. Turvey's army jobs are just as dead-end as those in civilian life. His routine infraction of rules and petty lawbreaking earn for him constant company punishment. He is a Parsifal, incapable of understanding any world that does not coincide with his own. An eternal bump-

kin, he is readily gulled by others, most of these more misguided than himself, to whom he looks for guidance and leadership. Thus, he is courtmartialed for being absent without leave because he impulsively follows a friend to Buffalo to spend the Christmas holidays with two women. He is sentenced to forty-five days detention, but this, as with the punishment he receives from further escapades, is not sufficiently onerous to destroy his good humor. Other characters in the book serve to set the stage for Turvey's purposeless, live-for-the-moment existence. Only when his best friend Mac is killed does Turvey begin to realize that only through his own efforts can he bring order to his life and achieve resolution.

Gillis MacGillis MacGillicuddy, Turvey's best friend and object of his quest, who runs into Turvey by chance in St. James Park in London. MacGillicuddy is a con artist who affects an upper-class accent to twist the Canadian army's confused social and hierarchical system to his advantage. Thus, through his wits and a little chicanery (he cheats on the officer candidate examination) he successfully manages to rise from an enlisted man to a lieutenant. As such, he arranges Turvey's transfer to him as his batman and jeep driver. Mac fulfills Turvey's idea of success, a factotum and operator who can challenge the system and win. War is difficult to control, however, and Mac is killed by artillery fire.

Peggy, Turvey's girlfriend and, later, fiancée, introduced to him by his friend Mac. She is a plump and charming young girl and makes Turvey feel like a man of romance and adventure. Their courtship seems a product of the same nonchalance that characterizes most of Turvey's associations. Yet a letter that she writes to Turvey, the correspondence reaching him three months late for Christmas (when he is a patient in a military hospital in England), brings them more closely together. Peggy, a force for order and common sense, characteristically tells Turvey that she cares about him by reminding him to change his socks when they get wet. Ensuing visits lead to a promise of marriage, which implies that Peggy will become a steadying influence in Turvey's life, helping him to end the nutty confusion and chaos that heretofore had bedeviled his existence.

Horatio Ballard, a private with the com-plexion of a celery root, strikingly adept at wheeling and dealing. He induces Turvey to take off to Buffalo, which leads to the charge of being AWOL. Later, in England, the irresponsible Ballard takes Turvey on another escapade in a stolen motorcycle, and Turvey is arrested again.

Sanderson, the alcoholic lieutenant charged with defending Turvey from the charge of AWOL. He does so in a drunken stupor.

Archibald McQua, a gloomy New Brunswicker, who leads Turvey into a field full of land mines.

Captain Airdale, a shy army psychiatrist who believes that the best way of diagnosing personality is through word association tests, but he gets turned on by suggestive words himself. He says that Turvey is suffering from temporary hysteria with a possible latent father-rivalry: Turvey had machine-gunned his own overcoat because it looked like a German paratrooper.

Wm. Laird Kleine-Ahlbrandt

TWENTY-SEVEN WAGONS FULL OF COTTON
A Mississippi Delta Comedy

Author: Tennessee Williams (Thomas Lanier Williams, 1911-1983)
Type of work: Play
Time of action: The 1930's or 1940's
First published: 1945

Flora Meighan, the young wife of Jake Meighan. Blonde, buxom, seductive, and mindless, Flora is childish and childlike, behaving like a petulant, demanding, spoiled child while exuding a vulnerability and dependence that make her a stereotypical female victim. Flora enjoys her husband's physical abuse and willingly accepts the role of baby to Jake's big daddy role; theirs is clearly a sadomasochistic relationship. Flora agrees to lie for Jake and provide him with an alibi when the neighboring cotton gin is destroyed by fire. She quickly reveals the lie under the questioning of Silva Vicarro, superintendent of the gin. Once Vicarro realizes Jake's guilt, he takes his revenge out on Flora, and she quickly becomes the victim of his sexual advances and physical abuse.

Jake Meighan, owner and operator of a cotton gin. A large, fat, greedy, ambitious, sixty-year-old man with all the mannerisms and class consciousness of a hardworking lower-middle-class Southerner, Jake proudly possesses his voluptuous young wife as a sign of his own power and sexuality, abusing her while he indulges her. As the play begins, he finds his business threatened by a rival cotton gin owned by the neighboring Syndicate Plantation. Jake sets fire to the rival cotton gin, forcing the superintendent, Silva Vicarro, to bring his cotton to Jake's gin, thus bringing together Vicarro and Flora who begin their adulterous relationship as the unwitting Jake supervises the ginning of Vicarro's cotton. So absorbed is Jake by the success of his plot, he fails to notice that while his cotton business has been saved, his wife, upon whom he dotes, has been lost to the younger man.

Silva Vicarro, superintendent of the Syndicate Plantation. Vicarro is of Latin descent, small, dark, intense, and intelligent. More clever than Flora, Vicarro quickly surmises from her conversation that Jake is the arsonist. His quick-tempered nature causes him to seek revenge on Jake, who has treated him with conspicuous condescension. Motivated by anger and a desire for revenge, he seduces Flora, who responds to his powerful physical aggression and abuse.

Jean McConnell

TWO FOR THE SEESAW

Author: William Gibson (1914-   )
Type of work: Play
Time of action: The late 1950's
First produced: 1958

Jerry Ryan, an attorney from Nebraska. A melancholy man of thirty-three, he fled Omaha and an unhappy marriage to start over in New York. Jerry owes much of his success to the intervention of others, especially his father-in-law, but he is now determined to do things for himself and for others. After meeting a young woman named Gittel at a party, the unlikely duo begins a nine-month-long rocky romance that is complicated by Gittel's unwillingness to let Jerry help her financially and by Jerry's emotional ties to his wife, which remain even after their divorce is granted. In the end, Jerry realizes that he still loves his wife and returns to Nebraska for another chance at life with her on his terms, not hers or her father's.

Gittel Mosca, a twenty-nine-year-old aspiring dancer who lives on unemployment insurance and income from various temporary jobs. She has spent much of her adult life as a victim, playing that role in a failed marriage and numerous doomed relationships. At first, she resists Jerry's willingness to help her, including his offer to pay rent on a loft Gittel wants to use as a rehearsal hall for a dance recital that could be her big break. Jerry eventually changes her mind about accepting help from others, and he makes her think, for the first time, about setting specific goals. When Jerry suspects her of sleeping with another man, they almost break off their relationship. Gittel's bleeding ulcer acts up, however, and Jerry nurses her back to health. Even though Gittel loves Jerry, she knows that he will never love her as he loves his ex-wife, so she decides that they should go their separate ways.

Gregory McElwain

TWO SOLITUDES

Author: Hugh MacLennan (1907-   )
Type of work: Novel
Time of action: 1917-1939
First published: 1945

Athanase Tallard, an elderly, French Canadian aristocrat, Seigneur of Saint-Marc-des-Érables, Member of Parliament. As a Federal politician, he is in an invidious position: Elected by French-speaking Catholic Quebec, he must work with English-speaking Protestants in Ottawa and is supporting national conscription, to which Quebec is opposed. A Catholic, Tallard is more intellectual, less biddable, less religiously observant than the local priest desires—but Athanase knows the Bishop. Tallard's second marriage has alienated him from his elder son. Attracted by the vision of industrial development and employment for St. Marc, Tallard mortgages his property to join a consortium headed by Huntly McQueen. The local priest, fearing change, quarrels with him and orders the parish to boycott him. Athanase moves to Montreal, defiantly becomes Protestant and sends his younger son to an English school. Having offended French Canadians, Tallard is useless to McQueen. Ruined, he dies, returning to the Catholic faith on his deathbed.

Kathleen Tallard, Athanase's second wife, a young Irish Catholic beauty, former hatcheck girl, mother of Paul. Kathleen Tallard cannot share her husband's political life, hates rural Quebec, and longs for urban distractions and male admiration. Nine years after Athanase's death, Kathleen marries an American businessman. Her character stresses the gap between Anglophones and Francophones even when religion is not an issue. She also contributes an English component to Paul.

Marius Tallard, son of Athanase and Marie Adèle, his first, pious, Quebecoise wife. Marius Tallard is attracted to his stepmother, detests his father's remarriage, and goes into hiding to escape conscription. He later becomes a lawyer, but his first concern is French Canadian politics.

Paul Tallard, son of Athanase and Kathleen. A brilliant student, his father's death and the Depression force Paul Tallard to play professional hockey and become a sailor. He returns to Canada determined to become a writer. Always an admirer of Captain Yard-

ley, he loves Heather Methuen and marries her. The product of a French English marriage and the husband of an English wife, bilingual himself, Paul embodies the ideal of an integrated Canada.

Father Emile Beaubien, a local priest in Saint-Marc, embodying the religion, culture, and antagonism to change characteristic of rural Quebec. Although he contributes to Tallard's destruction, Father Beaubien cannot stop McQueen, so Saint-Marc becomes a secular, modern community in spite of him.

John Yardley, a retired Nova Scotian sea captain, father of Janet, grandfather of Daphne and Heather, mentor to Paul Tallard after his father's death. Captain Yardley fulfills an old dream by buying land in Saint-Marc. Unprejudiced, intelligent, and sensitive, he is accepted by all though he speaks no French and is not a Catholic. Only his daughter Janet is ashamed of his unpretentious style. Paul and Heather love him and appreciate his wisdom. Captain Yardley retires finally to Nova Scotia, where he dies. Heather and Paul marry two days after the funeral. The captain epitomizes the human values that run counter to all barriers of status, religion and culture.

Janet Methuen, Yardley's daughter. A limited, insecure woman, resembling her English mother rather than her father, she is delighted to marry into the Methuen tribe, an old moneyed family in Montreal, pseudo-British and snobbish. Widowed by the war, Janet becomes socially ambitious for her daughters; however, she is stupid and unscrupulous. She betrays Marius Tallard to the authorities, seeks McQueen's help in separating Heather and Paul, and fakes a heart attack. She embodies all the pettiness, prejudice, and traditional English privilege that antagonize French Canada.

Heather Methuen, younger daughter of Harvey and Janet, a tomboy, independent thinker, and her grandfather's favorite. Always in rebellion against her mother's values, Heather wishes to be useful. She has socialist ideals, loves Paul, believes in his writing, and marries him, knowing that war is coming.

Huntly McQueen, a self-made man, creator and head of a powerful conglomerate, admirer of the Methuens—especially Janet. Huntly has private foibles (communing with his dead mother, for example), but his unremarkable appearance and his refusal to court publicity are protective coloration. Secretive, ruthless, pragmatic, and visionary, he is at the center of the Canadian power elite.

Jocelyn Creigh Cass

2001
A Space Odyssey

Author: Arthur C. Clarke (1917-   )
Type of work: Novel
Time of action: Three million years B.C. and A.D. 2001
First published: 1968

Moon-Watcher, a "man-ape" of the Pleistocene geologic era, hairy and muscular. Standing almost five feet tall, he is unusually tall for his dying race of cave-dwelling hominids and weighs more than one hundred pounds in spite of his tribe's usual lack of nourishment. Of the first creatures to take notice of the Moon, he is the only hominid in the world to stand erect and one of the few having a glimmer of intelligence. He discovers the New Rock, which is in fact a monolithic probe of an extraterrestrial intelligence. It studies him in particular and inspires him to use a stone to kill a warthog, then to kill another hominid. Moon-Watcher's tribe members become hunters to begin the evolution of Man.

Dr. Heywood Floyd, chairman of the National Council of Astronautics. A widower of ten years and father of three, he had completed one voyage to Mars and three to the Moon before returning to the lunar crater Tycho to see a recently uncovered monolith there.

David Bowman, first captain of the spaceship *Discovery.* At thirty-five years old, unmarried, and holding a Ph.D., he is a veteran astronaut with the curiosity of a generalist and an almost photographic memory who reads avidly and enjoys many styles of classical music. A caretaker of the ship and its three hibernating scientists until the planned rendezvous with Saturn, he has to disconnect the rebellious HAL, a computer, in order to complete the mission as he understands it. Once in orbit, he exits the ship in an exploratory pod to examine a free-floating monolith, then enters a Star Gate and is swept across time and intergalactic space until being transformed by extraterrestrials into the Star-Child.

Frank Poole, deputy captain of the *Discovery.* He is unmarried, like all the astronauts; experienced in his work; careful; and conscientious in sharing on-board duties with Bowman until Poole is murdered by HAL during an extra-vehicular activity in which he is engaged.

HAL 9000, an acronym for *H*euristically pro-grammed *AL*gorithmic computer, the brain and nervous system of the *Discovery.* Faster and more reliable than the human brain, HAL "thinks" intelligently, speaks, navigates the ship, and monitors the life-support systems of the three hibernating scientists. Unlike Bowman and Poole, HAL alone knows the true nature of the mission: to locate the source of the radio signals to the lunar monolith in Tycho. Created to be innocent and incapable of making errors, HAL tries to murder the humans on board when they threaten to disconnect HAL's brain, the equivalent of death. HAL fails to kill Bowman, however, who then disconnects HAL.

Clark G. Reynolds

TWO THOUSAND SEASONS

Author: Ayi Kwei Armah (1939-   )
Type of work: Novel
Time of action: 1000-1900
First published: 1973

The narrator, an omnipresent griot (poet-historian) and the voice of traditional African culture, specifically that of Ghana. Masculine in tone but speaking in the first person plural ("we"), the narrator is confident in his remembrance and in his interpretation of Anoa's prophecies as he traces the migration of his people from the deserts of Western Sudan to present-day Ghana. In recalling the collective experience and the principles of "the way," reciprocity and compassionate mutual respect, he also offers vivid, intimate, and detailed decriptions of "connectedness" among the people and with the land. Clearly charting the growth, decay, and transformation of cultural practices and values, he frequently employs rhetorical questions that reveal an obvious disdain for fragmented consciousness and religious dogmatism.

Anoa, the second prophetess bearing the name, living around A.D. 1000, who prophesies five hundred years (a thousand seasons) of cultural decline toward death and five hundred years of return to principles affirming life. Slender, supple, and of stunning beauty, her grace embodies her skills as a hunter. Her "deep" blackness reveals both physical strength and spiritual understanding. While gentle in manner, Anoa speaks in "two voices": one that is harassed and shrieking in her knowledge of impending doom for her people and one that is calm and encouraging, seeking to explore causes for the decline and creating hope for survival after the people's long suffering.

Isanusi, a learned counselor to Koranche, later exiled for his challenge to the king's authority. A master of eloquence and honest in his assessment of leadership, he refuses to flatter Koranche, who declares him mad when Isanusi reveals the king's secret alliance with the Europeans. Tired from suffering despair and loneliness from the people's loss of values, the slender teacher becomes rejuvenated by serving as mentor to and leader of a small group of young revolutionaries. After the revolt is in full force, Isanusi is betrayed by a messenger from the king and killed.

Idawa, the companion of Isanusi during his exile. Slender and graceful, the beautiful black woman is the ideal of physical strength and endurance as well as of compassionate, intelligent strength of mind and soul. When she chooses to marry Ngubane, a farmer, whom she loves, to avoid being coerced into marriage with Koranche, the king kills her husband within the year. Articulate and courageous, Idawa confronts Koranche with his own inferiority and rejects him with public contempt. After Isanusi has been exiled, she joins him in the forest.

Abena, a young woman who becomes the principal voice for the young rebels. Eloquent, beautiful, and brilliant, Abena is quick to grasp the various skills of initiation rituals. She is the greatest dancer in the village, and, in the ceremonial dance to choose mates, she dances her way to freedom, joining the rebels and rejecting Koranche's command for her to marry his son Bentum. When the rebels are betrayed and enslaved, her comprehension of Isanusi's wisdom helps the rebels endure their suffering before their escape. After the rebels return to Anoa, she leads them to victory over the colonists at Poano; at Anoa, she persuades Koranche to confess his crimes publicly and then executes him.

Koranche (kôr′ăn•chē), the King of Anoa who betrays African values to remain in power by allying himself with European slave traders and colonialists. Born an idiot in an incestuous dynasty, Koranche's sole skill consists of an uncanny ability to undermine the achievements of others, often destroying the fruits of their labor. As a child, he does not smile or cry, expressing himself in a dull, flat, constant stare. Breast-fed for five years and then vomiting at the sight of naked breasts thereafter, he does not walk until he is seven years old and does not talk until he is nine. Because he cannot complete the initiation rituals, he changes them for his son when he becomes king. Possessed by a numbing inner despair and emptiness in the self-knowledge that he is an utter fraud as an adult, Koranche learns to stay in power through mystification and pompous ceremony while surrounding himself with self-serving flatterers. He relies on the Europeans to enslave any who oppose him. Entirely dependent upon the people's gullibility, he continually betrays the Anoans, who come to fear his fraudulent power. As he ages, he becomes a very fat, deluded alcoholic, eventually executed by Abena.

Bentum, later renamed **Bradford George,** the son of Koranche, Prince of Anoa. Reared by Europeans in the colonized village of Poano and educated in Europe, Bentum is married to an older, crippled white woman to strengthen Koranche's alliance, but he lusts for Abena, who rejects him. Fat and stupid, he oversees the slave trading in Poano, marching children around the ground while he wears a blue cloak and a yellow wig. After his father is executed, Bentum, as Bradford George, becomes the colonial puppet king of Anoa.

Michael Loudon

TYPHOON

Author: Joseph Conrad (Jósef Teodor Konrad Korzeniowski, 1857-1924)
Type of work: Novella
Time of action: The 1890's
First published: 1902

Tom MacWhirr, captain of the steamer *Nan-Shan.* Dutiful, calculating, mechanical, mature, and effectual, the main character of the story does his job correctly although he does so without any manifest confidence from the men serving under him. That job is to take two hundred Chinese coolies to their destination of Fu-Chau and to do so directly and without delay. The obstacle to this plan is the typhoon, presenting MacWhirr with the central dilemma of the novella as he must decide whether to proceed straight into the hurricane or run from it. This latter choice would be a relinquishment of duty, which he cannot accept. In confronting the typhoon and surviving it, MacWhirr somehow comes to terms with all life's adverse universal forces.

The typhoon, a nameless hurricane that Captain MacWhirr must confront. Violent, strong, forceful, and controlling, the typhoon represents not only the power of nature but also all the adverse conditions that humanity must face and struggle against. The typhoon does not succeed in destroying the *Nan-Shan* and the men on board; however, it does not surrender the battle to MacWhirr so much as it simply ceases to struggle.

Young Jukes, the chief mate. Innocent and inexperienced to the evils of life and to the violence of nature, Jukes rightfully depends upon Captain MacWhirr for guidance, and he exactingly follows the orders of his superior. The central sections and the major portions of the plot unfold told from Jukes's perspective, though he is not the narrator. In following Captain MacWhirr's cold and calculating orders, Jukes realizes that he must be functional and mechanical in order to survive.

Solomon Rout, the chief engineer. Taller than anyone else on any ship he has served on, Old Sol's towering height accounts for his "habit of a stooping, leisurely condescension." As engineer, Rout is perhaps the most mechanical of men on board; his ability to follow MacWhirr's orders and to maintain a rather automaton-like existence helps assure the preservation of the ship.

The second mate, nameless and second in command of the *Nan-Shan*. A secretive loner who is "competent enough," the second mate has failed to master the subservience to duty, responsibility, and effectuality that Mac-Whirr has. He is an older, shabby fellow: one who is a ghost of what MacWhirr would become were he to fail. During the typhoon, the second mate loses his nerve and is unable to carry out his responsibilities.

The boatswain, first in charge of the crewmen on deck. Once described as an "elderly ape" and in another place as a "gorilla," the boatswain embodies raw strength, gruffness, and stupidity in human nature. Surprisingly,

Captain MacWhirr likes the boatswain, presumably because he knows he controls him and can put his strength to good use.

The steward, personal attendant to Captain MacWhirr. Unable to mind his own business, the steward reads Captain MacWhirr's personal mail to his family. Consequently, the reader is informed about the contents of these letters and MacWhirr's character is further revealed.

Two hundred Chinese coolies, these men exist in the story literally as cargo; they are returning to China after working several years abroad. They represent the thoughtless, purposeless mass of humanity, toward which MacWhirr feels his duty and responsibility as well as his contempt. Several of these die as the typhoon proceeds.

Carl Singleton

TZILI
The Story of a Life

Author: Aharon Appelfeld (1932-   )
Type of work: Novel
Time of action: The Holocaust, from the late 1930's to the mid-1940's
First published: Kutonet veha-Pasim, 1983 (English translation, 1983)

Tzili Kraus, a young, provincial Jewish girl. A plain, quiet, not very bright girl, Tzili is disliked by her family for her lack of intelligence. When the Nazi troubles begin, her family decides that she is so simple that no one will bother her, and so they leave Tzili behind when they try to make their escape. Though simple, Tzili has an innate sense of survival (such as saying that the town prostitute Maria, who is not Jewish, is her mother) that other Jews lack; no matter what troubles befall her, she goes on living in her undemanding, almost heedless, way—even when, near the end of the book, she sees Jewish survivors of concentration camps committing suicide around her. The novel follows her journey as she seems to survive accidentally, her pregnancy that ends in a stillborn

child, and finally, her decision to go to Palestine.

The old blind man, a man who sits in the fields all day. He gives Tzili some food but then tries to rape her.

The religious teacher, a Jewish tutor who is brought in by Tzili's family to teach her religion since they believe she is too stupid to learn anything more worthwhile. Although he did not feel affectionate toward Tzili, he was not really cruel to her, and so she remembers him as a kind man. The prayers she has learned from him serve to comfort her while she is hiding in the countryside.

Katerina, a dying old prostitute. Once a friend

of Maria, Tzili's "adopted" mother, Katerina takes Tzili in for the winter but then when Katerina becomes too ill to entice men, she tries to turn Tzili into a prostitute.

The old man and
The old woman, a couple who take Tzili in after she runs away from Katerina. The old woman beats Tzili, and the old man tries to rape her, so she flees them, too.

Mark, a Jewish man who has escaped from a concentration camp and who is hiding in the countryside. He and Tzili hide together in a bunker that he has dug. As Tzili matures, Mark is attracted to her, and Tzili becomes pregnant by him. The hiding takes a mental toll on Mark, and one day he leaves and never returns, presumably captured by the Nazis.

Linda, a fat Hungarian woman who was a cabaret performer. Linda helps keep up the spirits of the fatally depressed and guilt-ridden Jews who have survived the Holocaust. At one point, she forces the group of wanderers that Tzili has joined to go back for Tzili and carry her, when Tzili is heavily pregnant and unable to continue walking. At the end of the book, she joins Tzili for the voyage to Palestine.

The merchant, another Holocaust survivor. He helps to organize the men to carry Tzili on a stretcher when she can no longer walk, and he brings her milk. When Tzili starts having a problem with the pregnancy, the merchant goes from place to place trying to get her help. He is left behind, however, when the military ambulance finally arrives to take Tzili to the hospital.

The nurse, a young gentile Czechoslovak woman. She is Tzili's nurse in the hospital in Zagreb after Tzili's dead baby is surgically removed. With the nurse, Tzili strikes a chord of solidarity for the first time. Then, Tzili is moved away to make room for the sicker patients.

T. M. Lipman

UBU ROI

Author: Alfred Jarry (1873-1907)
Type of work: Play
Time of action: Unspecified
First produced: Ubu Roi, 1896 (English translation, 1951)

Père Ubu, the former King of Aragon, Captain of the Dragoons, Count of Sandomir, and, later, King of Poland. He is an obese, smelly grub, with an enormous paunch, who carries a walking stick in his right-hand pocket and uses a toilet brush as his scepter. As a grotesque parody of a petty official who usurps a position of power, he is vulgar, gluttonous, rapacious, untrustworthy, greedy, sadistic, cowardly, and stupid. His actions are impulsive, and his speech is a mixture of vulgar expressions, oaths, and repetitive phrases. He ruthlessly obtains the Polish throne, then recklessly abuses his power by killing off the nobility, usurping the power of the judiciary, and overtaxing the peasants. Unsuccessful in defending his kingdom against the Russians, he escapes to France.

Mère Ubu, Ubu's wife, a repulsive unattractive, foulmouthed woman who cooks her food in excrement. She goads Ubu into assassinating the Polish king and usurping the throne. Although just as vicious as Ubu, she knows the limits to which power can be wielded and is more practical than he in matters of politics. She tries to act independently of Ubu in stealing the royal gold, but her scheme is thwarted by Boggerlas.

Captain Macnure, an officer in the Polish army who agrees to assassinate the king. He

1631

is a parody of the honorable soldier who would rather split the king in half with his sword than poison him. Betrayed by Ubu, he joins the Russian Czar to wage war on Ubu, who eventually tears him to pieces in combat.

King Wenceslas, the good King of Poland who provides for his subjects. Rash and imprudent, he becomes an example of foolish credulity and heedless obstinacy when he attends the Grand Review unarmed and unprotected and is assassinated by Ubu's henchmen.

Queen Rosamund, Queen of Poland. Cautious and wary, she warns her husband not to attend the Grand Review, and, after he is assassinated, she dies of grief in her son's arms in a scene that parodies a melodramatic death scene.

Boggerlas, fourteen-year-old son of King Wenceslas who is wise to Ubu's schemes. He vows to avenge himself on Ubu for causing the death of his family. Fighting with great courage, he eventually reclaims the throne.

Tsar Alexis, the noble Czar of Russia who will not use treachery to win a victory. He joins forces with Macnure to defeat Ubu.

General Laski, a foolish general of the Polish army. He is more interested in the formality of parading than in battle tactics.

Palcontents, Ubu's henchmen, who kill King Wenceslas and his sons. Heads and Tails kill a wild bear without the help of Ubu, who watches and prays. After this incident, they desert him. Gyron, a Negro, is killed while helping Mère Ubu rob the crypt of the Polish kings.

Paul Rosefeldt

ULTRAMARINE

Author: Malcolm Lowry (1909-1957)
Type of work: Novel
Time of action: c. 1927
First published: 1933; revised, 1962

Eugene Dana Hilliot, the novel's center of consciousness, an upper-middle-class youth taking his first voyage as a deckhand. Sensitive, creative, half-Norwegian and half-English, out of place and out of his class among the crew, Hilliot is the only character (besides the ship, the *Oedipus Tyrannus*) to be described in any detail. He has an identity problem that mirrors that of the young first-time author, Lowry, whose own 1927 voyage to China Hilliot takes. Even his name is a compendium of references to Lowry's literary influences: Eugene O'Neill, Richard Henry Dana, and T. S. Eliot (the crew pronounce Hilliot's name "Illiot"). Hilliot wants both to be accepted as an "ordinary seaman" and to be extraordinary; at age nineteen, he has left boyhood behind but has yet to enter into adulthood. The voyage, his all-night "binge"

ashore at Tsjang-Tsjang, his challenge to Andy, and his acceptance as part of the group will allow him to come to terms with the bourgeois Merseyside past of which he has freed himself, his schoolboy love, and his sexual urges, and to forge himself an identity as a spinner of yarns and an expatriate (like his creator). Much of the novel is occupied with his interior monologues and dreams.

Andy, the "chinless wonder," ship's cook and focus of its social life, a dominating personality. The most memorable of the novel's sketchily drawn supporting players, tattooed and sensual, working-class Andy is nevertheless important not for what he is but for what he represents: a rival and alter-ego (he spends the night ashore with the prostitute Hilliot had fancied), a model for selfhood, and a father figure (he calls Hilliot "son" at the close of the novel) who can be left behind and surpassed.

Norman, the cabin boy, another rival and model. Easygoing, plucky, and eminently "normal," Norman performs the bathetically "heroic" act of rescuing a pigeon from atop the mainmast that Hilliot feels he should have attempted, the prize being the crew's applause and acceptance. He accompanies Hilliot on his binge and tour of the port sights: the cinema, the anatomical museum, and the bars. Concern for Norman (he loses his pigeon) draws Andy and Hilliot together.

Janet, Hilliot's innocent schoolboy love, to whom most of his monologues are addressed. Something of a cardboard cutout (the hometown madonna to the whore with whom Hilliot had contemplated losing his virginity), Janet is a soft, sweet, idealized representative of Hilliot's childhood values: His goodbye to her in Merseyside, finally related near the novel's close, has proved a decisive moment in Hilliot's life. He receives a letter from her only to lose it in a bar to an uncomprehending German, Popplereuter, who later forwards it. At the novel's close, Hilliot is mentally drafting his reply: an account of himself and his changes.

Joss Lutz Marsh

THE UNBEARABLE LIGHTNESS OF BEING

Author: Milan Kundera (1929-   )
Type of work: Novel
Time of action: The 1960's to the 1970's
First published: Nesnesitelná lehkost bytí, 1984 (English translation, 1984)

Tomas, a noted Czechoslovak surgeon and indefatigable philanderer. At the novel's pivotal chronological moment (the summer of 1968, when the Russians invade and occupy Czechoslovakia), Tomas is forty years old. He and his wife, Tereza, flee to begin a new life in Switzerland. After several months in Zurich, Tereza abruptly returns to Prague. The fact that Tomas follows Tereza suggests the depth of his love for his wife and homeland. There is, however, no corresponding commitment to fidelity. One of the keys to Tomas' character, to the pattern of his life, is his firm belief that love and sexuality have nothing in common. Thus, although he returns to Tereza, and truly loves her, his promiscuous womanizing continues. He also loves his country but will not participate in its destruction by the police-state apparatus. He twice refuses to retract a political essay he had published before the crackdown, he resigns his position at the clinic before the police have him fired and becomes a window washer. This job presents him with a certain freedom, or blissful indifference, and with

many new opportunities to practice his avocation: epic womanizing. There is a stubborn integrity at the core of his personality. Finally, when Tomas and Tereza choose to settle in the countryside and work at a collective farm, a kind of happiness settles over them. They are killed in a highway accident.

Tereza, a small-town waitress and autodidact who yearns for "something higher." Through a sequence of fortuities, she meets Tomas, follows him to Prague, and becomes his wife. Pursuing her new career as a photographer, she is caught up in the Soviet invasion, taking daring photographs, risking arrest, experiencing a happiness she has not known before. She initiates their move to Switzerland, just as she chooses to return. However insecure Tereza may feel, she does make choices and she lives up to the consequences of her choices. The mainspring of her character is her longing for beauty, for a world in which the soul will manifest itself and take precedence over the promiscuous and immodest flesh and over the view of the world—instilled in her by her mother—as a grim concentration camp of bodies. Driven and haunted by jealousy, compelled by and committed to fidelity, Tereza's unhappiness centers on her husband's sexual encounters with other women. Finally, when they have settled in the country and there is no longer a wide range of women for Tomas to pursue, Tereza knows the happiness for which she has longed, the satisfaction of her vision of "weight" through responsibility and fidelity.

Franz, a Swiss university professor. A gifted and successful scholar, he feels suffocated by his vocation. He has a "weakness for revolution," a fascination with leftist causes, and he remains intoxicated with the kitsch of the "Grand March," Kundera's name for the fantasy joining leftists and revolutionaries of all times. His personal life parallels his political life: His relationship with his wife is superficial, as is his affair with Sabina, his mistress, from whom he is separated by an abyss of misunderstanding. In Sabina's eyes, Franz, though he has physical strength, is a weak person. In the schematic presentation of character that drives the novel, Franz is an exemplar of "lightness."

Sabina, a Czechoslovak painter. Like Tomas and Tereza, Sabina flees her homeland, but she remains in a permanent state of exile in both a physical and a spiritual sense. She is a strong, liberated, sophisticated professional woman; a central figure in spite of her limited presence, she is mistress to both Franz and Tomas. She serves as a foil to define her lovers, yet she remains mysteriously superficial, profoundly unattached. The essence of her character is projected by her fascination with betrayal: She longs to betray everything, even her own betrayals. In the novel, she is the most sophisticated exemplar of "lightness"; she continues her drift westward until she ends up in California, alone, unattached, still living on the surface of things, successful and content with her life "under the sign of lightness."

The narrator, the central presence and voice. The narrator is probably the most engaging character. Whether regarded as the author's direct voice or as a compelling fictional device, the narrator delivers the rich and paradoxical political, philosophical, and erotic speculations that shape the novel and define each of the characters.

H. R. Stoneback

UNDER THE SUN OF SATAN

Author: Georges Bernanos (1888-1948)
Type of work: Novel
Time of action: The beginning of the twentieth century
First published: Sous le soleil de Satan, 1926 (*The Star of Satan*, 1927; better known as *Under the Sun of Satan*)

Germaine "Mouchette" Malorthy (má·lôr· tē'), a sixteen-year-old murderess and suicide. Small, nymphlike, and intense, she unashamedly sets out to seduce both Dr. Gallet and Jacques de Cadignan. Pregnant by the marquess, she threatens to expose him to public scorn and to the police if he does not agree to marry her. After Mouchette tells him that she is also the mistress of Dr. Gallet, however, he violently rapes her. She then shoots him in the throat, and it looks as though he committed suicide. She attempts also to black-

mail Dr. Gallet into performing an abortion, but he refuses. She lies for the sake of lying and enjoys watching others suffer; she will do anything to get her own way. Her final attempt at seduction is with the saintly Father Donissan, who immediately recognizes her demonic powers and offers her pity and forgiveness. She is so outraged by his generosity that she goes home and slits her throat.

Antoine Malorthy, the middle-aged father of Mouchette. A brewer by trade, he possesses all the manipulative cleverness of a northern French peasant. Although disturbed by the Marquess of Cadignan's sexual exploitation of his teenage daughter, he attempts to find ways by which the family can benefit financially from it. Antoine convinces the marquess that unless he makes some kind of monetary reparation for violating Antoine's daughter, Antoine will make the marquess' crime public.

Jacques de Cadignan (kȧ·dē·nȧṅ′), Mouchette's lover and an impoverished nobleman. A forty-five-year-old pleasure-seeking member of a dying nobility, he relentlessly pursues the young women of his area of the Artois. Although somewhat paunchy, he is a charming gentleman, with soothing manners and pale, icy blue eyes. He has been seduced by the nymphette Mouchette, who tells him that he has fathered her child. She insists that he marry her and rear the child as his own, but he refuses.

Dr. Gallet (gȧ·lä′), a middle-aged physician and member of the local Chamber of Deputies. He has become Mouchette's lover but is fearful of being found out. After Mouchette becomes pregnant, she insists that Dr. Gallet perform an abortion. He refuses on ethical grounds, but she threatens him with blackmail if he does not do as she wishes. After she commits suicide, he successfully keeps the facts of the situation quiet, thus protecting her family and himself. Everything he does is self-serving.

Father Donissan (dō·nē·sȧṅ′), the saintly Curé of Lumbres. He is a powerfully built, intellectually dull, inarticulate, awkward priest who is totally devoted to his parishioners. Because his natural instincts frighten him, particularly aspects of his bleak and violent nature, he flagellates himself, wears a hair shirt, and practices other techniques of self-mortification. In order to gain complete control over his feelings, he fasts and sleeps only a few hours each night. He is most fearful of the joy that spiritual pride may create within himself and leans heavily toward Jansenistic spiritualism. He is tempted by Satan himself when lost on a dark road late at night. He resists the consolations that Satan offers him and, as a result of his victory, attains the ability to read the souls of his parishioners, particularly in the confessional. He becomes a new Curé of Ars and spends the remainder of his life ministering to the souls of sinners. Mouchette commits suicide after he reveals the secrets of her soul to her.

Father Menou-Segrais (mĕ·noō′ sə·grä′), an aging canon of the parish of Compagne and spiritual director of Father Donissan. He is a clear-sighted, practical, though spiritual guide for Father Donissan. Although heir to a huge fortune, he has chosen the priestly life and devotes himself to the needs of his flock and to the younger priests in the diocese. He believes that Father Donissan has confronted Satan and urges him to seek temporary refuge in a monastery for further prayer and contemplation. He is in many ways responsible for Father Donissan's growing sainthood by urging him to pursue his spirituality in less masochistic ways and opening his heart to his parishioners.

Father Sabiroux (sä·bē·roō′), a priest in his fifties who is the pastor of the parish at Luzarnes. He befriends Father Donissan and believes in his miraculous powers, although he is skeptical at first. He is a former professor of chemistry in the minor seminary at Cambrai and leads a well-ordered and sober life.

Satan, or **Lucifer,** a figure who appears as a normal-looking, short, cheerful horse dealer who emerges out of the dark to guide Father Donissan to his destination. Father Donissan is immediately attracted to him and confides the secret of his soul to him. As Satan embraces him and declares his love for him, the young priest becomes violently aware that he is being kissed by Lucifer himself. The priest resists Satan's temptation and is empowered thereafter to read the souls of sinners. His victory over Satan comes as a result of the pity and love he expresses toward him.

Antoine Saint-Marin (săṅ mä·răṅ′), a

middle-aged wealthy intellectual. He is a famous author whose book, *The Paschal Candle*, is a scathing indictment of the mystical practices of the Catholic church. He has come to see the now-famous, aging Father Donissan and to prove to himself that his agnosticism is correct. Although he never meets the ag-

ing saint, his rationalistic skepticism is damaged somewhat by the moving stories he has heard about the holy pastor. He discovers the priest dead in his confessional at the conclusion of the novel.

Patrick Meanor

THE UNDERGROUND MAN

Author: Ross Macdonald (Kenneth Millar, 1915-1983)
Type of work: Novel
Time of action: The 1960's
First published: 1971

Lew Archer, the narrator, a private detective and former police officer who is middle-aged and divorced. Not a typical violent hard-boiled detective at all, Archer is more a questioner than a doer, humane and sensitive to clients, victims, and even criminals. He works by understanding and analyzing psychological states and family histories rather than collecting physical evidence.

Jean Broadhurst, his client, whose son is apparently kidnapped during a visit with his father to his grandmother's mountain cabin.

Ronny Broadhurst, her six-year-old son, who witnesses his father's death in the same place that Stanley aurally witnessed his own father's shooting fifteen years earlier.

Stanley Broadhurst, Jean's twenty-seven-year-old newly estranged husband, Ronny's father. Stanley was deeply affected as a child by the disappearance of his father, Leo, and has become obsessed with the need to search for him, neglecting his family as a result. He has recently stirred up interest in that search by putting an advertisement in the paper and offering a reward for information about Leo. His murder by pickax at his family's mountain cabin near the beginning of the novel leads eventually to the discovery that Leo was killed fifteen years earlier in the same place.

Elizabeth Broadhurst, the wealthy wife of

Leo Broadhurst, mother of Stanley, and grandmother of Ronny. A coldhearted daddy's girl, she is proud of her family's history. She shot Leo out of jealousy fifteen years earlier and believed that she had killed him.

Leo Broadhurst, a man who vanished fifteen years earlier, supposedly leaving his family to elope with Ellen Strome Kilpatrick and subsequently deserting her as well. In fact, Leo had been murdered the night before his planned departure. A chronic womanizer and the father of Susan Crandall, he blamed his infidelities on his wife's lack of attention to him. He had gone to the mountain cabin with Martha and Susan, was shot (but not fatally) by Elizabeth, and then was stabbed to death by Edna as he lay unconscious.

Edna Snow, Elizabeth's former housekeeper. She murdered Leo in revenge for the trouble he had caused Fritz and also in judgment of his infidelities, then murdered Stanley fifteen years later as he was about to discover his father's body and Edna's crime. A quick-moving gray-haired woman, she is accustomed to making excuses for Fritz and is overprotective of him.

Frederick (Fritz) Snow, Edna Snow's son and Elizabeth's gardener. In his middle thirties, with a moon face and a scar resembling a harelip, Fritz, along with Albert, took the blame and was punished for Leo's statutory rape of Martha Nickerson. Fritz suffered a nervous breakdown as a result and has been "emotionally immature" ever since. He lives with his mother and is both afraid of and dependent upon her.

Albert Sweetner, a former convict who was once a foster child of Edna Snow. He responds to Stanley's advertisement but is murdered by Edna before he can reveal the information that he and Fritz buried Leo's body for her.

Brian Kilpatrick, a real estate agent and the partner of Elizabeth Broadhurst in the Canyon estates development. He is a dangerously emotional man about forty-five years old. Out of jealousy caused by his wife's affair with Leo, he called Elizabeth to tell her that Leo and Martha would be in the cabin that night. He has been blackmailing Elizabeth ever since.

Ellen Strome, Brian's former wife and the former mistress of Leo Broadhurst. She went to Reno to obtain a divorce from Brian and wait for Leo, who never arrived. She has become a lonely woman content with her loneliness who spends her time painting. A former high-school teacher, she has stayed friendly with Martha, a former pupil.

Jerry Kilpatrick, a lanky boy of about nineteen, with long hair and a beard, hostile and emotional. He flees with Susan Crandall and Ronny Broadhurst after Stanley's murder.

Susan Crandall, the eighteen- or nineteen-year-old illegitimate daughter of Leo Broadhurst and the then-underaged Martha Nickerson. Susan accompanies Stanley and Ronny to the mountain cabin, panicking and fleeing with the boy after Stanley is murdered. She was present, as a three-year-old child, at Leo's murder. Though basically a good girl, she is confused and suicidal.

Lester Crandall, a shrewd and wealthy sixty-year-old man. He married Martha Nickerson when she was pregnant with Leo's child, Susan, and reared Susan as his own daughter.

Martha Nickerson Crandall, an attractive middle-aged woman who felt that she and her family did not belong in the wealthy world in which her husband wanted them to live. She has never told anyone that she was with Leo when he was shot.

William Nelles
Lori Williams

UNHOLY LOVES

Author: Joyce Carol Oates (1938-   )
Type of work: Novel
Time of action: The 1970's
First published: 1979

Brigit Stott, professor of English and the only novelist at the relatively prestigious Woodslee University, 256 miles north of New York City. Thirty-eight years old, thin, sharp-featured, and attractive in a mysterious way, Brigit has written two novels that have attained minor success, but her current work remains a tumble of notes and sketches. Separated from her abusive husband, whom she married when she was twenty-two years old, she begins an intense love affair with a musician on campus, just when she had hoped to

fall in love with the great visiting poet in residence, Albert St. Dennis. Her introspection, self-respect, and overwhelming desire to write novels, however, keep her from destruction in the painful romance; victoriously, she realizes that nothing in her life is inevitable.

Alexis Kessler, a thirty-two-year-old composer and pianist on the faculty at Woodslee University. Blond and beautiful, he has had numerous love affairs with both men and women. He is attracted to the mystery in

Brigit and, while they are together, wants to possess and transform her into a beautiful woman. Most of his peers feel intense animosity toward him, and it is only the Dean of Humanities' support that allows him to remain on campus. Meretricious and frustrated by an unrealized career, Alexis is pursued by unwarranted scandal and has an almost childlike inability to handle responsibility.

Albert St. Dennis, a seventy-year-old English poet in a one-year residence at Woodslee University. Known as the greatest living English poet, he has recently become a widower and looks and behaves like a confused and feeble old man. Yet, at his first poetry reading on campus, he is a critical success. Faculty members covet his attention and seek his opinions and insight, but his comments are often garbled and sententious, even though his career is based on impressive creativity and scholarship. His death, caused by a fire ignited from a cigarette he dropped when he passed out in a drunken stupor on his sofa, brings chaos and disorder to the entire English department.

Oliver Byrne, the attractive Dean of Humanities. Ambitious and egotistical, he views his current position as a stepping-stone on the path of an extremely successful career in academe. He regularly lists to himself the brilliant victories he has had, the latest and best of which was arranging the yearlong residency of Albert St. Dennis. Considering his wife, at best, a necessary inconvenience, he arranges a social life that will lead to the presidency of Woodslee or another major university.

Marilyn Byrne, the troubled wife of Oliver Byrne. She tries to create proper parties and a proper persona, but, as the year progresses, she fails more and more miserably, until she finally seeks divorce and hospitalization.

Warren Hochberg, the chairman of the English department. His one scholarly book, on John Dryden, belongs to the far distant past, and now he seems devoted to his administrative position. A dull man, he operates successfully in academic middle management.

Vivian Hochberg, the attractive and sophisticated wife of Warren Hochberg. Vivian, it is rumored, was in love with another member of the department, Lewis Seidel. For mysterious reasons, the relationship ended, but an emotional intimacy remains between the two of them.

Lewis Seidel, an influential faculty member and sometimes rival of Oliver Byrne. With the lengthy visit of Albert St. Dennis, Lewis had hoped to resurrect his flagging scholarly reputation with a book about the older man's work. Locked into a loveless marriage, but affable and social, he has liaisons with other women, but he is suffering increasingly from an unnamed pulmonary condition.

Faye Seidel, the wife of Lewis, who rightly feels unloved and out of place in the social group in which she is forced to remain.

Gladys Fetler, an older and very popular professor who is forced into retirement though remaining well-liked by students and members of the department, particularly Brigit.

Gowan Vaughan-Jones, the most highly acclaimed critic in the department, who gains the greatest benefits for his career from the visit of Albert St. Dennis. While eccentric and ingenuous, he is likable and unpretentious.

Leslie Cullendon, a James Joyce scholar who is dying from a mysterious degenerative disease that has forced him into a wheelchair. He is vitriolic, drunken, and insulting to everyone, including his wife; as a result, he is unliked and avoided by all.

Babs Cullendon, the long-suffering wife of Leslie. At parties, she either remains silent or complains of what she must endure in her life with Leslie.

Ernest Jaeger, a twenty-eight-year-old newly hired professor. Hardworking and grateful for his position, he still suffers the anguish of possible termination.

Sandra Jaeger, the beautiful, blonde twenty-four-year-old wife of Ernest. At first idealistic about her husband's bright future, she later becomes the lover of Lewis Seidel, in order to ensure her husband's termination and to combat boredom.

Vicki K. Robinson

THE UNICORN

Author: Iris Murdoch (1919-   )
Type of work: Novel
Time of action: The early 1960's
First published: 1963

Hannah Crean-Smith, nominally the mistress of Gaze Castle, a large and forbidding nineteenth century house situated near the black sandstone cliffs of West Ireland's coastline. Hannah, a lovely golden-haired woman no longer young, nor yet middle-aged, is restricted to the castle because of an indiscretion that she committed almost nine years before the story begins. Having married Peter Crean-Smith before she was twenty, she had a two-year affair with Philip "Pip" Lejour, a neighbor. Discovered by Peter, who was more frequently absent than present, she is said to have tried to kill him by pushing him over a cliff, after which she was imprisoned in the house and her husband left for New York; she has not seen him since, but he is rumored to be returning soon. Pampered and indulged for their own selfish purposes by the staff and a few other persons, Hannah nevertheless is a prisoner, arrested in time, fearful of the world outside the castle, and apparently content to live in an alcoholic haze, childlike and unchanging, like an enchanted princess.

Marian Taylor, in her late twenties, recently a schoolmistress, now a companion and tutor to Hannah Crean-Smith. Having decided that her relationship with Geoffrey would never go beyond affectionate friendship, Marian answered an advertisement that suggested change and adventure. She is astonished to learn that instead of a child or two whom she is to tutor, her charge is a beautiful woman of about her own age. Marian quickly overcomes her initial apprehension and is soon as devoted to this appealing, unusual personage as everyone else, apparently, in the household, all of whom play a role in keeping Hannah quietly content, dependent, and totally deprived of freedom. When a rescue attempt fails miserably, shaken by grief and acceptance, Marian decides to return to the world of reality.

Gerald Scottow, head keeper of the castle and of Hannah. Once Peter Crean-Smith's lover, he now holds young Jamesie Evercreech in a similiar thralldom. In his early forties, he is a big, handsome man, with a powerful, domineering manner slightly disguised by a courteous, reserved exterior. A local man, he is reputed to have supernatural powers commonly ascribed to the "fairy folk" of the region. His dominion over Hannah and the staff is absolute, even during his frequent and unexplained absences. Marian is both attracted to and repelled by him. Having incurred the hatred and anger of everyone through his cruel and brutal strength, Gerald threatens to take Hannah away with him after the aborted escape, but, before he can do so, she kills him with Pip Lejour's shotgun and then shortly thereafter takes her own life by drowning.

Denis Nolan, the clerk of Gaze, but more important, the most devoted of those who serve Hannah. Formerly, he was employed at Riders. Like Gerald Scottow, he is a local man, thought to have fairy powers. He is thirty-three, short, watchful, and taciturn. He performs services that cheer and entertain Hannah, such as singing in an astonishingly beautiful voice, dexterously cutting her hair, and bringing live creatures from outside for her to see, as she never leaves the house except on three disastrous occasions. He and Marian are united in their protective love for Hannah and their fearful hatred of Gerald, against whom Denis warns and advises Marian. Slowly, Marian begins to comprehend the strange circumstances surrounding life at Gaze. Only Denis seems to be single-mindedly and selflessly concerned for Hannah; when she dies, he leaves the castle, as does everyone else.

Jamesie Evercreech, a distant relation of Hannah, the chauffeur and Gerald's current lover. Five years ago, Jamesie tried to help Hannah escape but was stopped by Gerald, who whipped him and completely subjugated him to his own will.

Violet Evercreech, Jamesie's sister and the housekeeper of Gaze. Of an indeterminate age somewhere between forty and sixty, she is much older than Jamesie. She is thin and intense, perhaps a little mad, like everyone else at Gaze.

Effingham Cooper, a governmental department head, a frequent houseguest at Riders, where he visits his former tutor, and an egotistical pretender to Hannah's love, though he is essentially more curious and intrigued than truly concerned about her. Nevertheless, it is Effingham whom Marian enlists in her plot to release Hannah from her prison. He himself experiences an analogous adventure when he is almost drowned in a bog, from which he is magically rescued by Denis. At the end of the novel, Effingham leaves the area, relieved to be released from the spell that has held them all for a while and to which so many of them succumbed.

Alice Lejour, a horticulturist who once accused Denis of having tried to rape her, after which he was compelled to leave Riders. Later, she confesses that she had lied and that, as a matter of fact, it was she who tried vainly to get Denis to make love to her. She becomes a dear and solid friend to Marian during the turbulent and tragic events at the end of the novel.

Philip "Pip" Lejour, a journalist, poet, and owner of Riders, brother of Alice, and son of Max Lejour. Pip figures in the novel primarily as an important personage in Hannah's life when the two had an affair and were discovered by Peter Crean-Smith, and, at the end of the novel, when Pip comes armed with a shotgun to rescue Hannah. She refuses to leave with him, however, and Pip is reported to have killed himself accidentally while cleaning his gun.

Max Lejour, an elderly, weary classics scholar, father of Pip and Alice. While taking no part in the action of the story, Max is significant in his revealing conversations with several of the characters, particularly Effingham Cooper, his former pupil. He is the only person who seems to understand the whole mystery of Gaze, but his wisdom is of no help to anyone. He has remained aloof from Gaze all this while, yet it is to him that Hannah has left her entire property in a will that is a surprise to all the survivors except Alice, who realizes that it was only Max, who did not prey upon or interfere with Hannah, whom she really loved.

Natalie Harper

UNION STREET

Author: Pat Barker (1943-   )
Type of work: Novel
Time of action: Winter, 1973
First published: 1982

Kelly Brown, an eleven-year-old schoolgirl who lives with her older sister Linda and their mother. "Uncle" Arthur, the latest in a succession of her mother's male friends, also lives with the family for a while. A latchkey child who frequently skips school, Kelly has grown accustomed to deception and deprivation in order to survive. Although proud of her independence, Kelly still unconsciously clings to her mother, seeking her love and approval. When Kelly is raped, she is too afraid to tell anyone at first; her reactions only emerge later, in a screaming fit. Kelly cuts her hair as an act of self-mutilation and of aggression, and retreats into an obstinate isolation. Kelly also acts out her pain and anger through petty crime but is increasingly afraid of herself and what she might do.

Joanne Wilson, an eighteen-year-old bakery worker who wants for herself something different from what she observes around her. When she finds herself pregnant and unmarried, however, she gradually realizes that she is caught in the same trap. The pregnancy alienates her from her mother. Moreover, while communication with her resentful boyfriend, Ken, is never good, the couple feel themselves doomed to marry. Joanne is different enough from others to stand up for a co-worker, but her conformity is revealed through her relationship with the midget Joss. Joss is handsome and offers hospitality, a refuge, advice, and respect, but Joanne cannot imagine more than friendship because of his deformity.

Lisa Goddard, a young married woman with two boys (Kevin and Darren) and a third child on the way. She is often forced to cope alone because her unemployed husband Brian is always out drinking; he is often abusive when he does return home. Consequently, Lisa is frequently tired and desperate, and takes her anger and frustration out on the children, a reaction that horrifies her although she is unable to stop herself. The discovery that Brian has stolen money she was saving for the new baby finally gives Lisa the courage to take a stand, but it is short-lived, causing Lisa resentment and bitterness. The birth of her daughter in the new hospital does little to free her from this situation.

Muriel Scaife, a woman who works as a school cleaner while her husband John is on disability leave because of prolonged illness. The couple have a twelve-year-old son (Richard) and an older daughter (Sharon). Richard is clever, studious, and protective of his mother. Muriel's happiness is cut short by John's death. Coming to terms with this loss proves difficult for Muriel, who must continue to defend John to her mother and also support the family financially. In addition, Richard, who is also mourning his father, lapses into sullen uncooperativeness. Muriel's love, fortitude, and almost religious optimism finally effect a reconciliation, however, and she and Richard face an uncertain future together.

Iris King, a middle-aged home help. She lives with her husband, Ted, her daughter Brenda, who is sixteen, and her schizophrenic aunt, Laura. (Two other daughters, Sheila and Lindsey, already have families of their own.) Solidly built, Iris survives on tea, cigarettes, and adrenaline. To some, she appears vulgar, and she is quick to judge and gossip, but she can be counted on in a crisis and is a good neighbor to everyone. Although she works full-time, she keeps her own house spotlessly clean and cares about her reputation above all. Born in the worst part of town, Iris remains emotionally scarred for life by her childhood and is subject to fits of black depression. Because of these experiences, Iris is overprotective of her own children, and, when Brenda's pregnancy presents a crisis, Iris arranges for an illegal abortion to save face.

Blonde Dinah, a sixty-year-old prostitute who picks up men in pubs for whatever they can afford to pay. Although Dinah is physically run-down and lives in a sordid rented room, for men like George Harrison, a retired blast-furnace worker, sex with Dinah is a revelation.

Alice Bell, a widow in her mid-seventies who lives on social security. A staunch socialist, her two main fears remain the workhouse and a pauper's funeral. To avoid these supreme indignities, Alice clings to her independence and forgoes heat and food to save for her funeral. The double shame of poverty and her emaciated appearance at first isolated her from others, but, in time, she has come to trust and depend on the help of caring neighbors such as Iris King, her home help. In turn, Alice serves as a mother figure and discreet friend to many. After a stroke makes Alice even more helpless, her son decides to transfer her to the dreaded nursing home (formerly the workhouse), causing Alice to make one last gesture of independence.

Melanie C. Hawthorne

THE UNIVERSAL BASEBALL ASSOCIATION, INC., J. HENRY WAUGH, PROP.

Author: Robert Coover (1932-   )
Type of work: Novel
Time of action: The 1950's and the "UBA Years LVI and CLVII"
First published: 1968

J. Henry Waugh, fifty-six-year-old accountant for the firm of Dunkelmann, Zauber & Zifferblatt (German for "Obscurantist, Magic & Clock-face"). He is the creator ("J. Henry Waugh" is a play on "Jehovah") of the Universal Baseball Association, Inc., a paper-and-dice game baseball league consisting of eight teams, with twenty-one players each. With throws of three dice, the various combinations representing hits, errors, strikeouts, stolen bases, and other (fifty-six in all) of the standard activities and strategies of a baseball game, he plays out full seasons. He keeps complete records (earned-run averages, most valuable players, and so on) for each season and, in what is now Year LVI of the UBA, he has some forty volumes of records dating from Year IX. Henry's ballplayers, managers, owners, and chancellors become real people to him, and his creation takes over his life. Year CLVII represents either Henry's complete departure from his ordinary existence or the UBA's survival of its creator.

Lou Engel, Henry's coworker. He is a devoted but inept friend, whose corpulence attests his love of good food. He spends every Sunday evening at the cinema. He is the only person with whom Henry tries to share the UBA; however, during the single occasion on which they play, Lou is much more interested in recounting a film he has just seen than in playing Henry's intricate and highly detailed game. True to his name, which is a play on "Lucifer Angel," he messes up Henry's creation by spilling beer on the score sheets and record charts.

Hettie Irden, an aging B-girl. She is Henry's earthy (German *irden*) hetaera. Her lovemaking with Henry is described in the vocabulary of baseball: for example, "pushing and pulling, they ran the bases, pounded into first, slid into second heels high, somersaulted over third, shot home standing up, then into the box once more, swing away, and run them all again."

Horace Zifferblatt, director and sole surviving member of the firm of Dunkelmann, Zauber & Zifferblatt. He is Henry's employer, exacting and intolerant of laxity but not without some patience and consideration. Well aware of Henry's valuable competence, he puts up with Henry's tardiness and absenteeism as long as he can; ultimately, however, as Henry's preoccupation with the UBA causes him to neglect his work completely, Zifferblatt fires him.

Pete, a bartender, whom Henry calls **"Jake"** in his imposition of the UBA world upon the actual world. Jake Bradley is a UBA second baseman who retires to barkeeping.

Mitch Porter, a suave and stylishly competent restaurant owner, who serves Lou and Henry a gourmet meal of duck.

Benny Diskin, the son of a delicatessen owner. He makes regular deliveries to Henry.

Damon Rutherford, a rookie UBA pitcher for the Pioneers team. He is cool, gracious, and superbly talented. After he pitches a perfect game against the Haymakers, his creator (Henry) assumes the Damon Rutherford identity in a night of lovemaking with Hettie. In a game against the Knickerbockers, Damon is fatally beaned by pitcher Jock Casey in accordance with Henry's having thrown three consecutive triple ones with the dice.

Jock Casey, a rookie UBA pitcher for the Knickerbockers. He is gaunt and emotionless. After fatally (and, to all appearances, deliberately) beaning Damon Rutherford, he is himself killed in a subsequent game by a line drive to the mound, as Henry manipulates the death by deliberately setting up a third consecutive dice throw of triple sixes.

Royce Ingram, UBA catcher for the Pioneers. He hits the line drive that kills Jock Casey.

Brock Rutherford, all-time great UBA pitcher

and father of Damon and Brock II. He is fifty-six years old in Year LVI and is in the stands on Brock Rutherford Day when his son Damon is killed by a pitched ball.

Sycamore Flynn, UBA manager of the Knickerbockers and ancestor of Galen Flynn.

Barney Bancroft, UBA manager of the Pioneers. He is murdered after he becomes the ninth Chancellor of the UBA.

Raglan "Pappy" Rooney, UBA manager of the Haymakers, who lives to the age of 143.

Melbourne Trench, UBA manager of the seventh-place Excelsiors and ancestor of Paul Trench.

Hardy Ingram, descendant of Royce Ingram. In Year CLVII of the UBA, he plays the role of Damon Rutherford (equated with good) in the ritual Damonsday celebration.

Paul Trench, descendant of Melbourne Trench. In Year CLVII of the UBA, he takes the part of Royce Ingram in the Damonsday rite.

Galen Flynn, descendant of Sycamore Flynn. In Year CLVII of the UBA, he appears to have been assigned the role of Jock Casey (equated with evil) in the Damonsday rite.

Roy Arthur Swanson

THE UNNAMABLE

Author: Samuel Beckett (1906-1989)
Type of work: Novel
Time of action: The 1950's
First published: L'Innommable, 1953 (English translation, 1958)

The Unnamable, an unnamed disembodied voice seeking evidence of his own existence. He wonders if he has lived, will live, or does live. The Unnamable theorizes he was born of a wet dream in Bally, and he has no body, only syntax. Because he feels occasional pressure on his rump and the soles of his feet, however, he believes he might be seated, per-

haps in a crouched posture, hands on knees. Yet, he cannot move and is unable to blink or close his eyes, though he weeps. He sees only what is in front of him. He doubts that he even casts a shadow but cannot turn his head to see. Believing himself to be round and hard, he variously describes himself as an egg and a big talking ball. If he moves at all, he surmises that he moves in orbits or cycles that return him to his original place, thereby making verification of his movement impossible. His existence depends on words and presumably will cease when his narrative is done. His monologue is a compulsive babble in which he vaguely remembers having been other characters and decides that he will be someone called Mahood, then Worm. He has no sex, no possessions, no biography. He is trapped in time and space and becomes what he creates, for his life is solely the words he utters. He is essentially a mind in search of itself and is preoccupied with his own self-knowledge, although he despairs of knowing anything except in words.

Mahood, a lump who inhabits a jar outside a Paris restaurant opposite a horsemeat shop in the Rue Brancion. In the jar, Mahood seems suspended between life and death, and his only function appears to be as a display for the daily menu. Taken out once a week by the proprietress of the chophouse, he shrinks and sinks lower in the jar as she fills its bottom with sawdust. His head is covered with pustules and bluebottle flies and is shaded by a tarpaulin. Mahood is unable to move his head, for around his neck is a cement ring, a collar fixed to the mouth of the jar and encircling his neck just below the chin. He is able, however, to catch flies with his mouth. Before inhabiting the jar, Mahood returns from a tour abroad in order to visit his wife, parents, and eight or nine offspring. Upon arrival, he discovers his family dead of sausage poisoning, their bodies decomposing. He travels on crutches because he has but one leg and a homologous arm. Mahood is half-deaf and has a poor memory. Growing increasingly armless and legless, Mahood is transformed into Worm.

Worm, an amorphous consciousness evolved from Mahood. Worm is primarily concerned with probing his wormlike state. Worm is not clearly distinguishable from Mahood, because both are but manifestations of the Unnamable's desire for awareness.

Marguerite, also called **Madeleine,** caretaker of the jar. Every Sunday, she rids Mahood of excrement and rubs salt into his scalp. Perhaps because of her kindness, Mahood wonders if he might be related to her. Marguerite adorns his jar with colorful Chinese lanterns.

Basil, a detested fiction of the Unnamable who is rebaptized Mahood. The thought of Basil's face fills the Unnamable with hatred.

Malone, a figure seen in profile only from the waist up as he passes by the Unnamable. Although Malone is recognizable by his brimless hat and beard that hangs down in two twists of equal length, the Unnamable questions Malone's true identity.

Jerry W. Bradley

DER UNTERGEHER

Author: Thomas Bernhard (1931-1989)
Type of work: Novel
Time of action: 1981
First published: 1983

The narrator, an Austrian writer and former pianist from a well-to-do family, suffering from pulmonary disease. As the novel begins, the narrator has just attended the funeral of Wertheimer, one of his two best friends. He stops on the spur of the moment at an inn in the vicinity of his deceased friend's hunting lodge in Upper Austria. Feeling lonely, vulnerable, and somewhat guilty because of his recent neglect of Wertheimer, the narrator attempts to come to terms with his friend's suicide. This attempt leads him to explore the lifelong friendship and competition between him, Wertheimer, and a third pianist,

Glenn Gould, and to review the consequences of that relationship for each of the men's individual biographies. The three men met at the Mozarteum in Salzburg twenty-eight years before, studying under Horowitz. The narrator instantly recognizes Gould's musical genius and, not content to be second best, gives up music and, eventually, his beloved Steinway. The narrator turns to philosophy, although he never really understands what it is, and writing, although he never publishes his work. Eventually, he flees the narrow-minded dilettantism and social corruption he perceives in Austria for Madrid. The narrator is convinced that this change in locale protects him from inborn (Austrian) tendencies toward suicide and insanity, tendencies to which Wertheimer has succumbed. While in Madrid, the narrator starts a manuscript about Glenn Gould. Although he had thought it finally complete, he realizes now that it must be totally revised once again. The narrator's reminiscences are eventually interrupted by the landlady of the inn. From her and, later, from Franz Kohlroser, the narrator learns about Wertheimer's last few weeks of life. He proceeds to the hunting lodge, hoping—in vain—to be the recipient of Wertheimer's notes.

Wertheimer, an Austrian amateur philosopher and former pianist from a well-to-do family, the second of the three lifelong friends. Prone to failure, self-pity, madness, and despair, and suffering from pulmonary disease, Wertheimer is named the loser, or founderer (*der Untergeher*), by Gould. Wertheimer lacks a sense of his own unique identity, striving always to imitate other, more successful people. It is for this reason that his contact with Gould proves to be fatal. Like the narrator, Wertheimer recognizes the greatness of Glenn Gould immediately upon hearing him play at the Mozarteum. He follows the narrator's lead and exchanges his Börsendorf piano for a desk and his music for philosophy, jotting down aphorisms on hundreds of thousands of paper scraps only to burn them all just prior to his death. He writes a book called "Der Untergeher" but revises and corrects it so frequently that only the title remains. Ul-

timately, and in contrast to the narrator, all such survival tactics prove ineffectual. Whereas the narrator puts both physical (Madrid) and psychological (denial of desire to be a virtuoso) distance between himself and his former life as a concert pianist, Wertheimer continues to desire the virtuosity of a Glenn Gould and despairs when he cannot attain it. The immediate reason for Wertheimer's suicide seems to be his sister's marriage, which Wertheimer perceives as personal betrayal and abandonment and which prompts him to hang himself on a tree in front of her new home for revenge. The marriage, however, serves only as the final release of forces that began to destroy Wertheimer the moment he first heard Gould play. Gould's death at the age of fifty-one and at the height of his musical brilliance forces Wertheimer, the same age, to see his life as the failure that it is.

Glenn Gould, a Canadian American piano virtuoso (a real person, not merely a fictional character), the third of the lifelong friends and, like them, consumptive and rich. Described by the narrator as "the most clairvoyant of all fools," Gould is obsessed with making music and displays much of the eccentric behavior, for example constant humming, typical of the actual pianist. His favorite word is "self-discipline" and he is relentless in his pursuit of perfection, which to him means total effacement of the artist as subjective interpreter. Instead of mediating between composer and musical instrument, Gould strives to be the Steinway piano: "*Glenn Steinway, Steinway Glenn.*" After a total of only thirty-four concerts, he withdraws to the seclusion of a recording studio so as to safeguard his performance by any influence from the audience. Gould is most famous for the execution of Johann Sebastian Bach's *Goldberg Variations*, and it is this work that is first heard by the narrator and Wertheimer at the Mozarteum in Salzburg in 1953. It is this work that destroys their aspirations to greatness; it is clear from this point on that Gould is the triumphant one and that the narrator and Wertheimer are failures. The three friends see one another only two times after their summer together, two years later when Gould performs at Salzburg and in 1969 when the narrator and Wertheimer visit Gould for four and a half months in New York City. Thereafter, contact is maintained only through the recordings sent by the pianist to his two European friends. At the age of fifty-one, while playing the *Goldberg Variations*, Gould dies, but for the narrator and Wertheimer he lives on in his music. The final scene of the novel shows the narrator in Wertheimer's room as he plays the record lying ready on the open stereo: Gould's *Goldberg Variations*.

Wertheimer's sister, who lived in Vienna with Wertheimer for more than two decades. During this time he tyrannized her, forbidding her any contact with society and degrading her to a mere page turner. Finally, at the age of forty-six, she escapes her dungeon by marrying a rich industrialist named Duttweiler and moving to Switzerland.

Landlady, owner of the desolate and dirty inn where the narrator stops so as to visit Wertheimer's lodge. Although the narrator finds her to be vulgar and base, Wertheimer had an affair with the landlady. After ignoring the narrator's presence for some time, thereby allowing him extended time to reminisce, the landlady informs the narrator about Wertheimer's strange activities during the last weeks of his life.

Franz Kohlroser, one of Wertheimer's woodsmen. Franz, who has worked on the Wertheimer estate all his life, is worried now that the sister will totally change or even sell it. He provides the narrator a detailed account of events in the lodge during Wertheimer's final stay there. Most important, the narrator learns that Franz helped destroy the numerous notes written by Wertheimer that the narrator had hoped to acquire.

Linda C. DeMeritt

V.

Author: Thomas Pynchon (1937-   )
Type of work: Novel
Time of action: 1898-1956; primarily times of worldwide political crisis
First published: 1963

Benny Profane, a former Navy man and self-styled "schlemiel" who wanders purposelessly the streets of New York, Norfolk, and Malta. His chief activity is "yo-yoing" up and down the East Coast between New York and Norfolk. He has no goals and no value system and is incapable of loving or receiving love. Society around him is decaying, and his wandering simply keeps him continuously in motion to minimize the possibility of reaching a point of equilibrium. His last name, Sfacimento, means destruction or decay in Italian.

Herbert Stencil, son of Sidney Stencil, a British spy who had mysteriously lost his life near Malta in 1919. Herbert spends his life obsessively pursuing the mysterious V. He attempts to make some meaningful structure of the facts he obtains about V. as if he were a nonemotional historian. After searching in the sewers of New York, reading his father's diaries, and interviewing people about V., he avoids the possibility of actually succeeding in his quest, because to do so would end the search and leave him susceptible to the process of entropy.

V., a mysterious woman (and perhaps a place or even a fiction) who appears in various guises and in various places around the world, generally at a moment of crisis and upheaval. Some of her appearances are as Victoria Wren, Vera Meroving, Veronica, and the Bad Priest. She becomes increasingly mechanized and dehumanized, being a closed system subject to entropy with its resulting decay and disorder. She represents a dying society, personifying the forces that have sapped modern humankind's vitality and have made the world's people a "Sick Crew." She also seems to represent Henry Adams' theory of history as a mechanized twentieth century equivalent of Adams' Virgin or Venus.

Victoria Wren, a manifestation of V. as an eighteen-year-old girl in Egypt in 1898. In this guise, her innocence is emphasized, so she is seen as calm and incapable of being aroused by any emotion, as if she embodies some female principle that complements explosive male energy.

Vera Meroving, about forty years old, a manifestation of V. under siege in Africa in 1921. She has a glass eye containing a watch.

Veronica Manganese, a manifestation of V. in Malta in 1919, following the end of World War I. Seen wearing an evening cape and an elaborate bonnet, she has a reputation for being in the company of various revolutionary Italians and for being a wealthy troublemaker.

The Bad Priest, a manifestation of V. in Valletta, Malta, during World War II. Pinned under a falling timber during a bombing raid, she is slowly dismantled by some Maltese children. As V. has become more and more artificial, the children are able to remove a white wig, false teeth, a glass eye, a star sapphire in her navel, and artificial feet.

Mildred Wren, the stocky, myopic sister of Victoria Wren. Though she is plain, she is good. The sisters symbolize the terrible opposition between beauty and humanity.

Fausto Maijstral (mīzh·shträl′), another character that parallels Henry Adams. Both felt themselves moving toward inanimateness; both wrote journals; both recognize the futility of achieving order; and both turn to art in an attempt to save themselves from chaos. He appears in four stages: Fausto Maijstral I, before 1938, is a young man vacillating between politics and the priesthood. Fausto II emerges when his daughter Paola is born.

Fausto III was born on the Day of the 13 Raids of Malta during World War II. More than any other character, he approaches being nonhuman, like a stone. Fausto IV represents a level that reveals a slow return to humanity. An Irish Armenian Jew, he claims to be the laziest person in New York.

The Whole Sick Crew, a group that includes such characters as **Charisma, Fu, Melvin, Raoul** (rä·ōol′), **Winsome, Slab,** and sometimes **Paola.** The "Crew" represents decadence, especially among the younger generation. Purposelessly, they wander from one aimless party to another, indulging in drink and promiscuous sexual relationships.

Hugh Godolphin, explorer and discoverer of Vheissu, a mysterious polar underworld. Apparently a spy, he had engaged in a polar expedition that had been declared a failure, although he had survived. He is fifty-four years of age when he appears in Florence but is almost eighty in South Africa during a Bondel uprising. Father of Evan Godolphin, the two appear to represent a God the Father, God the Son, focusing on the perversion and deterioration of religion in the twentieth century.

Evan Godolphin, son of Hugh Godolphin, a British agent and World War I flying ace. As a youth, he was the leader of a nihilistic group called the League of the Red Sunrise. He is now a liaison officer in his middle thirties, sent on temporary duty with the Americans for some reconnaissance missions. On one mission, the top of his nose, part of one cheek, and half his chin were blown away. When all the physical attributes and his manner of speaking are brought together, there emerges a picture of a Christ figure, thus showing the kind of decadence and deterioration that religion has undergone in the twentieth century.

Rachel Owlglass, a short woman with long red hair that has strands of premature gray. She is a mothering person who, though kind to the Whole Sick Crew, is aloof from its decadence. An association with Rachel in the Bible may be intended. An occasional girlfriend of Benny Profane, she urges him, as a wanderer, to come home. She often pays the way for her roommate, Esther Harvitz, who takes unfair advantage of Rachel's kind nature. At other times, her own decadence comes to the fore.

Esther Harvitz, the twenty-two-year-old roommate of Rachel Owlglass who has plastic surgery to make her look less Jewish. Half the time, she is in control of her life; at other times, she is portrayed as a "victim" type. She habitually depends on Rachel Owlglass for financial support and sometimes borrows things without permission.

Paola Hod, née **Maijstral,** a woman who is separated from her sailor-husband, Pappy Hod. She assumes several identities, including that of a barmaid named Beatrice (possibly to be associated with Beatrice in Dante's *The Divine Comedy*). She is sometimes associated with the Whole Sick Crew; she appears as Ruby, a black prostitute, and may be one of a number of Puerto Rican girls in the novel. She is the daughter of Elena Ximxi, and, at one point, she seduces Mélanie l'Heuremaudit.

Dr. Shale Shoenmaker, an expensive plastic surgeon. He does plastic surgery on Esther Harvitz's nose to lessen her Jewish appearance and also tries to seduce her, emphasizing a trend toward inanimateness and perversion of sex.

Dudley Eigenvalue, D.D.S., a Park Avenue dentist who schedules dental sessions as if there were psychological connections with one's teeth. Ironically, Eigenvalue provides a contrasting figure to Stencil when he points out that the occurrence of cavities in several teeth does not constitute a connection among them, an approach opposite to Stencil's practice of trying to find connections with everything almost to the point of paranoia.

Hedwig Vogelsang, sixteen-year-old surrogate sister of V. who has white-blonde, hip-length hair. She is pursued by Mondaugan.

Mafia Winsome, a New York author who preaches a theory of heroic love that reduces love to lust. Her sympathetic characters are white; her villainous or comic characters are blacks, Jews, and South European immigrants.

Gouverneur "Rooney" Winsome, a native of North Carolina, one of the Whole Sick Crew. He is the husband of Mafia.

Josefina (Fina) Mendoza, sister of Angel and Kook, one of the Puerto Rican kids who urges Benny Profane, a sometime friend, to come home and to get a job. She was once something of a spiritual leader to a youth gang known as the Playboys.

Angel Mendoza, brother of Josefina and Kook Mendoza. He works under the street in the New York sewers with Geronimo.

DaConho, a Brazilian Zionist restaurant-bar chief at Schlozhauer's Trocadero in New York. He wants to fight Arabs in Israel and keeps a machine gun handy.

Mrs. Beatrice Buffo, owner of the Sailor's Grave bar. She hosts a "Suck Hour" from eight to nine on payday.

Beatrice, one of the guises of Paola Maijstral. She is a barmaid in the Sailor's Grave in Norfolk, and is "sweetheart" of the destroyer U.S.S. *Scaffold*.

Cesare, a sidekick of Mantissa. He slashes Sandro Botticelli's painting *Venus*. Sometimes, he thinks of himself as a steamboat and calls out "toot."

Clayton "Bloody" Chiclitz, a munitions king and president of Yoyodyne, a large defense contracting company that was once the Chiclitz Toy Company.

Geronimo, a friend of Angel with whom he works in the New York sewers. He likes to "girl-watch." He is also a friend of Benny.

Mélanie l'Heuremaudit (lər‑mō‑dā'), a

fifteen-year-old dancer whose name means "cursed hour." She is loved by V. and had a romance with her father. Representing the perversion of sex in modern society, she is killed when she is impaled on a pole while performing a dance.

Hugh Bongo-Shaftsbury, an Egyptologist who is wired, representing the increasing mechanization of humanity. He wears a ceramic hawk's head to represent an Egyptian deity.

Father Fairing, a priest, formerly of Malta, now in New York. He preaches Christianity to the sewer rats in Manhattan in the 1930's.

Kurt Mondaugan, a stout, blond engineer at the Yoyodyne plant on Long Island. He had worked in Germany developing weapons and is in South Africa in 1922 working on a project involving atmospheric radio disturbances.

Foppl, a leader in a military effort to put down the Bondel uprising against the Boers in South Africa. He had been with General Lothar von Trotha, who had led a systematic extermination effort against the Hereros and Hottentots in the Great Rebellion of 1904-1907. He held a "siege party."

Andreas, a Bondel beaten by Foppl, representing one of many kinds of destruction that have contributed to the deterioration of values in the twentieth century.

Mr. Goodfellow, a red-faced Englishman in his forties who is a British agent. He is suspected of being a spy because he looks like a street fighter but attends a consulate party.

Hanne Faherze, a stout, blonde, German barmaid described in a Faulknerian manner as possessing a cowlike calm, which is a positive asset in the beerhall where she is continuously around drunkenness, prostitution, and general immorality. She is unable to remove a triangular stain from a plate in a Pentecost-like experience. The name "Hanne" may be associated with Hansen's disease (leprosy), whose symptoms of inanimateness, paralysis, and waste parallel those of modern society.

Vernonica, a sewer rat in New York and possibly another manifestation of V. From what Benny Profane has heard, Vernonica was the only one of Father Fairing's parishioners whom the priest feels is worthy of having her soul saved.

Victoria Price

THE VAGABOND

Author: Colette (Sidonie-Gabrielle Colette, 1873-1954)
Type of work: Novel
Time of action: Six months during the early 1900's
First published: La Vagabonde, 1911 (English translation, 1955)

Renée Néré (nā·rā′), the narrator, a French mime and a dancer. Intelligent and largely self-aware, she divorced her husband after eight years of his adulteries and cruelties and has been struggling to support herself as a music hall performer in Paris for the past three years. She has also been a writer but rationalizes that she can no longer afford the time for writing. She is still an attractive woman at thirty-three but worries that she is aging and losing her good looks. Her bitter marriage has made her determined to keep her independence, despite her sense of loneliness and thwarted sensuality, but when she is devotedly pursued by an admirer, Maxime, she succumbs to his lovemaking and agrees to become his mistress and even wife, after completing an already planned six-week tour of the provinces. She discovers, however, that her free identity and a desire to create with words mean more to her than attachment to any man and breaks with him to remain a vagabond and pursue a career.

Maxime Dufferein-Chautel (dü·fĕr·rän′ shō·tĕl′), Renée's black-haired, long-lashed admirer, with tawny brown eyes and full red lips under his mustache. He is a wealthy, idle man-about-town whose mother runs the family estate in the Ardennes, leaving her youngest son free to pursue his pleasures. Handsome and thirty-three like Renée, he is much more conventional in his notions and far less quick-witted. He wants to marry Renée, settle down, and have children, and, though he tolerates her tour, he disapproves of it. He would prefer to load her with luxuries and cannot understand why she wants to work.

Brague (brä·gü′), Renée's mentor, partner, and comrade in vaudeville theater. Brague is a skilled and ambitious pantomimist, swarthy but with a clean-shaven Catalan face. Although authoritative and sometimes brusque in manner, he is genuinely fond of Renée and provides her with emotional support as well as professional guidance. He has arranged for the French tour and, to Renée's delight, for a South American one to follow it.

Hamond (hà·mōn′), Renée's old friend, a painter. A tall, thin, sickly man, he has also been disappointed by marriage but is not so cynical about love as is Renée. He acts as the go-between who formally introduces Maxime to Renée and encourages her to form a relationship.

Margot Taillandy (tī·yän·dē′), Renée's friend, the sister of her former husband. A warm-hearted woman with bobbed hair turning gray, Margot collects ailing Brabançon terriers to nurse them back to health and helps to support Renée with a monthly allowance to supplement her meager pay. Skeptical of Renée's determination to avoid love, she predicts that Renée must fall in love again because one cannot deny one's senses.

Jadin (zhà·dăn′), an empty-headed, unkempt eighteen-year-old singer, with light brown hair. Jadin has left the streets for the vaudeville theater and has become a success with her artless contralto, though she impulsively runs off with a lover. Just as casually, however, she returns to resume her stage career.

Bouty (boō·tē′), a slender vaudeville comic, with beautiful tender eyes. He is suffering from chronic enteritis and is gradually dying from the strain of performing while ill; he loves Jadin with silent devotion.

Harriet Blodgett

THE VALLEY OF DECISION

Author: Edith Wharton (1862-1937)
Type of work: Novel
Time of action: The late eighteenth century
First published: 1902

Odo Valsecca, cousin to the Duke of Pianura. Odo lives in neglect and poverty until, at age nine, his noble father dies and Odo is introduced to life at the duke's court. The contemplative Odo, influenced by the pageantry of the Church, desires to become a bishop. When the duke's young son becomes ill, however, and the heir-presumptive (the Marquess of Cerveno) dies, Odo becomes the heir-presumptive to the duke's throne. During his education as a nobleman, he learns philosophy, including the teachings of Voltaire, which are banned by the Church. Count Lelio Trescorre befriends Odo, but the Duchess of Pianura warns Odo that the count is really Odo's enemy and wants to discredit him.

Count Lelio Trescorre, the duke's arrogant

comptroller of finance and Master of the Horse. He has made himself indispensable to the court, and his engaging personality, handsome youthfulness, and sharp intellect allow him access to every area of political intrigue. The duchess is beholden to him for paying off her debts, which also made him popular with the tradesmen she had ruined. He immediately wins Odo's trust by engaging him in philosophical discussions. Yet, by letting Odo openly express his views, he endangers Odo to the Church. If Odo is discredited, Trescorre hopes to be appointed Regent of Pianura.

Maria Clementina, the Duchess of Pianura since the age of fourteen, when she married the duke. The fun-loving duchess, excessively rouged and jewelled in the French fashion, is neglected by the duke. She delights in reading books banned by the Church, merely to upset her religious husband. Her extravagant entertaining of all the pretty women and dashing spendthrifts of the court has led her to financial trouble. She is fond of Odo and helps him to escape Trescorre's plot against him.

The Duke of Pianura, a sickly, narrow-faced man, with a slight lameness that makes his walk ungainly. The duke cannot settle on one policy for governing his people. He leans first to one religion, then to another. After three months of marriage, he ignores his wife in favor of his young, pale cousin and heir-presumptive, the Marquess of Cerveno. When the Marquess loses favor with the duke, through

the manipulations of Count Trescorre, the duke takes the Countess Belverde as his mistress. When he realizes that his son is sickly, he sends for Odo, impressing upon him the necessity for strong religious beliefs rather than reform.

The Countess Belverde, a slender and graceful woman notorious for her cruel treatment of those serving her, though she maintains a piety toward the Church. At the court, on behalf of the duke, she entertains the more conservative members of the church and the nobility. The duke gives her a villa at Boscofolto, making her the Marchioness of Boscofolto.

Cantapresto, former primo soprano of the ducal theater of Pianura turned abate of the Church. He is Odo's servant. Cantapresto's acting ability and countless friends reveal to Odo yet another side of life. Cantapresto follows Odo carefully; so much so, that Odo thinks he is a spy.

Carlo Gamba, a hunchback servant at the palace, Count Trescorre's brother, and a member of the outlawed Illuminati. Found by a Jesuit priest at a foundling asylum, Gamba was educated to be a clerk. After the priest's death, the duke gave him as a servant to the Marquess of Cerveno. After Cerveno's death, Count Trescorre obtains a position for Gamba as an assistant to the duke's librarian. Gamba reveals to Odo the intrigues and political structure of the court.

Sandra Willbanks

VEIN OF IRON

Author: Ellen Glasgow (1873-1945)
Type of work: Novel
Time of action: 1900-1935
First published: 1935

Ada Fincastle, later **McBride,** a ten-year-old when the novel opens. Sensitive to people and nature, she instinctively understands that her role in life is to make the best of

every situation. Drawing heavily on the "vein of iron" that is the bloodline of her heritage (beginning with Great-Great Grandmother Martha Tod, who was held captive and married to a young chief by the Indians and then returned to civilized Christianity), Ada has a deep faith in the ultimate goodness of life and in the necessity to accept one's predestined fate. Growing up in Ironside, Virginia, she experiences disappointment, loss, and great happiness. Ada is the moral, financial, ethical glue that keeps the family from falling into chaos. Throughout the thirty-five years of her life that the novel chronicles, Ada is faithful to her heritage, her sense of what is appropriate, and her deeply felt understanding of the strength of love. As the novel ends, she moves Ralph, their son Rannie, and herself back to the manse in Ironside, believing that if they try, they will succeed.

Grandmother Fincastle, John's mother, Ada's grandmother, who is seventy as the novel opens. She is the strength holding the family together in the manse during the era of family poverty after John's dismissal from the pulpit. Deeply religious and a survivor, she believes that the Lord will provide and is content with what life gives. Of her nine children, only John and Meggie have survived to adulthood. Her consistency in activity and belief gives meaning to the Fincastle home. Despite her disapproval of Ada's pregnancy, she assists at the birth of Rannie. She dies after a fall in 1917.

John Fincastle, Ada's father, the fourth to carry the name, a world-renowned philosopher who has lost his pulpit for preaching Baruch Spinoza's god and not Abraham's. He is forty-four years old as the novel begins, unemployed, living in his family's manse, and writing on his (ultimately) five-volume philosophical opus. At the suggestion of Dr. Updike, the family physician and friend, he opens a school in one room of the manse and is able to maintain periodic payments on his insurance and the mortgage. His two years of study in England, mainly in the British Museum, have driven him away from the firm Presbyterian beliefs of his ancestors and mother. A loner for much of his life, he is able to accept things as they occur, even the early death of his beloved Mary Evelyn and the necessity to abandon the manse and move to Queensborough. In town, he becomes a bit more human, develops friendships that were denied to him in Ironside, and even stands with others in the breadlines. When he feels his own death coming, he slips away and returns to Ironside and dies early in 1935 at the manse, alone.

Ralph McBride, Ada's childhood playmate. Ralph is two years older than Ada. His family is even poorer than the Fincastles, but his mother has instilled in him the virtues of work and duty. Ada admires him from the beginning. When Janet Rowan's family accuses Ralph of fathering the child she is carrying and forces him to marry her, Ada is devastated. Ralph returns in 1913 for Mary Evelyn's funeral, and Ada promises to leave with him when he is free. In 1917, he and Ada spend a weekend in a cabin in the mountains, and Ada becomes pregnant. Ralph serves his time in France and comes home a different man, quieter, more morose, less optimistic. Janet divorces him, and now he and Ada are free to marry. Their time in Queensborough is a time of hardship and joy, a mixed bag of success and failure as the Depression forces him from temporary job to temporary job.

Meggie Fincastle, aged thirty-three at the beginning of the novel, John's unmarried sister and the de facto keeper of the house. Like her mother, she is a stabilizing force by virtue of her consistency and insistence on doing things as they must and need be done. Her beliefs are firm and unchangeable. A good Samaritan by nature, she helps whenever and however she can anyone who needs help.

Mary Evelyn Fincastle, a woman in her early forties as the novel begins. She is from similar pioneer stock to that of the Fincastles. Bright, sprightly, overly optimistic, and publicly cheerful, she is the sunshine in an otherwise often-dulled existence. She is slowly dying of an undisclosed illness, which claims her life in August, 1913. Her marriage to John was a good marriage, and his grief at her death and after is genuine.

Dr. Updike, aged forty at the beginning, the Fincastle family physician and friend. He takes care of Mary Evelyn in her illness, suggests to John that he start a school in the manse, and eventually buys the manse when the Fincastles have to leave.

William H. Holland, Jr.

THE VENDOR OF SWEETS

Author: R. K. Narayan (1906-   )
Type of work: Novel
Time of action: The 1960's
First published: 1967

Jagannath (Jagan), a manufacturer and seller of sweets in the mythical town of Malgudi in southern India. A prosperous widower, Jagan has almost reached the age of sixty, when Hindus are expected to enter into a life of detachment from worldly affairs. Deeply imbued with Gandhian values, he reads from *Bhagavad Gita,* lives ascetically, and engages in numerous dietary experiments. Yet, Jagan is a parsimonious and wealthy businessman who secretly counts his earnings in a daily ritual and hides his profits. He makes and sells a product that he thinks is bad for people but rationalizes that he uses the purest of ingredients. Jagan deeply loves his son Mali but is unable to understand or communicate with him. Repeatedly disappointed by Mali's behavior, he lacks the confidence to confront his son and solve the problems of their relationship. When pressed to invest in his son's business promotion, he tries avoiding Mali but finally must abandon his old way of life.

The Cousin, an unemployed man-about-town who survives by sponging off of others and ingratiating himself with his benefactors by offering them advice and the latest gossip. A contemporary of Jagan, The Cousin serves as the primary channel of communication between Jagan and his son Mali, and from him Jagan learns of Mali's plans and behavior.

Mali, Jagan's restless, modernistic son, who abandons his college studies, steals ten thousand rupees from his father's hidden cash box, and flies off to America for three years to learn how to write novels. He returns to India with Grace and tries to persuade his father to invest large sums of money in a joint venture with an American firm, which will create machines that can write stories. Mali has little love or respect for his father, considers his country and countrymen backward, and behaves in scandalously modern fashion.

Grace, Mali's half-Korean, half-American wife. She tries to be a good daughter-in-law and encourages Jagan to support Mali's business plans. Jagan discovers that it was Grace who wrote all the letters he received from America that he thought were written by his son. When Jagan learns from Grace that the couple has never married, he feels that his home has been tainted and isolates himself from both of them.

The Hair Dyer, formerly an apprentice to a master carver of temple statues, who dreams of carving two religious statues to complete his late master's unfinished work. He looks to Jagan to give him the financial support he needs to finish off the project. He supplies the new challenge and phase of life that will permit Jagan to end his old way of life.

Joseph Laker

VENUSBERG

Author: Anthony Powell (1905-   )
Type of work: Novel
Time of action: The mid-1920's
First published: 1932

Lushington, a young British journalist assigned to a nameless Baltic country on the eve of its political upheaval that may result in revolution. Intelligent but inexperienced, he is sorry to leave Lucy, with whom he is in love, but he is nevertheless vulnerable to the attractions of Ortrud Mavrin, whom he meets on the boat. He and Ortrud begin an affair that lasts throughout his stay in the Baltic. Lushington's approach to life is detached and uninvolved, which may explain why he is always at the furthest edges of the news stories he would like to cover. At last, the deaths of Ortrud and his friend da Costa seem to jolt him into consciousness, and, at the novel's end, he may be ready to court Lucy more actively.

Lucy, Lushington's attractive young mistress, a sometime actress. Although Lucy has been married twice, she is not particularly interested in men until, as Lushington's mistress, she meets da Costa, whom she finds attractive. Most of her letters to Lushington urge him to remind da Costa of her existence. Her disengagement is fully as great as Lushington's, however, and, at da Costa's death, she seems passive but willing to accept Lushington as a substitute.

da Costa, Lushington's friend and Oxford schoolmate. Somewhat livelier and more social than Lushington but no less disengaged, da Costa is an honorary attaché at the British legation of the Baltic state where Lushington is assigned. His death as a bystander during an assassination attempt on a military leader leaves Lushington and Lucy once more together.

Ortrud Mavrin, the beautiful and coolly flirtatious woman with whom Lushington falls in love during his foreign assignment. Dissatisfied in her marriage to a distinguished professor of psychology many years her senior, Ortrud has had a series of lovers. She is perfectly aware, however, that she will never leave her husband and child.

Panteleimon Mavrin, Ortrud's complacent but likable husband. Mavrin's knowledge of psychology has done little to attune him to his wife's restless state of mind; when he imagines that she may be in love with someone else, he confides to Lushington that he suspects da Costa.

Count Scherbatcheff, a Russian émigré who is vaguely in love with Ortrud. The numerous maladies from which he suffers at first seem only one more level of agony in an already painful life, but at last those illnesses cause his death, an event that begins to make Lushington and da Costa confront the reality of pain and loss.

Count Michel Bobel, a fraudulent Russian count. He surfaces at every turn, accompanied by disreputable women, borrowing money, and constantly trying to insinuate himself into society. Ironically, Lushington must share a cabin with him on his return voyage to England.

Pope, a valet shared by da Costa and Lushington. Pope is talkative, self-centered, and fond of platitudes. He uses his employers as a captive audience for his dull reminiscences. After da Costa's death, he goes to work for Cortney.

Curtis Cortney, third secretary at the American legation. Cortney has a puppyish enthusiasm for what he conceives to be the "old world" and an adolescent eagerness to believe every cliché concerning Europe and its quaintness; he thus contrasts with his blasé friends Lushington and da Costa.

Ann D. Garbett

VICTORIA

Author: Knut Hamsun (Knut Pedersen, 1859-1952)
Type of work: Novel
Time of action: The late nineteenth century
First published: 1898 (English translation, 1929)

Johannes, the miller's son, later a poet. At age fourteen, Johannes is immersed in nature. Birds, trees, and stones are all his friends. Imagination peoples his small realm with dwarfs and giants, kings and princesses. Emotional and sensitive, he suffers the misery of being the poor boy and servant when Ditlef and Victoria, children from the local manor house, wish to play. Even at fourteen, he adores Victoria, who at ten enchants him with her pretty appearance and gestures. His love for Victoria inspires him to write a series of successful books of love poems. His success, however, cannot clear away the misunderstandings, doubt, and pride that continue to bar his way to Victoria.

Victoria, daughter of the master and lady of the Castle. At ten Victoria is irresistible to Johannes, and as she grows older she becomes more lovely, graceful, and slender. Her deep blue eyes and wide slender brows lure the miller's son. As her childish affection for Johannes matures, Victoria disguises her love to save her mother. While the great success of Johannes and the death of Victoria's wealthy fiancé, Otto, might have freed the two lovers, a lack of frankness prevents their union. Hurt by Victoria's actions, Johannes proposes to Camilla hours before he learns of Otto's death. Misperception continues until Victoria's death, which comes not long after a tubercular attack. Death frees her not to call to him but to write him a letter and admit the depth and constancy of her love.

Camilla, the young child rescued from drowning by Johannes, later his fiancée. Where Victoria is complex, Camilla is simple and childlike. Cheerful, fair, and naïve, she holds no surprises for Johannes. Despite her engagement to Johannes, she falls in love with the uncomplicated and friendly Richmond.

Otto, a chamberlain's son. Wealthy and thoughtless, the young lieutenant is not one Victoria can love. His snobbish actions begin in childhood. The evening before he dies in a hunting accident, the jealous Otto strikes Johannes in the eye "by accident."

Master of the Castle, an improvident, partyloving man who allows the manor house to decline. Dependent upon his daughter's good marriage to restore his fortunes, the master destroys himself and the castle by fire when Otto dies.

Marlene Youmans

VIENNA: LUSTHAUS

Author: Martha Clarke (1944-   )
Type of work: Play
Time of action: The late nineteenth century
First produced: 1986

Vienna, a city at the turn of the century, the "character" that emerges from this group of tableaux, which are arranged so as to overlap, fade in and out, and even to take place simultaneously. The first one opens in a café with a couple waltzing while Hugo and Magda converse about a friend who, it seems, can fly through the air. There follows the description of the toilette of an elderly lady, then a woman's memory of an erotic encounter in India. A mother gives a lecture on deportment; a speaker tells of his daughter being drenched by an ornamental fountain. In an "Orchard Scene," a man carrying a tree branch has a homosexual encounter. A "River Scene" gives an impression of the Danube in the rain. In a return to the first tableau, the same couple speak "out of sync" about a visit to the Hofoper to see *Fidelio* and of the flying friend: a scene taken from Sigmund Freud's *The Interpretation of Dreams* according to the notes. There follows a woman reciting a list of "I don't likes" beginning with Johann Strauss. Streetgirls from Central Europe are listed. An elderly mother contemplates suicide. An anecdote follows of an eccentric aunt who always wanted to be dusted.

A speaker describes a black-and-white butterfly. Another tells of a rat seen in his lodgings: He unsuccessfully tries to strangle it. The whole ends with a discussion with a soldier on death. It is accompanied by music and mime: An old woman throws herself at a young man, nudes pose, a soldier in red is both himself and his horse. The purpose of the whole is to evoke the unconscious world of Vienna, the subterranean world that informed life in that time and place. Freud is omnipresent in the sexuality, in patriarchal figures, and in the association of sex and death. Notes refer to Freud's *Five Letters on Psychoanalysis*.

W. Gordon Cunliffe

THE VIOLINS OF SAINT-JACQUES
A Tale of the Antilles

Author: Patrick Leigh Fermor (1915-   )
Type of work: Novel
Time of action: 1902, as recalled from 1952
First published: 1953

Berthe de Rennes (bĕrt də rĕn), governess of the Serindan family, wealthy landowners living in Saint-Jacques. Berthe is an intelligent and independent-minded seventy-year-old Frenchwoman who is highly respected for her talents as a painter, pianist, and storyteller. At the time of the novel, she is retelling the events of her life when she was a young girl of eighteen fleeing from a poverty-stricken existence in France and settling into Saint-Jacques. As governess, she is privy to the romantic entanglements that develop between the other characters, in particular between Count Serindan's beautiful, young daughter Josephine and Governor Sciocca's son, Marcel. Berthe senses the calamity that will prevail if this love is revealed, for Josephine represents the social class of decorum and grace, while Marcel embodies the newly emerging political cry of liberation. Just as this class conflict is ready to surface, a volcanic eruption decimates the island, leaving, as almost by chance, Berthe as the lone survivor and, hence, the narrator of the events.

Count Raoul de Serindan (rä·ōōl′ də sĕr·ĭn·dăn′), a wealthy landowner whose Beauséjour is Saint-Jacques' most opulent estate. At once the symbol of hedonism and decadence as he parades through the crowds invited to his lavish balls and festivals, he also provides a portrait of a compassionate and sincere man, for, at the end of the novel, he has relinquished his political prejudices, invited the opposing Sciocca family to the Shrove Tuesday celebration, and, in doing so, has created some semblance of peace and goodwill throughout the island. His caring deeds earn for him the unofficial title Mayor of Plessis.

Sosthène de Serindan (sŏs·thĕn′), the count's oldest son, who is quite enamored of his governess, Berthe. While growing up under the tutelage of Berthe, he is well versed in the arts, and, as an adolescent, he falls in love with Berthe, or, more precisely, her charming aura. With the imagination and zest of youth, he hurls himself into the classic role

1656

of the pining lover who wails and threatens suicide, all because of unrequited love. At the end of the novel, he matures into a concerned brother stepping forward in an effort to save his sister Josephine from a doomed elopement.

Josephine de Serindan, the count's oldest daughter. Beautiful and noble, Josephine enters womanhood by falling in love with Marcel Sciocca, son of the rivaling liberal governor. Undaunted by this seemingly hopeless love, she is willing to proclaim her feelings and to sacrifice even her life to preserve them. At the end of the novel, she has decided to meet covertly with Marcel and flee aboard his yacht, where the two lovers intend to marry.

Anne-Jules de Serindan, the count's youngest son. Anne-Jules is a sprightly boy who represents the very best of childhood, in all its wonder. He learns his musical lessons,

tames mongooses, and entertains as a snake charmer.

Valentin Sciocca (sē′ō·kä), the French resident governor of Saint-Jacques. He represents the liberal attitudes that are slowly surfacing and threatening to challenge the traditional customs of the island.

Marcel Sciocca, the governor's son. With somewhat wily flirtations, he awakes passion in young and impressionable Josephine. At the Shrove Tuesday ball, he recklessly ridicules a portrait of Prince Louis and is then challenged to a duel.

British traveler-journalist, provides the introductory framework of the novel. While traveling through Mitylene, he interviews Berthe, inquiring about the almost-forgotten island of Saint-Jacques, and in the process, allows her to record her reminiscences.

Don DeRose

VIPERS' TANGLE

Author: François Mauriac (1885-1970)
Type of work: Novel
Time of action: 1930
First published: Le Nœud de vipères, 1932 (English translation, 1933)

Louis, a dying lawyer who comes to realize that his heart is a knot of vipers. Intelligent, cunning, greedy, unscrupulous, and incapable of love, Louis—as death approaches—writes a letter to be left to his wife. The letter, intended to explain his hatred for her and their children, becomes a diary of his dying days, a record of his life, and functionally an autobiography; ultimately, it becomes a confession of his spiritual journey to Christianity. The document rambles but is always coherent and organized as it records his misery as a miser; in writing it, Louis comes to see his own selfish and evil nature, and he is transformed.

Isa Fondaudège (fōn·dō·dĕzh′), Louis's wife.

Self-sacrificing to Louis and the children, Isa is a remarkably strong person in dealing with such a serpent as her husband. She lives with him by honoring the rule of not having conversation with him about anything important, by being subservient, and by being devoted to the Catholic church and her children. Stable, steady, and always dependable, she never does anything unpredictable in her life, except to shock everyone by dying before Louis.

Hubert, Louis's son, a stockbroker by trade. Cunning, greedy, and unscrupulous, Hubert is a nearly exact replication of his father, though perhaps not quite as smart. His main activity is to prevent Louis from disinheriting Hubert and his sister, and toward that end he contacts Robert, Louis's illegitimate son, and brings his half brother under his influence. These attempts are discovered by Louis, however, and they are ended. At the end, Hubert reads his father's letter only to fail to comprehend it, and he is left filling his father's shoes.

Geneviève, Louis's daughter. Geneviève is Hubert's female counterpart. She helps her brother plot against their father and is one of the little vipers who form this family of serpents.

Janine, Louis's granddaughter, Geneviève's daughter. At twenty-two years old, she is the only member of the family who comes to understand Louis and accept him. As a devout Christian, she forgives Phili, her husband, when he runs off with a music teacher. The family puts her in a nursing home, from which she escapes to be with Louis for the last three weeks of his life.

Robert, Louis's illegitimate son. A harmless store clerk by profession, Robert is too stupid to take Louis's money when it is offered to him as a revenge on Louis's legitimate children and heirs. Louis makes a lifetime settlement on him anyway, much to the dismay of Hubert and Geneviève.

Luc and
Marie, two other children of Louis and Isa. This brother and sister had died in youth; thus, as Louis thinks back on his life, he believes that he really had loved these two. In fact, he had sent Luc off to war to die, and Marie had died, it is suggested, because when she fell ill, Louis had her treated by a cheap practitioner rather than an expensive specialist.

Carl Singleton

THE VIRGIN AND THE GIPSY

Author: D. H. Lawrence (1885-1930)
Type of work: Novel
Time of action: The 1920's
First published: 1930

Yvette Saywell, a nineteen-year-old girl who has just returned home from school. A proud, spoiled girl, Yvette causes friction in the family because she does not take responsibility for her own actions. Like her sister, she is both attracted and repelled by the notion of having a relationship with a man. Because she does not like the "common" boys who are attracted to her, she decides never to fall in love. The candor of this "virgin witch" brings her both admirers and enemies. Because of her longing for freedom, she identifies more with the carefree gipsies than with the members of her own family. After her father reprimands her for visiting the Eastwoods, she becomes hard, detached, and revengeful; only the gipsy is able to reveal the mysteries of love to Yvette, thereby bringing her "back to life."

Lucille Saywell, Yvette's older sister and confidante. Unlike Yvette, this aristocratic-looking twenty-one-year-old not only takes care of household matters involving doctors and servants but also works at a job in town from 10:00 A.M. until 5:00 P.M. every day. Her insolence toward Granny and her belief that a girl should have flings and then marry at age twenty-six have much to do with Yvette's rebellion against her family and her involvement with the gipsy.

The rector, the father of Yvette and Lucille. Heavy and inert, this forty-seven-year-old man is fanatically afraid of the unconventional, which is why he prevents Yvette from visiting the Eastwoods. Although he still worships his departed wife, he is greatly disturbed by Yvette's similarities to this woman.

The Mater, the girls' grandmother, who is the matriarch of the household. Obese, bed-ridden, and nearly blind, this "toad-like" creature never does any harm, but her compulsive desire to control other people's lives interferes with the plans of Yvette and Lucille. After the great reservoir bursts, she drowns in the resulting flood.

Aunt Cissie, the rector's middle-aged sister. This pale, pious woman who eats very little has dedicated her life to serving the Mater. When Yvette steals from the money that Aunt Cissie has collected to commemorate the fallen heroes of World War I, Aunt Cissie's jealousy of the girl's privileged position in the family manifests itself in a torrent of insinuations and verbal abuse.

She-Who-Was-Cynthia, the girls' mother, who ran off years before with a younger man. Her freethinking qualities and blithe carelessness have been transferred to Yvette. Whereas the Mater and Aunt Cissie regard the girls' relation to this woman as a badge of shame, Yvette views her mother as a being from a higher, immortal world.

Joe Boswell, a gipsy who becomes Yvette's lover. Neat and dapper, almost rakishly so, he is, in Major Eastwood's words, a "resurrected man," having barely escaped death in World War I. Unlike Yvette, he is the master of himself and, therefore, is the only person who has any real power over her. At the end of the novel, he rescues Yvette from the flood and from her stifling view of love and sex. She is ultimately saved because of the gipsy's admonition to be brave in heart and body.

Mrs. Fawcett, a rich, Jewish divorcée. This thirty-six-year-old mother of two leaves her husband, a renowned engineer, for a man six years younger than she. Her nonconformist life-style attracts Yvette and repels the rector.

Major Eastwood, Mrs. Fawcett's lover and an admirer of the gipsy. Like the gipsy, he is a "resurrected" man who was literally dug out of the ground by his fellow soldiers. This handsome, athletic man also resembles the gipsy in his disdain for work and in his assertion that anyone who can really feel desire is a king. Because of his relationship with a rich woman who is younger than he, the major is viewed as a "sponge" by the rector.

Bob Framley, Yvette's friend and a member of the big, jolly, unruly Framley family. He accompanies Yvette on her holiday to Bonsall Head and assists in her rescue from the flooded house.

Leo, a friend of Yvette who is described by her as a "mastiff" among the "housedog" boys who court her. He proposes to Yvette, even though he is practically engaged to Ella Framley. It is Leo who honks the horn of his car and thereby brings the gipsy to Yvette's attention.

Lady Louth, friend of the Mater. The Mater insists that Yvette and her friends visit this awful woman during their trip to Bonsall Head.

Uncle Fred, the rector's middle-aged brother. This stingy and gray-faced man eats dinner with the Saywells periodically.

Alan Brown

THE VISIT

Author: Friedrich Dürrenmatt (1921-   )
Type of work: Play
Time of action: The mid-1950's
First produced: Der Besuch der alten Dame, 1956 (English translation, 1968)

Claire Zachanassian, one of the richest and most powerful women in the world and a former resident of Güllen. She is a sixty-three-year-old redhead smartly dressed in black;

a grotesque figure with an artificial leg and an ivory hand. Eccentric and extravagant, she rides around in a sedan chair, carries a coffin with her, owns a black panther, smokes cigars, and picks up and discards husbands at will. Once a wild and vivacious young girl in love with Alfred Ill, she lost a paternity suit against him through his deceit and left Güllen in disgrace to work in a brothel, where she was found by a millionaire. Incredibly wealthy, she has sought vengeance by buying up Güllen and shutting down its progress. Cold and menacing, she offers the town a large sum of money to kill Ill.

Alfred Ill, known as **Anton Schill** in the English translation, Güllen's leading citizen and the town's next mayor. He is a shabbily dressed, overweight, sixty-five-year-old shopkeeper with gray hair. As a young man, he had a passionate love affair with Claire but failed to meet his obligation to her when she became pregnant. Having bribed two witnesses to brand her a whore, he abandoned Claire and married Matilda to get Matilda's father's general store. When Claire offers money for his life, he feels secure that the town will support him. When he sees his townsmen spending lavishly on credit, however, he flees in panic but is stopped at the train station. Betrayed by his friends, stripped of his position of honor, and branded as a criminal, he courageously accepts the responsibility for what he has done to Claire and goes to his death with an air of tragic dignity.

The Mayor of Güllen, stodgy and long-winded. He is always trying to orchestrate events and create the appearance of propriety. Although the first to turn down Claire's proposal on humanitarian grounds, he is later seduced by wealth. Eventually, he threatens Ill to keep silent about the bounty on Ill's life and then gives Ill a gun so that he might commit suicide and save the town the messy business of executing him. Throughout the play, he changes from an inept and bungling politician to a snide and manipulative petty official.

The schoolmaster, a small-town teacher who

has turned down better offers because he has faith in Güllen's potential. The first to see Claire as a sinister figure, he is the one townsman who is truly outraged at Claire's proposal because it goes against all the cherished values of Western civilization. When reporters come to town, he wants to tell them the truth, and he urges Ill to fight for his life. Then, overwhelmed by temptation, he finds himself taking part in Ill's murder. Ironically, he gives a speech condoning Ill's murder as an act of justice, not a crime motivated by greed.

The priest, who has purchased new bells for the cathedral on credit. When Ill comes to him seeking sanctuary, he tells Ill to be concerned about his eternal life, not his earthly one. Strickened by pangs of conscience, he urges Ill to flee, for the temptation to kill him is too great.

The policeman, the town constable. When Ill asks for protection, he uses doubletalk to assure Ill that no harm will come to him, but Ill becomes suspicious of his hedging when he discovers that the policeman has bought a gold tooth. In the end, he takes a self-righteous and brutal attitude toward Ill.

Boby, Claire's eighty-year-old butler, who wears dark glasses. He was the chief justice who ruled against Claire in her paternity suit. She bought his services as a butler and lets him go after Ill is condemned to death.

Koby and
Loby, Claire's two talkative, overweight, and aging eunuchs, who are constantly repeating themselves. They are the two men bribed by Ill to swear that they slept with the young Claire. She tracked them down in Canada and Australia and had them blinded and castrated.

Roby and
Toby, two husky, gum-chewing gangsters from New York who act as Claire's porters and always speak in unison. Roby plays the guitar while Ill and Claire reminisce.

Mrs. Ill (Matilda), Ill's, thin, pale, worn-out, and embittered wife. When the money is promised, she refurnishes the general store and jubilantly buys a fur coat, thinking that everything will work out for Ill.

Ill's grown children, a daughter and a son.

They diligently seek work to aid the family until Claire's proposal drives the son to buy a new car and the daughter to play tennis and study literature. Before Ill goes to his execution, his children, along with their mother, drive out of town.

Paul Rosefeldt

VISITANTS

Author: Randolph Stow (1935-   )
Type of work: Novel
Time of action: 1959
First published: 1979

Alistair Cawdor, a patrol officer in the Australian protectorate of Papua New Guinea. Called **Misa Kodo** in the local pidgen, Cawdor is responsible for all aspects of central administration. His official duties, however, only add to the personal turmoil which has eroded his skill in the islands' maze of custom and responsibility. On the island of Kailuana, he becomes obsessed with an apparent cargo cult which worships extraterrestrial visitors. Considering evidence of spacecraft sightings, Cawdor finds what he considers to be his only chance for salvation: The returning aliens, it is said, will annihilate the "Dimdims" (whites) or will transform them into islanders; either possibility appeals to Cawdor. The one interpretation unbearable to him, that the apocalyptic cult is merely a political upheaval of an all-too-terrestrial kind, proves to be the case. With his hope for redemption dashed, Cawdor commits suicide rather than enforce the flawed and limited kinds of order which he represents officially, culturally, and personally.

Tim Dalwood, also called **Misa Dolu'udi,** Cawdor's nineteen-year-old assistant patrol officer. Although he is hindered by inexperience and ignorance of the local language, Dalwood's innate generosity makes him attractive to both whites and natives. He and Saliba begin an affair—necessarily exploitive and hopeless under the circumstances—which surprisingly develops into genuine

friendship. His enthusiastic study of local customs includes depths and sensitivities which seem uncharacteristic until his self-descriptions are taken as seriously as other characters' opinions of him. At that point, Dalwood emerges as a strong figure, capable of surviving the psychological upheavals of cultural interaction and helpful in directing, along with Saliba and Benoni, the transcultural affairs of modern Pacific society.

K. M. MacDonnell, entitled **MacDonnell of Kailuana** and called **Misa Makadoneli,** a planter who has lived on the island since 1915. The eccentric MacDonnell's cynicism and low expectations cover deep considerations of the personal and cultural interactions in which he participates. In Cawdor, MacDonnell recognizes equal intellectual range, but he is unable to argue the officer out of depression; he sees greater promise in Dalwood, whose open-mindedness and strength remind him of his own youth. At the onset of the native battles, MacDonnell withdraws: His age and position preclude involvement both in the political struggle and in his friend's sad decline.

Naibusi, MacDonnell's housekeeper and former lover. Rumored to maintain MacDonnell's security through sorcery, she is in fact a most alert witness to the complex interactions of natives and administrators. Her comments upon Cawdor's self-destructiveness and

Dalwood's assumption of authority provide a good measure of the whites' situation.

Saliba, Naibusi's teenaged assistant. Attracted to Dalwood, she nevertheless realizes that her prospects lie entirely on Kailuana. Although repelled by the whites' conduct—particularly when Dalwood kisses her in public—she is even more saddened by the violence among the natives; she ends the uprising by killing Metusela. Along with Benoni, Saliba represents a new, hopeful relationship between administrators and islanders.

Benoni, Dipapa's nephew and rightful heir; he has lost his position by having an affair with one of the chief's wives. Educated off the island in white-run schools, Benoni feels less threatened than most others by the values and customs of the whites. While his transcultural accommodation—not assimilation—continues to bring alienation and insecurity, Benoni proves to be a capable leader in the restructurings which follow the violence.

Dipapa, chief of Kailuana. Ancient, nearly immobile, yet still revered and powerful, Dipapa instigates the native violence through Metusela. His exact motive is not revealed; perhaps he desires to create proper conditions for the return of the "starmen," but he may want only a last show of force.

Metusela, the prophetic, possibly insane leader of the cargo cult and a provoker of violence. It is suggested, though not proven, that Metusela is actually Taudoga, the disappeared leader of a violent coup on another island. The spiritual basis of his nativist movement may be qualified by a simple lust for power.

Osana, a government interpreter. Unscrupulous and manipulative, Osana is detested by all on Kailuana. As the only character fluent in both English and the island dialect, his power lies in the ability to play one side against the other through threatened mistranslation.

Kailusa, Cawdor's servant. Pathetic and physically deformed, he is utterly reliant upon Cawdor; he commits suicide shortly after the death of his benefactor.

John Scheckter

THE VIVISECTOR

Author: Patrick White (1912-   )
Type of work: Novel
Time of action: c. 1900-1970
First published: 1970

Hurtle Duffield Courtney, a renowned Australian artist. He is sold at a young age to the wealthy Courtney family by his impoverished, prolific parents, the Duffields. This commerce in a human being provides the novel's main metaphor: Hurtle will be bought and sold many times more as an accomplished artist. Hurtle brings great hope to the Courtneys, who have one handicapped daughter; they throw all their energies into making Hurtle a suitable heir. Even at a young age, however, the selfish, egotistical qualities surface that will later contribute to his artistic genius. Hurtle ruthlessly uses people for his own artistic purposes: His family, friends, and lovers all provide fodder for his vision. Ironically, his quest is for purity and simplicity, a search for the color of God. As an artist, Hurtle is an iconoclast, tearing away at the pretensions and hypocrisy of the art world. To that end, he turns to the gritty, seamy, even grotesque side of life in order to produce his paintings. Hurtle has many affairs with women, all of which end badly because he uses and emotionally abuses them. Still, Hurtle is never entirely despicable: His honesty, although brutal at times, is admirable.

Alfreda Courtney and
Harry Courtney, the wealthy couple who adopt Hurtle. Alfreda is a pretentious, selfish woman who insists on Hurtle's calling her Maman and who exhibits incestuous tendencies toward him. Harry is a decent man and would dearly love to get close to his son but, in his blundering, male way, cannot.

Rhoda Courtney, the hunchback daughter of Alfreda and Harry, Hurtle's adoptive sister. Rhoda is intelligent and sensitive; as a child, she both resents and adores Hurtle. Her brother is repulsed by her, even though she also fascinates him: Her deformed body becomes his first artistic victim and his earliest artistic triumph. To a certain extent, Hurtle also fears Rhoda: She is perceptive enough to understand much about Hurtle and blunt enough to make him uncomfortable. When he finally leaves the Courtneys behind, Rhoda is the one person he misses. Many years later, he comes across Rhoda by chance. She has become a bag lady, collecting stinking horseflesh by day so she can feed street cats by night. Hurtle, as if to purge himself of guilt for his earlier treatment of Rhoda, persuades her to move in with him. Because Rhoda remains the one person who is completely honest with Hurtle, and from whom he has no secrets, they develop an extraordinary relationship. Rhoda provides Hurtle with both inspiration and exasperation.

Nance Lightfoot, a simple, warmhearted prostitute. Hurtle carries on an extended affair with Nance, whose amply endowed body provides him with fresh forms for his paintings. He transforms her curves into rocks and cheeses and enters upon a successful and productive period in his career. As much as he cares for Nance, however, he refuses to become attached to her. Ultimately, her accidental/suicidal death jars him into some belated self-reflection and humanity.

Olivia Davenport (Boo Hollingrake), a wealthy woman, a patron of the arts and a friend to both Rhoda and Hurtle. She first became acquainted with the Courtneys when she was a girl named Boo, and she is, in fact, Hurtle's boyhood crush. She surfaces again after many years as a socialite named Olivia who throws elegant dinner parties and collects Duffields even though she secretly despises them. She rejects Hurtle as a lover but tries to procure him for her own friend and lover, Hero Pavloussi. Olivia is charming and superficial and knows it, which is why she patronizes Hurtle.

Hero Pavloussi, Hurtle's lover, Olivia's friend, the wife of a wealthy Greek shipping magnate. Hurtle is attracted to petite, dark, exotic Hero but is also repulsed by her tragic Greek air. Theirs is a mutually destructive relationship: He uses her for his artistic needs and she lures him on a futile, depressing trip to Greece. Hero is victimized by herself as much as she is by Hurtle.

Kathy Volkov, a brilliant young pianist, Hurtle's neighbor and lover. In his old age Hurtle finds himself attracted to and seduced by the nubile young girl next door. She becomes his final source of inspiration and the one female capable of hurting him. When he first comes to know her, Kathy is all braids and limbs; still, she is not sexually shy. As she matures and achieves fame as a concert pianist, she discards Hurtle in selfish pursuit of her own goals. In Kathy, Hurtle comes up against an ego as large and ruthless as his own.

Susan Whaley

VOICES IN TIME

Author: Hugh MacLennan (1907–   )
Type of work: Novel

Time of action: 2039-2044, with flashbacks to the twentieth century
First published: 1980

John Wellfleet, the narrator, age seventy-six, a former hippie and teacher and the survivor of the "clean" bombs, which destroyed civilization. During the rebuilding of Metro (Montreal), the Wellfleet-Dehmel papers are discovered and André Gervais asks John Wellfleet to put them in order. The papers reveal the history of the twentieth century. Happy in his rediscovery of the past and his usefulness to a new generation, John dies in a cottage near the Gervais family.

André Gervais, a young French Canadian, discoverer of the papers, discoverer of John, and representative of the new generation eager to rebuild a civilization connected with the best the past can offer. He befriends Wellfleet, discovers his body, and narrates his death. Their friendship represents the renewed linking of the generations and the transmission of history and wisdom which results.

Timothy Wellfleet, John's older cousin, an advertising man and host of the 1970's television show *This Is Now*. Child of divorced parents and shaped by the novel *Catcher in the Rye*, Timothy rejects his conventional suburban life and family and his success in advertising for Esther Stahr and television. Apparently criticizing the capitalist system, his abrasive show is really a safety valve for it. Unprincipled showmanship leads Timothy falsely to accuse Dehmel of Nazism and leads to his murder. When Timothy discovers that his show has been canceled and his victim is the husband of his foster mother, he is distraught and disappears.

Esther Stahr, the Jewish coproducer of *This Is Now* and Timothy's mistress. Realizing Timothy destroys public men simply to entertain, she leaves him and the show before the Dehmel debacle.

Colonel Wellfleet, Timothy's father, a war hero and an archetypal male WASP of the Eisenhower period, rich, bewildered, and irrelevant in later decades.

Stephanie Wellfleet, John's mother, Timothy's foster mother, and the wife of Conrad Dehmel, a gentle, loving woman.

Conrad Dehmel, the second narrator, a German Egyptologist and historian. His narrative, written in German, is addressed to Stephanie and tells of his childhood in Freiburg with his gentle mother and grandfather, both musicians and cultured Europeans, of his father, a naval officer, and of his younger brother, Siegfried, a fanatical Nazi. Conrad foolishly marries stupid Eva Schmidt and takes her to England, where he is studying. The marriage fails. Subsequently he falls deeply in love with Hanna Enlich, a Jewish woman. In spite of her warnings, he returns to Adolf Hitler's Germany, where he is trapped, becoming director of an academic institute and working for an anti-Gestapo intelligence service. Finally he joins the Gestapo to help the Enlichs escape, but Eva Schmidt recognizes him and betrays him to her husband, Heinrich. Conrad breaks under Gestapo torture. The Allies liberate Dehmel from Belsen; he comes to North America and marries Stephanie. He appears on *This Is Now* to warn Canadians that casual violence, the manipulation of the economy and the society by hidden powers, and the absence of principle and restraint signal a civilization's collapse. When Timothy accuses him of Nazism, Dehmel walks off the show, but a Jewish viewer, confusing him with Heinrich, subsequently shoots him.

Hanna Enlich, Conrad's mistress, a cellist and member of the Jewish intelligentsia. Hanna returns to Nazi Germany as a Red Cross official to help her interned father. Though Conrad arranges their escape, they are captured and the Gestapo confronts them with Conrad. Understanding that under torture he has revealed their whereabouts, Hanna's last act is to explain they had already been captured, so the betrayal is unimportant.

Rear-Admiral Dehmel, Conrad's father, a

gunnery officer, technocrat, and unthinkingly obedient patriot. He is shattered by the defeat of 1914-1918, shamed by the Treaty of Versailles and seduced by Nazi promises. Though promoted in the rebuilt navy, he becomes disillusioned with Nazism. Accused of being privy to the officers' plot against Hitler, he is killed and his wife is taken by the Gestapo. He represents the German officer class.

Jocelyn Creigh Cass

VOLUNTEERS

Author: Brian Friel (1929-   )
Type of work: Play
Time of action: The 1970's
First produced: 1975

George, the site supervisor. A pompous, rather unlikable man, he has the most contact with the diggers. Nevertheless, he refuses to be entertained by their antics or concerned with their troubles. Most of the time he literally looks down upon them from a temporary office built above the excavation site. He is in constant conflict with Keeney.

Mr. Wilson, the guard. Professing a great understanding of criminal behavior, he is a no-nonsense, ostentatiously tough man in his sixties. Despite his loudly voiced concern over issues of crime and punishment, he is not a strong presence in the play: When he does appear, he is preoccupied with his young daughter's musical examination.

Des (Dessy the Red), an archaeology student. Nicknamed by the diggers, he is a serious young leftist of twenty. He likes to think of himself as more closely allied to the prisoners on the dig than to the professionals who supervise it. His small gestures of camaraderie—buying cigarettes and newspapers for the men—prove to be the extent of his aid to them, as he consistently fails to live up to his political and professional ideals.

Knox, a prisoner on the dig. A dirty, shambling man of sixty-five, but looking older, he is noteworthy among the men for his smell and his ill temper. He is frequently the butt of Keeney and Pyne's jokes. Reared in a fabulously wealthy and privileged home, he was left poor and useless after his father's death.

He subsequently found money and companionship as a message carrier for political subversives.

Butt, a prisoner on the dig. He is a solid, quiet man in his late forties, from the countryside. He looks after Smiler and is the only man on the dig who develops an objective, intellectual interest in the archaeological work. Throughout the play he is a model worker and a foil to the irreverent Keeney. It is Butt who makes the most significant gesture of rebellion when he smashes a highly valuable jug which is the prize find on the dig.

Smiler, a prisoner on the dig. In his midthirties, Smiler is a harmless, childlike man, appearing most of the time in a ridiculous tasseled hat, made an idiot by torture in prison. His disappearance from and later return to the dig precipitates Keeney's confession to the other diggers that they are marked for assassination by their fellow political prisoners. Smiler will, on occasion, begin speaking in his former idealistic voice before lapsing into vacuity.

Keeney, a prisoner on the dig. A sharp-tongued, energetic man in his forties, Keeney—along with his sidekick Pyne—keeps up a running series of jokes, insults, and limericks through much of the play. Once a leader in the Nationalist movement, he is the man who persuaded the others to join the dig, despite the threat of retaliation from the other political prisoners, and until he makes his revelation he is the only one who knows that they will all be killed. Keeney is obsessed with the Viking-era skeleton of a murdered man found on the dig and makes up a series of stories about the reasons for this man's death.

Pyne, a prisoner on the dig. A man in his thirties, he is a devoted follower of Keeney,

joining him and imitating him in his bantering. Pyne is less certain of himself than Keeney, however; sometimes even he is confused by Keeney's joking, and even more confused by his outbursts of anger. Finally, Pyne will have difficulty distinguishing Keeney's serious statements from his irreverent ones.

Heidi J. Holder

VOSS

Author: Patrick White (1912-   )
Type of work: Novel
Time of action: The 1840's
First published: 1957

Johann Ulrich Voss, a German immigrant to Australia, a botanist with a desire to become famous as an explorer during the golden age of nineteenth century exploration. Voss possesses the will of a Nietzschean superman, and he has settled on the goal of being the first to cross the Australian continent. Inspired by a historical figure, Ludwig Leichardt, whose obsession with crossing the Australian desert led to his death, the author presents Voss as a humorless and passionate idealist who sees the conquest of the Australian territory as both a personal triumph and a victory for the human spirit. Despite a natural arrogance and the fanatical dedication of the truly obsessed, Voss, a slender man with enormous capacities for planning and endurance, captures the imagination of many who meet him, including the Bonner family. Laura Trevelyan, Bonner's niece, finds him fascinating while resenting his pride and self-sufficiency. He wins her respect and undeclared love, and on his expedition, he believes he communicates with her telepathically. In the desert, Voss is betrayed by some of the members of his expedition and dies a tragic death, but not before learning a humility that softens his indomitable will. After Voss's death, his tragic enterprise is gradually transformed into a heroic legend, which Laura helps to create and perpetuate in her work as a teacher.

Edward Bonner, a Sydney merchant who has made a small fortune mainly through the sale of cloth. He is a stolid middle-class businessman who helps to finance Voss's expedition, though he does not fully understand why he is attracted by Voss's vision. Bonner enjoys being a patron and hopes that fame as well as financial advantage will result from Voss's venture.

Laura Trevelyan, Bonner's niece, who lives with the Bonners but is the family nonconformist. A beautiful young woman who is somewhat intellectual and contemptuous of conventional men, she has chosen to reject her childhood Christianity and considers herself a rationalist when she meets Voss; he perceives that she is in reality a believer with a concern for humility and compassion. Fascinated by his vision and drive, she falls in love with him, though neither she nor Voss will openly avow this passion. During his absence on the expedition, she writes long letters to him expressing her love and, like Voss, imagines that she communicates with him telepathically. After Voss's death and the failure of his quest, she chooses to live as a spinster and gains fame as a schoolmistress, while helping to create the legend of his heroism.

Harry Robarts, a simple young man who

follows Voss out of an inarticulate devotion and out of gratitude, because Voss treats him as a person of importance. At twenty, Robarts is physically strong but rather quiet and without intellect. He is willing to follow Voss to the end and in fact dies with him in the interior desert of Australia.

Frank Le Mesurier, another of Voss's faithful followers on the expedition, though he has seldom stuck to any purpose before he met Voss. A relatively young man, he has worked at several jobs in Australia without staying long at any, and he has even published a volume of indifferent verse. Though he has artistic ambitions, or pretensions, he has been a dilettante, lacking commitment to work or vision. Attracted to Voss because the German has an assurance of the significance of his vocation that Le Mesurier lacks, he hopes to find himself on the wilderness trek. Though he refuses to desert Voss, he is unable to sustain his courage when captured by a tribe of aborigines, and commits suicide.

Albert Judd, a former convict, now emancipated and a respectable farmer, is a responsible and steadying influence on the expedition. A strong and sensible middle-aged man, Judd has been tempered and humbled by his harsh years of penal servitude. Essentially, Judd is a man of material reality and common sense, and, despite his kindness toward Voss, finally mutinies after the death of Palfreyman, considering the expedition to be hopeless.

Palfreyman, a kindly but boring ornithologist who goes on Voss's expedition out of scientific curiosity. Constantly abstracted and devoid of egotism, Palfreyman practices a kind of benign Christian charity until murdered by an aboriginal tribesman.

Ralph Angus, the son of a wealthy landowner. He goes on the expedition seeking adventure and self-respect. Fairly honest, Angus finds that he is ultimately a practical man and becomes a friend of Turner, a former alcoholic and the least dedicated member of the expedition. Somewhat reluctantly, Angus follows Judd when the latter rebels against Voss.

Turner, supposedly a reformed alcoholic, who is primarily a man of the senses, experiencing life in the simplest epicurean terms. Somewhat reluctantly, Turner joins the expedition hoping to find his fortune, but his gross and vulgar views often annoy the others, even when they find them entertaining. Turner readily joins Judd's mutiny and abandons Voss to his fate.

Dugald, an elderly aboriginal guide who barely understands English. Entrusted by Voss with some important letters, including a love letter to Laura, Dugald sets off for the outpost of Jildra. After meeting some other tribesmen, he is persuaded to tear the letters to pieces and scatter them to the winds.

Jackie, a young aboriginal guide who accompanies Voss and his two remaining companions to their final encounter with a tribe of cannibals. Though Jackie feels bound to Voss by some inexplicable magic, he readily allows himself to be adopted by the tribe; to show his loyalty, he finally works up the nerve to murder Voss, and somewhat sullenly, Jackie cuts off Voss's head while the latter is sleeping.

Edgar L. Chapman

THE VOYAGE OUT

Author: Virginia Woolf (1882-1941)
Type of work: Novel
Time of action: c. 1906
First published: 1915

Rachel Vinrace, the twenty-four-year-old protagonist, an intelligent and sensitive but only informally educated young woman. She plays the piano beautifully and has considerable musical talent but is socially innocent and naïve, with a weak face and a hesitant character. An only child, she has led a very sheltered life, having been reared primarily by her two spinster aunts, her mother being dead and her father, Willoughby, a shipping magnate, being a very busy man of affairs. She has been kept ignorant of relations between men with women. When introduced through her aunt and uncle into the society of Santa Marina, which consists of a group of Englishmen vacationing at the local resort hotel, she meets and falls in love with Hewet after a series of encounters initiated by an afternoon climbing expedition and later a ball, culminating in their engagement during an expedition by boat up the river into the jungle. The main plot of the novel revolves around Rachel's metaphorical "voyage out" from innocence to experience, from her initially naïve and unreflective state to a greater intellectual sophistication, her first experience of love, and finally her death from a fever, possibly contracted on the journey up the river.

Helen Ambrose, Rachel's aunt, forty years old, tall and beautiful, not well educated formally but widely read and socially sophisticated. She and her husband, Ridley, a Cambridge scholar working on an edition of Pindar's odes, have left their two children with the grandparents in order to spend a winter and spring away from England at her brother's villa in Santa Marina, a coastal resort town in South America, presumably in Brazil. Having become interested in her niece during the literal "voyage out" to Santa Marina on the ship of her brother-in-law, who has business on the Amazon, she invites Rachel to stay with them rather than continue the voyage with Willoughby. Helen sets herself the task of helping Rachel learn about life and developing her character.

Terrence Hewet, who becomes Rachel's suitor and eventual fiancé, a young man with literary tastes who is vacationing in Santa Marina with his friend Hirst and attempting to write a novel. He is twenty-seven years old, tall and rather stout, with glasses. The only son of an English gentleman, he attended Winchester and then the University of Cambridge for two terms before leaving to travel, having an independent income (his father died when Hewet was ten) sufficient to allow him not to work. His role as the organizer of the climbing trip first brings him and Rachel together. Hewet is initially presented as a somewhat superficial character but becomes more sympathetic through his love for Rachel.

St. John Alaric Hirst, a friend of Hewet, twenty-four years old, a scholar and a Fellow of King's College, one of the most distinguished young intellectuals in England. He is in Santa Marina trying to decide whether to continue at the university or to become a lawyer. Young but unattractive, already stooped and very thin, he is uncomfortable with women and does not seem to get along well with Rachel. Helen initially has the plan of recruiting him to help with the project of her education by recommending books to her. He is attracted to both Helen and Rachel and for a while imagines that Rachel has fallen in love with him. His cynical nature is softened by the novel's end by his observation of his friends' love and by Rachel's affecting death.

William Nelles

A VOYAGE ROUND MY FATHER

Author: John Mortimer (1923-   )
Type of work: Play
Time of action: The 1930's to the 1960's
First produced: 1970

Father, a barrister in London. An antisocial man who takes refuge in his beloved garden every time a visitor threatens to disturb him, he seems sincerely to pity his son for having to go visit someone. Father collects the earwigs caught in his garden traps every evening and drowns them. His garden is his true passion, and the law is merely a way to earn a living—though he is very good at what he does. He is blinded from an accident while pruning an apple tree, yet he refuses to acknowledge that he is blind. His visual blindness also epitomizes his emotional blindness: He refuses to allow any emotional closeness between him and his son or him and his wife. A confusing yet fascinating character, it is not certain whether he has had several mistresses and smoked opium. He gets along with his grandchildren better than with his son.

Mother, a housewife. She caters to Father after he is blinded, taking care of him completely, even cutting up his food, but she never acknowledges his blindness either. She panders to her husband's every whim, including making marmalade, even though she hates doing it. She does not seem to be very sentimental or emotional; when her young son starts to cry, she apparently cannot believe or accept it. She is living in a rut, but one in which she means to stay. When she speaks about what she will do when her husband dies, she says she will stay in her home, because "someone has to see to the marmalade." Her main concern seems to be that no improper subject be discussed in general conversation.

Boy and
Son, a character who has two physical dimen-sions. He is called "Boy" when he is very young and "Son" when he is an adult. As a boy, he is bewildered and hurt by his parents' emotional aloofness. When he cries, his father merely tells him to say "rats," on the premise that "no one can cry when they're saying the word 'rats.' " When the boy is sent away to school, he finds that the school world is even stranger than home—complete with shell-shocked teachers who hallucinate that enemy attacks are taking place in the classroom and throw books at their students. The main facet of the young man's character is that as he evolves from a boy into an adult, he loses his softer side until, at the play's end, his wife, Elizabeth, accuses him of exhibiting the same inability to deal with seriousness that his father has.

Miss Cox and
Miss Baker, a lesbian couple who run a bookstore. The son makes friends with them while he is home during World War II. During a conversation, the women automatically assume that the son will join the Fire Service and become a writer, because that is what all their friends do.

Elizabeth, a scriptwriter who becomes the son's wife. Elizabeth is a beautiful brunette who is married when the son first meets her. She writes film scripts as part of the war effort. Elizabeth is an honest, open person; she disapproves of the mother, son, and father's charade about not mentioning his blindness. She is unhappy about the way her husband seems to have inherited his father's lack of being able to cope with serious issues.

T. M. Lipman

VOYAGE TO TOMORROW

Author: Tawfiq al-Hakim (1898-1987)
Type of work: Play
Time of action: The late 1950's and 309 years later
First published: Rihlah ila al-ghad, 1957 (English translation, 1984)

The first convict, a prominent physician and son of a physician, sentenced to death for murdering a patient, the husband of a woman with whom he falls in love. Although he has confessed to this crime of love at his trial, he later protests that the woman, misrepresenting her husband's character, encouraged him to kill the husband and, after they were married, betrayed him by establishing a relationship with his own defense attorney. He is obsessed with his wife and would like nothing better than a few minutes alone with her, he tells the prison doctor, to strangle her. When cut off from Earth (act 2) on the rocket trip and later when the rocket crashes (act 3) on a strange planet (where electrical charges, and not blood and hearts, energize him and his fellow space traveler), he still believes in emotions and in good and evil and treasures memories. Back on Earth (act 4), love remains important to him and causes his reincarceration at the end of the play.

The guard, who talks briefly with the first convict at the beginning of the play when the latter, expecting to face execution any day, is pacing back and forth in his cell nervously.

The prison doctor, respectful of the first convict's scientific knowledge and accomplishments in medicine, although he does not believe the latter's story about his wife's collusion with the defense attorney.

The warden, who visits the first convict twice (in act 1) to announce that his wife has come to see him and then that he may have a reprieve from his death sentence if he agrees to a proposal by the representative of a scientific agency. Upon accepting the proposal, the first convict is not thereafter allowed to see his wife.

The representative of a scientific agency, who comes to the first convict with a top-secret proposal, a scientific experiment consisting of a manned rocket to be sent into outer space with little chance of the men on board returning or surviving the journey. The first convict agrees to participate in the experiment as preferable to his imminent execution.

The second convict, the first convict's companion on the rocket (in act 3), an engineer specializing in electrical and atomic sciences. He too feels that death on the rocket is pref-

erable to death on earth. He had been sentenced to death for the murder of four older wealthy wives after being caught planning to do the same with a fifth wife. He married all of them for money to finance a beneficial engineering project. He also does not believe the first convict's story about his wife's collusion with the defense attorney. On the strange planet, the second convict worries about a life without work, events, and a future, and suggests suicide. The first convict's suggestion that they repair the rocket and attempt to return to Earth lifts his spirits. At the end of the play, he notes that the first convict has not changed in the three-hundred years that they have been away—and that the latter is again going to prison because of a woman.

The voice from ground control, which announces (in act 3) to the first and second convicts, as their rocket hurtles through space, that their contact with Earth will cease at five million miles' distance from Earth, in three minutes' time.

The first convict's wife, on the first convict's mind throughout the play but appears only on the strange planet (act 3), a realm where mental telepathy is possible, when the first convict is able to conjure up her image and show her, projected as if on a screen, to the second convict.

The blonde woman, assigned to the first convict when he and the second convict return (at the beginning of act 4) from outer space after three hundred years. As a member of the party of the future, she is suited to the second convict, who believes in materials and technological progress and attaches no importance to love. They will likely spend the rest of their lives together.

The brunette woman, assigned to the second convict. As a member of the party of the past, she is better suited to the first convict, who falls in love with her. She will likely treasure his memory once they are separated and he is sent in her stead to prison because of politically dangerous ideas stemming from a belief in the value of love.

The security man, sent with the robot, both in strange attire, to arrest the first convict and the brunette woman for having subversive thoughts and to give them a choice between "rays," by which their thoughts will be changed, and isolated confinement in the City of Quiet. They immediately choose the City of Quiet. Then, the first convict grapples with the security man when the latter tries to take the brunette woman away.

The robot, who accompanies the security man in his visit to the first and second convicts and the blonde and brunette women.

The voice from headquarters, which orders that the brunette woman be taken to the City of Quiet alone but then agrees to let the first convict take her place and finish his reports on his trip in space.

Michael Craig Hillmann

WAITING FOR THE BARBARIANS

Author: J. M. Coetzee (1940-   )
Type of work: Novel
Time of action: The late nineteenth or early twentieth century
First published: 1980

The Magistrate, an administrator of a territory belonging to an unnamed empire. The story's first-person narrator, an aging and somewhat decadent man, he explains that he has lived in the remote settlement for decades, where he has haphazardly and inefficiently carried out his administrative duties on behalf of the empire. Although he admits to his laziness, his fondness for young native girls, and his satisfaction with the old ways of imperialism, he still emerges an admirable and sympathetic character. When he comprehends the full extent of the cruelty condoned by the new regime that is determined to save the empire at any cost, he regrets his initial compliance with the Third Bureau's orders and rebels, then becomes a prisoner himself. At the same time, he searches for some significance in his own wasted life. In the light of the novel's allegorical overtones, the character of The Magistrate represents all men and women who face not only their inherent weaknesses but the forces of totalitarianism as well. At the story's conclusion, The Magistrate simply goes on living, however uneasily, and continues his struggle to find a clear pattern in the complexities of life.

Colonel Joll, an official in the mysterious Third Bureau, an arm of the Civil Guard that was created to protect the empire threatened by barbarians. This young officer specializes in torture and interrogation. An elegant sort with affectations in dress, manner, and speech, the colonel has come to terms with the demands made by the forces of evil set loose by a desperate government. Unlike The Magistrate, Joll does not question, only acts. Ultimately, though, he encounters defeat at the hands of the barbarians.

Warrant Officer Mandel, an assistant to Colonel Joll. He is a younger version of his superior officer: handsome and vain, sophisticated, cruel, spiritually vacuous, and, above all, blindly committed to the cause he serves. For The Magistrate, a man with a conscience, he feels neither sympathy nor pity. He displays his true colors by fleeing when it appears that Colonel Joll will not return from his expedition into the wilderness.

A young native woman, a victim of Colonel Joll's torture. She is stocky in build, quiet and long-suffering in nature, an innocent amid corruption. Blinded and crippled during her interrogation, she is rescued by The Magistrate, who nurses her to health, seduces her, and attempts to use her as a kind of expiation for his own part in the activities of the Third Bureau. The young woman gains a measure of nobility in her suffering.

Robert L. Ross

A WALK IN THE NIGHT

Author: Alex La Guma (1925-1985)
Type of work: Novel
Time of action: The 1950's
First published: 1962

Michael Adonis, a man of mixed race, in South African racial terminology "coloured"; in segregated Cape Town, he must live in the notorious District Six. He works irregularly and hangs about in cheap cafés, generally unemployed and existing on the fringes of crime. Although dressed in worn clothes, he moves with an air of jaunty, brash self-confidence. Fired for exchanging racist slurs with his white manager, he drinks himself into a mood combining bravado and self-pity. While drunk and burning with accumulated racial hate, he visits a white resident of the quarter, an old man, and murders him. Adonis rushes away, at first shocked and sobered by his horrendous yet futile crime. With a mixture of elation and hysteria, however, he soon rationalizes his deed and joins with real criminals in plans for an armed robbery. The story ends with Adonis cheerful and confident about his violent future.

Willieboy, another café lounger. In his dress and manner, he endeavors to present a smart image, taking pride in a prison sentence for assault. Nevertheless, he is as impoverished in money and spirit as the rest of his street acquaintances; he exists on menial jobs and small handouts. His background is commonplace: a mother who beats him without provocation to vent her frustration against his father, who, when drunk, straps both of them. He accidentally finds the body of the murdered old white man. Instinctively reacting to the rule that no nonwhite, even if innocent, should ever risk being involved with the law, he runs away but is recognized by the other tenants. Following their description, the police find him. He is cornered and shot. While dying, he has a final illumination that lives such as his are doomed from the start.

Constable Raalt, a policeman. Angry, tense, and arrogantly racist, he is indifferent to police regulations and legal restraints. Constant quarrels with his wife regularly reinforce his visceral rage and indicate its neurotic origin. Even his partner fears and deplores his pathological antagonism toward blacks. With threats, Raalt forces the tenement witnesses to identify Willieboy. Searching the streets, he triumphantly encounters his suspect and drives him into an alley. His more sensible partner is horrified when Raalt deliberately draws his revolver and shoots to kill, but he fears to challenge him. Even then Raalt refuses to call an ambulance, conversing at a café while his prisoner bleeds to death in the van.

Uncle Doughty, an aging Irishman, technically white, alcoholic and diabetic, married, illegally, to a nonwhite woman. Drink, malnourishment, and disease have ruined a once-handsome face. His skin is puffy and gray, his nose reddened, his teeth yellowed, his head bald. Once a recognized actor who played theaters in Great Britain and Australia, he now lives from one day to the next in a tenement legally reserved for "coloureds." From his rambling memory of playing Hamlet's father comes the title of the novel. Adonis kills him by smashing his head with a wine bottle.

Joe, one of the sad young people who live on the streets. His intelligence is low, but his nature has a strange sweetness. He has run away from home and manages to survive on the scraps the fishermen leave. Adonis is his hero because he has treated Joe kindly. In his halting way, Joe perceives and articulates deep truths, and his warning against Adonis mixing with the violent criminals is both wise and well-intentioned.

John Abrahams, a tenement dweller. He is induced by Raalt to describe the man he saw running from the murder. Other tenants violently abuse him for giving away anything to the hated police. He uses the familiar self-defense: that to survive one must not provoke authority.

John F. Povey

A WALK ON THE WILD SIDE

Author: Nelson Algren (Nelson Ahlgren Abraham, 1909-1981)
Type of work: Novel
Time of action: The early 1930's
First published: 1956

Dove Linkhorn, a red-haired, six-foot illiterate from Arroyo, Texas. After a brief affair with Terasina Vidavarri, he rides a freight train to seek his fortune in New Orleans. Convinced that anything can happen to someone who can make words from letters, Dove projects unsophisticated country innocence, but his principle of living is to do violence to anyone who tries to push ahead of him. On Perdido Street in New Orleans, Dove walks on the wild side with prostitutes, pimps, con artists, condom manufacturers, and petty criminals. With a pair of con artists, he joins a coffee-selling scam and a free beauty-treatment scam; later he assists a manufacturer of condoms and peddles salves while wearing a white suit with a pink-striped shirt, yellow suede shoes, and a hat with a matching yellow feather. In partnership with master pimp Oliver Finnerty, he becomes Big Stingaree, corrupter of supposedly innocent girls for a peep show. In Finnerty's house, Dove is scorned by Achilles Schmidt and attracted to Hallie Breedlove, both of whom figure prominently in his life. Dove is drawn to Hallie by a book; the two go away and live together during an idyllic period while he learns to read and questions her about history, until his insecurity about his ignorance dissolves and she secretly departs carrying his child. Caught in a raid back at Finnerty's, Dove spends time in jail, where he observes that he has found only suffering and degradation, but that those with the greatest troubles are always the ones most likely to help. After his release he is beaten and blinded by Schmidt. At the end of the novel Dove, feeling his way with a cane, returns to Arroyo seeking Terasina.

Fitz Linkhorn, Dove's father, a wild man of Scottish descent. Widowed with two sons, Fritz is reduced to cleaning cesspools and becomes a self-styled preacher. Estranged from his older son, allowing his younger son to grow up illiterate because the school principal is a Catholic, Fitz depends for inspiration on a whiskey bottle in his hip pocket as he harangues the townspeople in the square, preaching against vice and creating dire images of damnation for an audience that considers him crazy.

Byron Linkhorn, Dove's elder brother and Fitz's primary antagonist. Disillusioned and angry, wasting from tuberculosis, Byron straddles the cannon on the town square and taunts Fitz as he preaches. He dies during Dove's absence.

Terasina Vidavarri, the thirty-year-old Mexican owner of a run-down hotel, formerly a brothel. After holding herself aloof from men since a youthful experience with a brutal ex-soldier, Terasina is overcome by Dove's innocence. She has a brief affair with Dove and shares with him a picture book before telling him to leave.

Hallie Breedlove, a prostitute who is one-sixteenth black but lives as white. Tall and aloof, Hallie is a former schoolteacher once married to a white man who left her when their black child was born. After the child's death, Hallie turned to prostitution, but she has never accepted Finnerty as her pimp. Before Dove comes, she is Schmidt's lover.

Achilles Schmidt, a man with a powerful torso whose legs were severed by a train. A former wrestler and carnival worker, he moves about on a wooden platform mounted on skates. As a wrestler, Schmidt retained a gentleness, and as an embittered, legless cripple he scorns Dove's crude performance in peep shows. Violently angry over the loss of Hallie, he beats Dove unconscious and then calls for help. Schmidt is destroyed when onlookers send him and his platform thundering downhill until it crashes into a pole.

Kitty Twist, a seventeen-year-old runaway with straight brown hair. When Dove meets Kitty on the way to New Orleans, she leads him into a robbery from which he escapes while she is caught and sent to jail. Later,

when Kitty reappears in New Orleans with Finnerty, she is antipathetic toward Dove.

Oliver Finnerty, master pimp at Mama Lucille's. Shrewd, brutal, and arrogant, he claims to be five feet tall in cowboy boots and looks like an Australian fox with enormous ears. When one of his girls displeases him, he beats her on the nape of the neck, where bruises do not show.

Mama Lucille, technically a maid because the law forbids a black woman to manage a house employing white prostitutes, but actually the madam at Finnerty's house.

Rhino Gross, an obese, weak-eyed former obstetrician. With his wife Velma, Gross manufactures condoms in a back room covered with reddish dust. Dove briefly works as an errand boy for Gross and Velma and learns from their shrewdness.

Mary Ellen Pitts

THE WALL

Author: John Hersey (1914-   )
Type of work: Novel
Time of action: November, 1939, to May, 1943
First published: 1950

Noach Levinson, the ghetto archivist and historian, the "recorder" of the events of the novel. A small man in his early forties, Levinson is a messy-haired, intense intellectual, whose face is dominated by eyes made great by the magnification of steel-rimmed glasses. At times, the self-educated former shoemaker is cynical, even bitter about his poor family background, unattractive appearance, and lack of ties to his fellowman. He eventually finds human warmth and happiness, however, in the extended family of the ghetto. Levinson comes to serve as both the eyes and ears of the Warsaw Jewry, for he not only writes about what he sees, but he also listens unselfishly to those who need a sympathetic ear. With his fervor for Jewish literature and

sense of conviction, he comes to be regarded as ghetto orator as well. As the Nazi atrocities intensify and Levinson becomes monomaniacal about preserving the archives, he finally becomes the very creator of Jewish memories and thoughts. The ultimate turnaround in the character of the scholarly Levinson comes when, inspired by dedicated young Jews, he fights as a soldier of Israel. Then, almost a year after escaping through the sewers to safety, Levinson dies of pneumonia.

Dolek Berson, a thirty-two-year-old jovial, talkative drifter who becomes a highly responsible leader in the Jewish resistance. A big, gentle, but impatient man and a gifted pianist, he has reacted against his parents' demands for his high personal achievement as a way of meeting the German threat. Instead, he has restlessly followed a number of occupations, moved for a time with a company of tramps, and finally settled down to a life of ease and prosperity with his beautiful wife, Symka Berson, on his patrimony. As Nazi pressures increase, he works first as a bricklayer on the construction of the wall and then as a ghetto policeman. Gradually aligning himself with the radical resistance movement, he becomes firm, purposeful, and self-motivated. He proves to be a genius at finding safe routes and hiding places and maintaining lines of communication within the ghetto. As coordinator of such networks, Berson is equally esteemed by all factions of ghetto Jews as a humane genius who meticulously serves his fellow man. His bold defiance of his captors with guerrilla concerts on the concertina inspires his compatriots with a will to survive even as he is inadvertently left after their rescue to die in the sewers.

Rachel Apt, a serene, intelligent, well-proportioned young woman who, in spite of her ugly, parrotlike face, with its large nose and eyes set close together, rises to a position of leadership in the Jewish community because of her competence and boldness. Before the Warsaw ghetto years, she is totally overshadowed by her beautiful sister, Halinka Apt Mazur, whom their father obviously favors. After being painfully separated from her young brother, David Apt, Rachel experiences a brief period of vacillation and moodiness before finding a housemother position, in which she can fulfull her instinct for mothering. Once she goes into underground work, she is dubbed "Little Mother" of the Jewish Fighter Organization (Z.O.B.). Admired for her modest, fearless, kind, and selfless spirit, she sets the emotional tone for the whole group. As a group commander, she plays a profound role in the resistance. Near the end of the ghetto period, she has an affair with the widower Dolek Berson, which gives her a sense of freedom and happiness that, because of her ugly face, she might have never known under more pleasant circumstances.

Halinka Apt Mazur, the beautiful, fragile, flirtatious daughter of a wealthy Jewish defector who is attracted to men of power but marries a strong, handsome youth, Stefan Mazur, who is a Jewish ghetto policeman. After becoming a courier for the resistance and the mistress of the Hashomer leader, Zilberzweig, she suddenly ages and hardens in her will as well. Once dependent and submissive, she becomes obdurate in dangerous work outside the ghetto.

Mauritzi Apt, a prominent Jewish jeweler and art collector who attempts to buy favor for his children and finally escapes from the ghetto himself after undergoing plastic surgery to reverse his circumcision.

Pavel Menkes, a forty-year-old tall, somewhat rotund, jovial Jewish baker who devotes his services to the underground late in the resistance movement and dies fighting with the Z.O.B.

Rutka Mazur Apt, wife of Mordecai Apt and a Jewish courier on the Aryan side who gives birth to a son, Israel, in an underground bunker. A resourceful, lively, optimistic woman, she retains hope for the survival of Jewry even after her baby has been smothered in the bunker by a Z.O.B. leader because he cannot be quieted at a crucial moment.

Symka Berson, the attractive, delicate wife of Dolek Berson, who barely hangs on to life for a long period after suffering a serious case of typhus, only to be betrayed to the police by the quota-seeking Stefan Mazur, a member of her own extended ghetto family.

Janie Caves McCauley

THE WALL JUMPER

Author: Peter Schneider (1940-   )
Type of work: Novel
Time of action: The 1980's
First published: Der Mauerspringer, 1982 (English translation, 1983)

The narrator, an author who has lived in West Berlin for the last twenty years. Fascinated by the divisions and similarities between the two Berlins, he decides to write about someone who breaks the barrier separating East and West Berlin, a "wall jumper." He moves back and forth between the two cities, visiting friends and hearing their stories of such jumpers, which he blends into various fantasies. He discovers that each government molds the thought processes of its inhabitants to suit its peculiar social system. In the end, he finds that he cannot jump the wall inside his own mind.

Robert, a poet who has emigrated to West Berlin from East Berlin. A neighbor and friend of the narrator, he adapts quickly to life in his new home precisely because he is a Berliner. He has a cynical distrust of authority, finding a subtext in every act and a plan behind what seems to the narrator simple chance. He tells the narrator the stories of Mr. Kabe and Walter Bolle.

Lena, a former girlfriend of the narrator. She emigrated to West Berlin from East Berlin in 1961. During their relationship, she was suspicious of his absences and eventually became suspicious of everyone. He accompanied her on her first return visit to her family and realized she needed the security she had left on the other side of the wall. She meets with the narrator briefly in the present but talks mainly to Robert. The narrator is left to fantasize a one-sided conversation with her after she leaves.

Pommerer, an author living in East Berlin. He tells the narrator the stories of the three teenage cinema-goers and of Michael Gartenschläger. After signing a letter protesting a fine levied on a fellow author, he discovers that his telephone is often out of order and begins to think about leaving East Germany.

Gerhard Schalter, the narrator's first landlord in West Berlin. He claims that he is involved with a West German television correspondent based in Africa who wants to take her child and live with him but is prevented from doing so by her husband. As he loses hope in the future of that relationship, his appearance grows shabbier. He takes trips to East Berlin, where he discovers cheaper goods and friendlier people. Finally, he moves there.

Mr. Kabe, a welfare recipient in his midforties who becomes famous as a "border violator." Using a pile of rubble as a staircase up the wall on the West Berlin side, he jumped into East Berlin. He was imprisoned for three months and then returned to his home. After a vacation to Paris, paid for by the three months of welfare checks waiting for him, he returned and jumped again. The process was repeated. Following a failed attempt by the West German government to institutionalize him, he went on to jump the wall fifteen times.

Willy Wacholt,
Willy Walz, and
Lutz, three teenage boys who live close to the wall in East Berlin and jump it to see motion pictures in West Berlin. They love Westerns but not the West, at least not enough to emigrate during their twelve visits. The two Willys are apprehended at school after authorities read a West Berlin news account of their travels. By chance, Lutz escapes when a showing of *High Noon* in an East Berlin suburb is canceled and he goes to a late show in West Berlin. Wacholt is put in the army and Walz into a labor camp; Lutz becomes a lumberjack.

Walter Bolle, a border violator and spy. After being imprisoned for seven years for illegal border crossings, he was ransomed by West Germany in 1973 for 50,000 marks. Motivated by a desire to revenge himself on East Germany and to destroy the wall, he becomes a spy for the West against the East. Later, to magnify his revenge by means of disinformation, he also becomes a spy for the East against the West.

Michael Gartenschläger, a radical wall jumper who defaced the wall soon after its erection and burned property in East Berlin in protest of the wall. His freedom was purchased by the West German government after ten years in prison. He helped many people escape, but his greatest coup was dismantling two self-triggering robots that spray shrapnel at wall jumpers. While attempting to dismantle a third, he was shot by East German border guards.

Dora, the narrator's aunt in Dresden, a small, vivacious woman who lives in privileged, upper-middle-class surroundings. In telling the family history, she provides a link and a contrast between the old and new Germanys.

James W. Jones

THE WANDERERS

Author: Ezekiel Mphahlele (1919-   )
Type of work: Novel
Time of action: The late 1950's to the 1960's
First published: 1971

Timi Tabane, a black South African journalist who becomes an exile. Tabane, sensitive and idealistic, lives in the slums of Tirong, a black township in South Africa, and writes for the magazine *Bongo*. In Tirong he meets Naledi Kubu, a young woman who is convinced that her husband has been murdered at a slave farm labor camp. Risking arrest, Tabane travels with her to investigate the case. After publishing his exposé, Tabane, discouraged by the mild public response and disheartened by the prospects of progress in South Africa, leaves the country illegally. He accepts teaching positions in Iboyoru (Nigeria) and Lao-Kiku (Kenya), but he is deeply dissatisfied with the rootlessness of his existence and concerned by the rebelliousness of his eldest son, Felang. Ironically, Felang's death gives Tabane hope for the future, indicating to him that the younger generation may find a more assertive and effective path than he has.

Felang, Tabane's eldest son, who is killed with other African nationalist guerrillas by white farmers. Felang refuses to follow his parents' advice and runs away from home to join a rebel group that is fighting the South African government. He is murdered by white South African farmers along the border, and his body is thrown to the crocodiles. Felang shares his father's idealism but represents the new radicalism of African youth who are unwilling to wait for slow change.

Karabo, Tabane's wife. Beautiful, intelligent, and dignified, Karabo is unswervingly loyal to her husband, following him throughout his wandering exile, but she also demonstrates considerable independence. Her stamina, courage, and refusal to accept oppression or to allow it to beat her down make her an admirable complement to Tabane.

Steven Cartwright, Tabane's friend and the white editor of *Bongo*. Cartwright is Tabane's white counterpart. Repelled by the racism of his country, Cartwright struggles to disengage himself from his racist heritage. His love for the black woman Naledi is a conscious rejection of the code he has been taught. Like Tabane, Cartwright becomes disenchanted with the prospect of progress in South Africa, chooses exile, and suffers from a sense of homelessness. Cartwright marries Naledi but is killed while covering the Biafran revolution in Nigeria.

Sheila Shulameth, a white novelist who has an affair with Steven Cartwright. Although sympathetic to the plight of black Africans, she is still tied to the racist heritage that Cartwright seeks to escape. She represents the materially comfortable life that he abandons.

Naledi Kubu, a young black woman whose husband dies after enforced farm labor, who eventually marries Cartwright. At first, Naledi is a simple country girl, but her struggle to discover the truth of her husband's fate, her cautious initial rejection of Cartwright's advances, and her eventual marriage and exile turn her into a strong, sophisticated woman. After Cartwright's death, Naledi decides to stay in London and pursue a degree in nutrition.

Rampa Kubu, Naledi's husband, who is forced into slave labor. Tabane and Naledi discover that Rampa has been shanghaied, beaten, and dismissed before dying. Rampa exemplifies victims of South African racism, victims so numerous that their individual stories cause little concern.

Kofi Awoonor, the famous African author and Tabane's mentor in Iboyoru. Awoonor is an example of Mphahlele's tendency to mix historical and fictional characters. Tabane looks to Awoonor for inspiration and guidance.

Emil, Tabane's Austrian friend in Iboyoru. Emil is a companion with whom Tabane can commiserate about the subtle torments of exile.

Carl Brucker

WAR AND REMEMBRANCE

Author: Herman Wouk (1915-   )
Type of work: Novel
Time of action: 1941-1945
First published: 1978

Victor "Pug" Henry, a career naval officer serving as a captain at the outbreak of World War II. Deprived of a battleship command when the Japanese sink his ship at Pearl Harbor, Henry commands the USS *Northampton,* a light cruiser in the Pacific fleet, and participates in the Battle of Midway. He returns to shore duty, where his close association with President Franklin D. Roosevelt leads to his assignments in various posts both in Washington, D.C., and abroad, handling sensitive political and military matters. He travels to Russia to assist Harry Hopkins in negotiating Lend-Lease matters with Josef Stalin before returning to sea as a rear admiral in charge of a battleship division. His division participates in the historic battle of Leyte Gulf in the Philippines. During these turbulent years, Henry is struggling to salvage his marriage to his wife of a quarter century, and to deal with his growing feelings of love for his younger British friend, Pamela Tudsbury. Eventually, the Henrys are divorced, and Victor marries Pamela shortly before becoming naval aide to president Harry Truman.

Rhoda Henry, married to Victor Henry for more than twenty-five years but growing increasingly disenchanted with the marriage as she passes her fiftieth year. While her husband is at sea or abroad serving during World War II, Rhoda keeps house in Washington, D.C., participating in the limited social life there. For some time she agonizes over her relationship with businessman Palmer Kirby, with whom she has had an affair. She then meets Colonel Harrison Peters, whom she marries after divorcing Victor Henry.

Natalie Jastrow, an American Jew, thirty years old, living in Siena, Italy. Though married to Byron Henry, she stays with her uncle, noted historian Aaron Jastrow, who refuses to leave Siena despite advice to evacuate before the Nazis make it impossible to leave. Natalie finally persuades her uncle to leave, but because he is well known and she has her child with her, they are easily identified. She makes repeated attempts to engineer a return for all three to U.S. custody, but she finds herself being taken further into the Nazi circle: First they are detained in Italy, then they land in Germany, and eventually they are assigned to the Germans' model concentration camp at Thieresenstadt; there Natalie is coerced into working to trick representatives of the International Red Cross regarding the Nazis' real program for Jews. She is separated from her son and shipped off to Auschwitz, but she is rescued when Germany surrenders; after recuperating in Paris, she is reunited with Byron.

Pamela Tudsbury, assistant to her father, a noted journalist, and later assistant to Lord Bourne-Wilke of the British Air Corps. A woman of thirty, Pamela has fallen in love with fifty-year-old Victor Henry. She witnesses the fall of Singapore and is in North Africa when her father is killed. Unable to marry Victor, she becomes a military assistant in the British war effort. Her postings take her to both Moscow and Washington, D.C., where she meets Victor to renew her relationship. She is engaged briefly to Lord Bourne-Wilke, but his death from war injuries frees her just as Victor is divorced. She moves to Washington, where she realizes her ambition of becoming Mrs. Victor Henry.

Byron Henry, the second son of Victor Henry and a submariner in the Pacific fleet. Though married to Natalie Jastrow, he is separated from her and tries repeatedly to get reassigned to the European theater so that he may help her escape the Nazis. Aboard ship, he proves

a highly competent officer, becoming executive officer and eventually commander of a boat. Prolonged separation from his wife and repeated trips to his widowed sister-in-law's test his fidelity, but he manages to remain committed to his wife. After hostilities end, he is able to go to Europe to locate his missing child and reunite his family in Paris.

Aaron Jastrow, a noted historian. In his sixties, he believes that his status as an American will protect him from the Nazis' attempt to round up all Jews in Europe. He relies on a former student of his, Werner Beck, to protect him, only to learn that Beck is attempting to get him to collaborate with the Nazis. He is shipped off to various detention areas and at Thieresenstadt is beaten into submission and made to work for his captors. When he is no longer of use to the Nazis, he is shipped to Auschwitz and sent to the gas chamber.

Warren Henry, Victor Henry's eldest son, a career naval officer. Warren's assignment aboard the aircraft carrier USS *Enterprise* places him in the thick of the action at the Battle of Midway. He distinguishes himself in combat but is killed in the final sortie of the engagement, leaving behind a widow and a young son.

Madeline Henry, the Henry's only daughter and their youngest child. Just over twenty, she has secured a lucrative position as assistant to radio personality Hugh Cleveland, but the star's amorous advances put off her family. She eventually sees that this relationship will go nowhere; she returns home and takes up with an old beau, Simon Anderson, a naval officer. The couple marry and are transferred to Los Alamos, New Mexico—the site of the atom bomb testing.

Berel Jastrow, a prisoner in the Nazi concentration camp at Auschwitz. Though over sixty, Jastrow is healthy and cunning; he manages to get a job on a work crew and becomes involved in collecting evidence on atrocities at the camp. At an opportune moment, he escapes and makes his way first to the Soviet

Union and then to the West, where he delivers evidence to authorities who are able to make public the horrors of the Germans' treatment of Jews.

Werner Beck, a German diplomat. Formerly a student of Aaron Jastrow in the United States, Beck makes several gestures to guarantee the Jastrows their safety from persecution. He is intent on securing Aaron's services as a collaborator who can assure the world that the Nazis are not monsters; when Jastrow balks, Beck finds pressure being put on him, especially from Adolf Eichmann.

Harrison Peters, an Army colonel in his mid-fifties. Peters is a ladies' man in Washington, where he works on the top-secret Manhattan Project. He falls in love with Rhoda Henry and marries her when she is divorced from Victor. He plays a significant role in assembling the men and material for the successful testing of the atom bomb at Los Alamos.

Palmer Frederick Kirby, a widower in his fifties. An independent engineering consultant and manufacturer, Kirby helps the government build the successful atom bomb. After having an affair with Rhoda Henry, he sees the relationship die when she refuses to divorce her husband; he gives up his romantic interests and devotes his full efforts to the wartime effort.

Simon Anderson, a Naval Academy graduate and former classmate of Warren Henry. Working on research projects in Washington, Anderson makes the most of an opportunity to resume his courtship of Madeline Henry; they marry, to the delight of the Henry family. At work, his talents are recognized by superiors, who assign him to projects that involve him in nuclear research. As a result, he is reassigned to Los Alamos to assist with the testing of the first atom bomb.

Janice Henry, the wife of Warren Henry and the daughter of U.S. Senator Isaac LaCouture. She and her infant son reside in Pearl Harbor, Hawaii, while Warren is at sea. She is crushed by the news of Warren's death at Midway but stays in Hawaii to help the war effort. She has an affair with Carter Aster, whom she met through her brother-in-law Byron, but keeps the news from Byron because it becomes clear to her that he needs her emotional support in his struggle to learn the fate of his wife and child in Nazi Germany.

Carter ("Lady") Aster, a naval submarine officer. A fearless and clever warrior, Aster takes over the submarine from his inept commanding officer and establishes a reputation throughout the Pacific fleet for his exploits in sinking enemy ships. Ashore he takes up with Janice Henry, Warren's widow, though he has no genuine love for her. He is killed by enemy aircraft while his submarine is surfaced in hostile waters.

Armin von Roon, a major general in the German army. His assignment on the German General Staff places him in a position to witness the exploits of Adolf Hitler from close proximity, and his account of World War II from the Germans' perspective, written while he is imprisoned for war crimes, is interspersed with the story of the Henry family to give a portrait of grand strategy and to render a retrospective assessment of the growing derangement of Hitler as the war progressed.

Alistair Tudsbury, an internationally renowned British correspondent. His radio and newspaper accounts of the war outline the demise of the British empire. He is present at the fall of Singapore and is killed by a land mine while out with the British forces in North Africa.

Leslie Slote, an American diplomat. Formerly Natalie Jastrow's lover, he works to get Natalie and her uncle free from German control. As a result, he learns of the atrocities at the concentration camps and attempts to make the news public. Stymied by superiors, he becomes frustrated and quits the U.S. State Department; he joins the Office of Strategic Services and dies in France in operations incident to the D-day invasion.

Sammy Mutterperl, a Jew confined to Auschwitz. Because Sammy has earned the trust of his Nazi captors, he is allowed to lead a work crew; he recruits Berel Jastrow for his work party. Together they build many of the structures that will be used as gas chambers, all the while planning a breakout. Sammy dies trying to escape, after killing several of his guards.

Branch Hoban, a naval officer and commander of the submarine on which Byron Henry is serving when he sees his first combat. Though a stern disciplinarian and able commander in training, Hoban cracks under the pressure of combat and is relieved at sea by his executive officer, Carter Aster.

Philip Rule, a minor U.S. State Department official. Originally posted in Europe when World War II breaks out, he is eventually transferred to the Far East and is in Singapore when the Tudsburys arrive for a tour of British defenses there. He attempts to rekindle his old romance with Pamela Tudsbury, almost succeeding as he catches her in a weak moment when she is sure that she has lost Victor Henry forever.

Raymond Spruance, a naval rear admiral (later vice admiral) who commands the U.S. forces at the battle of Midway and later serves as Chief of Staff for Pacific Forces. Spruance shows exceptional courage and skill in managing naval forces at Midway, and prudence in the heat of battle, a trait that earns for him little respect from junior underlings but the grudging admiration of senior officers.

William "Bull" Halsey, a naval vice admiral and the hero of the American fleet in the Pacific. Sidelined with illness that keeps him from commanding the forces at Midway Island, Halsey takes the U.S. task force against the Japanese at Leyte Gulf in the Philippines; Victor Henry commands one of Halsey's battleship divisions there. Halsey's actions appear rash and chaotic to some of the senior officers, though the U.S. emerges victorious.

Adolf Eichmann, the Nazi officer responsible for implementing Hitler's plans to exterminate the Jews. He crosses paths with Natalie and Aaron Jastrow on several occasions, culminating in a meeting at the model camp at Thieresenstadt, where the Nazis try to persuade the International Red Cross that they are treating the Jews kindly. Eichmann brutalizes both Jastrows into cooperating with his scheme.

Laurence W. Mazzeno

THE WAR BETWEEN THE TATES

Author: Alison Lurie (1926-   )
Type of work: Novel
Time of action: 1969-1970
First published: 1974

Brian Tate, a political science professor at Corinth University in upstate New York. Born to a long line of social achievers, forty-six-year-old Brian is a dissatisfied and disappointed man. Because it is clear that his greatest accomplishment is to hold an endowed chair at a second-tier university, he suffers discontent in realizing that he will never be famous and important. While working on a new book, he is seduced by one of his students, Wendy Gahaghan, who convinces him that a physical relationship with her will abet the success of the book. After his wife, Erica, discovers the affair early in the novel, Brian agrees to break off the relationship. He does not quite do so, and Wendy eventually shows up in Erica's kitchen, crying and pregnant. Brian is then kicked out of the house by his wife, with whom he is reunited at the end.

Erica Tate, Brian's wife, a homemaker. Conservative, well-read, and alert, Erica's actions are usually guided by a sense of moral righteousness, a holdover from her Presbyterian childhood. Erica accepts Brian's initial affair with Wendy, but only on condition that he break it off. A few months later, Wendy visits Erica to apologize for her crimes against Erica and blurts out that she is pregnant. Erica takes Wendy under her own care, orders Brian to leave the house, then helps Wendy secure a then-illegal abortion. During Brian's absence from the house, Erica attempts an affair with Zed, a 1960's guru who runs a metaphysical bookstore. Her attempt fails, and at the end she invites Brian to come home.

Wendy Gahagan, Brian's student and mistress. Truly a flower child, something of a hippie, and gullible, Wendy serves the vague and naïve idealism of the era. She convinces herself that she is sacrificing herself to the arts and to humanity by repeatedly offering herself to Brian, and she becomes pregnant by him. Acting under pressure from both Brian and Erica, she has an abortion, only to become pregnant a second time at the end of the novel. (Brian may not be the father this time.) She is last seen heading west to join a commune with a young man who is her equal in gullibility.

Danielle Zimmern, Erica's best friend. Independent and divorced, Danielle is everything that Erica can become if she maintains her separation from Brian; as such, she is not much of a figure to emulate, for she is no happier without a cad for a husband than Erica is with one. Danielle is something of a failure as a mother, since she operantly— although perhaps not finally—hates her children. She has an affair with a veterinarian and accepts his first proposal of marriage with no real thought.

Sanford "Zed" Finkelstein, a former classmate of Erica, a 1960's guru and owner of the Krishna Bookshop. Zed is a social loner and something of a pariah; he has come to town because he knows Erica is there. He does meet her after she separates from Brian, and there are several attempts by them to have a physical relationship—all failures. Zed stands as a counterpart to Wendy, on the one hand, and to Danielle's new husband, on the other.

Carl Singleton

THE WAR OF THE END OF THE WORLD

Author: Mario Vargas Llosa (1936-   )
Type of work: Novel
Time of action: The late 1890's
First published: La guerra del fin del mundo, 1981 (English translation, 1984)

The Counselor, whose name is **Antônio Conselheiro,** a tall, thin, bearded man with fiery eyes, of mysterious identity and origins, who proclaims that he has been sent by God to become the lord of Canudos. This backlands mystic cloaked in a purple tunic begins to develop a following in the interior of the state of Bahia, Brazil. Predicting the end of the present world and the beginning of a new one, he gradually becomes a symbol and leader for those who remain committed to the monarchy. He preaches an errant Christian message of love, peace, and repentance; of death and judgment. He and several thousand of his followers establish a community at an abandoned cattle ranch called Canudos, where they plan to wait out the apocalyptic developments that he has predicted. Rejecting the advances of the encroaching republican civilization, they refuse to pay taxes and also shelter numerous backlands outlaws. The insecure new federal government eventually crushes this "revolt" in 1897.

Galileo Gall, alias of a Scottish-born utopian

anarchist and phrenologist. This libertarian intellectual views Canudos idealistically as a model of human fraternity, only superficially cluttered by religion. In his view, the Canudos movement is the beginning of a revolution which will ultimately end the tyranny of the state.

Epaminondas Gonçalves (gôn·säl′vəz), ruthless young leader of the Progressivist Republican Party and the ambitious editor of the *Jornal de Notícias*. He attempts to use the rebellion in the backlands to bring ultimate discredit to the remnants of the Empire.

Baron de Canabrava, an unscrupulous politician and head of Bahia's Autonomist Party. He represents the local elite, and in response to the attacks from both sides attempts to turn matters to his own favor by accusing the republicans of inciting the entire episode.

Rufino, a tracker and guide from Quijingue. A young, suspicious man with a thin, supple body and an angular, weather-beaten face, he has been hired by Galileo Gall to take the latter to Canudos.

The nearsighted journalist, an ugly, inept, and unnamed individual whose mission is to report on the campaign against Canudos. He breaks his glasses and cannot see anything during the destruction of the religious community, symbolically taking a myopic view of historical events. His character, one of the most memorable and believable in a novel devoted to the clash of monolithic social forces, performs a consistently subversive function in the narrative by indulging in self-parodying remarks. He also serves as one of Vargas Llosa's surrogate authors.

Jurema (zhōo·frä′mə), Rufino's young wife, Gall's victim, and the journalist's lover. Considered as nothing more than a domestic animal by Gall, she is raped by him in an intense scene of physical violence. Her rape underscores the relationship between sexual and political repression in the novel.

Genevieve Slomski

THE WARS

Author: Timothy Findley (1930-   )
Type of work: Novel
Time of action: 1915-1922, the 1970's
First published: 1977

Robert Ross, a second lieutenant in the Canadian Field Artillery during 1916-1917. As a boy, he feels somewhat distanced from his parents, and consequently he devotes himself to his congenitally deformed sister, developing very early in his life the desperate conviction that self-esteem must be measured by very personal, rather than conventionally public, standards. Inspired by Tom Longboat, an Indian marathon runner, he imposes a strict training regimen on himself, believing that his achievements in such an elemental sport will stand as a testament to his love for his sister. It is Ross's belief in his personal standards that leads to his attempts to save a group of war horses, actions that result in his disfigurement and ultimately his death.

Mr. and Mrs. Tom Ross, Robert's parents. Tom Ross is well-meaning, but he lacks the self-assurance to rally his family at times of emotional crisis. Robert's mother becomes a cynical alcoholic after her daughter Rowena is born with hydrocephalis. She views Robert's enlistment with bitter foreboding and, at one point while he is overseas, furiously leaves church in the middle of the service, disgusted by the generally accepted notion that religious fervor and patriotic zeal are compatible.

Lady Barbara d'Orsey, as physically beautiful as she is emotionally stunted. She ritualistically offers herself to a series of war heroes, as if believing that her fiercely sexual involvements with them function as some sort of classically symbolic corollary to their inevitable self-sacrifice in battle. When one of them is not killed but wounded so terribly that he is incapable of further combat, she makes a practice of visiting him in the hospital, accompanied by her new lover and presenting with a pointed silence a bouquet that serves as a coldly formal tribute to the fallen hero.

Lady Juliet d'Orsey, Barbara's younger sister. During Barbara's affair with Robert, she becomes infatuated with him, instinctively sensing the goodness and innocence that underlie his barely repressed turmoil. After his disfigurement, she becomes his constant, platonic companion.

Marian Turner, Robert's nurse at the frontline hospital where he is brought after he is burned. When she offers to administer a morphine overdose, he manages to communicate the simple response, "Not yet." She believes that he was a hero for daring to do what no one else dared.

Rodwell, in civilian life, an illustrator of children's books. Robert shares his dugout when he first comes to the front lines. In this dugout, Rodwell keeps a menagerie of small animals that he has rescued from the battlefield. Acutely sensitive, he writes truly touching letters to his daughter to maintain his sanity and finally to help her to cope with his death. He commits suicide after watching battle-wearied soldiers set fire to a cat.

Martin Kich

WATCH ON THE RHINE

Author: Lillian Hellman (1905-1984)
Type of work: Play
Time of action: 1940
First produced: 1941

Fanny Farrelly, the head of a distinguished Washington family. She eagerly awaits the return of her daughter, Sara, who has spent many years abroad with her German husband, rearing a family and helping him in his anti-Fascist efforts. Fanny disapproved of the marriage but is now anxious to make amends. She is out of touch with what has been happening in Europe, but she responds well to Kurt's explanation of his activities on behalf of the men and women who have opposed Hitler. Fanny is so moved by Kurt's humane efforts on behalf of his fellow human beings that she conspires with him in the murder of Teck de Brancovis, who plans to inform on Kurt to the German embassy.

David Farrelly, Fanny's good-looking son, who has struggled under the shadow of a famous father. David falls in love with Marthe de Brancovis and helps Kurt survive Teck's scheme against him.

Marthe de Brancovis, Teck's attractive wife, an American who has tired of her husband's gambling and generally dissolute life. She is a guest in Fanny's home and falls in love with her son David.

Teck de Brancovis, a Romanian nobleman who gambles away his funds and decides to turn in Kurt Muller to the German embassy, which is sure to pay Teck for his efforts. Teck is suave but contemptuous of Americans, including his hostess Fanny.

Kurt Muller, Sara's husband and the play's hero, a vulnerable man. His hands have been broken in torture, and he dreads returning to Europe, even though he knows that he must leave to rescue his compatriots who are in jail or are facing imminent extermination by the Nazis. Kurt is eloquent yet modest about his own role in history. He impresses Fanny with his sincerity and determination and is instrumental in arousing her awareness of the threat to civilization that Fascism poses.

Sara Muller, Kurt's dedicated wife, who has had to brook her mother's displeasure over her marriage. She wins Fanny over, however, with her dedication to Kurt and her family. Sara, in fact, articulates many of the emotions and opinions that Kurt keeps to himself. In this sense she is his interpreter, saying in her own words what it has meant to follow him and to dedicate herself to his cause.

Bodo, Kurt and Sara's precocious child. Like Sara, he often expresses in blunt fashion opinions about freedom and democracy that Kurt only implies in his manner and halting speech. Bodo injects some humor into the play with his youthful sense of importance.

Babette, the middle child in the Muller family. She is much like her mother, supporting the family's political commitment and feeling a solidarity with her father.

Joshua Muller, Kurt's son. As the oldest child in the family, he feels a special responsibility for carrying on his father's mission.

Carl Rollyson

THE WATCH THAT ENDS THE NIGHT

Author: Hugh MacLennan (1907-   )
Type of work: Novel
Time of action: The 1950's, with flashbacks to earlier in the twentieth century
First published: 1959

George Stewart, the self-effacing narrator, a part-time university lecturer and radio journalist, Catherine's husband and Sally's stepfather. George has known and loved the delicate Catherine since they were children together. Separated from Catherine by his aunt's ambitions and then his father's bankruptcy, he does not meet her again until, having put himself through college in Toronto, he returns to Montreal, only to find that she has married Jerome Martell. The unemployed George meets Nora, a Communist nurse, and, disillusioned with the politics and economics which produced the "dirty thirties," attends Communist rallies. Still loving Catherine, and admiring Jerome, he watches the marriage suffer from Jerome's increasing involvement in politics, his affair with Nora, and his departure for Spain. After Jerome's death is reported, George and Catherine marry and are happy until Jerome's reappearance triggers George's memories (which constitute much of the book) and a third embolism which nearly kills Catherine. The autumnal beauty of George and Catherine's life after this is

recognized as preparatory to their final separation. George's faithful love for Catherine, his affection (obviously reciprocated) for Sally, and his admiration for and understanding of Jerome indicate that he is both generous and just. His political acumen is evident in his work and in the analysis of his own and the younger generation; it can be seen also in his description of the 1930's and the mores of postwar Canada.

Jerome Martell, a brilliant surgeon, Catherine's first husband and a friend of George. Born the son of a cook in a lumber camp, Jerome at age ten escaped from his mother's murderer and was adopted by the Martells, an elderly, clerical couple. As a teenager in World War I, he bayonetted eleven men, lost his religious faith, and flung himself into medicine. Knowing Catherine had a damaged heart, he encouraged her to marry him and have a child, assured that his vitality would enable her to survive. Jerome's differences with the Montreal medical establishment are exacerbated by his appearance at a commu-

1685

nist rally with his mistress. He resigns to join the Spanish loyalists; later, fighting with the Maquis, he is captured and tortured by the Nazis and reported dead but is actually incarcerated in a concentration camp. Released by the Russians, he works in Siberia and China, returning to Canada after seventeen years to find his daughter grown and his wife remarried. After healing wounds inflicted seventeen years before and helping Catherine recover, he leaves for a remote medical practice. His vitality, his single-mindedness, his courage and his finally successful search for meaning in life make him a force in the lives of others. His names suggest both saint and warrior, and he is a powerful influence for good.

Catherine Stewart, later **Martell,** née **Carey,** the wife of both George and Jerome. She has suffered all of her life from a rheumatic heart, her mother's resentment, and her own inability to lead a normal life. Resenting Jerome's concentration on politics, she is reconciled with him before he leaves and supports herself and her daughter Sally until she remarries. Then she becomes a painter, trying to express an enjoyment of living intensified by her acceptance of death.

Sally Martell, Catherine and Jerome's daughter, a university student. She resents her father's defection and is in love with a fellow student, Alan Rowe. Both represent the younger generation.

Nora Blackwell, a Communist, a surgical nurse, the unfaithful wife of Harry, and Jerome's mistress. She dies, leaving a daughter whom Harry rears.

Arthur Lazenby, formerly a Communist and now a successful official who smooths Jerome's return. He owes his start to Jerome.

Giles Martell, an elderly, saintly Anglican clergyman. He and his wife Josephine reared Jerome.

Dr. Rodgers, the head surgeon at Beamis Memorial Hospital, the medical establishment personified.

Jocelyn Creigh Cass

THE WATCHMAKER OF EVERTON

Author: Georges Simenon (1903-1989)
Type of work: Novel
Time of action: The mid-1950's
First published: L'Horloger d'Everton, 1954 (English translation, 1955)

Dave Galloway, watchmaker and repairer with his own small shop in Everton, New York State, the novel's center of consciousness. Forty-three, a good citizen and an ordinary, happy man not much given to reflection, at the opening of the novel Dave has still to learn the "secret in men" which he hopes to communicate at its close to the grandson who will shortly be born to his imprisoned son. The alienation and purposelessness of the modern hero are registered in the details of his drab small-town existence: his lack of friends, his retreat from women, his clockworklike home habits and work routines. So contracted is his life that he depends almost entirely for love and recognition—for a very sense of self—on the son to whom he has been both father and mother since his wife Ruth left him fifteen years ago. Dave's bewildered attempt not simply to understand why Ben has stolen and murdered but also to assert the unbroken continuity and closeness of their relationship—in the face of the fact that Ben has severed his ties with the past and his father, refusing even to acknowledge his presence in court—results also in Dave's confronting his own deeply buried desire to rebel (which drove him to marry the town tramp) and that of his long-dead father. Through such a quasi-mystical sense of heredity, he can cling to a sense of identity with Ben.

Ben, Dave's sixteen-year-old-son. Quiet and self-possessed, a good son who has never given any trouble, and (until recently) a good student, one Saturday night Ben packs his suitcase, pockets a pistol bought from a school friend, steals his father's decrepit car, and picks up his girlfriend Miriam. The two head for Illinois, where they can legally be married. On the road, still close to home, Ben shoots a man for his car and a few dollars. Captured after an inconsequential shoot-out with police, tried, and imprisoned for life, Ben regrets nothing. Instead, he seems almost exultant, certainly callous, and suddenly adult: He has slept with Miriam, and he has imposed (if only for twenty-eight hours) his will on life.

Miriam, Ben's girlfriend. Small for her fifteen and a half years, and not strikingly attractive, Miriam commits herself to Ben as absolutely and exclusively as he to her, persistently refusing to let him take responsibility for the killing. In the months before their elopement, Dave discovers, Ben has lived more in the shabby Hawkins home—with its horde of badly behaved children, its slatternly mother, and drunken father—than in his own neat apartment.

Musak, Dave's one close friend, a solitary middle-aged cabinetmaker. A big man who nevertheless moves with silent grace, taciturn and sometimes cynical, Musak is something of a mystery to Dave even after years of friendship. It is while Dave is playing his regular Saturday night game of backgammon at Musak's place, over a bottle of rye, that Ben decamps with Miriam. After discovering Dave's loss, Musak comes to his apartment, for the first time—unquestioning, knowing how to deal with grief and disillusionment, helping Dave survive.

Wilbur Lane, the top-notch attorney Dave hires to represent his son. Lane is fat, busy, able, self-important, and well-connected. He dislikes Ben for his obstinate sanity (mental instability being the only plea that could possibly cut any ice with the court) and regards Dave as an insignificant nuisance who knows less of his son than the policemen who arrested him. Significantly, he reminds Dave powerfully of his successful businessman stepfather, Musselman, against whom as an adolescent Dave defined himself and because of whom he cut himself off from his mother and his past.

Joss Lutz Marsh

THE WATER HEN
A Spherical Tragedy in Three Acts

Author: Stanisław Ignacy Witkiewicz (1885-1939)
Type of work: Play
Time of action: Unspecified
First produced: Kurka Wodna, 1922 (English translation, 1968)

The Father, Albert Valpor (or **Wałpor** in some texts), a retired skipper of a merchant ship. He is an unflappable pessimist who does not believe human beings made much difference in the scheme of things. Still, he is rather impressed when his son Edgar kills Elizabeth Gutzie-Virgeling, who is referred to as the Water Hen, and he thinks that perhaps Edgar can make something important out of his life after all. Yet at the end of the play the revolution that takes place fails to impress Albert.

He, Edgar Valpor, Albert's good-looking, if inept, son. He is devoted to the Water Hen but balks at her insistence that he shoot her.

He wonders with whom he will be able to talk if he shoots her. He is finally persuaded by her arguments and actually kills her. He has no real convictions about life, and the murder does not affect him much. When his son Tadzio questions him about the murder, Edgar is unable to explain his motivations. Yet by the end of act 1, Edgar believes that he has created a family by acknowledging Tadzio and marrying Lady Alice. He is amazed when the Water Hen returns and is puzzled when she denies that Tadzio is her son. Because the Water Hen is convinced that he did not suffer because of her death, Edgar submits to the physical agony of a torture machine to demonstrate the reality of his feelings.

Tadzio, who claims to be Edgar's son and eventually convinces him that this is so. Yet by act 2, Tadzio has forgotten why Edgar is his father. Unlike the other characters, he tends to question why things are the way they are. In act 3, ten years later, Tadzio is much taken with the Water Hen, who is now beautiful and sensuous. Tadzio quarrels with his father Edgar, who has discovered him and the Water Hen in a violent embrace.

Duchess Alice of Nevermore (Lady Alice), blonde and beautiful and one of the objects of Edgar's affections. Alice is hostile toward the Water Hen because her first husband (also named Edgar) was obsessed with the Water Hen. Now married to Edgar Valpor, her first husband Edgar's friend, Alice counsels Tadzio not to question the nature of things because there are no answers. Alice's main interest seems to be in accumulating capital for the Theosophical Jam Company, her latest enterprise, and she is not much concerned with personal feelings. Yet, like Edgar, she believes that she must come to terms with the influence of the Water Hen on her life. When Edgar shoots the Water Hen for a second time, Alice tries to take the blame upon herself, although he will not let her do so.

The Water Hen, Elizabeth Gutzie-Virgeling, a confidante of Edgar and the object of Tadzio's affection and Alice's hostility. She dies twice in the play, each time apparently trying to make a difference in people's lives even as she expresses a sense of futility in trying to impress them. The Water Hen tends to think of herself as an illusion, a fiction that other characters, such as Alice's first husband Edgar, have created. The Water Hen also claims that she is a liar and that she does not really exist. Her Polish name, Elzbieta Flake-Prawacka, is a combination of the words *flaki* (tripe) and *prawiczka* (virgin), a fitting humorous name for a woman who is a bizarre combination of the down-to-earth (the guts of things) and the unbesmirched ideal.

The Scoundrel, Richard de-Korbowa-Korbowski, also known as **Tom Hoozey,** who resembles Edgar and is devoted to Lady Alice of Nevermore. Korbowski despises Edgar Valpor as a weakling and keeps insisting that Alice give him up.

Carl Rollyson

THE WATERFALL

Author: Margaret Drabble (1939-   )
Type of work: Novel
Time of action: The 1960's
First published: 1969

Jane Gray, the narrator, twenty-eight years old, the wife of Malcolm, mother of Laurie and Bianca, cousin of Lucy, and lover of James. She is a published poet and tells her own story. In order to evoke the importance and complexity of her love, she alternates between first-person and third-person narratives, telling of her shy and lonely childhood and of her drifting into an unhappy and violent marriage. She acknowledges her sexual beauty but is passive, hard-hearted, selfish, and frigid—"cold to the marrow." Although she rejects her husband Malcolm, she responds to James's confident persistence. With James, she experienced the "miracle" of orgasm, an experience rendered metaphorically by the "waterfall" of the title. Despite some reservations, she knows that this experience has changed her life. She is with James when he crashes his car but is not hurt. At the end, although she is still technically married to Malcolm, she and James remain lovers.

James Otford, Lucy's husband, a father of three, and Jane's lover. He is part-owner of a garage and drives sports cars recklessly both on the road and on the racetrack. His appearance is threatening—pale eyes, a hard face—yet his soft, gray-blond hair suggests the gentle, loving persistence and kindness by which he awakens Jane's sexuality. He is seriously injured in the automobile crash but recovers almost completely. At the end of the story, although he has not left Lucy, he is still intimate with Jane.

Malcolm Gray, the thirty-one-year-old husband of Jane and the father of Laurie and Bianca. He is a well-trained, ambitious, and successful professional guitarist and singer, and Jane falls in love with a song he sang. Their marriage fails in part because of his latent homosexuality. Frustrated with Jane's coldness, he beats her and leaves. After the automobile crash, his telling about Jane and James allows Lucy to find the lovers. He threatens to divorce Jane but does not.

Lucy Goldsmith Otford, James's twenty-eight-year-old wife, a mother of three and Jane's cousin. A Cambridge graduate, forceful and promiscuous, she works for a publisher. She has been a close friend of Jane since they were children, and Jane imitates her steps toward adulthood. After the crash, her discovery of the truth about Jane and James precipitates a change in all of their relationships. James eventually returns to her.

Laurie Gray, the three-year-old son of Jane and Malcolm. Jane sees him growing up like her—fated to be lonely.

Bianca Gray, a baby, the daughter of Jane and Malcolm. Her birth occasions James's first overnight stay with Jane.

Jane's parents, who are Mrs. Goldsmith's sister and the headmaster of a good but not first-rate boys' preparatory school. Jane describes them both as habitual name-droppers obsessed with social position. Jane says that her father's caustic wit masks a lack of intelligence. Most important, Jane believes that, between them, her parents caused her to retreat within herself—alone, unloved, and unloving. They disapprove of her and prefer Jane's younger, more normal sister, Catherine. At the end, Jane tells the reader that they are not as bad as she has said they are.

Mr. and Mrs. Otford, James's parents. He is a London businessman dealing in perfume. She, a Norwegian who works for Lucy's employer, is beautiful and has affairs. Although they are not rich, they live lavishly.

Mr. and Mrs. Gray, Malcolm's parents. They are Londoners; he is a tax official, and she is a restless, questioning little woman. They get along well with Jane's parents because they are so obviously from an inferior social class.

Mr. and Mrs. (Bridget) Goldsmith, Lucy's parents. Bridget is Jane's mother's sister.

George Soule

THE WATERFALLS OF SLUNJ

Author: Heimito von Doderer (1896-1966)
Type of work: Novel

Time of action: The 1870's to 1910
First published: Die Wasserfälle von Slunj, 1963 (English translation, 1966)

Robert Clayton, an engineer and the industrialist director of the Vienna branch of the British firm of Clayton & Powers, Ltd. At age twenty-eight in 1877, he marries Harriet and they honeymoon in the southeastern part of the old Austro-Hungarian Empire, including the town of Slunj and the waterfalls of the Slunjcica River in this remote area of Croatia. Upon their return to England, Robert's father informs them that he has arranged to open a branch factory of their agricultural machinery plant in Vienna to serve the southeastern provinces of the Empire. Robert, an efficient director, has a prosperous business established eighteen months later. Robert enjoys the social life of Vienna at the turn of the century after a respectful period of mourning following the death of his wife. He is an active, charming, and extroverted man who continues to bring success to his business and a host of people from various social circles into his home. Although thirty years older than his son, he is often mistakenly identified as a younger brother. Only a short while after he meets the vivacious Monica Bachler, then Donald's lover, Robert decides to marry her.

Donald Clayton, Robert's son, born in Vienna on May 10, 1878, exactly nine months after his parents visited the waterfalls of Slunj. He is sent to England when he is of school age to live with his grandfather, a typical Englishman who takes great interest in Donald's education. Donald's personality is the total opposite of his father's. He is incapable of responding to human emotions and actions and has a deathly fear of water in any form. When Monica Bachler tries to seduce him, he notices that it is raining outside and simply does not respond to her advances. Nevertheless, at age thirty-two while on an extended business trip, Donald decides that he should marry Monica, most likely because he thinks that a wife belongs to an orderly and well-appointed home. While in Slunj, a place his father has often praised for its beauty and vitality, Donald receives two unexpected letters. One comes from his father, announcing his intended marriage to Monica. The other letter comes from Monica, telling of her love for his father and her resolve to marry him, with the pernicious suggestion that she and Donald should remain friends. This news drives Donald to the waterfalls, where he climbs out on a rickety walkway. The handrail gives way, and he falls a short distance onto a protruding rock. His would-be rescuers find him dead. It is said that Donald did not die from the fall but from fright of the falling waters.

Monica Bachler (mōn'ē•kä bäk'lâr), at age thirty-seven in 1910, the director and engineer of a Swiss technical publishing firm that has just opened an office in Vienna. Upon her arrival in the capital, she falls in love with Donald immediately and pursues this relationship with unusual vigor. Donald, however, is incapable of responding to her amorous and sexual advances; he merely sits there, smokes his pipe, and smiles. While Donald is on a business trip to England, Monica is invited to the Clayton tennis parties, where she meets Chwostik, with whom she spends one evening fulfilling the unrequited love. There she also meets the "alive Donald," namely Robert Clayton. They fall in love and make plans to marry before Donald returns from another business trip.

Josef Chwostik (yō'zĕf shwō'stĭk), approximately thirty years old, the office manager and, later, business managing director and deputy director of Clayton & Powers in Vienna. Chwostik is the genius who makes the business a profitable enterprise. Although his educational background is very limited, he quickly learns English, Serbo-Croatian, and numerous other foreign languages that help him in business dealings for the firm in the multilingual and multinational Austro-Hungarian Empire. Even though his background is socially and materially disadvantaged, he learns respect and discretion and is included in the social life of his employer, serving as a highly trusted and respected member of Viennese society.

Zdenko von Chlamtatsch (zdĕn'kō fōn kläm' täch), in 1910 a fourteen-year-old schoolboy in Vienna. He and several school friends imitate the "Clayton Brothers," as Robert and Donald are called. The boys even form the Metternich Club, in which they affect a kind of dandyism not uncommon in Vienna at that time. Through Augustus, Robert Clayton's nephew, Zdenko becomes acquainted with the Claytons and is frequently invited to their tennis parties. His personality and behavior resemble those of Donald Clayton.

While on holiday at his aunt's home in Hungary, Zdenko goes riding and arrives at the waterfalls of Slunj just in time to witness Donald's fall and death.

Harriet Clayton, Robert's first wife and Donald's mother. She is an unassertive woman who prefers the rural life of horseback riding at her uncle's estate in England to the social life and engineering world of Vienna. Her husband and son rarely accompany her on these trips to England. She dies of tuberculosis in 1898 and is buried at Chifflington, England.

Thomas H. Falk

WATERLAND

Author: Graham Swift (1949-   )
Type of work: Novel
Time of action: The 1970's, with flashbacks to the eighteenth, nineteenth, and earlier twentieth centuries
First published: 1983

Tom Crick, a history teacher at a private secondary school in Greenwich, England, the spot where time can be said to begin. The narrator, in his mid-fifties, has been an instructor of history for thirty years and is being forced to retire because the authorities contend that history has little value in the modern world. In order to understand himself—his part in his wife's recent mental breakdown and in the deaths of his half brother Dick and boyhood friend Freddie Parr—and in response to his students' lack of interest in the more orthodox history of the French Revolution, Crick tells his students stories, stories from his own life and the life of his family in the Fen Country of Norfolk.

Mary Metcalf Crick, Tom's wife. Mary, also from the Fenlands, has been married to Tom for as long as he has been a teacher. Friends and lovers since childhood, while still in her teens the sexually precocious Mary becomes pregnant by Tom and has an abortion which renders her permanently sterile. After being a supportive teacher's wife and

working with the elderly for many years, Mary, believing that God wants her and Tom to have children, kidnaps a baby from a supermarket. The baby is quickly returned, but Mary no longer has any contact with reality and is admitted to a mental institution.

Dick Crick, Tom's older and retarded half brother. He is the offspring of Tom's mother, Helen Atkinson, from an incestuous relationship with her father, Ernest. Undeveloped both emotionally and intellectually, Dick is like his motorcycle, more machine than human. In the early 1940's, when in his late teens, he becomes attracted to Mary Metcalf and she to him. In his jealousy he kills sixteen-year-old Freddie Parr with an ale bottle, part of the legacy left to him by his true father, and then, fearing arrest, he commits suicide by drowning himself in the Fens' River Ouse.

Henry Crick, Tom's biological father but not Dick's, and the keeper of a lock on the Fens' River Leem. The Cricks are an old Fenland family, but never either wealthy or prominent. Injured physically and mentally in World War I, Henry is nursed back to health by Helen Atkinson. Aware of the Atkinson legacy, Henry attempts to spare Dick from the truth, but ultimately without success.

Helen Atkinson, Henry's wife and the mother of Tom and Dick. She is very beautiful, and her father turns to her for emotional and sexual consolation in his own disappointments. She dies when her sons are both young, but she passes on her father's legacy to their son Dick, a trunk filled with Ernest Atkinson's writings but also with bottles of strong ale.

Ernest Atkinson, Tom's grandfather and Dick's father and grandfather. The Atkinsons, a prominent Fenland family since the eighteenth century, founded their wealth and power on brewing ale. Emotionally affected by his family's history and the society's disasters, Ernest fathers a child on his daughter, a child whom he hopes will save the world. That child becomes the retarded Dick. After Helen's marriage to Henry Crick, which Ernest reluctantly accepts, he commits suicide.

Lewis Scott, the headmaster at Tom Crick's Greenwich school. Disturbed that Tom is not following the required curriculum of the French Revolution, and fearing the negative publicity created by Mary Crick's kidnapping incident, Scott wants Tom Crick to retire. A scientist by training, Scott sees no value in studying the past; to him the future is everything and history has no connection to it.

Price, a sixteen-year-old student in Tom's history class. Price also doubts the value of history, but, unlike Scott, Price sees no future. The world is threatened with imminent destruction, and Price fears that history cannot influence that end. Bright and challenging, Price becomes the focus of Tom's storytelling.

Thomas Atkinson, a brewer and the Fen Country's leading citizen during the first half of the nineteenth century. The Atkinson family reaches its apogee of fame and influence with the career of Thomas Atkinson; however, at that moment Thomas, in a fit of jealousy, strikes and permanently injures Sarah, his wife.

Sarah Atkinson, Thomas' young and beautiful wife. After being injured by her husband while in her thirties, she never recovers her mental health, although she lives for many, many years. Her demented presence hangs over the Atkinson family and the town for decades, even after her death.

Frederick Parr, sixteen years old, a friend of Tom, Mary, and Dick. Something of a braggart, Freddie is killed in 1943 by a jealous Dick after Mary, in order to spare Tom, intimates to Dick that it was Freddie who made her pregnant.

Eugene S. Larson

WATERSHIP DOWN

Author: Richard Adams (1920-　　)
Type of work: Novel
Time of action: The 1970's
First published: 1972

Hazel, one of the rabbits forced to leave Cowslip Warren when it is destroyed by encroaching civilization. He is a young buck rabbit who eventually matures into a wise leader of his warren at Watership Down. Hazel undertakes to guide the rabbits across country to safety; in the course of their travels, he outwits men, other beasts, natural disasters, and the evil dictator of Efrafa Warren, General Woundwort. Hazel's character is similar to those of such wiley tricksters of myth and folktale as Brer Rabbit, Coyote, Odysseus, and Robin

Hood. Eventually, Hazel establishes another warren on the Belt made up of rabbits from Watership Down and Woundwort's Efrafa Warren.

Fiver, the runt brother in Hazel's litter. This small rabbit is gifted with second sight. Although he is physically weaker than the others, Fiver can see the future, often one clouded in myth, allegory, and allusion. Fiver frequently falls into a troubled fit during which he dreams what will befall his rabbit band; these dreams presage encounters with enemies such as General Woundwort and farmers.

Bigwig, another Cowslip Warren rabbit who travels with Hazel to Watership Down. He is notable primarily for his physical strength, bravery, and willingness to defend his friends, Hazel in particular. Bigwig is instrumental in getting the rabbits of the Mark under General Woundwort's control to cooperate in Hazel's plan to liberate does for his warren at Watership Down. He also saves Hazel from the cat while they are at Nuthanger Farm trying to liberate the domesticated rabbits. It is Bigwig who deals the defeating blow to General Woundwort.

Kehaar, the seagull who, helped by Hazel's rabbit band shortly after its arrival at Watership Down, acts as their scout, looking for evidence of trouble, predators, and other rabbits. He periodically departs to go to the ocean but always returns to lend assistance to his friends. His odd accent adds comic relief to the story.

General Woundwort, the dictator rabbit of Efrafa Warren. This rabbit runs his warren like a military garrison. All that occurs there is unnatural behavior for rabbits. They are not allowed to interact with one another, to feed when they normally would, or to breed and frolic. Woundwort maintains a rigid control by a hierarchical system of officers and spies. Hazel and his rabbits fight Woundwort in order to liberate females for their warren. Woundwort is the personification of all that is unnatural in animal behavior. After Bigwig deals Woundwort a defeat, the rabbit disappears into the underbrush; he remains as a figure in the rabbits' mythology.

Prince El-ahrairah, the mythical founder and protector of the race of rabbits. His actions are recounted in tales that are interwoven throughout the story of Hazel and his band. Prince El-ahrairah is the emblem of all that is quintessentially rabbit: wiliness, cunning, playfulness, and a happy-go-lucky approach to life. The stories told about him by the rabbits mirror the predicaments and perils that Hazel's group faces as it struggles to make its way to Watership Down and establish a new warren there. These rabbit stories are the myths and legends that provide explanations for who they are, how rabbits came to be, and what their relationship to other races (species) is in their universe. Although El-ahrairah gradually takes on the character of the Supreme Being of the rabbit world, the stories that the rabbits tell about him reflect the current status of Hazel's group: If they are in danger, the story is serious; if they are secure, the tale is amusing and lighthearted.

The Black Rabbit of Inlé, a rabbit spirit who counsels El-ahrairah about the white blindness plague when he is in need of help.

Strawberry, a young rabbit who travels with Hazel's group and who eventually becomes an adviser in the Watership Down Warren.

Laurel, one of the domesticated black angora rabbits at Nuthanger Farm.

Boxwood, a domesticated black-and-white Himalayan rabbit at Nuthanger Farm and the mate of the female Haystack, also a Himalayan. Hazel and his rabbits rescue these rabbits from their domestic captivity.

Clover, a domesticated black angora rabbit liberated from Nuthanger Farm by Hazel's band.

Melissa E. Barth

WATT

Author: Samuel Beckett (1906-1989)
Type of work: Novel
Time of action: Probably between the two world wars
First published: 1953

Watt ("Christian name forgotten"), a servant in the Irish country house of Mr. Knott and subsequently an inmate of a mental institution. He is a "big bony shabby seedy knockkneed" man with a big red nose, rotten teeth, and red hair streaked with gray; the more conspicuous parts of his wardrobe include a hat found by his grandfather at the races, a coat bought by his father from a widow, a brown shoe found at the seashore, and a brown boot bought from a one-legged man with borrowed money. He walks with a swinging gait without bending his knees, his smile seems artificially composed, and he drinks only milk. Before coming to Mr. Knott's he had no fixed address, though he is described as probably a university man and as an experienced traveler. He mechanically obeyed whatever mysterious message summoned him to Mr. Knott's and obeys when his successor arrives and signals his departure. He is mostly uncommunicative and inarticulate, but he has had male friends and has even enjoyed some romances, at least one of them consummated. It is Watt's mental life which takes up the greater part of the book: He seeks "semantic succour" in naming accurately the objects around him, though even as commonplace an object as a pot gives him trouble. He seeks within his own mind explanations for the events that take place around him; he apparently solves the mysteries surrounding Mr. Knott's meals but fails to account for the visit of two piano tuners. Even when Watt settles on a hypothesis that satisfies him, he must first consider all the alternatives, however implausible, and later communicate them to Sam.

Mr. Knott, the owner of a country house that has been in his family for generations. His appearance varies daily, being now "small fat pale and fair," now "tall fat pale and dark," with endless variations; his wardrobe is also constantly changing. He is constantly moving about his room and constantly moving the furniture there. Otherwise his life is mechanically repetitious; he always has two live-in servants, one in charge of the ground floor and his meals, one in charge of the first floor and personal services. The meals are always the same; once a week Watt cooks a mixture of foods, drinks, and medicines, which is served cold to Mr. Knott for lunch and dinner, the leftovers (if any) being consumed by a famished dog. Mr. Knott sometimes walks in the garden; he apparently never communicates, though he makes mysterious noises and sings songs in an unknown tongue.

Sam, Watt's occasional companion in the mental institution. He is able to report the details of Watt's life with Mr. Knott—even though he sees Watt only when the weather is right for both of them, even though they converse while marching (Sam forward and Watt backward) between two barbed-wire fences, and even though Watt varies his delivery, sometimes inverting the order of words in the sentence, sometimes the order of the letters in the word, and invoking other variations as well.

Arsene, a servant whom Watt displaces, a "little fat shabby seedy juicy or oily bandy-legged man" who gives Watt a pessimistic account of the Knott establishment.

Erskine, a fellow servant, for whose mysterious dashes up and downstairs, and for whose mysterious responses to a bell in the night, Watt can find no satisfactory explanation.

Mrs. Gorman, Mr. Knott's fishwoman, with whom Watt necks every Thursday.

Mr. Graves, the unhappily married gardener, from whom Watt learns something of the Knott history.

Lynch, the name of an unhealthy and incestuous family paid by Mr. Knott to maintain a succession of famished dogs to consume his leftovers. Art and Con are the twin dwarfs who bring the dog to Mr. Knott's house each evening.

John C. Sherwood

THE WAVE

Author: Evelyn Scott (Elsie Dunn, 1893-1963)
Type of work: Novel
Time of action: April 11, 1861, to May 24, 1865
First published: 1929

Jefferson Davis, President of the Confederate States of America, a man small enough in stature to belie the authority invested in him and capable of seeing more with his one good eye than most men see with both. Very image-conscious, he is ashamed of his desire to flee once it becomes apparent that the Confederacy is doomed, and his fugitive status is difficult for his vanity to endure. He is eventually found secreted in a farmhouse near Irwinsville, Georgia, and awaits trial for treason against the United States of America at the end of the novel.

Abraham Lincoln, President of the United States of America. A tall, thin man with much presence, Lincoln is too proud to allow himself to show any humility in public. His determination and belief in predestination have brought him to the presidency, and they carry him through the difficult stance he has chosen to support in his actions against the Confederate States of America. Lincoln is assassinated at Ford's Theatre by John Wilkes Booth, who is captured while attempting to escape.

Robert E. Lee, a Confederate general. General Lee is a calmly tenacious man with a kindly eye and manner. Beloved by officers and enlisted men alike, he struggles with depressions and a love of privacy difficult for a leader to display with dignity. He is deeply religious and earns much of his reputation for kindliness and dignity through his efforts to persuade enlisted men of the importance of faith. Lee corresponds with General Ulys-

ses S. Grant during the fighting outside Richmond, and through this correspondence he obtains General Grant's respect. Lee is tricked into surrendering his Confederate Armies of Virginia to Grant after General Philip Henry Sheridan strategically contrives to make the numbers of the Union troops seem far greater than they are.

Ulysses S. Grant, a Union general, commander of the Army of the Potomac. A stocky, full-bearded man with pale eyes and oratorical abilities, he is nevertheless laconic in personal conversation. His popularity is a continual surprise to him, for he believes himself to be arrogant and shy. He spends his oratory abilities recruiting soldiers to the Union cause and later leads these same soldiers against Lee to the eventual surrender of Lee. Grant conducts himself superciliously during the surrender negotiations and formalities, and the whole affair of Lee's surrender leaves him determined never to spend as much energy on the man or the cause again.

Edwin George, a tobacco merchant and a Union spy from Tennessee. A handsome but coarse man with curly, graying hair, he believes himself to be wicked and accordingly distrusts and suspects fellow humans. He is undertaking an attempt to glean some information from a former lover and sister-in-law, Eugenia Gilbert. He is unaware that she has accepted a commission to become an abolitionist informer and hopes to extract similar information from him. Their meeting is warm with old attraction and rife with the inner conflict of their interests.

Eugenia Gilbert, an abolitionist spy. An older woman who appears more tired and haggard than her age should merit, she has become hypocritical and cares only for the money to be earned by spying. Her exploitation of her former lover Edwin George will probably be successful, for she unbalances him at their first meeting and secures a promise for a private meeting the following day.

Dickie Ross, a Confederate volunteer. Dickie is young, aflame with enthusiasm, and tired of his clerking position. He is in a rowboat on Charleston Harbor when the first shot is fired on Fort Sumter and responds with youthful, ignorant enthusiasm.

Percy, an attorney's scribe. Percy is unambitious, tedious, methodical, and fastidious about his health and manners. He is killed in a mob that is protesting the marching of Lincoln's troops through Baltimore.

Henry Clay, a little boy affected by the political pull between his Aunt Amanda's Confederate sympathies and his mother's Union sympathies. Henry is anemic, churlish, and frightened by the conflict between the women. He is unable to reconcile his love for both of them as they struggle to win his affections.

Franklin Rutherford and
Charlie, two Union soldiers. Franklin and Charlie are uneducated poor whites, basically well-meaning and patriotic. They become demoralized and embittered by the terrors of battle.

Mrs. Witherspoon, a member of the Confederate Ladies Aid Society. She is proud and falsely patriotic, reveling in the appearance of the mother worried about her soldier son's welfare. She experiences an awakening and her first real suffering when she receives news that her son George has been killed. Her false concern shows itself in indignity at not being the first to be told, before real grief overcomes her and she swoons.

Josie Kendricks, a member of the same Confederate Ladies Aid Society as Mrs. Witherspoon, and fiancée to George Witherspoon, Mrs. Witherspoon's oldest son. Josie is an emotional yet contained young patriot and the first person to receive the news that George Witherspoon has been killed.

James Witherspoon, Mrs. Witherspoon's youngest son and the late George Witherspoon's brother. Sensitive and unpatriotic, he is driven insane by the knowledge of his brother's death, since he wishes it could have been he and believes George has died a needless, worthless death.

Mose Elder and
Cat Foot Dawsey, two black "dirt-eaters" from Tennessee who shoot two men unawares. They are patriotic and have great feelings of guilt over their failure to enlist. They let these guilt feelings convince them their patriotic duty is to shoot the soldiers, who might be deserters. They shoot the two men without ever making their presence known.

Albert, a Union soldier. Albert is dutifully patriotic and servile, but he deserts when he is refused a leave of absence. He has received news that his sweetheart, Charlotte, can wait no longer for him, and in his desperation to get to her he becomes a deserter and the murderer of an innocent Negro.

Melinda and
Thomas, a couple aboard the blockade runner boat the *Atlantide*. Melinda and Thomas are wealthy idlers, concerned only with their own comfort and regarding the war as a great inconvenience. They are bound for the northeast coast, where Thomas plans halfheartedly to offer his services as a surgeon to the Confederate cause. They are in continual danger from the blockade searchers, and this danger lends them the only significance their lives contain.

Lee Shuck, a Union soldier. Lee is an average soldier, having enlisted out of a middleclass sense of duty. He is awaiting execution by his own commanders, however, for falling asleep while on sentinel duty, and he is bewildered and frustrated that his laxness is so seriously interpreted.

Mr. Samuel Wharton and
Mrs. Sadie Wharton, a Union couple in conflict about which side to support financially. They are self-righteous and vain about their ability to make financial contributions to any cause. Their son fought for the Confederacy, but Samuel wants to support the more official Union. Mrs. Wharton wants to support the Confederacy in memory of their son, and their arguments and ensuing alienations are terrible.

Gunner Renfield, a sailor aboard the *Itasca* during the assault near Fort Jackson. Gunner is an introspective and delicate individual. He is overcome by the horror of the battles and fails to save his shipmate and friend, Harry Dewey, when the *Itasca* is bombed and sinks.

Harry Dewey, another sailor aboard the *Itasca* during the assault near Fort Jackson. Harry is idealistically dependent upon the good will of his buddies and sentimentalizes their affections for him. When he is tossed overboard during the bombing of the *Itasca,* he relies on his friend Gunner Renfield and drowns when Gunner is too horrified to save him.

Parker, a Union soldier in New Orleans. Parker is an aggressive, alcoholic, and burly man unable to reconcile his dislike of his station with his sense of duty. He forces some Créole shopkeepers to sell him gin against their will, knowing that the sale of liquor to soliders is against the law of the federal government.

Hallie and
Her lover, two lovers who rendezvous during the young man's desertion. Hallie, a pretty and comely girl of about eighteen, is jaded and embittered by the war situation. Although she physically enjoys meeting her lover, she believes that the war has cheapened romance and forced her to accept a less romantic sort of involvement and commitment, a clandestine rendezvous instead of a marriage proposal.

Eloise Ducros, a young French girl. Eloise is cunning and poor, with barely attractive features hardened into ugliness by poverty. She has been jilted by her French lover and is forced, with Madame Ducros, her housemate, to take in Union boarders to support herself. Her sympathies are Confederate, and she is filled with self-loathing at the position to which she has sunk. She is particularly repulsed by one Lieutenant Fisk, who pays her romantic attentions and whom she cannot afford to anger.

Lieutenant Fisk, a Union soldier, vain, obese, and self-inflated. He is boarding in the house of Confederate sympathizers Madame Ducros and Eloise Ducros. Fisk is engaged in clandestine relations with Eloise, who despises him but receives his attentions because she and Madame Ducros need the money that Fisk gives to them.

Carrie, a rebel pickpocket. Carrie is twenty-nine, still attractive but becoming sullen and desperate, having come down in social station because of the war. Carrie kills a Yankee soldier in a fit of passionate hatred while trying to rob him.

Fanny May, a young Confederate mother. Fanny is dreamy, pale, and distant, living in a world apart since the death of her baby. The baby cost Fanny her health and most of her faculties, too. Despite Fanny's weak condition and the doctor's orders to stay in bed, Fanny and some friends drive out to the hills of Richmond to see the battle. They are shocked when they are shelled, and Fanny becomes even weaker.

Saunders, a plantation owner and a member of Morgan's cavalry. A short and stolid but agile man, Saunders is determined to hijack a train bearing Union soldiers and supplies to Hampton Junction. He succeeds in stopping the train so that the Confederates can attack and pilfer the supplies.

Smith, a wounded soldier of unknown loyalties. Smith is thin, slow-witted, and easily bewildered. He has been wounded unto death and dies slowly while crawling through a battlefield strewn with bodies from both armies.

Frazer, a Confederate deserter. Frazer is young, virile, and faithless. He is ashamed of his faithlessness as a pretense only, and given the chance to do so undetected, he deserts when he realizes that the Confederates are going to be defeated.

Miss Amanda and
Maude May, two Confederate spinsters. The sisters are proud and disdainful, thin, shrewish, and peaked looking. They have difficulty reconciling their pride with their situation, which requires them to beg their bread and sell their belongings for pittance. As a result, they spend most of their time deploring their situation and moanfully hoping the war will end.

Ann L. Postlethweight

THE WAY WEST

Author: A. B. Guthrie, Jr. (1901-   )
Type of work: Novel
Time of action: 1845
First published: 1949

Lije Evans, the thirty-five-year-old captain of a wagon train. A strong, large man with an easygoing manner, he goes west because of his strong conviction that Oregon should become part of the United States, not of England, and because he thinks that his son deserves a better chance. Although he does not actively seek the post, he is elected captain. Unlike his predecessor, Tadlock, Evans does not enjoy giving speeches, and he is compelled to make special provisions for the weaker members of the company. He feels like a whole man for the first time when he takes a stand against Tadlock, who wants to hang a thieving Indian. His awe of the wilderness culminates in Oregon, which he views as a fitting place for his grandson to be born.

Rebecca Evans, Lije's wife and the strongest of all the women. She reluctantly leaves her comfortable home in Missouri because she thinks that there are more opportunities for her son and husband in Oregon. Stout, assured, and unafraid, she sees it as her duty to suppress her own fears and disappointments and to help the weak ones, such as Judith Fairman and Mrs. Byrd. She is also a very insightful person who can predict how people will act and feel in certain situations, although she is occasionally baffled by the

behavior of her men. Because she wants to maintain harmony in her family, she decides not to tell Lije that Brownie is not the father of Mercy's child.

Brownie Evans, the seventeen-year-old son of Lije and Rebecca. At the beginning of the trip, he daydreams of performing heroic feats because he fears that he will never be as brave as Dick Summers, his idol. He proves himself, though, when he fights off the Indian dogs that are attacking his dog, Rock. Because he is a boy doing the man's job of taking care of the cattle on the journey, he matures quickly. By the end of the trip, he speaks to his father with the self-confidence of an adult as he tells Lije that he is going to marry Mercy and that he should take the lead wagon across the raging river.

Dick Summers, a mountain man and the pilot of the wagon train. His decision to go west with the company marks the end of his life as a farmer after his wife dies and the beginning of his return to the beaver country that he left eight years before. He takes a new pleasure at the awakening memory of beaver streams, squaws, and mountain men that he has known. His vast knowledge of frontier lore is indispensable to the pioneers, most of whom are not nearly as skilled in hunting, locating water, and dealing with the Indians. He is also the confidant of Lije and Brownie Evans, who constantly go to him for advice. Summers' fierce independence makes him unpopular with Tadlock, who rankles at his flagrant breaking of rules, such as the prohibition against drinking alcohol on the journey. Even though Summers pilots the company safely to Oregon, he does not share their enthusiasm for settling and returns to the frontier.

Henry McBee, dirty, shiftless, and poor. He sides with whoever is in power at the time. Because of his eagerness to carry out Tadlock's order to kill all the dogs in camp, McBee becomes Lije's enemy. Before leaving for California, McBee kills Lije's dog, Rock, so that he can have the "last laugh."

Mercy McBee, a pretty sixteen-year-old. Unlike her parents, she is kind, gentle, and hardworking. Seduced and impregnated by Curtis Mack, she agrees to marry Brownie, but only after telling him of her condition. She feels unworthy of Brownie and hopes that he has forgiven her.

Judith Fairman, the sickly wife of Charlie Fairman who works to the limits of her strength. She moves to Oregon in the hope that a change of climate will be good for her sickly son. Devastated by the loss of her son, she is sustained by the hope that her new baby will be a replacement for Tod.

Tod Fairman, the five-year-old son of Judith and Charlie Fairman. He no sooner recovers from the river fever that has plagued him all of his life than he dies from the bite of a rattlesnake.

Higgins (Hig), Fairman's hired man. Skinny, toothless, and ugly, Hig looks after Tod and entertains the pioneers with his sharp wit and his fiddle playing, although his ironic comments tend to disrupt the council meetings at times. He is also a deep thinker who

feels dwarfed by the vastness of the new land.

Curtis Mack, the frustrated husband of Amanda. He quits business and starts west to get things off his mind, namely his troubled marriage. The anger and disappointment that he feels from his wife's refusal to sleep with him drive him to commit the senseless murder of a Kaw Indian and to seduce the innocent, trusting Mercy. Mack tries to atone for his sin by staying behind with the single men and assisting with the dangerous task of driving cattle across the Dalles River.

Weatherby, an old preacher. He decides to go west because he is convinced that he has been chosen to spread the word of God. He forms an unlikely partnership with the harddrinking Summers, who provides him with food and shelter. The train comes to depend on the words that he speaks during council meetings, funerals, and weddings. He leaves the train shortly before they reach Oregon so that he can Christianize the Indians, who, he fears, are in danger of being corrupted by the encroaching white settlers.

Tadlock, the Illinois man who organizes the company. More educated than most of the pioneers, he has the skills of a politician and an organizer and is a firm believer in discipline and method. His egotistical desire to lead the first company to reach Oregon becomes intolerable when he refuses to slow the wagon train down for the benefit of the fever-stricken Martin. As a result, he is relieved of his command by the council. He joins a wagon train going to California because he believes that he will be more likely to realize his political ambitions there.

The Byrds, a weak, unfit family beset by misfortune. Mr. Byrd is visibly afraid of fording the raging river which causes his pregnant wife to pitch out of the wagon and to deliver her baby prematurely. Incredibly, Mr. Byrd apologizes when his wagon crashes off the mountain, even though Evans is responsible.

Alan Brown

WE

Author: Yevgeny Zamyatin (1884-1937)
Type of work: Novel
Time of action: The thirty-second century
First published: My, 1920-1921, written; 1927, corrupt text; 1952, complete text (English translation, 1924)

D-503, the narrator and the protagonist, a mathematician and builder of the spaceship *Integral*. At first, D-503 is a faithful follower of the Benefactor, the leader of a futuristic society, the One State. D-503 blindly believes that the One State is a just society, that individual freedom is a burdensome remnant of the distant past, and that the numbers, the inhabitants of the One State, live and work best in a collective state of contentment rather than happiness. He is happy to contribute to the export of the One State's ideas by way of the *Integral* to other possible worlds on distant planets. His metamorphosis begins when he meets, and falls in love with, a female number, I-330, who harbors dangerous ideas of individuality and personal freedom. He even promises to place at her disposal the spaceship in order to topple the government of the One State. D-503 discovers, to his horror, that he has developed a soul (an anathema in the materialistic, totally rational society of the One State); the hair growth on his hands is another indication of the suppressed, primitive side of his nature. He changes his mind at the last moment, upon discovering that I-330 does not really love him but only wants to use him and the spaceship. D-503 is an ironic caricature of an intellectual and a scientist who unquestioningly serves a totalitarian ruler, believing that the ruler is right in creating a collective frame of mind and in basing everything on a rational basis, excluding all emotions and spiritual values. D-503's wavering and an almost complete conversion, or a betrayal of reason, indicates the vulnerability of such convictions and the indestructibility of "the other half" of man's psyche, even after hundreds of years of brainwashing.

I-330, the woman with whom D-503 falls in love, a leader of the revolution. As the letter in her name hints, I-330 stands for individuality, infinity, and irrationality: individuality in protest against the deadening collectivism; infinity, refuting the finite world of the One State as a result of the final revolution which took place a thousand years ago; and irrationality, signifying the rebellion against the atrophying grip of reason based exclusively on mathematics. I-330 demonstrates that some individuals will eventually pierce the crust of conditioning and reject being nameless numbers. A strikingly beautiful woman, she uses her charms to assist the revolutionaries in their rebellion. Her failure in the end is only a temporary setback; eventual success is assured: If, after a thousand years of strict controls, a revolution was possible, what is to stop it the next time?

O-90, D-503's girlfriend and registered sexual partner. O-90 is assigned to D-503 after a careful examination of their hormones but is supposed to be shared by others. She falls in love with D-503, against the rules and scientific tests. She displays another forbidden sentiment, jealousy, of the love relationship between D-503 and I-330. A plump, less appealing woman than I-330, O-90 is nevertheless capable of genuine feelings. It is significant that during the rebellion she escapes to freedom across the border of the One State, carrying with her D-503's unborn child, thus assuring that in the future the numbers will become individuals again and live in freedom.

R-13, D-503's friend, who shares O-90 with him; he is poet laureate of the One State. Showing a striking physical resemblance to the greatest Russian poet, Alexander Pushkin, R-13 ostensibly serves the One State while secretly supporting the rebellion, as a clear indication that even the officially sanctioned artists cannot escape the lure of individuality and freedom. He dies together with I-330, but his poetry gives hope that free art can never be totally suppressed.

The Benefactor, the authoritarian leader of the One State. Elected "unanimously" for the fortieth time, he is devoid of a normal human countenance and is seldom seen acting like a human being. He is more of a myth, a symbol, almost an idea, the quintessential totalitarian leader, commanding total obedience and loyalty.

S-4711, a member of the Guardians. As his snakelike letter indicates, S-4711 is an omnipresent secret police agent, who seems to spy on everyone yet in the end sides with

I-330 and the rebels. That his fate at the end of the rebellion is not clear may be another indication of his elusiveness and insincerity.

U, a supervisor of the building in which D-503 lives. The only number without a number (D-503 omits her number lest he say something unflattering about her), she seems to have the sole duty of keeping an eye on D-503 as the builder of the *Integral*. In the course of her duty, she, too, falls in love with him, yet at the crucial moment of the rebellion, her sense of duty prevails and she reports D-503's complicity, ostensibly in order to save him from punishment.

Vasa D. Mihailovich

THE WEATHER IN THE STREETS

Author: Rosamond Lehmann (1901-   )
Type of work: Novel
Time of action: The early 1930's
First published: 1936

Olivia Curtis, twenty-seven, separated from her husband Ivor Craig. Olivia leads an impoverished semi-Bohemian life in London, where she shares a small house with her flighty cousin Etty Somers and works part-time for a pittance in the studio of a photographer and painter named Anna, one of a circle of artists and writers who form Olivia's present world. Called home by the serious illness of her father, Olivia takes a train to Tulverton, where the older Curtises live. In the dining car, she meets Rollo Spencer, whom she has not seen for ten years; they had met briefly at his sister Marigold's coming-out party and later at her wedding. Olivia is immediately and again attracted to Rollo and senses his fascination with her even though he cannot remember her name. The next day Olivia is invited to attend a small dinner party at the Spencers', after which Rollo drives her home, and the beginnings of what is to be an eight-month affair are evident.

Rollo Spencer, in his thirties, the handsome, self-assured, and prosperous son of Sir John

and Lady Spencer and the husband of Nicola Maude, a sickly and nervous woman, almost an invalid. Rollo is loving and generous with Olivia; he buys her flowers and jewelry, but they can never go to places where he might be seen and recognized, so their times together are spent in out-of-the-way pubs and small inns in country towns. A few times, Rollo meets some of Olivia's friends and enjoys them; he has a great capacity for pleasure.

Mrs. Curtis, Olivia's mother. Through Mrs. Curtis' questions and remarks, details of Olivia's life and personality are revealed. The reasons that Olivia cannot share her troubles with her mother and her sister Kate, married and with four children, are clear: The gulf between Olivia and her family is seen to be unbridgeable. Their conventional, kindly, superficial, and domestic outlook is in sharp contrast to Olivia's reserved, independent, and proud nature.

Lady Spencer, Rollo's mother, a woman

whom Olivia has always loved and admired because of a sense of congeniality of temperament and values. The older woman has always been fond of Olivia, whom she regards as her daughter Marigold's friend, but this relationship changes when Lady Spencer confronts Olivia, having learned from a very discreet source that Rollo and Olivia were seen together in Austria. Lady Spencer is instrumental in making Olivia perceive that the affair must end, yet the older woman also reveals that she is still fond of Olivia and concerned about her. The two lovers do meet again, but the thought of Lady Spencer, im-

placable and stern in her determination that her son's marriage to Nicola be preserved, helps Olivia in her anguished realization that Rollo's ability to play the double game is in direct contrast to her own single-minded and jealous love. Shortly afterward, Rollo is seriously hurt in a car crash, and Lady Spencer shows her kindness to Olivia by calling her to tell her about the accident and later to arrange a short and final visit to Rollo's house, where he is recuperating, the family being away for a few hours.

Natalie Harper

WEEDS

Author: Edith Summers Kelley (1884-1956)
Type of work: Novel
Time of action: The early twentieth century
First published: 1923

Judith Pippinger Blackford, the daughter of a Kentucky sharecropper who becomes another sharecropper's wife. The story begins when she is a little girl. She is a diamond in the rough, a child who stands out among the ignorant, overworked people who surround her because of her beauty, vitality, and strength of character. She displays artistic ability at an early age and obviously could have been successful in that field if she had had any opportunities. Instead, she is condemned like all the other girls to marry a poor farmer, with nothing to look forward to but drudgery and childbearing. When the story ends, she has had three children and one self-induced miscarriage. Her beauty has faded; her body is bent and coarsened by poverty and toil; her rebellious spirit has been broken, and she is resigned to her fate.

Jerry Blackford, Judith's sharecropper husband. This farmer's son is a strong, handsome man who loves and admires Judith, although he cannot fully understand her moods, lacking her intelligence and sensitivity. His main interest, like that of most of the men in the area, is raising tobacco and trying to climb out of poverty. A large part of this naturalis-

tic novel deals with the problems of tobacco growers over a period of good and bad years. The price of tobacco is high when weather conditions have caused a small crop; when there is favorable weather, the big yield drives tobacco prices down. The years of endless toil and disappointment gradually erode the Blackfords' affection for each other. At the end of the novel, the near-fatal illness of their youngest child brings them back together, making them realize that their fate is stamped and sealed. Like Adam and Eve in Genesis, their life of toil will be relieved only by whatever comfort they can give each other.

Jabez Moorhouse, an elderly farmhand who plays the fiddle at country socials. This wizened country philosopher is the counterpart of Judith, with whom he maintains a friendship throughout the novel. Jabez is the only other character who can see the beauty and mystery of nature and has the creative urge which that sensitivity inspires. His main regret in life is that he was never able to learn to play the violin as well as he knows himself to be capable of doing. Like Judith, his higher aspirations have had no chance of flowering in this grim, impoverished environment.

Lizzie May Pippinger Pooler, Judith's older sister, a sharecropper's wife. Lizzie May is also physically attractive, but she lacks the rare special qualities of her younger sister. When Lizzie May marries and begins bearing children, she accepts her role in life with unquestioning docility, lacking the imagination to see that things could be any different. Her main functions in the novel are to portray the typical farm wife and to serve as a foil to Judith's unique personality.

Dan Pooler, Lizzie May's sharecropper husband, a hardworking, unimaginative man who typifies the character and experiences of the average male in the region.

Luke and
Hat Wolf, a crude sharecropping couple, Judith and Jerry's closest neighbors. They, too, represent the typical farmers of the region.

At one point Judith discovers that Jerry, from whom she has become estranged, is having an affair with Hat. This further embitters her life and makes her feel more spiritually isolated than ever.

The Revivalist, a young traveling preacher. Judith is sexually captivated by this handsome young man because of his soulful eyes. For several months they have a clandestine love affair. She is ultimately disappointed to realize that he is a creature of surface appearances and does not really share her inexpressible yearnings for some transcendental reality. When she finds that she is pregnant with his child, she nearly kills herself in trying to induce a miscarriage. His function in the story is to highlight her unique spirit and her hopeless predicament in this blighted environment.

Bill Delaney

THE WELL

Author: Elizabeth Jolley (1923-   )
Type of work: Novel
Time of action: The early 1980's
First published: 1986

Hester Harper, an Australian rancher. A thin, flat-breasted, middle-aged woman with a lame leg, she is aware of having been a disappointment to her father, with whom she lives, because she was a girl, and an ugly, crippled one at that, instead of a boy. When she takes an orphaned teenager home with her, for the first time since the loss of her childhood governess Hester feels close to another human being. After her father's death, Hester neglects and then sells her land, planning to spend the money on luxuries for Katherine and for herself and determining never to let Katherine leave her. When the girl, driving fast in the dark, hits some object, presumably a man, Hester throws the body into her well in order to protect Katherine and to keep her. When she finds her money missing and learns that there has been a thief in the neighborhood, Hester as-

sumes that the money is in the well with the man, but she is willing to lose the money rather than to lose Katherine.

Katherine, an orphan. Almost sixteen when Hester meets her, she is a pretty, delicate-looking girl with thin blonde hair and a childish voice. Ingratiating and imaginative, she becomes a playmate for her employer, out of whom she can soon wheedle anything she wants. After the automobile accident, Katherine's sexual frustrations turn into an obsession. She is certain that the man in the well is still alive and that he must be released so that he can marry her. Even though Hester has the well covered, believing that the two women can return to their normal life together, it is obvious that Katherine has other plans. She seems to have some of Hester's missing cash. Moreover, she has insisted on having an unsavory girlfriend come to the ranch. It is obvious that she will not stay indefinitely with Hester.

Mr. Bird, a stock and station agent. A somewhat younger friend of Hester's father, he considers it his obligation to help Hester with business affairs after her father's death. Repeatedly he warns Hester about her reckless spending, which he accurately ascribes to her infatuation with Katherine. Although Hester sees him as a bore, after his death she discovers notebooks full of financial advice for her, proving that he has been her only real friend.

Mr. Harper, Hester's father. Although ill and dependent upon her, in old age he enjoys tyrannizing over his daughter. His lifelong indifference to her is evident in her memory of the events which took place years before, when he heartlessly banished her beloved governess and foster mother, who had had a miscarriage, the result of his seduction.

Mr. Borden, a neighboring rancher. A young, strong man, he buys Hester's house and then her land. It is at the party given to celebrate the purchase that Katherine discovers what she has been missing in her life with Hester, and it is after that party that Katherine has her accident.

Rosalie Borden, the wife of Mr. Borden. A plump, noisy young woman with an ever-increasing brood of children, to Hester she symbolizes the life from which her own ugliness has forever barred her. At the party, when Rosalie warns Hester that Katherine will and should leave her, she betrays her own distaste for the eternal spinster.

Rosemary M. Canfield Reisman

WHAT A BEAUTIFUL SUNDAY!

Author: Jorge Semprun (1923-   )
Type of work: Novel
Time of action: World War II
First published: Quel beau dimanche, 1980 (English translation, 1982)

Gerard Sorel, also known as **Sanchez, Camille Salagnac, Rafael Artigas, Rafael Bustamante, Larrea, Ramon Barreto,** and other pseudonyms, a Spaniard and Communist Party member who spent time in the Buchenwald concentration camp. He narrates his story and never reveals his real name. From a bourgeois background, yet well known and trusted in the Party underground, Gerard survives the prison camp because of the Party's place in its organization. He is an intellectual, or observer, by temperament, who constantly compares individuals, national groups, and times in history. His prison-camp experiences, especially the constant awareness of others' deaths, combined with his many identity changes and the changes, over the years, in the Communist Party line make him question the reality of his experiences and even of his existence.

Fernand Barizon, a Communist Party member from France, who survives Buchenwald with Gerard and discusses it with him fifteen years later. The meaning of his remark "What a beautiful Sunday!" is never articulated, though Gerard's memory of the statement resonates throughout the novel. Barizon is not an intellectual. He remembers his true and very physical love affair with a French garment union member, Juliette, and he has a zest for food and a desire for comfort. He is an extremely loyal friend. He never fully trusts the Party's insistence on organization, since he operates more from the heart.

Willi Seifert, assigned by the Nazi SS to be kapo of the Arbeitsstatistik (record-keeping department), had once been a member of the Communist Youth Movement. With his power in the camp, though he too is a prisoner, he is able to save Party members and others from extermination by assigning them to non-life-threatening jobs. He is a man of great personal authority, yet he is later frightened by Stalin's purges and he eventually disappears.

Henk Spoenay, a Dutch prisoner, is liaison between Seifert and the SS. He is the same age as Gerard, and they are friends.

Leon Blum,
Johann Wolfgang von Goethe, and
Johann Peter Eckermann, who are visualized by the narrator, Sorel. Blum, ironically, was not only a leader of the Socialist Party and the Popular Front, and therefore ultimately imprisoned on the premises of Buchenwald, but also the author of *Nouvelles*

Conversations de Goethe avec Eckermann. Some of the conversations in Blum's book were supposed to have taken place at Etters Hill, near Weimar, the site of Buchenwald.

Jehovah (Johann), one of the much-persecuted Jehovah's Witnesses at Buchenwald. He opens every conversation with Sorel by quoting a passage from the Bible which is appropriate to the moment.

Aleksandr Solzhenitsyn, the Russian dissident. He writes of the Stalinist gulag so that Sorel eventually realizes the parallel between the institutions of Communist labor camps and those of Nazi internment camps. Consequently, Sorel acknowledges the Russian Revolution as a historical catastrophe.

Anna R. Holloway

WHAT I'M GOING TO DO, I THINK

Author: Larry Woiwode (1941-   )
Type of work: Novel
Time of action: 1964
First published: 1969

Christofer (Chris) Van Eenanam (ē•nă′ năm), a graduate student in mathematics at the University of Chicago. At age twenty-three, he is still deeply unsure of his identity. His inability to resolve the conflicts within his personality, partially caused by the loss of his Catholic faith, undermines his relationship with Ellen Strohe even after their marriage. His feelings about her, and about virtually everything important to him, are deep but inconsistent. Always having to prove himself to himself, he is unable to provide Ellen the attention and understanding that she needs. After a three-year tumultuous relationship, begun when they were university students, they are married when Ellen becomes pregnant. The novel begins as they arrive at her grandparents' lodge in Northern Michigan, where they spend their honeymoon. During the summer, as Chris repairs the lodge, he struggles with his ambivalent feel-

ings about being a husband and prospective father.

Ellen Sidone Anne Strohe Van Eenanam, the pregnant wife of Chris. The twenty-one-year-old woman, brought up by her grandparents after the deaths of her parents in an accident, needs reliability and consistency in a lover to bring her out of her shell. She, too, is unsure of her feelings about him and about being a mother. Her pregnancy only increases her self-absorption, and Chris's ambivalence precludes his being sufficiently helpful.

Aloysius James Strohe, Ellen's grandfather and a wealthy brewery owner. A domineering, crafty, possessive, and insightful old man, Strohe recognizes the weakness in Chris but fails in his attempts to get Ellen to renounce him. His virtues are those of the Germanic, self-made, practical man. He has no patience with the equivocal personality of Chris or his interest in the abstractions of mathematics. He lets the young couple stay at the lodge in expectation that the experience will separate them.

Grandma Strohe, Ellen's Christian Scientist grandmother. Her inflexible morality allows no space for human error. She never forgives or forgets. Her rejection of Chris is absolute and her cruelty to Ellen in the name of religion is reprehensible.

Orin Clausen, a neighboring farmer, a coarse, provincial man with the rural mistrust of the unknown and the urban. Chris earns his respect by putting in a very hard day's work stacking Clausen's hay bales, but Clausen reminds Chris of the life as a farmer that Chris went to school to escape.

Anna Clausen, the widowed sister-in-law of Orin. Another example of rural isolation and its subsequent loneliness, Anna lives with her brother-in-law in a state of mutual antipathy as business partners. The young couple could give her pleasure merely by paying her a visit, but, caught up in themselves, they never do.

William J. McDonald

WHAT PRICE GLORY?

Authors: Maxwell Anderson (1888-1959) and Laurence Stallings (1894-1968)
Type of work: Play
Time of action: World War I
First produced: 1924

First Sergeant Quirt, the company's senior noncommissioned officer (NCO). He was Flagg's senior NCO in China when the captain was enlisted, and they had a disagreement over a woman which continues decades later. Quirt is brutal and dangerously self-confident, and he steals Flagg's girl after decking a drunken Irishman. In spite of Flagg's order, he refuses to marry the dishonored woman. At the battlefront, Quirt longs for action, so much so that he is seriously wounded in the foot and must return behind the lines. He escapes from the hospital and confronts Flagg; the two agree to a game of blackjack to decide their fate, but orders calling them back to the front force them to abandon their duel. Quirt serves as the essential soldier: a violent womanizer but always ready to answer a call to arms.

Captain Flagg, the company commander. Formally a corporal and a veteran of duty in both China and Cuba, Flagg is an alcoholic, which gets him into considerable difficulties. He does, at least, have some compassion for his woman, Charmaine, but it is frequently obscured by his drunken brawling, which leads to his imprisonment on an attempted manslaughter charge at one point in the play. He is also keenly aware of Quirt's abilities as a soldier, as well as Quirt's desire to usurp his command. A particularly touching scene occurs in act 2, when Flagg comforts a shell-shocked lieutenant. When he is sober, Flagg is a creditable leader who seems to be aware of the suffering inherent in war. In spite of these compassionate tendencies, he, like Quirt, does not hesitate when the call to arms is sounded.

Charmaine de la Cognac, described as a "drab," an attractive young woman who is the daughter of Cognac Pete, a local tavern keeper. She is quite liberal with her affections; in the opening scene, she worries over Flagg and his impending journey to Paris. In the next scene, she is passionately kissing Quirt. Anderson and Stallings use Charmaine as an example of the brutality and the callousness of the common soldier; they really care quite little about her and her situation. Not even the love of a beautiful woman will keep these men from hearing the call to arms.

Private Lewishon, a young Jewish recruit, who demonstrates that war can be brutal to the soldier as well as the civilian. He first appears in act 1, pleading with Flagg for re-placement identification tags. The captain dismisses him with a promise to replace the missing items but laughs at the young soldier's homesickness. The irony in this scene is revealed when Lewishon is mortally wounded in the attack on the wine cellar at the battlefront.

Richard S. Keating

WHAT THE BUTLER SAW

Author: Joe Orton (1933-1967)
Type of work: Play
Time of action: The 1960's
First produced: 1969

Dr. Prentice, a middle-aged psychiatrist. Prentice is an unscrupulous man who does not hesitate to use his position as a doctor to seduce his would-be secretary, Geraldine Barclay. He also refuses to tell the truth, despite the trouble that causes Geraldine with Dr. Rance. It was this same lustful lack of scruples that led him to interfere with an unknown chambermaid at the Station Hotel many years before, resulting in her conception of Geraldine and Nick.

Dr. Rance, a psychiatrist sent from the government to check up on how psychiatry clinics are being run. He is a brutal, power-mad doctor, and he tries to certify everybody as insane, though it is obvious that he is the only one who is truly mad.

Mrs. Prentice, Dr. Prentice's wife. During a brief stint as a chambermaid at the Station Hotel, she was raped in a linen cupboard during a power outage (hence her inability to recognize her attacker as her fiancé, Dr. Prentice). She is a blasé, disillusioned woman who belongs to a lesbian women's group. The failure of the Prentices' marriage is attributed to the fact that Mrs. Prentice refused to consummate their marriage during their wedding night in a linen cupboard.

Nicholas (Nick) Beckett, a page boy from the Station Hotel. Nick is an accomplished typist and blackmailer with an insatiable sex-ual appetite, exemplified by his attempted rape of Mrs. Prentice (his mother) and the accomplished molestation of "a section of the Priory Road School for girls" on the same night. He turns out to be Geraldine's twin brother and the Prentices' son.

Geraldine Barclay, an applicant for the position as Dr. Prentice's secretary. A young, attractive girl, she is trustful and believes in telling the truth. Though the only person with any morals (except, perhaps, for Sergeant Match), she gets the brunt of Dr. Rance's abuse, as when he cuts off all of her hair. Her ignorance of the whereabouts of Winston Churchill's missing body parts seems symbolic of her purity and naïveté. Ultimately, it is revealed that she is Nick's twin and the Prentices' daughter.

Sergeant Match, a policeman looking for Geraldine Barclay and Nicholas Beckett. His more important mission, however, is to find Geraldine and Sir Winston's missing parts; of lesser interest is his charge to find the molestor of the Priory Road schoolgirls. Having accomplished his main task, which is of national importance, Match has no qualms about forgetting everything else he has witnessed, though this willingness may be related to the large amount of narcotics that Dr. Prentice has given him.

T. M. Lipman

WHAT'S BRED IN THE BONE

Author: Robertson Davies (1913-   )
Type of work: Novel
Time of action: The mid-1980's in the framing fiction; from the mid-nineteenth century to 1981 in the body of the novel
First published: 1985

Francis Chegwidden Cornish, a Canadian art expert. The novel purports to tell what has been "bred in the bone" of Francis. Francis, who is from a wealthy but emotionally distant family, is a sensitive, intelligent boy. He teaches himself to observe carefully and to draw what he sees; he later discovers that his affinity in art is for the Old Masters and that he is false to himself when he tries to express himself in modern styles. His skill at observation makes him useful to the British intelligence service before and during World War II. He paints the myth of himself, an expression of what has made him what he is, in Old Master style; when the painting is discovered after the war, art experts dub it *The Marriage at Cana* and attribute it to the Alchemical Master.

The Daimon Maimas, Francis' personal attendant spirit, the guiding force in his life. It is he who has arranged Francis' life to make him what he is, though his control does not mean that Francis lacks freedom of choice.

The Lesser Zadkiel, the recording angel. His records provide the biography of Francis.

James Ignatius McRory (the Senator, Hamish), Francis' maternal grandfather. A Scottish Catholic, McRory has made a fortune in the timber business. His desire to rise socially leads him to debut his daughter at court in London. He is interested in photography and teaches Francis the effects of different angles and types of light on a subject. In his will, he leaves Francis a substantial sum of money and exempts him from entering the family banking business.

Major, later Sir Francis Cornish, Francis' father. The younger son in an old family, he agrees to marry the pregnant Mary-Jacobine

McRory after certain financial agreements are made. He is appointed president of his father-in-law's bank, a figurehead position. His real work is in intelligence, and he recruits Francis to follow him in that field.

Mary-Jacobine (Mary-Jim or Jacko) Cornish, née **McRory,** Francis' mother. A beauty, Mary-Jacobine makes her debut at the court of King Edward VII in 1903; on that night, she becomes pregnant with the child of a footman who reminds her of a famous actor. She later becomes the perfect society wife but spends little time with her sons.

Mary-Benedetta (Mary-Ben) McRory, Francis' great-aunt. Mary-Ben has the greatest hand in rearing Francis. She instills in Francis a romantic Catholicism and has him baptized a Catholic at age fourteen, though he has already been baptized a Protestant. Her collection of prints inspires Francis' interest in art.

Francis (the Looner) Cornish, Francis' elder brother. The Looner is mentally and physically handicapped because of Mary-Jacobine's attempts to end the unwanted pregnancy begun on her debut night. Francis' mother and father believe the Looner is dead; he is kept upstairs in his grandfather's house. His existence instills in Francis a compassion for the unfortunate.

Zadok Hoyle, a groom for the McRory family. Unknown to him and to the McRory family, he is the Looner's father. Zadok also assists the local undertaker by preparing bodies for burial. He allows Francis to watch him in the embalming process, teaching him a respect for individuals and the fragility of life.

Ismay Glasson Cornish, Francis' cousin and

later his wife. Francis at first believes her to be his dream woman, the woman who will complement his masculine nature with her feminine nature to make him whole. She tricks him into marriage to cover her pregnancy by another man, then leaves the child with her parents and joins her lover in Spain. The child and Ismay's family become a drain on Francis' finances. Ismay is a great believer in idealistic, unrealistic causes.

Tancred Saraceni, an art expert. He takes Francis as an apprentice and teaches him the style, physical composition (ingredients of paints), and iconography of Old Master paintings. He is casuistic about restoring paintings to look somewhat better than they did originally. He leaves Francis his fortune and his possessions.

Ruth Nibsmith, Francis' friend and lover. She casts Francis' horoscope seriously, wisely, and perceptively.

Aylwin Ross, a Canadian art critic. Francis' protégé, Ross becomes famous for his explication of *The Marriage at Cana,* unaware of its origin. He commits suicide after Francis

refuses to buy the painting for the Canadian National Gallery.

Victoria Cameron, the McRory's cook. She cares for the Looner and instills some hard, practical Calvinist values in Francis.

Dr. Joseph Ambrosius (J. A.) Jerome, the McRory family physician. Dr. J. A. recommends the false burial of the Looner, believing that knowledge of his existence will harm Francis.

Colonel ("Uncle") Jack Copplestone, Francis' contact in British Intelligence. He arranges Francis' positions as a spy to coincide with his art activities.

The Reverend Simon Darcourt, Francis' friend and biographer. In the frame fiction, he complains that he cannot find enough information to write Francis' biography properly.

Arthur Cornish, Francis' nephew and executor, a banker. he is worried by the whiff of scandal about Francis that Simon has brought to him.

Karen M. Cleveland

WHEN I WHISTLE

Author: Shusaku Endō (1923-   )
Type of work: Novel
Time of action: The 1960's
First published: Kuchibue o fuku toki, 1974 (English translation, 1979)

Ozu, an aging Japanese businessman. Entering his senior years, Ozu is a humble clerk, preoccupied with memories of his youth and greatly troubled by his increasing fear of the different moral vision animating the youth of postwar Japan, as exemplified in the unadorned avarice and ambition of his son, Eiichi. Nostalgic for an older, more disciplined, even militaristic Japan, he finds in the present a predatory industrial power immune to simple human compassion and idealism. His mental search recalls Nada Middle School and his impish friend Flatfish, who wiled away his

youth with Ozu, longing for female companionship. Both had sought the affection of the nubile, beautiful Aiko. Ozu's flashbacks and reveries of his youth and postadolescent contacts with Flatfish come crashing to a halt when he learns of Flatfish's death from a battlefield disease. He determines to search for Aiko to report this bad news. Finding her accidentally, as one of his son's terminal cancer patients, Ozu sees Aiko as merely one laboratory rat, prey to medical science's preoccupation with advanced objective knowledge at the expense of nurturing care and concern for individual persons. While locating Aiko's childhood home, now bulldozed in the name of progress, Ozu sinks into despair as his generation fades into the bleak sunset of Japan's moral resignation in the midst of its economic and technological triumphs.

Flatfish, Ozu's childhood and post-high school friend. Ozu's constant companion in the idyllic days before World War II, Flatfish is an undisciplined, unintellectual parody of Japanese manhood, always in trouble at the Nada Middle School, where he and Ozu met, and unconcerned about career advancement in his chosen employment. Irrepressible, frivolous, and hopelessly attracted to the young girls in his class and older ones, Flatfish surrenders any claim to scholastic prowess or responsible citizenship to remain an adolescent as long as he can. He tempers Ozu's basic reserved nature and teaches him to revel in the spontaneous and childish. Living only in Ozu's flashbacks, Flatfish is a vivid contrast to Ozu's son, Eiichi, in his free, unpretentious pursuit of joy and immediate fulfillment. Flatfish is the buoyant, unfettered spirit of Japanese manhood that has died in the aftermath of the wars. Ozu's discovery of his death triggers the novel's denouement as he seeks out the lovely Aiko to share his grief, only to discover more.

Eiichi, Ozu's son. Ambitious and without scruples, Eiichi is desperate to rise within the medical profession as a surgeon. He is completely identified with a grim, work-oriented Japan: driven, technological, spiritually barren, the epitome of Western imperialism that his father has fought to defeat. He finds his father's basic humanism debilitating and unprogressive, a needless sentimentality that impedes efficiency and his ultimate career goals. His reputation for callousness and insensitivity are well established when father and son are united by the illness of Ozu's beloved Aiko. Here their differing ethics are underscored and foregrounded. As his patient, Aiko represents to Eiichi (an aptly drawn representative of the new generation of Japanese professionals) only a convenient subject for an experimental cancer treatment, not a person deserving care, love, or basic dignity.

Aiko, a patient of Eiichi and the object of Ozu's adolescent infatuation. Aiko is a war widow and the living symbol to Ozu of all that is pure and authentic in the Japanese culture of his youth. She lives in the novel more as a memory or icon than as a living, breathing human being, trapped as she is in Eiichi's experimental cancer program. Her death signals to Ozu the final victory of technological imperialism over the tenderness and compassion representative of the Japanese character to him in his adolescence in prewar Japan.

Dr. Ii, a malevolent, unscrupulous doctor in the hospital where Eiichi serves. Dr. Ii is an imperious, natural product of postwar Japan's rigid determination to rise from the ashes of ignominy and defeat, experienced in using people and perfectly willing to prescribe worthless drugs for his patients if the pharmaceutical company which produces them continues to fund his research. As the dubious role model for Eiichi and other medical personnel, Dr. Ii manifests the greed and indifference to civility Ozu finds everywhere manifested in the new Japan.

Bruce L. Edwards

WHEN YOU COMIN' BACK, RED RYDER?

Author: Mark Medoff (1940-   )
Type of work: Play
Time of action: The late 1960's
First produced: 1973

Stephen "Red" Ryder, the graveyard clerk at a restaurant. A small, plain nineteen-year-old young man with brown hair, Stephen dresses in the style of the 1950's and has a tattoo on his arm that reads "Born Dead." Intense and unhappy, he feels stifled by the small New Mexico town in which he lives and has elaborate dreams of leaving, but he feels responsible for his ill mother. His dissatisfaction with his life is reflected in his negative relationships with others. His association with the cowboy hero Red Ryder serves to magnify his inability to mold his own life.

Angel, the daytime waitress. In her early twenties, Angel is overweight and plain. She lives with her mother and grandmother, and her life revolves around them, her job, and nights spent watching television with Lyle. She obviously cares about Stephen, and his departure at the end of the play is a devastating event in her life. Simple, sweet-natured, and vulnerable, she is a sympathetic character in the midst of the violence of the play.

Lyle Striker, the owner of the local gas station and motel. In his sixties, Lyle has a brace on one knee and walks with a crutch as the result of a stroke. None of this is a sign of weakness, however, and he remains an active and attractive man. He engages in a friendly rivalry with Stephen and has some feelings for Angel. Straightforward and likable, he is a sensible man of considerable inner strength who attempts to maintain an even keel, even in the midst of an upsetting situation.

Richard Ethredge, a textile import businessman. Confident and good-looking in his late thirties, Richard is attractive and graceful. Authoritative, manipulative, and somewhat condescending, particularly toward his wife, he is accustomed to being in control and in charge. His money and his attitude make him a primary target of the young man who invades the scene, and the shallowness of his strength makes him easy prey.

Clarisse Ethredge, a violinist and college professor. Also in her late thirties, Clarisse is reserved, shy, and quiet, largely as a result of her husband's dominance. In the action of the play, she reveals a repressed sexuality and strength of character that are not evident in early scenes.

Teddy, a young drifter and drug runner. Thirty years old, Teddy is a former GI with long hair, dressed in an army fatigue jacket. Teddy is intense, insulting, and violent, both physically and psychologically. He despises a world that he finds unacceptable in its weakness. Unpredictable in his behavior, he has an innate ability to reveal people's fears and desires and thus dominate them. His violence is without apparent purpose and occurs without any evident motivation. His sudden intrusion into the otherwise placid life of the play's characters is the force that motivates self-recognition and change.

Cheryl, Teddy's companion. Cheryl is busty and very attractive, no more than twenty, and dressed in jeans and a tank top. Submissive and basically silent through most of the play, she refuses to leave with Teddy at the end, exhibiting an independence and strength not previously revealed.

Mr. Carter, the owner of the restaurant. Mr. Carter is cheap, cantankerous, and totally devoted to his business. He is disdainful of other people and sees them only as tools for his own endeavors.

John C. Watson

WHERE HAS TOMMY FLOWERS GONE?

Author: Terrence McNally (1939-   )
Type of work: Play
Time of action: 1971
First produced: 1971

Tommy Flowers, a thirty-year-old dropout from St. Petersburg who has become a self-proclaimed urban revolutionary in New York City. Like his idols James Dean and Holden Caulfield, he sees himself as an outsider, defiant in the face of established authority, a confirmed malcontent who makes terrorist raids on an oppressively corrupt society and its stifling conventions. At first these attacks on conformity are pranks—shoplifting, defaulting on cabfare or the check for a meal, engaging in sex and drugs at any opportunity, alarming shoppers by announcing that there is a bomb in Bloomingdale's; but the menace becomes less playful after he manufactures a real bomb and carries it around Manhattan with him. He sets up in a ménage of misfits with Ben, Nedda, and his dog Arnold, but this surrogate family fails to satisfy his need for a community that allows individual expression. When Ben dies and Nedda flees for the security of the suburbs, Tommy, in a final aggressive (he would say redemptive) act, takes his bomb and wires it to go off in a telephone booth near a policeman.

Nedda Lemon, an aspiring cellist who has fled the suburbs for the promise of a career in New York City. What she finds instead is a mean, cold city that offers, at best, the prospect of being booked to play the Lord's prayer at Bar Mitzvahs in Brooklyn. Despondent, she meets Tommy in the ladies' room at Bloomingdale's where he discovers her stowing shoplifted goods in her cello case. She takes Tommy, Ben, and Arnold into her flat in the Village and for a while is content with this domestic arrangement, until Tommy's continued anarchic campaign to overturn the established order leads her to entertain fantasies of pipe-smoking doctors, station wagons, the whole scenario of suburban stability. Arrested when she returns to pay a check that Tommy has failed to pay, Nedda is incarcerated and must resort to her father for her rescue.

Jack Wonder, known as **Ben Delight,** an old has-been stage actor and panhandler. Ben and Tommy share a street corner where Ben rants about having spent his career in the shadow of Paul Muni, claiming that Muni got all the parts that rightfully should have been Ben's. He staunchly defends the stage against the screen, being ignorant of James Dean but having seen Tommy's disastrous stage performance in a minor Off-Broadway play. Ben precipitates one of Tommy's indictments of old age, but they are reconciled and move into Nedda's Village flat, where Ben passes his evenings endlessly reading *Variety.* He becomes ill and is taken to Bellevue, where he dies, which Tommy regards as yet another abandonment.

Arnold, Tommy's sheepdog, whom Tommy abandons to follow a sexy seventeen-year-old Californian to her hotel room. Left on the street alone, Arnold soliloquizes on the indecisiveness of his master while assuring the audience that he is not a talking but a thinking dog.

Thomas J. Campbell

WHO HAS SEEN THE WIND

Author: W. O. Mitchell (1914-   )
Type of work: Novel
Time of action: 1929-1937, during the Depression
First published: 1947

Brian Sean MacMurray O'Connal, ages four to eleven. A slight, lean, dark "black Scotch" boy, Brian is imaginative and always inquisitive about the rhythms of nature that he witnesses on the sweeping, beckoning, and now drought-ridden Saskatchewan prairie where he lives. By the age of eleven, Brian has experienced the deaths both of cherished pets and of beloved close family members, making him mature beyond his years. Always sensitive to the relentless patterns of birth and death around him, Brian perceives aspects of life about which his contemporaries Forbsie Hoffman and Artie Sherry comprehend little. Brian's sturdy independence makes his mother heartsick, but his independence and his extraordinary visionary capacity protect him somewhat from the harsh emotional blows he is dealt so early.

Gerald O'Connal, big and auburn-haired, Maggie's husband, Brian and Bobbie's father, and the town druggist. A quiet, serious man, as befits his respectable position in the town, Gerald is also gentle and sensitive. It is Gerald who solves the conflict between Brian and his grandmother over Brian's puppy Jappy, who shares Brian's wonder and respects his sorrow over the birth and death of a baby pigeon, who quietly finances his impoverished brother Sean's irrigation project, and who is his wife's model of the kind of person she wants their sons to be. Always concerned for others, he downplays persistent signs of his own ill health and dies suddenly at forty-three of gall-bladder disease.

Maggie MacMurray O'Connal, small, dark, pretty, and intense. She loves and admires her husband and cares fiercely about her sons, instilling in them a desire to be strong, worthy, and successful. Ordinarily a person who does not express her emotions, she nevertheless makes them evident on such occasions as the near-death of an infant Bobby and in her dignified but forceful defense of Brian to his sadistic teacher Miss Macdonald. Though she is devastated by her husband's death, her love and ambition for her sons is undiminished.

Margaret (Maggie) Biggart MacMurray, Maggie O'Connal's mother. Traveling west to homestead with her husband John in 1885, she led the pioneer's hard, challenging life, which she nevertheless loved, delighting still to tell her grandchildren about the old days. Now elderly, lame, and increasingly frail, she lives with her daughter's family, and at first she appears an authoritative figure to the small Brian. After Gerald's death, however, a mutual sympathy grows between grandmother

and grandson; each appreciates the other's independence and affinity for the natural world. At eighty-two, she dies of pneumonia, seeking the outdoor air at the last.

Sean O'Connal, Gerald's brother and his senior by fifteen years. A huge, profane redhead, never married, Sean loves his brother and his brother's family tenderly, having seen to Gerald's upbringing and education himself. A grain farmer devastated and embittered by the drought of the 1930's, Sean is a man of the future, vainly advocating conservationist ploughing, irrigation, and farming methods. After Gerald's death, he encourages Brian's growing interest in agricultural engineering, assuring the boy's future.

Young Ben, the half-wild, wholly unchecked son of the reprobate Old Ben, but really a true child of nature, a noble savage. The shockhaired, gray-eyed, broadcheeked Young Ben resists all efforts, both sympathetic and vengeful, to tame and educate him, preferring his natural habitat, the broad Saskatchewan prairie. He shares with Brian a compassion for helpless creatures, and he maintains an almost wordless, close, protective relationship with Brian. The Young Ben embodies a freedom of spirit that Brian perceives but cannot attain.

Mr. Digby, the elementary school principal, weathered-looking, with a shock of fair hair, very blue eyes, and threadbare clothing. Though improvident, Mr. Digby is a man of compassion and lively intellect, always doing his best to combat the small town's narrowness and bigotry. He releases the Young Ben from school, quietly financing the boy's few necessities after the Old Ben is jailed, and imperiling his own job in the process. He understands the needs of both his students and the many adults to whom he lends a sympathetic ear. Up to now a contented bachelor, he comes to love Ruth Thompson as a kindred spirit as well as a desirable woman.

Ruth Thompson, dramatically dark-haired and dark-eyed, a teacher at Digby's school. As compassionate as Digby, she takes overt action against injustice more readily than he does and vanquishes the town bully Mrs. Abercrombie. Breaking for the second time an engagement to the sardonic yet humane town doctor Peter Svarich, she will marry Digby instead.

Jill Rollins

WIDE SARGASSO SEA

Author: Jean Rhys (Ella Gwendolen Rees Williams, 1894-1979)
Type of work: Novel
Time of action: The 1830's
First published: 1966

Antoinette Cosway, later **Bertha Mason Rochester.** Antoinette and her story constitute a revisionist treatment of events culminating in her transformation into Charlotte Brontë's famed madwoman in the attic, Bertha Mason Rochester in *Jane Eyre*. Antoinette, the protagonist and narrator of approximately one-half of the story, reflects on her youth and the loneliness and isolation that she experienced as a white Créole child in the predominantly black West Indies. Having outlived most of her family, she halfheartedly submits to a marriage with the British Mr. Rochester that has been arranged by her stepbrother. In reality, this union is a business deal whereby Antoinette's inheritance is consigned to Rochester in return for his accepting responsibility for her. This latter point proves important as whispers and insinuations spread about Antoinette, her beautiful mother, and her younger brother, individuals thought to have "slept too long in the moonlight," who exhibit the madness supposedly present in all white Créoles. Antoinette's naïveté about life outside the West Indies contrasts sharply with Rochester's comparative worldliness. Her query to her soon-to-be husband reveals her troubled vulnerability—she speaks not of love or even romance but of rest: "Can you give me peace?" This attitude exposes a young woman who has deferred to the decisions of the men in her life—father, stepbrother, and husband—while depending on old and subservient women for what little emotional support and nurture she has received. She becomes a woman who cannot act and who is increasingly defined by men, as symbolized by Rochester's arbitrarily changing her name from Antoinette to Bertha. When her husband rejects her because of his growing preoccupation with her possible madness, Antoinette, denying her own resources, consults the black arts for a spell to bring love to their marriage. When this desperate attempt fails, she becomes blank, a shell destined for the profound madness chronicled in *Jane Eyre*.

Mr. Rochester, a young British gentleman, the second son of a proper English family who is forced by the law of primogeniture to secure his own fortune. His narration of the second half of the story recounts his arranged marriage to a beautiful but mysterious West Indian girl who brings to the union the fortune he seeks. Despite certain odd circumstances surrounding their marriage, only after receiving a revealing letter from a black man who claims to be a relative of his bride does Rochester realize why this marriage was so eagerly sought by her stepbrother. He also realizes that everyone but him is aware of the potential for madness that exists in his new wife's family. Sensing that he has been the victim of a duplicitous plot, Rochester expresses hatred for the deceptive beauty of the islands, a quality that he has come to associate with Antoinette as well. Seeking only his own sanity, he returns to England with Antoinette and conceals her with a nurse in the attic of his family home. Also on his return to England, he learns that both his father and his brother have died, thus ironically providing him with the fortune that he has needlessly already secured at great cost to himself and at even greater cost to Antoinette.

Annette Cosway Mason, Antoinette's mother, who was widowed at an early age. After Cosway's death, the family was very poor and lonely for five years. Determined to provide for her children and herself, Annette marries Mr. Mason and is happy for a time, but after the natives destroy her home and kill her son, Annette turns against Mason and tries to kill him. He places her in a separate house with servants as attendants. There her daughter witnesses the effects of madness—vivid impressions indelibly burned into Antoinette's mind.

Christophine Dubois, a native of Martinique given to Annette as a wedding present by her first husband. Christophine becomes the nurse of Antoinette and is the only person who consistently supports the lonely young woman. A colorful person given to expressing bromides of conventional wisdom, Christophine receives the news of the terms of Antoinette's marriage with the pronouncement, "All women . . . nothing but fools." A practitioner of voodoo, she refuses to use her black arts on Rochester until Antoinette has told him herself about her family secrets. In the end, Christophine's wisdom is not strong enough to save Antoinette.

Mr. Mason, Annette's second husband and Antoinette's stepfather. After Annette's demise, Mason attempts to care for Antoinette.

Pierre, the younger brother of Antoinette, who is afflicted with the family curse of madness. Their mother dotes on him much more than on Antoinette. Pierre is killed when natives set fire to the Mason home.

Aunt Cora, a relative of the Cosways who tries to protect Antoinette's rights and fortune upon learning of Richard's arranged marriage for Antoinette.

Richard Mason, Antoinette's stepbrother, who negotiates the marriage of Antoinette and Rochester.

Daniel Cosway, a black man who claims to be a relative of Antoinette. He writes a letter to Rochester telling him about the taint of madness that follows Antoinette's family.

Sandi Cosway, Daniel's half brother and a relative of Antoinette. Implications persist that Sandi and Antoinette are romantically involved.

Grace Poole,
Mrs. Eff, and
Leah, servants in the house in England in which Rochester confines Antoinette.

Lagretta T. Lenker

THE WIDOWER'S SON

Author: Alan Sillitoe (1928-   )
Type of work: Novel
Time of action: The early twentieth century to 1976
First published: 1976

Colonel William Scorton, the protagonist and a gunner during World War II. A straight-backed career soldier, he is rugged, tall, and authoritative. He is also very self-disciplined and organized, but rather pessimistic and solitary. Molded into the image of the perfect soldier by a father who never showed him the slightest affection, the military order and discipline of his twenty-five years in the army

has carried over into his civilian life, where he attempts to run his marriage and his career as if he were still in the army. Eventually he realizes that he was never really cut out to be a soldier. Despite the lack of emotion shown to him during his childhood and the blandness of his military career, he is a very passionate man, who feels things deeply and who yearns for a true, loving relationship. At first glance he falls head-over-heels in love with Georgina but never really understands that their marriage is doomed because they both are completely unable to express their emotions. Although he truly loves his wife, their marriage leaves them incomplete and yearning for something that neither of them has the emotional experience to comprehend. William's passions rise as he realizes that his wife is having an affair, causing their marriage to become a war zone and climaxing in an intensely emotional scene that results in William's suicide attempt. Rescued once again by his wartime friend Oxton, William finally realizes that there is nothing left of his marriage to save. He returns home to reestablish his relationship with his father and to sort out his thoughts and emotions before beginning his new career as a schoolteacher.

Sergeant Charlie Scorton, the widower of the title and William's father. Every inch the soldier, Charlie is tall, strong, and stubborn, and he has never exhibited any weakness during his eighty-three years. After watching his best friend die in the coal mines and attempting suicide, he decides to enter the army, a decision which results in his complete estrangement from his family. Feeling rather bereft of family and friends, he learns to cover his pain with a sort of icy indifference, which makes him an excellent soldier. Unfortunately he carries this coldness into his brief marriage and the rearing of his son. Although he loves his son very much and wants only the best for him, he really has no idea of how to behave with him, and so treats William as if he were a child soldier. Never realizing that his son might have needs or desires of his own, Charlie chooses his son's career for him, sending him off to military school as soon as possible. Living vicariously through William's military career, Charlie does not understand the reasons for William's resentment, nor does he recognize that he might not have done what was really best for his son. Living a rather lonely life, with only his sister Doris as company, he finally learns to accept William as an individual.

Georgina Woods Scorton, William's wife. Tall and fair, with piercing cold blue eyes, she too was reared in a military family. Restless in temperament, she attended boarding schools and spent her vacations with her grandmother. Never having seen a good example of married life, she must create her own ideas about marriage. Failing at this, and unhappy with the lack of emotion in her marriage, she is miserable and suffers from an inner despondency, and she eventually renews her acquaintance with an old lover as a form of release and rebellion. This, however, only becomes the catalyst for the explosion of her marriage into outright war, and she and William fight almost constantly. Eventually both she and William run out of passion and anger, and their marriage dissolves.

Sergeant Harold Oxton, William's batman during World War II. An extremely ugly man with false teeth, narrow eyes, a shapeless nose, and a lined face, he is a truly good person. Although a menace as a gunner, he is indispensable to William because of his common sense, his infinite stamina, and his blind loyalty. Completely devoted to his mother, he left home only twice, both times in order to fight against the Germans during the world wars. After his mother's death, he goes to work for William as a bouncer in a bowling alley and eventually meets and marries a nice German lady with whom he lives a happy, well-ordered life.

Brigadier "Jacko" Woods, Georgina's father. Tall, bony, and angular, the white-haired, blue-eyed Brigadier is restless but forceful, talented but volative, energetic but unpredictable. An excellent infantry officer, he is the only soldier who succeeded and became happy by making the army his career.

Susan V. Myers

WIELOPOLE/WIELOPOLE
An Exercise in Theatre

Author: Tadeusz Kantor (1915-   )
Type of work: Play
Time of action: Sometime after World War II, with flashbacks to World War I
First produced: 1980 (English translation, 1990)

Uncle Karol and
Uncle Olek, two of the author's maternal uncles. They are inseparable to the point that one will not go anywhere without the other. They do differ, however, in that Karol is very patriotic and believes in fighting (and dying) for one's country, while Olek is the type who believes in avoiding conscription at any cost. They serve as a kind of dark comic relief.

Uncle Staś, a Siberian deportee and another of the author's maternal uncles. Karol and Olek are so embarrassed by Staś's appearance—he looks like a busker wearing a tattered army uniform—that they decide to pretend that they do not know him.

Mother Helka (Helena Berger), also called **the Bride,** the author's mother. All dressed in white, she is dead at the time of the wedding, though in real life she lived long enough to have the author.

Father (Marian Kantor), the author's father, a soldier. He is also dead at the time of the wedding, and he is by turns reviled and welcomed by Helka's family.

Mad Aunt Mańka, an insane old woman. Another of the author's maternal relatives, she continually quotes biblical passages in a hysterical way, "as she periodically goes through a religious crisis."

Grandma Katarzyna, the author's maternal grandmother. Though she, too, is dead at the beginning of the play, she later comes alive, only to announce the timing of the crucifixion of Adas (a young recruit), the Priest, and Helka.

The Priest, Grandma Katarzyna's brother. Though dead, he performs the marriage ceremony for Helka and Marian. At the end, he is led away by the Little Rabbi, a character who appears only briefly.

The Photographer's Widow, the wife of the late town photographer, Ricordo. She serves double duty as the new town photographer and as a harbinger of death. She not only tends the dead bodies but also creates them by killing people with her camera-cum-machine gun.

T. M. Lipman

THE WIND
Attempted Restoration of a Baroque Altarpiece

Author: Claude Simon (1913-   )
Type of work: Novel
Time of action: The 1950's
First published: Le Vent: Tentative de restitution d'un rétable baroque, 1957 (English translation, 1959)

Antoine Montès, age thirty-five, who arrives in a small town to take possession of a vineyard inherited from a father whom he has never known. His mother had left the town and Antoine's father after she discovered him making love to the maid. Montès fires the bailiff, who refuses to uproot his own family from the property. Montès makes the acquaintance of several people in a town that generally rejects him: Rose (with whom he falls in love), Maurice, distant cousins, the notary, and a stranger whom he meets in a photography shop.

Maurice, a pretentious and nosy fertilizer salesman. He tries to befriend Montès and discovers that he is hiding stolen goods for Rose. He steals a note written by Cécile to Montès and tries to blackmail her father with it.

Cécile, the younger tomboyish daughter of Montès' distant relative. She breaks off her relationship with her fiancé as she becomes enamored of Montès and writes him a note. When she is found out by her older sister, she forces her former fiancé to make love to her.

Hélène, the older sister of Cécile. She discovers Cécile's relationship with Montès and is successful in thwarting Maurice's attempts at blackmailing their father. She informs the authorities about the stolen goods and Jep's role in the burglary by going to the prosecutor's house. She tells his wife that Rose had been in her employ. Having discovered Rose and Jep making love in her house, she dismissed Rose, who was then hired by the victims of the latest burglary.

The notary, who would like Montès to sell his property and leave the town. He believes, with the other people in town, that Montès is an imbecile for not doing so.

The social worker, who allows Montès to visit Rose's two orphaned children on the first Thursday of every month but discourages him from trying to adopt them.

The priest, who has received the stolen goods from Montès so that he might return them to the rightful owner.

Rose, a waitress in a very modest hotel. She and her two children are befriended by Montès. She confides in him and places in his care jewelry stolen by her husband.

Jep, a former boxer and Rose's gypsy husband. Once Hélène has informed on him to the authorities, he thinks that he has been betrayed by his wife, stabs her, and is later killed by the police in a scuffle.

Theresa, the older of Rose's daughters. She goes on a walk with Montès, during which they meet her father, who knocks him out in a fight.

The bailiff, an older man who lives on Montès' property with his wife and children. He does not want to leave the property when Montès returns to claim it. One of his daughters had been the father's mistress. In the lawsuit that ensues, the bailiff is awarded the property because of outstanding debts.

The prosecutor's wife, irate that she should be disturbed during dinner by Hélène. She believes that Hélène should have gone to her husband's office to inform him.

The narrator, a teacher and writer who becomes Montès' friend after they meet in a photography shop.

Peter S. Rogers

THE WIND FROM THE PLAIN, IRON EARTH, COPPER SKY, and THE UNDYING GRASS

Author: Yashar Kemal (Yaşar Kemal Gökçeli, 1922-   )
Type of work: Novel
Time of action: The 1950's or early 1960's
First published: Ortadirek, 1960 (*The Wind from the Plain,* 1963); *Yer demir, gök bakır,* 1963 (*Iron Earth, Copper Sky,* 1974); *Ölmez otu,* 1968 (*The Undying Grass,* 1977)

Halil Taşyürek, born in 1884, an eccentric old peasant who enjoys bemused toleration from others in his village. During the early twentieth century, he had served with Ottoman forces in Yemen, and he is wont to recall experiences from that period. He has some living relatives. He is regarded as something of a local oracle when it comes to foretelling the onset of the cotton harvesting season. In addition to squabbling with Meryemce along the way, he becomes involved in various escapades which seem to bolster his already colorful reputation. When he is implicated in a scheme to steal cotton at night, others vent their contempt by spitting on him in turn; yet genuine concern arises when he disappears for protracted periods. On one occasion, after formal religious services for the dead have been read over his name, he is found in the somewhat ignominious position of hiding in a grain crib. Later, he vanishes temporarily once more, in the course of another cotton-pilfering venture.

Meryemce, born in 1886, a woman with grown children of her own. She is no more able than Halil to undertake long journeys on foot, and so, when at the outset of the cotton season he wantonly pushes her from her family's horse, a spirited quarrel takes place that arouses lasting antagonism, which continues after the animal dies. She is determined where possible to hold her own in various confrontations, and she reflects with some bitterness on the ingratitude and lack of respect that others accord her; she resolves not to speak with those who have offended her. Religious convictions tinged with quaint folk beliefs also affect her outlook: She has faith in a white-bearded, black-eyed Allah, while a burial place popularly known as the forsaken graveyard fills her with trepidation.

Memet Taşbaş Efendi, an older man whom the others hold in veneration. His origins are partially shrouded in legend, much of which has been accepted by those around him. He has a wife whom the others regard with a certain envy mingled with awe. Taşbaş occasionally will go away, and stories sometimes make the round that he has gone to join forty saints and that his appearances are accompanied by seven balls of fire from on high. At times his actions seem calculated to dispel such notions: He is caught in the act during a melon-stealing effort, and he is briefly subjected to ridicule, but soon thereafter his intercession is sought in local controversies. Indeed, there is some tendency to believe that the earthbound Taşbaş has an ethereal counterpart who can minister to the distressed and the afflicted. In the end an apotheosis of sorts is achieved when he is found apparently drowned in a stream.

Zalaca, an older woman. She is prone to believe in odd portents, and she has unusual dreams that she believes have some prophetic overtones; at times she seeks out Sefer in an effort to obtain interpretations, though she does not entirely trust him. It is possible that her feelings about him finally surface in a vision that she relates to others, in which Taşbaş intervenes to take action against Sefer.

Sefer Efendi, the local Muhtar (mayor or headman). He holds a position of immediate authority over the villagers. He has two wives. In the field he would go attired in a fine coat, shirt, and necktie, with riding boots and a felt hat; often he carries a rifle over his shoulder and a whip in his hand. His methods, however, are sometimes oblique, and he employs hirelings to intimidate those whom he cannot easily subject to his personal control; he is capable then of dissembling and pretending to protect those against whom he is plotting. He does feel some constraints; in one episode, even after he has bribed a policeman to assist him in one of his intrigues, the man turns on him and beats him with a rifle butt. Sefer also must defer to other functionaries who have particular wealth and power. Because of Taşbaş's seemingly mystical powers, Sefer regards him as a particularly dangerous rival, and many of the Muhtar's schemes involve attempts to humiliate and undermine public confidence in the supposed saint. Elsewhere, Sefer hires a thug to beat Memidik, and he personally threatens the younger man as a means of underscoring his own standing. When in the end Memidik kills Sefer, the villagers respond with some approbation for this deed of vengeance.

Memidik Delibaş, born in 1940. His father died when he was six months old, and he was reared by his mother. He had performed his military service as a corporal in the engineering corps. He is also one of the two people in the village who have any knowledge of the written language. Although he is small in stature (he is one of the shortest men in the village) he is not easily brought to heel by the Muhtar or his hirelings. Once Memidik has been left bowed and bloody from an impromptu interrogation that Sefer has arranged, he seeks out the Muhtar in a series of efforts to lay him low. After a stabbing incident that remains somewhat murky, Memidik comes upon Sefer at intervals and fends off the Muhtar's threats. Other interludes feature relations with women; following a brief fling with a flighty and irresponsible housewife, he falls in love with Zeliha, and they experience deep and rewarding intimacy. Memidik later continues to stalk the Muhtar and leaves him dead after plunging his knife into him; yet, even after he has been sent to prison, others in the village, including Zeliha and Halil, visit Memidik and present him with gifts attesting their esteem.

Zeliha, a young woman who is about twenty years old. She is described as wily and alluring, with dark slanting eyes, firm breasts, and a trim figure. Although she seems shy and uncertain at first, she responds to Memidik's attentions with alacrity, and she remains loyally attached to him subsequently.

Adil Efendi, an official charged with tax collection. To play a trick on him, the villagers hide their possessions, which provokes an angry confrontation between Adil and Sefer.

Şevket Bey, a wealthy functionary. He had three brothers, all of whom were well off, and two sisters, one of whom was thought to be the wealthiest woman in the area. In his youth, Şevket Bey had killed three people, and he may have been implicated in the murder of another. At one time he had three wives, but a fit of temper prompted him to divorce all of them in one day. Of his six children, he arranged to have four of them educated at private schools in Istanbul. He is depicted as handsome but with a disquieting, unearthly quality; he has a tendency to walk in his sleep, and there is an untamed brutal side to his character. He disappears mysteriously on a dark night when Memidik encounters a figure who he thinks may be Sefer, and afterward it is thought that Şevket Bey has been killed.

Muttalip Bey, an important landowner. He represents the political party in power; he also has an impressive fleet of trucks and tractors. After he confers with Sefer, toward the end, he attempts to ingratiate himself among the villagers by passing out fifty-lira bills.

J. R. Broadus

THE WINDS OF WAR

Author: Herman Wouk (1915-   )
Type of work: Novel
Time of action: 1938-1941
First published: 1971

Victor "Pug" Henry, a career United States Navy officer. A short, physically fit man in his late forties, slightly graying, Henry has aspirations of becoming an admiral, perhaps even Chief of Naval Operations. He is a family man, though relations with his wife are sometimes strained. He takes an active interest in the lives of his three children. On the way to his post as naval attaché in Berlin, he meets the Tudsburys, father and daughter, leading to his developing a fondness for Pamela Tudsbury. His assignment in Berlin and the patronage of President Franklin Delano Roosevelt give him the opportunity to meet Adolf Hitler and Winston Churchill and to be present in Europe when World War II breaks out. Visiting Great Britain shortly thereafter, he finds himself taken along as an observer on a bombing run over Berlin. After completing his assignment in Berlin and returning to Washington, D.C., Henry carries out several important missions for the president; he is present at Roosevelt's historic meeting with Churchill in the North Atlantic and is posted to Moscow, where he meets Josef Stalin. Throughout, Henry repeatedly attempts to get assigned to sea duty; he is granted his wish, only to reach Pearl Harbor the day after the Japanese raid that sinks the battleship he was to have commanded.

Rhoda Henry, a Navy wife approaching fifty, still attractive. She is growing tired of the demands placed on the wife of a career officer and is suffering from a middle-age depression. Rhoda accompanies her husband to Berlin, where she meets Palmer Kirby, with whom she ultimately has an affair after the Henrys return to Washington. She attempts to hold the family together despite her own transgressions, keeping her infidelity a secret; she establishes a fine household in Washington that serves as a home for Victor Henry and the three children when they are not off serving abroad or working away from Washington.

Natalie Jastrow, a research assistant for her uncle, Aaron Jastrow, a noted historian. A lissome woman of thirty who has renounced her Jewish ancestry, she has led a wild life before settling down with her uncle in Siena, Italy. Initially devoted to Leslie Slote, she gradually falls in love with Byron Henry. With Byron, she visits Slote in Warsaw and witnesses German atrocities there; yet she has difficulty convincing her uncle to leave Italy. Separated from Byron, who has gone to submarine school in the United States, she finally begins a trek toward freedom, but the Germans block her way. She manages to meet

Byron in Lisbon; they marry there, but are quickly separated again. Natalie, now pregnant, tries even more earnestly to get her uncle to leave Italy, but nothing is successful. After giving birth to Louis Henry, she makes further attempts to evade the grasp of the Germans; nothing succeeds, however, and she is caught in Axis-occupied territory when the United States enters the war.

Byron Henry, a handsome, red-haired young man in his mid-twenties, unsure of his goals in life but ultimately pressed into military service just as the United States enters the worldwide conflict. Openly rebelling against his father, Byron travels to Europe to pursue a career in art; he secures a job as secretary to Aaron Jastrow and falls in love with co-worker Natalie Jastrow. Even though he and Natalie see the horrors of Hitler's invasion of Poland, he is unable to persuade her to leave her uncle as World War II breaks out in Europe; though they both go to Warren Henry's wedding in Florida, Natalie returns to Siena when Byron goes to submarine school. Byron manages to be reunited with Natalie in Lisbon, where his submarine docks briefly, and the two are married. The war separates them again, however, and Byron goes to the Pacific theater to serve aboard a submarine there.

Pamela Tudsbury, personal assistant to her father, Alistair Tudsbury. A woman approaching thirty, of decent figure and wholesome if not stunning beauty, she has devoted her life to aiding her father in promoting British nationalism through his newspaper and radio work. She accompanies him on worldwide trips, meeting Victor Henry aboard a ship bound for Berlin. She also travels with her father to the United States, Germany, Russia, and the Far East, crossing paths with Henry; she is captivated by the older man and falls deeply in love with him. She is present with Victor at the bombing of London and is with her father in Singapore when the Japanese invade and capture that Far Eastern stronghold of the British Empire.

Aaron Jastrow, a prominent American Jew

and an internationally known historian. Nearly sixty-five, Jastrow has authored numerous scholarly works, including *A Jew's Jesus*. He is in Siena completing a study of the Roman emperor Constantine and believes his renown as a writer will keep him safe from German harassment. Only reluctantly does he agree to leave Italy with daughter Natalie; his fame proves a stumbling block, however, as his movements are carefully monitored by German Gestapo agents, who track him to France and to Switzerland and who reach him just as he and Natalie are to leave clandestinely aboard a tramp steamer for Palestine. He returns to his villa in Siena to wait out the war.

Leslie Slote, a junior American diplomat. Once Natalie Jastrow's lover, Slote plays the role of jilted suitor as his assignments with the U.S. State Department take him to Berlin and then to Warsaw, where he assists in evacuating Americans when the Germans invade Poland. He is posted briefly to Moscow, then to Switzerland, where he is presented early evidence of Hitler's systematic extermination of the Jews. Slote tries to get his superiors in the State Department to pay attention to this information but repeatedly meets roadblocks.

Alistair "Talky" Tudsbury, a highly respected British radio and newspaper correspondent. Corpulent and aging, Tudsbury nevertheless commands a large audience in his native England and has the respect of journalists and politicians internationally. He travels throughout Europe, the United States, the Middle East, and the Far East, reporting on British preparations for all-out combat and on the conduct of operations in the various combat zones.

Madeline Henry, the Henrys' nineteen-year-old daughter, who leaves college to take a job in New York City as an assistant to radio celebrity Hugh Cleveland. She drifts into an amorous relationship with Cleveland, ignoring her family's repeated warnings. Concurrently, she rises in the entertainment world as a junior executive.

Warren Henry, the Henrys' oldest son. A Naval Academy graduate in his mid-twenties, handsome and committed to a career in the Navy, he enrolls in flight school and while there meets Janice LaCouture, the daughter of a Florida politician. They marry shortly before Warren gets his pilot's wings; he is then assigned to an aircraft carrier based at Pearl Harbor, Hawaii. Warren is considered a promising aviator by the higher-ups in the Navy. He is on patrol away from Pearl Harbor when the Japanese attack on December 7, 1941, but manages to return in time to engage in a dogfight over the island of Oahu.

General Armin von Roon, a German military professional and member of the German General Staff. Roon's account of World War II from the Germans' perspective is interspersed throughout the narrative of the Henry family saga. Roon gives both a sweeping assessment of Hitler's strategic campaigns and personal observations about the character of the Führer and his closest associates as the Germans sweep through western and central Europe and eastward into the Soviet Union.

Franklin Delano Roosevelt, President of the United States. Though crippled by polio, Roosevelt is a keen observer of world events and a shrewd political dealer. He calls on Victor Henry several times to gain the naval officer's assistance in dealing first with the Germans, then with the Russians. Roosevelt maneuvers carefully to satisfy both the American Congress (especially the isolationist elements) and the British, especially Churchill; he is clearly on the side of the Allies, though he manages to maintain a façade of neutrality. Throughout, the president is moving the United States into a wartime posture, anticipating the country's inevitable entry into the worldwide conflict.

Janice LaCouture, a young, blonde Florida beauty who marries Warren Henry. Though she comes from a wealthy family and is the daughter of a prominent politician, she cheerfully accompanies Warren to Pearl Harbor, Hawaii, and adapts to being a Navy wife. She bears a son, Victor, to carry on the Henry line. She is a witness at first hand to the

Japanese attack on Pearl Harbor on December 7, 1941.

Hugh Cleveland, a well-known American radio personality. Middle-aged and going to seed physically, he nevertheless commands a large listening public. His shows allow prominent political figures to give American listeners a sense of the growing tensions in Europe. At Madeline Henry's suggestion, he begins a touring amateur talent show that features American servicemen. Cleveland's failing marriage drives him to chase after other women, including the Henrys' daughter.

Palmer Frederick (Fred) Kirby, an engineer and manufacturer of technological equipment. A widower approaching fifty, Kirby meets the Henrys in Berlin and falls in love with Rhoda. His travels to New York and Washington give him opportunity to pursue his friendship with her, a friendship that culminates in their having an affair while Victor Henry is overseas. Business with the government and his expertise in manufacturing specialty items lead to Kirby's being recruited to work with the Manhattan Project to produce the atom bomb.

Berel Jastrow, a cousin of Aaron Jastrow, a Polish Jew residing outside Warsaw. Though in his sixties, Jastrow is able-bodied and adept at a number of occupations; he is also skilled at manipulating local government administrators. He manages to get his family out of Warsaw when the Germans invade, but he is eventually captured by the Nazis and placed in a concentration camp.

Avram Rabinovitz, a Jewish organizer who helps Jews wishing to escape the Nazis. He arranges for the Jastrows to leave Italy via a transport steamer and is disappointed when Aaron and Natalie refuse to go through with their escape. Nevertheless, he continues to work with them to help return them to U.S. custody.

Ted Gallard, a British fighter pilot. Engaged to Pamela Tudsbury, he participates in several dangerous missions and is eventually shot down over Germany. Wounded, he languishes in prison for a time and eventually dies of his injuries.

Carter ("Lady") Aster, a U.S. Navy executive officer on Byron Henry's submarine in the Atlantic. Aster proves to be highly competent but ruthless; he drives Byron to become a qualified submariner.

Ernst Grobke, a German submarine officer. About Victor Henry's age, Grobke becomes friends with Henry during the latter's journey to Berlin; he takes Henry to visit German submarine bases and introduces him to influential political figures within the Nazi regime.

Isaac LaCouture, a Florida politician. An isolationist who opposes Roosevelt's various programs to aid England and Russia against Germany, he is nevertheless pleased when his daughter marries Warren Henry and becomes a service wife. He uses what influence he has with the State Department to try to get Natalie Jastrow and her uncle out of Italy.

Wolf Stöller, a German businessman who supports Hitler. After inviting Victor Henry to several social affairs, he tries to recruit the American officer as a German spy.

Laurence W. Mazzeno

THE WINE OF ASTONISHMENT

Author: Earl Lovelace (1935-   )
Type of work: Novel
Time of action: The 1930's to 1951, with flashbacks to 1917
First published: 1982

Bee (Dorcas), a Spiritual Baptist preacher and a farmer. A dedicated, conscientious, and responsible leader, he struggles for years to keep his church alive despite a law prohibiting his sect's religious practices. He is strong, dignified, righteous, and long-suffering. Faced with increased official repression, the disintegration of his congregation, and the loss of his children's respect, he bravely but reluctantly breaks the law and endures the brutal consequences. Hopeful that black political representation will change the law, he works tirelessly for the election of Ivan Morton only to feel trapped, humiliated, and despairing when his trust is betrayed. Challenged by Bolo to restore the integrity of the community, Bee decides on violent, redemptive action but is circumvented when the police intervene. As the novel closes, religious freedom has been restored, but Bee is unable to recall the Spirit to his church. He feels that the Spirit still lives on in the steel band.

Eva, the dialect-speaking narrator of the novel, Bee's wife. A self-sacrificing, middle-aged black woman, she is devoted to her religion, her five children, and her husband, for whom she is a supportive confidante and moderating influence. Relatively uneducated but observant and worldly-wise, she believes that God has afflicted blacks with tribulations but given them the strength to bear and overcome their sufferings. She views brown-skinned people as tools of the whites while trying to understand and excuse Ivan Morton for betraying his past and his race. Despite Morton's example, she advocates education for her children as a way to escape poverty and powerlessness.

Bolo, a famous stickfighting champion and an estate laborer. Tall and slim, with a broad nose, high cheekbones, and full lips, he is the strongest and bravest man in Bonasse. A favorite of the village, he is good-natured, humorous, helpful, and sympathetic but begins to change when the war starts and ritual stickfighting is banned. With the arrival of American soldiers and easy money, many Trinidadians become hustlers and prostitutes, traditional values are forgotten, and Bolo becomes increasingly bitter and unimportant. Looking to Bee and his church to maintain the people's identity and integrity, Bolo tries to protect the congregation from police brutality, is badly beaten, and is jailed for three years. Upon his release, Bolo is appalled and heartbroken by the church's acquiescence in the ban on its traditional practices and by the general moral and political corruption. Enraged by their weakness, he deliberately antagonizes and terrorizes the villagers, hoping to provoke them into reclaiming their dignity and self-respect. He fails in his aim when he abducts two village girls and is fatally shot by the police.

Ivan Morton, a minister in the Legislative Council. Son of a poor black estate worker, he is respected as a teacher before turning to politics. He is ambitious, insensitive, self-serving, and cynical. Always seen as the hope of the village, he assumes the trappings of the old white plantocracy; he forgets his promises and rejects his past and the values of those who elected him. As a young man he impregnates and then abandons a local black girl and soon marries a light-skinned woman who speaks correct English. He further reveals his sense of social and racial inferiority when he urges the Spiritual Baptists to become "civilized" and states, "We can't change our colour . . . but we can change our attitude. We can't be white but we can act white." Nevertheless, to ensure black support Morton has religious freedom granted just before the next election.

Clem, also known as **Lord Trafalgar,** Bolo's friend, a chantwell. Lively, gregarious, and adaptable, he keeps his self-respect while taking advantage of the changes in Trinidad. Formerly a leader in traditional stickfight chants and bongo songs, he satisfies the demands of a new audience and becomes a calypso singer known as Lord Trafalgar.

Corporal Prince, a policeman. Tall, thickset, and powerful, he follows orders and zealously scourges Spiritual Baptist churches around the island. Hungry for promotion and taking pleasure in brutality, he ruthlessly persecutes other blacks, including Bee and his congregation, without compassion or understanding.

Mitchell, a laborer for the Americans, a snackette owner and political organizer. Loud-mouthed, dishonest, and corrupt, he is a thief, blackmarketeer, and moneylender who boasts of his wealth. He treats Bolo with disrespect and is punished as a result. He turns his talents to working for Ivan Morton.

Douglas Rollins

WINGS

Author: Arthur Kopit (1937-   )
Type of work: Play
Time of action: The 1970's
First produced: 1977, radio; 1978, staged

Emily Stilson, a retired aviatrix in her seventies. She suffers a stroke and is taken to a hospital, where she recovers over a two-year period. The play presents both her internal thoughts and her external behavior. Internally, she remains intact, though she is extremely confused as to what has happened to her and where she is. Thrown back on her memories, she reaches the conclusion that she is being held prisoner by unknown forces in a Romanian farmhouse disguised to look like a hospital following an aviation accident, and she interprets the doctors' questions as attempts to pump her for information. Although she believes herself to be lucid, nothing but gibberish emerges when she speaks. At moments when her thinking becomes jumbled, she returns to memories of flying and walking on the wings of airplanes. When she realizes that her ability to express herself does not match her ability to generate thought within herself, she becomes angry and reacts violently. This reaction, indicative of a desire to communicate with others, brings her out of herself somewhat and advances her therapy. She essentially learns to speak all over again. As her condition improves, more of her memories become conscious. Her son takes her to an aircraft museum, where she finds that her hands automatically manipulate the controls even though she cannot recall how to use them and forgets again as soon as she is no longer in physical contact with the plane. Talking with her therapist, she recounts an out-of-body experience in which she felt herself to be floating on the ceiling. As she speaks, the therapist disappears from her consciousness, which is taken over by a memory in which she is flying blind and lost, but nevertheless enjoying a feeling of freedom. The recollection ends with her walking out onto the wing of the aircraft and courageously facing the unknown—presumably her own death.

Billy, a stroke patient in his thirties. Billy is a member of Emily Stilson's therapy group. He owns a farm and is an expert cook, although he is not always clearly aware of his past. His response to the disabilities resulting from his stroke is to keep up a barrage of semicoherent chatter that prevents the therapist from pointing out deficiencies in his language skills and memory. During a therapy session, for example, he accuses the therapist of not having paid him for a cheesecake recipe he gave her, in an effort to put her on the defensive and make her the focus of the session.

Amy, the therapist who works with Emily Stilson, Billy, and other patients. She is extremely patient with and affectionate toward her patients: She encourages them to work through their disabilities and cheers each breakthrough. She negotiates Billy's efforts to deflect the therapy she offers him good-humoredly, and she gives Emily much personal attention, taking her outside and talking with her about her family and her past.

Philip Auslander

THE WINNERS

Author: Julio Cortázar (1914-1984)
Type of work: Novel
Time of action: The 1950's
First published: Los premios, 1960 (English translation, 1965)

Gabriel Medrano, a dentist and a womanizer, reflected by his dissatisfaction with life while on board the *Malcolm.* He allies himself with a group that does not accept the official explanation of why the passengers have not been given complete access to the ship: because of an outbreak of typhus among the crew's members. When Claudia Lewbaum's son Jorge becomes ill, Gabriel decides that the unsatisfactory response of the ship's authorities requires forcible entry into the restricted areas of the ship. He storms the radio room and forces the operator to send a message to Buenos Aires about Jorge's condition. The radio operator then kills Gabriel. The passengers are asked to sign a statement that Gabriel died of typhus instead of gunshot wounds.

Carlos López, a leftist high school Spanish teacher who refuses to believe that the passengers are being denied access to the entire ship because of an outbreak of typhus. He threatens one of the ship's officers that he will storm the other side of the ship if the restrictions on passenger movement are not lifted; he agrees with Gabriel Medrano about the need to send a radio message because of Jorge's illness. He is struck unconscious in the assault of the sailors' quarters and is returned to his room. He refuses to sign the official statement about the cause of Gabriel's death.

Persio, a short, bald, eccentric proofreader and aspiring writer. He is a dreamer who lives in a world of philosophical speculation. He is so engrossed in his own thoughts that he does not involve himself in the controversy among the passengers about their treatment on the ship.

Raúl Costa, a homosexual architect who tries to seduce Felipe Trejo. During his secret exploration of the other side of the ship, he steals three guns and ammunition from the sailors' quarters and then divides it among Gabriel Medrano, Carlos López, and himself. He helps Medrano and López storm the other side of the ship and, after shots are fired, finds Gabriel dead in the radio room. Like Carlos López, he refuses to sign the official statement about the cause of Gabriel's death.

Paula Lavalle (lä•vä'yĕ), an attractive redhead who writes poems and stories. Costa's close friend and traveling companion, she is courted by López. She also denies the official version of events on the ship.

Claudia Lewbaum, a divorced mother of Jorge. Her son's high fever precipitates the assault on the other side of the ship. Her budding friendship with Gabriel Medrano ends abruptly with his death.

Felipe Trejo (trĕ'hō), a high school student learning to deal with his sexual feelings. His fantasies of sexual conquest remained unfulfilled because there were no young ladies his age on board. Although contemptuous of homosexuality, it intrigues him. He rejects Costa's advances, only to be raped by a sailor, an incident he represses by fabricating a tale in which he seduced an insatiable Paula.

Dr. Restelli, a conservative colleague of Carlos López who teaches Argentine history. He speaks up for the passengers who accept the restrictions imposed by the ship's authorities. He organizes a passenger talent show to lift everyone's spirits and take their minds off the alleged outbreak of typhus among the ship's staff. He accuses those who challenge the authorities of trying to ruin the cruise for the others.

Don Galo Porriño (pō•rrĕ'nyō), a successful Galician businessman confined to a wheelchair. He speaks in defense of the authorities and considers those who were unwilling to submit to their demands to be guilty of insubordination and anarchy.

Evelyn Toft

WISE VIRGIN

Author: A. N. Wilson (1950-   )
Type of work: Novel
Time of action: The early 1980's
First published: 1982

Giles Fox, a blind scholar and librarian. Only forty-eight years old, his life is already dictated by habit: Every day he wears a gray suit, white shirt, and silk blue tie, and each dinner is a variation of cold meat, noodles, olives, and fresh fruit. He is obsessed by *A Tretis of Loue Heuenliche*, a medieval tract on virginity, and labors to produce the definitive edition of the text. Ironically, the content of the discourse concerns spiritual love, but by focusing solely on philology and linguistics, Giles fails to acknowledge the work's applicability to his own life.

Tibba Fox, Giles's daughter. An attractive, clever teenager with searching green eyes, Tibba leads two lives: At home, she assumes adult responsibilities by managing the house and caring for her blind father; at school, she is a popular but elusive coquette. Her favorite authors are Harold Pinter and Virginia Woolf, but she reads from Sir Walter Scott and Anthony Trollope to Giles every evening. To her, time is divided into B.C., before Mary's death, and A.D., All Desolation. Giles remarries when Tibba is thirteen, and Carol, his second wife, is perceived by Tibba as a rival. She puts a curse on her stepmother, asking God to kill her, and, within twenty-four hours, Carol is run over by a taxicab. Tibba is both shocked and pleased by this apparent power, but she never attempts to exercise it again.

Mary Hargreaves Fox, Giles's late first wife and Tibba's mother. Already deceased when the novel opens, Mary is remembered by Tibba as having hazel eyes, an oval face, and Vidal Sassoon hair. Her relationship with Giles is based primarily on physical attraction, and when she becomes pregnant out of wedlock, they feel forced into marriage. Resentment quickly arises on both sides, and Mary seeks, through numerous affairs, the attention and love she needs. After eight painful years of marriage, she and Giles develop a deeper love for each other, only to face Mary's death in childbirth.

Carol Fox, Giles's late second wife and nurse. Although described simply as beautiful, her Liverpudlian accent reveals her lower-class origins and explains why she marries Giles after only knowing him for a few weeks. A strong rivalry develops between Carol and Tibba for Giles's affection, but the tension is short-lived: Carol is hit and killed by a taxicab less than a year after being married to Giles.

Louise Agar, Giles's research assistant. Described as lumpish, with unshapely and columnar legs and a poor complexion, she has soft, thick hands and abundant long hair. In her mid-twenties, she still lives with her mother, her teddy bear, and her Winnie the Pooh poster. Although her research in diphthongs failed to produce a doctorate, she is one of the few individuals familiar enough with Giles's linguistic research to be of any use to him. Ironically hired by Tibba to serve as his professional assistant, eventually Louise and Giles fall in love.

Meg Gore, Giles's older sister. Having a rosy complexion and bright blue eyes, she tends to face her problems with determination and optimism. A bit of a busybody, she serves as a good support for Monty Gore, her husband, but tends to annoy Giles and Tibba by mothering them.

Monty "Ruddy G." Gore, Meg's husband and a housemaster at Pangham. A stereotypical teacher, Monty has short hair, glasses, and a caricatured Roman nose. Although in his fifties, he lusts for teenage girls, especially his niece Tibba, and until Piers Peverill, an unruly student, challenges his authority, he views life as an amusing joke.

Piers Peverill, Tibba's boyfriend and one of Monty's students. Charming, arrogant, and handsome, Piers is spoiled by his rich, divorced parents. He deliberately breaks Pangham's school rules, and Monty attempts to have him expelled on numerous occasions, but Piers's parents make sizable contributions to the proper people, and he is promptly reinstated.

Captain de Courcy, Tibba's fraudulent speech therapist. Having been court-martialed in the army and failing in theater work, he falsely proclaims to have a degree from the Royal Academy of Dramatic Art so that he can give voice lessons. Although Tibba's stammer does not improve, she spends numerous hours fantasizing about a life with de Courcy.

Coleen Maddy

THE WOMAN FROM SARAJEVO

Author: Ivo Andrić (1892-1975)
Type of work: Novel
Time of action: 1900-1936
First published: Gospodjica, 1945 (English translation, 1965)

Rajka Radaković (rī′kä rä·dă′kō·vĭch), a spinster from Sarajevo. Rajka is the quintessential miser, in a long line of similar characters in world literature. Her miserliness derives from a sense of insecurity, which came about primarily from her father's failure in business. Her father dies from grief, but not before advising his daughter to save at every step and to distrust people, because trusting people allows concern for others to govern one's life, which, in turn, makes one dangerously vulnerable. Rajka's bitter childhood experience stays with her all of her life. Taking over her father's business, she makes sure never to allow others to take advantage of her. Moreover, she denies herself every pleasure, isolates herself from people, even relatives. Eventually, her thrift and avarice become an obsession and grow to monstrous proportions. The excessive egotism, selfishness, miserliness, and lack of normal human drives in the end ruin her, along with everyone else with whom she associates. The author offers some plausible explanations for Rajka's behavior.

In addition to insecurity, a desire to avenge and redeem her father contributes heavily to her behavior. The remembrance of the past shapes her view of the world as basically evil, selfish, insensitive, and even cruel. Such a cruel world crushes soft and emotional people, like her father, but it bows before hard and resolute people, like herself. The only security people like Rajka can find is in money, and money becomes a god to which she is willing to sacrifice everything.

Obren Radaković, Rajka's father, a rich merchant from Sarajevo who goes bankrupt. In a very brief role (Rajka was only fourteen when he died), Obren leaves his daughter a weighty and even dangerous legacy, contained in a few guidelines: Do not trust people; depend only on your own strength and resoluteness; save as much as possible; never allow emotions to govern your life. Another lesson Rajka learns from her father's experience is that honest work alone is not enough for a successful life. Rajka's allegiance to her father borders almost on an Oedipus complex, all the more so since her mother is a very weak person.

Radojka Radaković (rä·doi′kä), Rajka's mother. The exact opposite of her husband, Radojka is a harmless, good-natured, but meek woman, weak in spirit and in body. As such, she is unable to offer Rajka any support, not even love, no matter how much she tries. She simply cannot comprehend her daughter and therefore stays out of her life, powerless to influence Rajka in any way.

Vladimir Hadži-Vasić (häd′zhē vä′sĭch), Rajka's favorite uncle. Only four years her senior, Vladimir enjoys life, likes beautiful things,

loves to give expensive gifts, and spends everything he can. Essentially a good-for-nothing, he stands for everything Rajka does not, and that is probably why she likes him better than any of her relatives. She even has motherly feelings and is exceptionally sentimental toward him, especially after his early death of tuberculosis at the age of twenty-three.

Rafo Konforti, a merchant from Sarajevo. A helpful and honest business partner, he helps Rajka learn the trade business, without taking advantage of her inexperience. He is swept away by the profound changes during World War I.

Vasa D. Mihailovich

THE WOMAN IN THE DUNES

Author: Kōbō Abe (1924-   )
Type of work: Novel
Time of action: 1955-1962
First published: Suna no onna, 1962 (English translation, 1964)

Niki Jumpei, a Japanese schoolmaster and amateur collector of insects. Thirty-one years old and ordinary-looking, Niki is a rather commonplace member of the conformist urban Japanese populace. In the city, he lives with a woman who is not a wholly fulfilling sexual partner. He is a creature of regular habits, appears to derive his sense of identity from the way that his society and his colleagues define him, and is not particularly individualistic or imaginative. Beneath this team-player exterior, however, Niki does harbor a few sparks of desire for individual difference and distinction; hence, he collects insects as a hobby. This hobby he has taken up in the hope that he will find a rare or hitherto unknown specimen of some insect and thereby earn for himself renown as an amateur entomologist. Niki also likes to toy with abstract theories about the nature of reality; he is similarly attracted to notions such as one which speculates that sand moves in waves like water (only, unlike water, sand desiccates). The novel opens on an August weekend in 1955 when Niki is out alone on

an insect-gathering trip among some sand dunes by the sea. What begins as a weekend outing eventually becomes a seven-year adventure as he becomes a guest of a village in the dunes, particularly of one woman in the dunes.

The Woman in the Dunes, who remains unnamed throughout the novel. About thirty years of age, she is small in build, pleasant in temperament. She is a widow and lives alone, having lost her husband and only daughter to a sand slide during a typhoon the previous year. She is a down-to-earth, sensual woman (who sleeps nude with only a towel to cover her face) and seems to have an intuitive, almost primal, grasp of the life force and a tenacious will to survive. Poor, unprepossessing, and unsophisticated though she be, she is not without dignity and spiritual beauty. Like the other inhabitants of this Kafkaesque dune village, the woman lives in a house at the bottom of a sand pit, and her only access to the outside world is a rope ladder suspended from the pit mouth, a ladder that can be retracted by the villagers. The village supplies her with a sense of community and the necessities of life, chief of which is water. An indefatigable and loyal worker, she in turn supplies the village council with quantities of the local salt-laced sand, which is illegally sold to dubious construction companies in the city. Niki is lured to her house by the villagers, who assign him to be her helpmeet. Through their life together, Niki learns to derive meaning from his existence—not by discovering an obscure insect but by realizing through their interaction a new sense of manhood, humanity, and community.

The Woman in the City, who also remains nameless, contrasts with the one in the dunes. The city woman is probably Niki's lover, possibly his wife. Sex between Niki and this woman is made uneasy by twinges of psychological rape and rendered discomfiting by feelings akin to a psychological venereal disease. Their coitus is deficient in libido and excessive in self-consciousness; Niki compares

it to punching off on some season ticket, and it is always performed through the prophylactic screening of condoms.

The Villagers of the Dunes, also anonymous, resembling a Greek chorus, Niki's captors and arbiters of his fate. They are motivated by the need of their community to survive; hence, they provide Niki as a mate to their woman. They are insular and uncaring of the larger society beyond their community, yet they have the redeeming qualities of peasantlike good humor, wisdom, and pragmatism. For example, when Niki escapes from the woman's pit only to become trapped in quicksand, the villagers rescue him ungrudgingly. Indirectly through the villagers and more directly through the woman, Niki learns to appreciate the difference between the bestial and the beautiful in sexuality, between the illusion of freedom and the true freedom in choice exercised, between rote conformity and individual meaningfulness in responsible human activity.

C. L. Chua

A WOMAN OF THE PHARISEES

Author: François Mauriac (1885-1970)
Type of work: Novel
Time of action: The early 1900's to World War I
First published: La Pharisienne, 1941 (English translation, 1946)

Louis Pian (pē•yăṅ′), a landowner, the illegitimate son of Marthe Pian and her first cousin, Alfred Moulis. The elderly narrator of the story, he is thirteen when it begins. He lost his beloved mother at age seven in a suicide "accident." When his sister Michèle and his best friend Jean fall in love, he is jealous of both of them and tries to keep them apart. He betrays a confidence by showing his stepmother a letter from his teacher M. Puybaraud to Octavia Tronche. Deprived of intimacy and sexual satisfaction himself (self-centered and dispassionate, he never marries), he resents and affects to despise it in others.

Brigitte Pian, Louis' stepmother and his mother's cousin, a pillar of the Church. She has dark eyes, big ears, a double chin, and long, yellow teeth with gold fillings. Although unlike Louis in her passionate temperament, she resembles him in being deprived of intimacy and sexual satisfaction and in reacting resentfully by trying to spoil it for others: Léonce Puybaraud and Octavie Tronche, Michèle Pian and Jean de Mirbel, Octave and Marthe Pian. She also delights in crushing opponents, such as Abbé Calou. Self-righteous, proud, hypocritical, she convinces herself that she is God's mouthpiece and enjoys the sadistic manipulation of people's lives. She over-compensates for feelings of sexual inferiority by an attitude of superiority and by her will to power. She persecutes the Puybaraud family and reduces them to dependence on her handouts, and she contributes to Octavie's miscarriage and death.

Marthe Pian, Louis' mother, who committed suicide when her lover, first cousin Alfred Moulis, terminated their affair.

Octave Pian, Louis' supposed father, a landowner. He wears a long mustache and is fond of eating and of hunting on his country estate. He is kind but weak and hesitant except on rare occasions, and frequently has been paralyzed into impotence by his love for his first wife, Marthe. He probably drank himself to death on reading the letters revealing his wife's affair with her cousin and Louis' probable illegitimacy. He loves his children, especially Michèle.

Michèle Pian, Louis' sister and only sibling, a year older than he. She has dark skin, a heavy lower jaw, white teeth, and pretty legs that she shows off whenever possible. She hates her stepmother for her domineering ways and her interference between herself and Jean de Mirbel, whom Brigitte succeeds in separating with her vicious insinuations.

M. Rausch (rōsh), a schoolmaster and a former member of the Papal guard. He has a scarred upper lip, a walleye, and yellow hair. He dresses carelessly, often in slippers, and is dirty. A harsh disciplinarian to his pupils, he is obsequious toward those in authority.

Abbé Calou (kȧ·lōō′), the parish priest of Baluzac (near the Pian estate). He has blue eyes, a large nose, good teeth, and big, hairy hands, and he is a head taller than Count Mirbel. He specializes in reforming rebellious boys, reputedly by harsh discipline but really by understanding, kindness, and trust. He tries particularly hard to help Jean de Mirbel but is punished for allowing Michèle to write to him.

Jean de Mirbel (mēr·bĕl′), a future landowner

of noble family, fifteen years old at the novel's beginning. He is handsome, dark-haired, has pointed white canine teeth, badly set. He adores his beautiful but selfish and indifferent mother and is bitterly disappointed at her using her visit to him to spend the night with a lover. He steals money from Abbé Calou and runs away with Hortense Voyod, the anticlerical lesbian wife of the local pharmacist.

Countess de Mirbel, Jean's mother. Slim, beautiful, and youthful, she has a slightly snub nose, heavy eyelids, sea-green eyes, and a charming contralto voice. She is hedonistic, insincere, manipulative, and self-centered: She lies about her adulterous activities. At odds with her husband, she wrote indiscreet letters that fell into the hands of her brother-in-law Count Adhémar de Mirbel. She uses the pretext of a visit to Jean to spend the night with her dramatist lover.

Count Adhémar de Mirbel, a retired colonel, seventy at the beginning of the story, Jean's uncle and guardian. He is tall, stout, and blue-eyed. He wants Jean to be disciplined harshly.

Léonce Puybaraud (pwē·bȧ·rō′), one of the twenty teachers at Louis' school of two hundred pupils. He is also general secretary of the local Catholic charities. His lack of qualifications makes him dependent on Brigitte Pian, who resents his love for Octavie Tronche and bullies him mercilessly. He marries Octavie, and buys for her a piano, which infuriates Brigitte, who is supporting them; he shares Octavie's dream of rearing children of their own.

Octavie Tronche, a teacher at a Catholic school sponsored by Brigitte Pian. She is flat-chested and has sparse, dull hair, small, colorless eyes, and pale lips; nevertheless, she is graceful, charming, and saintly. Brigitte hates her for enjoying the sexual fulfillment and (prospectively) the motherhood Brigitte herself has been denied. Thanks partly to Brigitte's persecution, Octavie loses her baby and dies in childbirth.

Hortense Voyod (vwoi•yō′), a landowner and the lesbian wife of a local pharmacist. She is blonde, freckled, and unattractive. Her private life runs afoul of Abbé Calous's interventions, and so she joins with the local school- teacher and his wife to plot against the priest. She runs away with Jean, who is young enough to be her son, to spite Calou.

Patrick Brady

WOMAN ON THE EDGE OF TIME

Author: Marge Piercy (1936- /   )
Type of work: Novel
Time of action: 1976 and 2137
First published: 1976

Consuelo (Connie) Camacho Ramos, a thirty-seven-year-old Mexican American woman whose early beauty has been erased by hard times and tragedy. Her first husband was killed, and her daughter was taken from her by the state's child welfare agency, but she is determined to survive. Once she used her mind at college; now she uses it to live with crushing poverty. She is fiercely loyal to what she has left of her family, a niece, and it is a fight with her niece's pimp that results in her entering a mental hospital. From there, Connie discovers a unique talent: She can commune with the future. With the help of Luciente, a woman from the future, she visits Mattapoisett, Massachusetts, in the year 2137 and is amazed by the utopian life that she finds there. Meanwhile, back in 1976, she battles the doctors who wish to perform neuroelectric experiments on her in a struggle that is fueled by the social consciousness that she is developing under Luciente's tutelage.

Luciente of Mattapoisett, a woman in her thirties with sleek black hair, black eyes, and bronze skin. She is from the year 2137 and, as a "sender," is able to contact receptive people from the past, such as Connie. Luciente works primarily as a plant geneticist, although, like everyone in her village, she shares in a number of other tasks as well. She is energetic, kind, and sensitive. She acts as Connie's guide and ambassador during her visits to Mettapoisett. In many ways, Luciente represents what Connie is capable of becoming but could never hope to be in the racist, sexist, class-conscious society of 1976.

Jackrabbit of Mattapoisett, an artist and one of Luciente's current lovers. He is a slender young man with curly, light brown hair. Long legs and a boundless appetite for life and love prompted him to choose the name Jackrabbit. He went mad as a teenager and was strengthened by the healing process. This bout with mental illness and the caring way in which his community responded stand in powerful contrast to Connie's predicament. Jackrabbit can be careless and irresponsible, but his silly, curious nature makes him a pleasure to know. Jackrabbit is killed while serving a voluntary six-month stint on defense.

Bee of Mattapoisett, a big-boned black man with a bald head. He is a chef and another of Luciente's current lovers. He reminds Connie of Claud, the boyfriend she had after she left her second, abusive husband. Connie and Bee make love one night in Mettapoisett.

Dolores (Dolly) Campos, Connie's twenty-two-year-old niece and a prostitute addicted to drugs. Unlike Connie, she is unable to see beyond a life of easy money and quick highs.

Geraldo, Dolly's handsome pimp and boyfriend. Geraldo admits Connie to Bellevue Hospital after she hits him over the head with a bottle in an attempt to stop him from attacking Dolly.

Luis (Lewis) Camacho, Connie's older brother and the owner of a plant nursery in New Jersey. Upwardly mobile, he has left his heritage behind by adopting the Anglicized name Lewis and marrying women who are successively more light-skinned and Anglo-looking. He has no sympathy for Connie's plight.

Gildina 547-921-45-822-KBJ, a young woman from the future, but a future that is vastly different from Luciente's. A series of operations and shots have given her a tiny waist, oversized hips and buttocks, and enormous, pointed breasts. She is a contract girl, assigned to a mid-level officer for two years of sexual services. Her existence is a stark reminder of what the future might bring.

Cash, the mid-level officer to whom Gildina is contracted. He has superneurotransmitters in his brain that are capable of turning him into a fighting machine. This technology is a refinement of the experiments planned for Connie.

Sybil, a practicing witch and Connie's friend at the mental hospital. She is tall, haughty, and strong.

Liz Marshall

THE WOMEN AT THE PUMP

Author: Knut Hamsun (Knut Pedersen, 1859-1952)
Type of work: Novel
Time of action: The late nineteenth century
First published: Konerne ved vandposten, 1920 (English translation, 1928)

Oliver Andersen, a man who lost a leg and possibly (the villagers speculate) something more in a mysterious shipboard accident. Lazy, self-seeking, and full of guile, Oliver is nevertheless charming and sympathetic. He drifts from job to job, never failing to capitalize on his handicap. With his wife, Petra, he rears a large family (though his paternity is questionable) and is much like a self-indulgent, boastful child himself. Fortune and misfortune alike leave Oliver unfazed for long; he squanders the gains from his spectacular salvage of a wrecked ship and from his discovery of the loot from the mail robbery, but his resiliency and cunning enable him time after time to turn misfortune to his advantage.

Petra Andersen, an attractive woman who is engaged to Oliver before his accident but who rejects him for Mattis the Carpenter when Oliver returns a cripple. Later she reconsiders and marries him, and shortly thereafter she bears a son. Her repeated "visits" to Scheldrup Johnsen, the wealthy double consul's son, and to lawyer Fredriksen, who holds the Andersens' mortgage, often save the family from financial ruin.

Frank Andersen, Petra's eldest son, introverted and academically brilliant. He studies languages at the university and eventually returns to the village as headmaster of the local senior school.

Abel Andersen, Petra's second son, a blacksmith. Called **the Squirrel** as a child, he is lively, industrious, and straightforward. His infatuation with Little Lydia and his unswerving determination to marry her despite her equally determined refusals offer some of the novel's more touching comic scenes. When she refuses his offer of a gold engagement ring that he has forged himself, he quickly and pragmatically gets engaged to a local farm girl, Louise, whom he soon marries.

C. A. Johnsen (Double Consul Johnsen), known as the **First Consul** until he becomes the town's only double consul. Wealthy and socially ascendant, Johnsen busies himself with more ponderous (though less concrete) duties than the running of his successful mercantile and shipping business, which he happily leaves to his clerk and his son. When his steamship sinks and is discovered to be uninsured, Johnsen is crushed by the prospect of financial ruin; when his son Scheldrup arrives and mysteriously manages to pay off the creditors, however, Johnsen revives and reassumes his role as unchallenged patriarch of the village.

Scheldrup Johnsen, the double consul's son. Frank, businesslike, and thoroughly "modern," Scheldrup travels extensively to foreign ports to learn the shipping business. Brown-eyed, amorous Scheldrup once got his ears boxed by Petra over something he whispered to her at a dance hall; not a few villagers suspect that he might have something to do with the surprising number of brown-eyed babies born in the village.

Fia Johnsen, the double consul's daughter, called **the Countess** for her refinement and artistic temperament. Attractive and accomplished, Fia prefers a life of moderation and calm to one of passion and rejects all of her several suitors, whom she rightly suspects of wooing her dowry as much as her. A talented but not brilliant artist, she is content to paint, travel, and act as a cultured hostess to her artist friends.

Frederiksen, a lawyer. Pompous and aspiring, Fredriksen is elected to the Storting (the Norwegian legislature), where he makes a name for himself by sponsoring a bill in direct conflict with the interests of his wealthy constituents. He energetically but unsuccessfully courts the daughters of the wealthiest villagers, thinking to win them with the suggestion that he may soon be appointed a government minister.

The Doctor, a rational, humorless, suspicious man. He takes vindictive pleasure in baiting others and fomenting trouble. In expounding genetic theory, he hints broadly that Scheldrup is the father of the inexplicable number of brown-eyed children in the village.

The Postmaster, a long-winded philosopher. He bores others with his interminable ramblings on human thought, enlightenment, and God. The trauma of the post office robbery leaves him a childlike, babbling madman.

Little Lydia, a childhood friend of Abel. Lighthearted and changeable, she resists his determined efforts to win her heart.

Catherine Swanson

THE WOMEN OF BREWSTER PLACE

Author: Gloria Naylor (1950-   )
Type of work: Novel
Time of action: Unspecified, but most likely during and after the 1960's
First published: 1982

Mattie Michael, a strong, elderly, unmarried black woman who reared a son before moving to Brewster Place. Mattie is the pivotal character in the novel. It is her own personal tragedies—her father's shame and rejection when he learns she is pregnant; the loss of her son, Basil, whom she loves dearly; the loss of her wordly possessions—that make her sensitive to the tragedies of others. She is the character who breathes life and hope into the dismal atmosphere of Brewster Place. At the end of the novel, Mattie is the first to begin tearing down the wall that makes Brewster Place a literal and figurative dead-end for its residents. In their symbolic protest and rage, she and the other women in the community join together to fight their condition instead of being ruled by it.

Etta Mae Johnson, Mattie's closest friend, an attractive woman who carries herself with pride. In Rock Vale, the town in which Mattie and Etta grew up, there was no place for a woman with Etta's rebellious, independent spirit. She refused to play by society's rules and spent most of her life moving to one major city after another, from one promising black man to another in the hopes that one of them would take care of her. Upon her return to Brewster Place, Etta learns that her friend Mattie can give her what she is searching for, things that no man has ever given her: love, comfort, and friendship.

Kiswana Browne (Melanie), a young black woman who rejects her parents' middle-class values, changes her name, and boasts of her African heritage. She is also an activist who organizes a tenants' association at Brewster Place. Kiswana, in her naïveté, believes that her mother is ashamed of being black because she leads a middle-class existence. Finally realizing that she and her mother are not so different, that they are both women who are proud of their heritage and who desire to improve the lot of future generations, Kiswana learns to be more tolerant to those whose life-styles are different from hers.

Luciela Louise Turner, a young married woman, the granddaughter of Eva Turner, the woman who befriended and sheltered Mattie years earlier. She constantly makes excuses for her husband's frequent absences from her and their month-old baby. When her husband learns that she is pregnant again, he threatens to leave her, and, in an attempt to prevent his leaving once more, she gets an abortion. When her daughter dies in a household accident, however, Luciela loses her connection with life and the ability to feel. She slowly begins to waste away. Mattie refuses to accept her friend's gradual suicide and rocks Luciela in her arms until Luciela is able to feel, to express her sorrow, and to return to life again.

Cora Lee, a young, unmarried high school dropout who continues to have babies because she loves children. After reluctantly agreeing to attend a performance of a William Shakespeare play with her children at Kiswana Browne's insistence, Cora Lee's outlook on life and motherhood begins to change. She realizes that her children are more than playthings, more than her baby dolls; they are human beings with needs and desires of their own.

Theresa, a lesbian who is Lorraine's lover. She has been with men (some of whom were kind, others cruel), but she is naturally drawn to women. In her direct and outspoken manner, she insists that being a lesbian means being different, by nature, from other people. It means being outside society, since society punishes those who are different so intensely. She prefers to ignore the straight world and socializes only with lesbians. She is jealous of Lorraine's friendship with Ben, the janitor.

Lorraine, a teacher who fears society's condemnation of her lesbian relationship with Theresa. Her view of what it means to be a lesbian is very different from Theresa's. She detests the word "lesbian" and insists that she is not different from other people. In the past, however, she has suffered more than Theresa for her choice. Her father disowned her, and she lost her teaching job in Detroit and fears that it could happen again. She and Theresa have moved many times because of her fears. She craves social acceptance and cannot accept being cut off from the community. Ben is the only one in the community who does not view her as being different. Becoming a scapegoat for the entire community's fears and prejudices, near the end of the novel she is brutally raped by a group of gang members.

Ben, the elderly alcoholic janitor of Brewster Place. He is a kind, gentle, and nonjudgmental man who sees some of his own daughter in Lorraine and who comforts her when she is rejected and ridiculed by the women of Brewster Place. Ben is killed by Lorraine when he appears in the alley where she has just been raped.

Genevieve Slomski

WOMEN OF MESSINA

Author: Elio Vittorini (1908-1966)
Type of work: Novel
Time of action: 1945-1946; epilogue, 1949
First published: Le donne di Messina, 1949; revised, 1964 (English translation, 1973)

The narrator, a character who is never named. His father worked for the railroad company, but this information is the only distinctive point about the narrator. He is the ordinary Italian who mourns for the past and discusses the changes wrought by the Fascist regime and World War II.

Uncle Agrippa, Siracusa's wandering father, an older man who is retired from the railroad company. For years, he has traveled throughout Italy, searching for his daughter. After many years of journeying, however, the object of his travels is no longer finding Siracusa but what he calls "the reunion": a perfect dimension in which human beings will understand one another without conflict. In addition, Agrippa's travels underline the subplot of the novel, which can be divided into three themes: the need for knowledge, the role of the individual in society, and the utopian "reunion."

Ventura, also known as **Ugly Mug,** a for-mer Fascist officer who lives anonymously in the village. He cannot forget the past, however, even while he is trying to adapt to the present. After Siracusa undergoes her "Teresa" transformation, Ventura is thereafter identified merely as "Teresa's husband."

Siracusa, Ventura's lover and Uncle Agrippa's daughter. She ran away during the war to search for a better world. Siracusa knows about Ventura's past and has forgiven him. With him she will undergo a symbolic metamorphosis, acquiring a new identity as Teresa.

Carlo the Bald, a former Fascist who is now working for the Italian government and who represents the new law. Carlo the Bald forces the addressing of the postwar moral dilemma regarding the punishment of former Fascists. His softer side is revealed when he sympathetically listens to Uncle Agrippa's tale of his search for his missing daughter while the two men are on a train together.

Rosaria Pipia

WOMEN OF TRACHIS

Author: Sophocles (c. 496-406 B.C.), translated by Ezra Pound (1885-1972)
Type of work: Play
Time of action: Mythic Hellenic prehistory
First produced: c. 435-429 B.C., Greek version; 1954, Pound's version

Daianeira (dā·ăn·ē'rä), also known as **The Day's Air,** or **Daysair,** the daughter of Oineus, the wife of the great hero Herakles. Powerfully alluring and aware of her beauty ("looks are my trouble"), she is unhappy as the action begins because her husband has been away from his family for some time. She admires him and finds him very attractive, but her love is tested when she learns that Herakles has sent a young woman captive to their home. In an attempt to remove any possibility of competition, she sends Herakles a love charm given to her by a centaur. When the potion turns out to be a deadly poison, she is driven mad with grief, and, when her son criticizes her, she feels completely deserted and decides to destroy herself.

Herakles (hĕr'ŭ·klēz), the son of Zeus, one of the greatest of the Greek heros, who has been condemned by the gods to carry out a series of labors, which keep him away from his wife and son. Headstrong ("he's capable of anything"), impulsive, very passionate, he is unbeatable by any man in combat but is susceptible to the lures of Eros. When the potion his wife sends him turns out to be a lethal mixture, he is driven mad with pain and anger. He appears for the first time late in the play, dressed in a "mask of divine agony," seeking a dignified death but too furious to be able to control himself. Ultimately, he is able to regain his heroic stature in his final instruction to his son.

Hyllos (hī′lōs), son of Herakles and Daianeira. He is loving and dutiful, obedient and respectful. He shares his mother's desire to see Herakles return home, but, when his father is poisoned, he blames his mother for the betrayal. Then, when he learns the truth, he is shattered by grief. Struggling against the overpowering emotion caused by the loss of his parents, he resolves to carry out his father's last request, to marry Iole, and to prove his devotion to his parent's legacy.

Iole (ī′ō•lā), daughter of Eurytus, a king, her name literally means "tomorrow," or the future. She caught Herakles' eye and he destroyed her father's capital city to get her. In his dying speech, he commands his son to marry her. She does not speak during the play, but her gestures register her sadness at her situation when Daianeira observes and questions her.

Likhas (lī′kŭs), family herald for Herakles and Daianeira. An honest, reliable, determined, and persistent man, he is totally faithful but not particularly sharp. He is killed by Herakles, who blames him for the work of the potion.

A messenger, a figure who is aware of the palace gossip and able to provide information beyond the official sources. He often disagrees with and chides the somewhat pompous Likhas. He is snide and cynical, even with the queen.

A nurse, or **housekeeper,** an old and tottery woman who is physically smaller than Daianeira. She provides information about actions (such as the suicide of Daianeira) that occur offstage.

Leon Lewis

THE WOMEN'S ROOM

Author: Marilyn French (1929-   )
Type of work: Novel
Time of action: Primarily 1968-1970, with extended flashbacks to the early decades of Mira's life
First published: 1977

Mira, a graduate student in the English department at Harvard who is the divorced mother of two sons. She is older than most of the other graduate students, having gone back to school at the age of thirty-eight, and yet it is the younger women who seem so much more comfortable with themselves. It is not until she becomes part of a small circle of friends at Harvard that she begins to see her personal life in terms of feminist politics; her consciousness is raised. From that perspective, she looks back at her earlier self with scorn. Although intelligent and a voracious reader, Mira accepted, almost without question, the limits put on her behavior and aspirations first by her parents and, later, by her husband. Married to a wealthy man, living in a beautiful house, dressed in lovely clothes, she considered herself successful—until her husband asked her for a divorce. At Harvard, she meets friends who help her learn to trust herself and to challenge the limits others place upon her.

Val, a graduate student in social science at Harvard and the divorced mother of a daughter. A year or so older than Mira, Val is tall, big-boned, flamboyant, and fleshy, and is known by her collection of capes from around the world. She talks loudly and authoritatively; at times, it seems as if Val has transformed every one of her experiences into theory. Val is more politically involved than the others. Eventually, her politics force her to take an uncompromising stand on women's rights, and she is killed as a result.

Isolde, an English graduate student at Harvard. She is in her mid-twenties, a lesbian, tall, very thin, with pale green eyes. She is central to the group, providing it with its source of creative energy. Iso is able to see the positive side of everyone. Mira, and others, often come to her when they need someone to talk to.

Ava, Isolde's lover for four years. Very shy, tall, and willowy, Ava leaves Iso to study dance in New York City.

Clarissa, an English graduate student at Harvard in her early twenties. Reared by liberal and educated parents, happy and content with herself, Clarissa seems to be the embodiment of what the others are striving for. Yet, clouds appear on her horizon: Her husband expects her to do all the housework even as she is studying for her doctoral orals.

Kyla Forrester, an English graduate student at Harvard in her early twenties. She is short, with long, straight red hair, wide blue eyes, and an oval face. A perfectionist, she smokes incessantly when nervous. Her husband's lack of support for her studies causes her to doubt herself, to drink too much, and to succumb to hysteria and weeping.

Christine (Chris) Truax, Val's teenage daughter. She is very close to her mother. Chris's rape, and her harsh treatment by the police and the courts, transform Val's politics irrevocably.

Ben Voler, Mira's lover, an expert on the (fictional) African country Lianu. Ben is in his mid-thirties, with a dark complexion and a large, round face. He is extremely supportive of Mira's work, until he gets the opportunity to return to Lianu.

Tadziewski (Tad), Val's lover. In his mid-twenties, Tad is fair, blue-eyed, gangly, and sensitive. He falls madly in love with Val. When she informs him that she will continue to have other lovers, he throws a hysterical jealous fit that ends the relationship.

Norm, Mira's husband, who is a physician. He is handsome but unfeeling and shallow.

Martha, Mira's friend during her years of marriage. Foulmouthed and refreshingly honest, Martha brags about her "built-in shit detector." She has returned to college and intends to go to law school. When her affair with her French professor ends, she attempts suicide and is never the same afterward.

Liz Marshall

THE WONDER-WORKER

Author: Dan Jacobson (1929-   )
Type of work: Novel
Time of action: c. 1950-1970
First published: 1973

Timothy Fogel, a psychotic individual who parallels the narrator. Beginning with his conception and ending with the murder of Susie, the narrative traces Timothy's development as a strange, isolated boy into a profoundly disturbed young man. As a child, Timothy believes he can transform himself into any inanimate form. Rejected by a young girl named Susie, young Timothy retreats into his subjective world, reveling in his meditative "power." As Timothy matures, so does his obsession with his "gift" and Susie until, in an effort to possess Susie completely, he murders her and her unborn child.

Gerhard Fogel, Timothy's father. A Jew who fled from Nazi Germany to settle in England, Gerhard is a commercial artist who leads a quiet, nondescript life. Although he is tortured by the possibility that Timothy is really Mr. Truter's son, Gerhard accepts the "arrangement" between his wife and landlord because of financial necessity. After his wife's death, Gerhard attempts to understand and help his son, to no avail. An underdog, Gerhard contrasts to his counterpart in the novel, the narrator's successful father.

Maureen Sullivan Fogel, Timothy's mother, a large Irishwoman with copper-colored hair and large, crooked teeth. A salesclerk in a tobacco shop, Maureen appears to be mentally handicapped in some way. She tells Timothy that, ever since she was rescued from the remains of a hotel destroyed by a German bomber, her mind has been damaged. Gerhard, attracted to her helplessness, marries her. After their marriage, Maureen continues working as a clerk, and, one day, unaware of her condition, Maureen gives birth to Timothy on the floor of Robinson's tobacco shop. Apparently for reasons of convenience, Maureen has a sexual relationship with the landlord, Mr. Truter. Maureen falls ill and dies when Timothy is a teenager.

Susie Sendin, a young woman with whom Timothy is obsessed. Susie's appearance seems average—light brown hair, hazel eyes, and a smattering of freckles on her nose—as does her personality, yet she becomes Timothy's entire world. Irritated and flattered by Timothy's attentions, she shuns his strange affection and dates other boys, which Timothy sees as betrayal. Susie falls in love with a married man, and, pregnant with his child, she is murdered by Timothy.

Laurence Sendin, Susie's brother and Timothy's friend. Laurence, an adolescent thief, confides in Timothy, and the two become partners of sorts. Through Laurence, Timothy develops a fascination for jewels, which, in his warped imagination, he ties into his "gift" and his desire for Susie. It appears that Timothy uses Laurence to become closer to his sister.

Mr. Truter, the Fogels' landlord. Mr. Truter, Maureen's lover, is possibly Timothy's father. It is implied that Mr. Truter exchanges rent for sexual favors from Maureen, and Timothy, who witnesses the two making love, is shunned by Susie and others because of his mother's scandalous relationship with the landlord.

Mabel, Susie's friend. At Susie's insistence, Mabel becomes Timothy's unlikely girlfriend. Although he despises the homely, overweight Mabel, Timothy courts her to spite Susie.

Elsie Brody Fogel, Gerhard's second wife. Heavily made-up with dyed-black hair, Elsie is a tacky, garrulous, and dull-witted woman who shows great curiosity in Timothy's peculiarities.

The narrator, Timothy's counterpart, who discovers that he is a patient in a mental institution. Paranoid and self-absorbed, the narrator harbors deep resentment toward his doctor and father. Fascinated with his own psyche, he creates his autobiography, the story of Timothy Fogel. According to the narrator's father, however, the pages of his book contain only scribbling.

The narrator's father, Gerhard's counterpart, who visits the narrator in the sanatorium. Unlike Gerhard, the narrator's father seems to be a successful, self-confident businessman, ashamed of his son's condition.

Dr. Wuchs, a psychiatrist treating the narrator. Dr. Wuchs is an immaculately dressed, well-respected professional. The narrator, however, suspects that he was a Nazi during the war and that his skills and motives are questionable.

Lisa S. Starks

WONDERFUL FOOL

Author: Shusaku Endō (1923-   )
Type of work: Novel
Time of action: 1957
First published: Osaka san, 1959 (English translation, 1974)

Gaston Bonaparte, called **Gas** for short, a native of the Savoy region in France and a descendant of Emperor Napoleon I. Having failed to qualify as a missionary priest in France, he has followed an inner call to journey to Japan to act out some nebulous missionary role despite his limited knowledge of Japanese. A gigantic man resembling a sumo wrestler, he has a long, horselike face, with sad eyes. Despite his size and his obvious strength, he is a coward who will not even defend himself against an attacker. Moreover, he is both a simpleton and a bungler. Yet, he is a man of peace, love, and compassion who seeks to aid any creature he sees suffering from misfortune, oppression, or a physical handicap, whether a man, woman, or dog; he is the "wonderful fool" of the novel's title.

Takamori Higaki, a young bachelor and university graduate who works in a bank in the Otemachi district of Tokyo and is a former pen pal of Bonaparte. He lives in the residential district of Kyōdō in Setagaya Ward, quite removed from the heart of Tokyo, with his mother and younger sister, who, to his annoyance, is in the habit of "policing" him. Although he takes his position at the bank seriously, after work he likes to make merry with friends in the amusement district of the city. He is a spendthrift and always lacking in funds. When Bonaparte arrives in Japan, the Higakis invite him into their home as a guest.

Tomoe Higaki, Takamori's younger sister, six years his junior, who is strong-minded, shrewd, a bad loser, and independent. She saves her money and invests it in the stock market. A university graduate, she studied Italian as well as typing and shorthand. She works for the Disanto Trading Company located in the Marunouchi Building across the street from Tokyo Station. Although she is very attractive, she resembles in her character the Japanese Amazon Tomoe Gozen of *The Tale of Heiki,* who rode to battle with her lord, Yoshinaka Kiso.

Takuhiko Osako, a business associate of Tomoe at the Italian trading company where she works. A grandson of Baron Osako, a member of the prewar nobility, he is a very thin man who wears rimless glasses and dresses with sartorial splendor, being unusually careful of his personal appearance. He is, however, effeminate in voice and manner. Although he courts Tomoe, she regards him strictly as a friend whom she dates on occasion.

Chōtei Kawaii, an old, emaciated Oriental diviner, formerly a teacher and school principal, who makes a meager living telling people's fortunes and writing love letters for women. He befriends Bonaparte.

Endō, a tubercular gangster with a face like General Tojo. A lone wolf and a "hit man" for the Hoshino gang of Tokyo, he is a pitiless killer who does what he likes without rancor or lament. A sniper in the army during World War II, he entirely lost faith in people and became a nihilist after his brother was executed at the end of the war for a war crime of which he was innocent. He trusts nobody nor anything but his Colt pistol. A university graduate, he speaks French.

Major Kobayashi, a land surveyor in the small city of Yamagata and a former army officer of the battalion in which Endō's brother served. A thin man in his early fifties, he has a ratlike face, very round eyes, and looks mean.

Richard P. Benton

WONDERLAND

Author: Joyce Carol Oates (1938-   )
Type of work: Novel
Time of action: 1939-1969
First published: 1971

Jesse Harte, later **Vogel,** and then **Pedersen,** a high school student who survives his distraught father's murder of the remaining Harte Family, during the Depression, in upper New York state. When his Grandfather Vogel pays his hospital bills, he agrees to be called Jesse Vogel and to live on the old man's remote farm, until placed in an orphanage. Dr. Karl Pedersen adopts him at age sixteen on condition that he now be known as Jesse Pedersen and prepare for a medical career. After a few years, however, Jesse cannot recognize his face as his own any longer and leaves to work his own way through medical school. By age twenty-four, he falls under the influence of instructor T. W. Monk, whose callous treatment of patients' bodies further confuses his sense of identity and worth. He breaks his engagement with nurse Anne-Marie Seton and, in order to be close to the distinguished doctor Benjamin Cady, marries Cady's daughter Helene. Remembering his own lost childhood, he can weep over hospitalized battered children. Yet, busily furthering his career and becoming involved with the mysterious Reva Denk, he ignores his two daughters' need for a father. As a result one daughter, Michelle, joins a drug commune in Canada. Awakened at last to how he has failed his family, Jesse follows her and buys her back from Noel, her onetime lover.

Dr. Karl Pedersen, a mystic and physician famous for instinctual diagnoses. He adopts Jesse as a substitute for his own children, both of whom are considered geniuses but neither of whom shows any promise in the field of medicine. As head of his own clinic as well as of his family, he is a completely domineering figure. What he considers necessary discipline his children maintain is an attempt to devour them. When Jesse finally runs away from the destructive demands of his adoptive father, Dr. Pedersen pronounces him dead.

Mary Pedersen, an ordinary woman who has become alcohol-addicted and obese because she cannot live up to her husband's standards of perfection. She enjoys Jesse because he alone is willing to talk to her. She joins him when, having seen in a mirror his own face as that of a fat stranger, he flees to Buffalo. Yet, weak-willed, she returns to Dr. Pederesen and to imprisonment within her widening flesh.

Hilda Pedersen, a brilliant thirteen-year-old who feels ugly in the eyes of her father. Knowing that she is a mathematical prodigy is little comfort to her in the face of his unconcealed rejection and her mother's reference to her as a freak. She is often on the verge of unconsciousness, torn between their dislike for her and the mystery of her wizardry.

Frederich Pedersen, Hilda's seventeen-year-old brother, who feels that his music composes itself. Unfortunately, his gift of special sensitivity is considered of no use to the world of medicine, and his father goes looking for a truer son in Jesse.

Talbot Waller Monk, also known as **Trick,** at thirty, a laboratory section man for Dr. Cady. He is capable of such bizarre insensitivities as eating a boiled portion of human flesh. He also writes poems in which no people appear. Although he suffers from a rheumatic heart condition, he attacks Jesse physically as if suicidal. He tells Helene that he is in love with her but, at the same time, says that love is illusory. He reappears in New York City, now a famous poet (author of the title poem, which prefaces the novel, and of another on the body's central nervous system, titled "Vietnam"). He has become a pathetic, unpredictable drug addict.

Dr. Roderick Perrault, Chief Resident at La Salle Hospital and a specialist in brain cancers. He takes Jesse as his apprentice, with expectations that Jesse will become his junior partner. He is interested in the possibility that a brain might be transplanted and, with it, the original mind still intact and operative. The issue, though a scientific one, affects Jesse's personal sense of shifting identity as well as the struggle within him between fate and free will.

Dr. Benjamin Cady, Helene's father, who argues that a mind, having memory and personality, is distinguishable as separate from the brain. He and Dr. Perrault seriously debate these differences and whether, after the body's death, certain brains should be preserved by the government for the good of the nation. His second marriage, at age sixty-seven, helps liberate Helene from a lifelong fixation on her father.

Helene Cady, a daughter who has been extremely close to her father since childhood. She wants Jesse to promise they will have at most one child. Later, she is tempted to abort their first daughter. Yet, after Michelle, their second daughter, is born, she weeps, feeling a failure because she cannot have more. With men other than her father, she has always felt

uncomfortable, and, at times, she is hostile toward the inner workings of her body.

Reva Denk, a stranger whom Jesse meets accidentally in 1956. He is immediately attracted to her. She resists him until she requires an abortion. He refuses but offers to father her unborn child because he likes to think that he is dedicated to life. He follows her to the commune where she lives with the father of that child and his wife. When Reva says his attention is suffocating, Jesse begins to slash himself with a razor blade.

Shelley Vogel, Jesse's daughter, who calls herself an unadopted baby in a letter written after she deserts her family. In 1969, she is bailed out of a county jail in Toledo, only to wander off again to Florida, Texas, Toronto. She is with Noel, a draft dodger on drugs, who has reduced her to a state of degradation in their Canadian commune. When Jesse finds her, she seems to be suffering from hepatitis and hunger. He refuses to let her die and rows her back to the United States in a fifteen-foot boat.

Noel, Shelley's companion in Canada. He finally agrees to sell her body back to Jesse at the same price he would pay for a corpse: five hundred dollars. He says that he once saved her from jumping off a bridge but that he has no personal feeling for her.

Leonard Casper

WOODCUTTERS

Author: Thomas Bernhard (1931-1989)
Type of work: Novel
Time of action: The 1980's, in retrospect, the 1950's
First published: Holzfällen, 1984 (English translation, 1987)

Unnamed first-person narrator, a writer who has recently returned to Vienna after twenty-five years in London. He is disgusted with himself for having accepted an invitation from the Auersbergers, met by chance in the street and well known to him in the 1950's. He had hoped to make a clean break

with his artistic past, which drove him to a nervous breakdown. He observes his fellow guests, many of whom he has already seen at the funeral of a suicide, Joana, that afternoon, while they were all waiting for the guest of honor, a famous actor. On leaving the Mozarteum in the 1950's, the narrator had had close emotional and artistic ties with Jeannie Billroth, also present and now a celebrated writer, before turning to the Auersbergers and Joana. He feels hatred for them all now for setting him on the artistic path through life. The narrator is asleep when the actor arrives, and his behavior is ungracious throughout, but by the end he takes a kinder view of Vienna.

Jeannie Billroth, a celebrated writer. She is the Austrian Virginia Woolf, according to the narrator, a writer of trash who has sold herself for state subsidies. In her youth, she was the first to take the narrator's poetry seriously, so that inevitably they now loathe each other, and he can note that she has grown fat and ugly. At Joana's funeral, she takes a collection to help with expenses but is generally abused for tastelessness. That evening, she addresses a naïve question to the actor and has to endure further insults.

Elfriede Slukal, professionally known as **Joana,** an unsuccessful choreographer, dancer, and actress from Kilb, Lower Austria, who has hanged herself. A country girl, pampered by her parents, she had set her sights on Vienna and was a member of the artistic circles attended by the narrator after he left Jeannie. She married a tapestry weaver, Fritz, and her beauty helped to make his studio world-famous. Seventeen years ago, Fritz ran away to Mexico with Joana's best friend, and she became bloated and drunken, trying for a time to earn a living with a "movement studio." Her last years were spent with a seedy former actor who vainly tried to cure her alcoholism.

Mr. Auersberger, a talented pianist and composer, a close friend of the narrator in the 1950's, and now his host. Of humble origins, he is a social climber who likes to impress by coarsely ill-mannered scenes (for example, complaining about the goulash after the funeral, removing his dentures in public) and embarrassing remarks. His evenings have often ended with broken glass and furniture. Now he is a bloated alcoholic, with a taste for young male writers.

Mrs. Auersberger, the woman who invites the narrator to the supper party. She is a social climber from the minor aristocracy; she and her husband live off their dwindling estates. Her artistic gatherings of twenty-five years ago horrify the narrator. Once a singer, she now has a grating voice and a shabby appearance, and she quarrels in public with her husband.

Actor from Vienna Burgtheater, a performer enjoying success as Ekdal in Henrik Ibsen's *The Wild Duck*. The guest of honor at the Auersbergers, he appears well after midnight for supper. He behaves in the manner of a self-centered celebrity, insulting Jeannie brutally when she asks him a question. The narrator describes him as a mindless ham, which is perhaps partly true. He departs, wishing he could live in peace like a woodcutter.

John, whose real name is **Friedrich,** a former actor turned commercial traveler, with a chronic cough, Joana's constant companion for the last eight years of her life. He gives a grisly account of Joana's death while the narrator is eating goulash. He met Joana at her foolish "studio" and attempted without success to cure her alcoholism. The narrator recognizes good qualities in John despite his appearance.

W. Gordon Cunliffe

THE WOODS

Author: David Mamet (1947-   )
Type of work: Play
Time of action: The 1970's
First produced: 1977

Ruth, a young woman seeking a romantic commitment from her reluctant lover. Spending a weekend at a cabin with Nick, trying to escape the pressures of the city, their jobs, and their obviously deteriorating relationship, she speaks incessantly in fragmented sentences and incomplete narratives. Fear of abandonment, loss, and decay are the central themes running through her conversation. What emerges is the gradual revelation of her psychological state: She is having problems controlling her rising hysteria and her need to make contact. After Nick's attack on her, she is able to withdraw emotionally from him and offer him a kind of a sexual nurturing for his childlike need.

Nick, an intensely troubled young man. For much of the play, he speaks very little, in contrast to Ruth's flood of language. His few comments contain the themes of fear of entrapment, fear of death, and fear of meaninglessness. When he feels the need to break through Ruth's romantic imaginings, he explodes and attacks her physically and sexually. When the assault fails and Ruth acknowledges the impossibility of her desires for a warm, committed relationship, Nick becomes increasingly vulnerable, frightened, and willing to express his emotional neediness. At the end, he comes to her arms as a child, and they cling to each other out of necessity, united by their mutual fears.

Lori Hall Burghardt

A WORD CHILD

Author: Iris Murdoch (1919-   )
Type of work: Novel
Time of action: The early 1970's
First published: 1975

Hilary Burde, linguist, former don, and minor bureaucrat, brother of Crystal, lover of Thomasina. A big, hairy, dark man, Hilary, now guarded and remorseful, irresistibly attracts the three women on whom the plot turns. An angry, unloved orphan, separated from his younger sister, Crystal, who represents goodness to him, Hilary escapes delinquency and despair only because of his talent for languages—thus he is a "word child," created by language, not love. Uninterested in what words mean, he seeks to learn the rules of grammar, which represent law to him. His fellowship at Oxford promises a decent life for him and his sister, until he becomes obsessed with Anne, wife of Gunnar Jopling, another don. Gunnar and Hilary both leave Oxford, the first to a successful career, the second to become a government clerk. In London, Hilary carefully limits his involvements; the rigid routine that mirrors his emotional state reserves an evening a week for each of his friends, two for Crystal. Gunnar's second wife asks Hilary to see her husband so that the past will no longer poison the present. Again, however, Hilary destroys both the woman he loves and Jopling's happiness. Yet, Hilary realizes that he is not solely responsible; all are in some degree victims of chance. He ceases to identify guilt and despair with penitence, and his new understanding means escape from the past. The measure of Hilary's growth is that this time he does not burden Crystal with what he has done but suffers alone. He also relinquishes his grip on Crystal so that she may marry.

Crystal Burde, Hilary's younger sister, self-sacrificing, simple, instinctively good. Crystal cares for Hilary after Anne's death, follows him to London, and warns him not to continue seeing Gunnar's wife. Gunnar had slept with Crystal on the night Anne died. She still cares for him but marries Arthur Fisch and plans a happy life in rural Yorkshire.

Gunnar Jopling, Oxford don, career civil

servant, Hilary's alter ego. Jopling is successful and happily married but equally obsessed by the past. Both of his wives die in accidents resulting from their attraction to Hilary; both deaths are precipitated by Gunnar's knowledge. Both Biscuit and Crystal love Jopling, and his relation to Burde is not solely one of hatred. Jopling conceals Hilary's part in both deaths, and both tragedies lead Gunnar to further public success.

Lady Kitty Jopling, Gunnary's second wife, the beautiful daughter of an Irish peer. She wants the child Jopling cannot give her and wishes Hilary to father a child, which she will claim is Gunnar's. Hilary is refusing when Jopling appears and Kitty is accidentally killed.

Thomasina Uhlmeister, a minor Scottish actress who is Hilary's jealous mistress, determined to marry him. She tells Jopling of Hilary's relationship with Kitty, thus precipitating the tragedy. It is unclear whether she and Burde will ever marry.

Arthur Fisch, an unprepossessing, good man who is a minor civil servant. He rescues drug addicts, loves Crystal and eventually marries her.

Biscuit, Lady Kitty's Eurasian maid, follower of Hilary, devoted to Jopling. Appearing as a mysterious agent of change in Hilary's life, she is actually gathering information and delivering messages for Kitty.

Jocelyn Creigh Cass

WORDS AND MUSIC

Author: Samuel Beckett (1906-1989)
Type of work: Play
Time of action: Unspecified
First produced: 1962, as a radio play

Croak, a character addressed as "lord" by Words; Croak, in turn, refers to Words and Music as his "balms" and "comforts" and, more familiarly, as Joe and Bob. Wearing carpet slippers and carrying a club, Croak arrives late, asks them to forgive his delay, and then announces the performance's first theme: love. He communicates his desires and, more often and more demonstrably, his displeasure, less by means of words than by means of sighs, groans, exclamations of anguish, and the peremptory thumping of his club. Disappointed by Words's disquisition on love, he calls on Music. Then (either because the playing does not please or because Words repeatedly interrupts Music), Croak changes the subject, first to age and later to "the face." His early gentleness soon gives way to tyrannical demands and ultimately to anguish as Words's speech conjures up for him the face of Lily (presumably the same face he saw earlier and that caused him to be late). As the performance gains momentum,

as Words and Music finally do play together as bidden, Croak becomes more and more their helpless, perhaps enraptured audience. At the end of this radio play, Croak is heard haltingly shuffling away, back to the tower—back into the silence—from which he first came.

Words, a character who is deferential toward his master, Croak, but imperious toward Music, with whom he is cooped up in the dark. Interested as he may be in pleasing the master who commands them to play together, Words appears more interested in gaining his master's sole favor by silencing Music, as if Words assumes that the two are at odds and so in competition with each other. Before the master's arrival, Words rehearses his speech on "sloth," and, when Croak announces that the theme is "love," Words simply repeats the same speech, substituting the word "love" for the word "sloth" wherever necessary. Neither his speech on love nor the next on age pleases Croak; however, with Music's help, the persistent Words, although still disdainful of his partner, does improve. His ragged speech turns into tentative song; consequently, and concurrently, his early imperiousness turns into gentleness. The earlier antagonism gives way to faltering cooperation and eventually to success. Working at last in concert with Music, Words composes the poem that silences the pair's demanding audience: Croak. Words, however, is shocked by Croak's sudden departure and unsuccessfully implores him to stay.

Music, played by a small orchestra. As the play begins, Music is tuning up, only to be peremptorily silenced by Words. Music here and through much of the play appears conciliatory, even "imploring." When Words's initial performances fail to please Croak, Music tries to help, suggesting possible directions, gently leading as well as unobtrusively accompanying a partner to whom Music is willing to grant ascendancy, or perhaps the illusion of ascendancy. Where Words appears cold, Music seems warm. Just at the point where Words begins to succeed, however, Music suddenly takes over, though whether in a sudden burst of enthusiasm or in retaliation for past wrongs is not at all clear. Less ambiguous and also more characteristic is Music's "brief rude retort" very near the end of the play; it may be the reason Croak departs. Its effect on the now "imploring" Words is more pronounced, as Music achieves this ironic triumph over his counterpart and nemesis.

Pause, the absence of sound and sense that Words and Music attempt to fill for Croak.

Lily, the woman whose face Croak saw on the stairs and that he now recalls as he listens to Words and Music.

Robert A. Morace

THE WORDS UPON THE WINDOW-PANE

Author: William Butler Yeats (1865-1939)
Type of work: Play
Time of action: The 1920's
First produced: 1930

Jonathan Swift, the eighteenth century satirist and poet, here a spirit called up in a séance. The ghost of Swift resembles the man at a more or less recognizable point in his life, during old age but before his descent into madness. In his two dialogues with the spirit forms of the women whom he loved, the satirist's wry cynicism has turned to bitterness and paranoia. In countering Vanessa's empassioned offer of marriage, he describes his own "disease of the blood" and the more general malaise of a debased humanity. Yeats's Swift is caught at that point in his late life where intellectual arrogance is waging a losing struggle with the social chaos that he believes is about to engulf him. His ghostly encounter with Stella, whose poem provides the "words" of the title, represents, however, a brief recurrence of the younger Swift, capable of redemption through intellectual grace and courage.

John Corbet, a graduate student at the University of Cambridge, a specialist in Swift's life and work. Corbet's initial skepticism about contact with the spirit world dissolves as the play progresses; the ghostly colloquies between Swift and Vanessa and between Swift and Stella persuade him that he has discovered the "mystery" behind Swift's celibacy. Although the revelation affords Corbet a measure of intellectual exaltation for its own sake, he also clearly views the discovery as a stepping-stone in his own scholarly advancement. To an extent, Corbet also serves as provider of literary background; his historical and critical asides to Dr. Trench and to Mrs. Henderson allow Yeats to supply his audience with facts about Swift's life and his relationships with Vanessa and Stella, insights crucial to an understanding of the play.

Dr. Trench, an elderly scholar, president of the Dublin Spiritualists' Association. Trench serves as the play's moral and intellectual pivot; like Corbet, he is an intellectual, a man of reason. Yet he has also become convinced of more ghostly realities, enabling him to glimpse the boundary between reason and passion. At the same time that he holds the overly emotional and superstitious impulses of the other séance participants in check, he also lends credibility to the séance's central action, the calling up of ghosts. As Corbet acts as dramatic channel for literary and historical information about Swift, Trench serves as an interpreter of spiritualist practice and Dublin legend.

Ester Vanhomrigh, called **Vanessa,** Swift's lover and protégé. Vanessa appears in the first of Swift's two dialogues with the women he loved. She describes her loyalty and passion to an obdurate Swift and rationally demands a reason for his refusal to marry. Why, she asks, has he raised her from her humble station, educating and "refining" her, if he does not love her? When Swift counters that he feels disgust at the prospect of siring children, she leaves him to his solitude.

Esther Johnson, called **Stella,** Swift's lover. The second of the women in Swift's life, Stella is more nearly his equal than Vanessa. In his brief scene with her, he describes his admiration for her intellectual excellence and specifically praises her poem to him. She is the representative of those women who are able to love "according to the soul," and, at least according to Swift, thereby possess greater happiness than those who experience bodily love. During the opening scenes of the play, Trench informs Corbet that the house in which the séance takes place was originally Stella's.

Mrs. Henderson, a simple Irishwoman, a medium through whom the spirits of Swift, Vanessa, and Stella pass. Mrs. Henderson's role is largely passive, serving first as a conduit for the exchanges between Swift and his lovers, then as ignorant reflector of Corbet's scholarly knowledge. In a very real sense, she is the stock figure of "old Ireland," the peasant woman to whom the movement of history and the rise of great individuals are nonsense. By the same token, she is both literally and metaphorically possessed by Ireland's past and by its madness. As the play ends, she is left alone; while she modestly goes about making tea, she simultaneously serves as the mouthpiece for Swift's tragic ravings.

Cornelius Patterson, a gambler. Bent only on the materialistic benefits of his contact with the "Other World," Patterson is the stereotype of the twentieth century materialist interested only in his own gain.

Abraham Johnson, an evangelist. Johnson futilely seeks to reconcile the reality of the spirit world with the teachings of Christianity. As ignorant as Mrs. Henderson is of Swift's importance, he is only able to see the writer as an embodiment of evil and must be restrained from disrupting the séance.

Mrs. Mallet, an experienced spiritualist. Like Patterson and Johnson, Mrs. Mallet's interest in spiritual contact lies in self-interest; unlike the two men, however, she is free from selfishness. Her principal aim is to contact her drowned husband; her longing for the beloved dead thus mirrors, in miniature, the larger themes of the play.

Miss Mackenna, another veteran spiritualist, secretary of the association.

John Steven Childs

THE WORKHOUSE WARD

Author: Lady Augusta Gregory (1852-1932)
Type of work: Play
Time of action: The 1900's
First produced: 1908

Michael Miskell, a pauper and current resident at the Workhouse. Michael is an old and disputatious peasant who spends his time talking to his former neighbor, who is now his fellow workhouse inmate, Mike McInerney. Michael seems determined to have the last word, to suffer the most, to come from the greatest family. In short, he is in a continual battle to defend his position against his old neighbor and fellow pauper. He is cunning and has the verbal skills to question the value of another's possessions or family while inflating his own situation. He rehashes old grudges and charges such as being bitten by Mike's dogs after returning from a fair day. Apparently that happened many years before, but Michael claims that it caused his downfall because he has been "wasting from then till now." Although their lives have been so closely tied together, his dearest wish is to be buried at a distance from his old neighbor. While he dismisses all troubles and obstacles with words, however, he is vulnerable to not having an opponent with whom to contend. When Mike McInerney indicates he is to leave with his sister, Michael poignantly asks if Mike is going "to leave me with rude people and with townspeople . . . and they having no respect for me or no wish for me at all." He needs someone to talk to because his life is talk, and, "with no conversable person," he is miserable.

Mike McInerney, an old farmer who has lost his land and been reduced to pauper status in the Workhouse. He spends his time defending himself against the assaults of Michael Miskell and making countercharges against his adversary. He does seem to have been better off in earlier years than Michael, but his strategies of attack and defense are quite similar to those of his opponent. He claims,

for example, that the banshee cries for the famous family of the McInerneys but never for the low Miskells. Their equal battle is turned in his favor by the arrival of his sister, Honor Donohue, with the invitation to join her in her seaside home. His victory does not lead to a final cry of triumph, however, and he softens his attitude to his old adversary by first offering him his pipe and then taking the unusual step of asking his sister to take Michael into the household. When she refuses, he is content to remain where he is; for all of its difficulties, a workhouse of continual verbal battles is preferable to a more regular but boring life without talk and the constant excitement of verbal battle. At the end of the play, they return to the battle that has been going on for so many years as Mike defends the house he has just rejected against Michael's attacks. Their battle finally exhausts words, and they resort to a final barrage of pillows, mugs, and whatever is within reach. Their relationship is a marriage of enemies that only death can dissolve.

Honor Donohue, an elderly woman, Mike's sister. She masks her need for a man in her home with a newfound charity to her impoverished brother. Though she is eager to have her brother help out in the house, she is not an obliging fool. When she is faced with the prospect of having two quarreling old men with her day and night, she proves as resilient as they are stuck in their ways. She immediately leaves them and goes off by herself with the clothes she had offered to Mike to seek "a man for my own." She is not interested in living through words and roles; the practical business of living comes first in the life of which she takes charge.

James Sullivan

THE WORKS OF LOVE

Author: Wright Morris (1910-   )
Type of work: Novel
Time of action: The 1880's to the 1930's
First published: 1952

Will Jennings Brady, a hardworking man who holds a number of jobs, but none for very long. A onetime handyman, night clerk in a hotel, hotel manager, chicken farmer, egg entrepreneur, and waybill sorter, he finally ends up as a department store Santa Claus. The son of Nebraska pioneers, orphaned at an early age, he lacks culture and education. A taciturn, kind, but naïve man who neither drinks, smokes, gambles, nor swears, he embarks on a quest that takes him from the desolate western plains to Omaha, then to California, and on to Chicago in search of his airy dreams of wealth, happiness, and love. Ironically, he attains none of these. Along the way, his fortunes briefly rise but mainly fall. As a husband and father, he is inept and incapable of understanding the needs of his family. After repeated failures, both as a businessman and family man, he turns Will, Jr., over to foster parents and heads for Chicago, where he dies penniless and alone, after falling into a sewage canal.

Ethel Czerny Bassett, a widow who marries Will Brady. A Bohemian immigrant, quiet and somewhat religious, she relies on Will's help after her husband, owner of the hotel where Brady works, dies. After marrying Brady, she goes with him on a honeymoon to Colorado Springs, but she spends her nights there rolled up in a sheet, afraid to consummate the marriage. After returning to Nebraska, she still experiences sexual problems. Although Brady provides her with many domestic amenities, including a large house, she does not sleep with him. After discovering Brady's affair with a cigar-counter girl in Omaha, she leaves.

Will Brady, Jr., a baby adopted by Will Brady after a runaway prostitute abandoned him on Brady's doorstep. Despite his father's ineptitude as a parent, Will, Jr., does well in school, joins the Boy Scouts, and cultivates a love for nature. Often perplexed by his father's odd behavior, he spends much of his time living elsewhere, mostly in foster homes.

Gertrude Long, Will Brady's second wife, a cigar-counter girl and a prostitute. The young and immature daughter of vaudevillian actors, she first meets Brady in a hotel in Omaha. Attracted initially by his good looks and unusual behavior, she lets the relationship develop and marries him, only to discover that he is no more able to fulfill her needs than he was able to fulfill those of his first wife. Brady, preoccupied with his dreams of riches and power, spends all of his energy tending to business. Meanwhile, she spends her time idly listening to phonograph records and going to cheap films. Although she pities Brady, she does not love him, and their relationship slowly disintegrates after she joins him in California and becomes a prostitute.

T. P. Luckett, the person in charge of the Union Pacific commissary in Omaha and an egg producer. A booster, he persuades Will Brady to give up his hotel job in Calloway and lends him money to move to Murdock to raise chickens for the carriage trade.

Rodney P. Rice

THE WORLD ACCORDING TO GARP

Author: John Irving (1942-   )
Type of work: Novel

Time of action: 1942 through the early 1970's
First published: 1978

T. S. Garp, a writer. Because his father dies before he is born, Garp grows up in a world created by his mother. As a result, he spends most of his life trying to create his own identity and never fully achieves one separate from that of his mother. He is educated at a private boys' school, where his mother is the head nurse; he goes to Europe after graduation and becomes closely involved in the darker side of life in Vienna. He returns home and marries the daughter of his wrestling coach, and while she teaches, he stays home and cares for the children and writes. He indulges in a series of affairs with other women but does little to hide the fact from his wife. He writes three books and loses a son in a bizarre car accident that maims his other son and castrates his wife's lover. He becomes the wrestling coach at Steering School, buys the Percy mansion, and, at age thirty-three, is shot to death by the youngest Percy daughter, now hopelessly insane.

Jenny Fields, a nurse. Jenny believes in evidence and results rather than emotions. Determined to have a child but having no desire to have a husband or to have anything to do with a man, Jenny has a very clinical one night encounter with a brain-damaged soldier, who dies shortly thereafter, and produces Garp. She subsequently takes a position at the Steering School so that Garp will have a proper education and goes about attending classes and reading voraciously so that Garp will have the benefit of her knowledge. After Garp is graduated, she goes to Vienna with him and there writes her autobiography, which becomes a feminist sensation. Her family home in Vermont becomes a haven for distressed women, and, eventually, she decides to enter politics. At a political rally, she is killed by a man dressed as a deer hunter.

Helen Holm, an English professor. Abandoned by her mother, Helen is brought up by her father, a wrestling coach. She becomes introverted and somewhat shy and is given to reading books. When her father takes a position at Steering School, Helen momentarily mistakes Jenny for her mother, who was also a nurse. She earns a Ph.D. at the age of twenty-three, becomes a college professor, marries Garp, and has two children. She has a number of affairs, the last being with Michael Milton, whom she accidentally castrates in a car accident. Eventually, she takes a position at Steering and outlives Garp by many years, dying in old age.

Ernie Holm, a wrestling coach. A small, neat man who is nearly blind, Ernie takes the position of wrestling coach at Steering School so that his daughter will have a good education. He fails to find out that Steering School is a boys' school until it is too late. He is the first friend Jenny Fields ever has, and it is because of him that Garp finds a sport in which he excels, a very important part of a Steering boy's life. He dies of a heart attack while masturbating at home at nearly the same time that Jenny is murdered, although the events of his death are kept very quiet. He is buried at Steering School the same day as Stewart Percy.

Dean Bodger, Dean of Steering School. A short-haired, muscular man, he is a brave and kindhearted individual who becomes a friend of Jenny Fields. His grasp of reality is a little off, but he means well, and it is he who rearranges the scene when Ernie Holm dies so that his daughter will not know what actually happened. He eventually dies while a spectator at a wrestling match.

Stewart Percy (Fat Stew), a Steering School history instructor. A large, florid man, he is noted for putting on a good appearance and doing nothing. While he holds the title of Secretary of Steering School, the only work he does for fifteen years is to teach a course entitled "My Part in the Pacific," which is nothing more than personal reminiscences of the war and how he met his wife, Midge Steering. As his wife was the last member of a very wealthy family, the marriage gave Stewart the leisure to do nothing. He develops a fierce antagonism toward Garp and even blames him for the death of his daughter Cushman. He dies the same day as Ernie Holm.

Cushman (Cushie) Pierce, a student. A pretty girl, she quickly develops disciplinary problems at school and is transferred to five different private girls' schools. Her problem is that she likes sex and is more than willing to participate in it. She seduces Garp and is his first sexual experience. She dies in childbirth with her first child.

Tinch, an English teacher. A frail man with a stutter, Tinch's only reputation with the student body of Steering School is for his very bad breath. He encourages Garp to write, and it is he who recommends that Garp and his mother go to Vienna. He fails to realize that his memories of the city are based on a visit in 1913 and that the city has changed. He eventually freezes to death after a fall in the winter coming home from a faculty party.

Charlotte, a prostitute. A tall, sad-faced woman, Charlotte tries to answer Jenny Fields's questions on lust and eventually develops a friendly, not always professional relationship with Garp. She plans to retire with the money that she has saved and move to Munich, where she hopes to marry a doctor who will take care of her. Instead, she becomes sick and enters an expensive private hospital outside Vienna. She dies at fifty-one, and her parting gift to Garp is two free encounters with the prostitutes who were her friends.

Harrison Fletcher, an English professor. Helen's colleague at the state university, Harrison has an affair with a student and then quickly drops her to have an affair with Helen. He is denied tenure because of his affair with the student, and he and his wife both move away although they remain friends of Garp and Helen. Eventually, he dies in an airplane crash while on vacation.

Alice Fletcher, a writer. Suffering from a severe speech impediment, Alice is aware of her husband's affair with his student. She appeals to Garp for help, and the result is that her husband transfers his attentions to Helen and Alice has an affair with Garp. She writes, but she cannot finish her novels. She wants the affair to continue, but Garp ends it after Helen ends her affair. Even after Alice and her husband move away, she still tries to rekindle her affair with Garp. She dies in an airplane crash with her husband.

Michael Milton, a graduate student. At age twenty-five, he is bright, thin, and tall, and he takes a course from Helen Holm because he has decided to have an affair with her. Helen finally succumbs, but she is overwhelmed with guilt and decides to end it. While consoling Michael over this decision, she accidentally bites off most of his penis when Garp's car plows into the one in which they are sitting. He loses the remainder of it during his subsequent hospitalization.

Roberta Muldoon, a former football player. A six-foot, four-inch former tight end, Roberta has had a sex change operation and becomes a fast friend of Jenny Fields. She lives in Jenny's house and acts as something of a bodyguard. Unable to maintain a relationship with a man, she still manages to become Garp's friend, and, when Jenny is murdered, she blames herself for not acting fast enough. After Jenny's death, she becomes the resident administrator of the Fields Foundation, which uses the money Jenny left to help women. She eventually dies after running on the beach.

Ellen James, a woman whose name is used by a group of radical feminists. As an eleven-year-old child, she was raped by two men who cut out her tongue so that she could not describe them. Instead, she wrote careful descriptions that led to their arrest and conviction. She meets Garp on an airplane after his mother's funeral and moves in with the family as her own family has recently died. She grows up to be a writer, and, while at first she hates the Ellen Jamesians who have their own tongues cut out in order to sympathize with her, she eventually befriends them.

C. D. Akerley

1751

THE WORLD MY WILDERNESS

Author: Rose Macaulay (1881-1958)
Type of work: Novel
Time of action: The years immediately following World War II
First published: 1950

Helen Michel, the handsome and sensuous widow of Maurice Michel and former wife of Sir Gulliver Deniston. In her early forties, curvaceous, with tawny eyes, dark hair, and classical features, she is highly sexed and quite attractive. Intelligent but indolent, well-educated, artistic, and unconventional, she lives in a secluded seaside villa in France, for amusement translating Greek, playing chess, and occasionally gambling compulsively. Maurice Michel has mysteriously drowned a few months earlier; Helen is stepmother to his son Raoul. Her own children are Richie and Barbary Deniston and the infant Roland Michel, on whom both she and Barbary dote. Because Maurice had for a time been considered a "collaborator" of sorts, attempting to coexist with the Germans after they occupied France, Helen is shunned by many neighbors. Much preferring her own company and that of Maurice's cousin Lucien Michel, a married man who becomes her lover after Maurice's death, she is grateful for their distance. As the novel begins, she seems detached from Barbary, sending her to spend time with Sir Gully in England; after Barbary's true parentage is revealed, Helen reclaims her, taking her back to France for the good of both mother and daughter.

Barbary Deniston, Helen's seventeen-year-old daughter by her second lover, a fact that is revealed at the end of the story. Small and young-looking, with olive skin, full lips, dark hair, and gray, slanting eyes, she always appears watchful and ill at ease. Although she trusts nobody, she worships Helen and has inherited her artistic ability. Caught in the tumult of World War II, she has joined the Resistance, engaging in anarchy almost casually and continuing to do so after the need has passed, accompanied always by her stepbrother Raoul. Barbary prefers wilderness to civilization because it provides better places

of refuge, her name indicative of her innocently barbarian nature. In London, she gravitates toward its "wilderness" of bombed-out ruins, teaming up again with Raoul, who has been sent by his grandmother to live with an uncle. After setting up a flat in the shell of an apartment building, she is drawn to a ruined church, where she performs daily penance. Although her father is wealthy, she prefers stealing as an act of rebellion against his conventional ways and his conventional new wife. As the story ends, the mystery of her penitence is solved: Her friends had drowned Maurice Michel. Unwilling or unable to prevent the murder (she was evidently tortured into providing information), she has suffered her own and Helen's grief. Her brush with death enables Helen to forgive and be reunited with her; because Barbary is illegitimate, Helen feels that only Barbary is really all hers.

Raoul Michel, Barbary's stepbrother, a boy in his mid-teens. Born of a marriage of convenience, he is small and olive-skinned, with large brown eyes and an often furtive air. Like Barbary, Raoul has joined the Resistance; unlike her, he appears not to suffer from having been allied with his father's murderers, although at the end of the story he truly grieves. Having been sent to London by his grandmother, who heartily disapproves of Helen Michel, he joins Barbary in the "wilderness" of London's ruins, but, after her accident, he decides to settle down and learn how to live in civilization.

Richmond (Richie) Deniston, Helen's eldest son, a man in his early twenties. Slim, well-educated, and elegant, he sees most of the world as Philistines, and he relishes civilization, fearing the encroachment of chaos. Although he had escaped from a prisoner-of-war camp and been smuggled back to England by the very Resistance of which Barbary is a part, he disapproves of his "wild" sister; his stilted worship of civilization contrasts with her fear of it. An admitted intellectual snob, he practices Catholicism only because he likes tradition.

Sir Gulliver Deniston, Helen's former husband, who is still in love with her but is now married to the much younger Pamela. A somewhat cynical lawyer, intelligent, and distinguished-looking but pale, he considers honor his guiding principal and is crushed to learn that Barbary is not really his child. Partly because he cannot fathom Barbary and

partly because of his hurt, he agrees to let Helen take her back to her "wild" life in France; because of his honor, he promises not to tell Richie of Barbary's parentage.

Pamela Deniston, Sir Gulliver's young second wife, mother of his son and expecting another child. Handsome and athletic, with clear skin and brown hair, she resents Barbary's invasion of her life and disapproves of her "barbarian" ways. Barbary senses her dislike and returns it in full measure, refusing to acknowledge her young half brother's existence.

Sonya H. Cashdan

A WORLD OF LOVE

Author: Elizabeth Bowen (1899-1973)
Type of work: Novel
Time of action: Two summer days in the early 1950's
First published: 1955

Antonia Montefort, a photographer in her early fifties, owner of the dilapidated Montefort manor in the south of Ireland. Antonia inherited the manor from Guy Montefort, her cousin, who was killed in action in World War I at the age of twenty. Antonia lives in London but occasionally visits the manor, where she is served by the Danbys: Fred runs the manor farm, and Lilia, his wife, manages the housework in a dilatory way. Antonia, having arranged their marriage, keeps them on the manor out of a sense of responsibility. Capricious and demanding, Antonia is indolent, caustic, and fearful of old age.

Jane Danby, the twenty-year-old daughter of Fred and Lilia. She is the favorite of her father and of Antonia, who has paid for her education. Exploring the attic one day, Jane finds a beautiful Edwardian dress and a packet of letters signed by Guy and tied in white ribbon. The recipient of the letter is not named, but they are clearly love letters and inspire Jane to speculate obsessively about the writer and the women to whom he was writing. She even imagines that his ghost is present

on a few occasions. She suspects that it was her mother, Lilia, to whom they were addressed, and Lilia does not deny it but does not read the letters. The mystery is solved at the end of the novel, when Jane burns the letters after discovering that they were not written to her mother. Jane tells Antonia of her discovery, but not Lilia. Then she goes off to Shannon Airport to meet Richard Priam, who is coming to visit Lady Latterly, a neighbor. As the passengers descend from the plane, Richard and Jane see each other and immediately fall in love.

Lilia Danby, a woman who was engaged to Guy Montefort when she was seventeen and beautiful but is now overweight, discontent, lazy, and ill-tempered. She has been a burden to Antonia since Guy's death because, but for that mischance, she would have inherited the manor instead of Antonia. She continues to dream of escaping but has long since lost the will to do so. She knows that Guy was unfaithful to her, as is her husband Fred, but, at the end of the novel, she seems to have undergone a kind of change, a renewal of energy, and is making an effort to reestablish a closer relationship with Fred.

Fred Danby, the illegitimate cousin of Guy Montefort and Antonia who was persuaded by Antonia to marry Lilia. He runs the manor farm with uncomplaining diligence but not much success for his efforts. His favorite daughter is Jane, but he is fair and civil to Maud, his younger daughter, and to his wife. He is reserved and slow to speak, resigned to his life and accepting of his obligations.

Maud Danby, twelve-year-old daughter of

Fred and Lilia. Maud lives in her own world, like each of the other characters, but while Jane's is inhabited by romantic notions and the ghost of Guy Montefort, Maud's contains an imaginary playmate named Gay David, a parody of Guy. Maud teases and torments everyone in the household with considerable ingenuity, thus provoking responses that help to reveal the thoughts and feelings of the other persons in the novel, to which she also contributes a tone of humor without in any way intending it.

Natalie Harper

A WORLD OF STRANGERS

Author: Nadine Gordimer (1923-   )
Type of work: Novel
Time of action: The early 1950's
First published: 1958

Tobias Hood (Toby), a publisher's agent. He has come from London to Johannesburg, South Africa, to work for a time in his family's publishing firm, Aden Parrot. Brown-haired and stocky, the Oxford-educated, twenty-six-year-old Toby is the first-person narrator of the novel. At odds with the liberal politics of his family, Toby comes to South Africa determined to see and do what interests him and not to be guided by social conscience. Through Hamish and Marion Alexander, he meets a group of privileged and luxury-loving white South Africans, including Cecil Rowe. He has an affair with Cecil, though he fails to make a serious commitment to her. Through Anna Louw, with whom he has a very brief affair, he meets Indians and Africans, including the black Steven Sitole, who becomes his closest friend. Toby finds himself slipping between two untouching worlds, the segregated white world and the world of the black townships. The death of Steven makes him face the changes that have shaped him since arriving in South Africa, where he now plans to stay indefinitely.

Steven Sitole (sǐ•tô′lä), formerly a journal-

ist, then an insurance agent. Tall, thin, elegantly dressed, Steven attracts many admirers. He has little stability, always moving from room to room, always pitting his wits against authority. A man of varied experience, he spent a year in England after the war and also earned a bachelor's degree from a correspondence college. Toby is drawn to him for his vitality, for the strength of his desire for a private life, while Anna Louw and Sam Mofokenzazi regret his political unconcern. Steven introduces Toby to the black townships and to his drinking companions. Finally, Steven dies tragically in a car accident, while fleeing from a police raid on a club.

Cecil Rowe, a former model who now rides show horses. The twenty-eight-year-old Cecil is slim and vividly attractive. Born in South Africa of English parents, she is the divorced and inattentive mother of a three-year-old son. Uncommitted, lacking direction, she often seems lost and fearful. She has an affair with Toby but is unaware of his friendship with Steven. Eventually, she plans to marry Guy Patterson.

Anna Louw (lōw), a lawyer who works for

the Legal Aid Bureau, taking up African causes. A short, dark-haired, young Afrikaans woman, she is divorced from her Indian husband. Bravely refusing to live according to the segregations imposed by white South African society, she is abandoned by her conventional family. She takes Toby to a party, where he meets Steven Sitole. Later, Toby sleeps with Anna out of friendship rather than desire. Finally, Anna is arrested for political action; Toby visits her while she is out on bail.

Sam Mofokenzazi (mô·fô·kĕn·zä′zē), a journalist for an African newspaper. Very short, Sam is described by Toby as having a "Black Sambo" face. A writer, jazz pianist, and composer, Sam is politically aware and also a responsible, stable family man. Toby is a frequent guest at the house of Sam and his wife Ella, often sleeping there, and becomes even closer to Sam after the death of Steven.

Hamish Alexander, one of the most powerful gold-mining millionaires in South Africa. Bald, red-faced, advanced in years, he relishes the privileges of his position. He and his wife Marion live at High House, an estate with swimming pool, tennis court, paddocks,

and exquisite gardens. He also breeds horses, and Cecil Rowe rides show horses for him.

Marion Alexander, wife of Hamish Alexander. Though Toby's mother and his great-uncle Faunce once knew her, they would now disapprove of her self-indulgent and exclusive way of life. Disguising her advancing age with elaborate dress and makeup, she is a fashionable and expert hostess to the large groups of people regularly gathering at the High House.

John Hamilton, a regular guest at High House. He helps Toby find his first flat in Johannesburg. An avid hunter, he takes Toby on a bird hunt into the bush.

Guy Patterson, a senior official in Hamish Alexander's mining group. A large man, thickened and lined with age, he is still handsome. Educated at Cambridge, a war hero, he joins the hunting party organized by John Hamilton. He shares Cecil's racial prejudice and will be able to offer her a life of material satisfactions.

Susan Kress

A WREATH FOR UDOMO

Author: Peter Abrahams (1919-   )
Type of work: Novel
Time of action: The 1950's
First published: 1956

Michael Udomo, a Panafrican who leads his country's opposition to colonialism. A central characteristic of Udomo is that, even while a doctoral student in England, he is devoted to his country's liberation. A major part of Udomo's character is his leadership of the rebel African People's Party on returning to Panafrica. As party leader and later as prime minister, Udomo's personality as a political rebel is revealed: He is opposed to tribalism, associating it with factionalism and colonialism; he is in favor of modernization of Africa; and he feels that to achieve this goal, help from the colonialists will be needed.

These characteristics are all-important in moving the plot along to other Panafricans' opposition to them. Udomo, therefore, is shown to be a charismatic leader who meets with conflict in his ideas of what constitutes building Panafrica after the end of colonialism.

Tom Lanwood, nearing sixty, a veteran revolutionary and political theorist from Panafrica. When Udomo is in England, Lanwood is his idol for his dedication to revolution. Yet, on Udomo's rise to power in Panafrica, when Lanwood returns, it is clear to Udomo that thirty years in England have made Lanwood woefully out of touch with the reality of the Panafrican situation. Lanwood, for example, feels total Africanization of workers is needed, while Udomo and Mhendi both feel European know-how is necessary, for the Panafrican people have not been adequately educated or prepared for total Africanization. Thus, Lanwood serves at least two purposes in advancing the plot: in showing Udomo's growth from idol-worshiper to leader who figuratively leaves his idol behind; and in making clear yet another difference of opinion Udomo faces with one of his Panafrican colleagues.

Selina, a powerful Panafrican revolutionary. Selina is central in being able to sway women to the side of the revolutionary forces. Yet, she is in opposition to Udomo on the questions of tribalism and Africanization. She is a staunch and uncompromising believer in both and believes that Udomo is moving much too slowly to achieve this end. Her disagreement with Udomo on this matter ultimately leads her to be in opposition to him.

David Adebhoy, a Panafrican revolutionary who, like Selina, initially supports Udomo but who agrees with Selina's views on tribalism and Africanization. Like Selina, Adebhoy ends up being in opposition to Udomo because of these matters.

Davis Mhendi, a revolutionary from Pluralia. Exiled in London as a result of a failed revolution, Mhendi returns to Africa after Udomo's rise to power in Panafrica. Mhendi is a staunch revolutionary, believing that until colonialism leaves Pluralia, he and those revolutionaries with him will do everything possible to disrupt everyday life in Pluralia—cut power lines and derail trains, for example. Mhendi represents the dedicated subversive. Yet, Abrahams makes it clear that the time has not yet come for this kind of revolutionary, as Udomo leads the Pluralian colonists to kill Mhendi, in order to keep whites helping Panafrica. Thus, Mhendi's presence reveals both Abraham's ideas of revolution and later shows that Udomo has been co-opted, to a degree, by white colonialists.

Paul Mabi, a Panafrican artist and revolutionary. Mabi becomes especially important to Udomo in Udomo's needing the support of the Panafrican mountain people, of which Mabi is one. Mabi thus comes to work quite closely with Udomo and is sympathetic to the pressures Udomo is under as a revolutionary leader.

Lois Barlow, Udomo's thirty-five-year-old white lover. At first haunted by her dead husband, Lois comes to fall in love with Udomo. During their relationship, Lois illustrates the tension between Udomo's private and political lives. Though Lois, for example, has a dream of being with Udomo forever, she realizes that his political work is more important to him and that she will someday have to let him go. Still, even as Udomo rises to power in Panafrica, he continues to be nostalgic about his interlude with her. Lois' presence in the novel helps to portray the emotional aspect of Udomo's life, in contrast to his political interests.

Maria, Mhendi's Panafrican lover. Her resemblance to his wife, who was killed after the revolution attempt in Pluralia, expedites his falling in love with her. As with Lois and Udomo, Maria's presence illustrates the importance of a political leader's private life.

Jo Furse, Lois' roommate. She briefly has an affair with Udomo, resulting in her pregnancy and abortion. This latter incident is the catalyst in Lois leaving Udomo.

Jane Davis

A WREATH OF ROSES

Author: Elizabeth Taylor (1912-1975)
Type of work: Novel

Time of action: A summer in the mid-1940's
First published: 1949

Camilla Hill, an unmarried school secretary in her late thirties, who usually makes no effort to enhance her pleasant-enough, blue-eyed looks and good figure. After years of lazy, serene summer holidays with her two closest friends and confidantes, Camilla is confronted this summer with their separate preoccupations: Frances Rutherford's with old age and despair, Liz Nicholson's with marriage and new motherhood. Resentful, alienated, and increasingly aware of her own encroaching middle age and her life's sterility, Camilla is quickly becoming waspish and bitter. Casting about for stimulation, she begins a curiously unpleasant, desultory near-affair with Richard Elton, whom she meets on the train to her holiday. Camilla is violently shaken from her emotional lethargy with Richard's revelation of his horrible secret, but it is not a happy awakening.

Frances Rutherford, in her seventies, once Liz's governess, now a painter and sometime pianist. Advancing old age, worsening rheumatism, and approaching death have all darkened Frances' vision; violence and inhumanity are now the subjects of her paintings, which once delicately reflected simpler, more pleasant details of life. Frances now feels she has wasted her life; her resentment is expressed in her brusque treatment of Camilla and particularly Liz, to whom she devoted much of her younger life. Her anger is somewhat softened by Morland Beddoes' sympathetic, devoted admiration so that she can finally accept her increasing need to depend on the others.

Elizabeth (Liz) Nicholson, in her thirties, girlish in appearance, restless and insecure as a married woman and mother. Absorbed in the care of her baby, Harry, she is nevertheless acutely aware of Frances' testiness, Camilla's jealousy, and the impulses that compel Camilla to pursue Richard Elton, whom Liz instinctively loathes. During the holiday, Liz reconciles herself to the compromises demanded in marriage and relaxes somewhat into motherhood, gaining maturity and becoming less self-absorbed.

Richard Elton, probably in his mid-thirties, movie-star handsome but perceptibly weak in character. Elton is able to overcome Camilla's initial indifference to him, first when they are drawn together by their mutual witnessing of a suicide at the train station, later with the image he creates of himself out of stories of wartime heroics, literary aspirations, and a brutal childhood—all false. He benefits also from Camilla's loneliness and yearning for a romantic relationship. In reality a sadist who has recently murdered a young woman, Elton desperately tries to hold self-knowledge and horror at bay, reaching out to Camilla as a woman too strong to harm. Having lost Camilla and increasingly unnerved by Morland Beddoes' scornful scrutiny, Elton finally commits suicide, leaping into the path of an approaching train as he and Camilla had seen the stranger doing.

Morland Beddoes, in his fifties, rumpled and plump, a well-established film director with a distinguished wartime military career. Captivated as a younger man by a painting of Liz by Frances, Morland has subsequently built a collection of Frances' work and has corresponded with her for years. Now he comes at last to meet Frances and stays to admire, to sympathize with, and to encourage her. Concerned for the happiness of all three women, Morland is especially disturbed by Camilla's reckless pursuit of Elton, whom he instantly recognizes as a man with something to hide. There is hope that Morland's own attraction to Camilla may bring an end to the isolation they have both felt to varying degrees.

The Reverend Arthur Nicholson, Liz's husband and Harry's father. Both the aura of his clerical authority and his overbearing masculinity have hemmed Liz in, provoking her petulance with him. He learns finally to accept her growth as an individual, no longer girlish and submissive as she was when he first knew and loved her.

Jill Rollins

THE WRECKAGE OF AGATHON

Author: John Gardner (1933-1982)
Type of work: Novel
Time of action: The sixth century B.C.
First published: 1970

Agathon, a philosopher and seer, originally a native of Athens but now living in exile in Sparta. Old, fat, and balding, Agathon is considered by some a wise man; by most, he is dismissed as a public nuisance who bothers decent citizens in the streets and rails at the established order of things. A philosopher in the Socratic mode, Agathon questions all conventions and refuses to accept the prevalent systems in society, politics, and thought. His sympathy with the oppressed Helots brings him into connection with their revolt against the Spartan tyranny, but in the end, Agathon is unable to translate his moral and philosophical feelings into practical, political applications. Still, the Spartan tyrant Lykourgos realizes that Agathon is implacably opposed to his own rigid and demanding system and imprisons the seer, hoping to break his will and demonstrate the supremacy of Spartan law. Agathon is reduced to remembering the events of his past, commenting upon the problem of the present, and trying to pass along what wisdom he commands to his young Helot disciple, Demodokos. Aided by the Helot rebels, Agathon escapes but soon dies of the plague while in hiding.

Demodokos, called **Peeker** by Agathon, a twenty-year-old Helot who was picked out by Agathon one day in the street to be his follower. Although Peeker finds much that is irritating, even despicable, about his master, he is unable to break away from Agathon and travels with him loyally, even into the midst of the Helot conspiracy and then into prison. Peeker is young, skinny, and often embarrassed to be in Agathon's company; he is shamed by his master's deliberately rude, often boorish behavior, and he cannot grasp many of the philosophical meanings of Agathon's baffling riddles. Still, as the novel progresses, Peeker matures, growing in strength as Agathon weakens, becoming more com-

passionate as Agathon sickens. In the end, Peeker travels to Athens to seek out Agathon's wife, Tuka, and to continue his master's philosophical quest.

Tuka, Agathon's wife. Now in her sixties, she was once a beautiful woman, Agathon's childhood sweetheart. When Agathon becomes embroiled in the Helot conspiracy and his ongoing struggle against Lykourgos, Tuka returns to her native Athens, unwilling to become part of Agathon's destruction. She is strong-willed and obsessive to the point of madness, a jealous woman whose fits of anger and fury alternate strangely with gentle, harp-playing behavior.

Iona, mistress of Agathon, a leader of the Helot revolt and wife of Dorkis. In her sixties, she is a clever, determined woman, still holding to the intense beauty she had when younger. For years she and Tuka conducted a running battle over control of Agathon; it has ended with neither of them winning. Although Iona has been Agathon's lover for years, she remains deeply devoted to her husband and to the cause of Helot freedom.

Dorkis, a Helot, friend to Agathon and husband of Iona. He is a pleasant, easygoing man in late middle age, seemingly mild in nature and perhaps even weak in character; he knows of Agathon's long-standing affair with his wife and seems to ignore it. Trusted by the Spartans as a loyal servant, Dorkis is actually a key leader in the Helot revolt and is known by the code name of "Snake." When the Spartans finally discover and capture him, he is tortured and killed. He shows great bravery in his death.

Lykourgos, tyrant and lawgiver of Sparta. A severe, one-eyed man in late middle age, he is remolding the Spartan state to be a military garrison devoid of artistic frills and intellectual curiosity. His set of laws is strict and inflexible, and his view of human society and the world lead inevitably to conflict with Agathon.

Michael Witkoski

XALA

Author: Ousmane Sembène (1923-   )
Type of work: Novella
Time of action: The early 1970's
First published: 1973 (English translation, 1976)

Abdou Kader Bèye, called **El Hadji,** a prosperous Senegalese businessman in his fifties, Muslim and a polygamist, with two wives and eleven children. Ousted from his first career as schoolteacher because of his union activities under the colonial regime, he prospers with the coming of independence, moving through a succession of business ventures, not always honest and sometimes exploiting the poor. Part of the rising native bourgeoisie, he is a member of the select Group of Businessmen of Dakar, as well as of several boards. Confident, ostentatious, pompous, he spends money lavishly on a Mercedes-Benz automobile and a chauffeur, villas for each of his spouses, European clothes, and, finally, the showy elaborate celebration of his third marriage. Someone has cast on him a spell, the *xala*, which makes him impotent, a disgrace in his society. Only at the end, when he has tried every means to remove the spell and correct his condition, when he has lost all—wealth, reputation, two of his wives, colleagues and friends, and property—does he learn that the spell was cast by a relative with whom he had dealt dishonestly years earlier.

The Beggar, unrecognized as a member of El Hadji Abdou Kader Bèye's clan. In spite of being picked up by the police frequently at El Hadji's request, the beggar returns consistently to the same spot opposite El Hadji's office, sitting cross-legged at the street corner and chanting in an annoying, piercing voice. It is he who finally brings about the downfall of El Hadji, to avenge his clan which El Hadji had robbed of property years before.

Adia Awa Astou, the first wife of El Hadji. An attractive woman approaching forty, Awa has habitually dressed in white since her visit to the Kaaba with her husband, as the devout Muslim she became at her marriage. In manner and speech she is reserved, dignified, and straightforward. Fidelity to her responsibility as spouse and as mother of her six children imposes restraint and self-denial as she copes with her husband's foolishness and her children's questions. A woman of great inner strength, she refuses the solution of divorce suggested by Rama, her oldest daughter. It is Astou, with Rama, who stands beside El Hadji in his final moment of humiliation.

Oumi N'Doye (n·doi'), the second wife of El Hadji. She is younger than and completely different from Adia Awa Astou. Dominated by Westernized taste, she thrives on French fashion magazines, a superficial social life, and extravagant spending. Because she really resents her position as second wife, jealousy and hatred of Awa motivate her demands for material advantages for her children and the elaborate measures she takes to keep El Hadji in her villa longer than the allotted time for polygamous marriage under Muslim law. When she realizes that El Hadji's bankruptcy will entail seizure of her villa, she removes everything to her parents' house before the creditor's agents arrive.

N'Gone (ngô'ně), the third wife of El Hadji. At age nineteen, N'Gone is pretty and pleasure-loving but has twice failed her examinations and cannot get a job. Her aunt proposes to find for her a wealthy husband. She is really a pawn, married off to El Hadji. Since he, because of the *xala*, cannot consummate the marriage, N'Gone returns eventually to her parents and associates with a young man of her own generation.

Yay Bineta, the twice-widowed paternal aunt of N'Gone. Physically unattractive and with a malicious expression in her eyes, this unfortunate busybody brings misfortune to others by her mischief. By flattery, cunning, and manipulation, she inserts N'Gone into the life and attentions of El Hadji, finally succeeding in arranging the marriage which precipitates his ruin.

Rama, the oldest daughter of El Hadji and Awa. A university undergraduate, active in movements to conserve African values and culture, such as the Wolof language, she also reveals modern revolutionary attitudes toward what should be changed. Close to her mother by affection and respect, she advises divorce but accepts her mother's decision against it.

Mary Henry Nachtsheim

THE YEAR OF LIVING DANGEROUSLY

Author: C. J. Koch (1932-   )
Type of work: Novel
Time of action: 1965
First published: 1978

Guy Hamilton, a correspondent for ABS, an Australian news agency. Tall and handsome, Hamilton was born in England but grew up in Singapore and Australia. He becomes one of the best newsmen in Jakarta, Java; he and Billy Kwan have a successful partnership as well as a friendship. He falls in love with Jill Bryant but nearly betrays her, a lapse which causes Billy to break off their friendship.

Jill Bryant, a secretary at the British embassy. Emotionally vulnerable because of a failed marriage and, later, a destructive affair, she is close to Billy Kwan, who is supportive but nonthreatening. She loves Guy and has become pregnant by him, but she believes Billy when he tells her that Guy has betrayed her.

Billy Kwan, a free-lance cameraman. A half-Chinese, half-Australian dwarf, Billy, though intelligent and caring, is obsessive and controlling, emotionally unstable. He chooses Guy as a friend and partner, helping him to get started in Jakarta. He idealizes Guy and Jill and believes that he has arranged their love affair; perhaps he has. He also idealizes President Sukarno, believing him to be the savior of his people. When Billy's delusion becomes apparent, he stages a political protest during which he is killed. He keeps dossiers on subjects and people; the narrator uses these to fill in the gaps in his own knowledge.

Wally O'Sullivan, a correspondent for a Sydney newspaper. The unofficial head of the press corps in Jakarta, the overweight Wally presides over the gatherings in the hotel bar. When Wally is deported because of his taste for Indonesian young men, it is generally believed that Billy betrayed him.

Pete Curtis, a Canadian journalist who works for *The Washington Post.* Curtis is Hamilton's main competition; they are friendly rivals. Curtis is not very sensitive to others and often visits Indonesian prostitutes.

Colonel Ralph Henderson, a military attaché at the British embassy. His *pukka sahib* demeanor suggests the remnants of the British Empire. He, too, is attached to Jill.

Kumar, Hamilton's Indonesian assistant. A member of the PKI, the Indonesian Communist Party, Kumar arranges a meeting between Guy and Vera Chostiakov. Kumar acutely perceives the Western advantages that his country lacks.

Vera Chostiakov, a cultural attaché at the Soviet embassy. She uses her sexual attractiveness to try to get information from Guy about a Chinese arms shipment to the PKI. Her play for Guy leads Billy to believe Guy false.

Sukarno, the Indonesian president. A charismatic man, he attempts to build a powerful Indonesian self-image but eventually loses

touch with his people and lets political schemes overtake him.

Ibu, an Indonesian woman. Ibu (which means "mother" in Indonesian) represents the poor for Billy, and her fate impels Billy to undertake his rebellion against Sukarno.

R. J. Cook, the narrator, a correspondent for a news agency. A divorced, lapsed Catholic, he becomes confessor, or confidant, to the members of the press corps. His knowledge of his colleagues combined with information from Billy's files allows him to write this account.

Karen M. Cleveland

THE YEAR OF THE DRAGON

Author: Frank Chin (1940-   )
Type of work: Play
Time of action: The 1970's
First produced: 1974

Fred Eng, a Chinese American travel agent and tourist guide, head of Eng's Chinatown Tour 'n Travel. The eldest son of Pa Eng, Fred is in his forties, unmarried and balding. Born in China and brought by Pa to San Francisco when an infant, Fred feels neither Chinese nor fully assimilated American Chinese. His job, which he despises, makes him conform to the American stereotype of the Chinese American, epitomized in the play by the American film character Charlie Chan. Though he must live and work in San Francisco's Chinatown, Fred hates the place. When in school, he apparently had promise as a writer, but he has lost sight of his dream to become one. Torn between his desire for his own life and his responsibilities to his family, Fred hates himself and the life he feels compelled to live. In the play's main action, the family members have gathered at their Chinatown home in San Francisco to celebrate the Chinese New Year, which is likely to be the dying Pa's last. Fred wants to get Ma and Johnny to leave San Francisco's Chinatown after Pa's death and move to Bos-

ton with Sis. He tries to get Pa to tell them to go, but the old man refuses and dies during a struggle with Fred. After his father's death, Fred remains in Chinatown, even though he hates it, because the San Francisco Chinatown is the only place he feels he belongs.

Pa (Wing Eng), the father of Fred, Sis, and Johnny and the honorary mayor of San Francisco's Chinatown. A stylish but conservative dresser, Pa is a China-born Chinese in his sixties. In the United States since 1935, he regards San Francisco's Chinatown as home. He is dying of a lung disease. As the play's action demonstrates, Pa is at times brutally autocratic and selfish, but he is loved by his children and wife. Pa clearly depends on Fred but also abuses him and considers him a failure. He refuses to see Fred as an individual and spurns Fred's request that he tell Johnny and Ma to move to Boston. Pa's love-hate relationship with Fred dramatizes the play's central conflict.

Ma (Hyacinth Eng), a Chinese American

in her middle or late fifties. Ma is Pa's second wife (his American wife) and the mother of Sis and Johnny. She is proud of being born and reared American and mission-school educated. Ma loves her home and family, fears change, but is aware that her family is drifting apart. Maniacally efficient, practical, and irrational, Ma attempts to escape moments of stress by going to the bathroom or bursting into song and dance. For Pa, whom she loves, she plays the role of a Chinese woman, though not successfully. Through Ma the audience discerns historical discrimination against Chinese in the United States.

Johnny Eng, the younger brother of Fred, a Chinese American in his late teens. Johnny is a Chinatown street kid, on probation for carrying a gun. Though an alienated youth, Johnny believes in the Chinese family. He wants to stay in Chinatown and help Fred with his tour business. He therefore resists Fred's attempts to make him move to Boston and live with his sister, Sis.

Sis (Mattie), a Chinese American, born in 1938, the married daughter of Ma and Pa Eng. Sis is middle-class in dress and manners. She has married a white American, has moved out of Chinatown, and is having commercial success in Boston as a Chinese cook, under the pseudonym Mama Fu Fu. She has just published a cookbook which promises to be a success. She hates Chinatown and has returned only at the request of her dying father. Sis is a fully assimilated Chinese American.

Ross, Mattie's Caucasian husband. A sincerely interested and admiring student of all things Chinese, Ross is aesthetic, supercilious, and pleasant. Unlike Ma, Fred, Sis, and Johnny, Ross reads Chinese. In the play's main action, Ross represents the majority white culture in the United States, which admires the Chinese culture yet does not understand the difficulties of the Chinese adjustment to life in the United States.

China Mama, an old woman and Pa Eng's China-born Chinese wife. She is Fred's biological mother, whom Pa left behind when he emigrated with Fred to the United States. Pa has brought China Mama to America so that he may die "Chinese." Near the end of the play, her presence incites Ma to try to act like a Chinese-born woman in order to please Pa Eng.

James W. Robinson, Jr.

YELLOW BACK RADIO BROKE-DOWN

Author: Ishmael Reed (1938-   )
Type of work: Novel
Time of action: 1801-1809
First published: 1969

The Loop Garoo Kid, a black circus cowboy, an American Hoo-Doo manifestation of Lucifer. His evil reputation, however, is unwarranted: He identifies himself as "the cosmic jester," an eternal pleasure principle. A member of the divine family, he is now sought by the Christian God as the only one to prevent the unhealthy domination of the eternal goddess, who appears variously as his former girlfriend Diane (the Roman goddess Diana) and the Virgin Mary.

Drag Gibson, a wealthy and powerful rancher,

Loop Garoo's nemesis. He started with nothing, riding drag (hence his name, though it also implies tranvestitism) for other cattlemen, but he amassed a fortune by his cunning and ruthlessness. Drag is also a supernatural character: The explorers Lewis and Clark appear near the middle of the novel and reveal that Drag has escaped from hell. His struggle with Loop Garoo is therefore a form of the eternal struggle between good and evil.

Mustache Sal, Drag's wife, formerly Loop

Garoo's girlfriend. Sal marries Drag in answer to a personal ad, motivated by inheriting his wealth. She crawls before Loop on the night before her wedding, begging to have sex with him. Instead, Loop brands a hell's bat on her abdomen.

Chief Showcase, an American Indian, Drag's lackey. A cousin of Cochise, Showcase is the last surviving Crow Indian and so is kept by Drag as a literal "Showcase." Yet while he plays the defeated primitive or noble savage before Drag, he first appears in a high-tech helicopter, rescuing Loop Garoo from Drag's minions. Chief Showcase is the first to recognize Loop as Lucifer, and he expresses the essential unity of the black and Native American causes and identities. His secret revenge on the white man is tobacco: With feigned civility, he offers a cigar to every enemy he encounters.

Field Marshall Theda Doompussy Blackwell, an army general. He is identified as President Thomas Jefferson's secretary of defense, though no such title existed in Jefferson's time. With Pete the Peek, he develops a plan to conquer the American West and set himself up as emperor. Theda is depicted as a stereotypical Pentagon hawk: He wheedles money from Congress through Pete the Peek and lavishes it on scientists (Harold Rateater and Dr. Coult) who develop new weapons for him.

Pete the Peek, a congressman, Theda's lover. He is called "The Peek" because he is a voyeur. Theda treats him as a stooge, apparently interested only in the federal appropriations Pete brings him.

Pope Innocent, putatively Loop Garoo's rival, to whom Drag appeals for help. Innocent recalls the days before Loop's estrangement from the Judeo-Christian God and pleads for him to return. The novel ends with Loop's reunion with Innocent on his ship bound for Europe. Because there were no popes named Innocent in the nineteenth century, this character is one of the many anachronisms in the novel, but he represents the ageless Church as partner/nemesis of Loop Garoo, rather than a historical individual.

John R. Holmes

YONNONDIO
From the Thirties

Author: Tillie Olsen (1912-   )
Type of work: Novel
Time of action: The 1920's
First published: 1974

Anna Holbrook, married to Jim and mother to Mazie, Will, Ben, the baby Jim, and baby Bess, born later in the story. Early in her life, Anna is as strong as a bull, with black eyes and black hair. After a move to a Dakota farm, she gives birth in March to Bess and develops health problems, culminating in a severe miscarriage when Bess is four months old; they have moved back to town in Colorado. She eventually feels better and is again in command of her children and her life. She tries to achieve a better life for her children, wanting them to secure an education and getting a library card for them. When she learns of the importance of hygiene and good diet, she attempts to provide these. She and the family enjoy good times in the country summer and out walking in Denver. At the end of the book, after a heat wave with the temperature in the hundreds for days, she notices that the "air's changen" and sees that tomorrow it will become tolerable. Anna is one of those referred to in the title, taken from the poem "Yonnondio," by Walt Whitman, which refers to those of whom eventually nothing remains, no picture or poem.

Jim Holbrook, Anna's blue-eyed husband and the father of the five children. He works in the dangerous coal mines in Wyoming. The hard life leads him to drink occasionally, but finally he takes his family to a Dakota farm. After a year of hard work, they get nothing and lose their animals. They then take the train to Denver, their hometown, from which they have been away seven years. Here Jim hopes for a job in the slaughterhouses, but first he works in the sewers, eventually getting a fine forty-five-cent-an-hour position. To him, a job is God, and praying is not enough. Because of his difficult circumstances, he is at times harsh to his wife and children, yet basically he is a loving husband and father.

Mazie Holbrook, the oldest of five children, between six and a half and nine years old during the story. A thin, now rather homely child, not doing well in school and often with a sadness in her heart, she is nevertheless effective at mothering the younger children, both at the beginning of the story and later when her mother is not well. Later in the story she is more independent, enjoying play and exploring the neighborhood. Partly because a crazed, drunken man almost kills Mazie, her father decides that the family will leave in the spring to be tenant farmers in South Dakota. There, Mazie shares the delights of clean, beautiful country life and begins school in the fall. Less happy in Denver, she eventually adjusts.

Will Holbrook, age five at the opening of the story. Later he is defiant to his mother and disrespectful to Mazie. Near the end of the book, he has, as with Mazie, a lust for sensation.

Alex Bedner and
Else Bedner, oldtime friends of the Holbrooks in Denver. He has now attained the high-skill job of a tool and die maker and thus a considerable rise in living standard. A piano in the living room and a stained-glass window are evidence of the Bedners' status. Unfortunately, they have no children. The Bedners serve as foils to the prolific but impoverished Holbrooks.

E. Lynn Harris

YOU CAN'T TAKE IT WITH YOU

Authors: George S. Kaufman (1889-1961) and Moss Hart (1904-1961)
Type of work: Play
Time of action: 1936
First produced: 1936

Penelope (Penny) Vanderhof Sycamore, a mother in her mid-fifties, the matriarch of a comic household, carefree and easygoing. Penny is someone who clearly loves her family and life itself. After a typewriter is mistakenly delivered to her, she drops her old hobby of painting and begins to write plays. Both she does very badly, but with style and good humor.

Paul Sycamore, Penny's husband and father of the Sycamore brood. Paul has given up ordinary work to construct fireworks in his basement. He often tries them out in the center of the living room. He intends to market them, but his plans never quite work out.

Paul is less involved in the lives of the children because he spends so much time in the basement.

Grandpa Martin Vanderhof, the patriarch and founder of the family's unconventional life-style. The Sycamore family clearly revolves around Grandpa, and his eccentric clear-sightedness saves the day more than once. One day Grandpa left work and never returned; he spends his life now in a more productive manner, throwing darts, attending commencements, and enjoying his family.

Essie Sycamore Carmichael, the elder married daughter. Essie splits her time between making new kinds of candy (successfully) and practicing to become a ballerina (unsuccessfully).

Ed Carmichael, Essie's husband. Ed plays the xylophone, operates an amateur printing press in the living room, and occasionally peddles Essie's candies.

Alice Sycamore, the younger daughter, in her early twenties. Alice is the only normal person in the Sycamore family. She works in an office on Wall Street and has no unusual hobbies. She is devoted to her outlandish family, however, and generally approves of their life-styles. Alice is very much in love with young Tony Kirby but afraid that their families will never get along.

Anthony (Tony) Kirby, Jr., Alice's fiancé, fresh out of college and the new vice president of his father's business, where Alice works. Tony finds the Sycamores delightful, in contrast to his stodgy family, although, like Alice, he is basically a very normal person.

Anthony Kirby, Sr., Tony's father. Mr. Kirby is a stereotypical Wall Street mogul: tired, worried, stiff, and bothered by indigestion. He is at first appalled by the antics of the Sycamores but comes to appreciate their "seize the day" attitude.

Rheba, the black maid. Entertaining in her own right, Rheba provides fairly objective commentary on the doings of the Sycamores.

Donald, Rheba's boyfriend. Donald is on relief and wanders around the Sycamore house in his bathrobe, but he, too, appears more normal than the white folks around him.

Mr. De Pinna, an iceman who came to make a delivery eight years before, fell under the Sycamores' spell, and has stayed ever since. Mr. De Pinna is Paul's assistant in the basement fireworks factory and models for Penny's paintings.

Evelyn Romig

THE YOUNG LIONS

Author: Irwin Shaw (1913-1984)
Type of work: Novel
Time of action: 1937-1945
First published: 1948

Christian Diestl, a former ski instructor, now a sergeant in the German army. Handsome, rugged, and cynical, he is determined to enjoy and to survive the war. Too worldly-wise to accept Nazi ideology but anxious to prosper, he enthusiastically fights in Germany's early victories and tastes the spoils of war. As the tide of battle turns against the Nazis, Christian prepares to save himself rather than die for a lost cause. Trapped in a concentration camp by a mutiny, he disguises himself as an inmate and kills a German officer to escape. As he flees toward Switzerland, he fatefully crosses the paths of two American soldiers.

Noah Ackerman, a university student drafted into the American infantry after Pearl Harbor. Born poor, physically slight, and Jewish, he is a target of suspicion and contempt. At boot camp he must fight his own platoon mates, who want a scapegoat for their prejudice and an outlet for their aggression. He emerges a tough, hardened soldier who performs heroically and skillfully in combat. He fights not so one nation can defeat another but so that ordinary citizens can live free of ideology. He is one of the soldiers whom Diestl ambushes and is killed.

Michael Whitacre, a successful film and stage writer with easy duty in a photography battalion. Well off, accustomed to comfortable living and cultured acquaintances, Michael enlists after a messy divorce but finds infantry life too demanding. Feeling only slight guilt, he uses his influence to gain a safer billet in the war effort. He is content to play soldier behind the lines in London while others fight and die. Injured in an air raid because he is drunk, he meets Noah and is moved by the man's loyalty to his platoon. Following Noah to France, Michael experiences real combat for the first time. After Christian kills Noah in the ambush, Michael stalks and slays the stormtrooper.

Hope Plowman, Noah's wife. She is a sensitive, sensible, sensuous woman attracted by Noah's sincerity and intelligence. Over the objections of her Protestant parents, she marries him. Through her, Noah learns to express his passionate, poetic nature. After his unit departs for Europe, she gives birth to their child.

Laura Whitacre, a beautiful actress married to Michael for several years. Like her husband before the war, she cares more for private pleasures than for politics. She regards the war as a rude intrusion into a comfortable life. During Michael's absence, she readily finds another man and files for divorce.

Gretchen Hardenburg, the wife of Christian's commanding officer. Left alone in Berlin, she lives a frantic life of self-indulgence; her beauty, sophistication, and availability quickly attract the attention of politicians and officers stationed in the capital. When Christian visits her to report that her husband has been seriously wounded, she takes him as a lover.

Johnny Burnecker, Noah's best friend in the platoon. A simple Midwestern farm boy, Johnny yearns only to go home and till the soil, as his ancestors have done. Admiring Johnny's sense of family and land, Noah treats him as his spiritual brother and fights fiercely to protect him. Johnny's death makes Noah bitter and reckless.

Colonel Colclough, Noah's superior. An officer by virtue of his birth and a stickler for rank, he is in charge of his men, but he does not lead them. Concerned neither for patriotism nor for his men, Colclough wants only for his unit to obey orders and perform well so that his own career will be enhanced.

Robert M. Otten

YOUNG TÖRLESS

Author: Robert Musil (1880-1942)
Type of work: Novel
Time of action: The late nineteenth century
First published: Die Verwirrungen des Zöglings Törless, 1906 (English translation, 1955)

Törless (tœr'lĕs), a young boy at the celebrated military boarding school "W" in a remote eastern town of the Austrian Empire. When Törless first arrives at the boarding school, he is homesick, writing letters home almost daily. Although a friendship with the youthful cadet Prince H. helps him to overcome this early personal problem, it is only when Törless becomes acquainted with two older classmates, Beineberg and Reiting, that he begins to resolve this crisis in his psychological development. Beineberg indirectly helps Törless to overcome the attendant and pain-

ful experiences of his awakening sexuality. Most important in the coming to adolescent consciousness, however, is his difficult and ambivalent homosexual relationship with his classmate Basini. Even though Törless is physically present during the torture of Basini and even receives some vicarious pleasure from the events, he seems to be intellectually separated from them. He is trying to come to terms with a confusion that does not allow him to exculpate the events he observes and feels with the intellectual world he is developing. No one on the faculty seems able to help him to articulate this dilemma. It is not until later, while under questioning about the Basini affair, that Törless suddenly recognizes the conundrum that has plagued him. He explains that there are things that are on some occasions seen with the eyes and at other times with the eyes of the soul. Having attained this insight, Törless decides to leave the boarding school.

Basini, another student. Basini is a boy who has all the personal characteristics of the physically and intellectually weak person. He is caught stealing money from the lockers of other students by Beineberg and Reiting, who take it upon themselves to punish him. Törless is involuntarily included in this conspiracy. For Törless, a period of immense confusion ensues, since he believes that the theft should be reported. Even more troublesome is the response of his parents, who are not outraged by the theft and suggest that Basini be given the opportunity to mend his ways in the future. The punishment takes place in a secret attic room where the three boys carry out a systematic plan of enslaving Basini. Each boy conducts a personal experiment with his slave, submitting Basini to brutality, humiliation, and egregious sexual demands. Basini is incapable of defending himself against his tyrannizers. As a final form of brutalization, it is decided to turn him over to the entire student body, where the masses will have the opportunity to annihilate Basini. Törless tries to warn him, but it is too late. Fearing the mass of tormentors, Basini turns himself in to the school authorities, who undertake an extensive inquest that results in his dismissal.

Beineberg (bī'nə·bârg), a young baron and student, two years older than Törless, dictatorial coconspirator in the Basini affair. Beineberg's father served as an officer in the British military in India, whence he returned with a somewhat perverted understanding of the Buddhist philosophy. The son attempts to apply these teachings by trying to wield spiritual powers over Basini. Through hypnosis, Beineberg hopes to initiate contact with Basini's lost soul and thereby cure him of his crime. Basini, however, rejects Beineberg's hypnotic suggestions and defeats the experiment, leading Beineberg to give him a wrathful beating. Beineberg's activities are not discovered by the school authorities, and he is able to remain and be graduated from the military boarding school.

Reiting, also two years older than Törless and the other dictatorial coconspirator in the Basini affair. Reiting is the instigator who promotes physical punishment of Basini. He rejects any suggestion from Törless that alternate means should be found to deal with the thief. In the secret attic room, Reiting takes considerable pleasure in torturing Basini and, after some time, proposes that Basini should be turned over to the entire school to suffer from the attacks of the masses. While Beineberg is conducting his spiritual experiments, Reiting's behavior produces an example of how large groups can effect mindless phsyical terror. Like his friend Beineberg, Reiting goes unpunished and completes his studies at the school.

Thomas H. Falk

ZAZIE IN THE METRO

Author: Raymond Queneau (1903-1976)
Type of work: Novel
Time of action: Thirty-six hours in the mid-1950's
First published: Zazie dans le métro, 1959 (Zazie, 1960; better known as *Zazie in the Metro*)

Zazie Lalochère (là·lō·shĕr'), a preteenage girl, nasty and precocious, clever and vulgar. She has come to Paris for the sole purpose of riding the subway. Unfortunately, the subway workers are on strike. Zazie spends her entire stay griping about life, causing havoc, and setting the people with whom she comes in contact at loggerheads, especially her uncle, Gabriel, whom she suspects of being a homosexual. When, finally, the subway resumes operation, Zazie is so exhausted from her escapades and partying that she misses the entire adventure, although her Paris weekend has nevertheless been a thrilling, eye-opening, and maturing experience.

Gabriel, under the stage name of **Gabriella,** a female impersonator and dancer in a gay nightclub. Tall and muscular, yet graceful, the thirty-two-year-old Gabriel considers his act art and himself an artist. While lacking sophistication, at times he waxes philosophical about life's transience. Alternately severe and indulgent with his niece Zazie, he plays his part in the madcap and unbridled events of tourism-gone-wild by inviting friends, acquaintances, and a busload of foreigners to share in the Paris-by-night activities.

Trouscaillon (troōs·cä·yoṅ'), also known as **Pedro-Surplus, Bertin Poirée** (pwä·rä'), and **Haroun al-Rations,** a man of many names and many callings: plainclothes policeman, traffic officer, flea-market vendor, child molester. For the middle-aged and still attractive Trouscaillon, forgetting his current name and putting on his disguises are done for fun and merriment. Nevertheless, he is quite ineffectual in his police functions, because he has neither police presence nor command of police jargon. He enjoys women of all ages, including young Zazie, but is at heart too fickle to remain faithful to any.

Marceline, a housewife, Gabriel's wife. A soft-spoken woman, she is very handsome and always well dressed, yet she never goes out, even to the neighborhood café. When she has trouble with Trouscaillon, however, she flees out her apartment window. Upon returning Zazie to her home, Marceline is called Marcel by Zazie's mother.

Charles, a taxi driver. He is Gabriel's best friend and serves as Zazie's guide, despite his very sketchy knowledge of the French capital. At age forty-five, he is still looking for the ideal woman, not realizing that she is right there in his favorite bar. Finally, he and Mado, the barmaid, marry, the cause for Gabriel and his guests to enjoy the carnival feast.

Madeleine (Mado) Ptits-pieds (ptē·pyä'), a barmaid. She is pretty and pleasant and marries Charles at last. Thereafter, she is seldom called by her diminutive and nickname, but by her given name, Madeleine.

Turandot (too·rän·dō'), a bar owner and Gabriel's landlord. He is gullible, good-hearted, and easily impressed.

Gridoux (grē·doo'), a cobbler. Probably in his fifties, he is nosy and arrogant. Along with Laverdure, he is the neighborhood philosopher.

Laverdure (lä·vĕr·door'), Turandot's parrot. Acting as a Greek chorus, he punctuates (and often deflates) the bar patrons' speech. His most famous one-line rejoinder is "Talk, talk, that's all you can do."

Madame Mouaque (moo·äk'), a middle-aged and homely but rich and snobbish widow who finds Gabriel, then Trouscaillon, irresistible. She joins the wedding party and, being too cantankerous and noisy, is gunned down by the riot police.

Jeanne Lalochère, Zazie's mother. She murdered her husband, allegedly because he tried to rape Zazie; more likely, she wanted to be free of him to pursue other men. She leaves her daughter with Gabriel to reconcile with her current lover.

Fyodor Balanovitch, a tour guide. A friend of Gabriel, he has become blasé over Pigalle nightclub acts and disinterested in the city's celebrated sights.

Pierre L. Horn

ZERO

Author: Ignácio de Loyola Brandão (1936-   )
Type of work: Novel
Time of action: The late 1960's
First published: 1974 (English translation, 1975)

José Gonçalves (gôn•säl′vĕz), also called **Zé,** a vagabond worker at odd jobs and later an assassin and subversive. At twenty-eight, he is small and unattractive, with a limp caused by a deformed foot. Though lacking the requisite self-assurance and drive, he once dreamed of being a singer. An avid reader, he is attracted to grotesques and oddities. Although seemingly apathetic, he is violent, feeling trapped, conscious of systematic oppression and his own mundane, captive life. José is relatively content as long as he retains his solitude, but when he marries, he is thrust into a confusing world that both beckons him and rejects him, threatening his individuality. In an atmosphere of rising political turmoil and violence, he is picked up and questioned regarding various small crimes. Bombarded by his wife Rosa, advertisements, and the government, he is pressured for material comforts. He begins robbing, then killing, and he gets what he wants, but it seems not to be worth it, especially when Rosa becomes estranged and ill and loses their child. After being harassed and brutalized by government officials, he finally joins the Communs, an antigovernment terrorist group. As the fight escalates, he wants only to escape everything. Betrayed and arrested, he is to be executed but escapes. He finally realizes that the group threatens his identity as much as does the oppressive government that he is fighting.

Rosa Maria, José's wife. Short and plump, she is seen as unattractive by José's friends. Reared as a good Catholic, she answers José's personal advertisement and they marry, though her people do not approve. Immediately she begins to pressure him for material comforts for them and their unborn child, especially for a house of their own. The difficulties they encounter render her sick and apathetic, and she aborts the child, then hemorrhages and returns to her parents, since José spends much time away as a terrorist. She is abducted by members of a cult and, in a grotesque ritual, is sacrificed as a means of ridding the earth of evil.

Gê, the leader of the Communs, a terrorist group. Self-sacrificing and charismatic, he is a well-known fighter with an obscure background, apparently a medical school graduate turned rebel. Surviving all attempts to capture or kill him, he walks into José's house one day and provides José with a possible outlet for his frustrations. With Gê's persuasion, José joins the group. Gê takes José under his wing and lectures him on the necessity of living for the group cause and not for individual action, a necessity that José never accepts.

Atila, Jose's friend and fellow subversive. His nickname derives from his tendency toward violence when drinking. His teaching degree proved useless when he refused to bribe officials for a position. He drives a bus, until José goes to join Communs, when he goes along for the fun. He joins in robbing and killing, is eventually caught and brutally tortured, but will not divulge information on the group and is finally released.

Malevil, José's friend and fellow subversive. A twenty-one-year-old student and a neighbor of José and Rosa, he is out of school because of military intervention there. Atila tells José that Malevil is the first case of reanimation after having been frozen. He works at a nightclub, but, when he is framed by the police and imprisoned, he joins Communs and the fight against oppression. When he becomes disillusioned with this as well, he betrays and identifies José in a scene much like that of Judas at Gethsemane.

Ige-Sha, a female African shaman. Searching for a person as a sacrifice for purifying the world from evil, she finds Rosa and executes her in a brutal ritual.

Carlos Lopez, a textile worker. A patriot with a sick son, he keeps running up against a bureaucratic government as he tries to find treatment. He is faithful, persevering in the face of all apathy, but when his son finally dies without care, he, too, turns against the system.

John S. Nelson

THE ZONE
A Prison Camp Guard's Story

Author: Sergei Dovlatov (1941-   )
Type of work: Novel
Time of action: The early 1960's
First published: Zona: Zapiski nadziratelia, 1982 (English translation, 1985)

Sergei Dovlatov, author not only of *The Zone* but also of a series of letters to its Russian émigré publisher, Igor Yefimov, reprinted at intervals throughout the novel. The letters act in part as a frame story but chiefly as a vehicle for direct comment by the author on the Soviet labor camp "archipelago" in which he served as an army guard from 1963 through 1965. His most important conclusion is that there is no fundamental difference between guards and prisoners (*zeks*).

Boris Alikhanov, a labor camp guard for special punishment cells, the fictional counterpart to Dovlatov. Tough and strong—more than six feet tall—he has three years of college and reads books. He is also part Jewish, but he does not advertise this fact. His friendships with a variety of guards and *zeks*, representing twenty Soviet nationalities, gradually teach him that even in the vast remoteness of a northern camp, life offers all that one needs to know about human existence. Alikhanov, the hard-drinking guard, suffers as much as the prisoners do. One night, horribly drunk on *zek* moonshine, he starts a big fight in the barracks and has to be tied up with telephone wire. In the morning he is escorted (by his best friend) into one of the very cells he has been guarding. Thus, the guard who has sympathized with the prisoners becomes a prisoner himself.

Lance Corporal "Fidel" Petrov, Alikha-nov's best friend. He is called "Fidel" because at a political lesson once, when asked to name a member of the Politburo, he said, "Fidel Castro." It is he who is told to escort Alikhanov to the stockade. On the way, Alikhanov simply walks off into the snow. Fidel threatens to shoot him, but Boris keeps walking. Finally Fidel begins to weep and tells Alikhanov that he can do what he wants, whereupon Boris returns to his escort, accepts his punishment, and saves Fidel from a similar fate.

Boris Kuptsov, a *zek* who refuses to work, an extreme individualist. One day, in front of Alikhanov, Kuptsov chops off his own hand with an ax. One realizes that Boris Alikhanov sees something of himself in Boris Kuptsov.

Captain Pavel Romanovich Egorov, a twelve-year veteran of the camps. He goes on leave to Sochi and brings back a bride, who suffers much in the married officers' quarters. When the barking from the kennels nearly brings her to hysteria, the captain goes out with his rifle and shoots Harun, the dog making the most noise. He returns proudly with the corpse.

Katya, Captain Egorov's wife. A graduate student sick of intellectuals, she found Egorov's honesty and bluntness refreshing. She is ashamed of herself for not being able to tolerate the freezing filth of the officers' quarters, but she cannot accustom herself to life in the far north.

Captain Tokar, an old veteran of the camps who loves only one living thing, his dog Brooch. The dog is killed, cooked, and eaten by the *zeks* one night at a party, to which Alikhanov, ambling along through "the zone," is invited. When Alikhanov learns the truth about the "cutlets" that the *zeks* are eating, he honorably informs Captain Tokar of the fate of his dog. Later, when Alikhanov is sent to the stockade, Captain Tokar cannot bring himself to rescind the order.

Donald M. Fiene

ZOO
Or, Letters Not About Love

Author: Viktor Shklovsky (1893-1984)
Type of work: Novel
Time of action: The 1920's
First published: Zoo: Ili, Pis'ma ne o lyubvi, 1923 (English translation, 1971)

Viktor Shklovsky, the narrator, a Russian novelist, literary critic, and political émigré living in Berlin after the consolidation of Bolshevik power in the Soviet Union. The narrator is in love with the woman to whom he writes the letters that form the novel; she does not reciprocate the narrator's feelings. She does, however, allow him to write to her as long as he does not write about his love. Because he cannot write what he wishes, he writes about what interests him: the theory of literature; literary friends in Berlin and in Russia whom he has left; descriptions of places; cars and the effect of technology on the world; the contrast between the life of bourgeois Europe, which Alya comes to represent, and the revolutionary culture to which he has become accustomed; and his bitter experience of exile. These topics reveal a man who values talent, wisdom, compassion, and magnanimity. He is ironic, witty, and imaginative, though he says that he is sick of wit and irony. He says that he is "sentimental" because he "takes life seriously." It gradually becomes clear that the narrator's passion for Alya is not so great as his passion for literature, as she is surely aware. In the last letter, he reveals his deep and enduring patriotism, asking his country to allow him to return home.

Elsa Triolet, also called **Alya,** a Russian woman and a writer. She has actually written the letters that bear her signature, but much of her characterization comes through Shklovsky's letters to her. She has been married to a Frenchman (André Triolet); they lived in Tahiti, a description of which (from one of her letters) she turns into a book somewhat later, authenticating her literary talent. The couple has parted, however, with him returning to Paris, her to Berlin. She refuses to love the narrator and says that she is "no *femme fatale* [but] . . . Alya, pink and fluffy." The narrator thinks that she treats men like toys and in letter 11 calls her an "utter woman." Her attitude toward clothes and buying things, however, leads him to call her "alien." He identifies her with the consumer-oriented, bourgeois European culture, entirely foreign to the cataclysmic experience of Civil War Russia from which she has escaped. He reasons, therefore, that she cannot understand and love the roughness of Russians with their unpressed pants in contrast to the European men in their tuxedos. In Alya's letter 19, however, she contradicts his characterization of her as alien by her description of her old nurse Stesha, who "loves the male sex," as a gentle and "completely warm" woman. Alya believes that she herself is like Stesha, whom the narrator realizes is profoundly Russian. The narrator calls Alya a "woman with no vocation," and she defines herself in letter 16 as "good for nothing." She has the ability to do many things, but she leaves the possibilities unused, like a package she has bought, brought home, and left unopened. She agrees with the narrator that wherever she goes, she knows "immediately what goes with what and who with whom," and she knows that she does not go with him. She shows him that he does not know how to write love letters and that he is more interested in his love and his art than in her. This rejection precipitates their break and the narrator's letter asking permission to return to Russia.

Martha Manheim

THE ZOO STORY

Author: Edward Albee (1928-   )
Type of work: Play
Time of action: A Sunday afternoon in summer, in the late 1950's
First produced: 1959

Peter, an executive for a publishing house. An average-sized and nearsighted man in his early forties, Peter has Catholic tastes and conservative dress; he is an upper-class representative of the Eisenhower years. His family life is predictably normal: a good wife, two daughters, two cats, two parakeets, and a nice apartment in the East Seventies of Manhattan. His attitude reflects his status: He is naïve, complacent, passive, proper, and a bit bored. His intention on this afternoon was to read quietly in Central Park. A stranger, Jerry, interrupts him with talk and then aggression. While Peter is slow to anger, Jerry's incessant prodding eventually drives him to pick up Jerry's knife. When Jerry impales himself, Peter exits the now-ending play with his previously established character destroyed by this chance and absurd encounter.

Jerry, an emotionally disturbed man in his late thirties. Anxious and angry about his bisexuality, poverty, and alienation, Jerry tries to make sense of his pain by walking from the New York Zoo looking for another human to confront. Finding Peter, he talks in a rambling yet intelligent way about the miseries of his life. His autobiography reveals his inability to relate to others, including the fellow residents of his rooming house on the upper West Side. In a final and suicidal attempt to give his life meaning, Jerry has on this day set out intent on creating the suicidal encounter which ends the play. By im-paling himself on a knife held by Peter, the paragon of the normal, Jerry at once makes contact with another human and challenges the bourgeois sense of social and moral order.

The Landlady, the caretaker of Jerry's rooming house. A lustful, obese, ignorant, and drunken woman, she, like her dog, makes unwanted advances toward Jerry. Presented in one of his narratives, she is the emblem of his disgust with humanity and the repulsiveness of his experiences.

The Dog, the landlady's canine friend. This black beast with a constant erection snarls and attempts to bite Jerry every time he enters or leaves his room. In an attempt to placate the monster, Jerry feeds it hamburgers and finally poisons the dog. When the dog recovers, Jerry is strongly drawn to the now-calmer animal. For a moment, he feels empathy for the dog that he has hurt. This violent love/hate foreshadows the play's final encounter between Jerry and Peter.

The queen, a black homosexual who occupies a flat in Jerry's building. This gay man lives with his door always open, never leaving except to go to the bathroom; he does nothing but model his Japanese kimono and tweeze his eyebrows. In Jerry's eyes, he becomes the image of an indifferent and supercilious god.

Daniel D. Fineman

ZOOT SUIT

Author: Luis Miguel Valdez (1940-   )
Type of work: Play
Time of action: The 1940's
First produced: 1978

El Pachuco, a mythical figure, the zoot-suited spirit of the Pachucos, alienated gangs of Mexican American youth living in the Los Angeles area. A rebellious, street-smart, young Chicano, El Pachuco is master of ceremonies of this play set in the World War II years, as well as a leading figure, chorus, and the alter ego of Hank Reyna. In his "cool" outfit (long jacket, baggy trousers, and lengthy watch chain), El Pachuco preaches, with bitter humor, fidelity to one's own culture and language and defiance of the Anglos. It is the Anglos, Americans not of Mexican origin, who seek to control the lives of his people (la Raza), robbing them of ethnic pride and manhood while exploiting them and discriminating against their brown skins.

Henry (Hank) Reyna, a twenty-one-year-old Chicano with Indian features, gang leader of the 38th St. Pachucos. Hank is arrested on the eve of joining the Navy, along with a number of other gang members, for the alleged murder of a Chicano one summer night in 1943 at a lakeside gathering spot and is convicted in a rigged trial. Rebellious, angry, and resentful of authority, which represents for him discrimination against Chicanos, Hank does nothing to placate those in control of his fate. Yet, though presenting an impenetrable façade to his persecutors and jailers, Hank is extremely confused about his own identity as an American in a country at war which regards him, too, as a foreign enemy. In his puzzled state, Hank seeks guidance from El Pachuco, who urges rejection of America and faith in his own heritage. After a successful appeal and release from prison, Hank remains uncertain whether integration into American life or rejection of it is the answer for himself and his people.

George Shearer, a dedicated yet realistic young public service lawyer. George volunteers to defend the Pachucos in their murder trial, convinced that they are victims of racial prejudice and irrational war hysteria. He finds, however, that before he can help them he must first overcome Chicano mistrust of him, since he is, in their eyes, just another "gringo." During a ludicrously one-sided trial, the judge badgers George mercilessly, making no effort at impartiality, while the Press convicts the young Chicanos in the pages of Los Angeles newspapers. When a guilty verdict is handed down despite his best efforts, George plans an appeal but is drafted into the Army before he can proceed.

Alice Bloomfield, an attractive young Jewish activist and leftist reporter who organizes the Pachucos' defense effort after their original conviction by raising funds and enlisting the support of American liberals, including prominent Hollywood figures. An uncertain relationship begins between her and Hank in the months she works in behalf of his cause. The gap between their backgrounds and Hank's alienation and anger and his commitment to Della, a Mexican American girl, make it unclear whether the two young people have a future together.

Rudy Reyna, Henry Reyna's hero-worshiping younger brother, who longs to don his own zoot suit, which for him is the symbol of manhood and defiance of Anglo hegemony. A marauding band of servicemen strip Rudy of his flamboyant zoot suit and his dignity as they rampage through the streets looking for brown-skinned "foreigners" who, they believe, do not sufficiently respect the American way of life in wartime.

Enrique Reyna,
Dolores Reyna,
Lupe Reyna, and
Della Barrios, Hank's family and girlfriend, who support and sustain him.

1773

The Press, the malevolent forces of yellow journalism which perpetuate feelings of Anglo racial superiority against Chicanos and incite injustices.

James E. Devlin

ZUCKERMAN UNBOUND

Author: Philip Roth (1933-   )
Type of work: Novel
Time of action: 1969
First published: 1981

Nathan Zuckerman, an American Jewish novelist who, thirteen years after his visit to a famous author in Roth's novel *The Ghost Writer,* has to cope with fame following the publication of his first successful novel. The novel, entitled *Carnovsky,* is based enough on Nathan's own experience that his family and friends are angry at his depiction of Jews in what they see as a peep-show atmosphere of perversion. The book has made Nathan both rich and famous, but he still struggles with the conflicts that result from the book's relationship to life, for he is taken to be the model of his lecherous protagonist Carnovsky, and his wife and family see themselves unflatteringly portrayed in his fiction.

Alvin Pepler, a former television quiz-show winner from a 1950's game show called *Smart Money.* He was caught up in the scandal that resulted when the show's producers persuaded him to lose so that a non-Jew, who had been given the answers, could win. Pepler is a former marine, a nonstop talker, and an expert in trivia, with a photographic memory. As the novel progresses, he increasingly becomes Zuckerman's double, or "secret sharer." Pepler "attaches" himself to Zuckerman, pesters him with talk about his own writing, and finally urges him to read his review of Zuckerman's own book. In its discussion of the complex relationship between life and art, the review reflects Nathan's own conflicts. Pepler argues that Zuckerman stole the character of Carnovsky from him—that indeed he, Pepler, is the model for Carnovsky.

Laura Zuckerman, Nathan's wife, a quiet and kind lawyer who aids and defends young men who escape the military draft by going to Canada. Nathan calls her a goody-good Pollyanna WASP who never says what is on her mind. Nathan no longer loves her and moves out after the publication of his novel, but he feels guilty that he does not love her.

Selma Zuckerman, Nathan's mother. Mrs. Zuckerman lives in Miami and is being implicitly threatened by an anonymous caller, who Nathan suspects is Alvin Pepler.

Caesara O'Shea, a glamorous film star from Ireland with a sad and seductive air, whom, according to the gossip magazines, Nathan is dating. Actually, Nathan has met her only once at a dinner party and has spent one evening with her. She leaves Nathan, however, to have an affair with Fidel Castro.

Victor Zuckerman, Nathan's father, a podiatrist, who has been disappointed in Nathan because of what he sees as Nathan's demeaning depiction of Jews. Victor is in a nursing home suffering from the effects of a stroke. His last word to Nathan before he dies is "Bastard."

Henry Zuckerman, Nathan's brother, a successful dentist. Nathan sees his brother as the tallest and handsomest of all the Zuckerman men. Because of Henry's kindly, gentle, doctorly manner, all of his patients fall in love with him, and he falls in love with his patients. Henry accuses Nathan of killing his father with his best-selling book.

Essie Metz, Nathan's cousin, an elderly woman who lives across the hall from Nathan's mother. Essie tells Nathan about Alvin Pepler, whom the family knew when Nathan was younger.

Gilbert Carnovsky, the central character in Nathan's controversial best-seller, a double for Nathan himself.

André Schevitz, Zuckerman's literary agent. André's gallant continental manner, his silver hair, and his European accent have earned for him the appellation "the Headwaiter,"

but in addition to being an agent, he is an adviser, confessor, and hand-holder to Zuckerman and a stable of film stars and novelists.

Rosemary Ditson, an elderly retired schoolteacher who lives alone in a basement apartment next door to Nathan's wife, Laura. Laura looks after Rosemary, and Rosemary loves her; she hates Nathan for his treatment of his wife.

Charles E. May

Cyclopedia
of
Literary Characters II

Indexes

TITLE INDEX

A ciascuno il suo. *See* Man's Blessing, A

À combien l'amour revient aux vieillards. *See* Splendors and Miseries of Courtesans, The

A maçã no escuro. *See* Apple in the Dark, The

Aaron's Rod (Lawrence), 1

Abbess of Crewe, The (Spark), 1

Abel Sánchez (Unamuno y Jugo), 3

Absurd Person Singular (Ayckbourn), 4

Abyss, The (Yourcenar), 5

Accident, The (Wiesel), 7

Accidental Death of an Anarchist (Fo), 8

Acolyte, The (Astley), 9

Acoso, El. *See* Manhunt

Acquainted with Grief (Gadda), 10

Across (Handke), 11

Across the River and into the Trees (Hemingway), 11

Ada or Ardor (Nabokov), 12

Adding Machine, The (Rice), 14

Aerodrome, The (Warner), 16

Affair, The. *See* Strangers and Brothers

After Many a Summer Dies the Swan (Huxley), 17

After the Banquet (Mishima), 19

After the Fall (Miller, A.), 20

Afternoon Men (Powell), 21

Âge de raison, L'. *See* Roads to Freedom, The

Age of Reason, The. *See* Roads to Freedom, The

Age of Wonders, The (Appelfeld), 22

Agents and Patients (Powell), 23

Agneau, L'. *See* Lamb, The

Agony and the Ecstasy, The (Stone, I.), 24

Ah Q cheng-chuan. *See* True Story of Ah Q, The

Ahasverus död. *See* Tobias Trilogy, The

Akatsuki no tera. *See* Sea of Fertility, The

All God's Chillun Got Wings (O'Neill), 26

All Green Shall Perish (Mallea), 26

All Men Are Enemies (Aldington), 28

All My Sons (Miller, A.), 29

All Our Yesterdays (Ginzburg), 31

All That Fall (Beckett), 32

Amadeus (Shaffer, P.), 33

Amant, L'. *See* Lover, The

Ambiguous Adventure (Kane), 34

America Hurrah (van Itallie), 36

American Buffalo (Mamet), 37

American Dream, An (Mailer), 38

American Dream, The (Albee), 39

Amerika (Kafka), 40

Amigo Manso, El. *See* Our Friend Manso

Among Women Only (Pavese), 41

Amortajada, La. *See* Shrouded Woman, The

Anatomy Lesson, The (Roth, P.), 42

Andorra (Frisch), 43

Andromeda Strain, The (Crichton), 44

Angel Pavement (Priestley), 45

Angels Fall (Wilson, L.), 47

Angle of Repose (Stegner), 48

Anglo-Saxon Attitudes (Wilson, Angus), 49

Angst des Tormanns beim Elfmeter, Die. *See* Goalie's Anxiety at the Penalty Kick, The

Animal Farm (Orwell), 51

Anne of the Thousand Days (Anderson, M.), 52

Anniversaries (Johnson, U.), 53

Annonce faite à Marie, L'. *See* Tidings Brought to Mary, The

Another Country (Baldwin), 55

Another Life (Trifonov), 57

Ansichten eines Clowns. *See* Clown, The

Antigone (Anouilh), 58

Apes of God, The (Lewis, W.), 59

Apple in the Dark, The (Lispector), 62

Apprenticeship of Duddy Kravitz, The (Richler), 63

Árbol de la ciencia, El. *See* Tree of Knowledge, The

Architect and the Emperor of Assyria, The (Arrabal), 65

Architecte et l'Empereur d'Assyrie, L'. *See* Architect and the Emperor of Assyria, The

Armies of the Night, The (Mailer), 65

Arms and the Man (Shaw, G.), 67

Around the World in Eighty Days (Verne), 68

Arrow of God (Achebe), 69

Arturo's Island (Morante), 70

As a Man Grows Older (Svevo), 71

As for Me and My House (Ross), 72

As the Crow Flies (Clarke, Austin), 74

Ashes and Diamonds (Andrzejewski), 75

Asiatics, The (Prokosch), 76

Aspern Papers, The (James, H.), 77

Assistant, The (Malamud), 78

Astillero, El. *See* Shipyard, The

Asya (Turgenev), 80

At Play in the Fields of the Lord (Matthiessen), 81

At Swim-Two-Birds (O'Brien, F.), 82

Aufstieg und Fall der Stadt Mahagonny. *See* Rise and Fall of the City of Mahagonny

August 1914 (Solzhenitsyn), 84

Aunt Dan and Lemon (Shawn), 86

Aunt Julia and the Scriptwriter (Vargas Llosa), 87

Aunt's Story, The (White), 88

Aura (Fuentes), 90

Auto-da-Fé (Canetti), 91

Autobiography of an Ex-Coloured Man, The (Johnson, J.), 92

Autobiography of Miss Jane Pittman, The (Gaines), 93

Autumn of the Patriarch, The (García Márquez), 95

Avalovara (Lins), 97

Aventure ambiguë, L'. *See* Ambiguous Adventure

Avgust chetyrnadtsatogo. *See* August 1914

Awake and Sing! (Odets), 98

Babel-17 (Delany), 99

Badenheim, 'ir nofesh. *See* Badenheim 1939

Badenheim 1939 (Appelfeld), 101

Baga (Pinget), 102

Balcon, Le. *See* Balcony, The

Balcony, The (Genet), 103

Bald Soprano, The (Ionesco), 105

Balkan Trilogy, The (Manning, O.), 106

Ballad of Peckham Rye, The (Spark), 108

Ballad of the Sad Café, The (McCullers), 109

Balthazar. *See* Quest of the Absolute, The

Banana Bottom (McKay), 110

Bang the Drum Slowly (Harris, M.), 112

Banjo (McKay), 113

Banya. *See* Bathhouse, The

Barefoot in the Head (Aldiss), 114

Barefoot in the Park (Simon, N.), 115

Bark Tree, The (Queneau), 116

Bàrnabo delle montagne. *See* Barnabo of the Mountains

Barnabo of the Mountains (Buzzati), 117

Barometer Rising (MacLennan), 118

Baron in the Trees, The (Calvino), 119

Barone rampante, Il. *See* Baron in the Trees, The

Barracks, The (McGahern), 121

Barrage contre la Pacifique, Un. *See* Sea Wall, The

Basic Training of Pavlo Hummel, The (Rabe), 122

Bass Saxophone, The (Škvorecký), 123

Bassaxofon. *See* Bass Saxophone, The

Bašta, pepeo. *See* Garden, Ashes

Bataille de Pharsale, La. *See* Battle of Pharsalus, The

Bathhouse, The (Mayakovsky), 124

Battle of Pharsalus, The (Simon, C.), 125

I

Beachmasters (Astley), 126
Beautiful and Damned, The
  (Fitzgerald, F.), 127
Beauty and Sadness
  (Kawabata), 128
Beautyful Ones Are Not Yet Born,
  The (Armah), 129
Becket (Anouilh), 130
Bedbug, The (Mayakovsky), 132
Beetlecreek (Demby), 133
Beggar in Jerusalem, A
  (Wiesel), 135
Beggar on Horseback
  (Connelly), 136
Beichte eines Toren, Die. See
  Confession of a Fool, The
Bell Jar, The (Plath), 137
Bellefleur (Oates), 138
Bend in the River, A
  (Naipaul, V. S.), 139
Bend Sinister (Nabokov), 141
Benefactors (Frayn), 142
Berlin Alexanderplatz
  (Döblin), 143
Beso de la mujer araña, El. See Kiss
  of the Spider Woman
Besuch der alten Dame, Der.
  See Visit, The
Beton. See Concrete
Betrayal (Pinter), 145
Betrayed by Rita Hayworth
  (Puig), 146
Beyond the Bedroom Wall
  (Woiwode), 147
Biedermann und die Brandstifter.
  See Firebugs, The
Big Knife, The (Odets), 150
Big Sleep, The (Chandler), 151
Billard um halbzehn. See Billiards at
  Half-Past Nine
Billiards at Half-Past Nine
  (Böll), 153
Billy Phelan's Greatest Game
  (Kennedy, W.), 154
Biloxi Blues (Simon, N.), 155
Bilvav yamim. See In the Heart of
  the Seas
Biodlares död, En. See Death of a
  Beekeeper, The
Birds Fall Down, The (West, R.),
  157
Birthday King, The (Fielding), 158
Birthday Party, The (Pinter), 159
Black Hermit, The (Ngugi), 160
Black Mischief (Waugh), 161
Black Prince, The (Murdoch), 162
Black Robe (Moore), 163
Black Thunder (Bontemps), 164
Blacker the Berry, The
  (Thurman), 166
Blacks, The (Genet), 167
Blaubart. See Bluebeard
Blé en herbe, Le. See Ripening
  Seed, The
Blendung, Die. See Auto-da-Fé
Blithe Spirit (Coward), 169
Blood Knot, The (Fugard), 169
Blood of the Lamb, The
  (De Vries), 170
Bloodsmoor Romance, A
  (Oates), 171
Bloody Poetry (Brenton), 172
Blue Bird, The (Maeterlinck), 173

Blue Boy (Giono), 175
Blue Mountains of China, The
  (Wiebe), 176
Blue Room, The (Simenon), 177
Bluebeard (Frisch), 178
Blues for Mister Charlie
  (Baldwin), 179
Bluest Eye, The (Morrison), 180
Boarding-House, The (Trevor), 182
Boesman and Lena (Fugard), 183
Bogmail (McGinley), 184
Bone People, The (Hulme), 185
Bonecrack (Francis), 186
Bonnes, Les. See Maids, The
Book of Bebb, The
  (Buechner), 187
Book of Laughter and Forgetting,
  The (Kundera), 190
Book of Lights, The (Potok), 192
Boquitas pintadas. See Heartbreak
  Tango
Borderline (Hospital), 193
Born in Captivity (Wain), 194
Bosnian Chronicle (Andrić), 195
Botchan (Natsume), 196
Bouts de bois de Dieu, Les.
  See God's Bits of Wood
Boys in the Band, The
  (Crowley), 197
Bread Givers (Yezierska), 198
Break of Noon (Claudel), 199
Bridal Canopy, The (Agnon), 200
Brief an Lord Liszt. See Letter to
  Lord Liszt
Brief Life, A (Onetti), 201
Brighter Sun, A (Selvon), 203
Brighton Beach Memoirs
  (Simon, N.), 205
Brighton Rock (Greene), 206
Browning Version, The
  (Rattigan), 207
Bruno's Dream (Murdoch), 208
Buchanan Dying (Updike), 209
Büchse der Pandora, Die. See
  Pandora's Box
Buenas conciencias, Las. See Good
  Conscience, The
Bull from the Sea, The
  (Renault), 831
Bullet Park (Cheever), 210
Burger's Daughter (Gordimer), 212
Buried Alive. See House of the
  Dead, The
Buried Child (Shepard), 213
Burmese Days (Orwell), 214
Burn, The (Aksyonov), 215
Burning Water (Bowering), 217
Burr (Vidal), 219
Bus Stop (Inge), 221
Bushūkō hiwa. See Secret History of
  the Lord of Musashi, The
Butley (Gray, S.), 222
Butt, Der. See Flounder, The
By Love Possessed (Cozzens), 223

Caine Mutiny, The (Wouk), 224
Caliban's Filibuster (West, P.), 225
Caligula (Camus), 226
Call, The (Hersey), 227
Cambio de piel. See Change
  of Skin, A
Camera Obscura. See Laughter in
  the Dark

Cancer Ward (Solzhenitsyn), 228
Cannery Row (Steinbeck), 231
Cantatrice chauve, Le. See Bald
  Soprano, The
Canticle for Leibowitz, A
  (Miller, W.), 233
Capricornia (Herbert, X.), 234
Captain Blackman
  (Williams, J.), 236
Captain with the Whiskers, The
  (Kiely), 237
Casa in collina, La. See House on
  the Hill, The
Casa verde, La. See Green
  House, The
Cassandra (Wolf), 239
Castello dei destini incrociati, Il. See
  Castle of Crossed Destinies, The
Castle of Crossed Destinies, The
  (Calvino), 240
Castle to Castle (Céline), 241
Cat, The (Colette), 243
Catcher in the Rye, The
  (Salinger), 244
Cathleen ni Houlihan (Yeats), 245
Cat's Cradle (Vonnegut), 246
Caucasian Chalk Circle, The
  (Brecht), 247
Caught (Green, Henry), 248
Cavaliere inesistente, Il.
  See Non-existent Knight, The
Caves du Vatican, Les.
  See Lafcadio's Adventures
Cenci, The (Artaud), 249
Centaur, The (Updike), 250
Ceremony of Innocence, The
  (Ribman), 252
Cette voix. See That Voice
Chain of Chance, The (Lem), 253
Chain of Voices, A (Brink), 254
Chairs, The (Ionesco), 255
Chaises, Les. See Chairs, The
Chambre bleue, La. See Blue
  Room, The
Chaneysville Incident, The
  (Bradley), 256
Change of Heart, A (Butor), 257
Change of Skin, A (Fuentes), 259
Changing Places (Lodge), 260
Changing Room, The (Storey), 261
Chant of Jimmie Blacksmith, The
  (Keneally), 262
Chatte, La. See Cat, The
Chemins de la liberté, Les. See
  Roads to Freedom, The
Chéri (Colette), 264
Cherokee (Echenoz), 265
Chevengur (Platonov), 266
Cheyenne Autumn (Sandoz), 267
Chiave a stella, La. See Monkey's
  Wrench, The
Chicken Soup with Barley
  (Wesker), 269
Chickencoop Chinaman, The
  (Chin), 270
Chiendent, Le. See Bark Tree, The
Chijin no ai. See Naomi
Child Story. See Slow Homecoming
Childe Byron (Linney), 271
Childermass, The. See Human
  Age, The
Childhood's End (Clarke,
  Arthur C.), 272

TITLE INDEX

Children of a Lesser God
(Medoff), 274
Children of Dune. *See* Dune
Trilogy, The
Children of Kaywana. *See* Kaywana
Trilogy, The
Children of Violence
(Lessing), 275
Children's Hour, The
(Hellman), 279
Chimmoku. *See* Silence
Chinese des Schmerzes, Der.
See Across
Chinese Wall, The (Frisch), 280
Chinesische Mauer, Die.
See Chinese Wall, The
Chosen, The (Potok), 281
Christ Stopped at Eboli (Levi, C.),
283
Chronicle of a Death Foretold
(García Márquez), 284
Ciascuno a suo modo. *See* Each in
His Own Way
Cien años de soledad. *See* One
Hundred Years of Solitude
Cinkos, A. *See* Loser, The
Cinquième Fils, Le. *See* Fifth Son,
The
Circle, The (Maugham), 286
Citadel, The (Cronin), 287
Cities of Salt (Munif), 287
Città e la casa, La. *See* City and the
House, The
Città invisibili, Le. *See* Invisible
Cities
City and the House, The
(Ginzburg), 289
City and the Pillar, The
(Vidal), 291
City Builder, The (Konrád), 292
Ciudad y los perros, La. *See* Time of
the Hero, The
CIVIL warS, the (Wilson, R.), 293
Clear Light of Day (Desai), 294
Clockwork Orange, A
(Burgess), 295
Closely Watched Trains
(Hrabal), 296
Cloud Howe. *See* Scots Quair, A
Cloud Nine (Churchill), 297
Cloven Viscount, The
(Calvino), 299
Clown, The (Böll), 300
Cock-a-Doodle Dandy
(O'Casey), 301
Coffin for Dimitrios, A
(Ambler), 303
Cognizione del dolore, La.
See Acquainted with Grief
Coin in Nine Hands, A
(Yourcenar), 304
Cold Storage (Ribman), 306
Collector, The (Fowles), 307
Color Purple, The (Walker, A.),
308
Colours in the Dark (Reaney), 309
Come Back, Little Sheba
(Inge), 310
Comedians, The (Greene), 311
Comforters, The (Spark), 312
Coming Up for Air (Orwell), 314

Comment aiment les filles.
See Splendors and Miseries
of Courtesans, The
Comment c'est. *See* How It Is
Como en la guerra. *See* He Who
Searches
Compagnie. *See* Company
Company (Beckett), 314
Company of Women, The
(Gordon), 316
Compromise, The (Dovlatov), 317
Concluding (Green, Henry), 318
Concrete (Bernhard), 319
Confederacy of Dunces, A
(Toole), 320
Confederate General from Big Sur,
A (Brautigan), 321
Confederates (Keneally), 322
Confession of a Fool, The
(Strindberg), 324
Confessions of a Mask
(Mishima), 325
Confessions of Nat Turner, The
(Styron), 326
Confessions of Zeno (Svevo), 328
Conformist, The (Moravia), 329
Conformista, Il. *See* Conformist,
The
Connection, The (Gelber), 330
Conscience of the Rich, The.
See Strangers and Brothers
Conservationist, The
(Gordimer), 331
Contesto, Il. *See* Equal Danger
Contractor, The (Storey), 333
Conversation in the Cathedral
(Vargas Llosa), 334
Conversazione in Sicilia.
See In Sicily
Coonardoo (Prichard), 335
Corn Is Green, The
(Williams, E.), 336
Coronation (Donoso), 337
Coronel no tiene quien le escriba,
El. *See* No One Writes to the
Colonel
Correction (Bernhard), 338
Corregidora (Jones, G.), 339
Corridors of Power. *See* Strangers
and Brothers
Coscienza di Zeno, La.
See Confessions of Zeno
Cosmos (Gombrowicz), 340
Count Julian (Goytisolo), 974
Country Girls, The. *See* Country
Girls Trilogy, The
Country Girls Trilogy, The
(O'Brien, E.), 341
Coup, The (Updike), 342
Coup de Grâce (Yourcenar), 344
Couples (Updike), 345
Cousin Bazilio (Eça de
Queiróz), 348
Cowards, The (Škvorecký), 349
Crimes of the Heart (Henley), 350
Cristo si è fermato a Eboli.
See Christ Stopped at Eboli
Crónica de una muerte anunciada.
See Chronicle of a Death Foretold
Crucible, The (Miller, A.), 351
Crusoe's Daughter (Gardam), 352
Crying of Lot 49, The
(Pynchon), 354

Crystal World, The (Ballard), 355
Curse of the Starving Class
(Shepard), 356
Custom House, The (King, F.),
357
Cuttlefish, The (Witkiewicz), 359
Cyclone, The. *See* Strong Wind

Da (Leonard), 360
Daiyon kampyōki. *See* Inter Ice
Age 4
Damballah. *See* Homewood
Trilogy, The
"Damma s sobachkoi." *See* Lady
with the Dog, The
Dämonen, Die. *See* Demons, The
Damskii master. *See* Ladies'
Hairdresser
Dance in the Sun, A
(Jacobson), 361
Dance of the Forests, A
(Soyinka), 362
Dangling Man (Bellow), 363
Daniel Martin (Fowles), 364
Dans le labyrinthe. *See* In the
Labyrinth
Dar. *See* Gift, The
Dark Child, The (Laye), 366
Darkness Visible (Golding), 367
Daughter of Earth (Smedley), 368
Day in the Death of Joe Egg, A
(Nichols), 370
Day of the Scorpion, The. *See* Raj
Quartet, The
Days of Hope. *See* Man's Hope
Days of the Turbins
(Bulgakov), 371
De Dónde son los cantantes.
See From Cuba with a Song
Dead, The (Joyce), 372
Dead Class, The (Kantor), 373
Dead Man Leading (Pritchett), 374
Dead Yesterdays. *See* All Our
Yesterdays
Dean's December, The
(Bellow), 375
Death and the King's Horseman
(Soyinka), 377
Death and the Lover. *See* Narcissus
and Goldmund
Death of a Beekeeper, The
(Gustafsson), 378
Death of Ahasuerus, The. *See* Tobias
Trilogy, The
Death of the Fox (Garrett), 379
Death on the Installment Plan
(Céline), 380
Deathwatch (Genet), 382
Debut, The (Brookner), 383
Decay of the Angel, The. *See* Sea of
Fertility, The
Defense, The (Nabokov), 384
Delicate Balance, A (Albee), 385
Demian (Hesse), 386
Democracy (Didion), 387
Demons, The (Doderer), 389
Denier du rêve. *See* Coin in Nine
Hands, A
Deptford Trilogy, The
(Davies), 390
Deputy, The (Hochhuth), 393
Dernier des Justes, Le. *See* Last of
the Just, The

Dernière Incarnation de Vautrin, La. See Splendors and Miseries of Courtesans, The

Deserto dei Tartari, Il. See Tartar Steppe, The

Design for Living (Coward), 394

Devils, The (Whiting), 395

Devotion (Strauss), 396

Dharma Bums, The (Kerouac), 397

Diario de la guerra del cerdo. See Diary of the War of the Pig

Diary of a Mad Old Man (Tanizaki), 398

Diary of the War of the Pig (Bioy Casares), 399

Different Drummer, A (Kelley, W.), 400

Dimanche de la vie, Le. See Sunday of Life, The

Dimitri Roudine. See Rudin

Dining Room, The (Gurney), 402

Dinner at the Homesick Restaurant (Tyler), 403

Dirty Linen and New-Found-Land (Stoppard), 404

"Disent les imbéciles." See "Fools Say"

Dispossessed, The (Le Guin), 405

Disprezzo, Il. See Ghost at Noon, A

Distant Relations (Fuentes), 406

Diviners, The (Laurence), 407

Division of the Spoils, A. See Raj Quartet, The

Dni Turbinykh. See Days of the Turbins

Doctor Copernicus (Banville), 409

Dog Beneath the Skin, The (Auden and Isherwood), 410

Dog Soldiers (Stone, R.), 411

Dog Years (Grass), 412

Dolina Issy. See Issa Valley, The

Dollmaker, The (Arnow), 414

Dom na naberezhnoi. See House on the Embankment, The

Don Goyo (Aguilera Malta), 416

Dona Flor and Her Two Husbands (Amado), 416

Donne di Messina, Le. See Women of Messina

Dôra, Doralina (Queiroz), 418

Dotazník, aneb modlitba za jedno mĕsto a přítele. See Questionnaire, The

Double, The (Dostoevski), 419

Down from the Hill (Sillitoe), 420

Dragon Can't Dance, The (Lovelace), 421

Dragon's Teeth. See Cousin Bazilio

Dream Journey, A (Hanley), 423

Dream on Monkey Mountain (Walcott), 424

Dream Play, A (Strindberg), 425

Dreambook for Our Time, A (Konwicki), 426

Dreigroschenoper, Die. See Threepenny Opera, The

Drömspel, Ett. See Dream Play, A

Drugaya zhizn'. See Another Life

Duel, The (Chekhov), 428

Dumb Waiter, The (Pinter), 429

D'un château l'autre. See Castle to Castle

Dune Messiah. See Dune Trilogy, The

Dune Trilogy, The (Herbert, F.), 430

Dune. See Dune Trilogy, The

Dusty Answer (Lehmann), 433

Dutchman (Baraka), 434

Dvärgen. See Dwarf, The

Dvoynik. See Double, The

Dwarf, The (Lagerkvist), 435

Each in His Own Way (Pirandello), 436

Earthly Powers (Burgess), 437

Eating People Is Wrong (Bradbury, M.), 439

Ebony Tower, The (Fowles), 440

Echoing Grove, The (Lehmann), 442

Ecstasy of Rita Joe, The (Ryga), 443

Eden End (Priestley), 444

Edible Woman, The (Atwood), 445

Educated Cat, The. See Life and Opinions of Kater Murr, The

1876 (Vidal), 446

Eighth Day, The (Wilder), 447

Einstein on the Beach (Wilson, R., and Glass), 449

Elsewhere, Perhaps (Oz), 450

Embers (Beckett), 451

Embezzler, The (Auchincloss), 452

Empire of the Sun (Ballard), 453

Emploi du temps, L'. See Passing Time

End of Bad Roads, The. See Splendors and Miseries of Courtesans, The

End of the Affair, The (Greene), 454

End of the Battle, The. See Sword of Honour

End of the World News, The (Burgess), 455

End Zone (DeLillo), 457

Endgame (Beckett), 458

Enemies (Singer), 458

Enfant noir, L'. See Dark Child, The

Engineer of Human Souls, The (Škvorecký), 460

English Teacher, The. See Grateful to Life and Death

Enrico IV. See Henry IV

Entertainer, The (Osborne), 461

Entertaining Mr. Sloane (Orton), 462

Envy (Olesha), 463

Epilogue. See Country Girls Trilogy, The

Equal Danger (Sciascia), 464

Equations of Love, The (Wilson, E.), 465

Equus (Shaffer, P.), 466

Erasers, The (Robbe-Grillet), 467

Erde und Feuer. See Silesian Tetralogy, The

Erste Polka, Die. See Silesian Tetralogy, The

Erwählte, Der. See Holy Sinner, The

Esmond in India (Jhabvala), 468

Espoir, L'. See Man's Hope

Este domingo. See This Sunday

Eva Trout (Bowen), 470

Eva's Man (Jones, G.), 471

Excellent Women (Pym), 473

Except the Lord. See Second Trilogy

Executioner's Song, The (Mailer), 474

Exit the King (Ionesco), 475

Exodus (Uris), 475

Explosion in a Cathedral (Carpentier), 477

Eye of the Storm, The (White), 478

Eyeless in Gaza (Huxley), 480

Ezra (Kops), 481

Fahrenheit 451 (Bradbury, R.), 482

Fair, The (Arreola), 483

Fairly Honourable Defeat, A (Murdoch), 485

Faith and the Good Thing (Johnson, C.), 487

Falconer (Cheever), 488

Familia lijana, Una. See Distant Relations

Family Happiness (Tolstoy), 489

Family Voices (Pinter), 490

Far Journey of Oudin, The. See Guyana Quartet, The

Far Tortuga (Matthiessen), 491

Farewell from Nowhere (Maximov), 492

Farewell, My Lovely (Chandler), 493

Farewell Party, The (Kundera), 494

Female Friends (Weldon), 495

Female Man, The (Russ), 496

Fences (Wilson, August), 498

Ferdydurke (Gombrowicz), 499

Feria, La. See Fair, The

Fiasco (Lem), 500

Fiddler's House, The (Colum), 501

Fifth Business. See Deptford Trilogy, The

Fifth Son, The (Wiesel), 502

Fin de Chéri, La. See Last of Chéri, The

Fin de partie. See Endgame

Final Mist, The (Bombal), 503

Final Payments (Gordon), 504

Financial Expert, The (Narayan), 505

Fire-Dwellers, The (Laurence), 506

Fire from Heaven (Renault), 508

Fire on the Mountain (Desai), 509

Fire Raisers, The. See Firebugs, The

Firebugs, The (Frisch), 510

Fireflies (Naipaul, S.), 511

First Circle, The (Solzhenitsyn), 512

First Love (Turgenev), 516

First Polka, The. See Silesian Tetralogy, The

Firstborn (Woiwode), 517

Fisher King, The (Powell), 518

Fixer, The (Malamud), 519

Flanders Road, The (Simon, C.), 520

Flaubert's Parrot (Barnes, J.), 521

Fliehendes Pferd, Ein. See Runaway Horse

TITLE INDEX

Flight to Canada (Reed), 522
Floating Opera, The (Barth), 524
Flounder, The (Grass), 525
Flowering Peach, The (Odets), 527
Fool for Love (Shepard), 529
"Fools Say" (Sarraute), 530
for colored girls who have
  considered suicide/when the
  rainbow is enuf (Shange), 531
Forbidden Forest, The
  (Eliade), 532
Forêt interdit, La. See Forbidden
  Forest, The
Fork River Space Project, The
  (Morris), 534
Foundation. See Foundation
  Trilogy, The
Foundation and Empire.
  See Foundation Trilogy, The
Foundation Pit, The
  (Platonov), 534
Foundation Trilogy, The
  (Asimov), 536
Fountain Overflows, The (West, R.),
  540
Four-Gated City, The. See Children
  of Violence
Fox, The (Lawrence), 541
Fragmented Life of Don Jacobo
  Lerner, The (Goldemberg), 542
Franchiser, The (Elkin), 543
Frankenstein Unbound
  (Aldiss), 544
Freedom of the City, The
  (Friel), 545
French Lieutenant's Woman, The
  (Fowles), 546
French Without Tears
  (Rattigan), 547
Friday (Tournier), 548
Friends and Heroes. See Balkan
  Trilogy, The
From Cuba with a Song
  (Sarduy), 550
From Here to Eternity (Jones,
  J.), 551
From the Terrace (O'Hara), 552
Fruits of the Earth (Grove), 554
Full Moon (Wodehouse), 555
Funeral Games (Renault), 557
Funnyhouse of a Negro
  (Kennedy, A.), 558
Fürsorgliche Belagerung. See Safety
  Net, The
Füten rōjin nikki. See Diary of a
  Mad Old Man
Futile Life of Pito Perez, The
  (Romero), 559

G. (Berger, J.), 560
Galileo (Brecht), 562
Games Were Coming, The
  (Anthony), 563
Garden, Ashes (Kiš), 564
Garden of Earthly Delights, The
  (Clarke, M.), 565
Garden of the Finzi-Contini, The
  (Bassani), 566
Garden Party, The (Havel), 567
Gargoyles (Bernhard), 568
Gates of the Forest, The
  (Wiesel), 570
Gaudy Night (Sayers), 571

Gazapo (Sainz), 572
Gemini (Tournier), 573
Generous Man, A (Price), 574
Gentlemen in England
  (Wilson, A. N.), 575
Geography of a Horse Dreamer
  (Shepard), 577
George Passant. See Strangers and
  Brothers
Geschichten Jaakobs, Die. See
  Joseph and His Brothers
Getting Out (Norman), 577
Ghost at Noon, A (Moravia), 578
Ghost Sonata, The
  (Strindberg), 579
Ghost Writer, The (Roth, P.), 580
Giardino del Finzi-Contini, Il. See
  Garden of the Finzi-Contins, The
Gift, The (Nabokov), 581
Gigi (Colette), 582
Giles Goat-Boy (Barth), 584
Ginger Man, The (Donleavy), 585
Giovanni's Room (Baldwin), 586
Girl Green as Elderflower, The
  (Stow), 587
Girl in Winter, A (Larkin), 589
Girl, 20 (Amis), 590
Girls in Their Married Bliss.
  See Country Girls Trilogy, The
Glance Away, A (Wideman), 591
Glasperlenspiel, Das. See Glass
  Bead Game, The
Glass Bead Game, The
  (Hesse), 592
Glass of Blessings, A (Pym), 594
Glengarry Glen Ross
  (Mamet), 595
Głos pana. See His Master's Voice
Go-Between, The (Hartley), 597
Goalie's Anxiety at the Penalty Kick,
  The (Handke), 598
God Bless You, Mr. Rosewater
  (Vonnegut), 599
God on the Rocks (Gardam), 600
God's Bits of Wood
  (Sembène), 601
God's Little Acre (Caldwell), 603
Gogo no eikō. See Sailor Who Fell
  from Grace with the Sea, The
Gold-Rimmed Eyeglasses, The
  (Bassani), 604
Golden Notebook, The
  (Lessing), 605
Golden Serpent, The
  (Alegría), 607
Gommes, Les. See Erasers, The
Good Apprentice, The
  (Murdoch), 608
Good Conscience, The
  (Fuentes), 610
Good Morning, Midnight
  (Rhys), 612
Good Soldier, The (Ford), 613
Good Terrorist, The (Lessing), 614
Good Woman of Setzuan, The
  (Brecht), 615
Goodbye Look, The
  (Macdonald), 616
Goodnight! (Tertz), 617
Gormenghast. See Gormenghast
  Trilogy, The
Gormenghast Trilogy, The
  (Peake), 618

Gospodjica. See Woman from
  Sarajevo, The
Gossip from the Forest
  (Keneally), 621
Grand Voyage, Le. See Long
  Voyage, The
Grania (Gregory), 622
Grateful to Life and Death
  (Narayan), 623
Gravity's Rainbow (Pynchon), 624
Great American Novel, The
  (Roth, P.), 626
Great Dune Trilogy, The. See Dune
  Trilogy, The
Great Fortune, The. See Balkan
  Trilogy, The
Great God Brown, The
  (O'Neill), 628
Great Ponds, The (Amadi), 629
Great White Hope, The
  (Sackler), 630
Green Card (Akalaitis), 631
Green House, The (Vargas
  Llosa), 632
Green Man, The (Amis), 633
Green Pastures, The
  (Connelly), 634
Grendel (Gardner), 637
Grey Granite. See Scots Quair, A
Grobnica za Borisa Davidoviča. See
  Tomb for Boris Davidovich, A
Group, The (McCarthy, M.), 638
Group Portrait with Lady
  (Böll), 641
Gruppenbild mit Dame. See Group
  Portrait with Lady
Guardian of the Word, The
  (Laye), 643
Guerra del fin del mundo, La. See
  War of the End of the World, The
Guerrillas (Naipaul, V. S.), 644
Guest for the Night, A
  (Agnon), 645
Gute Mensch von Sezuan, Der. See
  Good Woman of Setzuan, The
Guyana Quartet, The (Harris, W.),
  646

Habana para un infante difunto, La.
  See Infante's Inferno
Hadji Murad (Tolstoy), 649
Hairy Ape, The (O'Neill), 651
Hakhnasat kala. See Bridal
  Canopy, The
Ham Funeral, The (White), 652
Hamlet of Stepney Green, The
  (Kops), 653
Handmaid's Tale, The
  (Atwood), 654
Hapgood (Stoppard), 656
Happy Days (Beckett), 657
Harland's Half Acre (Malouf), 658
Harriet Said (Bainbridge), 658
Harrowing of Hubertus, The. See
  Kaywana Trilogy, The
Haru no yuki. See Sea of
  Fertility, The
Hasty Heart, The (Patrick), 660
Haute Surveillance. See Deathwatch
Hawaii (Michener), 661
He Who Searches
  (Valenzuela), 663
Headbirths (Grass), 665

CYCLOPEDIA OF LITERARY CHARACTERS II

Healers, The (Armah), 666
Heart of a Dog, The
   (Bulgakov), 667
Heartbreak House (Shaw, G.), 669
Heartbreak Tango (Puig), 670
Heat and Dust (Jhabvala), 671
Heidi Chronicles, The
   (Wasserstein), 673
Heimkehr der Fronttruppen.
   See November 1918
Heliga Landet, Det. See Tobias
   Trilogy, The
Hemsöborna. See Natives of
   Hemsö, The
Henry IV (Pirandello), 674
Her Privates, We (Manning, F.),
   675
Herland (Gilman), 676
Herzog (Bellow), 677
Hiding Place. See Homewood
   Trilogy, The
Hijo de hombre. See Son of Man
Hiob. See Job
His Master's Voice (Lem), 678
History (Morante), 679
History Man, The (Bradbury, M.),
   680
Ho teleutaios peirasmos. See Last
   Temptation of Christ, The
Hobbit, The (Tolkien), 681
Hojarasca, La. See Leaf Storm
Hōjō no umi. See Sea of
   Fertility, The
Holy Ghosts (Linney), 683
Holy Land, The. See Tobias
   Trilogy, The
Holy Place (Fuentes), 684
Holy Sinner, The (Mann), 685
Holzfällen. See Woodcutters
Homba. See Sea of Fertility, The
Hombres de maíz. See Men of Maize
Home-maker, The (Fisher), 686
Home to Harlem (McKay), 687
Homecoming, The (Pinter), 688
Homecomings. See Strangers and
   Brothers
Homewood Trilogy, The
   (Wideman), 689
Homme qui regardait passer les
   trains, L'. See Man Who Watched
   the Trains Go By, The
Homo Faber (Frisch), 692
Honorary Consul, The
   (Greene), 693
Honourable Schoolboy, The
   (le Carré), 694
Hopscotch (Cortázar), 695
Horacker (Raabe), 697
Horloger d'Everton, L'. See
   Watchmaker of Everton, The
Horseman on the Roof, The
   (Giono), 699
Hostage, The (Behan), 700
Hot l Baltimore, The
   (Wilson, L.), 701
Hotel du Lac (Brookner), 702
Hotel New Hampshire, The
   (Irving), 703
House Behind the Cedars, The
   (Chesnutt), 705
House for Mr. Biswas, A (Naipaul,
   V. S.), 706

House Made of Dawn
   (Momaday), 707
House of All Nations (Stead), 708
House of Blue Leaves, The
   (Guare), 710
House of the Dead, The
   (Dostoevski), 711
House of the Sleeping Beauties, The
   (Kawabata), 712
House on the Embankment, The
   (Trifonov), 713
House on the Hill, The
   (Pavese), 715
Householder, The (Jhabvala), 716
How Far Can You Go? See Souls and
   Bodies
How It Is (Beckett), 717
How Much Love Costs Old Men.
   See Splendors and Miseries of
   Courtesans, The
Hubertus. See Kaywana Trilogy, The
Huis clos. See No Exit
Human Age, The (Lewis, W.), 718
Humboldt's Gift (Bellow), 721
Hundejahre. See Dog Years
Hurlyburly (Rabe), 723
Hurry Home (Wideman), 724
Hurry on Down. See Born in
   Captivity
Hussar on the Roof, The.
   See Horseman on the Roof, The
Hussard sur le toit, Le.
   See Horseman on the Roof, The

I Am a Cat (Natsume), 724
"I Don't Have to Show You No
   Stinking Badges!" (Valdez), 726
I for One . . . (Sargeson), 726
I Like It Here (Amis), 728
I Never Promised You a Rose
   Garden (Green, Hannah), 728
I Will Marry When I Want (Ngugi
   and Ngugi), 729
Ice (Kavan), 730
Ice Age, The (Drabble), 731
Iceman Cometh, The
   (O'Neill), 732
If Beale Street Could Talk
   (Baldwin), 733
If He Hollers Let Him Go
   (Himes), 734
If Not Now, When? (Levi, P.), 735
If on a Winter's Night a Traveler
   (Calvino), 736
Ill Seen Ill Said (Beckett), 738
Illywhacker (Carey), 739
I'm Not Stiller (Frisch), 740
Imaginary Life, An (Malouf), 742
Immoralist, The (Gide), 743
Immoraliste, L'. See Immoralist, The
In a Free State (Naipaul, V. S.),
   744
In Sicily (Vittorini), 745
In the Beginning (Potok), 746
In the Castle of My Skin
   (Lamming), 747
In the Heart of the Seas
   (Agnon), 749
In the Labyrinth (Robbe-Grillet),
   750
In the Shadow of the Glen
   (Synge), 750

In the Time of Greenbloom
   (Fielding), 751
In the Wine Time (Bullins), 753
In Watermelon Sugar
   (Brautigan), 754
Inadmissible Evidence
   (Osborne), 755
İnce Memed. See Memed, My Hawk
Incident at Vichy (Miller, A.), 756
Increased Difficulty of
   Concentration, The (Havel), 757
Indian Summer (Stifter), 757
Indians (Kopit), 759
Indifferenti, Gli. See Time of
   Indifference, The
Infante's Inferno (Cabrera
   Infante), 760
Infernal Machine, The
   (Cocteau), 761
Inferno (Strindberg), 762
Inimitable Jeeves, The
   (Wodehouse), 763
Injury and Insult. See Insulted and
   the Injured, The
Innommable, L'. See Unnamable,
   The
Inquisitoire, L'. See Inquisitory, The
Inquisitory, The (Pinget), 764
Inspector Calls, An
   (Priestley), 765
Insular Possession, An (Mo), 766
Insulted and the Injured, The
   (Dostoevski), 767
Intensive Care (Frame), 769
Inter Ice Age 4 (Abe), 770
Interpreters, The (Soyinka), 770
Invention of Morel, The (Bioy
   Casares), 772
Investigation, The (Lem), 773
Invincible, The (Lem), 774
Invisible Cities (Calvino), 774
Invitation to a Beheading
   (Nabokov), 775
Iron Earth, Copper Sky
   (Kemal), 1718
Iron in the Soul. See Roads to
   Freedom, The
Ironweed (Kennedy, W.), 776
Island of Crimea, The
   (Aksyonov), 778
Islands in the Stream
   (Hemingway), 780
Isola di Arturo, L'. See Arturo's
   Island
Issa Valley, The (Miłosz), 781
Ivona, Princess of Burgundia
   (Gombrowicz), 782
Ivory Swing, The (Hospital), 784
Iwona, Księżniczka Burgunda. See
   Ivona, Princess of Burgundia

Jacob's Room (Woolf), 785
Jacques le fataliste et son maître.
   See Jacques the Fatalist and His
   Master
Jacques the Fatalist and His Master
   (Diderot), 785
Jahrestage. See Anniversaries
Jailbird (Vonnegut), 786
Jake's Thing (Amis), 787
Jalousie, La. See Jealousy
J. B. (MacLeish), 788
Jealousy (Robbe-Grillet), 790

TITLE INDEX

Jean le bleu. See Blue Boy
Jewel in the Crown, The. See Raj Quartet, The
Jill (Larkin), 790
Job (Roth, J.), 792
Joe Turner's Come and Gone (Wilson, August), 793
John Bull's Other Island (Shaw, G.), 794
Joke, The (Kundera), 795
Joseph and His Brothers (Mann), 797
Joseph, der Ernährer. See Joseph and His Brothers
Joseph in Egypt. See Joseph and His Brothers
Joseph the Provider. See Joseph and His Brothers
Joseph und seine Brüder. See Joseph and His Brothers
Jour, Le. See Accident, The
Journey into Fear (Ambler), 799
Journey to the Center of the Earth (Verne), 800
Journey to the Sky (Highwater), 801
Joy of Man's Desiring (Giono), 802
Joy of the Worm (Sargeson), 803
Juan sin tierra. See Juan the Landless
Juan the Landless (Goytisolo), 974
Jubiabá (Amado), 804
Jubilee (Walker, M.), 806
Judith Hearne. See Lonely Passion of Judith Hearne, The
July's People (Gordimer), 807
Jumpers (Stoppard), 808
Junge Joseph, Der. See Joseph and His Brothers
Just Above My Head (Baldwin), 809

Kalkwerk, Das. See Lime Works, The
Kamen no kokuhaku. See Confessions of a Mask
Kamera obskura. See Laughter in the Dark
Kangaroo (Aleshkovsky), 811
Kangaroo (Lawrence), 812
Kanthapura (Rao), 813
Karl and Rosa. See November 1918
Karl Marx Play, The (Owens), 815
Kaspar (Handke), 816
Kassandra. See Cassandra
Katar. See Chain of Chance, The
Kaukasische Kreidekreis, Der. See Caucasian Chalk Circle, The
Kaywana Blood. See Kaywana Trilogy, The
Kaywana Trilogy, The (Mittelholzer), 817
Keep the Aspidistra Flying (Orwell), 820
Keep Tightly Closed in a Cool Dry Place (Terry), 821
Keepers of the House, The (Grau), 822
Kein Ort. See No Place on Earth
Kenguru. See Kangaroo (Aleshkovsky)
Kepler (Banville), 823

Keys of the Kingdom, The (Cronin), 824
Khadzi-Murat. See Hadji Murad
Killdeer, The (Reaney), 825
Killer, The (Ionesco), 827
Killing Ground, The (Settle), 827
Kind of Alaska, A (Pinter), 829
Kindergarten (Rushforth), 829
Kindergeschichte. See Slow Homecoming
Kindheitsmuster. See Patterns of Childhood
King Jesus (Graves), 830
King Must Die, The (Renault), 831
Kingdom of This World, The (Carpentier), 834
King's Indian, The (Gardner), 835
Kinkakuji. See Temple of the Golden Pavilion, The
Kiss of the Spider Woman (Puig), 837
Kitchen, The (Wesker), 837
Klingsor's Last Summer (Hesse), 839
Klingsors letzter Sommer. See Klingsor's Last Summer
Klop. See Bedbug, The
Knekht, Der. See Slave, The
Know Nothing (Settle), 839
Kojinteki na taiken. See Personal Matter, A
Kompleks polski. See Polish Complex, The
Kompromiss. See Compromise, The
Konerne ved vandposten. See Women at the Pump, The
Kopfgeburten. See Headbirths
Korrektur. See Correction
Kōshoku ichidai otoko. See Life of an Amorous Man, The
Kosmos. See Cosmos
Kotlovan. See Foundation Pit, The
Krapp's Last Tape (Beckett), 837
Kuchibue o fuku toki. See When I Whistle
Kuntsnmakher fun Lublin, Der. See Magician of Lublin, The
Kurka Wodna. See Water Hen, The
Kurze Brief zum langen Abschied, Der. See Short Letter, Long Farewell
Kusamakura. See Three-Cornered World, The
Kutonet veha-Pasim. See Tzili

Ladies' Hairdresser (Grekova), 841
Lady Chatterley's Lover (Lawrence), 842
Lady Macbeth of the Mtsensk District (Leskov), 844
Lady with the Dog, The (Chekhov), 846
Lafcadio's Adventures (Gide), 847
Lamb, The (Mauriac), 848
Lanark (Gray, A.), 850
Landlocked. See Children of Violence
Langsame Heimkehr. See Slow Homecoming
Lao Ts'an youji. See Travels of Lao Ts'an, The
Largo Desolato (Havel), 851
Last Gentleman, The (Percy), 853

Last Incarnation of Vautrin, The. See Splendors and Miseries of Courtesans, The
Last Meeting of the Knights of the White Magnolia, The (Jones, P.), 854
Last of Chéri, The (Colette), 264
Last of the Just, The (Schwarz-Bart), 856
Last of the Red-Hot Lovers (Simon, N.), 857
Last Picture Show, The (McMurtry), 858
Last Temptation of Christ, The (Kazantzakis), 859
Last Things. See Strangers and Brothers
Laughing Boy (La Farge), 860
Laughter in the Dark (Nabokov), 861
Lawd Today (Wright), 862
Lazarus Laughed (O'Neill), 863
Leaf Storm (García Márquez), 864
Lean Lands, The (Yáñez), 865
Lear (Bond), 866
Leave It to Psmith (Wodehouse), 868
Lebensansichten des Katers Murr. See Life and Opinions of Kater Murr, The
Leçon, La. See Lesson, The
"Ledi Makbet Mtsenskogo uyez da." See Lady Macbeth of the Mtsensk District
Left Hand of Darkness, The (Le Guin), 869
Left-Handed Woman, The (Handke), 870
Legs (Kennedy, W.), 871
Lehre der Sainte-Victoire, Die. See Slow Homecoming
Lenz (Büchner), 872
Less than Angels (Pym), 873
Lesson, The (Ionesco), 875
Lesson from Aloes, A (Fugard), 875
Lesson of Mont-Sainte-Victoire, The. See Slow Homecoming
Letter to Lord Liszt (Walser), 876
Letting Go (Roth, P.), 878
Libro de Manuel. See Manual for Manuel, A
Lie of the Mind, A (Shepard), 879
Life, A (Leonard), 880
Life and Extraordinary Adventures of Private Ivan Chonkin, The (Voinovich), 881
Life and Opinions of Kater Murr, The (Hoffmann), 883
Life & Times of Michael K (Coetzee), 884
Life Before Man (Atwood), 885
Life Is Elsewhere (Kundera), 886
Life of an Amorous Man, The (Ihara), 888
Life of Man, The (Andreyev), 889
Light (Figes), 890
Light and the Dark, The. See Strangers and Brothers
Lime Works, The (Bernhard), 891
Lincoln (Vidal), 892
Linkshändige Frau, Die. See Left-Handed Woman, The

VII

Lion and the Jewel, The (Soyinka), 893
Lion Country. See Book of Bebb, The
Little Big Man (Berger, T.), 893
Little Girls, The (Bowen), 895
Little Hotel, The (Stead), 896
Lives of Girls and Women (Munro), 898
Living (Green, Henry), 899
Livre du rire et de l'oubli, Le. See Book of Laughter and Forgetting, The
Lizard's Tail, The (Valenzuela), 900
Local Anaesthetic (Grass), 902
Loitering with Intent (Spark), 903
Lolita (Nabokov), 904
Lonely Girl, The. See Country Girls Trilogy, The
Lonely Londoners, The (Selvon), 905
Lonely Passion of Judith Hearne, The (Moore), 907
Long Day's Journey into Night (O'Neill), 908
Long Dream, The (Wright), 909
Long Goodbye, The (Chandler), 910
Long Voyage, The (Semprun), 911
Long Way Around, The. See Slow Homecoming
Look at Me (Brookner), 912
Lookout Cartridge (McElroy), 914
Loot (Orton), 915
Loser, The (Konrád), 915
Losing Battles (Welty), 917
Lost Flying Boat, The (Sillitoe), 918
Lost Honor of Katharina Blum, The (Böll), 919
Lost Steps, The (Carpentier), 921
Lo-t'o Hsiang-tzu. See Rickshaw
Louis Lambert (Balzac), 922
Love and Salt Water (Wilson, E.), 923
Love Feast. See Book of Bebb, The
Love for Lydia (Bates), 924
Love in the Ruins (Percy), 925
Love Medicine (Erdrich), 927
Loved and the Lost, The (Callaghan), 928
Loved One, The (Waugh), 929
Lover, The (Duras), 931
Lu Ann Hampton Laverty Oberlander (Jones, P.), 932
Lubimow. See Makepeace Experiment, The
Lucinda Brayford (Boyd), 933
Luck of Ginger Coffey, The (Moore), 935
Lucy Gayheart (Cather), 936
Luna e i falò, La. See Moon and the Bonfires, The
Luther (Osborne), 937
Lydie Breeze (Guare), 938

Ma Rainey's Black Bottom (Wilson, August), 939
Machine infernale, La. See Infernal Machine, The
Macunaíma (Andrade), 940

Madman and the Nun, The (Witkiewicz), 941
Madman's Defense, A. See Confession of a Fool, The
Madman's Manifesto, A. See Confession of a Fool, The
Madmen and Specialists (Soyinka), 942
Magician of Lublin, The (Singer), 944
Magister Ludi. See Glass Bead Game, The
Magus, The (Fowles), 945
Maids, The (Genet), 946
Maître de la parole, Le. See Guardian of the Word, The
Makepeace Experiment, The (Tertz), 947
Making of Americans, The (Stein), 948
Makioka Sisters, The (Tanizaki), 950
Ma'kom a'her. See Elsewhere, Perhaps
Mal vu mal dit. See Ill Seen Ill Said
Mała apokalipsa. See Minor Apocalypse, A
Malign Fiesta. See Human Age, The
Malone Dies (Beckett), 951
Malone meurt. See Malone Dies
Man for All Seasons, A (Bolt), 952
Man fun Notseres, Der. See Nazarene, The
Man in the Holocene (Frisch), 954
Man Who Came to Dinner, The (Kaufman and Hart), 954
Man Who Cried I Am, The (Williams, J.), 956
Man Who Killed the Deer, The (Waters), 957
Man Who Loved Children, The (Stead), 958
Man Who Watched the Trains Go By, The (Simenon), 959
Man Who Would Be King, The (Kipling), 960
Man with the Golden Arm, The (Algren), 961
Man Without Qualities, The (Musil), 962
Mandelbaum Gate, The (Spark), 964
Man'en san'nen no futtoboru. See Silent Cry, The
Manhunt (Carpentier), 965
Mann ohne Eigenshaften, Der. See Man Without Qualities, The
Man's Blessing, A (Sciascia), 966
Man's Hope (Malraux), 967
Manticore, The. See Deptford Trilogy, The
Manual for Manuel, A (Cortázar), 969
Marat/Sade (Weiss), 971
Marbot (Hildesheimer), 973
Mariage d'amour, Un. See Thérèse Raquin
Marks of Identity (Goytisolo), 974
Marquise of O——, The (Kleist), 976
Marquise von O——, Die. See Marquise of O——, The
Marriage, The (Gombrowicz), 977

Martha Quest. See Children of Violence
Martian Chronicles, The (Bradbury, R.), 979
Maru (Head), 980
Mary (Nabokov), 981
Mary Olivier (Sinclair), 982
Mashenka. See Mary
Mask of Dimitrios, The. See Coffin for Dimitrios, A
Masks (Enchi), 983
Master and Margarita, The (Bulgakov), 984
"MASTER HAROLD" . . . and the boys (Fugard), 986
Master i Margarita. See Master and Margarita
Master of Go, The (Kawabata), 986
Master of the Mill, The (Grove), 987
Masters, The. See Strangers and Brothers
Matchmaker, The (Wilder), 988
Mątwe. See Cuttlefish, The
Mauerspringer, Der. See Wall Jumper, The
Maurice (Forster), 989
Meditación, Una. See Meditation, A
Meditation, A (Benet), 990
Meeting at Telgte, The (Grass), 991
Meijin. See Master of Go, The
Member of the Wedding, The (McCullers), 992
Memed, My Hawk (Kemal), 993
Memorandum, The (Havel), 995
Men at Arms. See Sword of Honour
Men of Maize (Asturias), 996
Mendiant de Jérusalem, Le. See Beggar in Jerusalem, A
Mensch erscheint im Holozän, Der. See Man in the Holocene
Menuhah nekhonah. See Perfect Peace, A
Meridian (Walker, A.), 997
Merry-Go-Round in the Sea, The (Stow), 998
Metafizyka dwugłowego cielęcia. See Metaphysics of a Two-Headed Calf
Metamorphosis, The (Kafka), 999
Metaphysics of a Two-Headed Calf (Witkiewicz), 1000
Météores, Les. See Gemini
Mickelsson's Ghosts (Gardner), 1001
Middle Age of Mrs. Eliot, The (Wilson, Angus), 1004
Middle Ground, The (Drabble), 1005
Middle of the Journey, The (Trilling), 1006
Middle Parts of Fortune, The. See Her Privates, We
Midnight's Children (Rushdie), 1007
Miguel Street (Naipaul, V. S.), 1008
Mikha'el sheli. See My Michael
Mimic Men, The (Naipaul, V. S.), 1010

VIII

Minor Apocalypse, A
(Konwicki), 1011
Minty Alley (James, C. L. R.), 1012
Miracle of the Rose (Genet), 1013
Miracle Worker, The
(Gibson), 1015
Miss Peabody's Inheritance
(Jolley), 1016
Missolonghi Manuscript, The
(Prokosch), 1018
Mr. Beluncle (Pritchett), 1018
Mr. Palomar (Calvino), 1020
Mr. Sammler's Planet
(Bellow), 1020
Mr. Sampath. See Printer of
Malgudi, The
Mr. Stone and the Knights
Companion (Naipaul, V. S.),
1022
Mrs. Bridge (Connell), 1023
Mrs. Caliban (Ingalls), 1024
Mrs. Stevens Hears the Mermaids
Singing (Sarton), 1025
Mrs. Warren's Profession
(Shaw, G.), 1026
Mobile (Butor), 1027
Model Childhood, A. See Patterns of
Childhood
Modification, La. See Change of
Heart, A
Moetsukita chizu. See Ruined
Map, The
Molloy (Beckett), 1028
Moment of True Feeling, A
(Handke), 1029
Monkey Grip (Garner), 1030
Monkey's Wrench, The
(Levi, P.), 1032
Monstre Gai. See Human Age, The
Month of Sundays, A
(Updike), 1033
Moon and the Bonfires, The
(Pavese), 1034
Moon for the Misbegotten, A
(O'Neill), 1035
Moon Is a Harsh Mistress, The
(Heinlein), 1036
Moonrise, Moonset
(Konwicki), 1037
Morning, Noon, and Night
(Cozzens), 1037
Morning Watch, The (Agee), 1039
Mort à crédit. See Death on the
Installment Plan
Mort dans l'âme, La. See Roads to
Freedom, The
Morte accidentale di un anarchico.
See Accidental Death of an
Anarchist
Morte d'Urban (Powers), 1040
Moses (Hurston), 1041
Mosquitoes (Faulkner), 1042
Mother and Two Daughters, A
(Godwin), 1043
Mother Courage and Her Children
(Brecht), 1046
Mother Night (Vonnegut), 1047
Mouchette (Bernanos), 1048
Mound Builders, The (Wilson, L.),
1049
Mountain and the Valley, The
(Buckler), 1051
Mousetrap, The (Christie), 1052

Moviegoer, The (Percy), 1053
Mudun al-milh: al-Tīh. See Cities of
Salt
Mulata (Asturias), 1054
Mumbo Jumbo (Reed), 1055
Murder of Roger Ackroyd, The
(Christie), 1056
Murderer, The (Heath), 1057
Murphy (Beckett), 1059
Mutter Courage und ihre Kinder. See
Mother Courage and Her Children
My. See We
My Brilliant Career
(Franklin), 1060
My Dinner with André (Shawn and
Gregory), 1061
My Heart and My Flesh
(Roberts), 1062
My Life in the Bush of Ghosts
(Tutuola), 1063
My Michael (Oz), 1065
My Name Is Asher Lev
(Potok), 1067
Mysterier. See Mysteries
Mysteries (Hamsun), 1068
Mysterious Stranger, The
(Twain), 1069

"Nabeg." See Raid, The
Nachdenken über Christa T.
See Quest for Christa T., The
Nachsommer, Der. See Indian
Summer
Nakanune. See On the Eve
Naked and the Dead, The
(Mailer), 1070
Naked Lunch (Burroughs), 1071
Name of the Rose, The (Eco), 1072
Naomi (Tanizaki), 1074
Napoleon Symphony
(Burgess), 1075
Narcissus and Goldmund
(Hesse), 1077
Narziss und Goldmund. See
Narcissus and Goldmund
Natives of Hemsö, The
(Strindberg), 1077
Natives of My Person
(Lamming), 1078
Natural, The (Malamud), 1080
Nazarene, The (Asch), 1081
Nectar in a Sieve
(Markandaya), 1082
Needle's Eye, The (Drabble), 1083
Nègres, Les. See Blacks, The
Neige était sale, La. See Snow Was
Black, The
Nemureru bijo. See House of the
Sleeping Beauties, The
Neshome Ekspeditsyes. See Shosha
Nesnesitelná lehkost bytí.
See Unbearable Lightness
of Being, The
Netochka Nezvanova
(Dostoevski), 1084
Never Come Morning
(Algren), 1085
New Day (Reid), 1087
New Life, A (Malamud), 1088
New Men, The. See Strangers and
Brothers
Ngaahika Ndeenda. See I Will Marry
When I Want

Niagara (Butor), 1089
Nickel Mountain (Gardner), 1091
Niezwyciężony i inne opowiadania.
See Invincible, The
Night (O'Brien, E.), 1092
Night and Day (Stoppard), 1093
Night and Day (Woolf), 1094
'night, Mother (Norman), 1095
Night Must Fall (Williams, E.),
1096
Night of the Iguana, The
(Williams, T.), 1097
Nightwood (Barnes, D.), 1099
Nine Tailors, The (Sayers), 1100
1934 (Moravia), 1101
Ninety-two in the Shade
(McGuane), 1102
Ningen shikkaku. See No Longer
Human
No Exit (Sartre), 1103
No Laughing Matter (Wilson,
Angus), 1104
No Longer at Ease (Achebe), 1105
No Longer Human (Dazai), 1107
No One Writes to the Colonel
(García Márquez), 1108
No Place on Earth (Wolf), 1109
Nœud de vipères, Le. See Vipers'
Tangle
Nome della rosa, Il. See Name of the
Rose, The
Non-existent Knight, The
(Calvino), 1110
Nord. See North
Norman Conquests, The
(Ayckbourn), 1111
North (Céline), 241
Not Honour More. See Second
Trilogy
Not Without Laughter
(Hughes), 1113
Nothing (Green, Henry), 1114
Nothing Happens in Carmincross
(Kiely), 1115
Nothing Like the Sun
(Burgess), 1116
Notre-Dame des Fleurs. See Our
Lady of the Flowers
Nouvelle Histoire de Mouchette.
See Mouchette
November 1918 (Döblin), 1117
Nuns and Soldiers (Murdoch), 1120

O Beulah Land (Settle), 1122
O, How the Wheel Becomes It!
(Powell), 1123
Oath, The (Wiesel), 1124
Obscene Bird of Night, The
(Donoso), 1125
Obsceno pájaro de la noche, El. See
Obscene Bird of Night, The
Occasion for Loving
(Gordimer), 1126
Occhiali d'oro, Gli. See Gold-
Rimmed Eyeglasses, The
October Light (Gardner), 1127
Octopus, The (Norris), 1129
Odd Couple, The (Simon, N.),
1130
Odd Woman, The (Godwin), 1131
Odin den Ivana Denisovicha. See
One Day in the Life of Ivan
Denisovich

Œuvre au noir, L'. See Abyss, The
Offending the Audience
  (Handke), 1132
Officers and Gentlemen. See Sword
  of Honour
Ogre, The (Tournier), 1133
Oh What a Paradise It Seems
  (Cheever), 1134
Oiseau bleu, L'. See Blue Bird, The
Oktiabr shestnadtsatogo
  (Solzhenitsyn), 1135
Old Blood, The. See Kaywana
  Trilogy, The
Old Devils, The (Amis), 1136
Old Man, The (Trifonov), 1138
Oldest Living Graduate,
  The (Jones, P.), 1139
Ölmez otu. See Undying Grass, The
Omensetter's Luck (Gass), 1140
On Heroes and Tombs
  (Sábato), 1142
On the Eve (Turgenev), 1143
On the Road (Kerouac), 1145
Once in a Lifetime (Kaufman and
  Hart), 1145
One Day in the Life of Ivan
  Denisovich (Solzhenitsyn), 1147
One Day of Life (Argueta), 1148
One Flew over the Cuckoo's Nest
  (Kesey), 1149
One Hundred Years of Solitude
  (García Márquez), 1150
One of Ours (Cather), 1154
One Way to Heaven (Cullen), 1155
Onnamen. See Masks
Open Heart. See Book of Bebb, The
Operetka. See Operetta
Operetta (Gombrowicz), 1156
Optimist's Daughter, The
  (Welty), 1157
Or, L'. See Sutter's Gold
Oreach nata lalun. See Guest for the
  Night, A
Orphée. See Orpheus
Orpheus (Cocteau), 1159
Ortadirek. See Wind from the Plain,
  The
Örtlich betäubt. See Local
  Anaesthetic
Osaka san. See Wonderful Fool
Ostře sledované vlaky. See Closely
  Watched Trains
Ostrov Krym. See Island of
  Crimea, The
Other Leopards (Williams, D.),
  1160
Other People's Worlds
  (Trevor), 1161
Otherwise Engaged (Gray, S.), 1161
Otoño del patriarca, El. See Autumn
  of the Patriarch, The
Ottepel. See Thaw, The
Où mènent les mauvais chemins.
  See Splendors and Miseries of
  Courtesans, The
Our Friend Manso (Pérez
  Galdós), 1163
Our Lady of the Flowers
  (Genet), 1164
Out of the Silent Planet. See Space
  Trilogy, The
Outer Dark (McCarthy, C.), 1166
Outsider, The (Sábato), 1167

Outsider, The (Wright), 1168
Oväder. See Stormy Weather
Ozhog. See Burn, The

Pagan Place, A (O'Brien, E.), 1169
Painted Bird, The (Kosinski), 1170
Painter of Our Time, The
  (Berger, J.), 1171
Palace of the Peacock. See Guyana
  Quartet, The
Palomar. See Mr. Palomar
Pan (Hamsun), 1172
Pandora's Box (Wedekind), 1173
Pantomime (Walcott), 1174
Paper Men, The (Golding), 1175
Paradiso (Lezama Lima), 1176
Paravents, Les. See Screens, The
Pardoner's Tale, The (Wain), 1178
Partage de Midi. See Break of Noon
Party Going (Green, Henry), 1179
Pasos perdidos, Los. See Lost
  Steps, The
Passage, The (Palmer), 1180
Passing (Larsen), 1182
Passing Time (Butor), 1183
Passion in Rome, A
  (Callaghan), 1184
Passion Play (Nichols), 1185
Path to the Nest of Spiders, The
  (Calvino), 1186
Patterns of Childhood (Wolf), 1187
Pauvre Christ de Bomba, Le. See
  Poor Christ of Bomba, The
Pearl, The (Steinbeck), 1188
"Pearl of the World, The."
  See Pearl, The
Pelican, The (Strindberg), 1189
Pelikanen. See Pelican, The
Penny for a Song, A (Whiting),
  1190
People Betrayed, A. See November
  1918
People of Hemsö, The. See Natives
  of Hemsö, The
People of the City (Ekwensi), 1192
Perelandra. See Space Trilogy, The
Perfect Peace, A (Oz), 1193
Perfect Spy, A (le Carré), 1194
Persecution and Assassination of
  Jean-Paul Marat as Performed by
  the Inmates of the Asylum of
  Charenton Under the Direction
  of the Marquis de Sade, The.
  See Marat/Sade
Persian Boy, The (Renault), 1195
Personal Matter, A (Oe), 1197
Pervaya lyubov. See First Love
Peščanik (Kiš), 1197
Petals of Blood (Ngugi), 1198
Petersburg (Bely), 1199
Petrified Forest, The
  (Sherwood), 1200
Pharisienne, La. See Woman of the
  Pharisees, A
Philadelphia, Here I Come!
  (Friel), 1202
Philadelphia Story, The
  (Barry), 1203
Photograph: Lovers in Motion, A
  (Shange), 1204
Physicists, The (Dürrenmatt), 1206
Physiker, Die. See Physicists, The
Picnic (Inge), 1207

Piknik na obochine. See Roadside
  Picnic
"Pikovaya dama." See Queen of
  Spades, The
Pilgrim at Sea. See Tobias Trilogy,
  The
Pilgrim på havet. See Tobias Trilogy,
  The
Pilgrimen. See Tobias Trilogy, The
Pincher Martin (Golding), 1208
Pitch Dark (Adler), 1209
Plaidoyer d'un fou, Le. See
  Confession of a Fool, The
Plains Song, for Female Voices
  (Morris), 1210
Planetarium, The (Sarraute), 1211
Play It As It Lays (Didion), 1212
Plenty (Hare), 1213
Plum Bun (Fauset), 1215
Pnin (Nabokov), 1216
Podrostok. See Raw Youth, A
Police, The (Mrożek), 1217
Policja. See Police, The
Polish Complex, The
  (Konwicki), 1218
Poor Christ of Bomba, The
  (Beti), 1219
Popiół i diament. See Ashes and
  Diamonds
Pornografia (Gombrowicz), 1221
Pornographer, The
  (McGahern), 1222
Portage to San Cristóbal of A. H.,
  The (Steiner), 1223
Porte étroite, La. See Strait Is the
  Gate
Portes de la forêt, Les. See Gates of
  the Forest, The
Portnoy's Complaint (Roth, P.),
  1224
Portrait d'un inconnu. See Portrait of
  a Man Unknown
Portrait of a Man Unknown
  (Sarraute), 1226
Possédés, Les. See Possessed, The
Possessed, The (Camus), 1227
Potting Shed, The (Greene), 1228
Prague Orgy, The (Roth, P.), 1229
Praisesong for the Widow
  (Marshall), 1230
Pravda (Brenton and Hare), 1232
Premios, Los. See Winners, The
Pretendent na prestol. See Pretender
  to the Throne
Pretender to the Throne
  (Voinovich), 881
Příběh inženýra lidských duší. See
  Engineer of Human Souls, The
Price, The (Miller, A.), 1233
Priglashenie na kazn'. See Invitation
  to a Beheading
Prime of Miss Jean Brodie, The
  (Spark), 1235
Primo Basílio, O. See Cousin Bazilio
Princess Iwona. See Ivona, Princess
  of Burgundia
Printer of Malgudi, The
  (Narayan), 1236
Prisoner of Grace. See Second
  Trilogy
Prisons (Settle), 1237
Private Lives (Coward), 1239
Promise, The (Potok), 281

Proper Marriage, A. *See* Children of Violence
Proshchanie iz niotkuda. *See* Farewell from Nowhere
Publikumsbeschimpfung. *See* Offending the Audience
Pylon (Faulkner), 1239

Quality of Mercy, A (West, P.), 1240
Quare Fellow, The (Behan), 1241
Quartet in Autumn (Pym), 1243
Que ma joie demeure. *See* Joy of Man's Desiring
Queen of Spades, The (Pushkin), 1244
Quel beau dimanche. *See* What a Beautiful Sunday!
Quer pasticciaccio brutto de via Merulana. *See* That Awful Mess on Via Merulana
Quest for Christa T., The (Wolf), 1245
Quest of the Absolute, The (Balzac), 1246
Questa sera si recita a soggetto. *See* Tonight We Improvise
Question of Power, A (Head), 1247
Questionnaire, The (Gruša), 1249
Quicksand (Larsen), 1250
Quiet American, The (Greene), 1252

Rabbit Is Rich (Updike), 1253
Rabbit Redux (Updike), 1254
Rabbit, Run (Updike), 1257
Radcliffe (Storey), 1257
Radiance of the King, The (Laye), 1258
Ragtime (Doctorow), 1259
Raid, The (Tolstoy), 1261
Raisin in the Sun, A (Hansberry), 1262
Raj Quartet, The (Scott, P.), 1263
Rakovy korpus. *See* Cancer Ward
Rashōmon (Akutagawa), 1265
Rat, The (Grass), 1266
Rat Man of Paris (West, P.), 1267
Rates of Exchange (Bradbury, M.), 1268
Rat's Mass, A (Kennedy, A.), 1269
Rättin, Die. *See* Rat, The
Ravishing of Lol Stein, The (Duras), 1270
Ravissement de Lol V. Stein, Le. *See* Ravishing of Lol Stein, The
Raw Youth, A (Dostoevski), 1271
Rayuela. *See* Hopscotch
Razor's Edge, The (Maugham), 1273
Real Thing, The (Stoppard), 1274
Rebel Angels, The (Davies), 1275
Rebellion in the Backlands (Cunha), 1276
Recherche de l'absolu, La. *See* Quest of the Absolute, The
Recognitions, The (Gaddis), 1277
Rector of Justin, The (Auchincloss), 1279
Red Pony, The (Steinbeck), 1281
Red Roses for Me (O'Casey), 1282
Regard du roi, Le. *See* Radiance of the King, The

Regenta, La (Alas), 1284
Reigen. *See* Ronde, La
Reino de este mundo, El. *See* Kingdom of This World, The
Reinvindicación del Conde Don Julián. *See* Count Julian
Removalists, The (Williamson), 1285
Reprieve, The. *See* Roads to Freedom, The
Restless Heart (Anouilh), 1286
Return of the Soldier, The (West, R.), 1288
Return to Región (Benet), 1289
Revenge for Love, The (Lewis, W.), 1290
Rickshaw (Lao She), 1291
Ride Across Lake Constance, The (Handke), 1292
Riders to the Sea (Synge), 1294
Rigadoon (Céline), 241
Right to an Answer, The (Burgess), 1295
Rigodon. *See* Rigadoon
Rihlah ila al-ghad. *See* Voyage to Tomorrow
Rimers of Eldritch, The (Wilson, L.), 1296
Ripening Corn, The. *See* Ripening Seed, The
Ripening Seed, The (Colette), 1297
Ripple from the Storm, A. *See* Children of Violence
Rise and Fall of the City of Mahagonny (Brecht), 1298
Rites of Passage (Golding), 1299
Ritt über den Bodensee, Der. *See* Ride Across Lake Constance, The
River Between, The (Ngugi), 1300
Road, The (Soyinka), 1302
Road to Mecca, The (Fugard), 1303
Roads to Freedom, The (Sartre), 1303
Roadside Picnic (Strugatsky *and* Strugatsky), 1306
Robber Bridegroom, The (Welty), 1307
Rock Cried Out, The (Douglas), 1309
Roi des Aulnes, Le. *See* Ogre, The
Roi se meurt, Le. *See* Exit the King
Romulus der Grosse. *See* Romulus the Great
Romulus the Great (Dürrenmatt), 1310
Ronde, La (Schnitzler), 1312
Room on the Hill, A (St. Omer), 1312
Rosencrantz and Guildenstern Are Dead (Stoppard), 1314
Rosshalde (Hesse), 1314
Route des Flandres, La. *See* Flanders Road, The
Royal Hunt of the Sun, The (Shaffer, P.), 1316
Royal Way, The (Malraux), 1317
Rubyfruit Jungle (Brown), 1318
Rudin (Turgenev), 1319
Ruined Map, The (Abe), 1321
Ruling Class, The (Barnes, P.), 1322

Runaway Horse (Walser), 1323
Runaway Horses. *See* Sea of Fertility, The
Runner Mack (Beckham), 1324

Sacred Families (Donoso), 1325
Sad idzie. *See* Trial Begins, The
Safety Net, The (Böll), 1326
Sailor Who Fell from Grace with the Sea, The (Mishima), 1328
Saint Jack (Theroux), 1329
Saint Manuel Bueno, Martyr (Unamuno), 1329
St. Petersburg. *See* Petersburg
St. Urbain's Horseman (Richler), 1330
Samurai, The (Endō), 1332
San Manuel Bueno, mártir. *See* Saint Manuel Bueno, Martyr
Sand Mountain (Linney), 1333
Sandcastle, The (Murdoch), 1334
Sapphira and the Slave Girl (Cather), 1335
Sarrasine (Balzac), 1337
Sasameyuki. *See* Makioka Sisters, The
Satin Slipper, The (Claudel), 1338
Saturday Night and Sunday Morning (Sillitoe), 1339
Sauvage, La. *See* Restless Heart
Save Me the Waltz (Fitzgerald, Z.), 1340
Saved (Bond), 1341
Sawbones Memorial (Ross), 1342
Scapegoat, The (Settle), 1343
Scenes from American Life (Gurney), 1345
Schlaflose Tage. *See* Sleepless Days
School for Fools, A (Sokolov), 1347
Schwanenhaus, Das. *See* Swan Villa, The
Scorched-Wood People, The (Wiebe), 1348
Scots Quair, A (Gibbon), 1349
Screens, The (Genet), 1352
Se non ora, quando? *See* If Not Now, When?
Se una notte d'inverno un viaggiatore. *See* If on a Winter's Night a Traveler
Sea of Fertility, The (Mishima), 1354
Sea of Troubles, A. *See* Sea Wall, The
Sea Wall, The (Duras), 1355
Search for America, A (Grove), 1356
Search for Signs of Intelligent Life in the Universe, The (Wagner), 1357
Seascape (Albee), 1359
Season of Adventure (Lamming), 1360
Season of Anomy (Soyinka), 1362
Second Coming, The (Percy), 1363
Second Foundation. *See* Foundation Trilogy, The
Second Man, The (Behrman), 1364
Second Trilogy (Cary), 1365
Secret History of the Lord of Musashi, The (Tanizaki), 1367

XI

Secret Ladder, The. *See* Guyana Quartet, The
Secret Sharer, The (Conrad), 1368
Seize the Day (Bellow), 1369
Seizure of Power, The (Miłosz), 1370
Self Condemned (Lewis, W.), 1371
Sem dnei tvoreniia. *See* Seven Days of Creation, The
Sembazuru. *See* Thousand Cranes
Semeynoye schast'ye. *See* Family Happiness
Señas de identidad. *See* Marks of Identity
Senilita. *See* As a Man Grows Older
Sennik Współczesny. *See* Dreambook for Our Time, A
Señor de Tacuru, El. *See* Lizard's Tail, The
Sent for You Yesterday. *See* Homewood Trilogy, The
Sentiero dei nidi di ragno, Il. *See* Path to the Nest of Spiders, The
Sentimental Journey, A (Shklovsky), 1372
Sentimental'noye puteshestviye. *See* Sentimental Journey, A
Separate Peace, A (Knowles), 1373
September Light. *See* Silesian Tetralogy, The
Septemberlicht. *See* Silesian Tetralogy, The
Serebryanny golub. *See* Silver Dove, The
Serious Money (Churchill), 1374
Serjeant Musgrave's Dance (Arden), 1375
Serment de Kolvillàg, Le. *See* Oath, The
Serpent and the Rope, The (Rao), 1377
Serpiente de oro, La. *See* Golden Serpent, The
Sertões, Os. *See* Rebellion in the Backlands
Setting Free the Bears (Irving), 1378
Setting Sun, The (Dazai), 1379
Settlers of the Marsh (Grove), 1380
Seven Ages, The (Figes), 1381
Seven Days of Creation, The (Maximov), 1383
Seven Madmen, The (Arlt), 1384
Severed Head, A (Murdoch), 1385
Sexual Perversity in Chicago (Mamet), 1386
Shadow of a Gunman, The (O'Casey), 1387
Shakespeare's Dog (Rooke), 1388
Shame (Rushdie), 1389
Shayō. *See* Setting Sun, The
Sheltering Sky, The (Bowles), 1390
Shikasta (Lessing), 1391
Shining, The (King, S.), 1393
Shipyard, The (Onetti), 1394
Shkola dlia durakov. *See* School for Fools, A
Short Letter, Long Farewell (Handke), 1395
Shosha (Singer), 1396
Shrouded Woman, The (Bombal), 1397
Shuttlecock (Swift), 1398

Sibyl, The (Lagerkvist), 1399
Sibyllan. *See* Sibyl, The
Siddhartha (Hesse), 1400
Siege of Krishnapur, The (Farrell), 1401
Siete locos, Los. *See* Seven Madmen, The
Sigismund (Gustafsson), 1403
Siglo de las Luces, El. *See* Explosion in a Cathedral
Sign in Sidney Brustein's Window, The (Hansberry), 1404
Silence (Endō), 1405
Silent Cry, The (Ōe), 1407
Silesian Tetralogy, The (Bienek), 1408
Silmarillion, The (Tolkien), 1410
Silver Dove, The (Bely), 1413
Silver Tassie, The (O'Casey), 1413
Simple Story, A (Agnon), 1415
Singapore Grip, The (Farrell), 1416
Sipur pashut. *See* Simple Story, A
Sirens of Titan, The (Vonnegut), 1418
Sister Mary Ignatius Explains It All for You (Durang), 1419
6,810,000 Litres d'eau par seconde. *See* Niagara
62: A Model Kit (Cortázar), 1420
Slaughterhouse-Five (Vonnegut), 1421
Slave, The (Singer), 1422
Śledztwo. *See* Investigation, The
Sleep of Reason, The. *See* Strangers and Brothers
Sleepless Days (Becker), 1423
Sleuth (Shaffer, A.), 1424
Slow Homecoming (Handke), 1425
Ślub. *See* Marriage, The
Small Changes (Piercy), 1426
Small Room, The (Sarton), 1427
Small World (Lodge), 1429
Smiley's People (le Carré), 694
Snail on the Slope, The (Strugatsky *and* Strugatsky), 1430
Snooty Baronet (Lewis, W.), 1432
Snow Country (Kawabata), 1433
Snow Was Black, The (Simenon), 1434
Sobache serdtse. *See* Heart of a Dog
Sobre héroes y tumbas. *See* On Heroes and Tombs
Solaris (Lem), 1435
Soldiers' Pay (Faulkner), 1437
Solid Mandala, The (White), 1438
Some Prefer Nettles (Tanizaki), 1439
Something Happened (Heller), 1440
Something Wicked This Way Comes (Bradbury, R.), 1441
Sometimes a Great Notion (Kesey), 1442
Son of Man (Roa Bastos), 1444
Song of a Goat (Clark), 1444
Song of Solomon (Morrison), 1445
Sonim de Geshichte fun a Liebe. *See* Enemies
Sophie's Choice (Styron), 1446
Sorrow Beyond Dreams, A (Handke), 1448

Soulier de satin, Le. *See* Satin Slipper, The
Souls and Bodies (Lodge), 1448
Sound of the Mountain, The (Kawabata), 1450
Sour Sweet (Mo), 1451
Source, The (Michener), 1452
Sous le soleil de Satan. *See* Under the Sun of Satan
Southpaw, The (Harris, M.), 1455
Space Trilogy, The (Lewis, C. S.), 1456
Speed-the-Plow (Mamet), 1458
Speedboat (Adler), 1459
Spell, The (Broch), 1460
Speranza (Delblanc), 1461
Spire, The (Golding), 1462
Splendeurs et misères des courtisanes. *See* Splendors and Miseries of Courtesans, The
Splendors and Miseries of Courtesans, The (Balzac), 1463
Spoilt City, The. *See* Balkan Trilogy, The
Spokoinoi nochi. *See* Goodnight!
Spöksonaten. *See* Ghost Sonata, The
Sport of the Gods, The (Dunbar), 1465
Sporting Club, The (McGuane), 1466
Spring Floods. *See* Torrents of Spring, The (Turgenev)
Spring Snow. *See* Sea of Fertility, The
Spy in the House of Love, A (Nin), 1468
Spy Who Came in from the Cold, The (le Carré), 1469
Stand, The (King, S.), 1470
Stanley and the Women (Amis), 1472
Star of Satan, The. *See* Under the Sun of Satan
Starik. *See* Old Man, The
Staring at the Sun (Barnes, J.), 1472
Starry Ticket, A. *See* Ticket to the Stars, A
Start in Life, A. *See* Debut, The
Stellvertreter, Der. *See* Deputy, The
Step. *See* Steppe, The
Steppe, The (Chekhov), 1474
Stiller. *See* I'm Not Stiller
Stone Angel, The (Laurence), 1475
Stopfkuchen. *See* Tubby Schaumann
Storia, La. *See* History
Stormy Weather (Strindberg), 1476
Strait Is the Gate (Gide), 1477
Stranger in a Strange Land (Heinlein), 1478
Strangers and Brothers (Snow), 1480
Streamers (Rabe), 1483
Strike the Father Dead (Wain), 1484
Strong Wind (Asturias), 1485
Stunde der wahren Empfindung, Die. *See* Moment of True Feeling, A
Subject Was Roses, The (Gilroy), 1486
Such Is My Beloved (Callaghan), 1487

Suddenly Last Summer
(Williams, T.), 1488
Suicide's Wife, The
(Madden), 1489
Sula (Morrison), 1490
Summer and Smoke
(Williams, T.), 1492
Summer of the Seventeenth Doll
(Lawler), 1493
Suna no onna. See Woman in the
Dunes, The
Sunday of Life, The
(Queneau), 1494
Sunlight Dialogues, The
(Gardner), 1495
Sunset Song. See Scots Quair, A
Surfacing (Atwood), 1498
Sursis, Le. See Roads to Freedom,
The
Survivor, The (Keneally), 1499
Sutter's Gold (Cendrars), 1500
Suttree (McCarthy, C.), 1501
Swamp Angel (Wilson, E.), 1503
Swan Villa, The (Walser), 1504
Sweet Bird of Youth
(Williams, T.), 1505
Sweet Dove Died, The (Pym), 1507
Sword of Honour (Waugh), 1508
System of Dante's Hell, The
(Baraka), 1510

Tade kuu mushi. See Some Prefer
Nettles
Take a Girl Like You (Amis), 1511
Takeover, The (Spark), 1513
Tales of Jacob, The. See Joseph and
His Brothers
Tali' al-shajarah, Ya. See Tree
Climber, The
Talley's Folly (Wilson, L.), 1514
Tango (Mrożek), 1515
Tartar Steppe, The (Buzzati), 1516
Taste of Honey, A (Delaney), 1517
Tea and Sympathy (Anderson, R.),
1518
Teahouse of the August Moon, The
(Patrick), 1519
Tell Me That You Love Me, Junie
Moon (Kellogg), 1520
Temple of Dawn, The. See Sea of
Fertility, The
Temple of the Golden Pavilion, The
(Mishima), 1522
Temptation (Havel), 1523
Ten North Frederick
(O'Hara), 1524
Tenda dos milagres. See Tent of
Miracles
Tennin gosui. See Sea of Fertility,
The
Tennis Players, The
(Gustafsson), 1525
Tennisspelarna. See Tennis Players,
The
Tent of Miracles (Amado), 1526
Tents of Wickedness, The
(De Vries), 1528
Terms of Endearment
(McMurtry), 1529
Terra Nostra (Fuentes), 1530
That Awful Mess on Via Merulana
(Gadda), 1532

That Hideous Strength. See Space
Trilogy, The
That Voice (Pinget), 1532
Thaw, The (Ehrenburg), 1533
Their Eyes Were Watching God
(Hurston), 1534
them (Oates), 1535
Theophilus North (Wilder), 1536
There Is a Tree More Ancient Than
Eden (Forrest), 1538
Thérèse Raquin (Zola), 1539
These Thousand Hills
(Guthrie), 1541
Thin Red Line, The (Jones, J.),
1542
Things Fall Apart (Achebe), 1544
Third and Oak: The Laundromat
(Norman), 1546
Third Factory (Shklovsky), 1546
Third Life of Grange Copeland, The
(Walker, A.), 1547
Third Policeman, The
(O'Brien, F.), 1548
This Side of Paradise
(Fitzgerald, F.), 1550
This Sporting Life (Storey), 1551
This Sunday (Donoso), 1552
Thousand Cranes
(Kawabata), 1554
Three-Cornered World, The
(Natsume), 1555
Three Lives (Stein), 1555
Three Marias, The (Queiroz), 1557
Three Sisters, The (Sinclair), 1558
Three Trapped Tigers (Cabrera
Infante), 1559
Threepenny Opera, The
(Brecht), 1560
Tía Julia y el escribidor, La. See
Aunt Julia and the Scriptwriter
Ticket to the Stars, A
(Aksyonov), 1561
Tidings Brought to Mary, The
(Claudel), 1563
Tierras flacas, Las. See Lean Lands,
The
Tiêta do Agreste. See Tieta,
the Goat Girl
Tieta, the Goat Girl
(Amado), 1564
Till We Have Faces (Lewis,
C. S.), 1565
Tilted Cross, The (Porter), 1566
Time and the Conways
(Priestley), 1567
Time of Hope. See Strangers and
Brothers
Time of Indifference, The
(Moravia), 1568
Time of the Hero, The (Vargas
Llosa), 1569
Time of Your Life, The
(Saroyan), 1571
Time Without Bells. See Silesian
Tetralogy, The
Tinker, Tailor, Soldier, Spy
(le Carré), 694
Tiny Alice (Albee), 1572
Tirra Lirra by the River
(Anderson, J.), 1573
Titan (Jean Paul), 1574
Titus Alone. See Gormenghast
Trilogy, The

Titus Groan. See Gormenghast
Trilogy, The
To Have and Have Not
(Hemingway), 1577
To Have and to Hold
(Johnston), 1578
To Kill a Mockingbird (Lee), 1580
To the Land of the Cattails
(Appelfeld), 1581
Tobacco Road (Kirkland), 1582
Tobias Trilogy, The
(Lagerkvist), 1583
Todo verdor perecerá. See All Green
Shall Perish
Told by an Idiot (Macaulay), 1585
Tomb for Boris Davidovich, A
(Kiš), 1586
Tonight We Improvise
(Pirandello), 1588
Tooth of Crime, The
(Shepard), 1589
Top Girls (Churchill), 1591
Torch Song Trilogy
(Fierstein), 1592
Tor-ha-pela'ot. See Age of Wonders
Torrents of Spring, The
(Hemingway), 1593
Torrents of Spring, The
(Turgenev), 1594
Tortilla Flat (Steinbeck), 1595
Tour du monde en quatre-vingts
jours, Le. See Around the World
in Eighty Days
Tower of Babel, The. See Auto-da-Fé
Towers of Silence, The. See Raj
Quartet, The
Towers of Trebizond, The
(Macaulay), 1596
Tra donne sole. See Among Women
Only
Tragédie du Roi Christophe, La. See
Tragedy of King Christophe, The
Tragedy of King Christophe, The
(Césaire), 1598
Traición de Rita Hayworth, La.
See Betrayed by Rita Hayworth
Transfiguration of Benno Blimpie,
The (Innaurato), 1599
Translations (Friel), 1600
Transposed Heads, The
(Mann), 1602
Travelling North
(Williamson), 1603
Travels of Lao Ts'an, The
(Liu E), 1604
Travesties (Stoppard), 1606
Travnička hronika. See Bosnian
Chronicle
Treasure Hunt. See Book of Bebb,
The
Tree Climber, The (Hakim), 1607
Tree of Knowledge, The
(Baroja), 1608
Treffen in Telgte, Das. See Meeting
at Telgte, The
Tremor of Intent (Burgess), 1609
Três Marias, As. See Three Marias,
The
Tres novelitas burguesas. See Sacred
Families
Tres tristes tigres. See Three Trapped
Tigers
Tretya fabrika. See Third Factory

Trial Begins, The (Tertz), 1610
Trick of the Ga Bolga, The (McGinley), 1612
Triptych (Simon, C.), 1613
Triton (Delany), 1614
Troops Return, The. *See* November 1918
Tropic of Cancer (Miller, H.), 1615
Trouble in Mind (Childress), 1616
Troubled Sleep. *See* Roads to Freedom, The
Troubles (Farrell), 1617
Trout Fishing in America (Brautigan), 1619
True Story of Ah Q, The (Lu Hsün), 1620
True West (Shepard), 1621
Tubby Schaumann (Raabe), 1622
Tueur sans gages. *See* Killer, The
Túnel, El. *See* Outsider, The
Turvey (Birney), 1623
Tutti i nostri ieri. *See* All Our Yesterdays
Twenty-seven Wagons Full of Cotton (Williams, T.), 1624
Two for the Seesaw (Gibson), 1625
Two Solitudes (MacLennan), 1625
2001: A Space Odyssey (Clarke, Arthur C.), 1627
Two Thousand Seasons (Armah), 1628
Typhoon (Conrad), 1629
Tzili (Appelfeld), 1630

Ubu Roi (Jarry), 1631
Ulitka na sklone. *See* Snail on the Slope, The
Última niebla, La. *See* Final Mist, The
Ultramarine (Lowry), 1632
Umarła Klasa. *See* Dead Class, The
Un día en la vida. *See* One Day of Life
Unbearable Lightness of Being, The (Kundera), 1633
Unconditional Surrender. *See* Sword of Honour
Under the Sun of Satan (Bernanos), 1634
Underground Man, The (Macdonald), 1636
Undying Grass, The (Kemal), 1718
Unholy Loves (Oates), 1637
Unhuman Tour. *See* Three-Cornered World, The
Unicorn, The (Murdoch), 1639
Union Street (Barker), 1640
Universal Baseball Association, Inc., J. Henry Waugh, Prop., The (Coover), 1642
Unizhennye i oskorblyonnye. *See* Insulted and the Injured, The
Unnamable, The (Beckett), 1643
Untergeher, Der (Bernhard), 1644
Utage no ato. *See* After the Banquet
Utsukushisa to kanashimi to. *See* Beauty and Sadness

V. (Pynchon), 1646
V kruge pervom. *See* First Circle, The
Vagabond, The (Colette), 1649

Valley of Decision, The (Wharton), 1650
Valse aux adieux, La. *See* Farewell Party, The
Városalapító, A. *See* City Builder, The
Vatican Swindle, The. *See* Lafcadio's Adventures
Vein of Iron (Glasgow), 1651
Vendor of Sweets, The (Narayan), 1653
Vendredi. *See* Friday
Vent, Le. *See* Wind, The
Venusberg (Powell), 1654
Verfolgung und Ermordung Jean-Paul Marats, dargestellt durch die Schauspielgruppe des Hospizes zu Charenton unter der Anleitung des Herrn de Sade, Die. *See* Marat/Sade
Verlorene Ehre der Katharina Blum, Die. *See* Lost Honor of Katharina Blum, The
Verratenes Volk. *See* November 1918
Verstörung. *See* Gargoyles
Vertauschten Köpfe, Die. *See* Transposed Heads, The
"Verwandlung, Die." *See* Metamorphosis, The
Verwirrungen des Zöglings Törless, Die. *See* Young Törless
Verzauberung, Die. *See* Spell, The
Veshniye vody. *See* Torrents of Spring, The (Turgenev)
Victoria (Hamsun), 1655
Vida a plazos de Don Jacobo Lerner, La. *See* Fragmented Life of Don Jacobo Lerner, The
Vida breve, La. *See* Brief Life, A
Vida inútil de Pito Pérez, La. *See* Futile Life of Pito Perez, The
Vie est ailleurs, La. *See* Life Is Elsewhere
Vienna: Lusthaus (Clarke, M.), 1655
Viento fuerte. *See* Strong Wind
Violins of Saint-Jacques, The (Fermor), 1656
Vipers' Tangle (Mauriac), 1657
Virgin and the Gipsy, The (Lawrence), 1658
Visconte dimezzato, Il. *See* Cloven Viscount, The
Visit, The (Dürrenmatt), 1659
Visitants (Stow), 1661
Vivisector, The (White), 1662
Voices in Time (MacLennan), 1663
Voie royale, La. *See* Royal Way, The
Volunteers (Friel), 1665
Volverás a Región. *See* Return to Región
Vorausset Zungen einer Erzählung. *See* Cassandra
Voss (White), 1666
Voyage au centre de la terre. *See* Journey to the Center of the Earth
Voyage Out, The (Woolf), 1667
Voyage Round My Father, A (Mortimer), 1668
Voyage to Tomorrow (Hakim), 1669
Vyrozumění. *See* Memorandum, The

Wagahai wa neko de aru. *See* I Am a Cat
Waiting for the Barbarians (Coetzee), 1671
Walk in the Night, A (La Guma), 1672
Walk on the Wild Side, A (Algren), 1673
Wall, The (Hersey), 1674
Wall Jumper, The (Schneider), 1676
Wanderers, The (Mphahlele), 1677
War and Remembrance (Wouk), 1678
War Between the Tates, The (Lurie), 1681
War of the End of the World, The (Vargas Llosa), 1682
Wariat i zakonnica. *See* Madman and the Nun, The
Wars, The (Findley), 1683
Wasserfälle von Slunj, Die. *See* Waterfalls of Slunj, The
Watch on the Rhine (Hellman), 1684
Watch That Ends the Night, The (MacLennan), 1685
Watchmaker of Everton, The (Simenon), 1686
Water Hen, The (Witkiewicz), 1687
Waterfall, The (Drabble), 1688
Waterfalls of Slunj, The (Doderer), 1689
Waterland (Swift), 1691
Watership Down (Adams), 1692
Watt (Beckett), 1694
Wave, The (Scott, E.), 1695
Way That Girls Love, The. *See* Splendors and Miseries of Courtesans, The
Way West, The (Guthrie), 1698
We (Zamyatin), 1700
Weather in the Streets, The (Lehmann), 1701
Weeds (Kelley, E.), 1702
Well, The (Jolley), 1703
What a Beautiful Sunday! (Semprun), 1704
What I'm Going to Do, I Think (Woiwode), 1705
What Price Glory? (Anderson, M., and Stallings), 1706
What the Butler Saw (Orton), 1707
What's Bred in the Bone (Davies), 1708
When I Whistle (Endō), 1709
When You Comin' Back, Red Ryder? (Medoff), 1710
Where Has Tommy Flowers Gone? (McNally), 1711
Who Has Seen the Wind (Mitchell), 1712
Whole Armour, The. *See* Guyana Quartet, The
Wide Sargasso Sea (Rhys), 1714
Widmung, Die. *See* Devotion
Widower's Son, The (Sillitoe), 1715
Wielopole/Wielopole (Kantor), 1717
Wind, The (Simon, C.), 1717
Wind from the Plain, The (Kemal), 1718

TITLE INDEX

Winds of War, The (Wouk), 1720
Wine of Astonishment, The
  (Lovelace), 1723
Wings (Kopit), 1725
Winners, The (Cortázar), 1726
Wise Virgin (Wilson, A. N.), 1727
Woman from Sarajevo, The
  (Andrić), 1728
Woman in the Dunes, The
  (Abe), 1729
Woman of the Pharisees, A
  (Mauriac), 1730
Woman on the Edge of Time
  (Piercy), 1732
Women at the Pump, The
  (Hamsun), 1733
Women of Brewster Place, The
  (Naylor), 1734
Women of Messina
  (Vittorini), 1736
Women of Trachis (Sophocles, trans.
  by Pound), 1736
Women's Room, The
  (French), 1737
Wonder-Worker, The
  (Jacobson), 1738
Wonderful Fool (Endō), 1740
Wonderland (Oates), 1741
Woodcutters (Bernhard), 1742
Woods, The (Mamet), 1743
Word Child, A (Murdoch), 1744
Words and Music (Beckett), 1745
Words upon the Window-Pane, The
  (Yeats), 1746
Workhouse Ward, The
  (Gregory), 1748
Works of Love, The (Morris), 1749

World According to Garp, The
  (Irving), 1749
World My Wilderness, The
  (Macaulay), 1752
World of Love, A (Bowen), 1753
World of Strangers, A
  (Gordimer), 1754
World of Wonders. See Deptford
  Trilogy, The
Wreath for Udomo, A
  (Abrahams), 1755
Wreath of Roses, A (Taylor), 1756
Wreckage of Agathon, The
  (Gardner), 1758
Wschody i zachody księżyca.
  See Moonrise, Moonset
Wunschloses Unglück. See Sorrow
  Beyond Dreams, A

Xala (Sembène), 1759

Yama no oto. See Sound of the
  Mountain, The
Year of Living Dangerously, The
  (Koch), 1760
Year of the Dragon, The
  (Chin), 1761
Yellow Back Radio Broke-Down
  (Reed), 1762
Yer demir, gök bakır. See Iron Earth,
  Copper Sky
Yonnondio (Olsen), 1763
You Can't Take It with You
  (Kaufman and Hart), 1764
Young Joseph, The. See Joseph and
  His Brothers
Young Lions, The (Shaw, I.), 1765
Young Törless (Musil), 1766
Yuki guni. See Snow Country

Zahradni Slavnost. See Garden
  Party, The
Zapiski iz myortvogo doma.
  See House of the Dead, The
Zashchita Luzhina. See Defense, The
Zazie dans le métro. See Zazie in the
  Metro
Zazie in the Metro
  (Queneau), 1767
Zbabělci. See Cowards, The
Zdobycie władzy. See Seizure of
  Power, The
Zeit ohne Glocken. See Silesian
  Tetralogy, The
Zero (Loyola Brandão), 1769
Žert. See Joke, The
Zhizn' cheloveka. See Life of Man,
  The
Zhizn'i neobychainye priklyucheniya
  soldata Ivana Chonkina. See Life
  and Extraordinary Adventures of
  Private Ivan Chonkin, The
Zona. See Zone, The
Zona sagrada. See Holy Place
Zone, The (Dovlatov), 1770
Zoo (Shklovsky), 1771
Zoo Story, The (Albee), 1772
Zoot Suit (Valdez), 1773
Ztížená možnost soustředění.
  See Increased Difficulty of
  Concentration, The
Zuckerman Unbound (Roth, P.),
  1774
Zvyozdnyi bilet. See Ticket to the
  Stars, A

AUTHOR INDEX

ABE, KŌBŌ
  Inter Ice Age 4, 770
  Ruined Map, The, 1321
  Woman in the Dunes, The, 1729
ABRAHAM, NELSON AHLGREN.
  See ALGREN, NELSON
ABRAHAMS, PETER
  Wreath for Udomo, A, 1755
ACHEBE, CHINUA
  Arrow of God, 69
  No Longer at Ease, 1105
  Things Fall Apart, 1544
ADAMS, RICHARD
  Watership Down, 1692
ADLER, RENATA
  Pitch Dark, 1209
  Speedboat, 1459
AGEE, JAMES
  Morning Watch, The, 1039
AGNON, SHMUEL YOSEF
  Bridal Canopy, The, 200
  Guest for the Night, A, 645
  In the Heart of the Seas, 749
  Simple Story, A, 1415
AGUILERA MALTA, DEMETRIO
  Don Goyo, 416
AKALAITIS, JOANNE
  Green Card, 631
AKSYONOV, VASSILY
  Burn, The, 215
  Island of Crimea, The, 778
  Ticket to the Stars, A, 1561
AKUTAGAWA, RYŪNOSUKE
  Rashōmon, 1265
ALAS, LEOPOLDO
  Regenta, La, 1284
ALBEE, EDWARD
  American Dream, The, 39
  Delicate Balance, A, 385
  Seascape, 1359
  Tiny Alice, 1572
  Zoo Story, The, 1772
ALDINGTON, RICHARD
  All Men Are Enemies, 28
ALDISS, BRIAN W.
  Barefoot in the Head, 114
  Frankenstein Unbound, 544
ALEGRÍA, CIRO
  Golden Serpent, The, 607
ALESHKOVSKY, YUZ
  Kangaroo, 811
ALGREN, NELSON
  Man with the Golden Arm,
    The, 961
  Never Come Morning, 1085
  Walk on the Wild Side, A, 1673
AMADI, ELECHI
  Great Ponds, The, 629
AMADO, JORGE
  Dona Flor and Her Two
    Husbands, 416

  Jubiabá, 804
  Tent of Miracles, 1526
  Tieta, the Goat Girl, 1564
AMBLER, ERIC
  Coffin for Dimitrios, A, 303
  Journey into Fear, 799
AMIS, KINGSLEY
  Girl, 20, 590
  Green Man, The, 633
  I Like It Here, 728
  Jake's Thing, 787
  Old Devils, The, 1136
  Stanley and the Women, 1472
  Take a Girl Like You, 1511
ANDERSON, JESSICA
  Tirra Lirra by the River, 1573
ANDERSON, MAXWELL
  Anne of the Thousand Days, 52
ANDERSON, MAXWELL, and
  LAURENCE STALLINGS
  What Price Glory?, 1706
ANDERSON, ROBERT
  Tea and Sympathy, 1518
ANDRADE, MÁRIO DE
  Macunaíma, 940
ANDREYEV, LEONID
  Life of Man, The, 889
ANDRIĆ, IVO
  Bosnian Chronicle, 195
  Woman from Sarajevo,
    The, 1728
ANDRZEJEWSKI, JERZY
  Ashes and Diamonds, 75
ANOUILH, JEAN
  Antigone, 58
  Becket, 130
  Restless Heart, 1286
ANTHONY, MICHAEL
  Games Were Coming, The, 563
APPELFELD, AHARON
  Age of Wonders, The, 22
  Badenheim 1939, 101
  To the Land of the Cattails, 1581
  Tzili, 1630
ARDEN, JOHN
  Serjeant Musgrave's Dance, 1375
ARGUETA, MANLIO
  One Day of Life, 1148
ARLT, ROBERTO
  Seven Madmen, The, 1384
ARMAH, AYI KWEI
  Beautyful Ones Are Not Yet Born,
    The, 129
  Healers, The, 666
  Two Thousand Seasons, 1628
ARNOW, HARRIETTE
  Dollmaker, The, 414
ARRABAL, FERNANDO
  Architect and the Emperor of
    Assyria, The, 65
ARREOLA, JUAN JOSÉ
  Fair, The, 483
ARTAUD, ANTONIN
  Cenci, The, 249

ASCH, SHOLEM
  Nazarene, The, 1081
ASIMOV, ISAAC
  Foundation Trilogy, The, 536
ASTLEY, THEA
  Acolyte, The, 9
  Beachmasters, 126
ASTURIAS, MIGUEL ÁNGEL
  Men of Maize, 996
  Mulata, 1054
  Strong Wind, 1485
ATWOOD, MARGARET
  Edible Woman, The, 445
  Handmaid's Tale, The, 654
  Life Before Man, 885
  Surfacing, 1498
AUCHINCLOSS, LOUIS
  Embezzler, The, 452
  Rector of Justin, The, 1279
AUDEN, W. H., and
  CHRISTOPHER ISHERWOOD
  Dog Beneath the Skin, The, 410
AYCKBOURN, ALAN
  Absurd Person Singular, 4
  Norman Conquests, The, 1111

BAINBRIDGE, BERYL
  Harriet Said, 658
BALDWIN, JAMES
  Another Country, 55
  Blues for Mister Charlie, 179
  Giovanni's Room, 586
  If Beale Street Could Talk, 733
  Just Above My Head, 809
BALLARD, J. G.
  Crystal World, The, 355
  Empire of the Sun, 453
BALZAC, HONORÉ DE
  Louis Lambert, 922
  Quest of the Absolute, The, 1246
  Sarrasine, 1337
  Splendors and Miseries of
    Courtesans, The, 1463
BANVILLE, JOHN
  Doctor Copernicus, 409
  Kepler, 823
BARAKA, AMIRI
  Dutchman, 434
  System of Dante's Hell,
    The, 1510
BARKER, PAT
  Union Street, 1640
BARNES, DJUNA
  Nightwood, 1099
BARNES, JULIAN
  Flaubert's Parrot, 521
  Staring at the Sun, 1472
BARNES, PETER
  Ruling Class, The, 1322
BARNSLEY, ALAN GABRIEL.
  See FIELDING, GABRIEL
BAROJA, PÍO
  Tree of Knowledge, The, 1608

BARRY, PHILIP
Philadelphia Story, The, 1203
BARTH, JOHN
Floating Opera, The, 524
Giles Goat-Boy, 584
BASS, ROCHELLE. See OWENS, ROCHELLE
BASSANI, GIORGIO
Garden of the Finzi-Continis, The, 566
Gold-Rimmed Eyeglasses, The, 604
BATES, H. E.
Love for Lydia, 924
BECKER, JUREK
Sleepless Days, 1423
BECKETT, SAMUEL
All That Fall, 32
Company, 314
Embers, 451
Endgame, 458
Happy Days, 657
How It Is, 717
Ill Seen Ill Said, 738
Krapp's Last Tape, 841
Malone Dies, 951
Molloy, 1028
Murphy, 1059
Unnamable, The, 1643
Watt, 1694
Words and Music, 1745
BECKHAM, BARRY
Runner Mack, 1324
BEHAN, BRENDAN
Hostage, The, 700
Quare Fellow, The, 1241
BEHRMAN, S. N.
Second Man, The, 1364
BELLOW, SAUL
Dangling Man, 363
Dean's December, The, 375
Herzog, 677
Humboldt's Gift, 721
Mr. Sammler's Planet, 1020
Seize the Day, 1369
BELY, ANDREY
Petersburg, 1199
Silver Dove, The, 1413
BENET, JUAN
Meditation, A, 990
Return to Región, 1289
BERGER, JOHN
G., 560
Painter of Our Time, A, 1171
BERGER, THOMAS
Little Big Man, 893
BERNANOS, GEORGES
Mouchette, 1048
Under the Sun of Satan, 1634
BERNHARD, THOMAS
Concrete, 319
Correction, 338
Gargoyles, 568
Lime Works, The, 891
Untergeher, Der, 1644
Woodcutters, 1742
BETI, MONGO
Poor Christ of Bomba, The, 1219

BIENEK, HORST
Silesian Tetralogy, The, 1408
BIOY CASARES, ADOLFO
Diary of the War of the Pig, 399
Invention of Morel, The, 772
BIRNEY, EARLE
Turvey, 1623
BIYIDI, ALEXANDRE. See BETI, MONGO
BLAIR, ERIC ARTHUR.
See ORWELL, GEORGE
BÖLL, HEINRICH
Billiards at Half-Past Nine, 153
Clown, The, 300
Group Portrait with Lady, 641
Lost Honor of Katharina Blum, The, 919
Safety Net, The, 1326
BOLT, ROBERT
Man for All Seasons, A, 952
BOMBAL, MARÍA LUISA
Final Mist, The, 503
Shrouded Woman, The, 1397
BOND, EDWARD
Lear, 866
Saved, 1341
BONTEMPS, ARNA
Black Thunder, 164
BOWEN, ELIZABETH
Eva Trout, 470
Little Girls, The, 895
World of Love, A, 1753
BOWERING, GEORGE
Burning Water, 217
BOWLES, PAUL
Sheltering Sky, The, 1390
BOYD, MARTIN
Lucinda Brayford, 933
BRADBURY, MALCOLM
Eating People Is Wrong, 439
History Man, The, 680
Rates of Exchange, 1268
BRADBURY, RAY
Fahrenheit 451, 482
Martian Chronicles, The, 979
Something Wicked This Way Comes, 1441
BRADLEY, DAVID
Chaneysville Incident, The, 256
BRAUTIGAN, RICHARD
Confederate General from Big Sur, A, 321
In Watermelon Sugar, 754
Trout Fishing in America, 1619
BRECHT, BERTOLT
Caucasian Chalk Circle, The, 247
Galileo, 562
Good Woman of Setzuan, The, 615
Mother Courage and Her Children, 1046
Rise and Fall of the City of Mahagonny, 1298
Threepenny Opera, The, 1560
BRENTON, HOWARD
Bloody Poetry, 172

BRENTON, HOWARD, and DAVID HARE
Pravda, 1232
BRINK, ANDRÉ
Chain of Voices, A, 254
BROCH, HERMANN
Spell, The, 1460
BROOKNER, ANITA
Debut, The, 383
Hotel du Lac, 702
Look at Me, 912
BROWN, RITA MAE
Rubyfruit Jungle, 1318
BÜCHNER, GEORG
Lenz, 872
BUCKLER, ERNEST
Mountain and the Valley, The, 1051
BUECHNER, FREDERICK
Book of Bebb, The, 187
BUGAEV, BORIS NIKOLAYEVICH. See BELY, ANDREY
BULGAKOV, MIKHAIL
Days of the Turbins, 371
Heart of a Dog, The, 667
Master and Margarita, The, 984
BULLINS, ED
In the Wine Time, 753
BURGESS, ANTHONY
Clockwork Orange, A, 295
Earthly Powers, 437
End of the World News, The, 455
Napoleon Symphony, 1075
Nothing Like the Sun, 1116
Right to an Answer, The, 1295
Tremor of Intent, 1609
BURROUGHS, WILLIAM S.
Naked Lunch, 1071
BUTOR, MICHEL
Change of Heart, A, 257
Mobile, 1027
Niagara, 1089
Passing Time, 1183
BUZZATI, DINO
Barnabo of the Mountains, 117
Tartar Steppe, The, 1516
BYRNE, JOHN KEYES.
See LEONARD, HUGH

CABRERA INFANTE, GUILLERMO
Infante's Inferno, 760
Three Trapped Tigers, 1559
CALDWELL, ERSKINE
God's Little Acre, 603
CALLAGHAN, MORLEY
Loved and the Lost, The, 928
Passion in Rome, A, 1184
Such Is My Beloved, 1487
CALVINO, ITALO
Baron in the Trees, The, 119
Castle of Crossed Destinies, The, 240
Cloven Viscount, The, 299
If on a Winter's Night a Traveler, 736

Invisible Cities, 774
Mr. Palomar, 1020
Non-existent Knight, The, 1110
Path to the Nest of Spiders,
The, 1186
CAMUS, ALBERT
Caligula, 226
Possessed, The, 1227
CANETTI, ELIAS
Auto-da-Fé, 91
CAREY, PETER
Illywhacker, 739
CARPENTIER, ALEJO
Explosion in a Cathedral, 477
Kingdom of This World,
The, 834
Lost Steps, The, 921
Manhunt, 965
CARY, JOYCE
Second Trilogy, 1365
CASEY, JOHN. See O'CASEY,
SEAN
CATHER, WILLA
Lucy Gayheart, 936
One of Ours, 1154
Sapphira and the Slave
Girl, 1335
CÉLINE, LOUIS-FERDINAND
Castle to Castle, North, and
Rigadoon, 241
Death on the Installment
Plan, 380
CENDRARS, BLAISE
Sutter's Gold, 1500
CÉSAIRE, AIMÉ
Tragedy of King Christophe,
The, 1598
CHALLANS, MARY. See
RENAULT, MARY
CHANDLER, RAYMOND
Big Sleep, The, 151
Farewell, My Lovely, 493
Long Goodbye, The, 910
CHEEVER, JOHN
Bullet Park, 210
Falconer, 488
Oh What a Paradise It
Seems, 1134
CHEKHOV, ANTON
Duel, The, 428
Lady with the Dog, The, 846
Steppe, The, 1474
CHESNUTT, CHARLES
WADDELL
House Behind the Cedars,
The, 705
CHILDRESS, ALICE
Trouble in Mind, 1616
CHIN, FRANK
Chickencoop Chinaman,
The, 270
Year of the Dragon, The, 1761
CHOU SHU-JÊN. See LU HSÜN
CHRISTIE, AGATHA
Mousetrap, The, 1052
Murder of Roger Ackroyd,
The, 1056

CHURCHILL, CARYL
Cloud Nine, 297
Serious Money, 1374
Top Girls, 1591
CLARÍN. See ALAS, LEOPOLDO
CLARK, JOHN PEPPER
Song of a Goat, 1444
CLARKE, ARTHUR C.
Childhood's End, 272
2001: A Space Odyssey, 1627
CLARKE, AUSTIN
As the Crow Flies, 74
CLARKE, MARTHA
Garden of Earthly Delights,
The, 565
Vienna: Lusthaus, 1655
CLAUDEL, PAUL
Break of Noon, 199
Satin Slipper, The, 1338
Tidings Brought to Mary,
The, 1563
CLEMENS, SAMUEL
LANGHORNE. See TWAIN,
MARK
CLUTHA, JANET PATERSON
FRAME. See FRAME, JANET
COCTEAU, JEAN
Infernal Machine, The, 761
Orpheus, 1159
COETZEE, J. M.
Life & Times of Michael K, 884
Waiting for the Barbarians, 1671
COLETTE
Cat, The, 243
Chéri, and The Last of
Chéri, 264
Gigi, 582
Ripening Seed, The, 1297
Vagabond, The, 1649
COLUM, PADRAIC
Fiddler's House, The, 501
CONNELL, EVAN S., JR.
Mrs. Bridge, 1023
CONNELLY, MARC
Beggar on Horseback, 136
Green Pastures, The, 634
CONRAD, JOSEPH
Secret Sharer, The, 1368
Typhoon, 1629
COOVER, ROBERT
Universal Baseball Association,
Inc., J. Henry Waugh, Prop.,
The, 1642
CORNWELL, DAVID JOHN
MOORE. See LE CARRÉ,
JOHN
CORTÁZAR, JULIO
Hopscotch, 695
Manual for Manuel, A, 969
62: A Model Kit, 1420
Winners, The, 1726
COWARD, NOËL
Blithe Spirit, 169
Design for Living, 394
Private Lives, 1239
COX, WILLIAM TREVOR. See
TREVOR, WILLIAM

COZZENS, JAMES GOULD
By Love Possessed, 223
Morning, Noon, and Night, 1037
CRAMPTON, MARY. See PYM,
BARBARA
CRAYENCOUR, MARGUERITE
DE. See YOURCENAR,
MARGUERITE
CRICHTON, MICHAEL
Andromeda Strain, The, 44
CRONIN, A. J.
Citadel, The, 287
Keys of the Kingdom, The, 824
CROWLEY, MART
Boys in the Band, The, 197
CULLEN, COUNTEE
One Way to Heaven, 1155
CUNHA, EUCLIDES DA
Rebellion in the Backlands, 1276
CZACZKES, SHMUEL YOSEF. See
AGNON, SHMUEL YOSEF

DAVIES, ROBERTSON
Deptford Trilogy, The, 390
Rebel Angels, The, 1275
What's Bred in the Bone, 1708
DAZAI, OSAMU
No Longer Human, 1107
Setting Sun, The, 1379
DELANEY, SHELAGH
Taste of Honey, A, 1517
DELANY, SAMUEL R.
Babel-17, 99
Triton, 1614
DELBLANC, SVEN
Speranza, 1461
DeLILLO, DON
End Zone, 457
DEMBY, WILLIAM
Beetlecreek, 133
DESAI, ANITA
Clear Light of Day, 294
Fire on the Mountain, 509
DESTOUCHES, LOUIS-
FERDINAND. See CÉLINE,
LOUIS-FERDINAND
DE VRIES, PETER
Blood of the Lamb, The, 170
Tents of Wickedness, The, 1528
DIDEROT, DENIS
Jacques the Fatalist and His
Master, 785
DIDION, JOAN
Democracy, 387
Play It As It Lays, 1212
DÖBLIN, ALFRED
Berlin Alexanderplatz, 143
November 1918, 1117
DOCTOROW, E. L.
Ragtime, 1259
DODERER, HEIMITO VON
Demons, The, 389
Waterfalls of Slunj, The, 1689
DONLEAVY, J. P.
Ginger Man, The, 585

DONOSO, JOSÉ
Coronation, 337
Obscene Bird of Night,
The, 1125
Sacred Families, 1325
This Sunday, 1552
DOSTOEVSKI, FYODOR
Double, The, 419
House of the Dead, The, 711
Insulted and the Injured,
The, 767
Netochka Nezvanova, 1084
Raw Youth, A, 1271
DOUGLAS, ELLEN
Rock Cried Out, The, 1309
DOVLATOV, SERGEI
Compromise, The, 317
Zone, The, 1770
DRABBLE, MARGARET
Ice Age, The, 731
Middle Ground, The, 1005
Needle's Eye, The, 1083
Waterfall, The, 1688
DUNBAR, PAUL LAURENCE
Sport of the Gods, The, 1465
DUNN, ELSIE. See SCOTT,
EVELYN
DURANG, CHRISTOPHER
Sister Mary Ignatius Explains It
All for You, 1419
DURAS, MARGUERITE
Lover, The, 931
Ravishing of Lol Stein,
The, 1270
Sea Wall, The, 1355
DÜRRENMATT, FRIEDRICH
Physicists, The, 1206
Romulus the Great, 1310
Visit, The, 1659

EÇA DE QUEIRÓZ, JOSÉ MARIA
Cousin Bazilio, 348
ECHENOZ, JEAN
Cherokee, 265
ECO, UMBERTO
Name of the Rose, The, 1072
EDMONDS, HELEN WOODS.
See KAVAN, ANNA
EHRENBURG, ILYA
Thaw, The, 1533
EKWENSI, CYPRIAN
People of the City, 1192
ELIADE, MIRCEA
Forbidden Forest, The, 532
ELKIN, STANLEY
Franchiser, The, 543
ENCHI, FUMIKO
Masks, 983
ENDŌ, SHUSAKU
Samurai, The, 1332
Silence, 1405
When I Whistle, 1709
Wonderful Fool, 1740
ERDRICH, LOUISE
Love Medicine, 927

FAIRFIELD, CICILY ISABEL.
See WEST, REBECCA

FARRELL, J. G.
Siege of Krishnapur, The, 1401
Singapore Grip, The, 1416
Troubles, 1617
FAULKNER, WILLIAM
Mosquitoes, 1042
Pylon, 1239
Soldiers' Pay, 1437
FAUSET, JESSIE REDMON
Plum Bun, 1215
FERMOR, PATRICK LEIGH
Violins of Saint-Jacques,
The, 1656
FIELDING, GABRIEL
Birthday King, The, 158
In the Time of Greenbloom, 751
FIERSTEIN, HARVEY
Torch Song Trilogy, 1592
FIGES, EVA
Light, 890
Seven Ages, The, 1381
FINDLEY, TIMOTHY
Wars, The, 1683
FISHER, DOROTHY CANFIELD
Home-maker, The, 686
FITZGERALD, F. SCOTT
Beautiful and Damned, The, 127
This Side of Paradise, 1550
FITZGERALD, ZELDA
Save Me the Waltz, 1340
FO, DARIO
Accidental Death of an
Anarchist, 8
FORD, FORD MADOX
Good Soldier, The, 613
FORREST, LEON
There Is a Tree More Ancient
Than Eden, 1538
FORSTER, E. M.
Maurice, 989
FOWLES, JOHN
Collector, The, 307
Daniel Martin, 364
Ebony Tower, The, 440
French Lieutenant's Woman,
The, 546
Magus, The, 945
FRAME, JANET
Intensive Care, 769
FRANCIS, DICK
Bonecrack, 186
FRANKLIN, MILES
My Brilliant Career, 1060
FRAYN, MICHAEL
Benefactors, 142
FRENCH, MARILYN
Women's Room, The, 1737
FRIEL, BRIAN
Freedom of the City, The, 545
Philadelphia, Here I
Come!, 1202
Translations, 1600
Volunteers, 1665
FRISCH, MAX
Andorra, 43
Bluebeard, 178

Chinese Wall, The, 280
Firebugs, The, 510
Homo Faber, 692
I'm Not Stiller, 740
Man in the Holocene, 954
FUENTES, CARLOS
Aura, 90
Change of Skin, A, 259
Distant Relations, 406
Good Conscience, The, 610
Holy Place, 684
Terra Nostra, 1530
FUGARD, ATHOL
Blood Knot, The, 169
Boesman and Lena, 183
Lesson from Aloes, A, 875
"MASTER HAROLD" . . . and
the boys, 986
Road to Mecca, The, 1303

GADDA, CARLO EMILIO
Acquainted with Grief, 10
That Awful Mess on Via
Merulana, 1532
GADDIS, WILLIAM
Recognitions, The, 1277
GAINES, ERNEST J.
Autobiography of Miss Jane
Pittman, The, 93
GARCÍA MÁRQUEZ, GABRIEL
Autumn of the Patriarch,
The, 95
Chronicle of a Death
Foretold, 284
Leaf Storm, 864
No One Writes to the
Colonel, 1108
One Hundred Years of
Solitude, 1150
GARDAM, JANE
Crusoe's Daughter, 352
God on the Rocks, 600
GARDNER, JOHN
Grendel, 637
King's Indian, The, 835
Mickelsson's Ghosts, 1001
Nickel Mountain, 1091
October Light, 1127
Sunlight Dialogues, The, 1495
Wreckage of Agathon, The, 1758
GARNER, HELEN
Monkey Grip, 1030
GARRETT, GEORGE
Death of the Fox, 379
GASS, WILLIAM H.
Omensetter's Luck, 1140
GELBER, JACK
Connection, The, 330
GENET, JEAN
Balcony, The, 103
Blacks, The, 167
Deathwatch, 382
Maids, The, 946
Miracle of the Rose, 1013
Our Lady of the Flowers, 1164
Screens, The, 1352
GIBBON, LEWIS GRASSIC
Scots Quair, A, 1349

GIBSON, WILLIAM
  Miracle Worker, The, 1015
  Two for the Seesaw, 1625
GIDE, ANDRÉ
  Immoralist, The, 743
  Lafcadio's Adventures, 847
  Strait Is the Gate, 1477
GILMAN, CHARLOTTE PERKINS
  Herland, 676
GILROY, FRANK D.
  Subject Was Roses, The, 1486
GINZBURG, NATALIA
  All Our Yesterdays, 31
  City and the House, The, 289
GIONO, JEAN
  Blue Boy, 175
  Horseman on the Roof, The, 699
  Joy of Man's Desiring, 802
GLASGOW, ELLEN
  Vein of Iron, 1651
GLASS, PHILIP, and ROBERT
  WILSON
  Einstein on the Beach, 449
GODWIN, GAIL
  Mother and Two Daughters,
  A, 1043
  Odd Woman, The, 1131
GOGGAN, JOHN PATRICK.
  See PATRICK, JOHN
GÖKÇELI, YAŞAR KEMAL.
  See KEMAL, YASHAR
GOLDEMBERG, ISAAC
  Fragmented Life of Don Jacobo
  Lerner, The, 542
GOLDING, WILLIAM
  Darkness Visible, 367
  Paper Men, The, 1175
  Pincher Martin, 1208
  Rites of Passage, 1299
  Spire, The, 1462
GOMBROWICZ, WITOLD
  Cosmos, 340
  Ferdydurke, 499
  Ivona, Princess of
  Burgundia, 782
  Marriage, The, 977
  Operetta, 1156
  Pornografia, 1221
GORDIMER, NADINE
  Burger's Daughter, 212
  Conservationist, The, 331
  July's People, 807
  Occasion for Loving, 1126
  World of Strangers, A, 1754
GORDON, MARY
  Company of Women, The, 316
  Final Payments, 504
GOYTISOLO, JUAN
  Marks of Identity, Count Julian,
  and Juan the Landless, 974
GRASS, GÜNTER
  Dog Years, 412
  Flounder, The, 525
  Headbirths, 665
  Local Anaesthetic, 902
  Meeting at Telgte, The, 991
  Rat, The, 1266

GRAU, SHIRLEY ANN
  Keepers of the House, The, 822
GRAVES, ROBERT
  King Jesus, 830
GRAY, ALASDAIR
  Lanark, 850
GRAY, SIMON
  Butley, 222
  Otherwise Engaged, 1161
GREEN, HANNAH
  I Never Promised You a Rose
  Garden, 728
GREEN, HENRY
  Caught, 248
  Concluding, 318
  Living, 899
  Nothing, 1114
  Party Going, 1179
GREENBERG, JOANNE.
  See GREEN, HANNAH
GREENE, GRAHAM
  Brighton Rock, 206
  Comedians, The, 311
  End of the Affair, The, 454
  Honorary Consul, The, 693
  Potting Shed, The, 1228
  Quiet American, The, 1252
GREGORY, ANDRÉ, and
  WALLACE SHAWN
  My Dinner with André, 1061
GREGORY, LADY AUGUSTA
  Grania, 622
  Workhouse Ward, The, 1748
GREKOVA, I.
  Ladies' Hairdresser, 841
GREVE, FELIX PAUL. See
  GROVE, FREDERICK PHILIP
GROVE, FREDERICK PHILIP
  Fruits of the Earth, 554
  Master of the Mill, The, 987
  Search for America, A, 1356
  Settlers of the Marsh, 1380
GRUŠA, JIŘÍ
  Questionnaire, The, 1249
GUARE, JOHN
  House of Blue Leaves, The, 710
  Lydie Breeze, 938
GURNEY, A. R., JR.
  Dining Room, The, 402
  Scenes from American
  Life, 1345
GUSTAFSSON, LARS
  Death of a Beekeeper, The, 378
  Sigismund, 1403
  Tennis Players, The, 1525
GUTHRIE, A. B., JR.
  These Thousand Hills, 1541
  Way West, The, 1698
HAKIM, TAWFIQ AL-
  Tree Climber, The, 1607
  Voyage to Tomorrow, 1669
HAMSUN, KNUT
  Mysteries, 1068
  Pan, 1172
  Victoria, 1655
  Women at the Pump, The, 1733
HANDKE, PETER
  Across, 11
  Goalie's Anxiety at the Penalty
  Kick, The, 598

  Kaspar, 816
  Left-Handed Woman, The, 870
  Moment of True Feeling,
  A, 1029
  Offending the Audience, 1132
  Ride Across Lake Constance,
  The, 1292
  Short Letter, Long
  Farewell, 1395
  Slow Homecoming, 1425
  Sorrow Beyond Dreams, A, 1448
HANLEY, JAMES
  Dream Journey, A, 423
HANSBERRY, LORRAINE
  Raisin in the Sun, A, 1262
  Sign in Sidney Brustein's Window,
  The, 1404
HARE, DAVID
  Plenty, 1213
HARE, DAVID, and HOWARD
  BRENTON
  Pravda, 1232
HARRIS, MARK
  Bang the Drum Slowly, 112
  Southpaw, The, 1455
HARRIS, WILSON
  Guyana Quartet, The, 646
HART, MOSS, and GEORGE S.
  KAUFMAN
  Man Who Came to Dinner,
  The, 954
  Once in a Lifetime, 1145
  You Can't Take It with You, 1764
HARTLEY, L. P.
  Go-Between, The, 597
HAVEL, VÁCLAV
  Garden Party, The, 567
  Increased Difficulty of
  Concentration, The, 757
  Largo Desolato, 851
  Memorandum, The, 995
  Temptation, 1523
HAXTON, JOSEPHINE.
  See DOUGLAS, ELLEN
HEAD, BESSIE
  Maru, 980
  Question of Power, A, 1247
HEATH, ROY A. K.
  Murderer, The, 1057
HEINLEIN, ROBERT A.
  Moon Is a Harsh Mistress,
  The, 1036
  Stranger in a Strange Land, 1478
HELLER, JOSEPH
  Something Happened, 1440
HELLMAN, LILLIAN
  Children's Hour, The, 279
  Watch on the Rhine, 1684
HEMINGWAY, ERNEST
  Across the River and into the
  Trees, 11
  Islands in the Stream, 780
  To Have and Have Not, 1577
  Torrents of Spring, The, 1593
HENLEY, BETH
  Crimes of the Heart, 350
HERBERT, FRANK
  Dune Trilogy, The, 430

HERBERT, XAVIER
  Capricornia, 234
HERSEY, JOHN
  Call, The, 227
  Wall, The, 1674
HESSE, HERMANN
  Demian, 386
  Glass Bead Game, The, 592
  Klingsor's Last Summer, 839
  Narcissus and Goldmund, 1077
  Rosshalde, 1314
  Siddhartha, 1400
HIGHWATER, JAMAKE
  Journey to the Sky, 801
HILDESHEIMER, WOLFGANG
  Marbot, 973
HIMES, CHESTER
  If He Hollers Let Him Go, 734
HIRAOKA, KIMITAKE.
  See MISHIMA, YUKIO
HIRAYAMA TŌGO. See IHARA,
  SAIKAKU
HOCHHUTH, ROLF
  Deputy, The, 393
HOFFMANN, E. T. A.
  Life and Opinions of Kater Murr,
  The, 883
HOSPITAL, JANETTE TURNER
  Borderline, 193
  Ivory Swing, The, 784
HRABAL, BOHUMIL
  Closely Watched Trains, 296
HUGHES, LANGSTON
  Not Without Laughter, 1113
HULME, KERI
  Bone People, The, 185
HURSTON, ZORA NEALE
  Moses, 1041
  Their Eyes Were Watching
  God, 1534
HUXLEY, ALDOUS
  After Many a Summer Dies the
  Swan, 17
  Eyeless in Gaza, 480

IHARA, SAIKAKU
  Life of an Amorous Man,
  The, 888
INGALLS, RACHEL
  Mrs. Caliban, 1024
INGE, WILLIAM
  Bus Stop, 221
  Come Back, Little Sheba, 310
  Picnic, 1207
INNAURATO, ALBERT
  Transfiguration of Benno Blimpie,
  The, 1599
IONESCO, EUGÈNE
  Bald Soprano, The, 105
  Chairs, The, 255
  Exit the King, 475
  Killer, The, 827
  Lesson, The, 875
IRVING, JOHN
  Hotel New Hampshire, The, 703
  Setting Free the Bears, 1378
  World According to Garp,
  The, 1749

ISHERWOOD, CHRISTOPHER,
  and W. H. AUDEN
  Dog Beneath the Skin, The, 410

JACOBSON, DAN
  Dance in the Sun, A, 361
  Wonder-Worker, The, 1738
JAMES, C. L. R.
  Minty Alley, 1012
JAMES, HENRY
  Aspern Papers, The, 77
JARRY, ALFRED
  Ubu Roi, 1631
JEAN PAUL
  Titan, 1574
JHABVALA, RUTH PRAWER
  Esmond in India, 468
  Heat and Dust, 671
  Householder, The, 716
JOHNSON, CHARLES
  (RICHARD)
  Faith and the Good Thing, 487
JOHNSON, JAMES WELDON
  Autobiography of an Ex-Coloured
  Man, The, 92
JOHNSON, UWE
  Anniversaries, 53
JOHNSTON, MARY
  To Have and to Hold, 1578
JOLLEY, ELIZABETH
  Miss Peabody's Inheritance, 1016
  Well, The, 1703
JONES, EVERETT LEROI.
  See BARAKA, AMIRI
JONES, GAYL
  Corregidora, 339
  Eva's Man, 471
JONES, JAMES
  From Here to Eternity, 551
  Thin Red Line, The, 1542
JONES, PRESTON
  Last Meeting of the Knights of the
  White Magnolia, The, 854
  Lu Ann Hampton Laverty
  Oberlander, 932
  Oldest Living Graduate,
  The, 1139
JOYCE, JAMES
  Dead, The, 372

KAFKA, FRANZ
  Amerika, 40
  Metamorphosis, The, 999
KANE, CHEIKH HAMIDOU
  Ambiguous Adventure, 34
KANTOR, TADEUSZ
  Dead Class, The, 373
  Wielopole/Wielopole, 1717
KAUFMAN, GEORGE S., and
  MOSS HART
  Man Who Came to Dinner,
  The, 954
  Once in a Lifetime, 1145
  You Can't Take It with You, 1764
KAVAN, ANNA
  Ice, 730

KAWABATA, YASUNARI
  Beauty and Sadness, 128
  House of the Sleeping Beauties,
  The, 712
  Master of Go, The, 986
  Snow Country, 1433
  Sound of the Mountain,
  The, 1450
  Thousand Cranes, 1554
KAZANTZAKIS, NIKOS
  Last Temptation of Christ,
  The, 859
KELLEY, EDITH SUMMERS
  Weeds, 1702
KELLEY, WILLIAM MELVIN
  Different Drummer, A, 400
KELLOGG, MARJORIE
  Tell Me That You Love Me, Junie
  Moon, 1520
KEMAL, YASHAR
  Memed, My Hawk, 993
  Wind from the Plain, The; Iron
  Earth, Copper Sky; and The
  Undying Grass, 1718
KENEALLY, THOMAS
  Chant of Jimmie Blacksmith,
  The, 262
  Confederates, 322
  Gossip from the Forest, 621
  Survivor, The, 1499
KENNEDY, ADRIENNE
  Funnyhouse of a Negro, 558
  Rat's Mass, A, 1269
KENNEDY, WILLIAM
  Billy Phelan's Greatest
  Game, 154
  Ironweed, 776
  Legs, 871
KEROUAC, JACK
  Dharma Bums, The, 397
  On the Road, 1145
KESEY, KEN
  One Flew over the Cuckoo's
  Nest, 1149
  Sometimes a Great Notion, 1442
KIELY, BENEDICT
  Captain with the Whiskers,
  The, 237
  Nothing Happens in
  Carmincross, 1115
KIMITAKE HIRAOKA.
  See MISHIMA, YUKIO
KING, FRANCIS
  Custom House, The, 357
KING, STEPHEN
  Shining, The, 1393
  Stand, The, 1470
KIPLING, RUDYARD
  Man Who Would Be King,
  The, 960
KIRKLAND, JACK
  Tobacco Road, 1582
KIŠ, DANILO
  Garden, Ashes, 564
  Peščanik, 1197
  Tomb for Boris Davidovich,
  A, 1586
KLEIST, HEINRICH VON
  Marquise of O——, The, 976

KLIMENTOV, ANDREI
PLATONOVICH. *See*
PLATONOV, ANDREI

KNOWLES, JOHN
Separate Peace, A, 1373

KOCH, C. J.
Year of Living Dangerously,
The, 1760

KONRÁD, GEORGE
City Builder, The, 292
Loser, The, 915

KONWICKI, TADEUSZ
Dreambook for Our Time,
A, 426
Minor Apocalypse, A, 1011
Moonrise, Moonset, 1037
Polish Complex, The, 1218

KOPIT, ARTHUR
Indians, 759
Wings, 1725

KOPS, BERNARD
Ezra, 481
Hamlet of Stepney Green,
The, 653

KORZENIOWSKI, JOSEF
TEODOR KONRAD.
See CONRAD, JOSEPH

KOSINSKI, JERZY
Painted Bird, The, 1170

KUNDERA, MILAN
Book of Laughter and Forgetting,
The, 190
Farewell Party, The, 494
Joke, The, 795
Life Is Elsewhere, 886
Unbearable Lightness of Being,
The, 1633

LA FARGE, OLIVER
Laughing Boy, 860

LAGERKVIST, PÄR
Dwarf, The, 435
Sibyl, The, 1399
Tobias Trilogy, The, 1583

LA GUMA, ALEX
Walk in the Night, A, 1672

LAMMING, GEORGE
In the Castle of My Skin, 747
Natives of My Person, 1078
Season of Adventure, 1360

LAO SHE
Rickshaw, 1291

LARKIN, PHILIP
Girl in Winter, A, 589
Jill, 790

LARSEN, NELLA
Passing, 1182
Quicksand, 1250

LAURENCE, MARGARET
Diviners, The, 407
Fire-Dwellers, The, 506
Stone Angel, The, 1475

LAWLER, RAY
Summer of the Seventeenth
Doll, 1493

LAWRENCE, D. H.
Aaron's Rod, 1
Fox, The, 541
Kangaroo, 812
Lady Chatterley's Lover, 842
Virgin and the Gipsy, The, 1658

LAYE, CAMARA
Dark Child, The, 366
Guardian of the Word, The, 643
Radiance of the King, The, 1258

LE CARRÉ, JOHN
Honourable Schoolboy, The;
Tinker, Tailor, Soldier Spy; *and*
Smiley's People, 694
Perfect Spy, A, 1194
Spy Who Came in from the Cold,
The, 1469

LEE, HARPER
To Kill a Mockingbird, 1580

LE GUIN, URSULA K.
Dispossessed, The, 405
Left Hand of Darkness,
The, 869

LEHMANN, ROSAMOND
Dusty Answer, 433
Echoing Grove, The, 442
Weather in the Streets, The, 1701

LEM, STANISŁAW
Chain of Chance, The, 253
Fiasco, 500
His Master's Voice, 678
Investigation, The, 773
Invincible, The, 774
Solaris, 1435

LEONARD, HUGH
Da, 360
Life, A, 880

LESKOV, NIKOLAI
Lady Macbeth of the Mtsensk
District, 844

LESSING, DORIS
Children of Violence, 275
Golden Notebook, The, 605
Good Terrorist, The, 614
Shikasta, 1391

LEVI, CARLO
Christ Stopped at Eboli, 283

LEVI, PRIMO
If Not Now, When?, 735
Monkey's Wrench, The, 1032

LEWIS, C. S.
Space Trilogy, The, 1456
Till We Have Faces, 1565

LEWIS, WYNDHAM
Apes of God, The, 59
Human Age, The, 718
Revenge for Love, The, 1290
Self Condemned, 1371
Snooty Baronet, 1432

LEZAMA LIMA, JOSÉ
Paradiso, 1176

LINNEY, ROMULUS
Childe Byron, 271
Holy Ghosts, 683
Sand Mountain, 1333

LINS, OSMAN
Avalovara, 97

LISPECTOR, CLARICE
Apple in the Dark, The, 62

LIU E
Travels of Lao Ts'an, The, 1604

LIU T'IEH-YUN. *See* LIU E

LODGE, DAVID
Changing Places, 260
Small World, 1429
Souls and Bodies, 1448

LOVELACE, EARL
Dragon Can't Dance, The, 421
Wine of Astonishment,
The, 1723

LOWRY, MALCOLM
Ultramarine, 1632

LOYOLA BRANDÃO, IGNÁCIO
DE
Zero, 1769

LU HSÜN
True Story of Ah Q, The, 1620

LURIE, ALISON
War Between the Tates,
The, 1681

MACAULAY, ROSE
Told by an Idiot, 1585
Towers of Trebizond, The, 1596
World My Wilderness, The, 1752

McCARTHY, CORMAC
Outer Dark, 1166
Suttree, 1501

McCARTHY, MARY
Group, The, 638

McCULLERS, CARSON
Ballad of the Sad Café, The, 109
Member of the Wedding,
The, 992

MACDONALD, ROSS
Goodbye Look, The, 616
Underground Man, The, 1636

McELROY, JOSEPH
Lookout Cartridge, 914

McGAHERN, JOHN
Barracks, The, 121
Pornographer, The, 1222

McGINLEY, PATRICK
Bogmail, 184
Trick of the Ga Bolga, The, 1612

McGUANE, THOMAS
Ninety-two in the Shade, 1102
Sporting Club, The, 1466

McKAY, CLAUDE
Banana Bottom, 110
Banjo, 113
Home to Harlem, 687

MacLEISH, ARCHIBALD
J. B., 788

MacLENNAN, HUGH
Barometer Rising, 118
Two Solitudes, 1625
Voices in Time, 1663
Watch That Ends the Night,
The, 1685

McMURTRY, LARRY
Last Picture Show, The, 858
Terms of Endearment, 1529

McNALLY, TERRENCE
Where Has Tommy Flowers
Gone?, 1711
MADDEN, DAVID
Suicide's Wife, The, 1489
MAETERLINCK, MAURICE
Blue Bird, The, 173
MAILER, NORMAN
American Dream, An, 38
Armies of the Night, The, 65
Executioner's Song, The, 474
Naked and the Dead, The, 1070
MALAMUD, BERNARD
Assistant, The, 78
Fixer, The, 519
Natural, The, 1080
New Life, A, 1088
MALLEA, EDUARDO
All Green Shall Perish, 26
MALLOWAN, AGATHA MARY
CLARISSA. See CHRISTIE,
AGATHA
MALOUF, DAVID
Harland's Half Acre, 658
Imaginary Life, An, 742
MALRAUX, ANDRÉ
Man's Hope, 967
Royal Way, The, 1317
MAMET, DAVID
American Buffalo, 37
Glengarry Glen Ross, 595
Sexual Perversity in
Chicago, 1386
Speed-the-Plow, 1458
Woods, The, 1743
MANN, THOMAS
Holy Sinner, The, 685
Joseph and His Brothers, 797
Transposed Heads, The, 1602
MANNING, FREDERIC
Her Privates, We, 675
MANNING, OLIVIA
Balkan Trilogy, The, 106
MARKANDAYA, KAMALA
Nectar in a Sieve, 1082
MARSHALL, PAULE
Praisesong for the Widow, 1230
MATTHIESSEN, PETER
At Play in the Fields of the
Lord, 81
Far Tortuga, 491
MAUGHAM, W. SOMERSET
Circle, The, 286
Razor's Edge, The, 1273
MAURIAC, FRANÇOIS
Lamb, The, 848
Vipers' Tangle, 1657
Woman of the Pharisees,
A, 1730
MAXIMOV, VLADIMIR
Farewell from Nowhere, 492
Seven Days of Creation,
The, 1383
MAYAKOVSKY, VLADIMIR
Bathhouse, The, 124
Bedbug, The, 132

MEDOFF, MARK
Children of a Lesser God, 274
When You Comin' Back, Red
Ryder?, 1710
MICHENER, JAMES A.
Hawaii, 661
Source, The, 1452
MILLAR, KENNETH. See
MACDONALD, ROSS
MILLER, ARTHUR
After the Fall, 20
All My Sons, 29
Crucible, The, 351
Incident at Vichy, 756
Price, The, 1233
MILLER, HENRY
Tropic of Cancer, 1615
MILLER, WALTER M., JR.
Canticle for Leibowitz, A, 233
MIŁOSZ, CZESŁAW
Issa Valley, The, 781
Seizure of Power, The, 1370
MISHIMA, YUKIO
After the Banquet, 19
Confessions of a Mask, 325
Sailor Who Fell from Grace with
the Sea, The, 1328
Sea of Fertility, The, 1354
Temple of the Golden Pavilion,
The, 1522
MITCHELL, JAMES LESLIE. See
GIBBON, LEWIS GRASSIC
MITCHELL, W. O.
Who Has Seen the Wind, 1712
MITTELHOLZER, EDGAR
Kaywana Trilogy, The, 817
MO, TIMOTHY
Insular Possession, An, 766
Sour Sweet, 1451
MOMADAY, N. SCOTT
House Made of Dawn, 707
MOORE, BRIAN
Black Robe, 163
Lonely Passion of Judith Hearne,
The, 907
Luck of Ginger Coffey, The, 935
MORANTE, ELSA
Arturo's Island, 70
History, 679
MORAVIA, ALBERTO
Conformist, The, 329
Ghost at Noon, A, 578
1934, 1101
Time of Indifference, The, 1568
MORRIS, WRIGHT
Fork River Space Project,
The, 534
Plains Song, for Female
Voices, 1210
Works of Love, The, 1749
MORRISON, TONI
Bluest Eye, The, 180
Song of Solomon, 1445
Sula, 1490
MORTIMER, JOHN
Voyage Round My Father,
A, 1668

MPHAHLELE, EZEKIEL
Wanderers, The, 1677
MROŻEK, SŁAWOMIR
Police, The, 1217
Tango, 1515
MUNIF, ABDELRAHMAN
Cities of Salt, 287
MUNRO, ALICE
Lives of Girls and Women, 898
MURDOCH, IRIS
Black Prince, The, 162
Bruno's Dream, 208
Fairly Honourable Defeat,
A, 485
Good Apprentice, The, 608
Nuns and Soldiers, 1120
Sandcastle, The, 1334
Severed Head, A, 1385
Unicorn, The, 1639
Word Child, A, 1744
MUSIL, ROBERT
Man Without Qualities,
The, 962
Young Törless, 1766

NABOKOV, VLADIMIR
Ada or Ardor, 12
Bend Sinister, 141
Defense, The, 384
Gift, The, 581
Invitation to a Beheading, 775
Laughter in the Dark, 861
Lolita, 904
Mary, 981
Pnin, 1216
NAIPAUL, SHIVA
Fireflies, 511
NAIPAUL, V. S.
Bend in the River, A, 139
Guerrillas, 644
House for Mr. Biswas, A, 706
In a Free State, 744
Miguel Street, 1008
Mimic Men, The, 1010
Mr. Stone and the Knights
Companion, 1022
NARAYAN, R. K.
Financial Expert, The, 505
Grateful to Life and Death, 623
Printer of Malgudi, The, 1236
Vendor of Sweets, The, 1653
NATSUME, SŌSEKI
Botchan, 196
I Am a Cat, 724
Three-Cornered World,
The, 1555
NAYLOR, GLORIA
Women of Brewster Place,
The, 1734
NGUGI, JAMES. See NGUGI WA
THIONG'O
NGUGI WA THIONG'O
Black Hermit, The, 160
Petals of Blood, 1198
River Between, The, 1300
NGUGI WA THIONG'O and
NGUGI WA MIRII
I Will Marry When I Want, 729

NICHOLS, PETER
Day in the Death of Joe Egg,
A, 370
Passion Play, 1185
NIIHARA, RYŪNOSUKE. See
AKUTAGAWA, RYŪNOSUKE
NIN, ANAÏS
Spy in the House of Love,
A, 1468
NORMAN, MARSHA
Getting Out, 577
'night, Mother, 1095
Third and Oak: The
Laundromat, 1546
NORRIS, FRANK
Octopus, The, 1129

OATES, JOYCE CAROL
Bellefleur, 138
Bloodsmoor Romance, A, 171
them, 1535
Unholy Loves, 1637
Wonderland, 1741
O'BRIEN, EDNA
Country Girls Trilogy, The, 341
Night, 1092
Pagan Place, A, 1169
O'BRIEN, FLANN
At Swim-Two-Birds, 82
Third Policeman, The, 1548
O'CASEY, SEAN
Cock-a-Doodle Dandy, 301
Red Roses for Me, 1282
Shadow of a Gunman, The, 1387
Silver Tassie, The, 1413
ODETS, CLIFFORD
Awake and Sing!, 98
Big Knife, The, 150
Flowering Peach, The, 527
ŌE, KENZABURŌ
Personal Matter, A, 1197
Silent Cry, The, 1407
O'HARA, JOHN
From the Terrace, 552
Ten North Frederick, 1524
OLESHA, YURY
Envy, 463
OLSEN, TILLIE
Yonnondio, 1763
O'NEILL, EUGENE
All God's Chillun Got
Wings, 26
Great God Brown, The, 628
Hairy Ape, The, 651
Iceman Cometh, The, 732
Lazarus Laughed, 863
Long Day's Journey into
Night, 908
Moon for the Misbegotten,
A, 1035
ONETTI, JUAN CARLOS
Brief Life, A, 201
Shipyard, The, 1394
O'NOLAN, BRIAN. See O'BRIEN,
FLANN
ORTON, JOE
Entertaining Mr. Sloane, 462
Loot, 915
What the Butler Saw, 1707

ORWELL, GEORGE
Animal Farm, 51
Burmese Days, 214
Coming Up for Air, 314
Keep the Aspidistra Flying, 820
OSBORNE, JOHN
Entertainer, The, 461
Inadmissible Evidence, 755
Luther, 937
OWENS, ROCHELLE
Karl Marx Play, The, 815
OZ, AMOS
Elsewhere, Perhaps, 450
My Michael, 1065
Perfect Peace, A, 1193

PALMER, VANCE
Passage, The, 1180
PATRICK, JOHN
Hasty Heart, The, 660
Teahouse of the August Moon,
The, 1519
PAVESE, CESARE
Among Women Only, 41
House on the Hill, The, 715
Moon and the Bonfires,
The, 1034
PEAKE, MERVYN
Gormenghast Trilogy, The, 618
PEDERSEN, KNUT. See HAMSUN,
KNUT
PERCY, WALKER
Last Gentleman, The, 853
Love in the Ruins, 925
Moviegoer, The, 1053
Second Coming, The, 1363
PÉREZ GALDÓS, BENITO
Our Friend Manso, 1163
PIERCY, MARGE
Small Changes, 1426
Woman on the Edge of
Time, 1732
PINGET, ROBERT
Baga, 102
Inquisitory, The, 764
That Voice, 1532
PINTER, HAROLD
Betrayal, 145
Birthday Party, The, 159
Dumb Waiter, The, 429
Family Voices, 490
Homecoming, The, 688
Kind of Alaska, A, 829
PIRANDELLO, LUIGI
Each in His Own Way, 436
Henry IV, 674
Tonight We Improvise, 1588
PLATH, SYLVIA
Bell Jar, The, 137
PLATONOV, ANDREI
Chevengur, 266
Foundation Pit, The, 534
PORTER, HAL
Tilted Cross, The, 1566
POTOK, CHAIM
Book of Lights, The, 192
Chosen, The, and The
Promise, 281

In the Beginning, 746
My Name Is Asher Lev, 1067
POUND, EZRA (trans.)
Women of Trachis, 1736
POWELL, ANTHONY
Afternoon Men, 21
Agents and Patients, 23
Fisher King, The, 518
O, How the Wheel Becomes
It!, 1123
Venusberg, 1654
POWERS, J. F.
Morte d'Urban, 1040
PRICE, REYNOLDS
Generous Man, A, 574
PRICHARD, KATHARINE
SUSANNAH
Coonardoo, 335
PRIESTLEY, J. B.
Angel Pavement, 45
Eden End, 444
Inspector Calls, An, 765
Time and the Conways, 1567
PRITCHETT, V. S.
Dead Man Leading, 374
Mr. Beluncle, 1018
PROKOSCH, FREDERIC
Asiatics, The, 76
Missolonghi Manuscript,
The, 1018
PUIG, MANUEL
Betrayed by Rita Hayworth, 146
Heartbreak Tango, 670
Kiss of the Spider Woman, 837
PUSHKIN, ALEXANDER
Queen of Spades, The, 1244
PYM, BARBARA
Excellent Women, 473
Glass of Blessings, A, 594
Less than Angels, 873
Quartet in Autumn, 1243
Sweet Dove Died, The, 1507
PYNCHON, THOMAS
Crying of Lot 49, The, 354
Gravity's Rainbow, 624
V., 1646

QUEIROZ, RACHEL DE
Dôra, Doralina, 418
Three Marias, The, 1557
QUENEAU, RAYMOND
Bark Tree, The, 116
Sunday of Life, The, 1494
Zazie in the Metro, 1767

RAABE, WILHELM
Horacker, 697
Tubby Schaumann, 1622
RABE, DAVID
Basic Training of Pavlo Hummel,
The, 122
Hurlyburly, 723
Streamers, 1483
RAO, RAJA
Kanthapura, 813
Serpent and the Rope, The, 1377
RATTIGAN, TERENCE
Browning Version, The, 207
French Without Tears, 547

REANEY, JAMES
Colours in the Dark, 309
Killdeer, The, 825

REED, ISHMAEL
Flight to Canada, 522
Mumbo Jumbo, 1055
Yellow Back Radio Broke-
Down, 1762

REID, VICTOR STAFFORD
New Day, 1087

REIZENSTEIN, ELMER
LEOPOLD. See RICE, ELMER

RENAULT, MARY
Fire from Heaven, 508
Funeral Games, 557
King Must Die, The, and The Bull
from the Sea, 831
Persian Boy, The, 1195

RHYS, JEAN
Good Morning, Midnight, 612
Wide Sargasso Sea, 1714

RIBMAN, RONALD
Ceremony of Innocence,
The, 252
Cold Storage, 306

RICE, ELMER
Adding Machine, The, 14

RICHLER, MORDECAI
Apprenticeship of Duddy Kravitz,
The, 63
St. Urbain's Horseman, 1330

RICHTER, JOHANN PAUL
FRIEDRICH. See JEAN PAUL

ROA BASTOS, AUGUSTO
Son of Man, 1444

ROBBE-GRILLET, ALAIN
Erasers, The, 467
In the Labyrinth, 750
Jealousy, 790

ROBERTS, ELIZABETH MADOX
My Heart and My Flesh, 1062

ROGERS, SAMUEL SHEPARD.
See SHEPARD, SAM

ROMERO, JOSÉ RUBÉN
Futile Life of Pito Perez,
The, 559

ROOKE, LEON
Shakespeare's Dog, 1388

ROSS, SINCLAIR
As for Me and My House, 72
Sawbones Memorial, 1342

ROTH, JOSEPH
Job, 792

ROTH, PHILIP
Anatomy Lesson, The, 42
Ghost Writer, The, 580
Great American Novel, The, 626
Letting Go, 878
Portnoy's Complaint, 1224
Prague Orgy, The, 1229
Zuckerman Unbound, 1774

RUSHDIE, SALMAN
Midnight's Children, 1007
Shame, 1389

RUSHFORTH, PETER
Kindergarten, 829

RUSS, JOANNA
Female Man, The, 496

RYGA, GEORGE
Ecstasy of Rita Joe, The, 443

SÁBATO, ERNESTO
On Heroes and Tombs, 1142
Outsider, The, 1167

SACKLER, HOWARD
Great White Hope, The, 630

ST. OMER, GARTH
Room on the Hill, A, 1312

SAINZ, GUSTAVO
Gazapo, 572

SALINGER, J. D.
Catcher in the Rye, The, 244

SAMSONOV, LEV. See
MAXIMOV, VLADIMIR

SANDOZ, MARI
Cheyenne Autumn, 267

SARDUY, SEVERO
From Cuba with a Song, 550

SARGESON, FRANK
I for One . . ., 726
Joy of the Worm, 803

SAROYAN, WILLIAM
Time of Your Life, The, 1571

SARRAUTE, NATHALIE
"Fools Say", 530
Planetarium, The, 1211
Portrait of a Man
Unknown, 1226

SARTON, MAY
Mrs. Stevens Hears the Mermaids
Singing, 1025
Small Room, The, 1427

SARTRE, JEAN-PAUL
No Exit, 1103
Roads to Freedom, The, 1303

SAUSER, FRÉDÉRIC LOUIS. See
CENDRARS, BLAISE

SAYERS, DOROTHY L.
Gaudy Night, 571
Nine Tailors, The, 1100

SCHMITZ, ETTORE. See SVEVO,
ITALO

SCHNEIDER, PETER
Wall Jumper, The, 1676

SCHNITZLER, ARTHUR
Ronde, La, 1312

SCHWARZ-BART, ANDRÉ
Last of the Just, The, 856

SCIASCIA, LEONARDO
Equal Danger, 464
Man's Blessing, A, 966

SCOTT, EVELYN
Wave, The, 1695

SCOTT, PAUL
Raj Quartet, The, 1263

SELVON, SAMUEL
Brighter Sun, A, 203
Lonely Londoners, The, 905

SEMBÈNE, OUSMANE
God's Bits of Wood, 601
Xala, 1759

SEMPRUN, JORGE
Long Voyage, The, 911
What a Beautiful Sunday!, 1704

SETTLE, MARY LEE
Killing Ground, The, 827
Know Nothing, 839
O Beulah Land, 1122
Prisons, 1237
Scapegoat, The, 1343

SHAFFER, ANTHONY
Sleuth, 1424

SHAFFER, PETER
Amadeus, 33
Equus, 466
Royal Hunt of the Sun, The, 1316

SHANGE, NTOZAKE
for colored girls who have
considered suicide/when the
rainbow is enuf, 531
Photograph: Lovers in Motion,
A, 1204

SHAW, GEORGE BERNARD
Arms and the Man, 67
Heartbreak House, 669
John Bull's Other Island, 794
Mrs. Warren's Profession, 1026

SHAW, IRWIN
Young Lions, The, 1765

SHAWN, WALLACE
Aunt Dan and Lemon, 86

SHAWN, WALLACE, and ANDRÉ
GREGORY
My Dinner with André, 1061

SHEPARD, SAM
Buried Child, 213
Curse of the Starving Class, 356
Fool for Love, 529
Geography of a Horse
Dreamer, 577
Lie of the Mind, A, 879
Tooth of Crime, The, 1589
True West, 1621

SHERWOOD, ROBERT E.
Petrified Forest, The, 1200

SHKLOVSKY, VIKTOR
Sentimental Journey, A, 1372
Third Factory, 1546
Zoo, 1771

SHU CH'ING-CH'UN. See LAO
SHE

SILLITOE, ALAN
Down from the Hill, 420
Lost Flying Boat, The, 918
Saturday Night and Sunday
Morning, 1339
Widower's Son, The, 1715

SIMENON, GEORGES
Blue Room, The, 177
Man Who Watched the Trains Go
By, The, 959
Snow Was Black, The, 1434
Watchmaker of Everton,
The, 1686

SIMON, CLAUDE
Battle of Pharsalus, The, 125
Flanders Road, The, 520
Triptych, 1613
Wind, The, 1717

SIMON, NEIL
  Barefoot in the Park,   115
  Biloxi Blues,   155
  Brighton Beach Memoirs,   205
  Last of the Red-Hot Lovers,   857
  Odd Couple, The,   1130
SINCLAIR, MAY
  Mary Olivier,   982
  Three Sisters, The,   1558
SINGER, ISAAC BASHEVIS
  Enemies,   458
  Magician of Lublin, The,   944
  Shosha,   1396
  Slave, The,   1422
SINYAVSKY, ANDREI. See TERTZ,
  ABRAM
ŠKVORECKÝ, JOSEF
  Bass Saxophone, The,   123
  Cowards, The,   349
  Engineer of Human Souls,
  The,   460
SMEDLEY, AGNES
  Daughter of Earth,   368
SNOW, C. P.
  Strangers and Brothers,   1480
SOKOLOV, SASHA
  School for Fools, A,   1347
SOLZHENITSYN, ALEKSANDR
  August 1914,   84
  Cancer Ward,   228
  First Circle, The,   512
  Oktiabr shestnadtsatogo,   1135
  One Day in the Life of Ivan
  Denisovich,   1147
SOPHOCLES
  Women of Trachis,   1736
SOYINKA, WOLE
  Dance of the Forests, A,   362
  Death and the King's
  Horseman,   377
  Interpreters, The,   770
  Lion and the Jewel, The,   893
  Madmen and Specialists,   942
  Road, The,   1302
  Season of Anomy,   1362
SPARK, MURIEL
  Abbess of Crewe, The,   1
  Ballad of Peckham Rye,
  The,   108
  Comforters, The,   312
  Loitering with Intent,   903
  Mandelbaum Gate, The,   964
  Prime of Miss Jean Brodie,
  The,   1235
  Takeover, The,   1513
STALLINGS, LAURENCE, and
  MAXWELL ANDERSON
  What Price Glory?,   1706
STEAD, CHRISTINA
  House of All Nations,   708
  Little Hotel, The,   896
  Man Who Loved Children,
  The,   958
STEGNER, WALLACE
  Angle of Repose,   48
STEIN, GERTRUDE
  Making of Americans, The,   948
  Three Lives,   1555

STEINBECK, JOHN
  Cannery Row,   231
  Pearl, The,   1188
  Red Pony, The,   1281
  Tortilla Flat,   1595
STEINER, GEORGE
  Portage to San Cristóbal of A. H.,
  The,   1223
STIFTER, ADALBERT
  Indian Summer,   757
STONE, IRVING
  Agony and the Ecstasy, The,   24
STONE, ROBERT
  Dog Soldiers,   411
STOPPARD, TOM
  Dirty Linen and New-Found-
  Land,   404
  Hapgood,   656
  Jumpers,   808
  Night and Day,   1093
  Real Thing, The,   1274
  Rosencrantz and Guildenstern Are
  Dead,   1314
  Travesties,   1606
STOREY, DAVID
  Changing Room, The,   261
  Contractor, The,   333
  Radcliffe,   1257
  This Sporting Life,   1551
STOW, RANDOLPH
  Girl Green as Elderflower,
  The,   587
  Merry-Go-Round in the Sea,
  The,   998
  Visitants,   1661
STRAUSS, BOTHO
  Devotion,   396
STRAUSSLER, TOMAS.
  See STOPPARD, TOM
STRINDBERG, AUGUST
  Confession of a Fool, The,   324
  Dream Play, A,   425
  Ghost Sonata, The,   579
  Inferno,   762
  Natives of Hemsö, The,   1077
  Pelican, The,   1189
  Stormy Weather,   1476
STRUGATSKY, ARKADY, and
  BORIS STRUGATSKY
  Roadside Picnic,   1306
  Snail on the Slope, The,   1430
STYRON, WILLIAM
  Confessions of Nat Turner,
  The,   326
  Sophie's Choice,   1446
SVEVO, ITALO
  As a Man Grows Older,   71
  Confessions of Zeno,   328
SWIFT, GRAHAM
  Shuttlecock,   1398
  Waterland,   1691
SYNGE, JOHN MILLINGTON
  In the Shadow of the Glen,   750
  Riders to the Sea,   1294

TANIZAKI, JUN'ICHIRŌ
  Diary of a Mad Old Man,   398
  Makioka Sisters, The,   950

Naomi,   1074
  Secret History of the Lord of
  Musashi, The,   1367
  Some Prefer Nettles,   1439
TAYLOR, ELIZABETH
  Wreath of Roses, A,   1756
TAYLOR, KAMALA PURNAIYA.
  See MARKANDAYA,
  KAMALA
TERRY, MEGAN
  Keep Tightly Closed in a Cool
  Dry Place,   821
TERTZ, ABRAM
  Goodnight!,   617
  Makepeace Experiment,
  The,   947
  Trial Begins, The,   1610
THEROUX, PAUL
  Saint Jack,   1329
THURMAN, WALLACE
  Blacker the Berry, The,   166
TOLKIEN, J. R. R.
  Hobbit, The,   681
  Silmarillion, The,   1410
TOLSTOY, LEO
  Family Happiness,   489
  Hadji Murad,   649
  Raid, The,   1261
TOOLE, JOHN KENNEDY
  Confederacy of Dunces, A,   320
TOURNIER, MICHEL
  Friday,   548
  Gemini,   573
  Ogre, The,   1133
TRAVERSO, DINO BUZZATI.
  See BUZZATI, DINO
TREVOR, WILLIAM
  Boarding-House, The,   182
  Other People's Worlds,   1161
TRIFONOV, YURY
  Another Life,   57
  House on the Embankment,
  The,   713
  Old Man, The,   1138
TRILLING, LIONEL
  Middle of the Journey,
  The,   1006
TSUSHIMA SHŪJI'. See DAZAI,
  OSAMU
TURGENEV, IVAN
  Asya,   80
  First Love,   516
  On the Eve,   1143
  Rudin,   1319
  Torrents of Spring, The,   1594
TUTUOLA, AMOS
  My Life in the Bush of
  Ghosts,   1063
TWAIN, MARK
  Mysterious Stranger, The,   1069
TYLER, ANNE
  Dinner at the Homesick
  Restaurant,   403

UNAMUNO Y JUGO, MIGUEL
  DE
  Abel Sánchez,   3

Saint Manuel Bueno,
Martyr, 1329
UPDIKE, JOHN
Buchanan Dying, 209
Centaur, The, 250
Coup, The, 342
Couples, 345
Month of Sundays, A, 1033
Rabbit Is Rich, 1253
Rabbit Redux, 1254
Rabbit, Run, 1257
URIS, LEON
Exodus, 475

VALDEZ, LUIS MIGUEL
"I Don't Have to Show You No
Stinking Badges!", 726
Zoot Suit, 1773
VALENZUELA, LUISA
He Who Searches, 663
Lizard's Tail, The, 900
VAN ITALLIE, JEAN-CLAUDE
America Hurrah, 36
VARGAS LLOSA, MARIO
Aunt Julia and the
Scriptwriter, 87
Conversation in the
Cathedral, 334
Green House, The, 632
Time of the Hero, The, 1569
War of the End of the World,
The, 1682
VENTSEL, YELENA
SERGEYEVNA.
See GREKOVA, I.
VERNE, JULES
Around the World in Eighty
Days, 68
Journey to the Center of the
Earth, 800
VIDAL, GORE
Burr, 219
City and the Pillar, The, 291
1876, 446
Lincoln, 892
VITTORINI, ELIO
In Sicily, 745
Women of Messina, 1736
VOINOVICH, VLADIMIR
Life and Extraordinary
Adventures of Private Ivan
Chonkin, The, and Pretender to
the Throne, 881
VONNEGUT, KURT, JR.
Cat's Cradle, 246
God Bless You, Mr.
Rosewater, 599
Jailbird, 786
Mother Night, 1047
Sirens of Titan, The, 1418
Slaughterhouse-Five, 1421

WAGNER, JANE
Search for Signs of Intelligent Life
in the Universe, The, 1357
WAIN, JOHN
Born in Captivity, 194
Pardoner's Tale, The, 1178
Strike the Father Dead, 1484

WALCOTT, DEREK
Dream on Monkey
Mountain, 424
Pantomime, 1174
WALKER, ALICE
Color Purple, The, 308
Meridian, 997
Third Life of Grange Copeland,
The, 1547
WALKER, MARGARET
Jubilee, 806
WALSER, MARTIN
Letter to Lord Liszt, 876
Runaway Horse, 1323
Swan Villa, The, 1504
WARNER, REX
Aerodrome, The, 16
WASSERSTEIN, WENDY
Heidi Chronicles, The, 673
WATERS, FRANK
Man Who Killed the Deer,
The, 957
WAUGH, EVELYN
Black Mischief, 161
Loved One, The, 929
Sword of Honour, 1508
WEDEKIND, FRANK
Pandora's Box, 1173
WEISS, PETER
Marat/Sade, 971
WELDON, FAY
Female Friends, 495
WELTY, EUDORA
Losing Battles, 917
Optimist's Daughter, The, 1157
Robber Bridegroom, The, 1307
WESKER, ARNOLD
Chicken Soup with Barley, 269
Kitchen, The, 837
WEST, PAUL
Caliban's Filibuster, 225
Quality of Mercy, A, 1240
Rat Man of Paris, 1267
WEST, REBECCA
Birds Fall Down, The, 157
Fountain Overflows, The, 540
Return of the Soldier, The, 1288
WHARTON, EDITH
Valley of Decision, The, 1650
WHITE, PATRICK
Aunt's Story, The, 88
Eye of the Storm, The, 478
Ham Funeral, The, 652
Solid Mandala, The, 1438
Vivisector, The, 1662
Voss, 1666
WHITING, JOHN
Devils, The, 395
Penny for a Song, A, 1190
WIDEMAN, JOHN EDGAR
Glance Away, A, 591
Homewood Trilogy, The, 689
Hurry Home, 724
WIEBE, RUDY
Blue Mountains of China,
The, 176
Scorched-Wood People,
The, 1348

WIESEL, ELIE
Accident, The, 7
Beggar in Jerusalem, A, 135
Fifth Son, The, 502
Gates of the Forest, The, 570
Oath, The, 1124
WILDER, THORNTON
Eighth Day, The, 447
Matchmaker, The, 988
Theophilus North, 1536
WILLIAMS, DENIS
Other Leopards, 1160
WILLIAMS, ELLA GWENDOLEN
REES. See RHYS, JEAN
WILLIAMS, EMLYN
Corn Is Green, The, 336
Night Must Fall, 1096
WILLIAMS, JOHN A.
Captain Blackman, 236
Man Who Cried I Am, The, 956
WILLIAMS, PAULETTE. See
SHANGE, NTOZAKE
WILLIAMS, TENNESSEE
Night of the Iguana, The, 1097
Suddenly Last Summer, 1488
Summer and Smoke, 1492
Sweet Bird of Youth, 1505
Twenty-seven Wagons Full of
Cotton, 1624
WILLIAMS, THOMAS LANIER.
See WILLIAMS, TENNESSEE
WILLIAMSON, DAVID
Removalists, The, 1285
Travelling North, 1603
WILSON, A. N.
Gentlemen in England, 575
Wise Virgin, 1727
WILSON, ANGUS
Anglo-Saxon Attitudes, 49
Middle Age of Mrs. Eliot,
The, 1004
No Laughing Matter, 1104
WILSON, AUGUST
Fences, 498
Joe Turner's Come and
Gone, 793
Ma Rainey's Black Bottom, 939
WILSON, ETHEL
Equations of Love, The, 465
Love and Salt Water, 923
Swamp Angel, 1503
WILSON, JOHN ANTHONY
BURGESS. See BURGESS,
ANTHONY
WILSON, LANFORD
Angels Fall, 47
Hot l Baltimore, The, 701
Mound Builders, The, 1049
Rimers of Eldritch, The, 1296
Talley's Folly, 1514
WILSON, ROBERT
CIVIL warS, the, 293
WILSON, ROBERT, and PHILIP
GLASS
Einstein on the Beach, 449

AUTHOR INDEX

WITKIEWICZ, STANISŁAW
  IGNACY
  Cuttlefish, The, 359
  Madman and the Nun, The, 941
  Metaphysics of a Two-Headed
    Calf, 1000
  Water Hen, The, 1687
WODEHOUSE, P. G.
  Full Moon, 555
  Inimitable Jeeves, The, 763
  Leave It to Psmith, 868
WOIWODE, LARRY
  Beyond the Bedroom Wall, 147
  Firstborn, 517
  What I'm Going to Do, I
    Think, 1705
WOLF, CHRISTA
  Cassandra, 239

No Place on Earth, 1109
Patterns of Childhood, 1187
Quest for Christa T., The, 1245
WOOLF, VIRGINIA
  Jacob's Room, 785
  Night and Day, 1094
  Voyage Out, The, 1667
WOUK, HERMAN
  Caine Mutiny, The, 224
  War and Remembrance, 1678
  Winds of War, The, 1720
WRIGHT, RICHARD
  Lawd Today, 862
  Long Dream, The, 909
  Outsider, The, 1168

YÁÑEZ, AGUSTÍN
  Lean Lands, The, 865

YEATS, WILLIAM BUTLER
  Cathleen ni Houlihan, 245
  Words upon the Window-Pane,
    The, 1746
YEZIERSKA, ANZIA
  Bread Givers, 198
YORKE, HENRY VINCENT.
  See GREEN, HENRY
YOURCENAR, MARGUERITE
  Abyss, The, 5
  Coin in Nine Hands, A, 304
  Coup de Grâce, 344

ZAMYATIN, YEVGENY
  We, 1700
ZOLA, ÉMILE
  Thérèse Raquin, 1539

CHARACTER INDEX

☉, 97
A, 1029
A., Bruno, 22
A . . . , 790
A. J., 1072
Aafaa, 943
Aaron, 167, 636, 1042
Aaron, Jimmy, 93
Aaronow, George, 596
Aaronson, Michael, 965
Ababio, 666
Abakumov, Victor
    Semayonovich, 514
Abalos, Andrés, etc., 337
Abashwili, Georgi, etc., 248
Abba, 1066
Abbey-Chillard, Miss, 897
Abbot, 393
Abbot, Richard (Dick), 1115
Abbott, Sally Page and
    Horace, 1128
Abd Umer, 1454
Abdi Ağa, 994
Abdulla, 1199
Abdullah, Mrs., 1123
Abel, 97, 707, 1525
Abena, 1628
Abercrombie, Sir Ambrose, 930
Abershaw, "Abb," 1291
Abigail, Don, 484
Abigail, Mother, 1471
Ableukhov, Nikolai Apollonovich,
    etc., 1199
Abo, 1073
Abrahams, John, 1672
Abram, 648
Abramowitz, Miriam Brener, 542
Abrasha, 1125
Abs, Jakob, 55
Abulafia, Dr., 1455
Academician, 215
Acatov, Arcady Arcadievich, 1347
Acatova, Veta Arcadievna, 1347
Accacio, Councilor, 349
Acey, 1431
Achakka, 813
Achilles, 239, 1311
Achterhang, Lottchen, 698
Ackerman, Noah, 1765
Ackermann, Paul, 1298
Ackroyd, Roger, etc., 1056
Activist, 535
Actor, 871
Actor from Vienna
    Burgtheater, 1743
Actress, 1312
Ada, 13, 452
Ada, Augusta, 272
Ada, Aunt, 1340
Adair, Crazy Bow, 111
Adair, Robin, 302
Adam, 395, 565, 636
Adam, Father, 1463
Adam Omatangu, 309
Adams, George, 319
Adams, Henry and Beatrice
    Mark, 1324
Adams, Robin, 1180

Adamson, Grigory Borisovich, 515
Adcock, Sparks, 918
Addams, Frankie, etc., 992
Addie, 452
Adebhoy, David, 1756
Adeia, 557
Adela, 645
Adelaida, 865
Adelantado, El, 921
Adele, 244
Adelmo of Otranto, 1074
Adenebi, 363
Adey, Max, 1179
Adil Efendi, 1720
Adler, Wilhelm, etc., 1369
Adolescent, 1614
Adolfo, Don, 485
Adolph, Father, 1069
Adonis, Michael, 1672
Adrian, 1449
Adriana, 338
Adriansen, Simon and Martha, 6
Adso of Melk, 1073
Adult, 1425
Aeneus, 239
Aengus, Brother, 74
Aeore, 82
Aesop, 1173
Afanasievich, Sergei, 57
Affie, 1372
Aftercliffe, Private, 1376
Aga, Mirza, 1433
Agabus the Decapolitan, 831
Agamemnon, 239
Agar, Louise, 1727
Agatha, 688
Agathe, 963
Agathon, 1758
Agboreko, 362
Agent, 965
Agilulf, 1110
Aglaonice, 1159
Agnes, 385, 425, 1070, 1186
Agni, Roland, 627
Agnita, 1313
Agnus Angst, 1358
Agrippa, Uncle, 1736
Aguilar, General Rodrigo de, 96
Agustin, Don, 1290
Ah Q, 1620
Ahasuerus, 1400, 1583
Ahime, Pa, 1362
Ai, Genly, 869
Aide-De-Camp, 378
Aiden, Miss, 959
Aigeus, 833
Aiko, 1710
Aina, 1192
Ainger, Dr., 77
Air Vice-Marshal, 16
Airdale, Captain, 1624
Aithra, 833
Ajax, 1491
Ajibala, Nigel, 1375
Ajoa, 667
Akamas, 833
Akbar, Ali, 1433
Akimovich, Akim, 712

Akissi, 1259
Akiva, 476
Akoub, 289
Akuebue, Ogbuefi, 70
Akukalia, Okeke, 70
Alan, 198, 1468, 1516, 1592
Alanin, Ensign Anatol
    Ivanich, 1261
Alaskawolf Joe, 1299
Albano, 1574
Albert, 724, 1696
Albert, Heinrich, 992
Albert ——, Mr., 308
Alberte, 117
Alberto, 1165, 1398
Albine, 1576
Albino, 708
Albinus, Albert, etc., 861
Alchemist, 240
Alcide, 744
Aldo, 1460
Aldridge, Mrs., 1256
Alec, 773
Alectryon, 719
Alejandrina, 484
Alevtina, 1432
Alex, 295
Alexander, 594, 1076, 1386
Alexander, Alex, 1180
Alexander, Dr., 141
Alexander, Father, 215
Alexander, Gilbert, 591
Alexander, Hamish and
    Marion, 1755
Alexander, L. D., 855
Alexander of Macedon, 1196
Alexander the Great, 508, 557, 1196
Alexander III of Macedon, 508
Alexander IV, 557
Alexandra, 2
Alexandros, 965
Alexandrov, Leonid, 584
Alexandrovna, Marya
    "Masha," 489
Alexis, Grand Duke, 760
Alexis, Tsar, 1632
Aley, 711
Alf, 719
Alfonso, 472
Alfonso, Don, 484
Alfred, 232, 425, 500, 942, 1312
Alfreda, 252
Alfyorov, Aleksey Ivanovich, 981
Ali Akbar, 1433
Ali-Pasha, 196
Ali Safa Bey, 994
Alia, 431
Alice, 354, 1382, 1538
Alice, Lady, 1688
Alice, Miss, 1572
Alicia, 1398
Alicia, Aunt, 583
Alida, 254
Alik, 1562
Alikhanov, Boris, 1770
Alima, 676, 942, 1135
Alisa, 215
Aliyu, 1363

All Pure, The, 95
Allen, Lee, 1039
Allington, Maurice, etc., 633
Alma, 632
Aloetta, Moses, 905
Alphendéry, Michel, 708
Alphonse, 1268
Alphonso, 309
Alpine, Frank, 78
Alston, Theodosia Burr, 219
Alter, Rabbi (The Slaughterer), 749
Alter, Rabbi (The Teacher), 749
Aluísio, 1558
Alva, 166
Alvarado, Benedición, 95
Alvarez, Madame (Inez), 583
Alvarez, Miss Cleothilda, 422
Alvear, 969
Alya, 1771
Alyoshka the Baptist, 1147
Ama, 667
Amabel, 588, 1179
Amah Wu, 1620
Amalric, 200
Amanda, 568
Amanda, Miss, 1698
Amaranta, 1152
Amaranta Úrsula, 1153
Amberley, Mary, 480
Ambie, 1170
Ambleside, The Reverend Harry, 358
Ambrose, Helen, 1668
Amelia, 805, 895, 1134
Amelia, Lady, 1222
American Legion commander, 1202
Americans, 288
Ames, Harry, etc., 956
Ames, Lucy, 453
Amos, 415, 1034
Amparat, Alain, etc., 243
Amrit, 470
Amsel, Eddi, 413
Amsel, Isaac, 1224
Amundsen, Ellen, 1381
Amuri, Zaki, 1362
Amusa, Sergeant, 377
Amy, 1725
Amyntor, 834
Ana María, 1397
Anagnos, Mr., 1016
Anan, 666
Anarchist, 1219
Anastasia (Stacey), 584
Anatolyevna, Elizaveta, 231
Ancestor, The Chief, 1064
Anchises, 239
Andersen, Oliver, etc., 1733
Anderson, Bert, 959
Anderson, Captain, 1300
Anderson, Dr. Robert, 1250
Anderson, Mrs., 755
Anderson, Palmer, 1386
Anderson, Simon, 1680
Andhaka, the blind one, 1603
Andozerskaja, Professor, 1135
André, 1061
Andreas, 1649
Andrée, 583
Andrew, 825
Andrew, Father, 444

Andrew (Andy), 780
Andrews, Polly, 640
Andrews, Shorty, 83
Andrews, Todd, etc., 524
Andri, 43
Andros, Nick, 1470
Andy, the "chinless wonder," 1632
Angel, 503, 1711
Angela, 1031, 1449
Angelica, 435
Angelina, 115
Angeline, 115
Angels, 566
Angie, 1591
Angiola, 305
Angstrom, Harry "Rabbit," etc., 1253, 1254, 1257
Angus, Ralph, 1667
Angustina, 1517
Anisie, 533
Anita, 726, 1398
Anita the Red, 55
Ann, 379
Anna, 31, 724, 1498
Anna, Sister, 942
Anna K, 884
Anna Maria, 715
Annabella, 253
Anne, 441, 671
Annie, 784, 1112, 1274, 1376
Annixter, 1129
Announcer, 1089
Annuka, 164
Anoa, 1628
Anonymous, Father, 1463
Ansa, Densu, 666
Anselm, 1279
Anselm, Father, 1463
Anselmo, Don, 632
Anshel, 135
Anstey, James, 913
Anstey, Lancelot, 589
Anstey, Mrs., 1161
Anthea, 383
Antheil, 412
Anthony, 16
Anthony, Dion, 628
Anthor, Pelleas, 539
Antigone, 58
Antigonos, 557
Antipater, 831
Antipatros, 509, 557
Anti-Philifor, 500
Antoine, 237
Antolini, Mr., 245
Antommarchi, Dr., 1076
Antonia, 1386, 1554
Antonio, 1397
Anubis, 762
Anwuanwu, 630
Aouda, 69
Apgar, John Day, 447
Aphranius, 985
Apollo, 251
Apollo, Marcus, 234
Apollonius, 1311
Aponte, Colonel Lázaro, 285
Aporat, Theo, 539
Apparition, 424
Appel, Milton, 43
Appia, 667
Appleby, Charles, 445
Appleby, Danil D., 100

Appleby, Frank and Janet, 347
Appleton, Dr. Harry, etc., 251
Appleyard, Elizabeth (Sweetie), etc., 1528
Applicant, First, 36
Applicant, Second, 36
Applicant, Third, 36
Applicant, Fourth, 36
Apt, Rachel, etc., 1675
Apthorpe, 1508
Aquarius the Monsterman, 1025
Aquila, Giancarlo D', 685
Aquilino, 633
Aquino, 694
Aquino, Dionisio "Nicho," 997
Ar-Pharazôn, 1412
Arab, 1572
Araba Jesiwa, 666
Aracil, Julio, 1609
Arago, Father R. P., 501
Aragonés, Patricio, 96
Aragorn, 1412
Arana, Ricardo, 1569
Arble, Iseult, etc., 471
Arcadio, etc., 1152
Arcati, Madam, 169
Arce, Juan María, 201
Archangel, 636
Archanjo, Pedro, 1526
Archbishop of Canterbury, 131, 809
Archbold, 1369
Archer, Helen, 777
Archer, Lew, 616, 1636
Archer, Major Brendan, 1417, 1617
Architect, 65, 402, 827
Architruc, 102
Ardell, 123
Arden, Ted, 1296
Ardengo, Mariagrazia, etc., 1569
Arévalo, Lucio, 400
Argaven XV, 870
Argentov, Nikodim Vasilievich, 217
Argo, Commdor Asper, 537
Argolo de Araújo, Nilo d'Ávila, 1526
Argyle, James, 1
Ariadny, 832
Ariel, 503
Arik, 215
Aristotle of Stagira, 509
Aristov, 712
Arkenholz, 579
Arkin, Margotte, 1021
Arkos, Dom, 233
Armagnac, Jean D', 396
Armand-Dubois, Anthime, 847
Armbruster, Brother, 234
Armenta, Clotilde, 285
Armstrong, Dollie, 50
Armstrong, Kate, etc., 1005
Arna, 1581
Arnaldo, 573
Arnheim, Herr Dr. Paul, 962
Arnica, 848
Arnold, 1712
Arnold, Ida, 206
Arnom, 1566
Aroni, 362
Arregui Paz, Valentin, 837
Arridaios, 557
Arsène, 1048, 1694
Artabazos, 1196
Artemis, 252

CHARACTER INDEX

Arthur, 104, 180, 405, 1515, 1521
Artie, 723
Artigas, Rafael, 1704
Artist, 887
Artworth, Sheila, 896
Aryeh, Penhas, 646
Asagai, Joseph, 1262
Asai, 358
Asamoa Nkwanta, 666
Ashburnham, Edward and Leonora, 613
Ashburton, Miss Flora, 1478
Ashe, William, 1470
Asher, John, 1224
Ashkenazy, Baron, 1260
Ashley, John Barrington, etc., 447
Ashley, Ralph, 1215
Asia, 1465
Asım, Sergeant, 995
Aspen, Lydia, 924
Asphalter, Lucas (Luke), 678
Aspinwall, Brian, 1280
Assad, Jimmy, 366
Assuntina, 71
Aster, Carter "Lady," 1680, 1723
Asterion, 833
Astolpho, 240
Astou, Adia Awa, 1759
Astrologer, 1070, 1384
Astrug, Boris Lvovich, 714
Asya, 80, 230
Atahuallpa, 1316
Atila, 1769
Atkins, Cora, etc., 1210
Atkins, Wilma, 1297
Atkinson, Helen, etc., 1692
Atkinson, Miss Maudie, 1581
Atreides, Paul, etc., 430
Atro, Dr., 406
Attorney, 425
Attorney, Prosecuting, 178
Atwater, William, 21
Atwell, Miss, 1013
Atwood, Henry and Deborah, 1428
Aubrey, Rose, etc., 540
Audebert, Philippe, 1298
Audri, 1615
Auerbach, Paul, 937
Auersberger, Mr. and Mrs., 1743
Augusta, Doña, 1177
Auguste, 381
Augusti, 1576
Augustin, 801
Aule, 1411
Aunt, 651
Aunt Dan, 87
Aunt Dot, 1597
Aunt Harriet, 402
Auntie, Woo Chow's, 663
Aura, 90
Aureliano Segundo, 1153
Aurore, 803
Austen, Uncle, 1258
Austin, 1421, 1621
Austin, Benny, 1213
Author, 218, 1117, 1594
Authors, 437
Auxilio, 550
Ava, 1738
Avdeev, Peter, 651
Avers, Raib, etc., 491
Avery, Shug (Lillie), 308
Avis, Buchanan Malt, 114

Awa, 526
Awoonor, Kofi, 1678
Axel, 324, 425
Axel/Son-in-Law, 1190
Axelrod, Moe, 99
Ayakura, Satoko, 1354
Ayers, Major, 1043
Ayuso, Professor, 976
AZ, 663
Azarael, 1160
Azazello, 985
Azcoitía, Don Jerónimo, etc., 1125
Azdak, 248
Azevedo, Professor, 1527
Aziz, 1066
Aziz, Aadam, etc., 1008
Azriel, 1124
Azureus, 141

Baako, Dr. Kofi James Williams, 1361
Baasie, 212
Babbo, 29
Babe, 1255
Babette, 511, 1685
Babichev, Andrei, etc., 463
Babs, 697
Babtchi, 646
Baby Johann, 816
Bach, Daniel, etc., 645
Bachani, 470
Bachir, 743
Bachler, Monica, 1690
Bachman, Ellie, 631
Bachofen, Linda, etc., 142
Badaloza, Admiral, 1080
Baden-Semper, Lady Carol, 1361
Bader, Shmuel, 747
Badger, 197
Badgery, Herbert, etc., 739
Baduhenna, 685
Baffin, Julian, etc., 162
Baga, 103
Baggins, Bilbo, 681
Baggins, Frodo, 1412
Bagley, Harry, 298
Bagnal, Barney, 1414
Bagnelli, Colette Swan Burger, 212
Bagoas, 557, 1195
Bailey, Ann and Rose, 1183
Bailey, Old, 718
Bailiff, 718, 1718
Baines, Guitar, 1446
Baines, Marylou, 1375
Bains, Mr., 1017
Baird, Jennifer, 433
Bakayoko, Ibrahima, 601
Baker, Miss, 1669
Baker, Miss Hermione, 318
Baker, Rena, 171
Bakul, 294
Balanovitch, Fyodor, 1768
Balcar, Dr. Anna, 757
Balcárcel del Moral, Jorge, 611
Bald Man, 1584
Baldo, 804
Baldry, Chris and Kitty, 1288
Balducci, Liliana, 1532
Balduíno, Antônio, 804
Baldy, 1007
Bale, Simon, 1092
Bale, The, 893
Ballad Singer, 546

Ballard, Horatio, 1624
Ballas, Jan, 995
Balli, Stephano, 72
Balmori, 573
Baloum, Samba, 1259
Baloyne, Yvor, 678
Baltazar, 781
Balthus, Fr., 356
Baltram, Edward, etc., 608
Balu, 506
Baluzac, Curé de, 849
Bama, 753
Banat, 799
Bancroft, Barney, 1643
Band, George, 1544
Bandele, 771
Bandit, 1014
Bandol, Sharli, 1268
Banford, Jill, etc., 541
Banjo, 113, 955
Banker, 1157
Banks, Ethel, 116
Banks, Joseph, 218
Banks, Rosie M., 763
Banks, Sir Gerald, 1172
Banner, Judge Goodwill, 1081
Bannon, Nora, 825
Banzin, Eberhard, 1505
Baptiste, 1079
Bar-El, Dr. Vered, 1453
Bar madam, 1108
Barach, Elie, 1224
Baraglioul, Julius de, etc., 847
Barbara, 192, 1500
Barbara, Sister, 942
Barbarka, 782
Barber, village, 1555
Barberini, Cardinal, 563
Barblin, 44
Barclay, Geraldine, 1707
Barclay, Wilfred Townsend, 1175
Bard, 682
Bardia, 1566
Barend, 255
Barfoot, Captain, 785
Barinaga, Santos, 1285
Baring, Tony, 434
Barizon, Fernand, 1704
Barker, Mrs., 39
Barlow, Christine, 287
Barlow, Dennis, 929
Barlow, Elsa, 1303
Barlow, Hector, 21
Barlow, Lois, 1756
Barnabo, 118
Barney, 719
Barnstorff, Edith, 1132
Baroka, 893
Baron, 313, 1173
Barons, Four English, 131
Barquentine, 621
Barr, Onum, 539
Barreira, Gustavo, 805
Barrell, Mr., 33
Barreto, Ramon, 1704
Barrett, Dr. Richard M., 488
Barrett, Nicole Baker, 474
Barrett, William (Will), etc., 1363
Barrett, Williston Bibb (Will), 853
Barrios, Della, 1773
Barron, Grace, 1024
Barry, 1342
Barry, Dr., 990

Barsut, Gregorio, 1385
Barth, Dr. Philippe, 254
Bartholomew, 906
Bartholomew, Reverend Errol, 931
Bartleff, 494
Bartlett, Paul Maxwell, 456
Bartley, 1294
Bartram, Mrs., 455
Bascombe, Betsy, 1076
Baseheart, Kitty Puss, 828
Basia, 1219
Basie, 454
Basil, 424, 1644
Basiliensis, Lusor "Joculator," 594
Basini, 1767
Bason, Wilfred, 595
Basque, The, 1177
Bassán, Bruno, 1142
Bassett, Ethel Czerny, 1749
Bassett, Mrs., 1492
Baston, Dr. Frederick, 1229
Batchelor, Barbie, 1265
Bateman, Glendon Pequod, 1471
Bates, 720
Bates, Louis, 439
Bates, Patrick, 496
Batista, Ricardo, etc., 1564
Batoki, Chief, etc., 1362
Batraga, Paul, 1494
Battista, Signor, 579
Baudouin, Father, 2
Bauman, Nikolaus, 1069
Baxter, Fred, 779
Baxter, Rupert, 869
Bayan, Oley, 132
Bayard, 756
Baylen, 596
Bayliss, Jim and Sue, 30
Baylor, 879
Bayo, 1193
Bazilio, 348
Beach Boy, 1521
Beadle, 374
Beaker, Sheikie, 896
Beals, Valentine, 518
Beamish, Henry, etc., 680
Beamish, Mary, 595
Bean, Sam, 1333
Beasley, Judith, 1358
Beatrice, 561, 1193, 1648
Beatrice, Great-Aunt, 297
Beatrice Two, 1193
Beatriz (Bea and Bé), 664
Beatty, Captain, 483
Beaty, 939
Beaubien, Father Emile, 1626
Beaugosse, Daouda, 602
Beauharnais, Rose-Josef-Marie
    de, 1076
Beaujo, 577
Beaulieu, Michel, 936
Beavis, Anthony, etc., 480
Bebb, Leo, etc., 188
Bébé, Toutout, 117
Bebe, Uncle, 1143
Bébert, 241
Beck, Mr., 757
Beck, Werner, 1680
Becker, Friedrich, 1118
Becket, Thomas à, 131
Beckett, Nicholas (Nick), 1707
Beckoff, Arnold, etc., 1592
Becky Lou, 1590

Becuccio, 42
Beddoes, Morland, 1757
Bedford, John, 1271
Bednar, Captain, 962
Bedner, Alex and Else, 1764
Bedouin workers at Harran, 288
Bedoya, Cristóbal (Cristo), 285
Bee, 1724
Bee of Mattapoisett, 1732
Beecham, Harold Augustus
    (Harry), 1060
Beecham, Nathan, etc., 917
Beevers, Ernest, 1568
Beevor, Beatrice, 540
Beezer-Iremonger, 601
Begbick, Leocadia, 1298
Beggar, 104, 1259, 1759
Beggar Woman, old, 315
Beggs, Judge Austin, etc., 1340
Begley, John, 1215
Begpick, Ladybird
    (Leokadia), 1298
Begum, 672
Behana, Madame, 1607
Behemoth, 985
Behrman, S., 1129
Beineberg, 1767
Beiters, Konrad, 920
Beizmenne, Erwin, 919
Bela, 685
Belcredi, Baron Tito, 675
Belhôtel, Dominique and
    Saturnin, 117
Belinda, 1361
Bell, Alice, 1641
Bell, Diana, 1536
Bell, Edwin, 368
Bell, Helen Bossier, 1060
Bell, John, 1543
Bell, Jonathan, 62
Bell, Latrobe, etc., 1045
Bell, Maisie, 1343
Bell, Theodosia, etc., 1062
Bella, 680, 736
Bellantoni, Polina, 1319
Bellati, 9
Bellboys, Sir Timothy, etc., 1190
Bellefleur, Leah, etc., 138
Bellette, Amy, 581
Bellew, Mr. and Mrs. John, 1182
Bellgrove, Professor, 620
Bellotti, Mrs., 702
Belmont, 237
Belochkin, Mira, 1217
Belqassim, 1391
Belsize, Inspector, 1097
Beluncle, Philip, etc., 1019
Belvedonsky, Isaac, 125
Belverde, Countess, 1651
Belyakova, Arina, 217
Belyashova, Nyura, 881
Bem, 717
Ben, 165, 366, 429, 1687, 1735
Ben Canaan, Barak, etc., 475
Ben-Ivan, 779
ben Sarah, David, 135
Benally, Ben, 708
Benasseraf, Gideon, 1224
Bender, Elmer, 412
Bendrix, Maurice, 454
Benedict, Father, 44
Benedict, Olivia and David, 913
Benedict, Patty, 150

Benedictine, Delta, 1395
Benefactor, 1701
Benenden, T., 47
Beniform, Flora, 680
Benítez, Don Pedro, 1554
Benjamin, 51
Benkowski, Casey, 1086
Bennett, 333
Bennett, Captain, 918
Bennett, James, 447
Bennie, 578
Benno, 350
Benno of Uppsala, 1073
Benoit, McCarthy, 1013
Benoni, 1662
Bensey, Pearl and Lov, 1582
Benson, Walter, 1496
Bentley, Mrs., etc., 72
Bentum, 1629
Benway, Doctor, 1072
Benziger, Natalie, 553
Benzon, Rätin, etc., 884
Beorn, 682
Beowulf, 638
Berbelang, 1056
Berchtold, Therese, 41
Beren One-hand, 1411
Berendeyeva, Klara Olsufievna, 419
Berengar of Arundel, 1073
Bérenger, 827
Bérenger the First, 475
Bérété, Fatumata, 644
Berezkina, Zoya, 132
Berg, Miriam, 1426
Bergdahl, Peter O., 534
Berger, Bessie, etc., 98
Berger, Ezra, etc., 450
Berger, Helena, 1717
Bergner, Elisabeth, 1293
Berlaimont, Jean-Louis de, 6
Berlingot, Madame, 174
Berlioz, Mikhail
    Alexandrovich, 985
Berman, Morrie, 155
Bermúdez, Don Cayo, 334
Bernadini, Dr. Emilio, etc., 1514
Bernard, 198, 405
Bernardino, Pedro, 485
Bernardo, 250
Bernardo, Messer, 435
Bero, Dr., etc., 943
Berry, John, etc., 703
Berryman, Captain, 541
Bersenev, Andrey Petrovich, 1143
Berson, Dolek, etc., 1674
Berson, Symka, 1675
Bert, 500, 614
Bert, "the Duke," 1093
Berthe, Aunt, 1212
Bertillon, Jules, etc., 708
Berto, 146, 1513
Berton, Giovanni, 118
Bertozzo, Francisco Giovanni Batista
    Giancarlo, 9
Bertram, 594, 852
Bertrand del Poggetto,
    Cardinal, 1074
Bérylune, 174
Besse, Martial, 1599
Beth, 879
Bethra, 400
Bethune, Brother, 918
Beti, 647

CHARACTER INDEX

Betty, 298, 470
Beuret, Professor Edmond, 141
Beutler, Herbert Georg, 1206
Bevans, Howard, 1207
Beveridge, Jack and Maria, 1428
Beverloh, Heinrich "Bev," 1327
Bey, Şevket, etc., 1720
Bèye, Abdou Kader, 1759
Beyl, Hannah, 397
Bezuidenhout, Piet and
  Gladys, 876
Bhakcu, 1010
Bhatta, 814
Bianetta, 1174
Biasse, Billy, 688
Bibbit, Billy, 1150
Biberkopf, Franz, 143
Bibicescu, Dan, 533
Bibikov, B. A., 520
Bicek, Bruno, "Lefty," 1086
Bichelonne, Jean, 242
Biddenhurst, Alexander, 165
Biddulph, Ms., 1375
Bidello, Dr. Jan, 942
Biedermann, Gottlieb, 510
Biegańska, Sophie, 1447
Biegański, Zbigniew, 1447
Big Anna, 1343
Big City, 906
Big Fanny, 671
Big Foot, 1009
Big Lambert, 952
Big Nurse, 1150
Biga, Chief, 1363
Biggs, Peter and Mrs., 659
Bigwig, 1693
Bihana, Madame, 1607
Bildad, 789
Bill, 1525
Billa, 698
Billposter, 426
Billroth, Jeannie, 1743
Billy, 527, 859, 1275, 1725
Billy Pop, 1105
Billyboy, 295
Bineta, Yay, 1760
Bingham, Teddie, 1265
Biondo, Jimmy, 872
Bird, 839, 1197
Bird, Harriet, 1080
Bird, Isabella, 1591
Bird, Mr., 1704
Bird, William Wagner, 182
Birgette, 1249
Biris, Petre, 532
Birling, Arthur, etc., 765
Birt, Sebastian, 318
Biscuit, 1745
Bishop, 104
Bishop of the Grand Plains
  Diocese, 1040
Bishops, 440
Bisland, Leota B., 1319
Bismarck, 1130
Bismillah, 332
Biswas, Mohun, etc., 706
Bittencourt, Marshal Carlos
  Machado de, 1277
Bittlesham, Lord, 763
Biye, 1363
Bjelke, Hans, 800
Black, Armour, 773
Black, Mr., 654

Black Antoine, 237
Black Aphrodite, 1462
Black Coyote, 268
Black Crane, 268
Black Herman, 1056
Black Jack, 1376
Blackbird of Derrycairn, 75
Blackett, Walter, etc., 1416
Blackford, Judith Pippinger,
  etc., 1702
Blackhouse, Tommy, 1509
Blackjap Kenji, 270
Blackman, 816
Blackman, Abraham, 236
Blackshirt, 61
Blacksmith, Jimmie, etc., 262
Blackwell, Field Marshall Theda
  Doompussy, 1763
Blackwell, Mélanie, 60
Blackwell, Nora, 1686
Blades, Zulu, 61
Blagodarjov, Arsenij, 1136
Blagodaryov, Arsenii, 85
Blain, Miss Maggie, 319
Blaine, Amory, etc., 1550
Blaine, Miriam, etc., 189
Blair, Paul, 656
Blaise, Julien, 1183
Blaise, Madame and Dr., 897
Blake, 1270
Blake, Rachel, 1336
Blakeley, Denis, 1258
Blalock, Danny, 324
Bland, William, 162
Blanka, 757
Blankensee, Mr., 1353
Blankenship, Ramsey
  Washington, 854
Blassenheim, Alan, 1003
Blatt, Monty, 270
Blau, Deborah F., etc., 728
Blaydon, John, etc., 751
Blazer, 216
Blazon, Father Ignacio (Padre
  Blazon), 392
Blechhammer, Schoolmaster, 1623
Bledyard, 1335
Bleibl, 1327
Blessing, Virgil, 221
Blicero, 624
Blick, 1571
Bligh, Betty, 61
Blimpie, Benno, 1599
Blind Man, 426
Blinnet, Mr., 610
Bliss, Buddy, 150
Bliss, Connie, 151
Bloch, 569
Bloch, Joseph, 598
Bloch, Shifra Puah, 459
Bloeckman, Joseph, 128
Bloggie, 61
Bloomberg, Anatole, 457
Bloomfield, Alice, 1773
Blore-Smith, 23
Blorna, Hubert and Trude, 919
Blossom, 660
Blount, Gilbert (Gil) and Eva, 1168
Blount, Theodora, 1045
Blount, Victoria, etc., 751
Blowick, Sergeant, 1613
Bludgeon, Joe, 1376
Blue Boy, 175

Blue Lady, 1585
Blum, 521
Blum, Katharina, etc., 919
Blum, Leon, 1705
Blume Nacht, 1415
Blundell, Superintendent, 1101
Bluntschli, Captain, 67
Boa, 1570
Boardman, Gillian (Jill), 1479
Boase, Will and Nigel, 209
Boatswain, 1079, 1630
Boaz, Dennis, 474
Bob, 37, 748, 1174, 1358
Bob, Uncle, 547
Bobby, 744, 1381
Bobel, Count Michel, 1654
Bober, Morris, etc., 79
Bobi, 802
Bobko, Efim, 618
Bobo, 538
Bobo, Mademoiselle Adélaïde, 168
Boby, 1660
Bobynin, 515
Boccaccio, 191
Boccarossa, 436
Boche, 1268
Bock, Martial, 266
Bocksfuss, Billy, 584
Bodden, Junior, 491
Bode, Else, 1005
Bodenland, Joseph (Joe), 544
Bodger, Dean, 1750
Bodice, 867
Bodine, Seaman, 626
Bodo, 1685
Boehling, Alexandra von, 159
Boesman, 183
Bogart, 1009
Boggerlas, 1632
Boggs, Billy and Murial, 684
Bogle, Paul, 1088
Bogolepov, Liza, 1216
Bohadlo, Dr., 350
Bohnenblust, Dr., 741
Bohun, Jeremy, etc., 803
Bok, Yakov, 519
Bokonon, 247
Bokov, Tolya, etc., 215
Bolensky, Professor, 812
Boles, Meg, 159
Boles, Petey, 160
Boleyn, Anne, 52
Boleyn, Daniel, 59
Boll, Sister Marta, 1207
Bolle, Walter, 1677
Bolling, John Bickerson
  "Binx," 1053
Bolo, 1010, 1724
Bolotka, Rudolf, 1230
Bolotov, Professor, etc., 1217
Bolt, Molly, etc., 1318
Bolton, 452
Bolton, Ivy, 844
Bolucra, Paul, 1494
Bom, 717
Bomber, 1208
Bonadea, 963
Bonamy, Dick, 785
Bonaparte, Gaston (Gas), 1740
Bonaparte, Napoleon, 1075
Bonaparte, Pauline, 835
Bonaval, Carlos, 991
Boncoeur, Remi, 1145

Bone, Everard, 473
Bones, Inspector, 809
Bongo-Shaftsbury, Hugh, 1649
Boniface, Father, 1040
Bonifacia, 633
Bonnard, Abel, 242
Bonnard, Madame, 896
Bonne-Mésure, Mademoiselle Francine de, 1533
Bonner, Edward, 1666
Bonneuil, Madame de, 703
Bonnie, 723
Bonny, 1031
Bono, Jim, 498
Bonser, 126
Bontchek, 503
Booker, Tim, 1003
Bookie, 1242
Bookkeeping Billy (Bill), 1299
Boon, Charles, 260
Boone, Peter, 18
Booth, John Wilkes, 892
Bora, Katherine von, 938
Bordeille, Captain, 1494
Borden, Mr., etc., 1704
Bordereau, Juliana, etc., 78
Bordwehr, General Stumm von, 963
Boreas, Nicholas, 115
Borenius, Mr., 990
Borgé, Isabelle, 1551
Borgesius, Katje, 625
Boris, 217, 1424
Bork, Ned, 1033
Bormenthal, Dr. Ivan Arnoldovich, 668
Boronai, 82
Bosoy, Nikanor Ivanovich, 985
Boss, 15, 1093
Bossier, Grandmother, 1060
Bostock, Pat, 1433
Bostwick, Dudley R., 1571
Bosun, Mrs., 62
Boswell, Joe, 1659
Bosworth, Dr. James McHenry, 1537
Botchako, 1014
Botchan, 197
Botrelle, Babe, 351
Botsford, Loretta, 1535
Botucat, Paul, 1494
Bourassa, Catherine (Midge), 1487
Bourne, 675
Bourrelier, Sergeant, 1494
Bouty, 1650
Bowen, Garnet and Barbara, 728
Bowles, Mrs., 483
Bowling, George, etc., 314
Bowman, David, 1627
Boxer, 51
Boxwood, 1693
Boy, 206, 391, 750, 1126, 1289, 1518, 1669
Boy, Gravedigger's, 867
Boy, young, 1170, 1614
Boy age fifteen, 756
Boy Blue, 748
Boy from the Island, 1242
Boy of nine, 394
Boyce, Humphrey, etc., 1507
Boyce, Rupert, 273
Boye, Mr., 1324
Boyer, 835

Boykin, Dallas, etc., 1309
Boyle, Chick, 351
Boyle, Master, 1203
Boyle, Mrs., 1052
Boys, The, 232
Boys, two young, 1613
Boys, young, 1614
Boysie, 204
Brabner, Janice, 1243
Braceweight, Mr., etc., 195
Bradamante, 1111
Bradford George, 1629
Bradley, 213
Bradley, Dr., 955
Bradshaw, Bennett T., 401
Brady, Caithleen (Kate), etc., 341
Brady, Nurse, 1223
Brady, Will Jennings, etc., 1749
Brague, 1650
Brahe, Dr. Tycho, 823
Braithwaite, Cecil Otis, etc., 724
Braithwaite, Edwin, 1243
Braithwaite, Geoffrey, etc., 522
Braithwaite, Maurice, 1552
Bramsom, Mrs., 1097
Brancovis, Marthe de, etc., 1684
Branden, Philip, 1356
Brandini, Carleto, etc., 418
Brandon, Constancia, etc., 1155
Brandy, 1358
Branly, Comte de, 406
Branom, Dr., 296
Brantley, Ethelred T., 327
Brasher, Phil, 115
Brass, 100
Brass, Mrs., 877
Brass Band, 1544
Brass Monkey, 1008
Bratter, Cori and Paul, 116
Braun, 1125
Brausen, Juan María, 201
Brave Man, 267
Brave One, 268
Braxton, 166
Bray, Harold, 585
Brayford, Lucinda, etc., 934
Breasley, Henry, 441
Breedlove, Hallie, 1673
Breedlove, Pecola, etc., 181
Brelle, Corneille, 1599
Brenda, 1339
Brennan, Bridget (Baba), etc., 341
Brennan O' The Moor, 1282
Brent-Oxford, John, 1392
Brentani, Amalia, 72
Brentani, Emilio, 71
Brentano, Clemens, etc., 1110
Brentwood, Pippa, 1428
Brett, Percy, 1484
Brettloh, Wilhelm, 920
Breugner, Peter, 1271
Brewer, Nadine, 1017
Brewster-Wright, Ronald and Marion, 5
Breydon, Mrs., etc., 1282
Brian (Bri), 370
Brickett Ranunculus, 585
Bricknell, Jim, 1
Bride, 378, 1717
Bride, young, 1614
Bridewell, Hannah, 1122
Bridge, 268
Bridge, Bonnie, 684

Bridge, India, etc., 1023
Bridges, Mr., 900
Bridget, 61
Brierley, Austin, 1450
Briggs, Lady "Snotty," 61
Brightwalton, Willy, etc., 610
Brinda, 506
Brinsley, 84
Brion, Ferdinand de, 242
Brisbey, Sergeant, 123
Brito, Bazilio de, 348
Britten, Lyle, etc., 180
Broadbent, Tom, 794
Broadhurst, Jean, etc., 1636
Brock, Raymond, 1214
Brocklebank, Mr., etc., 1300
Brodago, Paul, 1494
Broder, Herman, etc., 459
Brodie, 1274
Brodie, Dr. Valentine, etc., 455
Brodie, Miss Jean, 1235
Brodsky, Dr., 295
Brody, Joe, 152
Bromden, Chief, 1149
Bromley, Jerusha, 662
Brompton, Sir Ralph, 1510
Bronson, Edgar Beecher, 269
Bronstein, Lev Davidovich, 456
Brook, Sasha, 779
Brooke, Conway, 1063
Broome, Hilary, 260
Brother, 591, 1064
Brother, Elder, 594
Brother, Great-Grandfather's younger, 1407
Brother, Giulietta's, 977
Brother Bill, 462
Brother of the wife, 1321
Brother Rat, 1270
Brotherhood, Jack, 1195
Brott, A. K., 936
Brottin, Achille, 242
Brourne, Ursula, 1057
Brown, 311, 623, 1613
Brown, Alexander Theophilus, 810
Brown, Arthur, etc., 1438, 1482
Brown, Bailie, 1352
Brown, Berenice Sadie, etc., 992
Brown, Dr. Buddy, 926
Brown, Innis, 806
Brown, Jack "Tiger," etc., 1561
Brown, Jake, 687
Brown, Kelly, 1641
Brown, Laverne, 189
Brown, Minty, 1466
Brown, Mr., 1545
Brown, Pinkie, 206
Brown, Rectall, 1279
Brown, William, 1071
Brown, William A. (Billy), 628
Browne, Ethelbert, 1011
Browne, Kiswana, (Melanie), 1735
Browne, Mr., 373
Browne, Morgan, etc., 486
Brû, Valentin, 1494
Bruce, 311
Bruce, Dr., 910
Bruch, Walter, 1022
Bruckner, Ilse, 857
Brum, 23
Brumbach, Eddie, 1256
Brunelda, 41
Brunet, 1305

Brunies, Jenny, etc., 413
Bruno, 871
Brustein, Sidney and Iris, 1404
Bryant, 645, 649
Bryant, Jill, 1760
Bryant, William Cullen, 220, 447
Bryond, Bernard-Polydor, 1465
Bryson, Mavis Parodus, 1405
Bucephalus, 1196
Buch, Klaus and Helene, 1323
Buchanan, James, 209
Buchanan, John, etc., 1492
Buchanan, Lester, 1255
Buck, 1129
Buck, Billy, 1281
Buckhorn, Reverend Obediah,
    Senior, etc., 683
Bucolin, Alissa, etc., 1477
Bud, 1506
Budd, Norma, 552
Buddy, 492, 1501
Buendía, José Arcadio, etc., 1151
Bueras, Marujita, 1553
Buffalo Bill Cody, 759
Buffo, Mrs. Beatrice, 1648
Bugger, 1544
Bugsy, 113
Bukowski, Romuald, 781
Bulić, 304
Bulkaen, 1014
Bullock, Major Rupert, 1158
Bully, 296, 866
Bumpass, Usaph, etc., 323
Bunder, 195
Bundy, 165
Bunina, Zinaida Prokofievna
    (Zina), 668
Bunn, Jenny, 1511
Bunter, Mervyn, 1100
Buntline, Ned, 759
Buntui, 667
Buonaparte, Napoleon, 1075
Buonarroti, Michelangelo, etc., 24
Buque, Mme., 244
Burbridge, Buzzard, 1306
Burde, Hilary, etc., 1744
Burger, Rosemarie (Rosa), etc., 212
Burgess, Ted, 597
Burke, Dan, 751
Burke, Nora, 751
Burke, Tim, 1335
Burkett, Mrs., 443
Burkhardt, Otto, 1315
Burkin-Jones, Clare, 895
Burnecker, Johnny, 1766
Burns, Caleb, 1063
Burns, Mr., 1116
Burr, Aaron, etc., 219
Burrowes, A. H., 1058
Bursuc, 533
Burton, Banjo and Army, 115
Burton, Ben, 1203
Burton, Dr. Charles, 45
Burton, George, 1183
Buryan, John Thomas, 813
Busiccio, Aloysius, 1420
Bustamante, Rafael, 1704
Buster, 1114
Bustrófedon, 1559
Butcher, 100
Butler, 1573
Butler, Captain, 650
Butler, Sofia, 308

Butler, Theodore, etc., 891
Butley, Ben, etc., 222
Butt, 1665
Buturlin, Fyodor Borisovich, 779
Buyer, 1072
Buzdykin, Zheka, 216
Byelovzorov, Victor Yegorich, 516
Byer, Ruth Leonard, 1253
Byers, Rodolfo, 957
Byleveld, Marius, 1303
Byrd, Desiree, 1430
Byrd, Melanie, 261
Byrds, The, 1699
Byrne, Edna, 658
Byrne, Manus "Salmo," 1612
Byrne, Oliver and Marilyn, 1638
Byron, George Gordon, Lord, 173,
    271, 545, 1017
Byron, Lady, 272
BZ, 1213
Bzik, Wanda, etc., 1423

C, 1029
Cabrera, Gaspar Ruiz de, 484
Cabricarova, Milena, 460
Caddy, Lieutenant John, 802
Cadignan, Jacques de, 1635
Cadmore, Margaret, 980
Cady, Dr. Benjamin, etc., 1742
Cady, Gladys, etc., 136
Caesonia, 226
Cahel, Delia, 246
Cain, 635
Cain the Sixth, 635
Cajetan, 938
Cal, 225
Calac, 1421
Calazans, Professor, 1527
Calcott, 375
Calderón, Osvaldo Martínez
    de, 608
Caldicote, Dora, 473
Caldwell, 578
Caldwell, Duck, etc., 1007
Caldwell, George, etc., 250
Caliban, Tucker, 400
Caligula, 226
Caligula, Gaius, 864
Callahan, Billy Ray "Red," 1502
Callaway, Harold, 190
Callaway, Lew, etc., 1181
Callcott, Jack and Victoria, 813
Callendar, Annie, 680
Calli, 100
Callia, Lady, 539
Callie Lou, 415
Callifer, James, etc., 1228
Calou, Abbé, 1731
Calpurnia, 1580
Calvert, Roy, 1481
Calvin, 1319
Camacho, Luis (Lewis), 1732
Camacho, Pedro, 88
Cambo, Daniel, 710
Came with War, 860
Camel, 1598
Cameron, 647
Cameron, James, 732
Cameron, Victoria, 1709
Camilla, 1249, 1655
Camille, 1145
Camillo, 250
Camillo, Don, 1339

Camillon, Dr., 1361
Camish, Simon and Julie, 1083
Campanati, Hortense, etc., 438
Campanus, Bartholomew, 7
Campbell, 1209
Campbell, Aida "Anaydee"
    Hollinger, etc., 691
Campbell, David (Davie),
    etc., 1087
Campbell, Dr. Jeff, 1556
Campbell, Howard W.,
    Jr., 1047, 1422
Campbell, Kay, 1225
Campbell, Mattie, 794
Campos, Dolores (Dolly), 1732
Can, 43
Canaan, Barak Ben, etc., 475
Canaan, David, etc., 1051
Canabrava, Baron de, 1683
Canada, 1456
Canada, Eva Medina, 472
Cancer Man, 684
Candanga, 1055
Cándida, Doña, 1164
Candy, 993
Caneca, 560
Caneli, Carla, 1184
Canfield, Rogers, 683
Canhoto, Tadeu, 1527
Canino, Lash, 152
Cankerous other, 315
Cantabile, Rinaldo, 722
Cantapresto, 1651
Cantarelli, Antonieta Esteves,
    etc., 1564
Cantley, Gerald, 910
Cantwell, Richard, 12
Cap'n Dan, 631
Captain, 232, 418, 732, 906,
    1147, 1368
Captain, merchant ship, 1584
Car, Joseph, 426
Caramel, Richard, 128
Carballino, Angela, etc., 1330
Cardin, Dr. Joe, 279
Cardinal, 393, 1573
Carey, Catherine, 1686
Carl, 222, 578
Carla, 329
Carlo the Bald, 1736
Carlos, 338, 478
Carlos, Don, 416
Carlotta, 394
Carlsson, Johannes Edvard, 1077
Carlton, Beverly, 955
Carlton, Colonel Caleb, 269
Carlyle, 1483
Carmen, 104
Carmen, Purísima (Pura) del, 285
Carmichael, Essie Sycamore and
    Ed, 1764
Carmichael, Mike, 1542
Carmody, George, 681
Carmosina, Donna, 1565
Carnal, Lord, 1579
Carnehan, Peachey, 960
Carney, Donald, 156
Carnot, Madame, 721
Carnovsky, Gilbert, 1775
Caroline, 381
Carpenter, 44
Carpet Dealer, 616
Carpio, Fernanda del, 1153

Carr, Agnes, 82
Carr, Henry, 1606
Carral, Frank, 1357
Carrera, Rafael, 801
Carridge, Miss, 1059
Carrie, 1697
Carriere, Jacques, 709
Carrington, Imogen, 1586
Carroll, 647
Carson, Kit, 1572
Carson, Ruth and Geoffrey, 1094
Cartaret, Gwendolyn, etc., 1558
Carter, Captain Humphrey
  Cooper, 1432
Carter, Davis, 472
Carter, Faron, 1103
Carter, Hal, 1207
Carter, Kenny and Fiona, 1286
Carter, Mr., 1711
Carter, Rain, 1335
Cartright, Melinda McKarkle, 828
Cartwright, Steven, 1677
Cartwright, Walter, 29
Cartwright, etc., 914
Carver, Joseph, etc., 928
Casals, José, 146
Casewell, Leslie Margaret
  Katherine, 1052
Casey, Jem, 84
Casey, Jock, 1643
Casey, Margaret, 504
Casey, Teresa, 122
Cash, 1733
Cashman, Barney, 857
Cashtoc, 1054
Cass, 56, 115
Cassandra, 239
Cassie, 415
Castel, Juan Pablo, 1167
Casti-Piani, Marquis, 1174
Castillo, Martín del, 1142
Castle, Charlie and Marion, 150
Castro, Raul Nogueira de
  Albuquerque e, 97
Catalina, 533
Cate, 715
Cate, Decatur, 323
Cates, Jessie and Thelma, 1096
Catherine, 1160, 1220
Catherine, Lady, 973
Catherwood, Frederick, 801
Cathey, Doc, 1092
Cathleen, 909, 1294
Cathy, 299
Catlett, Jake, 828
Catlett, Jake and Essie, 1344
Catlett, Jeremiah, etc., 1122
Catlett, Johnny, etc., 840
Caton, Miss, 1508
Caulfield, Holden, etc., 244
Cava, Porfirio, 1569
Cavalieri, Tommaso de, 26
Cave, Rose, 182
Cavendish, Robert, 317
Cavidge, Anne, 1121
Cawdor, Alistair, 1661
Caxton, Ben, 1479
Ceballos, Jaime, etc., 611
Cecil, 1010, 1096
Cecil, Master, 1080
Cécile, 1718
Cecilia, 97, 255
Cecilia C., 776

Cecily, 1606
Cee, Jay, 137
Celedonio, 1285
Celestial, 1362
Celestina, 1530
Celia, 1421
Celie, 308
Céline, Ferdinand, 241
Celis, 676
Cellan-Davies, Malcolm and
  Gwen, 1137
Cemí, José (Joseíto), etc., 1176
Cenci, Count, etc., 249
Cerda, Amalia, 334
Ceres, 251
Cervantes, Miguel de, 1531
Cesare, 1648
Chabalier, Bernard, 212
Chaddha, Mr., 717
Chaikin, Freddy, 1213
Chairman, 1363
Chairman of the City Council, 133
Chalk, Bobby, 1361
Chalk, Esther and Vera, 457
Chalmers, Lawrence (Larry),
  etc., 616
Chaly, Maxim Petrovich, 231
Chamberlain, 405
Chamberlain, Art, 899
Chamellis, Mme de, 77
Champ, 778
Champion-Cheney, Arnold,
  etc., 286
Chani, 431
Channis, Bail, 539
Chantal, 104, 1494
Chantrapa, 1355
Chantry-Pigg, Father Hugh, 1597
Chao Mao-ts'ai, 1620
Chao T'ai-yeh, 1620
Chapin, Joseph Benjamin (Joe),
  etc., 1524
Chapin, Merle Meekins and
  Marcus, 1046
Chaplitsky, 1245
Chaps, First and Second, 852
Chapuys, 954
Char Nyuk Tsin, 663
Charcoal burner, 1029
Charisma, 1647
Charlebois, Odette, 988
Charles, 517, 743, 1768
Charles, Derek, 1313
Charles, Lieutenant, 15
Charles, Oncle, 1377
Charles, Uncle, 126
Charles, Victor, 926
Charleson, Sir Andrew, 1214
Charley, 754
Charley Popcorn, 271
Charlie, 897, 1359, 1696
Charlie, Young, 360
Charlotte, 353, 1274, 1751
Charmaine de la Cognac, 1706
Charteris, Colin, 114
Charwoman, 374, 1000
Chase, Elyot and Sybil, 1239
Chase, Gideon, 766
Chase, Lieutenant William, 268
Chase, Salmon P., 892
Chateau, Professor, 1217
Chatterley, Sir Clifford and Lady
  Constance, 842

Chauffeur, 871
Chave, George, 265
Chavez, Geo, 561
Cheeseman, Maria, 109
Cheeseman, Mr., 820
Cheeta, 620
Chef, 838
Chege, 1301
Chekalinsky, 1245
Chelmicki, Michael, 76
Chelnov, Vladimir Erastovich, 515
Chelyustnikov, A. L., 1587
Chen, 1451
Chen, Lin Fu, 228
Chentshiner, Celia and Haiml, 1397
Cheong, 1417
Chepa, 1552
Cheptsov, Stepan, 216
Chepurny, 267
Cherea, 226
Chéri, 264
Cherie, 221
Chernok, "Colonel" Sasha, 779
Chernyshevski, Nikolay, etc., 582
Chernyshevsky, 812
Cherry, 38
Cheryl, 1711
Chesney, Captain Conway, etc., 238
Chester, Reverend, 777
Chevre-Feuille, Jacques, 1341
Cheyenne, 1590
Chiang, Vera, 1417
Chiari, Lina, 305
Chichester-Redfern, Helen,
  etc., 1178
Chicken Number Two, 489
Chiclitz, Clayton "Bloody," 1648
Chid (Chidananda), 672
Chiddy, Grace Roche, 1573
Chief, 204, 808, 1012, 1160,
  1321, 1328
Chief Clerk, 1000
Chief-in-Town, 1302
Chief Joseph, 760
Chief of Police, 104, 1217
Chief of the Diallobé, 35
Chief Showcase, 1763
Chielo, 1545
Ch'ien Shao-yeh, 1620
Chierici, Elena, 72
Chiki, 1360
Chiklin, 535
Child, 742, 864, 871, 1167, 1426
Children, fourteen, 1334
Children's voices, 1608
Chimalpín, Mateo, 1055
China Mama, 1762
Chinaman, Old, 233
Chinese coolies, two hundred, 1630
Chinguala, Mariana, 608
Chipchase, Oliver, 23
Chipman, Phoebe, etc., 1309
Chiron, 250
Chisholm, Horace, 1135
Chisholm, Mr. and Mrs., 1201
Chisolm, Francis, 824
Chiung, 649
Chlamtatsch, Zdenko von, 1691
Chloe of the Dancing Bears, 127
Chomina, 164
Chomsky, Noam, 67
Chonkin, Ivan, 881
Chorus, 59

Chorus members, Sixteen, 449
Chorus of firemen, 511
Chorus of Men and Women, 272
Chostiakov, Vera, 1761
Chrabotzky, Emilia, 944
Chris, 720, 886, 1525
Chris-Kit, 720
Chrissy, 1358
Christa T., 1245
Christian, Paul, etc., 388
Christiane, 790
Christiani, Angela, 1010
Christiansen, Lena, 1181
Christine, 586
Christitsch, Johannes, 1501
Christophe, Henri, etc., 835, 1598
Christopher, 249, 1106
Christy, 33
Chrono, 1418
Chuang, Governor, 1605
Chubinov, Vassili Iulevitch, 157
Chucha, 560
Chudakov, 124
Chui, 1199
Chuikov, Vitaly Yegorovich, 217
Church, Corporal Jonathan
  (Johnny), 1238
Church, Soaphead, 181
Chūsaku, Matsuke, 1332
Chwostik, Josef, 1690
Ci, 941
Ciccio, Don, 1532
Cilly, 145
Cilsenenan, Jeriamiah, 1116
Cinci, Diego, 436
Cincinnatus C., 775
Cinto, 1034
Círdan, 1412
Cisovski, Stefan, 1370
Cissie, Aunt, 1659
Citizen Etcetera, 811
Citrine, Charles, etc., 721
City Mouse, 1502
Clackson, Faustina, 818
Claes, Balthazar, etc., 1246
Claims-Maier, 1505
Clair, Suzanne, etc., 355
Claire, 385, 914, 946, 1205
Claire, Ivor, 1509
Claire, Sister, 396
Clairemont, Claire, 173
Clancy, William de la Touche, 220
Clara, 446, 544, 570, 777, 897
Clara, Aunt, 1404
Clare, 316
Clare, Crispin, etc., 587
Clarence, 868, 1259
Clarice, 620
Clarendon, Antony, etc., 28
Clarinetist of the Marseilles Opera,
  Solo, 700
Clarissa, 1738
Clarisse, 962
Clark, Azalea, 1045
Clark, Lieutenant White Hat
  (Philo), 269
Clark, Rose, 819
Clark, Senator Samuel, etc., 987
Clark, Silly Willy, 753
Clarkson, Huntly, 89
Claude, 764
Clausen, Orin, etc., 1706
Clay, 434

Clay, Henry, 1696
Clay, Lady Leocadia, etc., 1000
Clay, Marion, 48
Clayton, Robert, etc., 1690
Cleary, John, etc., 1486
Clegg, Fredrick, 307
Cleghorn, Ma, 1351
Clegthorpe, Samuel, 809
Clem, 1724
Clémence, 381
Clemens, Brother, 685
Clement, 692
Clement, Karen Hansen, 476
Clementine, 1220
Clements, Laurence G., 1217
Cleon II, 537
Clerici, Marcello, 329
Clerk, 568
Clerricot, Miss, 182
Cleveland, Hugh, 1723
Clewes, Leland, 787
Clifford, Jane, 1131
Clifford, Tom, 421
Clinton, The Reverend E., 1283
Clipstone, Pete, 421
Clive, 297
Cloche, Madame Sidonie, 117
Clock, E. A., 182
Clocklan, Percy, 586
Close, Mister, 421
Clov, 458
Clover, 51, 1693
Clovis, Esther, 473, 874
Clown, 197, 1613
Clumly, Fred, etc., 1495
Cluveau, Albert, 94
Clyde, Mr., 321
Clytie, 415
Coal Heavers, 426
Cobb, Judge Jeremiah, 327
Cobby, 1031
Cobito, 147
Cock, Mysterious, 302
Cockerell, Jack, 1217
Cocklebury-Smythe, 405
Cocoa Princess, 1362
Códac, 1560
Codename Lazar, 1214
Cody, 577
Cody, Buffalo Bill, 759
Coffey, James Francis "Ginger,"
  etc., 935
Coffin, Jonathan, 1098
Coffin, William Sloane, Jr., 66
Coffman, Mrs., 311
Cognac, Charmaine de la, 1706
Cohen, Joss, etc., 276
Cohen, Mr., 64
Cojubul, Bastiancito, 1486
Coker, 1456
Cokes, 1483
Colbert, Sapphira, etc., 1335
Colclough, Colonel, 1766
Coldridge, Mark, etc., 278
Cole, Miranda, 1103
Cole, Walter, 37
Coleman, Alfred, etc., 1484
Coleman, Anne, 210
Coles, Anne-Marion, 998
Colet, Louise, 522
Colethorpe, Aileen, 358
Colin, 1342
Collector, 1401

Colley, 926
Colley, The Reverend James
  Robert, 1299
Collier, Slow, Pugnacious, and
  Earnest (Walsh), 1376
Collin, Jacques, etc., 1464
Collings, Trish, 1472
Collins, 291, 667
Colonel, 580, 660, 864, 1108, 3446
Colonel Lorenzo G——, 977
Colonna, Vittoria, 25
Colquohoun, Robert, 1350
Colston, Albert, 420
Colston, Leo, 597
Comes-in-Sight, 268
Commandant, 1079, 1363
Commander, 655
Commdora, 539
Commentator, 315
Commissioner of Police, 1160
Common Man, 954
Companions, 834
Comstock, Gordon, etc., 820
Concasseur, Captain, 312
Concettina, 32
Conchis, Maurice, 945
Condé, Prince Henri de, 396
Condé Babu, 643
Condomine, Charles and Ruth, 169
Condor, Jacinta, 1374
Conductor's assistant, 1608
Conegrund, Queen, 103
Congo Rose, 688
Conklin, Robert, 1296
Connage, Alec and Rosalind, 1551
Connel, Anna, 1184
Conners, Mrs. Harrison C., 247
Connolly, General, 162
Connor, Macaulay (Mike), 1203
Conover, Gertrude, 189
Conrad, 212
Conrad, Mrs., 559
Conroy, Gabriel, etc., 372
Conselheiro, Antonio, 1276, 1682
Consolação, Donna Carmosina
  Sluizer da, 1565
Constable, 1376
Constables, 9
Constance, 540
Constant, Adam, 709
Constant, Malachi, 1418
Constantine, 1475
Constantine, Eddie and Carol, 347
Consul, First, 1733
Contemporary, 280
Contenson, 1465
Control, 1469
Converse, John, 411
Convict, first, 1669
Convict, second, 1670
Conway, Judith, 1038
Conway, Mrs., etc., 1567
Cooger, J. C., 1442
Cook, The, 1047
Cook, Al, 1217
Cook, Captain James, 218
Cook, R. J., 1761
Cooley, Benjamin, 812
Coonardoo, 335
Cooper, 1059
Cooper, Effingham, 1640
Coote, Mrs., 315
Coote, Rufus George, 1612

Cootes, Edward, 869
Cope, Carryl, 1427
Copeland, Grange, etc., 1547
Copernicus, 409
Copplestone, Colonel ("Uncle") Jack, 1709
Cora, 620, 733, 1173
Cora, Aunt, 1715
Cora Lee, 1735
Coral, Miss, 729
Coram, Rob, 998
Corbet, John, 1746
Corbett, Myna, 457
Corcoran, Jesus Maria, 1596
Corday, Charlotte, 972
Corday, Sylvia, 1325, 1326
Corde, Albert, etc., 375
Cordelia, 867
Cordingley, Belle, 127
Cordingley, District Agent, 126
Corentin, 1465
Corey, Giles, 352
Corinne, 520, 1613
Corman, Billy, 1375
Cornelius, 1081
Corner, James Pendennis "Chatty," 1509
Corniflet, 103
Cornish, Arthur, 1276
Cornish, Francis Chegwidden, etc., 1708
Cornwall, Duke of, 867
Corporal from Torreón, Mexico, 1596
Corrado, 715
Corral, Cayetano, 991
Corregidora, Ursa, 339
Corró, Lídio, 1527
Cors, Doctor, 234
Cortez, Señora Teresina, 1596
Cortney, Curtis, 1654
Cosburg, Lorena, 684
Cosgrove, Billy, 1041
Cosi, 1485
Cosini, Zeno, etc., 328
Cosme, Don, 478
Costa, Raúl, 1726
Costello, Ivan, 1213
Cosway, Antoinette, etc., 1714
Cotes, Petra, 1153
Coulagot, Mademoiselle Marianne, 216
Coulmier, 972
Counihan, Miss, 1059
Counselor, 1682
Count, 1121, 1312
Count F——, 977
Countess, 1105, 1734
Courage, 992
Courteney, Sir Samson, etc., 161
Courtial des Pereires, Roger-Martin, 381
Courtland, Miss Adele, 1158
Courtney, Hurtle Duffield, etc., 1662
Cousin, 1186, 1653
Cousin, The Dead, 1064
Cousin of Chole, 484
Cousins, Hilda, 1503
Coutts, Barry, 421
Coverdale, Merle, 109
Cowboy, 198, 330
Cox, Miss, 1669

Coyón, 485
Crabb, Jack, etc., 893
Craig, Etty, 187
Craig, Malcolm and Priscilla, 111
Craig, Uncle, 899
Craigan, Mr., 899
Crail, Miss, 1470
Crandall, Susan, etc., 1637
Crane, Edwina, 1263
Crane, Helga, 1250
Crane, Maria, 828
Crane, Max, 1490
Cranes, The, 834
Crang, Stephen, 28
Cranmer, Thomas, 953
Cranston, Amelia, 1537
Cranton, Nobby, 1101
Craon, Pierre de, 1563
Crawford, Beth, 672
Crawford, Milo, 855
Crawford, Miss Stephanie, 1581
Crawford, Nanny, 1534
Crawford, R. T. A., 1482
Crawford, Sonny, 858
Crawley, Peter John, 257
Crazy Bow Adair, 111
Creamhair, Lady, 585
Crean-Smith, Hannah, 1639
Crecy, Adelaide de, 209
Credo, Ruggiero di, etc., 305
Creed, Emmett, 457
Creighton, Margaret, 1251
Creighton, Mr., 748
Creon, 58
Cres, 464
Crespi, Pietro, 1152
Crespo, Tomás, 1284
Cresspahl, Gesine, etc., 53
Creuzot, M., 165
Crevy, Angela, 1180
Crew, The Whole Sick, 1647
Crewe, Leslie, 109
Crewe, Sir Francis, etc., 411
Crews, Tony, 167
Crick, Alicia, 1033
Crick, Tom, etc., 1691
Criddle, 165
Cripla, Aunt, 573
Cripple, 943
Cristo, 648
Croak, 1745
Croaker, 585
Crocker-Harris, Andrew and Millie, 207
Croconyan, 265
Croft, Gerald, 765
Croft, Nancy, 1331
Croft, Staff Sergeant Sam, 1071
Crofts, Sir George, 1027
Cromarty, Sir Francis, 69
Crompton, Father, 455
Cromwell, General Oliver, 1238
Cromwell, Thomas, 53, 953
Crook, General Braided Beard (George), 269
Croom, Nancy and Arthur, 1006
Crooner, 1093
Cross, Anthony, 1215
Cross, Faith, etc., 487
Cross, Nadine, 1471
Crouch, 809
Crouch, Joseph, 791
Crouchback, Guy, etc., 1508

Crow, 1590
Crow of Achill, 74
Crowe, Letty, 1243
Crownbacker, Marvin, 1224
Croxley, James and Eleanor, 1185
Crozier, Lief, 1349
Crubog, 185
Cruickshank, Ivor, 423
Cruikshank, Leola, 392
Crunch, 810
Crusoe, Robinson, 549
Cruz, Agata and Nicanor, 27
Cruze, John "Jack," 1290
Crystalsen, 142
Cuban Exile, 92
Cubbage, Rod, 1124
Cubbs, 61
Cuckold, 489
Cucurucu, 972
Cué, Arsenio, 1560
Cukrowicz, Doctor, 1489
Culafroy, Louis, 1165
Cullen, Tom, 1471
Cullendon, Leslie and Babs, 1638
Cullinane, Dr. John, 1452
Cummings, Diana, 1210
Cummings, General Edward, 1070
Cumnor, John, 78
Cuney, Aunt, 1231
Cunningham, Candace (Candy), etc., 343
Cunningham, Molly, 794
Cunningham, Pearl, 1493
Cunningham, Phineas, 228
Cuno, Harry, etc., 609
Cuppy, Ellen "Gypsy," etc., 923
Curator, 921
Curl, Jack, 1364
Curly, 975
Currie, Hagar, 1475
Curtis, 918
Curtis, Brian, 548
Curtis, Michael, etc., 1473
Curtis, Olivia, etc., 1701
Curtis, Pete, 1760
Cusan, 465
Cuscianna, Donna Caterina Magalone, 284
Custer, General George Armstrong, 894
Cusumbo, 416
Cuthbert, Father, 576
Cutler, 940
Cutler, Maggie, 955
Cutler, Mrs. Maggie, 383
Cutrer, Kate, etc., 1053
Cutright, Daisy, 828
Cyprian, 7

D. B., 245
D. B. da Silva, 296
D. E., 54
D-503, 1700
Da, 360
Dabbasi, 288
Dach, Simon, 991
DaConho, 1648
da Costa, 1654
Dad, 1399
Dadda, 462
Daddy, 39
DaddyGene, 592
Dadier, Jeannine, 497

Dagenham, Charles, 1598
Dahl, Poul and Katrina, 1252
Dahlberg, O. P., 534
Daianeira, 1736
Daibutsu, 1339
Daily, Lincoln Agrippa, 113
Daimon Maimas, The, 1708
Dain son of Nain, 682
Dajcher, Menachem
  Nachmanovich, 735
Dale, Jim, 899
Dalhart, Vernon, 1529
Dallas, Francis, 61
Dalleray, Madame Camille, 1298
Dalwood, Tim, 1661
Daly, Lady, 1472
Daly, Mr. and Mrs., 415
Dalziel of Meiklebogs, 1351
Damfo, 666
Damon, Cross and Gladys, 1168
Damroka, 1267
Dan, 32, 1096
Dan, Aunt, 87
Dan the Prince, 135
Dana, 632
Danby, Jane, etc., 1753
Dance, Nichol, 1103
Dancey, Henry, 471
Dancing Master, 1346
Dangerfield, Sebastian Balfe,
  etc., 585
Dani, 916
Daniel, 504, 807, 906
Danielle, 87
Daniels, May, 1146
Daniels, Sam, etc., 1309
Daniels, Steve, 876
Danilech, 515
Danilov, Alexander
  Pimenovich, 1138
Danny, 1595
Danticus, 410
Dany, Mademoiselle, 827
Danzig, 23
Danziger, Nat, 151
D'Aquila, Giancarlo, 685
Dara, Micheal, 751
Darcella, Cécile, 258
Darcourt, The Reverend
  Simon, 1275, 1709
D'Arcy, Bartell, 373
Darcy, Thayer, 1550
Darell, Bayta, etc., 537
Darius, 1196
Dark, G. M., 1442
Dark Girl of Long Alley, The, 1186
Dark Lady, 1117
Darlene, 321, 723
Darling Daintyfoot, 1165
Darling Jill, 604
Darmolatov, A. A., 1588
Darrell, Larry, 1273
Dartigelonghue, Xavier, 848
Darwin, Sir Leonard, 1214
Daryalsky, Pyotr, 1413
Das, Bim, etc., 294
Das, Ila, 510
Da Silva, 647
Datchet, Mary, 1095
Date, His Lordship,
  Masamune, 1332
D'Aubain, Anne-Marie, 1313
Daugherty, Martin, etc., 155

Daughter, 1190, 1227, 1346
Daughter, O. B. G.'s, 585
Daughter, Old Woman's, 1520
Daughter, Sears's eldest, 1134
Daughter, Slocum's, 1441
Daughter-in-law, Ryzak's, 742
Daughter of Indra, 425
Daumler, Kitty, 364
Dave, 1162
D'Avenat, Cesar, 196
Davenport, Olivia, 1663
Daventry, 421
David, 586, 780, 784, 1498, 1592
David, Sean, 1205
David, Uncle, 747
Davidov, 1125
Davidovich, Boris, 1586
Davidson, 1209
Davidson, Margaret, 1481
Daville, Jean Baptiste-Étienne, 195
Daville, Madame, 196
Davis, Boaz and Ann, 1127
Davis, Jefferson, 1695
Davis, Joel, 180
Davis, Mathew L., 221
Davis, Millie, 1617
Davis, Roger, 780
Davis, William O'Brien
  (Billy), 935
Davison, Helena, 639
Davna, 196
Davoren, Donal, 1387
Davost, Daniel, 164
Dawes, Marion, 956
Dawes, Senator, 759
Dawood, Maulana, 1390
Dawsey, Cat Foot, 1696
Dawson, 1096
Dawson, Cliff, etc., 753
Dawson, Leonard, 1154
Day, Herald Newton, 111
Dayo, 744
Day's Air, The, 1736
Daysair, 1736
Deacon, Geoffrey, 1101
Dead, Macon, etc., 1445
Dead Woman, 901
Dean, Eliza, 1280
Deans of Philosophy, Theology,
  Medicine, and
  Jurisprudence, 426
Death, 575, 1160
Death (The Great Bald
  Madame), 550
Debbie, 1275
Debicki, 427
Deborah, 38, 792, 829, 1115
de Brito, Major Febronio, 1277
De Candia, Pedro, 1317
December, 885
Décidément, 175
De Ciz, 200
Decker, Bo, 221
Declan, Father, 1170
De Coster, Julius, 959
de Courcy, Captain, 1728
Deer of the Seventh Fire, 997
Deever, Ann and George, 30
Defouqueblize, 848
de Grazia, Ed, 66
de Hahn, Hans, 77
Dehinwa, Komolola, 771
Dehmel, Conrad, etc., 1664

Dehning, Henry, etc., 949
Deifendorf, Ray, 252
Deigh, Agnes, 1279
Dejean, Monsieur, 603
Dekker, Francis, 1
de la Barra, José Ignacio Saenz, 96
Delacroix, Dinah, 895
Delahunt, Effie, etc., 1051
Delamarche, 41
Deland, Flora, 1537
Delaney, Doc and Lola, 310
de la Paz, Professor Bernardo, 1036
de la Rochepozay, 396
Delarue, Mathieu, etc., 1303
Del Colle, Antonio, 118
Delibaş, Memidik, 1720
Delight, Ben, 1712
Deliliers, Eraldo, 605
Del Lago, Alexandra, 1506
Dellinger, David, 66
Delmar, Nicholas, 612
Delmiro, Raimundo, 418
Delmont, Léon, etc., 257
Delmore, Julia Sanders and
  Jake, 1179
Deltoid, P. R., 295
Demakin, Isola, 1362
Demian, Max, 386
Demmie, 722
Demodokos, 1758
Demoke, 363
Demons, 396, 566
Demoyte, 1335
Dempsey, Robin, 1430
Dempster, Mary, 392
Dempster, Paul, 391
Denham, J. W., 1295
Denham, Ralph, 1095
Denis, 1220
Denise, 674
Deniska, 1475
Denisovich, Ivan, 1147
Deniston, Barbary, etc., 1752
Denk, Reva, 1742
Denman, Leroy, 1319
Denne, Cornet Henry, 1238
Denning, Audrey, 1251
Dennis, 915, 1449
Dennis, Orin, 275
Denny, Dr. Philip, 287
Dennys, 1313
Densu Ansa, 666
Dentist, 902, 1362
de Pas, Fermín, 1284
De Pinna, Mr., 1765
Deputies, Two, 1202
Deputy Director, 1523
Der, 1148
Derain, Madame, 1049
Derby, Edgar, 1422
de Reixach, Charles, 520
Derek, 1441
Derkum, Marie, etc., 300
de Romeiro, Linda, 1576
Derrick, Magnus, etc., 1129
Dersingham, Howard Brompart,
  etc., 46
de Rubempré, Lucien, 1464
Dervish, 1608
Des, 1665
Deschampsneufs, Champ, etc., 1011
Desconocida, La, 194

Des Fossés, Amédée Chaumette, 196
Deshee, Mr., 636
Designori, Plinio, 593
Desmond, 265, 880
Despierre, Andrée Formier, etc., 177
Dessy the Red, 1665
Detective, 1607
Detillion, Max, 376
Detweiler, Helen, etc., 224
Deuneh, 994
Deverel, Lieutenant, 1300
Devers, Lathan, 537
Devi, 1603
Devi, Miss, 1610
Devil, 984
de Villenoix, Pauline, 922
Devine, Dick, 1457
de Vine, Helen, 571
Deviser, 315
Devlin, Michael, 720
Devlin, Sarah, 1618
Devore, Daisy Diana Dorothea, 15
Dewar, Cleva, 1132
Dewdney, Edgar, 1349
Dewers, Norman and Ruth, 1111
Dewey, Harry, 1697
Deweys, The, 1491
Dewis, Father, 214
DeWitt, Elizabeth (Libby), 878
Dexter, Caleb, 478
Deyssel, Captain Pieter Van, 549
Dezauzay, Miriam, 1313
Diakonov, Count Nikolai Nikolaievitch, 157
Diakonova, Countess Sofia Andreievna, 157
Diali, Eze, 629
Diallo, 1259
Diallo, Samba, 34
Diamond, John Thomas "Legs," etc., 871
Dian, 1576
Diana, 43, 441, 1485, 1583, 1594
Diarist, 484
Diarmuid, 623
Diaz, Juan, 369
Diccon, 1579
Dick, Hopping, 111
Dickel, Fayrene Atkins, 1211
Dida, Old Mother, of Ponte Porzio, 306
Didine, 1495
Didion, Joan, 388
Diederitz, Anna Sergeevna von, 846
Diestl, Christian, 1765
Dieter, 412
Digby, Mr., 1713
Digby, The Reverend Doctor Daniel, 1480
Digger, 660
Diggs, David, etc., 134
Dignitaries, Court, 979
DiGorro, Dagger, 914
Dikeledi, 980
Dilbin, Thomas, etc., 781
Dill, Dr. Tihamer, Jr., 679
Dillion, Billy, 388
Dillon, Barney, 365
Dillon, Meg, 700
Dim, 295

Dimble, Cecil and Mrs., 1458
Dimka, 1562
Dinah, Blonde, 1641
Dingleman, Jerry, 64
Dining Room Table, 402
Dino, 715
di Nolli, Marquis Charles, 674
D'Invilliers, Thomas Parke, 1550
Dioki, 1259
Dionisia, 417
Diop, Mademoiselle Étiennette-Vertu-Rose-Secrète, 167
Dios, Juan de, 1599
Diotima, 963
Diouf, Samba Graham, 168
Dipapa, 1662
Director, 550, 567, 1119, 1523
Director of the Play, 125
Dirge, Captain, etc., 836
Diskin, Benny, 1643
Ditcher, 165
Ditson, Rosemary, 1775
Divers, 1014
Divine, 1165
Divisionists, 1072
Divney, John, 1549
Dixon, Hugh, etc., 384
Djemila, 1353
Djuna, 1469
Dmitri, 778
Dmitrievna, Marya, 650
Dōami, 1368
Dobbs, Dr., 546
Dobie, Martha, 279
Doc, 232, 1590
Dockwiler, Victoria, 552
Doctor, 44, 393, 475, 569, 577, 578, 699, 750, 864, 885, 977, 1173, 1362, 1734
Doctor, prison, 1670
Doctor, white, 1189
Doctorow, Robert, 237
Dodd, Ethelbert Cuthbertson "Cubby," 1038
Dodd, Graham, 462
Dode, 1445
Dodge, 213
Doe, Revisson, 904
Dog, 1772
Dogherty, Fern, 899
Doherty, Elizabeth (Lily), 545
Doherty, Father William, 47
Dokusen, Yagi, 725
Dolgoruky, Arkady Makarovitch, etc., 1272
Dolittle, Maud, 988
Doll, Don, 1544
Dolly, 33, 422, 988
Dolores, 976
Dolphus, 918
Dolu'udi, Misa, 1661
Domenica, 1510
Domineer, Father, 302
Domingo, 1317
Dominguez, 1253
Dominick, 1600
Dominique, 849
Don Rogelio de la Flor, 285
Doña María La Matraca, 485
Donald, 198, 1468, 1765
Donaldson, Flora, 212
Donissan, Father, 1635
Donna, 723

Donne, 646
Donnelly, Hugh "The Proker," 1612
Donohue, Honor, 1748
Donohue, Miss, 444
Donsell, Ramona, 677
Dontsova, Dr. Lyudmila Afanasyevna, 229
Doogan, Kate, etc., 1202
Doorkeeper, 425
d'Or, Alice, 359
Dora, 338, 773, 1677
Dôra, 418
Doralina, 418
Doran, Barney, 795
Dorcas, 1724
Doreen, 137
Dores, Maria das, 418
Dorfû, 343
Dorina, 1589
Dorine, 1427
Doris, 753, 926
Dorkis, 1758
Dorn, Lydia Nikolaevna, 981
Dornick, Dr. Gaal, 539
Doronin, Rostislav Vadimich, 514
Dorothy, 880, 1024
d'Orsey, Lady Barbara, etc., 1683
Dorwin, Lord, 536
Dosen, Father Tayama, 1522
Doss, Arul, 506
Dot, Aunt, 1597
Dottie, 904
Dotty, 460
Doubletree Mutt, 1281
Doudou, 602
Doughty, Uncle, 1672
Douglas, Dougal, 108
Douglas, The Honorable Joseph Edgerton, 1479
Douglas, Mildred, 651
Douglas, Monica, 1235
Douglas, Richie, 1483
Douglass, Ned, 93
Dove, Chipper, 704
Dovlatov, Sergei, 317, 1770
Dowd, Johnny, 1494
Dowell, John and Florence, 613
Dowling, Elizabeth, 791
Dowling, Father Stephen, 1487
Dowling, Sicca, 1045
Downes, Celia (Cis), 423
Downey, Ella, 26
Dowzard, 1283
Doyle, Laurence, 795
Draeger, Jonathon, 1443
Dragon, 637
Drake, Augusta, 49
Drama critics, five, 437
Dravot, Daniel, 960
Dreamer, 931
Dreiman, Sam, 1396
Drendorf, Heinrich, etc., 757
Dritto, 1187
Driver, Jake, 1179
Drogo, Giovanni, 1516
Drozdov, Lisa, 1228
Druce, Vincent R., 109
Drucker, Sasha, 107
Drumm, Desmond, 880
Drumm, Dolly, 880
Drumm, Mr., 360
Drummer, 1594

Drummond, The Reverend, 1156
Drumont, Father, 1219
Drunkard, 978
Drunkards, 979
Druzyaev, 714
Dubber, Miss, 1195
Dubois, Christophine, 1715
Dubois, Lucille, 1087
Dubose, Mrs. Henry Lafayette, 1581
Dubrovsky, Alexis, 1444
Dubrow, Don, 37
Duce, Il, 482
Duchesne, Jay, 1024
"Duchess, the," 1567
Duckett, 1375
Duckworth, Elma, 222
Duclos, 1080
Ducros, Eloise, 1697
Dudu, 799
Dufferein-Chautel, Maxime, 1650
Duffet, Marcelle, 1304
Duffy, Creighton, 553
Duffy, Leonard, 1089
Duffy-Goya, Edwina, 456
Dugald, 1667
Duggan, Tom, 342
Duk, Dr., 1364
Duke, 863
Duke, Stanley, etc., 1472
Dukes, Tommy, 844
Dull Gret, 1591
Dull Knife, 268
Dumont, Gabriel, 1348
Dumontet, Louis, 1227
Duncan, 446
Duncan, Robert, 1350
Dunkel, Ed and Galatea, 1145
Dunlavin, 1241
Dunlop, Rosie, 1529
Dunn, Ellie, etc., 669
Dunn, Jim, 331
Dunstaple, Louise, etc., 1402
Duperret, 972
Dupigny, François, 1417
Duplessis, Professor Alain, 384
Dupont, Daniel, etc., 468
Dupret, Mr., etc., 900
Durack, Frank, 342
Durdu, Mad, 994
Dureepah, 720
Durelle, Yvette, 64
Durga, 1603
Durham, Clive, etc., 989
Durieu, Jean, 258
Durkfeld, 1375
Durrant, Timmy, etc., 785
Durrell, Paul, 956
Dussie Mae, 940
Duszek, 1219
Dutch, 1455
Dutton, Elvira (Vyry), etc., 806
Duval, Kitty, 1571
Dvanov, Alexander, etc., 266
Dwarf, 435
Dy, 249
Dyke, 1130
Dykes, Judy, 1019
Dymond, Ruby, 115
Dymov, 1475
Dympna, 1283
Dyomka, 230
Dyrsin, Ivan Salivanov, 515

Dysart, Martin, 467
Dzhugashvili, Iosif Vissarionovich, 513
Dziobak, 1423
Dzugashvili, Iosif Vissarionovich, 513

Eagle of Knock, 74
Eaglets, 74
Eales, Eamonn, 185
Eärendil, 1412
Earl, 1205
Earl of the Hauberk family, Fifth, 19
Earle, Judith, etc., 433
Earline, 1056
Eastlake, Elinor "Lakey," 640
Eastman, Walter, 767
Eastwood, Major, 1659
Eaton, Raymond Alfred, etc., 552
Ebanks, Athens, 491
Ebenhöh, Frau, 569
Ebert, Friedrich, 1119
Ebiere, 1445
Eborebelosa, 440
Eccles, Jack and Lucy, 1257
Eckerbusch, Dr. Werner, 697
Eckermann, Johann Peter, 1705
Ed (Eddie), 462
Ed, the "facilitator," 788
Eddie, 232, 529, 723, 1515
Eddoes, 1010
Eddy, 1577
Edelman, Samuel, 543
Edelman, Stanley Albert, 1045
Eden, Desmond, 492
Edge, Miss Mabel, 318
Edgely, Miss, 1017
Edie, 1359
Edith, 169, 1029, 1343
Editor, 772
Edmée, 264
Edmund, 252
Edna, 386
Edogo, 70
Édouard, 603, 827
Édouard, Uncle, 381
Eduardo, 1134
Edumu IV, King, 343
Edward, 298, 852, 1010, 1449, 1622
Edward, Uncle, 500
Edwards, Calvin, 1045
Edwards, Molly, 384
Edwards, Rob, 442
Edwige, 191
Eeada, 1283
Eele, Major, 182
Eenanam, Christofer (Chris) Van, etc., 1705
Eff, Mrs., 1715
Effendi, Bahadir, 1607
Efor, 406
Efua Kobri, 667
Egbo, 771
Egorov, Captain Pavel Romanovich, 1770
Egret, The, 901
Eguchi, Yoshio, 712
Ehem, Regina, 823
Ehrendorf, Captain Jim, 1417
Eichmann, Adolf, 394, 1681
Eierkopf, Dr., 585
Eigenvalue, Dudley, D.D.S., 1648

Eiichi, 1710
Eiko, Tanizaki, 1451
Einhorn, Billy, 711
Einstein, Albert, 1206
Eisen, 1021
Eisenring, Willi, 511
Eitel, Rudi W., 1505
Ekwefi, 1545
El Adelantado, 921
El-ahrairah, Prince, 1693
Elaine, 322, 874
Elbereth, 1410
Elbert, Donald Merwin, 1471
Eldar, 651
Elder, Mose, 1696
Elders, 161
Eleanor, 466, 505, 1516
Elendil, 1412
Elfstone, 1412
Elias, 1009
Eliav, Dr. Ilan, 1453
Eliezer, 7
Eliezer bar Zadok, Rabbi, 1454
Elihu, 1363
Eliot, Meg and Bill, 1004
Eliot, Sir Lewis, etc., 1480
Eliphaz, 789
Elisabeth, 693
Elise/Mother, 1189
Elizabeth, 259, 316, 322, 1247, 1584, 1669
Ella, 359, 606, 1012
Ellador, 676
Ellelloû, Colonel Hakim Félix, 343
Ellen, 298, 1002
Ellis, 180, 357
Ellis, Steve, 56
Elly, 816
Elmer, Fanny, 785
Elrond, 682
Elrond Half-elven, 1412
Elsa, 1384
Elsbeth, 115
Elton, Richard, 1757
Elvenking, 682
Elvira, 169, 715
Elwë, 1411
Emanuel, 96
Ember, 141
Embezzler, 1242
Emerson, 357
Emerson, Jude, 939
Emil, 1678
Émile, 244
Emilian, 1311
Emilie, 144
Emily, 446
Emina, Larisa Nikolayena, 515
Emma, 145, 252, 1170, 1312
Emmeline, 735
Emmie, 776
Emmy, 1437
Emory, 198
Emperor, 65, 1407
Empress of Blandings, The, 556
Endō, 1740
Enemy, 268
Eng, Fred, etc., 1761
Engel, Lou, 1642
Engelbaum, Golda, 856
Engels, Friedrich, 816
Engineer, Indian, 1032
Engineer, Second, 652

Englishman, 258
Eni, 798
Enlich, Hanna, 1664
Ennis, Jerome, 1045
Ennis, Kate, 1209
Enno, 612
Enoch, 415
Enright, Geoffrey, 439
Enrique, Luis, 285
Envoy, 104
Enzian, 625
Enzkwu, Jaja, 956
Ephraim, 1133
Ephraim, Reb, 201
Epp, David, etc., 176
Eppes, Reverend, 327
Epstein, Arnold, 156
Erastovich, Nikolai, 1138
Erdmann, Greta, 626
Erdosain, Augusto Remo, 1384
Ergueta, Eduardo, 1384
Eribó, 1560
Erichson, Dietrich, 54
Eriksen, D. K. (Delia), 1050
Erlich, Mrs., 1155
Ermanno, Professor, 567
Ermelinda, 63
Ermengarde, 989
Ermolkin, Boris, 882
Ernest, 395
Ernesti, Ernst Heinrich, 1206
Ernestine, 1166
Ernesto, 202
Ernie, 331
Ernst, 871
Erskine, 1694
Erskine, Mr., 820
Eru, 1410
Erzberger, Plenipotentiary
   Matthias, 621
Esau, 300
Escolástica, Aunt, 1143
Esenbeck, Nees and Lisette
   von, 1110
Eshuro, 362
Esme, 1278
Essie, 1371
Essman, Boris, 493
Esteban, 477
Estel, 1412
Estela, 338
Estella, 130
Estelle, 1025, 1134
Estersweh, 413
Estete, Miguel, 1316
Estévez, Julieta, 760
Esther, 147, 528, 944, 1278
Estraven, Therem Harth rem
   ir, 869
Estrella, 901, 966
Estrella, La, 1560
Esuman, 667
Etchepare, Juan Carlos, etc., 670
Etelvina, 761
Etermon, Mr. and Mrs., 141
Ethelred, King, 252
Etherington, Mrs., 1375
Ethredge, Richard, etc., 1711
Etienne, 697
Etsuko, 950
Eugene, 1248, 1516
Eugenia, 1516
Eukie, 925

Eulalia, Marchioness, 1157
Eunice, 420
Eurydice, 1159
Eurydike, 557
Eustace, 764
Ev, Aunt, 1016
Eva, 144, 191, 1173, 1724
Eva, Frau, 387
Evandale, Christian, 163
Evans, 587, 1618
Evans, Albert Gallatin (Lat),
   etc., 1541
Evans, Bullhead, 1498
Evans, Dixie, 151
Evans, Lije, etc., 1698
Evans, Miss Amelia, 109
Evans, Morgan, 336
Evason, Janet, 497
Eve, 1031, 1160, 1462
Evenwrite, Floyd, 1443
Evercreech, Jamesie, etc., 1640
Everett, etc., 1296
Evers, Vemon Dilbert, 491
Evpraksein, Pavel, 882
Evrard, Simonne, 972
Ewbank, etc., 333, 1258
Ewell, Nellie, 1492
Ewell, Robert (Bob) E. Lee,
   etc., 1580
Ewka, 1170
Executioner, 104
Executor, 478
Eyes of Xangô, 1526
Eyre, Leonora, 1507
Ezana, Michaelis, 343
Ezechiele, 745
Ezekiel, 299
Ezeulu, 69
Ezinma, 1545

F. Alexander, 295
Faber, 483
Faber, Walter, 692
Fabrikant, C. D., 1089
Factualists, 1072
Fadigati, Dr. Athos, 605
Faehmel, Robert, etc., 153
Fagot, 985
Faherze, Hanne, 1649
Fähmel, Robert, etc., 153
Fahrenkopfs, The, 1099
Fain, Jen, 1459
Fairchild, Dawson, 1042
Fairing, Father, 1649
Fairman, Judith, etc., 1699
Fairsmith, Ulysses S., 627
Fairy, Good, 83
Falcon, Pierre, 1348
Falcone, Antonio (Tony), etc., 177
Falk, Maxy, 567
Falterle, 1575
Family of eight, 616
Fandiño, Obdulia, 1285
Fanny, Aunt, 724
Fanny May, 1697
Fanshawe, Maud, 988
Fantom, Doug, 1233
Fanych, Fan, 811
Farber, Binnie, 1521
Farías, Don, 485
Farina, Paolo, 305
Farmer, Gladys, 1154
Farmer, Madame Hélène's, 803

Farmer, Prosper Valley, 1334
Farnham, Mattie, 687
Farnham, Pamela (Pammie), 61
Farnsworth, Jerome, etc., 1255
Farr, George, 1437
Farragut, Ezekiel, etc., 488
Farrall, Arturo, 399
Farraluque, 1177
Farrant, Geoffrey, 445
Farrell, Senior Constable, 263
Farrelly, Fanny, etc., 1684
Farris, Elinor, 898
Farrow, Jacy, etc., 858
Farrow, Sam, 547
Fat Gret, 526
Fat Stew, 1750
Fatface, 216
Father, 22, 402, 443, 871, 1226,
   1260, 1345, 1346, 1669, 1687, 1717
Father, Alex's, 295
Father, Camden's, 1241
Father, David's, 587
Father, Hearer's, 315
Father, Henry's, 451, 1092
Father, Jaromil's, 887
Father, Libertino Faussone's, 1032
Father, man's, 889
Father, Menelao's, 573
Father, Mickelsson's, 1002
Father, Miloš', 297
Father, Misako's, 1440
Father, Mr. Sumata's, 1520
Father, Mizoguchi's, 1522
Father, Mohammed's, 648
Father, Mouchette's, 1048
Father, Skelton's, 1103
Father, T's, 916
Father G., 1244
Father-in-law, Bird's, 1197
Father of the Baby, 1584
Fatimah, 1117
Fatta, Maghan Kön, 643
Fatty the Booky, 1299
Fatumata Bérété, 644
Faulk, Maxine, 1098
Faulkner, Dr., 17
Faussone, Libertino, 1032
Faustine, 772
Faustino, Don, 484
Fava, Andrés, 969
Favorite, The, 893
Fawaz, 288
Fawcett, Mrs., 1659
Faxe the Weaver, 870
Fay, Becky, etc., 826
Faye, 615
Fëanor, 1411
Featherstone-Haugh, 115
Febo, 42
Febo, Polo, 1530
Federner, Anna, 1556
Fedotovna, Anna, 1244
Fedri, 44
Fedukin, 1587
Fedya, 779, 846
Feet, 1351
Feffer, Lionel, 1021
Fehnern, Mr., 920
Feinman, Colonel H. I., 1240
Feinschreiber, Sam, 99
Feinstein, Dulcie, 1439
Feitelzohn, Morris, 1396
Felang, 1677

Felice, 20, 687
Felicity, 193, 885
Felicity, Sister, 2, 1489
Felipe, 243, 1530
Felipe the Fair, 1531
Felipillo, 1317
Felleti, Maria, 9
Fellow, Other, 1242
Fellow, Quare, 1241
Fellowes, Judith, 1098
Fellowes, Miss, 1180
Fender, Dr. Robert, 787
Fennel, Robin, etc., 589
Fennick, "Buckle," 507
Fenwick, 648
Fenwick, Charles, 1538
Ferdinand, 140, 380
Ferguson, Jinny, 109
Fermín de Pas, 1284
Fernand, 266
Fernanda, Princessa, 1157
Fernandez, Carlos, 1088
Fernández, Nélida Enriqueta, 670
Fernando, 971, 1398
Ferndale, Julia, 1161
Ferrand, 756
Ferrante, 1584
Ferrauto, Silvestro, etc., 745
Ferreira, Christovao, 1406
Ferrer, 44
Ferrer, Roberto, 1325
Ferret, The, 342
Ferret, Vinca, 1297
Ferromonte, Carlo, 593
Ferwalter, Mrs., 55
Fetler, Gladys, 1638
Fetyukov, 1147
Feuille Morte, 1421
Feverstone, Lord, 1457
Feyos, Swiss Cheese, 1046
ffoulkes-Corbett, Dorothea, 1597
Fiammetta, 436
Fidel, 573
Fidencio, Don, 484
Fiedler, 1469
Fielding, Emma, 439
Fielding, Roger, 1215
Fields, Jenny, 1750
Fierling, Anna, 1046
Fierro, Concha de, 485
Fife, Geoffrey, 1543
Figlow, John, 1496
Filchenko, Tamara (Toma), 217
Filipovich, Andrei, 419
Filippov, Lieutenant, 882
Fillmore, 1616
Filomena, 29
Fincastle, Ada, etc., 1651
Finch, Jean Louise "Scout,"
    etc., 1580
Finch, Jennifer, 1428
Fingers, 577
Finglas, Inspector Tom, 1283
Fingo, Brother, 233
Fink, Mike, 1308
Finkelstein, Sanford "Zed," 1682
Finley, Boss, etc., 1506
Finley, Mrs., 73
Finn, 622
Finnerty, Oliver, 1674
Finney, 1002
Finney, Nick, 1093

Finnian Shaw, Lord Osmund
    Willoughby, etc., 60
Finnucane, Martin, 1549
Finny, 1373
Finoola, 1283
Finsberg, Julius, etc., 543
Finzi-Contini, Micòl, etc., 566
Fiona, 846
Fior, 1157
Fiori, Jack, 1329
Fire Chief, 105
First Communion, 1165
First Corinthians, 1446
Firulet, Baron, 1156
Fisby, Captain, 1519
Fisch, Arthur, 1745
Fischer, 1477
Fischer, Sabine, 1327
Fischer, Siegfried, 91
Fischer, Theodor, 1069
Fischerle, 91
Fish, Father, 1039
Fishbond, Jamestown, etc., 1538
Fisher, Huntley, etc., 1241
Fisher, Jeanette, 857
Fisher, Pop, 1080
Fisk, Lieutenant, 1697
Fistula, 1523
Fitt, Miss, 33
Fitzgerald, Adrian Casimir, 546
Fitzgerald, George, 1039
Fitzpatrick, 333
Five, Mr. and Mrs., 15
Five Past Twelve, 906
Fiver, 1693
Fix, 68
Fixer, 15
Flachsbinder, Johannes, 410
Flagg, Captain, 1706
Flagg, Randall, 1471
Flaggler, Dr., 1093
Flam, Ruth (Ruthy), 1331
Flanders, Jacob, etc., 785
Flannery, Michael (the
    Nigger), 1170
Flatfish, 1107, 1710
Flatfoot, 636
Flaubert, Gustave, 521
Flaxman, 821
Flay, Mr., 619
Fleischman, Laura, 190
Fleisher, Von Humboldt, 722
Flesh, Ben, 543
Fletcher, etc., 361
Fletcher, Harrison and Alice, 1751
Fletcher, Muriel, 421
Fletcher, Robin, 29
Fleurissoire, Amédée, 848
Fleury, Annie, 55
Fleury, George, 1402
Fleury, Madame, 1155
Flight-Lieutenant, 16
Flingus, Bunny, 710
Flint, Dr. Luther, etc., 836
Flint, Paul, 914
Flint, Polly, etc., 352
Fliss, Aviss, 1089
Flod, Anna Eva, etc., 1078
Flood, Dora, 232
Flood, Galton, etc., 1058
Flood, Nora, 1099
Flor, Don Rogelio de la, 285
Flor, Dona, 417

Florence, 17
Florinda, 785
Flory, John, 214
Flounder, The, 525
Flowers, Jack, 1329
Flowers, Tommy, 1712
Flowers Playing, 957
Floyd, Dr. Heywood, 1627
Flynn, Sycamore, etc., 1643
Foch, Field Marshall
    Ferdinand, 621
Foción, Eugenio, etc., 1177
Fogarty, Joe "Speed," 872
Fogel, Timothy, etc., 1738
Fogg, Phileas, 68
Fogler, Tess, 507
Fokusov, Academician, 216
Foley, Bishop, 1488
Foley, Chuck, 929
Foley, Miss, 1442
Foley, Rebecca, etc., 1232
Foley, Slate, 1333
Follett, Horace, etc., 59
Folliot, Gilbert, 131
Fomich, Piotr, 736
Fomorowski, Louie, 961
Fondaudège, Isa, 1657
Fonny, 734
Fonso, 715
Fontaine, 66
Fontaine, Suzie, 1233
Fontana, Father Riccardo, etc., 393
Fontanelle, 867
Fool, 35
Foppl, 1649
Foran, Teddy, etc., 1414
Forbes, Duncan, 844
Ford, Bob, 291
Ford, John, 1395
Ford, Josephine, 1
Foresight, Minnie, 874
Forest Father, 362
Forester, General, 100
Forrester, Gene, 1373
Forrester, Kyla, 1738
Forrester, Sheldon, 1617
Forsyth, Colonel, 760
Forsyth, Wilmet, etc., 594
Fortescue, 1467
40s, 523
Fortnum, Charley and Clara, 693
46, 1511
Fosnacht, Peggy, etc., 1256
Foster, 1283
Foster, Dr., 1024
Foster, Leland, 1485
Foster, Mr., 748
Foster, Roger, 544
Foster, Rupert, etc., 486
Fotheringham, 22
Foucauld, Father, 976
Four, Mr. and Mrs., 15
Foustka, Dr. Henry, 1523
Fowler, Frank, etc., 705
Fowler, Thomas, 1252
Fox, 936, 1565
Fox, The, 541
Fox, Benny, 1343
Fox, Charlie, 1459
Fox, Digby, 874
Fox, Giles, etc., 1727
Fox, Philippe, 172
Fox, Policeman, 1549

Foxe, Brian, 480
Foxe, Miss, 1507
Foxhill, Miss, 1489
Fracastoro, Girolamo, 410
Framley, Bob, 1659
Fran, 674
France, Florent, 1287
Frances, 1603
Francine, 970
Francis, 1031
Francisco, 707
Franck, 790
Françoise, 178, 496
Frank, 361, 978, 1552, 1603
Frankenstein monster, 544, 545
Frankie, 232, 879
Frankie Machine, 961
Franklin, Jesse, 872
Franklin, Mr., 275
Franta, 495
Franz, 259, 1312, 1634
Franz, Victor, etc., 1233
Franziska, 871
Frary, Dr., 151
Fraser, Honoria, 1027
Fraser, Nick and Alix, 913
Frau N., 397
Frayling, Charles, etc., 600
Frayne, Mrs. Kendall, 1365
Frazer, 1698
Freak, 441
Fred, 655, 1025, 1182, 1342, 1398, 1574
Fred, Uncle, 420, 1659
Freddy, 779, 1578
Frederick, 52, 1221
Frederiksen, 1734
Fredrik, 1190
Fredrik, Karl, 1477
Freeman, 1497
Freeman, Ernestina, 547
Freeman, Yeruham, 645
Freie, Viktoria, 297
Fremont, Katherine (Kitty), 476
French, 405
French, Garnet, 898
French, John, etc., 690
Frenchman, Little, 699
Frere, Jean, 709
Freud, 704
Freud, Dr. Sigmund, 456
Freund, Willard, 1091
Frewen, Alan, 107
Frey, Dorcas, 1214
Freytag, Robert (Bobby), 42
Frida, 675
Friday, 549
Frieberg, Hans, 912
Fried, Dr. Clara, 729
Friedlander, Lisa, 674
Friedmaier, Frank, etc., 1434
Friedman, Matt, 1514
Friedrich, 1743
Friend, 623
Friesen, Jakob, IV, etc., 176
Frígilis, 1284
Frisco, Mr. Hugh, 1526
Fritsche, Lieutenant Colonel
  Dr., 394
Fritz, 397
Fritz, Onkle, 158
Fro, 891
Froad, Lionel "Lobo," 1160

Froats, Ozias "Ozy," 1276
Frobisher, Dr., 208
Frobisher, Ronald, 1430
Froman, Americy, 1063
Frome, Debbie, etc., 1017
Fronesis, Ricardo, etc., 1177
Frosby, 1375
Frost, Lilly, 586
Frost, Mark, 1043
Froulay, Liane von, etc., 1575
Froulish, Edwin, 195
Fruit-Norton, Elliot, 1233
Fruitozov, L. P., 217
Frummet, 201
Fu, 1647
Fuchs, 340
Fuchs-Forbes, Alistair, 926
Fuchsia, Lady, 619
Fuecht, Mrs., etc., 1127
Fuentes de Guardado, Guadalupe
  (Lupe), etc., 1148
Fugger, Benedicta, 7
Fuhr, Nicholas, 139
Fuller, Mabel, 434
Fumiko, 129
Funnyhouse Lady, 559
Funnyhouse Man, 559
Furber, Cedric, 1372
Furber, The Reverend Jethro, 1140
Furey, Michael, 373
Furii, 729
Furlow, Jeremy, 794
Furomoto, 358
Furriskey, John, 83
Furse, Jo, 1756
Fury, Tom, 1442
Fusako, 1451
Fushía, 633
Fussholdt, Professor and Mitzi, 101
Fyfe, Julian, etc., 433
Fyodor, 668
Fyodorich, 217
Fyodorovna, Nadyezhda, 428

G., 560, 747, 916
Gaber, 1029
Gabilan, 1281
Gabriel, 635, 1554
Gabriel (Gabriella), 1768
Gabriel Archangel, 1165
Gabriel, Father, 427, 1501
Gabrielle, 191
Gabrielle, Sister, 396
Gad, Lieutenant Colonel, 135
Gagin, 80
Gahagan, Wendy, 1682
Gaillard, Eugene, 342
Gajapathy, 623
Galactic Jack, 1590
Galahad, 906
Galano, 464
Galant, 255
Galateo, 300
Galbraith, Milly, 770
Gale, Essy, 1559
Galileo Galilei, 562
Galitsky, Cate Strickland
  Patchett, 1044
Gall, Galileo, 1682
Gallagher, Dolly, 988
Gallagher, Jane, 245
Gallagher, Jimmy, 1298
Gallagher, Matt and Terry, 346

Gallagher, Roy, 1071
Gallard, Ted, 1723
Gallelty, 183
Gallet, Dr., 1635
Gallia, 1135
Gallindo, Josette, 799
Gallo, 715
Gallo, Jacob, 865
Gallo, Teresa and Mentina, 1032
Gallogher, Mr., 1388
Galloway, Dave, 1686
Gálvez, A., 1394
Galvez, Don Mucio, 485
Galya, 812, 842, 1562
Gamallo, etc., 1289
Gamba, Carlo, 1651
Gambeson, Kelly, 788
Gamboa, Lieutenant, 1570
Gamesh, Gil, 626
Ganchuk, Nikolai Vasilievich,
  etc., 714
Gandalf, 681, 1412
Gangart, Dr. Vera
  Kornilyevna, 229
Gangut, Vitaly Semyonovich, 778
Ganin, Lev Glebovich, 981
Ganz, Aunt Leah, 1067
Ganz-Crispin, Dr. Jenia, 1066
Garabito, Rómulo, etc., 866
Garay, Félix Mejía, 485
Garcia, 968
García Grande, Señora de, 1164
Garcin, Joseph, 1103
Garden, Aubrey, etc., 1585
Gardeners, Negro, 1090
Gardiner, Eunice, 1235
Gardner, 223
Gardner, Frank, etc., 1027
Gardner, Mrs. Vinnie, etc., 825
Gardnor, Ruth, 965
Garesche, Leon, 1038
Garfield, James, 447
Garinati, 468
Garland, Prudence, etc., 556
Garnsey, Mrs., 755
Garp, T. S., 1750
Garpe, Francisco, 1406
Garrison, Minny, 753
Gartenschläger, Michael, 1677
Gaspar, 996
Gaspard de Cesara, 1576
Gaston, 838, 1153
Gates, Lily, etc., 899
Gathoni, 730
Gatiel, 721
Gatti, Mindy, 87
Gaunt, Miss, 1236
Gavriel, 570
Gavrila, 1171
Gay, 232
Gayheart, Lucy, etc., 936
Gdalia, 135
Gê, 1769
Geary, Sam, 336
Geat Hero, 638
Geer, Reginald (Rex), etc., 453
Geiger, Arthur Gwynn, 152
Geiser, 954
Gelnhausen, Christoffel, 991
Gemini, Father, 87
General, 95, 104, 411, 732, 1157,
  1218, 1262
General K——, 977

Generalessa, 120
Generalississimo, 901
Genet, Jean, 1014, 1164
Genevieve, 859, 1658
Genki Nagayama, 20
Gensir, Squire, 111
Gentleman, 1477
Gentleman, Old, 1435
Gentleman, Young, 1312
Gentlemen, 1157
Gentlemen, Two Old, 360
George, 36, 104, 180, 632, 861, 995, 1009, 1012, 1665
George, Amelia, 818
George, Bradford, 1629
George, Edwin, 1695
George, Heinrich, 1293
Georges, 520
Georgie, 295, 1474
Georgina, 296
Gerace, Arturo, etc., 71
Gerald, 1031
Geraldine, 166
Geraldo, 1732
Gérard, 911
Gerard, Brother Francis, 233
Gerasimovich, Illarion Pavlovich, 515
Gerda, 598, 1190, 1477
Gerhardt, Lieutenant David, 1154
Gerhardt, Paul, 992
Germaine, 1616
Geronimo, 1648
Gerry, 299
Gersbach, Valentine (Val), etc., 677
Gershenson, Rav, 283
Gershon, 1423
Gerstein, Kurt, 393
Gertie, 102
Gertrude, Lady, 619
Gertrude, Sister, 2
Gertrudis, 202
Gervais, André, 1664
Geschwitz, Countess Martha von, 1174
Getkrepten, 697
Getliffe, Sir Francis, etc., 1481
Geyrenhoff, Councillor Georg von, 389
Ghani, Naseem, 1008
Ghost, The Homeless, 1064
Ghost, The Smelling, 1064
Ghost of Aldo Campione, 778
Ghost of Howard Allen, 778
Ghost of Katrina Daugherty, 777
Ghost of King Laius, 762
Ghostess, The Television-handed, 1064
Ghosts of Kathryn, Michael, and Gerald Phelan, 777
Ghosts of the Ninth Town, 1064
Giant, 667, 1584
Gibarian, 1436
Gibbon, Reverend Stuart, 1350
Gibbs, Donald, etc., 343
Gibbs, Ferguson, 265
Gibbs, Gabrielle, 1341
Gibilisco, Doctor, 284
Gibson, Drag, 1762
Gibson, Tom, 1466
Gicaamba, 730
Giese, Tiedeman, 410

Giesebrecht, Ekki, 481
Gigi, 583
Gigi, Tanti, 376
Gigolo, 1090
Gil, Professor, 1370
Gilbert, Eugenia, 1696
Gilbert, Peter, etc., 208
Gilberte, 583
Gilchrist, Miss, 700
Gilda, 394
Gildina 547-921-45-822-KBJ, 1733
Giles, George, 584
Giles, Therphilio, 1058
Gillane, Michael, etc., 246
Gillayley, Joseph Kakaukawa (Joe), etc., 185
Gillespie, Duncan and Caroline, 1343
Gillespie, Gimp, 185
Gillette, Bunny, 753
Gilley, Pauline and Gerald, 1089
Gillian, 791
Gilligan, Joe, 1437
Gilling, Joan, 138
Gillum, Hobe, 1039
Gilmore, Gary, etc., 474
Ginger, 114
Ginotta, Pete, 1043
Giovanni, 435, 586, 1584
Girardi, Rita "Bubbles," 1226
Girl, 104, 580, 653, 701, 731, 1600
Girl, Cain's, 635
Girl, English, 1100
Girl, redheaded, 887
Girl, Tobacco Shop, 1241
Girl, village, 1074
Girl, Young Newlywed, 530
Girl in restaurant, 598
Girl of five, 394
Girls, two young, 1614
Gisa, Dona, 417
Gisela, 572
Gisella, 41
Gitano, 1281
Gitlin, Azariah, 1194
Giula, 330
Giulietta, 976
Giuma, 31
Giuseppe, 679, 699
Giustino, 32
Giusto, 1584
Gladis, 970
Gladishev, Kuzma, 882
Gladys, 910
Glaeson, Annie, 203
Glahn, Lieutenant Thomas, 1172
Glanz, Zahn, 1379
Glazier, 426
Gleason, 1375
Gleb, 778
Glebov, Vadim Alexandrovich, 713
Gleeman, Professor, 141
Glendenning, 333
Glick, Mr., 1066
Globov, Vladimir Petrovich, 1611
Glogauer, Herman, 1146
Gloria, 43, 1557
Glossop, Honoria, 764
Glover, Captain, 667
Glowko, Sergeant, 427
Glutton, 839
Gnar, King, 103
Goat, 1308

Goat-boy, 584
Goat Lady, 1092
Goats, 585
Gobseck, Esther, 1464
God, 379, 634
Goddard, Lisa, 1641
Godfrey, Inspector, 1199
Godolphin, Hugh, etc., 1647
Godoy, Colonel Gonzalo "Chalo," 996
Gods, three, 615
Godunov-Cherdynstev, Fyodor Konstantinovich, etc., 582
Godwin, Mary Wollstonecraft, 545
Goethe, 191
Goethe, Johann Wolfgang von, 1705
Gold, Liz, 1469
Goldberg, Nat, 159
Goldbook, Alvah, 398
Golden, Clarence, 189
Golder, Joe, 771
Goldie, 529, 631
Golding, Jeff, 1162
Goldmund, 1077
Goldsmith, 699
Goldsmith, Frannie, 1470
Goldsmith, Mr. and Mrs. (Bridget), 1689
Goldstein, Joey, 1071
Goldstein, Leah, 740
Gollum, 682
Golspie, James, 45
Golspie, Lena, 46
Golubev, Ivan, 881
Golyadkin, Yakov Petrovich, Sr., etc., 419
Gombrowicz, Witold, 1221
Gomez, 970, 1305
Gomez, Mattias, 648
Gonçalves, Epaminondas, 1683
Gonçalves, José, 1769
Gonen, Michael, etc., 1065
Gonzales, Mr., 321
Gonzalez, Rosa, etc., 1492
Goodchild, Sim, etc., 368
Goodcountry, John, 70
Goodfellow, Mr., 1649
Goodman, Paul, etc., 66
Goodman, Theodora, etc., 88
Goodwin, Dr., 1357
Goodwin, Les, 1213
Goole, Inspector, 765
Goosey, 114
Gordo, 805
Gordo, Pedrito, 1527
Gordon, 1043
Gordon, George, 924
Gordon, George. See Byron, George Gordon, Lord.
Gordon, Howard, 936
Gordon, Michael, etc., 282
Gordon, Richard and Helen, 1577
Gore, Geoffrey, 1526
Gore, Meg and Monty "Ruddy G.," 1727
Gorgui, Seck, 1165
Gorin, 157
Gorman, Marcus, 872
Gorman, Mrs., 1694
Gorman, Rachel, etc., 1051
Gornotsvetov, 981
Gorov, Eskel, 537

Gort, 1360
Goryachev, Kapitolina (Kapa), 883
Goryanchikov, Alexander
Petrovich, 711
Gosta, 1287
Gotama, 1401
Gotobed, Maddie, 404
Götten, Ludwig, 919
Gottwold, 1404
Gould, Bobby, 1458
Gould, Glenn, 1645
Gould, Hubert "Safecracker," 1056
Governor, 168, 1129, 1243
Govind, 707
Govinda, 1401
Gowda, Patel Rangè, 814
Goyi, 943
Goyo, 996
Grabot, 1318
Grace, 221, 370, 1653
Grace-Groundling-
Marchpole, 1509
Gracey, Nicola, 924
Gracie, 1030
Grady, 309
Grady, Delbert, 1393
Grady, Jeremiah, 939
Graf, Miss Petra, 263
Graff, Hannes, 1378
Graham, 799
Grahame, Mr., 1249
Grales, Mrs. (Rachel), 234
Gram, 310
Gramp, 309
Gran Maestro, 12
Granberry, Myra, 1538
Grandfather, 403, 1281
Grandfather, Miloš', 297
Grandfather, T's, 916
Grandier, Urbain, 395
Grandlieu, Mrs., 645
Grandma, 39
Grandmama, 530
Grandmother, 530
Grandmother, Eliezer's, 8
Grandmother, O.'s, 126
Grandmother, T's, 916
Grandson, 530
Grandson, Visagie's, 885
Grandson of Alvaro and
Chepa, 1553
Granger, 483
Granger, Bill, 1253
Granger, Paul, 702
Granham, Miss, 1300
Grania, 622
Granny Martin, 1382
Grant, Ulysses S., 447, 1695
Grantlik, Anita, 55
Grass, John, 759
Grass Sandal, 1452
Grasse, Marcellus de, 453
Graves, Mr., 1694
Gray, Allegra, 473
Gray, Claude, 1039
Gray, Jane, etc., 1688
Gray, Jenny, 1235
Gray, T. R., 326
Grayle, Mrs. Lewin Lockridge, 494
Grayne, Olivia, 1096
Grays, Mr., 564
Grazia, Ed de, 66
Great Figurehead, 974

Great-Grandfather, Miloš', 297
Great Lombard, 745
Greatorex, Jim, 1559
Greatton, Doreen, 1339
Greaves, Wodie, 491
Green, April, 701
Green, Dr. Ed, 706
Green, Miss, 590
Green, Mr., 654
Green, Saul, 607
Green, The Reverend Mr.
Pleasant, 1251
Green, William, 1106
Green Eyes, 382
Green Lady, 1457
Green Pope, 1486
Greenbaum, Emanuel, 1066
Greenbloom, Horab, 752
Greene, Peter, 584
Greenfell, Doctor, 226
Greenfield, Graham, etc., 819
Greensleave, Bruno, etc., 208
Greenstreet, Eve, 788
Greenwald, Lieutenant Barney, 225
Greenway, Aurora, 1529
Greenwood, Esther, 137
Greenwood, Mrs., 137
Greggson, George, etc., 273
Gregor, 570
Gregorio, Don, 802
Gregorius, 686
Gregorovius, Ossip, 697
Gregory, 773, 821, 1521
Gregory, André, 1061
Gregory, Captain Al, 153
Gregovich, Sergeant, 1520
Gregson, Agatha, 763
Greidinger, Aaron, 1396
Grendel, 637
Grenfel, Henry, 541
Grésigne, Philippe, 1306
Gret, Dull, 1591
Greta, 115
Gretchen, 800
Gretel, 1267
Grethel, 1462
Grey, Anne, 1250
Grey, Dr. Díaz, 202, 1394
Grey, Everard, 1061
Grey, Margaret Allington, 1288
Grey, Miranda, 307
Grey, Monica, 1365
Gridoux, 1768
Grierson, Doctor, 238
Griffith, Jasmine, 167
Griffon, Neil, etc., 186
Grigham, Horace, 1123
Grigorss, 686
Grigson, Adolphus, etc., 1388
Grimald, Duke, 685
Grimble, Reverend, 1343
Grimes, Ed, 807
Grimpen, Mr. and Mrs., 423
Griot, Johnny, 237
Griscam, David, 1280
Griscam, Jules, 1280
Griselda, Patient, 1591
Grisson, Mother, 1461
Grivet, 1541
Groan, Titus, 618
Grobke, Ernst, 1723
Grodek, Wladyslaw, 304
Groener, General, 1120

Groenewegel, Adriansen van,
etc., 817
Grøgaard, Johannes, 1068
Grogan, Dr., 547
Groom, 1614
Gross, Josef, 995
Gross, Rhino, 1674
Grossman, Larry, 747
Grosvenor, Gerald (Gerry), 935
Grotius, Dr. Michael, 679
Group, Jen's, 1460
Grover, Red, 855
Groves, Becky, 674
Groves, Cora, 1297
Grubeshov, Attorney, 520
Grumpus, 360
Grün, Dr. Ephraim, 942
Gruner, Angela, etc., 1021
Grunewald, Felix, etc., 159
Grusha, 247
Gruyten, Leni, etc., 641
Gruzdev, Dr. Nikolai
Maximovitch, 1224
Gryphius, Andreas, 992
Guaraldi, Giuseppe, etc., 289
Guard, 382, 475, 885, 1670
Guardado, José "Chepe," etc., 1148
Guardian angel, 860
Guardian Angel, Prouheze's, 1338
Guards, Three, 59
Gude, Martha, 1069
Gudelia, 685
Guerin, Roger and Bea, 346
Guest, 645
Guest, Angus, 1
Gueuse-Pardon, Madame
Félicité, 168
Gugolevo, Katya, 1413
Gui, Bernard, 1073
Guiccioli, Countess Teresa, 1018
Guide, 15
Guildenstern, 1314
Guillam, Peter, 694
Guillaume, 587
Guimarães, Dona Flor dos,
etc., 417
Guimarán, Pompeyo, 1285
Guimiez, Alain, etc., 1211
Guinea, Philomena, 137
Guiness, Nurse, 670
Guisepe, 806
Gulab, 469
Guly, Lyudmila, 216
Günderrode, Karoline von, 1109
Gunn, Morag, etc., 408
Gunn, Victoria, 610
Gunnarsen, Haldar and Vera, 1504
Gunter, Betty June, 524
Gupak, 1384
Gurchenko, Sanya, 215
Gurduloo, 1111
Gurney, Sir Charles, etc., 1322
Gurov, Dmitrii Dmitrich, 846
Guru Brahmin, 931
Gurudeva, 1011
Gus, 429, 1043
Gustafsson, Lars, 1525
Gustav, 325
Gustave, 1508
Gustavinho, 806
Guta, 1557
Guthrie, Chris, etc., 1349
Gutzie-Virgeling, Elizabeth, 1688

Guy, Mr., 422
Guy from Semur, 911
Guzmán, 1531
Guzmán, Commandante Rufino, 81
Gwen, 420
Gwendolen, 131, 1606
Gwyon, Wyatt, etc., 1277
Gyp, 1340
Gypsy, 756
Gyula, 8
Gyurkicz, Imre von, 390

H. R. H. The Prince, 378
Haas, Dr., 912
Habakkuk, Charlie, 19
Habersack, Lilian, 178
Hachilah, Dr., 721
Hackl, Cornelius, 988
Hadassah, 1066
Hadji, El, 1759
Hadji Murad, 649
Hadley, Brinker, 1374
Hadži-Vasić, Vladimir, 1729
Haecker, Mr., 524
Haemon, 58
Haffigan, Tim, etc., 795
Haffner, Arturo, 1384
Hag, Old, 1001
Hagar, 1446
Hagen, Herman, 1217
Hagino, Mrs., 197
Hagood, 1240
Hair Dyer, 1653
Hajem, 289
Haki, Colonel, 303
Hakim, Larry, 460
Hal, 36
HAL 9000, 1627
Hale, Abner, etc., 662
Hale, Fred, 206
Hale, Reverend John, 352
Halie, 213
Halil, 1066
Hall, Dr. Mark, 45
Hall, Maurice, etc., 989
Halleck, Gurney, 432
Haller, Fritz, 799
Halliday, Eve, 868
Halliday, Michael, 121
Hallie, 1697
Halloran, Mrs., 913
Halloran, Dick, 1393
Halloway, J. P. "Jack," 779
Halloway, Will, etc., 1441
Hally, 986
Halm, Helmut and Sabina, 1323
Halsey, William "Bull," 1681
Ham, 528, 636
Hamada, 1075
Hamanaka, Momoko, 1355
Hamid, Abdul, 1055
Hamille, Ironman, 564
Hamilton, Alexander, 220
Hamilton, Berry, etc., 1465
Hamilton, Freddy, 964
Hamilton, Guy, 1760
Hamilton, John, 1755
Hamish, 1708
Hamm, 458
Hamm, Gene and Frances, 1310
Hammer, Paul, etc., 210
Hammond, David, 1500
Hammond, Joyce Emily, 1235

Hammond, Valerie, 1551
Hamond, 1650
Hampel, Alexander, 1195
Hampton, Dr. Freddy, 287
Hampton, Reverend M., 1402
Hampton, Skip, etc., 855, 933
Hananiah, 749
Hancock, Alexandra Finch, 1581
Hancock, Len and Vee, 1172
Hand, Laurel McKelva, 1158
Hands, Georgie, 1386
Handsome, The, 1249
Hanema, Piet, etc., 345
Hangman, 1242
Hank, 198
Hannah, 646
Hannigan, Daisy, 157
Hans, 838, 937
Hansel, 1267
Hansen, Mr., 18
Hapgood, Elizabeth, etc., 656
Hapsburg, Duchess of, 558
Har Dayal, 469
Harappa, Iskander, etc., 1389
Harcamone, 1014
Hard Case, 1242
Hardcaster, Percy, 1290
Hardcastle, Fairy, 1458
Harden, Jane, 1556
Hardenburg, Gretchen, 1766
Harder, T. Stedman, 1035
Hardin, Gaybrella Hollinger,
   etc., 691
Hardin, Salvor, 536
Harding, Dale, 1150
Harding, René and Hester, 1371
Härdtl, Anna, 320
Hardwigg, Professor, 800
Hardy, 902
Hare, Jenny, 1026
Hari, 1403
Harish, Reuven, etc., 450
Harismann, Reuven, 450
Hark, 327
Harkness, Gary, 457
Harkness, George, 752
Harkonnen, Vladimir, 431
Harland, Frank, etc., 658
Harlow, Frances (Frankie) and
   Gerald, 1033
Harner, 517
Harold, 198, 720, 986
Harold, Sir, 1353
Haroux, 912
Harp, Mr. and Mrs., 1343
Harper, Hester, etc., 1703
Harper, Mister, 400
Harpo, 308
Harrani townspeople, 288
Harras, 414
Harras, Doctor, 242
Harriet, 659, 1024
Harrington, Ann, etc., 1490
Harris, 906
Harris, Charles "Dill" Baker, 1580
Harris, David, 1519
Harris, Hattie, etc., 26
Harris, Jim, 26
Harris, Mr., 1058
Harris, Niles, etc., 47
Harrison, Alice, 735
Harrison, Cuthbert (Guppy), 1241
Harrison, David, 237

Harrison, Miss, 1075
Harrison, Thelma, 1254
Harrogate, Gene, 1502
Harry, 386, 672, 800, 1342, 1571
Harshaw, Jubal E., 1479
Hart, Orin, 683
Harte, Jesse, 1741
Hartley, Miss, 1251
Hartmann, 1288
Hartmann, Marika and Wolfgang
   von, 561
Hartshorn, Priss, 640
Haruspica, 641
Harvitz, Esther, 1648
Haryk, 350
Hasan, 1433
Hasekura, Rokuemon, 1332
Hassan, 62, 647, 1160
Hassan, Ali, 1072
Hassan, Khazna al-, 289
Hat, 1009
Hatçe, 994
Hatcher, 1506
Hatfield, Clara, 819
Hathal, Miteb al-, 288
Hathaway, 979
Hathaway, Anne, 1116, 1389
Hathorne, Judge, 352
Haug, Theresa, 878
Haupt, Erbert, 242
Haupt, Kattrin, 1046
Hausbotcher, Claudius-
   Octavian, 1431
Havel, Ernest, 1154
Haven, C. K. Dexter, 1203
Havistock, Horace, 1280
Hawat, Thufir, 432
Hawden, Frank, 1061
Hawk, 472, 1470
Hay, John, 892
Hayano, Olavo, 98
Haydon, Bill, 695
Haydon, Mrs., 1557
Hayes, Sally, 245
Hayes-Rore, Mrs., 1251
Hayim, Reb, 645
Haynes, 773, 1012
Haywood, Jessica, 335
Haze, Lolita, etc., 905
Hazel, 180, 232, 1031, 1692
He, 426, 889, 1687
Head, 362
Headmaster, 623
Healy, Mr. and Mrs., 263
Hearer, 315
Hearn, Lieutenant Robert, 1070
Hearne, Judith, 907
Heasman, Carol, 223
Hecht, Garnet, 139
Heckethorn, Julius, 97
Heckler, 1506
Hector, 239
Héctor, 146
Hector, Virginia, etc., 585
Hecuba, 239
Hedda-of-the-Speckled-Teats, 585
Hedgehog, 315
Hedron, Professor, 141
Hedwig, 698
Hedwiga, Princess, 884
Heegan, Harry, etc., 1414
Hegarty, Michael Joseph, 545
Hegemon, 984

Hei, Miss, 1252
Heilmann, 1174
Heine, Dr. Helga, 926
Heiserova, Mrs., 350
Heiss, 66
Held, Truman, 998
Helen, 369, 1209, 1517, 1604
Helen, Aunt, 782, 1346
Helena, 996
Helene, 1213
Hélène, 618, 1420, 1718
Helford, Joan, 1568
Helga, 23, 393
Helicon, 226
Helka, Mother, 1717
Hella, 985
Helstrom, Bron, 1614
Hemmer, Mar, 1026
Hench, Simon, etc., 1162
Henchman, Saul, 518
Hencke, Joachim, etc., 693
Henderson, Colonel Ralph, 1760
Henderson, Evelyn, 1180
Henderson, Mrs., 1388, 1747
Henderson, Timmy, 94
Hendler, Hubert and Helga, 1327
Henestrosa, Fray Pedro de, 921
Heng, Mr., 1252
Henia, 1221
Hennesey, James, 156
Henreid, Lloyd, 1471
Henri, 232, 258
Henrietta, 1161
Henry, 132, 327, 451, 978, 1274
Henry, Meridian, etc., 179
Henry, Victor "Pug,"
  etc., 1678, 1720
Henry II, 130
Henry IV, 674
Henry VIII, 52, 953
Hephaestion, 1196
Hephaestus, 251
Hephaistion, 508
Heracopoulos, Nato, etc., 718
Herakles, 1736
Herald, 972
Herb, 1201
Herbert, 792
Herbert, Melanctha, 1556
Herbert, Meredith, 644
Hercules, 327
Herder, Dr. Paul, 1322
Herdsmen, 1584
Heredia, etc., 407, 971
Hereira, Mrs., 1010
Hermann, 839, 1244
Hermann, Dinah Burkett, etc., 442
Hermelinda, 98
Hermenilda, 98
Hermit, 1357
Hermitage, Giles, 1178
Hernandez, Captain, 968
Hernandez, Father Rafe, 1128
Hernández Guardado,
  Adolfina, 1148
Herndon, Langley, 1169
Herndon, Renée, 1134
Hero, 104
Herod (the Great), 831
Herold, David, 892
Herr Afrika, 816
Herrera, Abbé Carlos, 1464
Herriot, Eduard, 1588

Herrold, G., 585
Hersey, Roscoe, 228
Hersh, Jacob (Jake), etc., 1330
Hersland, David, etc., 949
Hertha, 598
Hertzlinger, Boze, 1201
Herz, Paul, etc., 878
Herzog, Moses Elkanah, etc., 677
Hesse, Anton, 277
Hessie, 1092
Hession, Nora, 184
Hester, 255
Heuremaudit, Mélanie l', 1648
Heurtebise, 1159
Heurtevents, The, 744
Hewet, Terrence, 1668
Hewitt, Donald, 1156
Heybrook, Lord, 548
Hezdrel, 636
Hickey, 733
Hickman, Lydie, etc., 938
Hickman, Theodore, 733
Hickok, James Butler (Wild
  Bill), 894
Hickok, Wild Bill, 759
Hicks, Ray, 412
Hicks, Virginia (Ginny) Page,
  etc., 1128
Hig, 1699
Higa Jiga, Miss, 1520
Higaki, Takamori, etc., 1740
Higgins, 1699
Higgins, Doc, 863
Higinio, 971
Hignam, Claire and Robert, 1180
Higueróa, Doctor, 11
Hilbery, Katharine, etc., 1094
Hilda, 10, 1118, 1574
Hill, Camilla, 1757
Hill, Meridian, 997
Hillier, Denis, 1609
Hilliot, Eugene Dana, 1632
Hilly, 249
Hillyard, Miss, 571
Hilti, Dr., 1174
Hilton, Jack, 1169
Himalaj, Szarm, etc., 1156
Himalay, Count Charmant,
  etc., 1156
Himiko, 1197
Himmelstein, Sandor, 678
Hindenburg, General Oskar
  von, 1120
Hing Kheng Fatt, Chop, 1329
Hinkfuss, Doctor, 1588
Hinsley, Sir Francis, 930
Hinton, Frances, 912
Hipólita, 1385
Hippo, 1221
Hippolyta, 832
Hippolytos, 833
Hippolytus S., 1221
Hiroshi, 1440
Hirschkop, 66
Hirst, Richard, 383
Hirst, St. John Alaric, 1668
Hirt, Professor August, 393
Hisamatsu, Keiko, 1355
Hissen, Fanny, 949
Hitchcock, Mrs., 1376
Hitchhiker, Old, 544
Hitchhiker, Young, 544
Hitler, Adolf, 812, 1223

Hoban, Branch, 1681
Hobart, Helen, 1146
Hobbs, Roy, 1080
Hochberg, Warren and
  Vivian, 1638
Hod, Paola, 1648
Hodge, Taggert Faeley, etc., 1495
Hoe, Mildred, 211
Hoenikker, Dr. Felix, etc., 246
Hoff, Marcus, 151
Hoffbach, Baron Nicholas von,
  etc., 158
Hoffman, Captain, 242
Hoffman, Professor, 756
Hoffmann, 1462
Hogan, Jason, 810
Hogan, Josie, etc., 1035
Hogarth, Mervyn, etc., 313
Hogarth, Peter E., 678
Hogg, Georgina, etc., 313
Hokaida, Mr., 1520
Holberg, Jack, 9
Holbrook, Anna, etc., 1763
Hold, Jack, 1271
Holga, 20
Holger I, 1327
Holiday, Kerry and Burne, 1551
Holland, Heidi, 673
Holland, Jack, 342
Holland, Tom, etc., 924
Höller, 339
Hollier, Clement, 1275
Hollinger, May, etc., 691
Hollingrake, Boo, 1663
Holloway, 452
Holloway, Miss, 590
Holly, 1319
Holly, Catharine, etc., 1489
Holly, Seth and Bertha, 793
Holm, Helen, etc., 1750
Holme, Rinthy and Culla, 1166
Holmes, Alpha Omega, 488
Holmes, Captain Dana and
  Karen, 551
Holmes, Jack, 1240
Holmes, Kerewin, 185
Holmes, Mycroft, 1036
Holsclaw, Arlene, etc., 577
Holst, Gerhardt, etc., 1435
Holstius, 89
Holy Healey, 1242
Holy Sinner, 686
Holzpuke, 1327
Homeless, 984
Homer, Mr., 444
Honda, Shigekuni, 1354, 1355
Honest Lil, 781
Hong Kong Dream Girl, 271
Hood, Tobias (Toby), 1754
Hooded Figure, 1001
Hooker, 1388
Hooligan, Mary, 1092
Hoopoe, 1454
Hooven, 1130
Hoozey, Tom, 1688
Hopcroft, Sidney and Jane, 4
Hope, 1012
Hope, Edith, 702
Hope, Harry, 732
Hopewell, Diana, 1016
Hopit, Ivona, 783
Hopkins, Clifford, 826
Hopkins, Mr., 1401

L

Hopping Dick, 111
Horacker, Cord, 698
Horn, Franz, etc., 876
Hornby, 829
Horowitz, Mrs., 747
Horpach, 774
Horricker, Wharton, 1022
Horse, 452, 1159
Hortensia, 334
Horton, Emma and Thomas
    "Flap," 1529
Horty, 62
Hoschédé, Alice Raingo, etc., 890
Hoshio, 1407
Hoss, 1590
Höss, Rudolph Franz, 1447
Hotta, 197
Houbova, Mrs., 1523
Houlihan, Cathleen ni, 246
Houngan, 1361
Hourican, Conn, etc., 501
Housekeeper, 1737
Houston, Ely, 1168
Howard, Alan, 548
Howard, Donald, 1482
Howard, Thomas, 953
Howe, Professor August and
    Cynthia, 1049
Howells, Marge, 878
Howells, Mary, 249
Howkins, Gus and Daphne, 1178
Howland, William, etc., 822
Hoxworth, Rafer, etc., 662
Hoyle, Zadok, 1708
Hoyt, Titus, 1010
Hrma, Miloš, 296
Hrobek, Oldrich, 1230
Hrothgar, 637
Hsiang-tzu, 1291
Hsiao Fu Tzu, 1292
Hsiao Niku, 1620
Hu Niu, 1292
Hua, 779
Huang Jen-jui, 1605
Huang Ying-t'u, 1605
Huasanga, 1054
Hub, 778
Hubbard, Mrs. Emma, 211
Hubbard Squash, 197
Huben, Leslie, etc., 81
Hubert, 1011, 1657
Hubička, Ladislav, 296
Hudson, 755
Hudson, Thomas, 780
Hufnagel, Count, 1157
Hugenberg, Alfred, 1174
Huger, Allison (Allie), etc., 1364
Hugh, 597
Hughes, Lucy, 1403
Hugo, 191
Hugonin, 1599
Hugues, Victor, 477
Huia, 799
Huismans, Father, 140
Humbert, Humbert, 904
Huml, Dr. Eduard and Vlasta, 757
Hummel, 580
Hummel, Al, etc., 251
Hummel, Pavlo, etc., 122
Humpage, William, 1191
Humph, 1432
Huniady, 427
Hunidei, Mr., 1174

Hunn, James, 472
Hunt, Alonzo, etc., 734
Hunt, Billy, 779
Hunt, Leigh, 1018
Hunt, Olive, 1428
Hunted, The, 965
Hunter, Allende, etc., 1167
Hunter, Bob, 1169
Hunter, Doc, 1342
Hunter, Elizabeth, etc., 478
Hunter, Frank, 208
Hurlecka, Aunt, 500
Hurst, Private, 1376
Hurtado, Andrés, 1608
Hurvitz, Hirshl, etc., 1415
Hury, Jacques, 1563
Husband, 426, 731, 1312, 1346, 1607
Husband, O-Nami's former, 1555
Husband, White, 1090
Hushabye, Mrs. Hesione (Hessy),
    etc., 669
Hustav, 142
Hutchins, George, 194
Hutchinson, Nowell, etc., 1472
Hwang Ti, 280
Hyberry, Wallace, 263
Hyde, Angelica, etc., 453
Hyder, Raza, etc., 1390
Hyland, Jerry, 1146
Hyllos, 1737
Hyman, Bennie, 728
Hyoi, 1458
Hyperides, 719
Hyrcan IV, 359

"I," 116
I, 1222
I, Dreaming, 646
I-330, 1700
Iacofleff, Massimo, 306
Ibbot, Barney, 1493
Ibrahim-Pasha, 196
Ibu, 1761
Ibuki, Tsuneo, 983
Ichmenyev, Natalia "Natasha"
    Nikolaevna, 768
Ichmenyev, Nikolai Sergeyitch, 768
Icrista, Aunt, 573
Ida, 698
Idaho, Duncan, 432
Idawa, 1628
Idiot Prince, 1531
Idoine, 1577
Iffley, Sir Edgar, 50
Ige-Sha, 1769
Iglésia, 520
Ignatievna, Paulina, 216
Ignatius, 783
Ignatius, Sister Mary, 1419
Ignatyev-Ignatyev, Yury, 779
Ignatz, 646
Iguarán, Ursula, 1151
Igumnova, Anna
    Konstantinovna, 1138
Igwu, 630
Ii, Dr., 1710
Iinuma, Shigeyuki, etc., 1354
Ikagin, 197
Ikechi, 629
Ikemefuna, 1545
Ikhnaton, 798
Ikuua wa Nditika, 730
Ill, Alfred, etc., 1660

Ilóm, Gaspar, 996
Ilse, 10
Ilsebill, 525
Ilúvatar, 1410
Imbrie, Elizabeth, 1204
Imitation Foreign Devil, 1620
Imker, Minna, 1120
Immelmann, Art, 925
Inamura, Yukiko, 1554
inBOIL, 754
Inchcate, 107
Incremona, 914
Inder Lal, 672
Indian, First, 218
Indian, Second, 218
Indian Sahuaripa, 485
Indian Woman, Old, 444
Indians, two, 1594
Indira, 470
Indu, 716
Industrialist, 569
Inez, 1145
Infant Prodigy, 1601
Ingalls, Miss, 534
Ingestree, Roland, 392
Ingram, Geoffrey, 1518
Ingram, Royce, etc., 1643
Ingravallo, Francesco, 1532
Innkeeper, 44
Innocent, 783
Inoue, 1406
Insarov, Dmitry Nikanorovich, 1144
Inspector, 274, 506
Intellectual, 258
Interrogator, 764
Interrogee, 764
Intruder, 1289
Inverarity, Pierce, 354
Ioanna, 377
Iole, 1737
Iona, 1758
Ippolito, 32
IQ, 1363
Ira, 1083
IRA Officer, 701
Irawaddy, 1083
Íraz, 995
Irden, Hettie, 1642
Irena, 350
Irenäus, Fürst, 884
Irene, 560, 773, 1035, 1163
Irène, 381
Iribarne, María, 1167
Iridescent, 1362
Irinka, 57
Iriyise, 1362
Irma, 103
Irons, Agnes, 1291
Irulan, 431
Irvin, 940
Irving, Washington, 221
Isaac, 1558
Isaacs, Solomon, 1070
Isabel, 259, 500, 864, 1530
Isaías, Don, 485
Isan, 327
Isanusi, 1628
Ishida, Lord, 1332
Ishii, 663
Isildur, 1412
Ismène, 58
Isobel, 783
Isolde, 1738

Istra, 1565
Itakura, 951
Italian, 259
Itani, Mrs., 950
Itsuko, 399
Iturrioz, Dr., 1609
Iva, 364
Ivan, 1079, 1357
Ivanov, Benjamin, 779
Ivanova, Darya Petrovna, 668
Ivanovich, Alexander, 1200
Ivanovich, Rodrig, 776
Ivanovna, Elizaveta, 1245
Ivanovna, Karolina, 419
Ivascu, Irina, 533
Ives, Mr., 926
Ivona, 783
Ivors, Molly, 373
Ivory, Marcia, 1243
Ivy, 692
Iya Agba, 943
Iya Mate, 943
Iyaloja, 377
Izmaylov, Boris Timofeyevich,
etc., 845
Izmaylova, Katerina L'vovna, 844

J. B., 788
Jabaal, 1454
Jack, 87, 278, 296, 777, 792,
1334, 1340
Jack, Mr., 519
Jack-Lackwit, 1495
Jack the Ripper, 1174
Jackie, 701, 1201, 1667
Jackie, the "Samaritan," 719
Jackie Smolders, 262
Jackmin, Bing, 457
Jacko, 1708
Jackrabbit of Mattapoisett, 1732
Jacks, Albert, 1491
Jackson, 952, 1426
Jackson, Andrew, 220
Jackson, Eva, etc., 1296
Jackson, General, 1403
Jackson, Geoffrey and Eva, 5
Jackson, Jake and Lil, 862
Jackson, Nurse, 1013
Jackson, Reba Love, 692
Jackson, Ronald, 12
Jackson, Thomas "Stonewall," 323
Jacob, 98, 797, 1423
Jacob, Senator Edward, 40
Jacobo, 573
Jacobs, Mrs. Sally, etc., 384
Jacobs, Molly, etc., 606
Jacobson, 394
Jacobus, 332
Jacobus, Father, 593
Jacqueline, 258
Jacques, 587, 786
Jadin, 1650
Jaeger, Ernest and Sandra, 1638
Jaffe, Sid, 878
Jaga, 43
Jagan, 1653
Jagannath, 1653
Jago, Paul, 1482
Jaguar, 1570
Jahn, Ludvik, 795
Jake, 787, 879, 1209, 1642
Jakub, 495
James, Ellen, 1751

James, Hilda, etc., 727
James, Parnell, 180
James, Taylor "Warm-Gravy," 1539
Jamie, 10, 701
Jan, 191
Janaki, 1083
Jandira, 1557
Jane, 161, 644
Janet, 886, 1633
Janey, 1467
Janice, 420, 993
Janine, 1658
Jannings, Emil, 1293
Jannson, Sune, 379
Jansen, Sasha, 612
Jap, 267
Japheth, 528, 636
Jara, Cristóbal, etc., 1444
Jaromil, 887
Jaros, Joe, 112
Jaroslav, 796
Jashormit, 720
Jasker, Chad, 1050
Jason, 577
Jasper, 577, 614
Jaspers, 821
Jastrow, Natalie, etc., 1679, 1721
Java Jim, 836
Javaroo, 1030
Javes, 1030
Javier, 259
Javo, 1030
Javotnik, Siegfried (Siggy),
etc., 1378
Jay, 1469
Jaybird, 331
Jaz, 813
Jazinski, Leon, 348
Jean, 175, 1334
Jean-Pierre, 441
Jean-sans-tete, 1495
Jeanine, 1591
Jeanne of the Angels, Sister, 395
Jeannette, 1288
Jebel, 100
Jeddan, Mufaddi al-, 289
Jeeves, 763
Jefferson, Bert, 955
Jefferson, Jack, 630
Jefferson, Thomas, 220
Jeffrene, 340
Jeffy, 340
Jehovah, 1705
Jehu, 1542
Jehubabel, 1454
Jelkes, Hannah, 1098
Jenkins, 440
Jenkins, James, 1183
Jenkinson, Doctor, 576
Jennings, 647
Jennings, Elizabeth (Liz), 1115
Jennings, Vandyck, 676
Jenny, 43, 61, 1289, 1298
Jep, 1718
Jepp, Louisa, 313
Jeremiah, 836
Jernigan, Roger, etc., 1045
Jerome, Dr. Joseph Ambrosius (J.
A.), 1709
Jerome, Eugene Morris, 156, 205
Jerome, Father Fernand, 164
Jerry, 33, 137, 145, 1772
Jesiwa, Araba, 666

Jesse, 322, 631
Jessica, 431, 632
Jessie, 1031
Jesting Squaw's Son, 861
Jesus, 559, 685, 830, 859, 1270
Jesús Jiménez, José de, 560
Jesus of Nazareth, 1081
Jethro, 1041
Jetzer, Helene Mathilde, 179
Jew in his seventies, Old, 756
Jewel, 1014
Jewett, Helen, 219
Jewish Pumpkin, The, 1225
Jezebel, 730
Jiggs, 1240
Jiguê, 941
Jill, 674, 791
Jilson, Robin, 518
Jim, 340, 402, 454, 614, 632,
1185, 1460
Jiménez, José de Jesús, 560
Jimmie, 62, 1091, 1248
Jimmy Jack, 1601
Jimmy Tomorrow, 732
Jin, 1407
Jirouskova, Nadia, 460
Jo, Monsieur, 1356
Joan, 1604
Joan, Pope, 1591
Joana, 805, 1743
Joanna, 349, 497
Joanna Regina, 1531
Jocasta, 761
Jocelin, 615, 1462
Jocelyn, 561
Jochanan, 1082
Jody, 489
Joe, 26, 274, 296, 415, 446,
657, 734, 1203, 1471, 1498, 1549,
1571, 1672
Joe, Rita, etc., 443
Joey, 587, 689
Johann, 1705
Johann, Baby, 816
Johannes, 1267, 1655
Johar, 289
John, 246, 253, 1171, 1468, 1743
John, Belasco "Fisheye," 422
John, Father, 1040
John, Uncle, 1346
John the Carpenter, 867
Johnnie, 499
Johnny, 828, 978
Johns, Ellen, 1351
Johns, Ephraim, 423
Johns, Lewie, 1574
Johnsen, C. A., etc., 1733
Johnsen, Double Consul, 1733
Johnson, 1552
Johnson, Abraham, 1747
Johnson, Albert (Al), 863
Johnson, Alberta (Bertie) and
Deedee, 1546
Johnson, Albertine, 927
Johnson, Avatara (Avey), etc., 1230
Johnson, Blackie, 925
Johnson, Edith, 134
Johnson, Esther, 1747
Johnson, Etta Mae, 1734
Johnson, Gwendolyn, 167
Johnson, Harry, 374
Johnson, Hubert H.
"Skeeter," 1255

Johnson, Johnny, 133
Johnson, Lionel Boyd, 247
Johnson, Mattie, etc., 1155
Johnson, Myrtle, etc., 465
Johnson, Patsy, etc., 1297
Johnson, Rose, 1556
Johnson, Sister, etc., 1114
Johnson, Uwe, 55
Johnson, Yogi, 1593
Johnson-Hansbury, Brigadier, 546
Johnston, Harriet Lane, 210
Johnston, Susan, 673
Johnston, Wallace, 1578
Johor, 1391
Joktan, 1453
Joll, Colonel, 1671
Jolly, Father, 1488
Jonas, 792
Jones, 755
Jones, Abednego (Ab), 1502
Jones, Alice, 1024
Jones, Alpha, etc., 148
Jones, Bert, 900
Jones, Burma, 321
Jones, Captain Osborne, 524
Jones, Dr. Lionel Jason David,
   D.D.S., D.D., 1048
Jones, Emory, 155
Jones, Eric, 56
Jones, Harry, 152
Jones, Januarius, 1438
Jones, Jenny, 1298
Jones, John Goronwy, 337
Jones, "Major," 311
Jones, Miss, 306
Jones, Mr., 51
Jones, Mr. Lasker, 990
Jones, Mrs., 1248
Jones, Mother, 1345
Jones, Richard, 423
Jones, Robert, 734
Jones, Robert Stanley, 1456
Jonny, 379
Jopling, Gunnar and Lady
   Kitty, 1744
Jordan, 648
Jordan, Del, etc., 898
Jordan, Nelly, etc., 1187
Jorge, 348, 478
Jorge of Burgos, 1073
José, Celso, 485
José Arcadio, etc., 1151
Josefina, 1395
Joseph, 362, 363, 378, 420, 782,
   797, 859, 1157, 1199, 1201, 1270,
   1301, 1356
Joseph, Lebert, 1231
Joseph of Emmaus, 831
Joseph II, 34
Josephine, 1076, 1222
Josephine (Jo), 1517
Josephine (Joe), 370
Josh, 1043
Joshua, 298, 636, 1042
Joshua, Benjamin Eleazar bar, 233
Joshua, Brother, 234
Josie, 632
Joss, 1031
Joubert, Madame and
   Monsieur, 1155
Jourdain, Maurice, 982
Jourdan, 802
Journalist, nearsighted, 1683

Journalists, 411
Journeyman, 44
Joy, 755, 1161
Joyboy, Mr., etc., 930
Joyce, 1502, 1591
Joyce, James, 1606
Juan, 1420
Juan, Don, 1531
Juana, 1188
Juana la Loca, 1531
Juanita, 180
Juanito, 1433
Juard, Dr., and his wife, 468
Juba, 165
Jubban, 111
Jubiabá, 805
Judas Iscariot, 859, 1081
Judd, Albert, 1667
Judd, Ash, 324
Jude, 1491
Judge, 104, 168, 546
Judith, 1382, 1395
Jukes, Young, 1629
Julia, 303, 386, 394, 1219, 1311, 1505
Julia, Aunt, 88
Julian, 29, 1031, 1572
Julián, Count, 975
Julián, Fray, 1531
Julienne, 1575
Juliet, 784
Juliette, 475
Julius II, 359
July, 807
Jumpei, Niki, 1729
Jumper, Sir Archibald
   (Archie), 809
Jumpers, 809
Juno, 620
Jupiter, 117
Jurema, 1683
Jürgen, 871
Just-Marrieds, 1090
Justine, 426
Justus, 1246

Kabe, Mr., 1676
Kabitzke, 1424
Kable, Eric and Valerie, 1500
Kabonyi, 1301
Kadidia, 1174
Kadidja, 1353
Kadishman, Avraham, 1066
Kadmin, Nikolay Ivanovich, 231
Kadmina, Yelena
   Alexandrovna, 231
Kadongolimi, 343
Kafi, 1433
Kagan, Issak Moiseyevich, 515
Kagle, Andrew (Andy), 1441
Kahn, Jacob, 1068
Kahn, Sarah, etc., 269
Kailusa, 1662
Kaiser, 648
Kakabsa, Leonhard, 390
Kalaycı Osman, 994
Kaletsky, Izzie, 740
Kali, 1083, 1603
Kalick, Herbert, 301
Kalinova, Eva, 1230
Kalman, 62
Kalman, Rav Jacob, 282
Kalmar, Hugo, 732
Kaltammer, Jarl F., 1505

Kaltenborn, General von, 1133
Kamala, 1401
Kamalamma, 815
Kamananda, 1603
Kamau, 1301
Kamchatka, 779
Kamensky, Alexander
   Gregorievitch, 157
Kamienski, Michael, 1371
Kamiko, 226
Kammerling, Rudolph, 1146
Kamnitzer, Yoram, 1065
Kanakoa, Keoki, etc., 661
Kaname, 1439
Kandaurov, Oleg Vasilevich, 1138
Kandid, 1431
Kaneda, Mr., etc., 725
Kang Pi, 1605
Kangaroo, 812
Kanoot, 62
Kantor, Marian, 1717
Kantor, Tadeusz, 374
Kao Shao-yen, 1605
Kapsreiter, Anna, 389
Kapturak, 793
Karabo, 1677
Karaun, 1362
Karega, 1199
Karel, 190
Karellen, 272
Karen, 1241, 1459, 101
Karl, 920, 1312
Karl, Tatiana, 1271
Karla, 695
Karlinsky, Yury, 1611
Karlovna, Katerina "Katya," 490
Karlovna, Polina, 1138
Karol, 1221
Karol, Uncle, 1717
Karp, Julius, 79
Karsch, 55
Kash, Callie, 1541
Kashiwagi, 1522
Kashpaw, Marie Lazarre, etc., 927
Kaskiwah, 837
Kaspar, 157, 816
Kassandros, 557
Katarzyna, Grandma, 1717
Katasia, 341
Kate, 1185, 1358
Katerina, 1630
Katharina, 28
Katherine, 517, 978, 1161, 1703
Kathleen, 8, 1210
Kathy (Kath), 462
Katie, 112
Katriel, 135
Katsuko, Wada, 770
Katsumi, Professor, 770
Katya, 212, 1611, 1770
Katya, Princess, 1085
Katz, Mr., 701
Kauffman, Julius, 1043
Kaufmann, Christopher, 873
Kaul, Nanda, 509
Kavalerov, Nikolai, 463
Kavanagh, Mervyn, 1115
Kawai, Jōji, 1074
Kawaii, Chōtei, 1740
Kay, 333, 1270
Kaywana, 817
Kazbeki, Arsen, 248
Kazu Fukuzawa, 19

Kazuko, 1379
Kearns, Larry, 880
Kearns, Mary, 880
Keating, Anthony, 731
Kee Mun Ki, etc., 663
Keeble, Lady Constance, 868
Keefer, Lieutenant Thomas, 225
Keegan, "Father," 795
Keeney, 1665
Keff, 1379
Kehaar, 1693
Kei-boy, 951
Keil, Professor, 1133
Kein, Lionel (Li) and Isabel, 60
Keith, Ensign Willis Seward, 225
Kelcey, etc., 534
Kell-Imrie, Sir Michael, 1432
Keller, Helen, etc., 1015
Keller, Joe, etc., 29
Kelly, Alison, 945
Kelly, Augustine (Gus), 193
Kelly, Barney, 38
Kelly, Celia, etc., 1059
Kelvin, Kris, 1435
Kementari, 1411
Kemp, 462
Kemp, John, etc., 790
Ken, 180
Kendal, 262
Kendrick, Granma, etc., 415
Kendricks, Josie, 1696
Kendry, Clare, 1182
Kenji, 270
Kennington, Dr., 1083
Kenny, 262, 1083
Kenosi, 1248
Kent, Earl of, 253
Kentaurs, 834
Kenworthy, Dr. Wilbur, 931
Keora, Mr., 1520
Kepka, Jan Chrysostom, etc., 1249
Kepler, Johannes, etc., 823
Kerimoğlu, 994
Kerner, Joseph, 656
Kerr, Ellen and Alison, 1236
Kervinski, Sergeant, 292
Kessler, Alexis, 1637
Kessler, Alice and Ellen, 1293
Ket, Charles, 235
Keter, Jakob, 192
Keuschnig, Gregor, 1030
Kevin, 838
Kevin, Father Kev, 926
Keyston, Joseph (Joey), 222
Kgosana, Marisa, 212
Khakimova, Klara, 217
Khan, Badè, 814
Khanna, Mr., 717
Khlopov, Captain Pavel
  Ivanovich, 1261
Khoja, Govind, 512
Khuschbertieff, Georges, 1377
Khvastishchev, Radius
  Apollinarievich, 215
Kibbee, Madge Atkins, etc., 1210
Kich, Pont, 125
Kichijiro, 1406
Kidalla, 811
Kiddemaster, Edwina, etc., 175
Kielland, Dagny, 1069
Kien, Dr. Peter, 91
Kien, George, 92
Kienbaum, 1622

Kiga, 713
Kiguunda, 729
Kikuko, 1451
Kikyō, Lady, 1367
Kilbannock, Ian, 1509
Killainen, Annie, 55
Killed a Navajo, 861
Killer, 827
Killicks, Logan, 1534
Kilpatrick, Brian, etc., 1637
Kim, 1186
Kimberly, Lorna, 769
Kimmer, Saul, 1621
Kimura, Private, 454
King, 1001, 1458
King, Dr. Hughie, 1160
King, Iris, 1641
King, Julius (Kahn), 485
King of Babylon, 635
King of Spain, 1339
Kingfisher, Arthur, 1430
Kinkaid, Colonel J. C., 855
Kinkaid, Colonel J. C., etc., 1139
Kino, 1188
Kinská, Countess, 297
Kinu, 1451
Kinuko, 1451
Kinuthia, 1301
Kinze, Lothar, 124
Kioi wa Kanoru, Ahab, 730
Kirako, Haruno, 1075
Kirby, Anthony (Tony), Jr.,
  etc., 1765
Kirby, Palmer Frederick, 1680,
  1723
Kirby, Paul, 73
Kirby, Stella, etc., 444
Kirilin, Ilya Mihalitch, 428
Kirilov, Alexey, 1228
Kirk, Howard, etc., 680
Kirnberger, Professor, 366
Kirsi the Swede, 1527
Kitchen, Campbell, 167
Kito, Makiko, 1354
Kittredge, George, 1204
Kitty, 717
Kitzinger, David and Jane, 142
Kiwi, 660
Kiyo, 197
Klara, 981
Klein, Edna, 275
Klein, Honor, 1386
Kleist, Heinrich von, 1109
Kleopatra, 557
Kleppmann, R. V., 1497
Klima, etc., 494
Klimentiev, Lieutenant
  Colonel, 514
Klimuk, Gennady (Gena)
  Vitalevich, 58
Klinger, Menasha, 722
Klingsor, 839
Klipspringer, 343
Klüber, Karl, 1595
Knack, 658
Knapp, Evangeline (Eva), etc., 686
Knauer, 387
Knecht, Joseph, 592
Knife-Grinder, 745
Knight, 35, 938
Knight, Alabama Beggs, etc., 1340
Knight, Mr., 836
Knight, Sheila, 1480

Knight, Sir Sydney and Lady
  Rose, 1567
Knobel, 741
Knott, Mr., 1694
Knott, Wyoming, 1036
Knowell, Douglas, 276
Knox, 1665
Knox, Professor William, 357
Knuchel, Helene Mathilde, 179
Knut, The Finn, 62
Knyazev, Yegorushka, 1474
Ko, Drake, 695
Kobayashi, Major, 1740
Kobialka, 1012
Kobri, Efua, 667
Koby, 1660
Koch, Ilse, 912
Kochan, 325
Kochetov, Vitaly, 948
Kodadek, Fireball, 1086
Kodo, Misa, 1661
Koffritz, Renata, 722
Koga, 197
Kohlroser, Franz, 1646
Koi-san, 950
Kojak, 1471
Kojran, Tadeusz, 1218
Kokabiel, 721
Kokol, 972
Kol, 226
Kola, 771
Kolin, 981
Kolley Kibber, 206
Koltovsky, Boris Lvovich, 642
Koltun, Grisha, 217
Kolya, 842
Komako, 1434
Komarov, Oleg, 1217
Koncheyev, 582
Konforti, Rafo, 1729
Koningrijk, Jan and Marta, 115
Konrad, 891
Konstantine, Bonifacy, 1086
Konwicki, 1011
Konwicki, Tadeusz, 1037, 1218
Koomson, 130
Kop, 226
Kopeida, 499
Kopenkin, Stepan, 267
Kopfhalstam, 226
Koppernigk, Nicolas, etc., 409
Koranche, 1628
Korbowski, Richard de-
  Korbowa-, 1688
Kornhoer, Brother, 234
Koroteyev, Dmitri, 1534
Koroviev, 985
Korsak, Miss Malvina, etc., 426
Korvin, 427
Kosmonopolis, Princess, 1506
Kossecki, Antoni, etc., 75
Kossof, Hymie, 270
Koster, 1184
Kostka, 796
Kostoglotov, Oleg
  Filimonovich, 228
Kostya, 842
Kotonu, 1302
Kotrly, 1523
Kovaleva, Professor Marya
  Vladimirovna, 841
Kozlova, Serafima Petrovna, 948
Kozlowski, Stan, 1496

Kraft, George, 1048
Krainer, 570
Kram, 718
Kramer, Pop, 251
Kramm, Antonia, 1424
Krapp, 841
Krateros, 1196
Kratz, Bucky, 1346
Kraus, Tzili, 1630
Kravitz, David "Duddy," etc., 63
Kravitz, Duddy, 1331
Kreder, Herman, 1557
Kregg, Melinda Lacey, etc., 840
Kreisler, Johannes, 883
Kremer, Julius, 857
Kress, 123
Kress, Krazy, 1456
Kretzer, etc., 242
Kreuzer, Dr., 1229
Krieble, Karel, 757
Krim, 718
Krings, Sieglinde (Linde),
  etc., 903
Kripalsingh, 1011
Krishna, 623
Krisskt, 720
Krista, 816
Kromer, Franz, 387
Kromer, Fred, 1435
Krondrashev-Ivanov, Hippolyte
  Mikailich, 514
Kronkite, Irma, 1208
Kronos, 251
Kroust, Mildred, 1255
Krug, Adam, etc., 141
Krumbholz, Therese, 91
Krupa, Jasiu, 427
Krupp, 1571
Kruppenbach, Fritz, 1257
Krupskaya, Nadya
  (Nadezhda), 1606
Krusnayaskov, Feodor, 77
Kruzek, Alberta (Albertine or
  Albertynka), 1156
Krystyna, 191
Kuba, 646
Kublai Khan, 775
Kubu, Naledi, etc., 1678
Kucorra, Maria, 527
Kudeyarov, 1413
Kugako, 399
Kühl, Horst Hermann, 124
Kulanich, Steve, 73
Kulanski, Eddie, 747
Kulken, Rodriguiz, 1224
Kumar, 1760
Kumar, Hari, 1263
Kun, 215
Kundera, Milan, 190
Kungu Poti, 1174
Kunitser, Aristarkh
  Apollinarievich, 215
Kunthi, 1083
Kunz, 1394
Kuptsov, Boris, 1770
Kurbiella, Agnes, 526
Kurimoto, Chikako, 1554
Kurnatovsky, Yegor
  Andreyevich, 1144
Kuroda, Noboru, etc., 1328
Kurtewitz, Konradine von, 120
Kushami, Sensei, 725
Kutunda, 343

Kuvetli, 799
Kuzenkov, Marlen
  Mikhailovich, 778
Kuzitski, S. J., 1091
Kuzmichov, Ivan, 1474
Kwan, Billy, 1760
Kwinto, Peter, 1370
Kyin, U Po, 214
Kyūsuke, Nishi, 1332

Labarthe, Néstor, 399
LaBas, PaPa, 1055
Lace, Nate, 543
Lacey, Beverley, etc., 1343
Lacey, Jonathan, etc., 1122
Lacey, Sally Crawford, 841
Lachaille, Gaston, 583
Lachie, 660
Lackersteen, Elizabeth, 214
Lackeys, 1157
LaCouture, Janice, etc., 1722
Lacroix, Paul, 35
Lacy, Nell Cockburn, 1238
Ladies, 1157
Ladies, Two, 653
Ladislaus, 1157
Lady, Most Royal, 35
Lady, The Super, 1064
Lady-Apple, 1165
Lady Astor, 1520
Lady Blues, 1593
Lady from the Soviet Union, 385
Lady Green, 1608
Lady in Blue, 531
Lady in Brown, 532
Lady in Green, 531
Lady in Orange, 531
Lady in Purple, 531
Lady in Red, 531
Lady-in-White, 1298
Lady in Yellow, 531
Lady of the House of Trade and
  Justice, 1079
Lady X, 702
Laevsky, Ivan Andreitch, 428
Laforgue, Father Paul, 163
Lagos, Horacio, 203
Laidlaw, Marjory, 851
Lajide, 1192
LaJoie, Stuart Rene, 1037
Lake, Kenneth, etc., 547
Laki, Rabbi, 1454
Lakshmi, 469, 1378
Lakunle, 893
Lal, Dr. V. Govinda, 1022
Lal, Inder, 672
Lal, Madan, 506
Lal, Ram, 510
Lal, Sohan, 716
Lalochère, Zazie, etc., 1767
La Maga, 696
Lamartine, Lulu Nanapush,
  etc., 927
La Matraca, Doña María, 485
Lamb, Peter, 1047
Lambert, 1613
Lambert, April, 674
Lambert, Big, 952
Lambert, Freddy, 259
Lambert, Louis, 922
Lambert, Rabbi Milton, 459
Lambie, Ma, 204
Lamont, Antony, 83

Lamont, Gary, 518
Lampl, Heidi, 97
Lamport, Percy, 1372
Lanark, 850
Lancewood, Damon, 788
Lancey, Captain, 1601
Landau, Dov, 476
Landau, Nathan, 1447
Landau, Richard, 306
Lander, Richard, 503
Landlady, 652, 1646, 1772
Landlady, Sarah's, 559
Landlord, 652
Landolph, 675
Lane, Jimmy, 1114
Lane, Wilbur, 1687
Lanfranc, Pat, 934
Lang, Carter, etc., 1213
Lang, Miriam, 1403
Langley, David, 1598
Langmann, Dr., 102
Langsam, Dr., 1416
Lansing, Breckenridge, etc., 448
Lánská, Mrs., 297
Lánský, 296
Lanty, Count de, etc., 1337
Lanwood, Tom, 1755
Lao Ts'an, 1604
Laoutaro, Oraga "Mamusia,"
  etc., 1276
Lapidus, 254
Lar, 881
Lariosik, 372
Larivière, Ida, 14
Larrea, 1704
Larry, 198, 204, 1025
Lars, 1403
Larsen, E., 1394
Larsen, Knut, etc., 369
Lartigue, 1168
Laserowitz, Dr. Sam, 679
Lashkov, Pyotr Vasilievich,
  etc., 1383
Laskell, John, 1006
Laski, General, 1632
Las Torres, Paquita de, 1024
Lasunskaya, Darya Mikhaylovna,
  etc., 1320
Laszlo, 1172
Lathbury, Mildred, 473
Latimer, Charles, 303
Latnah, 113
Latter, Nina, etc., 1365
Latunsky, 985
Lauchen, George Joachim
  von, 409
Lauda, 774
Lauder, Harold Emery, 1470
Lauger, 501
Laughing Boy, 860
Laundrei, Kommandant, 115
Laura, 150, 497, 561, 1010
Laura G., 1403
Laurana, Professor Paolo, 967
Laurel, 1592, 1693
Laurent, 1540
Laurent, Inspector, 468
Laurie, 816, 1597
Laurie, Hubert, 1097
Lavalle, Paula, 1726
Lavender, 895
Lavenza, Elizabeth, 545
Laverdure, 1768

Laverty, Dale, etc., 933
Lavezzoli, Signora, 605
Lavin, Father, 1161
Lavin, Janos and Diana, 1171
Law, Mrs., 1452
Lawler, Edward, 1003
Lawrence, 1615
Lawson, Catherine (Cat), 340
Lawson, Clarence, 108
Lawson, Edward (Eddie), etc., 591
Lawson, John, etc., 690
Lawyer, 1572
Lay-Brother, Little, 1584
Laye, Camara, 366
Layton, Sarah and Susan, 1264
Lazar, Guy, 810
Lazarus, 233, 1239
Lazarus of Bethany, 863
Lazenby, Arthur, 1686
Lazhenitsyn, Isaakii, 85
Lazhenitsyn, Isaakij, 1136
Lazzaro, Paul, 1422
Leach, 330
Lead actors, four, 449
Leadbelly, 816
Leader, 134
Leader of the Elders, 160
Leading Lady, 437, 1589
Leading Man, 1588
Leah, 528, 1125, 1715
Leamas, Alec, 1469
Lear, 866
Lear, Mark, 996
Lear, Mr., 720
Leary, Blanche, 706
Leavitt, Dr. Peter, 44
Lebeau, 756
Lebedev, Vyacheslav
  Nikolaevich, 842
Lebyatkin, Maria, 1228
Le Cato, Jonathan (Jon), 1038
Le Croce, Signor Palmiro,
  etc., 1589
Ledbetter, Huddie, 816
Ledbetter, Leroy, 926
Lederer, Grant, III, 1195
Ledesma, Ernestinho, 349
Leduc, 756
Ledwidge, Helen, etc., 480
Lee, 271, 1621
Lee, Bull, 1145
Lee, Lana, 321
Lee, Robert E., 1695
Lee, Tom, etc., 1518
Lee, Wickie, 1045
Lee, William, 1072
Lee, Yohan, 539
Lee Chong, 232
Leech, Olive, etc., 1493
Leechfield, Stray, 523
Leeds, James, 274
Leela, 623
Leeming, Belle, etc., 1499
Lees, Murray Ferney, 1476
LeFabre, Mary Agnes, 94
Lefranc, Georgie, 382
Leftwich, Thelma (Tel), 828
Legett, William, 220
Leggatt, 1368
Legionnaire, 1202
Le Grand, Pierre, 116
LeGuen, Father Jean-Martin, 1220
Lehntman, Mrs., 1556

Leibush, 749
Leiden, Arthur, 192
Leiden, Inge (or Isis) von, 242
Leiden, Rittmeister von, 242
Leigh, Jocelyn, 1578
Leigh, William, 1329
Leighton, Miss, 1146
Leila, 1353
Leinsdorf, Count, 963
Leistle, Hortense, 1505
Leiterman, 66
Leitón, Don, 416
Lejour, Alice, etc., 1640
Lekach, Zeftel, 944
Lekh, 1170
Leland, Harry, etc., 401
Lemaire, Germaine, 1212
Le Mesurier, Frank, 1667
Lemon, 86
Lemon, Iris, 1081
Lemon, Nedda, 1712
Lemon, Sydney (Syd), 1195
Lemos, Oscar, 970
Lemuel, 952
Lemulquinier, 1247
Len, 296, 1296, 1341
Lena, 183, 341, 1446, 1676
Lenartovich, Sasha, 85
Lenchen, 816
Lenin, 1606
Lenin, Vladimir Ilich, 1136
Lenka, 1188
Lennox, Terry, etc., 910
Lenny, 689
Lenz, Jacob Michael Reinhold, 872
Leo, 317, 394, 1659
Léo, 1533
Leocadia, 1312
Leon, 681
Leon, Henri, 709
Leona, 56
Leonard, 1503
Leonard, Father Cyprian, 316
Leonard, Ruth, 1257
Leonid, 735
Leonid, Father, 779
Leonidovich, Lev, 230
Leonora, 86
Leopold, 537
Leopolda, Sister, 928
Leopoldina, 349
le Page, Anna, 1512
le Page, Kate, 1286
Lepatofsky, Charles, 1003
Lepellier, Elwin "Leper," 1373
Leregas, 1177
Lermontov, 191
Lerner, Dr., 679
Lerner, Jacobo, etc., 542
Leroi, 1510
Le Rossignol, Jean-Pierre, 874
Le Roux, Lambert, etc., 1232
Lesbian-Ape, 60
Lesje, 886
Leslie, 904, 1002, 1359
Leslie, Sim, 1351
Leslie, Uncle, 1473
Lester, Jeeter, etc., 1582
Lester, Rick, 376
Lestrade, Corporal, 424
Lestrade, John, etc., 1313
Leticia, 1176
Leto II, 431

le Tor, Mrs., 183
Lettner, Joseph, 1299
Letunov, Pavel Evgrafovich,
  etc., 1138
Leung, James (Jimmy
  Ahmed), 644
Lev, Asher, etc., 1067
Levee, 939
Levene, Shelly, 596
Levenson, James D., 1527
Leventhal, Dr., 913
Levi, Carlo, 283
Levi, Dolly, 988
Levi, Matthu, 984
Levielle, Financial Counselor, 389
Levin, Karen, 193
Levin, Seymour, 1088
Levinski, Pavel Yurevich, 736
Levinson, Noach, 1674
Levitt, Calhoun, etc., 1310
Levy, David (Davy), etc., 653
Levy, Ernie, etc., 856
Levy, Gus and Mrs., 321
Lewand, Veronica (Vero), 902
Lewbaum, Claudia, 1726
Lewis, 906, 1458
Lewis, Bill, 701
Lewis, Cecil, 732
Lewis, George, 1146
Lewis, Nora (Nor), 1030
Lewishon, Private, 1707
Leyroud, Père, 126
Lezhnev, Mikhaylo
  Mikhaylych, 1320
Lezo, 1378
l'Heuremaudit, Mélanie, 1648
Lhomond, Erick von, 344
Li Po, 839
Libuschka, 992
Lica, 1164
Licario, Oppiano, etc., 1177
Lidenbrock, Axel, etc., 800
Lie Detector, 1468
Lieb, 733
Lieb the Lion, 570
Liebenau, Harry, 413
Lieber, Emmanuel, 1223
Liebknecht, Karl, 1119
Lieutenant, 1353
Lifer, 1242
Lifshitz, Yonatan, etc., 1194
Light, 175
Lightfoot, Maria, etc., 166
Lightfoot, Nance, 1663
Ligre, Henry Maximilian, etc., 6
Likhas, 1737
Likhodeyev, Styopa, 985
Likhutin, Sergy and Sophia, 1200
Lil, 1093
Lili, 241
Lilli, 830
Lillian, 180, 1031
Lillie, 446
Lilly, Rawdon, 1
Lily, 206, 372, 890, 945, 1358, 1451,
  1614, 1746
Lily, Aunt, 541
Lily Moon, 541
Lin, 299
Lin Fu Chen, 228
Lin To, 616
Lina, 329
Lincoln, Abraham, 523, 1695

Lincoln, Abraham and Mary Todd, 892
Lincoln, Hella, 587
Lind, Jurgen, 392
Lind, Katherine, 589
Linda, 317, 745, 1631
Linde, Dr., 948
Lindner, Karl, 1263
Lindstedt, Niels, 1380
Line, 735
Lingk, James, 596
Linkhorn, Dove, etc., 1673
Lino, 329
Lippanchenko, 1200
Lippmann, Lotte, 479
Lippschitz, Annie "Lippsie," 1195
Liputin, 1228
Liquefactionists, 1072
Lisa, 1569
Liscov, Master Abraham, 883
Listener, 1089
Lister, William Galahad "Blister," 556
Liszt, Dr. Horst, 877
Litko, Bernard (Bernie), 1387
Little, Richard "Bingo," etc., 763
Little Big Man, 893
Little Boy, 1259
Little Darling, 1312
Little David, 237
Little Finger Nail, 268
Little Harp, 1308
Little Horse, 894
Little Lydia, 1734
Little Miss, 1312
Little Mother, 1377
"Little Winds," The, 34
Little Wolf, 267
Lituma, 632
Livingstone, Tom, etc., 769
Liz, 755, 869, 1027, 1507
Liza, 1183, 1361, 1574
Llorente, Señora Consuelo, 90
Lloyd, Arthur, 1500
Lloyd, Barnette, 351
Lloyd, Maggie, 1503
Lloyd, Teddy, 1236
Lo, 1452
Loby, 1660
Lochore, Mrs., 61
Lockhart, Jamie, 1308
Lodgers, Three, 1000
Loeb, Annie, 1435
Loew, Gregory, 345
Loewe, Hans, 716
Loftus, Canon, 184
Logan, Betsy, 1135
Logan, Brother, 1114
Logan, Christie, etc., 408
Logan, Senator, 759
Loggins, Dr. Dan and Dr. Jean, 1050
Lokyar, Robbie, 1238
Lola, 21
Lolita, 761, 905
Lomas, Trevor, 108
London, Bishop of, 253
Lone Ranger, 271
Long, 651
Long, Geoffrey, 703
Long, Gertrude, 1749
Long Rob of the Mill, 1350
Longridge, Piers, 595

Lonoff, E. I. and Hope, 581
Lonstein, 970
Lonval, Léa de, 264
Loomis, George, 1091
Loomis, Herald, etc., 793
Loop Garoo Kid, The, 1762
Loos, Idelette de, 7
Lopez, Carlos, 1726, 1770
López, Enrique, 976
Lopez, Trinidad, 334
López de Ceballos, Adelina, 611
Loran, Gershon, 192
Lorbeer, Harry, 534
Lord, 1334
Lord, Tracy, etc., 1203
Lord Chamberlain, 783
Loreius, 97
Lorencova, 1523
Lorene, 551
Lorenheim, 821
Lorenzo, 180
Lorenzo, Juan Manuel, 611
Loretta, 1096
Lorimer, Becky, 826
Loring, Linda, 911
Loris-Melikov, Captain Count Mikhail Tarielovich, 650
Lorraine, 879, 1735
Loser, Andreas, 11
Lotaria, 738
Lotte, 101
Lotus Blossom, 1519
Lotus Flower, 550
Lou, 21, 753, 1031
Lou Ann, 327
Louis, 131, 341, 1533, 1657
Louis the Cruel, 839
Louise, 20, 23, 1214, 1239, 1440, 1477, 1591
Louise, Sister, 103, 396
Louka, 67
Loukoum, Norbert, 242
Lourdes, 338
Lousse, 1029
Louth, Lady, 1659
Louw, Anna, 1754
Louw, Ignatius "Nasie," 362
Lovell, Mary, 1208
Lover, Hallie's, 1697
Lover, protagonist's, 504
Lover, Sibyl's, 1400
Lovett, Jack, 388
Lovisi, Old Giulio, 305
Lowe, Austin, 1365
Lowe, Julian, 1437
Lowe, Sir Hudson, 1076
Lowell, Robert, 66
Lowther, Gordon, 1236
Loxias, P., 163
Lozelle, Agnes, 152
Lu Ann, 932
Lubey, Lydia and Frank, 30
Lubijova, Marisja, 1268
Luc, 1658
Lucas, 782, 938
Lucas, Asmodeu, 418
Lucas, Lindsey, 1472
Lucas, Sam, 1155
Luccani, Dr. Lothar, etc., 394
Luce, Eva de, 158
Lucero, Adelaido, 1485
Luchnikov, Andrei Arsenievich, etc., 778

Lucie, 350
Luciente of Mattapoisett, 1732
Lucifer, 1635
Lucille, Mama, 1674
Lucio, 1102
Luckett, T. P., 1749
Lucrezia, 290
Lucy, 238, 446, 852, 1654
Lucy, Lady, 1382
Lucy, Miss, 1506
Lucy, Mistress, 1117
Lud, 1358
Lüders, Otto, 145
Ludi Magister Josephus III, 592
Ludmilla, 737, 970
Ludovic, 1509
Ludovico, 1531
Ludwig, Prince von and zu Turm und Parvis, 1001
Luigi, 805, 1575
Luis, 1398
Luisa, 897
Luísa, Old, 805
Luise, Frau, 80
Luiza, 348
Luke, 655
Luke, Sir Walter, 1482
Lula, 434
Lullo, 742
Lulu, 160, 1173
Lulú, 1608
Lumley, Charles, 194
Lumumba, Patrice, 558
Lundgren, Carol, 152
Lunina, Tatyana (Tanya), 778
Lupton, Timothy, 576
Lurie, David (Davey), etc., 746
Lushin, 517
Lushington, 1654
Lusty, Alma and Will, 652
Lutchman, Vimla, etc., 511
Luther, Martin, 937
Luthien Tinuviel, 1411
Luton, Edward (Teddie), 286
Lutz, 1676
Luxemburg, Rosa, 1120
Luzhin, Aleksandr Ivanovich, etc., 384
Lyamin, Fyodor Ignat'yevich, 846
Lyamshin, 1228
Lydell, The Reverend David, 1244
Lydgate, Gertrude, etc., 874
Lydgate, Miss, 571
Lydia, 255, 275, 601
Lydia, Aunt, 655
Lydie, 938
Lygher, Boris Yevdokimovich, 216
Lygher-Cheptsova, Nina, 216
Lykourgos, 1758
Lyle, Mrs., etc., 1391
Lyman, Dr. Gerald, 221
Lyn, 1358
Lynch, 1695
Lynch-Gibbon, Martin, 1385
Lynx, 455
Lyons, 498
Lysias, 1565
Lysimachus of Akarnania, 509

M'Swat, Mr. and Mrs. Peter, 1061
Ma, 309, 748, 1355, 1761
Ma Mla May, 215
Ma Rainey, 940

Maanape, 941
Maas, Mrs. Oedipa, etc., 354
Mabbott, Alcestis and Geoffrey, 788
Mabel, 1739
Mabi, Paul, 1756
Mac, 142, 793
Mac the Knife, 1560
McAffie, Mrs., 1372
MacAindra, Stacey Cameron, etc., 506
MacAlpin, Marian, 445
McAlpine, James, 928
Macandal, 835
McAndrew, Murray, 226
MacAusland, Elizabeth (Libby), 639
McBee, Ewell, 1364
McBee, Henry, etc., 1699
McBride, 327
McBride, Ralph, etc., 1652
Mc Call, 226
McCall, Charlie, etc., 155
McCann, Dermot, 160
McCarthy, 1571
McCaskerville, Margaret (Midge) Warriston, etc., 609
McCatt, Dr., 774
McClellan, Clarisse, 482
McClintoch, Graham, 1512
McCone, Alexander Hamilton, 787
MacConnell, Brian, 502
MacCool, Finn, 83
McCormick, Tadpole, 340
McCrae, 555
McCreadie, Mr., 263
MacCruiskeen, Policeman, 1549
MacDonald, Colonel Archibald, 802
Macdonald, Dwight, 66
Macdonald, Sir John Alexander, 1348
Macdonald, Sophie, 1273
MacDonnell, K. M., 1661
MacDonnell of Kailuana, 1661
McDougall, William, 1349
McEvoy, Major, 1520
McGarrigle, Persse and Peter, 1429
MacGillicuddy, Gillis MacGillis, 1623
McGing, 185
McGloin, Pat, 732
McGoffin, Miss, 1156
McGrath, Phoebe, 740
MacGregor, G. E., 935
Macgregor, Mary, 1235
Macgregor, Mr., 215
MacGuinness, 420
Machal, Emil, 757
MacHardie, James, 553
Macheath, 1560
McHenry, Arthur, 1524
Machi, The, 901
Machin, Arthur, 1551
Machojón, Tomás, etc., 996
Maciel, Antonio Vicente Mendes, 1276
McInerney, Mike, 1748
McIvor, 1350
Mack, 232
Mack, Curtis, 1699
Mack, Edvarda, etc., 1172
Mack, Harrison, etc., 524

Mack, Runnington (Runner), 1324
MacKarkle, Gideon, 1238
McKarkle, Hannah, etc., 827
Mackay, Hugh, 999
Mackay, Miss, 1236
McKechnie, Mr., 820
McKelva, Judge Clinton, etc., 1158
MacKendrick, 261
Mackenna, Miss, 1747
Mackenzie, Big Alec, 119
McKenzie, Professor Ian, 1372
Mackinsen, Pamela, 960
McKyle, 1322
McLachlen, Lachlen, 660
McLash, Frank, etc., 235
McLaurin, Alan, etc., 1309
McLean, Captain, 1519
McLeavy, etc., 915
McLennan, Hamish, 1233
Macleod, 203
McMackin, Imelda, etc., 1612
McMahon, Fay, 915
Macmann, 951
McMurphy, Randle, 1149
MacMurray, Margaret (Maggie) Biggart, 1713
McNab, Dr., 1402
McNabb, Bishop Hamish, 825
McNair, Clem, 1181
McNeil, Jenny, 365
McNeil, Lonnie Roy, 855
McNullis, Father, 1613
Macnure, Captain, 1631
McPhail, Rob, etc., 1432
MacPhellimey, Fergus (The Pooka), 83
McPherson, 729
MacPherson, John, 64
McQua, Archibald, 1624
McQueen, Huntly, 1627
Macrae, Neil, 118
McRae, Neil, 136
Macrain, Elspeth, 610
McRaith, Dan, 408
Macrob, Tormod, 720
McRory, James Ignatius, etc., 1708
MacShilluck, Reverend Edward, 1352
McTavish, Alistair, 1508
McTeazle, 405
MacTeer, Claudia, 181
MacTeer, Frieda, 181
Macunaíma, 940
McVarish, Urquhart, 1276
MacWhirr, Tom, 1629
Macy, Marvin, 110
Madam President, 901
Madame, 947, 1341, 1498, 1499
Madame, The Great Bald (Death), 550
Madame-la-Reine, 175
Madame R., 1268
Madame Tortoise, 362
Madden, James, 907
Maddy, 32
Madeleine, 258, 1644
Madge, 1202
Madhuri, 469
Madison, Claire, 1395
Madison, James, 220
Madison, Oscar, 1130
Madison, Robert (Bob), 863
Madureira, Dr. Teodoro, 417

Madurga, Miss, 307
Mafolo, Len, 1127
Mag, 1029
Magalone, Luigi, 283
Magda, 648
Magdalena, 782, 1446
Magdalena, La, 194
Magdalena (Magda), 1505
Mageeba, President, 1094
Magelone, 1174
Maggie, 20, 1173, 1523
Maggs, 657
Maghan Kön Fatta, 643
Magician, Head, 636
Magiot, Dr., 312
Magistrate, 444, 1402, 1671
Magnificent, The, 95
Magnifico, Il, 25
Magnifico Giganticus, 538
Magnin, Colonel, 968
MaGrath, Lenny and Meg, 350
Mahan, Sailor, 302
Mahesh, 140
Mahmilji, Dr. Suhbi al-, 289
Mahon, Donald, etc., 1437
Mahoney, Jim, 1298
Mahood, 1644
Maia, 1565
Maiberling, Count Alfred, 622
Maid, 875, 1312, 1607
Maiden, Miss Sibyl, 1430
Maier, Helmut, 1505
Maijstral, Fausto, etc., 1647
Mailer, Norman, 66
Maimas, The Daimon, 1708
Maingot, Jacqueline, etc., 548
Mainwaring, Hugo, etc., 1005
Mainwaring, Professor Felix Byron, 874
Mainz, Lena, 1557
Maire, 1601
Maisie, 1013
Maitland, Bill, 755
Majcinek, Francis and Sophie, 961
Maji, 673
Major, 756, 1385
Maka, Orfée, 1567
Makadoneli, Misa, 1661
Makak, 424
Makargin, Major General Pytor Afanasyevich, 514
Makarov, Volodya, 463
Makepeace, Eddy, 791
Makepeace, Leonard (Lenny), 947
Makkar, 217
Makropoulos, Dimitrios, 303
Malachi of Hildesheim, 1073
Malchios, P. D., 226
Malcolm, Sergeant, 357
Maleldil the Younger, 1458
Malevil, 1769
Malevsky, Count, 516
Malfenti, Giovanni, etc., 328
Mali, 1653
Malika, 1353
Malinowski, Dominic, 782
Malins, Freddy, etc., 373
Malka, 135
Malkolmov, Gennady Apollinarievich (Genka), 215
Malkuson, Nathan, 192
Mallet, Mrs., 1747
Mallindaine, Hubert, 1513

CHARACTER INDEX

Mallory, Jane, etc., 365
Mallow, Hober, 537
Mallow, Tom, 874
Malloy, Moose, 494
Malloy, Sam and Mrs., 233
Malmert, Camille, 243
Malmstrom, Bill, 1499
Malnate, Giampiero, 567
Malone, 951, 1644
Malone, Mr., 1388
Malone, Walter, 929
Maloney, 1222
Maloney, Cor Mogaill, 185
Maloney, Mary, 586
Malopo, Willie, 986
Malorthy, Germaine "Mouchette," etc., 1634
Malory, The Reverend Julian, etc., 473
Malskat, Lothar, 1267
Malter, Reuven, etc., 281
Maltravers, Peter, etc., 24
Malty, 114
Mama, 29, 340, 734, 1262
Maman, 887
Mambo, 1469
Mami, 203
Mammy Barracuda, 523
Mamurin, Colonel Yakov Ivanovitch, 515
Man, 37, 104, 129, 558, 827, 889, 1600, 1613
Man, Blind, 943
Man, Dead, 363, 580
Man, dim, 1029
Man, Fat, 1003
Man, Lame, 750
Man, Nice young, 544
Man, old, 11, 201, 255, 1237, 1631
Man, old blind, 1630
Man, Old Character, 1589
Man, security, 1671
Man, Unemployed, 616
Man, unnamed, 1265
Man, Young, 40, 634, 652, 1124
Man Alone, Young, 1090
Man in the Iron Mask, 515
Man in Tecali, 1332
Man Kee, 1452
Man-man, 1009
Man Next Door, 613
Man of the World, 888
Man of Thirty, 1242
Man on the gilded bed, 124
Manatee, Mr., 826
Mancebo, Antonia, 332
Manchek, Major Arthur, 45
Mancuso, Angelo, 321
Mandel, Arnold, 1225
Mandel, Warrant Officer, 1671
Mandelbaum, Professor, 102
Manders, Laurence, etc., 312
Mandrake, 1116
Mandrova, Sonya, 267
Mandy, 1594
Mandy, Aunt, 1155
Manfredi, 1
Mangan, Alfred "Boss," 670
Manganese, Veronica, 1647
Mangini, 1589
Manhood, Flora, 479
Maniac, 8
Mańka, Mad Aunt, 1717

Manley, Mrs., 319
Mann, Frau, 1100
Mannaei, 719
Manners, Al, 1617
Manners, Daphne, 1263
Manners, Geraldine, 433
Manners, Gwendaline, 1017
Mannie, 1036
Mannock, Willie, 720
Mannoury, 395
Manor, Skelly, 1297
Mansfield, Lydia Strickland, etc., 1044
Manso, Máximo, etc., 1163
Manson, Andrew, etc., 287
Manson, Gloria, 910
Mantee, Duke, 1201
Manuel, 911, 967, 970
Manuel, Don, 483, 1330
Manuela, 1164
Manus, 1601
Manus, Brother, 74
Manvekar, Anand, 369
Manwë, 1410
Maple, Gramp, etc., 1201
Maples, 755
Maplestead, Rick, 999
Marama, 661
Marango, Mr., 838
Marat, Jean-Paul, 971
Marbot, Sir Andrew, 973
Marcel, 1079
Marcel, Étienne, 116
Marceline, 743, 1768
Marcello, Abbe, 1462
March, Charles, etc., 1481
March, Ellen (Nellie), 541
Marchais, Jean, 1501
Marchand, 756
Marchbanks, Miss, 319
Marchetti, 1165
Marco Polo, 775
Marcos, 922, 969
Margaret, 28, 378, 628, 660, 754, 783
Margarethe, 1267
Margarita, 984
Margarita del Campo, 760
Margayya, 505
Marge, 412, 1359
Margherita, 72
Margie, 733
Margolin, Archibald (Archie), 60
Margrave, Jeff, 676
Margret, 1070, 1190
Marguerite, 852, 1644
Marguerite, Queen, 475
Maria, 570, 913, 995, 1756
Maria Augusta, 1557
Maria da Gloria, 1557
Maria dos Reis, 805
María Griselda, 1398
Maria José, 1557
Maria-Veronica, Mother, 825
Marian, 1399
Marianne, 548, 870
Marie, 310, 324, 875, 1358, 1533, 1658
Marie, Queen, 475
Marie-Laure, 265
Marie-Thérèse, 242
Mariella, 647
Marigold, 163

Mariko, 1523
Marina, 317, 1611
Mariner, 1412
Marinette, 1494
Mario, 88, 338, 1521
Marion, 302
Maris, Stella, 450
Marjorie, 496, 1243
Mark, 721, 1002, 1031, 1631
Marketa, 191, 796
Markovich, Caesar, 1147
Marks, Sonia, 1132
Marlene, 1591
Marloe, Francis, 163
Marlowe, Philip, 151, 493, 910
Marlusha, 778
Marnal, Alexandre, 258
Marquez, Dolores, 194
Marquis, Italian, 490
Marquise of O——, 976
Marrast, 1421
Marriott, Lindsay, 494
Mars, 1311
Mars, Eddie and Mona, 152
Marsh, Margaret, etc., 600
Marshall, John, 220
Marshfield, The Reverend Thomas, etc., 1033
Marsili, Ludovico, 562
Marston, 752
Marta, 1170
Martell, Jerome, etc., 1685
Marter, Hilke, etc., 1379
Martha, 808, 886, 1738
Marthe, 776, 802
Marthraun, Michael, etc., 301
Marti, Enriqueta "Queca," 202
Martial, Paul and Lucienne, 35
Martim, 63
Martin, 101, 216, 298, 530, 1031, 1399, 1484
Martín, 865
Martin, Christopher Hadley "Pincher," 1208
Martin, Daniel (Dan), etc., 365
Martin, Gertrude, 1182
Martin, Granny, 1382
Martin, Joe and Rita, 204
Martin, Jonathan, 1223
Martin, Letitia, 571
Martin, Mr. and Mrs. Donald, 105
Martin, Shago, 39
Martinez, 708
Martínez, Corporal, 1148
Martinez, Julio, 1071
Martínez de Calderón, Osvaldo, 608
Martiniano, 957
Martins, Miss Helen, 1303
Martlow, Charlie, 675
Maru, 980
Marukakis, N., 304
Marva, Miss, 925
Marvin, Professor Alan, 681
Marvy, Duane, 626
Marx, Carlo, 1145
Marx, Karl Heinrich, 815
Mary, 103, 105, 319, 831, 859, 981, 990, 1082, 1270, 1342, 1600
Mary Agnes, 309
Mary Appenzeller, 585
Mary-Ben, 1708
Mary Jane, 373

Mary-Jim, 1708
Mary K., 390
Mary L., 1571
Mary Magdalene, 860, 1082
Mary of Bethany, 831
Mary of Migdal, 1082
Mary Rose, 316
Mary the Hairdresser, 831
Maryk, Lieutenant Stephen, 224
Marylou, 1145
Masamune Date, His
  Lordship, 1332
Masao, Horiki, 1107
Masataka, Yakushiji Danjō, 1367
Masefield, Dr. Viola, 440
Masha, 216, 297
Mashka, 216
Maskers, 281
Mason, Annette Cosway, etc., 1715
Mason, Cynthia, 136
Mason, Jill, 467
Mason, Kate, 1286
Mason, Roger, 1463
Massa, Donato José, 671
Masseur, 1445
Massot, the shepherd and his
  wife, 175
Masta Fa, 779
Master, 786, 984
Master of Ceremonies, 133, 636,
  1259, 1599
Master of the Castle, 1655
Masters, Rickie, etc., 442
Masters, Will, 222
Masterson, Mike, 627
Masuilis, 782
Mat, 1291
Match, Sergeant, 1707
Mate, Chief, 1368
Mate, Monster's, 545
Mate, Second, 1368
Matefi, 70
Mater, 1659
Matera, Benjamino (Mino), 1538
Matern, Walter, etc., 413
Mateu, Don, 1291
Matfield, Lilian, 46
Mathers, Phillip, 1549
Mathieu, Monsieur and Madame
  Camille, 1049
Mathilda, Miss, 1556
Mathilde, 441
Mathis, 800
Matiana, 866
Matilda, 325
Matriarca, 573
Matriarch, 1382
Matrons, Two, 359
Matryona, 1413
Matsugae, Kiyoaki, 1354
Matter, Karl, 144
Matthew, 860
Matthews, Donnie, 1002
Matthews, Hallam, 1191
Matthews, Quentin, etc., 1104
Matthias, 830
Mattie, 1762
Maturin, Isabel Bradley and
  Gray, 1273
Matzerath, Oskar, 1266
Maud, 298
Maude May, 1698
Maudsley, Marian, etc., 597

Maugham, W. Somerset, 1273
Maulsby, Sarah Abbott, 1225
Maunciple, Miss Virginia, 18
Maunoir, Jim-Jacques, 588
Maurice, 382, 1157, 1718
Mauricio, 572, 1326
Maurier, Jacques de, 342
Maurier, Mrs. Patricia, 1042
Maurya, 1294
Maus, Johannes, 1118
Mavrin, Ortrud, etc., 1654
Mavrocordato, Prince, 1018
Max, 415, 689, 1275, 1405
Maxey, Captain Harris (later,
  Colonel), 1155
Maxim, Gifford, 1006
Maximilian, Father, 2
Maximovich, Georgii, 58
Maximovitch, Nikolai, 519
Maxson, Troy, etc., 498
Maxted, Mr., 454
Maxwell, Isaac, 487
May, 529, 564
May, Andrew, 1232
May, Aunt, 1278
May, Ma Hla, 215
Maya, 1553
Maybury, Diana, 634
Maybury, Wilfred, 818
Mayer, 254
Mayer, Wiletta, 1616
Maynard, Mr., 277
Mayo, Ida, 1574
Mayor, 865, 1376
Mayor of Güllen, 1660
Mayor of B., 897
Mazur, Halinka Apt, 1675
Mazur, Yasha, 944
Mead, Lester, 1485
Meade, Hazel, 1037
Meakin, Mrs., 820
Mealey, Anselm, 824
Meares, John, 218
Mechanical Hounds, 483
Meche, 1553
Meck, Gottlieb, 145
Medardo, Viscount of
  Terralba, 299
Medea, 834
Medici, Lorenzo de', etc., 25
Medina, Franco de, 1599
Medium, 623
Medrano, Gabriel, 1726
Medusa, 1248
Medvedev, 1347
Mee Lan, 280
Meena, 505
Meers, Sylvia, 591
Meeuwissen, Corrie, etc., 829
Meg, 879, 1508
Mehmed-Pasha, 196
Mehring, 332
Meidanov, 517
Meidling, Wilhelm, 1070
Meighan, Flora and Jake, 1624
Meir, Rabbi Yosef, 749
Meitei, 725
Mela, Grandmother, 1177
Melancholy Ruffian, 1384
Meleager, 557
Melinda, 1696
Melkor, 1410
Mellings, Alice, etc., 614

Mellon, Lee, 322
Mellors, Oliver, 843
Melody, 165
Melquíades, 1150
Melvin, 1647
Melvyn, Sybylla Penelope,
  etc., 1060
Members of the Audience, 1589
Meme, 865, 1153
Memed, İnce (Slim), 993
Men, First and Second, 852
Men, tiny old, 860
Men, Two Wise, 1270
Men, young, 1613
Men with Machine-Guns,
  Three, 104
Ménalque, 743
Mendel, 735
Mendel, Rabbi Yehudal, 749
Mendelsohn, Solly, 904
Méndez Ruda, Doña Munda, 1177
Mendiola, Álvaro, 974
Mendoza, Josefina (Fina),
  etc., 1648
Mendoza, Mrs., 24
Menelao, 572
Menestheus, 834
Menkes, Pavel, 1675
Menou-Segrais, Father, 1635
Mentira, José, 485
Menuchim, 792
Menzies, Archibald, 218
Mephos, 226
Mercator, Vladko, 779
Mercedes, Ana, 1527
Merchant, 1631
Merchant, Cloth, 700
Mercy, Max, 1080
Merg, Heinrich, 1299
Meridian, 997
Merlin, 1115, 1458
Merode, 319
Meron, John, 193
Meroving, Vera, 1647
Merrick, Ronald, 1264
Merrison, 1375
Merryweather, 657
Merrywin, Nora, 381
Merten, Joseph, 1110
Mertz, Zina, 582
Merumeci, Leo, 1569
Merwe, Piet van der, 254
Meryemce, 1719
Mesa, 200
Meshkov, Temosha, 779
Mesía, Alvaro, 1284
Messenger, 302, 1737
Messengers, Two, 789
Messiah ben David, 1081
Messire, 984
Mestwina, 526
Meta, 1623
Metcalf, Major, 1052
Metellus, 1599
Meterstein, Mr., 1146
Methuen, Janet, etc., 1626
Methwold, William, 1008
Metty, 140
Metusela, 1662
Metz, Essie, 1774
Metz, Professor, 955
Metzger, 355

Mews, Sir Byron "Chimpy,"
   etc., 1500
Mexico, Roger, 624
Mezalyansova, Madame, 125
Mezy, Monsieur Lenormand
   de, 835
Mhani, 808
Mhendi, Davis, 1756
Mi Tzŭ, 616
Mibs, 881
Michael, 61, 197, 1065, 1205,
   1449, 1502
Michael, Mattie, 1734
Michael K, 884
Michael of Cesena, 1073
Michaelis, 844
Michaels, 821
Michaud, 1540
Michel, 743, 912
Michel, Helen, etc., 1752
Michelangelo Buonarroti, 24
Michele, Bobbi, 857
Michelle, 191
Michie, Maisie, 804
Mick, 844, 1214
Mickelsson, Peter J., 1002
Mickey, 21, 26, 123, 723
Middleton, Gerald, etc., 50
Midget, The, 1068
Midwife, 977
Miehlau, Sibylle, 527
Mientus, 499
Mieze, 144
Mignon, 1461
Mignon-les-Petits-Pieds, 1165
Migulin, Sergei Kirillovich, 1138
Mikamé, Toyoki, 983
Mike, 880, 1036, 1342
Mike the Mouth, 627
Mikhailovna, Aleksandra, 1085
Mikhaylych, Sergey, 490
Mikheev, 1347
Mikheyev, Saviely, 493
Mikit, Lieutenant, 1250
Miksha, 1587
Mikulin-Pechbauer, Professor
   Edward, 1000
Miland, Irmgard, 1461
Milbaum, Princess, 102
Milch, Dr. Jacob, 646
Mildred, 1058
Mildred, Sister, 2
Miles, 1449
Miles, General Bear Coat (Nelson
   A.), 269
Miles, Sarah, etc., 454
Milillo, Doctor, 284
Military Chaplain, 1047
Milkmaid, 580
Milkman, 1445
Millbanke, Annabella, 272
Miller, 569, 1496
Miller, Gerda, 1132
Miller, Henry, 1615
Miller, James, 480
Miller, Julia, etc., 809
Miller, Nick, 1343
Millie, 701
Millikin, Moira, 681
Millington, Miss, 1023
Millionaire, 92
Mills, Dan, 348
Milly, 708

Milne, Jacob, 1094
Miltiades, General, 1509
Milton, Michael, 1751
Milyaga, Captain, 882
Mimi, 632
Mimosa I, 1166
Mimosa II, 1165
Mineyko, Zygmunt, 1219
Mingo, 165
Minister, 465
Minister Q., 957
Minkoff, Myrna, 321
Minnie, 1521
Minnies, Major, 672
Minogue, Ward, 79
Minoru, Mimaki, 951
Minos, 834
Mira, 1737
Mira, Tiakinga Meto, 186
Mira-masi, 294
Miranda, Francisca Xavier, 419
Mirbeau, Octave, 890
Mirbel, Jean de, etc., 1731
Mirbel, Jean de and Michèle
   de, 849
Mirek, 190
Mirella, 1553
Miriam, 203, 792, 831, 863, 1042,
   1423, 1687
Mirza Aga, 1433
Mis, Ebling, 539
Misako, 1439
Mishari, Emir Khaled al-, 288
Miskell, Michael, 1748
Miss Billie, 472
Miss Mother, 1502
Missionary, 168
Missouri, 1158
Mr. Albert ——, 308
Mr. Gentleman, 342
Mr. . . . , 1588
Mrs. . . . , 1589
Mita, 146
Mitani, Kikuji, 1554
Mitchell, 1725
Mithrandir, 1412
Mitka, 1171
Mitrani, León, 542
Mitterer, Josef von, 195
Mitty, Fred, 47
Mitzelbach, Grete, 41
Mitzi, 350
Miyoshi, 951
Mizoguchi, 1522
Mizushima, Kangetsu, 725
Moadine, 677
Möbius, Johann Wilhelm, 1206
Mockford, James, 937
Moeding, Walter, 920
Moeller, 799
Moffat, Miss Lily Christabel, 336
Mofokenzazi, Sam, 1755
Mohammed, 647, 1160
Mohammed, Dhris, 304
Mohansingh, Imbal, 564
Moine, Mademoiselle, 1533
Moira, 319, 655
Moktir, 743
Mola, Rosetta, 41
Moleka, 980
Molina, Luis Alberto, 837
Moll, 952
Mollie, 51

Molloy, 1028
Molloy, Irene, 988
Molly, 978
Molomo, Dan, 1248
Molteni, Riccardo and Emilia, 578
Molyneux, Colin and Sheila, 143
Mom, 1621
Momina, 41
Mommbrekke, Lucy, 375
Mommina, 1589
Mommy, 39
Momoko, 1407
Mona, 1616
Monahan, Sean, 398
Monceau, 756
Mondaugan, Kurt, 1649
Monegro, Joaquín, etc., 3
Monet, Claude, etc., 890
Monica, 702
Monican, Susie, 1414
Monique, 838
Monk, Colin, 770
Monk, Talbot Waller, 1741
Monkey, The, 1225
Monkiewicz, Father, 782
Monod, Guy, 697
Monseigneur, 700
Monsewer, 700
Monsieur, 947
Monsieur C. K., 303
Montag, Georg, 1409
Montag, Guy, etc., 482
Montague, Harold, 1313
Montana, Hall, etc., 809
Montaner, 1609
Montani, Angelo, 118
Montanza il Toro, Lodovico,
   etc., 436
Montefort, Antonia, 1753
Montero, Felipe, 90
Montero, Lola, 1304
Montès, Antoine, 1717
Monzano, Papa, 247
Moody, Elvira, 472
Moon, Junie, 1521
Moon, Lily, 541
Moon, Meriwether Lewis, 81
Moon-Watcher, 1627
Mooney, 828
Moore, Duane, 858
Moore, Duncan, 1281
Moore, George and Dorothy, 808
Moore, Isabel, etc., 504
Moore, Roger, 1483
Moore, Tom, etc., 327
Moore, Vivaldo, 56
Moorhouse, Jabez, 1702
Moors, Patricia, etc., 1456
Moorthy, 814
Moosbrugger, 963
Mor, William, etc., 1334
Mora, Gaspar, 1444
Mora, Marta, 1325
Moraïtis, 89
Moran, 182, 733
Moran, Jacques, 1028
Moran, Jacques (the
   younger), 1029
Morato, Don Alvaro, 1290
Morazan, Francisco, 802
More, Billy, 836
More, Dr. Thomas, 925
More, Sir Thomas, 53

More, Sir Thomas, etc., 952
Moreira Cesar, Colonel
  Antonio, 1277
Morel, 772
Morelli, 42, 696
Morello, Chuck, 733
Morello, Delia, 436
Moreno, Delia, 437
Moresby, Port and Kit, 1390
Moretti, Lauro, 1513
Morgan, 1009, 1127
Morgan, Dorothy, 1138
Morgan, Emma Lou, 166
Morgan, Harry and Marie, 1577
Morgan, Jane Lightfood, 166
Morgan, Senator, 760
Morgana, Fulvia, 1429
Morgenstein, Saul, 1604
Morgoth, 1410
Moriarity, Maurice P., 1093
Moriarty, Dean, 1145
Moriuw, 1382
Morkan, Kate, etc., 372
Morneen, Sheila, 1282
Morpeth, Miss, 913
Morrel, Jean, 273
Morris, Arthur, 1115
Morrison, Harry, 1233
Morrissey, Lipsha, 927
Morrow, Cecil, 1116
Morse, Dixie, 108
Morse, Mr., 701
Mortar, Lily, 280
Mortimer, 1433
Mortimer, Miss Julia Percival, 917
Mortin, Alexandre, etc., 1532
Morton, Blanche, etc., 205
Morton, Colonel Henry, 524
Morton, Ivan, 1724
Morton, Paul, 420
Morty, Uncle, 99
Mory, Angèle, 1215
Mosca, Gittel, 1625
Moses, 51, 635, 1041, 1475
Moses, Trinity, 1299
Moshe, 1124
Moshe, Rabbi, 749
Mosher, Ed, 732
Moss, Dave, 596
Motel-Keeper, 36
Mother, 21, 22, 44, 92, 191, 360,
  559, 578, 1189, 1260, 1345, 1346,
  1352, 1380, 1669
Mother, Aina's, 1192
Mother, Alex's, 295
Mother, Becker's, 1118
Mother, Camden's, 1241
Mother, Eva's, 472
Mother, G.'s, 748
Mother, Grendel's, 637
Mother, Helga's, 1251
Mother, Inder Lal's, 672
Mother, Jaromil's, 887
Mother, Katherine's, 727
Mother, Lenny's, 948
Mother, Menelao's, 573
Mother, Miloš', 297
Mother, Mizoguchi's, 1522
Mother, Mouchette's, 1048
Mother, Offred's, 655
Mother, Prem's, 716
Mother, protagonist's, 1169
Mother, Richard's, 1039

Mother, Ryzak's, 742
Mother, Skelton's, 1103
Mother, T's, 916
Mother, The Flash-eyed, 1064
Mother, Tom's, 780
Mother Courage, 1046
Mother-in-law, Bird's, 1197
Mother Jones, 1345
Mother Meakin, 820
Mother Peep, 827
Mother She, 1502
Mott, Joe, 732
Mouaque, Madame, 1768
Mouche, 921
Mouchette, 1048
Mougre, 103
Mountain, Stanley, 936
Mountain Bride, 1461
Mouse, The, 441
Moustique, 424
Moutelik, Bertie, 350
Mowat, Stephen, 1351
Moynihan, James, 502
Mozart, Wolfgang Amadeus, 34
"Mucho" Maas, 355
Mucius, 227
Mudge, First Lieutenant
  Zachary, 218
Mudito, 1125
Muerte, 991
Mugwumps, 1072
Muhammad, Abdu, 289
Muhra, 647
Mui, 1451
Mukhachov-Bagrationsky,
  Sergeyevich, 216
Mulata, The, 1054
Mulcahy, Father, 505
Muldoon, Roberta, 1751
Mule, The, 538
Muleteer, 801
Mulge, Dr. Herbert, 18
Mullcanny, Tim, 1283
Mullen, Walt, 1497
Muller, Barbara, etc., 823
Muller, Kurt, etc., 1684
Müller, Beate/Trude, etc., 1102
Mulqueen, Eustace, 62
Mulrooney, Mike, 1455
Mulvaney, Gerda, 1132
Mulvaney, Nancy, 913
Mumbo, 895
Mummy, 580
Mums, 959
Munda, Grandmother, 1177
Mundt, Hans-Dieter, 1469
Munira, Godfrey, 1198
Munn, Homir, 538
Murano, 1302
Murchison, George, 1263
Murderers, Three, 444
Muriel, 316
Muriel, Auntie, 886
Murkett, Webb, etc., 1253
Murkins, Gladys Matthews, 1105
Murphy, 1059, 1618
Murr, Kater, 883
Murray, 1131
Murray, Alison, etc., 731
Murray, Angela, etc., 1215
Murray, Charles, 1468
Murray, Doctor Angus, 119
Murray "The Goose," 872

Musak, 1687
Musclewhite, Biff, 1056
Musgrave, Serjeant, 1376
Musgrove, Clement, 1307
Mushari, Norman, 599
Music, 1746
Music, Susanna, 1161
Music Master, 593
Music teacher, 452, 1049
Mussolini, Benito, 482
Mustache, 746
Mustache Sal, 1762
Mustafa, 779
Mustian, Milo, etc., 574
Muswell, Aunt Sarrie, 323
Mut, 798
Mut-em-enet, 798
Mute, 280
Muthoni, 1301
Mutterperl, Sammy, 1681
Muzzlehatch, 620
Mwawate, 807
Mxenge, Fats, 212
Myself, 550
Myshin, Major, 514
Myshlaevsky, Viktor
  Viktorovich, 371
Mytyl, 174
Myuller, Zoya Nikitishna, 1144

Nabokov, Vladimir
  Vladimirovich, 1216
Nacar, 573
Nacho, 96
Nacht, Blume, 1415
Nadelashin, Junior Lieutenant, 515
Nadezhda, 1012
Naegeli, Liselotte, 392
Nagel, Johan Nilsen, 1068
Nagg, 458
Nagoa, 1259
Naibusi, 1661
Naifu, The, 1332
Nailles, Eliot, etc., 210
Nair, Shivaraman, 784
Nan, 1
Nanapush, Gerry, 927
Nancy, 886, 1336, 1359
Nanda, 1602
Nanette, 1494
Nantauquas, 1579
Naoji, 1380
Naomi, 898, 1074, 1225
Napier, Rockingham (Rocky),
  etc., 473
Napoleon, 51
Narayan, 470
Narcense, 117
Narcissus, 1077
Nardi, 1589
Narota, Tommy, 126
Narrow Nose, 861
Narumov, 1245
Nasar, Santiago, 284
Nash, 918
Nastya, 535
Natalya, 217
Nathan, 1082
Nathan, Abe and Mildred, 366
Nathaniel, 517
Nathanson, Reb Yudel, 200
Nathanson, Reb Yudel, 201
Natividade, 98

Nava, 1431
Navazio, Elaine, 857
Navoni, Alfredo, 664, 901
Nawab, 672
"Nawnim," 235
Nazareno, Leticia Mercedes
    María, 95
N'Deye Touti, 602
N'Doye, Oumi, 1759
Ndugire, Samuel, 730
Neary, 1059
Ned, 1203, 1460, 1507
Nedokoro, Mitsusaburo (Mitsu),
    etc., 1407
Neehatin, 164
Nègre Ange Soleil, le, 1165
Negro Angel Sun, 1165
Negro-Sarah, 558
Negus, The, 969
Neige, Madame Augusta, 168
Neighbor, First, 161
Neighbor, Second, 161
Neighbors, Three, 1445
Neighbour, 1242
Neilan, Kit, 548
Neill, Althea, 828
Neill, Ann Brandon, 840
Neill, Daniel, 1345
Nélida, 399
Neljapäev, Jaan, 549
Nell, 458, 1185, 1591
Nellie, 1281, 1346
Nelson, 327
Nemuro Haru, etc., 1321
Nené, 670
Nenè, 1589
Nephew, Joe's, 415
Néré, Renée, 1649
Nervo, Guillermo "Mito," etc., 684
Nerzhin, Gleb Vikentyevich, 512
Nesselrode, Lidochka, 779
Nestor, 1133
Nestorius, Walter, 658
Nettie, 308
Nettles, Professor Leopold, 852
Nettleship, Horace, etc., 575
Neubauer, 698
Neuenburger, Herr, 179
Neumann, Baruch David, 1588
Neumiller, Otto, etc., 147
Neuwirth, 1523
Nevada, 1205
Nevels, Gertie, etc., 414
Nevermore, Duchess Alice of, 1688
Neville, Philip, 703
Neville, The Reverend Mr.
    A. J., 263
Nevins, John, 1617
Newby Family, 263
Newman, James (Jimmy), 400
Newspaperman, Unnamed, 960
Newton, Isaac, 1206
Neyarky, Alik, 216
Nezvanova, Anna
    "Netochka," 1084
N'Gone, 1759
Ngugi, Jim, 837
Nibsmith, Ruth, 1709
Nicholas of Morimondo, 1074
Nicholas I, 650
Nicholas II, 1136
Nicholson, Elizabeth (Liz), 1757
Nicholson, Richard, 982

Nicholson, Terry O., 676
Nick, 655, 1571, 1744
Nicke, 379
Nickles, 789
Nicodemon, Rabbi, 1081
Nicol, Brenda, 474
Nicola, 67
Nicolaas, 255
Nicolás, Fray, 707
Nicole, 1421
Nicoll, 555
Nicolo, 1579
Niece, 310, 966
Niemand, Fritz Jemand von, 1447
Nifty Louie, 961
Nigel, 1244
Night Brother, 1452
Nightingale, R. E. A., 1482
Nightshade, Jim, 1442
Nijo, Lady, 1591
Niki Jumpei, 1729
Nikolaevna, Zinaida (Zina), 519
Nikolayevna, Anna, 80
Nilssen, Peter, 1251
Nilsson, Axel, 486
Nimier, Roger, 242
Nimmo, Nina, etc., 1365
Nino, 679
Nissen, Reb Abraham, 459
Nizza, Fray Marcos de, 1317
Njooki, 730
Nkwanta, Asamoa, 666
N. N., 80
No Mustache, 746
Noaga, 1259
Noah, 421, 528, 635
Noah Webster, 918
Noble, Maury, 128
Nocio, 464
Nock, Dr. Hubert, 727
Noel, 885, 1742
Nolan, Denis, 1639
Nolan, Doctor, 138
Nollins, Radley, 1333
Nonnie, Aunt, 1506
Nonno, 1098
Noonan, Richard (Dick), 1307
Nora, 1035, 1295
Norden, Van, 1616
Nordhoff, Charles, 447
Nordstöm, Erik, 1078
Norishige, Oribenshō, 1367
Norm, 1738
Norman, 1243, 1633
Norman, Alan, 410
Norman, Sarah, etc., 274
Noronha, Felicidade de, 349
Norris, 152
Norris, Sophie and Charlie, 1137
North, Duke of, 867
North, Theophilus (Teddy), 1536
Northrup, Charlie, 872
Norton, Simon, 1414
Norvegov, Pavel Petrovich, 1347
Noske, Gustav, 1120
Notary, 1718
Noth, Helga, etc., 1047
Nounoune, 264
Novak, 1230
Novara, Domenico Maria de, 410
Novelist, Spanish, 1268
Novitsky, David, 62
Novo-Sila, 779

Novosiltsev, Count, 779
Novotny, Molly, 961
Noyocki, Eilif, 1046
Nucingen, Baron Frédéric de, 1464
Nugent, Michael, 1003
Nulty, Lieutenant, 494
Numa, The, 991, 1289
Numi, Alberico de', 6
Nun, 699
Nunnery, George, 22
Nunnery, Susan, 21
Nunziata, 71
Nuper, Ollie, 1497
Nurse, 1737
Nurse, Rebecca, 352
Nuša, 561
Nuta, 200
Nuti, Baron, 437
Nuto, 1034
Nuttall, Reg, 222
Nwadika, John, 70
Nwaka, 70
Nwoye, 1545
Nyambura, 1301
Nyaneba, 667
Nye, Dr. Eugene Albert, 678
Nymphea alba, 1347
Nyobi, 160

O., 125
O-90, 1700
Oakenshield, Thorin, 682
Oakhart, General Douglas O., 626
Oakley, Maurice, etc., 1465
Oba, Elesin, 377
O'Balacaun, Roory, 1283
Oban, Willie, 732
Obd, Tome, 183
Oberlander, Lu Ann Hampton
    Laverty, etc., 932
Oberlin, Johann Friedrich, etc., 873
Obi, 1106
Obierika, 1545
Obika, 70
Obispo, Dr. Sigmund, 18
Obregón, Father, 612
O'Brian, Jack, 1299
Obsle, 870
O'Byrne, Canon Mick, 1203
Ochi, Tofu, 725
O'Connal, Brian Sean MacMurray,
    etc., 1712
O'Connor, Dr. Matthew, 1099
Octopus, 779
Odell, Danby, 209
Odette, 126
Odilón, 484
Odoaker, 1310
O'Doherty, Mary and Cyril, 1223
O'Donnell, Gareth, etc., 1202
O'Donnell, Hugh Mor, 1601
Oduche, 70
Oedipus, 761, 834
Oetsu, Lady, 1368
Ofeyi, 1362
Offenbach, Emily, 1084
Officer, 425
Officer of Dragoons, 1376
Officers, Five Young
    Aviation, 1589
Offred, 654
Ofglen, 655
O'Gara, Consolata, etc., 1612

Ogé, Doctor, 478
Ogilvie, Alec (Ake), 1351
Oglethorpe, Ellen, 925
Oglethorpe, Nancy, 190
Oguki, Sono, 678
O'Hara, Sean and Eileen, 1290
O'Hara, Wally, 1405
O'Hare, Lieutenant Bernard
    B., 1048
O-Haru, 951
O-hisa, 1440
Ohls, Bernie, 153, 911
Oitana, Clelia, 41
Ojuobá, 1526
O'Keefe, Kenneth, 585
Okehi, Eze, 630
Okeke, Clara, etc., 1106
O'Kelly, Liam, 546
O'Kelly, Manuel Garcia, 1036
Oki, Toshio, 128
Okoli, The Honorable Sam, 1107
Okonkwo, 1545
Okonkwo, Michael Obiajulu,
    etc., 1106
Okubata, 951
Olan, 280
Olaya de Cemí, Rialta, etc., 1176
Old African, 184
Old Jack, 257
Old Liu, 1291
Old Lodge Skins, 894
Old Luísa, 805
Old Madam, 1090
Old Magdala, 1361
Old Mahailey, 1154
Old Major, 51
Old Man, 529, 943, 1600
Old Man in the Loo, 373
Old Man Exhibitionist, 374
Old Man Repeater, 374
Old Man with a Bike, 373
Old Married Couple, 1090
Old Martin, 1316
Old Mother Dida of Ponte
    Porzio, 306
Old Students, 373
Old Woman, 1520
O'Leary, Father, 720
Olek, Uncle, 1717
Olga, 495, 1170
Olguin, Father, 707
Olías de Cuervo, Visitación, 1285
Oliphant, Catherine, 873
Olive, Earl, 1467
Olive, Miss, 422
Oliveira, Horacio, 696
Oliver, 360
Oliver, Henry, 906
Oliver, Sir Quentin, etc., 903
Olivi, 329
Olivia, 309
Olivier, 1541
Olivier, Mary, etc., 982
Ollershaw, Ern, 195
O'Looney, Mary Kathleen, 786
Olsen, Axel, 1251
Olsen, Veronica (Ronnie), 1487
Olson, Jack, 1467
Olumba, 629
Olunde, 378
Olympias, 557
Olympias of Epirus, 508
Omange, 161

Omatangu, Adam, etc., 309
Ombrellieri, Dalmacio, 773
Omensetter, Brackett, 1140
Omi, 325
Ommu, 1353
Omura, Mr., 1520
Ondariva, Violante (Viola), 120
One I told you, the, 969
One, Mr. and Mrs., 15
One-Eye, 557
One-Eyed Larry, 303
O'Neil, Scripps, 1593
O'Neill, Moira, 907
Ong, John and Bernadette, 347
Ong, Mabel, 1024
Oosthuizen, Captain, 885
Openshaw, Guy and Gertrude, 1121
Optimistenko, 124
Or, Alice d', 359
Orator, 256
Orderly, 660
Oresanu, Sophie, 108
Oreshchenkov, Dr. Dormidont
    Tikhonovich, 230
Orestovna, Olda, 1135
Orion, 692
Orkay, Géza von, 390
Orlando, 330
Orlik, Professor, 141
Orlov, 712
Ormeau, Constantine, 471
Ormerod, Julian, 1512
O'Rourke, Harry, 767
Orphan girl, 1080
Orpheus, 1159
Orsenigo, Cesare, 393
Orsey, Lady Barbara d', etc., 1683
Orsini-Rosenberg, Count Franz, 34
Orsino, 250
Ortiz, Captain, 1516
Orual, 1565
Orukorere, 1445
Orya, 86
Osako, Takuhiko, 1740
Osana, 1662
Osanyin, 362
Osborne, 1181
Oscar de Andrade Guimarães,
    General Arthur, 1277
O'Shea, Caesara, 1774
Oshii, 663
Oshira, Mr., 1520
Oskolupov, Foma Guryanov, 514
Ossadnik, Ulla, etc., 1409
Osterman, 1130
O'Sullivan, Wally, 1760
Oswald, Abbot, 253
Oswestry, 420
Ota, Mrs., etc., 1554
Otaké, 986
Otford, James, etc., 1689
Otis, Uncle, 724
Otto, 394, 1655
Otway, Cassandra, 1095
Oudin, 647
Our Lady of the Flowers, 1164
Ovchinnikov, Anton, 714
Overseer, 748
Ovid (Publius Ovidius Naso), 742
Owen, 1601
Owen, Oscar, 203
Owens, Clifford, 261
Owens, Madge, etc., 1207

Owens, Sybela, 692
Owens, Tommy, 1388
Owlglass, Rachel, 1647
Oxalá, Rosa de, 1527
Oxarthes, 1196
Oxencroft, Gretchen Shurz, 211
Oxenham, Mrs., 702
Oxford, Miss, 1521
Oxhead, 1196
Oxton, Sergeant Harold, 1716
Oyarsa, 1458
Oyo, 130
Ozenfant, Professor, 851
Ozores, Ana, 1284
Ozu, 1709
Ozzie, 420

Pa, 309, 309, 748, 1542, 1761
Pa Tsong, 1621
Pablo, Juanita del, 931
Pabst, Angelica, 1429
Pac, Count, 427
Pacelli, Eugenio, 393
Pachuco, El, 1773
Packer, Pee Wee, 777
Pàcori, Zamira, 1532
Paddy, 651, 1031
Padgett, 572
Padishah, 719
Padma, 1008
Padre, 1402
Padrutt, Andrea, 179
Paduk, 141
Paek Sun-gi, 1407
Paepke, Hilde, 54
Páez, Bartolomé, 1553
Páez, Francisco Catalino, 671
Pagano, Eduardo, 1345
Page, Anna le, 1512
Page, Clara, 1551
Page, Dr. Edward, etc., 287
Page, James, etc., 1128
Pai Chü-jen, 1620
Pajasek, 1256
Pajehú, 1276
Pakhomov, Viktor
    Aleksandrovich, 618
Pal, 265
Pal, Dr., 506
Palcontents, 1632
Palegari, Donna Livia, 436
Palegari, Doro, 436
Palemon, 957
Palfreyman, 1667
Palissier, Jérôme, etc., 1477
Palmer, Dr., 1134
Palomar, Mr. and Mrs., 1020
Palver, Arcadia, etc., 538
Paly, Major, 217
Pam, 1341, 1359
Pamela, 255, 300, 779
Pan, Abdul, 720
Pancho, Grandfather, 1143
Pandalevsky, Konstantin
    Diomidych, 1320
Pangall, etc., 1463
Panov, Kirill, 1306
Pansetta, 1114
Pant, 215
Pantelei, Pantelei
    Apollinarievich, 215
Panteleone, 1595
Panteley, 1474

Pantelyusha, 215
Panthous, 239
Pantik, 215
Panton, Linda, 1241
Paola, 1647
Papa D., 180
PaPa LaBas, 1055
Papenbrock, Louise, etc., 54
Paphnatius, 942
Pappa, 538
Pappenheim, Dr., 101
Papps, Lily, 1429
Papuans, Six, 1001
Paquita, 147
Paraclydes, Xenophon, 1598
Paradise, Sal, 1145
Paravicini, Mr., 1053
Parbury, Miss Veronica, 590
Parchment, William, 491
Pardi, Angélo, 699
Pardo, Ambrosio, 334
Paredes, Juana, 542
Paredros, The, 1421
Parents, Sibyl's, 1400
Pariag, Boya, 422
Paris, Memo, 1080
Park, Alice, 1214
Parker, 1057, 1697
Parker, Charlie, 926
Parker, David, 1004
Parker, Miss, 383
Parkhill, Sam, 979
Parkinson, Robert "Rotter," 1372
Parkinson, Rudyard, 1430
Parkis, Alfred, etc., 455
Parkoe, Dora, 1097
Parks, Estelle, 1128
Parlabane, John, 1275
Parmigian, Joseph, 306
Parodus, Gloria, 1405
Parr, Antonio, 187
Parr, Frederick, 1692
Parris, Reverend Samuel, 352
Parritt, Don, 733
Parrott, Frank, etc., 89
Parson, 1376
Parsonby, Jeremy (Jimmy), 982
Parsunke, Emilie, 144
Partenie, Ciru, 533
Particulars Joe, 1302
Partridge, Olive, 1573
Parvati-the-witch, 1007
Parvay, Rosalie, 1231
Parvis, Angus, 500
Parvis, Mirabella, 1001
Pascoe, Susan Matthews, 1105
Pascual, 1290
Pasetti, 579
Passant, George, 1481
Passepartout, Jean, 68
Passer, 192
Pastor, 161
Paszkowski, Albert, 1221
Pat, 614
Patch, Anthony, etc., 127
Pateman, Kitty, 1483
Patient Griselda, 1591
Paton, Captain Ralph, 1057
Patriarch, 95
Patrician, Old, 227
Patricianello, 1000
Patricio, 970
Patrick, 700

Patrone, Peter, 673
Patterson, Cornelius, 1747
Patterson, Guy, 1755
Paul, 167, 333, 403, 426, 838, 862, 1498, 1358
Paul, Jaimie, 443
Paula, 1102, 1201
Paula, Doña, 1284
Paulina, la Gallina sin Pico, 485
Pauline, 754, 829
Paulo, Dom, 233
Pause, 1746
Pavel, Sergeant, 1125
Pavlo, 1147
Pavlou, Katina, 89
Pavloussi, Hero, 1663
Pavlovich, Zakhar, 266
Pavlovna, Vera, 1138
Pawling, Henry, 802
Pawn, The Invisible and Invincible, 1064
Paxton, Kathleen, etc., 1497
Payne, Dennis, 1233
Paz, Valentin Arregui, 837
Peabody, Dorothy, etc., 1016
Peace, Sula, etc., 1491
Peaches, 1511
Peachum, Jonathan Jeremiah "Beggar Boss," etc., 1561
Peake, Horace "Potty," 1101
Peake, Morgan, etc., 923
Peanut, 810
Pearl, 733
Pearl, Nat, 79
Pearson, Bradley, 162
Pearson, Bruce, 112
Pearson, Bruce William, Jr., 1456
Pearson, John, 1002
Pearson, Mr. and Mrs., 47
Peasants, 566
Peckham, Charlotte Thom, 1038
Peckham, Lewis, 1364
Pedal, 952
Pedal, Lady, 952
Pedersen, Jesse, etc., 1741
Pedigree, Mr. Sebastian, 367
Pedrick, Reverend Horace, 348
Pedro de Henestrosa, Fray, 921
Pedro-Surplus, 1768
Peeker, 1758
Peel, Maureen, 182
Peet, 648
Peggy, 83, 403, 1031, 1624
Peider, 44
Peiksva, Father, 782
Pelagio, Don, 1338
Pelham, Morris, 1500
Peloux, Frédéric, etc., 264
Pelumpton, Mr. and Mrs., 46
Pelzer, Walter, 642
Pembroke, Ralph, 439
Pena, Fausta, 1526
Peña, Manuel, 1163
Peñaloza, Humberto, 1125
Pendleton, Jill, 1255
Pendrake, Mrs., 894
Penfold, Mark, 874
Penny Whistle, 1589
Penrose, Jocelyn, 442
Penrose, Julius, etc., 223
Pentacost, Candida (Candy), 828
Pentacost, Jarcey, 1122
Pentecost, Martha Loomis, 793

People in and around Sirancy, France, 765
Pepe, 663
Pepler, Alvin, 1774
Pepper, 1430
Pepper, Harry, 116
Peranzules, Alvaro, 974
Percy, 918, 1696
Percy, Captain Ralph, 1578
Percy, Stewart, 1750
Perdikkas, 557
Père Jean, 175
Pereira, Lindinalva, 805
Pereira, Mary, 1008
Pereires, Roger-Martin Courtial des, 381
Peret, Louise, 355
Perez, Colonel, 694
Perez, Dominic and Catalena, 648
Pérez, Mortal, 550
Pérez, Pito, etc., 559
Perillo, Nikolai Gorimirovich, 1347
Peritas, 1196
Perken, 1318
Perkins, Corporal Thankful, 1238
Perkins, Madge, 735
Perraj, Rito, 1486
Perrault, Dr. Roderick, 1742
Perron, Guy, 1265
Perrot, Bastian, 594
Perry, Matthew, 588
Persephone, 834
Persio, 1726
Perturber, Professor John R., Jr., 1526
Pesah, Rabbi, 749
Pestalozzi, Corporal, 1532
Petacci, Claretta, 482
Petain, Marshall, 242
Pete, 180, 295, 1342, 1642
Pete the Peek, 1763
Petepre, 798
Peter, 102, 445, 568, 838, 860, 1209, 1399, 1772
Peter, Father, 1070
Peter, Saint, 1334
Peters, 1470
Peters, Harm and Dörte, 665
Peters, Harrison, 1680
Peters, M. A., 1324
Peters, Margot, 861
Peters, Mr., 303
Petersen, Frederik, 303
Peterson, Carl, 1072
Petherbridge, Jenny, 1100
Pétion, 1599
Petkoff, Catherine, etc., 67
Petra, 1284
Petrarch, 191
Petrov, Lance Corporal "Fidel," 1770
Petrovitch, Ivan, 768
Petrovna, Ekaterina, 1611
Petrus, Jeremías, etc., 1394
Petrushka, 420
Petrushkin, 668
Petworth, Angus, etc., 1268
Petyusha, 217
Petz, Hans Albrecht, 1195
Peverell-Watson, Renee, 1045
Peverill, Piers, 1728
Peyrade, 1465
Pfaff, Benedikt, 91

Pfardentrott, Thon Taddeo, 233
Pfeifer, Herr, 178
Pfeiffer, Leni, 641
Ph.D., 511
Phaedra, 833
Pharaoh, 165, 635
Pharmacist, old, 1108
Phee, Felicity, 681
Phelan, Francis, etc., 776
Phelan, William (Billy), etc., 154
Phelps, Mrs., 483
Phelps, Reverend, 180
Phelps, Rufe, 855
Phibbs, Mary, 1019
Phil, 723, 1426
Philifor, 500
Philip, 783, 1468
Philip II, 508
Philip III, 557
Philipot, Henri, 312
Phillip, 575
Phillip, Jackson, 1175
Phillips, Gilbert, 375
Phillips, Queenie, 540
Philomen, 1013
Philomène, 1049
Phineas, 1373
Phipps, Ben, 108
Phipps, Tristram and Gillian, 1290
Phoebe, 366
Phoebus, Lord, 60
Phoibee, Pollo, 1530
Phokus, 142
Phosphorescent Woman, 124
Phosphoridos, 1311
Photographers, Three, 104
Phuong, 1252
Phylax, 1311
Phyllis, 336
Physician, 1109
Pian, Brigitte, 849
Pian, Louis, etc., 1730
Pianura, Duke of, 1651
Piccolino, 435
Pickpocket, Negro, 1021
Pickpockets, 1157
Pickwort, Hedgepinshot
    Mandeville, 61
Pierce, 123
Pierce, Cushman (Cushie), 1751
Pierce, Ellie, 189
Pierpoint, 59
Pierquin, 1247
Pierre, 521, 775, 1079, 1715
Pierrot, 1014
Pietersen, Morris and
    Zachariah, 169
Pietro, 1241
Pigasov, Afrikan Semyonych, 1320
Pigeon, Gwendolyn and
    Cecily, 1131
Pigeonnier, Madame, 117
Piggott, Diana "Dicey," 895
Piggott, Fola, etc., 1360
Pilate, 1446
Pilate, Pontius, 984
Pilgrim, 233, 1225, 1531
Pilgrim, Billy, etc., 1422
Pilitzky, Adam and Theresa, 1423
Pilkings, Simon, etc., 377
Pilkington, Mr., 52
Pilman, Dr. Valentine, 1307
Pilon, 1596

Pim, 717
Pimber, Henry and Lucy, 1141
Pimko, Professor T., 499
Pin, 1186
Pina, 1553
Pindi, 82
Pineda, Martha, 312
Ping, Tom, 1541
Pingaud, Inspector, 254
Pinteados, 1079
Pinto, Dr. Zèzinho, 1527
Pioggi, Rocky, 733
Piojosa Grande, 996
Piontek, Valeska, etc., 1408
Piovasco di Rondò, Cosimo,
    etc., 120
Piper, Arthur, 249
Piper, Hanna, 692
Pippa, 394
Pirate, 1596
Pirate Captain, 1584
Pirenne, Dr. Lewis, 536
Pires Ferreira, Lieutenant Manuel da
    Silva, 1276
Pirie, Lady Viola, etc., 1004
Pirithoos, 833
Pirobutirro de Eltino, Gonzalo,
    etc., 10
Pissani, 9
Piston, 103
Pistorius, 387
Pither, Phyllis, 653
Pittheus, 833
Pittman, Miss Jane, etc., 93
Pivner, Otto, 1278
Pizarro, Francisco, 1316
Place, Humphrey, 108
Plant, Tabitha (Bita), 110
Plantier, Félicie, 1478
Plarr, Doctor Eduardo, 693
Platon, 720
Plavnikov, Vitaly, 842
Player, 1314
Plaza, Juan, 608
Plessington, Eloise, 1510
Plimsoll, Tipton, 556
Plitplov, Doctor, 1269
Plowmain, Sarah, 610
Plowman, Hope, 1766
Plowman, Richard, 710
Pluck, Sergeant, 1549
Pludek, Hugo, etc., 567
Plum, 1492
Plummer, Zeddy, 688
Plunkett, Matthew, 60
Pnin, Timofey Pavlovich, 1216
Pobedonosikov, 124
Pochintesta, 78
Podduyev, Yefrem, 230
Podgorski, Frank, 76
Podtyagin, Anton Sergeevich, 981
Poet, 234, 425, 484, 922, 1312,
    1499, 1570
Poetry Readers, Two, 102
Poilisheh, 79
Point, Max, 610
Pointsman, Ned, 624
Poirée, Bertin, 1768
Poirot, Hercule, 1056
Pokey, 134
Pokler, Franz and Leni, 625
Pokriefke, Tulla (Ursula), 414
Pola, 697

Polanco, 1421
Polemon, 719
Police Sergeant, 1218
Policeman, 599, 940, 966, 1660
Polidori, Dr. William, 173
Polish Lina, 145
Pollit, Samuel Clemens (Sam),
    etc., 958
Polly, 1449
Polly, Aunt, 825
Polozov, Maria Nikolayevna,
    etc., 1595
Polpoch, 972
Polya, 125
Pomaré, Odile, 243
Pomarici, 1589
Pomeray, Cody, 398
Pomeroy, Rooster, etc., 575
Pometti, 1589
Pomfret, John, etc., 1114
Pomme d'Api, 1165
Pommerer, 1676
Pompeia, 864
Ponce, Peta, 1126
Ponyets, Limmap, 537
Ponyrev, Ivan Nikolayevich, 984
Pooka, The (Fergus
    MacPhellimey), 83
Pookins, 1346
Poole, Frank, 1627
Poole, Grace, 1715
Poole, Stanley, 46
Pooler, Lizzie May Pippinger and
    Dan, 1703
Poor Old Woman, 246
Pop-Pop, 1600
Pope, 131, 1654
Pope, Mrs., 1244
Pope Innocent, 1763
Pope Pius XII, 393
Popinga, Kees, 959
Popo, 1009
Popper, Herman and Ruth, 858
Poppy, Axel H., 1195
Porch, Dame Mildred, 162
Porcupine, 197
Pordage, Jeremy, 17
Porriño, Don Galo, 1726
Portagee, Big Joe, 1596
Portago, Conde, 779
Porten, Henny, 1293
Porteous, 314
Porteous, Lord (Hughie), 286
Porteous, Nora Roche, etc., 1573
Porter, Alexander Thornton
    (Lex), 553
Porter, Doc, 351
Porter, Mitch, 1643
Porters, Six, 1001
Portnoy, Alexander, etc., 1225
Portway, Canon Reginald, 50
Poseidon, 649
Poskrebyshev, Lieutenant General
    Aleksandr Nikolyevich, 513
Postmaster, 1734
Potiphar, 798
Potopov, Andrei Andreyevich, 515
Potter, Ann Randolph, 828
Potter, Harlan, 911
Potter, Joseph, 720
Potter, Kenneth, 184
Potter, Mrs., 1229
Pottier, Yvette, 1046

Potts, Helen, 1207
Potts, Olin, 855
Poulet, Robert, 242
Poulsifer, Étienne, etc., 1267
Poulteney, Mrs., 547
Poulter, Mrs., 1438
Pound, Ezra, etc., 481
Poundamore, Heather, 235
Powell, 1361
Powell, Dr. Judith, 257
Powell, Minnie, 1388
Powell, Mrs., 897
Powell, Rachel, 1216
Powers, Dorothy (Dot), 1168
Powers, Margaret, 1437
P. R. Deltoid, 295
Prabhakaran, 784
Prader, 44
Praed, 1027
Praise-Singer, 377
Pratt, Mrs., 224
Preen, Miss, 955
Prem, 716, 784
Prema, 350
Prentice, Dr., etc., 1707
Prentice, Geoffrey "Pirate," 625
Prentis, etc., 1398
Preobrazhensky, Professor Philip
    Philippovich, 668
Prescott, Francis (Frank),
    etc., 1279
President, Ol' Time, 759
Presley, 1129
Press, The, 1774
Pressoir, Charlot, 1361
Prest, Mrs., 78
Prestino, 437
Prettiman, Mr., 1300
Preveza, Irana, 304
Prewitt, Private Robert E. Lee, 551
Prey, Easy, 1090
Prey, Percy de, etc., 14
Priam, 239
Price, 1692
Price, Jason, 1123
Prideaux, Jim, 695
Priest, 44, 258, 444, 546, 943,
    1079, 1157, 1660, 1717, 1718
Priest, High, 636
Priest, Jesuit, 1339
Priest, The Bad, 1647
Priest of the temple, 1400
Priest of Ungit, 1566
Prieto, Anselmo and
    Magdalena, 1325
Prime, Guy, etc., 452
Prince, 435
Prince, Corporal, 1724
Prince, H. R. H. The, 378
Princess Bili di Rovino, 897
Princess de Lascabanes, 479
Princess Quaw Quaw
    Tralaralara, 523
Princip, Katya, 1269
Principal, 578
Pringle, Harriet and Guy, 106
Pringle, Raymond, 21
Prinz, 414
Priscilla, 1244
Prison Chaplain, 295
Prisoner, 1217
Prisoners, Young, 1242
Prisoners A-E, 1242

Prisypkin, Ivan, 132
Pritchard, Captain Hans (later
    Colonel, General), 538
Priya, 744
Procession, 1270
Proctor, Colonel Stamp, 69
Proctor, John, etc., 352
Producer, 1089
Prof, 1036
Profane, Benny, 1646
Proferansov, Savely Kuzmich,
    etc., 947
Professor, 133, 875, 1157, 1302
Professor Rom Rum, 1269
Prokofievna, Alexandra, 57
Prokopovich, Annie, 464
Prologue, 59
Prometheus, 251
Prompters, Three, 817
Prophet, 636
Propter, Mr. William, 17
Proshka, 267
Prospect, Aldrick, 421
Prosser, Gabriel, 164
Prosser, Sergeant-Pilot
    Thomas, 1473
Prosser, Thomas, 165
Prostitute, 1312
Protagonist, 503, 1169
Protagonist, Unnamed, 965
Prothero, Donald, 678
Prothero, Mary "Pokey," 640
Protos, 848
Prouheze, Doña, 1338
Prouza, Jan, 460
Provo, Lois, etc., 574
Provocación, 991
Prst, Veronika, 460
Prudence, 249
Prunesquallor, Dr., etc., 620
Prushevsky, 535
Pryanchikov, Valentine (Valentulya)
    Martynich, 515
Prynne, Amanda, etc., 1239
Prynne, Mrs., 361
Prynne, Ms., 1034
Przyballa, Lina, 145
Psmith, Ronald Eustace, 868
Psyche, 1565
Ptits-pieds, Madeleine
    (Mado), 1768
Ptolemy, 509, 558, 1196
Publisher, 871
Publius Ubonius, 97
Pucinski, Murray "The
    Goose," 872
Puget, Lt. Peter, 218
Puig, 968
Pukhov, Andrey, etc., 1534
Puli, 1083
Pulley, 718
Pullman, James, 718
Pultoric, Tiger, 1086
Pumpkin, The, 1225
Pums, Herr, 145
Punt, Larry, 1233
Puntschu, 1174
Pup, The, 865
Pupil, 875
Purdy, Colonel, 1519
Pureco, Father, 560
Pusey, Iris, etc., 702

Putbus, Count Malte Moritz
    von, 1461
Putnam, Thomas, 352
Putney, Bishop of, 1233
Puybaraud, Léonce, 1731
Pye, Albert, 249
Pylaszczkiewicz, 499
Pyle, 1201
Pyle, Alden, 1252
Pym, Della, 139
Pym, Magnus Richard, etc., 1194
Pyne, 1666
Pyramus, 1311
Pythagoras, 922

Quackenbush, Cliff, 1374
Quadra, Don Juan Francisco de la
    Bodega y, 218
Quadri, Professor, 330
Quaid, Mrs. Dorothy, 610
Quaife, Roger, 1482
Quakatz, Andreas, 1622
Quapp, 390
Quarantine Officer, 425
Quare Fellow, 1241
Quaritch, Neil, 1351
Quarrier, Martin, etc., 81
Quast, Rodrigo, 1174
Queeg, Lieutenant Commander
    Philip Francis, 224
Queen, 103, 168, 1772
Queen, Else, 1350
Queen, Young, 131
Queen Bee, The, 472
Queen Honeybee, 308
Queen Mother, 131
Queen of Clubs, 241
Quelch, Queenie, 804
Queluz, Skipper Dário, 1565
Quentin, 20, 1091
Quest, Martha, etc., 275
Quicksilver Nick, 836
Quickskill, Raven, 523
Quigley, Father Francis
    Xavier, 908
Quilty, Clare, 905
Quimi, Don Goyo, etc., 416
Quince, Michael, 1233
Quinn, 1399
Quinn, James, 1466
Quintanar, Víctor, 1284
Quirino, Laurindo, 418
Quirke, Superintendent John
    James, 122
Quirt, First Sergeant, 1706
Quist, Peter, 142

R., 191, 916
R-13, 1700
Raalt, Constable, 1672
Rabbi, old, 102
Rabbit, 1253, 1254
Rabbit of Inlé, Black, 1693
Rabette, 1576
Rabinovich, Dr. S. Y., 1611
Rabinovitz, Avram, 1723
Rabinowitz, Lynne, 998
Rabinsky, Jossi, etc., 475
Raccamond, Aristide, 709
Race, Naomi, 22
Rachel, 529, 798, 964, 1125,
    1463, 1474
Rachel (Mrs. Grales), 234

Rack, Philip, 14
Radaković, Rajka, etc., 1728
Radcliffe, Leonard, etc., 1258
Radcliffe, Maggie, etc., 1513
Radek, Captain, 356
Radley, Arthur "Boo," 1580
Radovich, Dushan, 515
Ragin, David, 1405
Raglan, "Squire" Josiah
    Devotion, 1122
Ragman, 1502
Ragnal, Larry, 421
Ragpicker, 1502
Rahel, Sister, 641
Raider, Faye, 1319
Railey, Frank, 1063
Raimbaut, 1111
Rainbow, Dorothy Irey, 1573
Rainey, Dr., 534
Raisl, 519
Raj, 470, 716
Raj, Guru, 506
Raj, Mr., 1295
Rajah, 648
Raji, 289
Raka, 509
Ralegh, Sir Walter, 379
Ralph, 151, 180
Ralston, Mollie and Giles, 1052
Ram, 647
Ram Nath, 469
Rama, 1377, 1760
Ramaillet, 912
Ramaswamy, K. R., 1377
Ramatoulaye, 601
Ramdez, Yusif (Joe), etc., 965
Ramèges, Albert, 1318
Ramírez, Antonia Josefa, 671
Ramirez, Delores Engracia
    "Sweets," 1596
Ramírez, María Romelia, 1149
Ramírez Trueba, Antonio, 975
Ramos, Consuelo (Connie)
    Camacho, 1732
Ramos, Ignacio, 608
Ramos, Professor, 1527
Ramsay, Dunstable, 391
Ramseur, Gus, 323
Ramsey, Alexander and Ella, 1499
Ramsey, Phil, 1346
Ramsey-Eyes, 854
Ramundo, Ida, 679
Rance, Dr., 1707
Ranceville, 115
Randall, Jack, 421
Randall, Lieutenant, 494
Randall, Nell, etc., 365
Rangamma, 814
Ransom, 1456
Ransome, Dr., 454
Ransome, Marius, 595
Raoul, 1647
Rapallo, Mrs. Elsie, 89
Raphael, 191, 1160, 1220
Raphael, Madame, 191
Rappaport, Dr. Saul, 678
Rappaport, Mr., 1370
Raquel, 202
Raquin, Thérèse, etc., 1539
Rara, 103
Raresh, Valeria, 376
Rashad, 692
Rashaverak, 274

Rashed, Ibn, 288
Rasmussen, Shelly, 49
Rat, 1266
Rat, Brother and Sister, 1270
Rat Man of Paris, 1267
Ratched, Nurse, 1150
Ratface, 1436
Rathor, Savithri, 1377
Rations, Haroun al-, 1768
Ratna, 815
Ratner, Julius, 60
Ratti, Marius, 1460
Rauh, Baptist, 1505
Raul, 1558
Rausch, M., 1731
Ravelston, Philip W. H., 820
Ravi, 470, 1237
Ray, 113, 688, 753
Ray, Mr., 1357
Raycroft, Dorothy, 128
Raye, 631
Raymond, 140, 559
Raymond, Geoffrey, 1057
Raymond, Sam, 1184
Raymond, Veronica, etc., 1361
Raynard, Jules, 93
Raynell, 499
Rea, 1311
Reader, 550, 737, 1090
Reader, Other, 737
Readers, 1089
Reasoner, Alice-Jael, 497
Reba, 1446
Reba, Dr., 27
Rebbe, The Ladover, 1068
Rebeca, 1151
Recep, Sergeant, 994
Record Head, 962
Rector, 16, 1658
Red, 92, 753, 810, 1456
Red Cloud, 268
Red Cudgel, 1452
Red Man, 861
Red Shirt, 197
Red Wolf, 1186
Reddick, Maxwell (Max), etc., 956
Redfearn's Tommy, 585
Redfield, Irene ('Rene) Westover,
    etc., 1182
Redival, 1566
Redman, Stuart, 1470
Redpath, Herman, 190
Reed, Mary Jane, 1225
Reed, Nancy, 366
Reede, Tim, 1121
Reegan, Elizabeth and
    Sergeant, 121
Reese, 1502
Referee, 1590
Reg, 1112
Regan, Vivian Sternwood, etc., 152
Regan, Warder, 1242
Reganhart, Martha, 878
Regina, 426, 504, 1504
Reid, Constance, 843
Reid, Hilda, 844
Reilly, Ignatius J., etc., 320
Reilly, Nora, 795
Reimer, Samuel, etc., 176
Reinhold, 144
Reinhold, Lissi, 1505
Reinosa, Candelario, 996
Reis, Maria dos, 805

Reiss, Ed, 1592
Reiting, 1767
Reixach, 521
Relatives, Four, 653
Remedios, Pedro, 767
Remedios the Beauty, 1152
Remi, 160
Remigio of Varagine, 1074
Remington, Alice, 767
Removalist, The, 1286
Rena, Cenzo, 31
Rena, Manuel, 958
Renaissance, Elzevira Davidovna,
    etc., 132
Renata, 12, 757
Renata Remedios, 1153
René, 338, 612, 1015
Renfield, Gunner, 1697
Renfrew, Dorothy (Dottie), 639
Renfro, Jack, etc., 917
Rennes, Berthe de, 1656
Renton, Monsignor, 1041
Reo, Oscar, 777
Representative of a scientific
    agency, 1670
Resident, 378
Restelli, Dr., 1726
Restif, 242
Reuben, 415, 798
Reuttinger, Susana, 823
Reval, Conrad de, etc., 344
Revel, Jacques, 1183
Revivalist, 1703
Révora, Dante, 400
Rex, 296
Rex, Axel, 862
Rexford, Lucky, 585
Rey, Leandro, 399
Reyna, Henry (Hank), etc., 1773
Reynolds, Laura and Bill, 1518
Rheba, 1765
Rheingold, Herr, 579
Rheticus, 409
Rheya, 1436
Rhoades, Lola, etc., 925
Rianzares, Doña Petronila, 1285
Ribeiro, Father Joaquim, 767
Ricardo, 1397
Ricardo, Don, 435
Rice, Archie, etc., 461
Rice, Bernard, 907
Rice, Dr. Albert, 136
Rice, Mrs. J. J., 1114
Rice, Sister Bessie, 1583
Rich, Richard, 953
Richard, 61, 132, 1039, 1599
Richards, Clementine, 1251
Richards, Jem, 1556
Richardson, 924
Richardson, Jake and Brenda, 787
Richardson, Michael, 1271
Richelieu, Cardinal, 396
Riches, President, 464
Richmond, Clemmie, 61
Richmond, Toby, 1051
Rick, 296
Rickward, Edith (Ricky), 965
Ricky, 43, 1096
Rico de Peña, Doña Javiera, 1164
Riding master, 452
Ridley, Ernest, 656
Ridpath, Rufus, 376
Riedel, Heinz, 1119

Riel, Louis, etc., 1348
Riemeck, Karl, 1470
Rifkin, Dr., 1002
Rigate, John, 720
Rigault, Estelle, 1104
Riley, Harry, 261
Rima, 851
Rimon, Rami, 451
Rimsky, Grigory Danilovich, 985
Rina, 1186
Riordan, Anne, 493
Riose, General Bel, 537
Ripamilán, Cayetano, 1285
Ripert, Christian, 266
Risach, Baron Gustav von, 758
Risley, 990
Rita, 905, 1031
Ritchie-Hook, Ben, 1509
Riton-la-Noie, 1014
Ritter, Mrs. Valerie, 1432
Ritu, 672
Rivas, Father León, 693
Rivenburg, Willard, 1039
Rivera, Alessandro, etc., 186
Rivers, Clementine, etc., 733
Rivers, Jack, 1001
Rivers, Olivia, etc., 671
Roarty, Tim, 184
Roaster, The, 1031
Rob, 1286
Robal, Aurelio, 1289
Robarts, Harry, 1666
Robbie, 271
Robbins, 115
Robert, 1658, 1676
Roberts, 38, 145, 615, 885, 1014
Roberts, Annjelica (Annjee), 1113
Roberts, Marion "Kiki," 872
Robichaux, Claude, 321
Robinson, 41, 423
Robinson, Taft, 457
Robinson, Tom and Helen, 1580
Robison, James, 1488
Robot, 515, 1671
Robson, Poll, 1004
Roby, 1660
Robyn, Patricia (Pat), etc., 1043
Rocca, Michele, 437
Roche, Father Urban, 1040
Roche, Peter, 644
Rochefide, Madame de, 1337
Rochepozay, De la, 396
Rochester, Bertha Mason, etc., 1714
Rock, Lucian, 939
Rock, Mr., etc., 318
Rockaway, Leo, 1471
Rockoffer, Paul, 359
Rocky, 1015
Rocky's girl, 1014
Rodas, 1317
Rodgers, Dr., 1686
Rodgers, James (Sandy), etc., 1113
Rodgers, Owen, etc., 237
Rodichev, 231
Rodion, 776
Rodney, William, 1095
Rodricks, Jan, 273
Rodrigo, Don, 1338
Rodrigues, Sebastian, 1406
Rodríguez, Fanny, 1553
Rodwell, 1684
Roe, Richard, 248
Roethling, Dr. Gervinus, 1224

Rogas, Inspector, 464
Roger, 104, 896
Rogers, Commander, 548
Rogers, Marie, etc., 368
Rogers, Milton, 929
Rogers, Mimosa, 236
Roguski, John Llewellyn, 1456
Rohan, 774
Roithammer, 339
Roitman, Major Adam
    Veniaminovich, 514
Rojack, Stephen Richard, 38
Rokuemon Hasekura, 1332
Rola, 362
Roland, 240, 849, 971
Rolf, 741
Rolfe, John, 1579
Rom Rum, Professor, 1269
Roma, Richard, 596
Romanoff, Princess Cecilia, 721
Rombal, Aurelio, 1289
Romero, Matías, etc., 607
Rominov, Avraham, 451
Romney, Dr., 679
Romo, Dr., 27
Romulus Augustus, 1310
Romus, 427
Ron, 100
Ronald, 697
Ronberry, Miss, 337
Rondò, Corradino di, etc., 120
Rondón, Dolores, 550
Ronnie, 270, 578
Roo, Aunt, 658
Rookwood, Barberina, 518
Roon, Armin von, 1680, 1722
Rooney, 1484
Rooney, Mr. and Mrs., 32
Rooney, Raglan "Pappy," 1643
Roos, Anneliese, 97
Roosevelt, Franklin Delano, 1722
Root, Arnold, 595
Rootham, Margaret Matthews, 1105
Roper, Edwin, 1609
Roper, Jim, 553
Roper, William, 953
Rosa, 1505
Rosa Maria, 1769
Rosalind, 632
Rosamond, 1308
Rosamund, 540
Rosamund, Queen, 1632
Rosario, 338, 818, 921
Rosario, Wanda, 1427
Rosas de Vives, Josefina, 1552
Roscio, Dr., etc., 967
Rose, 97, 207, 919, 946, 1313, 1718
Rose, Caroline, 312
Rose, Frau Lina and Oskar, 1206
Rose, Ma, 254
Roseboro, Virgil, 64
Rosedá, Rosenda, 805
Rosello, Dean, etc., 967
Rosemarie, 1581
Rosemary, 1270, 1386
Rosen, Gabriel, 193
Rosenbaum, Scoop, 673
Rosenberg, Dr. Proinsias, 788
Rosencrantz, 1314
Rosencrantz, Lieutenant, 1261
Rosenfeld, Toni, 1581
Rosewater, Eliot, etc., 599
Rosie, 1171

Rosine, The Penitent, 104
Ross, 1762
Ross, Aylwin, 1709
Ross, Constable Neville, 1285
Ross, Cora, 1483
Ross, Dickie, 1696
Ross, Lethe, 1063
Ross, Robert, etc., 1683
Rosselli, Gemma, etc., 1595
Rossi, Herr, 179
Rossignol, 972
Rossignol, Jean-Pierre le, 874
Rosskam, Old, 777
Rossman, Karl, 40
Rostenkowski, Steffi, 1086
Rostovitch, Philomena, 1420
Roth, Constance Fox, 346
Rothermal, Tom, 553
Rotzoll, Sophie, 527
Rouet, Doctor, 1462
Rougemont, 303
Roundtree, Neville St.
    Michael, 1345
Rouse, Mrs. Alice, 1013
Roussellin, Madeleine (Mado),
    etc., 1377
Roustam, 1462
Rout, Solomon, 1629
Roux, Clément, 306
Roux, Jacques, 972
Rovino, Princess Bili di, 897
Rowan, Laura, etc., 157
Rowan, Nigel, 1264
Rowcliffe, Steven, 1559
Rowe, Cecil, 1754
Rowena, 156
Roxane, 558, 1197
Roy, 16, 1131
Royce, Enid, 1154
Royland, 408
Rozier, Jeanne, 960
Rozilda, Dona, 417
Rua, Rory, 185
Ruan, Jorge, etc., 991
Rubal, Aurelio, 1289
Rubanski, Lyudmila, 981
Ruberto, Alberto, 1184
Rubin, Jerry, 66
Rubin, Lev Grigoryvich, 513
Rubinstein, Something
    Something, 296
Ruby, 578, 1201
Rudd, Howard, 683
Rudin, Dmitri Nikolaich, 1320
Rudolph, 320
Rudolph, Emperor, 824
Rudore, Chloe Evans, etc., 496
Rudy the Kraut, 777
Ruel, 1041
Rufel, Professor, 141
Rufford, Nancy, 614
Rufino, 1683
Ruiz, Cornelia, 1596
Ruiz, Emilio, 991
Rukmani, 1082
Ruku, 1082
Rulag, 406
Rule, Philip, 1681
Rumbal, Aurelio, 1289
Rumfoord, Winston Niles and
    Beatrice, 1418
Rupf, Caesar, 1311

Rusanov, Pavel Nikolayevich, etc., 229
Rusanova, Avieta Pavlovna, etc., 230
Rusch, Margarete, 526
Ruska, 514
Russel, Dr. Paul, 8
Russell, Elizabeth, 1057
Ruta, 38
Rutenspitz, Krestyan Ivanovich, 419
Ruth, 402, 688, 921, 1449, 1744
Rutherford, Damon, etc., 1643
Rutherford, Frances, 1757
Rutherford, Franklin, 1696
Ruthmayr, Friederike, 390
Rutta, Air Force Lieutenant von, 394
Rutta, Baron von, 393
Rutuola, Swami, 211
Ruzena, 494
Ryan, Bubba, 1493
Ryan, Father, 720
Ryan, Jerry, 1625
Ryan, Liz, etc., 505
Rybkin, 812
Ryden, Tom, 575
Ryder, Japhy, 397
Ryder, Sir Evelyn, 1224
Ryder, Stephen "Red," 1711
Rylands, 590
Rysio, 1012
Ryumin, Sergeant, 217
Ryynänen, Dr. Rudolf, 877
Ryzak, 742

S-4711, 1701
Saavedra, Doctor Jorge Julio, 694
Sabas, Don, 1109
Sabashnikov, Petya, 779
Sabata, Dr., 350
Sabeth, 693
Sabina, 1468, 1634
Sabine, 521
Sabiroux, Father, 1635
Sabler, Samson Apollinarievich (Samsik), 215
Sabul, 406
Saburaov, 1534
Sacayón, Hilario, 997
Sachiko, 950
Sachs, Connie, 695
Sad Sam, 1455
Sadako, 226
Sade, Marquis de, 971
Sadie, 10
Sadiku, 893
Sado, 650
Saffi, Clarissa, 25
Sage, Krystyna (Christie), 779
Sagoe, Biodun, 771
Saha, 243
Sahib, 744
Saïd, 1352
Sailors, Four, 1001
St. Dennis, Albert, 1638
Saint Germain, Count, 1245
Saint-George, Lord, 571
St. John, Angela, 708
St. John, Mary, 553
St. Leonhard, Gallen von, 1378
Saint-Marin, Antoine, 1635

Saint-Nazaire, Edgar-Hélas Ville de, 168
Sakagawa, Kamejiro, etc., 663
Sakami, Keiko, 129
Sakini, 1519
Sala, Elena, 202
Salagnac, Camille, 1704
Salazzo, Sammy, 1135
Salcombe, Lord Luke of, 1482
Saldívar de Etchepare, Leonor, 671
Salesgirl, 871
Saliba, 1662
Salieri, Antonio, 33
Salim, 140
Salla, Teacher von, 569
Sally, 102, 789, 879
Salmon, Freddie, 1291
Salmon of Assaroe, 75
Salo, 23, 102, 1418
Salome, 1308
Salomon, Hesther, 467
Saltport, Maxwell "Black-Ball," 1539
Saltskin, Solly, 961
Saltz, Ben and Irene, 347
Salubi, 1302
Salvador, Don (Don Salva), 484
Salvador, Mickey, 1496
Salvadora, La, 194
Salvatore, 1074
Salway, 126
Salway, Gavi, 126
Sam, 327, 331, 564, 689, 986, 1615, 1694
Sam, Eduard, 1197
Sam the Lion, 858
Samadhi, 1603
Samazeuilh, Antoine, 77
Samba Baloum, 1259
Sameshkin, 793
Samitzky, Leon, 101
Sammael, 719
Sammler, Artur, etc., 1020
Samoylenko, Alexandr Daviditch, 428
Sampath, 1237
Sampson, Samuel "Philo," 422
Samsa, Gregor, etc., 999
Samson, 1302
Samson, Robert, Sr., etc., 94
Samsonov, Alexander Vasilich, 84
Samsonov, Vladimir (Vlad), etc., 492
Samuel, 1283
San Román, Bayardo, 285
Sanae, 358
Sanchez, 1704
Sánchez, Abel, etc., 3
Sánchez, Manuela, 95
Sanders, Brian, 1500
Sanders, Cliff, 1179
Sanders, Dr. Edward, 355
Sanderson, 1624
Sanderson, Alex, 925
Sanderson, Peggy, 928
Sandra, 777, 1025
Sands, Alice, 420
Sands, Gus, 1081
Sandy, 1204
Sanford, William, etc., 447
Sang Picker, 1333
Sangirgonio, Dominic, 1496
Sango, Amusa, 1192

Sanin, Dimitry Pavlovich, 1594
Sanja, 1136
Sankar, 815
Santee, 577
Santiaga, Luisa, 285
Santina, 1035
Santis, Mary de, 479
Santosh, 744
Sanya, 85
Saposcat, 952
Sapphira, 1335
Saraceni, Tancred, 1709
Sarah, 8, 403, 445, 789, 1112, 1360, 1601
Sarah, David ben, 135
Sarah, Lady, 1382
Sarajobalda, 1486
Saranoff, Major Sergius, 68
Sarella, 1589
Sargent, Frank, 49
Sarrasine, Ernest-Jean, 1337
Sarte, Marcella Ardeati, etc., 304
Sarti, Andrea, etc., 562
Sartorius, 1436
Sasaki, Nurse, 399
Sasha, 157, 266, 513, 1079
Sastri, 506, 624
Sastri, Belur Narahari, 814
Satan, 984, 1069, 1635
Satanael, the Devil, 719
Satters, 718
Satterthwaite, 718
Saunders, 1697
Saunders, Cecily, 1437
Saunders, Daniel (Danny), etc., 281
Saunders, Davina, 1162
Saunders, Dr., 672
Saunders, Herman, 1511
Saunders, Mrs., 298
Saurau, Prince, 569
Sauron, 1410
Saussure, 254
Savage, Eleanor, 1551
Savaget, General Claudio do Amaral, 1277
Savant, Alex, 996
Savigny, Friedrich Karl and Gunda von, 1110
Savio, Francesco, 437
Savl, 1347
Sawatzki, Inge, 414
Saxe, Priscilla and Roger, 163
Say Tokyo Kid, 1302
Saywell, Yvette, etc., 1658
Scaife, Commissioner, 66
Scaife, Muriel, 1641
Scales, Alton, 1405
Scali, Giovanni, 969
Schaad, Felix Theodor, etc., 178
Schaffner, Moira, 926
Schalter, Gerhard, 1676
Scham, Eduard, etc., 564
Schamm, 142
Schatz, Paul, 1505
Schaumann, Heinrich "Tubby," 1622
Scheidecker, Sebastian, 873
Scheidemann, Philip, 1119
Scherbatcheff, Count, 1654
Scherbaum, Philipp "Flip," 902
Scherer, Vera, 1534
Scheumel, Hertha, 920

Schevitz, André, 1775
Schicklgruber, Davigdor, 710
Schigolch, 1174
Schill, Anton, 1660
Schiller, Lawrence, 474
Schiller, Richard (Dick), 905
Schilling, Otto, 291
Schillings, Anna, 410
Schimmelpfennig, Father, 150
Schlaggenberg, Kajetan von,
    etc., 389
Schlank, Dr. Heinrich, 721
Schlosser, 99
Schlottau, Heinz, 903
Schlumbermayer, 24
Schmidt, Achilles, 1674
Schmidt, Alma, 551
Schmidt, Jakob, 1299
Schmitz, Sepp, 510
Schneider, Ed, 358
Schnell, Dutch, 112
Schnell, Herman H., 1455
Schnier, Hans, etc., 300
Schoenhof, Elizabeth and
    Nate, 886
Schoenwalder, Christine, 1208
Scholara, 1242
Scholarship Holder, 966
Schomburgh, 647
Schön, Dr. Alva or Alwa, 1173
Schönner, Adolf, 920
Schoolgirl, 101
Schoolmaster, 1660
Schoppe, 1576
Schreiber, Lisa, 503
Schrella, Alfred, 154
Schroubek, Richard, 396
Schrutt, O., 1379
Schuhart, Redrick (Red), etc., 1306
Schuldiener, Shosha, 1396
Schultz, Mr., 931
Schumann, Ernestine, 721
Schutz, Dr., 101
Schuyler, Charles (Charlie), 219
Schuyler, Charles Schermerhorn,
    etc., 446
Schwander, Herr, 179
Schwiebel, George, 722
Sciocca, Valentin, etc., 1657
Scipio, 226
Sciss, Harvey, 773
Scorton, Colonel William,
    etc., 1715
Scott, 1467
Scott, General John, 165
Scott, Hector, 1529
Scott, Ida, 56
Scott, Lewis, 1692
Scott, Luke, 1331
Scott, Reuben, 794
Scott, Rufus, 55
Scott, Thomas, 1348
Scottow, Gerald, 1639
Scotty, 1506
Scoundrel, 1688
Scribbin, Mr., 183
Scroop, Leander, 1233
Scrope, Henry, 28
Scudder, Alec, 989
Scudder, Dr. George, 1506
Sea, 452
Seal, 1370
Seal, Basil, 161

Seal, Leon, etc., 563
Seaman, Jane, 1428
Sear, Kennard and Hedwig, 585
Searcy, Horace, 323
Sears, Judith (Judy), 1617
Sears, Lemuel, 1134
Sears, Lilly, 1519
Seaton, Arthur, 1339
Sebastian, 349
Sebastian, Clement, 937
Sebastián, Doctor Daniel, 1289
Sebastiana, 300
Sebetka, Lucie, 796
Sechita, 531
Second Mate, 1630
Secretary, 568, 809
Secretary of the Industrial Workers
    of the World, 652
Seducer, Vile, 1090
Seeker, The Gold, 1385
Seelig, Hugo, 199
Sefer Efendi, 1719
Segal, Solly, etc., 654
Segovie, Julia Julie
    Antoinette, 1494
Segre, Davide, 680
Seidel, Lewis and Faye, 1638
Seifert, Irmgard, 902
Seifert, Willi, 1704
Seigals, The, 717
Seiko, Mr., 1520
Seitaro, Kumagai, 1075
Sekachev, Vladimir, 1138
Sekoni, 771
Selbig, Dr. Ernest, 442
Seldon, Dr. Hari, 536
Selena, 1031
Selig, Rutherford, 794
Selina, 1756
Selincourt, George, 1191
Selkirk, Alexandra, 1211
Sellers, Poppy, 46
Sello, 1248
Selridge, Roy, 156
Selvam, 1083
Selversen, Peter, 1026
Semi-dozen, 1362
Semple, 791
Sempleyarov, Arkady
    Apollonovich, 985
Semyonovich, Prokofy, 230
Semyonovna, Tatyana, 490
Senator, 1708
Sender, 1347
Sender of Winds, 1347
Senders, 1072
Sendin, Susie, etc., 1739
Seneca, 974
Senhora, 418
Senka, 85, 1136
Señor, El, 1530
Señora, 44
Señora, La, 1530
Senta, 414
Sentoryen, 720
Sepulchrave, Lord, 619
Serafin, 1290
Serebro, Igor Yevstigneyevich, 217
Serebyanikov, Vadim, 216
Serena Joy, 655
Sereno, Daniel, 1305
Sergeant, 303, 632, 1353
Sergeev, Colonel, 778

Sergei, 493
Sergey, 845
Sergio, 976
Serguine, Ivich, etc., 1304
Serindan, Count Raoul de,
    etc., 1656
Serjeant, Jean, 1473
Sermak, Sef, 539
Serpent, 565
Serrano, Inez, 1104
Servant of the oracle, little, 1400
Service, Willie, 61
Servière, Charlotte and Paula, 1110
Seryozha, 618, 1611
Seth, 161
Sethji, 717
Setsuko, 358
Settin of Kalgan, Lord, 538
Seven-for-Eight, Afanasy, 217
Sevenswords, Doña, 1339
Severance, Nell, etc., 1503
Severinus of Sankt Wendel, 1073
Severjan, Father, 1136
Seward, William, 892
Sewerman, 395
Seymour, Alan, 1207
Seymour, Jean-Marc, 194
Shablinsky, Mikhail "Misha"
    Borisovich, 317
Shadbold, Geoffrey F. H., etc., 1123
Shadrack, 1491
Shaft, Edna, 222
Shakagov, Captain of the Combat
    Engineers, 514
Shakespeare, William,
    etc., 116, 1389
Shakil, Omar Khayyam, etc., 1389
Shakuntala, 468
Shamil, 649
Shanaar, 302
Shanahan, Paul, 83
Shannon, T. Lawrence, 1098
Shanti, 1237
Shaper, 637
Shapiro, 1102
Shapiro, Danny, 1386
Shapiro, Fred, 265
Sharfman, Rav Tuvya, 747
Sharik, 668
Sharikov, Polygraph Polygraphovich
    (Sharik), 668
Sharon, 648
Sharovkyan, 668
Sharp, Phoebe, 1507
Sharpe, James, 813
Shashava, Simon, 248
Shatov, Dasha and Maria, 1228
Shatov, Ivan, 1228
Shaughnessy, Artie, etc., 710
Shaw, Lord Osmund Willoughby
    Finnian, etc., 60
Shaw, Ronald, 291
Shawcrosse, Philip, 438
Shaybo, 1242
Shchyogolev, Boris Ivanovich, 582
She, 426, 664, 738
She-Who-Was-Cynthia, 1659
Shearer, George, 1773
Sheba, 343
Shebeko, Dim, 778
Shedman, Nancy, etc., 683
Sheffield, 421
Sheila, 122, 370

Sheill, Queely, etc., 1566
Sh'eira, Naim, 288
Sheldon, Lorraine, 955
Shelgrim, 1130
Shelley, Grace, 1322
Shelley, Mary, 173
Shelley, Percy Bysshe, 173, 545, 1018
Shelly, 214
Shelomo, Rabbi, 749
Shem, 528, 636, 675
Shemariah, 792
Shen Te, 615
Shen Tung-tsao, 1605
Shen Tzu-p'ing, 1605
Shenstone, Mrs. Anna, 286
Shepherd, 514, 1270
Shepherd, Old, 762
Shepherd, Rita, 617
Sheppard, 773
Sheppard, Dr. James and Caroline, 1056
Sheppard, Katherine, 727
Sheppard, Mossely, 165
Sherban, George, etc., 1391
Sheridan, Joyce, 1541
Sheriff, 1202
Sherman, Nickie and Lila, 1528
Sherriff, Marion, 899
Shervinsky, Leonid Yuryevich, 371
Shevardina, Tinatina, 217
Shevek, 405
Shibalo, Gideon, 1127
Shields, Seumas, 1388
Shigalov, 1228
Shillingsworth, Oscar, etc., 234
Shimamura, 1433
Shin, Mrs., 616
Shingo, 1450
Shiny, 92
Shioda, O-Nami, etc., 1555
Shipley, Hagar, etc., 1475
Shiraishi, Lord, 1332
Shirlee, 816
Shirley, 755
Shiva, 1007
Shivaraman Nair, 784
Shizuko, 1107
Shklovsky, Viktor, 1771
Shklovsky, Viktor Borisovich, 1546
Shlemskaya, Aleksandra, 1075
Shmuel, 519, 1124
Shoba, 140
Shockley, Albert, 1393
Shoemaker, 748
Shoenmaker, Dr. Shale, 1648
Shor, Reb Vovi, 201
Shorty, 26, 1248
Shotover, Captain, 669
Showalter, Mahlon, 1256
Shrdlu, 15
Shridaman, 1602
Shu Fu, 615
Shubin, Pavel Yakovlevich, 1143
Shuck, Edwin (Eddie), 1329
Shuck, Lee, 1696
Shug Avery (Lillie), 308
Shui Ta, 615
Shuichi, 1450
Shukov, 1147
Shulameth, Sheila, 1678
Shulepa, 714

Shulepnikov, Lev Mikhailovich, 714
Shulubin, Alexey Fillipovich, 230
Shumann, Roger, etc., 1240
Shūsai, 986
Shusgis, 870
Shushani, 1433
Shuttlecock, 1399
Shvonder, 668
Si Slimane, 1353
Sib, 62
Sibgatov, Sharaf, 230
Sibyl, 1400
Sibylla, 685
Sibylle, 741
Sickenger, Clarence and Martha Ann, 1139
Sid, 720
Siddhartha, 1400
Sideri, Ileana, 532
Sidi, 893
Sidneys, First and Second, 852
Sidonie, 613
Siebenschein, Grete, 390
Siegfried, Captain, 243
Siemian, 1222
Sigismund III, 1403
Sigrid, 912
Silbergleit, Arthur, 1409
Silenski, Clarissa, 56
Silenski, Richard, 56
Silent One, The, 1171
Siles, Tempy, 1113
Silicate, Agent, 217
Silk, Lord Ben, 1233
Silva, 375
Silva, D. B. da, 296
Silver, Prince, 270
Silvester, 216
Silvestre, 1560
Silvestro, 71
Silvia, 1035, 1398
Simas, Elisa Esteves, etc., 1564
Simek, Dr., 913
Simeon, 831, 860, 1224
Simeoni, 1517
Simha-the-Dark, 502
Simmer, Otto von, 242
Simmonds, Dave, 270
Simmonds, David, 703
Simmonds, Sergeant Dan, 1285
Simmons, Henry, 1537
Simon, 783, 831, 922
Simon, Ann, 1482
Simonetta, Signora, 394
Simpkins, Mother Bess, 691
Simpson, Carolyn, 1319
Simpson, Perry Garvey, 1456
Simpson, Sam "Bub," 1080
Simrock, Karl and Ruth, 1424
Sims, Chris, 910
Sinai, Saleem, etc., 1007
Sinclair, Emil, 386
Singer, 443
Singer, Mendel, 792
Singers, Four, 972
Singh, Pratap, 1378
Singh, Ranjit Ralph Kripal, etc., 1010
Singh, Sardar Ranjit, 369
Singh, Talvar, 369
Sings Before Spears, 860
Sinisterra, Frank, 1279

Sinyavsky, Andrei Donatovich, etc., 617
Siphon, 499
Siracusa, 1736
Sirin, Colonel, 343
Siriysky, Father Christopher, 1474
Siromakha, Arthur, 515
Sis, 734, 1762
Sisovsky, Zdedek and Olga, 1230
Sissl, 736
Sisson, Aaron, etc., 1
Sissy, 827
Sister, Rudolph's, 320
Sister, Wertheimer's, 1646
Sister Mary, 1419
Sister Rat, 1270
Sister Salvation, 331
Sita, 1602
Sitole, Steven, 1754
Sittina, 344
Sitting Bull, 759
Six, Mr. and Mrs., 15
64, 1511
Skaggs, 1466
Skeel, Miss Elspeth, 1538
Skelton, Brooke, 408
Skelton, Thomas, etc., 1102
Skidler, Gedaleh, 735
Skidmore, Thomas, 220
Skinner, 546
Skinny, 334
Skocopole, Prema, 460
Skorko, Tadzio, 1012
Skotoma, Fradrik, 141
Skreta, 495
Skripkin, Pierre, 132
Skully, Egbert, 586
Skuziak, Olek, 1222
Slab, 1647
Slade, 968
Slade, Hugh, etc., 505
Slade, Larry, 732
Slagg, Mrs., 621
Slank, Leonard "Len," 446
Slape, Mrs., 183
Slater, 357
Slater, Nick, 1497
Slattery, Mike, 1524
Slave, 104, 1569
Sleep, Asnetha, 1567
Sleeping Beauty, First, 713
Sleeping Beauty, Second, 713
Sleeping Beauty, Third, 713
Sleeping Beauty, Fourth, 713
Sleeping Beauty, Fifth, 713
Sleeping Beauty, Sixth, 713
Sleeth, Monsignor, 825
Slim Girl, 860
Slimane, Si, 1353
Slime, Mr., 748
Sloane, Clere, 167
Sloane, Mr., 462
Slobber, 238
Slocum, Mr., 33
Slocum, Robert (Bob), 1440
Slomer, Mr., 1552
Slonim, Betty, 1396
Slose, Vanake, 870
Slote, Leslie, 1680, 1722
Slothrop, Tyrone, 624
Slotzker, Nahum, 102
Slow Drag, 940
Sludden, 851

Slug, 100
Slukal, Elfriede, 1743
Slušný, 297
Smales, Bamford (Bam), etc., 807
Small, Otto, 996
Small, William, etc., 591
Smart, Weeper, 675
Smasher, 1281
Smaug, 682
Sméagol, 682
Smeaton, Camden, etc., 1240
Smeeth, Herbert Norman, etc., 46
Smiler, 1665
Smiley, Bill, 1233
Smiley, Coy, 151
Smiley, George and Ann, 694
Smiricky, Daniel, 460
Smiricky, Danny, 349
Smith, 1698
Smith, Donald A., 1349
Smith, Doobie, 1525
Smith, Doris, 1161
Smith, Earle Banning, 1456
Smith, Elena "Nellie," 769
Smith, Father Rinaldo, 926
Smith, Gordon Hugh, 1526
Smith, Harold and Marcia, 347
Smith, Jack, etc., 36
Smith, Jack Tom, 553
Smith, Jenny, 1298
Smith, John Jacob (Jake), 1299
Smith, Miguel Moreno, 491
Smith, Mr. and Mrs., 105
Smith, Mrs. Horace, 1257
Smith, Peter, 1517
Smith, Polidorio, 1567
Smith, Raymond, 397
Smith, Robert, 651
Smith, The Reverend James, 1546
Smith, Valentine Michael
  (Mike), 1478
Smith, William Abel, etc., 311
Smith, Word, 626
Smitheram, Dr. Ralph, etc., 617
Smithson, Charles, 546
Smitty, 626, 631
Smolders, Jackie, 262
Smolinski, Sara, etc., 199
Smolka, 1225
Smothers, Maudel, 1114
Smythe, Richard, 455
Snake, The, 514
Snake Sutt, 539
Sneak, 866
Sniffer, 1007
Snoots, 1432
Snooty, 1432
Snoozer, 1346
Snotnose, 1007
Snow, 1436
Snow, Edna, etc., 1636
Snowball, 51
Snowdon, Miss, 1017
Soames, Henry, 1091
Soaphead Church, 181
Soat, 1375
Social worker, 1718
Socorro, 550
Sofía, 477, 1398
Sofia Butler, 308
Sofía de la Piedad, Santa, 1152
Sogolon, 643
Soichi Yamazaki, 20

Sokolnikov, General Alyosha
  Sergei, 89
Solange, 946, 1165
Solar, Ramón del, 1325
Solaris, 1436
Soldier, 44, 299, 746, 1312
Soldier, Lone, 750
Soledad, 560
Soliman, 835, 964
Solis, L'Abbé de, etc., 1247
Solly, 331
Sologdin, Dimitri
  Aleksandrovich, 513
Soloman, Deborah (Deb), 1387
Solomon, 1475
Solomon, Gregory, 1234
Solzhenitsyn, Aleksandr, 1705
Somel, 677
Someone in gray, 889
Somers, Richard Lovat and
  Harriet, 812
Something Something
  Rubenstein, 296
Somnambulist Prostitute, 374
Son, 22, 178, 310, 1064, 1190, 1346,
  1353, 1669
Son, Sibyl's, 1400
Son, Slocum's older, 1441
Son-in-Law, 1190
Sonetka, 846
Songford, Grace, 496
Sonia, 144, 1102
Sono Oguki, 678
Sonoko, 325
Sonya, 490
Sookdeo, 204
Sophie, 1382, 1447, 1604, 916
Sophie Loy, 1029
Sophronie, 415
Sor Matteo, 1034
Sorcerer, 900
Sorel, Gerard, 1704
Sorger, Valentin, 1425
Sorniani, 72
Sorokin, Elfrida, 376
Sotero, Dr., 27
Soto, Hernando de, 1316
Soul Emperor, 809
Sourdust, 621
Souris, 424
Southampton, Earl of, 1117
Souza, Frank de, 1508
Souza, Major Damiao de, 1527
Spalding, Abe, etc., 554
Spangler, Dewey, 376
Sparks, Kitty, 1132
Sparky, Private, 1376
Sparrow, 961
Sparrow, Jeremy, 1579
Speaker, 133
Speakers, Four, 1132
Specialist, 943
Spectators, 437
Spector, Carl, 684
Speed, 1131
Speedy, 491
Speedy, Captain Andrew, 69
Speier, Ada Malfenti, etc., 328
Speight, Jimmy, 1352
Spencer, Angela, etc., 1618
Spencer, Melissa, 155
Spencer, Rollo, etc., 1701
Spender, John, 979

Spengler, 1467
Sphynx, 761
Spicer, 206
Spielman, Max, 584
Spigliano, John, 878
Spike, The, 1615
Spina, Marchioness Matilda, 674
Spiridon, 515
Spirit, unnamed female, 1076
Spitz, General, 1510
Spock, Dr. Benjamin, 67
Spoenay, Henk, 1705
Spot, Hanon, 1233
Spotted Tail, 760
Sprague, Theodosia and
  Caleb, 1003
Springer, Bessie, 1254
Springer, Old Man, 1255
Spruance, Raymond, 1681
Spurius Titus Mamma, 1311
Spyhole, 1363
Squaw, 1594
Squeak, 309
Squealer, 51
Squier, Alan, 1201
Squire, 17, 337
Squirrel, 1733
Srinivas, 1236
Srulik, 1194
Stack, Malachi, 989
Staël, Madame Germaine de, 1076
Stag of Leiterlone, 74
Stage manager, 437
Stahr, Esther, 1664
Stainface, 1007
Staithes, Mark, 481
Stakhov, Nikolay Artem'yevich,
  etc., 1144
Stakhova, Yelena Nikolayevna,
  etc., 1143
Staley, Major, 457
Stalin, Josef, 811
Stalin, Joseph V., 513
Stamm, Gisela, 179
Stamp, Victor and Margaret, 1290
Stamper, Hank, etc., 1442
Stams, Baron Bodo von, 1537
Stan, 719
Standish, Patrick, 1512
Stangeler, René von, 389
Stanhope, Sophy, etc., 367
Stankiewicz, Walter, 786
Stanley, 1157, 1279
Stanley, Mrs., 1249
Stanley, Rose, 1235
Stanleys, The, 955
Stanton, Edwin, 892
Stanton, Vernor, 1467
Stapanov, Boris Sergeyevich, 514
Stapps, 1076
Star-Man, 1590
Starbuck, Walter F., etc., 786
Starck, Agnes, etc., 1477
Stark, 23
Stark, Jessica, 1002
Starks, Joe (Jody), 1535
Starr, Herbert, 1372
Starr-Smith, Bertram, 61
Starusch, Eberhard, 902
Staś, Uncle, 1717
Stateira, 558
Statue of Benjamin Franklin, 1619
Staunton, Percy Boyd, etc., 391

Staupitz, Johann von, 938
Stavrogin, Nicholas, etc., 1227
Stavros, Charlie, etc., 1254
Stead, Dowie, 263
Steadiman, Felix and Budgie, 1269
Steergard, 501
Steerpike, 619
Stefan, 871
Stefano, Doctor Mirko, 1565
Stein, Getzel, 1416
Stein, Harry, 1331
Stein, James, 1544
Stein, Julio, 203
Stein, Lol Valerie, 1271
Steinbauer, Jenny, 1043
Steinbock, Tolya von, etc., 215
Steinherz, Ludmilla, 1174
Stella, 1747
Stencil, Herbert, 1646
Stennett, Ted and Evelyn, 1005
Stepanov, Oleg, 778
Stephen, 934, 1313
Stephens, John Lloyd, 801
Stephens, Knolly, 645
Sterling, Hattie, 1466
Stern, Thomas, 277
Sterne, Edward, 1191
Sternwood, General Guy de Brisay, etc., 152
Stettler, Monika, 1206
Stevens, Clement (Clem), etc., 423
Stevens, F. Hilary, 1025
Stevenson, Stony, 1419
Stevo, Carlo, 305
Steward, 1079, 1630
Stewart, 1460
Stewart, Charlie, 1488
Stewart, George, etc., 1685
Stierle, Benedikt, 877
Stig, Uncle, 1404
Stiggins, 1063
Stiles, Albert, 1063
Stiles, Lottie, etc., 1333
Stilgar, 432
Stiller, Anatol Ludwig, 740
Stiller-Tschudy, Julika, 741
Stillwood, Esmond, 469
Stilson, Emily, 1725
Stilwell, Jessica (Jessie) and Tom, 1126
Stingo, 1447
Stitch, Julia, 1509
Stock, Willi, 313
Stöckl, Max, 1505
Stoever, 773
Stoker, 40
Stoker, Maurice, 584
Stokes, Jill, 1005
Stokesay, Dollie, etc., 50
Stöller, Wolf, 1723
Stolnitz, Dora, 1397
Stomil, 1515
Stone, Dr. Jeremy, 44
Stone, Mr. and Mrs., 654
Stone, Neil, 1427
Stone, Richard and Margaret Springer, 1022
Stoneham, Carla, 729
Stoner, Lester, 1485
Storey, Clark, 1364
Storey, Jerry, 899
Storm, 1543
Stormalong, Jack, 589

Stormgren, Rikki, 272
Störzer, Friedrich (Fritz), 1622
Stott, Brigit, 1637
Stovall, Curly, 917
Stoyte, Mr. Jo, 17
Strack, Count Johann von, 34
Strahan, Charles (Chae), 1350
Straight, Judge Archibald, 706
Strang, Alan, etc., 467
Strange, Arline, 166
Stranger, A Pale Blonde, 588
Stranger, Sandy, 1235
Strangers, Three, 1167
Sträubleder, Alois, 920
Strauss, Toni, etc., 1581
Stravinsky, Professor, 985
Strawberry, 1693
Strayhorn, Lemuel, 692
Streamline, 863
Street, Judith, 1006
Strether, Wulfstan, 728
Stretter, Anne-Marie, 1271
Strickland, Nell Purvis, etc., 1043
Striker, Lyle, 1711
Strohe, Aloysius James, etc., 1705
Stroller, Corrinna, 711
Strome, Ellen, 1637
Strong, Catherine (Kay) Leiland, 638
Strong, Charley, 1280
Strudelmacher, Jan, 216
Struthers, Willie, 813
Stryker, Dr. Kenneth, 926
Stu, 1037
Stuart, James, 380
Stubbe, Lena, 527
Studdock, Mark and Jane, 1457
Studdy, 182
Student, 191
Student, French, 1219
Studzinsky, Alexander Bronislavovich, 372
Stuff, 1507
Sturdyvant, 940
Styofa, Auntie, 231
Sub, 914
Suberu, 1363
Sue, 587
Sukarno, 1761
Sukey, 1105
Sula, 1491
Sullavan, Gary, 1420
Sullivan, Annie, 1015
Sullivan, Paul, 291
Sulphurides, 1311
Sumaoro, 643
Sumata, Mr., 1520
Summerbee, Cheryl, 1430
Summers, Dick, 1698
Summers, Lieutenant, 1300
Summerson, Harriet (Hallie), 1428
Sundiata, 643
Sunlight Man, 1495
Sunster, Maria Theresa, 1178
Superbrain, 334
Surgeon, 1079
Surin, Édouard, etc., 573
Surkont, Casimir, etc., 781
Surveyor, 893
Susan, 36, 180
Susana, 970
Sushilov, 711
Susie, 87, 704

Susila, 623
Sussex, Earl of, 253
Susy, 688
Sut, 1501
Sutcliffe, Mr., 982
Sutherland, Bruce, 477
Sutt, Jorane, 539
Sutter, John Augustus and Anna, 1500
Suttree, Cornelius, etc., 1501
Suzana, 852
Suzanne, 1356, 1541
Suzi, 23
Sužuki, Tojuro, 725
Suzy, 701
Svatá, Virginia, 296
Svensson, Irene, 460
Swallow, Charles (Chick) and Crystal, 1528
Swallow, Philip, etc., 260, 1429
Swami, 716
Swami Havananda, 836
Swamp Woman, 487
Swan, Deirdre, 874
Swanlake, Jessica, 625
Swanson, 679
Swarze, Dorothea, 526
Sweeney, Lizzy and Con, 1203
Sweeny, King, 83
Sweet Girl, 1312
Sweet Young Lady, 1312
Sweet Young Miss, 1312
Sweet Young Thing, 1312
Sweetner, Albert, 1637
Swelter, 619
Sweyn, King, 253
Swieten, Baron Gottfried Van, 34
Swift, Jonathan, 1746
Swille, Arthur, 523
Swint, Pluto, 604
Sybil, 1733
Sycamore, Penelope (Penny) Vanderhof, etc., 1764
Sydney, Rosemary, 1207
Sylvester, 940
Sylvester, Dr., 679
Sylvester, Eaton, 1232
Sylvia, 422, 563, 1100
Symonds, Diane, 1419
Szafir, 427
Szczepanski, Peter, 1121
Szczuka, Stefan, 75
Szretter, Julius, 76

T, 915
Tabaha, Don, 47
Tabane, Timi, 1677
Tabari, Jemail, 1452
Tabidgi, 262
Tadlock, 1699
Tadziewski (Tad), 1738
Tadzio, 1688
Taeko, 950
Taichiro, 129
Taiila, 1362
Taillandy, Margot, 1650
Tainui, James Piripi (Piri), etc., 186
Taite, Jessie, 1414
Takanatsu, Hideo, 1440
Takeichi, 1108
Takver, 406
Taladis, 303
Talas, 303

CHARACTER INDEX

Talberg, Yelena Vasilyevna, etc., 371
Talbot, Edmund, 1299
Talbot, Fleur, 903
Talbot, Mary and Tom, 233
Talbott, Rowena, etc., 595
Talita, 696
Tall, Gordon, 1544
Tall Boy, 204
Tallard, Athanase, etc., 1626
Talley, Sally, 1514
Talleyrand-Perigord, Charles-Maurice Cardinal, 1076
Talliaferro, Ernest, 1043
Taloufa, 114
Tam Lum, 270
Tamatoa VI, 661
Tamina, 191
Tamiroff, Reuven, etc., 502
Tamkin, Dr., 1369
Tancred, Jack Arnold Alexander, 1322
Tanizaki Eiko, 1451
Tankic, 1269
Tanner, Flight Lieutenant, 544
Tanomogi, 770
Tanpinar, Dr. Halide, 1597
Tanty Bessy, 906
Ta-Phar, Pharaoh, 1041
Taplow, John, 207
Tar Baby, 1491
Tara, 294, 706
Tarde, Thérèse, etc., 1287
Tardieu, Michel, 1430
Tariq, 975
Tarkington, Newton, 811
Tarozaemon, Tanaka, 1332
Tarver, Mr., 900
Taşbaş Efendi, Memet, 1719
Tashiro, 1321
Taşyürek, Halil, 1719
Tat, Roger, 193
Tate, Brian and Erica, 1681
Tate, Brother, etc., 691
Tate, Mary, 361
Tate, Wesley, etc., 356
Tate de Lysle, Gabriel, 1079
Tateh, 1260
Tatsuo, 950
Taube, Karl, 1587
Taufiq, 1392
Taupe, Old, 117
Tavendale, Ewan, 1349
Tavendale, Young Ewan, 1350
Tavira, Juliana Conceiro, 349
Tayle, Lily, 1432
Taylor, 357
Taylor, Felicitas Maria, etc., 316
Taylor, Marian, 1639
Taylor, Mr., 1092
Taylor, Owen, 152
Tazol, 1054
Tchitcherine, 625
Teach, 37
Teacher, 43, 130, 444
Teacher, religious, 1630
Teagle, Hank, 151
Teague, Walter, 66
Teapot, 1567
Tecún, María, 997
Ted, 720
Teddy, 689, 1711
Tee Bob, 94

Tegularius, Fritz, 593
Teinosuke, 950
Teissières, Édouard, 1478
Tekla, 1397
Teku, 1224
Telegraph linemen, two, 1201
Tell, 1421
Telrico, 134
Temma, Tirza, 1423
Tempe, Mark, 500
Temple, Alberto Fernández, 1570
Templeton, Elliott, 1273
Tenczara, "One-Eye," 1086
Tenn, Richard, 1183
Tennyson, Persis, 1537
Teodora, Princess, 435
Tepano, Juan, 483
Terblanche, Richard, etc., 212
Terence, Mrs., 1097
Teresa, 700, 1145, 1570
Tereza, 1633
Teri, 916
Ternera, Pilar, 1152
Teroro, 661
Terry, 332, 1145
Tertz, Abram, 617
Teru, 1367
Terukatsu, 1367
Tetsu, 1108
Tetzel, John, 938
Tewce, Ainsley, 445
Thames, Father Oswald, 595
Thanatogenos, Aimée, 930
Thanthalteresco, 274
Thaw, Duncan, etc., 850
Thaxter, Pierre, 722
Thé, General, 1252
Théo, 117
Theoderich, 1311
Theodora, Sister, 1111
Théodore, 1533
Theodorescu, 1610
Theotoky, Maria Magdalena, 1275
Theresa, 23, 1718, 1735
Therese, 1361
Theseus, 832
Théus, Pauline de, 699
Thief, 104
Thiele, Arthur, 877
Thierno, 35
Thin, Pauline, 1513
Thin Elk, 268
Thingol, 1411
Thoday, William, etc., 1101
Thoko, 1248
Thomas, 258, 1419, 1696
Thomas, Joe, 1169
Thomas, Matthew, 784
Thomas, Mutt, 339
Thomas, Owen, 1002
Thomas, Peter and Muriel, 1137
Thomas, Ruth and Ed, 1129
Thomas, Tristram W., 1217
Thompson, Al, 1519
Thompson, Cornet, 1238
Thompson, Judge, 1501
Thompson, Ruth, 1713
Thompson, Will, etc., 604
Thoni, 160
Thorensen, etc., 355
Thorkill, 253
Thorlakson, Thor, 507
Thorne, Arabella, 1017

Thorne, Freddy and Georgene, 346
Thornton, Gerald, 1568
Thornton, Sir Frederick, 261
Thorpe, Sir Henry, etc., 1101
Those Who Came, 1347
Three, Mr. and Mrs., 15
Threepwood, Clarence, etc., 555
Threepwood, The Honorable Freddie, 868
Thrush, Old, 682
Thulja, 252
Thunderjet, Patrick, 216
Thurley, Robert, 591
Thursley, Joan, 481
Thurston, Cora, 167
Thwaite, Arthur, etc., 353
Thwaites, Mrs., etc., 1040
Ti Noël, 835
Ti Pao, 1620
Tibe, Pemmer Harge rem ir, 870
Tiberius Caesar, 864, 1531
Tick, 631
Ticket Taker, 966
Ticklepenny, Austin, 1060
Tides, Virgil, 683
T'ieh Pu-ts'an, 1604
Tieta, 1564
Tiffauges, Abel, 1133
Tiflin, Jody, etc., 1281
Tiger, 203
Tigler, Kathleen Fleisher, 722
Tigre, 424
Tikhomirov, Leonid, 947
Tilden, 213
Tilden, Samuel, 447
Tilford, Mary, etc., 279
Tillotson, Blake, 1428
Tim, 1485
Timoteo Teo Timoteo, 1055
Timothy, 1116
Tims, Beryl, 904
Tina, 1358, 1581
Tinbergen, 1347
Tinch, 1751
Tindall, Milo, 1425
Tinker, 1166
Tinklepaugh, Tacky, 1003
Tinuviel, Luthien, 1411
Tiny, 489, 592, 753
Tippis, Arnold Tyler, 488
Tiptoft, Dr. Lorna, 518
Tiresias, 762
Tish, 733
Tishchenko, Semyon Gavrilovich, 948
Tito, 594
Tituba, 351
T'Mwarba, Dr. Markus (Mocky), 100
Toad, The, 141
Tobias, 385, 1583
Toby, 1660
Tocky, 235
Todd, James B., 228
Todd, Scilla, etc., 1374
Toff, anonymous, 1093
Toganō, Mieko, etc., 983
Tokar, Captain, 1771
Tokugawa, Ieyasu, 1332
Toledo, 940
Tolland, James, 447
Tolley, Sarah, etc., 134

Tolliver, Abigail Howland Mason, etc., 822
Tolm, Fritz, etc., 1326
Tolroy, 906
Tolson, Victor (Vic), 1258
Tom, 271, 780, 985, 1031, 1112, 1203, 1248, 1571
Tomas, 1633
Tomchak, Zakhar, etc., 85
Tomchek, Forrest, 722
Tomlin, Lily, 1358
Tomlinson, Marie, 1107
Tomlinson, Tony and Grace, 1022
Tommy, 33, 660
Tomsky, Pavel, 1245
Tonks, Mrs., 755
Tonnerre, Jules "Skinner," etc., 408
Tonto, 271
Tony, 934
Tony, Uncle, 1181
Tonyá, 1445
Toole, Jimmy, 1039
Toomey, Kenneth Marchal, etc., 437
Toomey, Merwyn J., 156
Tophel, 226
Torelli, etc., 1596
Torg, 720
Törless, 1766
Tormie, 720
Torona, Natalie, etc., 758
Torpille, La, 1464
Torrance, Jack, etc., 1393
Torrance, Pearl, etc., 769
Torrismund, 1111
Tortshiner, Masha, etc., 459
Tosamah, John Big Bluff, 708
Toshie, 193
Tötges, Werner, 919
Tothero, Marty, 1257
Totina, 1589
Toto, 146
Totsuka, 20
Tott, Israbestis, 1141
Tours-Minières, Baron des, 1465
Toussaint, Anatole, 891
Touti, N'Deye, 602
Toutout, Bébé, 117
Tower, Sergeant, 123
Townsend, Mrs. Rosanna, 219
Toyama, 1321
Toyber, Yona, 1415
Trabatta, Cavaliere, 11
Trachtenberg, Sheina Solomonova, 1347
Trackers, The, 1189
Tracy, Albert, 1577
Tracy, William, 1204
Trafalgar, Lord, 1724
Tragedians, 1314
Traherne, Susan, 1214
Traian, 377
Traitor, 966
Trajella, Don Giuseppe, 284
Tramp, 751
Trant, 249
Traphagen, Berwyn Phillips, 1456
Traphagen, Red, 113
Trapp, Bill, 133
Trashcan Man, 1471
Trask, Jean, 617
Traugutt, Romuald, 1219

Traum, Philip, 1069
Trave, Thomas von der, 593
Traveler, 696
Traveler-journalist, British, 1657
Travelling Salesman, 258
Travis, Joseph, 327
Treadup, David, etc., 227
Trease, Big Jim, 1352
Treasurer, 97
Tree, Hilma, 1130
Tree-Man, 565
Treece, Paul, 353
Treece, Stuart, 439
Trejo, Felipe, 1726
Trelawney, Dr., 299
Trelawney, Edward John, 1018
Trellis, Dermot, 82
Trellis, Orlick, 83
Tremaine, Mike, 1140
Trench, Dr., 1747
Trench, Melbourne, etc., 1643
Trépat, Berthe, 697
Trescorre, Count Lelio, 1650
Trevelyan, Laura, 1666
Trevor, 262
Trewe, Harry, 1174
Trewhella, William James, 813
Trezevant, Mr., 327
Tricardio, 572
Trick, 1741
Trimbell, Gene, 1615
Trimble, Willy, 918
Trimingham, Viscount, etc., 597
Trimmer, 1508
Trincant, Phillipe, etc., 396
Trindade, Ascânio, 1564
Triolet, Elsa, 1771
Triple T., 585
Tripping, Geli, 626
Tritt, Victoria May, 465
Trixie, Miss, 321
Trollope, Mrs. Lilia, 896
Trom, 1566
Tronche, Octavie, 1731
Trooper of Dragoons, 1376
Trotsky, Leon, 456
Trotter, Detective Sergeant, 1052
Trotts, Mother Abigail Freemantle, 1471
Trouble-shooter, 1363
Trouscaillon, 1768
Trout, Eva, etc., 470
Trout, Kilgore, 599, 1422
Trout Fishing in America Shorty, 1619
Trowbridge, Dr. Whitmore, 224
Troy, Virginia, 1508
Truax, Christine (Chris), 1738
Trude, 101
Trudy, 1358
Truit, Lena, etc., 1297
Trujillo, Epifanio, etc., 865
Truman, 167
Trumble, Letty, 127
Trumper, 748
Truscott, 915
Truscott, Kelso, Q. C., 1322
Truscott, Pam, 1017
Truslove, Linda, 1019
Trust, Angela Whitling, 628
Truter, Mr., 1739
Truttwell, John, etc., 617
Tryon, George, 705

Ts'ao, Mr., 1292
"Tsar," 659
Ts'ui-huan, 1605
Tsukazaki, Ryuji, 1328
Tsuneko, 1108
Tsurukawa, 1522
Tsuruko, 950
Tsutsik, 1396
Tu Fu, 839
Tucker, Barnaby, 989
Tucker, Daniel, 1322
Tucker, Honeyboy, 1087
Tucker, Rex "Fishbelly," etc., 909
Tucker, Richard (Rick) Linbergh, etc., 1176
Tudor, Elizabeth, 380
Tudsbury, Pamela, etc., 1679, 1721
Tuia, 799
Tuka, 1758
Tull, Pearl Cody, etc., 403
Tull, Rebecca, 1333
Tullio-Friole, Marchesa, 1513
Tullius Rotundus, 1311
Tulloch, Dr. Willie, 825
Tulsi, Mai, 707
Tunja, Harry de, 645
Tunner, 1391
Tupe, Mr., 900
Turandot, 1768
Turati, 385
Turbin, Alexei Vasilyevich, etc., 371
Turgis, Harold, 46
Turk, 311
Turnbull, Cordelia Prescott, 1280
Turnbull, Mary McGregor, 1045
Turner, 1667
Turner, Luciela Louise, 1735
Turner, Marian, 1684
Turner, Mrs., 1535
Turner, Nat, etc., 326
Turnstyle, Eva Bartok, 1361
Turonok, Henry Franzovich, 317
Turpitz, Siegfried von, 1429
Turquoise, 450
Turvey, Thomas Leadbeater "Tops," 1623
Tutsi, 1093
Tuttle, Noah, 223
Twa, Mollya, 100
Twining, Harriet, 21
Twinkletoes, 592
Twist, Kitty, 1674
Two, Mr. and Mrs., 15
Two Bows, 861
Tyche, 97
Tyler, Mr., 33
Tylette, 174
Tylo, 174
Tyltyl, 174
Tynan, Charlie, etc., 360
Typhoon, 1629
Tyrone, 472
Tyrone, James, etc., 908
Tyrone, James, 1035
Tyte, Francis, 1161
Tyurin, 1147
Tzara, Tristan, 1606
Tzili, 1630

U, 1701
U Po Kyin, 214
Ubertino of Casale, 1074
Ubonius, Publius, 97

CHARACTER INDEX

Ubu, Père and Mère, 1631
Udomo, Michael, 1755
Uehara, 1380
Ueno, Otoko, 128
Uffe, 379
Uganda, Duchess of, 1156
Ugly, 1456
Ugly Edith, 426
Ugly Mug, 1736
Ugoye, 70
Uhlmeister, Thomasina, 1745
Uiko, 1522
Ukrainian Man, 421
Ulbán, 975
Ulfsdatter, Sign, 7
Ulick, 722
Ullman, Stuart, 1393
Ulmo, 1411
Ulrich, 962
Ulyan, 975
Ulybin, Osip Ivanovich, 736
Uma, 470
Umberto, 561
Umer, Abd, 1454
Una, 122
Unachukwu, Moses, 70
Uncle, 84, 1223
Uncle, Pito Pérez's, 560
Uncle Benny, 898
Uncle from Shizuoka, 725
Uncle Robin, 523
Underhill, Dr. Thomas, 634
Underhill, Emma, 740
Undershaft, 22
Underwood, Freddie, etc., 370
Underwood, Larry, 1470
Unferth, 638
Ungar, Felix, 1131
United States, 1028
Unk, 1418
Unnamable, 1643
Unnamed, 665
Unoka, 1545
Upchurch, Jonathan Adams, 835
Updike, Dr., 1653
Upjohn, Isolde, 1123
Uprichard, Dymphna, 752
Ur, 1453
Uragami, 987
Urbaal, 1453
Urbach, Dr., 1067
Urbano, 485, 975
Urfe, Nicholas, 945
Uriel, 1454
Urmilla, 204
Ursula, 1070
Useppe, 679
Utsugi, Mr. Tokusuke, etc., 398
Utterword, Lady Ariadne (Addy), etc., 669
Uyuyu, 82

V., 916, 1646
Vacasour, Miss, 1027
Vachousek, 460
Vadastra, Spiridon, 533
Vail, Lawrence, 1146
Val, 1432, 1737
Valentin Arregui Paz, 837
Valentina, 1622
Valentine, Basil, 1279
Valentinov, 385
Valento, Velma, 494

Valenzuela, Luisa, 901
Valeria, 905
Valet, 168, 1104
Valino, 1034
Valkovsky, Alexei "Alyosha" Pyotrovitch, etc., 768
Vallon, Léonie, 264
Valpor, Albert, etc., 1687
Valsecca, Odo, 1650
Valsen, Red, 1071
Valverde, Fray Vincente de, 1317
Valya, 464
Vanamee, 1130
Vanbruik, Charles, 555
Van Buren, Martin, 220
Vancouver, George, 218
Van Dam, Mr., 1346
Vandergelder, Horace, 988
Vanderhof, Grandpa Martin, 1764
Vandervane, Sir Roy, etc., 590
Vane, Frederick, etc., 934
Vane, Harriet, 571
VanEenanam, Christofer (Chris), etc., 1705
Vaneleigh, Judas Griffin, 1566
Vanessa, 1747
Vangreen, Jason, 820
van Groenwegel, Adriansen, etc., 817
Vanhomrigh, Ester, 1747
Van Huysen, Flora, 989
Vannec, Claude, 1317
Van Rossum, Father Gerard, 974
Van Roy, 1015
Vanselow, Captain, 622
Vanwinkle, Colonel Nicholas, 1537
Vanya, 428
Varda, 1410
Vardoe, Maggie, etc., 1503
Varenger, Mr., 530
Varenukha, Ivan Savelievich, 985
Varlamov, 1475
Varrells, The, 139
Varya, Aunt, 217
Vasca, 1317
Vasile, Spiru Gheorghe, etc., 533
Vasilievna, Maria, 618
Vasilievna, Olga, 57
Vásquez, José, 560
Vassiliou, Rose and Christopher, 1084
Vasudeva, 1401
Vaughan, Barbara, 964
Vaughan-Jones, Gowan, 1638
Vaughn, Granny, 917
Vaught, Chandler, etc., 853
Vautier, Abel, etc., 1478
Vautrin, 1464
Vayle, James, 1251
Vbasti, 720
Vea, 406
Veen, Ivan (Van), etc., 13
Vegallana, Marquis and Marchioness of, 1284
Vei, 941
Velasco, Padre Vrais Luis, 1332
Velasco, Victor, 116
Veli, 994
Velosipedkin, 124
Velvel, 135
Venable, Violet, 1488
Venables, Commander Hugo, 24

Venables, The Reverend Theodore and Agnes, 1100
Venables, Thomas Orpen, 182
Venantius of Salvemec, 1073
Venceslau Pietro Pietra, 941
Venere, Giulia, 284
Venitequa, Carola, 848
"Venticelli," The, 34
Ventress, 355
Ventura, 1736
Venturi, Luke, 507
Venus, 251
Vera, Miguel, 1444
Veraguth, Johann, etc., 1314
Veraswami, Doctor, 214
Vercors, Violaine, etc., 1563
Vere, 1598
Verelst, 22
Verever, Miss, 47
Verkhovensky, Stepan Trofimovich, etc., 1227
Verlaine, 191
Verlaine, Maria, 292
Vermeulen, Brandt, 213
Vernede, 62
Verneuil, Lucien, 971
Vernon, Phil, 658
Vernonica, 1649
Veronica, 194
Veronique, 266, 848
Verrall, The Honourable Lieutenant, 214
Verri, Rico, 1588
Vershoyle, Gould, 1587
Versilov, Andrei, 1272
Vescovi, Francesco, 1516
Vesper, Paul, 10
Veuillet, M., 244
Viadomsky, Pan, 1081
Vicar of Pressan Ambo, 411
Vicario, Angela, etc., 284
Vicarro, Silva, 1625
Vice-Chancellor, 440
Victor, 415, 1562
Victor, Gilbert, 752
Victor, Inez Christian, etc., 387
Victor, Siegfried, 61
Victoria, 298, 1655
Victoria Regina, Queen, 559
Vidal, 1220
Vidal, Don Isidro, etc., 399
Vidal Olmos, Alejandra, 1142
Vidavarri, Terasina, 1673
Vielle, 103
Vienna, 1655
Vieuxchange, 1433
Vigan, Le, 241
Vigilance, 647
Vigot, 1252
Vigue, La, 241
Vilca, Lucas, 607
Villa, Buddy, etc., 726
Village, Clément, 1165
Village, Dieudonné, 167
Villagers of the Dunes, 1730
Villalba, Crisanto, 1444
Villeroy, 1015
Vilma, 1523
Vince, 213
Vincent, Mrs., 454
Vinelander, Andrey, etc., 14
Viney, 1016
Vinnie, 1131

Vinrace, Rachel, 1668
Vio, Thomas de, 938
Violet, 1450
Violeta, 1553
Violeta del Valle, 760
Violinist, 449
Vip, The, 971
Vipess, The, 971
Virajá, Dr. Silva, 1527
Virgilius, Father, 74
Virginia, 562
Virgins, Three, 446
Virginsky, 1228
Viriato, 805
Vishalakshi, 1377
Vishvanathan, 717
Visitor, Sibyl's, 1400
Vissarionovich, Roman, 776
Visser, Manus, 304
Vitalyevna, Serafima
   (Simochka), 514
Vitória, 63
Vitzliputzli, Liesl, 392
Vivaldi, Antonio, 482
Vivaldi, Carlo, 680
Vives, Alvaro, 1552
Viziru, Stefan and Ioana, 532
Vlaciha, Olin, 1250
Vladi, Marina, 216
Vläntsch, Ruodlieb von der, 389
Vogel, 721
Vogel, Clara, 1381
Vogel, Corinne, 179
Vogel, Jesse, etc., 1741
Vogelsang, Hedwig, 1648
Vogg, David, 1020
Voice, 315, 762
Voice, Female, 33
Voice from ground control, 1670
Voice from headquarters, 1671
Voice 1, 490
Voice 2, 490
Voice 3, 490
Voices, Mixed group of, 530
Voldemar, Vladimir Petrovich,
   etc., 516
Voler, Ben, 1738
Volkbein, Felix, etc., 1099
Volkmar, 345
Volkov, Kathy, 1663
Volodin, Innokenty
   Artemyevich, 514
Volodya, 779
Volpe, Ema de, 27
Volpini, 72
Voltaire, 191
Volyntsev, Sergey Pavlych, 1320
Von Berg, Wilhelm Johann, 756
Von Dönhof, 1595
Vonghel, Anna Dempster, 722
Von Koren, "Kolya," 428
Vonnegut, Kurt, Jr., 1422
von Stroheim, Erich, 1293
von Turpitz, Siegfried, 1429
Von Vampton, Hinckle, 1055
von Winterfeldt, General
   Detlev, 622
von Witte, General, 779
von Zahnd, Fräulein Doktor
   Mathilde, 1206
Vorontsov, Prince Mikhail
   Semenovich, etc., 649

Vorontsova, Princess Maria
   Vasilyevna, 650
Vorotyntsev, Georgii
   Mikhalych, 84
Vorotyntsev, Georgij
   Mikhailych, 1135
Voshchev, 535
Vosk, Father (Colonel), 975
Voss, Johann Ulrich, 1666
Voss, Richard, 1206
Vostokov, Colonel Vadim, 778
Vote, Robin, 1099
Voyod, Hortense, 1732
Vulbo, 572
Vulindlela, Zwelinzima, 212
Vyazemskaya, 668

Wacholt, Willy, 1676
Wack, 521
Waczelrodt, Lucas, 409
Wada, Uncle, 1380
Wade, Johnston, 322
Wade, Roger, etc., 911
Wade, Walter, 1053
Wadsmith, Miss Mary, 1556
Wagner, Dick, 1094
Wago the Leopard-Killer, 629
Wain, Jefferson, 705
Wain, Penelope, etc., 119
Wainwright, Alexander, 273
Wainwright, Rodney, 1430
Waiter, 756, 1062
Waitzmann, Ruprecht, etc., 158
Waiyaki, 1301
Walburga, Sister, 2
Wald, Waldemar, 722
Walden, Rena, etc., 705
Walden, Ty Ty, etc., 603
Walewska, Princess Marie, 1077
Walk-Man, 1058
Walker, Beth Phail, etc., 1426
Walker, Bynum, 793
Walker, Coalhouse, Jr., 1260
Walker, Patrick, 802
Walker, Susan, 1146
Walker, The Reverend Lane, 1128
Wall, Mrs., 684
Wall, Sergeant, 123
Wallace, Peter, 1291
Wallach, Gabriel (Gabe), 878
Wallach, Reuben, 1291
Wallas, 468
Walldorff, Professor Ernest, 942
Waller, Lilly, 466
Wally, 558, 1061
Walpor, Albert, etc., 1687
Walpurg, Alexander, 941
Walsh, Ken, 261
Walt, 1092
Walter, 962, 1297
Walters, Alan and Clara, 1610
Walterson, Nathaniel (Nat), 1208
Walz, Willy, 1676
Wanda, 1502
Wanderhope, Don, etc., 170
Wandering Jew, 233, 1400, 1583
Wang, 615
Wang Lai-hu, 1621
Wangeci, 730
Wanja, 1198
Wapter, Leopold, 581
Ward, Lyman, etc., 48
Warda, 1353

Warden, 578, 731, 1243, 1670
Warden, Second Lieutenant
   Charles, 107
Warden, Sergeant Milton
   Anthony, 551
Warder, Chief, 1243
Warder Donelly, 1243
Warder 2, 1243
Ware, Randall, 806
Warieda, 336
Warner, 667
Warner, Christopher, etc., 791
Warren, 1521
Warren, Mary, 352
Warren, Peggy, 769
Warren, Professor, 1003
Warren, Vivie and Mrs. Kitty, 1026
Warwick, John, 705
Washington, Dr. John, etc., 256
Washington, George, 220
Watchett, Gerry, 481
Watchman, 1058
Water Hen, 1688
Waterlow, Rosemary, 820
Waters, Elsie, 314
Waters, Johnny, 1213
Waterton, Richard, 29
Wates, Ben, 656
Watkin, Lisa, 209
Watler, Byrum Powery, 491
Watson, Daddy, 1503
Watson, Meg, etc., 1351
Watson, Phoeby, 1535
Watt, 1694
Watt, Bessie, etc., 335
Watty, Mrs., etc., 337
Watzek-Trummer, Ernst, 1379
Waugh, J. Henry, 1642
Wayne, Chance, 1505
Wealtheow, 638
Weary, Roland, 1422
Weatherby, 1699
Weatherby, Jane, etc., 1114
Weaver, Alun and Rhiannon, 1136
Weaver, Charles and Diane, 1552
Webb, Charles, 724
Webb, Matthew, 1416
Webber, Joan, 1387
Webber, Roo, 1493
Webber, Stanley, 159
Weber, Constanze, 34
Webster, Aaron, 1455
Webster, Clarence, 811
Webster, J. G. L., 313
Wechsel, Hirst, 115
Wedekind, Georg Christian, 1110
Wedge, Veronica (Vee), etc., 556
Wee Willie Winkle, 1008
Weeks, Gabriel, 1131
Wehmeier, 1575
Wehrfritz, 1576
Weinand, Brother, 938
Weiss, Ruth, etc., 383
Weisskopf, Mr., 1146
Weissman, Misu, 533
Weissmann, Captain, 624
Weldon, Reverend Arthur, 1154
Wellfleet, John, etc., 1664
Welling, The Reverend
   Michael C., 357
Wellington, Archibald
   Absalon, 167
Wells, Calliope (Callie), etc., 1091

Welsh, Edward, 1542
Weltman, Jenny, 266
Wemyss, First Sea Lord
  Rosslyn, 622
Wenceslas, King, 1632
Wendall, Loretta, etc., 1535
Weng, 648
Wenthien, Dr. Konrad, 665
Wentworth, Hugh, 1183
Wentworth, Margaret (Peggy), 1195
Wenzel, 1461
Wertheimer, 1645
Wesley, 1571
Wessells, Captain Little Flying
  Dutchman (Henry W.), 268
West, David, 1043
West, John Henry, 993
West, Judith, 73
West, Miriam, 1309
Westbrook, Harriet, 173
Westerby, Jerry, 694
Westin, Lars Lennart, 378
Weston, Dr., 1457
Westphalen, Jenny von, 816
Wetchy, 1461
Wetjoen, Piet, 732
Wexford, Jane, 999
Weygand, General Maxime, 621
Weymann, Charles, 561
Whale, General, 1510
Wharton, Samuel and Sadie, 1697
Wheat, Lafcadio, 323
Wheeler, 1300
Wheeler, Claude, etc., 1154
Whipple, Dora, 323
Whipple, John, 662
Whit, 415
Whitacre, Michael and Laura, 1765
Whitbread, 791
Whitcomb, Micah Elihue, 181
White, Mr., 654
White, Sam, 1497
White Paper Fan, 1452
Whitehead, Margaret, 328
Whiteside, Sheridan, 955
Whiteside, Sister, 1114
Whitman, Elizabeth "Foxy" and
  Ken, 345
Whittingdon, Dick, 59
Whittman, Ishmael, 236
Whyborn, Naomi, 769
Whymper, Bill, 1023
Wicked Cobra, 1526
Wickersham, Mrs., 449
Wicks, Freddy, 1604
Widow, 1091
Widow, Photographer's, 1717
Widower, 1090
Widower, Negro, 1091
Wienis, Prince Regent, 536
Wieser, 891
Wife, 426, 889, 1346, 1607
Wife, Bird's, 1197
Wife, Carpet Dealer's, 616
Wife, Colonel's, 1109
Wife, first convict's, 1670
Wife, Gálvez's, 1394
Wife, Gravedigger's Boy's, 867
Wife, Innkeeper's, 786
Wife, Konrad's, 891
Wife, Noah's, 636
Wife, prosecutor's, 1718
Wife, Rector's, 16

Wife, Slocum's, 1441
Wife, Steward's, 1080
Wife, Surgeon's, 1080
Wife, T's, 916
Wife, White, 1090
Wife, Young, 1312
Wife of Colonel Lorenzo
  G——, 977
Wife of the Sergeant-
  Provocateur, 1218
Wigbaldy, Greta, 171
Wigga, 526
Wiggen, Henry Whittier, etc., 1455
Wiggin, Henry "Author," etc., 112
Wilbur, 233
Wilcox, Humphrey, etc., 384
Wild Bill Hickok, 759
Wild Bill Hickok, 894
Wild Hog, 268
Wilder, Captain, 979
Wildflower, 633
Wildhack, Montana, 1422
Wildsmith, Arthur, 62
Wilenski, Lou, 1488
Wilfrid, Father, 1040
Wilhelm, Tommy, etc., 1369
Wiligis, 685
Wilkes, Albert, 690
Wilkins, 836
Wilkins, Major Frank, 896
Wilkins, Mr. Robert, 897
Wilkinson, James, 220
Wilkinson, Roger, 957
Will, 1460
Willard, Buddy, 137
Willard, Jim, 291
Willard, Slug, 83
Willett, Robert Courtland van
  Caulaert, 456
Willi, Vater, 877
William, 886
William of Baskerville, 1072
William the Conqueror, 1375
Williams, 774
Williams, Abigail, 351
Williams, Aunt Hager, etc., 1113
Williams, Beth, 441
Williams, Clink, 1333
Williams, David, 440
Williams, Goose, 112
Williams, Leslie A., 700
Williams, Nathan "Slim," 863
Williams, Sandra Wentworth, 785
Williams, T. T., 993
Williamson, John, 596
Willie, 122, 657, 781, 1571
Willie, Uncle, 1204
Willieboy, 1672
Willing, Jerome and Nell, 687
Willis, 327
Willis, Cousin Lymon, 110
Willis, Mr., 1433
Willis, Richard, 109
Willoughby, Carey, 440
Willoughby, Tom, 1402
Wills, Edweena, 1537
Willson, David, etc., 401
Willy, 145, 1031
Willy the Booky, 1299
Wilsden, Brenda "Brownie,"
  etc., 610
Wilson, Annie, 572
Wilson, Bertila, etc., 542

Wilson, Billy, 1483
Wilson, Joanne, 1641
Wilson, Mr., 1665
Wilson, Ron, 929
Wilson, Warren K., 935
Wilson, Woodrow, 1071, 1119
Wimsey, Lord Peter Death
  Bredon, 571, 1100
Win, 1591
Winburn, Brenda, 1003
Winckler, Christian, 698
Wincobank, Len, 732
Wind, Dr. Liza, etc., 1216
Windgrave, Matty "Septimus," 367
Windrave, Matty "Septimus," 367
Windrod, Mary, etc., 1297
Windrove, Matty "Septimus," 367
Windwebel, Victor, 698
Winemiller, Alma, etc., 1492
Winifrede, Sister, 2
Winkler, Vernon, 507
Winner, Arthur, Jr., 223
Winner, Clarissa, etc., 224
Winnie, 657, 1340
Winslow, Godfrey, 1482
Winsome, etc., 1647
Winston, 1058
Winter, Josiah, 1371
Winter, Lucy, 1427
Winter, William, 1296
Winterbottom, 1296
Winterbottom, Captain T. K., 69
Winters, Francesca, 1184
Winters, Goodwin "Stale-
  Bread," 1539
Winterwade, Cedric, 1123
Wirtanen, Major Frank, 1047
Wisbeach, Mrs., 820
Wischow, Herbert, 144
Wiseman, Eva, 1043
Wishrop, 647
Witchdoc, 900
Withenshaw, 405
Witherspoon, Mrs., etc., 1696
Witherspoon, Nathaniel (Turner),
  etc., 1538
Witnesses, Three, 444
Witold, 340
Witt, 1544
Witt, Alec, 376
Wluiki, Lafcadio, 847
Wohl, Isaac, 1291
Wohlmeyer, Seppi, 1069
Wojtys, Kulka, etc., 341
Woland, 984
Wolf, Luke and Hat, 1703
Wolfe, "Doctor," 544
Wolff, 837
Wolfie, 82
Wolfsleach, 1389
Wolgast, 929
Wolin, 1371
Wolper, Naomi Lutz, 722
Wolseley, Sir Garnet, 667
Wolsey, Cardinal Thomas, 53
Wolsey, Thomas Cardinal, 953
Woltersheim, Else, 920
Woman, 37, 104, 161, 559, 713, 750,
  870, 1600
Woman, blonde, 1670
Woman, brunette, 1670
Woman, Character, 1589
Woman, Dead, 363

Woman, elderly, 1614
Woman, Fat, 97
Woman, intense young, 1062
Woman, nameless old, 1266
Woman, old, 256, 1631
Woman, Old Black, 966
Woman, young married, 1614
Woman, young native, 1671
Woman Alone, Young, 1090
Woman at Blatherdene cottage garden, 421
Woman Behind the Window, 374
Woman from Gradenberg, 569
Woman in the City, 1730
Woman in the Dunes, 1729
Woman with a Basket, 1585
Woman with a Mechanical Cradle, 374
Woman with white scarf, 1294
Woman's Dress, 268
Wonder, Jack, 1712
Wondrak, Willi, 1409
Wong, 697
Wong, M. and Mme., 1214
Wong, Rydra, 99
Wood, Bernard, 1162
Wood, Henry, 781
Woodcock, Luther, 237
Woodful, 126
Woodrow, Ken, 292
Woodruff, Sarah, 547
Woods, Brigadier "Jacko," 1716
Woods, Janie Crawford Killicks Starks, etc., 1534
Woods, Jimmy, 278
Woods, Mrs. Agnes, 353
Woods, Piney, 113
Woodville, Nina, 1365
Wooster, Bertram (Bertie), 763
Wordlaw, Aunt Hattie Breedlove, 1538
Words, 1745
Wordsworth, B., 1009
Worm, 1644
Worried Little Woman, 259
Worthington, Georgie Enthoven, 443
Worthington, Henry Dodd (Hank), etc., 1037
Worthington, Lizzie, 695
Wortman, Billy Bob, 933
Would-be literary figure, 437
Woundwort, General, 1693
Woyke, Amanda, 526
Wray, Julia, 1180
Wren, Christopher, 1052
Wren, Victoria, etc., 1647
Wright, Charles, 375
Wright, Helene, 1491
Wright, Karen, 279
Wright, Nel, 1491
Wright, Shiner, 249
Wriothesley, Henry, 1117
Wriste, Richard (Rick or Ricky), 1610
Writer, 1030
Wu, Johnny, 228
Wu Ma, 1620
Wu Tsiang, 281
Wuchs, Dr., 1739
Wulf, Anna Freeman, 605
Wut, Gottlub, 1379
Wyatt, Sarah, 787

Wyburd, Arnold, 479
Wyckoff, Miss Norine, 1537
Wyeth, Maria, 1212
Wyke, Andrew, 1424
Wykowski, Joseph, 156
Wylie, 1059
Wylinski, Herr, 1120
Wyner, Sidney, 1521
Wynn, May, 225
Wynn, Thomas, 1217
Wyoh, 1036
Wytwyl, Doctor Amalia von, 142

Xa, 1318
Xantes, Father, 82
Xavinha, 419
Ximenes, Colonel, 968

Yakamoto, 226
Yakimov (Yaki), Prince, 107
Yakonov, Anton Nikolayevich, 513
Yakov the Timid, 135
Yakovlevich, Pavel, 1200
Yakovlevich, Vitold, 779
Yale, Samuel Delbert, 1455
Yamamoto, Professor, 770
Yancsi, 1125
Yandell, Douglas, 590
Yang Sun, etc., 615
Yank, 651, 660
Yankee Jack, 523
Yannes, 921
Yanovsky, Professor, 141
Yardena, 1066
Yardley, John, 1626
Yashoda, 784
Yasuko, 1450
Yasunaga, Toru, 1355
Yavanna, 1411
Yavor, Dov, 736
Yefimov, Yegor Petrovich, 1085
Yegey, 870
Yegorov, Spiridon Danilovich, 515
Yegorovich, Philip, 216
Yehudah of Kerioth, 985
Yellow Singer, 861
Yellow Swallow, 268
Yemelyan, 1474
Yen, 123
Yesenin, 191
Yeshua Ha-Nozri, 984
Yevgenievna, Galina, 57
Yic, Goyo, 996
Ying Chan, 1355
Yoko, 1434
Yolland, Lieutenant George, 1601
Yonosuke, 888
Yosef, Rabbi Shmuel, 749
Yoshikawa, 197
Yoshiko, 1108
Youdi, 1029
Youkoumian, Krikor, 162
Young Ben, 1713
Young Marrieds, 258
Young Martin, 1316
Youngblood, 1501
Younger, Lena, etc., 1262
Younger Bear, 894
Younghusband, Aunt Frances, etc., 353
Youthful, Zutka, etc., 499
Yoyo, 82
Yozo, 1107

Yozō, 1332
Ysé, 200
Yü Hsien, 1605
Yü Tso-ch'en, 1605
Yuan Ming, 1292
Yueh, Doctor, 432
Yuken Noguchi, 19
Yuki, 1406
Yukiko, 950
Yukio, 1434
Yumí, Celestino, 1054
Yurka, 1562
Yusuf, 650
Yves, 56
Yvette, 140

Z. Dolin, 296
Zabala, Catalina, 1054
Zaccheus, 1362
Zachanassian, Claire, 1659
Zacharia, 1220
Zackerman, Zac, 1374
Zadkiel, The Lesser, 1708
Zadok, 1454
Zadok, Rabbi Eliezer bar, 1454
Zaehner, Elfrida, etc., 376
Zagreus, Horace, 59
Zalaca, 1719
Zambelli, Cardinal, 131
Zambinella, La, 1337
Zapp, Morris, 1429
Zapp, Morris and Désirée, 260
Zappala, Salvatore "Zappy," 48
Zarri, Angiolina, 72
Zaruski, Kazimierz, 944
Zasyekin, Princess, etc., 516
Zatsyrko, Vadim, 230
Zauberbilt, Frau, 101
Zauze, Doctor, 1347
Zava, 677
Zavala, Don Fermín, 334
Zavala, Father, 484
Zavala, Santiago, 334
Zawistowska, Sophie, 1447
Zaworski, Jerzy, 1195
Zazie, 1767
Zbarski, Magda, 944
Zbingden, Otto, 594
Zdena, 190
Zé, 1769
Zé Camarão, 805
Ze Sampaio, Dona Norma de, 417
Zeba, 635
Zebedee, 859
Zednicek, Councillor, 297
Zeit, Theodore (Theo), 353
Zelger, Veronica, 1327
Zeliha, 1720
Zemanek, Helena, etc., 796
Zenkai, Father Kuwai, 1522
Zeno, 6, 328, 1311
Zentgraf, Erna, 877
Zerchi, Dom Jethrah, 234
Zero, Mr. and Mrs., 14
Zesen, Philipp von, 992
Zeus, 251
Zhachev, 535
Zhbankov, Mikhail Vladimirovich, 318
Zhuravliov, Elena (Lena) Borissovna, etc., 1533
Ziegenhals, Plinius, 594

CHARACTER INDEX

Ziegler, Janet "Nezzie"
   Christian, 388
Ziemlich, Mina, etc., 1415
Zifa, 1445
Zifferblatt, Horace, 1642
Zilberantsev, 217
Zimmerman, Louis M., 251
Zimmern, Danielle, 1682
Zinn, John Quincy, etc., 171
Zipporah, 636, 1041
Zissu, Stella, 533
Zizi, 762

Zodman, Paul J., 1453
Zogg, Rosalinde, etc., 178
Zoika, Silly, 217
Zoila, 760
Zommer, Rachel, etc., 646
Zoo Director, 132
Zophar, 789
Zosh, 961
Zoya, 229
Zuckerman, Nathan, etc., 42, 581,
   1230, 1774

Zuess, Sammy, 225
Zulena, 1183
Zulma, 803
Zuno, Ezequiel, 611
Züpfner, Heribert, 301
Zürn, Gottlieb and Anna, 1504
Zusia, Rebbe, 1125
Zuss, Mr., 789
Zutkin, Bernard, 957
Zuzarte, Juliao, 349
Zvuvium, Baal B., 1404